Warman's
English &
Continental
Pottery & Porcelain

3RD EDITION

Susan & Al Bagdade

Published by

krause
publications

700 E. State Street • Iola, WI 54990-0001
Telephone: 715/445-2214

Please call or write for our free catalog.
Our toll-free number to place an order or obtain a free catalog is 800-258-0929
or please use our regular business telephone 715-445-2214
for editorial comment and further information.

Library of Congress Catalog Number: 91-50430

ISBN: 0-87341-641-4

Printed in the United States of America

Photos: On the cover is a jardiniere, 7" h, 14-1/4" H-H, "HenRiot Quimper" mark, c1922, $1,250; from the collection of Susan and Al Bagdade, Northbrook, Ill. Pictured on the back cover are a vase, 15-3/4" h, "HenRiot Quimper France" mark, c1926, $2,800, also from the collection of Susan and Al Bagdade; and a figure, 11-1/2" h, 10-1/2" l, Ernst Wahliss, Teplitz, c1890, $2,500, from the collection of Raven and Dove, Wilmette, Ill.

Photo credits: Photos on the front and back covers by Charles J. Bagdade; author photo by Sig Nielsen.

CONTENTS

ACKNOWLEDGMENTS

This book would not have been possible without the cooperation of hundreds of antiques dealers who allowed us to gather information and photograph their wares at antique shows and in their homes and shops.

A special thank you goes to the auction houses in the United States and London that provided subscriptions to their extensive catalogs. The authors express sincere gratitude to auctioneers Leslie Hindman of Chicago; Terry Dunning of Elgin, Illinois; and Mike Clum of Rushville, Ohio, who allowed us to photograph auction properties.

Judith Anderson of Americana, Ltd. of Chicago; Smith and Ciffone of Kenilworth, Illinois; and Lucie and Bob Reichner of Wilmette, Illinois, were exceptionally generous in allowing us into their homes for private photo sessions.

Mark Wilkinson of Christie's South Kensington deserves an extra special thank you for all his help securing catalogs covering the newest "hot" categories.

A special debt of gratitude must go to Rich Kleinhardt for drawing the pottery and porcelain marks for all three editions, as well as to Donna Bagdade, who drew the marks for our newest categories in the third edition.

Additional thanks to Randi Schwartz, who once again allowed us to invade her private collection of majolica, as well as her shop, The Raven and Dove, to photograph examples for this book's cover. We also wish to thank Charles Bagdade for once again photographing our cover.

Al's partner in dentistry, Burt Turek, must be thanked for taking on the lion's share of work at the office, and for his infinite patience while Al made innumerable phone calls, did research, and delved through auction catalogs.

We also want to thank our new editor at Krause Publications, Kris Manty, for all her help in editing this third edition.

PREFACE TO THE THIRD EDITION

For the first edition of *Warman's English and Continental Pottery and Porcelain,* we worked closely with our mentor and friend Harry Rinker, who held our hands every step of the way, and Warman's publishers Stanley and Katherine Greene, who introduced us to the book publishing world.

When the time came for the second edition, Warman had been sold to Wallace-Homestead, a division of Chilton Books, which was owned by ABC Cap Cities. After we began work on the third edition, Wallace-Homestead was acquired by Krause Publications, and we moved on to our third and newest publisher.

Many changes have occurred in the world of antiques since we started writing our first book in 1983. We have been through a series of computers, both desktop and laptop, a multitude of computer programs, and have finally graduated to Windows 95, the Internet, faxes and E-mail. What used to take weeks to get by mail, we now receive in a matter of minutes.

In order to keep up with changes in the antiques marketplace, we have added categories for Chintz china, Burleigh Ware jugs, and Charlotte Rhead for this edition. Vincennes has been added to Sevres, Nantgarw has joined England-General, Switzerland has been retired, and Mennecy now resides in France-General since there was not enough material available for these to warrant separate categories.

In each book, we have utilized all new price listings and descriptions–more than 10,000 items. All the photos are new to this third edition, and some new marks have been added. Museums, histories, reference books, collectors' clubs, collecting hints, and especially reproduction alerts have all been updated and verified.

To all our faithful readers who were continually asking for a new edition since they called our book "the bible" for pottery and porcelain, we present our third edition. We appreciated all the kind and generous comments and hope our readers are pleased with our new effort. As always, we invite comments which can be sent to us in care of our publisher, Krause Publications.

Susan and Al Bagdade

Northbrook, Illinois

PREFACE TO THE SECOND EDITION

For the second edition, decisions were made concerning certain categories that needed to be added, changed or amended. Readers will be pleased to find the Blue Onion Pattern, Relief Molded Jugs, Staffordshire Blue and White, as well as additional Sevres information.

Imperial St. Petersburg has been incorporated into Russia-General, Plymouth now resides in England-General, and Zurich is at home in Switzerland-General. Bernard Moore has been retired.

More importantly, users of our first edition should note that this edition contains *entirely* new pottery and porcelain examples, more than 12,000 in total. All the photographs are *new for this edition,* and additional marks have been added, along with dates for all the original marks.

As with the first edition, we invite readers to send their comments to us in care of our new publisher, the Wallace-Homestead Book Company.

We appreciated the generous remarks from readers of our first edition, and think they will be pleased with this new and improved effort.

Susan and Al Bagdade

Northbrook, Illinois

PREFACE TO THE FIRST EDITION

For the past few years, we have been writing "Answers on Antiques," a column that appears in *The Antique Trader Weekly.* We realized that many of the questions we received related to English and continental pottery and porcelain. Our readers wanted to know: What is it? When was it made? How much is it worth?

As we did our research, we realized how little information was available from American publishers about English and continental pottery and porcelain. The books that did exist were published by European firms, most notably the Antique Collectors' Club in England. They were expensive, difficult to obtain, and focused on the European market. The English antiques price guides reflected foreign prices and did not contain helpful introductory material to a collecting category that is now the hallmark of the American antiques prices guides.

A void existed, and we decided to fill it.

This book represents a true division of labor. Al was in charge of the 16,000 data entries and their prices. Susan wrote more than 200 histories of the companies and categories listed in the guide. Both weathered the numerous crises involved with writing one's first book on a brand new computer.

Everywhere we turned in gathering information for this book, whether it was to a member of the staff of a large auction house or to a small antiques shop owner, we found encouragement for our efforts. We also queried these individuals about what type of information they felt should be included. This book is not only a response to their needs, but to their numerous requests as well.

When we started to work on this book, Harry L. Rinker, our editor, suggested that a book has a far longer gestation time than a child, involves more work, and is much harder to deliver. We wish we could say that he was wrong. But, alas, he was right. We only hope that the final product brings you as much joy as our two real children and this adopted child in book form does to us.

Susan and Al Bagdade

Northbrook, Illinois

Part One:

How to Use This Book

ORGANIZATION OF THE PRICE GUIDE

Listings: More than 200 categories and sub categories dealing with English and Continental pottery and porcelain are listed alphabetically in this price guide. Most categories refer to a single manufactory. A general category by country includes smaller firms that are not dealt with individually.

Every effort has been made to make the price listings descriptive enough so that specific objects can be identified by the reader. Emphasis has been placed on examples being sold in the marketplace today. Some harder to find objects were included to provide a full range in each category.

History: Every category has a capsule history that details the founding of the company, its principal owners, the nature of its wares, the patterns utilized, and general information available on the specific company. Notes about marks are included in the history, collecting hints, or a marks section.

References: Reference books are listed whenever possible to encourage the collector to learn more about the category. Books are listed only if there is a substantial section on the specific category being considered. Included in the listing are author, title, publisher, (if published by a small firm or individual, we have indicated "privately printed"), and date of publication or most recent edition.

Some of the books listed may be out of print and no longer available from the publisher; these will usually be available in public libraries or through inter-library loan. Readers also may find antiques book dealers at antiques shows, flea markets, and advertised in trade papers and journals. Search services are another source for out-of-print books. Many dealers provide mail-order services. Since the second edition, the Internet is a new source for searching for hard-to-find books.

Periodicals: In addition to publications of collectors' clubs, there are numerous general-interest newspapers and magazines that devote considerable attention to pottery and porcelain. A sampling includes the following:

Antique Monthly, P.O. Drawer 2, Tuscaloosa, AL 35402

Antique Review, P.O. Box 538, Worthington, OH 43085

Antique Showcase, Amis Gibbs Publications, Ltd. Canfield, Ontario, Canada NOA1CO

Antique Trader Weekly, P.O. Box 1050, Dubuque, IA 52004

Antique Week, P.O. Box 90, Knightstown, IN 46148

Antiques and Collecting, 1006 S. Michigan Avenue, Chicago, IL 60605

Antiques and The Arts Weekly, 5 Church Hill Road, Newtown, CT 06470

Antiques (The Magazine Antiques), 551 Fifth Avenue, New York, NY 10017

China and Glass Quarterly, David & Linda Arman, P.O. Box 39, Portsmouth, RI 02871

Collector News, Box 156, Grundy Center, IA 50638

The Daze, P.O. Box 57, Otisville, MI 48463

Maine Antique Digest, P.O. Box 645, Waldboro, ME 04572

New York-Pennsylvania Collector, Drawer C, Fishers, NY 14453

Porcelain Collector's Companion, Dorothy Kamm, P.O. Box 7460, Port St. Lucie, FL 34985

Southern Antiques & Southeast Trader, P.O. Box 1550, Lake City, FL 32055

Warman's Today's Collector, 700 East State St., Iola, WI 54990

West Coast Peddler, P.O. Box 5134, Whittier, CA 90607

Museums: Museums are listed if significant collections in the category are on display. Many museums have large collections of pottery and/or porcelains, but did not provide a listing for inclusion in this book.

Collectors' Clubs: All collectors' clubs have been verified to be active. Addresses are listed for membership information. Some clubs have regional and local chapters. English clubs listed welcome American members.

Reproduction Alert: Where reproduction alerts are listed for a particular category, the collector should be extremely careful when purchasing examples. Some reproductions are unmarked; the newness of their appearance is often the best clue as a reproduction. We recommend strongly that collectors subscribe to Antique & Collectors Reproduction News, P.O. Box 12130, Des Moines, IA 50312-9403 to receive current information on reproductions. Antiques newspapers also provide news of reproductions when they appear in the marketplace.

Collecting Hints: This section calls attention to specific hints if they are applicable to a category. Clues also are given for spotting reproductions when known.

Additional Listings: When more than one category is covered by a specific listing, other listings are added to help the reader find additional information.

Marks: When pottery and porcelain ware are marked, we have included representative marks for that manufactory. However, to see the full range of marks used by a firm, one must consult one of the marks books listed in the bibliography.

Photographs: We have used representative photographs for each category. However, to see a full range of examples, one must consult one of the specialized books listed for that category.

DERIVATION OF PRICES USED

The majority of the prices listed in this book was derived from "on site" inspection which required a good deal of shoe leather and gasoline, but provided a realistic feel for what ceramics are selling for in the marketplace. The prices reflect what the collector should pay for an item, i.e. the retail price.

Antiques shops, antiques and flea markets, antiques shows and antiques malls from all sections of the country were a major source for prices. The explosion of antiques malls, as well as mega-malls in the last few years, has placed a large number of antiques under one roof; this allows for comparison shopping. Prices were also obtained from the smaller sized antiques shows, as well as major international expositions and other shows in varying ranges.

Auction houses located in the United States, London and the continent were a source for upper level ceramics, but were also useful for middle and lower range material in some instances. Specialized auctions have increased in number and provided pricing material for collectors with specific interests. Those pieces derived from auction houses are denoted with an (A) preceding the price in the listings and represent the actual hammer price along with the buyer's premium where applicable.

Antiques newspapers, antiques magazines, and antiques journals were a rich source of information. Antiques dealers' price lists, both generalized and specialized, were used extensively in deriving prices for numerous categories.

Since the second edition of this price guide, the Internet has become a major marketplace for buying and selling ceramics. Many dealers maintain Web sites with constantly changing inventories, and these sites were utilized for comparative pricing. Numbers of these sites located worldwide should expand significantly over the next few years and, as a result, a larger number of collectors will visit these sites to shop for their collections. It also allows for comparison shopping in the comfort of the home. Auction houses have also found the Web and are utilizing this media to supplement their printed catalogs. It may come to pass that a collector can build or add to a collection without ever leaving his or her home.

When conflicting prices occurred for similar pieces, an additional source was sought which included consulting with ceramics specialists to confirm or reject a specific item's value.

It is unlikely that the collector will be able to match exactly a specific piece with listings in this price guide. Each category represents a range of examples and prices from each manufactory. It should act as a *guide* to the collector, rather than an absolute determination of what a collector would have to pay to purchase a specific piece.

CONDITION OF WARES

Condition plays an important role in determining the value of ceramics. Porcelain and pottery from the early periods, i.e. 16th to 18th century, and rare pieces are less affected pricewise by condition than the more recent ceramic examples. One would be less concerned about missing fingers on a figure by the Meissen modeler Kaendler than by the same damage found on a 19th or 20th century Dresden "lace" figure. Availability is the key word.

Middle and lower priced pieces that are damaged should not be overlooked completely. In some cases, they may act as a "filler" piece for a collection until a better example becomes available. However, these damaged pieces should reflect a lower price than a fine example. The price should be directly proportional to the extent of the damage. As an example, tin-glazed earthenware often shows signs of wear along the rim. Glaze flakes in this area are to be expected. However, glaze flakes affecting the central design are less acceptable, even if they are smaller in diameter.

Outright chips also should be reflected by a lower price. Under-the-rim chips are more tolerable than those on the surface or at a margin. Major defects such as breaks, cracks, fades in the design, pieces missing (knobs, handles, covers, etc.) or heavy cuts in the glaze greatly diminish the value of a piece. Remember that an age crack is still a crack and should be treated as such. It is wiser to spend extra dollars to purchase the best examples available.

Repaired examples should be evaluated critically. A reglued handle detracts considerably from the value of a piece. A professionally restored handle may be more acceptable to the collector. Casual examination of a piece may not show the location or extent of a repair.

Changes in the glaze, brilliance, and texture and slight variations in the decorative colors are often signs of a repair. By examining the inside of a hollow figure, a repaired fracture may be quite visible since inside cosmetics were often overlooked during inferior restorations. It behooves the buyer to examine a piece carefully under a strong light or black light before purchasing the piece since repaired merchandise is difficult to return when discovered at a later time.

THE CARE AND FEEDING OF CERAMICS

Ceramics by nature are fragile and should be treated with the utmost care. Dirt and dust are natural enemies to all ceramics and should be removed whenever encountered. The natural impulse is to plunge the dirty object into a sinkful of hot, sudsy water and give it a good "once-over." This is the wrong procedure to follow. Care was used in selecting this piece; care should also be used in the cleaning process.

Visual examination of the piece is the first step. Check for obvious repairs, hairline cracks, and crazing, as these factors require additional care when cleaning the piece. It is important to know what the piece is made of, as this also controls the method of cleaning. Unglazed ceramics are washed differently than glazed examples.

Set aside a work area that is uncluttered and near running water. A textured towel makes a good work surface and adds support for the piece. Remove loose dirt and dust with a soft brush, such as an artist's brush. Never use a stiff brush since this can disturb surface decorations. Proceed slowly and carefully, especially around projections and handles. A good portion of the grime can be removed in this manner. In addition, pieces with hairlines will less likely soak up dirt when the washing process starts.

A solution of mild soap in lukewarm water with ammonia (1 oz. of ammonia to 10 ozs. of water) is an ideal working solution. Enough soap should be added to bring forth suds. Cotton swabs or balls dipped into the solution and applied gently to the surface will loosen and remove years of grime. Stains such as grease and unknown stains should be approached with caution.

On vertical pieces such as figures, begin at the top and work toward the base. Constantly change the wash water, as it tends to become dirty with use. Continually rinse away the soapy solution using clean water and cotton swabs. Never use abrasive materials such as scouring or soap pads or harsh detergents. Unglazed ceramics such as earthenware and bisque should be wiped with moist, soft swabs.

Though the dishwasher is a handy device for commercial dishware, it is a not a friend to early ceramics. Hot water and strong detergents can dissolve water soluble glue joints and remove surface decorations. Pieces with metal bases should not be immersed in water. This is true especially for ormolu.

Never use bleach. This material is harmful to certain types of decoration. In addition, bleach can cause a stain to spread rather dramatically. Dry pieces with equal care using cotton swabs or linen towels. A hair dryer can be a handy tool for getting into hard to reach areas. If stains are persistent, are of unknown origin, or if a glue joint separates, it is wise to consult a professional restorer.

Once the pieces are clean, storage is the next consideration. Certain precautions apply. All pieces must be dried thoroughly before storing. When stacking plates, always keep the same sizes and shapes together. Tissue or felt should separate each plate. Cups should be hung from plastic-coated hooks or stored individually. Never stack cups or bowls since this tends to damage surface decorations.

Plate hangers serve a purpose, but should be used with discretion. Always use the proper size. Too large a hanger will not support the piece properly. Hangers that are too small put excessive pressure on a piece. Wrap the wire projections in plastic tubing. This helps protect the rim glaze.

For additional hints on the care of ceramics, consult one of the following books: Frieda Kay Fall, *Art Objects: Their Care and Preservation,* Museum Publications, 1967; Albert Jackson & David Day, *The Antiques Care & Repair Handbook*, Alfred A. Knopf, 1984; Judith Larney, *Restoring Ceramics,* Watson-Guptill Publications, 1975; Judith Miller, *Care & Repair of Everyday Treasures: A Step-By-Step Guide to Cleaning & Restoring Your Antiques & Collectibles,* Putnam Pub Group, 1997; Mette Tang Simpson, Ed. & Michael Huntley, Ed. *Sotheby's Caring for Antiques: A Guide to Handling, Cleaning, Display and Restoration,* Antique Collectors' Club, Ltd. 1996; V.P. Wright, *Pamper Your Possessions,* Barre Publishers, 1972.

STATE OF THE MARKET

After several years of relative inactivity, it appears that there is some new life in the antiques ceramics field. Dealers are reporting "modest" sales across the board, which is not just designer driven as has been the case in the recent past, but rather caused by new collectors entering the field and existing collectors adding to their collections under the star of a relatively strong economy. Fortunately, some of this spendable income is being directed toward the acquisition of English and continental pottery and porcelains.

The mid to late 1990s found a decided lack of upper-level material such as Vincennes, St. Cloud, Nantgarw, and museum quality Meissen, Sevres, and Vienna, which was so prevalent during the buying spree of the 1980s. Much of this caliber material now resides in collections and those few examples that do come up for auction, are selling at or above their pre-auction estimates. A Nantgarw plate featuring birds at a fountain sold at an eastern auction for $2,702, nearly ten times the pre-auction estimate. A large collection of pate-sur-pate drew an international audience with a monumental Louis Solon decorated Minton vase walking off with an astounding $55,200 hammer price. Quality continues to sell well, but quality is scarce.

Art Deco ceramics continue to capture the spotlight. This is probably due to the crossover effect of Art Deco collectors vying for the same examples that excite ceramics collectors. Susie Cooper, Charlotte Rhead, and Clarice Cliff have all been the subject of specialized auctions at Christie's South Kensington in England. Clarice Cliff material was highlighted by a small, conical "Orange Roof" pattern sugar sifter that went to a collector for $3,040, and another sifter in the "Orange Tree and House" pattern that crossed the block at $3,387. Amazing prices for pieces that stand about 5 1/2" high! Complete coffee and tea services potted by Susie Cooper Enterprises also sold well, though incomplete and slightly damaged examples did not fare as well.

While Art Deco ceramics are selling well, the same is not true for their cousins in the Art Nouveau category. This once popular material has remained fairly dormant, and Amphora, Teplitz, Goldscheider, and Royal Dux are often passed when brought up for consideration at auction. The shelf life is also fairly long for these categories, as antiques dealers report very spotty sales for these manufactories.

One of the new categories added to the third edition is Burleigh Ware jugs, which has really jumped in popularity. The large variety of sizes, shapes, colors, and subjects have attracted an enthusiastic following, and these pieces rarely remain unsold for extended periods of time. Prices should continue to climb for better examples, especially those with crossover appeal such as the Tennis Player example.

Another darling of collectors is the seemingly endless variety of Chintz china that has captured the fancy of collectors and decorators alike. Chintz china rose rapidly in price once it was discovered by collectors and, for the most part, has remained at this high level. Dealers who specialize in Chintz report fairly strong and constant sales, especially for unusual patterns, shapes, and combinations such as stackable teapots and complete breakfast sets. Prices are still stable for ordinary patterns and shapes, and this has tended to draw new collectors into the field. Beginning collectors often become advanced collectors, and the relatively small quantity of the unusual pieces may drive prices even higher. This is one field that bears watching.

The untimely death of Princess Diana has seen a wealth of commemorative ceramics hit the market. Future gains are highly unlikely for these new pieces, but dealers are finding an eager market for older examples such as wedding objects that featured the Princess. How long this fascination will last and what effect it will have on the original pieces bears watching.

Blue and white appears to be the colors of choice in the transfer printed ceramics field. Dealers are reporting strong sales of Historic Staffordshire featuring American views, Blue Onion, and the always popular Romantic Staffordshire. Flow Blue is fairly stable with early patterns and unusual forms selling much better than later Victorian examples.

One area that continues to remain stagnant is that of Staffordshire figures that were so popular during the 1980s. Part of this is due to the large number of reproductions that have flooded the market; buyers are tending to shy away from these pieces. A few exceptions occurred when rarer forms came up for consideration. An unusual bocage group of a hunter, dog, and bird sold recently for $5,980, but, for the most part, these figural groups sell in the three-figure range or are passed. As a result, there are bargains to be had. Knowledge is the key to success in this area.

Quite the opposite is true for 18th century Wedgwood and the popular Fairyland luster. Wedgwood and Bentley examples are very strong, and dealers handling Wedgwood feel that this strength is indicative of the quality and rarity of the material. An example of Wedgwood's popularity was found in the hammer price of $19,950 for a dessert plate from the Frog Service of Catherine the Great. In the same price range was a three-color jasper and crystal candelabra that found a buyer for $13,800. Both were sold as part of the successful Skinner auction of the Kanter collection.

Folk art ceramics are also showing well. Though Quimper has plateaued at a very high level, well-potted examples continue to find buyers. Mocha and spatter are showing strength as witnessed by an Earthworm pattern wash basin that sold for a record $11,500, and a Rainbow spatter pitcher that crossed the auction block for $14,850. Well-colored pieces and unusual forms and designs are very "hot" at present and should continue for the next few years. This was apparent when the Harlan Miller collection was offered by the Conestoga Auction Company. Good examples are fairly rare and when they do come into the marketplace, price does not seem to be a factor.

Though there is a large amount of Czechoslovakian material available, and most of it is waiting to be discovered, the artist signed hand painted examples are much in demand. These brightly colored Art Deco pieces should continue their upward trend as more and more collectors discover this material.

Boxed lots of Austrian, Czechoslovakian, and Bavarian dinnerware continue to be one of the best kept secrets on the market. Many of these incomplete sets are selling in the three-figure range—a far cry from what new dinnerware place settings are commanding. Some of these sets can be augmented by using replacement services or by haunting antiques show and markets for elusive serving pieces. Whatever the scenario, this quality porcelain has graced many a table and should continue to do so in the future.

Part Two:

Pottery and Porcelain Listings

Abbreviations used in the listings

C	century
circ	circular
d	diameter
dbl	double
dtd	dated
emb	embossed
ftd	footed
ground	background
h	height
H-H	handle to handle
hex	hexagonal
horiz	horizontal
irid	iridescent
irreg	irregular
l	length
med	medium
mtd	mounted
mts	mounts
#	numbered
no.	pattern number
oct.	octagonal
pr	pair
prs	pairs
rect	rectangular
sgd	signed
SP	silver plated
sq	square
vert	vertical
w	width

ABC AND MAXIM WARE

Staffordshire, England and Continental, 19th Century

History: Nineteenth century English ABC plates from Staffordshire are not considered great works of art, but are quite collectible. They were made in soft paste by many potteries, most of whom did not mark the plates with a factory mark.

ABC plates were designed to teach a child letters and numbers. In addition, knowledge of important people, places, or things also was transmitted via these plates at mealtimes.

ABC plates were made in 44 different sizes, ranging from 4 inches to the large size of approximately 9 inches. Usually the alphabet was on the rim of the plate, either applied (transferred) or embossed (raised). The center of the plate usually had a scene of people, domestic or wild animals, birds, sports, occupations, places, months, military, Indians or some other type of design transferred onto it.

When the picture was transferred to the plate and fired, the basic color was added as well. When additional colors were used, the plate had to be fired one or more additional times depending on the number of colors.

ABC plates also were made in Braille for the blind child. These are quite rare today.

Some English ABC plates were marked with the diamond British Registry mark from 1812-1883, while some marks were transferred, stamped, or pressed onto the soft paste.

English Staffordshire soft paste alphabet mugs are difficult to find in perfect condition. Mugs were cylindrical with a thick wall. Usually two or three consecutive letters appeared with transfer illustrations. Some mugs had a capital and lower case letter with an illustration. Others had just one letter that was used to begin a short verse. Very few mugs were marked. Subjects included animals, children, birds, rhymes, and stories, and just letters of the alphabet with an illustration.

Benjamin Franklin's *Poor Richard's Almanac* was the source for many of the maxims and moral lessons used on maxim ware. Biblical passages and nursery rhymes also were used on these plates to present a message to the child.

Plates are most frequently encountered. Teapots, cups, bowls, and porringers also carried lessons for the young. Most of the maxims were illustrated with transfer printed pictures that helped make the lesson more palatable. Some were hand painted, but most were multicolored transfers. The same maxim or rhyme frequently was illustrated by various manufacturers, each using a slightly different drawing.

Manufacture of ABC plates and cups began about 1890 in Germany, much later than in England. The examples were made in hard paste and were thinner and whiter than the Staffordshire pieces. Decals were used in place of transfers on the German wares. The alphabet was usually embossed and sometimes trimmed with gilt. Subjects included chickens, cats, animals, and people.

References: Mildred & Joseph P. Chalala, *A Collector's Guide to Plates, Mugs & Things,* Pridemark Press, 1980; Irene & Ralph Lindsay, *ABC Plates & Mugs,* Collector Books, 1997.

Collectors' Clubs: *ABC Collector's Circle,* Joan M. George, 67 Stevens Avenue, Old Bridge, NJ 08857, $25 per year for quarterly newsletter.

Collecting Hints: Interest in ABC plates has increased dramatically in the past five to ten years. Make certain the transfers are in good to very good condition. Avoid pieces that are seriously cracked or crazed.

Bowl, 5 5/8" d, multicolored transfers of reindeer, hen, parrot, soldier, children, and basket of vegetables in center, multicolored alphabet border, Austria 28.00

Mug

2 1/8" h, "Franklin's Maxim-Slough Like Rust Consumes Faster Than Labor Wears," black transfer 165.00

2 1/4" h, PQR, child flying kite, blue transfer 98.00

2 3/8" h

"G was a gamester" and "H was a hunter," blue transfer with red and yellow accents, hairline 200.00

Q & R, teacher quizzing students or reverend blessing child, purple transfer with green and blue accents 135.00

2 1/2" h

Children sitting at table in cartouche, letters "G" and "H," red transfer, (A) 116.00

E & F, red letters, black transfers of man holding lion's paw or friar with Christ, tan ground 110.00

"Franklin's Maxim-Little Strokes Fell Great Oaks," man with ax, blue-gray transfer 155.00

2 3/4" h

Bird perched on branch, printed alphabet on side, brown transfer with blue accents 245.00

"K's a Kitten that plays with a ball," black transfer. 185.00

Letter V and vulture in forest setting, green transfer 200.00

2 7/8" h, DEF letters and children playing shuttlecock, pink transfer 165.00

Plate

4" d, green accented emb griffin in center, raised alphabet border, c1810 . 350.00

5" d

Children playing with marbles, black transfer, pink rim, raised alphabet border, chip 165.00

Conundrum, 3 boys catching same fish, answer on reverse, black transfer, blue and green accents, raised alphabet border 385.00

Franklin's Proverbs, "Silks and Satins," room setting center design, red, green, blue, and yellow, raised alphabet border 150.00

Two men and 2 women seated at table, multicolored, raised alphabet border 165.00

5 1/8" d, boy selling newspaper, red transfer, raised alphabet border 75.00

5 3/16" d, woman and children having picnic, black transfer, red, green, yellow, and blue accents, raised alphabet border, (A). 70.00

5 1/4" d

Franklin's Proverbs

"He That By The Plow Would Thrive Himself Must Either Hold Or Drive," man behind 2 horses plowing, black transfer with red and blue accents, raised alphabet border, green lined rim 225.00

"Three Removes Are As Bad As A Fire, A Rolling Stone Gathers No Moss," woman seated in wagon with belongings, man loading wagon, black transfer with blue, red, and yellow accents, raised alphabet border, red lined rim 225.00

"The Sentinel," boy sleeping on drum, dog at side, black transfer, raised alphabet border, red rim with raised loop design 275.00

5 3/8" d

Franklin's Proverbs, "Three Removes are as bad as a fire," black transfer with polychrome accents, raised alphabet border, "imp Meakin" mark, (A). 135.00

"Pretty Polly," black, blue, red, green, and yellow, raised alphabet border 185.00

"Stilt Walking," black transfer with polychrome accents, raised alphabet border, "imp Meakin" mark, (A) . . . 135.00

5 1/2" d

"Franklin's Maxim, Constant Dropping Wears Away Stone And Little Strokes Fell Great Oaks," boy chopping tree, black transfer with green, red, and blue accents, molded leaf border, green lined rim. 95.00

"Ready For A Ride," 2 children in buggy, multicolored, raised alphabet border 145.00

5 5/8" d

"Brighton Beach Pavillion," red transfer, raised alphabet border . 235.00

Franklin's Maxim, black transfer of "He that by the plow," emb floral border, red lined rim, "BW & CO." mark 85.00

5 3/4" d, "The Blind Girl," multicolored, raised alphabet border 150.00

5 7/8" d

"Harry Baiting Is His Line, For To Fish He Doth Recline," brown transfer with red, yellow, and blue accents, raised alphabet border, "imp Elsmore & Son" mark 169.00

"Zebra Hunt," 2 hunters chasing horses, black transfer with green, tan, blue, and red accents, raised alphabet border 145.00

6" d

Brown transfer of 2 girls with hurdy gurdy or tambourine, gold skirt, red skirt, green base, raised alphabet border, "imp Edge Malkin" mark 155.00

"Catch It Carlo When I Throw & Bring It To Me Ere We Go," 2 children and dog, multicolored, raised alphabet border. 195.00

James Garfield, blue transfer, raised alphabet border 110.00

"Royal Standard," military raising of flag, brown, green, red, and orange, raised alphabet border, "imp Edge Malkin" mark, c1875. . . . . . . 165.00

Transfer of dog in center, Braille alphabet border, unmkd 45.00

"That Girl Wants The Puppy Away But Its Mother's Looks Say Nay," black transfer with green and red accents, raised alphabet border, "ELSMORE and FORSTER" mark 195.00

6 1/16" d

Comic scene of black man baking and "Why Would This Pastry Chef Make

Plate, 6 3/8" d, red transfer, "imp Adams" mark, $185.

Plate, 6 7/8" d, magenta, brown, and green transfer, raised alphabet border, $145.

A Good Soldier?" reverse with "Because He Seems To Stand The Fire Well," black transfer with blue and green accents, raised alphabet border, red lined rim, (A) 190.00

Shepherd and dog, black transfer with red, yellow, and green accents, raised alphabet border, red lined rim, (A). 120.00

6 1/8" d, "Archery," black transfer with yellow, blue, and green accents, raised alphabet border, red lined rim, (A)110.00

6 3/16" d, "President Abraham Lincoln," black transfer with blue, yellow, and green accents, raised alphabet border, (A). 520.00

6 1/4" d

"Franklin's Proverbs, Keep Thy Shop and Thy Shop Will Keep Thee," multicolored transfer of storekeep and stores, raised floral border, green lined rim, c1851. . . . . 150.00

Pink, yellow, and green floral decal in center, raised alphabet border, gold striped rim, (A). 35.00

"Sign Language," green transfer, dk red inner line border, raised alphabet border, "Aynsley & Co. Longton" mark. 295.00

6 3/8" d, "AESOP'S FABLES-THE COCK AND THE FOX," black transfer with green and red accents, printed alphabet border. 275.00

6 5/8" d

"A Sioux Indian Chief," brown transfer, raised alphabet border 175.00

Comic scene of man in suit wading, fox hunt in bkd, red transfer, raised alphabet border, hairline, (A) . 100.00

6 11/16" d, "Brighton Beach Bathing Pavillion," red, brown, green, and blue 100.00

6 3/4" d

Hex, "Franklin's Maxims, Want of Care does us more damage Than want of Knowledge," multicolored transfer,

raised flowerheads on border, red rope rim 155.00

Two men on horseback in hunt scene, blue transfer, raised alphabet border, (A) 88.00

6 7/8" d

Children in runaway dog cart, blue transfer, raised alphabet border 195.00

Riders on jumping horses, blue transfer, raised alphabet border 125.00

7" d

Christmas scene of Santa, tree, angel and donkey, raised alphabet border, c1880 . . . . 165.00

"February," man with ax, brown transfer, raised alphabet border . 170.00

"Horses for Sale or Hire," barn and sign, multicolored, raised alphabet border. 185.00

"How Glorious is Our Heavenly King Who Reins Above the Sky, How Shall a Child Presume To Sing His Dreadful Majesty," child kneeling and praying, angels overhead, black transfer with blue, green, red accents, red striped rim, raised alphabet border. 168.00

"January," man with sheep, multicolored, raised alphabet border 170.00

Multicolored transfer of mother duck wearing hat, holding baby duck, yellow alphabet border, "Wood & Sons" mark 16.00

"Nursery Rhymes, Old Mother Hubbard," multicolored transfer, blue printed alphabet border 95.00

"Oriental Hotel," black transfer, raised alphabet border 120.00

"Playing at Lovers," boy and girl dressed as adults, black transfer with red, green, and yellow accents, raised alphabet border. 195.00

"Poor Richard's Proverbs," plough in center, "Plough deep while sluggers sleep and you shall have corn to sell and keep," red transfer, raised alphabet border 140.00

Rooster and chicks, multicolored transfer, raised alphabet border . . 45.00

"Swing, Swong," boy on swing, multicolored transfer, raised alphabet border. 195.00

"The Village Blacksmith," multicolored, raised alphabet border. 135.00

Two children feeding geese, black transfer with blue, brown, red, and green accents, raised alphabet border 200.00

7 1/8" d, "Paul and Virginia," multicolored transfer, raised alphabet border 125.00

7 3/16" d, "Nations of the World, Japanese," brown transfer, blue, yellow, and red accents 110.00

Plate, 7 1/8" d, brown transfer, blue accents, British reg. mark, $195.

7 1/4" d
"Bible Pictures, The Destruction of Pharaoh," brown printed scene and alphabet with polychrome accents 195.00
Brown jaguar in green foliage, brown transfer printed alphabet borde r 195.00
"Crusoe Rescues Friday," brown transfer with green, brown, blue accents, "B.P.Co." mark 165.00
"Look Not Into God's Decrees But Into His Commandments," pink transfer, raised alphabet border 185.00
"Nations of the World, Greek," brown transfer with blue, yellow, and brown accents. 145.00
"Nations of the World, Wallachian," brown transfer, figure wearing blue cloak. 165.00
"Nursery Tales, Little Jack Horner," 8 sided cartouche, brown printed alphabet 300.00
"RED RIDING HOOD AND HER SUPPOSED GRANDMOTHER," brown transfer with red, yellow, and blue accents, brown printed alphabet border, "B.P.Co." mark. 235.00
Two horsemen and brick wall, purple transfer, raised alphabet border 169.00
Walking elephant, blue transfer, raised alphabet border 230.00
7 3/8" d
"Crusoe at Work," brown transfer with blue and yellow accents, brown printed alphabet border 225.00
"Crusoe Finding The Foot Prints," brown transfer with multicolored center, brown printed alphabet border 225.00
"Oriental Hotel," red, brown, green, and blue, raised alphabet border 75.00
7 1/2" d
"Aesop's Fables, The Fox and the Grapes," green, brown, maroon,

and purple, printed alphabet borde 225.00
"Boy and Pony," red transfer, black alphabet transfer on border, (A) 125.00
Boy with mandolin, bird on fence, red transfer, raised alphabet border, c1860. . . . . 155.00
"Chinonca Watching The Departure Of The Cavalcade," brown transfer, raised alphabet border 185.00
Diamond shaped center with "Horses For Hire," brown transfer with blue, green, and red accents, raised alphabet border 165.00
"Dost Thou Love Life Then Do Not Squander Time There Will be Sleeping Enough in the Grave," men drinking outside tavern, brown, pink, and green, raised alphabet border, magenta lined rim, c1880s 195.00
Leopard crouched on branch, green and brown, printed borde r 180.00
Man hunting on foot with gun and dogs, brown transfer, raised alphabet border, c1890 . . . . 155.00
Polychrome scene of "Marine Railway Station, Manhattan Beach," raised alphabet border 175.00
Rider falling off of horse, red transfer, raised alphabet border 185.00
Train emerging from tunnel, multicolored, raised alphabet border 145.00
Two little girls with lambs, blue transfer, raised and printed alphabet border, red lined rim 120.00
Two seated children eating grapes, blue transfer, raised alphabet border 145.00
7 5/8" d, "Iron Pier Length 1000 Feet. West Brighton Beach," brown transfer with red, blue, and green accents, raised alphabet border 245.00
7 3/4" d
Calendar and clock design, blue transfer, "Charles Allerton & Sons" mark, c1890. . . . . 145.00
"F's For The Fowls And The Farm...," scene of animals inside barn, blue transfer, raised alphabet border 185.00
"The Golden Crested Wren," yellow, blue, green, and white, raised alphabet border 210.00
7 7/8" d, "Young Artist," brown transfer with green, blue, and yellow accents, brown printed alphabet border 120.00
8" d
"American Sports," "Base Ball-Out On The Third Base," green transfer, raised alphabet border 395.00
"Experience Keeps A Dear School, But Fools Will Learn In Other," multicol-

ored, magenta lined inner border, raised alphabet border. . . . 195.00
Man whipping horse, multicolored, raised alphabet border. 175.00
8 1/8" d, polychrome scene of boy on waterfall, raised alphabet border 150.00
8 1/4" d
"Crusoe at Work," brown transfer with yellow and blue accents, "B.P. & Co. Tunstall" mark 110.00
Fox and goose, multicolored transfer, raised alphabet border. 120.00
Man climbing on horse in diamond center, brown transfer, raised alphabet border. 225.00
Organ grinder and 3 children, blue transfer, raised alphabet border, c1860 . . . . 155.00
8 5/16" d, "Crusoe Viewing The Island," brown transfer with orange and blue accents, printed alphabet border 150.00
8 1/2" d
Diamond center with child painting, artists on border, brown transfer with green and red accents, raised alphabet border 168.00
Hunter, fox, and horse, green, red, and brown, raised alphabet border 150.00

ADAMS

Burslem, Staffordshire, England 1770 to Present

The Adams family established themselves in Burslem. The first potter was William Adams, but this name was used repeatedly throughout the Adams' history. Eventually there were Adams potteries in seven different locations. Most of the potteries, if they marked their works, simply used the name "Adams."

William Adams Brick House, Burslem and Cobridge 1770-c1820

He produced blue–printed wares with chinoiserie patterns early in the 1780s. They were probably not marked. Two of his potteries were lent to other potters among whom were James and Ralph Clews in 1817.

William Adams
Greengates, Tunstall,
c1779-1805 (1809)

Blue–printed wares were made. They were the first pottery in Tunstall to do so. William died in 1805, but the works were continued by trustees. Benjamin, his son, took over in 1809.

William Adams
Stoke-on Trent
1804-1819

Large quantities of blue and white transfer wares were made both for the home market and for export to America. In 1810, William, his son, joined the partnership and three other sons joined soon after. The company was then called "William Adams & Sons."

Benjamin Adams
Greengates, Tunstall,
1809-1820

Benjamin used the impressed mark "B. Adams." He continued making blue-printed wares.

William Adams and Sons
Stoke-on Trent
1819 to Present

William Adams died in 1829; William, his eldest son, took over. In 1834, the Greenfield pottery was added to the firm. The Stoke factory was closed in 1863. The Greengates pottery was added to the group in 1858. William Adams joined the Wedgwood Group in 1966.

Adam's Rose
1820s-1830s

This pattern was named for its maker William Adams & Sons of Stoke-on-Trent. It consisted of a border of large red roses with green leaf sprigs on a white ground.

G. Jones & Son, England, produced a variation known as "Late Adam's Rose." The colors were not as brilliant. The background was a "dirty" white.

References: A.W. Coysh, *Blue-Printed Earthenware 1800-1850,* David & Charles, 1972.

Bowl, 6 1/4" d, Calyx Ware, blue and iron red floral in center, 3 floral sprays on inner border, blue lined center, shaped rim with gilt dentil margin 15.00

Chamber Pot, 2 1/2" d, green and red Adam's Rose design, scalloped rim, (A). 330.00

Coffee Pot, 12" h, red and green stenciled sprigs, white ground, black trimmed knob, handle, and spout, c1810 . . . . 675.00

Coffee Server, 9 1/2" h, "Cries of London-New Mackeral" 300.00

Creamer, 5 3/8" h, scene of 3 people in front of English buildings, dk blue transfer, wishbone handle, "imp Adams" mark, (A)
. . . . 165.00

Cup and Saucer
Green and red Adam's Rose design, black stripe on rims, (A) 140.00
"The Sower" pattern, red transfers, c1830
. . . . 55.00

Cup and Saucer, Miniature, beehive design, brown transfers 75.00

Dinner Service, 8 plates, 9 1/8" d, 8 plates, 8" d, 8 plates, 7 1/8" d, 8 plates, 6" d, 8 fruit dishes, 5 3/4" d, 8 butter chips, 3 3/16" d, 8 cups and saucers, gravy boat, rect vegetable dish, 7 5/8" l x 5 1/2" w, rect vegetable dish, 8 1/4" l x 6" w, 2 rect vegetable dishes, 9 1/8" l x 6 5/8" w, 2 vegetable dishes, 10 1/8" l x 7 5/8" w, 2 rect platters, 11" l x 8 1/8" w, rect platter, 14 1/4" l x 11 1/8" w, oct cov vegetable dish, 9 7/8" H-H, oriental pattern, blue transfers, chips and hairlines, (A) 950.00

Dish, 6" H-H x 3 3/4" w, rect, "Cries of London-Ten Bunches a Penny Primrose"
. . . . 50.00

Mustard Pot, 2 1/4" h x 3 3/4" d, straight sides, green and red Adam's Rose design, shaped handle, (A) 1,705.00

Pitcher
4" h, Calyx Ware, red stylized flowerheads and green stylized leaves, pale blue ground, band of red crisscross on border. 45.00
5" d, green and red Adam's Roses design, scalloped rim, (A) 110.00

Pitcher, 9 1/2" h, "Calyx Ware," gilt outlined purple flowers, rust trim, purple feather on spout, cream ground, $75.

Pitcher, 7 1/2" h, "Standing Rock Picturesque, Wisconsin Dells" and "The Narrows, Wisconsin Dells" on reverse, multicolored transfers, $75.

4 1/8" h, "Cries of London-Ten Bunches a Penny Primroses" 55.00
5 1/8" h, "Cries of London-A New Love Song Hapenny A Piece" 100.00
5 3/8" h, "Mr. Bumble and Mrs. Corney taking tea" and "Mrs. Gummidge casts a damp on our departure," green transfers with blue, yellow, red, and green accents, gold pearlized accents on collar and handle and orange striping, "Illustrations From David Copperfield, Dickens, Made in Great Britain" and "Adams, England" marks, chip on spout
. . . . 75.00
6 1/8" h, center green jasper type band with white cameos of classic figures separated by hanging arches, top dk green band with molded leaves, base with band of diamonds, cream ground
. . . . 115.00
7" h
Green and red Adam's Rose design, shaped handle, (A) 358.00
Ironstone, white with ribbed base, "Minuet" pattern, black transfer of girl on bridge on sides, "Real English Ironstone, Wm Adams & Sons Minuet" mark 85.00
9" h, "Marriage and Engagement" design, black transfer 695.00
9 1/2" h, lobed body, green, red, and blue Adam's Rose design 390.00

Plate
6 7/8" d, green and red Adam's Rose design, scalloped rim with molded beaded band, "imp Adams" mark, (A) 75.00
7 1/4" d, red, blue, green, and brown floral center, green basketweave border, "Adam's Tunstall" mark, (A) 45.00
8" d
"English Scenic" pattern, 3 cows and castle, brown transfer 28.00

Green and red Adam's Rose design, scalloped rim with molded beaded band, "imp Adams" mark, pr, (A) 120.00

8 1/2" d

Oct

"Cries of London-Do You Want Any Matches" 40.00

"Cries of London-Strawberrys Scarlet Strawberrys" 69.00

"Oliver Twist-Oliver Amazed At The Dodger Mode of Going To Work," green transfer with orange and yellow accents 40.00

Red, green, and black Adam's Rose design, "imp Adams" mark, (A) 40.00

"The Sea" pattern, red transfer 80.00

8 7/8" d, people in boat on lake, English villa and trees in bkd, dk blue transfer, "imp Adams" mark, ft rim chip (A) 248.00

9" d

"Shakespeare Series-Sir John Falstaff," black transfer with blue and green accents, orange border 32.00

Titian Ware, "Brocade" pattern, border of orange flowerheads, blue, purple, and yellow leaves 18.00

9 1/8" d, Calyx Ware, sm pink flowerhead in center, sm purple and mauve scattered flowers, border of pink swags, pink diamond design rim 22.00

9 1/4" d, 2 turbaned men in foreground, middle eastern city in bkd, bunches of flowers on border, dk pink transfer, shaped rim, "imp Adams" mark 85.00

9 1/2" d, green and red Adam's Rose design, plain scalloped rim, unmkd, (A) 85.00

10" d

"Italian Scenery" pattern, 2 men in gondola, woman seated on shore, castle in bkd, gray transfer with red and green accents, relief molded pinecones and leaves on border, cream ground, gilt lined rim 19.00

Titian Ware, HP poppy design . . 55.00

Twelve sides, Calyx Ware, HP floral and leaf spray on lt green ground, red fishscale border 20.00

10 1/4" d, green and red Adam's Rose design, scalloped rim with molded beaded band,(A) 165.00

10 3/8" d, "Cherub" pattern, pr of flying putti in center, dk blue transfer, "imp Adams Warranted Staffordshire and eagle" mark, (A) 310.00

10 1/2" d

"Cries of London-Turnips and Carrots" 50.00

Green and red Adam's Rose design, scalloped rim with molded beaded

band, "imp 20/Adams" mark, pr, (A) 220.00

10 3/4" d, "Cries of London-Knives, Scissors, and Razors to Grind" 55.00

Platter

13 11/8" l, Titianware, pink luster band of leaves, border of molded fruit and leaves 175.00

13 3/8" l x 11 1/4" w, green and red Adam's Rose design, scalloped rim with molded beaded band, "imp Adams" mark, (A) 550.00

13 1/2" l, "The Sea" pattern, red transfer 330.00

14" l, Calyx Ware, "Carolynn" pattern 75.00

15 1/2" l x 12 /8" w, blue molded beaded, acanthus, and palm design rim, "imp Adams, Warranted Staffordshire and eagle" mark,(A) 85.00

20" l x 16 1/2" w, green and red Adam's Rose design, scalloped rim, "imp Adams" mark, (A) 1,320.00

Soup Plate, 8 5/8" d, blue-gray print of steam powered sailing ship in center, blue int band, 2 blue bands on rim 210.00

Teabowl and Saucer, red flower with green leaves, blue buds, black stripe on rim, "imp Adams" mark, chips, (A) 65.00

Teapot

7" h, Titian Ware, bulbous shape, band of dk red, purple, and blue flowers and green leaves on top and lid, green lined rims and handle, green and tan knob, cream ground 35.00

7 3/4" h, "Sharon" pattern, sheet design of clovers, brown transfer 65.00

Tumbler, 3 1/2" h, "Cries of London-Do You Want Any Matches" 35.00

Vegetable Bowl, 8 3/4" d, "Mazara" pattern, "William Adams & Sons" mark 20.00

AMPHORA

Turn-Teplitz, Bohemia
1892 to Present

History: Hans and Carl Riessner, Rudolf Kessel and Edward Stellmacher started the Amphora Porzellan Fabrik in 1892 for the manufacture of earthenware and porcelain. This pottery was established at Turn-Teplitz, Bohemia (now the Czech Republic). It produced mostly porcelain figures and Art Nouveau styled vases that were widely exported. Many of the wares

were hand decorated. They marked their wares with a variety of stamps, some incorporating the name and location of the pottery with a shield or a crown.

Edward Stellmacher left Amphora to start his own company from 1905-1912. The factory was then named "Riessner & Kessel Amphora Werke" until Kessel left in 1910. When Carl died in 1911, it left Hans Riessner as the sole proprietor. World War I and the Depression affected the company as it decreased in size, and finally faded out during World War II.

They used the Art Nouveau style on their original forms and decorations. Molded animals were applied to the vases in the form of leopards, panthers, frogs, salamanders, lions, various birds, alligators, monkeys, bats, mice, and elephants. Vases depicting sea life were some of their best works. Paul Dachsel and Alfred Stellmacher were excellent designers for Amphora. Portrait vases were also made. A tremendous variety of glazes was utilized.

After World War I, there were less designs and glaze experimentation. Stoneware pieces were made with hard enamel designs using Egyptian or Art Deco motifs. Before WWI, Bohemia was part of the Austro-Hungarian empire so that the name "Austria" may have been used as part of the mark. After WWII, the name "Czechoslovakia" may be part of the mark.

The Amphora Pottery Works was only one of a number of firms that was located in Teplitz, an active pottery center at the turn of the century.

Museum: Antiken Museum, Basel, Switzerland.

Basket

4" h x 7 1/2" l, gold textured ground and center overhead handle, green relief molded leaves and blue-green grapes on side 175.00

9" h, red and white enamel dot cartouche with red and yellow enamel flowerheads and green leaves on med blue ground on side, dk blue textured ground, 2 med blue wing side handles, overhead handle with swirls. 325.00

Box, 6" d x 6" h, relief molded poppies, mauve, tan, and lt green textured ground, gilt trim, flower bud knob 340.00

Ewer

5 1/2" h, yellow stylized roses, pink teardrops, green leaves, band of blue centered yellow daisies on rose red band, 2 cream bands, rose red handle, gold outlined rim, imp mark 225.00

8" h, Egyptian, center medallion of lt and dk brown bust of Egyptian, lt and dk blue enamel cartouche, med blue ground with yellow Egyptian birds, dk blue trim 425.00

Figure

12" l, figural tan curled leaf with gold swirled edge, figural green to cream shaded rooster with gold head and tail 385.00

12 3/4" h x 13 1/4" l, standing work horse with molded harness and collar, gold tones, "imp crown, Amphora in oval, and Austria in oval" mark, (A) 230.00

14" l, gray, blue, and pink gloss glazed game bird, rosy base, "Blue oval Amphora-Made in Czechoslovakia" mark 750.00

15 3/4" h, standing woman holding pitcher in hand, bowl on head, dk green and gold trimmed flowing classical robe, gold accents, circ base, "imp Austria, Amphora, crown and 4941/38" mark, (A) 180.00

Pitcher

6 3/4" h, pink, blue, and green floral garland, raised gold basket with cascading pink roses hanging from blue and green floral wreath, raised matte olive green leaves at top and handle with pink bird attached to rim, matte gold beaded base, cream ground 285.00

10" h, figural seated cat, cream ground, gray spots, red bow on neck, black tail handle, "Amphora Austria" mark 145.00

10 1/2" h, figural bird on shoulder, tail forms handle, dk blue and white accents, tan glazed tapered body, "Czechoslovakia, Amphora, Wien" mark, pr 1,250.00

13 1/2" h, pink enameled cartouche of red, white, and blue enameled dancing woman, yellow leaves on matte blue ground, green jewels on base, blue figural dragon handle 795.00

Planter

7 1/2" h, figural Dutch girl in yellow hooded cape, holding green wicker basket on base, cream and gilt accents, (A) 125.00

11" l x 6" h, stylized rooster, cobalt outlined sq head and tail, tan body with pink cabouchons on border, green enameled zigzag line with blue dots 390.00

13" l x 5 1/2" h, center band of pink and gold flowerheads with blue raised jewels with gold luster centers, textured gold ground, raised gold drippings and circles 1,675.00

Vase

5 1/2" h, blue, red, and green marbled stones, gray textured ground, dk blue enameled vert lines, cobalt lined rim with raised enameled pink and green dots 195.00

6" h, cylinder shape, flared rim, white, blue, green and orange enameled flowerheads on border, black enameled

vert stripes and rim, tan matte textured ground 110.00

6 1/2" h, applied pinecones, red leaves, green stems, mottled tan ground 350.00

6 3/4" h, 6 sides, ftd, reticulated band of green and white diamonds at top, diamond band at base, pitted green ground 475.00

7" h, tapered cylinder shape, mottled blue center band with red, yellow and dk blue flowerheads and green leaves, brown textured ground, dk blue rim and ft 230.00

7 1/2" h, baluster shape with 2 handles, relief molded with leaves and scrolling foliage in green and blue with gilt, (A) 200.00

7 3/4" h, ball shape with 4 flat open handles extended from body, pale pink roses, blue-green leaves, cream ground, "imp crowned Amphora Austria" mark 650.00

8 1/8" h, bulbous base, narrow neck, Robin's egg blue base, 4 gold diamond shapes, moss green faceted neck 375.00

8 3/4" h

Applied purple grapes, pink luster leaves, blue-green irid ground 250.00

Blue floral design, cobalt rim, dbl handles 165.00

Four side handles from base to neck, joined on neck, red enameled cherries, blue flowerheads with yellow centers and red dots, cream ground with tan speckle, imp mark 295.00

9" h

Baluster shape, scrolling branch handles, sides painted with Art Nouveau style profile of woman with flowing hair in green and brown, leaves and berries on rim, (A) 745.00

Panel of enameled seated Greek warrior and young boy, gray-brown textured ground with enameled pink flowerheads, green squares and streaks 350.00

Squat base, trumpet neck, green vert bands separated by lt brown swellings, dk brown ground, cream vert bands on neck, matte finish 675.00

9 1/2" h

Raised glazed white flowers with raised gilt border, cobalt to lt blue shaded ground, "EW" mark, c1905 . . . . 550.00

Teardrop-shaped body, flared neck, relief flowerheads with cobalt accents and jeweled centers, gold body, pierced top, curved horn-type handles 950.00

White, purple, and blue enameled jewels in molded teardrops, matte blue glaze 475.00

9 3/4" h

Applied pink and white roses, pearlized green and white ground, c1905 . . . . 425.00

Jeweled flowers, slate gray and cream ground, salamander handles, "imp Austria, Amphora and crown" mark 395.00

10" h

Bulbous body, straight neck, yellow, brown, and white enamel owl on side, blue, gray, and green enameled geometrics, blue and green textured ground, green and blue enameled diamonds on neck 490.00

Waisted shape, enameled red, blue, and yellow hanging bellflowers, green leaves, lt brown textured ground, brown rim lines, green, white and red geometrics on ft 325.00

10 3/8" h, HP lg red irises from green pod, blue-green and green leaves on base, single iris on reverse, gold scrolling on neck, shaped rim, gold scrolled handles 595.00

10 1/2" h

Applied grapes and leaves, lt green and cobalt glazes, 2 sm handles on shoulder 400.00

Wide base to tapered cylinder body, slightly flared rim, enameled blue, yellow, and green-blue kingfisher, pink band with stylized white and lt blue flowerheads and green leaves on base, blue-green spotted ground, enameled triangles on neck, "Amphora Czechoslovakia" mark 195.00

11" h

Bulbous shape, slender flared neck, ftd, 2 handles on side, 4 sm handles on neck, 2 raised overlapped leaves, pink, green, and blue, "imp crowned Austria Amphora" mark, (A) 460.00

Figure of child on side, applied pink rose, gray luster basketweave ground 450.00

Ftd, 2 side handles, gold irid overall relief design of leaves, spotted green glaze, "imp Amphora, 3946" mark, (A) 518.00

11 1/2" h, bulbous base, flared neck, folklore rooster spout and handle, Prussian blue and chrome yellow details on metallic bronze ground, mkd 895.00

11 3/4" h

Bulbous shape, spread ft, rolled rim, cream center band with gilt outlined green trees, raised gold birds on shoulder, dk tan beading on squiggles on border, matte gold raised "Xs" and lines on rim and ft, gilt handles with cascading rope 650.00

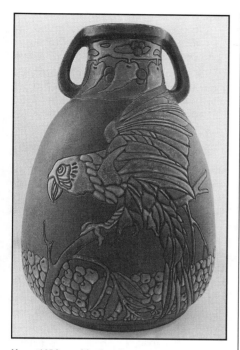

Vase, 16" h, multicolored parrot, gray-green ground, "Amphora, Austria, and crown" mark, $650.

Swollen cylinder shape, flared rim and ft, cream carved relief of stag in landscape, lavender ground, gilt accents, "imp Amphora, Austria, crown" mark, pr, (A) 690.00

White slip outlined gold geometrics, 8 cabochons on shoulder, (A)
. . . . .1,870.00

12" h, applied white and maroon flowers, tan and green basketweave body, gold rope handles, lustered accents
. . . . 400.00

12 1/4" h

Cylinder shape with rolled rim, blue-gray outlined panels of relief molded stylized landscape scene on front, 2 peasants sowing seeds on reverse, blue, green, brown, and gilt, (A) 340.00

Enameled med and dk blue standing storks, mottled textured orange-brown ground, 2 sm dk green handles on neck, "Amphora Made in Czechoslovakia" mark 395.00

13" h, spread ft, narrow base, wide shoulder, pink flowerform rim, applied figural Art Nouveau woman in green luster gown seated on shoulder, green and gold lustered leaves, orange-red flowerheads, imp mark 1,195.00

13 1/2" h, bulbous shape, molded grapes and leaves on green irid basketweave ground, 2 handles 725.00

14 1/8" h, wide base, narrow neck, straight handles molded to sides, molded pelican heads on base, raised jewels and dots, maroon and gold luster finish, white int 1,800.00

15" h

Applied leaves and flowers, matte green and yellow, chips . . . 600.00

Cylinder shape, 4 organic style leaf handles at base, bands of hand formed applied flowers and buds, purple and pearlized glazes
. . . . 2,400.00

16" h, Art Deco, enameled tulips, butterfly, and dragonfly in circ panels, mottled blue ground, 2 handles. 475.00

16 3/4" h, overall lt pink blossoms and buds on matte green glaze, applied flowerheads to base, thin handles from base to shoulder, "Amphora and 3438" mark, repair to handles
. . . . 1,350.00

Vase, Cov, 8" h, brown and tan enameled bust of woman on front, burning candles on reverse in circ cartouche with red and white enameled hearts, gray textured ground with red and blue enameled leaves, 2 loop handles, "imp AMPHORA" mark 225.00

ANGELICA KAUFFMANN

Switzerland
1741-1807

History: Marie Angelique Catherine Kauffmann (1741-1807), a Swiss artist, worked primarily in a neo-classical style. Many artists copied her original paintings and used them on hand decorated porcelains during the 19th century.

Charger, 13" d, multicolored center scene of seated classical woman with 2 attendants and cherub in sq gold cartouche with raised dots, med green ground with gilt overlay, sgd "Kauffmann" 175.00

Cooler, 4" h, gold outlined center cartouche of woman in chair in palace with 2 attendants and Cupid, cobalt base shaded to lt blue top with gold overlay, gold spattered handles, sgd "Kauffmann," "Victoria, Austria" mark
. . . . 75.00

Plaque

8 1/2" d, classical scene in colors, pierced for hanging, sgd "Kauffmann," blue shield mark 50.00

11 3/4" d, coupe shape, multicolored center scene of classic maidens and Cupid, dk green and ivory border with gold scrolls, flowers, and curlicues, sgd "Kauffmann," "Victoria Austria" mark
. . . . 88.00

Pass Cup, 7" h, multicolored cartouche of classical women and cherub, 3 applied gold scrolled handles, 3 gold paw feet, gold borders, sgd "Kauffmann," "Victoria AG" mark, repair to handle 225.00

Plate

5 3/4" d

Center scene of 3 dancing maidens, Cupid playing lute, gold border, sgd "Kauffmann" 12.00

Four maidens in Temple of Venus, gold border, sgd "Kauffmann" 15.00

6" d, 2 classical women and Cupid dancing in meadow, shaded cobalt border with gilt overlay, gilt rim, sgd "Kauffmann". 28.00

8 1/2" d, center scene of classical woman dancing with cherub, woman playing tambourine in colors, lt green band, molded shell edge with lt green accents, gold scrolled stenciled design, sgd "Kauffmann," "Victoria, Carlsbad, Austria" mark, (A). 40.00

8 5/8" d, center scene of Cupid, chariot, and 3 maidens in classic gowns, multicolored, magenta border with gilt foliate designs and 3 cartouches of floral sprays, cream rim with gilt leaves, sgd "Angelica Kauffmann," "Imperial Crown China Austria and crown, wreath and Austria" marks 550.00

9 3/4" d, center with multicolored scene of lady and attendants, Cupid, blue border with gold design, sgd "Kauffmann"
. . . . 50.00

10" d, multicolored transfer of 2 classical women, green emb border, gold inner border, pierced for hanging . . . 135.00

Teapot, 7" h, classical scene of couple in period clothes, floral and gold trim, sgd "Kauffmann" 165.00

Vase

5 1/2" h, multicolored scene of 3 maidens dancing in meadow in raised gilt cartouche, dk green and red panels with raised gold and stenciled designs, cream ground, pink and gold twist handles, sgd "Kauffmann," blue shield mark. 85.00

Plate, 9" d, multicolored center, maroon border, sgd "Kauffmann," $125.

10" h, flattened ovoid shape, flared ruffled rim, 2 handles on shoulder, center white oval of multicolored scene of maidens dancing with baton and tambourine in forest, roses on reverse, green ground with gold stenciled overlay, gold sponged int rim, sgd "Kauffmann" 65.00

AUSTRIA

1884 - 1909

AUSTRIA

16th Century to Present

History: Salzburg was the center of peasant pottery or pottery stove making during the 16th and 17th centuries. These wares were similar to those being made in Germany at the same time. Sometimes they were colored with tin enamels. Factories in Wels, Enns, and Steyr also made this type of pottery ware.

Peasant pottery, known as "Habaner ware" or Hafner ware, was decorated in an unsophisticated style with flowers, animals, and figures. These faience wares were made in Salzberg and Wels during the late 17th century. Most were used locally.

The only porcelain being produced in the early 18th century was made by a Vienna factory founded by Claudius I Du Paquier in 1718 with assistance from Meissen workers. This was the second factory in Europe to make hard paste porcelain. The factory was sold to the Austrian State in 1744.

Many of the later Austrian porcelain factories such as Schlaggenwald, Klosterle, Prague, Dallwitz, Pirkenhammer, and Elbogen were classified with Bohemia porcelain because of their location.

A number of porcelain factories originated in the 19th and 20th centuries to make utilitarian and decorative porcelains. These included Brux, Frauenthal, Turn, Augarten, Wienerberger, Spitz, and Neumann.

In 1897, the Vienna Secession Movement provided a stimulus to Austrian ceramics. A group of young painters, sculptors, and architects desired to overthrow conservatism in the arts and design and revolutionize taste. Moser and Peche were designers of tableware and decorative porcelains associated with this movement.

In 1903, Moser and Peche founded the Wiener Werkstatte, an association of artisans, along with porcelain maker Joseph Bock. They made innovative designs in both shape and pattern. Michael Powolny and Berthold Loffler founded the Wiener Keramik Studio in 1905 which produced advanced tablewares and figure designs in earthenware and porcelains. Products included black and white majolica, generally decorated with Cubist inspired geometrical patterns from designs by J. Hoffmann, D. Peche, and Powolny. Figures were modeled by Loffler and Powolny. Art Nouveau and Art Deco designs were utilized. The products of the Wiener Keramik Studio became the foundation for the international Modern Movement that developed after World War I.

References: George Ware, *German and Austrian Porcelain*, Lothar Woeller Press, 1951.

Museums: Osterreisches Museum fur Angewandtekunst, Vienna, Austria; Vienna Kunsthistoriches Museum, Vienna, Austria.

Bowl

8" l x 6" w, HP dk brown acorns and leaves, beige ext ground, orange lustered int, 4 gold feet, "M.Z. Austria" mark
.... 189.00

10" d, Art Nouveau style, ring of pink water lilies and green leaves on int, inner border of hanging pink water lilies and green leaves, shaped gold rim, "green M.Z. Austria" mark 35.00

10 1/2" d
HP bunches of violets, green leaves, yellow shaded ground, wide gold rim, "Austria" mark........ 60.00

Int center multicolored scene of couple in period clothes in meadow, woman sleeping, dog at feet, man with basket of flowers, scattered magenta, red, and yellow flowers, scroll molded ground, wave border with gold circles, sgd "Boucher" 45.00

Box, 6 1/2" l x 4" w x 1 1/2" h, rect with shield shaped top section, purple florals in shield, raised molded florals on lt green ground, gilt trim........................ 70.00

Cake Plate
11" H-H, single pink rose and green leaves in center, border band of pink roses and green leaves, rim of hanging stylized gold flower buds, "M.Z. Austria" mark
.... 25.00

11 1/2" H-H
Open handles, dk green, maroon, cream, and gray starburst design, gold trim 95.00

Orange poppies, gold trim 30.00

Candelabrum, 10" h, 2 sockets on top arm with molded grapes under sockets, loop handles from midstem to base, matte med green finish........................ 250.00

Charger
11 1/2" d, center painted with Orpheus leading Euridyce out of underworld in

conc gilt, green, and claret bands with gilt foliate scrolls and geometric diamonds, "blue shield and Orpheus In Der Underwelt" marks,(A) 920.00

13 3/8" d, multicolored center scene of 2 women in period gowns seated in garden, third braiding hair, inner border of gold heart swags, border of joined ovals of pink roses and green leaves reserved on cobalt ground with gilt stenciled flowers, sgd "Carl Larson"..... 210.00

Chocolate Set, pot 12" h, 6 cups and saucers, oval reserves of busts of woman with long flowing hair on brown shaded ground, green to white shaded bodies with gold stenciled floral design, gold scrolled handles and knob, "Elbogen, Austria and Imperial Austria" marks, (A) 475.00

Compote, 5" h x 8 5/8" d, "Alhambra" pattern, red, green, tan, and gold 135.00

Cracker Jar, 5 1/4" h, red, yellow, and purple bouquets on white ground, arrowhead handles and knob 85.00

Cream Pitcher, 4 3/4" h, figural elk head, brown shades, "Austria" mark....... 42.00

Cup and Saucer, Cov, rect reserve of painted scene of classical couple and attendant, burgundy ground with gilt pendants, foliate scrolls and band of turquoise arches, "blue shield" mark, (A) 460.00

Dessert Plate, 6" d, transfer of pink and green rose swag with gold stenciled floral swags, dk green band on rim with gold stenciled florals, scalloped edge, "Wheelock China, Austria," set of 10,(A)..................... 80.00

Dinner Service, Part, 11 dinner plates, 10" d, 9 salad plates, 8 1/2" d, 10 dessert plates, 7 1/2" d, 7 cups, 8 saucers, border of white flowers and sm pink rose swags, green hanging swags, molded indented dots on rim, gilt outlined rim, Victoria Austria 100.00

Dish, 9 3/4" l x 7" w, transfer of purple lily of the valley and greens on green to yellow shaded ground, wide gold indented border, "Eagle Austria" mark...................... 45.00

Dresser Tray, 12 3/4" l, oval, HP bunches of violets on sides, lt purple inner band, cream ground, gold lined rim.............. 50.00

Ewer, 11 3/4" h, painted cherries with blue-green shadow leaves, gold netted panels, blue cloudbursts on base, gold lined rim, gold ribbon handle 225.00

Ewer and Stand, ewer, 11 1/2" h, stand, 12 1/2" d, painted stork and snail on side, frog and spider on reverse, owl under spout, stand with painted butterflies, sgd "Radler & Pilz," Vienna, Austria 250.00

Figure
9" h, standing young woman wearing black bonnet, fur-trimmed brown coat, hands in muff, spray of pinecones from arm, Busch & Ludescher 770.00

13" h, woman with raised arms, black lace evening gown, cranberry red cape, (A) 460.00

13 1/8" h, seated lion on rect plinth, orange glaze, Augarten, (A) 930.00

17" h, musicians, boy seated on chair, blue pants, white shirt, flowered vest and hat, playing flute, girl seated in chair, white blouse, blue vest, mauve skirt, yellow flowered apron, blue ribbon in blond hair, holding tambourine, missing baton, late 19th C, pr, (A) 847.00

19" h, nude flapper girl with multicolored cape draped over arms and shoulder, (A) 2,875.00

28 3/4" h, standing blond haired nude putto holding blue, red, lavender, and yellow flower bouquet, floral and leaf green circ base, Wiener Keramic, c1905-12, (A) 500.00

Jug, Cov, 10" h, tin glazed, polychrome figural standing owl with molded scrolling crest on torso, late 18th C, (A) 402.00

Pitcher

6" h, straight sides, green apples and leaves, tan to green shaded ground, black handle, "blue Victoria Austria" mark. 28.00

12 1/2" h, HP purple flowers, orange and yellow leaves, gold accents, Vienna 235.00

Plate

6 3/8" d, handle at top, HP yellow roses yellow and green shaded ground, gold molded scalloped rim and handle, "M.Z. Austria" mark, (A) 10.00

8 1/2" d, lady in garden setting in center, multicolored, turquoise border with gold accents 65.00

9" d

Bunches of lily of the valley and wide green leaves with gray shadowing, cream ground, wide gold banded rim, "M.Z. Austria" mark 26.00

HP purple, gray, and dk green flowers, cream ground. 85.00

9 1/2" d, brown bust of German Shepherd dog, white ground, band of pink, green, and brown clover on border, "M.Z. Austria" mark 38.00

9 3/4" d

Painted scene of Venus blindfolding Cupid, wide lt pink border reserved with brown panels gilt with animals and sm blue panels with gilt urns, "blue shield" mark, late 19th C, (A) 403.00

Sm scattered pink tinged green roses in center, lg bouquet of pink tinged green roses and stems on border with sm sprays, molded drop on outer border 38.00

9 7/8" d, HP black, blue, red, and brown butterfly in center on pale yellow ground, lt blue border with sm bunches of pink roses, green buds joined by green stems, gilt lined rim, "blue Victoria Austria" mark 15.00

Plate, 10 1/2" d, multicolored portrait, auburn hair, raised gold flower and trellis border, green rim, sgd "F. Tenner," (A) $747.

Platter

15 1/2" l, red roses, dk green ground, gold rim. 65.00

18 7/8" l x 12 5/8" w, rect, bluish-gray chrysanthemums, molded straight ribbons at corners, "AUSTRIA" mark. . . . 45.00

Punch Bowl, 14" d x 6 3/8" h, with undertray, HP pink, red, and yellow roses on int and ext, gold striped rim and base, tray with 4 paw feet, molded gold accented scroll designs, "green Vienna Austria, crown and rampant lion, and red Vienna Hand painted China" mark, (A). 300.00

Relish Dish, 11" l x 7" w, 3 lobes, pink dogwood blossoms with raised enameled centers, green buds and leaves on border, shaded tan to cream ground, matte gold loop handle on center rim, "green M.Z. Austria and eagle" mark 65.00

Serving Dish, 12" H-H, purple and magenta florals in center, 4 pierced sections on border with interspersed florals, gilt rim 62.00

Serving Plate, 11 5/8" d, wide salmon band with gold splotches, molded scalloped rim, "Loraware, Made in Austria" mark, (A). 15.00

Tankard, 5 1/4" h, yellow band with gray, lt blue and red parrots on green branch, dk brown lower band, brushed gold body bands and handle, Imperial Austria 68.00

Tobacco Jar, 5 1/2" h, relief molded dk and lt brown owl on front, brown, green leaves, brown shaded ground 75.00

Tray, 9" l x 6" w, rect, 2 lg red flowers in center and lily of the valley, shaded orange ground, molded border with black dots, molded handles. 20.00

Tureen, Cov, 12" H-H, garlands of roses design. 50.00

Urn, 21 1/4" h, ovoid shape, gilt lined reserve of green, blue, brown, and white courting couple on front, reverse with smaller scene, gilt foliate decoration on body, parcil gilt neck, ft, and scrolling handles, "blue shield, crown, Vienna, Made in Austria" mark 690.00

Vase

7" h x 7" d, Wiener Werkstatte style, 3 open panels of flowers and birds, 3 raised center rings, curdled red-orange ground 495.00

7 1/8" h, bulbous shape, handles from shoulder to ribbed neck, purple and white orchids, green ferns on front, shaded yellow ground, gold trim 20.00

9 1/4" h

Blue and white scene of 2 seated classical women, one holding bust in raised gold cartouche, cobalt ground with gold outlined raised molding and gold overlay, 2 handles from shoulder to neck, "gold shield" mark 60.00

Tapered shape, flared ball neck, man in red jacket, woman in blue dress, jumping brown horses over fence, shaded base, blue cloud shaded top 195.00

Waisted cylinder form, Vienna style painted reserve of classical maiden holding vase of apple blossoms, gilt decorated white ground, (A). 615.00

9 1/2" h, relief of blue, green, and brown curvilinear designs, white ground, "Made in Austria" mark, (A) 110.00

12" h

Art Nouveau style, indented sides, donut shaped neck, scalloped rim, orchid in white reserve front and reverse, pink ground, gold rococo accents and tracery, gold fancy handle. 95.00

Cylinder shape, flared top and base, HP pink and yellow roses, green leaves, blue and pink shaded ground, gold band at rim with scroll design, "Vienna Austria" mark, (A). 50.00

Tapered shape, sq base, HP pink-red roses with gold accents, gold trimmed rim and base, c1895 . . . . 175.00

14" h, dbl handles, multicolored pastoral scene of cows, water, and mountains 195.00

15 3/4" h, ftd base, ovoid body, flared rim, 2 handles from shoulder to neck, lg white and pink rose transfer with shaded green leaves, olive green handles, neck and ft with red and yellow accents, "Royal Wettina, Made in Austria" mark, (A) 88.00

18 1/2" h, flattened straight sides, 4 sm feet, flowerform opening, purple flowers, raised white enameled sm flowers, matte cream ground, matte orange top and base with gold molded accents, 2 gilt and lt green scroll and leaf form handles, "red Royal Wettina, Made in Austria" mark 165.00

20" h, slender ovoid shape, spread circ ft, foliate handles on shoulder, trumpet neck, pink and green painted sprays of gladiolus, streaked blue and pink ground with powder gilt patches, ivory neck and ft with gilt designs, pr, (A) 650.00

Vegetable Bowl, Cov

10 1/2" H-H x 6" h, gilt outlined tan and green geometric border, white ground, gilt trim, "crowned Vienna Austria" mark. 85.00

12 3/3" H-H, "Princess" pattern, gold outlined band of sm pink roses on rims, "green M.Z. Austria" mark 20.00

Wall Mask

4 1/2" h, terra cotta, woman with stylized features, blond curly hair with green scarf on head, (A) 308.00

9 1/4" h

Pottery, modeled as young woman with eyes closed, orange hair, Keramos, (A). 400.00

Terra cotta, bust of Art Deco woman, red hat, pale blue face with red cheeks, yellow canary on cheek, (A). 425.00

BAVARIA

Bayreuth, Bavaria
c1713-1852

History: By the 18th century, many factories were established in the Bavarian region. Bauscher at Weiden produced utility wares, some of which featured cobalt blue ornamentation. J.N. Muller at Schonwald supplied painted and unpainted utility wares. Other factories operating in Bavaria included Schuman, Thomas, and Zeh, Scherzer and Company.

J. G. Knoller founded the Bayreuth factory in Bavaria and produced faience and brown glazed wares with silver, gilt, and engraved decorations. The finest work was done from 1728 until 1745.

Bayreuth brown glazed wares were a lightly fired reddish earthenware covered with a manganese brown or red glaze. Yellow glazed wares were lighter in body and were covered with a buff or pale yellow

glaze. About 1745 Frankel and Schrock took over and started to make porcelain. J.G. Pfeiffer acquired the firm, later selling it in 1767.

After 1728, the pottery and porcelain pieces were marked frequently. The mark consisted of the initials of the place and the owner, along with the painter's mark.

Museum: Sevres Museum, Sevres, France.

Tirschenreuth
1838 to Present

The Tirschenreuth Porcelain Factory was established in 1838 and made tablewares, utilitarian and decorative porcelains, figures, and coffee and tea sets. In 1927, the company was acquired by the Porcelain Factory Lorenz Hutschenreuther in Selb.

Additional Listing: Hutschenreuther.

Ashtray, 4 1/4" l, rect, pink rose medallion and gold tracery, wide maroon border with gold flowers and lattice, "Bavaria, Schumann, Arzberg, Germany" mark 8.00

Bowl

8" d, orange cherries and green leaves, reticulated border, white scalloped rim with gilt trim, "CS Bavaria" mark
. . . . 22.00

8 1/2" d, 3 lg white roses, green thorny stems and leaves in center, relief design with orange and green lustered finish on rim 48.00

9" d, red and white roses, scalloped rim, "RC Bavaria" mark 75.00

9 1/4" d

HP white lilies with purple and rust red accents, tan to green shaded ground, gilt rim, "P.S. A.G. Bavaria" mark. 23.00

Red sliced apple, 2 apples and brown nuts in center, swirled green to pink lustered border 28.00

9 3/8" d, multicolored transfer in center of 18th C couple in garden setting with stone wall and castle in bkd, orange luster inner border, pierced lattice rim
. . . . 45.00

10 3/4" H-H, HP lg white and pink roses, sm gold flowers, dk green to brick red shaded ground, floral relief molded rim, open handles, "Regina Z.S. & Co. Bavaria" mark 95.00

Cake Plate

8 3/4" d, open handles, center multicolored floral transfer and gold "Give us this day our daily bread," shaded purple irid flowers on border with gold stenciling, scalloped rim, "red Bavaria" mark, (A) 30.00

10 3/4" H-H, 2 lg orange poppies in center, wide blue border, gold stripe on rim, "Z.S. & Co. Bavaria" mark, (A)
. . . . 20.00

11" H-H, sq, yellow daisies and orange-red poppies in center, cobalt border with gilt overlay, open white handles 69.00

Cake Set

Master plate, 9 3/8" d, 6 plates, 5 7/8" d, multicolored center scene of classic figures with Cupid resting head on female's lap, gold stenciled floral inner border, wide gold border with molded swag designs, "Bavaria and eagle" marks 45.00

Master plate, 10 3/8" H-H, 6 plates, 6" d, blue and green peacock on inner lt blue border with raised enameled yellow centered pink flowerheads, sgd "J. Stocker," "BAVARIA" marks. . . . 125.00

Casserole, Cov, 11" H-H, band of green flowerheads and sm red sqs joined by green stems with sm red flowerheads on borders, gold lined rims, gold outlined handles and knob, "P.T. Bavaria and shield" mark
. . . . 30.00

Celery Tray

11 1/2" l x 5 1/2" w, pierced handles, pink and white roses and leaves, white ground, band of dk green and gold tracery 50.00

12 1/4" l, multicolored 3 masted sailing ship in center, pearlized lustered ground, blue lined rim, "green Z.S. & Co. Bavaria" mark 35.00

12 3/8" l x 6" w, oval, yellow and pink rose with green leaves on white, green to pink shaded ground, gold stenciled floral border, gold banded rim, "Mignon, Z.S. & Co. Bavaria" mark, (A) . . . 18.00

Charger

11 1/2" d, multicolored stag in center, maroon and cobalt border, pierced for hanging, "blue shield and Bavaria Germany" marks, pr. 170.00

11 5/8" d, center multicolored scene of period couple seated in garden, man presenting bouquet to woman in gilt dot cartouche, dk red inner border with gilt stenciled pendants, outer border of series of U-shaped gilt dot panels of courting couples, sgd "Fragonard"
. . . . 100.00

Chocolate Set, pot, 8 1/2" h, 4 cups and saucers, 4 serving plates, 6" d, lg red poppies on shaded green to cream ground, gold lined rims, "Z.S. & Co. Bavaria" marks 275.00

Chop Plate, 12 1/2" d, lg pink and white rose transfer in center, sm roses on border, gold lined scalloped rim, "PM in wreath, Bavaria" mark, (A) 15.00

Cider Pitcher, 5" h, HP yellow flowers, green leaves, cream ground, dull gold handle
. . . . 175.00

Coffeepot

9 3/8" h, lg pink roses, green stems and leaves, lt blue to yellow shaded ground, gold rim, handle, and knob, Tirschenreuther 87.00

10 1/4" h, purple and red wreaths hanging from blue ribbon on upper border, draped green, gold lined rims . . . 35.00

Coffee Set, pot, 9 1/4" h, creamer, cov sugar bowl, melon ribbed with scrolling, lg multicolored florals, gold trim and rim 110.00

Cookie Jar, 6 1/2" h, windmill, buildings, and houses, green trees and grass, pastel bkd 110.00

Cookie Plate, 9 3/4" H-H, red strawberries and green loganberries, gold outlined rim, open handles 12.00

Cracker Jar, 6" h, white snowball flowers, shaded green ground, gold hanging flowerheads from border, shaped rim, twisted flowerhead knob 130.00

Creamer and Sugar Bowl, Cov

Creamer, 3 1/2" h, sugar bowl, 5 1/8" h, molded arch panels, side panel with pink roses and green leaves, gold overlay, lt blue-gray luster ground, gold accented bases and handles, "red BAVARIA" marks 48.00

Creamer, 4 1/2" h, sugar bowl, 5 1/2" h, molded arched panels with orange centered white water lilies, pearl luster ground, shaded orange rims with relief molded drop 35.00

Sq hourglass shape, cream ground, band of blue flowers on creamer, band of pink flowers on sugar bowl, gold handles, "Favorite, Bavaria" marks 50.00

Cup and Saucer, blue luster ext, mother of pearl int, black handle and rim, "Bavaria" mark, set of 6 . . . . 60.00

Cup and Saucer, Demitasse, pedestaled, relief scrolled body, pink flowers, green leaves, gold trim on int and ext, shaded pink to blue ground, scrolled handle 10.00

Dish

7 1/2" l, yellow and gold florals, shaded green leaves, lavender flowers, white to blue shaded ground, gilt trimmed open handle, gilt rim, "green PT, shield Bavaria" mark 30.00

12" l x 5" w, Rosie O'Neil winged Kewpies, "Z.S. & Co. Bavaria" mark 145.00

Ewer, 13 5/8" h, enameled pink and yellow ground, green shaded ground, gilt trim, "Bavaria" mark, (A) 100.00

Figure, 11" h, boy in lt green vest, red trousers, girl in green flower print dress, seated on brown rock oval base 435.00

Gravy Boat, 8" l, with attached undertray, rim band of sm pink roses and green hanging leaf swags from gray line and dot band, "Paul Muller, Selb, Bavaria" mark 18.00

Hair Receiver, 4 3/4" d, white and pink roses, green leaves, tan shaded ground, "green J.S. Bavaria" mark 35.00

Hatpin Holder, 5" h, corset shape, brown pinecones and needles, "BAVARIA" mark 88.00

Pitcher

5 1/4" h, straight sides, molded wave base, overall orange lustered glaze . . . 35.00

5 1/2" h, molded arch with 2 blue peacocks with green tails standing on green mountain ledge with magenta flowers, ribbed rim with orange luster 24.00

6 3/4" h

Cylinder shape, silhouette of period dancing couple, multicolored and black transfer, molded neck with orange pearlized finish 95.00

Overall blue splashed glaze, molded chevrons on base 40.00

Planter, 4" h x 5 1/4" d, 3 gold feet, dk red lower band, beaded blue middle band, cream band at top with yellow, blue, and red flowers, green leaves 25.00

Plate

6" d, multicolored center scene of period couple walking or dancing, raised gold cartouche, shaded light to cobalt ground, cobalt border with raised gilt leaves and florals, scalloped rim, "P M Bavaria" mark, pr 30.00

7 5/8" d, red and green strawberries, green leaves, gold outlined rim, "Louise Bavaria" mark 40.00

8" d, pastel fruit, ivory ground, "Sevres Bavaria" mark 95.00

8 1/4" d

Lg purple plums, lg yellow and green leaves, brown to green shaded ground, gold lined rim, "Favorite Bavaria" mark 28.00

Two bunches of blue lily of the valley on green stems, pink shaded ground 22.00

8 3/8" d

Multicolored center scene of king with shield in boat pulled by swans, women on shore, lt green ground,

Plate, 10" d, gilt rim, pierced rocaille gilt and polychrome floral cavetto, green ground with orange, yellow, purple, and magenta flowers and alternating panels of multicolored courting scenes, "Schumann Bavaria" mark, $190.

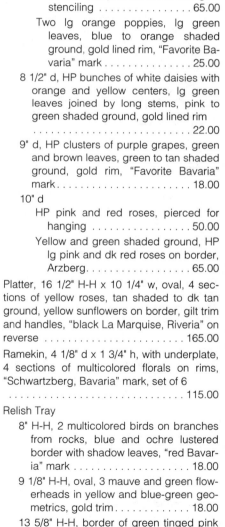

Spittoon, 5 1/2" h, 7 3/4" d, lg orange and purple flowers, gold outlined leaves, molded swirled body, blue-green shaded ground, "J.S. Bavaria" mark, $90.

gold stenciled inner border, maroon border with pierced holes and gold stenciling 65.00

Two lg orange poppies, lg green leaves, blue to orange shaded ground, gold lined rim, "Favorite Bavaria" mark 25.00

8 1/2" d, HP bunches of white daisies with orange and yellow centers, lg green leaves joined by long stems, pink to green shaded ground, gold lined rim 22.00

9" d, HP clusters of purple grapes, green and brown leaves, green to tan shaded ground, gold rim, "Favorite Bavaria" mark 18.00

10" d

HP pink and red roses, pierced for hanging 50.00

Yellow and green shaded ground, HP lg pink and dk red roses on border, Arzberg 65.00

Platter, 16 1/2" H-H x 10 1/4" w, oval, 4 sections of yellow roses, tan shaded to dk tan ground, yellow sunflowers on border, gilt trim and handles, "black La Marquise, Riveria" on reverse 165.00

Ramekin, 4 1/8" d x 1 3/4" h, with underplate, 4 sections of multicolored florals on rims, "Schwartzberg, Bavaria" mark, set of 6 . . . . 115.00

Relish Tray

8" H-H, 2 multicolored birds on branches from rocks, blue and ochre lustered border with shadow leaves, "red Bavaria" mark 18.00

9 1/8" H-H, oval, 3 mauve and green flowerheads in yellow and blue-green geometrics, gold trim 18.00

13 5/8" H-H, border of green tinged pink roses with green leaves, dk green shaped rim with gold overlay, "J & C. Bavaria" mark 95.00

Tea Set

Pot, 5" h, creamer, cov sugar bowl, dk blue trumpet shaped flowers from long green stem, gold trim, "Seltmann Bavaria" marks 48.00

Pot, 6 3/4" h, paneled, creamer, cov sugar bowl, "China Blau" pattern, blue oriental floral transfers, "Seltmann, Bavaria" marks 85.00

Vase

6 3/4" h, ovoid shape, HP red, pink, and yellow roses on shaded ground, gold banded rim, pr, (A) 85.00

9 1/2" h, ovoid shape, flared rim, HP purple florals, yellow to green shaded ground, orange int on neck, gold rim, "Z.S. & Co. Bavaria" mark, (A) 75.00

11 3/4" h, swollen cylinder shape, flared neck and ft, HP green, red, and purple bunches of grapes, green leaves, dl green neck 95.00

Vegetable Bowl

8" sq, multicolored floral bouquet in center, wide yellow inner border, white open lattice work rim, "R.C. Bavaria" mark 75.00

8 1/4" sq, int with Art Deco style yellow, pink, and red flowerheads in dbl black line cartouche, lt tan ground, gold accented pierced rim, Schumann, Bavaria 295.00

BELGIUM- GENERAL

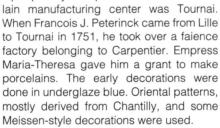

1751-1891

1751-96

History: Belgium's principal pottery and porcelain manufacturing center was Tournai. When Francois J. Peterinck came from Lille to Tournai in 1751, he took over a faience factory belonging to Carpentier. Empress Maria-Theresa gave him a grant to make porcelains. The early decorations were done in underglaze blue. Oriental patterns, mostly derived from Chantilly, and some Meissen-style decorations were used.

In 1763, Duvivier joined the factory as chief painter and added Sevres-style decorations, adopting the Louis XVI style in 1780. The principal background colors were bleu de roi and yellow. Figures and groups also were made in biscuit and glazed porcelain.

When Peterinck died in 1799, the factory experienced difficulties. Peterinck's descendants continued production until 1815 when the firm went bankrupt. Henri de Bellingnies reopened the factory in 1817 and managed it until 1850. Porcelains with a blue ground, similar to earlier styles, were made. The Boch brothers of Luxembourg purchased the factory in 1850. They made creamwares until 1891.

Francois Peterinck's son Charles established a second factory for stoneware production at Tournai that operated from 1800 to 1855.

Plate, 8 1/8" d, black transfer, $65.

Another smaller porcelain center in Belgium was in Brussels and its suburbs. Several factories operated on a small scale, mostly as decorating workshops utilizing the Paris style of decoration.

Museums: Chateau Mariemont, Brussels, Belgium; Musee du Cinquantenaire, Brussels, Belgium.

Bowl

5 1/2" d, ftd, band of red gaudy flowerheads and blue and green leaves on ext 45.00

9 1/8" d, red and green Adam's Rose type pattern, "Manufacture Imperial Royal, Nimy, Fabrication Belge, Made in Belgium" mark 35.00

Charger, 15 3/8" d, center scene of old woman reading book, floral and leaf border, blue transfer, shaped rim 125.00

Ewer, 11" h, center cartouche of blue peacock with green, yellow, and brown feathers on tan ground outlined in indented gold, mottled blue-green ground with gilt trim, gold outlined spout, ribbed handle with gold lines, 6 gold circles on base 85.00

Jardiniere and Stand, 44" h, raised medallions, cobalt, brown, and green mottled and streaked ground, rim repair, chips, (A) 495.00

Plate

8 1/8" d, Napoleon on horseback in center and "Le Ge'al Massena Devant Zurich, Decembre 25 1799," border with Napoleonic crests, black transfer 65.00

8 3/8" d, hunters in woodland setting, black transfer, shaped rim 32.00

9 1/4" d, HP lg red rose in center, green leaves, blue buds and stems, red striped rim, "Manufacture Imperiale Royale, Nimy, Fabrication Belge, Made in Belgium" mark, (A) 20.00

Sauce Boat, 9 1/2" l, with undertray, molded swirls, scattered blue sprays, overhead handle, Tournai, (A) 253.00

Soup Plate

10 5/8" d, painted stylized flowerhead in center with scattered leaves and flower-

heads, design zigzag border, red, green, blue, and yellow, "Made in Belgium" mark, (A) 55.00

10 7/8" d, lg HP green and red floral rosette in center with red flowers and green leaves, blue design spatter florets, yellow and red striping on inside of bowl, wide red and green spatter sawtooth border flanked by dk blue stripes, red striped rim, "Manufacture Imperiale Royale Nimy and Fabrication Belge, Made in Belgium" marks, pr, (A) 125.00

Vase

4" h, round, green and red circ flowers, cobalt ground 85.00

4 1/2" h, squat shape with 2 loop handles, molded beatles design and blue streaks on brown drip glaze . . . 175.00

5 3/4" h, free-form, 2 side twist handles, brown, yellow, and green drip ground, blue drip on neck 65.00

6 1/2" h, pinched waist, turquoise drip, red flambe ground, "Ceramic Bruxelles" mark 130.00

7" h

Dbl loop shape, beige gloss drip glaze, cobalt ground 65.00

Oval shape, lg loop handles, orange rim with brown drip and white crackle ground, "imp BELGIUM and Made in Belgium" mark 30.00

8" h, wide body, narrow neck, 2 handles, chocolate brown drip glaze, cobalt ground 65.00

8 5/8" h, 2 side loop handles from base to neck, red centered yellow, red, and blue enameled daisies, mottled tan and orange ground, orange-brown stripes on handles, artist sgd 125.00

9 1/2" h, flat base, slim bulbous body, rolled rim, streaky cream-gray drip glaze over red glazed body 45.00

11 3/4" h, baluster shape, sq base, gilt winged female herms handles, painted named scene of "*Vue de Hotel de Ville de Bruxelles*" or "*Vue de L'Eglise de Ste Gudule a Bruxelles*" in gilt chased borders reserved on gilt ground, reverse with chased trophies on gilt ground, "F. Faber A Bruxelles" mark, Brussels, c1825, repairs, pr, (A) 8,050.00

13" h, stoneware, cobalt flying storks before white clouds, "Hand Made Belgium" mark 195.00

BESWICK

Staffordshire, England
Early 1890s to Present

Beswick Ware.
MADE IN
ENGLAND
1936

History: James Wright Beswick and John, his son, acquired the Gold Street Works in Longton, Stoke-on-Trent in 1896. They made utilitarian and ornamental wares, but are best known for their series of figures of horses and domestic pets. All of their animals are created with utmost accuracy and attention to details. In 1918, the Beswicks added the Warwick China Works in Longton.

After James Beswick died in 1920, John took over the firm. In 1934, John was succeeded by John Ewart Beswick, his only son. John Ewart worked along with Gilbert Ingham Beswick. They expanded the firm and increased their reputation for excellent equestrian figures. The firm was called John Beswick Ltd. from 1936.

The firm continued to expand by acquiring the site of Williamson & Son's factory in 1945 and Thomas Lawrence's site in 1957. They were converted to a public company in 1957.

Since neither Ewart or Gilbert had a successor to take over, they sold the firm to Royal Doulton Tableware Ltd. in 1969. Their reputation for figures of animals continues to the present day.

Beswick's best known models of horses are part of the "Connoisseur Series." Though the "Connoisseur Series" was developed in the early 1970s, it incorporated figures that had been made many years before. Cats, dogs, farm animals, birds, wildlife, and figures identified with children's literature such as *Winnie the Pooh*, *Alice in Wonderland*, and the works of Beatrix Potter have been modeled by Beswick.

The Beswick name is stamped on most pieces, but the earliest examples are unmarked. Every item made since 1933 is assigned a model number.

References: Diana & John Callow, *The Charlton Standard Catalogue of Beswick Animals, 2nd Edition*, Charlton Press, 1996; Diana & John Callow, *The Charlton Standard Catalogue of Beswick Pottery*, Charlton Press, 1997; Jean Dale, *Royal Doulton Beswick Jugs, Third Edition*, Charlton Press, 1995; Jean Dale, *Royal Doulton Beswick Storybook Figurines, Third Edition*, Charlton Press, 1996; Harvey May, *The Beswick Collectors Handbook*, Kevin Francis Publishing Ltd. 1986; Harvey May, *The Beswick Price Guide, 3rd Edition*, Francis Joseph Publications, 1995; Doug Pinchin, *Beatrix Potter & Bunnykins Price Guide*, Francis Joseph Publications, 1995.

Collecting Hints: It is usually best to start a collection by selecting a specific theme or subject.

Alice in Wonderland Figures
  1 1/2" h, Cheshire Cat 635.00
  3 1/4" h, Gryphon. 165.00
  3 3/4" h, King of Hearts 75.00
  4" h
    Dodo. 285.00
    Queen of Hearts 75.00
  4 1/4" h
    Frog Footman 285.00

    Mad Hatter. 265.00
    Mock Turtle 195.00
  4 3/4" h
    Alice. 295.00
    Fish Footman 285.00
Animals
  3 1/4" h, Lakeland Terrier, matte finish
  . . . . 35.00
  3 3/4" h, Penguin, with walking stick, #803
  . . . . 35.00
  4" h, Dachshund, begging, black and tan, #1461 . . . . 40.00
  4 1/4" h, Lolopy Dog, blue glaze, #454 . . . . 95.00
  4 1/2" h, Hereford Calf, brown and white, #854 . . . . 85.00
  4 3/4" h, West Highland Terrier, #2038 . . . . 125.00
  5" h
    Blue Jays, #925. . . . . 90.00
    Persian cat, standing, white glossy finish, #1898 . . . . 42.00
  5 1/4" h, Spotted Appaloosa pony, #1516 . . . . 295.00
  5 1/2" h
    Boxer, "Blue Mountain Greta," #1202 . . . . 95.00
    Bulldog, "Basford British Mascot," #965. . . . . 110.00
  5 3/4" h
    Cardinal, #927. . . . . 52.00
    Collie, "Lochinvar of Ladypark," #1791 . . . . 65.00
    Tanager, red, #928 . . . . 90.00
    Wire Hair Terrier, "Talavera Ramulus," #963. . . . . 130.00
  6" h
    Greyhound, "Jovial Roger," gloss finish, #972 . . . . 130.00
    Parakeet, #930 . . . . 48.00
    Pheasant in Flight, #849 . . . . . 125.00

Figure, 3 1/4" h, Ribby and Patty Pan, multicolored, Royal Albert mark, $35.

  6 1/2" h, Bull Terrier, "Romany Rhinestone," white finish, #970 . . . . . . 75.00
  7" h, Great Dane, "Ruler of Oubourgh," #968. . . . . 130.00
  8 1/2" h, Old English Sheepdog, gray and white, #453. . . . . 150.00
Beatrix Potter
Character Jug
  3" h
    Jeremy Fisher, #2960, (A). . . 76.00
    Old Mr. Brown, #2959, (A) . . 75.00
    Peter Rabbit, #3006 . . . . 60.00
  4" h, Jemima Puddleduck, #3088 . . . . 125.00
Cup and Saucer, Benjamin Bunny, "Royal Albert" mark 16.00
Figures
  1 1/4" h, Timmy Willie Sleeping, brown stamp 125.00
  2 1/4" h, Jemima Puddleduck Made a Feathered Nest, brown stamp 65.00
  2 1/2" h
    Flopsy, Mopsy, and Cottontail, gold stamp 159.00
    Old Mr. Pricklepin, brown stamp 135.00
  2 3/4" h
    Babbity Bumble, Royal Albert stamp 80.00
    Diggory Diggory Delvet, brown stamp 49.00
    Hunca Munca, gold stamp 150.00
    The Old Woman in a Shoe, brown stamp 65.00
  3" h
    Anna Maria, #1851, gold stamp, (A) 335.00
    Miss Moppet, gold stamp 150.00
    Old Mr. Brown, gold stamp 150.00
  3 1/4" h
    Appley Dappley, gold stamp 275.00
    Mrs. Tiggywinkle
      Brown stamp 50.00
      Gold stamp 210.00
    Ribby, brown stamp 35.00
    Samuel Whiskers, brown stamp 45.00
    Thomasina Tittlemouse, brown stamp 125.00
    Tom Thumb, brown stamp 115.00
  3 1/2" h
    Amiable Guinea Pig, brown stamp 450.00
    Hunca Munca Sweeping, brown stamp 60.00
    Johnny Townmouse with bag, brown stamp 30.00
    Little Pig Robinson Spying, Royal Albert stamp 100.00

Mrs. Tittlemouse, brown stamp
. . . . 75.00
Tabitha Twitchet, brown stamp
. . . . 65.00
Tabitha Twitchet and Miss Moppet,
brown stamp 200.00
Tom Kitten, gold stamp. . . . 210.00
Tom Kitten and Butterfly, brown
stamp 175.00
3 3/4" h
Aunt Pettitoes, brown stamp
. . . . 35.00
Benjamin Bunny Sat on a Bank,
brown stamp 65.00
Chippy Hackee, brown stamp
. . . . 85.00
Mr. Rabbit and Bunnies, brown
stamp 75.00
Cottontail, brown stamp 50.00
Ginger, brown stamp 650.00
Mr. Jeremy Fisher Digging, brown
stamp 195.00
Poorly Peter Rabbit, #2560, brown
stamp 79.00
Samuel Whiskers, brown stamp
. . . . 65.00
Sir Isaac Newton, #2425. . . 500.00
Squirrel Nutkin
Brown stamp 40.00
Gold stamp 115.00
Timmy Tiptoes, gold stamp
. . . . 175.00
4" h
Cecily Parsley, gold mark . . 325.00
Duchess with pie, style two, brown
stamp 200.00
Goody and Timmy Tiptoe, brown
stamp 195.00
Lady Mouse, gold stamp . . 120.00
Little Pig Robinson, gold stamp
. . . . 325.00
Pig-Wig, gold stamp 350.00
Simpkin, brown mark 550.00
4 1/4" h
Pigling Bland, gold stamp
. . . . 225.00
Mr. Benjamin Bunny, 2nd version,
brown stamp 50.00
Mrs. Rabbit, oval gold stamp
. . . . 245.00
4 1/2" h
Peter Rabbit, brown and white rabbit, dk blue coat 110.00
Pickles, brown stamp 280.00
4 3/4" h
Fierce Bad Rabbit, brown stamp
. . . . 50.00
Foxy Gentleman, gold stamp
. . . . 150.00
Jemima Puddleduck, gold stamp
. . . . 135.00
Plaque, 7 1/2" h, Peter Rabbit, #2650
. . . . 85.00
Plate, 4" d, Jeremy Fisher, "Royal Albert"
mark 13.00

Jug, 11 1/2" h, magenta, turquoise, mustard yellow, and brown, cream ground, c1930s, $595.

Celery Tray, 12 1/2" l, 2 raised red flower-heads at end, molded leaf ground shaded green to white. 58.00
Character Jug
Barnaby Rudge, small, #1121 . . . . 50.00
Micawber, 1st version, large, #310
. . . . 65.00
Navy-HMS Wink, large, #736, (A)
. . . . 177.00
Robert Burns, large, #1045. . . . . 245.00
Sairy Gamp, large, #371 . . . . 55.00
Scrooge, large, #372 . . . . 50.00
Cheese Dish, Cov, 7" l x 6" w x 4 1/4" h, slant top, molded red and yellow flowers, green molded leaf ground, blue flowerhead knob, "imp BESWICK" mark. 58.00
Creamer and Sugar Bowl, Tony Weller, #674, Micawber, #674 . . . . 40.00
Disney Figures
2 3/4" h, Pigglet, gold stamp. 80.00
3" h
Owl, brown stamp 45.00
Tigger, brown stamp 75.00
3 1/4" h, Kanga, brown stamp. . 65.00
4 3/4" h, Christopher Robins, 1st version 125.00
Figure
3 1/2" h, Dusty Mole, #1155, David Hand Animaland, (A) 495.00
3 3/4" h, Oscar Ostrich, #1154, David Hand Animaland. 495.00
4" h, Ginger Nutt, #1152, David Hand Animaland, (A) 390.00
4 1/4" h, Dinkum Platypus, #1148, David Hand Animaland, (A) 285.00
4 1/2" h, Anglund Girl with Doll, #2293
. . . . 175.00
5 3/4" h, Farm Boy, #912. . . . . . . 750.00
6" h, Goose Girl, #905 . . . . 750.00
Jug, 8" h, Falstaff, #1126 . . . . 145.00
Mug, 4" h, Falstaff, #1127. . . . . 45.00

Pitcher
7 1/4" h, blue drip, yellow ground, matte finish. 95.00
7 5/8" h, molded neck rings, pastel blue, tan, and yellow streaks and whites splashes, matte finish 95.00
Plaque, 14" l, Seagull, white, black, and yellow, gloss finish, #658/1 . . . . . 45.00
Salt and Pepper, Sairy Gamp, #689, Micawber, #690. . . . . 58.00
Teapot
5 3/4" h, Sairy Gamp 99.00
6" h, Peggoty, #1116 . . . . 99.00
Vase, 11 1/4" h, swollen cylinder shape, green, black, and pink painted and sgraffito abstract columns and polka dots 125.00

BING AND GRONDAHL

Copenhagen, Denmark
1853 to Present

History: The Bing and Grondahl Porcelain Factory was established in Copenhagen in 1853 when Frederich Grondahl left the Royal Copenhagen Porcelain Manufactory due to an artistic disagreement and joined with M.H. and J.H. Bing. The Bing brothers provided the business expertise, while Grondahl was the artistic force.

About one and one-half years after the company started, Grondahl died. The Bings hired top designers and decorators to continue fabricating utilitarian and art wares. In 1886, the firm first used under-glaze painting. Previously, the firm manu-factured pieces with "biscuit" or overglaze porcelain decorations.

In 1895, the first Christmas plate was is-sued. A seven-inch blue and white plate utilizing the underglaze technique is made every year with the molds being destroyed after Christmas to prevent later restrikes. From 1910-1935, Easter plaques also were issued.

Several great artists were employed by the company such as J.F. Willusmen, Effie Hegermann-Lindercrone, Fanny Garde, Haus Tegner, Kai Nielsen, and Jean Gauguin. In 1914, stoneware was made for the first time. Soft paste porcelain began in 1925. In 1949, a new factory was built for producing dinnerwares.

Every piece of Bing and Grondahl work is signed with either the artist's name or ini-tial. While today's collectors know Bing and Grondahl primarily for its figurals and annu-al Christmas plates, the company still pro-duces a porcelain line.

Reference: Pat Owen, *The Story of Bing & Grondahl Christmas Plates*, Viking Import House, Inc.1962.

Figure, 8 1/2" h, dk blue scarf, lt blue jacket, white apron, green dress, #2233, $475.

Museums: The Bradford Museum, Niles, IL; Metropolitan Museum, New York, NY.

Cake Plate, 11" H-H, lt blue clematis, dk blue leaves, blue to white shaded ground, #101A 50.00

Compote, 9 5/8" d, gold accented white seagulls, blue to gray shaded ground, relief molded overlapped clouds, #206 . . . . . 70.00

Figure
   4" h, 2 seated children reading book, girl in dk blue dress, boy white pants and shirt, brown jerkin, #1567 . . . . . 155.00
   5" h
      Kneeling child, holding stomach, white glaze, #2208 . . . . 95.00
      Seated cat, gray, white chest, tan inner ears, #1876 . . . . 165.00
   5 3/8" h, seated boy in blue overalls, holding shoe in hand, #2275 . . . . . . 155.00
   5 1/2" h, parrot on limb, blue and mauve, #2019 . . . . 120.00
   5 3/4" h, seated Siamese cat, brown and black, blue eyes, #2308, "B. & G. Castle" mark 120.00
   8" h, "The Long Dress," white, tan, and green young girl holding hem of dress 215.00
   9 1/2" h, seated old man reading book, girl standing at side, blue and gray shades, oct base, #2037 VI, (A) 75.00
Vase
   3 1/2" h, white lily of the valley, blue shade ground, #157-5012 . . . . 32.00
   5 1/2" h
      Stoneware, carved panel of shepherd and sheep, maroon and gray-green matte glaze, artist sgd 165.00
      Two gilt trimmed white seagulls, blue to gray shaded ground, raised overlapping clouds, #678 . . . . 55.00
   6 3/4" h, flat sides, white dogwood blossoms, dk brown gnarled branch, lt blue ground, #260-5239 JC 95.00

Vase, 7 1/8" h, "JULEN 1918" on base, blue shades, (A) $100.

   7" h, swollen cylinder shape, blue and gray sailboat reflected in dk and lt blue and gray waves, shaded blue sky, #B356-251 . . . . 175.00
   7 3/8" h, landscape, green and brown trees, white winding road, gray mountain bkd, #8692-251 NN 175.00
   8 1/4" h
      Bulbous shape, slightly flared rim, brown farmhouse with dk red roof, green puffy trees, green and brown ground, shaded blue sky, #602-5249 . . . . 195.00
      White English roses, lt blue ground 195.00
   8 1/2" h, white Egret-type bird feeding chicks in nest, blue to gray shaded ground 185.00
   9 1/2" h, swollen cylinder shape, brown, green, pink, and blue butterflies on blackberry bushes, blue to white shaded ground, #6750/2 . . . . 225.00
   9 5/8" h, bulbous cylinder shape, lg white magnolias, brown leaves at base, pink accents, med blue ground, pr, (A) 616.00
   10" h, bulbous body, flared rim, white and tan florals and gray-green leaves, blue shaded ground, #8607/368, c1915 . . . . 275.00

BISQUE

English/Continental 1750 to Present

History: Bisque, or biscuit china, is white, marble-like, unglazed hard porcelain or earthenware that has been fired only once. The composition of the body and the firing temperature are most important to achieve the matte, porous surface of the figure. Since there is no glaze or decoration, the

surface has to be completely free of imperfections. Razor-sharp modeling of details is made possible by the absence of glaze.

Bisque figures first were produced around 1751 at Vincennes and Sevres in France. They became very fashionable. Many French porcelain factories during the latter part of the 18th century added them to their product lines. Bisque figures also were made at Meissen in Germany.

Beginning in 1773, Derby was the principal manufacturer of bisque figures in England. Bisque figures in soft paste porcelain have a great smoothness to the touch and a warm soft tone.

About 1850 German factories produced bisque dolls. Delicacy of coloring and realism of features could be achieved with this material. In the late 1850s, France also started producing bisque dolls. Both French and German factories manufactured bisque dolls in the image of children rather than ladies during the 1880s. They were called "bebes," even though they depicted girls from about 8 to 12 years old.

Most bisque examples are unmarked.

Museums: Bayerisches National Museum, Munich, Germany; Victoria & Albert Museum, London, England.

Box, 10 1/4" h, figural seated black man in black striped yellow shorts and pink jacket, seated in armchair, Germany, (A) 120.00

Centerbowl, 8 3/4" h, pierced body, figural cherub tripod feet, white, France, (A) 575.00

Cigar and Match Holder, 7 1/4" h, figural seated hunter in green jacket, gray trousers, gray hat with green band, begging dog on base, rifle at feet, lg and sm open tree trunks, Germany, chips and overpaint, (A) 50.00

Fairy Lamp, 6 3/4" h, figural 3 story house, white brick, red roof 600.00

Figure
   4 5/8" h, black man with arms raised, lt blue trousers, pink vest, and red shoes, seated on barrel, Germany, (A) 65.00
   5 1/2" h, bust of musketeer, blue, gold, and brown trimmed blue tunic, brown hat, lt blue plumes, circ base, unmkd, (A) 35.00
   5 5/8" h, girl holding doll, seated in lg chair, long pink and yellow dress, gold trimmed, unmkd, (A) 35.00
   6" h
      Boy in yellow coat, gray breeches, girl in mop hat, yellow dress, both under umbrella 135.00
      Standing boy wearing brown hat, lt blue pants, pink and white shirt, lt blue scarf, hands in pockets, brown books, lt tan base 24.00
   7 1/2" h, seated Red Riding Hood, orange hood and cape, holding yellow basket with pink and green flowers, sm HP red

Figure, 7 3/4" h, blond hair, lt blue or pink clothes, green and brown base, "blue R in diamond" mark, Germany, $295.

and green floral sprigs on dress, brown and yellow wolf, (A) 50.00

8" h x 9" l, women in 18th C dress holding tea cup, reclining on ornate chair, feet on stool, purple, pink, and lt green dress with gold accents, oval scrolled base, (A) 75.00

8 1/4" h, standing boy in purple shorts, standing girl in blue trimmed white dress, yellow bonnet with blue ribbon, lt brown umbrella on metal shaft, oval base, Germany 55.00

8 5/8" h, standing "Mr. Pickwick" in white trousers, lt green waistcoat, and black hat or "Mrs. Bardell" wearing lt orange dress, lt green shawl, and green bonnet, gold relief beading, labeled bases, Germany, pr, (A) 30.00

9 3/4", 10" h, standing boy in pink and gold trimmed white waistcoat, blue knee breeches and shoes, playing horn, standing girl wearing blue trimmed white blouse, yellow bow, pink skirt, blue shoes, holding music book, chip on horn, pr, (A) 60.00

10 3/8" h, Kate Greenaway-style standing girl wearing eyeglasses, pink blouse, white dress and apron, white and pink bonnet, holding book, gold accents, Germany, (A) 40.00

10 1/2" h, young man cutting wheat, white and pink, unmkd 48.00

11" h

Bust of period man, blond hair, blue eyes, gray hat with flowers, tan vest,

pink florals on shirt, blue base, France 295.00

Period man in powdered wig, maroon waistcoat, blue overcoat, woman in pink and blue ball gown, holding rose, blue and yellow striped circ base, France, pr 425.00

11 1/2" h, standing brown haired boy, blue jacket, purple striped trousers, holding lg blue edged envelope under arm, standing blond haired girl, purple jacket, lt blue collar, flowered yellow dress, hand in muff, green and brown mottled base, Germany, pr 650.00

12 1/2" h, seated Cupid or Psyche, blue glazed base with gold trim and French saying, Sevres. c1872, chips and repairs, pr, (A) 1380.00

13 1/8" h, man or woman in 18th C French clothes, man holding mandolin, woman with fan overhead, blue and pink with HP pink floral sprigs and gold beading, green and brown shaded circ scrolled and floral base, pr, (A) 50.00

13 1/2" h, standing young boy holding basket, lavender coat with yellow ribbon, blue striped short pants, lt blue hat with yellow ribbons and blue band and feathers, France 195.00

16 1/4" h, bust of 18th C lady wearing sm hat, circ base, France, c1785-95 . . . . 2,200.00

25" h, 25 1/4" h, standing youth in pink lined lt blue jacket, yellow sash, pink trousers with raised gold dots, holding fishing net, young girl in pink bodice, lt yellow skirt, lt blue sash, raised gold flowers and dots, holding barrel under arm, circ brown rock base, Austria , pr 495.00

Flower Holder, 3 1/2" h x 4" l, reclining boy in blue shaded clothes, lying on blue rock base with white and green moss, blue and white bucket for flowers 39.00

Game Tureen, 5 3/8" h x 8 1/4" l, cov with figural reclining white shaggy dog with brown and black trm, holding bone, green blanket, gold basketweave base, France 550.00

Nodder, 5 1/2" h, seated oriental man in pale blue robe, pink hat, holding staff, seated oriental female in pink gown, holding stringed instrument, Germany, pr 450.00

Planter, 6 3/4" h, standing boy in pink sailor suit, blond hair, holding coiled rope, brick planter with anchor at side 46.00

Plaque, 9 5/8" l x 4 7/8" h, rect, white cameos of classic female figures with statue, blue ground, Sevres, c1810, (A) 1,610.00

Vase

4 3/8" h, oval, figural rooster, hen, and chicks or ducks and ducklings on rim, green and gold swag body, lt blue and gold scrolled base, Germany, pr (A) 50.00

5" h, figural Santa Claus with basket on back, long white coat with lt blue and

pink trim, lt blue hood, Germany, (A) 40.00

5 1/2" h, trumpet shape lt yellow, purple, and gold tree trunks, figural children in purple, pink, and red clothes, Germany, chip in base, pr, (A) 25.00

5 5/8" h, cornucopia shape, woman in purple and gold accented dress holding flower garland seated on rect base, France, chips, (A) 35.00

6 3/4" h, figural bust of Indian chief, dk brown jacket, yellow, red, and green trim, white feathered headdress with black edge, Germany 125.00

8 1/4" h, figural classic man in pale pink coat, blue scarf, flowered trousers, holding basket of multicolored applied flowers, 2 vases in bkd, gold trim, scroll molded base, France 135.00

8 7/8" h, figural child stretching, white dress, green trim, one green trimmed white sock, lt brown wicker chair in bkd, Germany, (A) 70.00

BLUE ONION

German
c1730 to Present

English/Continental
1800s to Present

MEISSEN

AFTER 1882

History: The Blue Onion or bulb pattern was started in Meissen, Germany about 1728 and was based on a Chinese aster pattern from the late Ming dynasty. After Horoldt perfected the underglaze blue paint technique in 1739, the onion pattern took on its more familiar form. This pattern really had nothing to do with onions. The flower in the center has been described as a chrysanthemum, peony, or aster. The bulbs or fruits on the border were not onions either, but resembled pomegranates and peaches. In later years, they resembled onions more closely.

More than 60 European and oriental manufacturers copied the onion pattern and called it by a variety of names. In German, the pattern is called "Zwiebelmuster."

The pattern underwent various changes and was produced in tremendous numbers. It was less expensive to make and could be painted by less experienced workers.

The Royal Prussian Manufactory in Berlin was one of the most serious competitors utilizing the onion pattern from the 18th to the 20th century. It utilized the scepter mark.

Popularity increased in the second half of the 19th century, and the onion pattern appeared on other items such as pots, boxes, tablecloths, and napkins.

Most of the onion pattern pieces available today were made after 1865. Some examples have a gilt edge, or the fruits and plants are heightened with gold or red contours.

Some of the European manufacturers produced blue onion stoneware in addition to their porcelain examples. Since the pattern was not copyrighted, it could be used by any factory. To protect the actual Meissen examples, the factory utilized the crossed swords mark in the lowest part of the bamboo cane about 1888. Pieces without this mark date before 1888.

Carl Teichert's factory combined with Melzer's as the Meissen Stove and Fireclay Factory and copied the Meissen onion pattern exactly. It hand painted its copies. In 1882, it registered a trademark with the name "Meissen" that caused much confusion. Other factories were established that used similar marks to add to the confusion. There were disputes with Meissen over the marks. Another popular producer of the onion pattern was L. Hutschenreuther, who printed the pattern rather than hand painting it since they produced it in quantity for everyday use.

The Meissen Stove and Porcelain Factory acquired a factory in Eichwald Bohemia which later became B. Block's factory. He continued to produce the onion pattern.

Additional changes in the factory and borders put the Block factory in Czechoslovakia after 1918 but they still utilized marks that caused confusion. With World War II, more changes occurred and the factory came under German jurisdiction.

After WWII, the factory returned to Czechoslovakia and with other factories became Duchsovsky Porcelain. This Dubi branch continued to make the onion pattern.

After 1900, Meissen added "MEISSEN" to its mark impressed into the piece before firing and then glazed over it. "Made in Germany" was printed in blue under the glaze for export pieces. Other factories in Germany and abroad also copied the onion pattern in both porcelain and stoneware. Examples are available from English, French, Japanese, Austrian, and Czechoslovakian manufactories.

Ashtray, 5" d, "blue X'd swords" mark . 80.00

Bowl

6 1/2" d, "blue oval MEISSEN" mark 45.00

7 7/8" d, scalloped rim, "MADE IN GERMANY in oval" mark 55.00

8 1/8" d, reticulated flowerhead border, "blue MEISSEN" mark 275.00

8 1/2" d, reticulated, "blue X'd swords" mark 395.00

Cake Stand, 4" h, 8 1/4" sq, pedestal base, "B.W.M. & C. MEISSEN" mark 325.00

Candlestick, 6" h, "blue X'd swords" mark, pr 130.00

Cheese Dish, 9 1/4" d, "blue X'd swords Germany" mark, (A) $75.

Candy Dish, 4 3/4" l, rolled handle, "blue X'd swords" mark 75.00

Celery Tray

9 1/4" l, "blue MEISSEN in oval and star" and imp marks 145.00

11 3/4" l x 4 7/8" w, molded swirl designs on sides, gold accented scalloped rim, "Sontag & Sons, Tettau" mark, (A) 65.00

Cheese Dish, 9 1/4" d, "blue X'd swords, Germany" mark, (A) 80.00

Coffee Server, 11 1/2" h, leaf molded and flowerhead knob 375.00

Compote, 14" h, 2 tier, swirl base, reticulated borders, c1860 . . . . 1,050.00

Cup and Saucer, Demitasse, Staffordshire, c1886 . . . . 40.00

Cutting Board, 10" l x 6" w, (A) 160.00

Dish

12" d, "blue X'd swords and dot" mark, (A) 375.00

13 3/8" d, "blue X'd swords" mark, c1770, chip, (A) 385.00

Egg Cup, 3 1/2" h, "blue X'd swords" mark 75.00

Fish Platter

21 5/8" l, gold rim 775.00

24" l, "blue X'd swords" mark, c1880 . . . . 895.00

Hot Plate, 7" d, sloping rim, "green FAM, tower and Bonn" mark 20.00

Inkstand, 12" l x 8 1/2" w x 3 1/2" h, dbl cov wells on scalloped rimmed tray 1,400.00

Invalid Feeder, 2 1/4" h x 3" d, side handle, gold accents, "blue X'd swords" mark, (A) 20.00

Pitcher, 4 1/4" h, "TK and shield" mark 45.00

Plate

6" d, "blue oval MEISSEN" mark . . . 35.00

6 1/2" d, "blue X'd swords" mark . . 40.00

7" d, open work border of flowerheads, "MEISSEN in oval and star" mark 175.00

8 1/4" d, "blue MEISSEN in oval and star" mark 45.00

8 1/2" d, Cauldon, set of 6, (A) . . . 100.00

8 3/4" d, "blue MEISSEN" mark, (A) 50.00

9 1/2" d, gold striped rim, "red KPM" mark, set of 6, (A) 50.00

10" d, "blue oval MEISSEN" mark 75.00

Platter

12 1/4" l, Johnson Brothers, (A) 65.00

13" l x 10" w, "blue X'd swords" mark 295.00

15" l x 12 1/2" w, scalloped raised flange, "blue X'd swords" mark, (A). . . . 500.00

20" l, "blue X'd swords" mark 550.00

21" l x 15" w, oval, "blue X'd swords" mark 320.00

Salt Box, 5 3/8" h, wood top, brass hinges, pierced for hanging, "black Salt" on front, "G.M.T. & Bro., Germany" mark, (A) . . 115.00

Sauce Boat

9" l, with attached undertray, open flowerhead knob, "blue MEISSEN and GERMANY" marks. 225.00

9 1/2" l, with attached undertray, 2 side handles, "blue X'd swords" mark, (A) 125.00

Serving Dish, Cov, 11" d, molded scrolled border, cut out handles, flower form knob, Germany, (A). 69.00

Soup Plate, 8 1/2" d, Cauldon 59.00

Soup Tureen, 15 1/2" H-H, "blue X'd swords" mark, (A) 395.00

Strainer, 5" d, wood handle, chine hook on bowl, (A) 75.00

Sugar Bowl, Cov, 4 3/4" h 22.00

Sweetmeat Dish, 14 1/2" d, 4 sections, overhead twist handle, "blue X'd swords" mark, (A) 225.00

Tazza, 5 1/4" h x 8 1/4" d, pierced border with 3 sm cartouches of flowers 495.00

Teapot, 7 3/4" h, floral knob, "MEISSEN in oval and star" mark 165.00

Tea Tile, 6 1/2" d, Schoenau, Huttensteinach 145.00

Tray, 17 1/2" l, oval, "blue X'd swords" mark 195.00

Vegetable Bowl, Cov

9 1/2" d, Villeroy and Boch, c1900 . . . . 100.00

11 1/2" l, rect, "blue MEISSEN" mark, (A) 100.00

13 1/2" H-H, "blue X'd swords" mark, (A) 125.00

BOCH FRERES KERAMIS

La Louviere, Belgium 1841 to Present

History: The Boch Freres factory at La Louviere, called Keramis, was founded in 1841 by Victor and Eugene Boch and Baron J.G. Nothomb. Previously, the Boch brothers were associated with the Villeroy and Boch concern.

The designs of Alfred William Finch, an English artist, and Marcel Goupy, a French artist, were produced at the Keramis factory. Finch signed vases, dishes, jugs, and candlesticks featuring a rough, red earthenware body covered with slip and glazed in ochre, blue, bottle green, or fawn along with incised linear decoration and dots of light colored glaze in the Art Nouveau style.

Marcel Goupy made earthenware services decorated in ochre and blue for the Keramis factory. His pieces usually were signed.

Tiles were made from the 1880s at a branch factory in France. The Keramis factory also produced earthenware and stoneware similar to Staffordshire wares. Imitations of Delft china were produced along with Rouen and Sevres copies.

Museum: Museum voor Sierkunst, Ghent, Belgium.

Bowl, 4 1/2" d, "Dentelle" pattern, fans and rosettes, red transfer 55.00

Box, 2 5/8" h, sq, green stripes with magenta circles and black centers, yellow ground 300.00

Jardiniere, 8" h, vert bands of black and blue enameled flowerheads, blue banded rim and base, white crackle ground, (A) 250.00

Lamp Base, 12 1/4" h, black and cream crackle alternating panels on shoulder and base, center body with geometric panels of rust and gold sunburst 225.00

Planter, 11 3/4" l, rect, ftd, Persian blue crackle glaze, (A) 100.00

Vase

5" h, bulbous shape with sm flared rim, blue outlined yellow flowerhead and green centered orange flowerhead, stylized blue leaves, yellow shoulder with vert blue stripes, cream ground, smooth finish 145.00

6" h, blue enameled stained glass outline filled with green and yellow enamel, gray crackle ground 435.00

6 1/4" h, yellow spiraling flowerheads suspended from black drip from rim, hanging bluebells, smooth white ground 250.00

6 1/2" h, bulbous, yellow, blue, and turquoise stylized flowerheads and leaves, cream crackle ground, dk blue band on rim, (A) 150.00

6 3/4" h, white body with black vert stripes and dots, yellow shoulder with dk red, white, and black stylized flowerheads 450.00

7 1/2" h, swollen shape, dk brown stylized flowerheads and overlapping half circles, tan ground with brown shading, gunmetal int and ringed base, Charles Catteau 800.00

7 3/4" h, bulbous base, stepped shoulder, blue enameled basket with brown, dk blue, and yellow flowerheads, turquoise and blue leaves, cream crackle ground

panels with med blue ovals and dk blue diamonds, dk blue rim 475.00

8" h

Bulbous with molded horiz raised rings, Persian blue crackle glaze, (A) 50.00

Narrow base, wide shoulder, narrow rim, vert bands of yellow and dk blue flowers on turquoise ground, white crackle body, (A) 200.00

8 1/2" h, gourd shape, "Soleil Bleu," yellow flowerhead with med blue swirled leaves, dk blue accents, vert med blue wavy stripe, blue oval dots, gray crackle ground 825.00

9" h

Gourd shape, "Roses Stylisees," brown centered green and blue enameled flowers, dk blue enamel swirls, turquoise vert stripes, gray crackle ground, blue rim . . . 825.00

Swollen cylinder shape, dk brown panels with stylized dk brown outlined cream leaves, cream crackle ground, sgd "Catteau" . . . 1,100.00

9 1/2" h

Art Deco building shape, Art Deco yellow and black enameled geometric design, cream crackle ground, "Keramis/Made in Belgium" mark, (A) 1,045.00

Bulbous base, slender neck, turquoise vert straight and wavy lines and dots, white crackle ground, turquoise lined rim and base. 325.00

9 3/4" h, ovoid shape, brown and black circles, brown vert wavy lines, white crackle ground. 325.00

10" h

Bulbous, dk blue, turquoise, black, and yellow abstract floral design, white

Vase, 13 1/2" h, eggshell birds, blue and turquoise striped ground, yellow line borders, "Made in Belgium, Bausch Firienze LaLouviere, Catteau" mark, (A) $1,035.

crackle ground, dk blue neck, (A) 495.00

Flared rim, bulbous shape, dk red and black stylized vert florals, white crackle ground, dk red line in shoulder, pr 775.00

10 1/8" h, 2 handles, yellow, purple, and tan flowers, magenta ground, brown sanded textured neck, gold accents, turquoise int 220.00

10 3/8" h, ovoid shape, incised and enameled blue, turquoise, green, and yellow glazed long tailed birds in exotic foliage, (A) 465.00

10 3/4" h, bottle shape, white and blue grapes and green leaves, dk green and brown flambe ground, "Gres Keramis" mark, (A) 450.00

11" h, turquoise and white vert stripes, turquoise and dk blue hanging circles, yellow crackle ground between, cream crackle ground on neck with yellow circles and lt and dk blue drops connected by black lines, sgd "Catteau," pr 1,500.00

12" h, ovoid shape, lg black walking elephants and palm trees, crimson ground, C.H. Catteau, (A) 1,600.00

12 3/8" h, ovoid shape, red centered yellow petaled and red petaled stylized flowerheads, green and blue foliage, vert bands of green, red, and blue geometrics, white ground, (A) 233.00

12 3/4" h, ovoid shape, green, red, and blue overlapped flowerheads, white crackle ground. 425.00

13" h, fluted body, alternating brown enameled stylized rising suns, (A) 550.00

14" h, lt and dk blue enameled flowerheads and stems, cream crackle ground, pr 3,800.00

17 1/4" h, flared body, Secessionist stylized yellow, black, and turquoise vert designs, white crackle ground, Charles Catteau, (A) 1,100.00

BOHEMIA-GENERAL

Germany Late 1700s to Present

History: Franz Anton Haberditzel pioneered the Bohemian porcelain industry. In 1789, along with 25 partners, he established a factory in his native Rabensgrun near Schlaggenwald. Johann Gottlieb Sonntag of Rudolstadt was the technical director. When Haberditzel died in 1792, Sonntag carried on. The company disbanded in 1793 due to the unsatisfactory nature of the porcelain.

The first successful porcelain factory in Bohemia was started by Johann George

Paulus and Georg Johann Reumann at Schlaggenwald. Production initially was limited to earthenware because their patent to produce porcelain was refused in 1793 as a means of protecting the porcelain production in Vienna. Louise Greiner acquired the firm in 1800, enticed workers to move from Meissen in 1808, and received a regional patent in 1812. After 1876, the firm became Haas and Czizek.

Johann Nikolas Weber established a porcelain factory at Klosterle in 1794. This firm was rented by Christian Noone in 1799 to distribute Volkstedt porcelain. In 1820, Count Thun assumed management of the factory. Karl Venier, as director, improved the quality of the porcelain and produced examples that were gilded richly. Important sets, such as the "Empire" set (1851) and the "Thun" service (1856), and fine figures were made during his tenure.

Christian Noone set up a new factory near Carlsbad. After Noone died in 1813, Anton Hladik took over. There was a succession of owners. The factory eventually was sold to Johann Schuldes.

Johann Wenzel, Karl Kunerle, Josef Longe, and Josef Hubel started a factory in Prague in 1795. At first stoneware was made. Later the plant became the largest porcelain factory in Bohemia. In 1800, the firm was called Hubel and Company. It was sold to J.E. Hubel in 1810 who took in his son in 1820. Many figures were made during the 1840s for the wealthy bourgeois of Prague.

Friedrich Hocke established the Pirkenhammer factory in 1803 near Carlsbad. He sold out to Johann Fischer and Christof Reichenbach in 1811. By 1830, this was a fine Bohemian porcelain factory. All kinds of subjects were used on their porcelains: views, flowers, mythological, antique, and allegorical themes. Lithophane bedside lamps, dessert dishes, vases, and figures were made.

Christian Fischer became managing director in 1831. Fischer bought out Reichenbach in 1846. From that date until 1853, Reichenbach was the sole proprietor. In 1853, Ludwig von Mieg, Reichenbach's son-in-law, entered the business. The name was changed to Fischer and Mieg from 1857 to 1918 and used after both Fischer and Mieg died. After 1875, the wares became less important artistically and more practical. In 1918, the firm operated at Branch Pirkenhammer by Opiag. The name eventually was changed to Epiag and existed until 1945.

By the mid-19th century, there were 30 new porcelain factories in Bohemia. Forty-three factories existed by the end of the century.

Reference: E. Poche, *Bohemian Porcelain,* Artia, 1954.

Museums: Industrial Art Museum, Prague, Czechoslovakia; Museum of Bohemian Porcelain in the State Castle Klosterle, Czechoslovakia.

Box, 7 1/2" l x 6" w, egg shape, Art Nouveau style red and yellow flowerheads and ribbons on dk green glaze, "Eichwald" mark . 265.00

Dinner Service, tureen, cov, ftd, 2 loop side handles, 8 1/2" h, sauceboat and stand, 7 1/2" w, 2 salad bowls, 9" sq, rect butter dish, 8 3/4" w, 18 plates, 10" d, 12 soup plates, 10" d, 12 plates, 8 1/4" d, 12 plates, 6 3/8" d, 2 platters, 13 5/8" l, 12 plates, 10" d with painted scenes of various fish in sea, gilt scrolled inner border, border with panels of gilt loose bouquets in scrollwork cartouches with gilt phoenix heads reserved on green ground with gilt arabesques, Pirkenhammer, (A) 8,050.00

Figure, 18 3/8" h, "La Fortune," classical draped young woman, 6 pointed star on forehead, arm raised holding flowers, kneeling on winged wheel, hex base with gold and green accents, sgd "T. Schoop," "imp BB" mark, B. Bloch & Co., (A) 370.00

Plate

   6" d, multicolored classical scene of 2 classical maidens and man in garden, gold inner border with raised dots, blue border, Pirkenhammer 65.00

   7" d, center with pink rose transfer, lt green border, gold striped scalloped rim, "Sommer & Matschak, Schlaggenwald" mark,(A) 10.00

   7 7/8" d center motif of multicolored fruit, emb gilt rim, cream ground, Pirkenhammer, set of 6 . . . . 200.00

   Soup Bowl, 7 7/8" d, band of yellow, magenta, and purple flowers, green leaves and stems on border, cream ground, gold lined rim, Pirkenhammer. . . 10.00

Tobacco Jar

   7 1/2" h, terra cotta, figural barrel, dog head on lid, multicolored, "Made in Bohemia" mark, chips and repair, (A) 179.00

Plate, 8 3/4" d, polychrome center, magenta and blue floral border, set of 6, 3 women, 3 men, $2,800.

   8 1/4" h, terra cotta, figural pipes wrapped in sash, cov of man drinking beer, multicolored, "Made in Bohemia" mark, (A) 223.00

Teapot, 5 1/4" h, pedestal base, HP pink florals on shoulder, gold painted base, pedestal, spout, and handle, gold rim and knob, Oscar & Edgar Gutherz, (A). 35.00

Vase

   5 1/2" h, brown figural open flower, yellow and pink side blossoms, modeled green leaves, brown rock base, "Lippert & Hass, Schlaggenwald" mark . 285.00

   14" h, Art Nouveau style fruit form, mottled green glaze with raised flowers and jewels, serpent handles, c1905-10, (A) 175.00

BOW

East End of London, England
c1741-1776

1760 - 76

History: The Bow factory, one of the earliest English porcelain factories, was located in what is now the East End of London from c1741-1776. Mostly utilitarian wares that imitated the imported Chinese porcelains were made; underglaze-blue designs also were made. Bow's porcelains were the soft paste variety, incorporating a high percentage of bone ash in the paste mixture.

In the 1760s and 1770s, numerous decorative figures and animal models were made. The back usually had a square hole to hold a metal candle holder. Bow figures were press molded and thick walled.

Bow pieces of the 1760s are not marked with a true factory mark. They usually have the painter's mark or a reference number painted under the base. Later pieces often have an anchor and dagger mark painted in red enamel.

Bow porcelains found a willing audience in American buyers. Many pieces were exported. American clay also was utilized to manufacture some of the wares.

References: Elizabeth Adams & David Redstone, *Bow Porcelain,* Faber & Faber, 1981; Anton Gabszewicz & Geoffrey Freeman, *Bow Porcelain,* Lund Humphries, 1982; Egan Mew, *Old Bow China,* Dodd, Mead & Co.1909; H.Tait, *British Museum Catalogue of the 1959 Bow Exhibition*, Faber & Faber.

Museums: British Museum, London, England; Victoria & Albert Museum, London, England; Fine Arts Museums, San Francisco, CA.

Bowl, 6 1/4" d, pierced overlapping ring border, applied florets, enamel painted flowers and sprigs on int, c1765, (A) 633.00

Butter Boat, 3 3/8" l, molded overlapping leaves, loop handle, int painted with sm multicolored floral sprays, rose feathered rim, c1765, repaired hairline 450.00

Candlestick, 9 3/4" h, figural winged Cupid wearing flower garland reaching for blue-crested bird in branches, molded green leaves and flowers, rococo scrolled base accented with plum, blue, green, and gilt, quiver and dog on base, blue and gilt accented socket and bobeche, c1765, pr 6,850.00

Coffee Cup and Saucer, blue "Golfer and Caddy" pattern, c1758, (A) 475.00

Dish

7 7/8" d, enamel painted scattered roses, peonies, and tulips, fluted border, gilt dentil shaped rim, "iron red anchor and dagger" mark, c1765 . . . . . . .2,550.00

10 5/8" l, rect with cut corners, oval reserve of Chinese water scene, border with 4 fan reserves of oriental landscapes and 4 rd reserves of flowers, powder blue, c1765, (A) 690.00

Figure

2" h, sphinx seated facing right, scroll molded mound base, white glaze, c1750, damages and repairs, (A) 585.00

3 1/2" h, goldfinch, iron red patches on black head, puce back, black tail, black and yellow wings, seated on flowered branch, c1760, repairs, pr 1,950.00

5" h

Seated Harlequin in red flowered shirt and puce point hat holding bagpipe, seated Columbine in rose-pink bodice, flowered skirt, and flat puce hat holding hurdy-gurdy, c1756, pr, repairs and neck reglued . . .2,850.00

Standing putto, blue and plum sash, flower garlands around head and chest, holding yellow basket of flowers, flower strewn base, c1762 . . . . 975.00

Figure, 6 3/4" h, "Neptune," rust sash with yellow floral int, purple shaded plumed bird, $1,900.

6 1/4" h

Standing youth, bagpipe under arm, hound at feet, white glaze, repairs 400.00

White flower pot with painted flower bouquets, horiz raised ribbing, multicolored figural flowers and green leaves from pot, c1760, pr 3,750.00

6 3/4", 7 1/4" h, Fall modeled as male wearing lion skin, leaning on tree trunk, applied grape lusters, sleeping putto at feet, Spring modeled as female wearing flowered dress, pink cape, holding flower, leaning on tree stump with applied flowers, raised puce and blue accented rocaille molded base with applied flowers, c1765, pr, (A) 920.00

7" h, man carrying pack on back, white glaze, repairs 400.00

7 1/2" h, Cybele, standing, holding cornucopia of fruit, brown hair, flowered gown, rose-pink edged cloak, brown lion curled at feet, c1758, restored hand 1,450.00

10" h, figure of woman in flowered dress, holding cloak overhead, eagle on rt side, pierced scroll molded rect base, c1765, damages, (A) 585.00

Pickle Dish, Leaf Shape

3" l, blue painted fruiting vines, serrated rim, c1765, (A) 270.00

3 3/4" l, molded veins on ext, painted bouquets and sprays on int, rose feathered serrated rim, c1765, repairs . . . 450.00

Salt, 7 5/8" w, molded scallop shell on base of shell covered coral, white, c1755, chips and cracks, (A) 920.00

Sauceboat, 7 3/4" l, blue printed chinoiserie pattern, band of flowerheads on int border, c1765 . . . . 600.00

Sweetmeat Dish, 6 1/4" h, figural seated market woman in puce cape, blue-lined yellow dress, flowered skirt, beside lg bucket, glass in hand, rocaille molded base, c1760, (A) 322.00

Urn, 6 3/4" h, molded rose-pink, turquoise, and carmine female masks, blue painted flowers, rose-pink and carmine swirled feet, pyramid of white flowers w/green leaves on top, red anchor and dagger mark, pr . . . 3,550.00

Vase, Cov, 7 5/8" h, tapered baluster shape, painted multicolored enamel floral branches from blue rocks, diapering on shoulder and rim, pointed finial, c1750, pr 3,400.00

BRISTOL

**Bristol, England
c1749-1752, soft paste**

c1770-1781, hard paste

1770-81

History: Soft paste porcelain called "Lund's Bristol" was made in Bristol, c1749-52. Pieces show a strong Chinese influence. There usually was no factory mark. Hence, it is easily confused with early Worcester porcelains. In 1752, the Worcester Porcelain Company, under Dr. John Wall, purchased the Bristol soft paste factory and relocated it at Warmstry House in Worcester.

In 1770, a second porcelain factory at Bristol was established by William Cookworthy. This venture made hard paste porcelain, rather than soft paste. Richard Champion continued the factory between 1774 and 1778. A group of Staffordshire potters bought Champion's patent for hard paste porcelain and formed the New Hall Company, closing the Bristol factory in 1781.

Bristol porcelains of the 1770-78 period are rare. Tea services, dessert services, and dinner wares were made with simple floral patterns. Some gilding was used. Figures and vases were decorated with florals too. The factory is best known for its oval biscuit floral encrusted plaques.

Much Bristol porcelain was unmarked. Sometimes a cross in blue was accompanied by a painter's or gilder's mark. Copies of Dresden crossed swords were used on some Bristol pieces.

References: F.S. Mackenna, *Cookworthy's Plymouth & Bristol Porcelains*, F. Lewis, 1947; F. Severne, *Chapmion's Bristol Porcelain*, F. Lewis, 1947; Dr. B. Watney, *English Blue & White Porcelain of the 18th Century*, Rev. Ed. Faber & Faber, 1973.

Museum: Gardiner Museum of Ceramic Art, Toronto, Canada.

Collecting Hints: Fake Bristol porcelains often bearing the cross mark with a date are in the marketplace.

Bottle, 8 1/2" h, continuous oriental landscape with lg chrysanthemum heads, scrolling design on rim, blue and white, c1750 . . . 525.00

Charger

11 3/4" d, Adam and Eve, polychromed, blue dash border, c1720 . . . . 2,500.00

12" d

Center scene of man standing with boy, balcony overhead, border with oval panels of leaves, crisscross and dots between, blue and white, c1720-60, pr 2,100.00

Lg twisted tree branches with stylized flowerheads in center, flowerheads, leaves and stems from ground on border, blue and white, c1770, (A) 460.00

12 1/8" d, 2 oriental figures in front of twisted tree in center, branches with chrysanthemum heads and leaves on border, blue and white, c1770 . . . . 500.00

13" d, oriental man seated on ground holding fishing pole, rock with tree sprouting at side, mountains at top, blue and

white,
c1730-40 . . . . .1,150.00

13 1/4" d

Center scene of man standing on dock, man in boat, border of shaped panels with stylized flowers, criss-cross and dots between, blue and white 1,300.00

Red, blue, and green florals from cornucopia in center, flowers in compartments on border, c1745
. . . . 850.00

13 1/2" d, center with Chinese landscape and hillside pagoda, inner border of alternating crisscross panels and scrolling geometrics, border with plants issuing from rocks, blue and white, c1750 . . . . 450.00

14 3/8" d, center leafy stem with 2 stylized flowerheads, flowerheads and leaves on border, blue and white, c1740-60
. . . . .1,650.00

Dish

9" d, "Cracked Ice" pattern, blue and manganese 1,350.00

10 1/8" d, blue center scene of 2 fishermen in boat, terraced hills in bkd with houses and trees, bianco sopra bianco border of white flowerheads, c1760, (A)
. . . . 259.00

13 1/2" d, blue center design of oriental house with weepingwillow tree, manganese "Cracked Ice" border with 3 oval reserves of oriental house and weeping willow tree, c1760, (A) 633.00

Inkstand, 6" l, rect, 4 sm feet, oriental bridge in landscape scene, blue and white,
(A) 561.00

Mug, 7 1/8" h, polychrome stylized peacock with lg stylized flowerheads and insects, scroll design on rim, dot handle, mid-18th C, repairs, (A) 403.00

Plate

7 3/4" d, blue painted crane standing in marsh, border of stylized flowers, blue-white glaze, c1720, (A) . . . 460.00

Plate, 9 1/4" d, med blue design, lt blue ground, c1760-80, $300.

8 3/4" d, oriental scene of man standing over child, stylized bushes and balcony, border of panels of stylized flowers reserved on crisscross and dot pattern, red, blue, yellow, green, and manganese, rim chips, (A). 297.00

8 7/8" d, manganese, yellow, and blue of man and pagoda, bianco sopra bianco scalloped border, (A) 2,200.00

9" d

Blue painted poet Arion as child holding lyre astride swimming dolphin, sailboats in bkd, c1750, (A)
. . . . .1,610.00

Lt blue ground, blue center scene of oriental village, fisherman on dock, and boat, bianco sopra bianco border-band of white flowerheads, fruit, and leaves, hairline and chips,
(A) 192.00

Underglaze blue with green and red enameled overall floral design, gilt accents, Champion, (A) . . . 193.00

Punch Bowl

10 3/8" d x 4 1/2" h, ftd, oriental scene of cottage, mountain, and lake on ext, int band with geometrics, blue and white, c1740-60 . . . . 1,350.00

12" d, int blue painted with flowering plant in border of alternate panels of whorl and hatch, ext painted with band of floral and foliate lambrequins and plants in blue, iron red, and green, c1730,
(A) 7,130.00

Wet Drug Jar, 7 1/4" h, blue and white baroque design, label on reverse, (A) . . 578.00

BRITISH ROYALTY COMMEMORATIVES

Staffordshire, England
1600s to Present

PARAGON
BY APPOINTMENT
FINE CHINA
MADE IN ENGLAND
REG¹
1932

History: British commemorative china dates from the 1600s, although the early pieces were rather crude in form and design. When transfer printing was developed about 1780, the likeness of the king or queen was much improved.

With coronations or jubilee celebrations of England's royalty, a great number of souvenir wares appeared on the market to commemorate the occasion. This practice started in earnest with the coronation of Queen Victoria and has been in use ever since.

Most of these wares were manufactured in the Staffordshire district of England. Many small potters, finding a ready market for these souvenir products, produced them well in advance of any upcoming celebration. At times this was premature. The number of pieces prepared for the corona-

tion of Edward VIII is an excellent example. With his abdication of the throne, the coronation ware quickly became abdication ware. Since large quantities were produced and sold previously, wares for this event that never happened are not scarce.

It was not long before the major houses such as Minton, Royal Doulton, Aynsley, and Wedgwood began producing commemorative wares. Plates, jugs, pitchers, and tea sets were the popular pieces.

Transfers and decals that often featured busts of the king or queen and the consort graced most pieces. Other royal symbols used on the pieces included: crowns, dragons, royal coats of arms, national flowers, swords, scepters, dates, messages, and initials.

Some items were issued in limited quantities and are very desirable, but much of the materials prepared for coronation and jubilee celebrations were mass produced and are readily available.

From 1887-1937, the Golden Jubilee period through the coronation of George VI are the most popular periods for collecting royal commemoratives. Queen Victoria's commemoratives are the single most popular theme for collectors due to her populatory and longevity. For her Diamond Jubilee there was great quantities of memorabilia made since she was the longest reigning monarch in English history.

References: M.H. Davey & D.J. Mannion, *Fifty Years of Royal Commemorative China 1887-1937,* Dayman Publications, 1988; Douglas H. Flynn & Alan H. Bolton, *British Royalty Commemoratives,* Schiffer Publishing Ltd.1994; Lincoln Hallinan, *British Commemoratives,* Antique Collectors' Club, 1995; Josephine Jackson, *Fired for Royalty,* Heaton Moor, 1977; Peter Johnson, *Royal Memorabilia,* Dunestyle Publishing Ltd.1988; John May, *Victoria Remembered, A Royal History 1817-1861,* London, 1983; John & Jennifer May, *Commemorative Pottery 1780-1900,* Heinemann, 1972; David Rogers, *Coronation Souvenirs & Commemoratives,* Latimer New Dimensions Ltd. 1975; Sussex Commemorative Ware Centre, *200 Commemoratives,* Metra Print Enterprises, 1979; Geoffrey Warren, *Royal Souvenirs,* Orbis, 1977; Anthony B. Zeder, *British Royal Commemoratives With Prices,* Wallace-Homestead, 1986.

Collectors' Clubs: Commemorative Collectors Society, 25 Farndale Close, Long Eaton, United Kingdom, NG 10 3PA, $25.00 per year, *Journal of the Commemorative Collectors Society*; Royalty Collectors Association of North America, 30 E. 60th St., Suite 803, New York, NY 10022; $15.00 per year, annual newsletter.

Museums: Brighton Museum, Brighton, England; London Museum, Kensington

Palace, London, England; Victoria & Albert Museum, London, England.

Collecting Hints: Some collectors specialize in just one monarch, while others include several different ones. Another approach is to collect only pieces for special occasions, such as coronations, jubilees, marriages, investitures, births, or memorials. Others specialize in one specific form such as mugs, teapots, spoons, etc.

Newsletter: *The Commemorative Collector,* Douglas H. Flynn, P.O. Box 294, Lititz, PA 17543-0294, quarterly, $18.00 per year.

Edward VII

Beaker, 4 3/4" h, "The King's Coronation Dinner," purple profile portraits of Edward and Alexandra in crowned cartouche, Royal Doulton 99.00

Dish, 3 1/4" d, bone china, Silver Wedding Anniversary 1888, multicolored and HP crown, ribbons, and feathers, WH Goss 195.00

Jug

5 1/2" h, bone china, Coronation, multicolored half portraits of Edward and Alexandra in crowned wreath, gold accents, Austria 125.00

8 1/4" h, Coronation, brown busts of Edward and Alexandra, brown transfer, sepia ground, "Coronation of King Edward VII-1902" on base, dk brown neck, Royal Doulton 295.00

Medallion, 3 3/4" h, bisque, white portraits of Edward and Alexandra wearing crowns, Sevres, chip 80.00

Mug

2 3/4" h, "Coronation Memorial 1902," brown tone portraits of Edward and Alexandra and ground decorations, staining 49.00

3 1/4" h

Bone china, Coronation, sepia and multicolored portraits of Edward and Alexandra, crest, and flags, flowers on reverse and int, gold trim, RH & SL Plant 105.00

Multicolored busts of Edward and Alexandra with ribbon with "Enthroned in the Hearts of their People," brown "Presented By The Town of Penrith, Coronation Day June 26, 1902" on reverse, gold rim 65.00

Plate

8 1/2" d, Coronation, multicolored half portraits of Edward and Alexandra, Royal crest above, rose blossoms on border, molded vert ridging, gilt shaped rim 79.00

10 1/4" d, dk brown portrait of Edward, shaded brown ground, gold rim, Ridgway, crazing 105.00

Edward VIII

Box, 5 1/2" d, Coronation, raised band of "King Edward VIII Coronation 1937" on top band, national flower on base, crown on front, salt glazed green and blue on cream ground, Moorcroft, (A) 442.00

Cereal Bowl

6 3/8" sq, sepia bust of Edward and multicolored flags on border, ER VIII on opposite border, blue lined rim, "Made in England" mark 35.00

7 3/4" d, Coronation, sepia bust of Edward surrounded by multicolored flags, Coronation date below, list of Commonwealth above and black *"Porridge,"* gold lined rim 75.00

Dish, 5 1/2" d, white relief profile of Edward, med blue ground, crown over portrait and commemoration, J. & G. Meakin 49.00

Loving Cup, 3 1/2" h, bone china, multicolored Royal crest and commemoration, gold trim, brown figural lion handles, Paragon 148.00

Mug, 3 1/4" h, bust of Edward surrounded by Dame Laura Knight circus animals, multicolored, Woods Ivory Ware. 59.00

Plate

6 1/2" sq, semi-circular corners, Coronation, sepia bust of Edward with multicolored Royal Arms around portrait at top, 2 sm flags on opposite side, gold rim, unmkd 35.00

10 1/2" d, bone china, Coronation, brown tone profile of Edward surrounded by multicolored flags, HP accents, flags and names of Empire countries on border, Cauldon 149.00

Elizabeth

Beaker, 4" h, bone china, Coronation, brown portrait of Elizabeth, multicolored wreath, gold trim, Royal Doulton 79.00

Bell, 4 1/4" h, Silver Jubilee, multicolored Royal crest on front, previous monarchs on reverse, gold crown handle, Aynsley . . . 39.00

Butter Dish, Cov, 3" h, Coronation, brown profile, multicolored flags, blue trim, Sandland Ware, crazing 115.00

Cup and Saucer, Coronation, sepia portrait bust of Elizabeth and multicolored Royal Arms, "June 2, 1953, Coronation" under portrait, "Royal Grafton Bone China, Made in England" mark 35.00

Dish

4 1/2" d, bone china, Coronation, multicolored "ER," flags, and horns, gold trim, 4 sm handles, Paragon 25.00

5" d, Coronation, bone china, crenelated body, brown tone portrait, multicolored flags, lt green ground, Aynsley. . 33.00

5 1/2" H-H, Coronation, bone china, brown tone portrait of Elizabeth, multicolored flags, gold trim, Aynsley 33.00

Figure, 5 1/2" h, Coronation, white bisque bust of Elizabeth, glazed lt blue circ base, gold trim, Foley 95.00

Loving Cup, 3 1/4" h, bone china, Silver Jubilee, multicolored Royal crest on front, kings and queens of England on reverse, gold trim, molded branch handles, Aynsley 52.00

Mug

2 3/4" h, "HRH Princess Elizabeth," sepia crowned portrait of Elizabeth, gold rim, crazing, 1937 . . . . 105.00

3" h, bone china, Coronation, multicolored and gold arms design, gold lion handle, gold cipher and crown on reverse, Paragon 85.00

4" h, bone china, Silver Jubilee, multicolored and gold Royal crest, gold base band, Spode 69.00

4 1/4" h, Coronation, raised white overlapping profile busts of Elizabeth and Philip, lt blue ground, blue band on int rim, Burleigh Ware 59.00

5 3/4" h, 2 twist handles, Coronation, black transfer of Elizabeth on horseback in leaf roundel, "Here's a health unto Her Majesty" below, pink trim and "1953," Royal Doulton, (A) 150.00

Pin Dish, 4" l x 3" w, bone china, Coronation, multicolored portrait bust of Elizabeth, ivory ground, gold trim, Royal Crown Derby . . .47.00

Plate

7 3/4" d, ironstone, Silver Jubilee, red, white, and blue profile of Elizabeth and flags, Silver Jubilee information on border, Adams 20.00

8 1/4" d, bone china, Silver Jubilee, sepia portrait bust of Elizabeth, multicolored flags and accents, silver trim, Royal Sutherland 21.00

8 1/2" sq, Coronation, sepia frontal bust of Elizabeth, multicolored Royal Arms, "Coronation, June 2nd, 1953," gold trimmed border, molded design on rim, "Royal Alma" mark 35.00

8 3/4" sq, Coronation, bust of Elizabeth in center, ER and crown overhead, oak leaves, acorns, Royal crest, crown and flags of Ireland and England on border, red transfer, John Maddock & Sons Ltd 24.00

10 1/2" d

Coronation, multicolored crowned portrait bust of Elizabeth in center, cobalt border with gold overlay, gold emb rim, Aynsley 295.00

Silver Jubilee, HP multicolored arms of England in center, gold trim, cartouches of Balmoral, Conway, and Windsor castles and crowns on blue border, gold shaped rim, Longton Hall 385.00

Tea Plate

5 1/2" d, oct, birth, bust of Elizabeth and "H.R.H. Princess Elizabeth," sepia

transfer, "By special permission of HRH Duchess of York" on reverse, red and gold lined rim, Paragon 235.00

6 1/4" d, bone china, Royal Tour 1953-54, sepia portrait busts of Elizabeth and Philip, multicolored floral border, gold rim, Roslyn 89.00

Teapot, 4 /4" h x 8 1/2" l, bone china, Princess Elizabeth Birth, scattered multicolored HP flying birds and floral sprigs, blue trim, "For H.R.H. the Duchess of York for Princess Elizabeth" on base, Paragon 395.00

Tea Service, 7 piece, pot, 3 1/2" h, creamer, 2" h, sugar bowl, 2 1/2" d, 4 cups and saucers, bust of Princess Elizabeth, sepia transfers, gold lined trim, Wadeheath, c1937, crazing 475.00

Tea Set, pot, 5" h x 8 1/2" w, white cameo of bust of Elizabeth in wreath on front, Prince Philip on reverse, creamer, cov sugar bowl, "ER" in wreath on front, Royal arms on reverse, stiff leaf bands on cov rims, dk blue jasper ground, Wedgwood 475.00

Tumbler, 4 1/8" h, Coronation, multicolored transfer of bust of Elizabeth and flags, "ER" and crown on reverse, cream ground, "British Pottery Manufacturers Federation" mark 38.00

George V

Beaker

3 1/2" h, bone china, Coronation, multicolored portraits of George, Mary, Prince Edward, flags, and flowers, gold rim, lithophane of George on base . . 255.00

4" h, Silver Jubilee, sepia portraits of George and Mary, multicolored flags, crest, and wreath, silver trim 59.00

4 1/8" h, Coronation, brown crown over "M," "Coronation 1911," brown bust of George in crowned cartouche, Royal Doulton 195.00

Bowl, 8 1/2" d, oct, Silver Jubilee, sepia portraits of George and Mary, multicolored flags, gold rim, fading 22.00

Cup and Saucer, bone china, Coronation, sepia portraits of George and Mary, multicolored wreaths and flags, battleship George I and dreadnought George V on sides of portraits, HP accents, Aynsley 59.00

Dish, 6 1/2" l x 4" w, fan shape with molded streaks, multicolored crest with HP accents, gold rim, Late Foley Shelley 49.00

Loving Cup, 10 1/4" h, Silver Jubilee, white profile busts of George and Mary on yellow ground reserved on green textured ground with multicolored flags and musicians, brown wrapped green handles and rim, Royal Doulton 650.00

Mug

2 3/4" h, molded swirl body, Coronation, multicolored portraits of George and Mary, "Long May They Reign" in banner, "Crowned June 22, 1911" below, multicolored flags of Empire at sides 125.00

3" h

Coronation, green portraits of George and Mary and wreath, Windsor and Holyrood Castles on sides, "Presented by Mrs. Johnstone" on ribbon below Windsor, green transfers, Booths Silicon China 105.00

Silver Jubilee, brown tone portraits of George and Mary, Arms of Stockport on reverse, gold trim, commemoration on base, Royal Doulton 65.00

3 1/2" h

Coronation, portraits of George and Mary in wreath, cypher, crown, and date on reverse, green transfers, Royal Doulton 79.00

Silver Jubilee

Blue tone profile portraits of George and Mary and sawtooth border, "Bowdon Urban District" on reverse, chip on rim 42.00

Brown tone profile portraits of George and Mary, multicolored Royal arms, crown, "May 6th 1935" on reverse, silver trim, Nelson Ware 59.00

Pitcher

3" h, Coronation, sepia portrait busts of George and Mary surrounded by multicolored flags of the Empire, "June 22, 1911" under portraits, banner with Long May They Reign, gold lined rim". 85.00

5 1/8" h, Coronation, multicolored portrait of George, "Coronation 1911," crown over initials, Royal Doulton 175.00

Plate, 7" d, Coronation, multicolored bust of George in uniform, gold crown and "Coronation 1911" overhead, gold cypher below, shaped rim, Royal Doulton 85.00

George VI

Beaker, 4 1/4" h, egg shape, ftd, Coronation, multicolored crown over date, shaded blue-green ground, Moorcroft 595.00

Bowl, 10" d, South African Visit, orange, green, and yellow Royal crest and dates, gray ground, gold rim, crowns on ext 295.00

Cup and Saucer

Bone china, Coronation, portraits of George and Elizabeth, Princess Elizabeth and Margaret on reverse and saucer, brown transfers, Shelley . . . 89.00

Coronation, sepia portraits of George and Elizabeth and multicolored Royal crest, crest on saucer, gold trim, Aynsley 95.00

Mug

3" h, Coronation, individual sepia portraits of George and Elizabeth, multicolored flags and crown, gold trim, Bovey Pottery Devon. 35.00

3 1/2" h, multicolored Royal crest, gold trim, "From Capt. And Mrs. Stewart Liberty-May 12th 1937" on base, unmkd 69.00

Plate, 7 1/2" sq, Coronation, sepia portrait of George VI, multicolored flags, gold lined rim, "L. & Sons Ltd Henley, Made in England" mark, $60.

Plate

8" d, sepia busts of George and Elizabeth, multicolored flags, scenes of London in bkd, gold wreath with "To Commemorate The Visit Of Their Majestys King George VI and Queen Elizabeth To Canada And The United States Of America May 1939," yellow border, Royal Winton 35.00

8 1/4" d, oct, Coronation, sepia portraits of George and Elizabeth, multicolored flags, busts of Princess Elizabeth and Margaret in corners, Alfred Meakin 49.00

8 1/2" sq, Coronation, sepia bust of George on blue ground cartouche, "May 1937," blue rim, "Woods Ivoryware Eng" mark 24.00

8 3/4" d, family portrait, sepia transfer, emb floral border, red sawtooth rim, Alfred Meakin 79.00

Scuttle Mug, 4 3/8" h, Coronation, sepia portraits of George and Elizabeth, multicolored crown and flags, dtd 1937 . . . . 60.00

Tea Set, pot, 5 1/8" h x 8 3/4" l, Coronation, white cameo of crowned bust of George VI or Elizabeth in wreath, creamer, cov sugar bowl with monogram of king or queen, rampant lion and unicorn on reverse, white laurel wreath banding, dk blue ground, "Wedgwood, Made in England" marks, (A) 75.00

Tumbler, 3 1/2" h, Coronation, sepia busts of George and Elizabeth in multicolored flag cartouches 30.00

Royalty, miscellaneous

Bell

5" h, 80th Birthday, Queen Mother Elizabeth, color portrait on front, Castle of Mey on reverse, gold trim 43.00

5 1/4" h, Wedding, multicolor portraits of Charles and Diana in crowned cartouches, arms on reverse, gold trim, Crown Staffordshire 45.00

Dish

4" d, Prince William Birth, white cameos of Charles and Diana over Royal crest, lt blue jasper ground, Wedgwood . 28.00

4 1/4" d, Wedding of Prince and Princess of Wales, white cameo bust of Charles or Diana, white band of stiff leaves on border, lt blue jasper ground, Wedgwood, 1981, pr. 53.00

4 3/4" d, bone china, Investiture of Prince of Wales, sepia portrait of Charles, multicolored cartouche and flags, gold rim, Coronet 33.00

7" sq, bone china, Princess Margaret Canada Visit, brown portrait in center, gold leaf and berry band border, gold shaped rim, Aynsley 235.00

7 5/8" d, black transfer of bust of Queen Caroline and *Long Live Queen Caroline*," pink luster stripes and rim, (A) 200.00

Figure, 3 1/2" h, bone china, bust of Prince or Princess of Wales, HP natural colors, Royal Staffordshire, pr. 75.00

Jug

6 1/2" h, 1858 Wedding, black transfer of Princess Royal and Prince of Prussia, multicolored florals, German royal palace on reverse, blue and copper luster zigzag cartouche and borders . 295.00

7" h, Coronation, puce printed half portrait of William IV and Adelaide, crown in reserve of roses, thistles, and shamrocks and "KING WILLIAM IV AND QUEEN ADELAIDE CROWNED SEP. 1831" on front, (A) 195.00

Jug, Cov, 5 7/8" h, puce transfers of Prince Alfred standing before sailing ships beneath "IN MEMORY OF PRINCE ALFRED'S VISIT TO JAMAICA" on front, "SECOND SON OF OUR GRACIOUS QUEEN VICTORIA" and "LONG LIVE ALBERT AND THE ROYAL FAMILY" reserved in palm trees on sides, (A) . .1,232.00

Loving Cup, 3" h, bone china, 80th Birthday, Queen Mother Elizabeth, gold portrait bust, gold and multicolored crowned Royal crest, gold figural lion handles, Paragon 83.00

Plaque, 5 1/4" h x 4 1/2" w, rect, raised profile bust of Queen Caroline and "Q & C," pink luster beaded frame, (A) 375.00

Plate

7 1/2" d

Black transfer of "THE LITTLE JOCKEY" and young prince riding hound, border relief molded with ALBERT EDWARD PRINCE OF WALES BORN NOV 9 1841," (A) . . . 300.00

Pearlware, relief molded bust of George IV in blue and red uniform and yellow shoulder combs, yellow ribbon with "George IIII," molded border of blue and pink crowns, red ribbons, and green leaves with pink thistles, (A) 462.00

8" d, multicolored portrait of Queen Mother Elizabeth, wide gold border with scrolling overlay, Royal Worcester 99.00

Soup Plate, 8 1/2" d, multicolored relief busts of George IV or Caroline, crowns and ribbons on border, Scotland, restored, pr. . . . 1,995.00

Vase, 6 1/8" h, tapered, black printed Robert Hancock type bust of George III, reverse with figures walking in Italianate landscape, Worcester, (A) 2,156.00

Victoria

Bowl, 5 1/2" d, Victoria and Albert, multicolored and pink luster trim, c1840s 79.00

Cup and Saucer, Diamond Jubilee, black transfer of bust of Victoria, HP flowers and banner 225.00

Figure

7 1/4" h, parian, bust of Victoria, sq base, "imp Turner & Wood Stoke" mark 265.00

11 5/8" h, stoneware, Victoria seated on throne, brown salt glaze, Doulton Lambeth, (A) 2,945.00

Jug

4 1/4" h, 1887 Jubilee, raised beige profile portrait of Victoria and decorations, raised flowers on sides, med brown ground, beige int, base chip . . . 79.00

7" h, stoneware, Diamond Jubilee, white relief bust of Victoria, Royal coat of arms, titled ribbon, green glazed ground, Copeland late Spode, (A) 165.00

7 1/4" h, stoneware, Diamond Jubilee, relief portraits of Queen in 1837 and 1897 and "She Wrought Her People Lasting Good," slip decorated date and title on banding on neck, blue, green, and brown glazes, sgd "Emily Partington," Doulton Lambeth, (A) 288.00

Loving Cup, 7" h, bone china, Diamond Jubilee, multicolored transfer of flags of England, Scotland, and Ireland, HP accents, gold trim, flowers on int, Aynsley, restored 695.00

Mug

3" h, Diamond Jubilee, multicolored and HP crest, flags, and wreaths, gold trim, emb body, Aynsley 149.00

4" h, black transfer of bust of queen Victoria and British flag, "1837-1897," wording for anniversary on reverse, gray ground, "Wood & Hulme, Burslem" mark 135.00

Pitcher, 5 3/8" h, 1887 Jubilee, multicolored portrait of Victoria and "Jubilee of Her Majesty the Queen 1887," curved vert orange textured panels, "Made in Germany" mark . . . 150.00

Plate

6 1/4" d

Coronation, crowned bust of Victoria and "VICTORIA REGINA and coronation dates," purple transfer, emb floral border, Dillwyn Swansea 1,275.00

Proclamation, crowned bust of Victoria and "VICTORIA REGINA" and dates, dk brown transfer, emb floral border 1,075.00

8 1/2" d, bust of Victoria, banner with Whom God Preserve," flowers and thistles at sides, black transfer 155.00

9 1/2" d

Diamond Jubilee, blue shield with "To Commemorate The 60 Years Reign of Her Majesty Queen Victoria June 20, 1897" gold cartouche with raised gold dots, multicolored flags and elephant with Empress of India on shaded yellow ground with raised curlicues, gold splashed rim, British reg number. 199.00

Oct, Golden Jubilee, portrait of Victoria in rect, florals and "June 20, 1886," black transfer, worn gilt rim . 145.00

10 1/4" d, Diamond Jubilee, bust of Victoria in center surrounded by flags and "June 22, 1897" overhead, border banner with "Queen Victoria's Diamond Jubilee Alderman A. S. Tomson Mayor," blue-green transfer 175.00

BURLEIGH WARE JUGS

Middleport Pottery, Burslem, England 1931-1950s

History: This firm was started as Hulme and Booth in 1851 and became Burgess and Leigh in 1877. Their new factory was built at Middleport in 1889. The company remained in the hands of these two families until the death of R.S. Burgess, when it passed to the Leigh family who are still the owners. Burgess and Leigh became a Limited Company in 1919. It is still located in Middleport.

Charlotte Rhead worked at Burgess and Leigh from 1926-1931, where she trained a team of tube liners. She then moved on to A.G. Richardson.

Burleigh Ware was an important aspect of English Art Deco ceramics. During the 1930s, it produced the geometric, embossed, and hand painted yellow earthenware "flower jugs" that became very popular and were eagerly collected. Ernest Bailey, as an apprentice modeler in 1931, made the Squirrel, Parrot, Dragon, Kingfisher, Flamingo, Harvest (a rabbit in a corn stalk), Highwayman, and Pied Piper jugs. The elaborately molded figural handle formed the main subject of the jug while the body had appropriate decoration to coordinate with the handle.

Another designer of many jugs was Charles Wilkes who added Butterfly, Budgerigar, Village Blacksmith, and Stocks in 1938. Later, Coronation, Tally-ho (a hunting scene), and Sally in the Alley were made.

A series of larger sports people jugs also were made including the golfer, cricketer, and the tennis player, but less of these were made. Jugs were made in a variety of sizes and often in several colorings.

The usual mark is a beehive with leaves around it and "Burleigh Ware Made in England."

References: Judy Spours, *Art Deco Tableware,* Rizzoli International Publications, 1988; Howard and Pat Watson, *Collecting Art Deco Ceramics, 2nd Edition,* Wallace-Homestead, 1997.

Collecting Hints: Burleigh Ware jugs are sought by collectors of Art Deco ceramics, as well as by collectors who are just interested in the jugs for their subject matter or design.

Jug
  5 1/2" h
    Blue and green figural Kingfishe
    . . . . 475.00
    Rabbit in haystack, brown, yellow, and green 235.00
  6 3/4" h, brown branch handle, molded grapes on yellow ground body, orange and brown leaves on base 325.00
  7" h
    Blue, green, and yellow figural parrot handle, molded green scorpian, and blue and yellow butterfly, yellow ground, orange int, c1930 . . 295.00
    Green branch handle, raised brown kangaroos on sides, yellow flowers, dk blue dash rim 795.00
  7 1/4" h
    Brown figural fox handle, yellow ground with band of brown stemmed bushes, dk blue dash rim 400.00
    Relief molded figure of rabbit in bound corn, polychromed, (A) 150.00
    Rock Garden, figural orange flowerhead handle, raised orange tulips, blue and mauve flowers, gray stepped base, yellow body 575.00
  7 1/2" h, orange and black figural parrot handle, orange and black butterfly, yellow ground with orange accents at top and base 395.00
  7 5/8" h, figural golfer in plaid pants and hat teeing off, painted fairway on yellow ground, crack on base, (A) 625.00
  7 3/4" h
    Black, brown, and orange Dick Turpin handle, brown raised village with brown fence, green trim, yellow body 425.00
    Orange dragon handle with black claws, yellow ground 450.00
  7 7/8" h
    Figural handle of female tennis player, polychrome landscape . . .1,500.00
    Figural squirrel handle, painted brown tree branch, green leaves, yellow ground, (A) 125.00
  8" h, Coachman, polychrome, tan-gray running coach, brown and green forest,

Pitcher, 9 1/2" h, pink dress, yellow vest, green coat, black pantaloons, brown brick, green window, brown lantern handle, "Sally in the Alley" on base, c1940, $279.

    yellow ground, dk blue dash rim 750.00
  8" 1/2" h
    Bird of Paradise, blue, yellow, and orange-red figural bird handle with green stem onto molded green and brown leaves, cream and green bamboo body 425.00

    "GRETNA" on handle, "The Runaway Marriage," relief of blacksmith making ring for couple, polychromed 375.00
    "Village Blacksmith," relief of blacksmith in blue top, brown apron working at anvil, raised blue-green flowerhead border, brown branch handle 375.00
  8 3/4" h, orange, green, yellow, blue, and brown figural Pied Piper blowing horn handle, gray castle with red windows, yellow ground, green int, dk blue dash rim 475.00
  9" h, Aesop's Fables, blue figural stork handle with orange legs, dk blue relief of fox on side with red tongue, green ground with horiz ribbing 450.00
  9 1/4" h, Flamingo, raised orange and black flamingo, raised vert green leaves with sm red flowers, yellow ground, orange-brown flower stem handle 585.00

  10 1/4" h
    Aesop's Fable, green figural stork handle, raised fox on side, green ground with horiz ribbing . . . 395.00
    Handle modeled as swooping kingfisher and branch ending in spread leaves, polychromed, (A) . . . 250.00

CAPODIMONTE

Near Naples Italy 1743-1759
Buen Retiro, near Madrid, Spain 1760-1812

c1760 - EARLY 20™ C

History: Capodimonte was a royal palace in Naples, where a porcelain factory was established in 1743. Charles III, the Bourbon King, and his Queen, who had brought quantities of porcelain from Meissen, were the founders. The factory produced primarily soft paste porcelain in a milky white color for the court.

Guiseppe Gricci was the chief modeler. His specialties included religious subjects (madonnas, pietas, and holy water stoups,) snuff boxes, and mythological figures. Gricci was in charge when the factory created an entire room for the king that featured porcelain panels in high relief decorated in chinoiserie and which can be viewed today at the Museo di Capodimonte in Naples. Pieces usually were marked with the armorial fleur-de-lys of the Bourbon family.

When Charles inherited the throne of Spain and became king in 1759, he moved the factory and workers to Madrid with him. Gricci, now signing his works Jose Gricci, also made the transition. The new factory, located on the palace grounds, was called Buen Retiro. They continued to make soft paste porcelains similar to those made at Capodimonte including elaborate tablewares, centerpieces, flowers and figures. Sometimes the factory used the Bourbon fleur-de-lys mark. An attempt to make hard paste porcelains was made shortly before the factory closed.

When Ferdinand IV governed Italy in 1771, he revived the royal factory. Styles were influenced by a classical revival, inspired by the unearthed treasures at Pompeii. Best known are the pieces decorated with mythological reliefs.

After 1807, the factory declined and closed several years later. In 1821, the molds and models were sold to the Ginori factory at Doccia.

Museums: Metropolitan Museum of Art, New York, NY; Museo di Capodimonte, Naples, Italy; Woodmere Art Museum, Philadelphia, PA.

Reproduction Alert: Many factories in Hungary, Germany, France, and Italy copied Capodimonte examples. Many of the pieces on the market today are of recent vintage. Many reproductions are made with the red mark underglaze.

Bell, 4" h x 3" d, winged cherubs, gold arched scrolled and foliate handle, gold banded body, "GB Capodimonte 1535/366 Italy" mark, (A) 25.00

Box

6" h x 6" w, molded polychrome mythological scenes and masks, (A) 288.00

7" l, shaped rect form, top and sides relief of figures in garden, (A) 460.00

Bureau Box, 2 5/8" d, relief of cherubs on island on cov, cherub and floral design on sides, cast brass rims and hinge, (A) . . 40.00

Center Bowl, 14 1/4" H-H, oval, polychrome band of frolicking cherubs on ext, yellow ground, gold floral design on int, lt yellow and green scroll handles, 4 scroll ft, "Italy" mark. 115.00

Centerpiece, 11" h, 12 classic female figures in gilt flowing draped garb, pedestal bases with gilt lion masks, 2 rect sectioned planters with gilt lion masks, 2 curved divided planters with gilt lion masks, gold rims, (A) 4,600.00

Coffee and Tea Service, coffeepot, 8" h, teapot, 5" h, lid replaced, cream jug, cov sugar bowl, 4" h, 6 teacups and saucers, 6 demi-

Ewer, 16 1/2" h, polychrome, "gold crown over blue dash" mark, (A) $375.

Urn, 10" h, polychrome neo-classical figural scene, gilt rim, gilt garland band, relief molded horned satyr masks and garlands, faux marble and acanthus pedestal, plinth base, pr, (A) $850

tasse cups and saucers, polychrome classic scenes, gilt accents, (A) 1,000.00

Figure

4" h, standing young Bacchus holding grapes in hand, basket of grapes in other hand, gold sash across waist, green leaves in ears, green leaves in bkd, gilt scroll molded base 150.00

10" h x 9" l, female figure in puce and blue eastern garb, seated on brown seated camel, gold crown, "crowned N" mark 3,500.00

Plaque

5 1/2" d, polychrome semi-nude lovers in garden setting, gold trim, pierced for hanging. 9.00

12" d, polychrome relief center scene of wolf and Romulus and Remus, rolled white and green floral pierced border 225.00

Plate, 8 1/2" d, polychrome relief of woman burned at stake in center with classical figures at sides, hanging floral swags on border, gilt dentil shaped rim, "blue crowned N" mark 250.00

Stein, .3 L, multicolored battle scene around center, puce drape on ft and rim, porcelain lid with lion finial, (A) 444.00

Tankard, 9 3/4" h, body molded with polychrome landscape with figures of Bacchus over gilt beaded band and molded floral flared base, molded polychrome finial of putto seated on lion skin holding gilt cup with floral swags and gilt bows, winged female head and torso handle ending in green serpent legs, "blue N and crown" mark, (A) . . 550.00

Urn, 16 1/2" h, campana shape, relief molded and polychromed center band of classic warriors in landscape, "blue crowned N and

Handpainted France" mark, pr, (A) 1,495.00

Urn, Cov, 15 1/4" h, polychrome relief of frolicking cherubs, molded ram's head handles, figural knob, "crown and N" mark, (A) 577.00

Vase

4 1/2" h, cylinder shape, flared rim, multicolored relief classic battle scene, gold int rim design, "crown N" mark, (A) 154.00

9" h, narrow trumpet shape, multicolored cherubs at activities on body, "gold crowned N" mark 385.00

11" h, molded nude and semi-nude Grecian women, pastel colors 130.00

23 3/4" h, ovoid shape, narrow neck, flared rim, overall painted scene of 5 winged cherubs dancing with pink floral garlands, black spotted and lt brown and yellow figural snake handles with lion mask terminals, yellow and black foliate lined rim, base bolted to shaped base, (A) 1,250.00

CARLSBAD-GENERAL

Bohemia, now Czechoslovakia 1848 to Present

History: Carlsbad and the vicinity surrounding it was the center of the Bohemian porcelain industry. Many factories used the name Carlsbad in their marks despite the fact that they were not located in the city itself. The factories manufactured household and decorative porcelains and gift items.

Opiag, Austrian Porcelain Industry AG changed its name to Epiag after Bohemia was removed from the Austrian Empire at the end of World War II to become part of the newly created state of Czechoslovakia. Epiag was nationalized after WWII.

Bone Dish, 6 1/4" l lt yellow roses, green leaves, brown stems, scrolled body, gold rim, "Carlsbad, Made in Austria" mark, set of 6 . . . . 88.00

Bowl, 11 1/2" d, multicolored center scene of ladies and child with musical instruments, heart-shaped reticulation 195.00

Cake Plate

10" H-H, multicolored center of 3 cherubs by river, blue molded swirl border, gold outlined shaped rim, Victoria Carlsbad 20.00

11 1/4" H-H, multicolored center scene of 3 maidens in green and peach gowns, Cupid with harp, burgundy border with gold overlay 215.00

Cake Set, master plate, 10 1/2" H-H, 6 plates, 6 7/8" d, centers with multicolored scenes of children eating fruit, mother of pearl luster ground, dk red borders, gold trim, "gold Carlsbad Czechoslovakia" marks.... 295.00

Chocolate Pot, 9" h, portrait of Phillipe de Orleans, cobalt ground, "Victoria Carlsbad" mark 275.00

Console Bowl, 13" l x 4 1/2" w x 7 3/4" h, HP gold and applied flowers, pink and yellow ground, "Carlsbad, Austria" mark. . . . 275.00

Cracker Jar, 8 1/4" h, multicolored transfer of scene from "Rosalind" in forest setting, brushed gold rim. 70.00

Creamer, 4 7/8" h, transfer of purple, blue, and white violets, cobalt shaded to white ground, gilt shoulder, rim, and scrolled handle, "Victoria, Carlsbad, Austria" mark, (A) 25.00

Cup and Saucer, pink rose design with green leaves and yellow scrolling, molded shell design with gold splotches on rims, "Carlsbad China, Made in Austria and W" mark . . 10.00

Cup and Saucer, Demitasse

   Gold outlined molded shell pattern with sm pink and yellow roses, shaded cobalt ground, fancy gold handle, set of 6
   . . . . 425.00

   Rambling pale pink flowers, lt brown leaves and stems, gold rims, "blue Carlsbad, Austria" mark 15.00

Dish, 7 3/8" l x 5 1/2" w, oval, multicolored cherub transfer in center, pink border with purple and gold accents, molded scroll border, "Victoria, Carlsbad, Austria" mark, (A) 25.00

Ewer

   9 1/2" h, blue and yellow enameled poppies, blue and pink enameled ground, gold ivy figural pierced handle . 195.00

   14" h, polychrome floral spray, gold relief accents, (A) 65.00

Jardiniere, 5" h x 8" l, modeled overlapped gold outlined purple and green irid leaves, pink int, 4 feet, "Carl Knoll, Carlsbad, Made in Austria" mark. 275.00

Nappy, 5 3/8" d, pink daisies, green leaves, gold trim, scalloped, "L.S. & S. Carlsbad" mark, set of 4. . . . . 14.00

Oyster Plate, 5 wells

   8 1/4" d, molded shell outlines, purple flowers, sm yellowheads and leaves, white ground 165.00

Dresser Set, tray, 11 1/2" l, 7 3/8" w, ring tree, cov box, candlesticks, 7 3/4" h, pink, yellow, and red flowers, green leaves, white ground, "Victoria Carlsbad" marks, $275.

8 1/2" d, HP brown flowers in each well, white ground 75.00

Plate

   6 3/4" d, sm pink rose floral spray in center, scattered sprays, border of bunches of garden flowers, gold band of leaves and hanging flowerheads, scalloped rim. 8.00

   7 1/4" d, yellow and white pansies and lily of the valley in center, pink border with raised vert lines. 10.00

   8 3/8" d, multicolored transfer of 2 angels with blue and green ribbons, yellow border with gold overlay, gold geometric band rim, "blue Victoria Carlsbad Austria" mark. 20.00

   9" d, multicolored transfer of 2 cherubs sleeping on red sash in clouds, vert beading with scattered sprays, reticulated border with gold outlined raised molding and ovals of garden flowers
   . . . . 55.00

Platter

   15 1/2" l, scattered bunches of pink roses, brown leaves, molded scroll border, gold shaped rim 25.00

   17 1/4" l x 11 3/4" w, pink dogwood blossoms, brown stems, sm lt blue leaves
   . . . . 119.00

Talc Shaker, 5" h, egg shape, HP yellow daffodils with green and brown accents, gilt trim, matte finish, c1890s 65.00

Toast Rack, 9" l, 5 bar, sm blue forget-me-nots, green leaves, twisted bars, "blue Victoria Carlbad" mark 45.00

Tray, 11 1/8" l, brown transfer of farm and stream, scattered dogwood blossoms and branches, pink border, gold outlined white molded handles, "Imperial Karlsbad" mark
. . . . 35.00

Vase

   3 1/4" h, multicolored scene of women and Cupid in garden, maroon ground with gold accents. 45.00

   5 3/4" h, flat sides, 2 sm gilt accented handles, multicolored Cupid with blue palette, gray heart, and raised gold arrow, raised gold outlined cartouche, matte cream ground, "blue Victoria Carlsbad" mark 60.00

   7 1/8" h, Art Nouveau style orange flowerheads on dk green stems, med green ground, "Carlsbad Austria" mark
   . . . . 138.00

   10" h, raised gold flowers, berries, and leaves, cream ground, gold scaled dolphin handles, gold divided rim, brushed gold accents, "Victoria Carlsbad" mark
   . . . . 160.00

   10 1/4" h, bulbous body, flared lip, 2 figural snake handles, gold outlined purple and lt green violets, matte cream ground 125.00

   12" h, white florals, blue ground, "Carlsbad Austria" mark 200.00

Vegetable Bowl, Cov, 12" H-H, rect, sprays of purple daisies with yellow centers, blue-green leaves, brown branches, gold trimmed handles and knob 75.00

CARLTON WARE

Stoke-on-Trent, Staffordshire, England c1890-1992

c 1894

History: Staffordshire porcelain and earthenware were produced at the Carlton Works, Stoke-on-Trent, by a firm that traded as Wiltshaw and Robinson from about 1890. Carlton Ware became the factory's trade name in 1894.

In the early 1920s, luster wares were made in 12 colors and were one of the main lines of the factory between the two world wars. Vases, bowls, ginger jars, wall plaques, dishes, and potpourri holders in classic shapes were decorated with a variety of patterns including Egyptian, Byzantine, Persian, Chinese, Japanese, and Art Deco styles. Motifs included angel fish, birds of paradise, waterlilies, butterflies, bluebirds, sunbursts, shooting stars, and lightning flashes.

Due to the complex nature of the luster process, luster pieces comprised the luxury end of Carlton Ware's production. Luster pieces often had mother-of-pearl interiors. Background colors could be marbled, mottled, bubbled, or splashed. Enameled paint and gilding enriched the surface of the pieces.

In the mid 1920s, novelty earthenware was introduced including the cruets that were characteristic of this firm. Jampots were made in the shape of fruit, small figurines were made, along with napkin rings. Advertising and promotional items were made as well as china commemoratives and crested wares.

Following the takeover of Birks, Rawlins & Company in 1920, china production was expanded to teawares in floral patterns such as "Delphinium," "Springtime," and "Sunshine" that utilized hand painting and transfer printing.

Embossed salad ware was made from the 1920s in green and red until 1976 when regulations about lead paint eliminated the red color that was utilized for the tomatoes and lobster claws. A tremendous variety of shapes was made in this embossed ware.

In 1929, Carlton Ware introduced oven to table utilitarian wares with banding in three colors.

The most collectible Carlton Ware lines are the floral embossed pieces based on leaf and flower shapes. "Oak Tree" from 1934 in blue and cream was made for plaques, vases, jugs, candleholders, bookends, match holders, and cruets. "Garden Ware" from 1935 was made in similar objects and also matte glazed. "Handcraft" was a less expensive version of the luxury luster examples.

Highly glazed lines included "Buttercup," "Waterlily," "Apple Blossom," "Wild Rose," "Foxglove," "Primula," and "Poppy."

After World War II, Carlton Ware had major improvements and expansions. Designs became more sophisticated in two tone colors with more exotic flowers motifs. In 1967, Arthur Wood & Sons took over the factory and expanded the export trade. Fruits replaced flowers as a popular theme.

With the 1980s recession, Carlton Ware finally stopped production in 1992.

Most products are marked with a circular printed mark with W & R/STOKE ON TRENT enclosing a swallow and topped by a crown until about 1927. "Made in England" was added in the early 1900s. Later a variety of script marks was used.

References: Francis Salmon & others, *Collecting Carlton Ware,* Francis Joseph Publications, 1994; Judy Spours, *Art Deco Tableware,* Rizzoli, 1988.

Collectors' Club: Carlton Ware Collectors International, Helen and Keith Martin, P.O. Box 161, Seven Oaks, Kent TN15 6GA England, Membership: $55.00, four magazines per year, *The Carlton Times.*

Collecting Hints: Collectors have given their own names to many patterns where the names are not known. Most patterns can be identified by pattern number, but some patterns were made in several background colors so the same numbers are repeated.

Basket, 4 3/4" h, "Primrose" pattern, molded puce, red, and yellow flowers, molded basketweave ground, mint green int. 159.00

Beaker, 5 1/2" h, Rouge Royale, gold spiderweb, enameled green, yellow, and orange flowers and leaves, cream int with gilt rim
. . . . 225.00

Bowl

   7 1/2" l, molded red tomatoes, green leaves, molded veined leave base shaded yellow to green 55.00

   9 1/2" l, "Lily of the Valley" pattern . . 45.00

   9 3/4" l, shell shape, molded rolled handle, multicolored corabell flowers on border, cobalt and gilt rim 270.00

   10" d, Rouge Royal, enameled exotic bird, butterflies, and trees, gold accents, 3 gold peg feet, 3 open sections on rim
. . . . 495.00

   10" l x 8 1/4" w, Vert Royale, enameled white, yellow, orange, and gold exotic birds, lavender, orange, yellow, and green trees, gold trim and border
. . . . 225.00

   10 1/4" d

      "Red Devil" pattern, standing red devil, multicolored stylized flowers, gilt trim, turquoise ground, (A)
. . . . 6,200.00

      "Tutankhamun" pattern, printed and painted design with gilt accents, matte black ground, (A) . . . 745.00

   12 3/8" d, pedestal base, red and yellow Gerbina daisies, green leaves and grasses, lt green ground, gold trim
. . . . 395.00

   13 3/8" l, rect, inverted rim, 4 feet, "Handcraft," painted pink, blue, and ochre fan shaped flowers from wavy cross, white ground 195.00

Centerpiece Bowl, 6 1/2" h x 13 1/4" l x 6 1/2" w, gold flying ducks and irises, black ground, gold shaped handles, pedestal base with gold feet 920.00

Charger

   12 5/8" d, "Midnight Oak" pattern, relief molded brown tree trunk, lt brown foliage, blue circ ground, (A) 125.00

   15 3/8" d, "Handcraft," "Daisy" pattern, orange, mauve, red, yellow, and white flowers, matte blue ground, (A) 619.00

   15 1/2" d, orange, yellow, lt blue, gilt, and red painted stylized flowerheads, yellow luster ground, green rim, (A) . . 619.00

Coffee Service

   Pot, 6 5/8" h, milk jug, cov sugar basin, 6 cups and saucers, printed and painted oriental temple scene, gilt accents, cream ground, pattern #4328, (A)
. . . . 465.00

   Pot, 7 1/2" h, milk jug, cov sugar basin, 6 cups and saucers, Rouge Royale, green enameled and gilt printed fruiting vine design, pattern #4385, (A) 532.00

   Pot, 7 7/8" h, milk jug, sugar basin, 6 cups and saucers, printed and painted Chinese man and dragon, yellow ground, gilt accents, pattern #3660, (A)
. . . . 698.00

Coffee Service, Part

   Pot, 7" h, milk jug, sugar basin, 3 cups, 4 saucers, orange luster ground, gilt accents, (A) 230.00

   Pot, 7 5/8" h, milk jug, sugar basin, 5 cups, 6 saucers, gilt printed courting couple in roundel, matte black ground, (A)
. . . . 90.00

Cookie Jar, 6 1/2" h, emb dk pink water lilies on sides, lt yellow ground, green handles and flower bud knob 175.00

Cruet Set, 5 1/8" w, golfing figure in blue cap and pants, green jacket, salt, pepper, and mustard pots as cov white golf balls, green base, (A) 388.00

Cup and Saucer, "Australian" ware, yellow poppy design 65.00

Cup and Saucer, Demitasse, gold wading birds in pond, burgundy luster ground 85.00

Dish

   5 1/8" l, leaf shape, "Australian" ware, pink molded flowerhead at end, cream ground 25.00

   9 1/2" l, leaf shape, molded mauve and white flowerheads on green leaves, pale yellow leaf molded ground, brown rect stem handle 60.00

   10 1/4" l, oval, orange, black, and gold enameled swimming fish, molded coral shaped handle, mottled gray-green ground 95.00

   12 1/4" H-H, oval oval, Art Deco landscape, black tree with pale green hanging foliage and red and black flowerheads, yellow and black bkd, mottled orange luster handles and ft, mottled yellow and black underside
. . . . 375.00

   13" d, 3 section, "Australian" ware, green magnolia, yellow ground 65.00

Figure

   5 1/8" h, golfer, polychromed, John Hassall design, (A) 293.00

   8 1/4" h, standing lady, yellow, green, blue, and pink ribbed skirt, floral apron, black bodice, repairs, (A) 673.00

Inkstand, 2 1/4" h x 8" l, gold "Egyptian Fan" pattern, cobalt ground 600.00

Jar, Cov

   8 1/4" h, "Handcraft," pink flowers, gray and black branches, mottled blue ground, satin finish, gold foo dog knob
. . . . 395.00

   9" h, paneled, Kang-Hsi, gold oriental house, trees, and boat, pink, aqua, green enameled accents, dk blue ground, gold foo dog knob 395.00

Ginger Jar, 7 3/4" h, "Rouge Royale," enameled white and multicolored flowers, shaded green leaves, burgundy luster ground, "Carlton Ware Made in England Trademark" mark, $595.

Jug

7" h, handle modeled as figural toucan, yellow and red beak, black body, cream rim, red Guinness label, lt brown base, (A) 1,425.00

12 1/4" h, "Oak Tree" pattern, brown, green, and yellow relief of tree, leaves and acorns, peach horiz ribbed body 195.00

Pitcher, 8 1/4" h, "Rabbits at Dusk" pattern, printed and painted green and brown design, orange luster ground, green int, (A) . . 442.00

Plaque

12 5/8" d, "Hydrangia" pattern, blue and pink relief molded flowerheads with green foliage, white ground, (A) 300.00

13" d, "Rabbits at Dusk" pattern, painted green and brown tree and foliage, rabbits on ground, orange luster ground, (A) 850.00

Plate, 5 3/4" d, yellow and purple flying long-tailed bird, yellow outlined lavender and purple starburst, sm blue flowers on border, gold rim, satin finish 85.00

Potpourri Jar, Cov

4" h, Rouge Royal luster, enameled bird and flowers on sides, gold trim, pearlized int 165.00

7 5/8" h, green, orange, and gold enameled Chinese house, lavender and yellow trees, lavender, blue, and orange flowers, gold trim, dk blue ground 495.00

9 3/4" h, gold outlined reserves of multicolored enameled oriental buildings on satin black ground on body and cov, yellow body ground 475.00

Powder Jar, 5 1/8" h, pedestal base, "Jazz" pattern, gold and red geometrics, dk blue ground, gold rosebud knob, (A) 892.00

Relish Tray, 14" l, rect, 3 section, 3 raised trumpet shaped flowers and green leaves, in center section, green painted stalk in end sections 100.00

Salad Bowl, 9 1/2" d, with serving spoon and fork, "Australian" Ware, molded green leaf ground, 2 raised red tomatoes 50.00

Tankard, 3 3/4" h, polychrome relief of Puritan hanging from gallows, reverse inscribed "There are several reasons for drinking," (A) 132.00

Tazza

7" d, "Gum Nut" design, HP Gum Nut flowers, leaves, and nuts, green and maroon cream mottled ground. . . . 195.00

7 1/4" d, gold outlined stylized blue and pink flowerheads, green stems, pale green ground, gold rim 225.00

Tea For Two, pot, 5 7/8" h, milk jug, sugar basin, 2 cups and saucers, "Glamour" pattern, Modern shape, matte black finish, gold handles, bases, spout, and knob, (A). . . . 495.00

Tea Service, pot, 7 1/2" h, milk jug, cov sugar basin, 6 cups and saucers, 6 side plates, Vert Royale, gilt lined rims, (A) 460.00

Tea Tile, 6" d, blue floral design, white ground 36.00

Tray, 10 1/4" H-H, oval, Rouge Royale, pale blue kingfisher bird, white and yellow water lilies, green pads, white and purple grapes and leaves. 175.00

Vase

5" h, bulbous shape, orange, blue, yellow, and gold enameled exotic trees and flowering landscape with 2 flying long-tailed birds, mottled blue ground 300.00

5 7/8" h, ovoid, "Fantasia" pattern, orange, yellow, green, and red painted geometric flowers, gilt accents, matte blue ground, pattern #3405, (A) 744.00

6" h, cylinder shape, flared rim, 2 cartouches of pixies blowing bubbles on pearlized ground, orange luster body, matte black int 600.00

7" h

Flowers and hummingbirds, blue luster ground. 295.00

Gold and multicolored enameled birds and flowers, maroon luster ground, gold shaped rim, pearl luster in 240.00

7 1/2" h

Ovoid, printed and painted heron flying past stylized flowering tree, gilt accents, cream ground, (A) . . 283.00

Yellow, green, orange, and blue paneled fan and flowerheads, clouds of dots, gilt trim, mottled red ground, #3558. . . . . 920.00

10 1/2" h, "Persian" ware, 3 Persian servants attending ruler in open Persian building, multicolored enamels with gilt trim, palm trees, animals, and birds, dk blue ground 395.00

11" h, bulbous middle, cylinder neck, flared rim, multicolored enameled and gilt oriental scene of 2 ladies in boat with man paddling, oriental temple on shore, mottled blue ground, pearlized int 425.00

11 3/8" h, everted rim, "Handcraft," "Fan Flower" pattern, blue, purple, and yellow painted design, white ground, (A) 567.00

Vase, Cov

9 1/4" h, multicolored lustered oriental temple scene on front gold outlined flowers, man and woman sitting at table on reverse, blue luster ground 395.00

16 1/8" h, baluster shape, printed and painted flying bird of paradise over flowers and foliage, gilt accents, red luster ground, gilt foo dog on cov, (A) 300.00

Wall Pocket, 12 1/4" h, modeled pink flower spray with green leaves, (A) 300.00

C **S**

2775-90   c 1775-1790

CAUGHLEY

Royal Salopian Porcelain Manufactory
Shropshire, England
c1775-1799

History: Thomas Turner, who received his training at the Worcester porcelain factory, converted an existing pottery at Caughley in Shropshire in 1772 to make possible the manufacture of porcelain products. He developed a uniformly smooth, transparent glaze that lent itself well to the transfer printed decorations. Basic Caughley porcelain had a white soapstone body.

Blue and white ware with printed transfer decorations in a Chinese design was the chief item of manufacture. The "willow pattern," c1780, and the "Broseley dragon" were two of the most characteristic and popular Caughley patterns. Sometimes the Caughley blue and white china was painted in underglaze blue as well as transfer printed. The china often was enriched with bands of gilding.

Turner established a London warehouse called the "Salopian China Warehouse" in 1780 for the sale of Caughley chinaware. Tablewares, tea and coffee services, and other utilitarian items were the chief Caughley products. Few decorative pieces were made.

In 1870, Turner brought back several French china decorators leading to a greater variety in decoration. Turner sent some of his porcelain pieces to be gilded and enameled at the Chamberlain factory at Worcester. By 1796 hard paste porcelain was introduced.

The factory was taken over by John Rose of nearby Coalport in 1799 and continued to offer whiteware for decoration at London and Coalport until its closing in 1814.

References: G.A. Godden, *Caughley & Worcester Porcelains, 1775-1800*, Herbert Jenkins, 1969.

Museums: Clive House Museum, Strewbury, England; Metropolitan Museum of Art, New York, NY; Victoria & Albert Museum, London, England.

General

Bowl

5 5/8" d, ftd, red and underglaze blue oriental scene of house in landscape, (A) 77.00

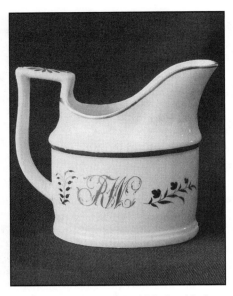

Creamer, 4" h, overglazed gold design, black florals, c1810.

6" d, "Waiting Chinaman" pattern, blue and white, c1750 . . . . 225.00

9 1/2" d, int blue printed with chinoiserie house on hill in gilt line, ext blue printed with fisherman and figures in landscape, int rim with blue printed stylized flowers and scale diapers, c1775, (A) 288.00

Dessert Plate, 8" d, center painted with 4 blue floral sprigs in cavetto decorated with floral garlands, blue edged scalloped rim, "blue S" mark, (A) 185.00

Dish

8" sq, beaded band around gilt accented floral spray reserve, gilt accented cobalt border, late 18th C 250.00

10 3/4" l, elongated heart shape, blue scattered floral sprigs, blue lined rim, (A) 148.00

Pitcher

3 3/4" h, blue printed "Pleasure Boat" pattern. 375.00

7 1/2" h, leaf molded body, blue printed bouquets of garden flowers, mask spout, scroll handle with thumbrest, c1785, (A) 460.00

8" h, floral design, blue transfer, molded design on body, hairline, (A) . . . 193.00

Teabowl and Saucer, fluted, saucer with gold flower in center in gold band, gold, pink, blue, yellow, and green flowerheads, serrated rim 240.00

Teapot, 5" h, globular shape, underglaze blue and gilt flower sprays and border banding, molded scrolling on spout and handle, c1790, (A) 460.00

Tea Service, Part, teapot, barrel shape, milk jug, 2 sugar boxes, 2 slop bowls, 9 cups, 4 saucers, saucer dish, fluted, underglaze blue and gilt flower sprigs, border bands of quartered ovals, late 18th C 385.00

Salopian

Bowl

6" d, ftd, green, rust red, olive green, and orange transfer of shepherdess and piper in forest setting 300.00

6 1/2" d, multicolored transfer of classic figures and florals on int and ext, c1780-90 . . . . 325.00

6 5/8" d, ext with oriental waterfall, boat, and pagoda, int with center pagoda, floral spray border, polychrome, (A) 330.00

Cider Mug, 6" h, multicolored transfer of classical figures and florals, compass rose with initials on front, c1780-90, chip 650.00

Creamer, 2 3/4" h, squat shape, figural livestock in landscape scene, floral border, polychrome, (A) 440.00

Cup and Saucer

Oriental scene of figures, pagoda, and landscape, polychrome, (A) . . . 248.00

Scalloped edge, figural livestock in landscape scene, floral border, chips, (A) 358.00

Cup and Saucer, Handleless

Black and gray transfer of people in landscape scene with buildings, blue trim 165.00

"Chinese" pattern, ext view of mountain landscape, figures, and stream, polychrome, (A) 220.00

Cottage, castle, figure, and landscape view, brown transfers, (A) 275.00

Girl with sheep, barn in bkd, acorn, leaf, and floral border, polychrome, rim chip, (A) 385.00

Sheep in meadow, castle and cottage scene, floral border, polychrome, chip, (A) 358.00

Miniature, black deer with brown spots near stream, yellow thatched cottage in bkd, border bands of deer 300.00

"Queen Victoria" pattern, brown transfer with yellow, blue, and green accents, (A) 150.00

Dish, 4 3/4" d, 3 pheasants in shrub, blue transfer, "S" mark 200.00

Jug, 5" h, blue, rust, and black transfer of fishing before castle, Salopian, $295.

Sweetmeat Dish, 6 1/4" d, blue printed, (A) $495.

Pitcher

3 1/4" h, oriental scene of 2 figures in garden with birds and flowers, polychrome, (A) 220.00

4" h

Barrel shape, spotted deer design, polychrome transfer 450.00

Squat shape, robin, florals, and foliage design, polychrome, gray ground, base chip, (A) 165.00

5 3/4" h, rd ft, Goldfinch design, polychrome transfer 450.00

Plate

6 3/4" d, center with urn of flowers on table, border of 3 cartouches of flowers, brown transfer with tan, blue, and yellow accents, (A) 220.00

7 1/4" d

Acorn, floral, and foliate design, Roman key border, polychrome, blue rim, (A) 330.00

Oriental scene of figures, pagoda, and landscape, polychrome, orange-brown border, (A) 358.00

7 1/2" d

Exotic bird and floral spray in center, floral and leaf border, polychrome, (A) 330.00

Oriental scene of boat in river with pagoda-like buildings on shore, green transfer, (A) 110.00

8" d, oriental couple in garden setting, yellow, salmon, and blue peonies, ground of sm green dots, black and green curlicues with yellow centers, black geometrics on rim 225.00

8 1/4" d, center harvest scene of man with wheat, woman and cottage in bkd, floral spray border, polychrome, (A) . 302.00

8 5/8" d, couple gleaning wheat in wheatfield, flowerhead border, gray-green transfer, (A) 50.00

Sugar Bowl, Cov

3" h, figural livestock in landscape scene, floral border, polychrome, (A) . . 550.00

4 3/4" h, squat shape, 2 sm handles, robin, floral, and foliage design, polychrome, gray ground, lid repair, (A) 110.00

Teapot, 5 1/2" h

Globular shape, underglazed blue printed oriental pagoda scene in lake landscape, band of chevrons on spout, gilt accents, "blue S" mark, c1785, (A) 460.00

Squat shape, robin, floral and foliage design, polychrome, gray ground, rim chips, (A) 495.00

Waste Bowl, 5 3/4" d, pearlware, vases of flowers, peony and fence design, blue transfer, gilt accents, restored, c1775, (A) .. 80.00

CAULDON

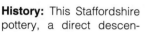

Shelton, Hanley, England
1905-1962

History: This Staffordshire pottery, a direct descendant of the Ridgway potteries, operated from 1905 to 1920 at Cauldon Place, Shelton, Hanley. After John Ridgway dissolved his partnership with William, his brother, in 1830, he operated the Cauldon Place Works. A wide variety of china and earthenware was made including utilitarian and decorative pieces.

Ridgway sold to T.C. Brown-Westhead, Moore & Company in 1855. Brown-Westhead, Moore & Co. (1862-1904) became Cauldon Ltd. in 1905. From 1920 to 1962, the firm operated as Cauldon Potteries, Ltd. at which time it became known as Cauldon Bristol Potteries, Ltd. It was eventually acquired by Pountney & Co. Ltd. of Boston in 1962.

Bowl, 5 1/4" d, ftd, red, blue, and yellow floral hanging swags on border, turquoise curlicues, brown honeycomb printed ground, gold shaped rim 25.00

Chamberstick, 3" h x 6" d, scattered sm red flowers, rim of sm red and blue flowers, gold trim 75.00

Cup and Saucer, lt blue shaded borders with gold ivy design, entwined handle, "Cauldon Ware, Brown, Westhead, Moore & Co., Staffordshire, England, Bailey, Banks & Biddle, Philadelphia" mark, (A) 20.00

Jardiniere, 6 1/4" h, continuous scene of church and village, blue transfer, silver luster rim 225.00

Plate

8 3/4" d, 6 different multicolored fruit in center, lt blue, pink, turquoise, lt green, yellow, or white reticulated borders, gilt trim, "Potters to her Majesty, England" marks, set of 12 .... 1,850.00

9 1/2" d, gilt foliate cavetto, scalloped blue and gilt rim, set of 11, (A) 161.00

Plate, 10 1/2" d, banded and stamped parcil gilt and cobalt border, "green Cauldon China England" mark, set of 12, (A) $715.

10 1/2" d, multicolored apples and blossoms designs, early 20th C ... 110.00

11 1/4" d, red, yellow, blue, and purple flower spray in center, green leaves, molded scroll border, molded shaped rim, set of 12 .... 100.00

Teapot

4 3/4" h, pink and lt blue swirls and bands of florals on rims and base, hanging trellises of florals 98.00

9 3/4" h, ftd, acanthus leaf on scrolled handle, lid, collar, and base, red, blue, and yellow flowers, green leaves, sm pink floral sprigs on sides, gold striped base, collar, handle, and lid, "Cauldon, England" mark, (A) 55.00

Turkey Set, platter, 18" l, 9 plates, brown transfer of turkey in center, foliate borders, (A).......................... 575.00

CHANTILLY

1725 - 1800

Chantilly, France
1725-c1860

History: The Chantilly factory, established in 1725 in the Chantilly district of France, produced soft paste porcelain. The first manager of the works was Ciquaire Cirou who worked under the guidance and influence of the Prince de Conde. The factory's original purpose was to copy old designs rather than initiate new ones.

Conde's love for Japanese porcelain dictated that the first products assume the form and color of the classic Japanese porcelains. In order to achieve the strong colors of the Japanese palette, a milky glaze was developed to present a satisfactory surface for decoration.

In addition to the Japanese designs, many of the popular Meissen designs and decorations were imitated. The factory also made soft paste of old silver pieces. A lobulated body form characterized Chantilly porcelain of this period.

By the mid-18th century, the opaque glaze was replaced with a more transparent type. The decorative style now shifted to imitating the porcelains from the Sevres factory. This second glaze gave a softer look to the finished products. "Chantilly Sprig," a sketchy type blue floral motif, appeared about this time. Table services, statuettes, writing paraphernalia, and boxes and jars for the ladies dressing table were the staple products of the factory.

About 1800, the factory ceased operation. Several other factories in the area picked up the production of the most popular Chantilly designs in hard paste porcelain. These pieces were characterized by a soft pastel coloring and dull surface finish, contrasting with the early products of the original factory. They are classified under the general heading of "Chantilly."

References: W.B. Honey, *French Porcelain of the 18th Century*, Faber & Faber, 1950; George Savage, *Seventeenth & Eighteenth Century*, Hamlyn Publishing Co. Ltd.1969.

Museums: Fine Arts Museums, San Francisco, CA; J. Paul Getty Museum, Los Angeles, CA; Musee Conde, Chantilly, France; Musee des Arts Decoratifs, Paris, France; Victoria & Albert Museum, London, England; Wadsworth Atheneum, Hartford, CT.

Bowl, 8 3/4" d, lobed, blue painted scattered carnations and insects, basketweave molded rim, "blue hunting horn" mark, c1755, set of 3, (A) 1,344.00

Cooler, 5 3/4" h, cylinder shape with dragon handles, painted dragon, loose bouquet tied with yellow ribbon and scattered flowers in Kakiemon colors, reeded gilt bronze ft mount, c1740, cracks and repairs, (A) 6,900.00

Ecuelle and Stand, 9 3/4" l, lobed oval shape, puce, green, yellow, blue, and iron red painted sm bouquets and scattered flowers, blue accented pink ribbon tied paired scroll knob,

Bowl, 8 3/4" d, blue and white, "blue hunting horn" mark, $395.

"blue hunting horn" mark, c1770, cracks and repairs 1,250.00

Figure

14 3/4" h, Cinderella and Prince, Prince in yellow lined lt blue coat, pink flowered pantaloons, holding red shoe, Cinderella in pink gown, blue overgown, brown and pink chair, pink cushion, c1873, pr 1,350.00

21" h, woman with mandolin, polychrome, (A) 115.00

Holy Water Font, 17 1/4" h, figural winged angel in clouds seated on rim of scallop shell supported by flying putto, white, c1750, restored, (A) 3,450.00

Mug, 2 5/8" h, barrel form, underglazed blue and multicolored floral sprays, "blue horn" mark, (A) 300.00

Plate

9 1/4" d, blue sprig pattern, basketweave molded border, blue lined rim, c1755, set of 12, (A) 2,760.00

10 1/8" d, blue painted scattered ferns and flowers, basketweave molded border, c1755, set of 3, (A) 1,345.00

Pot-De-Creme, spiral molded, stylized blue foliate design, "blue horn" mark, pr . . 275.00

Teapot, 4 1/2" h, lobed oviform, faceted handle, flat loop and scroll handle, painted grapevines from banded hedges, rat climbing hedge in Kakiemon colors, silver mts, c1740, (A) 11,500.00

CHARLOTTE RHEAD

Tunstall, England 1912-1960

c. 1920s

History: Charlotte Rhead came from a family of designers that was connected to English potteries since the 18th century. She was trained by her father Frederick and her brothers with her sister Dolly. Charlotte joined her father at Wood and Sons in 1912 and remained there until 1926. Her works were not signed while she worked at Wood. Popular patterns from that period were "Seed Poppy" and "Pomona." Charlotte also worked for a Woods' subsidiary, Ellgreave Pottery and created "Lottie Rhead Ware" there.

Tube lining became Charlotte Rhead's signature while she worked at Burgess and Leigh from 1926 until 1931. She trained workers at this firm to execute her designs with tube lining techniques. Charlotte designed tablewares and sandwich sets at Burgess and Leigh such as "Paisley" pattern for tablewares and the Richmond shape for sandwich sets.

Charlotte made many successful patterns for Burgess and Leigh such as "Florentine," "Sylvan," "Garland," and "Laurel

Band." All her works from this time were signed "L. Rhead" along with the Burleigh Ware backstamp. Charlotte often wrote the "C" of her signature as an "L" with a long underline since she preferred to be known as Lottie. The number in the mark refers to the pattern. Fruits and flowers were the central motifs of her patterns. She also experimented with luster during this time.

The pattern "Carnival" was done in bright colors to compete with patterns from Clarice Cliff, Susie Cooper, and inexpensive Czechoslovakian imports coming into England at this time.

In 1931, Charlotte Rhead moved on to A.G. Richardson (Crown Ducal) and remained there for more than a decade where her artistic and technical influences were seen in their ceramics. Although she designed a range of tablewares and utilitarian pieces, she is well known for her art ware and tube-lined designs for lamp bases, vases, bowls, and wall chargers called Rhodian ware.

Charlotte experimented with various glazes and lusters. Some patterns had a mottled effect such as "Persian Rose" and "Granada." In 1936, her snow glaze was used on "Foxglove" and "Wisteria." "Stitch" and "Patch" were produced by trainees from Rhead designs and were never marked with the Rhead signature. Other patterns included "Byzantine," "Persian Rose," and "Golden Leaves." Most other patterns have the Richardson trademark "Crown Ducal" with a tube-lined "C. Rhead."

During World War II, there was a large drop in pottery production, and in 1942 Charlotte was unemployed. She then worked for Harry Wood with a new range of tube lined wares for H.J. Wood Ltd. Most of these examples were made for export during and immediately after the war. Although Charlotte died in 1947, her designs continued to be made until 1960.

References: John Barlett, *English Decorative Ceramics 1875-1939*, Kevin Frances Publishing, 1989; Bernard Bumpus, *Charlotte Rhead: Potter & Designer*, Kevin Frances Publishing, 1987; Susan Scott, *Charlotte Rhead Ceramics*, <u>Antique Trader Weekly</u>, Aug. 31, 1994; Judy Spours, *Art Deco Tableware*, Rizzoli International Publications, 1988.

Basket, 5 3/4" h x 5 1/2" d, brown tube lined yellow and orange flowers and brown leaves, swirl lines, tan ground, indent for handle terminal, gilt rim, "Bursley Ware Charlotte Rhead England" mark 295.00

Bowl

6 7/8" d, oct, "Dragon" pattern, red, green, blue, and gilt oriental dragon on int, yellow int border, Bursley Ware, (A)
. . . . 200.00

9 5/8" d, band of corn and foliage over geometric band, green, yellow, and blue, (A) 160.00

9 7/8" d, oct, blue, green, and orange painted fan motifs between diamond borders, orange mottled ground, pattern #4908, Burleigh Ware, (A)
. . . . 265.00

10" d

Green, tan, orange, and copper Art Deco style flowers, mottled beige ground, Crown Ducal body . 235.00

Orange, green, gray, and tan tube lined flowers, beige satin ground, Crown Ducal body 225.00

11 1/4" d, "Benares" pattern, bands of blue stylized flowerheads, green chains, orange-brown curlicues, dk brown ground, Bursley Ware 85.00

Charger

11 7/8" d, painted green band of stylized foliage, mottled orange ground, (A)
. . . . 375.00

12 1/2" d, blue spider web design in center, border band of yellow and orange leaves and green leaves, cream ground, pattern #5623, Crown Ducal, (A) 250.00

12 5/8" d, center band of orange and bronze interlocking "S" shapes, border of band of orange and bronze interlocking "S" shapes, cream ground, Crown Ducal, (A) 285.00

13" d, green, blue, and yellow stylized floral pattern, #3052 . . . . 450.00

14 3/8" d, border of band of oranges, leaves, and flowerheads, orange, yellow, blue, and green, mottled orange ground, pattern #TL.5, (A) 355.00

17 3/8" d, center band of stiff leaves, blue, yellow, and brown painted stylized flowers and foliage, orange ground, pattern #5983, Crown Ducal, (A) 495.00

18 3/4" d, brown stylized castle, orange road, blue hills, hanging red flowerheads and brown and blue leaves, orange-yellow ground, Bursley Ware, (A) 975.00

Dish, 11 3/4" l, elliptical shape, orange, green, blue, and yellow flowers, fruit, and foliage, mottled orange ground, pattern #TL.5, (A) 355.00

Ewer

9" h, dk blue and lt purple stylized florals and foliage, mottled cream ground, pattern #TL.14, Bursley Ware, (A). . 265.00

15 1/4" h, brown outlined orange and yellow flowers on lower section, brown lined squares and curlicues, tan rim and base 495.00

Jug

5 3/4" h, multicolored leaf design, gray ground, green trim 360.00

6 1/4" h, ovoid, purple, yellow, pink, and green painted band of fruiting vine, mottled blue ground, pattern #5391, (A)
. . . . 142.00

Dish, 9" H-H, raised green flowers, brown leaves, orange and yellow scrolling, tan ground, brown luster handles, Bursley Ware, $195.

7 1/2" h, tapered shape, "Wisteria" pattern, pink, purple, and green, white ground, pea green int and base, pattern #4984, (A) 400.00

8 5/8" h, ovoid, everted rim, band of green and orange overlapping chevrons, mottled orange ground, (A) 215.00

10" h, painted stylized orange-yellow and blue daisies, brown stems and green foliage, green handle, pattern #TL.37, Bursley Ware, (A) 442.00

Pitcher, 9 1/2" h, yellow and red flowers on yellow ground, tan trim and handle, slip loop design on top and base, luster glaze, #TL95 Bursley Ware. 360.00

Plaque, 14 3/8" d, painted stylized orange peonies and chrysanthemums, blue stylized leaves, black fan-shaped panels, white ground, pattern #1419, (A) 495.00

Plate

7 1/2" sq, mottled orange over yellow center, border of orange and black stacked geometrics, orange lined rim. . . . 95.00

10 1/2" d, tan, orange, and dk brown geometric pattern, #4926 . . . . 430.00

12 1/4" d, "Byzantine" pattern, yellow, green, and blue, turquoise ground, rim chip, (A) 150.00

Tankard, 7" h, "Wisteria" pattern, green, pink, and yellow, white ground, pattern #4954, Crown Ducal, (A). 168.00

Tazza, 7 1/2" H-H, painted band of stylized purple and blue flowers and foliage, white ground, pattern #TL.43, Bursley Ware, (A) 225.00

Vase

4 1/2" h, horiz lobed body, 2 dbl handles, tan and green acorns and oak leaves, lt tan ground, matte finish. 58.00

5 1/8" h, orange and brown "Indian Tree" design, mottled yellow-beige ground, Crown Ducal body. 175.00

7" h

Bulbous shape, center band of gray outlined green and black waves and tan dots, tan body bands, green rims. 225.00

Swollen shape with flared top, horiz ribbing, center band of cream outlined brown and orange wave design, brown dots, orange rim with brown dots, orange base, "*Rhead*" mark 195.00

8 5/8" h, single handle, horiz ribbing, "Manchu" pattern, red, yellow, and green on mottled green ground, Crown Ducal, (A) 142.00

9" h, pink, aqua, and lavender flower and geometric pattern, aqua top and base, #TL76 Bursley Ware 440.00

10 1/4" h

"Byzantine" pattern, center band of red, blue, and yellow painted stylized flowerheads and foliage, orange ground, applied lug handle, pattern #2681, Crown Ducal, (A) 336.00

Single handle, painted bands of orange and bronze luster interlinking "S"s, (A). 160.00

10 1/2" h, swollen cylinder shape, purple and orange-yellow stylized flowerheads on green leaves and stems in wavy brown and orange lined trellis, green banded leaf border, green rim and ft, mottled cream ground, pattern #6016, Crown Ducal, (A) 175.00

c 1752-1769   1769-84

CHELSEA

London, England
c1745-1769

History: As early as 1745, soft paste porcelains were being manufactured at Chelsea in London, one of the most famous English porcelain factories. Nicholas Sprimont, originally a silversmith, was manager of the factory for most of its history. Chelsea porcelains were the most richly decorated of English 18th century ceramics. Pieces were ornate and made for the higher class market.

Various periods of Chelsea porcelain are classified according to the anchor-like mark. But before these were used, there was an incised triangle mark, c1745, and a painted mark of a trident piercing a crown.

From 1749 to 1752, a "raised-anchor" mark was used. This mark was relief molded on a small applied oval pad. Porcelains of this period have the tin-added glaze and mostly are decorated with oriental motifs or simple, floral designs.

The "red-anchor" period (1752-56) has the anchor painted directly on the porce-

lain. Small light colored "moons" can be seen on these porcelains when held up to the light.

Animal fables and botanical studies were characteristic of this period along with florals and oriental motifs.

The Chelsea "gold-anchor" period dates between c1786 and 1769. Porcelains of this era were richly decorated and ornately gilded. The glazes tend to be thickly applied. The anchor period dates are only approximations. More than half of all Chelsea porcelains had no mark at all.

William Duesbury of the Derby factory purchased the Chelsea factory in 1770. The wares of the 1770-1784 period are called "Chelsea-Derby." Because of the interaction of these two factories and the interchange of molds, clay, and workmen, it is difficult to distinguish between the Chelsea and Derby porcelains of this period. Further complications resulted when Duesbury used the Chelsea gold anchor mark on some Derby pieces. A "D" and anchor mark also was used, as was a crowned anchor mark. By 1784 the last of the Chelsea works was demolished and the molds and workers transferred to Derby.

References: John C. Austin, *Chelsea Porcelain at Williamsburg*, Colonial Williamsburg Foundation, 1977; John Bedford, *Chelsea & Derby China*, Walker & Co.1967; Yvonne Hackenbroch, *Chelsea and other English Porcelains, Pottery and Enamel in the Irwin Untermyer Collection,* Harvard University Press, 1957; William King, *Chelsea Porcelain*, Benn Brothers, 1922; F. Severne Mackenna, *Chelsea Porcelain, The Triangle & Raised Anchor Wares,* F. Lewis, 1948; F. Severne Mackenna, *Chelsea Porcelain, The Red Anchor Wares*, F. Lewis, 1951; F. Severne Mackenna, *Chelsea Porcelain, The Gold Anchor Period,* F. Lewis, 1952.

Museums: Colonial Williamsburg Foundation, Williamsburg, VA; Fine Arts Museums, San Francisco, CA; Fitzwilliam Museum, Cambridge, England; Gardiner Museum of Ceramic Art, Toronto, Canada; Henry E. Huntington Library & Art Gallery, San Marino, CA, (gold anchor); Museum of Fine Arts, Boston, MA.; Seattle Art Museum, Seattle, WA; Victoria & Albert Museum, London, England; Wadsworth Atheneum, Hartford, CT; Walters Art Gallery, Baltimore, MD.

Reproduction Alert: Samson made copies of Chelsea pieces, but these were generally marked as copies. Many forgeries and imitations are seen every year bearing red or gold anchors.

Basket, 5 1/8" d, int painted with multicolored florals, raised green leaves on int border, pierced border with sm yellow flowerheads at intersections on ext, c1760 . . . . . . 3,000.00

Figure, 8 1/4" h, white, gold trim, restored, unmkd, $900.

Bowl, 6 1/8" d, Meissen-style painted pastoral scene of farmer leaning on ox, recumbent sheep on ext, scattered sprigs on reverse, foliate rim, c1755, damage, (A) 739.00

Dessert Dish, 8 1/4" l, shell shape, painted botanical flower sprays, turquoise edged rococo shell end, red-brown shaped rim, "red anchor" mark, c1758, pr 6,400.00

Dish

7 1/2" l, leaf shape, painted fruit in center, mauve veining, brown and mauve branch handle, red anchor mark, pr 7,500.00

8 1/8" d, puce, iron red, and yellow painted bouquet of tulips and flowers, scattered flowers, brown edged shaped rim, "red anchor" mark, c1755, (A) 253.00

9" l, puce crane with purple and yellow exotic birds, painted insects, gold outlined shaped rim, gold molded shell handle, "gold anchor" mark 225.00

9 5/8" l, painted purple and yellow rose and loose bouquet in center, molded green leaves on border with puce veins and pink undersides, "red anchor" mark, c1755, (A) 805.00

11 1/8" l, leaf shape, painted puce tulip in center, puce veining, green rim, puce figural stem, white scalloped basket molded edge, "puce anchor" mark, c1758, (A) 633.00

11 3/8" l, kidney shape, painted branches of fruit and insects, brown rim, "brown anchor" mark, c1760, chips and repairs, pr, (A). 230.00

Figure

6" h, d, drummer, lt green jacket, puce pantaloons, white stockings, black hat, drumsticks in hands, drum at side, flower encrusted circ base, "imp R" mark, restored, (A). 925.00

7 1/4" h, harvester standing in puce jacket, blue hat, flowered trousers, holding rake, water barrel on bk, companion in

Figure, 8 3/4" h, purple jacket, yellow dress, iron red, black, and green trim, gilt scrolled base, "gold anchor" mark, $1,100.

white bodice, flowered dress, magenta plumed blue hat, holding wheat sheaf under arm, rake in hand, gilt scroll molded bases, "gold anchor" marks, c1765, restored, pr, (A) 2,772.00

8 7/8" h, hunter in gold rimmed green hat, fur lined puce coat, gilt floral red breeches, brown and black boots, holding dead game and gun, female companion in gilt rimmed feathered hat, blue vest, fur lined puce jacket, gilt and red flowered white skirt, hound at side, gilt reserve scroll molded and flower encrusted bases, "gold anchor, imp R" marks, c1765, pr, (A) 2,618.00

10 5/8" l, "Hogarth's Dog Trump," right and left modeled lying dog on shaped base, white glaze, c1747-50, pr, (A) 81,700.00

Flower Holder, 9 1/2" h, figural seated fisherman in green hat, lt mauve coat, iron red breeches, open pierced basket between knees, 1758, (A). 518.00

Inkwell, 6" h, dbl, standing winged Cupid with basket wells at sides, oval base, white with blue accents. 425.00

Pipe Tamper, 3 5/8" h, modeled bust with brown hair and ruffle, tapered pedestal with orange, yellow, and blue lines, blue flower on base, c1780 . . . . 2,250.00

Plate

8 1/4" d

Center painted with exotic birds in branches, border shaped with gilt cornucopia pattern of scroll and flowers on dk blue ground, gilt dentil rim, "gold anchor" mark, (A) 1,000.00

Tray, 10 1/2" l, magenta, red, yellow, and gray bird, lt blue and gold border, "brown anchor" mark, $1,500.

Painted multicolored spray of fruit, leaves, and berries with insects and fruiting branches, brown and green feather molded rim, "red anchor" mark, c1760, pr, (A) 585.00

8 1/2" d, silver shape, painted exotic birds on green and brown foliage, 3 molded rose-pink and gilt shells on border, painted leaf on reverse, "gold anchor" mark, repaired 1,850.00

9" d, pastel bouquets and florets, gilt and blue fluted scrolled edged rim, "gold anchor" mark 600.00

9 5/8" d, Kakiemon style and palette, center painted with white and gilt outlined alternating peach and white paneled rosette in scalloped surround, border with Chinese style butterflies, flowering prunus, and bamboo, scalloped rim, "iron red anchor" mark, c1755, (A) 368.00

10" d, painted standing peacock with tree at left, scattered flowers, shaped rim, "gold anchor" mark 820.00

Sauce Boat, 7" l, oriental form, modeled cupped leaf, concave lobes, pink stem and green leaf feet, green stem handle with leaves and applied multicolored flowers, painted floral sprays on int and ext, "red anchor" mark, c1756 . . . . 2,250.00

Scent Bottle, 2 5/8" h, figural seated pug, black outlined fur, mound base painted with scattered sprigs, gilt dentil rim, gilt metal mts, c1755, restored, base crack. 700.00

Sweetmeat Stand, 6 5/8" h, figure of rustic man in puce jacket, flowered trousers, holding rect basketweave box, companion with child on bk, blue-green jacket, flowered skirt, holding rect basketweave box, flower encrusted tree trunks, gilt scroll molded base, "gold anchor" marks, pr, repairs, (A) 2,618.00

Teabowl and Saucer, oct, multicolored painted bouquets and insects with scattered sprays, c1760, (A). 308.00

Vase, 10" h, painted lily of the valley on body, molded design on shoulder and neck design, gold curlicue handles on shoulder 95.00

CHILDREN'S WARE

English/German
Late 17th C to Present

History: Initially miniature English china dinnerware sets were made primarily to furnish miniature decorative rooms. By the late 19th century, the emphasis shifted. Most of these dinnerware and tea sets now were made as children's playthings. They served a dual purpose, first as playthings and second as a means of teaching the social graces to children in families of means.

Children's dinnerware sets were made in two basic sizes. One size was used by children to entertain their friends. A smaller size was used when playing with dolls. Various designs were used on these sets, including historical scenes, moral and educational phrases, botanical lessons, and art works of famous illustrators.

Children's feeding dishes, often divided into sections, were made during the late 19th and early 20th century, and used for children's meals. Many have a unit to hold hot water to keep the food warm during the meal. These dishes were designed with colorful animals, nursery rhymes, and children's activities to make mealtime fun for the child.

German children's dishes also were designed with rhymes, animals, children, and florals. Paints, decals, and lusters were used in abundance on these dishes. Among the leading German manufacturers was the R.S. Prussia factory of Schlegelmilch.

References: Maureen Batkin, *Gifts for Good Children Vol. 2,* Richard Dennis, 1996; Doris Anderson Lechler, *Children's Glass Dishes, China, & Furniture,* Collector Books, 1983; *Volume 2,* 1986; Doris Anderson Lechler, *English Toy China,* Antique Publications, 1990; Lorraine May Punchard, *Child's Play,* published by the author, 1982; Lorraine Punchard, *Playtime Pottery and Porcelain from Europe and Asia,* Schiffer Publishing Ltd. l996; Noel Riley, *Gifts for Good Children, Vol. 1,* Richard Dennis, 1991; Margaret & Kenn Whitmyer, *Children's Dishes,* Collector Books, 1984.

Collectors' Club: Toy Dish Collectors' Club, Shelley Smith, Box 159, Bethlehem, CT 06751; Membership: $25.00, Quarterly newsletter.

Bank, 3 5/8" h, yellowware, figural cottage, black outlined roof, door, windows, and "For My Dear Girl," (A) 660.00

Bowl, 5" d, multicolored decal of Little Bo Peep in center, border of cat, dog, crawling child and toy with gold *"Baby,"* "green Germany" mark 69.00

Bureau Set, tray, 6 1/8" l x 4 7/8" w, oval, "Little Miss Muffet," 2 candlesticks, 3" h, "Little Boy Blue" or "Rock-A-Bye Baby," ring holder, and cov box, 2" d, "Little Betty Blue," green striped rims, chips, (A) 220.00

Canister Set, 3 canisters, 3 1/2" h, "BARLEY," "OATMEAL," and "SUGAR," 4 canisters, 2 1/2" h, "SPICE," "ALLSPICE," "CLOVES," and "CINNAMON," 2 bottles, 4 1/4" h, "OIL" and "VINEGAR," black lettering, blue stiff leaf border, white ground, Germany 450.00

Cereal Bowl, 6" d, little boy and girl holding flowers seated in meadow, floral chain rim, blue transfer, Alfred Meakin 12.00

Chamber Pot, 6" d x 4" h, pearlware, "Wild Rose" pattern, blue transfer, c1820 . . 375.00

Coffee Service, pot, 6" h, creamer, cov sugar bowl, 6 plates, 5 1/2" d, 6 cups and saucers, multicolored stick drawings of children, Beyer & Boch, Rudolstadt 600.00

Coffee Service, Part, pot, 5 3/4" h, creamer, cov sugar bowl, 4 plates, 5 1/4" d, 3 cups and saucers, multicolored Happifats designs, Royal Rudolstadt 350.00

Cup and Saucer

　Boy and girl cowboys, yellow and blue, Royal Rudolstadt 55.00

　"Little Red Riding Hood," brown transfers with red, yellow, green, pink, and brown HP accents, "Where are you going to My Pretty Maid? I'm going to Grandma's Sir She Said" gold striped handle and rims, "brown The Foley China, England, RD. 397893" mark, (A) 125.00

Cup Plate

　3 1/2" d, children at play, rust-brown transfer, "imp Wood" mark 75.00

　3 7/8" d, children playing with hoop, purple transfer, unmkd. 110.00

　4 1/2" d, "A Ride on a Donkey," blue transfer, raised floral border, early 19th C 110.00

Feeding Dish

　5 1/2" d, 2 birds in clothes perched on branch in center, children's toys on border, "red Made in Czechoslovakia" mark 65.00

　6 1/4" d

　Multicolored decal of 3 Dutch children in center, automobiles and "BABY" on rim, Czechoslovakia. 55.00

　Robinson Crusoe, man with hand on desk, blue top, black pants, green globes around scene, raised design on border, blue inner and outer lines, shaped rim, c1860 . . . . 125.00

　6 3/8" d, Peter Rabbit and Mr. McGregor, multicolored, Wedgwood 45.00

　6 1/2" d

　Child with Boo-Boos on seesaw, sgd "Mabel Lucie Atwell," Shelley 145.00

　Multicolored decal of dog biting crochet mallet in boys hand, "blue BABY" and toys on rim, "Made in Czech" mark 75.00

　7" d, 5 scenes of children at play and work in blue, rust, yellow, and orange, 4 multicolored florals, scenes repeated on

Mug, 2 3/4" h, brown transfer, $275.

ext, white ground, rust red lined rim, Royal Rudolstadt 65.00

7 1/2" d, mint green slant sides, multicolored decal of 2 children washing clothes at stove, Germany 60.00

8" d

　Multicolored scene of boy leading donkey with 7 Boo-Boos, Shelley 175.00

　Three section, yellow horse with gray mane, flying bird, or floral bunch in sections, yellow and blue banded rim, Susie Cooper. 128.00

Mug

　2 1/4" h

　"For My Dear Girl," black transfer, pink luster trim 225.00

　Oriental figure standing by river with stone bridge, blue transfer . . 120.00

　"Remember Me," "A Present," or "Think of Me" in gold, pink luster trim, set of 3 . . . . 135.00

　2 3/8" h, pearlware

　American eagles on shells, "PROSPER/FREEDOM" in cartouche on front, red transfers, (A) 440.00

　"Ann," geometric rim, black transfer, applied leaf tip handle 185.00

　Black transfers of "Washington/His Country's Father" and bust on side, reverse with "Fayette/The Nations Guest" and bust, American eagle and "Republicans Are Not Always Ungrateful" on front, black lined rim, chip on base, (A) 1,540.00

　"November" and mother doctoring child, geometric design on rim, black transfer, c1840 . . . . . . 255.00

　2 1/2" h

　"A Present For James," man and woman in landscape with fences, trees, and house, purple transfer, blue lined rim and outer border, c1820 . . . . 38.00

"A Present For John" in shield, reverse with seated man and woman, cattle in bkd, blue transfer 200.00

"A Present For Joseph," scrolls and dots, blue transfer, green sprigs, pink luster leaf sprigs and rim, c1840 . . . . 185.00

Cock Robin and verse, black transfer with multicolored accents . . 185.00

Farmer with sheep and farmhouse, blue transfer 95.00

"The Beggar's Petition," dog and cat, seated woman, multicolored transfer 175.00

"To Washington, the Patriot of America," red transfer 425.00

2 3/4" h

Cattle in landscape setting, black transfer, white ground, early 19th C, (A) 35.00

"Deer Stalking," polychrome of dogs, hunters, and deer, c1830 . . . 140.00

"MARIA" in oblong geometric cartouche, black transfer, chips, (A) 46.00

"Silks and Satins Scarlet and Velvets Put Out The Kitchen Fire" on rim, black transfer with green, blue, and red accents 145.00

3" h, boy standing in boat, blue transfer with red and green accents 195.00

Mush Set, milk pitcher, bowl, plate, Cat and Fiddle decals, Germany 150.00

Plate

4" d, Cinderella and shoe, brown transfer 20.00

4 1/4" d, "PEACE," lion, cow, and shepherd in center, zigzag inner border, flowers, fruit, and leaves on border, blue transfer 450.00

5" d, 3 boys greeting each other, black transfer, raised floral border, early 19th C 115.00

5 3/8" d, "A Trifle for Margaret" in wreath cartouche, black transfer, polychrome relief flowers on border, "imp Wood" mark, (A) 180.00

5 1/2" d

Punch and Judy design, red transfer, Allerton, early 20th C 85.00

"Turkish Courier" design, green transfer, emb flower border 155.00

5 5/8" d, creamware, "Tiger Hunt," multicolored, relief molded leaf border, c1800 . . . . 45.00

6" d

"Juvenile Companions-The Young Anglers," black transfer, molded basketweave border, (A) 65.00

Oct, "Joseph's Two Dreams," multicolored, emb flowerhead border pink luster rim 95.00

6 1/8" d

"My Pretty Bird," girl with bird on wrist, black transfer, emb floral border 125.00

"The Little Nurse," girl holding doll, black transfer, emb floral border 125.00

6 1/4" d

"FOR MY NEPHEW," blue transfer, border with red, blue, and green dots 350.00

Kitchen scene with Robert Burns verse, black transfer, relief rim 75.00

6 3/8" d, black transfer of monkey holding tail out to growling dog, brown, blue, and red accents, "Don't You Wish You May Get It" under design, raised wheat, flowerheads, and lily of the valley on border, "J. & G. Meakin" mark . 145.00

6 5/8" d, "UNCLE TOM'S CABIN-PRAYER MEETING IN UNCLE TOM'S CABIN," black transfer with blue and red accents, molded flowerhead border 175.00

7 3/8" d, "Infancy," 4 sm children surrounded by flowers and birds, black transfer, relief molded flowerheads on border, "imp ALBION" mark 135.00

7 1/2" d, "SACRED HISTORY of JOSEPH and his BRETHREN," black transfer, molded flowerhead border 32.00

7 3/4" d

"The First Step" design, brown transfer, Bailey & Ball 195.00

"Very Good Fun is Blind Man's Bluff, If You Play It With Spirit And Not Rough," scene of children playing game, purple transfer with yellow and red accents, relief molded flowerhead border 68.00

Soup Tureen, 5 3/4" h, 6" d, attached undertray, with ladle, blue florals, white ground, curled handles, France 85.00

Teapot, 4 1/2" h, "Cinderella on her way to the ball," red transfer, British reg mark . . 145.00

Tea Set, 3 piece, pot, 5 1/8" h, creamer, cov sugar bowl, sq handles, red diamond design spatter band, blue striping, "Staffordshire England" marks, chips, (A) 150.00

Tea Service

4 piece, teapot, 3 1/2" h, creamer, 2 3/4" h, 2 handleless cups and saucers, green and blue Rainbow spatter, repairs, (A) 1,100.00

5 piece, teapot, 4" h, creamer, 3" h, cov sugar bowl, 3" h, 2 cups and saucers, transfers of red raspberries and green leaves, star knobs, unmkd 165.00

7 piece

Teapot, 4 7/8" h, creamer, cov sugar bowl, 4 cups and saucers, gold "Merry Christmas" and Santa Claus holding tree with children, pink luster rims, Germany 275.00

Teapot, 6 3/4" h, creamer, cov sugar bowl, 4 mugs, multicolored decal of children eating, Thuringia . . . 85.00

9 piece, teapot, creamer, sugar bowl, 6 cups and saucers

Children playing instruments, Germany 225.00

Overall blue spatter, (A) 605.00

10 piece

Miniature, ironstone, teapot, 4 1/4" h, creamer, cov sugar bowl, handled cake plate, 6 cups and saucers, molded scroll design with gold, pink, and purple florals and brown leaves, gold accented rims and handles, chips, (A) 110.00

Teapot, creamer, 4 cups and saucers, 4 plates, Dutch Children pattern 165.00

11 piece

Teapot, 5 3/4" h, creamer, cov sugar bowl, 4 plates, 5 1/4" d, 4 cups and saucers, gold sprigs with blue florets, gold banded rims, Germany, chips and hairlines, (A) 95.00

"Stag" pattern, blue transfers, Allerton, c1880 . . . . 595.00

Teapot, 6 1/4" h, creamer, cov sugar bowl, 4 cups and saucers, 4 plates, 5" d, multicolored decals of children at play, pea green lustered borders, Germany 275.00

12 piece

Teapot, 5 1/4" h, creamer, cov sugar bowl, waste bowl, 4 cups and saucers, 4 plates, 5 1/2" d, overall brown spatter, "Staffordshire England" marks, (A) 88.00

Teapot, creamer, cov sugar bowl, waste bowl, 4 cups and saucers, 4 plates, Wagon Wheel pattern 1,200.00

13 piece, teapot, creamer, cov sugar bowl, 5 cups and saucers, 5 plates, colored fruit and florals, beaded luster finish, Germany, c1900 . . . . 245.00

14 piece, teapot, 5 3/8" h, creamer, cov sugar bowl, 5 plates, 5 1/4" d, 5 cups and saucers, Punch design, red transfers 525.00

15 piece, teapot, creamer, cov sugar bowl, 6 cups and saucers, 6 tea plates, Kate Greenaway pattern 395.00

16 piece, teapot, 3 3/4" h, creamer, cov sugar bowl, waste bowl, 6 cups and saucers, 6 plates, 4 3/4" d, girl and goat design, red transfers, "Edge Malkin & Co." marks 800.00

CHINTZ CHINA

Stoke-on-Trent, Staffordshire, England 1880s-Present

History: The earliest chintz wares date back to the1800s when transfer printing was popular. Today's collectors seek chintz china that was made from the 1930s to the 1960s.

Royal Winton Stoke-on-Trent, England 1886-Present

History: The Grimwade brothers firm was founded in 1885 by Leonard, Edward, and Sidney Grimwade at Winton Pottery in Stoke-on-Trent. They immediately started adding additional companies and built a new pottery. In 1900, they changed the name to Grimwades, Ltd. By 1913, they were one of the largest pottery firms in the area.

Royal Winton was the pre-eminent producer of chintz china since it made more than 60 different patterns from the late 1920s until the 1960s. The early chintz china patterns were tightly grouped, small floral patterns reminiscent of chintz fabrics.

"Marguerite" was Royal Winton's first pattern made in 1928. The chintz pattern was applied by the lithographic process. Many patterns were similar to each other. The pattern name was often incorporated into the back-stamp, while the name impressed in the body of the piece was a shape name.

In 1931, "Delphinium" was added, 1932 saw "Summertime," and by 1936 there were "Queen Anne," "Cranstone" "Sweet Pea," and "Hazel." Shapes included Ascot, Norman, Countess, Athena, and Rose Violet. Nearly all the chintz pieces that came in a tremendous variety of sizes and shapes were marked. Chintz china was earthenware, not expensive china.

Cake plates, trays, salt and pepper sets, teapots, vases, honey pots, sugar bowls, creamers, cruet sets, nut dishes, divided sweet meat dishes, plates, cups and saucers, and platters were made in the delightful and colorful chintz patterns.

Pattern names were mostly taken from English garden flowers, girls' names, or places. Some chintz patterns were used by several firms with different names. Factories were always looking to create new shapes as well as patterns.

Highly sought out Royal Winton examples include breakfast sets, condiments, teapots, and unusual sizes and shapes in the popular patterns. Black background patterns such as "Hazel," "Majestic," "Balmoral," and "Florence" are very desirable.

During World War II and until 1952, the British government restricted potteries from making products with a design; they could only make undecorated ware. Some decorated ware was made for export only.

In 1964, the pottery was taken over by Howard Pottery Company of Shelton, but the Royal Winton name was retained. From that time on, there were a succession of owners, but the Royal Winton name continued.

Crown Ducal Tunstall, England 1915-1974

History: A. G. Richardson developed its first chintz motifs in earthenware in 1918 under the Crown Ducal name after it bought out the Gordon Pottery. Its designs fell between the early Victorian and later tightly patterned, all over florals.

In 1922, the company introduced tennis or hostess sets (trays with cups) followed by console sets, 10-inch candlesticks with a matching bowl in 1923. Next in line was a 12-inch lily bowl with a black matte interior.

Numerous Crown Ducal chintz patterns were made including "Florida" in 1925, "Primrose" in 1936, "Peony" in 1937, "Pansy" in 1938, and "Priscilla" in 1940.

A.G. Richardson was acquired by Enoch Wedgwood Ltd. of Tunstall in 1974, and this firm was taken over by the Wedgwood Group in 1980 and renamed Unicorn Pottery.

James Kent Longton, England 1897-Present

History: James Kent took over the Old Foley Pottery at Longton in 1897 and renamed it James Kent, Ltd. Popular patterns were "Du Barry" and "Hydrangea." This firm was bought by M.R. Hadida Fine Bone China Ltd. in the 1980s.

Elijah Cotton Ltd. (Lord Nelson) Hanley, England 1889-1981

History: This firm operated at Nelson Pottery in Hanley starting in 1889. "Black Beauty" and "Green Tulip" were its most popular chintz patterns. The chintz patterns at this firm were never applied to handles or spouts since this required special skills.

W.R. Midwinter, Ltd. Burslem, England 1910-Present

History: "Springtime," "Lorna Doone," and "Brama" were the most popular chintz patterns at W.R. Midwinter. In 1968, this firm merged with J & G Meakin Ltd. and was taken over by the Wedgwood Group in 1970.

Shelley Potteries, Ltd. Longton, England 1872-1966

History: This firm began in 1872 as Wileman & Company and became Shelley Potteries, Ltd. in 1925. In 1966, it was taken over by Allied English Potteries and acquired by Doulton & Company in 1971. These companies formed Royal Doulton Tableware Ltd.

This company made chintz patterns on earthenware bodies before World War II, but after the war, it only made bone china chintz. Black ground patterns were the most popular.

Additional English potteries that made chintz ware included: Barker Brothers, Ltd. Brexton, Empire Porcelain Co. Ltd., Ford & Sons, Myott Son & Co., Wade & Co., and Wood & Sons, Ltd.

References: Linda Eberle & Susan Scott, *The Charlton Standard Catalogue of Chintz, 1st Edition,* Charlton Press, 1996; *2nd Edition,* Charlton Press, 1997; Bonnie Heller, Joy Humphrey, & Felicity Finburgh, *Chintz By Design,* Chintz International, 1997; Muriel Miller, *The Chintz Collectors Handbook,* Krause Publications, 1998; Muriel Miller, *Collecting Royal Winton Chintz,* Frances Joseph Publications, 1996; Jo Anne Welsh, *Chintz Ceramics,* Schiffer Publishing Ltd. 1996.

Collectors' Clubs: The Chintz Collectors' Club, P.O. Box 50888, Pasadena, CA 91115, $40, Quarterly newsletter; Chintz Connection, P.O. Box 222, Riverdale, MD 20738, $25, Quarterly newsletter; Royal Winton International Collectors' Club, Ken Glibbery, Dancer's End, Northall, Bedfordshire, LU6 2EU England, $50, Bi-monthly newsletter.

Reproduction Alert: Chintz patterns have been copied in Germany, Czechoslovakia, and Japan. Examples marked "Erphila" come from Germany and Czechoslovakia. Japanese chintz called Mano and Halton wares copied Royal Winton patterns.

Royal Winton is reproducing the "Julia" pattern in a stacking teapot in a limited edition of 1,000, and the "Florence" pattern in an 11-inch octagonal footed vase in a limited edition of 2,000.

Collecting Hints: Be sure to check that sets are always complete and that the patterns match–not just similar patterns. Check to make sure finials have not been reglued, and check for chips on spouts of tea and coffeepots. Check to see if the lithographs have been applied properly, and the patterns match up. Some pieces in the same pattern vary in color over the years they were made. Since this is earthenware and not bone china, check the crazing in the glaze.

Collectors seek out either a particular pattern in a number of shapes, or they pick a particular shape such as a stacking teapot and collect as many patterns as possible. Patterns and shapes affect the price of chintz pieces. Different examples are more or less desirable in different parts of the country. Some of the most desirable examples include wall clocks, musical boxes, wall pockets, breakfast sets, and small, unusual pieces such as a stand with eggcups and tiny salt and pepper sets.

Biscuit Jar
    5 7/8" h, "Queen Anne" pattern, Athena shape, SP cov and handle, Royal Winton (A) . . . 375.00
    7" h, "Marguerite" pattern, Royal Winton 375.00

Bonbon Dish
    4" d, "June Festival" pattern, Royal Winton 25.00
    5 1/4" d, "Du Barry" pattern, James Kent 50.00

Bowl
    5 1/2" d, "Florence" pattern, Royal Winton 75.00
    8" d, "Rosalynde" pattern, scalloped, James Kent 175.00
    9" l, oval, "Summertime" pattern, Royal Winton 125.00
    10" l x 8 1/2" w, oval, "Marguerite" pattern, scalloped rim, Royal Winton . . . 195.00
    14" d, "Victoria" pattern, Royal Winton 175.00

Box
    5" l x 3 5/8" w x 2 1/4" h, "Queen Anne" pattern, Royal Winton 95.00
    5 1/2" l x 3 3/4" h, "Pekin" pattern, black ground, Royal Winton 125.00

Bread Tray, 12" l x 6" w, "Summertime" pattern, Royal Winton 295.00

Breakfast Set
    Teapot, 4 3/8" h, creamer, open sugar bowl, toast rack, cup, tray, 9 1/4" l, "Summertime" pattern, Royal Winton 1,550.00
    Teapot, creamer, open sugar bowl, cup, toast rack, cup, tray, "Cheadle" pattern, Royal Winton 1,475.00

Bud Vase, 5 1/4" h, "Marina" pattern, Lord Nelson 120.00

Butter Dish, Cov
    5 1/2" sq x 2 1/2" h, "Spring Glory" pattern, black ground, Royal Winton . . . 265.00
    6 1/2" l x 3 3/4" h, rect, "Summertime" pattern, Royal Winton 250.00

Butter Pat, 3 1/4" sq, "Old Cottage" pattern, Royal Winton 40.00

Cake Plate
    8 3/4" sq x 6" h, "Queen Anne" pattern, chrome center handle, Royal Winton 75.00
    11" H-H, "Summertime" pattern, Royal Winton 120.00
    12" d, "Pekin" pattern, black ground, Royal Winton 250.00

Cake Stand, 8" sq x 2" h, "Royalty" pattern, Royal Winton 185.00

Charger
    12 d
       "Pelham" pattern, Royal Winton 195.00
       "Queen Anne" pattern, Royal Winton 190.00
    15 1/2" d, "Chelsea" pattern, Erphila Czechoslovakia 350.00

Cheese Dish, Cov
    4" h x 6 3/4" l, "Chinese Rose" pattern, Leighton Pottery 350.00
    6" l, slant top, "Summertime" pattern, Royal Winton 365.00

Coffeepot
    6 1/2" h, "Rosalynde" pattern, Lord Nelson 345.00
    6 5/8" h, "Sweet Pea" pattern, Albans shape, Royal Winton, (A) 620.00

Coffee Service, pot, 7 1/4" h, milk jug, sugar basin, 6 cups and saucers, "Paisley" pattern, Greek shape, Royal Winton, (A) 590.00

Compote
    2 1/2" h x 6 1/2" d, "Queen Anne" pattern, Royal Winton 69.00
    3" h x 6" d, "Marguerite" pattern, Royal Winton 165.00
    3 1/4" h x 10" l x 9 1/4" w, "Queen Anne" pattern, Royal Winton 95.00

Coffee Service, pot, 8 1/2" h, creamer, sugar bowl, 8 cups and saucers, "Melody" pattern, Shelley, $995.

Condiment Set, 2 1/2" h, salt, pepper, mustard pot, tray, "Nantwich" pattern, Royal Winton 175.00

Cream and Sugar, open creamer, 2 1/4" h, sugar bowl, 3 1/2" h, "Summertime" pattern, Royal Winton 135.00

Creamer, 3" h, "Spring" pattern, Countess shape, Royal Winton 120.00

Cream, Sugar, and Tray
    Tray, 9" l, "Hazel" pattern, Royal Winton 2,220.00
    Tray, 9 1/2" l x 3" w
       "Black Beauty" pattern, Lord Nelson 375.00
       "Rose Time" pattern, Lord Nelson 225.00

Cup and Saucer
    "Ascot" pattern Crown Ducal 70.00
    "Balmoral" pattern, Royal Winton . . 145.00
    "Black Beauty" pattern, Lord Nelson 85.00
    "Briar Rose" pattern, Lord Nelson . . 65.00
    "Delphinium" pattern, Royal Winton 75.00
    "Du Barry" pattern, James Kent 70.00
    "Floral Feast" pattern, Royal Winton 85.00
    "Green Daisy" pattern, Shelley . . . 60.00
    "Hazel" pattern, black ground, Royal Winton 65.00
    "Heather" pattern, Lord Nelson . . . 90.00
    "Julia" pattern, Royal Winton 110.00
    "Kinver" pattern, Royal Winton 125.00
    "Majestic" pattern, Royal Winton . . 165.00
    "Marguerite" pattern, Royal Winton 85.00
    "Maytime" pattern, Shelley 95.00
    "Melody" pattern, Shelley 79.00
    "Nantwich" pattern 165.00
    "Old Cottage" pattern, Royal Winton 65.00
    "Poppy" pattern 85.00
    "Rosetime" pattern, Lord Nelson . . . 85.00
    "Rosina" pattern 75.00
    "Royal Brocade" pattern, Lord Nelson 38.00
    "Spring Glory" pattern, Royal Winton 115.00
    "Summer Glory," Shelley 150.00
    "Summertime" pattern, Royal Winton 65.00

Cup and Saucer, Demitasse
    "Du Barry" pattern, James Kent . . . 110.00
    "English Rose" pattern, Royal Winton 75.00
    "Hazel" pattern, Royal Winton 100.00
    "Rosetime" pattern, Lord Nelson . . . 85.00

Dessert Bowl, 5" d, "Rosalynde" pattern 55.00

Dish
    10 5/8" l, canoe shape, "Florence" pattern, Royal Winton 350.00
    11 1/4" l x 5" w, 3 section, "Old Cottage" pattern, Royal Winton 150.00

12" l x 10" w, diamond shape, "Melody" pattern, Shelley 275.00

Egg Cup, 2" h, "Marguerite" pattern, Royal Winton 50.00

Egg Set, 6 5/8" w, 2 egg cups, shakers, tray, "Sweet Pea" pattern, Royal Winton, chip, (A) 217.00

Jam Pot, with liner, "Marina" pattern, Lord Nelson 90.00

Jam Set, 4" h, 3 piece, "Sweet Pea" pattern, Royal Winton 295.00

Jug

4" h, "Hazel" pattern, Royal Winton 450.00

4 3/4" h, "Sweet Pea" pattern, Duval shape, Royal Winton, (A) 232.00

5" h, "Marguerite" pattern, Royal Winton 325.00

5 1/2" h, "Chinese Rose" pattern, Leighton Pottery 400.00

6 1/4" h, "Royal Brocade" pattern . 225.00

Milk Pitcher, 6 1/2" h, "Marina" pattern, Lord Nelson

. . . . 270.00

Muffin Dish, Cov, 7 1/2" d, "Welbeck" pattern, Royal Winton, (A) 620.00

Mustard Jar, Cov, 2 1/2" h, "Summertime" pattern, Royal Winton 185.00

Nappy, 5" d, ruffled, "Du Barry" pattern, James Kent 145.00

Nut Dish, 3" d, shell shape, "Esther" pattern, black ground, Royal Winton . . 65.00

Nut Set, dish, 6 1/2" H-H, scoop, 2 sm dishes, "Summertime" pattern, Royal Winton . 225.00

Pitcher

4" h

"Marina" pattern, Lord Nelson . . 75.00

"Royal Brocade" pattern, Lord Nelson 140.00

5" h, "Marguerite" pattern, Royal Winton 195.00

5 1/2" h, "Clyde" pattern, Royal Winton 195.00

6 1/2" h, "Green Tulips" pattern, Lord Nelson 450.00

Plate

5" sq

"Marion" pattern, Royal Winton . 75.00

"Sweet Pea" pattern, Royal Winton 100.00

"Welbeck" pattern, Royal Winton 165.00

6" d

"Du Barry" pattern, James Kent . 65.00

"Royal Brocade" Lord Nelson . . 65.00

6" sq

"Chelsea" pattern, Royal Winton 125.00

"Sweet Pea" pattern, Royal Winton 65.00

"Summertime" pattern, Royal Winton 25.00

"Queen Anne" pattern, Royal Winton 28.00

6 1/2" d, "Du Barry" pattern, James Kent 60.00

7" d

"Heather" pattern Lord Nelson . 75.00

Oct, "Blue Chintz" pattern, Crown Ducal 150.00

"Rapture" pattern, James Kent . 90.00

7" sq

"English Rose" pattern, Royal Winton 125.00

"Florence" pattern, Royal Winton 275.00

"Hazel" pattern, Royal Winton . 100.00

"Kew" pattern, Royal Winton . . . 85.00

"Victorian" pattern, Royal Winton 95.00

7 3/4" sq, "Queen Anne" pattern, Royal Winton 35.00

8" d

"Du Barry" pattern, James Kent 98.00

"Green Daisy" pattern, Shelley 140.00

"Maytime" pattern, Shelley . . . 100.00

"Melody" pattern, Shelley 145.00

"Summer Glory" pattern, Shelley 48.00

8" sq

"Floral Feast" pattern, Royal Winton 100.00

"Julia" pattern 185.00

"June Festival" pattern, Royal Winton 85.00

"Old Cottage" pattern, Royal Winton 60.00

"Summertime" pattern, Royal Winton 40.00

"Sweet Pea" pattern, Royal Winton 82.00

9" d

Oct

"Blue Chintz" pattern, Crown Ducal 175.00

"Ivory Chintz" pattern, Crown Ducal 110.00

9" sq

"Estelle" pattern, Royal Winton 155.00

"Hazel" pattern, Royal Winton . 195.00

"Kew" pattern, Royal Winton . . 155.00

"Orient" pattern, black ground, Royal Winton 100.00

"Summertime" pattern, Royal Winton 125.00

9 1/4" d, "Du Barry" pattern, James Kent 95.00

10" d

"Persian" pattern, Royal Doulton 150.00

"Rosalynde" pattern, James Kent 105.00

10" sq

"Estelle" pattern, Royal Winton . 95.00

"Hazel" pattern, Royal Winton . 185.00

"Old Cottage" pattern, Royal Winton 90.00

"Summertime" pattern, Royal Winton 195.00

Stacked Teapot, 5 1/2" h, "Chelsea" pattern, multicolored florals, black ground, "Royal Winton Grimwades Made in England" mark, $900.

Platter

10" l x 7" w, oval, "Old Cottage" pattern, Royal Winton 100.00

11" l, "Cheadle" pattern, Royal Winton 245.00

Sandwich Tray, 11" H-H, "Royalty" pattern, Royal Winton 135.00

Sauce Dish, 5 1/4" d, "Fireglow" pattern, Royal Winton 30.00

Shakers, 2 1/2" h, "Pekin" pattern, Royal Winton, pr 48.00

Soup Bowl, 8" d

"Summertime" pattern, Royal Winton 85.00

"Sweet Pea" pattern, Royal Winton 95.00

Stacking Tea Set

5 1/2" h

"Chelsea" pattern, Royal Winton 900.00

"Sweet Pea" pattern, Royal Winton 750.00

6" h

"Clyde" pattern, Royal Winton 425.00

"Royal Brocade" pattern 450.00

Sweet Dish, 5" sq, "Du Barry" pattern, James Kent 45.00

Tea For Two, pot, 4 3/4" h, milk jug, sugar basin, 2 cups and saucers, "Spring" pattern, Ascot shape, Royal Winton, (A) 698.00

Teapot

5" h

"Hazel" pattern, 4 cup, Royal Winton 650.00

"Marguarite" pattern, Norman shape, Royal Winton 475.00

"Pekin" pattern, 2 cup, Royal Winton 250.00

"Summertime" pattern, Norman shape, Royal Winton 475.00

5 3/4" h, "Queen Anne" pattern, Royal Winton 495.00

Tennis Set, 9 1/4" l, "Summertime" pattern, "Royal Winton Grimwades Made in England" mark, $125.

6" h, "Summertime" pattern, Royal Winton
. . . . 725.00
6 1/2" h, 4 cup size
"Du Barry" pattern, James Kent
. . . . 650.00
"Rosalynde" pattern, James Kent
. . . . 685.00
Tea Set, pot, creamer, sugar bowl, "Apple Blossom" pattern, James Kent 595.00
Tennis Set
7 1/2" l, "Sweet Pea" pattern, Royal Winton, (A) 295.00
7 5/8" l, "Marion" pattern, Royal Winton
. . . . 135.00
Toast Rack
4 1/2" l, 3 bar
"Marion" pattern, Royal Winton
. . . . 395.00
"Sweet Pea" pattern, Royal Winton, (A) 325.00
7" l, 5 bar, "Marquerite" pattern, Royal Winton 225.00
Tray
3 1/2" sq, "Du Barry" pattern, James Kent
. . . . 110.00
8" l x 6 3/4" w, "Summertime" pattern, Royal Winton 245.00
9" l x 7" w, "Hazel" pattern, Royal Winton
. . . . 175.00
10" l x 7" w, "Sweet Pea" pattern, Royal Winton 225.00
11" l, 3 section, "Kinver" pattern, Royal Winton 295.00
12" l x 7" w, "Summertime" pattern
. . . . 215.00
13" l, "Marina" pattern, Lord Nelson
. . . . 95.00
Tray, 4 Section, 12" l, "Old Cottage" pattern, Royal Winton 135.00
Trivet, 6" d, "Floral Feast" pattern, Royal Winton 85.00
Vase
3 1/2" h
"Chelsea" pattern, Royal Winton
. . . . 195.00
"Summertime" pattern, Royal Winton
. . . . 185.00
3 3/4" h, "Clyde" pattern, Royal Winton
. . . . 80.00

5" h
"Peony" pattern, Royal Winton
. . . . 175.00
"Rapture" pattern, James Kent
. . . . 175.00
5 1/2" h, "Old Cottage" pattern, Royal Winton 160.00
6 1/2" h, "Queen Anne" pattern, bulbous shape, Royal Winton 185.00
9" h, "Chinese Rose" pattern, Albion Pottery 450.00
11" h, "Ivory Chintz" pattern, Crown Ducal, pr, (A) 435.00

CHOISY-LE-ROI

Seine, France
1804 to Present

c 1836 -1900

History: This French factory produced porcelain and white earthenware at Choisy-le-Roi in Seine, France from 1804. First, table services and toilet sets that featured French views or classical scenes printed in red or black were made here. Later, relief decorative motifs were added.

The factory began making earthenware about 1830. Black transfer prints were used with occasional touches of color. After 1860, more relief work was used, and some pieces were glazed with brilliant colors. Majolica wares were made with careful glazing and naturalistic colors. Other works included tiles and trompe l'oeil pieces in the form of ducks, pigs, and plates of asparagus or oysters.

Beginning in 1836, the factory traded as Hautin and Boulanger. Marks incorporated Choisy, or Ch le Roy, or HB & Cie. The factory still remains in operation.

Bowl
5 3/4" d, ftd, raised purple and yellow pansies, green leaves on ext, cream ground 80.00
6" d, center band of blue and red flowerheads and green leaves 50.00
8" d, vert ribbed int, cobalt center, yellow and cobalt splashed int border, gold trim, cream ext 70.00
Plate
7 1/2" d, "Le Debate," black transfer, purple transfer border of French symbols
. . . . 35.00
7 5/8" d, "La Ranlieue a Paris-No. 10," man lying on shelf, black transfer with orange, green, and blue accents, orange and black floral border 70.00
7 3/4" d
"Fruits et Legumes," "6. La Noix Genant Sur Le Moment," scene of 2 men lying under tree, black transfer, purple transfer border design of fruits and vegetables 47.00

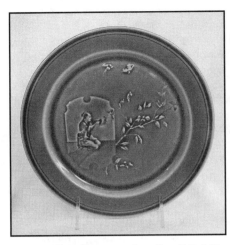

Plate, 8 1/2" d, olive green glaze, "imp H.B. & Cie Choisy Le Roi" marks, $45.

"La Bonne Voie" series, black transfers, blue transfer printed vine borders, "imp HB CHOISY" marks, set of 7 . . . . 180.00
"Le Langage des Fleurs" series, man giving flowers to woman, black transfers, blue transfer printed geometric borders, set of 5 . . . . 175.00
Relief of fruiting branch and leaves, overall green tin glaze 65.00
Scenes of life of Christ, black transfers, borders of blue transferred geometrics, set of 12 . . . . 325.00
8" d, French classical scenes, black transfers, yellow ground, "P & H Choisy" mark, set of 8, (A) 1,886.00
8 1/8" d, "Adieu" pattern, standing man and lady seated at table, black transfer with polychrome accents, "Porcelaine du Choisy" mark, (A) 55.00
8 1/4" d, French puzzle, black transfer, molded floral border, blue lined rim
. . . . 36.00
8 3/4" d
Lt and dk brown hen pecking ground, green chicks on ground, white sky with lt blue buildings in bkd, shaped rim, majolica-type glaze 155.00
Lg rose red Chanticleer rooster in center, green leaves, rose red swirls on border, white ground 10.00
Relief design of gray rabbits, green ground, pale blue house and trees in bkd 125.00
9 1/8" d, dk red, green, and yellow stylized rooster in center, dk red foliage on border, mkd. 42.00
9 1/2" d, majolica, green fern fronds, red flowers, brown ground, Greek key border, pr, (A) 385.00
Teapot, 7 1/2" h, green, gold, and brown pseudo-oriental designs 300.00
Vase
7 5/8" h, majolica, brown flower over green leaves, brown base, applied snail, (A) 100.00

8" h, upper band of green glaze, gloss black lower section with enameled and gilt butterflies 395.00

CLARICE CLIFF

WILKINSON LTD
ENGLAND
c1930

Burslem, England
1925-1963

History: Clarice Cliff, 1899-1972, began her training at Stoke-on-Trent at age 13 when she joined the staff at A.J. Wilkinson, Ltd. Royal Staffordshire Pottery at Burslem. They acquired the adjoining Newport factory along with a huge supply of undecorated bowls and vases that were assigned to Clarice Cliff to decorate. She utilized vivid colors and eccentric Art Deco designs with chunky, angular shapes that contrasted sharply with the flowing lines of the earlier Art Nouveau period. Cliff became art director of A. J. Wilkinson, Ltd. in 1930.

Cliff's earthenwares were gay, colorful, and all hand painted. Circles, squares, colored bands, diamonds, conical shapes, and simple landscapes were incorporated in the designs. Pattern names included: "Applique," "Bizarre," "Fantasque," "Gay Day," "Latonia," "Lodore," "Ravel," and the most popular "Crocus." These patterns were all mass produced and achieved tremendous popularity in both England and America.

Shapes also had special names such as: Athens, Biarritz, Chelsea, Conical, Daffodil, Iris, Lotus, Lynton, Stamford, and Trieste. A customer could order the shape that he wanted decorated with the pattern of his choice. Many novelty pieces such as flower holders, vases, inkwells, candlesticks, cruet sets, bookends, umbrella stands, and even a ceramic telephone cover all were made in Clarice Cliff designs.

Clarice Cliff used several different printed marks, each of which incorporated a facsimile of her signature and usually the name of the pattern.

In 1965, Wilkinson was bought by Midwinter. Midwinter merged with J & G Meakin in 1968. In 1970, Meakin was absorbed by the Wedgwood Group.

References: Richard Green & Des Jones, *The Rich Designs of Clarice Cliff,* Rich Designs, 1995; Leonard Griffin, *Taking Tea with Clarice Cliff: A Celebration of Her Art Deco Teaware,* Pavilion Books, 1996; Leonard Griffin & L & S Meisel, *Clarice Cliff: The Bizarre Affair,* Adams, 1988; Howard Watson, *Collecting Clarice Cliff,* Kevin Francis, 1988; Pat and Howard Watson, *Clarice Cliff Price Guide, 1st Edition,* Kevin

Francis Publications, 1995; Peter Wentworth-Shields & Kay Johnson, *Clarice Cliff,* L'Odeon, 1976.

Collectors' Club: Clarice Cliff Collectors Club, Leonard R. Griffin, Fantasque House, Tennis Drive, The Park, Nottingham NG7 1AE Great Britain. Membership: £55, *Review,* three times a year, *Newsletter,* six times a year.

Museum: Brighton Museum, Brighton, England.

Reproduction Alert: 1993 Wedgwood reproductions in limited editions of 500 patterns were: Sliced Circle, May Avenue, Orange Roof Cottage, Trees and Houses, Carpet and Lighting which were issued as sugar dredges priced at $125 each.

Fakes are also appearing on the market.

In 1985, Midwinter produced a series of "limited edition" reproductions marked with a 1985 backstamp. In 1997, Clarice Cliff reproductions included two Stamford shape teapots each with a different design on either side–Summerhouse with Tennis and Red Roofs with Apples, based on the originals from the book "*Taking Tea with Clarice Cliff.*" They have a full commemorative backstamp and are in a strictly limited edition.

Two of Clarice Cliff's figurines from the "Age of Jazz" from 1930 are the piano player and banjo player and the couple dancing are being reproduced by Pastimes of England. The reproductions are cast as one piece instead of with blocks as the old ones were done.

Collecting Hints: Unmarked pieces of Clarice Cliff china are rare. The large number of back stamps that were used leads to confusion in dating examples.

"Bizarre" (1928-1937) and "Fantasque" (1929-1934) are the most actively sought patterns. "Crocus" is the most popular pattern she ever created which was started in 1928.

There is a big demand for regular tableware items such as tea sets, vases, and fruit bowls, but decorative wares such as wall plaques and her lotus jugs are also big sellers.

Ashtray, 4 3/4" w, "Orange Battle" pattern, (A). 428.00

Biscuit Barrel
    5 7/8" h, "Orange Autumn" pattern, shape #335, (A). 570.00
    6 1/4" h, "Crocus" pattern, shape #336, (A). 428.00

Bowl
    6 5/8" d, stepped, "Latona Red Roses" pattern, red and black, Latona white ground, (A) 535.00
    7 1/2" d, "Forest Glen" pattern, black, blue, green, and red landscape design,

"Hand Painted, Bizarre by Clarice Cliff" mark, (A) 690.00
8 5/8" d
    "Delecia Pansies" pattern, (A) . 357.00
    "Windbells" pattern, (A) 267.00
8 7/8" d, oct, "Rhodanthe" pattern, (A) 230.00
Bowl, Cov, 7 1/2" H-H, "Odeon" pattern
    . . . . 450.00

Candlestick
    2 1/8" h, "Coral Firs" pattern, shape #331, pr, (A). 532.00
    3 1/2" h, mushroom shape, "Autumn Crocus" pattern, pr 1,100.00
Charger, 13" d, "Rhodanthe" pattern, lg orange, yellow, and brown flowerheads and stems, (A) 863.00
Coffeepot, 7 5/8" h, "Capri" pattern, Lynton shape, (A) 338.00

Coffee Set
    Pot, 6 5/8" h, milk jug, sugar basin, 6 cups and saucers, "Delecia Citrus" pattern, Conical shape, (A). 4,278.00
    Pot, 7 1/2" h, milk jug, sugar basin, 6 cups and saucers, "Brookfields" pattern, Lynton shape, (A) 2,495.00
Console Set, bowl, 5 3/4" d, 2 candlesticks, Bizarre, orange, yellow, and blue geometrics, (A) 400.00
Creamer, 3 1/2" h, "Tonquin" pattern, multicolored transfer 25.00

Cup and Saucer
    "Autumn Crocus" pattern. 165.00
    "Coral Firs" pattern, Conical shape 345.00
Dish, 9" l x 7 1/2" w, rect, center depression, "Old Somerset" pattern, multicolored cottage with blue, orange, yellow and purple flowers and fence at rt, flowers at lt, yellow ground, blue rim, "The Biarritz Royal Staffordshire Great Britain Old Somerset" mark. 42.00
Gravy Boat, 8" l, with attached undertray, "Charlotte" pattern, purple transfer. . . . 75.00
Jam Pot, 4 1/4" h, "Autumn Crocus" pattern, orange ground, green rims, "Bizarre and Clarice Cliff" marks. 275.00

Jug
    5" h, "Ravel" pattern, jade green and orange cubist style flowers, Perth shape
    . . . . 370.00
    5 7/8" h, "Forest Glen" pattern, Athens shape. 155.00
    6 1/2" h
        "Applique Avignon" pattern, red and black banding, (A) 1,605.00
        "Tennis" pattern, Conical shape, (A). 2,208.00
    11 1/2" h, Lotus, "Melons" pattern, band of black, blue, yellow, lavender, and green stylized melons over wide orange lower band, "Hand Painted Fantastique by Clarice Cliff" mark, (A) 1,495.00
    11 7/8" h, "Fantasque Bizarre-Summerhouse" pattern, red bands, single handle Lotus Shape, (A) 3,210.00

12" h, Lotus

Dbl handles, "Lightning" pattern, hairline, (A) 2,576.00

Single handle

"Forest Glenn" pattern, (A)
. . . . .1,931.00

"Inspiration Persian" pattern,
(A) 2,760.00

Pitcher

4 1/2" h, 6 1/4" h, 7" h, "Charlotte" pattern, olive brown transfer, set of 3 . . . 135.00

6 1/8" h, "Tonquin" pattern, blue transfer
. . . . 95.00

10" h, "My Garden" pattern, red, yellow, and orange foxglove handle, green leaves, lt brown ground, chip . . 350.00

Plaque

9 1/4" d, "My Garden" pattern, pierced for hanging 175.00

12 3/4" d, Bizarre ware, orange, yellow, green, and brown relief flowerheads, white ground, hairlines 500.00

13 1/2" d, "Trallee" pattern, thatched roof design, (A) 2,024.00

16 1/2" l x 4 3/4" h, rect, Bizarre ware, pink, blue, and brown relief flowerheads, lt brown ground, (A) 325.00

Plate

5 1/2" d, fluted rim, black outlined blue, green, orange, and yellow geometric design, orange border, (A) 428.00

6 1/2" d, oct, "Clematis" pattern, (A)
. . . . 392.00

6 3/4" l x 5 5/8" w, rect with round center, roses, purple flowers, dk green leaves in center, brown thorny branches and gray leaves on border, cream ground, "The Biarritz, Royal Staffordshire" mark
. . . . 155.00

8 1/2" d

Cream ribbed circles, border of mottled lavender and turquoise ribbing, "hp Bizarre Wilkinson Ltd England Clarice Cliff" mark 40.00

"Sunkisses," bananas. 70.00

Plate, 10 1/2" l, "Biarritz," green, rose, and yellow flowers, brown branches, cream ground, "The Biarritz Clarice Cliff" mark, $595.

9" d

"Applique Etna" pattern, yellow, red, and black banding, (A) . . . 1,604.00

"Comets" pattern, orange and green bands, (A) 847.00

Dk brown transfer of Mutiny on the Bounty ship in center with blue-green waves, border of sailing scenes, mkd 42.00

"Persian" pattern, bands of radiating green outlined blue, purple, and yellow stylized foliage, (A) . . . 1,514.00

9 7/8" d, "Blue Chintz" pattern, blue banding, (A) 623.00

10" d, "Applique Caravan" pattern, gypsy wagon scene, (A) 2,576.00

10 3/4" d, man paddling red canoe in lake, forest on sides, med blue dimpled border, "Confederation Series Canada" on reverse 75.00

Platter, 15 1/2" l x 12" w, "Tonquin" pattern, brown transfer 40.00

Preserve Pot

3 1/8" h, "Summerhouse" pattern, cylinder shape, (A) 855.00

4 3/8" h, "Coral Firs" pattern, Bonjour shape, (A) 392.00

Rose Bowl, 6 1/4" h, 4 sq feet, "Latona Stained Glass" pattern, Latona white ground, Conical shape, (A). 295.00

Sandwich Set, tray, 11 3/4" l oct , 6 side plates, "Crocus" pattern, (A) 500.00

Sugar Sifter

4 7/8" h, "Alton" pattern, Bonjour shape, (A) 885.00

5 1/2" h

"Blue Firs" pattern, (A). 1,619.00

"Honolulu" pattern, (A) 2,024.00

"Liberty" pattern, yellow, orange, red, and black horiz bands, (A) . 638.00

"Orange Roof Cottage" pattern, Conical shape, (A) 3,040.00

"Orange Trees and House" pattern, green drip, Conical shape, (A)
. . . . 3,387.00

5 3/4" h, "Napoli" pattern, Conical shape, (A) 567.00

Teapot, Conical Shape

4 3/4" h, "Applique Windmill" pattern, chip on spout, (A) 3,922.00

6 3/4" h, "Honolulu" pattern, (A) . 2,392.00

Tea Set

Pot, 5" h, milk jug, sugar basin, Bizarre stylized multicolored flowers on base, spouts, and knob, Stamford shape, (A) 428.00

Pot, 5 1/8" h, milk jug, sugar basin, "Pine Grove" pattern, Trieste shape, (A)
. . . . 570.00

Tea Set-Duo

Pot, 4 3/4" h, milk jug, sugar basin, side plate, 2 cups and saucers, yellow, orange, and black stripes, Stamford shape, (A) 1,248.00

Pot, 5 1/2" h, milk jug, sugar basin, side plate, 2 cups and saucers, "Taormina" pattern, Bonjour shape, (A) . . 1,960.00

Trio, Cup, Saucer, Side Plate

"Coral Firs" pattern, Conical shape, (A) 570.00

"Fantasque Bizarre-Autumn" pattern, Conical shape, (A) 392.00

Vase

2 3/4" h, ovoid, band of green outlined orange and brown triangles, orange border bands, (A) 355.00

5" h, "Delicia Citrus" pattern, orange, yellow, blue, and green citrus fruit, white ground, shape #341, "Delecia, . . Hand Painted, Bizarre by Clarice Cliff" mark, (A) 575.00

6" h

Ftd, wide flat base, trumpet shaped neck, flared rim, Bizarre ware, green, orange, purple, and tan geometrics, green int 725.00

Stepped shape, "Sliced Fruit" pattern, yellow, orange, and black, (A)
. . . . 690.00

6 1/8" h

"Fantastique Bizarre-Floreat" pattern, band of orange flowerheads, green and white leaves, black ground, wide orange border stripes, shape #264, (A) 496.00

"Orange House" pattern, black roofed orange house, lime green, black, and red stripes, Meiping shape, (A). 1,950.00

6 1/4" h, ball shape, "Clouvre" pattern, lg yellow, red, and mauve flowers on mot-

Vase, 7 3/4" h, raised yellow flowers, blue leaves, dk brown and green branches and stems, mint green int, "Newport Pottery 990 Clarice Cliff" mark, $325.

tled violet ground, shape #370, (A) 4,278.00

6 5/8" h, "Applique Idyll" pattern, Double Bonjour shape, (A). 2,140.00

7 1/4" h, "Autumn" pattern, band of blue, black, yellow, lavender, brown, and orange stylized trees, orange ground, shape #342, "Fantasque, Hand Painted, Bizarre by Clarice Cliff" mark, (A) 1,265.00

7 5/8" h, stepped shape, "Delecia" pattern, blue and purple drip, red ground, shape #369A, (A). 713.00

7 7/8" h, cylinder body, flared ft, ball neck, "Double V" pattern, orange V's, green leaves, yellow ground, orange and green banding with black stripes, shape #368, (A). 500.00

8 1/4" h
"Applique Caravan" pattern, red and black banding, shape #264, (A) 3,565.00

"Red trees and House" pattern, red banding, shape #362, (A) .3,896.00

8 5/8" h
Cylinder shape, everted rim, "Delecia Pansies" pattern, shape #195, rim restored, (A). 445.00

"Latona Dahlia" pattern, mauve, green, and blue flowerheads and zigzags on pink ground, shape #360, (A) 1,514.00

9 1/2" h, "Moonlight" pattern, green and yellow banding, Isis shape, (A) 2,675.00

10 7/8" h, "My Garden" pattern, orange and yellow flowers, black leaves on base, mushroom ground, "My Garden-Bizarre Ware 664 Wilkinson, Ltd" mark. 650.00

12 1/4" h
"Cafe au Lait Autumn" pattern, mottled green ground, Maiping shape, (A). 4,635.00

Green and yellow figural budgies, cream ground. 410.00

"Summerhouse" pattern, red trim, Meiping shape, c1931, (A) 8,832.00

Wall Mask, 6 7/8" h, "Marlene," Art Deco style woman's face with curly hair, green, yellow, and red, pr, (A) 1,063.00

CLEWS

Cobridge Works, Staffordshire, England 1818-1834

c1818-1834

History: James and Ralph Clews were Staffordshire potters who operated the Cobridge Works from 1818 to 1834. They were known for the fine quality of their blue transfer-printed earth-enwares, mostly made for the American market. American views used on their wares were taken from contemporary prints. In addition, designs were taken from books, e.g. the Clews series of *Dr. Syntax* and *Don Quixote*. Plates also were made from the comic pictures drawn by Sir David Wilkie. The company's English views consisted chiefly of castles, abbeys, and cathedrals.

Reference: N. Hudson Moore, *The Old China Book*, Charles E. Tuttle Co. Second printing, 1980.

Museums: Cincinnati Art Museum, Cincinnati, OH; Metropolitan Museum of Art, New York, NY.

Collecting Hints: The two most famous patterns by Clews are "Landing of Lafayette" and the "States." The "Landing of Lafayette" pattern contains an extremely large number of accessory pieces.

Bowl
6 1/2" d, "Christmas Eve," dk blue transfer 400.00
12" d
"Bird of Paradise" pattern, red transfer 355.00
Vase of flowers design, dk blue transfer, "imp Clews" mark, (A). . 468.00

Creamer
4" h, "Basket and Vase" design, blue transfer, molded rim 245.00
4 1/2" h, "Water Girl" pattern, girl at well with dog, flower and scroll border, dk blue transfer, hairline 400.00

Cup and Saucer, Handleless
Basket and urn with flowers, blue transfers, "imp Clews" mark, (A). 94.00
Three children with hooded basket holding dog, dk blue transfers. 235.00

Cup Plate
3 1/2" d, "Christmas Eve," dk blue transfer 325.00
4 1/4" d, "Coronation" pattern, floral design, med blue transfer. 155.00

Jug, 3 3/4" h, rect, black basalt, press molded floral relief, (A) 230.00

Plate
5 1/2" d, "Letter of Introduction," Wilkie's, Designs, dk blue transfer 250.00
6" d, beehive design, dk blue transfer 65.00
6 3/4" d, "Christmas Eve," dk blue transfer 165.00
7" d, overall floral design, black transfer, raised scalloped rim, imp mark . 40.00
7 7/8" d, "Playing at Draughts," dk blue transfer 250.00
8" d, "Dr. Syntax Star Gazing," medium blue transfer 350.00
8 1/8" d, HP heavy set mauve and yellow oriental man seated before bouquet of

Plate, 6 5/8" d, "Christmas Eve," med blue transfer, "imp CLEWS" mark, $125.

flowers and fence, lg overall red and mauve flowerheads and dk brown branches with exotic birds, red lined rim, c1820, pr. 440.00

8 1/4" d, "Sancho, the Priest and Barber," dk blue transfer, hairline 110.00

8 7/8" d, "Christmas Eve," dk blue transfer, "Clews Warranted Staffordshire, crown and Christmas Eve From Wilkie's Designs" mark, (A) 80.00

9" d
"Meeting of Sancho and Dapple," dk blue transfer 250.00
"The Valentine," medium blue transfer 350.00

10" d
"Dr. Syntax Reading His Tour," med blue transfer, unmkd 140.00
"Dr. Syntax Taking Possession," med blue transfer, imp "CLEWS" mark 130.00

10 1/2" d, "Solar Rays," black transfer 65.00

Platter
16 1/2" l, English hunt scene, shell border, dk blue transfer, "imp Clews" mark, repairs, (A) 468.00
17" l, "The Valentine," dk blue transfer, (A) 1,210.00
19" l x 14 1/2" w, "Dr. Syntax amused with Pat in the pool," blue transfer . . . 750.00

Soup Plate
9 3/4" d, "Pancho Panza at the Boar Hunt," blue transfer 350.00

Tureen, 16" l, "The Letter of Introduction" and "Rabbit on the Wall" patterns, dk blue transfers, leaf handles, "imp Clews" mark, repairs, (A) 3,740.00

COALPORT

Severn Gorge, Shropshire, England c1796 to Present

History: After John Rose completed his apprenticeship at Caughley, he established a pottery at Coalport in Shropshire in 1796. Rose expanded his original factory with the purchase of Caughley in 1799. His original soft paste formula eventually was superseded by bone china ware.

By 1822, molds, models, and some key personnel were acquired from the South Wales porcelain manufacturers at Swansea and Nantgarw and incorporated into the Coalport factory. In 1820, John Rose won a Society of Arts medal for his lead-free glaze.

The most characteristic type of Coalport porcelains are the distinctive rococo style flower-encrusted decorative pieces called "Coalbrookdale." "Indian Tree," first made in 1801, and "Hong Kong," made c1805 are two tableware patterns that are still popular to this day.

John Rose died in 1841. Production at Coalport continued under Thomas Rose, his son, W.F. Rose, his nephew, and William Pugh. The influence of Sevres was reflected in the style and decoration of table and ornamental wares made during the mid-19th century.

In 1885, the Bruff family took over. The Coalport firm was sold to Cauldon Potteries Ltd. in Staffordshire in 1923 and moved to the Staffordshire area in 1926 along with many of the workers.

By 1936, both Coalport and Cauldon became part of Crescent potteries at Stoke-on-Trent. In 1958, Coalport was acquired by Brain of Foley China and preserved its separate identity. Many traditional patterns and lines were revived. In 1967, Coalport became part of the Wedgwood group. The Coalport name continues on a line of modern china products.

References: G. Godden, *Coalport and Coalbrookdale Porcelains,* Praeger, 1970; Compton MacKenzie, *The House of Coalport, 1750-1950,* Collins, 1951; Michael Messenger, *Coalport 1795-1926,* Antique Collectors' Club, 1995.

Museums: Cincinnati Museum of Art, Cincinnati, OH; Coalport China Works Muse-um, Ironbridge Gorge Museum Trust, Shropshire, England; Victoria & Albert Museum, London, England.

Basket, 7" h, pink ground, encrusted polyanthus, cowslips, and carnations on sides, rim, and handle, Coalbrookdale 795.00

Cabinet Cup and Saucer
    Gilt leaf design, white jewels, dk red ground 150.00
    Underglaze blue swallows and bamboo reserved on gold ground 175.00

Center Bowl, 10 1/4" d, "Pageant" pattern, stylized enameled purple, yellow, and blue chrysanthemums, swirling purple stems, green leaves on int and ext, gold rim. 155.00

Coffee Can and Saucer
    Enameled graduated turquoise jewels on beaded gilt ground between raised gilt chevron borders, branch handle, dtd 1893, (A) 500.00
    Quatrefoil shape, painted with 4 lake district scenes in gilt foliate cartouches on can and saucer, pattern #A9631, green crown mark, c1885, (A) 650.00

Cream Jug, 4 1/4" h, multicolored scene of stone bridge and lake on front, middle band of pale green in scrolling panels, body with scrolling designs 175.00

Cup and Saucer
    King's Ware, "Fisherman" pattern, blue oriental scene with gold trim. 16.00
    "Sabrina" pattern, floral urns and gargoyles, blue transfers, gold rims . .35.00

Cup and Saucer, Demitasse
    Molded alternating rib and scale vert bands, yellow or cream ground, gold int, gold center on saucer, gold striped rims, scroll molded handles and foliate terminals, mkd, pr, (A) 25.00
    Turquoise trim, jewels, gold ground, fancy handle. 135.00

Dessert Service, 2 compotes, 2" h, compote, 4 1/2" h, 12 plates, 9" d, pink, blue, orange, and yellow enameled florals with green leaves, black and gold feathered border 985.00

Desert Service, Part, 2 cov ice pails, 12 1/2" h, with liners, 3 compotes 5 1/4" h, with stands, 4 platters, 10" l, oval, 18 plates, 8 3/8" d, painted pink flowers in conc gilt and turquoise bands, border with band of painted flowers, c1820, (A). 6,900.00

Dessert Tureen, 6 3/4" h x 9" l, with undertray, oval, vert panels of green and orange leaves and florals and cobalt and gilt leaves, florals interspersed with cobalt ground, gilt leaves and lg rust and gilt mons, white and gilt handles and knob, c1820 . . . . 795.00

Dinner Service, Part, cov tureen, 12" H-H, bowl, 12" H-H, 2 cov sauce tureens with stands, 12" H-H, 43 dinner plates, 9 7/8" d, 14 platters, 10 7/8"-21" l, molded and gilt ribbon tied flowered branches with dbl foliate C-scrolls on wide pink border and bands, int rims with gilt diamonds, scrolls, and bellflowers, c1825, (A) 12,600.00

Plate, 9" d, blue and gilt, "green crown, Coalport England Leadless Glaze" mark, set of 16, (A) $770.

Dish
    8 5/8" d, shell shape, "King's" pattern, Imari palette of flowering tree in stylized foliate border, c1820, pr, (A) 483.00
    9 1/2" d, shell shape, center painted with garden flower sprays, gilt C-scroll inner border, dk blue border with flower sprays, gilt lined rim, gilt scroll and scallop handle, c1820, pr, (A) . . . 1,694.00
    10 3/8" H-H, HP violets and blue ribbons, lt blue relief scroll scalloped rim and handles 45.00

Dish, Cov, 9" d, orange, green, and blue bird and oriental style flowers on int of bowl and cov, green outlined open knob, borders with molded flowerheads and stems, cream ground. 30.00

Pitcher, 4 1/8" h, elongated oval shape, gold band with rust and gold leaves and lines, gold bands on rim, gold trimmed handle. c1803-7, John Rose 195.00

Plate
    7 1/4" d, "Canton" pattern, black transfer with red, yellow, and green flowers 18.00
    8 1/4" d, center painted with landscape view of Edinburgh Castle or Holyrood Castle in gilt surround, brown border, gilt rim with gilt spears, gilt metal frame, c1855, pr, (A) 1,035.00
    8 3/4" d, underglaze blue and enameled iron red, gilt, and green Imari pattern of flowering plants, c1820, set of 18, (A) 3,000.00
    9" d
        HP fruits, scalloped gold border, sgd "Gosling" 150.00
        Painted floral cartouche, green border, gadrooned and foliate molded rim, set of 6, (A) 345.00
    9 1/2" d, sm painted mountainous lake scene in gilt foliate scroll lozenge reserved on lt yellow ground, shaped border with molded shells, scrolls, and strapwork in gilt and enamels, c1885, pr, (A) 2,070.00

10 1/2" d, etched gilt and cobalt border, set of 10, (A) 690.00

Scent Bottle, 4" h, flat based spherical shape, gilt ground with graduated enameled jewels, scalloped ivory band on shoulder with red centered florets, orb stopper with gilt metal mts, pattern #V.2068, green crown mark, c1905, (A) 1,495.00

Service Plate, 10 1/2" d, gilt foliate border on yellow ground, set of 12, (A) 633.00

Soup Plate, 10" d, oriental style cobalt and gilt twisted tree in center with iron red and gilt flowerheads, cobalt and gilt stylized seated bird, border of cobalt stems and orange-red flowerheads, c1820, pr 550.00

Tea Canister, 5 3/4" h, waisted circ shape, hanging pink loops with gilt designs, gilt ground with turquoise enameled jeweling, c1900, (A) 920.00

Teapot

5" h, wide center chased gilt band with enameled turquoise jewels, pink borders with gilt geometrics, acanthus molded spout, handle, and knob, pattern #T1774, dtd 1893, (A) . . .2,100.00

6 1/4" h, oval shape, Imari style underglaze blue, iron red, and gilt floral and fan designs, pattern #819, (A) 575.00

Tea Service, Part, teapot and stand, 6 1/4" h, squat shape, sugar basin, waste bowl, 6 teabowls, 6 coffee cans, 6 saucers, band of orange-red peony heads and birds, willow trees, gilt accents, gilt striping and rims, Anstice, Horton, and Rose, c1810. . . . .3,450.00

Vase

5 1/2" h, overall turquoise cabochons on gilt ground, band of red centered gilt flowers on lt yellow ground on shoulder, stemmed ft with canted sq base, "green crown mark", c1905, pr, (A) . .1,265.00

8 1/4" h, circ ft, ovoid body, narrow neck, flared rim, raised gilt quatrefoil cartouche of painted fruit in landscape reerved on pink ground with radiating gilt sunbursts, powdered gilt rim, 2 gilt scrolled handles, sgd "F.H. Chivers," dtd 1907, (A) 1,380.00

8 3/4" h, campana shape, gilt and white figural swan handles, circ ft, raised gilt outlined shield panels of raised gilt leaves and swirled stems on white ground, gilt body with enameled turquoise jewels, white ground neck and ft with gilt accents, c1900, (A) . . . 633.00

14" h, campana shape with sq base, polychrome flower encrusted body and handles with Cupid and bird, gold accents, Coalbrookdale, chips 2,850.00

Vase, Cov, 19 1/4" h, painted en grisaille center band of Athena and Zeus and attendants on lt blue ground, gilt accented gadrooned cov, lower body, and ft on magenta ground, c1861, (A) .3,680.00

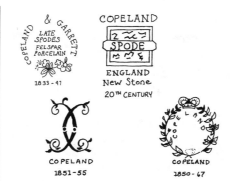

COPELAND-SPODE

London and Stoke-on-Trent, England
1833 to Present

(See Spode for early history)

History: William Copeland died in 1826, and Josiah Spode II died in 1827. In 1833, William Taylor Copeland bought the Spode share in the London showroom and warehouse as well as the Spode Factory. Copeland took Thomas Garrett, a London colleague, as a partner and the firm was known as Copeland & Garrett from 1833 to 1847.

About 1842, Copeland's statuary porcelain body was developed and achieved success. Statuary porcelain, a major new art product, was sponsored by the new Art Unions. Many competitors adopted it, renaming it "Parian." Copeland statuettes, portrait busts, and other objects dominated the market until 1914. Production was halted after that date.

The name Spode was subordinated to that of Copeland after 1847, but the high standards of quality in all its products both in design and execution were maintained. The Spode Factory has held Royal Warrants from 1806 to the present time. The Spode Factory survived many difficult times, constantly striving to maintain its reputation as the producers of fine ceramic wares.

In 1966, the Copeland family sold the firm to the Carborundum Company Ltd., which injected much needed capital to help the firm compete with the other English pottery and porcelain companies. In 1970, the bicentenary year of the firm's establishment, the name of the company was changed back to Spode to honor the founder. In 1976, Spode joined with the Worcester Royal Porcelain Company to form Royal Worcester Spode.

Up to 1833, the name "Spode" referred to the period during which the two Josiahs controlled the company. From 1833 onward, "Spode" referred to the Spode Factory irrespective of ownership. From about 1842 to 1880, the name Spode seldom appeared on its products. Remember all Copeland & Garrett and Copeland wares were Spode factory productions.

Copeland & Garrett: 1833-1847

Copeland: c1847-1970

Spode: 1970-Present

References: See Spode.

Museums: See Spode.

Beverage Set, pitcher, 8" h, 6 tumblers, 4" h, white cameo of tavern scene, blue jasper-type ground, (A) 150.00

Bowl, 9 1/4" sq, "Spode's Tower" pattern, blue transfer 169.00

Cake Plate, 11" H-H, "Spode's Tower" pattern, blue transfer 200.00

Cereal Bowl, "Spode's Tower" pattern, blue transfer 22.00

Charger, 12 1/2" d, brown enameled "Ross Castle, Killarney," sgd "W. Yale" 175.00

Coffee Pot

7 1/2" h, "Spode's Tower" pattern, blue transfer 175.00

9" h, "Spode's Tower" pattern, red transfer 340.00

Creamer, 3 7/8" h, white cameo band of classic figures, molded swag band on shoulder, blue jasper ground, incised geometrics on rim and base, molded shell on spout, "imp Copeland, England" mark, (A) 125.00

Cup and Saucer

"Buttercup" pattern, Spode yellow buttercups, sm blue flowers, molded design on border 12.00

"Daisy" pattern, molded band of daisies, overall white glaze, "Copeland Late Spode" mark 12.00

"Ermine Centurion" pattern, blue transfer 40.00

"June" pattern, panel of red and green exotic bird, molded floral side panels, "Copeland Late Spode" mark . . . 22.00

"Spode's Aster" pattern, polychromed transfer 18.00

"Spode's Cowslip" pattern, multicolored floral and basketweave bands, "Copeland Late Spode" mark 38.00

Vignettes of puce painted figures in landscape, lt yellow bands festooned with roses, c1860 . . . . 285.00

Cup and Saucer, Demitasse

"Du Barry" pattern, ribbed body, red roses and stems, green leaves 20.00

"Hazel Dale" pattern 45.00

"Mandarin" pattern, red transfer, fluted body, Spode Copeland, set of 4 . . . . 140.00

"Old Chicago Scenes" pattern, black transfer, set of 6 . . . . 85.00

"Wicker Dale" pattern 45.00

Dessert Dish, 12 1/4" l, oval, center with multicolored English coastal scene, pink border with molded gilt rim, Copeland and Garrett, c1833-47 . . . . 495.00

Dinner Service, Part

Four plates, 12" d, 4 plates, 10" d, 4 cups and saucers, 4 berry bowls, 4 dessert plates, 4 handled soup bowls with underplates, "Spode's Ermine" pattern, overall blue ermine tails, "Copeland Spode, Spode's Ermine" marks. 350.00

Eighteen plates, 10 1/2" d, 17 soup plates, 10 1/2" d, 28 plates, 9" d, 15 bouillon cups, 18 saucers, border band of gilt stylized flowerheads alternating with seeded panels, pattern #Y1470, Spode-Copeland, (A) 1,955.00

Eighteen plates, 10 5/8" d, 14 plates, 9" d, 10 plates, 7 3/4" d, 24 saucers, 6 1/4" d, 5 side plates, 6 1/4" d, soup plate, 9" d, 4 platters, 17 3/8" l, center painted with multicolored loose bouquets in blue spearhead cartouche, green vermiculite border with scattered flowers, egg and dart beaded rim, (A) 1,840.00

Ewer, 15 1/2" h, baluster shaped body, swan molded lip, cattail handle, reserve with ships at sea in molded cattail border, gilt accented shaped ft molded with cartouches, restored, 19th C, (A) 230.00

Figure, 7 7/8" h, "Cries of London-Cherry Seller," woman standing by barrow, (A) . . 141.00

Milk Barrel, 4" h, "Spode's Tower" pattern, blue transfer 135.00

Pancake Server, 7" h, 11 1/4" d, ftd, bands of blue and gold stylized flowers, gold trim on handles and knob, dtd 1852, "Copeland Late Spode" mark 290.00

Pass Cup, 5 1/4" h, stoneware, white relief of band of dancing women, hanging swags, green ground, tan body and 2 handles, "Copeland Late Spode, England" mark, (A) 112.00

Pitcher

4 1/2" h, multicolored ethereal forest scene on front, lt yellow ground, white vert panels on base, raised gold scrolling, Copeland and Garrett, c1833-47 . . . . 285.00

Pitcher, 6" h, gray-white cameos, med blue ground, c1875, $175.

Plate, 7 1/2" d, "Italian" pattern, blue transfer, "Copeland Spode's Italian England and imp Copeland and crown" marks, $65.

5 1/2" h, stoneware, white relief of rugby game, grasses on border, brown glazed body, (A) 247.00

6 1/2" h, "Spode's Fitzhugh" pattern, green transfer, floral molding, crossed twig handle 85.00

7" h, stoneware, cream relief of hunting scene, brown ground, (A) 112.00

Plaque, 9 3/8" sq, painted yellow and red roses, buds, and greens in glass pedestal bowl on marble table, "red COPELAND AND GARRETT and crown" mark, (A) . . . 1,540.00

Plate

6 1/2" d, "Spode's Tower" pattern, blue transfer 14.00

7 3/4" d, "Mayflower" pattern, red flowers and green leaves in center, purple floral transfer border, molded reeded rim 45.00

8 1/2" d, leopard, bird, and butterfly, brown tree with green and tan leaves, tan molded body, c1847-67 . . . . . . 28.00

9" d, swimming fish in seaweed, inner border of swags, scalloped border with diamond design, blue transfer, c1870, set of 4 . . . . 100.00

9 1/2" d

"Historic Sites-Roche Hermitage" pattern, brown transfer with polychrome, Copeland Spode . . . 55.00

"Spode's Tower" pattern, blue transfer 32.00

9 3/4" d, "The Three Wisemen," 3 figures in scroll, scattered birds and flowers, flowerhead border, brown transfer . . 35.00

10" d

Blue, orange, red, brown, and black oriental interior design, red drape and flowerhead border, "imp COPELAND" mark, c1840-60 . . . . . 32.00

Plain center, apple green border with cartouches of shells, exotic birds, and flowers, gilt accented foliate rim, Copeland and Garrett, (A) . . . 58.00

10 1/4" d

"Buttercup" pattern, yellow buttercups, blue flowers, inner basketweave border, yellow buttercups, blue flowers, and molded design on border, Spode 30.00

Wide blue border band surrounded by emb gilt bands of geometrics, Spode Copeland, set 12, (A) 690.00

10 1/2" d

Purple, green, and dk red peacock and florals in center, scalloped border, "Copeland Late Spode" mark 35.00

"Severn" pattern, village and river scene, red transfer 35.00

"Spode's Tower" pattern

Blue transfer 37.00

Pink transfer 23.00

Platter

12 3/4" l x 9 1/4" w, "Spode's Castle" pattern, blue transfer, Copeland & Garrett, c1833-47 . . . . 330.00

18 1/2" l, Scottsmen standing on bridge, scroll border, lt blue transfer . . . 225.00

Potpourri Jar, 4 1/2" h, white cameos of putti, brown ground, white lizard handles, 19th C 325.00

Punch Bowl, 11" d x 6" h, with stand, continuous landscape scene with floral bouquets, green transfers, Copeland and Garrett 850.00

Serving Dish, 11" l, oval, green flowers in basket in center, ruffled rim, Copeland-Spode 75.00

Soup Bowl, 9 1/4" d, "Spode's Tower" pattern, blue transfer 49.00

Soup Plate, 9" d, Imari pattern, cobalt and gold onion bulb with cobalt, iron red, and gilt flowerheads, cobalt rim with pink and gold flowerheads, c1860 . . . . 115.00

Teapot

3" h, baluster form, gilt accented anthemion and floral decoration, (A) 25.00

10" h, "Spode's Tower" pattern, red transfer 490.00

Tray, 13 5/8" l, 7 3/8" w, "Spode's Tower" pattern, red transfer 45.00

Turkey Set, Part, platter, 23" l, oct, 9 plates, 10 5/8" d, underglaze blue with brown and black transfer of lg walking turkey in center, hanging floral swags on borders, "Copeland Spode England" mark, (A) 1,705.00

Vegetable Bowl

9 1/4" sq, sheet transfer of green flowerheads, brown stems and buds, "Copeland Spode" mark 30.00

10" l, rect, ftd, "Spode's Tower" pattern, blue transfer 90.00

Warming Dish, 9 5/8" d, HP oriental scene of blue and purple chrysanthemums, stylized red and black fence, purple swag rim with stylized flowerheads, "Copeland and Garrett, Late Spode" mark 98.00

Waste Bowl, 5" d, "Spode's Tower" pattern, blue transfer 139.00

COW CREAMERS
**Staffordshire, England
2nd half 18th C to mid 19th C
Delft, Holland
c1755**

History: Cow creamers were cream jugs in the shape of a cow. There was an oval hole opening in the top of the back of the cow for filling the creamer. The spout was the mouth with the curved tail serving as a handle. Historically, most filling holes had lids. Today they frequently are missing.

Some cow creamers had a seated milkmaid alongside the creamer. The earliest earthenware cow creamers were made in Staffordshire during the second half of the 18th century.

English cow creamers were made in Whieldon ware, creamware, Prattware, and many other ceramic types. Large size versions often were called cow milk jugs. Cow creamers in tin-glazed ware, c1755, were made at Delft, Holland.

Museum: City Museum and Art Gallery, Stoke-on-Trent, Hanley, England.

Covered

4 3/8" h

Blue spatter standing cow and seated calf, brown and yellow trim, oval lined base, horns restored, cov missing, (A) 715.00

Brown-red splotches, silver lined base with raised green grass 600.00

4 3/4" h, brown sponging, white ground, horn damaged, (A) 138.00

5" h, orange and brown brushed spots, brown horns and muzzles, nursing calf, green washed rect base with cut corners, c1810 . . . . .2,800.00

5 1/4" h, ochre and black sponging, seated milkmaid, green oct base with black and ochre sponging 1,425.00

5 3/8" h, dk brown crescents on cream ground, seated milkmaid in ochre dress, England, repairs to tail, horns, and ear 1,650.00

Covered, 5" h, 6 1/2" l, green, rust, and chartreuse florals, gold horns, iron red and mustard striped base, unmkd, (A) $207.

5 1/2" h

Brown and purple luster spots, Swansea, c1840.00 . . . . 1,550.00

Pearlware, gray and ochre sponging, seated milkmaid in yellow dress, green base 1,825.00

Splashed yellow and olive green body with olive spots, shaped green base, (A) 437.00

Sponged black and ochre vert stripes, black horns, tail, and knob, oval blue sponged base with ochre and white seated milkmaid in black hat, (A) 920.00

Sponged yellow brown spots, white ground, shaped green base, seated milkmaid in green dress, yellow-brown hat, (A) 633.00

5 3/4" h

Jackfield, black glaze 250.00

Pink and black sponging, calf on black and green sponged white base, c1790 . . . . 1,425.00

6" h x 7 1/2" l, orange-brown spotting, seated milkmaid in yellow hat, gray blouse, lavender skirt, cracks in tail . . . 195.00

6" l, splashed pink luster, Swansea type, restored, (A) 250.00

Open

4 1/4" h, seated on haunches, orange body, black horns and tail handle, Czechoslovakia 40.00

5" l x 3 1/2" h, standing, tan body, black hooves, Germany 35.00

5 1/2" l x 3" h, standing, brown body, black hooves and accents, Germany 60.00

7" l

Seated on haunches, white body, black accents 35.00

Squatting on front and back legs, red floral transfer, Clarice Cliff 75.00

7 1/4" l, standing brown cow, "imp Germany" mark, (A) 25.00

7 1/2" l

3 3/8" h, recumbent, blue sailboat scene, white ground, (A) 30.00

5" h, standing, blue sailboat on side, blue splashed body, white ground, Germany 145.00

Open, 3 3/8" h, 7 1/2" l, rust glaze, unmkd, (A) $35.

Open, 4" h, 7 1/4" l, blue shades, unmkd, (A) $45.

Seated on haunches, white, unmkd 150.00

8" l, seated on front and rear feet, white glaze, unmkd 125.00

8 1/2" h, standing red-brown and white cow, young man at tail holding green basket on head for milk, cobalt jacket, red striped breeches, spotted calf seated on green base, c1860 . . . . 995.00

10" l, standing, molded udder and teats, dk brown shading, unmkd 245.00

CREAMWARE

English/Continental
c1740 to Present

History: Creamware (cream-colored earthenware) provided a fine form and thin body in addition to a clean and brilliant glaze. Creamware made no pretense to imitate porcelain in color, form, or decoration. Yet, it found a ready acceptance in the market place.

Creamware was made from the beginning of the 18th century. The materials were identical to those used to make salt glaze. The principal difference was that creamware was fired at a lower temperature and glazed with lead.

In 1740, Enoch Booth of Tunstall in Staffordshire invented a fluid glaze that provided a brilliant, transparent cream color. Thomas Whieldon and Josiah Wedgwood both used this glaze. By 1760, enameled decoration was being added to the creamware glaze. Derbyshire, Liverpool, Yorkshire, and Swansea also produced creamware products.

Creamware was improved in 1768 by introducing china clay and china stone from Cornwall into the body and glaze. This resulted in creamware that was paler in color, plus lighter and more brilliant in the glaze.

Since there was much interchange and copying of ideas among a number of potteries, similarities in both the body and glaze were found. Hence, it was quite difficult to assign early creamware to a particular factory since most creamware was unmarked prior to that manufactured by Wedgwood.

Creamware was the main product in England between 1760 and 1820. It supplanted the manufacture of white salt glaze by c1780. Creamware's prominence during these years provided the death blow to tin-glazed earthenware in England and on the continent. From c1760, English creamware was exported to nearly every European country.

Many Staffordshire potters left England and established factories in France, thus threatening the faience factories and undercutting the sale of porcelains. The European factories turned to the manufacture of creamware in self defense.

Reference: Donald Towner, *Creamware,* Faber & Faber, 1978.

Museums: Castle Museum, Norwich, England; Cincinnati Art Museum, Cincinnati, OH; City Museum & Art Gallery, Hanley, Stoke-on-Trent, England; Victoria & Albert Museum, London, England.

Continental

Plate, 8" d, woman seated on rock formation, man kneeling in front placing shoe on foot in exotic garden setting, border band of stylized palm fronds, dk brown transfer, "imp Gien" mark, 19th C 125.00

Pot, Cov, 7 1/2" h, 3 relief molded lion masks on sides, tripod base formed from 3 curved strips with molded lion's paws, Paris, c1810 . . . . 1,500.00

Wine Coaster, 2 1/4" d, cylinder shape, arched column pierced sides, beaded rim, pr 750.00

English

Basket, 10 1/2" H-H, oval, pierced gadrooned sides inset with circlets, band of pierced hearts and diamonds above, pierced shell handles, Yorkshire, c1780, pr, (A) . . 1,265.00

Basket and Stand

   5 1/4" l, oval, lobed, scalloped rim pierced and molded w/husk swags, twisted han-

dles ending in floral and foliage terminals, c1780 . . . . 1,850.00

   9" l, oval, flared shape, entwined rope twist handles with molded flower terminals, molded winged female masks over drapes and laurel swags and scrolling leaves, pierced sides, feather molded rims, c1780-1800, (A) 925.00

   9 7/8" l, ribbed base, flared top pierced w/diamonds and hearts, dbl twisted entwined handles ending in flower and foliage terminals, trompe l'oeil simulated pierced dots in center, Leeds, c1785 . . . . 2,500.00

Bowl and Stand, 8 3/4" h, w/ladle, body and cov w/radiating lobes, pierced cov, multipetaled floral finial, pierced stand rim w/bellflower garlands, ladle w/pierced bowl and reeded handle, c1785, Leeds 2,550.00

Candlestick, 2 7/8" h, faceted stem, flared top, compressed ball base on lobed flaring ft, feathered rim, c1775, crack in base 1,500.00

Chestnut Basket, 8 1/8" h, molded intersecting scrolls, husk garlands, and acanthus leaves, pierced upper section, flower finial, twisted dbl entwined handles, imp "WEDGWOOD" mark, c1775 . . . . 3,850.00

Chocolate Cup, 2 3/4" h, cylinder shape, reeded entwined dbl strap handle w/flower and foliage terminals, c1785 . . . . 650.00

Cup and Saucer, Handleless, band of HP red flowers, green leaves, brown stems, dk brown striped rim, int of cup with dk brown chain, (A) 90.00

Custard Cup, 3 1/4" h, ribbed body and cov, grooved ear handles, ball knob, imp "WEDGWOOD" mark, c1775 . . . . 1,250.00

Dessert Dish, 9 1/2" d, lobed, flattened pierced rim with molded scrolls and bellflowers, scallop and point rim with raised line, c1780, pr 850.00

Egg Drainer, 2 7/8" d, pierced geometric design, concave gadrooned rim, twisted handle, c1780 . . . . 450.00

Figure

   3 7/8" h, Spring, standing woman with garland of flowers, white ground with green splashed drapery, Staffordshire, c1770, (A) 575.00

   5 7/8" h, youth wearing formal coat, shirt w/ruffled collar, knee breeches, black eyes, holding drapery filled w/molded flowers, Devonshire, c1785 . . 1,450.00

   6" h, recumbent doe, brown spots, cream body, green grass mound base, Staffordshire, c1805, repairs, (A) 518.00

   8 1/2" h, "Narcissus," standing youth, overall white, 19th C 695.00

Fish Mold, 8 1/4" d, stepped, sides pierced with lozenge, c1790, (A) 210.00

Flower Frog, 9 1/2" h, figure of Psyche sitting on rock holding staff, Wedgwood . . . 375.00

Hot Water Plate, 9 3/4" H-H, reeded handles with leaf terminals, c1790, (A) 210.00

Jam Pot, Cov, 3 1/2" h, bulbous shape, loop handle, ball knob, white glaze, c1760 . . . . 225.00

Jug, 8" h, baluster shape, beak spout, strap handle, black printed portrait of Lord Nelson and "Here's our old friend, and success to the Peace Makers. Here's a health to brave Nelson, Old England's Boast, The Hero of the Nile, Let this be our toast" in cartouche, reverse with Nelson's ship, trumpeting angel under spout, Staffordshire, c1805, (A) 1,265.00

Mug

   3 5/8" h, bell shape, enamel painted chinoiserie figures in temple, blue, yellow, and green accented grooved entwined dbl strap handle, flower and foliage terminals, 1770 . . . . 1,150.00

   3 3/4" h, cylinder shape, horiz ribbing, ribbed entwined dbl strap handle, flower and foliage terminals, c1780 . . . . 1,150.00

   5 3/4" h, cylinder shape, polychrome floral sprigs, mid 18th C 350.00

Oil and Vinegar Stand, 10 1/2" h, figural warrior in center, 2 pierced and diamond molded holders on base, late 18th C, Yorkshire, feather missing, (A) 747.00

Pepper Castor, 3 1/4" h, pear shape with spreading ft, pierced dome, turned finial, c1780 . . . . 1,950.00

Plate

   8 1/4" d, orange and black flower design in center and border design, (A) . . . 40.00

   8 3/4" d, pierced heart diapers in molded bellflower garlands, c1790, (A) 200.00

   9" d, center with pagoda reserved on stylized flowers and foliage in Imari colors, molded daisies on border, Wedgwood, set of 12, (A) 805.00

   9 1/4" d, "Personages" pattern on border, black transfer, scalloped rim, "imp

Continental, Plate, 8" d, dk brown transfer, "imp Gien" mark, $125.

England, Plate, 8" d, "incised beehive" mark, (A) 35.

WEDGWOOD" mark, early 20th C, set of 9, (A) 115.00

9 5/8" d, central gold shield with black star hung from pink ribbons, flower garlands at side, banner w/"PAX OPTIMA RERUM EST." below, scalloped shell border, c1780, pr 1,100.00

9 3/4" d, black transfer of American sailing ship on green enamel water, pr, (A) 440.00

Platter, 18 1/8" l, oval, "Bedford Vine" pattern, brown enameled design on border, Wedgwood, late 18th C, (A) 75.00

Sauceboat

5 1/2" l, quatrefoil shape, elongated gadrooning on bottom, feathered rim, reeded dbl strap handle with flower and foliage terminal, c1780 . . . . 750.00

7 1/8" w, with undertray, lozenge shape, rocaille molded with acanthus, shell handles, feather molded rim, Staffordshire, c1770, pr, (A) 1,035.00

Sauce Tureen, 8" l, with ladle, enameled brown laurel border, Wedgwood, 18th C, (A) 125.00

Sugar Bowl, Cov, 3 7/8" d, applied trailing fruiting vine and flowers, mottled brown glaze, gilt accents, bird knob, Staffordshire, c1760, restorations, (A) 345.00

Sweetmeat Dish, 4 1/2" l, molded pectin shell, "imp WEDGWOOD" mark, c1785 . . . . 450.00

Sweetmeat Tazza, 2" h x 5 1/4" d, molded pectin shell, truncated cone foot, green translucent stripes, c1780 . . . . .1,900.00

Tankard, Cov, 7 1/4" h, cylinder shape, button knob on cov, white glaze, c1780-1810 .295.00

Teabowl and Saucer, beaded bowl rim and saucer center, green translucent vert striping, c1775 . . . . .1,050.00

Tea Caddy

4 3/4" h, rect, red painted farmhouse and red fencing flanked by green trees, mauve hills in bkd, molded shell shoulder, red interlocking "S" pattern on rim, Wedgwood, c1770 . . . . 265.00

5 1/4" h, cylinder shape with tapered shoulder, red and green enamel floral bunches hanging from swags, domed cov with round knob, (A) 750.00

Teapot

4" h, globular, applied trailing fruiting vines, crabstock handle and spout, bird knob, 3 paw feet, mottled brown glaze, restorations, Staffordshire, c1760, (A) 690.00

4 3/4" h, cylinder shape

Molded acanthus spout, ribbed handle, (A) 385.00

Transfer printed and painted "The Prodigal Son Receives his Patrimony" and "The Prodigal Son Taking his Leave" on sides, cov rim, shoulder, and foot with molded band of key pattern, gilt accents, flower knob, William Greatbatch, c1775, (A) 2,070.00

5" h, globular, dbl twist handle, flower knob, worn gilt floral spray on sides, c1770, (A) 374.00

5 1/4" h

Black and red enameled stylized bird on branch on sides, relief molded beaded rim, c1770, restored, (A) 430.00

Male and female figures drinking in landscape setting on front, "Long may we live, happy may we be, blest with content, and from misfortunes free" on reverse, black transfers, Wedgwood, c1770, (A) 632.00

5 1/2" h, "Harlequin and Columbine Discovered in an Arbor by Pierrot," on front, similar scene on reverse, black transfers with polychrome enamels, restorations, Greatbatch, c1780, (A) . . 920.00

5 3/4" h, cylinder shape with stepped shoulder, translucent vert green and yellow stripes with brown dotting, leaf molded spout, dbl entwined handle, Leeds, c1780, (A) 2,645.00

Tea Service, Part, coffeepot, 10" h, baluster shape, teapot, 4 1/8" h, globular shape, teapot, 3 3/4" h, cylinder shape, cream jug, 3 1/2" h, cov sugar bowl, 4" h, tea caddy, 4 3/4" h, arched rect shape, tea caddy, 5" h, cylinder shape, mug, 3 3/4" h, mug, 2 5/8" h, plate, 9 3/4" d, 7 teabowls and saucers, enameled red roses with green leaves and loose bouquets, England, c1780, (A) 4,830.00

Tureen

6 5/8" h, blue floral sprig on sides, blue drip borders and rims, blue accented floral knob an dbl handles, "Neale & Co." mark, repairs, (A) 220.00

8" l, lobed melon shape, pierced cov with pomegranate knob, attached serrated leaf molded and veined base with flowers at stem, c1785, knob reglued 2,950.00

CREIL

Seine-et-Marne and Oise, France 1784-1895

CREIL
LM & CIE
MONTEREAU
1841-1895

History: About 1784, the Englishman Bagnad in association with M. de St. Cricq-Cazeaux established a factory for the manufacture of English style earthenware. These two founders united with Montereau during the early 19th century, forming a firm that continued until 1895.

The Creil factory was the first French pottery to use transfer printing on earthenware. Transfer views of Paris, French chateaux, portraits of important people, English country houses, fables of La Fontaine, and paintings of religious or allegorical subjects in monochrome graced white or cream colored ware. Porcelain never was made.

Marks were either stamped in the paste or stenciled. They . included Creil et Montereau or LM & C.

Box, 3 1/2" h x 5 1/2" l, rect, blue printed oriental birds and branches, blue diamond rims, c1880 . . . . 500.00

Coffeepot, 8 1/2" h, black transfers of pr of classical busts on sides, band of branches and leaves with grotesque mask on top, band of compass roses on base, black striping on rim and ft, figural birdhead spout 985.00

Cup, Miniature, child jumping rope, black transfer, cream ground, (A) 25.00

Cup and Saucer, "Brouette" and man with wheel barrow, fort in bkd on cup, 2 men in landscape and floral border on saucer, black transfers, yellow ground, c1800 . . . . . 175.00

Jar, Cov, 6 1/2" h, village scenes, black transfer, yellow ground, (A) 517.00

Pitcher, 8" h, Toby-type, figural fat man in red coat, black hat, flesh colored face and hands, "green CREIL ET MONTEREAU, DEPOSE" mark 225.00

Plate

6 1/2" d, center with couple dancing and "Les Sports No. 7 Dancing," black transfer, vine border, blue transfer, "C.M. Depose Creil et Montereau" mark. 15.00

7 1/2" d, center with cartoon of dueling scene, black transfer, geometric border, blue tranfer, "B. & Co. Depose Creil et Montereau" mark, and "UN DUEL EST SOUVENT FATAL AUX CANARDS" on reverse 12.00

7 3/4" d, "Combat de Puente Colorado," floral and shield border, black transfer, "Creil et Montereau" mark 25.00

8" d

Black transfers of named scenes from French Revolution, yellow ground, set of 5, (A) 747.00

"Garde Municipale de la VII de Paris," soldier on horseback, 2 soldiers on ft, multicolored transfer, c1820, imp mark 245.00

"La Lune de Miel," man and woman seated on sofa, geometric border, purple transfer scalloped rim, "Creil et Montereau" mark, c1890 . . 35.00

"Le Vieux Celibataire," black transfer, cream ground, "Montereau" mark, c1820 . . . . 425.00

"Rigolades No. 1-Comment Marie Enore Un Nouveau Soldat?" ovals and geometrics on border, black transfer, "Creil et Montereau" mark 40.00

8 1/8" d, farmer and wife in field, polychrome transfer, floral border . . . 55.00

8 1/4" d

Center scene of men fishing, arched bridge, trees, and house in bkd, flowerhead and leaf border, brown transfer, yellow ground, "imp Montereau," (A) 286.00

8 1/2" d

Black transfer of Willow-type pattern of pagoda and bridge, yellow ground, c1820 . . . . 350.00

Creamware, black transfer of puzzle of love, band of trailing interlaced flowers, "imp MAU," c1800, set of 9, (A) 600.00

"Dame de Mallorca," polychrome transfer, "imp CREIL" mark . . 55.00

Hunter in period clothes shooting, black transfer, cream ground 155.00

8 5/8" d

Black transfer of French proverbs in diamond center, yellow border, set of 6 .2,000.00

Brown transfer of "Henry IV Jouant Avec Ses Enfants," brown floral transfer on border, "imp Montereau" mark, rim wear, (A) 35.00

8 3/4" d, "Rebus No. 6" proverb, 3 sections of soldier, sword swallower, and date test, grapevine border with 2 men drinking, blue transfer 45.00

9" d, "Observetoire Royal A Paris," band of flowerheads on border, black transfers 150.00

9 3/4" d, black transfer of map of France in center, scenes on France on border, cream ground, set of 8, (A) 414.00

Platter, 14" l, "Arnos Grove" in center, black transfer, cream ground, repaired, (A). . 52.00

Soup Bowl, 9 1/2" d, black transfer

Louis XVII in center, grape border, sepia ground, (A) 70.00

"Partage Des Tresors De Dagobert," grapevine border, cream ground, "imp CREIL" mark 65.00

Soupiere, 11 1/4" d, with undertray, Henri IV and Duc DeBerry on lid, Madame Duchess D'Angouleme on body, black transfers, cream ground, (A) 467.00

Tureen, 11" h x 14 1/2" H-H, with undertray, "Vue de L'hotel de Ville de Paris-Prise du cote de la Place," reverse with "Vue de la Barriere

Plate, 8 1/2" d, black transfer, cream ground, "imp Creil" mark, $375.

du Tome-Faub Dt. Antoine de Paris," "Vue du Chateau de la Mal. Maison" on undertray, floral border, black transfers, black striped rims, cream ground, c1815. . . . . 2,950.00

c1890

1878-90

CROWN AND ROYAL CROWN DERBY

Osmaston Road, Derby, England 1876 to Present

History: Edward Phillips, formerly of the Royal Worcester Company, established the Royal Crown Derby Porcelain Company, on Osmaston Road in Derby in 1877. This new company had no connection with the original Derby works. By 1878, the new factory was producing earthenwares called "crown ware" in addition to porcelains.

The new Derby porcelain was richly decorated in the old "Japan" patterns featuring reds and blues along with rich gilding very much in the manner of the earlier Derby porcelains. Additionally, the new Derby company produced ornamental forms including figures and highly decorated vases and services.

The year 1890 marked the beginning of the Royal Crown Derby period when the company was appointed manufacturers of porcelain to Queen Victoria and "Royal Crown Derby" was added to the trademark.

Desire Leroy was the most distinguished artist employed by Royal Crown Derby. He trained at the Sevres factory, went to Minton in 1878, came to Royal Crown Derby in 1890, and stayed until his death in 1908. His most successful contribution was the use of white enamels painted over rich dark blue ground in the style of Limoges enamels. He exhibited a great versatility of design and remarkable use of colors. His lavish designs usually featured birds in landscape, fruits, flowers, and occasional figures. He also added gilt embellishments.

In 1904, toy shapes were produced that attracted the attention of miniature collectors. Figures were made in the late 1920s and early 1930s. During the post-war period, Arnold Mikelson modeled lifelike birds and animals.

In 1935, the Royal Crown Derby company purchased the small King Street works which had been established by some

former Derby workers in 1848. This provided a link with the original Derby factory founded by William Duesbury in the mid 18th century.

References: F. Brayshaw Gilhespy, *Crown Derby Porcelain,* F. Lewis Ltd. 1951; F. Brayshaw Gilhespy & Dorothy M. Budd, *Royal Crown Derby China*, Charles Skilton Ltd. 1964; John Twitchett & Betty Bailey, *Royal Crown Derby,* Barrie & Jenkins, Ltd. 1976.

Museums: Cincinnati Art Museum, Cincinnati, OH; Gardiner Museum of Ceramic Art, Toronto, Canada; Royal Crown Derby Museum, Osmaston Road, Derby; Derby Museums & Art Gallery, The Strand, Derby; Victoria & Albert Museum, London, England.

Collecting Hints: Royal Crown Derby continues production to the present day as part of Royal Doulton Tablewares Ltd. From 1882 onward, all Crown Derby can be dated. A year cypher appears under the trademark, the key for which can be found in Geoffrey A. Godden's *Victorian Porcelain*, Herbert Jenkins, 1961.

Bottle, 7 1/2" h, with stopper, bulbous body, straight neck, raised enameled decoration and gilt foliate designs, yellow ground, Royal Crown Derby, c1894, (A) 345.00

Cake Plate, 8 1/2" sq, Imari pattern in cobalt, iron red, and gilt, pattern #5244, Royal Crown Derby. 95.00

Creamer, 3 1/8" h, bone china, blue and white oriental figures in landscape, gilt trim, Royal Crown Derby 20.00

Cup and Saucer, red floral transfer, cobalt and gilt trim and rims, Royal Crown Derby, (A) 20.00

Cup and Saucer, Demitasse

Cylinder shape, Imari pattern, saucer with cobalt and gilt garden urn with flowers in center, iron red flowerheads, cup with alternating white vert panels with iron red flowerheads and cobalt panels with gilt trim, Crown Derby 75.00

Overall pink roses and gold leaves, Royal Crown Derby, set of 4 . . . . 300.00

"Vine" pattern, Royal Crown Derby . 24.00

Dish, 10 1/4" l x 8 1/2" w, Imari pattern, underglaze blue, iron red, salmon, and gold floral and foliate pattern, Royal Crown Derby, early 19th C, pr, (A) 259.00

Ewer

8" h, raised gilt reserve of polychrome florals, pink ground, raised gold scrolling, vert lines on base, Royal Crown Derby, c1892, (A) 258.00

11 1/2" h, raised gilt birds and floral motif on yellow ground, green ground neck and base with gilt and red designs, Crown Derby, (A) 7,000.00

12 1/2" h, raised gilt and iron red bird and foliate design, mottled blue ground,

Figures, 7 1/8-7 1/2" h, "Earth, Water, and Air," lt blue, dk blue, yellow, pink, and red, gold accented bases, "iron red crown, X'd batons and D" marks, set of 3, (A) $320.

pierced handle, Crown Derby, c1888, (A) 690.00

13 3/8" h, Turkish style terra cotta glazed bands and panel trim with overall raised gilt foliate designs, yellow ground, pierced flat handle with mons, Crown Derby, c1890, (A) 978.00

13 1/2" h, overall gold floral design, gilt trim, cream ground, reticulated handle, Royal Crown Derby 395.00

Figure, 7 7/8" h, "The Fishwife," multicolored, modeled by Locke, Royal Crown Derby, (A) 247.00

Jar, Cov, 7 1/4" h, raised gilt floral and vine swags, pink ground, gilt rims with beading, Royal Crown Derby, c1894, (A) 805.00

Loving Cup, 4 3/8" h, waisted shape, gilt wild flowers, grasses and raised ornaments, pink ground, (A) 150.00

Menu Holder, 5 1/8" h, Delftware, painted boats on calm seas, scroll molded rim, Royal Crown Derby, pr, (A). 240.00

Plate

8 1/2" d, "Red Aves" pattern, Royal Crown Derby 20.00

8 5/8" d, black scene of "Lake Avernus, Italy" named on reverse in gilt oct cartouche, gilt border bands with gilt designs between on white ground, Royal Crown Derby 250.00

9 1/2" d, iron red, blue, and gold Imari style flowers, Royal Crown Derby, set of 12, (A) 632.00

Saucepan, Cov, 2" h, Imari colors and gilt florals and scrolls, pattern #1673/6299, Royal Crown Derby, pr, (A). 770.00

Service Plate, 10" d, gilt swag border, cream ground, Royal Crown Derby, set of 12, (A) 375.00

Urn, 2 3/4" h, Imari pattern and colors, 2 sm gilt handles, pattern #1512/6299, Royal Crown Derby, (A) 216.00

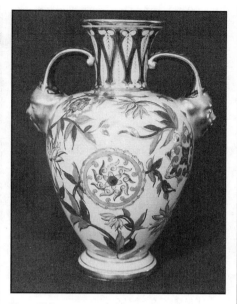

Vase, 6" h, magenta and orange florets, gold outlined leaves, pink ground, cobalt trimmed neck, gold handles, Crown Derby, $850.

Vase

4 1/2" h, multicolored floral bouquets in gold cartouche, yellow ground, Royal Crown Derby 110.00

8 1/2" h, gilded leaves and flowers, pink ground, 3 handles, Royal Crown Derby 350.00

Vase, Cov

4 3/4" h, squat shape, raised gilt bird and floral design, pink ground, white and gilt loop handles with gilt mask terminals, Crown Derby, c1889, (A) 690.00

12" h, bulbous shape, ftd, apple green ground, gilt painted leaves and flowers, raised irreg gilt band with fruit and bows, gilt trimmed curved horiz handles on shoulder with raised gilt fruit and leaf designs, raised gilt wavy line on base, Royal Crown Derby, c1891. . . 3,800.00

CROWN DEVON

Stoke-on-Trent, England
1870 to 1982

History: S. Fielding and Co. Ltd. established a pottery at Stoke-on-Trent, England in 1870. This Staffordshire factory produced a wide variety of products including majolica wares, terra cotta wares, and earthenwares for domestic use.

Abraham Fielding acquired the pottery soon after it began. Its "majolica argenta" was a white body and glaze introduced in the early 1880s. The wares were decorated with high temperature colors and designs in relief.

After majolica fell out of fashion, it was replaced by vellum–a range of pale, bis-cuit-colored ware with gilding and hand painted floral or topographical patterns that was made until World War I. A huge variety of patterns was made in cream and ivory grounds. "Royal Devon" was the most popular pattern made in vellum. Other "Royal" patterns included "Essex," "Sussex," "York," "Scotia" and "Suffolk."

From 1913, luster wares were sold under the trade name Crown Devon, including works done in the Art Deco style. In the early 1920s, the lusterware was made for the higher end market, and embossed salad ware, tableware and novelty items were made for the lower end market. Crown Devon Art Deco patterns included "Aztec," "Espanol," "Moresque," "Mattajade," "Mattajung," "Fairy Castle," and "Rustic Lustrine."

Figurines were made from 1919 for more than a decade. In addition to animals and birds, there were figurines of Gainsborough Girl, War Officer, Italian woman and man, Grecian lady and numerous others. Kathleen Parsons made Art Deco figures in the late 1920s and 30s of Spring, Gina, Caroline, Ballerina, Old Kate, Flapper Girl, Bathing Girl, and Windy Day, plus others.

In 1932, son Arthur Ross Fielding took over and added a range of musical pottery including the John Peel Series, Widdicombe Fair, Auld Lang Syne, Daisy Bell, and Ilkla Moor Baht. Tankards, jugs, cigarette boxes, and salad bowls were designed which, when lifted, played popular tunes. He also made Art Deco colors and shapes with vivid patterns of stylized fruit and flowers, many of which had dark backgrounds.

After World War II, Reginald Fielding took over, and modern shapes and sharp contemporary color contrasts were used. Crown Devon also made souvenir and commemoratives wares, as well as Christmas plates and Cries of London plates.

After a fire in 1951, it was the beginning of the end for Crown Devon. After 1967, Fieldings were no longer involved in the operations. The factory closed in 1982, a victim of the recession.

Marks used were an impressed "FIELDING" and "SF & CO" printed with the title of the pattern.

References: Ray Barker, *The Crown Devon Collectors Handbook, First Edition,* Francis-Joseph Books, 1997; Susan Hill, *Crown Devon,* Jazz Publications, 1993; Irene & Gordon Hopwood, *The Shorter Connection,* Richard Dennis, 1992.

Collecting Hints: The 1920s and '30s pieces are sought after by collectors. There is a lot of interest in luster pieces, as well as mattajade and mattasung.

Jug, 8" h, musical, multicolored relief horse and cart scene, "The Irish Jaunting Car" and "Muckross Gates" at top, "Kilarney" verse on side, $185.

Bowl

> 10 5/8" w, elliptical, pedestal, printed and painted Chinese landscape in colors, red luster ground, (A) 53.00

> 11" l, oval, pedestal base, fluted rim, painted green, orange, and black geometric banding, gilt accents, paper label, (A) 90.00

Cheese Dish, Cov, 7" l x 5 3/8" h, slant top, "Spring" pattern, red and blue flowers and urn, scattered ivy, tan shaded ground . 85.00

Chocolate Pot, 8" h, "Indian" pattern, ribbed sides, cobalt and peach flower and leaf design, gold accents, cream ground, cobalt handle, "S.F. & Co." mark 150.00

Egg Dish, 5" h, figural rooster handle at end, brown shades with orange comb, dish with 3 egg wells, cream ground with green striped rim 75.00

Jug, musical

> 4 1/2" h

>> "Auld Lang Syne," polychrome relief of men in tavern drinking 85.00

>> "Widdicomb Fair," multicolored relief of travelers 95.00

> 6 1/8" h

>> "JOHN PEEL," mauve coat, black hat, holding riding crop, poem on side, brown riding crop handle. . . . 70.00

>> "ON ILKLA MOOR BAHT' AT," "Courting Mary Jane, Then We Shall Ha' To Bury Thee," boy and girl walking in field, 3 raised ducks on green band near rim, green handle with purple feathery leaves. 365.00

Mug, 4 1/8" h, pub scene with See All, Hear All, Say Now't," blue transfer. 75.00

Pot, 3 1/8" h, "Tartan Series," Mackenzie plaid on side, floral bunch on reverse, gold lined rim 28.00

Plate, 10 1/2" d, Art Deco style blue red, yellow, and green overlapping triangles and circles, cream ground, (A) 200.00

Tankard, 6 1/8" h, corset shape, polychromed relief tavern scene on side, "Auld Lang Syne" and poem on reverse, cream ground, green stalk handle with purple flowers. 95.00

Vase

> 5 1/4" h, brown dot outlined trees with green, orange, and yellow leaf puffs, matte tan ground with lt brown drip, 2 sm handles 125.00

> 6 1/4" h, bulbous base, trumpet shaped neck, molded brown branches with molded blue, yellow, and red flowerheads, molded dot pink ground . 65.00

> 11 1/4" h, multicolored florals and crest design on front, florals on reverse, shaded tan ground with lt orange accents, raised gold outlined leaf design on base, curved ribbed neck, 2 matte gold handles, matte gold rim 75.00

> 12" h, printed and painted Pegasus, maroon luster ground, gold tracery 225.00

C. TIELSCH-GERMANY

Silesia, Germany; now Walbrzych, Poland 1845-1945

History: Beginning in 1845, the C. Tielsch and Company factory located at Altwasser made household, hotel, and decorative porcelain, along with coffee and tea sets. The C.M. Hutschenreuther Company in Hohenberg acquired most of the stock of Tielsch in 1918 and merged the factory with its own. Hutschenreuther continued using the C. Tielsch name until after WWII.

Bowl

> 11 1/2" d, shaded peach colored roses, buds, green leaves, gilt trim, flowing blue ground, self handles, ruffled rim 245.00

> 13 1/2" H-H, dk red rose, blue forget-me-nots, yellow and red garden flowers in center, gold outlined vert panels on border with sprigs, gold outlined molded open handles. 48.00

> 14" l, oval, red and yellow roses and green leaves in center, gold swag inner border, crimped outer border with gold wash 65.00

Cake Plate, 10" H-H

> Purple and white lilacs, temple in bkd, gold outlined rim and handles . . 38.00

> White lilies, green ground, "C.T. Altwasser" mark 59.00

Charger, 12 1/2" d, HP white lilies, "C.T. Altwasser Germany" mark 160.00

Creamer and Cov Sugar Bowl, gold striped rims and handles, "C.T. Altwasser, eagle and Germany" mark 10.00

Serving Dish, 13 3/4" w, red lobster, gold florals on white ground, "blue C .T. Germany" mark, $45.

Cup and Saucer

> HP red, purple, blue, yellow, and green florals, gold accents, molded scrolled designs, scroll handle, "C. Tielsch & Co." mark, (A) 30.00

> Molded shell design, HP yellow, purple, red, green, blue, and gold florals, gold striped rim, "C.T. and eagle" mark, (A) 45.00

> Purple floral sprig transfer with green leaves, gold stripe on scalloped rims and handle, "C.T. and eagle" mark 10.00

> White daisies and lg purple flowers, molded scroll feathered ground, gold sponged border and handle, "C.T. eagle" mark 20.00

Cup and Saucer, Demitasse, peach, pink, blue, and green floral transfer, molded scrolling, gold striped scalloped rim on saucer, gold stenciled floral design on cup int rim, "green C.T. eagle, red Made in Germany" mark, pr, (A) 20.00

Dresser Tray, 10 3/4" l x 8" w, dk pink roses and green leaves, raised scalloped border with gilt corners, "C.T. Germany" mark . 85.00

Pin Dish, 7 1/2" l x 4 1/4" w, rect, 4 pink roses and green leaves, shaded white to lt brown ground, scalloped rim, gold trim on inner edge, "green C.T. eagle" mark 25.00

Pitcher, 7" h, multicolored floral spray with white and pink chrysanthemums, relief scrolled body, flower on handle, gold rim, "C.T. Germany" mark 65.00

Plate

> 6" d

>> HP yellow iris, "C.T. Altwasser Germany" mark 28.00

>> Pink roses, green leaves, emb scalloped rim 8.00

>> Red and white roses and green leaves on border, shaped rim, "C.T. eagle" mark 8.00

> 6 1/8" d, 2 open pink and white lilies, 2 wide green leaves at base, shaded dk green to lt green ground with mint green panel, gold lined rim, "C.T. Altwasser Germany" mark 15.00

> 7" d, lg purple plum, green and purple leaves in center, border of 6 gold out-

lined molded swags, "C.T. eagle" mark
. . . . 10.00

7 3/4" d, lg bunch of purple flowers in center, 2 sm bunches at sides, relief design on border. 15.00

8" d, yellow banded border with gold scrolled floral design, gold banded scalloped rim, "blue C. Tielsch and green Made in Germany" marks, (A) 20.00

8 1/2" d, blue forget-me-nots, yellow wheat, gold outlined pierced lattice border, "blue C.T. eagle" mark 15.00

8 3/4" d, bunch of purple chrysanthemums in center, shaded green ground, relief molded border with raised gold rim, "C.T. Germany and eagle" mark . 15.00

9 1/2" d, lg white lilies, orange stems, sm blue flowers, shaded ground and "Give Us This Day..," gold rim, "C.T. Altwasser, Silesia" mark. 28.00

9 5/8" d, purple and yellow orchids in center with sm garden flowers, gold inner border, sm garden flowers and relief molding on border, lt yellow ground, "C.T. Germany and eagle" mark . 25.00

Platter, 11 1/4" H-H, floral sprig in center, purple flowers on border, gilt scalloped rim and handles, "C.T. Germany" mark 55.00

Serving Dish

12 1/4" l x 11 3/4" w, open handle at end, bunches of purple and pink violets with raised white enameled dot centers, scalloped raised rim with gilt ribbed depressions on border, "C.T. eagle" mark
. . . . 55.00

14" l, dbl leaf molded, center handle, gold geometrics, pink border 145.00

Vase

4 1/2" h, decal of 18th C couple in colors, scattered flowers on reverse, molded design on base, rim with band of garden flowers and gold geometrics, "C.T. Germany and eagle" mark 25.00

8 1/2" h, red flowers, green leaves, lt gray ground, 2 gold handles, "C.T. Altwasser Silesia" mark 80.00

10 1/4" h, tree trunk form with 2 sm handles, pink roses, green leaves, tan to brown shaded ground, "C.T. eagle" mark. 70.00

CZECHOSLOVAKIA-GENERAL

1918 to Present

History: In 1918, the Czechs and Slovaks became free of Austro-Hungary domination and were granted their own country, Czechoslovakia. Portions of the regions of Bavaria, Bohemia, Moravia, and Austrian Silesia made up the new country. Bohemia, now the metropolitan area of Czechoslovakia, was the chief ceramic producing area in the Austro-Hungarian empire in the 19th century.

A variety of china wares was made by the many Czechoslovakia factories, among which were Amphora in Egyptian and Art Deco styles and Erphila Art Pottery. Decorative items such as flower holders and wall pockets in the form of birds were produced. Creamers, salt and peppers, and napkin rings were made in interesting shapes. Kitchen or cereal sets and complete dinner sets, with pattern names such as "Iris," "Royette," "Royal Bohemia," "Ivory Rose," and such kept factory production high.

The Karlsbad Porcelain Factory "Concordia" Brothers Lew & Co. operated from c1919 until 1937. From 1939 until 1945, the factory was operated by Winterling & Co. It was nationalized in 1945 and merged with the former Count Thun's Porcelain nationalized factory in Klosterle. Several other factories such as Meierhofen, Alp, and Altrohlau merged with Epiag in Karlsbad about 1939. This merged firm was nationalized in 1945.

Between 1871 and 1940, B. Bloch & Company made table, household, and decorative porcelain and earthenware, some in the onion pattern. After 1920 the name was changed to the Eichwald Porcelain and Stove Factory Bloch & Co., then to the Eichwald Porcelain Stove and Tile factory for the period from 1940 until 1945.

Most items are stamped "Made in Czechoslovakia" with an ink stamp.

References: Dale & Diane Barta & Helen Rose, *Czechoslovakian Glass and Collectibles, Book II,* Collector Books, 1997; Ruth A. Forsythe, *Made in Czechoslovakia*, Richardson Printing Corp.1982; Ruth A. Forsythe, *Made in Czechoslovakia, Book 2,* Antique Publications, 1996.

Collectors' Club: Czechoslovakian Collectors Guild International, P.O. Box 901395, Kansas City, MO 64190. Newsletter.

Bank, 4" h, figural comic bird, white with orange and yellow accents, "Erphila Czechoslovakia" mark. 45.00

Basket

5" h, paneled pearlized lustered body, piecrust border with black lined rim, "Made in Czechoslovakia" mark. 25.00

5 3/4" h, pleated body, orange to yellow shaded ground, blue lined rim . . 36.00

Berry Bowl, 5 3/8" d, mauve roses and buds with green leaves, relief molded rim with green shading 9.00

Beverage Set, pitcher, cov, 11 1/2" h, 4 tumblers, stylized blue and yellow flowers and khaki green leaves, cream ground, black rims, black and cream handle, "Erphila Art Pottery Czechoslovakia" marks. 250.00

Bonbon Dish, 8 1/2" sq, 4 sections with black transfers of dancing couples, black outlined shaped rim and center handle, "Erphila Czechoslovakia" mark. 45.00

Bowl

7 5/8" sq, gold, orange, green, and gray peacock in center, white, green, orange, and yellow florals, chain link int rim, green edge, florals on ext, "M.Z. Altrohlau CM-R Czechoslovakia" mark
. . . . 42.00

9" d, blue and green stenciled basket of fruit in center, stenciled florals in lozenges on border, "Made in Czechoslovakia" mark 18.00

9 1/2" d, folded rim, HP yellow, purple, and pink oriental style flowers, orange-red ground, black int 80.00

Bud Vase

5" h, red, blue, and green figural parrot on green 3 hole tree stump, "Made in Czechoslovakia" mark. 15.00

5 3/4" h, tapered cylinder shape, 2 vert brown handles, lg open magenta flowers, stylized green vert stems at side, "Made in Czechoslovakia" mark
. . . . 50.00

Butter Dish, Cov, 7 3/4" d x 3 3/4" h, with drain, violets and green leaves on rim and sides of dome, gold knob and trim, "T.K. Thun" mark
. . . . 90.00

Candlestick

2 1/2" h x 5 1/4" d, peasant art, blue and orange flowers, yellow ground, black outlined nozzles, finger holes in base, circ ft, "J. Mrazek, Made in Czechoslovakia" mark, pr 245.00

4 3/4" h, orange luster with black stripes on rim and base, pr 28.00

Canister Set

4 piece set, 8 1/4" h, black checkerboard design with center lozenge with "TEA, BARLEY, SUGAR, COFFEE, or OATMEAL," cream ground 200.00

12 piece set, 6 canisters, 8" h, " OATMEAL, SUGAR, COFFEE, TEA, RICE, and BARLEY," 4 canisters, 4 1/2" h, " NUTMEG, GINGER, CLOVES, and ALLSPICE," 2 bottles, 9 1/2" h, "OIL and VINEGAR," black labels, fluted sides, band of blue stylized flowerheads on borders 285.00

Centerpiece Vase, 7" h x 10" H-H, flat sides, multiple graduated ball handles, white glaze, "Royal Crown Czechoslovakia" mark
. . . . 295.00

Charger

11 3/4" d, center scene of church, stone bridge, and waterfall, multicolored transfer, wide gold inner band, gold stenciled daisies on border, dbl gold bands on rim 40.00

12" d, cream center, black outlined brown circ band, yellow and cream shading, orange, blue, and black stripes, brown rim, matte finish, "Erphila, Czechoslovakia" mark 95.00

Console Set, center bow, 10" l x 2 1/2" h, 2 candlesticks with sq bases, Art Deco style turquoise ground with raised white drapes, knobbed corners. 120.00

Creamer

3 3/4" h, blue-black sailboats and shadows on water 22.00

4" h, figural sailor and rope handle, blue shaded uniform, "Erphila, Made in Czechoslovakia" mark 48.00

Cup and Saucer

Blue luster ext, orange luster int, black angular handle. 5.00

HP black honeycomb, orange stylized flowerheads, blue and yellow striped rims 55.00

Demitasse Service, coffeepot, 8 1/2" h, creamer, cov sugar bowl, 4 cups and saucers, multicolored florals, gilt trim, white ground, basketweave borders, gilt trimmed handles, "TK Thun Made in Czech" marks 98.00

Egg Cup, 3 3/4" h, band of fruits and flowers on border between brown bands, gold trim, "Victoria Czechoslovakia" mark 10.00

Figure, 9 7/8" h, terra cotta, peasant woman with hands on hips, yellow scarf, (A) . . 62.00

Flower Pot, 4 1/2" h, center orange-yellow band with raised multicolored exotic bird, purple bands top and base 55.00

Mug, 5" h, peasant art, multicolored flowers, orange ground, black handle, set of 4 260.00

Oyster Plate, 9 3/4" d, hex, 6 molded shell wells, gold lined rim 95.00

Pitcher

2 3/4" h, ribbed panels, lt green and gold luster, dk green trim and handle, "P.A.L.T. Czechoslovakia" mark . 18.00

3 1/4" h, figural barrel, brown vert bands, black horiz stripes, lt brown body 20.00

3 1/2" h, orange luster body, black handle and rim, "CZECHOSLOVAKIA" mark 16.00

4 1/2" h, figural parrot, orange with yellow front, black eyes, orange beak, orange and green handle 65.00

4 3/4" h, figural bird, orange and yellow, lt blue feathers, green lined rim . . . 79.00

5" h

Multicolored decal of classical maidens by lion head fountain, yellow to green shaded ground, gold trimmed handle and rim 50.00

Paneled, multicolored decal of Arabs and camels, orange ground, green rim 60.00

6 3/4" h, HP yellow, orange, and blue flowers, black trim 60.00

7 1/2" h

Art Deco style brown herringbone pattern, ivory ground, (A) 137.00

Orange, black, and gray geometrics, white int, c1930 . . . . 395.00

8" h

Black Greek key design, orange ground. 75.00

Figural exotic bird, black and yellow accents, pale yellow ground, "Ditmar" mark, (A) 150.00

8 1/8" h, wavy bands of blue, tan, cream, and orange, black handle, cream int, "Ditmar Urbach Made in Czechoslovakia" mark 195.00

8 1/4" h

Brown and cream mottled glaze, orange drip band at middle, aqua rim, seahorse handle 150.00

Molded orange pears, purple grapes, green leaves, red border, black striped rim, "black Made in Czechoslovakia" mark 65.00

8 1/2" h, figural Toucan, red beak, yellow body, black and red trim, "Erphila, Czech" mark 395.00

9" h, figural goat head, black and red accents, yellow ground, "Erphila, Czech" mark 750.00

Planter, 4" h

5 1/2" l, figural swan, white body with red and black accents, "Made in Czechoslovakia" mark. 28.00

Cylinder shape, molded side ring handles, 4 sm feet, multicolored scene of farmhouse, flowers in front, dk brown to yellow shaded ground, brown int . . 40.00

Plate

6 1/4" d, center multicolored scene of barn, stream, and meadow in gilt dash cartouche, purple berries and green leaves at side, ivory ground on border, gilt lined rim, "MZ Altrohlau Czechoslovakia" mark 14.00

7 1/4" d, purple thistle in center with bouquet of yellow daisy, sm red roses, and green leaves, iron red inner border, iron red outlined shaped rim 16.00

7 1/2" d, HP yellow center with black inner border, lg orange, mauve, and blue flowerheads with stylized green leaves, black lined rim 35.00

8 1/4" d, band of blue flowers, red centers, raised white dots, white ground with lt blue and lt pink shading, gilt rim, "Epiag Czechoslovakia" mark 25.00

8 1/2" d, multicolored scene of period couple in center, burgundy ground, geometric border 12.00

10 3/4" d, floral spray of garden flowers in center, band of garden flowers on border, set of 12 . . . . 225.00

Salt box, 6 3/4" h, band of pink and purple flowers, green leaves on black ground on base, black "SALT" on front, pearl luster ground, gold trim, wood cov 58.00

Vase, 7 1/8" h, yellow centered red flowers, green leaves, black ground, red lined rim, cream int, "Czechoslovakia Hand Painted" mark, $325.

Soup Bowl, 7 1/2" d, blue, green, and red exotic bird on branches with flower, 4 floral bunches on border 7.00

Syrup Jug, Cov, 5 1/2" h, pearl lustered base, orchid top, black lined rims. 32.00

Teapot

4" h, purple and cream flowers on sides, green leaves, shaded orange ground, black lined handle 20.00

4 1/2" h, yellow luster body, black handle and trim 30.00

7 3/8" h, lg red rose, purple orchid and garden flowers on sides, gold net design on rims 48.00

Tea Set

Pot, 3 1/2" h, creamer, cov sugar bowl, pearl luster body, black lined rim, black handles and knobs 35.00

Pot, 6" h, creamer, cov sugar bowl, HP oval reserve of blue, yellow, and maroon flowerheads on green ground, painted red bodies, black handles, spouts, and knobs 325.00

Pot, 6 1/2" h, squat shape, creamer, 4 3/4" h, cov sugar bowl, 5" h, gold lined band of lg pink roses, sm blue, rust, and purple flowers, green leaves, white ground 125.00

Pot, 7" h, milk jug, cov sugar bowl, oval shape, porcelain, Art Deco style printed gilt, black, and purple stylized geometrics, (A) 50.00

Tray, 9 1/2" H-H, HP orange, red, yellow, purple, and blue flowers, green ground . . . 50.00

Vase

4 1/2" h, blue, black, and white geometric pattern with green hanging fans, orange ground, 2 sm handles 45.00

4 5/8" h, bulbous, 2 sm handles, brown, black, and blue marbleized glaze 28.00

5" h

Fan shaped top, purple, orange, and mauve tulips, orange shaded border and base, vert ribbing 45.00

Figural yellow, orange, and blue bird on side of green shaded tree trunk body, "red Made in Czechoslovakia" mark 25.00

5 1/4" h, tapered shape, flared rim, yellow and purple flowerheads on lt yellow to blue shaded ground, rect reticulated handles,pr 40.00

5 1/2" h

Bulbous base with blue and orange stripes, cylinder shaped neck with lg yellow and blue flowers 65.00

Pinched shouldered, black squared handles, black rim, blue-gray lustered glaze, "Made in Czechoslovakia" mark 22.00

5 3/4" h, campana shape, black scene of children and deer, yellow ground, raised black chevrons on shoulder, molded curlicues on neck 45.00

6" h, dbl gold side scrolls, white ground 85.00

6 1/4" h, cylinder shape, lg orange poppy, green leaves, cream ground, raised orange horiz bands and rim 80.00

7" h, bulbous base, cylinder neck with loop handles, yellow and brown stylized flowerheads and green leaves on yellow scale, black neck and handles, matte finish, "Made in Czechoslovakia" mark 115.00

7 1/2" h, urn shape with 2 brown trimmed swan handles, lt orange, green, and brown scene of man in boat on front, castle on reverse in pentagon cartouches, raised green base shaded to yellow, ribbed orange top, "Made in Czecho" mark................... 20.00

8" h

Black silhouette of courting couple in blue dash cartouche, cream ground, blue ftd base and neck 50.00

Vase, 7 3/4" h, black outlined blue flowers, yellow-gold ground with white enamel dots, "Czechoslovakia Hand Painted" mark, $375.

Tapered body, flared ribbed rim, 3 sm feet, multicolored transfer of period man playing bagpipe to woman lying in field, gold design on reverse, dk rust borders top and base, 2 sm handles on shoulder 28.00

10" h

Bulbous shape, straight neck, molded side handles, black molded face on front, orange ground, black molded geometric base 120.00

Orange and beige marbled pattern, mkd 95.00

10 1/2" h, tapered cylinder shape, 2 squared handles on sides, shaded red roses and green leaves on front, pink, blue-green, and yellow shaded ground, gold trim, "red CZECHOSLOVAKIA" mark 45.00

13 1/4" h, HP gold, black, white, and green paisley design with gray outlined blue circles interspersed, black rim, "Ditmar Urbach, Made in Czech" mark . 650.00

Vegetable Bowl, 9 1/4" sq, brown transfer of man driving oxen over bridge, relief molded border with brown transfers of farm people in corners, gold rim 24.00

Wall Pocket

7 5/8" h, flat cone shape, HP multicolored flowers, gloss white ground, orange rim 65.00

8" h, rust and pastel figural parrot on grape cluster 45.00

DAVENPORT

Longport, Staffordshire, England 1794-1887

History: John Davenport and family established their factory in 1794. Earthenware, ironstone, porcelains, caneware, black basalt, and glass were made. Few of the early examples were marked. Porcelains were not manufactured until 1805-1810. The earliest Davenport porcelains were marked with the word "Longport" in red script.

About 1825, Davenport teawares and dessert services came under the influence of the rococo revival. The shapes of pieces resembled the Coalport forms of this period. Landscape decorations were used frequently.

Porcelain painted plaques were decorated both at the factory and by independent artists about 1860-1880. Earthenware table services for use on ships became a specialty product. Colorful Japan patterns were produced in the Derby manner in the

1870s-1880s. These were a specialty of the Davenport factory. The firm ceased operation in 1887.

References: T.A. Lockett, and Geoffrey A. Godden, *China, Earthenware & Glass, 1794-1884*, Random Century, 1990.

Museums: British Museum, London, England; Cincinnati Art Museum, Cincinnati, OH; Hanley Museum, Stoke-on-Trent, England; Liverpool Museum, Liverpool, England; Victoria & Albert Museum, London, England.

Compote, 9 1/8" d, red, green, and yellow orchid in center, pink rim 165.00

Cup and Saucer, Handleless, "Hawthorn" pattern, blue transfers, (A) 96.00

Dessert Service, Part, reticulated basket, 13 3/4" H-H, ftd, 2 cov sauce tureens, 7 1/2" d, with fixed stands, 2 dishes, 11" H-H, sq, 2 dishes, 10 1/8" H-H, lozenge shape, 3 dishes, 12" H-H, rect, 10 plates, 9" d, painted flower sprays in centers, wide orange borders with gilt flowers an foliate scrolls, molded gilt rim reserved with paired flowerheads, c1830, (A) 2,300.00

Dinner Service, Part, 2 oval tureens with stands, 14" w, 3 oval cov vegetable dishes, 11 1/2" w, oval ftd bowl, 11" w, 3 sauce tureens with stands, 8" w, 11 platters, 10 5/8"-20 1/2" l, 18 plates, 10" d, 18 soup plates, 10" d, 16 plates, 8 5/8" d, border of iron red flowerheads reserved on blue-green band suspending alternating gilt lappet and spear designs, pattern 1451, c1850, (A) 5,750.00

Dish, 9 1/2" l, molded cobalt and gilt handle at end, oriental style gilt outlined blue, yellow, green, and red exotic birds, orange-red chrysanthemums, pink and magenta flowerheads on scrolling branches, "blue Davenport Stone China, anchor" mark,c1820 .... 295.00

Inkwell, 2 3/8" h, enameled floral medallions on blue ground with gilt decorations, molded lion mask handles, early 19th C, pr, (A) 460.00

Jug, 5 7/8" h, "The Litchfield Jug," black outlined white Greek warriors, orange ground,

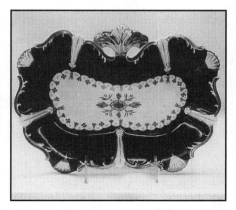

Dessert Service, 2 ftd dishes, 11" l, 7 3/4" w, 9 plates, 9 1/2" d, green border with gilt florals and molded shells, "Davenport and anchor" marks, (A) $287.

white handle, "The Litchfield Jug" mark, c1850 . . . . 395.00

Plate

9" d, Chinese red flowerheads, blue inner border and rim with red accent, c1844 . . . . 150.00

9 1/4" d, gold center medallion, magenta and gold scalloped rim, anchor mark 27.00

9 1/2" d, "Hawthorn" pattern, bouquet of hawthorn in center, 3 bunches on border, blue transfer, (A) 55.00

10" d, "Muleteer" pattern, man riding mule, C-scroll and flower border, blue transfer 100.00

10 1/2" d, "Indian Festoon" pattern, red, green, and yellow bower and flowers in center, green floral transfer on border 125.00

Platter

13 3/8" l, oval, Imari pattern, pink, gilt, and cobalt base with iron red flowerheads, border of iron red and gilt designs 225.00

15 1/2" l x 12" w, rect with cut corners, white, green feather edge rim, mkd 185.00

18 3/4" l, rect with cut corners, center scene of Chinese junk before lg house, willow trees on shore, floral border, blue transfer 675.00

19" l x 15" w, rect with cut corners, "Mon Filla" pattern, med blue transfer 195.00

Sauce Tureen, Cov, 8 1/4" H-H, with underplate, iron red, cobalt, and gilt "Japan" pattern, gilt curved horiz handles, pr, (A) 1,450.00

Soup Plate, 8 3/4" d, sm sprig in center, band of orange-brown and blue flowerheads, blue and orange-brown stylized acorns, green and brown foliage on border, "imp Davenport" mark, (A) 220.00

Soup Tureen

13 3/4" H-H, with undertray, Stone China, bird and floral design, blue transfer and polychrome accents, gilt lion mask handles, c1810, hairlines, (A) 1,610.00

15" l x 9 1/2" h, "Java" pattern, flowers, bird, and fruit, blue and white . . 395.00

Vase, 8 1/2" h, campana shape, painted sprig of azalea in gilt etched panel on front, puce, blue, iron red, and yellow ground, gilt lion's mask handles, c1805-1810, (A) 1,610.00

Vegetable Bowl, Cov, 12" l, Imari pattern, cobalt, iron red, and gilt panels, gilt outlined handle on cov and molded leaf terminals 275.00

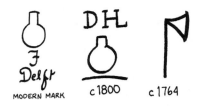

MODERN MARK   c1800   c1764

DELFT, DUTCH AND ENGLISH

**Holland
c1613 to Present**

**Bristol, Lambeth, and Liverpool, England
1690-1790**

Dutch

History: Tin enamel ware was first manufactured in Delft about 1613 as a result of Italian potters immigrating to Holland and bringing the techniques with them. Prior to this, the Dutch relied heavily on the Dutch East India Company's importing Chinese porcelains to fulfill their china needs.

When the imported supply was reduced, through disruption of the trade routes, the local Dutch pottery industry thrived. Idle breweries were refitted as potteries. By the mid 1600s, more than 30 pottery manufacturers were operating out of the defunct breweries making imitations of Chinese and Japanese porcelains in blue and white tin glazed wares. A transparent lead glaze was added as a "flashing" or overglaze to make the tin enamel copies closely resemble Chinese porcelain.

Two types of blue and white wares were made. The first type featured blue and white motifs in the monochrome Chinese style. The blue and white motifs of the second type included Dutch subjects such as landscapes, windmills, sailing ships, portraits, Bible stories, views of towns, and other "series" plates. The prime period of production for both types of blue and white wares was 1640-1740. Other towns in Holland also produced blue and white in addition to Delft. Few pieces are found with identifying maker's marks.

After 1700, more polychrome wares were produced in tones of copper green, iron red, and yellow. Japanese Imari wares were the source of inspiration for the polychrome wares. In addition to plates, tiles, vases, and other dishes, Delft potters also specialized in novelties such as shoes, cow milk jugs, violins, and small figures especially of animals.

The decline of Dutch Delft was accelerated by the introduction of Wedgwood's creamware in the second half of the 18th century. In addition, the works of Meissen

and Sevres surpassed the tin glazed wares from Delft. By the beginning of the 19th century, the number of pottery manufacturers in Delft was reduced to three.

Today only one of the original producers of Delftwares remains in operation. De Porceleyne Fles began producing pottery in 1653. This firm was saved from bankruptcy in 1870 by Joost Thooft. To make the company competitive, Thooft made some changes in the manufacturing process, among which was importing white baking clay from England. Each piece is marked with the logo of De Porceleyne Fles, Joost Thooft's initials, and the initials of the decorator.

English

History: Tin enamel pottery came to England from Antwerp in the Netherlands in the 16th century. At first the tin glazed earthenware was called "galley-ware." The name changed to Delftware in the mid-18th century because of its similarity to Dutch Delft products. English Delft production was centered in Bristol, Lambeth, and Liverpool after strong beginnings in London in the mid-17th century.

At Lambeth, apothecary wares, barber basins, and puzzle jugs were among the most popular forms produced. In Bristol, the glaze had a more bluish tone. Plates, bowls, and flower holders with a naive treatment predominated. Liverpool Delft with its harder body resembled Chinese porcelains more closely than those made elsewhere. By 1790, tin enamel glaze wares fell into decline in England due to the rise of Wedgwood's creamware.

References: John C. Austin, *British Delft at Williamsburg,* Decorative Arts Services, 1994; John Bedford, *Delftware,* Walker & Co.1966; Frank Britton, *London Delftware,* Jonathan Horne, 1987; Carolene Henriette De Jonge, *Delft Ceramics,* Praeger, 1970; H.P. Fourest, *Delftware,* Rizzoli,1980; F.H. Garner & Michael Archer, *English Delftware,* Faber & Faber, 1972; Ivor Hume, *Early English Delftware from London and Virginia*, The Colonial Williamsburg Foundation, 1977; Diana Imber, *Collecting European Delft and Faience*, Praeger, 1968; Anthony Ray, *English Delftware Pottery in the Robert Hall Warren Collection*, Boston Book & Art Shop, 1968.

Museums: Ashmolean Museum, Oxford, England; Fitzwilliam Museum, Cambridge, England; Gemeente Museum, Arnhem, Holland; Gardiner Museum of Ceramic Art, Toronto, Canada; Henry Ford Museum, Dearborn, MI; Hius Lambert van Meerten Museum, Delft, Holland; Musees Royaux d'art et d'Historie, Brussels, Belgium; Prinsenhof Museum, Delft, Holland; Rijksmuseum, Amsterdam, Holland; Royal Factory

"De Porceleyne Fles" Collection, Delft, Holland; Sheffield City Museum, Sheffield, England; The Colonial Williamsburg Foundation, Williamsburg, VA; Victoria & Albert Museum, London, England; William Rockhill Nelson Gallery of Art, Kansas City, MO.

Reproduction Alert: The old Dutch wares have been copied as souvenirs and are quite popular with the foreign traveler. Be careful not to confuse these modern pieces with the older examples. There are many reproductions on the market particularly from 1960 to the present day. Both new and old marks are generally in blue under the glaze. Many new pieces have made up marks that are not used on older pieces.

Many 16-inch Delft platters were invented for interior decorators and antique reproduction wholesalers and have been made for over thirty years. Examples with the marks **Delfts** are less than 30-40 years old. New pieces are transfer decorated and not hand painted with visible brush strokes.

Dutch

Barber Bowl

9 3/4" d, center starburst, border paneled with squiggles and crisscross design, blue, red, and green polychrome, c1700-50 . . . . 395.00

11 1/4" w, basin blue painted Chinese style with cranes in flowering plants, fluted border with hanging floral sprays, indented rim, "blue ax and check" mark, c1750, (A) 1,840.00

Bowl

8 3/4" d, with attached strainer, flowers issuing from fence, vert bushes, flowerheads, scattered floral sprays on int, blue and white, hairlines and repair, (A) 468.00

9" d, int painted with dbl blue lines, ext painted with blue florals and vines, 18th C, (A) 138.00

9 3/8" d, flared shape, blue "Anno 1671" on int in conc blue bands, ext painted with blue chinoiserie scenes of figures in landscapes, (A) 2,990.00

11 5/8" d, molded shell rim, white glaze, c1700, (A) 600.00

12" d, oriental landscape in center with person and building, wavy rim pattern with dots, blue and white, (A) . . 550.00

Box, 17" h x 12 1/4" w, figural house, 4 floral finials and floral and leaf reserve, paneled sides and front with putti, fishscale roof with figure looking out from arched spandrel, foliate bands at top of body, continuous int scene of tea party with molded relief mask, bun feet, blue and white, 18th C, (A) 2,300.00

Candlestick, 7 1/2" h, bell shaped base, bobiche on center body, white glaze, c1680, repairs 1,200.00

Charger

12" d, oriental waterside landscape with lg flowering tree in foreground, stylized leaf and geometric border, blue and white, (A) 192.00

12 1/2" d, lg dk blue peacock and tulips in center, tulip heads, swirls, and geometrics on border, dk blue and white, c1800 . . . . 1,250.00

12 5/8" d, bowl of flowers with peacock feathers behind, bold cloud-like patterns on border, blue and white, yellow rim, (A) 825.00

13" d, manganese and blue central building, clouds, and plants, border with floral sprays in compartments, (A)
. . . . 605.00

13 3/8" d, blue painted scrolling foliage around central rosette, border reserved with oval panels of pseudo-Chinese symbols on crosshatched band, late 18th C, (A) 231.00

13 1/2" d

Busts of William and Mary, "K.V.B.T.-MA. K.IN-," framed in curtain swags, band of stylized foliage on border, blue and white, late 17th C, extensive repairs, (A) . . . 740.00

Tulip head in center, 6 radiating ovals with geometrics from center, loops and half circles on rim, blue ground, white designs, Johannes Van Duyn, c1764-77, chips. 1,200.00

William III in center, stylized tulips on border, polychrome, c1688-1710
. . . . 2,650.00

13 3/4" d, blue painted flowering tea plant before fence in center, shaped border with stylized floral lappets, late 18th C, (A) 460.00

14" d

Blue and white center scene of house on hill, lake in foreground and willow trees, border of groups of ovals and stylized leaves and stems
. . . . 650.00

Polychrome scene of shade tree and fence, scattered floral sprays on border, (A) 550.00

Coffeepot, 10 1/2" h, fluted conical shape, L-shaped spout, scroll handle, ball feet, blue painted chinoiserie design of open peacock in flowering plants, reverse with flowering plants and rocks, domed cov with lion finial, "blue LVE/2/0" mark, c1700-10, (A)
. . . . .4,830.00

Cruet, 5 1/2" h, overall stylized floral design, dot marked handle, "S" scroll joins spout to body, blue and white, 18th C, (A) . . . 920.00

Dish

8 1/4" d, stylized landscape, molded cavetto with rays, plants on border, molded rim, blue and white, (A)
. . . . 302.00

12 1/4" d, blue lined star design in circle in center, cavetto of stylized blue flowerheads, border of compartments with

straight lined starbursts separated by panels of blue squiggles, white ground, c1780, (A) 230.00

12 3/8" d, blue, brick red, yellow and green painted insects over flowering branches, terrace over stylized rockwork, crosshatched inner border with roundels, border with band of diapering and panels of devices, mid-18th C. . 150.00

Garniture, vase, cov, 15 1/2" h, baluster shape, 2 vases, 13 1/2" h, dbl gourd shape, painted underglaze blue and yellow and green enameled peacocks, butterflies, and birds in flowering Chinese garden, shoulder with lappets reserved with a flower, stiff leaves on flared ft, c1680, (A) 26,450.00

Inkstand, 9 3/4" l, cov center pot, raised rim, blue and white landscape scene, floral, and insect designs, late 18th C, (A) 460.00

Inkwell, 4 1/2" h, heart shape, 3 holes, white flowers, blue ground, (A) 495.00

Jar, 5" h, flowers and leaves issuing from rocks, vert panels with curlicues, blue and white, chips, pr, (A) 715.00

Pitcher, 7 3/4" h, blue figural monkey seated on haunches, brown tail handle, wearing brown hat, yellow banana spout, blue crisscross base. 2,000.00

Plaque, 24" h x 21" w, HP Dutch farm scene with windmill in bkd, cartouche and face in lower section, molded border, blue and white, pierced for hanging, "script Fl" mark,
late 19th C 850.00

Plate

8 1/2" d, vase of flowers in center with insects, leaf and floral border, blue and white, set of 5, (A) 825.00

8 3/4" d, center scene of resting horse, stylized florals on inner and outer border, blue, green, red, and brown, mid 18th C, hairline. 185.00

9" d

Dutch inscription in floral cartouche, floral swags on border, blue and white, (A) 192.00

Floral bouquet in center, flowers and leaves on border, manganese, green, iron red, and blue, (A). 605.00

Flower spray in center, arched cavetto, checkerboard design border, brown, red, yellow, blue, and green polychrome, mid 18th C, rim chip
. . . . .250.00

Hanging basket of flowers, lined scrolls on border, med blue on lt blue ground, orange rim. 400.00

Man seated under tree playing flute, squiggle and bud border, blue, green, and white, c1750. . . . 250.00

Oriental building with trees, leaf band border, blue and white, c1780
. . . . .295.00

Polychrome oriental bridge scene in center, blue acanthus leaf border, chips, (A) 275.00

Yellow and white urn in center with hanging blue handles on or-

Plate, 9" d, polychrome decoration, "blue AK" mark, late 18th C, $235.

ange-yellow ground, pencil drawn cobalt and lt blue flowerheads, green leaves, border of orange, red, cobalt, and yellow half flowerheads, 18th C 500.00

9 1/8" d, center with flowers from stylized vase, paneled geometric border, blue and white, c1750 . . . . 185.00

10" d, blue painted stylized flowers, piecrust rim, 19th C, (A) 77.00

Posset Pot

8 3/4" h, painted underglaze blue and green, yellow, and iron red enameled cranes in marsh with flowering plants, blue dash handles, c1680, (A) 5,520.00

10" h, polychrome floral and foliate designs, dash and dot handles, c1770, (A) 1,495.00

Punch Bowl, 11 5/8" d x 65/8" d, lg and sm circles of flower sprays reserved on crisscross and geometric ground, blue and white, c1680-1720, hairlines 2,950.00

Puzzle Jug, 8 1/4" h, baluster form, mouth with 3 spouts, neck with 3 pierced trellis cartouches, blue painted gallant and woman on river bank, mandolin and flute player in foliate cartouche, 18th C, (A) 8,050.00

Sauceboat, 8 1/4" l, blue applied scroll handle, fluted flared lip, blue transfer of oriental scenes in panels, hairline, (A) 440.00

Saucer Dish, 8 3/4" d

Bowl of flowers in center, geometrics and leaves on border, blue, manganese, iron red, and yellow, (A) 330.00

Figure of standing woman with bough in hand, flowing hair, wash ground, blue and white, (A) 467.00

Soup Plate, 8 3/4" d, vase of flowers in center, "X's," floral cartouches on border, blue and white 195.00

Spice Dish, 7" d, int divided into compartments, ext blue painted with hanging lambrequins and flowers, 5 bun feet, "blue CM and asterisk" mark, c1780, (A) 748.00

Strainer Bowl, 9 1/8" d, 3 sm feet, scattered flowerheads in center, border of hanging swags with flowerheads, blue and white, chips, (A) 517.00

Tankard, 6 1/2" h, cylinder shape, manganese and blue stylized trees and foliage design, hinged pewter lid, 18th C, (A) 863.00

Teabowl and Saucer, blue painted seated Chinese man in quatrefoil cartouche on ext of cup and int of saucer, crimped rims, c1680, (A) 748.00

Tea Caddy, 5 7/8" h, paneled, blue and floral decorations, diapered corners, scalloped base, "MVS 1750" on base, (A) 550.00

Teapot, 5 1/2" h, globular gadrooned shape, blue painted Chinese style center band of oval panels on flowers reserved on scrolling ground, scattered flowers on cov, shoulder and base, blue dash handle and spout, c1720, (A) 2,990.00

Tobacco Jar, 10" h, quatrefoil of "SIVILIE" flanked by standing Indians, blue and white, later brass cov, (A) 1,870.00

Tulipiere

11 3/8" h, baluster form with central oct aperture and 2 conc tiers of apertures modeled as bull's head, overall blue stylized flowers and scrolls, early 18th C, (A) 10,925.00

38" h, hex colonnade base, 5 tiers with flower apertures molded as fish heads supported on molded bird heads, pyramid finial, ball feet, blue geometrics and outlines, pr, (A) 12,650.00

Vase

6 3/8" h, baluster shape, lg flowerhead from stem, scattered floral sprays, banded ft and rim, manganese and white, (A) 345.00

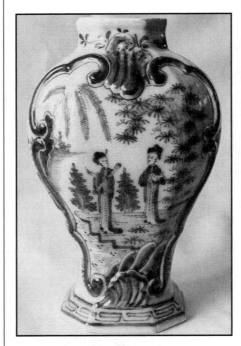

Vase, 9" h, dk blue designs, white ground, "blue claw" mark, mid-18th C, pr, $1,280.

9" h, trumpet shape, polychrome bust of William of Orange or Mary, flowerheads and squiggles, pr, (A) 431.00

9 3/4" h, rect body, flared ft and neck, molded shells and foliage, underglaze flowers and scrolls, blue and white 525.00

11 3/4" h, oct bulbous form, tapered garlic neck, blue painted flowers and shrubs, early 19th C, pr 385.00

20 3/4" h, fluted oct garlic shape, polychrome flowering plants and birds, De Porceleyne Klaeuw, pr, (A) . . 6,325.00

Vase, Cov

14 5/8" h, molded scroll and flowerhead panel, blue painted oriental figures in fenced garden with flowers and foliage, dog finial, white ground, (A) . . . 400.00

20" h, oct, paneled, blue and white period lovers in coastal landscape, scrolled borders, figural foo dog knob, 18th C, chips, (A) 1,035.00

Whistle, 2 3/4" h, yellow, green, and blue standing figural dog, rect base, pr, (A) 170.00

English

Bottle, 8 3/4" h, center exotic trees with scattered flowers and flowerheads, flower sprays, blue and white, Lambeth, (A) 385.00

Bowl

8 1/8" d, blue and ochre painted busts of King William and Queen Mary of Orange, "WMR" overhead, London, c1690, (A) 12,650.00

9" d, ftd, blue and white oriental landscape design with ducks, Lambeth, chips, (A) 358.00

Butter Pot, Cov, 2 5/8" h, scattered floral sprays, blue and white, pr, (A) . 230.00

Charger

12 1/4" d, standing figure of Flora in wooded landscape, blue and white, c1730-60 . . . . 1,650.00

13" d, blue seated Chinese fisherman in landscape setting extending through border, c1740, (A) 374.00

13 1/4" d, blue, green, yellow, and iron red painted flowering branch and insect, border of half flowerheads and leaves, Lambeth, c1740, (A) 185.00

13 5/8" d, vert leaves in circle in center, stylized flowerheads and leaves on inner border repeated on outer border, blue and white, orange enameled rim, Wincanton, c1760, (A) 633.00

Dish, 12 3/8" l, oval, fluted, center geometric and leaf design, hanging lambrequins on border, blue and white, Lambeth, chips, (A) 440.00

Drug Jar, 7 1/4" h, oval cartouche with angels and flowers surrounding "U.RUB.DESI," blue and white, London, c1770, (A) 863.00

Flower Brick, rect

5 1/2" l, central aperture with 3 rows of holes, sides blue painted with chapel,

Plate, 8 3/4" d, orange, blue, green, and iron red, Lambeth, c1730, $625.

fence, and stylized plants, serpentine ft, Lambeth, mid 18th C, (A) 500.00

8 1/4" l, rope twist upper edge, painted overall blue flowering arabesques and stylized carnations, London, c1750, (A) 2,760.00

Inkwell, 5" w, star shape, molded lion masks on 3 points, blue dash rim, white ground, c1640-70 . . . . 695.00

Jar, 6 1/2" h, blue and white oriental style landscape and flower design, chips, (A) . . 248.00

Plate

8 1/2" d

Blue and purple house in landscape scene, bianco sopra bianco border, Lambeth, (A) 275.00

Iron red and green accented blue and white crown over "AR," conc blue bands, rim of band of blue entwined scallops, London, c1702-14, (A) 6,325.00

Polychrome walking peacock standing under tree with sponged leaves and ground, mid-18th C, rim chips, (A) 1,840.00

8 3/4" d, overall farm scene, blue and white, c1760 . . . . 285.00

8 7/8" d

Blue, green, and manganese painted windmill in center, stylized flowers on border, blue-white glaze, Lambeth, c1770-80, (A) 655.00

Building in landscape with sponged trees, blue and white, (A) . . . 935.00

Red, yellow, blue, and green oriental style flowers and birds in center, scattered floral sprays on border, Lambeth, (A) 330.00

9" d

Blue center scene of birds perched on flowerheads and leaves, scattered flowerheads and leaves on border, c1740, pr, (A) 316.00

Iron red, yellow, manganese, and underglaze blue "Fazackerly" design of lg flowerhead and meandering flower sprays, chips, (A) 165.00

Lg tree in center with hanging foliage, flying birds in formation, and fencing, border of 3 compartments of florals or 3 compartments of crisscross pattern, blue and white, c1740, pr 800.00

Parrot perched on branches beside rockwork, border of stylized flowers and pine cones, polychrome, Lambeth, c1760, rim chips, set of 3, (A) 693.00

Sprays of flowers issuing from flowerhead on terrace, half flowerheads and scattered sprays on rim, blue, green, yellow, and manganese, Lambeth 330.00

Stylized flower bud and leaves in center, bud and leaf border, blue and white, (A) 138.00

Yellow, green, blue, and red oriental scene with bridge and bushes, blue sawtooth rim, Lambeth, (A) . 341.00

9 1/8" d, overall oriental landscape with houses, birds flying in formation, bushes in foreground, manganese, blue, and yellow, Lambeth, repaired, (A) . 330.00

10" d, scattered oriental flowers and chrysanthemum in center, border with 4 lozenges and geometrics and crisscross pattern between, blue and white, c1750 . . . . 215.00

10 1/4" d, biblical scene in center with tablet and "MAT:2.IV. 1752," geometric and floral border, blue and white, (A) 770.00

10 5/8" d, oriental coastal landscape scene, man fishing in boat, trees and pagodas in bkd, blue and white, c1760, (A) 259.00

Posset Pot, 7 1/4" h, floral bouquets on body, band of geometrics on rim, striped loop handles, blue and white, mismatched lid, Lambeth, hairlines, (A) 1,650.00

Pot, Cov, 4" h, 2 handles, blue and white bird and floral designs, mid 18th C, rim chip, (A) 546.00

Punch Bowl

10 1/2" d, ext with floral bunches and scattered floral sprays, lined rim, blue and white, Wincanton, c1730-60 . . 2,350.00

11 3/4" d, manor house, sm houses front and back, pile of boulders and trees on ext, band of curlicues on int, blue and white, c1750-70 . . . . 4,250.00

12" d, blue painted int design of flowering plants, border of repeating dbl diamonds, circles, and rosettes, ext in blue, iron red, and green panels of flowering plants separated by trilobed trellis panels, Lambeth, c1720, (A) . 5,750.00

Wall Pocket, 7 3/4" h, molded white cornucopia base, blue and white molded cherub head on border, repairs and chips, (A) . . . 1,100.00

Wine Jug, 5 3/4" h, bottle shape, blue "WHIT, 1657" over blue squiggle, white ground, London, (A) 8,625.00

DE MORGAN, WILLIAM

Chelsea, England
1872-1881

Merton Abbey,
near Wimbledon, England
1882-1888

Sand's End Pottery,
Fulham, England
1889-1907

History: William De Morgan, 1839-1917, was primarily a designer and decorator, not a potter. He purchased many tile blanks from commercial firms, e.g. Architectural Pottery Company to decorate with his own designs. In 1872 De Morgan established a pottery in Chelsea to produce his own underglaze blue tiles while experimenting with other colors such as red luster. In the mid-1870s he used the Persian colors purple, blue, and green for decorating tiles and ornamental vases. William Morris, De Morgan's friend, influenced his design motifs in areas such as flowers, birds, fish, ships, or mythical beasts.

In 1882, De Morgan moved to Merton Abbey near Wimbledon. He still made tiles, but increased his output of jugs, bowls, and globular vases. In partnership with Halsey Ricardo, an architect, he moved to Sand's End Pottery at Fulham in 1888. Together they produced pottery, tiles, panels, and murals. De Morgan's pottery body was lightly fired, rather granular, and well suited to the ornamental nature and broad designs of his work. Vases were decorated in the "Isnik" style with the strong Persian colors. Although some pieces showed an Art Nouveau influence, De Morgan was associated with the Arts and Crafts Movement during the Sand's End Pottery period. The more important decorators to work for De Morgan were: Charles and Fred Passenger, James and John Hersey, and Joe Juster. Their initials usually appeared with the standard factory marks on their works.

De Morgan was the first English potter to rediscover the secrets of older luster decoration. Later lusters used by Pilkington (see Tiles) are related to De Morgan's successful experiments in the 19th century.

After 1892, De Morgan lived much of the time in Italy due to illness. In 1898, his partnership with Ricardo ended, and the showroom closed. De Morgan reorganized and took into partnership the artists Charles and Fred Passenger and his kiln master, Frank Iles. The factory stopped making its own pots and bought biscuit wares from Carter and Co. of Poole. The factory closed in 1907. De Morgan gave permission to the Passengers to continue using his designs.

References: Julian Barnard, *Victorian Ceramic Tiles,* Mayflower Books, 1972; John Catleugh, *William De Morgan Tiles,* Van Nostrand Reinhold Co.Inc.1983; W. Gaunt & M.D.E. Clayton Stamm, *William De Morgan,* N.Y. Graphic Society, 1971; Martin Greenwood, *The Designs of William De Morgan,* Richard Dennis Publications, 1989.

Museums: Art Institute of Chicago, Chicago, IL; Battersea Old House, London, England; Castle Museum, Norwich, England; City Art Gallery, Birmingham, England; City Museum & Art Gallery, Stoke-on-Trent, England; Fitzwilliam Museum, Cambridge, England; Leighton House, Kensington, England; William Morris Gallery, Walthamtow, England; Victoria & Albert Museum, London, England.

Bowl, 12 1/2" d, pedestal base, ext with Persian style flowers and foliage over band of plumes, int with band of "S" scrolls and hearts, turquoise, blue, and white, (A)
. . . . .1,960.00

Charger

14" d, ruby luster Persian flowers in pot, reverse with band of stylized bellflowers, "imp star" mark, (A) 2,495.00

14 1/18" d, ruby luster Persian flowers in pot, rim with overlapping scale frieze, reverse with band of foliage motif, (A) 1,960.00

Tile

6" sq

Green painted owl catching mouse, white ground, "imp DM 98" mark (A). 855.00

Metallic brown and purple emb lions, circ flower mark, (A) 275.00

Yellow, pink, and green stylized flowerheads and leaves, (A) 275.00

6 1/8" sq, blue painted classical lion, white ground, (A) 623.00

Vase, 8 1/4" h, bottle shape, Moorish style brass glaze outlined dk and lt blue-gray blossoms and leaves, cobalt ground, "F.P." mark, (A) 1,800.00

DENMARK-GENERAL

1759 to Present

History: Louis Fournier, a Frenchman, made soft paste porcelain in Denmark from 1759 to 1765. These wares had a yellow tone with a dull glaze and were decorated with flowers and cupids in the French style. The principal products were tablewares.

Franz Muller made the first hard paste porcelain in Denmark in 1773. From 1779 until his death, Muller managed the Royal Porcelain Manufactory in Copenhagen. Furstenberg and Meissen models were copied. Anton Carl Luplau, master modeler, came from Furstenberg to work in Denmark. His strawflower pattern in underglaze blue achieved tremendous popularity.

Neo-classical decorations were used on the majority of Copenhagen porcelains. Gustav Hetsch served as managing director of the Royal Porcelain Manufactory about 1815. During the 1830s, many state services were designed for the royal residences. Denmark's national sculptor Berthel Thorwaldsen made numerous sculptures and reliefs during the 1840s. Copies of his works were made in biscuit porcelain, and these statuettes sold extensively. Christian Hetsch continued his father's neo-classical style at the Royal Porcelain Manufactory, but enhanced the pieces with colorful decorations, relief, and gilt.

Financial problems occurred after 1850. By 1868, the factory was Royal in name only. It was privately owned. In 1882, the firm regained some prominence when it merged with the Faience Alumina factory which had been established in Copenhagen in 1863. Philip Schou served as manager.

Arnold Krog became artistic director in 1885. He reinstituted the original strawflower ornamentation and designed new tableware shapes. Krog's revival of underglaze blue decoration utilizing the strawflower and other patterns started a prosperous period for Copenhagen. Animal sculptures were introduced by Carl Liisberg in 1888.

The Bing and Grondahl factory was the second factory established in Copenhagen. Starting in 1852, the sculptor Hermann Bissen produced biscuit statuettes and reliefs based on the same models as the Royal Porcelain Manufactory. Harold Bing became managing director in 1885. He appointed Pietro Krohn as artistic direc-

Figure, 9" h, "Girl From Amager," dk brown skirt, blue scarf, flowered belt, tan skirt, "DJ Copenhagen" mark, $675.

tor in 1886. Krohn's greatest design was the "Heron Service" where the heron appeared on each piece.

Museum: Royal Porcelain Factory, Copenhagen, Denmark.

Bowl, 7 1/2" sq, relief of fish, matte brown glazed ground, Marselis, (A). 150.00

Bud Vase, 4 1/2" h, bulbous body, lg red flowerhead, gray crackle ground, gold lined rim, Dahl Jensen 69.00

Chalice, 8" h, figural bust of woman's head, green, yellow, and brown, gray ground, Bjorn Winbald 125.00

Charger, 10 3/4" d, lg floral spray in center, half flowerheads on border, black transfer, shaped rim, "R.A.M. Copenhagen" mark 60.00

Dessert Service, master bowl, 12 3/4" d, 6 plates, 8" d, multicolored bird in center of master bowl, multicolored fruits or nuts on plates, wide orange-brown border band 290.00

Figure

5" h x 6 1/2" l, Bedlington Terrier, blue and gray, Dahl Jensen 300.00

7" h, seated cat, gray, Dahl Jensen 145.00

8 1/2" h, terra cotta, "Venus", sq base, Kai Nielson. 888.00

Inkwell, 4" h, freeform, turquoise drip glaze, stone ground 75.00

Potpourri Jar, 4 7/8" h x 6 3/4" d, HP blue tulips on sides, blue band of diamonds on border, blue geometrics and lines on cov, pierced sides and cov 34.00

Plaque, 10 1/2" d, relief molded biscuit of winged Minerva carrying 2 sleeping children, flying owl at side, or winged Venus and Cupid flying, lt green, Copenhagen, pr, (A) . 225.00

Vase

6 1/2" h, green reticulated neck, piecrust rim, black glaze 110.00

7" h, bulbous shape, dk blue flowerheads with yellow centers, brown outlined green leaves, cream ground, blue lined base and rim, "Copenhagen Denmark" mark. 75.00

Wall Plaque, 9 1/2" h x 12" l, figure riding fawns, maroon, gray, and green glazes, "Denmark" mark, pr, (A) 468.00

1820-40

1782-1825

DERBY

Derby, England
1755 to Present

History: William Duesbury I opened the Derby works at the Nottingham Road factory in 1755. Tablewares and ornamental wares were produced. Chinoiserie designs, exotic bird paintings, and blue and white patterns were the favorite design motifs. Derby had no factory mark before Duesbury purchased the Chelsea factory.

In 1769, Duesbury acquired the Chelsea factory and transferred some of the extremely skilled craftsmen from Chelsea to Derby; 1770 witnessed the production of the first biscuit or unglazed porcelain and figure groups. Originally developed at the Sevres factory about 1752, biscuit figures were to make Derby famous.

In 1784, Duesbury closed the Chelsea works, moving the remainder of the craftsmen to Derby. Duesbury died in 1786, and William Duesbury II, his son, assumed control.

Between 1786 and 1797, under the guidance of Duesbury II, the Derby factory became a major British pottery. Great advances were made in body, glaze, potting, and decoration. A tremendous variety of lavishly decorated objects was made. Added to the popular floral patterns were landscapes, maritime subjects, and hunting scenes. Duesbury's group of painters and craftsmen were among the finest in England during the 18th century.

In 1795, Duesbury took Kean as his partner. Duesbury died in 1791. Kean continued to produce landscape and marine subjects, but the quality of the body and the glaze deteriorated. Robert Bloor leased the factory in 1811 and then took over completely. The shapes tended to be larger, utilizing flamboyant gilded decoration as a reflection of the current tastes. The Japan or Imari patterns with their rich colorings and lavish use of gold typified the period. Imari patterns that started about 1770 are still being produced. Many figures were also modeled during the Bloor period. Bloor experienced a long illness during which the factory declined. He died in 1846. In 1848 the factory was sold.

The Nottingham Road factory closed. Several of the potters and painters began manufacturing china at King Street, trading as Sampson Hancock until the eventual merger with Royal Crown Derby in 1935. Utilitarian wares were made with an emphasis on the popular Japan and Imari designs. This small factory is the link to the claim of continuous china production in Derby.

References: F.A. Barrett & A.L. Thorpe, *Derby Porcelain 1750-1848*, Faber & Faber, 1971; Gilbert Bradley, *Derby Porcelain 1750-1798,* Seven Hills Books, 1992; F.B. Gilhespy, *Derby Porcelain*, Spring Books, 1961; Dennis Rice, *Derby Porcelain - The Golden Years, 1750-1770,* Hippocrane Books, 1983; John Twitchett, *Derby Porcelain, The Illustrated Dictionary,* Antique Collectors' Club, Ltd. 1997.

Collectors' Club: Derby Porcelain International Society, Membership Secretary, The Old Barracks, Sandon Road, Grantham, Lincolnshire NG31 9AS England, £25 Membership, quarterly newsletter, journal, occasional essays.

Museums: See Crown & Royal Crown Derby.

Bough Pot

7 1/4" l, pierced cov, painted multicolored floral bouquet of spring flowers in rect cartouche flanked by gilt trellis pattern with stylized flowerheads, foliate molded scroll handles, 4 scroll molded feet, Bloor Derby, c1825, restored cov, chips, pr, (A) 4,025.00

10 7/8" l, demi-lune shape, painted "Villa of Mecenas, Italy" named on base, reserved on gold ground with painted flowers, band of iron red and gilt molding on neck and ft, bracket handles, "blue crown, X'd batons, and D" mark, c1805, (A). 2,300.00

Cream Jug, 2 3/8" h, painted chinoiserie scene of pagoda flanked by rockwork and pines, int with boulder and grasses, brown lined rim, c1760, (A). 2,464.00

Cup and Saucer

Painted iron red, pink, and green scrolling foliage, gilt accents, "iron red crown, X'd batons and D" mark, pr, (A) . 75.00

Peach pink border bands with gilt drops and red circles, rounded dentil inner border on cup, saucer with gilt outlined well, c1810 . . . . 78.00

Cup, Cov, with stand, relief molded gilt edged white flowerhead of overlapped petals on cup base and center of stand, cobalt border with gilt flowerheads, 2 gilt handles, Chelsea Derby, c1770, restored, (A) 246.00

Dessert Dish, 10 1/2" l, lozenge shape, center with gilt floral sprig in oval cartouche, gilt scrolling leaf border over pink acanthus border over gilt swag border, scalloped gilt rim, pr. 495.00

Dessert Service, serving dish, 12 1/4" l, scalloped, 2 plates, 9" d, gilt inner chain with blue, green, and yellow sprigs, gilt rims, undulating iron red, cobalt and green border of stylized floral chain, "iron red crown, X'd batons and D" marks, c1820 . . . . 975.00

Dessert Service, Part, cov sauce tureen, 8 3/4" l, with stand, 2 dishes, 11 1/2" w, oval, 2 dishes, 9 3/4" w, lozenge shape, 11 plates, 8 3/4" d, wide peach borders with gilt foliate scrolls, "iron red crown, X'd batons and D" marks, c1810, (A) 1,050.00

Dish, 9 7/8" l x 7 1/4" w, diamond shape, green scattered floral bouquets and sprigs, gilt lined and dentil rim, "gilt anchor and D" mark, Chelsea-Derby, c1775 . . . . 425.00

Figure

3 1/4" h, squirrel seated on haunches, nut in paws, collar with ring, orange coat, polychrome trim, circ mound base, (A) 632.00

4" h

Autumn, young girl with grapes in hair, yellow bodice, flowered underskirt, holding basket of fruit, green bocage with grapes, gilded scroll base, c1760 . . . . 850.00

Spring, putto in yellow and turquoise sash with iron red band, blossoms on head, wreath of flowers in hand, floral and foliage base, patch marks, Chelsea-Derby, repair to fingers 1,250.00

5 1/4" h, "Pale Family," fruit sellers, man with turquoise top, iron red breeches, female with turquoise top, flowered skirt, both seated holding basket of grapes, rococo base with turquoise and gilt accents and scattered flowers, c1758, repairs, pr 2,500.00

6 1/8" h, standing shepherd with flower in hand, pink hat, lt yellow coat, striped waistcoat, iron red breeches, gilt accents, leaning on flower encrusted stump, hound at side, mound base, c1765, chips and repairs. 300.00

6 1/4" h, "Mansion House Dwarf," pink pantaloons, yellow flowered waistcoat, blue hat, circ base with applied flowers, (A) 275.00

7" h, shepherd in pink hat, puce lined yellow coat, playing recorder, female wearing yellow cap, flowered skirt, holding flowers, lamb at feet, turquoise accented rocaille molded base, c1765, pr, (A) 1,380.00

9" h, birdcatcher and companion, man in puce jacket, turquoise hat, flowered pantaloons, holding bird nest, companion in yellow bodice, flowered dress, puce sash at waist, holding birdcage, flower encrusted tree stumps, scroll molded gilt line reserve base, c1765, pr, (A). 1,848.00

13" h, "John Wilkes," standing man in gilt trimmed white suit, puce sash over shoulder, leaning on podium with "Bill of Rights," seated putto on base with book, ringing bell, gilt scroll molded base, c1765. . . . . .1,700.00

Flask, 5 3/4" h, pear shape, flower encrusted, polychrome and gilt, c1820, pr, (A) . . 385.00

Flower Pot and Stand, 7 1/2" h, flared shape, continuous painted scene of cattle by river, castle in bkd, horiz loop handles on base, gilt band of scrolling foliage and pamettes on base, "iron red X'd batons and D" mark, c1805, (A) 2,530.00

Ice Pail, Cov, 10 5/8" H-H, iron red, cobalt, and gilt "Japan" pattern honeycomb panels, "iron red crown, X'd batons, and D" mark, c1810, pr, (A) 1,450.00

Plate

8 1/2" d, painted loose flower sprays and scattered sprigs, brown line shaped rim, c1770, set of 3, (A). 462.00

9 1/4" d, cartouche of "Mme DuBarry" in center, mauve dress with white trim on gray bkd, floral and turquoise bands with gilt, gilt rim 95.00

9 3/4" d, oriental style underglaze blue, iron red, and gilt birds on branches in flowering tree beside banded hedges, gilt rim, "iron red crown X'd batons and D" mark, c1820, set of 14, (A) .2,070.00

10" d

Oct, oxblood red, turquoise, gold, and blue design in Persian manner, set of 10 . . . . .6,500.00

Painted named specimen flower in center, blue border with gilt lines, gilt gadrooned rim, "iron red crown and D" mark, Robert Bloor, c1835, chips and repairs, set of 10 . . . . .3,950.00

Potpourri Vase, 6" h, globular shape, painted carnations, pansies, and garden flowers, blue ground, gilt rims, gilt masks applied to edge, tripod paws, pointed knob, pierced cov, "iron red crown and D" mark, Robert Bloor, c1830, knobs restored, pr. 1,400.00

Sauceboat, 6 3/4" l, molded overlapping leaves with painted flower bouquets, stalk handle with leaves, flowers, and fruit, green rim, c1755, (A). 500.00

Sauce Tureen

5 1/2" h x 8 1/2" h, with underplate, lobed, pink roses, gilt paw feet, gilt handles and lion mask terminals, "red X'd batons" mark, c1815, pr 1,400.00

6 1/2" h x 8 5/8" l, with undertray, oval shape, raised flared ft, pointed loop handles, leaf molded terminals, painted named oval views of "Near Woolwich,"

Vegetable Dish, Cov, 11" sq, "King's" pattern, gold and iron red florals, cobalt trim, $600.

"Southampton" on reverse, "Lake Agnano, Italy" on undertray in gilt lines,, wide mint green band between gilt lines, lower line with gilt swags, egg and darts, and flowerhead pendants, "blue crown, X'd batons, dots and D" marks, c1800 . . . . 2,750.00

7 7/8" l, oval, spread pedestal ft, green ground with painted named scenes of Atholl, the river Ferg and Roslin in gilt oval cartouches, gilt stem knob with scrolling foliage, early 19th C, repairs, (A). 154.00

Serving Dish

9 3/4" l x 9 1/2" w, gold center circle, pink roses with dk pink centers and green leaf border, gilt trim, serrated rim with raised end handle, "red crown, X'd batons and D" mark 595.00

11 3/8" d, Japan pattern, Imari colors with gilt trim, c1865, pr, (A) 316.00

Sweetmeat Dish, 4 1/2" h x 6 1/2" d, 3 molded scallop shells with blue floral sprays, blue cell form border, shell center handle, shell encrusted trefoil base, c1760-70, chips 1,800.00

Teapot, 7 1/4" h, blue banding with gilt vinework and trim, pattern #59, late 18th C, (A). . 488.00

Vase

3 1/2" h, bottle shape, painted bouquets and scattered sprigs, gilt chevron border, gilt line rim, "iron red crown, X'd batons and D" mark, (A). 200.00

4 1/2" h, HP multicolored enameled titled landscape of "Dryburgh Abbey" or "Barnard Casthe" in raised gilt cartouche, raised gilt foliate designs on reverse, white ground, squared gilt handles, c1865, pr, (A). 1,380.00

6 1/4" h, everted pierced basketweave border with raised yellow flowerheads, 2 molded masks in multicolored encrusted floral wreaths, band of green molded leaf frills, panted insects on base and body, c1765, repairs, (A) 225.00

6 1/2" h, campana shape, painted baskets of flowers on ledge in gilt surround, dk blue ground with gilt scrolls and accents, 2 vert handles, c1820, pr, (A) . . .633.00

12 3/4" h, campana shape, white body, cobalt ground, gilt scrolled foliate framed panel of enameled floral arrangement on table, side handles, pr, (A). . . . 2,760.00

DERUTA
Near Perugia, Italy
Late 15th Century to Present

History: A large pottery industry was established at Deruta near Perugia, Italy. Metallic luster decorations in a golden mother-of-pearl iridescence and ruby colors were used on the polychrome wares utilizing special firing techniques. Deruta also was known for the excellence of its border patterns usually encircling a central motif of a bust or heraldic arms.

At first yellow colored pieces outlined in blue were prominent at Deruta. Later wares included olive green shades. Large dishes were made, some with raised decorations.

Today Deruta produces souvenir wares for tourists.

Museums: Gardiner Museum of Ceramic Art, Toronto, Canada; Victoria & Albert Museum, London, England; Wadsworth Atheneum, Hartford, CT; Wallace Collection, London, England.

Albarello, 8 1/2" h, majolica, polychrome armorial over drug label in laurel wreath, reverse with "1568" on shoulder, cracks and chips, (A) 2,697.00

Charger, 15" d, basin painted with multicolored shaped shield in conc bands of geometric patterns, stylized flowerheads and zigzags on border, (A) 633.00

Cruet, 8" h, painted "Gothic script IHS" in buds, and floral designs, flanked by vert bands of buds, band of scales below, early 16th C, (A). 3,450.00

Dish, 9 3/4" d, shell molded, multicolored painted winged putto in landscape in center, border of grotesque figures and arabesques, mid 17th C, (A) 978.00

Plaque, 16 3/8" d, painted and lustered profile of Alexander the Great in Helmet, inscribed band with "ALESANDERO M," border with alternating panels of foliate, scale, and stripe designs, c1520, (A) 40,250.00

Dish, 6 1/2" l, 2 1/2" h, ftd, blue, yellow, and cream design, blue border, $550.

c 1902-1929

DOULTON AND ROYAL DOULTON

DOULTON OF LAMBETH

Lambeth, near London
1815-1956

1880-1902

History: In Lambeth, near London, John Doulton founded the Doulton Lambeth pottery in 1815. Utilitarian salt glazed stonewares were the mainstay. When John Watts joined the firm, it became known as Doulton and Watts (1820 1853). Stoneware barrels, bottles, spirit flasks, and jugs were produced in vast quantities.

Henry Doulton, John's second son, joined the firm in 1835. His inventiveness led to the application of steam to drive the potter's wheel, placing Lambeth Pottery ten years ahead of the other potteries. Architectural terra cotta and garden ornaments were added to the catalog. Production of stoneware drainpipes, conduits, and other sanitary wares also began.

The Lambeth School of Art, under John Sparkes' direction, became associated with the Doulton wares. Through Sparkes, George Tinsworth began working with Doulton in 1866. Hannah and Arthur Barlow, students at the school, joined Doulton in 1871. They made pots with incised decorations worked directly into uncoated clay. During the next 20 years, the number of artists and designers grew; 250 artists were at work by 1885. The monogram, initials, or signature of the artist appeared on the piece; often the assistants' initials appeared too. In 1887, Queen Victoria knighted Henry Doulton for his achievements in the advancement of ceramic art.

Sir Henry died in 1897; Henry Louis Doulton succeeded his father. In 1899, the family company became Doulton & Co. Ltd. During the 20th century, reductions took place in the production of artist signed pieces from Doulton Lambeth. By 1925, only 24 artists were employed. Leslie Harradine did excellent stoneware figures of Dickens' characters. He also modeled spirit flasks of contemporary politicians.

During the 1920s and 1930s, collectors' pieces in simple shapes, subtle colors, and uncluttered decorations were made. A large range of commemorative wares also was produced. Agnete Hoy, working at Lambeth from 1951-1956, achieved fame for her cat figures. She used salt glaze techniques and developed a new transparent glaze. In 1956, production ceased at the Doulton Lambeth pottery.

1882-1902   1882-1902

DOULTON OF BURSLEM

Staffordshire, England
1877 to Present

History: In 1877, Henry Doulton acquired the Nile Street pottery located in Burslem, Staffordshire, from Pinder, Bourne & Co. The name was changed to Doulton & Co. in 1882. Beginning in 1884, porcelains of the highest quality were manufactured. Simple, inexpensive earthenware tablewares also were made. A large group of artists under the direction of John Slater assembled at the Burslem factory.

Doulton's china was exhibited at the Chicago Columbian Exposition in 1893. Charles Noke, who joined the company in 1889 and became one of the most important workers at Burslem, exhibited his vases. Many Noke figures portrayed contemporary people as historical personages. His early achievements included Holbein, Rembrandt, and Barbotine wares plus a popular range of flasks, jugs, and other shapes in subdued colors. Rouge Flambe was perhaps the most important ware introduced by Noke. He became art director in 1914. Noke also used many oriental style dragons in high relief.

Other notable artists included Percy Curock, Daniel Dewsbury, Edward Raby, and George White. They used many experimental glazes including Chang ware, Chinese Jade and Sung. Doulton artists often used nature as their theme. Flowers, animals, especially farms animals such as cows and goats were utilized. Many landscapes were also hand painted.

At the Burslem factory, a tremendous amount of tablewares was produced. In addition to the earthenwares, fine bone china ornamented in gold and frequently exhibiting elaborate designs also was manufactured. In 1901 King Edward VII granted the Royal Warrant of appointment to Doulton. From that point on, they used the word "ROYAL" to describe their products.

Royal Doulton Figures

Nearly all of Royal Doulton figures are made at the Burslem factory. Three basic ingredients, china clay, Cornish stone, and calcined bone ash, were blended together with water to make a fine body able to withstand the high temperature firings needed to produce a superfine, yet strong translucent ceramic body. Figurine subjects included child studies, street sellers, and historical, literary, or legendary characters in large and miniatures sizes.

In 1913, Royal Doulton began marking each new figurine design with an "HN" number. Harry Nixon was the artist in charge of painting the figures. The "HN" numbers refer to him. "HN" numbers were chronological until 1949 after which blocks of numbers were assigned to each modeler. More than 2,000 different figures have been produced. New designs are added each year. Older designs are discontinued. There are approximately two hundred designs in current production.

Character and Toby Jugs

Character jugs depicted the head and shoulders; Toby Jugs feature the entire figure either standing or seated. Noke revived the old Staffordshire Toby tradition in the 20th century by modeling characters based on songs, literature, legends, and history. The first jugs were produced by Noke in 1934. Large jugs measure 5 1/4" to 7 1/2," small jugs 3 1/4" to 4," miniatures 2 1/4" to 2 1/2," and tinies 1 1/4" tall or less. The shape and design of the jug handle aids in establishing the age of a jug. For a brief period, all seated Tobies were discontinued. Production of the seated Tobies began again in 1973.

Series Ware

Series Ware, created by Charles Noke, used a large number of standard blank shapes decorated with a selection of popular characters, events, and illustrations. A series ranged from two to three to as high as 20 scenes.

A variety of printing techniques was used on Series Ware. Transfer printing from engraved plates and lithography supplemented with hand coloring was one technique. The block printing and silk screening techniques produced denser, more colorful images. A photographic process captured famous views and characters.

Series Ware production was interrupted by WWII. However, a revival of decorative plate production led to the Collectors International plates during the 1970s, featuring plates for special holidays such as Valentine's Day and Christmas and designs by international artists.

Today, Doulton and Company is the largest manufacturer of ceramic products in the UK. Minton, Royal Crown Derby, Ridgway, Royal Albert, Royal Adderley,

Colclough, Paragon, John Beswick, and Webb Corbett are all part of the company.

References: Jean Dale, *The Charlton Standard Catalogue of Royal Doulton Beswick Figurines, 5th Edition*, The Charlton Press, 1996; Richard Dennis, *Doulton Character Jugs*, Malvern Press, 1976; Michael Doulton, *Discovering Royal Doulton*, Swan Hill, 1994; Desmond Eyles & Richard Dennis, *Royal Doulton Figures Produced at Burslem, Staffordshire 1892-1994*, Richard Dennis Publications, 1994; Desmond Eyles, *The Doulton Burslem Wares*, Royal Doulton & Barrie Jenkins, 1980; Desmond Eyles, *The Doulton Lambeth Wares*, Hutchinson, 1975; Louise Irvine, *Royal Doulton Bunnykins Collectors Book*, Richard Dennis, 1993; Louise Irvine, *Royal Doulton Limited Edition Loving Cups & Jugs*; Louise Irvine, *Royal Doulton Series Ware, Vol. 1 & 2, Vol. 3 & 4*, Richard Dennis, 1980, 1984; Ralph & Terry Kovel, *Kovels' The Illustrated Price Guide to Royal Doulton*, Crown, 1980; Katherine Morrison McClinton, *Royal Doulton Figurines & Character Jugs*, Wallace-Homestead, 1978; Kevin Pearson, *The Doulton Figure Collectors Handbook*, Kevin Francis Publishing Ltd. 1988; Doug Pinchin, *The Beatrix Potter & Bunnykins Price Guide*, Francis Joseph Publications, 1995; Doug Pinchin, *The Doulton Figure Collectors Handbook, 4th Edition*, Francis Joseph Publications, 1996; Francis Salmon, Ed. *The Character Jug Collectors Handbook, Sixth Edition*, Francis Joseph Publications, 1995.

Gallery: Sir Henry Doulton Gallery, Doulton Fine China Nile Street Pottery, Burslem, England.

Collectors' Club: Mid-America Doulton Collectors, P.O. Box 483, McHenry, IL 60060. Annual membership: $20.00 per year, Newsletter: 6 per year; Royal Doulton International Collectors Club, Minton House, London Road, Stoke-on-Trent ST4 7QD, England. Annual membership: $50.00 per year, Quarterly magazine.

Newsletter: Character Jug Report, Box 5000, Caledon, Ontario, LONIC0, Canada; Collecting Doulton, P.O. Box 310, Surrey TW9 1 FS, UK. Bi-Monthly magazine; Doulton Divvy, Quarterly magazine, Betty J. Weir, P.O. Box 2434, Joliet, IL 60434.

Doulton of Burslem

Biscuit Jar, 7" h, stoneware, cylinder shape, brown, blue, and white geometric design, etched metal cov, c1879. . . . . 400.00

Bowl

  9" sq, blue and white roses, stems, and buds, gold accents 325.00

  9 1/2" d x 5 1/2" h, ftd, relief design of gold and silver flowers, beige ground, ribbed body. 350.00

Ewer, 10 1/2" h, brown bird of paradise on off-white ground, sgd "GD," c1880s . 350.00

Gravy Boat, 8 1/2" l, with undertray, "Sorrento" pattern 62.00

Jardiniere, 10" d, blue daffodils, white ground, gold rim, c1890s 300.00

Pass Cup, 6 1/2" h, 3 panels of HP roses, cobalt and gold body, gold molded angel resting on elbow at handle terminal, sgd "RA". . 1,250.00

Plate, 8 1/2" d, HP Japanese style pink, gold, and black flowers, cream-white ground, scalloped rim, set of 8 . . . . 300.00

Vase

  3 3/4" h, "Hyperion Ware," HP pate-sur-pate type white flowers with green and blue leaves, pink bone china ground, gold int on neck. 450.00

  4 1/4" h, squat shape, ruffled top, white flowers and berries, green leaves, tan and beige shaded ground, gold trim on sides 95.00

  8" h, urn shape, HP floral design on front and reverse, blue and gold bands with beads of white flowers, cobalt and gold handles, sgd "FM & MV," Doulton Slater's Patent. 650.00

  12 1/4" h, gold outlined HP chrysanthemums, 5 gold bands on neck, c1880s 450.00

Vegetable Bowl, 9 1/4" d, "Malvern" pattern 18.00

Doulton of Lambeth

Biscuit Jar, 7" h, stoneware, blue and brown geometric design, etched metal lid, 1879 . . . . 400.00

Ewer, 6 1/4" h, stoneware, pinched sides, lt brown body, blue and green applied beading and incised foliate scrolls, cobalt bkd . .275.00

Jug

  4 1/4" h, white hunting scene, cobalt and brown ground, c1925 . . . . 95.00

  6 1/2" h, blue oriental design, brown top, tan base, strap handle, c1891-1910 . . . . 395.00

  8 1/2" h, relief of figures on tan to brown ground and "Good Is Not Enough The Best Is Not Too Good" 250.00

  10 1/2" h, incised lion grooming in landscape, blue glazed stiff leaf border, Hannah Barlow, 1878, (A). 747.00

Pass Cup

  6 1/2" h, 3 handles, incised blue designs of birds in natural settings, dk cream ground, Hannah Barlow 1,250.00

  6 3/4" h, stoneware, 3 handles, relief of men in tavern, running dogs, tan base, dk brown top, SP rim, "Doulton Lambeth, England No. 5722" mark, dtd 1898, (A). 127.00

Pitcher

  6 1/2" h, stoneware, imp sm gold stars, dk green, white, and turquoise enameling, mottled brown handle and inner neck 325.00

10 1/4" h, stoneware, etched and relief design of geometrics and raised balls, multicolored, SP top rim and lid, (A) .110.00

13" h, stoneware, bust of Lord Nelson in uniform, brown salt glaze finish, Doulton and Watts, (A) 316.00

Plaque, 17" d, faience, HP scene of cows and farm girl, Hannah Barlow, c1880. . . 1,750.00

Toby Jug, 13 7/8" h, stoneware, man holding jug seated astride barrel, dk brown top, tan base, salt glaze, restored brim, (A). . . 431.00

Umbrella Stand, 25" h, yellow leaves, mottled blue ground, brown horiz bands, "stamped Doulton Lambeth" mark, (A) 1,000.00

Vase

  3" h, bulb shape, stoneware, aqua and white floral design, buff and brown ground, ear handles, "Slaters Patent" mark. 225.00

  7" h, moon flask form, 2 sm loop handles on should, faience, polychrome floral decorations, c1875, (A) 173.00

  7 1/4" h, narrow base, bulbous body, short neck, flared rim, salt glazed stoneware, blue and white slip decorated foliate design, brown ground, Eliza Simmance, c1883, (A) 315.00

  8 1/2" h, incised horse profiles in blue glazed foliate cartouches on mottled brown ground, blue and green foliate border, Hannah Barlow, (A). . . . 575.00

  11" h, white beaded green hearts, mottled blue ground, brown neck with green int 300.00

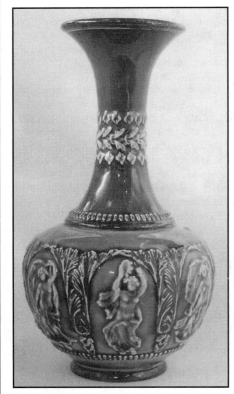

Vase, 7 3/4" h, tan shades, blue trim, "Doulton Lambeth" mark, $450.

14" h, "Persian" pattern, blue and white florals 295.00

16 1/4" h, central incised frieze of grazing cows, blue outlines on textured tan ground, blue and dk brown glazes with white floral and foliate borders, Hannah Barlow, (A) 632.00

20" h, 3 quatrefoil reserves with incised cobalt and brown scenes of goats, brown scrolls on cobalt ground, raised enameled jewel borders, Hannah Barlow, c1891-1902, repairs, pr 5,000.00

Royal Doulton

Animal Figures

Airedale, K5 . . . . 250.00
Alsatian, HN 1117 . . . . 175.00
Antelope, HN 2064 . . . . 180.00
Boxer, HN 2643 . . . . 125.00
Bull Terrier, K14 . . . . 325.00
Chestnut Shire, HN 2623 . . . . 650.00
Chow, K15 . . . . 130.00
Cocker Spaniel Puppy in Basket, HN 2585 . . . . 80.00
Cocker Spaniel with Pheasant, HN 1028 . . . . 175.00
Collie, HN 1058 . . . . 145.00
Dalmatian, HN 1114 . . . . 225.00
Doberman Pinscher, "Rancho Dobe's Storm," HN 2645 . . . . 135.00
Drake, standing, green, HN 807 . . 135.00
Elephant, HN 2644 . . . . 150.00
English Setter, HN 1050 . . . . 150.00
English Setter with Pheasant, HN 2529 . . . . 375.00
Fox, seated, flambe, #14 . . . . 145.00
German Shepherd, HN 1116 . . . . . 150.00
Gray Gude Mare, HN 2570 . . . . . . 350.00
Irish Setter, HN 1056 . . . . 165.00
Labrador, HN 2667 . . . . 175.00
Mallard, HN 2556 . . . . 290.00
Monkey, HN 2657 . . . . 175.00
Owl, flambe, #2249 . . . . 650.00
Peacock, HN 2577 . . . . 250.00
Penguin, K22 . . . . 200.00
Persian Cat, white, HN 2539A 250.00
Pointer, HN 2624 . . . . 375.00
Rabbit, crouching, HN 2592 . . . . . 120.00
Rhinoceros, 9" h, 17" l, Rouge Flambe, #615 . . . . 875.00
Salmon, Leaping, Rouge Flambe, #666, (A) 431.00
Sealyham, "Scotia Stylist," HN 1032 . . . . 250.00
Scottish Terrier, K18 . . . . 125.00
St. Bernard, lying, K19 . . . . 90.00
Tiger, flambe, HN 2646 . . . . 795.00
Welsh Corgis, K16 . . . . 45.00
Wire Fox Terrier, K8 . . . . 75.00

Bowl

10" d, oct, "Poppy" pattern, pink and yellow flowers, green vert stems, "black Royal Doulton England" mark, (A) 250.00

11" d, pedestal base, Sung, blue, purple, and yellow painted bird of paradise, mottled flambe ground, Charles Noke, (A) 1,705.00

Brambly Hedge Figures

3 1/4" h
Basil, DBH14 . . . . 75.00
Catkin, DBH12 . . . . 75.00
Clover, DBH16 . . . . 40.00
Mr. Apple, DBH2 . . . . 40.00
Mr. Toadflax, DBH10 . . . . 40.00
Old Mrs. Eyebright, DBH9 . . . . 75.00
Old Vole, DBH13 . . . . 75.00
Wilfred Entertains, DBH23 . . . . 75.00

Bunnykins

Cup and Saucer
Benjamin Bunny, Royal Albert mark 16.00
"The Engagement," Royal Albert mark 10.00
Feeding Dish, 6" d, Mr. Piggley's Store 130.00
Figures
2 1/2" h, Jogging Bunnykins, DB22 60.00
2 3/4" h, Aerobic Bunnykins, DB40 105.00
3" h, Partners in Collecting, DB151. 39.00
3 1/4" h
Billie and Bunty Bunnykins Sleigh Ride, DB4 . . . . 25.00
Busy Needles Bunnykins, DB10 . . . . 48.00
3 1/2" h
Boy Skater Bunnykins, DB152 . . 21.00

Figure, 4" h, Bunnykins, Master Potter Bunnykins, $150.

Figure, 4 1/2" h, Bunnykins, Father, Mother, and Victoria Bunnykins, $40.

Buntie Bunnykins Helping Mother, DB2 . . . . 45.00
Christmas Surprise Bunnykins, DB146 . . . . 30.00
Harry the Herald, DB49 . . . . . 125.00
3 3/4" h
Ace Bunnykins, DB42 . . . . 140.00
Billie Bunnykins Cooling Off, DB3 . . . . 160.00
Lollipopman Bunnykins, DB65 . . 50.00
Master Potter Bunnykins, DB131 . . . . 90.00
Rise and Shine Bunnykins, DB11 . . . . 115.00
Tally Ho! Bunnykins, DB12 . . . . 55.00
4" h
Bathtime Bunnykins, DB148 . . . . 25.00
Bogey Bunnykins, DB32 . . . . 80.00
Bride Bunnykins, DB101 . . . . . . 25.00
Brownie Bunnykins, DB61 . . . . . 45.00
Grandpa's Story Bunnykins, DB14 . . . . 325.00
Mr. Bunnykins Autumn Days, DB5 . . . . 200.00
Paperboy Bunnykins, DB77 . . . . 50.00
Rainy Day Bunnykins, DB147 . . . 25.00
Schoolmaster Bunnykins, DB60 . . . . 40.00
4 1/4" h
Cook Bunnykins, DB85 . . . . 45.00
Nurse Bunnykins, 2nd version, DB74 . . . . 21.00
4 1/2" h
Family Photograph Bunnykins, DB1 . . . . 120.00
Groom Bunnykins, DB102 . . . . . 25.00
Milkman Bunnykins, DB125 . . . 160.00
Mr. Bunnybeat Strumming, DB16 . . . . 135.00
Uncle Sam Bunnykins, DB50 . . . 25.00
Oatmeal Bowl, 6" d
"Bath Night" 40.00
"Family in the Garden" 45.00
"Story Time" 65.00

Plate

4" d, Jeremy Fisher, Royal Albert mark
. . . . 13.00

6" d, "Letter Box" 60.00

6 1/2" d, "Visiting the Cottage," sgd
. . . . 30.00

7" d
"Camp Site" 24.00
"Space Rocket Launch" 24.00

7 1/2" d
"Bathtime". 15.00
"Dressing Up". 15.00
"Golfing" 75.00
"Mr. Piggly's Store". 40.00
"Orange Vender" 15.00
"Pillow Fight," sgd, c1940 . . . . 185.00
"Ticket Office". 60.00
"Washing". 60.00
"Watering The Flowers" 65.00

8" d, "Flying Kites" 35.00

8 1/4" l x 6 1/2" w, "Art Class" 85.00

8 1/2" d
"Christmas Tree," sgd, "A" mark
. . . . 185.00
"Conducting the Orchestra," sgd, "A"
mark 125.00
"Getting Dressed," sgd, "A" mark
. . . . 200.00

Trio, "Trio," Royal Albert. 28.00

Chalice, 8 1/2" h, Chang, molton white, yellow, and red glazes, red, green, and blue ground, "Chang, Royal Doulton, Noks, NC" mark
. . . . .3,500.00

Character Jugs

Anne Boleyn, large, D6644 . . . . 80.00
Anne of Cleves, large, D6653
Ears down. 100.00
Ears up 255.00
Apothecary
Large, D6567 . . . . 150.00
Small, D6574 . . . . 50.00
Arriet
Mini, D6250 . . . . 60.00
Tiny, D6256 . . . . 190.00
Athos, small, D6439. . . . . 50.00
Aud Mac
Large, D823 . . . . 65.00
Mini, D6253 . . . . 40.00
Bacchus
Large, D6499 . . . . 70.00
Mini, D6521 . . . . 45.00
Beefeater
Large, "ER" pink handle, D6206
. . . . 100.00
Mini, "GR" handle, D6251 . . . . . 60.00
Cap'n Cuttle
Mid, D5842. . . . . 165.00
Small, D5842, A mark. 84.00
Capt. Hook, small, D6601 . . . . 300.00
Cardinal, large, D5614. . . . . 140.00
Catherine Par, large, D6664 . . . . . 130.00
Cavalier, large, with goatee, D6114
. . . . 40.00
Chief Sitting Bull/George Armstrong
Custer, large, Antagonist series, D6712

Blue eyed version 125.00
Brown eyed version. 250.00
Clown, large
Brown hair, D5610. . . . . 3,200.00
Red hair, D5610 . . . . 2,650.00
White hair, D6322 . . . . 1,200.00
Confucius, large, flambe, D7003 . 219.00
Dick Turpin
Mini, D6128 . . . . 60.00
Small, D6535 . . . . 50.00
Don Quixote, small, D6511 . . . . . . 55.00
Falconer
Large, black and white striped hat,
D6533 . . . . 80.00
Small, D6540. . . . . 50.00
Falstaff, small, D6385 . . . . 50.00
Farmer John, small, D5789, A mark
. . . . 105.00
Fat Boy
Mid, D5840 . . . . 215.00
Tiny, D6142 . . . . 150.00
Fortune Teller, mini, D6523. . . . . . 325.00
Gladiator, small, D6553 . . . . 425.00
Goaler, small, D6577 . . . . 65.00
Gone Away
Mini, D6545 . . . . 50.00
Small, D6538. . . . . 50.00
Grant and Lee, large, Antagonists Series,
D6698 . . . . 340.00
Gulliver, large, D6560. . . . . 525.00
Jane Seymour, large, D6646 . . . . 100.00
Jarge, large, D6288, A mark. 259.00
John Peel
Mini, D6130 . . . . 50.00
Tiny, D6259 . . . . 175.00
King Henry VIII, 2 handles, large, D6888
. . . . 699.00
Lawyer
Large, D6498. . . . . 99.00
Mini, D6524 . . . . 65.00
Small, D6504. . . . . 52.00
London Bobby, raised emblem, D6744
. . . . 110.00
Lobster Man, large, D6617 . . . . . . 120.00
Mad Hatter, small, D6602 . . . . . . 100.00
Mephistopheles, with verse, large, D5757
. . . . .2,750.00
Mikado, large, D6501 . . . . 625.00
Mr. Pickwick, Mid, D5839 . . . . . . 165.00
Old Charlie, tiny, D6144 . . . . 110.00
Old Salt, mini, closed arm version, D6557
. . . . 55.00
Owl Mac, small, D5828. . . . . 250.00
Paddy, tiny, D6145 . . . . 110.00
Parson Brown
Large, D5486. . . . . 120.00
Small, D5529 . . . . 70.00
Punch and Judy, large, D6946 . . . 625.00

Jug, Robin Hood, large, D 6527, $125.

Regency Beau, large, D6559 . . . . 950.00
Robin Hood
1st version, mini, D6252 . . . . . . 65.00
2nd version, mini, D6541 . . . . . 45.00
Robinson Crusoe
Large, D6532 . . . . 70.00
Small, D6539 . . . . 50.00
Ronald Reagan, large, D6718 . . . . 395.00
Sairey Gamp
Mini, D6045 . . . . 40.00
Tiny, D6146 . . . . 110.00
Sam Weller
Mini, D6140 . . . . 60.00
Tiny, D6147 . . . . 110.00
Santa Claus, large
Candy cane handle, D6840 . . . 400.00
Reindeer handle, D6675 . . . . . 120.00
Scaramouche, small, D6561 . . . . . 475.00
Sleuth, mini, D6639 . . . . 55.00
Ugly Duchess
Mini, D6607 . . . . 245.00
Small, D6603 . . . . 295.00
Uncle Tom Cobbleigh, D6337 . . . . 325.00
Vicar of Bray, large, D5615, A mark
. . . . 280.00
Viking, mini, D6526 . . . . 125.00

Figures

Adrienne, HN 2152 . . . . 175.00
Affection, HN 2236. . . . . 139.00
Afternoon Tea, HN 1747 . . . . 275.00
Alice, HN 2158. . . . . 135.00
Anna, HN 2802 . . . . 160.00
Auctioneer, HN 4988 . . . . 155.00
Autumn Breezes, HN 2131 . . . . . . 300.00
Balloon Man, HN 1954. . . . . 188.00
Bathing Beauty, HN 3156 . . . . 325.00
Biddy Penny Farthing, HN 1843 . . 200.00
Blacksmith, HN 2240. . . . . 175.00
Blithe Morning, HN 2065 . . . . 335.00
Bluebeard, HN 2105 . . . . 425.00

Figure, Betsy, HN 2111, $295.

Figure, Midsummer Noon, HN 2033, $495.

Buddies, HN 2546 . . . . 220.00
Carpet Seller, open hand version, HN
    1464 . . . . 995.00
Cerise, HN 1007 . . . . 200.00
Charlie's Aunt, HN 35 . . . . 650.00
Chic, Reflection Series, HN 2997 . 185.00
Christmas, red, HN 1910 . . . . 500.00
Christmas Morn, HN 1992 . . . . . . 160.00
Christmas Parcels, HN 2851 . . . . . 275.00
Clarinda, HN 2724 . . . . 215.00
Cleopatra, HN 2868 . . . . 1,700.00
Coppelia, HN 1952 . . . . 575.00
Country Lass, HN 1991 . . . . 215.00
Dancers of the World-Philippines,
    HN 2439 . . . . 695.00
Day Dreams, HN 1731 . . . . 212.00
Deborah, HN 2701 . . . . 385.00
Dinky Do, HN 1678 . . . . 100.00
Dorcas, HN 1491 . . . . 495.00
Eleanor Provence, HN 2009 . . . . . 625.00
Eliza, green, HN 3798 . . . . 85.00
Elizabeth I, HN 3099 . . . . 249.00
Embroidering, HN 2855 . . . . 245.00
Ermine Coat, HN 1981 . . . . 275.00
Falstaff, HN 2504 . . . . 200.00
Farmer's Wife, HN 2069 . . . . 470.00
Fat Boy, HN 2096 . . . . 365.00
First Dance, HN 2803 . . . . 225.00
Flirtation, Reflection Series, HN 3071
    . . . . 185.00
Flower Seller's Children, HN 1342 . 275.00
Genevieve, HN 1962 . . . . 260.00

Good King Wenceslas, HN 2118 . 495.00
Good Morning, HN 2671 . . . . 235.00
Gossips, HN 2025 . . . . 395.00
Grandma, HN 2052 . . . . 250.00
Harriet, blue, HN 3795 . . . . 100.00
Janice, HN 2022 . . . . 650.00
Jester, HN 2016 . . . . 295.00
Jovial Monk, HN 2144 . . . . 180.00
Julia, HN 2705 . . . . 125.00
June, HN 1947 . . . . 1,100.00
Kristy, HN 2381 . . . . 175.00
Lambing Time, HN 1890 . . . . 135.00
La Sylphide, HN 2138 . . . . 418.00
Leading Lady, HN 2269 . . . . 225.00
Lilac Time, HN 2137 . . . . 265.00
Little Boy Blue, HN 2062 . . . . 220.00
Love Letter, HN 2149 . . . . 550.00
Lunch Time, HN 2485 . . . . 185.00
Lynne, HN 2329 . . . . 175.00
Lyric, HN 2757 . . . . 80.00
Madonna of the Square, HN 2034 650.00
Make Believe, HN 2225 . . . . 130.00
Maureen, M 84 . . . . 1,000.00
Mermaid, HN 97 . . . . 600.00
Miss Demure, HN 1402 . . . . 195.00
Miss Fortune, HN 1897 . . . . 495.00
Miss Muffet, HN 1937 . . . . 285.00
Mr. Pickwick, HN 2099 . . . . 400.00
My Love, HN 2339 . . . . 375.00
My Pet, HN 2347 . . . . 160.00
New Bonnet, HN 1728 . . . . 875.00
Newsboy, HN 2244 . . . . 450.00
Nicola, HN 2839 . . . . 384.00
Officer of the Line, HN 2733 . . . . 195.00
Old Balloon Seller, HN 1315 . . . . 188.00
Old Mother Hubbard, HN 2314 . . 495.00
Olga, HN 2463 . . . . 270.00
Once Upon A Time, HN 2047 . . . . 375.00
Orange Vendor, HN 72 . . . . 900.00
Organ Grinder, HN 2173 . . . . 700.00
Pantalettes, M15 . . . . 450.00
Parson's Daughter, HN 564 . . . . . 475.00
Patchwork Quilt, HN 1948 . . . . . . 270.00
Paula, HN 2906 . . . . 160.00

Pearly Boy, HN 2035 . . . . 100.00
Pearly Girl, HN 2036 . . . . 100.00
Peggy, HN 2038 . . . . 95.00
Philippa Hainault, HN 2008 . . . . . 625.00
Polly Peachum, M21 . . . . 450.00
Prized Possessions, HN 2942 . . . . 500.00
Punch and Judy Man, HN 2765 . . . 310.00
Rita, HN 1448 . . . . 1,095.00
River Boy, HN 2128 . . . . 195.00
Rose, HN 1369 . . . . 70.00
Rosebud, HN 1983 . . . . 450.00
Rowena, HN 2077 . . . . 525.00
Royal Governor's Cook, HN 2233 . 475.00
Sailor's Holiday, HN 2442 . . . . 335.00
Shy Anne, HN 65 . . . . 3250.00
Spring Morning, HN 1922 . . . . 350.00
Stitch in Time, HN 2352 . . . . 150.00
Summer's Day, HN 2181 . . . . 375.00
Sweet & Twenty, HN 1298 . . . . . . 225.00
Sweet Lavender, HN 1373 . . . . . . 800.00
Taking Things Easy, HN 2677 . . . . 145.00
The Gaffer, HN 2053 . . . . 275.00
The Mask Seller, HN 2103 . . . . . . 240.00
Tinkerbelle, HN 1677 . . . . 100.00
Tootles, HN 1680 . . . . 115.00
Treasure Island, HN 2243 . . . . . . 135.00
Uncle Ned, HN 2094 . . . . 420.00
Upon Her Cheeks She Wept, HN 59, (A)
    . . . . 4,030.00
Veronica, HN 1517 . . . . 350.00
Wee Willie Winkle, HN 2050 . . . . . 300.00
Wigmaker, HN 2239 . . . . 175.00

Jar, Cov, 7" h, Chang, curdled crackle white, red, and yellow flambe glazes, poppy pod knob, "painted Royal Doulton, Chang, Noke" mark, reglued knob, (A) 1,500.00

Loving Cup, 7 3/4" h, The Village Blacksmith
. . . . 950.00

Plaque, 9 1/2" h x 7 1/2" w, oval, "Babes in Woods," 2 little girls and pixie, blue shades
. . . . 1,500.00

Plate

6 7/8" d, "Little Tom Tucker, Sang for his supper," "Royal Doulton, England, Copyright Nursery Rhymes and imp Colingwood, England" mark, (A)
. . . . 40.00

9 1/2" d

George Washington portrait, garland border, blue transfer 125.00

Poppy ware, Art Nouveau style blue, green, and yellow poppies, white ground, set of 6 . . . . 275.00

Series Ware

Bowl, 9" l x 7 3/4" w, "Bill Sykes," sgd "Noke" 150.00

Charger, 13" d, "Under the Greenwood Tree-Friar Tuck Makes Merry" . . 275.00

Jug, Square

Old Curiosity Shop, D5584 . . . . 275.00

Plate, 6 1/8" d, Series Ware, "Coaching Days," $55.

Pickwick Papers, D5756. . . . . 325.00

Pitcher, 6" h, "Shakespeare-Wolsey"
. . . . 165.00

Plate

9 1/4" d

"Old English Inns-Roger Solemel
Cobbler" 85.00

"Professionals"

"The Mayor" 75.00

"The Squire" 65.00

10" d

"A Widow and Her Friends"

"A Message From the Outside
World" 100.00

"She Finds That Exercise Does
Not Improve Her Spirits"
. . . . 100.00

"Old English Inns-The Leather Bottle" 90.00

"Old English Scenes-Roger Solemel Cobbler" 80.00

10 1/2" d

"Doctor Johnson-Dr. Johnson at the
Cheshire Cheese" 75.00

"Early Motoring-Bloody Money",
landscape border 150.00

"The Artful Dodger," D5175 110.00

"The Bayeux Tapestry-Landing of
Pevensey" 60.00

"The Mayor-In A Man's World,"
D6283 . . . . 75.00

Platter, 13 1/2" d, An Old Jarvey . . . 88.00

Teapot

6 1/2" h, Old Salt, D6818 . . . . . 225.00

7" h, Old Charley, D6017 . . . .1,475.00

Tea Service, pot, 8" h, pot, 6" h, creamer,
4" h, sugar bowl, 6" l, 12 cups and saucers, demitasse, "Reynard the Fox" pattern. 900.00

Vase, 4 1/2" h, Fagin, sgd "Noke" . . 95.00

Toby Jugs

Best is Not Good Enough, #6107
. . . . 325.00

Cliff Cornell, brown suit, green, black, and
blue tie. 300.00

Jester, D6910 . . . . 100.00

Jolly Toby, #6109 . . . . 70.00

Old Charlie, #6069 . . . . 155.00

The Standing Man, large, blue coat, brown
vest, brown salt glazed body, somber
face, #8572, (A) 345.00

Winston Churchill

Large, D6171. . . . . 125.00

Medium, D6172. . . . . 75.00

Small, D6175 . . . . 40.00

Vase

3 3/4" h, 5" l, pillow shape, "Babes in
Woods," girl with crying baby, blue
shades, gold rim. 600.00

5 1/2" h, "Babes in Woods," girl picking
flowers. 695.00

6 1/2" h, bulbous shape, Sung, cobalt, fire
red, and amber blotches, (A) . . 425.00

6 3/4" h

Cylinder shape, spread base, rolled
rim, "Babes in Woods," woman shel-
tering child from snowstorm, blue
shades. 665.00

Spherical, Chang, lime green, gold,
crackled white, and red volcanic
glazes on dk red ground, "black
Noke, Chang, Royal Doulton, England, HN" mark, (A). 2,000.00

7" h, ovoid shape, Flambe, silhouette of
desert landscape, crimson red ground,
"stamped ROYAL DOULTON, FLAMBE,
MADE IN ENGLAND" mark, (A) 225.00

8" h, sq vert sq shape, "Titanium" ware, HP
seagulls and waves, c1921 . . . 895.00

9" h, "Babes in Woods," girls with witch
. . . . 1,050.00

9 1/2" h, bulbous base, cylinder neck,
flambe, blue, green, and yellow veined
and mottled glazes, (A) 172.00

10 1/2" h

Baluster shape, Sung, red and cobalt
streaked lustered flambe glaze,
"ROYAL DOULTON/MADE IN EN-
GLAND/ NOKE/ FM/SUNG" mark,
(A) 600.00

Blue and green stylized flowers, mottled brown ground, green base,
#BB7 5828. . . . . 275.00

11 1/4" h

Flared rim, red and blue flambe gloss
glaze, (A). 325.00

Tapered cylinder shape, Sung, mottled
blue and red glazes, sgd "Noke,"
(A) 402.00

13" h, bulbous shape, flared rim, Sung,
black outlined Arabian street scene,
ruby red glaze, "stamped Royal Doul-

ton/Made in England/Flambe/Moorish"
mark, (A) 1,100.00

DRESDEN

Germany
1694 to Present

History: Two men, working for Augustus II
Elector of Saxony, rediscovered the technique to make hard paste porcelain of the
oriental type. Count Tschimhaus, who began his research in 1694, was joined by Johann Bottger, an alchemist, in 1701. At first
they produced a red stoneware. By 1709,
Bottger was producing white porcelain.
Tschimhaus did not live to enjoy their success, having died in 1708. The king established the Royal Saxon Porcelain Factory in
Dresden in 1710 and then moved it to Meissen one year later.

During the 18th century, Americans and
English used the name "Dresden china" for
the porcelain ware produced at Meissen.
This has led to much confusion. Dresden,
the capitol of Saxony, was better known in
18th century Europe than the city of Meissen, 15 miles away. In addition, Meissen
products were sold in Dresden, Hence,
Dresden became a generic term for all porcelains manufactured and decorated in the
city of Dresden and its surrounding environs, including Meissen.

In the mid-19th century, about 30 factories were operating in the city of Dresden
producing and decorating porcelains in the
style of Meissen wares. Marks were adopted which were similar to the crossed
swords of the original Meissen factory.
Many simply faked the Meissen mark.

Helena Wolfson and her successors imitated AR Meissen porcelain between 1843
and approximately 1949. Her firm had a
large staff of painters trained to imitate the
18th century porcelain. Wolfson also purchased "white" china blanks from the Meissen factory and had them decorated by her
own staff of painters and gilders. After
much litigation, Wolfson was forced to
abandon the AR mark. About 1880 the firm
adopted a mark using the word "Dresden"
with the letter "D" surmounted by a crown.

Meyers and Son was the greatest rival of
Wolfson in the production of imitation Meissen porcelains. They used the crossed

swords with an "M" to mark their examples. Franziska Hirsch, another copiest, used a mark similar to that of Samson, the French potter, on her Meissen and Vienna imitations made between 1894 and 1930.

The porcelain factory of Carl Thieme of Potschappel produced rococo imitations of Meissen pieces from 1872 until 1972 often marketing them as Meissen 18th century figures. They also produced household, table, and decorative porcelains, knick knacks, souvenirs, and gift articles, all decorated in the Meissen and Vienna styles.

A "Dresden style" came into being when four decorators, Richard Klemm, Donath and Co., Oswald Lorenz, and Adolph Hamann, all registered the same mark in 1883. The mark was a crown with "Dresden" underneath in blue. Later this group altered their marks. Eight other decorators then used the "Dresden" and the crown mark.

Donath and Co. produced porcelain in the Meissen and Vienna styles from 1872 until 1916. The company merged with Richard Klemm's decorating workshop for three years. In 1918, the firm became the Dresden Art Department of C.M. Hutschenreuther, continuing in that relationship until 1945. Adolph Hamann, another member of the "Dresden style" group, operated a porcelain decorating workshop from 1866 until 1949. It was acquired by Heinrich Gerstmann in 1933 and continued with its earlier name.

Franz Junkersdorf, A. Lamm, Henfel and Co., Anton Richter, Max Robra, Wilhelm Koch, and others had decorating workshops from the last quarter of the 19th century and extending into the 20th century. All of these firms imitated Meissen porcelains.

Museums: Bayerishes National Museum, Munich, Germany; Kunstgewebe Museum, Berlin, Germany; Museum fur Kunst und Gewerbe, Hamburg, Germany; Staatliche Porzellansammlung, Dresden, Germany.

Additional listings: See Hutschenreuther.

Basket, 14 1/2" l, gilt outlined overhead handle with applied pink roses and green leaves at terminals, ivory ground, gilt outlined rim 45.00

Bowl
9 1/4" d, 4 red roses and buds on stems, gold outlined reticulated swirl border 35.00
11 3/8" H-H, purple, yellow, and orange Meissen style flowers in center with scattered sprays, vert fluted body, relief molded flowerheads at twist handle terminals, pink and gold outlined border 145.00

Cache Pot, 8" h, painted multicolored floral bouquets on sides, molded handles, figural bouquet of multicolored flowers at top, late 19th C, pr 1,650.00

Cake Stand, 4 3/4" h x 12" d, ring of red roses and green leaves, cobalt cavetto, gold trimmed open lattice work with 3 panels of multicolored flowers, Schumann 395.00
Candelabra, 16 1/2" h, 4 arm, figural classic female holding stem, multicolored applied flowerheads on arms, chips, pr 1,650.00
Candlestick, 4 1/2" h, urn form socket, spread ft, pierced latticework and painted floral sprays, set of 4, (A) 540.00
Celery Tray, 11 1/2" l, magenta, purple, and yellow carnations and green leaves in center, molded border with gold sponging . . . 49.00
Charger, 11 1/2" d, scattered pastel floral sprigs, gold outlined reticulated border 325.00
Creamer, 4 5/8" h, bulbous base, cylinder top, vert pleating, HP yellow, orange, pink, blue, green, and red floral design, gold stenciled rim and handle, "Dresden, Germany" mark, (A). 55.00
Cup and Saucer
Flared shape, HP yellow, pink, blue, purple, and green floral design, gold swag design on scalloped rim, Richard Klemm. 25.00
Quatrefoil shape, HP Watteau scenes and floral sprays, reticulated border on saucer, wishbone handle, c1890 . . 345.00
Cup, Cov, 2 handles, multicolored painted hunting scenes, Pottschappel, (A). . . . 75.00
Dish, 6 3/4" l, branch handle, leaf shaped, painted multicolored Meissen style flowers in center, gold hanging pendant rim 95.00
Dish, Cov, 12" H-H, cov with alternating panels of HP courting scenes on white ground, florals on cobalt ground, leaf shaped handles, dbl twist knob, Richard Klemm 450.00
Figure
5" h x 7 1/2" l, 3 females with musical instruments, pink and white lace dresses with applied flowers 475.00
5 1/8" h, boy feeding geese, blond hair, blue jacket, pink pants, applied greens in basket, gold trimmed base . . 145.00
5 3/8" h, young boy in lt blue jacket, flowered vest, red striped pants, feeding yellow and gray geese, gold trim, Carl Thieme 135.00
7 1/4" h, "The Senses," modeled as crowned maidens in classical dress holding bird, lute, flower basket or dog at base, polychromed, rococo scrolled base, "blue X'd swords" mark, set of 5, (A). 1,610.00
7 1/2" h x 7 1/2" w, peasants harvesting grapes with lg basket, polychrome 265.00
8" h
9 1/2" l, young boy, 3 young girls holding hands dancing in circle, polychromed outfits, scroll molded base with painted and applied flowers 950.00
10" l, young brown haired boy in brown short pants, holding black and white

dogs by gray leashes, green and brown rocky base 750.00
9 1/8" h, seated period man holding bagpipes, seated maiden holding flowers, applied flowers on oval base, polychrome and gilt, "Dresden" mark, chips, (A) 220.00
11" h, 2 brown haired cherubs in purple or green sashes hanging onto brown and white goat's beard, figural multicolored fruit garland across goat's back 1,200.00
Jar, Cov, 5" h, figure of seated ballerina in yellow bodice, lace skirt with applied flowers on cov, white ground 125.00
Luncheon Service, 6 plates, 8 3/8" d, 6 plates, 5 3/4" d, 6 cups and saucers, HP purple, red, yellow, green, and blue florals in center with sm bouquets on border, gold swag design below gold accented scalloped rim, Richard Klemm, (A) 850.00
Plaque, 9" d, comic scene of black chef and cook standing in field, multicolored, shaped rim 225.00
Plate
8 3/4" d, HP floral spray in center, reticulated border with oval reserves of HP florals, scalloped rim, Carl Thieme, pr, (A) 125.00
9 3/8" d, 2 fan shaped panels of 18th C couple, 2 fan shaped panels of pink fretted diamond designs, gilt scroll cavetto, pierced border, shaped rim, "blue X'd swords" mark, late 19th C, set of 3 . . . . 450.00
Powder Box, 3 3/4" l x 2 1/4" h, ftd, cartouche of Fragonard scene of couple in grass, lt blue-green ground, gilt trim, raised gold border 65.00

Plate, 7 1/4" d, magenta and blue flower border, orange and raised gilt in center, (A) $50.

Sweetmeat Dish, 9 1/4" w, 2 scroll molded recesses with painted flowers, scrolling center handle, gilt accents, (A) 230.00

Teapot, 6" h, globular shape, applied florals and leaves surrounding figural landscape and floral panels, Carl Thieme, (A) . . . 402.00

Urn, Cov, 23" h, oval gilt cartouche of HP scene of 2 classic women sewing in garden, cobalt body with gilt scrolling accents, circ stepped base, 2 sm curved handles on shoulder, crown type knob, damages, (A) . 385.00

Vase, 9 1/2" h, ovoid shape, sq socle, ram handles, painted multicolored baskets of roses under swags of laurel, gilt accents, pr, (A) 400.00

Vase, Cov

   10" h, ovoid shape, printed and painted panels of courting couples on body and cov in gilt scrolled cartouches, blue ground panels with painted flower sprays, pr, (A) 695.00

   28 1/2" h, baluster shape, painted vignettes of amorous couples in park in flower encrusted surround, encrusted flowers on body, trailing fruiting vine on ft, figural mythological figural handles, domed cov with figural mythological figure and encrusted flowers, "blue T over anchor" mark, late 19th C, pr, (A) 2,990.00

   42" h, with stand, campana shape, painted allegorical scene on center and base, applied multicolored flowers, figural Cupids seated on shoulder, base, and cov, flower encrusted twist handles, painted crest on cov with crown, Pottschappel, pr, (A) 18,400.00

ENGLAND-GENERAL

Porcelain
1700 to Present

History: Before the 1740s, porcelains available in England were of Chinese or Japanese origin and were imported by the British East India Company. Many early English pottery manufacturers tried to duplicate oriental porcelains and the continental porcelains of Meissen and Sevres, but achieved only limited success.

The earliest English porcelains date about 1745 and were made at the Chelsea factory. This porcelain was the soft paste type. By the mid-18th century, production of soft paste porcelain was well established at Bow and Chelsea. Other factories, including Bristol, Longton Hall, Derby, Worcester, Liverpool, and Lowestoft soon followed. The English factories were private enterprises, not subsidized by royal families or princely households as were those on the Continent.

Soft paste was fragile. Hot liquids could crack it. Sometimes it collapsed or lost its shape in the kiln. Efforts were mounted to find a material that was more stable in the kiln and durable. The Bow factory tried adding ash of calcined bones. Bristol and Worcester incorporated a soapstone paste to their mix to strengthen their porcelains.

Many credit William Cookworthy of Plymouth with the rediscovery of the Chinese method of hard paste porcelain manufacture in England about 1768. He made hard paste type porcelain at Plymouth for only two years, 1768-70. In 1771, he moved to Bristol.

Pieces from the Plymouth pottery have an oriental influence. Some under-the-glaze blue designs are enhanced with over-the-glaze enamels. Figurines and animal and bird groups also were made. The second Josiah Spode of Stoke developed bone china by adding bone ash to the ingredients of hard paste porcelain. This "bone" china led to the development of cream colored earthenware. Based on the hard paste rediscovery and Spode's bone china, England became a major supplier to the world wide market.

Pottery
17th Century to Present

History: Early pottery wares in England included stoneware, Delftware, slipware, and salt glaze ware. Potters such as Thomas Toft, John Dwight, and the Elers were among the principal manufacturers.

During the early 17th century, Staffordshire became the center of the pottery industry due to an abundant supply of coal, availability of clays and adequate transportation to the marketplace. Astbury, Whieldon, and the Woods experimented with all forms of earthenwares from figure groups with colored glazes to numerous types of vessels and dishes. Earthenware production dominated the first half of the eighteenth century.

As the newly perfected cream colored earthenwares introduced by Josiah Wedgwood in the 1760s came to the forefront, Staffordshire salt glazed wares started to go out of fashion. Numerous Staffordshire makers such as the Turners, Elijah Mayer, Palmer and Neale, Wilson of Hanley, Leeds, William Adams of Tunstall, and Josiah Spode of Stoke copied Wedgwood's cream colored earthenwares. They also imitated Wedgwood's black basalt, jasper, and cane colored stoneware. Spode introduced the manufacture of blue printed earthenwares.

During the 1800s, lusterwares became popular with the Staffordshire potters. New techniques in the early 19th century included overglaze transfer printing and ironstone china. Underglaze blue printing was developed in the first half of the 19th century.

Figures, depicting all sorts of people and animals, were made during the 1800s by John Walton, Ralph Salt, and Obadiah Sherratt. During the reign of Queen Victoria, earthenware cottage mantelpiece figures were decorated in enamels and some gilding. Underglaze blue was the most important color used. Sampson Smith was the principal manufacturer. Pot lids were another 19th century product with decorations in polychrome underglaze.

Other pottery firms making utilitarian and decorative wares during the 19th century included H.& R. Daniels, Miles Mason, W. Ridgway & Co., Cauldon Place Works, John Davenport, Job Meigh, Lakin & Poole, Mintons, and Doulton of Lambeth.

Since the late 1800s, the studio potter had become important in England. This movement was a reaction against the emphasis on mass produced pieces. The studio potter usually threw his own wares with the glazing and decorating done either by himself or under his supervision. The first of the studio potters was William de Morgan and the Martin Brothers. Bernard Leach of the St. Ives Pottery made stoneware influenced by early Chinese and Japanese wares. The studio potters used many tradiional methods of manufacture such as tin glaze, salt glaze, slipware, agate ware, and sgraffito work.

Patent Office Registration Marks: From 1842 until 1883, many manufacturers' wares were marked with the "diamond mark" which was an indication that the design or form of the piece was registered with the British Patent Office and protected against piracy for three years. The mark could be applied by either printing, impressing, or applying a molded piece of clay. Pottery and porcelains were in Class IV. In the diamond the numbers or letters in each corner were keyed. A ceramic marks book is necessary to decipher the mark and discover the date the design was registered with the Patent office. After 1884 the diamond mark was replaced by a registry number.

References: Cyril G.E. Bunt, *British Potters & Pottery Today*, F. Lewis Publishers, 1956; J.P. Cushion, *English China Collecting for Amateurs*, Frederick Muller, 1967; B. Watney, *English Blue & White Porcelain, Rev. Ed.* Faber & Faber, 1973.

Museums: British Museum, London, England; City Museum & Art Gallery, Stoke-on-Trent, England; Cranbrook Academy of Art Museum, Bloomfield Hills, MI; Gardiner Museum of Ceramic Art, Toronto, Canada; Norwich Castle Museum, Norwich, England; Victoria & Albert Museum, London, England.

Additional Listings: Adams, Beswick, Bisque, Bow, Bristol, Carlton Ware, Caughley, Cauldon, Chelsea, Clews, Coalport, Copeland-Spode, Creamware, Crown & Royal Crown Derby, Davenport, Delft, De Morgan, Derby, Doulton, Flow Blue, Ironstone, Jackfield, Leeds, Liverpool, Longton Hall, Lowestoft, Lusterware, Majolica, Martin Brothers, Mason, Meakin, Meigh, Minton, Mocha Ware, Moorcroft, New Hall, Pot Lids, Pratt, Ridgway, Rockingham, Royal Worcester, Salt Glaze, Slipware, Spode, Staffordshire, Stoneware, Swansea, Wedgwood, Whieldon Ware, Willow Ware, Enoch Wood, Ralph Wood, Worcester.

Ale Mug, 4 1/2" h, earthenware, baluster shape, loop handle, unglazed, c300 AD
. . . . 750.00

Bough Pot, Demi-Lune Shape

8" w, pierced cov, painted bouquets of purple, blue, and yellow flowers and green leaves reserved in gilt line cartouche on yellow ground, lower band of flutes painted with red and blue flower sprays, c1820, chips and cracks, pr, (A) .6,900.00

8 3/4" w, 3 everted bough holes on cov, painted bouquet on black ground in gilt lined and scrolling vine rect cartouche on front, single painted flower in oval gilt carouche on sides in fluted pilasters, gilt gadroons on base, c1820, (A)
. . . . .2,300.00

Bowl

2 1/2" h x 5 3/4" d, ftd, band of brown, blue, and orange enameled hearts and "BRANDY" on int, band of green, orange, and brown enameled florals on ext, hairline, (A) 220.00

8" d, mottled blue glaze, Pilkington, c1913
. . . . 245.00

12" d, painted birds perched on branches with flower bouquets on int and ext, wide claret red band on ext rim with gilt scrolls, rocaille, and monogram, crack, c1840, (A) 863.00

Butter Tub, Cov, 6" H-H, with undertray, molded basketweave body, green glaze, reclining cow knob, 18th C, (A) 920.00

Cottage Ware, Butter Dish, 4 3/4" h, 6 3/4" l, HP brown and yellow, "Keele St. Pottery Company" mark, $100.

Cane Handle, 3 1/8" l, porcelain, cylinder shape with bulbous head, painted flower sprays in gilt molded cartouches on body, head painted with city view of bridge and buildings, c1830, (A) 340.00

Chamber Pot, Cov, 11" d x 11 1/2" h, painted multicolored bouquet of garden flowers, lg raised gilt trimmed leaves, scattered sm bouquets, white ground, gold flower form knob, gold outlined leaf handle 2,500.00

Coffee Pot, 9" h, lighthouse shape, glazed redware with engine turned chevron pattern, domed cov, spout, and handle with molded basketry, c1765 . . . . 4,500.00

Compote, 7 1/4" h x 14" H-H, multicolored scene of man riding horse on stone bridge, mountains in bkd, green borders with molded gilt trim, molded white handles with gilt accents. 435.00

Cottage Ware

Biscuit Jar, 7 1/2" h, wicker handle, Price Brothers, c1920s. 95.00

Butter Dish, Cov, 4 3/4" h 100.00

Cracker Box, Cov, 4 3/8" h, Price Brothers
. . . . 90.00

Creamer

3 1/2" h, green cottage, orange roof, Royal Winton 115.00

4 1/2" h, Kensington, England. . 35.00

Cup and Saucer, Price Brothers. . . 35.00

Jam Jar, 2 1/2" h, Kensington, England
. . . . 35.00

Milk Pitcher, 7 1/4" h, "Price Brothers, England" mark 75.00

Mug

3 1/4" h, Price Brothers, England, set of 6. . . . . 195.00

5" h, Price Brothers, England . . 48.00

Pitcher, 10" h 65.00

Teapot

6 1/2" h, Kensington, England
. . . . 45.00

8 1/2" h, Kensington, England
. . . . 65.00

Tea Set, pot, 6 3/4" h, creamer, cov sugar bowl, "imp Devon Cobb" mark
. . . . 195.00

Cup and Saucer, bone china, purple thistles from green pods, brown thorny stems, green leaves on int and ext, gold lined rims
. . . . 16.00

Cup and Saucer, Miniature, painted pink roses, gilt lined rims, (A) 75.00

Dessert Plate, 9" d, center HP multicolored design of 3 roses in leaves and ferns, dk pink border with gilt jewel designs, c1850s, set of 10 . . . . 1,000.00

Dessert Service, Part

Two compotes, 10 1/4" H-H, ftd, 3 dishes, 11 5/8" H-H, oval, 12 plates, 9 1/8" d, painted looses bouquets in centers, gray shaped borders with gilt accented relief molded flowerheads and beading, c1850, (A) 3,450.00

Two compotes, 10 1/2" H-H, ftd, 8 plates, 9" d, centers painted with different bo-

tanicals, green border of band of stylized ivy leaves and geometrics, gilt shaped rims, c1860 . . . . 2,150.00

Two dessert stands, 5" h, 8 plates, 9" d, each painted with named different scenes of lochs, castles, and bridges, Loch Lomond, Kilchurn Castle, Point Aberglaslyn, and Chepstow Castle, turquoise borders with gilt trim . . . 950.00

Dinner Service, Part, platter, 13" l, oval, 9 plates, 10 3/8" d, 9 plates, 8" d, 8 plates, 6 1/2" d, cream jug, 5" h, 8 cups and saucers, border of blue entwined ribbon and gilt leafy stems, "Tiffany & Co., New York" marks, (A). . .529.00

Figure

10" h, Chelsea style, shepherd playing pipe, recumbent dog at feet, companion with flowers in apron, lamb at feet, flowered bocage bkd, turquoise and gilt rocaille molded scroll base, "iron red anchor" mark, pr, (A) 1,955.00

13 1/4" h, seated cat, gilt and enameled florals on blue blanket on back, green glass eyes, c1900, leg repair, (A)
. . . . 920.00

Hot Water Jug, Cov, 4 5/8" h, with underplate, solid buff, brown, and gray agate clay, loop handle, button knob, c1770, cracks, (A)
. . . . 345.00

Inkstand, 4 1/4" h, circ, solid buff and brown agate clay, pierced for 3 quills, stripes on sides, c1770, (A) 288.00

Jug, 7 1/2" h, bust of Wellington, "imp Wellington/Died Sept. 14 1852" on front, Rockingham glaze 295.00

Mug, 2 7/8" h, earthenware, bell shape, loop handle, cream glaze with brown dots and streaks, spread ft, c1760 . . . . 1,250.00

Planter, 8 1/4" h, modeled in relief as baby's head in bonnet and collar, bronze glaze, Bretby, (A) 195.00

Plate

8 1/2" d, painted bouquet in border of molded foliage and 6 sm floral reserves, gilt dentil scalloped rim, Nantgarw, c1820, (A) 633.00

8 1/2" sq, oct, porcelain, red, blue, pink, green, and gilt gaudy floral design with fencing, (A) 110.00

9" d, printed and painted panels of birds and flowers reserved on blue scale ground, pierced border, pr, (A)
. . . . 262.00

9 1/4" d, "Dragon in Compartments" pattern, gilt and polychrome enamel, early 19th C, hairlines, set of 4, (A)
. . . . 2,990.00

9 1/2" d

Oct, earthenware, ochre edged brown dotted crossing bands, molded diamond shapes on border, cream ground, c1760, repair to corner, pr 3,600.00

Porcelain, center stylized foliate reserve, cobalt border with gilt acanthus design, scrolling gilt accented foliate rim, 19th C, (A) 125.00

9 7/8" d, multicolored birds and birdbath design, raised enameled and gilt floral border, Nantgarw, early 19th C, (A) 3,737.00

Platter

11" l, 13" l, 16 3/8" l, 17 1/8" l, "Verona" pattern, blue-green transfer, "Verona, F. & Sons" mark, nested set of 4. . . . 375.00

21" l, oval, "Kyota" pattern, maroon, yellow, and black, Bates, Gildea, & Walker 675.00

Serving Dish, 9 3/4" H-H, rect, porcelain, HP water landscape in center, gilded branch border. 225.00

Soup Plate, 8" d, HP standing oriental figure, gilt border of stylized anthemion and scroll, c1805, pr, (A) 1,035.00

Spill Vase, 4 1/4" h, flared cylinder shape, painted sea shells in rect gilt reserve flanked by gilt seeding and foliage, gilt flower on reverse, lt blue ground, c1815, pr, (A) 1,380.00

Tea Canister, 5 1/4" h, rect, earthenware, cream molded cauliflower florets at top, curved modeled green leaf base, c1765, replacement cov. 1,650.00

Teapot

3 1/2" h, squat shape, black glazed redware with applied scrolling fruiting vine, crabstock handle and spout, bird knob, 3 paw feet, c1770, restored cov, (A) 460.00

3 5/8" h, unglazed redware, spherical shape, applied birds, flower sprays, and scrolls, straight spout, ear handle, c1760 .1,950.00

4 1/8" h, earthenware, cream colored molded cauliflower florets on top, modeled curved green leaves on base, cauliflower spout, floret knob, scrolled handle with split terminal, c1765 . . . . .5,200.00

6 3/4" h, oval shape, multicolored enameled scene of oriental figures in court-

yard setting, c1800, chips, (A) 288.00

Tea Service, pot, 4 3/4" h, milk jug, sugar basin, 6 cups and saucers, 6 side plates, "Streamline," painted green, brown, and blue overlapping leaf design, celadon ground, Poole Pottery, (A) 215.00

Tea Service, Part, pot, 7 3/4" h, cream jug, 4 3/4" h, cov sugar bowl, 6 7/8" h, waste bowl, 5 1/8" d, 10 cups and saucers, 10 cake plates, 6 1/4" d, 2 plate, 10 3/8" sq, porcelain, centers with gilt wreath around rosette, borders of band of pink cabbage roses and gilt leaves, gilt dentil rims, late 19th C, (A). 1,150.00

Vase

4 1/2" h, squat body, pinched neck, flared rim, "Sunstone," crystalline copper and amber flambe glazes, Pilkington, pr, (A) 500.00

5 1/2" h, bottle shape, reserves of birds and butterflies on claret red ground, pr, (A) 100.00

6" h, ovoid shape with rolled rim, lustered turquoise and mustard flambe glazes, "stamped RUSKIN, ENGLAND, 1924," (A) 250.00

6 5/16" h, ewer shape, HP green, blue, red, and yellow polychromes, gold accents, textured ground, brown sq handle with gold accents, scalloped rim, imp English registry mark, (A) 45.00

6 1/2" h, crater shape, painted continuous landscape with ruins, gilt spray below painting, gilt foliate handles, gilt rim, gilt bands on ft, Nantgarw, c1820, (A) 460.00

7" h, globular shape, 3 cylinder necks, enameled blue and brown flowers and stems, mottled gray and blue ground, "black painted Elton" mark, (A) 200.00

8" h, baluster shape, narrow neck, blue-green drip glaze 195.00

8 1/2" h, baluster shape, frothy lt green and lt blue flambe glazes, "imp P. Royal Lancastrian, Made in England, 2462" mark, Pilkington, (A) 125.00

8 5/8" h, shouldered cylinder shape, tan leaping gazelle, blue and green stylized leaves, yellow and blue bands on rim, pattern TZ, Poole Pottery, (A) . . 620.00

10 1/2" h, dumbbell shape, center band of yellow daisies, mustard ground, dk green body, pr 130.00

11" h, flat base, slender neck, sm flared rim, dk red drip glaze, Pilkington, c1913 . . . . 295.00

22" h, dumbbell shape, applied figural dragon on side, Persian blue glaze, Bermantoff 750.00

Waste Bowl, 4 1/2" d, dk red and brown solid agate, flared lip, applied ft rim, c1750 . . . . .2,650.00

Teapot and Stand, 9 1/2" h, "Meashan Ware," "A Present To A Friend," multicolored enameled flowers, brown ground, c1870, $695.

FAIRINGS AND TRINKET BOXES

Locket, Elbogen, Germany Possneck, East Germany c1840 -1900s

Staffordshire, England

History: Fairings, common during the Victorian era, were small porcelain groups of gaily colored human and animal china figures designed to catch the eye with their humor and sentimentality. One figural, captioned, "The last in bed to put out the light," shows a man and woman bumping heads as they jump into bed while a lighted candle stands on a table nearby. "Five o'clock tea" features humanized cats at a tea party. Fairings were made to be given away as prizes or purchased at English fairs.

Fairing themes include courtship and marriage scenes, events in the lives of the people, war, politics and the law, children at work and play, and animals behaving like people. Most fairings had inscriptions written in English. Often these were naive or intended to be risqué.

Colors mainly were shades of pink and blue with the inscriptions in black or gold. Early examples were usually 3 1/2 inches to 4 1/2 inches high with plain, undecorated bases. Gilt was used sparingly. After 1890, the colors became more garish.

Fairings were made of white heavy paste. Most had numbers incised or impressed beneath their bases, though the earliest and best examples had no numbers.

Although fairings were associated with English fairs, they were actually made by German makers Springer and Oppenheimer of Locket, Elbogen, Germany which is now part of the Czech Republic, and Conta and Boehme of Possneck, Germany.

Trinket boxes usually had a utilitarian purpose. They were designed to hold pins, rings, watches, or other trinkets after being taken home from the fairs. Early boxes usually were not marked, but by the late 1860s there were incised or scratched numbers.

The marks on boxes made by Conta and Boehme and Springer and Company were similar. Conta and Boehme had an arm holding a sword in an enclosed shield, while Springer had a bent elbow in a shield crest with a crown. Conta and Boehme porcelain boxes had identifying numbers on the base or underside of the cover. Most of the boxes were exported to England and America.

Box styles included bureaus or dressers, figurals, baskets, furniture and others. Some had fairing type subjects in a variety of sizes. Many boxes had mirror frames.

Boxes could also be a combination of bisque and glazed finishes. Conta and Boehme made more than four hundred different designs for boxes. Fairing boxes were captioned on the front base or side in English. When fairs became less popular, boxes were sold in gift shops and other stores.

Some boxes were also match boxes with a striker on the underside of the cover. Otherwise the design is the same as a trinket box. Beginning in the 20th century, production and interest declined and nearly ceased during World War I. The factory finally closed in 1931.

Small English Staffordshire porcelain trinket boxes were sold at fairs and seaside resorts. They ranged in size from about 3-5 inches in length and usually were several inches tall. The lids were decorative and featured subjects similar to the fairings from Germany. Many had animals or children on them. Most were white and had gilt trim.

References: Margaret Anderson, *Victorian Fairings & Their Values,* Lyle Publications, 1975; W.S. Bristowe, *Victorian China Fairings,* A & C Black, 1964; Nancy Neely, *Victorian Fairing Boxes,* <u>Antique Trader Weekly,</u> March 9, 1994; Janice and Richard Vogel, *Victorian Trinket Boxes,* PoBneck Publishing Co.1996.

Museums: Strong Museum, Rochester, NY.

Reproduction Alert: There are an increasing amount of fairings being reproduced in England and sold as original Conta and Boehme pieces. These examples have captions printed in black caps and have numbers on the solid bottom from the 1800 series. They also have a crude copy of the mark. Reproductions are also coming from Germany and Japan.

Collecting Hints: Boxes in mint condition with the original gold and paint command the highest prices. Make sure the top and bottom actually match each other.

Fairings

3" h, "Returning at one o'clock in the Morning," polychromed, Conta & Boehme 95.00

3 1/8" h x 2 3/4" w, "Emancipation," woman in lt blue skirt, black blouse, seated in chair, smoking cigar, rd table with mug and ashtray with 3 cigars, sq base with gold accents, repair to mug handle, (A) 120.00

3 1/4" h x 3 1/4" l, "The Last in bed to put out The light," white night clothes, black top on bed, florals on table and orange candle
. . . . 295.00

3 3/8" h, "Returning At One O'Clock In The Morning," woman spanking man over chair, canopy bed in bkd, polychrome. 265.00

3 1/2" h, 3 1/2" l, "*Who is coming?*" man in lt blue jacket, pink striped pants, woman in gold dotted white gown, blond hair, gold trimmed base, c1850, $295.

3 1/2" h

3 1/2" l, "Alone at Last," yellow wall, white and lt blue bed, man in black pants, woman in white dress with blue and rust trim, 2 men in black suits, woman in pink dress with white apron behind wall
. . . . 475.00

"Returning at one o'clock in the Morning," woman in white dress with green and rust dots, man in blue coat and striped pants, tented bed, gilt trim 179.00

3 3/4" h

3 1/2" l

"Looking Down Upon His Luck," man in white outfit, lilac jacket, woman in white outfit, lilac apron, blue blanket, gilt trim, blue trimmed base, "Made in Germany" mark 250.00

"Sarah's young man," woman in bkd in pink jacket, young girl in floral dress, standing man in lt blue coat, tan pants, man under table in purple coat, gilt trim, "Made in Germany" mark, c1880-90 . . . . 275.00

"The Child's Prayer," child seated in bed praying, gilt accented nightshirt, red, purple, and green sprigs on blanket, blue pillow, doll at side, green dress over end of bed, chips, (A) 55.00

3 7/8" h x 3 7/16" w, "A doubtful case," shoemaker examining woman's shoe at workbench, purple, green, blue, and red polychromes, gold accents, rect base, (A). 75.00

4" h x 3 3/8" d, "The Welsh Tea Party," 3 ladies seated at table, black hats, rose red dresses, 2 tree trunks in bkd 110.00

4 1/8" h x 3 1/2" l, "Wedding Night," woman in yellow skirt, man in rust vest, lt blue robe, black clock, gilt trim, c1850 . . . . 295.00

4 1/4" h x 3 1/2" l, "Kiss Me Quick," man in lt blue coat, woman in white dress with orange

and dk yellow flowers, rust top, white and gilt trimmed bed and base, c1850 . . . . . . 295.00

4 1/2" h, "Five O'Clock Tea," 3 cats on top, 2 below, white and gray, gilt trim, Germany
. . . . 185.00

Trinket Boxes

1 7/8" h, draped Victorian table with teapot, creamer, cup and saucer, white ground, gold trim, Conta & Boehme, c1850-70 . . . . 125.00

2 1/8" h x 2 1/4" l, modeled hooded christening cradle with sleeping child, openwork hood with applied star rosettes, arched pierced rim around base, gold accents, (A) 60.00

2 3/8" h, boy seated in black boat, yellow hat, holding oar 110.00

2 1/2" h

Pearlized brown wicker coach base with pink luster accented wheels, cov with baby in pink luster dress lying in coach under blue and yellow pearlized blanket, doll and cat at side, Staffordshire, (A) 160.00

Victorian green table top with draping and teapot, creamer, sugar bowl, 2 cups and saucers, Conta & Boehme, c1840-60 . . . . 165.00

2 3/4" h, 3 spot, boy with basket of flowers reclining on grass, green, red, brown, and lavender, Conta & Boehme, c1860-90
. . . . 250.00

3" h

4 1/4" l, basket shaped base, cov with lying child and black and white cat and orange ribbon, purple blanket, green bed with orange molded ribbon, gold edging, Staffordshire, (A) 170.00

4" h, 3 1/2" l, green and blue coverlet, red and blue clothes, brown posted bed, "*Shall We Sleep First Or How*" on base, $225.

Bureau shape with mirror, drum and horn on top, white with gold trim 90.00

3 1/8" h x 2 3/4" l, figural guardian angel over child in bed on cov, floral rosettes, pink and green polychrome, gold accents, molded ivy and beading on base 125.00

3 1/4" h, bureau with brown coffee grinder, coffee pot, and funnel on top with blue-lined mirror frame, gold trim, c1850-90 . . . . 125.00

3 3/4" h

Ladies hand holding box cov, white ground with gold accents, Conta & Boehme, c1850-70. . . . . 275.00

Lady in blue and orange jacket paddling boat on legged dresser with mirror frame, gilt and blue trim, Conta & Boehme, c1860-70. . . . . 225.00

Woman seated on hill, holding child, 3 sm kittens, leaf and acorn molded rect base, brown, green, black, orange, and purple, c1860-80 . . . . 350.00

4" h

Commode with concave shell design, pilasters, and molded lion heads accented in blue and gold, cov with gilt accented oval mirror, cov with seated young girl in pink dress with green bow, holding blue ball, doll at feet, (A) 160.00

Commode with mirror frame, blue and gold pitcher, washbowl, and glass on top, c1860-70 . . . . 200.00

"The Child's Prayer," blond haired child sitting in bed with doll and red pillow, Staffordshire 125.00

Three spot, man in red jacket, blue breeches, lady in cobalt and pink gown sitting at table playing checkers, lady standing behind, Conta & Boehme, c1860-90 . . . . 250.00

4 1/8" h, standing figure of Napoleon and horse on cov, molded branch, leaf and basketweave base, white with gold accents 175.00

4 1/4" h

2 3/4" l, figural ftd washstand, cov with pitcher and bowl, mirror frame, dk blue and gold accents, mirror missing, (A) 75.00

Bisque eagle on top, white glazed box with gilt trim, c1850-60 . . . . 125.00

Little girl in green top, flowered skirt, yellow hat, seated on mirrored bureau top, flanked by vases of flowers, green swags and orange trim on base 145.00

4 3/8" h x 3" l, figural fireplace, lid with rooster and sm boy, oval scrolled mirror frame, box forms fireplace hearth, dk blue, orange, green, lt blue, and gold accents, mirror missing, (A). 160.00

4 3/4" h

Bisque Ulysses Grant standing next to horse, glazed rect box, white with gold accents 288.00

Molded bureau base with green, gold, and orange accented shell and scrolls, rd gold accented mirror on cov with 2 girls sitting on edge in pink and gold or lt blue and gold, Conta & Boehme, (A) 95.00

4 7/8" h

Figural child and dog seated on bureau top, blue, red, and gold, white body 295.00

Open purple clam shell with child's head peeking out on bureau top, gold accents 185.00

5" h x 2 3/4" l, figural child in cradle with gold accented rosettes on cov, green, pink, and orange, molded ivy and beading on base, (A) 90.00

5 1/4" h, white figure of girl reclining on elbow against wine cask, holding grapes overhead, blue jasper sides with gilded grape clusters, unmkd 275.00

5 3/4" h, full figure, colonial lady in blue jacket and purple gown seated at piano, colonial man in blue jacket and orange breeches, gold trim, Conta & Boehme, c1860-80. . . . 375.00

5 7/8" h x 3 3/4" l, figural pump organ, keyboard, music book, and arched mirror on cov, base forms organ with 2 petals and rosettes, pink, blue, green, and brown polychrome accents, gold trim, (A) 70.00

6 5/8" h x 4 5/8" l, figural sideboard, mantel clock, 2 vases, and oval scrolled mirror on cov, sideboard base, lt green, and gold accents, (A) 65.00

FISCHER

Herend, Hungary c1839 to Present

MF
1880

History: Moritz Fischer established a porcelain manufactory at Herend, Hungary about 1839. His factory was noted for the high quality of its reproductions of Chinese porcelains and 18th century European porcelains from Meissen, Vienna, Capodimonte, and Sevres. Reticulated vases, ewers, and chimney ornaments also were made in very bright enamel colors, almost majolica-like in appearance. Oriental patterns such as famille rose, famille verte, and Imari decorations were imitated by Herend craftsmen. They employed no independent designers, only craftsmen. Every piece was hand painted.

When the Imperial Vienna factory closed in 1864, Fischer received the right to use the patterns and models selected by Emperor Franz Joseph for continued use. These old Vienna molds and patterns were marked with a beehive. Many wares were exported to the United States.

Fischer was raised to the nobility and used the name Farkashazi in 1865. Fischer was succeeded by his sons. The factory

Vase, 8 1/4" h, brown-red and gold accents, dk red ground, $1,250.

failed in 1874 and then underwent a series of changes in ownership.

New prosperity was achieved under Jeno Farkashazi, the grandson of Moritz. The factory was taken over by the state in 1948. The factory continues to produce hard paste porcelain dinnerware, vases, and figures similar to those of Meissen and Sevres.

Herend porcelain is still produced today. Although figures are very popular, Herend is most known for its tablewares. Patterns are never discontinued, so it is always possible to order replacements.

Museum: Victoria & Albert Museum, London, England.

Bottle, 28 1/2" h, canteen shape, 4 side holders for rope, 2 feet, Iznik design, dk red, blue, and med blue enameled flowerheads, gold leaves, border of gold, blue, red, and green flowers and stems, blue enameled stones and red flowerheads, pink and blue enameled stones on sides 7,500.00

Jug, 10 3/4" h, oriental style multicolored enameled flowers, butterflies, and fans, gold outlined trim. 198.00

Pitcher

9 3/4" h, blue and pink panels with gilt accented raised pointed seashells, flowered border top and base, "blue Fischer Budapest" mark 225.00

12" h, pink painted flowers, cream ground, pierced cabochons, gold dots on neck, figural mask handle, "blue J. Fischer, Budapest" mark 650.00

Planter

9 1/2" H-H, boat shape, int with matte gold outlined magenta and turquoise tile pattern on tan ground, raised turquoise and magenta dots, matte outlined raised leaves, ext with raised designs and cobalt, green, and yellow flowers and dots, reticulated band curved at

Vase, 12 7/8" h, med blue leaves, gold reticulation, pale blue ground, $375.

each end, lt green and brown rolled rim, "Fischer Budapest" mark 395.00

19" H-H, painted green and brown flowerheads, cream ground, green and brown reticulated raised diamonds around base, "blue J. Fischer, Budapest" mark 1,650.00

Teapot, 5" h, globular shape, cartouche of yellow rose and green leaves on white ground, brown and red mottled body, floral knob 925.00

Vase

10 1/4" h, bulbous base, slightly flared straight neck, heavy enameled yellow sunflower with green seeded center, blue enameled leaves on mauve, cream ground, lt purple dots, raised yellow flowerheads on neck with pink dots, turquoise striped serrated rim and middle 295.00

13" h, moon flask shape, 2 loop handles on shoulder to rim, Iznik design of red flowerheads and green vines on cream ground, gold brocade ground on sides, base, and handles, "Fischer J. Budapest" mark, c1882 . . . . 850.00

14 1/2" h, lg reticulated gold oriental design, tapestry flowers with raised beaded bkd, dbl handled with raised blue beading, mkd 650.00

15 3/8" h, raised gold cartouche with yellow flowers on magenta ground, raised gold stems with raised red, orange, and

blue flowerheads, cream ground, brown vert loops around neck with orange enameled jewels, triangular base 350.00

FLOW BLUE

**Staffordshire, England
Early Victorian 1835-1850s**

Mid Victorian 1860s-1870s

Late Victorian 1880s, 1890s, and the early 1900s

History: "Flow" or "Flowing" Blue was developed for commercial consumption in the 1820s by Josiah Wedgwood. Other well-known makers included W.T. Copeland, Samuel Alcock, and William Davenport. Flow Blue was being marketed in many countries including France, Germany, Holland, and the U.S. The peak production period was from the mid-1800s to the early 1900s.

The Flow Blue process occurred when a transfer printed design, originally in cobalt oxide, received volitizing agents such as lime of chloride or ammonia causing the pattern to "bleed" during the glaze firing stage. The cobalt when first applied was brown in color and changed to a deep blue during the firing. The degree of flowing varied considerably with some designs barely discernible while others showed a slight hazing of the pattern.

The earliest patterns were Oriental in style and named in most cases by the manufacturer. These names often are found incorporated with the maker's mark. Scenics and florals were popular during the Victorian period. Some Art Nouveau designs were produced. Most designs were applied by transfers. In some cases, hand painted designs were done.

Though some of the designs were registered, it was not unusual to find the same name used by two different companies for two entirely different designs. Manufacturers also had a habit of changing design names. More than 1,500 patterns were

manufactured during the peak years of Flow Blue production.

Early Flow Blue was characterized by a dense coloration. Later pieces had a softer look to them. By the mid-Victorian era, colors, as well as gold embellishments, were added to enhance the designs.

Many early examples were made of stoneware, but porcelain and semi-porcelain also served as bodies for the Flow Blue patterns. By the later half of the 19th century, semi-porcelain was the material of choice. The designs of this period usually were sharper and cleaner. The body design was more elaborate.

Back stamps usually provided the pattern name and initials or name of the maker. Often the location of the factory was included. Transfer marks outnumber all other types. Marks with a pattern name date after 1810.

References: Sylvia Dugger Blake, *Flow Blue,* Wallace-Homestead**,** 1971; Robert Copeland, *Spode's Willow Pattern and Other Designs After the Chinese*, Rizzoli, 1980; Mary Gaston**,** *The Collector's Encyclopedia of Flow Blue China*, Collector Books, 1983, values updated 1996; Mary Gaston, *Collector's Encyclopedia of Flow Blue, 2nd Series,* Collector Books, 1994, values updated 1996; Veneita Mason, *Popular Patterns of Flow Blue China with Prices,* Wallace-Homestead, 1982**;** Jeffrey B. Snyder, *A Pocket Guide to Flow Blue,* Schiffer Publishing, Ltd. 1995; Jeffrey B. Snyder, *Flow Blue, A Collectors Guide to Pattern, History & Values,* Schiffer Publishing, Ltd. 1992; Jeffrey B. Snyder, *Historic Flow Blue,* Schiffer Publishing, Ltd. 1994; Petra Williams, *Flow Blue China, An Aid to Identifications,* Fountain House East, 1971; Petra Williams, *Flow Blue China 11,* Fountain House East, 1973; Petra Williams, *Blue Flow China & Mulberry Ware, Rev. Ed.* Fountain House East, 1981.

Collectors' Clubs: Flow Blue International Collectors' Club, Inc. P.O. Box 205, Rockford, IL 61105; $30 annual dues, bi-monthly newsletter, *Blueberry Notes.*

Museums: Margaret Woodbury Strong Museum, Rochester, NY.

Reproduction Alert: New Flow Blue has been manufactured by Blakeney Pottery Limited in Stoke-on-Trent since 1968. Objects are termed "Victorian Reproductions" and are made with large blue roses in many forms. Evidence shows that some of these items have been sold as old.

A reproduction barber bowl is marked "Made in China" with a paper label. Pitcher and bowl sets are also being reproduced. Some pieces have an enormous backstamp with "Victoria Ware" and "Ironstone."

Collecting Hints: The center for collecting Flow Blue is in the United States. Even though the vast majority of Flow Blue was made in England, the English do not attach much antique value to Flow Blue since it was mass produced, transfer decorated, and inexpensive. Since most was exported to the U.S. during the 19th century, it is not prevalent in the English market.

Miniatures and children's dishes are scarce in Flow Blue since not many examples were made. Art or decorative items are harder to find than ordinary table and utilitarian wares.

"Abbey" pattern
  Grill Plate, 1 1/4" d, Petrus Regout, Maastricht 70.00
  Jam Jar, 5" h, slotted lid, George Jones 275.00
  Plate
    7 1/2" d, George Jones 30.00
    9" d 50.00
  Platter, 11 1/2" l 150.00
  Soup Plate, 9 1/4" d, Petrus Regout 50.00
  Syrup Pitcher, 6" h, George Jones 195.00
  Teapot, 4 3/4" h, recessed lid, George Jones 375.00
"Agra" pattern
  Bone Dish, "F. Winkle & Co." mark, set of 8 . . . . 395.00
"Alaska" pattern
  Plate
    8" d 50.00
    10" d, "W.H. Grindley" mark 75.00
"Albany" pattern
  Butter Dish, Cov 295.00
  Butter Pat 28.00
  Cup and Saucer 65.00
  Plate
    4" d 23.00
    5" d 23.00
    10" d 80.00
  Platter
    12" l 135.00
    14" l 165.00
  Vegetable Bowl, Cov, 10" l, oval, "Johnson Brothers" mark 345.00
"Alton" pattern
  Milk Jug, 6 3/4" h, pewter lid, "Keeling & Co." mark 495.00
"Amour" pattern
  Platter, 15" l x 11 1/4" w 575.00
"Amoy" pattern
  Dessert Dish, 5 1/8" d, paneled rim, Davenport 150.00
  Plate
    9" d 115.00
    10 1/2" d, Davenport 125.00
  Platter, 20" l 1,395.00
  Soup Plate, 10 1/2", Davenport . . . 250.00
  Sugar Bowl, Cov, 8 1/2" h 650.00
  Teapot, 10" h, paneled 995.00

"Anemone" pattern
  Platter, 22" l x 17" w 895.00
"Arabesque" pattern
  Plate, 11" d 165.00
  Platter, 15 3/4" l x 12 1/4" w, (A) . . 213.00
  Sauce Dish, 5" d, "T.J. & J. Mayer" mark 145.00
  Teapot, "T.J. & J. Mayer" mark . . 1,450.00
"Arabic" pattern
  Plate, 8" d, "W.H. Grindley" mark 15.00
"Arcadia" pattern
  Cup and Saucer 85.00
  Plate, 10" d 69.00
  Platter, 16 1/2" l x 12" w, oval . . . 195.00
"Argyle" pattern
  Cup and Saucer, "W.H. Grindley" mark 80.00
  Fruit Dish, "W.H. Grindley" mark . . . 40.00
  Plate
    7 1/2" d 60.00
    9" d, "W.H. Grindley" mark 80.00
    10" d 110.00
  Platter
    13" l 165.00
    19 1/4" l 495.00
  Vegetable Bowl
    10" l, oval, "W.H. Grindley" mark 100.00
    10 1/2" d, "W.H. Grindley" mark 130.00
"Astoria" pattern
  Bowl, 9 1/2" d, "N.W.P." mark 150.00
  Cup and Saucer, "N.W.P." mark . . 145.00
"Athol" pattern
  Plate, 9" d 85.00
"Aynsley" pattern
  Plate, 9" d, gold trim 55.00
"Azalea" pattern
  Biscuit Jar, 9" h, gold trimmed handles and finial 225.00
  Dresser Tray, 12 1/2" l x 9 1/2" w, Bourne & Leigh, c1897 . . . . 175.00
"Bamboo" pattern
  Platter, 16 3/4" l x 13 7/8" w, Alcock, c1845 . . . . 595.00
"Beatrice" pattern
  Bowl, 6" d, Cauldon 25.00
"Beaufort" pattern
  Platter, 14" l x 10" w 175.00
"Beauties of China" pattern
  Plate, 7 1/4" d 110.00
"Beauty Roses" pattern
  Plate, 8" d 12.00
"Belport" pattern
  Platter, 17" l, Maddock 195.00
"Brooklyn" pattern
  Butter Pat 35.00
  Platter, 13" l x 9" w 300.00
"Brunswick" pattern
  Cup and Saucer 80.00
  Plate, 9" d, Wood and Sons 75.00
"Brush Stroke" pattern

Creamer, "Daisy Seven Petals" design 385.00
  Cup and Saucer, Handleless, "Snow Flake" design 175.00
  Plate, 10" d, "Grapes and Leaves" design 175.00
"Burmese" pattern
  Plate, 8 1/2" d 50.00
"California" pattern
  Plate, 10" d, "P.W. & Co." mark . . . 90.00
"Cambridge" pattern
  Plate, 10" d, Meakin 80.00
"Campion" pattern
  Chamber Pot, Cov, 8 1/2" h x 11 1/2" w 485.00
"Canton" pattern
  Cream Pitcher, 5" h, Maddock, c1850 . . . . 495.00
  Cup and Saucer, Handleless, Maddock 150.00
  Sugar Bowl, 8" h, oct, tab handles, spots on int, Maddock 550.00
"Carlton" pattern
  Platter, 14 1/4" l x 13 1/2" w, "Samuel Alcock" mark 595.00
  Soup Plate, 10 1/4" d 175.00
"Cashmere" pattern
  Cup and Saucer, Handleless 250.00
  Platter
    13" l 695.00
    16" l 850.00
    19" l x 15 1/2" w 1,850.00
"Chapoo" pattern
  Milk Pitcher, 6 3/4" h, bulbous shape, John Wedgewood, (A) 892.00
  Plate
    6 1/4" d, John Wedgewood . . . 145.00
    10 1/2" d, John Wedgewood . . 245.00
  Platter, 15 3/4" l x 12 3/4" w, John Wedgewood 625.00
  Soup Plate, 10 3/4"d, John Wedgewood, c1850, (A) 175.00
  Teapot, 9" h, primary form, (A) . . . 460.00
  Waste Bowl, 6 1/4" d, John Wedgewood, (A) 575.00
"Chen-Si" pattern
  Cup and Saucer, Handleless, Meir 250.00
  Platter, 10 1/2" l x 8" w, Meir 425.00
  Waste Bowl, 14 panels, 5 1/4" d, Meir, hairline and chips 345.00
"Chiswick" pattern
  Tureen, 13" w x 7" h, Ridgway 325.00
"Chusan" pattern
  Cup and Saucer, paneled, Clementson, c1840 . . . . 495.00
  Milk Pitcher, 8" h 550.00
  Muffin Dish, Cov, 10 1/4" H-H, 4 1/2" h, twisted twig knob 750.00
  Pitcher, 9" h, polychromed 175.00
  Plate
    8 1/4" d, "P.W. & Co." mark . . . 60.00
    10 1/2" d, scalloped, Morley, c1850 . . . . 235.00

Platter, 13 1/3" l x 10 1/8" w, Holdcroft
. . . . 395.00
Soup Plate, 10 3/8" d, Morley. 75.00
Teapot, 9 1/2" h, 6 sided Gothic, Clementson, c1840 . . . . 995.00

"Claremont" pattern
Gravy Boat. 140.00
Plate, 10" d. 85.00

"Clarence" pattern
Plate, 10" d, "W.H. Grindley" mark. . 85.00

"Clayton" pattern
Butter Pat. 20.00
Cup and Saucer. 80.00
Platter, 14 1/2" l 145.00

"Cleopatra" pattern
Teapot, 9" h, acorn knob, "E. Walley" mark
. . . . .1,400.00

"Clifton" pattern
Bowl, 10" d, gold trim, "W.H. Grindley" mark. 135.00
Vegetable Bowl, Cov, 12" H-H x 7" h, "W.H. Grindley" mark. 320.00

"Coburg" pattern
Plate, 10 1/2" d. 125.00
Platter, 17 3/4" l x 13 3/4" w, fluted, scalloped corners, crazing, Edwards
. . . . 895.00
Sugar Bowl, 7 1/2" h, 8 sided Gothic shape, restored, Edwards 400.00

"Colonial" pattern
Creamer. 50.00
Cup and Saucer. 65.00
Gravy Boat. 85.00
Plate, 8 7/8" d. 80.00
Platter, 14" l x 10" w 250.00
Sugar Bowl, Cov 50.00
Vegetable Bowl, Cov, 10" H-H x 7" h
. . . . 250.00

"Conway" pattern
Bowl
8 3/4" d, "N.W.P." mark. 125.00
9" d. 125.00
Cake Plate, 9 1/8" d, embossed border, scalloped rim, "Wood & Son" mark
. . . . 145.00
Plate
8" d 75.00
9" d 65.00
10" d, "N.W.P." mark. 75.00
Platter
10 1/2" l x 8" w 95.00
10 3/4" l x 8" w, oval, "N.W.P." mark
. . . . 150.00
Soup Plate, 9" d 80.00

"Dahlia" pattern
Vegetable Bowl, Cov, 10 1/4" d x 7" h, oct 850.00

"Daisy" pattern
Berry Bowl, 4 3/4" d, Burgess & Leigh
. . . . 35.00
Butter Dish, cov, 8" d, Burgess & Leigh
. . . . 275.00
Butter Pat, Burgess & Leigh 40.00
Cup and Saucer, Burgess & Leigh . 80.00

Plate, 10" d, Burgess & Leigh. . . . 110.00
Platter, 16" l x 11 3/4" w, oval, Burgess & Leigh. 260.00
Soup Bowl, 8 7/8" d, Burgess & Leigh
. . . . 55.00

"Delph" pattern
Bowl, 9" d, "Wood & Son" mark . . . 69.00
Cereal Bowl, 6 3/8" d 30.00
Platter, 18 1/2" l x 15 1/4" w, well and tree, crazing, Minton 650.00
Vegetable Bowl, 10 3/8" d, scalloped emb edges, Bourne & Leigh, c1892. 175.00

"Delft" pattern
Soup Tureen, 13" l x 8 1/2" w x 7 1/2" h, "Brownsfield Guild Pottery Society" mark 475.00

"Doreen" pattern
Chamber Pot, Cov, 9" d 260.00

"Dorothy" pattern
Bowl, 9 1/2" d 95.00
Platter, 15" l 125.00

"Dresden" pattern
Pancake Dish, 8 1/2" d, 4 vents . . 125.00
Plate, 9 3/8" d 50.00
Platter, 11 1/2" l x 8 1/6" w, "Saxony" mark
. . . . 95.00

"Duchess" pattern
Cup and Saucer, Demitasse. 28.00
Plate, 9 1/2" d, "W.H. Grindley" mark .70.00

"Dudley" pattern
Milk Pitcher, 6 1/2" h, pewter lid, Bishop & Stonier, c1891. . . . . 525.00
Platter, 19" l 225.00

"Dunbarton" pattern
Butter Pat 25.00

"Dundee" pattern
Cereal Bowl, 6 1/2" d, Ridgway . . . 45.00
Plate, 8" d, Ridgway 48.00
Platter, 12 3/4" l x 8 1/2" w. 100.00

"Eclipse" pattern
Butter Pat, "Johnson Brothers" mark
. . . . 50.00
Plate
6" d 42.00
10" d 85.00

"Fairy Villas" pattern
Bowl, 6 1/2" d 65.00
Butter Pat 50.00
Plate
8 3/4 d 65.00
10 1/2" d 135.00

"Fairy Villas II" pattern
Plate, 10 1/2" d 75.00

"Fandora" pattern
Plate, 10" d 80.00

"Fern" pattern
Soup Plate, 10 1/2" d, "W. ADAMS" mark
. . . . 125.00

"Florida" pattern
Berry Dish, 5" d 50.00
Egg Cup 140.00
Plate
7" d, "Johnson Brothers" mark . 52.00

8" d, "Johnson Brothers" mark . . 65.00
9" d, "Johnson Brothers" mark . . 80.00
Vegetable Bowl, Cov, 12" d, "Johnson Brothers" mark. 250.00

"Formosa" pattern
Cake Stand, 11 3/4" h x 3" h, hairline
. . . . 650.00
Plate, 9 3/4" d, Mayer. 85.00
Tea Set, lighthouse shape, 8 sides, pot, 8 1/2" h, creamer, cov sugar bowl, Mayer, (A) 920.00

"Gainsborough" pattern
Bowl, 9" d 95.00

"Geisha" pattern
Cake Set, master plate, 10 1/4" H-H, 4 plates, 6 3/4" d, scalloped rims, gold trim, "Ford & Sons" marks, c1893
. . . . 285.00
Pitcher, 4" h, Ford & Sons 275.00
Plate, 7" d, "Ford & Sons" mark . . . 40.00
Waste Bowl, 5 3/4" d, Ford & Sons
. . . . 160.00

"Geneva" pattern
Plate, 10" d, "N.W.P." mark 85.00

"Gironde" pattern
Cup and Saucer. 69.00
Plate, 8 3/4" d 65.00
Platter, 17 1/2" l 395.00

"Gothic" pattern
Platter, 18" l x 14" w 895.00
Vegetable Bowl, Cov, 9 1/4" d, oct, with pedestal, Furnival 950.00

"Granada" pattern
Gravy Boat, with undertray, Alcock
. . . . 175.00
Vegetable Bowl, 10 1/2" d 135.00

"Haarlem" pattern
Butter Pat 45.00

"Haddon" pattern
Cup and Saucer, "W.H. Grindley" mark
. . . . 90.00
Pitcher, 5" h, "W.H. Grindley" mark
. . . . 395.00
Plate, 10" d. 60.00
Vegetable Tureen, Cov, 10 1/2" l, oval, scalloped base, "W.H. Grindley" mark
. . . . 495.00

"Hamilton" pattern
Butter Pat. 45.00
Coffee Pot, 8" h, John Maddock . . 895.00
Cup and Saucer. 45.00
Gravy Boat, Maddock 95.00
Plate, 10" d. 80.00
Platter, 15" l x 10 1/2" w 225.00

"Hindustan" pattern
Cup and Saucer, Handleless, Maddock
. . . . 235.00
Plate, 10 3/4" d 225.00
Platter, 18" l x 14" w 850.00
Soup Plate, 10 3/4" d 185.00
Vegetable Bowl, 9 1/2" d 295.00

"Hizen" pattern
Plate, 10 1/4" d, Ashworth 85.00

Platter, 15 1/2" l, Ashworth 285.00

"Holland" pattern
  Platter
       10 1/2" l x 8" w, "Johnson Brothers"
        mark 75.00
       15 1/2" l 425.00
  Vegetable Bowl, 9" d, "Johnson Brothers"
    mark 125.00

"Honc" pattern
  Plate, 8 3/4" d, Petrus Regout 115.00

"Hong" pattern
  Platter, 15" l 495.00

"Hong Kong" pattern
  Cream Pitcher, 5 1/4" h 450.00
  Sugar Bowl 750.00
  Teapot, 8" h 850.00
  Vegetable Bowl, 8 1/2" l x 6 3/4" w, Meigh
    . . . . 395.00
  Vegetable Bowl, Cov, oct
    9 1/2" d 995.00
    10 1/2" d 1,000.00

"Indiana" pattern
  Platter, 16" l 475.00
  Soup Plate, 10 1/4" d 95.00

"Indian Jar" pattern
  Creamer, 5 1/2" h, Furnival 750.00
  Soup Plate, 10 1/2" d, 12 panel rim
    . . . . 250.00
  Vegetable Bowl, Cov, 10" d, oct, pedestal
    base 975.00

"Iris" pattern
  Creamer 85.00
  Platter, 116 1/2" l x 12" w 195.00
  Vegetable Bowl, 9 1/4" l 50.00

"Jenny Lind" pattern
  Bowl, 8" d 250.00

"Jewel" pattern
  Plate, 9" d 80.00

"Keele" pattern
  Butter Pat 45.00
  Vegetable Bowl, 8 1/8" l x 5 3/4" w, oval,
    scalloped edge, "W.H. Grindley" mark
    . . . . 175.00

"Kelmscott" pattern
  Platter, 18" l 225.00

"Kinworth" pattern
  Bowl, 5 1/2" d, "Johnson Bros." mark
    . . . . 19.00
  Plate, 6 1/4" d, "Johnson Bros." mark
    . . . . 21.00

"Kyber" pattern
  Bowl, 9" d, "ADAMS" mark 135.00
  Cup and Saucer, Handless, Meir, c1850
    . . . . 225.00
  Gravy Boat with undertray, "ADAMS" mark
    . . . . 250.00
  Plate
    6" d, "ADAMS" mark 75.00
    9" d, "ADAMS" 95.00
    10" d, "ADAMS" mark 110.00
  Platter, 10" l x 7 1/4" w 275.00
  Salad Bowl, 9 1/4" d, with undertray, oct
    .3,450.00

Soup Plate, 9" d, gold rim 90.00
Soup Tureen, with undertray, oct, 1 1/2"
  qt, ... 3,400.00
Teapot, 7 3/4" h, restored 950.00
Vegetable Bowl, 10 1/4" l x 7 3/4" w, rect
  with clipped corners 295.00

"Lahore" pattern
  Vegetable Dish, 10 1/2" d 95.00

"Lakewood" pattern
  Cereal Bowl, 6 1/2" d, "Wood & Son" mark
    . . . . 65.00

"Lancaster" pattern
  Bowl, 6 1/4" d, "Lancaster, New Wharf Pot-
    tery, England" mark, (A) 20.00
  Cup and Saucer, "N.W.P." mark . . . 65.00
  Gravy Boat, 3 7/8" h x 8 1/2" l, oval, scroll
    handles, "Lancaster, New Wharf Pot-
    tery, England" mark, (A) 60.00
  Plate, 9" d, "N.W.P." mark 60.00
  Platter, 12" l x 9" w 300.00
  Soup Plate
    8 3/4" d, "W.E. Corn" mark 65.00
    9 1/2" d 50.00

"Lawrence" pattern
  Platter, 16" l, scalloped edge 250.00

"Leicester" pattern
  Plate, 9" d 100.00

"Le Pavot" pattern
  Bone Dish, "W.H. Grindley" mark . . 75.00
  Platter, 16" l x 11" w 285.00
  Vegetable Bowl, 9" l, oval, "W.H. Grindley"
    mark 175.00

"Limoges" pattern
  Plate, 8" d, "Wood & Son" mark . . . 45.00

"Linda" pattern
  Butter Pat 55.00
  Plate, 8" d 40.00

"Lobelia" pattern
  Platter, 20" l, Phillips, c1834, hairline
    . . . . 350.00

"Lois" pattern
  Bowl, 10" d 95.00
  Plate, 9" d, New Wharf Pottery 80.00
  Soup Plate, 9" d, New Wharf Pottery
    . . . . 85.00

"Lonsdale" pattern
  Bowl, 5 1/4" d 45.00
  Cup and Saucer 75.00
  Plate, 8" d 65.00

"Lorne" pattern
  Plate
    7" d 55.00
    8 3/4" d, "W.H. Grindley" mark . . .75.00
    9 1/2" d 85.00
  Platter
    14" l x 10 1/2" w 135.00
    16" l 250.00
  Vegetable Dish
    9 1/4" l x 6 1/2" w, "W.H. Grindley"
    mark. 110.00
    10" l x 7" w 125.00

"Lorraine" pattern
  Butter Pat 55.00

Bowl, 5 3/4" l x 4 1/4" w 50.00

"Lotus" pattern
  Comport, 9" d x 4 3/4" h, Dimmock .595.00
  Platter, 14" l x 10 1/2" w 195.00

"Lucerne" pattern
  Butter Pat, "N.W.P." mark 35.00

"Lyndhurst" pattern
  Platter, 12" l x 8 3/4" w, oval "W.H.
    Grindley" mark 120.00

"Madras" pattern
  Cup and Saucer, Demitasse 125.00
  Gravy Boat 15.00
  Milk Pitcher 350.00
  Plate
    6 1/4" d 60.00
    8 1/2" d 65.00
    9 1/2" d 95.00
    10" d, "Royal Doulton" mark 95.00
  Platter
    17 1/4" l 795.00
    18" l x 14" w 350.00
  Soup Plate, 8 1/2" d 95.00
  Toothbrush Holder, 4 1/2" h, flared top
    . . . . 350.00

"Mandarin" pattern
  Platter, 18" l x 13 1/2" w, oval, gadrooned
    rim, Pountney, c1900 . . . . 295.00

"Manhattan" pattern
  Berry Bowl, Alcock 35.00
  Butter Dish, 8" d, self handles 375.00
  Butter Pat, Alcock 45.00
  Soup Plate, 9" d 50.00

"Manilla" pattern
  Pitcher
    5" h 550.00
    8" h 650.00
    12 3/4" h 1,200.00
  Plate
    6 3/4" d, "P.W. & Co." mark . . . 175.00
    7 3/4" d, "P.W. & Co." mark . . . 195.00
    8 1/2" d, dk blue transfer, "P.W. & Co."
    mark 120.00
    9 1/2" d, "P.W. & Co." mark . . . 145.00
    9 3/4" d, "P.W. & Co." mark . . . 195.00
  Platter
    12 3/4" l x 9 1/4" w, "P.W. & Co." mark
    . . . . 395.00
    15 3/4" l x 12" w, "P.W. & Co." mark
    . . . . 850.00
    20" l 1,095.00
  Teapot, 9 1/2" h, 8 sides 1,050.00
  Vegetable Bowl, 9" l x 6 3/4" w 285.00
  Waste Bowl, 5 7/8" d, "P.W. & Co." mark
    . . . . 550.00

"Marechal Niel" pattern
  Berry Bowl, 4 7/8" d, "W.H. Grindley"
    mark 45.00
  Butter Dish, Cov, 7 3/4" d, with drain, "W.H.
    Grindley" mark 375.00
  Butter Pat 55.00
  Cup and Saucer 95.00
  Plate
    7" d 35.00

8" d 55.00
8 7/8" d 50.00
Platter
12 1/2" l x 9" w, "W.H. Grindley" mark
. . . . 175.00
14 1/2" l x 10 1/2" w, "W.H. Grindley"
mark 150.00
Soup Plate, 8 7/8" d 50.00
Sugar Bowl, Cov, 6" h 235.00
Vegetable Bowl, 9 1/4" l, oval 125.00
Vegetable Bowl, Cov, 11 1/4" H-H, oval,
"W.H. Grindley" mark. 325.00
"Marie" pattern
Tureen, 10 3/4" H-H x 6 1/2" h 650.00
"Margot" pattern
Creamer, "W.H. Grindley" mark. . . 190.00
"Marlborough" pattern
Butter Pat 55.00
"Meissen" pattern
Cereal Bowl, 6" d 30.00
Plate, 8" d 45.00
"Melbourne" pattern
Creamer, 3 1/2" h, Grindley 295.00
Platter
14" l x 10" w 275.00
16" l x 11" w, gold trim 375.00
18" l x 12 3/4" w 425.00
Sugar Bowl, Cov, 4 1/2" h 295.00
Vegetable Bowl, 9" l, oval 125.00
"Melrose" pattern
Platter, 16 1/4" l x 12" w 395.00
Soup Plate, 10 1/4" d, Doulton. . . . 95.00
Vegetable Bowl, Cov, 11" H-H. . . . 225.00
"Monarch" pattern
Vegetable Bowl, Cov, 9 1/2" d, fluted
. . . . 425.00
"Mongolia" pattern
Berry Bowl 55.00
Cup and Saucer. 105.00
Plate
6 1/2" d 60.00
8" d 80.00
9" d 95.00
10" d 105.00
Platter, 14" l 320.00
"Montana" pattern
Bowl, 5" d 35.00
Plate, 10" d 55.00
"Montrose" pattern
Soup Plate, 10 1/4" d 110.00
"Muriel" pattern
Plate, 9" d 50.00
"Nankin" pattern
Pitcher, 4 1/8" h, bulbous shape, applied
handle, F. & R. Pratt. 395.00
Platter
10" l x 7 3/4" w, oval, Ashworth
. . . . 165.00
13 3/4" l x 11" w, oval, Ashworth
. . . . 325.00
15 1/2" l x 12 1/2" w 265.00
"Navy" pattern
Plate, 8" d. 80.00

"Neapolitan" pattern
Plate, 10" d, "Johnson Bros." mark
. . . . 49.00
"Ning Po" pattern
Dessert Dish, 5 1/4" d, paneled rim, Hall
. . . . 150.00
Teapot, 8 1/2" h, primary shape, Hall,
c1845, (A) 460.00
"Non Pariel" pattern
Berry Bowl, 5" d, "Burgess & Leigh" mark
. . . . 50.00
Bone Dish 75.00
Bowl, 8 3/4" d, "Burgess & Leigh" mark
. . . . 85.00
Cake Plate, 10" d 185.00
Creamer, 5" h 249.00
Plate
6" d 50.00
6 3/4" d 65.00
8 1/2" d 85.00
10" d 95.00
Platter
13 1/4" l x 11" w, Burgess & Leigh
. . . . 295.00
15 1/2" l x 12 3/4" w 395.00
Vegetable Bowl, Cov, 13" d 395.00
"Norfolk" pattern
Plate, 10" d 50.00
"Normandy" pattern
Plate, 10" d, Johnson Brothers . . . 100.00
Platter
13 1/2" l 165.00
14 1/4" l x 10 1/2" w, Johnson Brothers
. . . . 295.00
Soup Plate
8" d, "Johnson Brothers" mark . 85.00
8 1/2" d, "Johnson Brothers" . . . 88.00
Vegetable Bowl, 8 1/2" d, "Johnson Broth-
ers" mark. 135.00
"Orchid" pattern
Chocolate Pot, 10 1/2" h, "Maddock &
Sons" mark 235.00
"Oregon" pattern
Creamer, 5 3/4" h, pumpkin shape, 1845,
(A) 403.00
Milk Pitcher, 6 1/4" h, bulbous shape, May-
er, c1845, (A) 748.00
Plate
7 1/2" d, 14 sides. 68.00
9 1/2" d, "T.J. & J. Mayer" mark, set of
7, (A) 440.00
Platter, 17 3/4" l x 13 3/4" w, Mayer, c1845,
(A) 288.00
Relish Dish, 9" l, curled handle, Mayer
. . . . 215.00
Teapot, 8 1/2" h, primary single line shape,
Mayer 1150.00
Vegetable, 10 1/2" l, rect, Mayer. .575.00
Waste Bowl, 6 1/4" d, paneled, Mayer
. . . . 475.00
"Oriental" pattern
Berry Bowl
5" d 45.00
5 3/4" d 50.00

Comport, 12" d x 4" h, Alcock . . 1,250.00
Plate
6" d 20.00
7 3/4" d, Ridgway 60.00
9" d 25.00
9 3/4" d 30.00
Vegetable Bowl, Cov, 11" H-H, rect, scal-
loped, Ridgway 695.00
"Ormonde" pattern
Platter, 10 3/8" l x 8 1/4" w, Alfred Meakin,
c1891. . . . . 165.00
Vegetable Bowl, 9 3/4" l, oval, Alfred
Meakin, c1891 . . . . 165.00
"Osborne" pattern
Berry Bowl, 5 1/4" d, "W.H. Grindley" mark,
c1900. . . . . 35.00
Bowl, 8" l, Ridgway 54.00
Cup and Saucer, Demitasse 75.00
Plate
8" d 42.00
8 7/8" d, "W.H. Grindley" mark . . 55.00
9 3/4" d, Ridgway, c1905 . . . . . 50.00
Platter
14" l x 10" w 84.00
18 1/4" l x 13 3/8" w 500.00
Vegetable Bowl, 12" H-H, oval, "W.H.
Grindley" mark 140.00
"Oxford" pattern
Plate
8" d, Johnson Brothers, c1900 . . 70.00
9 3/4" d, Alfred Meakin 80.00
10 1/2" d, Burgess & Leigh. 65.00
Platter, 17 1/2" l x 13 1/2" w, Ford & Son,
c1900. . . . . 375.00
"Pagoda" pattern
Plate, 10 1/2" d, "S. & K. Co." mark . 98.00
"Panang" pattern
Cup and Saucer, Handleless, Ridgway
. . . . 245.00
"Paris" pattern
Plate
8" d 50.00
9" d 65.00
10" d 85.00
"Pekin" pattern
Bowl, 10" d, "Royal Staffordshire Burslem"
mark. 195.00
Chop Plate, 11 7/8" d, Albert Jones & Co
. . . . 250.00
Milk Pitcher, 7 3/4" h, tapered sides, Wood
& Sons, c1907 . . . . 375.00
Plate
8" d 80.00
9" d 75.00
10 1/4" d, Wilkinson, gold accents
. . . . 150.00
Platter, 15 1/2" l x 11 7/8" w, rect with cut
corners, Dimmock, c1845 . . . . 395.00
Vegetable Bowl, 9 1/2" d, Wilkinson
. . . . 225.00
"Peking" pattern
Pitcher, 5 3/8" h, primary shape, Podmore,
Walker & Co., c1850 . . . . 450.00

"Pelew" pattern
    Cup and Saucer, Handleless. 135.00
    Plate
        7 1/2" d, Challinor 100.00
        9 7/8" d 115.00
    Teapot, 10" h, lighthouse shape, Challinor, repaired lid, (A) 403.00
"Penang" pattern
    Cup and Saucer, Handleless, Ridgway
    . . . . 195.00
"Persian" pattern
    Platter, 16" l x 12" w 295.00
"Poppy" pattern
    Butter Dish, Cov, "W.H. Grindley" mark
    . . . . 200.00
    Creamer and Sugar Bowl 200.00
    Gravy Boat with undertray, "W.H. Grindley" mark 150.00
    Plate, 10" d, "W.H. Grindley" mark
    . . . . 55.00
"Raleigh" pattern
    Bowl, 6" d, gold rim, "Semi Porcelain, England, Burgess & Leigh, Middleport Pottery, Burslem, Raleigh, Rd. 393237" mark 25.00
    Plate
        6 1/8" d, gold rim, "Semi Porcelain, England, Burgess & Leigh, Middleport Pottery, Burslem Raleigh Rd 393237" mark 25.00
        8 1/2" d 60.00
        9 7/8" d, gold rim, "Semi Porcelain, England, Burgess & Leigh, Middleport Pottery, Burslem, Raleigh, Rd. 393237" mark 45.00
"Regal" pattern
    Bowl, 10" d, "Bishop & Stonier" mark
    . . . . 85.00
"Regent" pattern
    Soup Plate, 8 3/4" d 85.00
"Rhine" pattern
    Platter, 21 1/2" l x 17" w, well and tree, Dimmock 1,100.00
"Richmond" pattern
    Butter Dish, Cov, 4" h x 8 1/2" H-H . . 150.00
    Plate, 9 1/4" d, "Johnson Bros." . . . 135.00
"Rose" pattern
    Bone Dish, set of 4 . . . . 160.00
    Plate, 8" d 80.00
"Royal Blue" pattern
    Bone Dish 95.00
"Royston" pattern
    Creamer 40.00
    Gravy Boat with undertray 45.00
    Plate, 10" d, 12 sides, Johnson Brothers
    . . . . 65.00
    Platter, 14" l 50.00
"Sabroan" pattern
    Dessert Dish, scalloped 125.00
    Milk Pitcher 795.00
    Platter, 20" l 700.00

"Savoy" pattern
    Plate, 8" d, Johnson Brothers, c1900
    . . . . 40.00
    Soup Bowl, 7 1/2" d, Johnson Brothers, c1900 . . . . 45.00
    Vegetable Bowl, 9" l, oval, Johnson Brothers, c1900 . . . . 85.00
"Scinde" pattern
    Berry Dish, 5 1/8" d, J. & G. Meakin
    . . . . 95.00
    Bowl, 9 3/4" d, T. Walker, c1847 . . 350.00
    Butter Dish, with drain 1,100.00
    Coffeepot, 11 1/2" h, T. Mayer, (A)
    . . . . 1,150.00
    Cup and Saucer 95.00
    Plate
        9" d 125.00
        10 1/2" d 170.00
    Platter
        13" l x 10 1/2" w 285.00
        14" l 395.00
        15" l x 12 1/2" w, J. & G. Meakin
        . . . . 750.00
        16" l 495.00
        20" l 1,150.00
    Sauce Dish, 5" d 60.00
    Soup Tureen, 14" h x 15 1/2" H-H, with undertray 6,250.00
    Teapot, 9 1/2" h, primary shape, Alcock, c1840, (A) 575.00
    Waste Bowl 500.00
"Seaweed" pattern
    Cup and Saucer, Handleless 175.00
"Sevres" pattern
    Bowl, 9" d, "Wood & Son" mark . . . 45.00
    Butter Pat, "Wood & Son" mark . . . 20.00
"Shanghai" pattern
    Cake Plate, 9 3/4" d 175.00
    Compote, 9 7/8" d x 4 3/4" h, "W.H. Grindley" mark 350.00
    Plate
        6" d 38.00
        7 1/2" d 125.00
        9 7/8" d, "W.H. Grindley" mark
        . . . . 110.00
    Platter
        16" l x 12" w, "W.H. Grindley" mark, c1891, crazing on reverse
        . . . . 225.00
        17 1/2" l 395.00
    Teapot 495.00
    Waste Bowl, 5 1/2" d 250.00
"Shapoo" pattern
    Cup and Saucer, Handleless, 12 panels
    . . . . 225.00
    Pitcher, 6" h 280.00
    Plate
        6 3/8" d 110.00
        8 1/2" d 125.00
        9 1/4" d 130.00
    Platter, 12 1/2" l x 9 1/2" w, T. & R. Boote
    . . . . 395.00
    Teapot, 9 5/8" h 975.00

Plate, 7 1/4" d, "Spinach" pattern, "Maastricht" mark, (A) $15.

"Siam" pattern
    Soup Plate, 10 1/2" d, Clementson . . 65.00
"Sobraon" pattern
    Berry Bowl, 5 1/8" d, paneled 85.00
    Soup Plate, 10 1/2" d 150.00
    Sugar Bowl, Cov, 7" h, pumpkin shape
    . . . . 695.00
    Teapot, 8 1/4" h, pumpkin shape, 8 panels
    . . . . 1,250.00
"Spinach" pattern
    Cup and Saucer 85.00
"Splendid" pattern
    Cup and Saucer 65.00
"Stanley" pattern
    Bone Dish, "Johnson Bros." mark . . 60.00
    Butter Dish, Cov, "Johnson Bros." mark
    . . . . 350.00
    Butter Pat, "Johnson Bro." Mark . . . 35.00
    Creamer, "Johnson Bros." mark . . 150.00
    Cup and Saucer 75.00
    Gravy Boat with undertray, "Johnson Bros." mark 140.00
    Plate
        7" d, "Johnson Bros." mark 55.00
        8" d, "Johnson Bros." mark 65.00
        8 3/4" d, "Johnson Bros." mark . . 65.00
    Platter, 12 1/2" l, "Johnson Bros." mark
    . . . . 185.00
    Sauce Dish, 5" d, "Johnson Bros." Mark
    . . . . 40.00
    Soup Bowl, 7 1/2" d, "Johnson Bros." mark
    . . . . 55.00
    Sugar Bowl, Cov, "Johnson Bros." mark .
    . . . . 150.00
    Vegetable Bowl, Oval
        8" l, "Johnson Bros." mark 95.00
        9" l, "Johnson Bros." mark 95.00
        10" l, ftd 125.00
"St. Louis" pattern
    Bone Dish, 6 1/4" l, Johnson Brothers, c1900 . . . . 60.00
    Bowl, 8 1/2" d, gold trim 110.00
"Temple" pattern
    Dessert Dish, 5 1/2" d, paneled rim, Podmore Walker, c1850 . . . . 175.00

Plate, 8 5/8" d. 165.00

Platter, 14" l x 10 5/8" w, Podmore, Walker, c1850. 650.00

"Thistle" pattern

Plate, 9" d. 55.00

"Ting Hae" pattern

Cup and Saucer, Holdcroft 195.00

"Tivoli" pattern

Soup Tureen, 13 1/2" l x 8 1/2" h, "R.H. & S." mark 225.00

"Togo" pattern

Butter Pat, set of 4 . . . . 96.00

Plate, 9" d. 75.00

"Tokio" pattern

Creamer and Sugar Bowl, creamer, 4" h, sugar bowl, 5" d, Ford & Sons . . 235.00

Plate, 6 3/4" d. 29.00

"Tonquin" pattern

Bowl, 10" d. 175.00

Plate

8 5/8" d, Heath 135.00

9 1/4" d, Heath 120.00

Soup Plate, 9 1/2" d, Heath 225.00

Vegetable Bowl, Cov, 11" H-H, J. Meir & Son. 595.00

"Touraine" pattern

Bacon Platter, 10 1/2" l, Alcock . . . 125.00

Bone Dish, 6" l 135.00

Butter Dish, Cov. 285.00

Coffee Cup and Saucer. 145.00

Creamer, 4 1/2" h. 145.00

Cup and Saucer. 80.00

Gravy Boat, 8 1/2" l, "Touraine, Semi-Porcelain, Henry Alcock & Co., Ltd, England, Rd No. 329815" mark, (A) 130.00

Plate

6 1/2" d 70.00

7 3/4" d 75.00

8 3/4" d 60.00

9" d 80.00

Platter

12 1/2" l x 8 1/2" w, Stanley. . . . 245.00

14 3/4" l x 10 1/4" w, oval, "Touraine, Semi-Porcelain, Henry Alcock & Co. Ltd, England, Rd. No. 329815" mark, (A). 180.00

Sauce Dish, 4 7/8" d, "Touraine, Semi-Porcelain, Henry Alcock & Co., Ltd, England, Rd. No. 329815" mark, set of 6, (A) 100.00

Soup Plate

9" d 85.00

10" d 160.00

Sugar Bowl, Cov, 6 1/4" h 525.00

Teapot, 7 1/2" h, restored lid 1,050.00

Vegetable Bowl

9 1/4" H-H 165.00

9 3/4" l, Stanley. 125.00

9 7/8" d, Henry Alcock, (A) 85.00

Vegetable Bowl, Cov

10 1/2" l, oval 395.00

11 3/4" l, oval, "Touraine, Semi-Porcelain, Henry Alcock & Co., Ltd, En-

gland, Rd. No. 329815" mark, (A) 270.00

Waste Bowl, 5 7/8" d, "Touraine England" mark 275.00

"Trent" pattern

Cup and Saucer, "N.W.P." mark. . . 65.00

"Tyrolean" pattern

Charger, 12 1/2" d, Ridgway. 175.00

Unknown Patterns

Biscuit Barrel, 5 1/2" h, 4 panels of flow blue pansies, gilt trim and scrolls between panels, emb neck and base, SP rim, handle, and cov. 850.00

Cracker Barrel, 5 1/2" h, fluted base, sm dk blue flowers and leaves on lt blue ground, gilt traces, SP rim, handle, and lid 850.00

Ewer, 5" h, cobalt poppies, gold trim on top and ornate handle 75.00

Pitcher, 6 3/4" h, violets with long stems and leaves on lower section, cobalt handle, gold accents, pewter lid. 450.00

Platter, 19 1/2" l x 15 3/4" w, oval, well and tree, lg center medallion, flowing blue stylized flowers overpainted with rust, dk rust rim. 975.00

Sugar Shaker, 5" h, sprigs of holly 285.00

Teapot, 5" h, oval shape, berries and leaves design, gold flecking. . . 600.00

Vase, 6 7/8" h, sq bulbous body, slender neck, fruit in sq basket and front, flowers, sprigs, and leaves 365.00

"Venice" pattern

Casserole, Cov, 10" d, "Wood & Son" mark 200.00

Plate, 8" d, "Wood & Son" mark . . . 65.00

Platter, 18" l x 13 3/4" w, scalloped rim, gold accents, Johnson Brothers, c1895 . . . . 235.00

"Vermont" pattern

Berry Dish, 5" d. 35.00

Butter Pat 55.00

Platter, 10" l x 7 1/2" w, Burgess & Leigh 110.00

Soup Plate, 8 7/8" d, Burgess & Leigh 55.00

Vegetable Bowl, 9" l, oval, Burgess & Leigh. 145.00

"Verona" pattern

Plate, 10" d 85.00

"Versailles" pattern

Plate

7 3/8" d, fluted, gilt scalloped rim 65.00

9 1/2" d, fluted scalloped rim gilt edge 75.00

10 1/2" d, Furnivals, c1894 . . . . 95.00

Platter

16" l x 12 7/8" w, oval, scalloped 325.00

18 1/4" l x 14 3/4" w, oval, gilt scalloped rim 475.00

Sauce Tureen, 7 1/2" H-H, with undertray and ladle. 695.00

Soup Plate, 10 1/2" d 90.00

Tureen, 13" H-H, with undertray, gilt rims 995.00

"Victoria" pattern

Vegetable Bowl, 10" d, Wood & Son 150.00

"Virginia" pattern

Butter Pat. 55.00

"Waldorf" pattern

Bowl, 9" d 125.00

Creamer. 425.00

Cup and Saucer. 110.00

Milk Pitcher 1,095.00

Plate

6" d 50.00

9" d 85.00

Platter

11" d 100.00

16" l 375.00

Soup Plate, 9" d, New Wharf Pottery 125.00

Waste Bowl 240.00

"Warwick" pattern

Vegetable Bowl

8" l, oval, Johnson Brothers . . . 175.00

9 3/4" l, oval Johnson Brothers 225.00

"Watteau" pattern

Berry Bowl 45.00

Bone Dish, Doulton 65.00

Bowl, 9" d, "N.W.P." mark 125.00

Casserole, Cov, 12" l 225.00

Cup and Saucer, Demitasse 110.00

Pitcher

2 3/4" h 275.00

7 3/4" h, gold trim 675.00

Plate

10" d 75.00

10 1/2" d 75.00

Platter

13 1/2" l 195.00

16" l x 12 1/2" w, chips 450.00

Punch Bowl, 18" d, Doulton 2,300.00

Soup Bowl, 8 1/4" d 85.00

Soup Plate, 10 1/4" d 95.00

Sugar Bowl, Cov, 6" h 450.00

Teapot, gold trim 995.00

"Whampoa" pattern

Compote, 12 1/2" d x 6 1/2" h, looped and woven handles, (A) 575.00

Ginger Jar, 8" h, Mellor & Venables, crazing 1,150.00

Platter, 20 3/4" l x 17 1/4" w, well and tree, Mellor & Venables, (A). 1,265.00

Vegetable Dish, Cov, 11 1/4" d, gold accented handles and knob, (A). . 288.00

"Willow" pattern

Biscuit Barrel, 6" h, scalloped body, fluted shoulder, "Bridgless" example, SP lid and handle, Wiltshaw & Robinson, c1894 . . . . 695.00

Plate, 7 3/4" d, Keeling. 68.00

Toothbrush Holder, 5" h, Doulton. . 265.00

"Yedo" pattern
Cup and Saucer. 65.00
Plate
8 3/8" d, Ashworth 65.00
9 1/2" d, Ashworth 80.00
10 3/8" d, Ashworth 80.00
Platter
12 3/4" l x 9 1/4" w, Wilkinson . . 195.00
15 3/8" l x 12 1/2" w, gold edge Ashworth. 395.00
Soup Plate, 10 1/4" d, Ashworth . . . 95.00

FRANCE-GENERAL

Rouen
1673-1696

Louis Poterat, a faience maker, was granted a patent to make the earliest French soft paste porcelain at Rouen in 1673. The decorations were dark blue in the style of faience ware with lambrequins and gadroons. Relief work appeared on the body of pieces such as salt cellars, mustard pots, and vases. Poterat died in 1696.

Lille
1711-1817

Barthelemy Dorenz and Pierre Pelissier established a soft paste porcelain factory in Lille in 1711. Pieces were decorated with Chinese designs. Leperre Ducot began manufacturing hard paste porcelains in 1784. The French Dauphin became a patron of the factory in 1786. The dolphin was chosen as the factory's mark.

Strasbourg
1721-1781

Charles Hannong, who started a porcelain factory in Strasbourg in 1721, manufactured clay pipes and stoves that were decorated in relief and glazed. For a short time he was a partner with Johann Wachenfeld who came from Meissen. Together they made faience and porcelain wares. In 1724, a second factory was established in Haguenau.

Hannong transferred the factories to his sons, Paul Antoine and Balthasar, in 1732. Between 1745 and 1750 hard paste porcelains were produced that were decorated in red and pale gold. Adam Lowenfinck arrived from Hochst in 1750 and became co-director of the porcelain factory. He brought the rococo style and introduced flower painting to Strasbourg.

By 1753, Paul Hannong assumed control of both factories. When Louis XV of France ordered him to dismantle his porcelain factory and demolish his kilns, Paul Hannong went to Frankenthal. As a result, early Strasbourg ware and Frankenthal ware resembled each other.

By 1766, Joseph-Adam, Hannong's son, tried to re-establish a hard paste porcelain factory in Strasbourg. Opposition by the authorities forced its closure in 1781.

Sceaux
1748-1795

Under the patronage of Duchess de Marne, the architect de Bay established a porcelain factory that was managed by Jacques Chapelle. The firm's soft paste porcelains were decorated with exotic birds, flowers, and cupids in the fashion of the Louis XVI period. The factory closed in 1795.

Niderviller
1754-1827

Baron Beyerle established a faience factory in 1754. Porcelains were produced by 1765. When opposition arose from the Sevres potters, Beyerle took Count de Custine into partnership in 1770 because of his influence at the French Court. On Custine's death, the factory was sold to Claude-Francois Lanfrey and continued until 1827. Tea sets, tablewares, and services were made and decorated in the manner of Sevres.

Paris area

The majority of French hard paste porcelains available in today's market was made at numerous small factories in the Paris area. Production of porcelain began in the early 18th century.

Museums: Frick Collection, New York, NY; Louvre, Paris, France; Musee des Arts Decoratifs, Paris, France; Musee des Beaux-Arts et de la Ceramique, Rouen, France; Musee National de Sevres, Sevres, France; Victoria & Albert Museum, London, England; Wadsworth Atheneum, Hartford, CT.

Additional Listings: Chantilly, Choisy-le-Roi, Creil, French Faience, Limoges, Malicorne, Old Paris and Paris, Quimper, Saint Cloud, and Sevres.

Box
2 3/8" d, painted loose bouquets, blue lined rim, figural cherry knob, "incised D.V." mark, Mennecy, c1770, (A) 300.00
9 1/2" d, HP scene of period courting couple on cov, cobalt border with gilt scrolls and dots, sgd "C Rochette," c1890 . . . . 950.00

9 3/4" l x 6 1/2" w x 4 3/4" h, Sevres style, top painted with gallant, companion and maid in gilt emb foliate wreath, corners molded and gilt with foliate scrolls, sides with watery landscapes in molded and gilt foliate cartouches, blue ground, int with loose bouquets, "gilt chateau" mark, late 19th, (A) 2,760.00
Bud Vase
6 3/4" h, wide body, narrow rim, Art Deco style blue, turquoise, and white drip over orange and yellow drip body 295.00
8 3/8" h, bulbous body, sm tapered neck, lg stylized flowerheads with green enameled centers, black outlined gray leaves, mottled gray ground, green int, sgd "L. Dage" 395.00
Butter Dish, Cov, 7 1/4" d, sm pink florals and green leaves, rim design of black geometrics and gold trim, gold handle 35.00
Cache Pot
3 5/8" h, black transfer of 2 boys building fire and "script L'Hiver," reverse with black transfer of women putting produce in baskets, children at side and "script L'Automne," black outlined crenelated rim, molded lion head and ring handles on sides 125.00
6 1/2" h, scattered mauve and purple flowerheads, bands of gilt diamonds, gilt lined rim, gilt outlined molded side handles, "Made in France" mark . . . 225.00
9" h, rect, panels painted with alternating fruit and floral still lifes, gilt scrollwork on sides and base, green ground, pierced gilt rim, 4 paw feet, Jacob Petit, pr, (A) 2,990.00
Candlestick, 7 3/4" h, tulip shaped top, blue forget-me-nots, white ground, "blue X'd arrows mark," pr 350.00
Charger
17" d, center with HP romantic scene of 2 women in walled garden, blue border with gilt accents and 4 oval panels of polychrome florals, brass mtd rim, late 19th C, (A) 770.00
18" d, porcelain, lt blue and gold lobed geometric in center, blue lambrequin border with blue, red, and yellow flowerheads. 2,500.00
19 3/4" d, porcelain, painted red birds with black wings on berried branches, gold ground, "imp black B & CIE" mark, c1889. . . . . 2,500.00
Chocolate Pot, 9" h, pink flowers, pink and gold ground, dtd 1891 . . . . 195.00
Coffee Can and Saucer
Cup with painted Flora reclining in woodland, gilt accents, blue ground, saucer with center and 2 border lozenges of flowers, gilt trim, blue ground, "blue interlaced L's" mark, (A) 400.00
Sevres style, circ portrait medallion of Marie Louise or Hoche in titled tooled gilt foliate cartouche, band of tooled stylized anthemion, saucer painted with

Cake Plate, 11" H-H, blue-gray transfer, "Windmill, Nord, Orchies, Moulin des Loups & Humage France" mark, $75.

Figure, 13 3/4" h, brown haired man, turquoise jacket, mauve pantaloons, gilt trim, blond haired woman, white gown w/gilt trim, lt blue and pink flowers, orchid overgrown, med blue and gilt bases, "blue D & T, anchor" marks, c1880, pr, $2,800.

trophies and gilt tooling, green ground, late 19th C, pr 700.00

Coffee Service, Part, pot, 9" h, cov hot milk jug, 6" h, cov sugar bowl, 5" h, 12 cups and saucers, Empire style transfer printed portraits of Napoleon and Josephine in shaped cartouches reserved on green ground with bands of flowers and gilt anthemion, (A) 1,495.00

Cup, Sevres style, green ground with raised gilt fleur-de-lys under bands of beads 100.00

Cup and Saucer, printed and painted spray of flowers reserved in gilt cartouche, yellow ground, set of 6 . . . . 225.00

Cup and Trembleuse Saucer, Sevres style, painted men at work at quayside in gilt cartouche, blue ground with gilt ovals and geometrics, "blue interlaced L's" mark 250.00

Decanter, 10" h, figural humorous man, blue coat, holding yellow bag and orange umbrella, gray hat stopper, Robj, (A) 90.00

Dessert Service, Part, 3 compotes, 9" d x 2 3/4" h, 11 plates, 9 1/8" d, centers HP with different garden flowers, blue borders with HP garden flowers in diamond reserves joined by gold chain and striping, gold scalloped rims, unmkd, (A) 160.00

Dish, 9 1/2" l, shell molded, gold floral sprays and shell outline, "gold FRANCE" mark 20.00

Ewer

10" h, oval cartouches of enameled classical scenes, ruby red ground with silver gilt scrolling foliage and putti, lg scrolled foliate handle, late 19th C 5,000.00

Figure

9" h, standing troubadour with bagpipes, companion holding music book, turquoise ground, gilt accents, "blue interlaced L's" marks, pr, (A) 437.00

9 7/8" h, "Winter" and "Spring," modeled as busts of young girls, "Winter" with green head kerchief, brown hair, "Spring" with wreath of multicolored flowers in blond hair and around neck,

gilt accents, waisted socle bases, pr, (A) 308.00

11 1/4" h, terra cotta, naked reclining young peasant girl, wearing blue spotted kerchief, corn sheaf over leg, (A) 462.00

14 1/2" h, standing penguin, white glaze, "France HD 1307" mark, (A) . . . 115.00

20 3/8" l, pottery, Art Deco style cream crackle glazed reclining nude Diana with bow and brown hound and doe at side, green and brown mottled base, (A) 535.00

Jam Service, 9 7/8" l, 2 cov pots attached to tray, painted scattered flowers, blue line and gilt dash borders, gilt dentil rims, 1772, (A) 805.00

Jar, Cov, 5 1/8" h, cylinder shape, button knob, painted scattered floral sprays, blue line and gilt dash rim, "blue interlaced L's and V" mark, set of 3, (A) 748.00

Jardiniere, 14" h x 18" d, bombe shape, everted rim with molded gilt stiff leaves, gilt outlined blue painted trellis on body, flowering bunches at intersections, "blue interlaced L's" mark, late 19th C, (A) 3,910.00

Oyster Plate, 8 1/8" d, 6 brown outlined lt blue molded wells, gold striped scalloped rim, set of 4, (A) 170.00

Pitcher, 13" h, straight sides, sprays of garden flowers on yellow ground, dk brown borders 25.00

Planter, 14" d x 6" h, oval, green and red Art Deco style birds on branches, dashes on border, "Monterey" 100.00

Plate

8" d

"A L'Eglise," wedding scene, black transfer, blue swirled border, Gien 28.00

"Les Dejuner Comiques-Le Malade," sick man with medicine, black transfer, molded purple swirl border, Gien .50.00

Multicolored transfer in center of colonial man astride horse in stream farm in bkd, 3 bunches of red, blue, and yellow flowers and meandering stems on border, relief molded line rim. 30.00

Sevres style, painted 2 young lovers in various landscapes, scalloped pink and gilt metal rims, "interlaced L's with S and Chateau de Versailles" marks, fitted case, (A) . . . 1,265.00

9" d, HP

Cupid hunting in woods, shaped gold rim, sgd "F. Furlaud" 100.00

Pink carnations and roses, blue scalloped rim, pr. 45.00

9 1/8" d, "Gentlemens Club," 4 men in room setting, scrolling cartouche, black transfer, molded panel border, "imp Porcelaine a la Perle J.F." mark 65.00

9 1/4" d, Sevres style, painted portrait of Mme. De Pompadour or Mme. De Montespan, named on reverse in looped ribbon surround with flower garlands, border of 4 oval panels of flowers in gilt foliate cartouches on pink ground, "blue interlaced L's and gilt crowned cypher" mark, 19th C, pr, (A) 161.00

Sauce Tureen, 9" h, 3 paw feet, 3 mask handles, floral knob, white glaze. 135.00

Serving Dish, 11" l, rect, 4 sections, 2 outer sections with red and blue bachelor buttons, middle sections with garden flowers, green lined rim. 24.00

Snuff Box, 2 3/4" l, rect, basketweave body with painted scattered flowers on ext, int with painted flower bouquet and scattered flowers, silver mts, "puce D.V." mark, Mennecy, repairs and cracks, (A). 207.00

Soup Plate, 9" d, "Fleurette" pattern, blue transfer, Gien. 55.00

Sugar Bowl, Cov, 4 1/2" h, painted scattered cornflower sprigs, gilt fruit knob, Clignancourt-Paris, c1790, (A) 368.00

Tea and Coffee Service, Part, teapot, 5 1/8" h, coffeepot, 7 1/2" h, with gilt metal hinge, cov sugar bowl, 4 coffee cans and saucers, puce and iron red scrolls with flower swag, gilt beaded swags, c1790, chips, (A). . 1,840.00

Tea Service, Part, pot, 5" h, cov sugar bowl, 6 cups, 4 saucers, 5 plates, Art Deco style with disc handles and knobs, overall black glaze, chips, (A). 1,550.00

Tete-A-Tete, Part, cov sugar bowl, 5" h, 2 cups and saucers, tray, 12 1/4" w, Sevres style, painted Louis XVI court portraits and looses bouquets in gilt foliate border reserved on turquoise ground, "blue interlaced L's" mark, late 19th C, (A) 368.00

Urn

9 1/2" h, campana shape, Sevres style gilt bordered reserve of painted portrait of

Napoleon or Josephine, dk red ground with gilt urns, foliage, scrolls, and vines, trophies on reverse, gilt metal garland rim, gilt metal swan handles, gilt metal plinth base, 19th C, pr, (A) . . .1,955.00

23" h, bulbous shape with buttressed handles, blue, green, and caramel flambe crystalline glaze, Pierefonds, repaired hole, (A) 850.00

Urn, Cov, 22" h, Sevres style, inverted baluster form, raised panel of multicolored scene of goddess and cherubs, landscape on reverse, cobalt ground with gilt floral and filigree, figural caryatid handles, gilt bronze base, (A) 2,415.00

Vase

4 3/4" h, porcelain, reticulated neck, brown triangular leaves, gold-yellow ground, "incised Mougin, Nancy" mark 550.00

6" h, cylinder shape, black sailboat on blue-black sea, mottled blue sky, black rim, matte finish, artist sgd 165.00

7 1/2" h, tapered shape with base handles, emb arrowroot leaves, amber, pink, and blue matte crystalline flambe flowing glaze, "imp C. Greber, France" mark, pr, (A). 400.00

10 1/8" h, pottery, baluster shape, 2 C-scroll handles with leaf terminals, sprigged portrait medallions of king or queen in egg and dart and foliate scroll frame, reverse with foliate scroll motif, overall tan, 19th, pr, (A). 690.00

10 1/4" h

Dbl gourd shape, slender neck, enamel decorated lustered purple, green, and gun metal peacock feathers, "slip Robalbin, Paris, Laurent" mark, (A). 1,400.00

Porcelain, flared conical shape, gray-brown enameled relief of cicada in landscape, yellow to orange glazed ground, c1930 . . . . . 495.00

10 1/2" h, bottle shape, flared rim, black incised curlicues, gloss brown ground, (A) 450.00

11 3/4" h

Cylinder shape, Aesthetic Movement, Chinese dragon decoration under Persian blue gloss glaze, brass bamboo mts, drilled base, "TH. DECK" mark, pr (A) 2,200.00

Dbl gourd shape, incised conc rings, turquoise green and white drip on gunmetal ground, "imp PRIMAVERA, MADE IN FRANCE, 13691" mark, (A). 345.00

12" h, bulbous tapered body, slender neck, flared rim, blue drip over wisteria glaze, Pierrefonds 395.00

12 3/4" h, campana shape, 4 oval panels with en grisaille painted landscapes in blue enamel tied ribbons, molded green leaf and red berry swags from gilt slugs, yellow ground with blue sprigs, gilt gadrooned lower section, yellow socle,

faux red marble base, everted rim with molded green stiff leaves, Niderville, c1790, pr, (A) 6,325.00

21" h, urn shape with flared ft and rim, center pink band with painted scenes of classic warriors or women in garden, gold banding, chips, pr, (A) . . 1,300.00

Vase, Cov

8 1/4" h, Sevres style, shouldered cylinder shape, turquoise ground reserved with oval gilt cartouches of multicolored flying birds on front, floral bouquets on reverse, chinoiserie style gilt bronze ft, cov, and foo dog handles, pr, (A) 430.00

8 3/4" h, dolphin handles, gilt floral designs surrounding central oval cartouche of enameled flower basket, blue ground body, (A). 489.00

14 1/8" h, Sevres style, painted and printed scene of 18th C courting couple in gilt oval cartouche, blue ground, late 19thC, pr. 155.00

21 1/2" h, Sevres style, painted reserve of woman holding grapes above putto in gilt rocaille cartouche with pink and blue diapering, yellow ground, gilt scrolls on reverse, ormolu vine handles and base, (A) 1,150.00

22 1/2" h, Sevres style, multicolored scene of period couple walking in landscape in elaborate gilt surround, dk blue ground with gilt foliate and stiff leaf designs, domed cov with berry knob, ormolu scroll handles and base, sgd "B. LeBrun," pr 1,450.00

33 5/8" h, Sevres style, painted scene of peasant mother and 3 children reserved in gilt foliate cartouche on turquoise ground, lakeside scene on reverse, ormolu mtd handles, base, and trim, sgd "Quentin," "blue interlaced L's" mark, late 19th, (A) 2,760.00

FRANKENTHAL

Palatinate, Germany
1755-1799

1762-1793

History: Paul Hannong established the Frankenthal hard paste porcelain factory in 1755, with the consent and patronage of the Prince Elector Karl Theodor of Palatinate. Previously Hannong worked at Strasbourg, France, 65 miles south of Palatinate.

Dinner services and accessory pieces were marketed along with biscuit and decorated figures, some of which were excellent artistically. The rococo style dominated and was similar to that appearing on Vincennes-Sevres pieces. Frankenthal decorators used a full range of colors along with the Vienna style of raised gilt work. Classical and natural themes proved the most popular.

Despite high quality pieces, the company suffered from financial difficulties. In

1762, Karl Theodor purchased the factory and personally supervised its operation. Modelers Luck and Melchior fashioned figural pieces of note. Nevertheless, the company failed in 1799. Nymphenburg acquired the Frankenthal molds to reproduce the old forms. The Nymphenburg factory used the blue lion mark and "CT" with a crown on their pieces made from Frankenthal molds.

Frankenthal's 44 years of production were the shortest production period experienced by a major German porcelain manufacturer. However, Frankenthal's high quality and variety of products produced during this brief period were enough to rank it among the greatest of the German factories.

Reference: George Ware, *German & Austrian Porcelain*, Crown, Inc. 1963.

Museums: Bayerisches National Museum, Munich, Germany; Museum fur Kunst und Gewerbe, Hamburg, Germany; Schlossmuseum, Berlin, Germany; Victoria & Albert Museum, London, England.

Coffee Pot, 9" h, painted birds perched on branch, marshy landscape, scattered flowers, puce diaper border with gilt edging, pine cone knob, J-shaped handle, c1755, restruck knob, (A) 1,035.00

Figure

4 1/4" h, painted and parcil gilt putto wearing tricorn hat, ragged breeches, carrying staff, mid-18th C, restored, (A) 150.00

5 5/8" h, Neptune, gray hair and beard, white lined puce drapery, walking with hippocamp, gilt accented rococo scroll base, c1765, restorations . . . 1,250.00

6" h, gardener's companion, standing girl wearing wide brimmed hat, blue laced bodice, puce striped and flowered skirt, circ scroll base, "blue crowned CT and 84" mark, c1784, gardener's tools missing, (A) 5,175.00

Cream Jug, 4" h, mauve and purple flowers, green leaves, brown lined rim and outlined feet, "blue crowned CT" mark, $975.

Monteith, 11" l, oval, waved rim, painted birds and green diapering, scrolling leaf handles, late 18th C, (A) 2,990.00

Tea Service, Part, teapot, slop basin, oval fluted serving dish, globular cov sugar box, coffee cup, 2 teacups and saucers, painted brown and ochre sprays of roses, tulips, or carnations, band of open ovals and dots on border, 1775-1777, (A) 3,234.00

1738 - c 1790

c1827

1758 -1788

1740-60

FRENCH FAIENCE

Nevers c1632-1800

Rouen 1647-c1800

Moustiers 1670-1800

Marseilles 1677-c1800

Strasburg 1721-1780

History: Faience, a porous pottery, was lightly fired earthenware that was painted and then covered with an opaque stanniferous glaze. Tiny particles of tin oxide suspended in the glaze provided the characteristic white, opaque nature of the pottery.

Italian potters migrated to France in the 1600s, first to Nevers, and later to Rouen, Moustiers, Marseilles, and other pottery centers. In **Nevers,** the potters transformed the Italian majolica tradition into something distinctively French. The Nevers potters developed a Chinese style employing oriental subjects and the Chinese blue and white color scheme. They also added a richly intertwining border pattern of leaves and flowers. Nevers was the leader during the 17th century.

In the third-quarter of the 17th century, four main schools, Rouen, Moustiers, Marseilles and Strasburg, developed. **Rouen** faience was characterized by "decor rayonnant," a richly intricate pattern of stylized leaves and florals which adorned the outer border, cascading in swags around a central flower burst that was adapted from the delicate lace and iron work of the mid-18th century rococo patterns. Polychrome chinoiserie styles also were introduced.

Moustiers derived its early system of decoration from Nevers. The pioneer was Pierre Clerissy (1679-1739). The Chinese influence is in evidence in pattern design, form, and the blue and white palette. The use of "grotesques," fantastic human or animal figures in scenes of wild vegetation, added excitement to the pieces.

In 1677, Joseph Clerissy came from Nevers to **Marseilles.** The Marseilles potters used border patterns that were heavier than at Moustiers. Landscape panels, acanthus leaves, or birds with foliage followed the Nevers style.

Strasburg faience was influenced by the rococo motifs from Rouen. In 1748-1749, a group of artists who had worked at Meissen arrived in Strasburg from Hochst. They applied enamel painting techniques, giving the wares a more German than French appearance.

Before the French Revolution, faience factories were thriving. After the revolution and the treaty of commerce between England and France, English potters flooded the market with their industrial pottery that was cheaper to make, lighter in weight, easier to transport, and less liable to chip or crack under heat. This pottery appealed to both wholesale dealers and the public. The French factories experienced great difficulties competing. Many factories closed. By 1850, the French pottery industry was practically extinct.

References: Diana Imber, *Collecting European Delft and Faience,* Frederick A. Praeger, 1968; Arthur Lane, *French Faience,* Faber and Faber, 1970; Millicent S. Mali, *French Faience,* United Printing, 1986.

Museums: Musee Ceramique, Rouen, France; Musee des Arts Decoratifs, Paris, France; Victoria and Albert Museum, London, England.

Reproduction Alert: Collectors of French faience should be very wary of imitations being made in large quantities in modern day Paris. Genuine French faience is rare and only is offered for sale when a famous collection is dispersed.

Barber Bowl, 11 1/2" l x 8 1/4" w, black centered yellow daisies and green leaves in bowl, blue chain rim, (A) 193.00

Bell, 4" l, black painted cat on front, "Aux Cycles du chat noir" below, stylized blue snowflake and red and blue flowers on reverse, blue sponged loop handle, (A) 176.00

Bough Pot

4 1/2" h x 6" w, bombe chest shape, drawer fronts and corners painted with brown and purple, blue, green, and yellow flowers and foliage on sides and between drawer fronts, purple outlined apertures, chips, (A). 115.00

7" w, fluted, flared semicircular shape, painted oriental style flowering branches and butterflies in colors, lobed rim, "black G" mark, c1750, restored, (A) 462.00

Bowl

8 3/4" sq, cut corners, "V" and crown in center, hanging drapes on border, blue, Gien 235.00

11 1/2" d, polychrome stylized figure of man with top hat, hanging floral swags from rim, scalloped rim, early 19th C, (A) 300.00

Box, 14 1/2" l, rect, Chinese style molded relief of masks, roundels, and foliage on body, cov painted and molded river scene, gilt accents, St. Clement, late 19th C, (A) 431.00

Candlestick

6 3/8" h, figural standing dog, curled tail handle, raised green and blue and yellow and blue swirls, yellow flowerheads and blue dots, white body, gray outlined feet and haunches, nozzle on turned head with blue lines and red dots, Rouen. 145.00

11 1/2" h, standing figural bearded lion, aqua body, lavender, brown, and yellow accents, St. Clement 385.00

Charger

14" d, painted blue, yellow, and purple flower and leaf arrangement, cavetto with series of roundels with yellow flowers, parallel yellow lines, cream ground, (A) 115.00

15" d

Rust, blue, yellow, and green floral center, inner border with 5 blue dots and floral sprigs, blue scalloped rim, Nevers, c1850 . . . . 525.00

Silver shape, border of painted loose sprays of yellow and green flowers and sprigs, "G & LO" mark, Moustiers, 18th C, (A). 493.00

Dish, 14 1/2" d, multicolored exotic bird, insects, and floral sprays from cornucopia, lt blue ground, indented rim, "HT" mark, Rouen, 18th C, damaged 450.00

Egg Cup, 2 1/2" h, yellow, red, green, and cobalt Rouen drape design, unmkd, (A). . 60.00

Flower Frog, 3 1/2" h x 6" l, figural standing pig, red, yellow, and green painted flower sprays, blue dashed snout, blue ears, blue dots, white ground, sgd "Mosanic," c1880 . . . . 225.00

Jug, Cov

5" h, baluster shape, polychrome floral sprays, blue banded trim lines, 19th C 150.00

9 1/2" h, baluster shape, puce trimmed green design of floral landscape with male figure blowing horn, flanked by wild bird and animal, Moustiers, 18th C, chips and repairs, (A) 518.00

Milk Jug, Cov, 5" h, pear shape, loop handle, beak spout, pink putti in clouds in green surround on front, pink garlands and sprays on sides, (A) 58.00

Pitcher, 12 1/2" h, figural standing duck, red and green feathers, black beak, (A) . . .88.00

Plate, 9" d, magenta and yellow robe, blue pants, green umbrella, mauve rim, Luneville, c1850, $225.

Planter, 6 1/4" h x 7 1/2" w, with liner, quatre-lobed, painted landscape of lake with boats, trees, and church, "JEAN" mark 1,900.00

Plate

8 1/2" d, oct, painted walking peasant man with walking stick in field, blue acanthus border, shaped rim, Desvres, c1920, (A) 275.00

9" d, yellow and red vase with lg purple and orange flowers, sitting on green, purple, and orange stand, orange sun ray border, green lined shaped rim, Nevers 210.00

9 1/4" d

Blue and green flower spray in center, scattered green buds, sm floral spays on border, unmkd 53.00

Blue and white band of stylized foliage and swags and coat of arms with tassels on border, Moustiers, c1775, (A) 123.00

9 1/2" d, crest in center, red, green, blue, and yellow-orange hanging baskets, geometrics, and lambrequins on border, Moustiers 125.00

9 3/4" d

Painted multicolored oriental figure at fence with brown boulders, molded compartments on border with painted insects, iron red shaped rim, 18th C, pr 1,250.00

Spray of flowers in oval panel under trailing sprays of roses, pink dentil lobed rim, early 19th C 230.00

9 7/8" d, hexafoil shape, puce tulip, green leaves, scattered sprays, Joseph Hannong, Strasburg, (A) 123.00

10" d, divided, blue single strokes with yellow-gold flower strokes, cream ground, blue lined rim, "Faiencerie on naing Made in France and rooster" mark, set of 6 . . . . 185.00

11" d, painted Cupid and Psyche in center, dk red vert streaked border, (A) 748.00

Platter

11" l x 9 1/2" w, rococo shape, peasant man seated on wooden fence, ft on rock, church in bkd, molded cobalt, red, yellow, and green rococo border, pierced for hanging, Desvres, c1920, (A) 405.00

14 3/4" l, oval, green, orange, and blue dancing middle eastern couple in center, paneled border with green, orange, and blue flowers and fencing, shaped rim, Moustier, c1750 . . . . 2,400.00

Puzzle Jug

6" h, molded purple grapes and green leaves on upper half, French verse on lower half, blue striped ft, blue top, "PB" on base 200.00

7 3/4" h, pierced neck with florets above polychrome flowers and insects surrounding fruiting vine crest, "HB" mark, (A) 375.00

Salt, 2 1/2" h x 3" w, dbl, figural duck, cobalt head, yellow and black beak, painted florals on breast and wings, (A) 93.00

Salt and Pepper, 5 1/2" h, figural male peasant with baskets on pole over shoulder, lt blue cap, cobalt jacket, rose red pants, yellow stockings, brown clogs, dk orange poles, green sponged baskets with red flowers and leaves, Desvres, (A) 150.00

Sauce Tureen, cov, 7 1/2" w, lozenge shape, 2 side handless, painted green and black cottage, ruins, and landscape vignettes, green and black lined rims, c1779, (A) . . . 1,150.00

Snuff Bottle, 3 1/2" d, spray of cobalt flowers and buds, green leaves, yellow tulip, blue banded sides, blue dot border, Rennes, (A) 300.00

Spice Box, 2 3/4" h, trefoil shape, paw feet, floral knob, cartouches of polychrome floral baskets with florals and scrolling vine borders, repairs, Rouen, 19th C, (A) 316.00

Tureen, 9 1/2" h, pedestal base, vert brown and yellow sponged stripes, yellow and blue banded rims, green loop handles, cov with vert brown and yellow sponged stripes, circ reserve with black "Joseph Boutilliez," yellow and green fruit knob, 19th C, (A) 483.00

Vase

9 1/4" h, bulbous base, slender neck, cartouche of couple in period clothes or woman with distaff and dog, arabesques and leaves, blue and magenta, Nevers, c1880 . . . . 525.00

9 3/8" h, blue design of putto with quiver of arrows, scattered florals, pale blue glaze, loop handles, 3 paw feet, unmkd 1,500.00

21" h, figural fluted cornucopia, circ base with bracket feet, blue painted Rouen style foliate scrolls, scattered flowers, and insects, pr, (A) 2,300.00

Wall Pocket, 13" h, overlapped cone shape, multicolored cornucopia design with scattered butterflies and insects, (A) 412.00

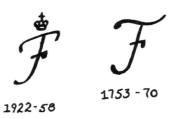

1922-58   1753-70

FURSTENBERG

Brunswick, Germany
1747-1859 Royal-State

1859 to Present-Private

History: The Furstenberg factory was founded in 1747 in the castle of Karl I, Duke of Brunswick, primarily to satisfy his vanity. Six years passed before porcelain was produced in 1753. The technique came from artists who left Hochst. Raw materials for the paste and glaze had to be imported from a great distance. By 1770 the porcelain paste closely approximated that made at Meissen.

Many figures were modeled, but the amount of production was not great. The figures imitated figural molds and decorations produced at Meissen and Berlin. English styles from Bow, Wedgwood, and Chelsea, and Sevres from France also were copied. After 1760, Frankenthal vases became famous. China services and various utilitarian and decorative wares were competitive with those produced by other 18th century factories.

The period of 1770 to 1790 was the golden age at the Furstenberg factory. Materials improved considerably, additional enamel colors were utilized, and gilding was employed in the border patterns. After 1775, neo-classical influences appeared.

During the French occupation, Brunswick was part of the Kingdom of Westphalia ruled by Napoleon's brother, Jerome Bonaparte. The factory became the Royal Porcelain Manufactory from 1807 to 1813. After Napoleon's defeat, Brunswick regained its independence. In 1813, the former name was restored. The factory continued to produce tablewares, decorative porcelains, figures, and coffee and tea sets.

In 1859, Furstenberg was leased by the Brunswick government. Private ownership took over again in 1876. The company was reorganized as a joint stock company and named Furstenberg Porcelain Factory AG. Today, the factory still manufactures a

Charger, 14" d, polychrome enameled designs, c1780, $5,500.

great variety of vases, tablewares, and other porcelains.

Reference: George A. Ware, *German & Austrian Porcelain*, Crown, Inc.1963.

Museums: Museum fur Kunst und Gewerbe, Hamburg, Germany; National Museum, Stockholm, Sweden; Victoria and Albert Museum, London, England.

Coffee Pot, 7 3/4" h, pear shape, rocaille molded beak spout, painted loose bouquets, entwined berried vine and pink ribbon on shoulder, "blue F" mark, c1770, (A) . . 288.00

Figure, 5 1/2" h, swan spreading wings, natural colors, "blue script F" mark, (A) . . . 115.00

Potpourri Jar, 11 3/8" h, oviform shape, painted continuous landscape with figures, ruins, and bridge between molded and gilt scrolls, panels of landscape vignettes and pierced section, flower knob, c1760, repairs 3,500.00

Teapot, 4" h, globular, painted with vignettes of figures in landscapes, gilt foliate scrolls on shoulder, silver replaced cov with ball knob, "blue script F" mark, c1760, (A) 420.00

GALLE

Nancy, France
1874-1904

1846 -1904

History: Emile Galle, a leading designer and manufacturer of art glass, first made faience in Nancy, France in 1874. Later he experimented with both stoneware and porcelain. Galle's decorations included heraldic motifs and scenes that resembled Delft ware. A series of souvenir dishes was made to commemorate the Franco-Prussian War.

Glazes used were flowing and opaque in nature. Sometimes several colors were mixed together. Most of the forms were simple in design.

Victor Prouve, an artist friend of Galle, provided designs for figures of bulldogs

and cats. The most popular figures were painted yellow with blue hearts and circles, black and white with pale indigo blue, or beige with pink and green decorations of naturalistic flowers. Green glass eyes were used. Prouve's designs were used for candlesticks of heraldic lions and grotesque and fantastic ducks, fox, owls, swans, and parakeets. Plant designs of dandelions, chrysanthemums, and orchids were used in Art Nouveau style decorations that duplicated Galle's work on glass.

All of Galle's ceramics were marked with the impressed initials E.G. Em. Galle Faiencerie de Nancy, or some version of his signature.

Museums: Bowes Museum, Barnard Castle, Durham, England; Musee des Arts et Metiers, Paris, France.

Collecting Hints: Galle faience now is prevalent in the American antiques market. Cat, parrot, and dog figures are seen in various colors and sizes. Sets of plates, three sectioned dishes, tureens, wall vases, and inkwells are eagerly sought. Large candlesticks with figures of lions are among the most expensive pieces.

Bowl
  5" l x 4" h, 4 sm feet, boat form with molded blue scrolling, painted landscape and castle, "E. Galle, Nancy" mark, (A) 575.00
  8 1/2" l, rect, 4 paw feet, red and gilt low relief of heraldic lion and swirling foliage, "Rouge" mark, (A) 492.00

Cabinet Vase, 5" h x 6 1/2" l, figural melon, red and purple bachelor buttons on ext, cream ground, green stem handle, "E. Galle Nancy" mark 650.00

Candlestick, 16 3/8" h, figural heraldic lion holding tower and shield aloft, scrolling oval base, blue tones on white, "Galle Nancy editeur, St. Clement, Lorraine" mark, pr, (A) 1,605.00

Plate, 8 3/4" d, brown, red, green, and cream glazes, "E.G. E. Galle Nancy Edward VI H. Holbein" mark, (A) $350.

Cup and Saucer, blue heraldic motif with thistle on cup, blue "Non Inutus Premor" on saucer, white ground, "Galle a Nancy, St. Clement" mark, (A) 143.00

Figure
  9 1/2" h, architectural form, molded scroll and floral decoration, painted yellow, dk red, and green bird on base, "Galle, Nancy" mark, (A) 488.00
  13" h, cat, black trimmed blue decorations, yellow enameled ground, glass eyes, restorations, (A) 230.00
  Jug, 5 1/8" h, faience, twisted baluster shape, scroll handle, painted fleur-de-lys, gilt accents, mkd, restored spout 275.00

Pitcher, 7 5/8" h, baluster shape, incised brown, blue, gray, and silver foil berried holly, "Noel, Noel" incised on neck, "EG and cross" mark 700.00

Planter
  13 3/8" l, tapered rect form, painted polychrome scene of 18th C coach scene at coach house, leaves and berries on reverse, green ground, "EG cross, depose, E. Galle Nancy" marks, damages, (A) 264.00
  14" l x 7" h, figural fighting rooster, tan-brown head, dk orange-brown comb, white wing feathers with yellow and brown accents, green and purple tail feathers, clutching egg in claw, "imp *Emile Galle Nancy*" mark 3,450.00
  18 1/2" l x 7 1/2" h, 4 feet, slip painted multicolored Barbotine fox hunt scene, Charles Volkmar, "EG" mark, (A) 1,500.00

Teapot, 8 3/4" h, blue geometrics and zigzags on shoulder, lt and dk blue rope twist overhead handle, offset knob, white ground 775.00

Tureen, 10 1/4" l, faience, 4 foliate feet extend to handles, domed cov with molded crossed onions and artichoke knob, 4 panels of blue

Vase, 4 1/2" h, blue, red, and green flowers and swags, white ground, "Galle France" mark, (A) $165.

painted landscape scenes, "blue E. Galle Nancy" mark, (A). 920.00

Vase

7 1/2" h, bulbous body, tapered cylinder neck, brown, yellow, green, and gold enameled stylized foliage design, "E. Galle, Nancy" mark, (A). 374.00

8 1/4" h x 8 1/4" w, dbl diamond shape, multicolored relief of fox, stork and bottle, and spider in web, dk blue borders with gold dashes, lustered gold sides with blue splashes, mkd 3,200.00

Wall Pocket, 13" h, molded semi-circular basket, pink and gray floral sprays, pink dash border, pink outlined rope twist hanger, "pink Galle Nancy, blue St. Clement" mark 400.00

GAME PLATES AND SETS

English/Continental
c1870-1915

History: Game plates and sets, usually including a large platter, serving plates, and a sauce or gravy boat, were popular between 1870 and 1915 both in England and on the Continent. They are specially decorated plates used to serve game and fish. Subjects utilized by the makers included all types of game birds, quail, snipe, pheasants, mallards, etc. and fish.

Among the principal French manufacturers were Haviland and firms in Limoges. Makers in England included Crescent and Sons, Mason, Royal Doulton, Wedgwood, and Royal Worcester. Factories in Bavaria, Villeroy and Boch in Germany, and Royal Vienna in Austria also made game plates and sets.

Reproduction Alert: Game plates were imported to the United States by reproduction wholesalers and giftware distributors during the 1970s and 80s. The new pieces are full color transfers that were also used on urns, vases, and compotes in addition to plates. These carry Germany and Austrian backstamps as well as facsimile signatures. Beware of gold trim that is too shiny.

Fish Set

Platter, 17 1/4" l x 12" w, 10 plates, 8 1/2" d, HP fish on green, orange, and yellow ground, brushed gold trim. 650.00

Platter, 19 3/4" l, 12 plates, 9 3/4" d, sauce boat with attached underplate, 6 different black and tan fish and sea grasses, lt blue to blue-green shaded ground,

Fish Set, platter, 23 1/2" H-H, 12 plates, 7 3/8" sq, multicolored fish in center, different fish on each plate, gold rim, "CFH/GDM" marks, (A) $375.

sculpted borders, gilt rims, Wallendorf, Germany. 925.00

Platter, 21" l

9 plates, 8 1/2" d, sauceboat with undertray, HP reserves of leaping trout, seaweed border with heavy gold accents, Limoges 990.00

10 plates, 8 1/4" d, multicolored swimming fish in centers, roses and gold trimmed rims, Austria 895.00

Platter, 22" l, sauce boat with stand, 12 plates, 8" d, 12 bone dishes, 7 1/2" l, polychromed swimming fish in center, gold outlined shaped rims, unmkd 595.00

Platter, 24" l, 10 plates, 9 3/4" d, painted swimming fish in seaweed, green, brown, and rose floral borders, indented rims, sgd "L. Martin," Haviland, c1900 . . . . 1,350.00

Platter, 24 1/2" l

9 plates, 9" d, pr of swimming fish in green, pink, and yellow sea plants, paneled border with molded magen-

Plate, 9" d, multicolored bird in forest setting, lt blue and mauve bkd, molded matte gold border, "MR France" mark, set of 6 different birds, $390.

Plate, 9 3/4" d, brown and green fish, seaweed and red dots, molded shell border, gold outlined rim, Bing and Grondahl, set of 11, (A) $144.

ta and gold designs, "Crescent China, England" marks 900.00

10 plate, 9 1/4" d, sauceboat, pr of swimming fish, 2 purple iris, maroon, brown, and gold bkd, molded gold border with white molded handles, "L.R.L. France" dbl marks 1,250.00

Platter, 24 3/4" l, 12 plates, 8 5/8" d, sauceboat with undertray, 9" l, multicolored swimming fish, pink borders with raised gold swags, "blue Victoria Carlsbad" marks. 575.00

Game Set

Platter, 18" l, oval, 12 plates, 8 1/4" d, cream dish, 7 1/2" l, enameled central scene of pheasants in various poses, raised gilt foliate rims, Haviland, Limoges, (A) 1,495.00

Platter, 19" l, 8 plates, 9 1/2" d, multicolored game birds in meadow with lake, raised gold weeds, pink borders with molded panels, shaped rococo gold rims, sgd "Roche, N." 900.00

Plaque

11 1/2" d, multicolored walking quail in field, gilt scrolled rim, pierced for hanging, "E.S. Germany, Prov. Saxe" mark 145.00

11 5/8" d, lg brown bellowing moose in woods in center, dk blue shaded border with gold overlay, pierced for hanging 38.00

13 1/4" d, pr of antlered deer or pr of does, multicolored forest setting, gold rococo rim, sgd "Dubois," Limoges, pr 845.00

13 5/8" d, HP pr of pheasants in meadow, shaded yellow, blue, green, and brown ground, sgd "Luk," "green B & H, Limoges, France" mark, (A). 70.00

14" d, PUG, multicolored hanging fish and lobster, gold rim, #1044-9025, Mettlach, (A) 375.00

14 1/8" d, printed and painted multicolored scene of 3 flying mallards over irises,

gilt accents, red luster ground, Carlton, (A) 465.00

14 1/4" d, 2 quail and 3 chicks in meadow, multicolored, emb border, gilt rim, pierced for hanging, Limoges . . 195.00

14 1/2" d, PUG

Multicolored flying ducks over marsh, gold rim, #1044-9030, Mettlach, (A) 347.00

Multicolored flying pheasant in meadow, gold rim, #1044-9032, Mettlach, (A) 385.00

Plate

8 3/4" d, HP brown standing quail in green and tan landscape, white ground, inner border of yellow flowers and green leaves, raised outer border with gilt leaves, shaped rim, "C.T. and eagle" mark 55.00

8 7/8" d, HP brown flying woodcock, lt blue to brown shaded ground, molded border, shaped rim, artist sgd, "green B & H Limoges" mark 75.00

9 1/2" d

HP flying quail or pr of pheasants on ground, pastel pink, blue, and cream bkd, gold rococo border, Limoges, pr 225.00

Multicolored woodcock in field, dk green shaded ground, relief molded drops on rim, "black Petrus Regout sphynx" mark 75.00

Polychrome enameled single fish under hanging seaweed, molded foliate and gilt border, France 165.00

Quail walking in field, multicolored, matte brown border with raised design, "black Petrus Regout sphynx" mark 75.00

9 3/4" d

Blue grouse, brown grouse in shaded green field, shaded brown border, brown lined rim, Bavaria. 22.00

Brown, green, and blue bird standing on ground, brown and cream shaded bkd, irreg relief molded and gold trimmed border, pierced for hanging, Limoges. 38.00

Multicolored pheasant standing in field, green shaded border, wide swirl molded gold rim with dentil edge, "red Bavaria" mark. . . . 49.00

10" d, wild boar in colors, Limoges 150.00

10 1/4" d, 2 brown and gray quail in field with blue and purple flowers, yellow and green shaded ground, gold molded rim, Limoges 165.00

Platter, 15 1/4" l x 12 1/8" w, oval, multicolored transfer of antlered deer fighting, cobalt border with gold stenciling, gold striped rim, unmkd, (A). 50.00

Tray

14 1/2" l x 9 5/8" w, oval, 2 ducks in flight over lake, Roman gold handles, artist sgd. 250.00

18 1/2" l x 12" w, HP bird in flight, purple flowers, grasses, and daisies, green to lavender shaded ground, gold rococo rim, Limoges 230.00

GARDNER

Verbiki, near Moscow, Russia 1766-1891

ГАРДНЕРЪ

EARLY 19TH CENTURY

History: Francis Gardner founded his factory in 1766. He brought experienced European potters and decorators to Russia. Utilitarian wares, artistic objects, and articles for sale at fairs comprised the production.

Floral motifs and pastoral scenes were favored. Many dinner sets were made on commission. The Gardner family controlled the factory until 1891 when it was acquired by the Kuznetsov family.

The initial "G" or name "Gardner" was used as the mark.

Reference: Marvin Ross, *Russian Porcelains,* University of Oklahoma Press, 1918.

Museum: Hermitage, Leningrad, Russia.

Bowl, 7" d

Blue ground with white oval panels of multicolored flowers 195.00

With underplate, raspberry red ground with white leaves, white oval panels with multicolored floral bouquets . . . 250.00

Figure, 9" h, white blouse, cream jerkin, multicolored floral wreath, iron red underlayer, black boots, $1,200.

Figure, 9 1/2" h, gray-brown jacket, blue kerchief, pink skirt, white bag with blue dots, green ground, $1,400.

Cup and Saucer, overall polychrome florals, gilt paneled rim on saucer, gilt int and handle on cup, 19th C, (A) 238.00

Figure

4 1/2" h, kneeling Middle Eastern man, white turban with purple flowers, gray beard, green flowered shirt, purple trousers, blue lined white cape, blue flowered prayer box on gilt tasseled green pillow, purple oriental rug, rect base 365.00

7" h, bisque

Cossack seated on bench playing concertina, black hat and boots, beige coat, lavender shirt, blue pants 425.00

Standing baker in long white coat, dk brown hat, blue striped trousers, holding brown cake in hand 250.00

10 3/4" h, bisque, Cossack dressed in lt blue jacket and gold dotted pants, wearing ice skates, female peasant in white blouse, pink dress, and lt blue underdress, gold trim, holding scythe and next to wheat stack, rococo molded base, pr 1,550.00

Plate, 11" d, garden scene in center, blue transfer, white ground, 19th C, pr, (A) 302.00

Teacup, cobalt glaze with gilt geometric rim, c1910, (A) 75.00

Teapot, 5 3/4" h, ball shape, center gilt lined cartouche of painted garden flowers on white ground, raspberry red body, white handle and knob, mid 19th c 295.00

GAUDY DUTCH

J & R. Riley
1802-1828

Staffordshire, England c1810-1830

History: Staffordshire pottery with a Gaudy Dutch motif was made for the American trade and experienced wide popularity from c1810-1830. White earthenwares, mostly plates and teawares, were made by a number of Staffordshire potters among whom were Riley and Wood. Painted patterns included: Butterfly, Grape, King's Rose, Oyster, Single Rose, Strawflower, Urn, War Bonnet, etc. Dominant colors were cobalt blue, bright yellow, green, red, and pink.

References: Eleanor J. Fox and Edward G. Fox, *Gaudy Dutch*, privately printed, 1970; Sam Laidacker, *Anglo-American China Part 1*, Keystone Specialties, 1954; Earl F. Robacker, *Pennsylvania Dutch Stuff*, University of Pennsylvania Press, 1944; John A. Shuman, III, *The Collector's Encyclopedia of Gaudy Dutch & Welsh*, Collector Books, 1998 values.

Collectors' Club: Gaudy Collector's Society, P.O. Box 274, Gates Mills, OH 44040.

Museums: Henry Ford Museum, Dearborn, MI; Philadelphia Museum of Art, Philadelphia, PA; Reading Art Museum, Reading, PA.

Reproduction Alert: Cup plates, bearing the impressed mark "CYBRIS," have been reproduced and are collectible in their own right. The Henry Ford Museum has issued pieces in the Single Rose pattern, although they are of porcelain and not soft paste.

Bowl
    3 1/4" d, ftd, lg red Carnation on ext with green leaves, repairs and overglaze, (A) 175.00
    6 3/8" d, ftd
        "Oyster" pattern on ext, brown lined rim, (A) 1,475.00
        "Single Rose" pattern, crack and repairs, overglazed, (A) 125.00
Coffeepot, 11 3/4" h, domed shape, "Single Rose" pattern, (A) 9,350.00
Creamer
    3 3/4" h, "Single Rose" pattern, (A) 550.00
    4" h, squat shape, "Double Rose" pattern, (A) 1,073.00
    4 1/8" h, " War Bonnet" pattern . . . 600.00
    4 1/4" h
        "Grape" pattern, brown polychrome rim, (A) 1,150.00
        "Sunflower" pattern, (A) 715.00
    4 1/2" h, oval body, arched handle, "Grape" pattern, brown lined rim, (A) 1,200.00

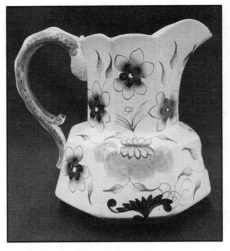

Pitcher, 8 3/4" h, "Carnation" pattern, blue and iron red, green handle, (A) $258.

Cup and Saucer, Handleless
    "Butterfly" pattern, tripalmate leaf in center, (A) 1,400.00
    "Dove" pattern, (A) 550.00
    "Grape" pattern, mismatched, (A) 248.00
    "Single Rose" pattern, brown lined rim, base chips, (A) 775.00
    "Sunflower" pattern, brown lined rims, repaired rim, (A) 500.00
    "Urn" pattern, (A) 303.00
    "War Bonnet" pattern, red lined rim, (A) 1,000.00
Cup Plate, 4 3/8" d, "Double Rose" pattern, hairline, (A) 220.00
Dish
    6" d, "Urn" pattern, (A) 220.00
    8 1/4" d, "War Bonnet" pattern, (A) 715.00
    9 3/4"d, "Double Rose" pattern, (A) 715.00
Pitcher, 5 1/2" h, "Grape" pattern, handle restored 1,400.00
Plate
    5 1/4" d
        "Double Rose" pattern, hairline, (A) 200.00
        "War Bonnet" pattern, (A) 660.00
    5 5/8" d
        "War Bonnet" pattern, hairline, (A) 160.00
    5 3/4" d
        "Dove" pattern, repaired rim, (A) 175.00
        "Sunflower" pattern, brown polychrome rim, (A) 925.00
    6 1/4" d
        "Grape" pattern, cobalt lined rim, repairs to rim, (A) 300.00
    6 3/8" d
        "Single Rose" pattern, brown lined rim, (A) 775.00
        "Sunflower" pattern, brown lined rim, (A) 800.00
    6 1/2" d
        "Dove" pattern, (A) 900.00

Plate, 8 1/4" d, "Sunflower" pattern, $875.

    "Single Rose" pattern, brown lined rim, (A) 700.00
    7" d, "Grape" pattern, (A) 743.00
    7 1/8" d, "War Bonnet" pattern, red lined rim, repaired, (A) 525.00
    7 1/4" d, "Double Rose" pattern, scalloped rim, (A) 700.00
    7 3/8" d, "Butterfly" pattern, wear, (A) 110.00
    7 1/2" d
        "Carnation" pattern, (A) 160.00
        "Dove" pattern, (A) 850.00
        "Oyster" pattern, chip on reverse, (A) 523.00
    7 3/4" d, "Double Rose" pattern, glaze loss, wear, (A) 120.00
    8" d, "Butterfly" pattern, (A) 990.00
    8 1/4" d
        "Grape" pattern, (A) 298.00
        "Urn" pattern, (A) 908.00
        "War Bonnet" pattern, (A) 750.00
        "Zinnia" pattern, "imp Riley" mark, (A) 990.00
    8 3/8" d
        "Butterfly" pattern, blue banded border with yellow squiggled line, (A) 850.00
        "Carnation" pattern, brown polychrome rim, (A) 1,050.00
    8 1/2" d
        "Grape" pattern, paint touch up 375.00
        "Single Rose" pattern, (A) 688.00
    9 1/4" d
        "Single Rose" pattern, brown polychrome rim, hairline and scratches, (A) 350.00
    9 3/4" d
        "Grape" pattern, (A) 1,045.00
        Lg red Carnation, yellow and green leaves, sm red flower with yellow center, brown lined rim, (A) 1,300.00

Tea Set, pot, 6 1/4" h, creamer, sugar bowl, "Carnation" pattern, repairs, $2,100.

"War Bonnet" pattern, red lined rim, (A)................1,250.00

9 7/8" d

Lg red Carnation, green leaves, red flower with green center, cobalt border band with yellow oval and dot design, crack and repairs, (A) 425.00

"Oyster" pattern, repaired rim and overglazed, (A).......... 300.00

10" d

"Double Rose" pattern, (A).... 715.00

"Single Rose" pattern, (A) 990.00

"Sunflower" pattern........1,100.00

Soup Plate

8 1/4" d, "Grape" pattern, brown polychrome rim, (A) 950.00

9 3/4" d

"Double Rose" pattern, (A)...1,595.00

"War Bonnet" pattern, red polychrome rim, (A) 1,600.00

10" d, "Single Rose" pattern, brown polychrome rim, (A) 1,300.00

Sugar Bowl, Cov, 5 1/2" h

"Oyster" pattern, repaired, (A).... 500.00

"Single Rose" pattern, repair to lid, (A) 660.00

Teabowl and Saucer

"Dove" pattern, brown polychrome rim, chip, (A)................... 1,250.00

"Urn" pattern, chip on base, (A) .. 950.00

Teapot

5 1/2" h, "Double Rose" pattern, repairs, (A) 412.00

5 3/4" h

9 5/8" l, rect, C-shaped handle, "Dove" pattern, chips, (A) 8,000.00

9 3/4" l, rect, C-shaped handle, "Oyster" pattern, chips and wear, (A) 3,000.00

Squat shape, "War Bonnet" pattern, extensive repairs, (A) 100.00

5 7/8" h x 10 1/4" l, squat shape, "Single Rose" pattern, repairs to hairlines and chips, (A) 400.00

6" h x 11 1/4" l, squat shape, wishbone handle, "Grape" pattern, crack in spout, (A) 600.00

6 1/4" h

9" l, round body, flared gallery rim, C-shaped handle, acorn knob, "Sunflower" pattern, brown lined gallery rim, chips, (A) 5,000.00

9 1/2" l, round body, flattened gallery, C-scroll handle, molded shell on spout, "Dove" pattern, acorn finial, chips, (A)............. 5,000.00

10 1/2" l, sq shape, wishbone handle, flower knob, "Double Rose" pattern, (A) 1,760.00

11 1/4" l, oval, scalloped rim, arched handle, scrolled knob, "War Bonnet" pattern, hairline, (A)...... 3,630.00

Waste Bowl, 6 3/8" d, "Dove" pattern, (A) 660.00

GAUDY IRONSTONE

Staffordshire, England
1850-1865

History: Gaudy Ironstone was produced in the Staffordshire district between 1850 and 1865. Edward Walley's "wagon wheel" was a popular Gaudy Ironstone design similar to the design of Gaudy Welsh. Walley, who worked at Villa Pottery in Cobridge, utilized bright colors and floral designs to give a country or folk character to his pieces.

While some of the examples used the same colorations as Gaudy Welsh, other pieces used varying shades of red, pink, and orange with light blue and black accents. Some designs utilized copper luster, while others did not. The flow blue technique also was used on some Gaudy Ironstone pieces.

Collectors' Club: Gaudy Collector's Society, P.O. Box 274, Gates Mills, OH 44040

Bowl, 5 1/4" d, "Strawberry" pattern, (A) 138.00

Coffeepot, 10 1/2" h, "Seeing Eye" pattern, scrolled handle, pear shaped knob, imp English registry mark, repairs, (A) 450.00

Cup and Saucer, lg copper luster flowerheads, cobalt leaves and sm iron red leaves, shaded dk blue ground 110.00

Cup and Saucer, Handleless

Morning Glory pattern, copper luster outlined cobalt leaves 285.00

Paneled

Cobalt and copper luster urn, red flowerheads, cobalt leaves with copper luster trim............... 185.00

Floral pattern, red and green HP flowers with gold luster and yellow accents, underglaze cobalt leaves, gold lustered rims, (A).... 200.00

"Strawberry" pattern, red and green strawberries, underglaze cobalt leaves, gilt trim 160.00

Mug, 4 1/4" h, cylinder shape, lg hanging cobalt and luster leaves, red hanging flower-

heads and stems, blue shaded ground 215.00

Pitcher

5 1/2" h, paneled, "Pinwheel" pattern 550.00

6 1/2" h, copper luster maple leaves, sm green leaves, copper luster stem, lt blue pebble ground, pink luster bands on base, copper luster rim 485.00

8 1/4" h, paneled, lg iron red and cobalt flowerheads, lg cobalt leaves from base, sm mauve leaves 495.00

8 1/2" h, paneled

Lg cobalt leaves with copper luster outlines and stems, lustered rim and base 675.00

"Strawberry" pattern, (A) ... 1,045.00

8 3/4" h, "Carnation" pattern, serpent handle, (A) 258.00

Plate

6 3/4" d, cobalt and copper luster chrysanthemum-type flowerheads, copper luster rim, "Staffordshire, England" mark 125.00

7 3/4" d, 12 sides, "Strawberry" pattern, gold accented red and green strawberries with underglazed cobalt leaves, pink and green polychrome floral border, (A)..................... 225.00

8" d, border of lg red, green, blue, and black floral design, "lion and unicorn" mark, (A) 45.00

8 1/2" d

Green, red, purple luster, and underglaze cobalt flowerheads and leaves, center flowerhead, "imp Ironstone" mark, (A) 140.00

Lg straw brown flowerhead in center, cobalt stem, iron red flowerheads, cobalt and gold splashes, unmkd 75.00

"Morning Glory" pattern, cobalt and copper luster flowers, green leaves 235.00

Plate, 8" d, "Blinking Eye" pattern, iron red, cobalt, green, and copper luster, c1840, $325.

"Pinwheel" pattern, 12 sides, red flowerheads, cobalt and copper luster
leaves 175.00
"Urn" pattern, blue and green,
(A). 220.00
8 5/8" d, bunches of grapes, cobalt and
copper luster leaves, molded border,
c1845. . . . . 145.00
8 3/4" d, 12 sides, "Strawberry" pattern,
red and green strawberries, underglazed cobalt leaves 325.00
9 1/4" d
10 sides, iron red flowerheads and
green leaves, lg cobalt and gilt
leaves, border of iron red and cobalt
flowers, copper luster rim, shaded
blue ground 145.00
12 sides, "Urn" pattern, mauve flowerhead, luster and cobalt urn, red flowerheads 125.00
"Seaweed" pattern, blue, red, and luster seaweed design 150.00
9 1/2" d, 10 sides, "Poppy" pattern, red
flower, cobalt, and luster center, purple
rim 150.00
9 3/4" d, 12 sides, urn and flowers design
in red, pink, green, and underglaze blue
(A) 138.00
10" d, "Half Strawberry" pattern, hairline
. . . . 250.00

Platter
13" l
Cobalt vase of flowers in center with
yellow veined cobalt leaves and iron
red flowers, tan table and iron red
fence, border of iron red flowerheads and luster, green leaves,
shaded blue ground. 295.00
Gaudy floral pattern, yellow transfer
with red, green, black, and underglaze cobalt accents, (A). . . 385.00
14 7/8" l, oval, red, blue, green, and yellow
gaudy floral pattern, black transfer of
rabbits, frogs, and florals on border,
(A) .1,100.00
15 1/2" l x 12" w, "Strawberry" pattern,
(A) 605.00
Soup Plate, 9 1/2" d, 10 sides, lg cobalt and
luster leaves and tendrils, (A) 110.00
Vegetable Bowl, 9 1/8" l, rect with cut corners,
cobalt berries and leaves, copper trim, sm red
flowers and green leaves, copper luster rim
. . . . 295.00
Waste Bowl
5 3/8" d, "Seeing Eye" pattern, (A)
. . . . 200.00
5 1/2" d, "Strawberry" pattern, hairline,
(A) 110.00

GAUDY WELSH

England, Wales
1820-1860

History: Gaudy Welsh, manufactured between 1820 and 1860, was produced for
the working class people in England and
Wales. It traced its decorative motifs to
Japanese Imari. Gaudy Welsh was identified by its colors of underglaze cobalt blue
(often in panels), rust (burnt orange), and
copper luster on a white ground, plus its
decoration which most often was floral, although trees, birds, or geometric forms
were sometimes used. The body can be
earthenware, creamware, ironstone, or
bone china.

Swansea and Llanelly were the two areas in Wales where the Gaudy Welsh motif
began. At least four firms in Newcastle and
two Sunderland firms copied the design to
their wares. However, it was the Staffordshire potteries at Stoke-on-Trent that produced the greatest amount of Gaudy
Welsh.

Grape leaves, panels, cartouches,
fences, and flower petals appeared repeatedly in Gaudy Welsh designs and reflected
the oriental influence. Many patterns had
names indicative of the design, e.g. "Tulip,"
"Sun Flower," "Grape," and "Oyster," while
other names were more fanciful and bore
little resemblance to the decorative motif.
True Gaudy Welsh had the cobalt portion of
the design under the glaze and the additional enamel colors including the lusters
over the glaze. In addition to the bold colorations of cobalt, orange, and luster decorations, pieces can be found with shades
of green and yellow highlights added. As
many as 300 designs have been identified.

Tea cups and saucers were made more
than any other forms. Most Gaudy Welsh
designs were painted on the inside of the
cups. Tea sets, jugs, bowls, and miniatures
were produced in smaller quantities.

Much of the Gaudy Welsh was unmarked. Design and techniques allowed
some pieces to be traced to specific companies.

References: John A. Shuman, III, *The Col-
lector's Encyclopedia of Gaudy Dutch &
Welsh,* Collector Books, 1998 values;
Howard Y. Williams, *Gaudy Welsh China*,
Wallace-Homestead 1978.

Collectors' Club: Gaudy Collector's Society, P.O. Box 274, Gates Mills, OH 44040.

Museums: Royal Institution of South
Wales, Swansea, Wales; St. Fagen's Welsh
Folk Museum, near Cardiff, Wales; Welsh
National Museum, Cardiff, Wales.

Reproduction Alert: Gaudy Welsh has
been reproduced during this century by
several Staffordshire potteries. The most
prolific was Charles Allerton & Sons
(1859-1942), who specialized in jugs in the
"Oyster" pattern. The orange-red pigment,
often streaked and uneven, is the sign of a
reproduction.

Compote, 5" h, 9" d, "Grape" pattern, blue, green,
lavender, and iron red, (A) $287.

Bowl
6" d, "Grapes" pattern 115.00
6 1/4" d
Ftd, "Dogwood Flower" pattern .225.00
"Sunflower" pattern. 110.00
Cake Plate, 9 1/2" H-H, "Oyster" pattern
. . . . 98.00
Creamer
4" h, "Wagon Wheel" pattern 130.00
4 1/2" h, "Oriental" pattern 265.00
Cup and Saucer
"Anemone Varient" pattern 190.00
"Asia" pattern. 120.00
"Columbine" pattern 75.00
"Dimity" pattern 100.00
"Drape" pattern 100.00
"Feather" pattern 100.00
"Flower Basket" pattern 125.00
"Flower Basket II" pattern 125.00
"Grape" pattern 75.00
"Honeysuckle" pattern 75.00
"Pinwheel" pattern 135.00
"Tulip" pattern 75.00
Mug
2" h, "Grape" pattern 125.00
2 1/2" h
"Columbine" pattern 135.00
"Grape" pattern 155.00

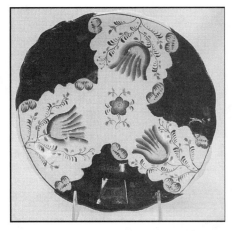

Plate, 9 1/2" d, "Tulip" pattern, blue, yellow, and
iron red, $45.

2 3/4" h, "Grape" pattern 135.00
4" h, "Oyster" pattern 250.00
Pitcher
   3 3/4" h, "Oyster" pattern 75.00
   5" h, orange "Church" pattern 595.00
   5 1/2" h, "Grape" pattern 265.00
   7 1/2" h, orange "Church" pattern . .475.00
Plate
   5" h
      "Grape" pattern 45.00
      "Herald" pattern, rope handle
      . . . . 385.00
   5 1/2" d, "Oyster" pattern 25.00
   6" d
      "Tulip" pattern. 45.00
      "Urn" pattern. 65.00
   8" d, "Oyster" pattern 65.00
   8 1/4" d, "Pinwheel" pattern 250.00
   8 7/8" d, "Oyster" pattern 85.00
   9" d, 12 sides, "Rocking Urn" pattern,
      c1840. . . . . 295.00
Punch Bowl, 10" d, "Grape" pattern . . 550.00
Soup Plate, 9 1/4" d, "Grape" pattern on border, Allerton. 85.00
Sugar Bowl, Cov, "Tulip" pattern, (A) . .385.00
Teapot
   7 1/4" h, "Columbine" pattern 365.00
   11 1/4" h, "Poppy" pattern, gallery top
   . . . . 600.00
Vegetable Bowl, 12" l, "Oyster" pattern
. . . . 335.00
Waste Bowl, 5" d, "Tulip" pattern, paint wear
. . . . 85.00

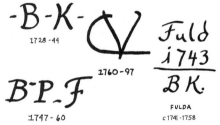

GERMAN FACTORIES-MINOR

History: Many small, but highly important, factories were established in the German provinces during the last half of the 18th century. Some were started by princes, but the majority were private commercial enterprises.

Ansbach
Hesse, 1758-1860

Under the patronage of Hohenzollern Margrave Alexander of Brandenburg and with the help of workers from Meissen, this porcelain factory was established in 1758 in connection with an old faience works. In 1762, the firm moved to a hunting castle at Bruckberg. Fine pieces were made during the rococo period, c1775. The factory was sold to private interests in 1807 and continued to make a variety of wares until 1860.

Wares imitated those made at Berlin, Meissen, and Nymphenburg. Exotic groups and figures, white and painted decorative and utilitarian wares, especially coffeepots, souvenir plates, monogrammed cups and saucers, and silhouette medallions were made. The principal mark in the c1760 to 1785 period was an "A" of varying sizes and shapes.

Bayreuth
Bavaria, Germany
1899-1920

Siegmund Paul Meyer's factory produced utilitarian and hotel porcelains. The firm changed its name to First Bayreuth Porcelain Factory in 1920, continuing to make ovenproof pots and coffee machines.

Fulda
Hesse, 1765-1790

This factory was established for the Prince-Bishop of Fulda in 1765. The predominant decorative style was from the late rococo period. The products resembled those manufactured at Frankenthal. The main subjects of the figures were shepherds, children, ladies, cavaliers, and comedians positioned on rococo trellises. The factory mark in underglaze blue was a double "F" with or without a crown. A few pieces were marked with a cross.

Gotha
1757-1782

Wilhemn von Rotberg established this factory in 1757. His cream-colored paste had a translucent glaze. Products included coffee sets, tea sets, and decorative porcelain figures. At first, the rococo style was predominant. Later the Louis XVI and neo-classical styles were used. Underglaze blue marks were first an "R" and then "R-g" and "G." The factory survived until 1782.

Kassel
Hesse, 1766-1788

Friedrich II founded the factory. It made attractive tablewares with underglaze blue decoration and some simple figures. The mark was a lion or "HC" in underglaze blue.

Kloster Veilsdorf
1760 to Present

The factory was established in 1760 under the patronage of Friedrich Wilhelm Eugen. Tablewares and decorative porcelains, coffee sets, tea sets, and figures were made. The typical decorations were large freely painted purple, red, and yellow flowers evolving from thread-like stems. The underglaze blue monogram "CV" was used, occasionally supplemented with a coat of arms. After 1799, the mark became a three-leaf clover.

Limbach
1772 to Present

Gotthelf Greiner established this factory in 1772. Porcelains were decorated primarily in blue and purple tones. Figures were rustic subjects and small town people. The marks "LB" or crossed "L's" were applied on the glaze in red, purple, or black. About 1787, an underglaze blue cloverleaf mark was used. Later cloverleaf marks were purple, black, or red.

Greiner and his five sons acquired other factories such as Grossbreitenbach in 1782 and Kloster Veilsdorf in 1791. From 1797 to 1850, G.Greiner's Sons made utilitarian and decorative porcelains and figures.

Thuringian Factories
From 1757

Nine hard-paste porcelain factories were established in the Thuringian region. The three main ones were Gotha, Kloster Veilsdorf, and Volkstedt-Rudolstat. (see Volkstedt-Rudolstat)

Wallendorf
1764-1833

Johann W. Hammann established this factory in 1764. The first products had rococo style decoration. Later dinner services were made in formal styles. Pastoral and street scenes in monotones of purple, brown, black, and gray tones featured figures of rural characters. The factory's mark was an underglaze blue "W." In 1833 the factory was sold to Hutschenreuther, Kampfe, and Heubach.

Reference: George W. Ware, *German & Austrian Porcelain,* Crown, Inc. 1963.

Museums: Bayeriches Nationalmuseum, Munich, Germany; Gardiner Museum of Ceramic Art, Toronto, Canada; Museum fur Kunst und Gewerbe, Hamburg, Germany; Schloss Museum, Berlin, Germany; Victoria & Albert Museum, London, England.

Bayreuth

Plate, 10 1/4" d, painted loose bouquet in center and sm bouquets, brown lined foliate rim
. . . . 150.00

Stein, 9 1/2" h, faience, purple, yellow, and blue stylized flowerheads, green leaves, blue sponging on sides, blue striped ft and rim, pewter lid, (A) 1,800.00

Tankard, 9" h, cold painted basket of flowers in foliate bands, pea green ground, pewter lid, c1735, (A) 275.00

Fulda

Flask, 4 3/4" h, cylinder shape, manganese sponged trees in continuous landscape, c1750, neck repair 125.00

Plate, 8 7/8" d, faience, blue painted pear with stylized foliage, early 18th C, (A) 200.00

Gotha

Plate, 11 7/8" d, HP scene of figures on bluff over valley and "Gotha" or view of "Reinhards-brunn" named on reverse, gilt diaper panels alternating with molded gilt floral cartouches on border, gilt shaped rim, c1875, pr, (A) 1,725.00

Hannau

Charger, 11 1/2" d, Delft, molded chrysanthe-mum flower head form, center with oriental man holding book, each border petal with ori-ental man or flowerheads, blue and white, c1660-90. 1,950.00

Jug, 7 7/8" h, pear shape, blue painted bird on mound beside tree, house in landscape on re-verse, blue scrolls on handle, white ground, c1720, (A) 430.00

Kassel

Vase, Cov, 17 1/4" h, oviform, agate body with draped gilt swags suspended from rings, handles on shoulder, figural widow knob, sq basalt base, c1778, pr, (A) 8,395.00

Kloster-Veilsdorf

Figure, 12 3/8" h, bust of Furst Ludwig Friedrich Carl Hohenlohe-Oehringen or Soph-ie Amalie Caroline, white glaze, waisted so-cle, sq base, c1770, pr 4,500.00

Figure, 7" h, 6 3/4" w, peach-pink blouse, lt purple sleeves, green flowered overdress, gilt trim, dtd 1762, $1,650.

Tea Caddy, 5 1/2" h, rect, chamfered shoul-ders, painted loose bouquets and scattered sprigs, replaced domed filigree cov, c1770 . . . . 1,800.00

Thuringia

Cup and Saucer, painted mythological scenes on band of blue and gilt beading, bor-der with blue and gilt cornucopia spilling flow-ers, (A) 95.00

Stein, 9 1/2" h, faience, HP blue, white, and yellow overlapped stylized flowerheads, green leaves, blue ferns on front, purple trees on sides, pewter ft and lid, 18th C, (A) 1,155.00

Wurzburg

Coffee Cup and Saucer, painted grosbeak on branch on cup, bird on saucer, gilt vert spear borders, c1780. . . . . 2,200.00

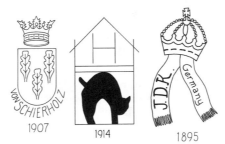

GERMANY-GENERAL

Pottery
15th Century to Present

History: Some of the earliest forms of Ger-man decorative pottery were made by the Hafner or stove-makers. The stove tiles of the 15th century were covered with a green lead glaze. Later 16th century stoves con-tained tiles of yellow, brown, and white clays or with tin-glaze over red clay bodies. Hafner wares also included large vessels or jugs made in Nuremberg.

In 1712, Marx and Hemman first made tin-glazed earthenwares. They continued in a series of partnerships until 1840. Most of the wares were decorated in blue with ba-roque style scrolls, foliage, or strapwork. Subjects encompassed landscapes, heral-dic shields, and biblical or mythological scenes.

Hamburg faience came in the period of the second quarter of the 17th century. Pear-shaped jugs decorated with a coat-of-arms in a blue motif were best known.

The most prolific center of German faience was at Hanau, near Frank-fort-am-Main, from 1661 until 1806. The wares imitated Delftware. Many Chinese forms were copied. At first only blue deco-ration was used. By the early 18th century, wares were decorated with landscapes

and biblical scenes in a variety of colors. Naturalistic flowers in enamel colors domi-nated the mid-18th century wares.

Ansbach, Bayreuth, Erfurt, Frankfort-am-Main, Kassel Proskau, and Schrezbeim were other areas where faience factories were es-tablished.

Porcelain
16th Century to Present

History: In Germany, there were many small principalities which competed with each other in establishing porcelain facto-ries. Each developed an individual style. There was no royal monopoly in Germany as there was in France since there was no unified Germany.

In addition to the major German facto-ries of Berlin, Frankenthal, Furstenberg, Hochst, Ludwigsburg, and Meissen, at least 20 minor manufactories were estab-lished in the German provinces during the last half of the 18th century. Some of these include Ansbach, Fulda, Gera, Gotha, Grossbreitenbach, Gutenbrunn, Llmenau, Kassel, Kelsterbach, Kloster Veilsdorf, Lim-bach, Ottweiler, Rauenstein, Volkstedt, and Wallendorf.

Though some of these factories were established by princes, most were formu-lated as private commercial enterprises to make wares that could be sold competi-tively. For the most part, these wares cop-ied works of the major German factories, such as Frankenthal and Meissen, etc. The majority of the minor factories were able to continue operation despite changes in ownership, economic disruptions, and competition from larger firms, especially those established in the 19th and 20th cen-turies that were close to the source of raw materials.

Independent painters developed soon after the establishment of the Meissen fac-tory about 1720. Porcelains painted by these independent decorators in their homes or studios were known as Hausmal-erei. The painters were designated as Hausmaler. Hausmalers were experienced painters of faience and other ceramics. The large porcelain factories feared their com-petition. Hausmalers obtained Meissen and Vienna blanks and painted them as they wished. Ignaz Bottengruber of Breslau was best known of the independent deco-rators. Hausmalers were active for about 40 years during the mid-18th century.

A smaller group of factories was in oper-ation during the last half of the 18th cen-tury. These included Baden-Baden, Blanken-hain, Eisenberg, Ellwangen, Hanau, Hoxter, Schney, and Tettau. Only Tettau still oper-ates today.

Germany was in the forefront of the hard paste porcelain industry. Many new factories, making high quality utilitarian and decorative porcelains, were established during the 19th and 20th centuries. Most of these 19th and 20th century factories, approximately 200 of them, were concentrated near the source of porcelain's raw materials, i.e. the central and eastern regions of Germany, (mainly North Bavaria, Thuringia, Saxony, and Silesia). Among the dominant factories are Sitzendorf, Rosenthal, Schumann, Hutschenreuther, and Heinrich. Factories located at Altwasser, Passau, Plaue, Potschappel, Rudolstadt, and Selb concentrated on the production of utilitarian and decorative porcelains.

Reference: William B. Honey, *German Porcelain*, Faber & Faber, 1947.

Museums: Arts & Crafts Museum, Prague, Czechoslovakia; Bayerishes National Museum, Munich, Germany; Kunstgewerbe Museum, Berlin, Germany; Metropolitan Museum of Art, New York, NY; Museum für Kunst und Gewerbe, Hamburg, Germany.

Additional Listings: Bavaria, Bohemia, Carlsbad, C.T. Germany, Dresden, Frankenthal, Furstenberg, Heubach, Hochst, Hutschenreuther, KPM, Ludwigsburg, Minor German Factories, Meissen, Nymphenburg, Rosenthal, Royal Bayreuth, Royal Dux, Rudolstadt, Schlegelmilch, Sitzendorf, and Volkstedt.

Basket

   5 1/8" d, white open crisscross body, basketweave base, raised pink roses and blue flowers on sides, gilt line rim
   . . . . 55.00

   11" h x 12 1/4" l, relief molded white basketweave body, applied white and pink roses and green leaves, applied figural cherubs at sides of handle, gilt lined center handle, gilt rim and base, Schierholz and Sohn, c1880-90. . . . . 550.00

Berry Set

   Master bowl, 8" d, 6 bowls, 4 3/4" d, transfer of pink and peach roses, pink borders, molded beaded scalloped rims, (A) 50.00

   Master bowl, 8 3/4" d, 8 bowls, 5 1/4" d, bunches of yellow and pink roses with green leaves, white ground, scalloped rim with raised dots on int, lt yellow and blue irid on int rim, "P K Silesia" marks
   . . . . 75.00

Bowl

   9" d

      Lg white and pink rose, green leaves, purple lilacs in center, stenciled blue-gray leaves and shadow foliage on inner border, luster finish, "three crowns Germany" mark
      . . . . 25.00

      Vert ribbing, lg red roses and multicolored garden flowers in center, orange luster and white ground,

Bowl, 9 1/4" d, red and yellow roses, green leaves, shaded green border with gold stenciling, $68.

molded fleur-de-lys and beaded border, wavy rim 25.00

   9 3/8" d, lg white and red-pink rose joined by green stems and leaves, shaded brown to cream ground, gold rim, Kloster Vessra, c1937 . . . . 55.00

   9 5/8" d, paneled, lg mauve chrysanthemums, shaded yellow to green ground, chain of gold with red roses from rim
   . . . . 25.00

   10" H-H, sm orange flowers and green leaves in center, border of lg orange and white flowers and green buds, molded curlicue drop on rim, gold outlined handles, Silesia 18.00

   10 5/8" d, red speckled yellow tiger lilies on int border, green leaves, joined by green stems, perforated border, molded lt yellow stylized flowerhead and dot rim. 25.00

   10 7/8" d, peaches transfer, irid yellow, purple, and blue border, molded scalloped rim, "Germany in oval" mark, (A)
   . . . . 40.00

   11" d, transfer of white and pink rose on shaded green ground, molded scroll and floral border, gold accented scalloped rim, C. & E. Carstens, (A) . 45.00

Bud Vase, 7 1/2" h, ovoid, multicolored scene of young man presenting bouquet to woman in meadow in gold dot cartouche on dk green panel with raised gold stenciling, sgd "Fragonard," 2 vert dk red panels on sides, dk green panel on reverse with gold stylized flowerheads, "gold crown, G and Germany" mark
. . . . 65.00

Bureau Box, 2" d, multicolored scene of period man and woman in forest, green pearlized sides, brass rims and hinge, "incised Germany 7757" mark, (A) 38.00

Butter Dish, Cov, 8 3/8" d, with drain, border band of yellow and green sunrise design and suspended pink roses, gold knob, Silesia
. . . . 32.00

Cake Plate, 10" H-H, mother of pearl luster center, black outlined orange luster border, sm molded handles 28.00

Candelabrum, 31 3/4" h, standing figure of musketeer in plumed hat, aqua jacket, pink pantaloons or plumed hat, red jacket, gray striped hose, holding 5 arm candelabrum with molded masks and jewels, foliate scroll arms, and gadrooned nozzles, waisted circ base with scroll feet, c1900, pr, (A) 2,070.00

Candlestick, 12" h, modeled as classical maid and child, gadrooned sq base, applied flowerheads, polychrome with gilt accents, (A)
. . . . 185.00

Canister Set

   8 piece, 4 canisters, 8" h, COFFEE, BARLEY, RICE, and FARINA, 4 canisters, 4 5/8" h, CINNAMON, CLOVES, PEPPER, and ALLSPICE, gold labels, band of multicolored florals on borders, molded designs on rims and bases 170.00

   11 piece, 4 canisters, 9" h, 5 canisters, 5 1/4" h, oil, vinegar, 11" h, dk blue stylized flowerheads with dark red centers, vert band of yellow flowers, black names 265.00

   14 piece, 6 sq canisters, 7 1/2" h, 6 sq canisters, 4 1/2" h, 2 sq bottles, 10 1/2" h, windmill scenes, blue transfers
   . . . . 225.00

Centerpiece Bowl, 16 3/4" l x 11" w, vert pierced sides, pink and blue floral swags, gilt outlined molded drape on ext, Von Schierholz 650.00

Chocolate Pot

   6 1/4" h, painted purple flower bouquets around body, band of flowers and herringbone design on borders, chip on spout 200.00

   10" h, dk pink and yellow roses, green leaves, blue florals, lobed shaped base, raised molded designs on rim, worn gold trim, "Made in Germany" mark
   . . . . 75.00

   10 1/4" h, paneled body, 2 multicolored exotic birds in pink flowering branches, purple lustered border 25.000

   11" h, scattered red carnations, green leaves, sm blue flowers, gold sponging,

Chocolate Set, pot, 10 1/4" h, 6 cups and saucers, yellow roses, brown to yellow shaded ground, $250.

molded swirls, molded swirl knob, Krister, Waldenburg. 125.00

Console Set, 9 3/4" h, oval basket with applied flowerheads, gold reticulated rim, painted scattered florals on int, supported by 4 figural cherubs, oval base with applied flowers, Von Schierholz 2,350.00

Creamer and Cov Sugar Bowl, pink rose and lily of the valley transfers, shaded pearlized ground, gold accented rims and handles, scalloped rims. 23.00

Creamer

3 7/8" h, red floral transfer, green shaded ground, scrolled handle, scalloped rim, C.A. Lehmann & Son, (A) 30.00

4" h, enameled seated fat man in red vest, lt brown trousers, purple cape, brown bowler hat, dk green mottled ground, c1910-25 . . . . 125.00

6 1/4" h, black spotted figural handle, cream ground, "Erphila Fayence Germany" mark 65.00

Cup and Saucer

Blue and gold outlined molded "SISTER" on cup, HP gold flowers, gold banded rims, (A) 20.00

Gold and vine molded "Forget me not" on white to cobalt shaded ground, gold int, gold striped handle and rims, "Made in Germany" mark, (A) 12.00

White calla lilies, green to purple lustered ground 8.00

Cup and Saucer, Miniature, Meissen style reserve of painted European harbor scene, mauve pink ground, gilt scroll borders, late 19th, (A). 75.00

Dresser Set

Candlestick, 7" h, hatpin holder, cov hair receiver, sm cov box, lg cov box, tray, 11" l x 8" w, oval, lg yellow roses, gold trim on cream ground with turquoise shading 295.00

Cov box, hair receiver, tray, 10 1/4" l x 7 1/4" w, pink and purple roses in brown basket with twisted handle, pink ribbons with yellow flowers and green leaves on border, white ground 75.00

Ewer, 24" h, tapered cylinder shape, molded satyr mask and grapes on base, molded grapes and vines on body, Art Nouveau maiden formed molded handle, brown and amber glazes 270.00

Figure

1 1/2" h, snowbaby on wooden skis, pink cheeks, "Germany" mark. 115.00

2 5/8" h, bisque, seated Kate Greenaway girl, lt blue dress, pink sash, white bonnet with pink ribbon, (A) 20.00

4" l, baby's shoe, applied white flowers, lt blue ground, Elfinware. 45.00

4 1/2" l, 3 1/2" h, 2 pink pigs in shaded gray purse 75.00

6" h, porcelain, green speckled frog in pink shorts, folding orange umbrella, lettuce leaf base, c1890 . . . . 525.00

6 1/8" h, busts of Royal children, yellow lined multicolored costumes and caps, gilt accents, scroll molded bases, "blue AR" marks, 19th C, pr, (A) 616.00

7" h, young girl kneeling, white polka dot dress, applied pink florals in hair, Wallendorf. 65.00

8 7/8" h, seated woman sewing, white gown over red bodice, brown chair, blue hat with pink ribbon hangs from chair 275.00

9 1/4" h, 4 putti freeing 2 pigeons from cages, red or blue sashes, oval rocky mound with applied florals, gilt accents, (A) 650.00

13 1/8" h, standing Spanish dancer, pink and puce layered skirt, holding castanets, oval base, gilt accents . . . 300.00

14" h, seated panther, white glaze, (A) 345.00

Grill Plate, 8" d, blue "Delft" design . . . 20.00

Hatpin Holder, 7" h, roses design, white ground, "Germany" mark 90.00

Hot Milk Jug, Cov, 6 1/4" h, pear shape, wishbone handle, painted bouquet and smaller scattered sprays, bud knob, "imp H, incised P" marks, mid-18th C 225.00

Hot Plate, 6 1/2" d

Three purple irises, orange and blue luster border, 3 crowns Germany. 22.00

Three white roses and lt blue flowers in center, cream shaded ground, gold curlicues on border and rim 35.00

Yellow and white water lilies reflected in water, blue and orange luster border with molded geometrics 32.00

Jar, Cov, 5" h, bell shape, pink, peach, and cream rosebuds, applied leaves, Schierholz, chips. 110.00

Match Striker, 4 1/2" h, porcelain, brown figural bust of devil holding lt blue cards, white cloak, E. Bohne & Sohne, chips and repairs 150.00

Milk Pitcher, 6 5/8" h, vert black stripes, black outlined blue dots, brown and green dashes on border, "Made in Germany" mark. . 35.00

Mirror, 12 1/4" h, oval, flower encrusted, 2 putti holding floral wreaths, polychrome and gilt, Plaue, (A) 277.00

Mug, 5 1/2" h, HP lg pink and purple roses on shaded green, yellow, and pink ground, sgd "C. Rene," Habsburg mark, (A) 30.00

Nodder, 7 1/8" h, woman holding fan, lt blue and gold conical hat, white dress with cobalt and gold accents, HP facial features, (A). 100.00

Pickle Dish, 9 3/4" l, shaded pink roses in center, 4 sets of roses and shadow leaves on border, lt orange open handles. 15.00

Pincushion Doll, 3 1/4" h, gray hair with blue ribbon, yellow ruffled dress, "Germany" mark 100.00

Pitcher, 5 1/4" h, Friarware, friar in brown robe eating dinner, lt brown shaded ground, scalloped shaped rim and base, "Germany" mark, c1900 . . . . 35.00

Plaque

3" h, oval, painted portrait of young woman in eastern dress, polychrome, 19th C, (A) 493.00

7 1/8" h x 5 1/8" w, rect, porcelain, painted seated sleeping rotund man before dinner table, sgd "Wagner," (A) . . . 575.00

7 1/2" h x 5" w, rect, titled "Wieder Leer Nach," HP scene of monk in cellar looking at empty tankard, "Made in Germany" mark, framed, (A). 2,178.00

Plate

7 1/4" d, HP portrait of 16th C woman in ermine trimmed dk blue jacket, jeweled necklace, lg purple hat with white plumes, gold ground, mtd in frame, (A) 35.00

8" d, multicolored farm scene with 2 sheep, thatched house and stream, brown and green shaded ground 30.00

8 1/4" d, multicolored transfer in center of young boy in 18th C clothing kneeling before young girl holding fan, lt blue ground, molded scroll border, gold lined rim 55.00

8 1/2" d, pale yellow border band with gilt cartouche of multicolored period couple in garden, gold banded rim with dots 30.00

9" d, black outlined center mural of reindeer in snow by stream, farm house across stream, splashed yellow luster border, black lined rim, "black Made in Germany in circle" mark 25.00

9 1/2" d, enameled pr of birds on branch with blossoms, molded lattice border with insects in 4 compartments, gilt shaped rim, "AR" mark, c1900, set of 12, (A) 748.00

Potpourri Vase, Cov, 11 3/8" h, shouldered tapered cylinder shape, arched quatrefoil base, pierced cov with ring handles, blue painted relief molded scrolling flowers and branches, applied multicolored putti on shoulder, Plaue, pr, (A) 540.00

Punch Set, bowl, 14" H-H, 10 mugs, 3 5/8" h, dk green roundels with raised named castle scenes, raised green and brown leaves and stems, cream ground, brown figural castle knob, molded grapes and leaves on cov 275.00

Relish Tray

8 5/8" l, peach and red rose transfer in center, orange luster border with panels of gold stenciled lattice design, molded handles 28.00

11 1/2" l x 4 3/4" w, open handles, red and yellow rose transfer, green shaded ground, shaded pink and yellow border with gold accents and stenciled gold florals, scalloped rim, "IPP and Germany" mark, (A) 30.00

12 1/2" H-H, lg yellow and white roses in center, yellow roses at ends, orange luster border with beaded rim, "PK, tent, Silesia" mark 35.00

Vase, 8 3/4" h, dk green ground, gold trim, gold handles, Ludwig Wessel, "Imperial Bonn Germany" mark, $150.

Salt, 3 1/2" d, leaf shape, multicolored floral sprays, gold scrolls, brushed gold rim, "Elfinware Germany" mark 20.00

Serving Dish, 12 1/4" H-H, mauve thistle flowers, thorny leaves, gilt outlined molded rim and closed handles. 38.00

Shaker, 4 1/8" h, figural standing Kate Greenaway girl, long white dress, dust cap, gold accents, (A). 20.00

Sugar Bowl, Cov, 6" h, pink clover head and snowballs, pearlized ground, gray-blue base
. . . . 55.00

Tankard, 6 7/8" h, baluster shape, gray body incised and glazed in blue with interlocking stylized scrolling motifs "Derersete Zug, Nie Lang Genug" title, pewter lid (A). 139.00

Tea and Coffee Service, Part, coffeepot, 11" h, teapot, 8 1/2" h, cream jug, 6 1/2" h, sugar bowl, cov, 6 3/4" h, 12 cups, 9 saucers, overall dotted red and green florals, black handles with molded floral terminals, late 19th C
. . . . .2,000.00

Teapot, 5 3/4" h, squat shape, red stoneware, silver gilt mounts, early 18th C 1,200.00

Vase

5 1/8" h, HP orange, purple, and blue single stroke vert wavy stripes, purple, yellow, and blue single stroke flowerhead, gray single stroke ground, black wavy rim, "Gobelin, triangle" mark . . . 125.00

7 1/2" h

Bulbous shape, band of blue leaves on shoulder, ivory ground, Max Lauger
. . . . 200.00

Waisted baluster shape with short integral handles, green banding with red and turquoise jewels, textured silvered ground, jewel missing, pr, (A) 123.00

8 1/2" h

Bulbous, enameled green and brown spreading trees, dk blue ground, Max Lauger, rim repair 550.00

Figural, 19th C woman in yellow dress, yellow bonnet with blue ribbon, ruffled pantaloons, fluted vase
. . . . 75.00

10" h, tapered cylinder shape, stepped rim, 4 lg red roses and green leaves, shade brown ground 150.00

12" h, hex baluster shape, drabware body, 2 arched rope twist handles ending in bearded peasant figures, ozier molded neck, applied buff figures of dancing couples on body, flowering foliate scrolls on mouth, shoulder, and lower section, mid 19th C, pr, (A). . . . 920.00

13 3/4" h, baluster shape, polychrome oval rustic view, blue ground with scrolling and floral sprays, pr, (A). 70.00

16" h

Art Nouveau style, tapered cylinder shape with ftd bulbous base, rim molded with mask of water sprite with flowing water falling on maiden from water lilies, brown and ochre shades, sgd "K. Lahl," "imp JMH" mark, (A) 123.00

Bottle shape, painted maiden in thin blue gown, seated in landscape in gilt foliate cartouche, band of gilt Greek key and foliage on neck, gilt scrolling foliage on base, lt green lustered ground, "gilt RPM" mark, c1880, (A) 2,900.00

23 1/4" h, swollen body, flared neck and rim, spread ft, sq base, panel of enameled "Madonna and Child with St. John the Baptist" or "The Annunciation," scenic landscapes on reverse, gilt ground with stiff leaves and acanthus borders, 19th C, repairs, pr, (A) 9,200.00

Vase, Cov

5" h, ovoid shape, painted multicolored flower bouquets in gilt scrolling diaper and dot cartouche panels, pr . . 225.00

20 1/4" h, baluster shape, applied overall rows of yellow centered white flowers, cov, finial, and side handles modeled with colored birds perched on branches with blue mayflowers, "blue X'd swords" mark, c1880, (A) 3,450.00

Wall Mask, 7 7/8" h, stylized woman's face, orange-brown face, turquoise kerchief with yellow flowered braid, (A) 154.00

GINORI

Doccia, near Florence, Italy
1737 to Present

History: In 1737, the Ginori family established a factory to manufacture porcelain and earthenware at a villa in Doccia, a few miles from Florence. Marquis Carlo Ginori, the founder, operated the factory until 1757. Carlo Ginori's management was known as the "first period."

Stencil decorated dark blue plates, teapots, coffeepots, and cups were the earliest wares. Ginori produced many examples of snuff boxes, extremely popular in the 18th century, in a variety of shapes and decorations. Sculptures and large reliefs depicting mythological or religious subjects also were made.

In 1757, Lorenzo, his son, took over. This is the "second period." Lorenzo introduced an imitation Sevres blue ground, and strong use of colors. He continued making figurals in the rococo style.

Anton Maria Fanciullacci served as director from 1791-1805, the "third period," changing the designs to reflect the Empire style. In 1792, the manufacture of creamware helped subsidize the production of porcelain.

Doccia was the only Italian pottery that survived and prospered during the 19th century. It remained in the control of the Ginori family. Around 1821 the Doccia factory acquired Capodimonte molds from the Naples factory and continued production. Ginori used the Old Naples mark on these examples.

Lorenzo Ginori II took charge in 1848. The firm started to make lithophanes, majolica, and egg-shell porcelains. A large number of pieces was decorated with urban scenes enclosed within a shield shaped reserve on a white ground in the classical style. The crowned "N" mark was used on some of the wares. Industrial ceramics for the electrical industry also were manufactured on a large scale.

In 1896, the firm incorporated with Societa Ceramica Richard in Milan to become Societa Ceramica Richard-Ginori. The Art Nouveau style was introduced. In addition to modern forms and decorations, some traditional motifs such as cockerels, narrative reliefs, and tulip motifs continued to be used.

Early Ginori porcelains were frequently not marked. During the third period, the "F" or "PF" incised marks appeared. In the 19th century, "G," "Ginori," or a "N" crowned and impressed was used. The present mark is "Richard-Ginori" with a crown.

References: Arthur Lane, *Italian Porcelain,* Faber & Faber, 1954; Francesco Stazzi, *Italian Porcelain,* G.P. Putman's Sons, 1964.

Museums: Doccia Museum at Sesto Fiorentino, Florence, Italy; Fitzwilliam Museum, Cambridge, England; Metropolitan Museum of Art, New York, NY; Victoria & Albert Museum, London, England.

Basket, 10 1/2" l, HP floral sprays on int and ext, reticulated fan sides, "Ginori, Italy" mark 295.00

Bookends, 6 5/8" h, modeled as stylized elephant, lt green glaze, pr, (A) 292.00

Dish, 6 3/8" H-H, oval, majolica, painted green stylized flowerhead on cobalt ground in center, painted griffins and heads on border, molded shell handles, "blue crown Ginori" mark 48.00

Plaque, 16 3/8" h x 6 3/4" w, Pre-Raphaelite woman in green robe with gold drape, wreath of green leaves on head, emptying jug, blue and green ground, vine of pink flowers, "TEMPERANTIA" in banner at base, framed, (A) 690.00

Plate

    8" d, Hp thistle design 20.00

    9 3/4" d

        "La Bevta," blue, green, red, and brown couple dancing, white ground, (A) 330.00

        Multicolored fish in center, different fish on each, flower and sea grass on

Soup Bowl, 7 7/8" d, gold center, brown band, gold rim, "Richard Ginori Italy" mark, set of 12, $240.

border, white ground, "Richard Ginori Italy" mark, set of 6. . . . . 100.00

Serving Dish, 11" H-H, gilt outlined orange-rust, and blue florals in center, border with band of basketweave, band of paneling, and rust florals, gilt rosettes, and rectangles between, gilt scalloped rim, "Richard Ginori, Italy" mark 23.00

Soup Plate, 9 1/4" d, "Stresa" pattern, multicolored pagoda, blue mountain in bkd, green crisscross rim with floral ovals 16.00

Teapot, 8" h, Art Deco style blue, green, yellow and rose dancing couple on green bkd, cream body, rust and black edged cov, "S. Christoford, Made in Italy" mark. 195.00

Vase

    4 1/2" h, cylinder shape, everted rim, ftd, black ground with bands of gold outlined cells with dot in center, sgd "Gio Ponti," (A) 230.00

    4 3/4" h, HP peaches, artist sgd . . 275.00

    7 1/2" h, Asian style bridge and willow trees silver overlay on cream ground, c1920, "Richard Ginori" mark, (A) 165.00

    15 1/4" h, rd body, spread ft and base, flared rim, majolica, multicolored crests on front and reverse, relief of bows and face on neck, applied figural satyr handles, blue int, "blue crown, Ginori" mark 900.00

Wine Pot, 11 5/8" h, majolica, ogee body with mask spout, painted mythical beasts and satyrs, (A). 100.00

GOEBEL

Rodental, Bavaria, Germany 1871 to Present

1935

History: In 1871, Franz and William Goebel, father and son, applied for a permit to manufacture porcelain in the village of Oeslau near the city of Coburg. When Duke Ernst II of Saxe-Coburg intervened, the permit finally was granted in 1879. The firm, F.D. & W. Goebel Porcelain Works, began manufacturing dinner services, milk pitchers, beer steins, and egg cups.

When Franz died in 1909, William expanded the porcelain dinnerware and figurine business into an export-oriented concern. Max-Louis, William's son, took over in 1912 when William died. Max-Louis introduced many new porcelain figurine designs and added a ceramic figurine line as well. Frieda, wife of Max-Louis, Franz, son of Frieda and Max-Louis, and Dr. Eugene Stocke, Frieda's brother, assumed control when Max-Louis died in 1929.

Franz Goebel first saw Sister Maria Innocentia Hummel's sketches in 1934. In March 1935, the first "M.I. Hummel" figure

was made. These were an immediate success, especially in America.

During WW II, the Goebel works concentrated on the manufacture of dinnerware for the domestic market. A few figurines were made. When the United States Military Government of Germany lifted the wartime embargo and gave permission for production and exportation of "M.I. Hummel" figurines and other objects in 1946, a rapid recovery was accomplished by this firm.

When Franz died in 1969, the management of the company transferred to Wilhelm, his son, and Ulrich Stocke, Eugene's son. They continued expansion of the company and acquisition of other factories.

Today the Goebel factories manufacture high quality porcelain dinnerware for the home and export markets. In addition to the popular Hummel series, they manufacture figurine series that include Disney characters, birds, animals, and Friar Tuck monks. A collector's plate series also is made. There is a wide variety of Friar Tuck and Cardinal Tuck versions: salt and pepper shakers, cookie jars or biscuit barrels, banks, and cruets were all made.

Marks: There are six trademarks by Goebel. They are called "Trademark 1," "Trademark 2," etc. and also referred to as "crown," "bee," "stylized bee," "3-line," "Goebel bee" and "Goebel." Trademark 1, the crown trademark is the oldest mark; Goebel or Trademark 6 is the current one.

Trademark information is generally stamped on the bottom of the piece. Mold numbers and often the year the item was sculpted are incised on the bottom. Mold numbers are an accurate method of identifying pieces.

References: Eric Ehrmann, *Hummel,* Portfolio Press Corp.1976; John F. Hotchkiss, *Hummel* Art 11, Wallace Homestead, 1981; Thomas E. Hudgeons, III, Ed., *The Official Price Guide to Hummel Figurines and Plates,* House of Collectibles, 1980; Carl F. Luckey, *Hummel Figurines and Plates,* 5th Edition, Books Americana, 1984; Robert L. Miller, *M.I. Hummel: The Golden Anniversary Album,* Portfolio Press, 1984; Wolfgang Schwatlo, *W. Goebel Porzellan, Part I: Figurines,* Sammlerverlag Schwatlo GmbH, 1996; Lorie A. Wuttke, *Fired Up over Friar Tuck,* Antique Trader Weekly, December 17, 1997.

Collectors' Clubs: Friar Tuck Collectors Club, P.O. Box 262, Owego, NY 13827, Membership: $18.00, Quarterly newsletter; Goebel Networkers, P.O. Box 396, Lemoyne, PA 17043, $15.00 per year, quarterly newsletter.

Museum: Goebel Museum, Tarrytown, NY.

Cream and Sugar Set, creamer, 4"h, sugar bowl, 4 3/4"h, tray, 7"l, Friar Tuck, brown robes, flesh faces, brown lined rim on tray, "blue V and full bee" mark, $125.

Bank, 4 3/4" h, Friar Tuck 160.00

Beer Mug, 5" h, Friar Tuck, stylized bee mark
. . . . 50.00

Box, 5 3/4" h x 5 1/4" d, figural black, brown, and cream bird knob, cream ground . 115.00

Calendar, 3 1/2" h, Friar Tuck, W. Germany
. . . . 115.00

Clock, 7" h, Brad the Clockmaker, Co-Boys
. . . . 225.00

Cookie Jar, 9 11/2" h, Friar Tuck, barefoot
. . . . 525.00

Creamer, 2 1/2" h, Friar Tuck, full bee mark
. . . . 22.00

Decanter, 10 3/4" h, modeled as cello player with purple nose, orange jacket, yellow trousers, head forms stopper, (A) 100.00

Egg Timer, 3" h, single, figural Friar Tuck, #104, 3 line mark. 50.00

Figure

2" h, Friar Tuck. 50.00
3" h

4 1/8" l, Colonial woman, 2 men and sedan chair, white glaze, #GM506, crown and bee mark 125.00

Angel in pink dress with stars, stylized bee mark 38.00

Owl with wings spread, brown, white breast, #38307-07, "Goebel, W. Germany" mark 35.00

3 1/4" h, seated Persian cat, white with green eyes. 30.00
3 3/4" h

Man blowing horn, carrying lantern, brown coat, green hat, #13907-09, "Goebel, W. Germany" mark
. . . . 60.00

Red haired boy facing red poodle, Charlot Byj, 3 line mark 25.00
4" h

"She Loves Me," boy with daisy and dog, Norman Rockwell, #213, 3 line mark 275.00

"Strike," child bowling, Charlot Byj, #1
. . . . 80.00

4 3/8" h, chimney sweep in black outfit, carrying ladder, riding pig. 75.00

4 1/2" h

"Eek" dog tugging little girl's dress, Charlot Byj 65.00

"The Roving Eye," Charlot Byj, #2
. . . . 80.00
5" h

"Shear Nonsense," Charlot Byj, #5
. . . . 135.00

"The Kibitzer," #23, Charlot Byj, 3 line mark. 85.00

5 1/4" h, "Sleepy Head," blond, Charlot Byj, #11 . . . . 80.00

5 1/2" h, boy proposing to girl, polychrome, Nasha, #8, crown and bee mark 350.00
6" h

Boy playing harmonica, polychrome, Nasha, #6/A, bee mark 250.00

Boy sitting with straw hat, #5, Nasha, crown mark 350.00

Little veterinarian, boy pouring medicine for dog, Norman Rockwell, #201. . . . . 450.00

6 1/4" h, 2 parakeets on branch, green and yellow or blue and white, "W. Goebel, W. Germany, V and bee, CV95" and "Wellensittich Budgerigar Perruche ondulee" paper label, (A) 30.00

6 1/2" h, Madonna and child, brown bisque faces and hands, #HM70, "crown WG" mark 55.00

7" h, Poodle, gray 75.00
7 1/2" h

"Lisette," white gown, brown hair, Huldah, stylized bee mark 250.00

"Love Bugs," white glaze, Charlotte Byj, BYJ 64 . . . . 125.00

Seated woman with halo, child at side, white, HX 246, stylized bee mark
. . . . 100.00

8" h, "Sepp the Drunkard," Co-Boy. 65.00

8 1/4" h, swallow on branch base, natural colors, "Goebel, W. Germany, V and bee" and "W. Goebel, Rotelschwalbe, Red-rumped Swallow, Hirondelle rousse" paper label, (A). 25.00

8 3/8" h, woman dressed in long gray skirt, white and blue mottled fur jacket, rd purple hat, white plumes, carrying black walking stick with gold ball handle, "Goebel W. Germany 16 282 21, 78" mark, (A) 50.00

Liqueur Tot, 2" h, Friar Tuck, "Goebel, W. Germany" mark 45.00

Mug

1 1/2" h, Friar Tuck 34.00

2 1/2" h, Friar Tuck, brown robe, full bee mark, (A) 25.00

4 1/2" h, barrel shape, nude figural handle, white glaze, crown mark. 88.00

Mustard Pot, 3 3/4" h, Friar Tuck with toes
. . . . 45.00

Pepper Shaker, 2 1/2" h, figural Friar Tuck, full bee mark 32.00

Perfume Lamp

6 1/2" h, begging dog, full bee mark
. . . . 350.00

8" h, hiker in lederhosen 250.00

Pitcher

2" h, Cardinal Tuck, red robe, #141 3/0, stylized bee mark. 250.00

2 1/2" h, Friar Tuck, cross-eyed, bee mark
. . . . 35.00

4" h, Cardinal Tuck, stylized bee mark
. . . . 150.00

5" h, Cardinal Tuck, stylized bee mark
. . . . 275.00

Salt Shaker

2 3/4" h, Cardinal Tuck, stylized bee mark
. . . . 125.00

3" h, Friar Tuck, full bee mark 24.00

Stein, .5 L, figural Friar Tuck, full bee mark, (A)
. . . . 331.00

Tumbler, 2" h, red hearts, #L/MUN16B, set of 4 . . . . 20.00

Wall Mask, 12 1/2" h, stylized woman, orange face, blond hair, dk blue hat scarf on head, green collar, (A) 231.00

Wall Pocket, 11" h, figural partly opened umbrella, black glaze, incised crown mark, c1930s. 75.00

Water Pitcher, 7" h, figural Friar Tuck . . 125.00

GOLDSCHEIDER

Vienna, Austria
1885 to Present

History: Friedrich Goldscheider founded the Goldscheider Porcelain and Majolica Factory in 1885. Goldscheider's family owned a factory in Pilsen, Czechoslovakia, along with decorating shops in Vienna and Carlsbad. Decorative earthenwares and porcelains, faience, terra cotta, and figures were made.

Regina Goldscheider and Alois Goldscheider, her brother-in-law, ran the firm from 1897 until 1918. They made figures along with sculptured vases in the Art Nouveau style. Regina's sons, Walter and Marcel, took control in 1920 and adopted styles prevailing in Vienna during the 1920s.

The factories experienced several name changes both before and after World War I and II. Following Hitler's invasion of Austria, the family left and settled in Trenton, New Jersey, in the early 1940s. They established a factory in Trenton and made art objects and tablewares.

After World War II, Marcel Goldscheider established a pottery in Staffordshire, England to manufacture bone china figures and earthenware. The company's mark was a stamp of Marcel's signature.

Figure

3 7/8" h, 2 stylized foals, cream crackle glaze with turquoise mane, neck, and base, (A) 93.00

4 1/2" h, terra cotta, bust of young woman with stylized features, orange curly hair, green scarf around neck, circ black base, (A) 215.00

6 1/2" h, standing woman in purple flowered white hoop skirt, blue-green jacket, flowered hat, holding parasol, Austria 55.00

7 5/8" h, stylized terrier, orange glaze with black accents, sgd "Meisinger," (A) 185.00

9 1/4" h, bust of stylized young woman with green and orange wavy hair, tulip under chin, oval base, mkd, (A). 539.00

9 1/2" h, standing young girl in green beret, green plaid dress, looking back at black and white terrier at feet, black oval base, (A) 642.00

9 7/8" h, bust of stylized young woman with orange curly hair, green scarf around neck, holding apple in hand, circ wooden base, pr, (A) 215.00

10" h, standing African girl, late 19th C gown, straw hat at side, glazed earthenware, "imp C GOLDSCHEIDER" mark, (A) 630.00

11" h, nude woman with seated dog, yellow, gray, and peach glazes, (A) 1,495.00

11 3/8" h

Standing naked woman wrapped in flowered white gown with gray tassels, domed oval black base, mkd, (A) 770.00

Young woman in floral sprig gray and yellow dress, lg yellow bonnet, facing wind, circ base 325.00

12 1/2" h, "Butterfly Girl," standing girl, brown hair, raised blue skirt with black centered pink flowers, green leaves, black and white striped sleeves, lt green base, Austria mark, c1930 . . . . .1,535.00

13 3/4" h, young Negro child holding blue and yellow sash astride tan walking camel, domed oval base, mkd, (A) 616.00

14 1/2" l, Art Deco style woman in lt blue trousers with dk blue dots, blue wide brimmed hat, seated in brown canoe,

Figure, 16" h, white glaze, sgd "K. Lorenzl", $3,250.

black and white terrier on rim, (A) 605.00

14 3/4" h, nude young girl standing on one ft with bent knee, long braids, brown glaze, (A) 428.00

16" h

Art Deco style dancing woman, leg, raised, holding skirt hem, cream with purple skirt with dk purple flowers, Vienna. 1,295.00

Standing woman in long blue flowered dress, hand on hip, hand holding lg blue hat, gray and white Borzoi at side, oval black base, chips and repairs, (A) 1,693.00

17 1/2" h, "Salome," standing figure in red trimmed black streaked dress, sgd "Lorenzl," c1920 . . . . 3,500.00

19 7/8" h, Pierot and Columbine, standing man in black trimmed white clown suit playing brown mandolin, brown haired woman in pink flowered dress with dk pink shawl, pink slippers, standing on blue and red floral ottoman with white drape, gray base, artist sgd . . 2,200.00

20" h, dancing woman in pink gown with floral decorated border 950.00

Lamp Base, 4 1/2" d, spherical, Wiener Werkstatte style green, red, and violet cross pattern, yellow ground, (A) 55.00

Vase

8 1/8" h, thistle form, angular handles, stylized red flowers and green foliage, yellow ground, (A) 310.00

8 7/8" h, thistle form, stylized leaf and heart motifs in blue and white glazes, black ground with orange banding . . 500.00

Wall Mask

7 1/4" h, woman's face, dk brown hair, red lips, oatmeal face, (A) 275.00

8" h, terra cotta, stylized young woman with green and yellow scarf around hair, holding apple to face, mkd, (A) 170.00

8 1/4" h, terra cotta, woman's face with blue curly hair, white face with red lips, green and yellow scarf on base, (A) 642.00

10 1/2" h, terra cotta, stylized young woman with green hair, black ribbon on neck, mkd, (A) 462.00

13 1/2" h, terra cotta, stylized young woman with green curly hair, holding black mask on side of face, mkd, (A) . 739.00

GOSS AND CRESTED WARE

Stoke-On-Trent, England 1858-1930

History: William Henry Goss founded the Goss China Company in 1858 at Stoke-on-Trent. Goss began producing a fine grade parian which was used for figural groups, busts of famous people both past and present, pierced baskets, and a variety of other items. Terra cotta tobacco jars and wine vases decorated with transfers also were produced. Goss developed a method of imbedding colored glass into the parian body to make "jewelled" vases, patenting the technique in 1872. Fine tea services appeared in his catalog by 1880.

In 1883, Adolphus, William's son, joined the firm. William's aggressiveness helped launch the company into new and profitable fields. It was William who introduced crested china.

Victorian England had increased leisure time and great accessibility to the seacoast and resort areas. These vacation sites were perfect for the introduction of inexpensive souvenir items. Adolphus, much to the chagrin of William, produced and marketed the now famous white glazed souvenir pieces complete with enameled decorations and coats of arms of various towns and resorts. The technique was simple. A paper transfer was applied to the glazed body, and the colors were hand painted in the design. These heraldic souvenirs were an instant success. Shops were established in the resort areas to sell Goss crested china. Other factories quickly imitated the Goss crested ware.

In 1893, Goss China began producing miniature full color buildings, duplicating every detail of the original buildings from which they were modeled. Expansion was necessary to meet the demands for the

Goss products. Victor and Huntley, Adolphus' sons, became partners in 1900. Goss china even published its own journal, "Goss Records," to promote its products.

The company suffered during the Great Depression. Its assets were sold to Cauldon Potteries in 1929. Cauldon began the manufacture of figurines of young girls similar to the Royal Doulton figurines. Coalport China Co. purchased the rights to Goss in 1945; Ridgway and Adderly took control in 1954. The company currently is part of the Royal Doulton organization.

Other manufacturers of crested ware in England were: Arcadian, Carlton China, Grafton China, Savoy China, Shelley, and Willow Art. Gemma in Germany also made crested wares.

References: Sandy Andrews, *Crested China*, Milestone Publications, 1980; Sandy Andrews & Nicholas Pine, *1985 Price Guide to Crested China*, Milestone Publications, 1985; John Galpin, *Goss China*, 1972, published by author; Nicholas Pine, *Goss China: Arms, Decorations & Their Values, Rev. Ed.* Milestone Publications, 1982; Nicholas Pine, *The Concise Encyclopedia & Price Guide To Goss China*, Milestone Publications, 1989.

Collectors' Clubs: Goss Collectors Club, The Secretary, 4 Khasiaberry, Walnut Tree, Milton Keynes, MK77DP, England. Membership: £18. Monthly newsletter; The Crested Circle, 42 Douglas Road, Tolworth Surbiton, Surely KT6 7SA, England. Membership: £7. Bimonthly magazine and *Crested Circle* Annual Magazine. This circle covers the products of W.H. Goss, Arcadian, Carlton, Grafton, Shelley, and Savoy factories and commemoratives from the different factories.

Collecting Hints: Early Goss pieces tend to be heavier and less perfectly rounded than later pieces, gilding tends to come off easily if rubbed, and a heavy mold line is often apparent. By 1890-1900, the molding technique was improved and resulted in a thinner, more precise mold. Gilding also was of better quality and did not rub off easily. Greater color and more precision was used in the application of the coats of arms transfers.

Aberdeen Bronze Pot, City of Edinburgh crest, Goss 30.00

Alnwick Celtic Sepulchral Urn, 4 1/4" h, Goss 32.00

Bideford Ancient Mortar, Folkstone crest, Goss 55.00

Box, 3 3/4" d, sides relief molded with rope twist between reeded bands, applied flower encrusted knob, painted in colors, Goss, (A) 67.00

Brixworth Ancient Cup, Filey crest, Goss 30.00

Canary Ancient Jarra, Bergen crest, Goss 32.00

Canterbury Leather Bottle, Gourock crest, Goss 28.00

Charger, 13 1/2" d, Arms of Winchester College in center, dbl gilt bands, red and green "Manners Makyth Men" on border, molded petal rim, Goss 525.00

Cheese Dish, mini, The Island & Royal Manor of Portland crest, Goss 60.00

Chester Roman Vase, Cork crest, Goss 18.00

Chichester Roman Urn, sepia transfer of Windsor Castle, Goss, (A) 14.00

Colchester Famous Vase, Walton-on-Naze crest, Goss 22.00

Cottage, 28 3/4" l, The Old Maid's Cottage, Lee, Devon, glazed, Goss, (A) 69.00

Cream Jug
  Big-lipped
    Barnstable crest, Goss 25.00
    Beaumaris crest, Goss 20.00
  Melon, small, City of Leicester crest, Goss 25.00
  Ribbed, Manor of Dramber crest, Goss 40.00
  Taper
    Medium, Windsor crest, Goss . . 25.00
    Small, Lynton crest, Goss 24.00

Creamer and Sugar Bowl, Kingston, Canada crests, Shelley 95.00

Cup and Saucer, Edinburgh crest, Shelley 65.00

Cup and Saucer, Low Melon, small
  Farnham crest, Goss 25.00
  Faversham crest, Goss 25.00
  Margate crest, Goss 20.00

Dart Sack Bottle, Hastings crest, Goss 30.00

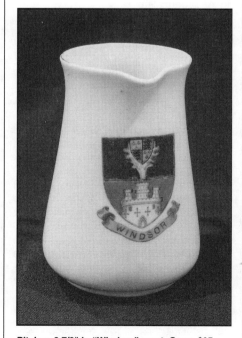

Pitcher, 3 7/8" h, "Windsor" crest, Goss, $25.

Devon Oak Pitcher, Warwick crest, Goss 18.00

Ewer, 3 1/8" h
  Batley crest, Arcadian 8.00
  Blandford Forum crest, Arcadian . . . 8.00

Exeter Vase, City of Worcester crest, Goss 20.00

Fountain Abby Cup, Sheringham crest, Goss 20.00

Glastonbury Bowl, See of Llandaff crest, Goss 20.00

Goodwin Sands Carafe, Royal Arms of Scotland crest, Goss 20.00

Hamworthy Lamp, Llandudno crest, Goss 35.00

Harrogate Ewer, City of Edinburgh crest, Goss 22.00

Irish Mather, Glasgow crest, Goss 30.00

Irish Wooden Noggin, Oakham crest, Goss 30.00

Japan Ewer, See of Exeter crest, Goss 38.00

Jug, 2 1/8" h, City of Bristol crest, Model of Jug about 600 years old found in the ancient moat of Scarborough, Arcadian 10.00

Kettle, 2 1/4" h, Battle Abbey crest, model of ancient kettle dredged up near Hastings, Carlton 10.00

Las Palmas Covered Jarra, Haslemere crest, Goss 45.00

Leiston Abbey Pitcher, Goss
  Flamborough crest 21.00
  Freshwater crest 21.00

Lichfield Jug, Eastbourne crest, Goss 18.00

Lincoln Vase, Dorchester crest, Goss 25.00

Louth Ewer, City of Wells crest, Goss . . 25.00

Loving Cup, 2 1/4" h, 3 handles, Arms of Ireland, Goss 45.00

Mug, mini, single handle
  Battersea crest, Goss 15.00
  Deal crest, Goss 16.00

Musselburg Urn, Cork crest, Goss 24.00

Newcastle Roman Jug, Abergele crest, Goss 20.00

Norwegian Bucket, 2 1/2" h, Goss 20.00

Ostend
  Bottle, City of Exeter crest, Goss . . . 28.00
  Vase, See of York crest, Goss 22.00

Painswick Roman Pot, City of Victoria, British Columbia, Goss 20.00

Penmaenmawr Urn, Las Planches Montreux crest, Goss 15.00

Pitcher, 3 1/8" h, Killarney crest, Florentine 10.00

Plate
  5" d, Bagware, Hastings crest, Goss 22.00
  6" d
    Flintshire crest, Goss 20.00
    Newquay crest, Goss 20.00

Portland Vase, 2" h 10.00

Ramsey Cinerary Urn, Worthing crest, Goss
. . . . 38.00

Reading Jug, See of Lincoln crest, Goss
. . . . 20.00

Seaford Urn, Sussex crest, Goss 30.00

Shakespeare's Jug, Shakespeare's Arms
crest, Goss 65.00

Southampton Pipkin, Highworth crest, Goss
. . . . 24.00

Southwold Jar, Glasgow crest, Goss . . 15.00

Staffordshire Tyge, single handle, Ancient
Port of Minehead crest, Goss 10.00

Stockport Plaque Stone, Stow-on-the-Wold
crest, Goss 75.00

Stockton Salt Pot, Cheddar crest, Goss
. . . . 30.00

Swindon Vase, lg, Swindon crest, Goss
. . . . 75.00

Swiss Vinegar Bottle, Lytham crest, Goss
. . . . 45.00

Tresco Brazier, Clacton-on-Sea crest, Goss
. . . . 45.00

Tresvannack Urn, Ayr crest, Goss 38.00

Trio, Cup, Saucer, side plate, Leeds crest,
multicolored, Foley 45.00

Tumbler, mini, See of Worcester crest, Goss
. . . . 15.00

Vase

2 1/8" h, dbl handles, City of Wells crest,
Foley 10.00

2 1/4" h, Seal of Minster, Carlton . . . 22.00

2 3/8" h
Lutterworth crest, model of Roman
vase found near Canterbury,
Arcadian 8.00

Stockton on Tees crest, Arcadian
. . . . 10.00

8 5/8" h, bottle type, single handle, enameled spray of forget-me-nots, Goss, (A)
. . . . 35.00

Teapot, 5 1/8" h, Bagware, "Buckinghamshire"
and "Arms of Wycombe" crests, turquoise
handle, "Published By Symond's Brothers High
Wycombe" and Goss marks, $195.

Ball, Crinkle Top
Cambridge University crest, Goss
. . . . 22.00

City of Wells crest, Goss 18.00

Hastings crest, Goss 18.00

Wide Taper, Lewes crest, Goss . . . 25.00

Walmer Roman Vase, Harrogate crest, Goss
. . . . 18.00

York Roman Urn, East Sussex County Coun-
cil, Goss 20.00

GOUDA

Gouda, Holland 17th Century to Present

MADE IN

Zuid Holland

c1897

History: Gouda and the surrounding areas of Holland have been producing Dutch pottery wares since the 17th century. Originally Delft-type tin glazed earthenwares were manufactured along with the clay smokers' pipes.

When the production of the clay pipes declined, the pottery makers started producing art pottery wares with brightly colored decorations. These designs were influenced by the Art Nouveau and Art Deco movements. Stylized florals, birds, and geometries were the favorite motifs, all executed in bold, clear colors. Some Gouda pieces have a "cloisonné" appearance.

Other pottery workshops in the Gouda region included Arnhem, Plazuid, Regina, Schoonhoven, and Zenith. Utilitarian tartan wares, vases, miniatures, and large outdoor garden ornaments also were included in the product line.

Reproduction Alert: With the recent renewal of interest in Art Nouveau and Art Deco examples, reproductions of earlier Gouda pieces now are on the market. These are difficult to distinguish from the originals.

Bowl

4 3/4" d, red outlined yellow, blue, and green Art Deco style geometrics, matte black ground, "Favorite Konin Kluk Gouda" mark 85.00

6 3/4" d, blue and white shields, rust and brown leaves, lt olive ground with blue bands, black body, house mark
. . . . 195.00

7" d, black outlined brown and tan leaves, green and yellow birds, sm gold circles and shields, tan ground, brown scalloped rim, semi-matte finish, "103 Ruturo, Hand Painted Goedewaagen, Holland" mark 80.00

9 1/2" d, center band of red and steel blue half flowerheads on gold ground, matte

ext, green crystalline int, "Rhodian Holland" mark, c1920 . . . . 185.00

Box, Cov, 5" d x 4 1/2" h, rust, blue, and green fan shapes with cream and yellow dots, matte black ground, "Regina Gouda Holland" mark 165.00

Candlestick, 12" h

Gold, gray, blue, and turquoise swirling geometrics, metallic green ground, house mark, pr 395.00

Rust red, blue, and yellow geometrics, lt green ground, black vert stripes, black bobiche, matte finish, house mark, pr
. . . . 940.00

Chamberstick

2 1/4" h, 6 1/2" d, clusters of gold and rust outlined blue flowerheads, black and gold ext, brown handle, satin finish
. . . . 110.00

3" h x 6" d, matte gold outlined rust, brown, yellow, turquoise, and lavender leaf designs, black border, base, and handle, socket with blue and rust accents, matte finish, Piso Gouda 165.00

Charger, 15 3/4" d, lg blue and orange-yellow flowerheads in center, brown leaves, orange and brown curling tendrils, red and tan flowerheads on border, pink accents, olive green swirled rim, (A) 248.00

Compote

6 1/2" h, rust flowerheads, gold circles, black body with blue stripes and dots, matte finish, house mark 225.00

6 3/4" h, bands of blue with rust centered cream squares, black ground, gold rim, int with blue pentagons with blue outlined rust and tan florals, gold circles, matte finish, "Berga, house, Gouda Holland" mark 225.00

Dish

8 1/4" l, overall blue, rust, and yellow teardrops and curlicues, lg teardrops on border with gold leaves, dk tn ground, olive rim, semi-matte finish, house mark
. . . . 85.00

9 1/2" d, ftd, 5 blue and mauve tops with lines and dots and yellow squiggles, yellow border with white streaks
. . . . 325.00

Flower Pot, 4" h, cream, black, and rust heraldic shapes, rust rim with painted green and gold scalloped edge, black int, matte finish, "Betty B, house, Holland" mark 120.00

Inkwell, 3 1/4" h, oct, dk red and blue morning glory flowers, green, brown, and yellow ground, gloss glaze, "Gouda, Made in Holland" mark 395.00

Jar, Cov, 19 1/2" h, cloisonné Persian floral design, blue and gold, acorn knob, "1054, Cloisonné, Gouda, Holland, IL, Y" mark, (A)
. . . . 800.00

Pitcher

4" h, bulbous shape, loop handle, turquoise, red, yellow and blue Art Deco geometric design, matte black ground
. . . . 55.00

Vase, 5" h, orange and gold flowerheads, turquoise rim, dk blue ground, matte finish, house mark, $425.

5 1/2" h, bulbous shape, matte black ground with lg red enameled dots and gold outlined blue teardrops, gold lined handle, gold Gouda house mark
. . . . 110.00

6 3/4" h, bulbous shape, overall lt green gloss glaze, c1902 . . . . 55.00

9 1/4" h, blue, white, gold, yellow, and brown Art Nouveau design, green ground, matte finish, house mark
. . . . 190.00

Planter, 7 1/2" h, flared shape, raised green leaves with yellow lines, brown wood textured ground, green int, "Royal Zuid Gouda" mark
. . . . 95.00

Plate

9 1/2" d, center with olive centered rust flower, bordered by chartreuse outlined green and turquoise leaves on cream ground, black border with scalloped rust int design, matte finish, "Modia Gouda Plated Oud Gouda Zuid Holland, house" mark 165.00

9 7/8" d, Art Deco style cobalt and yellow flowerhead in center, turquoise, red, and green stylized leaves, brown trim on border and rim, cream ground, satin finish 165.00

Shoe, 6" l, Dutch style, blue and green florals, black ground, unmkd 35.00

Tobacco Jar, 8 3/4" h, orange, blue, brown, and turquoise overlapping waves, cobalt ground, gloss finish, "MASS, house" mark
. . . . 300.00

Vase

3 3/4" h, green, mauve, purple, aqua, and orange stylized flowers and leaves, black ground, gloss finish, "Regina"
. . . . 175.00

4 1/2" h, indigo, white, and green stripes, black ground, house mark 65.00

5" h, ball shape, blue trimmed iron red and yellow flowerheads, stylized yellow and blue flowers, yellow rim, green int, gloss glaze, house mark 98.00

6 1/8" h, squat shape, slightly flared neck and rim, white center band with red, blue, and green stylized flowerheads and scrolling leaves bordered by bands of triangles, matte black base and neck 110.00

6 1/4" h, compressed ovoid form, cylinder neck, cylinder handles from shoulder to neck, green, blue, purple, and yellow stylized dandelions, cream ground, (A) 345.00

7" h

Bulbous shape, green, rust and gilt mushroom shapes on cream ground, border with orange and rust circles on blue ground, black base and int, matte finish, "Bagirmi, X Bi2, house, Y.R. Holland Gouda" mark
. . . . 125.00

Matte green floral design with silver overlay 350.00

7 1/2" h, tapered narrow base to wide shoulder, matte gold outlined blue, lavender, rust, and green geometrics, matte black base, geometric bands on top and base, house mark 200.00

8" h, bulbous body, flared trumpet neck, dull black and brown body stripes, red and turquoise enamel banding, "Splendid Holland, house" mark 195.00

8 1/4" h, 4 buttress handles, dk green and purple stylized flowers, gloss glaze, house mark, (A) 345.00

8 3/4" h, bulbous shape, lt tan, mustard yellow, blue, and black geometrics, mustard yellow and blue-black stripes on top and base, irid blue handles and int, "444 L C, Aqer, house, Zuid Gouda" mark 350.00

9 5/8" h, squat shape, overhead loop handle, purple, blue, raspberry, yellow, and green stylized poppies, (A) . . . 403.00

10 1/4" h, rust and blue fan and geometric designs, gold hanging spearheads, blue and orange dot and wave bands, matte glaze, "Candia Gouda Holland" mark 225.00

10 1/2" h, globular body, tapered slender neck, loop handles from shoulder to neck, purple, green, and yellow stylized irises, pr, (A) 345.00

11" h, flared and tapered top, rust stylized blossoms, orange outlined orchid blossoms, green-yellow ground with lt blue accents, matte finish, Schoonhaven
. . . . 1,200.00

11 1/2" h, slender shape with flared rim, dull gold outlined blue, cream, rust, and orange geometrics, black ground and int 225.00

19" h, blue and mustard stylized "Eagles," emerald green ground, gloss finish, "Goedenwaagen" 475.00

H&C°
L
c1885

CFH
GDM
FRANCE
c1891

HAVILAND

Limoges, France
1842 to Present

History: David and Daniel Haviland, two brothers, had a china import business in New York. When traveling to France in search of china, David decided to remain in Limoges, the leading center for the manufacture of pottery. By 1842, David and his family were firmly established in Limoges. David supervised the purchasing, designing, and decorating of stock for export from several Limoges companies. In 1865, he acquired a factory in Limoges to produce porcelains directly. Instead of sending whiteware to Paris to be decorated, David established studios at his own factory. He hired and trained local decorators.

In 1852, Charles Field Haviland was sent by Robert Barclay Haviland, his father, to learn the business from Uncle David. Charles Field married into the Alluaud family who owned the Casseaux works. When Charles Field took over, the mark used on the whiteware was "CFH."

Charles Edward and Theodore, sons of David Haviland, entered the firm in 1864. By 1878, the Haviland factory was the largest in the Limousin District. When David died in 1879, the firm passed into the hands of his two sons. A difference of opinion in 1891 led to the liquidation of the old firm. Charles Edward produced china under the "Haviland et Cie" name. After Charles died in 1922, his firm lost its significance and went out of business in 1931. Theodore started his own factory, "La Porcelaine Theodore Haviland," that produced china until 1952.

In 1875, Charles and Theodore Haviland founded a faience studio in Paris that was headed by Bracquemond, the famous engraver. This Auteuil Studio gathered together the greatest artists and decorators of the period. The entire French china production at the end of the 19th century was influenced by this studio's output.

William David, son of Theodore, took over in 1919. William David's three sons, Theodore II, Harold, and Frederick, eventually became involved. Members of the Haviland family, all direct descendants from the founder David Haviland, always have directed the French firm in Limoges. Each has chosen to retain their U.S. citizenship.

Marks: Until 1870, only one back mark was used for the "H & Co." or the Haviland & Co. After that time, two back marks were used–one for the factory where a piece was made and the other for the factory in which the piece was decorated. Department stores, hotels, railroads, and restaurants that placed special orders received individual marks.

All the whiteware marks were under the glaze. The decoration back marks were over the glaze. Various colorings used in the back marks designated different periods in the Haviland factory production. Pattern names often appeared on many older sets between the whiteware and decorating marks.

References: Jean d'Albis & Celeste Romanet, *La Porcelain de Limoges*, Editions Sous le Vent, 1980; Mary Frank Gaston, *Haviland Collectibles & Objects of Art,* Collector Books, 1984; Mary Frank Gaston, *The Collector's Encyclopedia of Limoges Porcelain,* Collector Books, 1980; G.T. Jacobson, *Haviland China: Volume One & Volume Two*, Wallace-Homestead, 1979; Arlene Schleiger, *Two Hundred Patterns of Haviland China, Books I-V*, published privately, Omaha; Nora Travis, *Haviland China, The Age of Elegance,* Schiffer Books, 1997; Harriet Young, *Grandmother's Haviland,* Wallace-Homestead, 1970.

Collectors' Club: Haviland Collectors Internationale Foundation, Dept. AT 96, P.O. Box 802462, Santa Clarita, CA 91380-2462. Membership: $30.00, Quarterly newsletter, Annual convention.

Collecting Hints: The term "blank" refers to the whiteware piece before any pattern decoration has been applied. A blank can be a simple, all white finished glazed piece. Blanks can be smooth or have embossed edges and designs in the whiteware itself. Decorations and gold trims were applied later.

One must know both the blank number and the pattern number to make an exact match of a Haviland piece. The width and placings of the gold trims also exhibited tremendous variety and must be checked carefully.

Haviland matching services use Arlene Schleiger's reference books to identify patterns. Xerox a plate on both sides and indicate colors of the patterns when sending a sample to a matching service.

Monsieur Jean d'Albis, Haviland & Company historian, believes that more than 20,000 patterns were created and produced by artists of the company. Many old patterns have been discontinued, but Haviland Limoges porcelain dinnerware still is being made and sold in department and specialty stores.

In addition to the popular floral pattern tablewares, collectors of Haviland also should be alert for the art objects and richly decorated tableware and the unique non-tableware items that the company also manufactured.

Bone Dish, 6" l, leaf shape, blue, green, and brown floral transfer, "red Haviland & Co., Limoges and green H & Co./L" marks, set of 10 (A). 30.00

Bouillon Cup and Saucer, gold flowers and bows, cream to green shaded ground, magenta and gold scalloped rim, 2 gold handles, "Haviland, France" mark 30.00

Cake Set, cake tray, 14 1/2" l x 9 1/4" w, 11 plates, 7 1/4" d, brown and green floral sprays and leaves 175.00

Celery Vase, 6 1/4" h, molded swirls, bouquet of white, green, and dk red flowers and stems, c1900 . . . . 50.00

Chocolate Set

Pot, 8 3/4" h, 6 cups and saucers, sm pink roses and green leaves at top, pastel green to ivory shaded ground, gold handles, c1897 . . . . 650.00

Pot, 10" h, 4 cups and saucers, wreaths of pink roses, Theodore Haviland. 425.00

Pot, 10 1/4" h, creamer, sugar basin, tray, 15 3/4" d, 4 cups and saucers, tan and brown pine cone and green leaves, shaded cream to green to lavender ground, scalloped rims on saucers and rim and base of pot, gilt lined rim on tray, "red Haviland France" marks 695.00

Pot, 11" h, 6 cups and saucers, bands of sm pink roses, gold trim, gold bow knot knob, "CFH/GDA" marks 1,200.00

Creamer and Cov Sugar Bowl, "Springtime" pattern 75.00

Cup and Saucer

"Moss Rose" pattern, plain blank, gold line trim, "H.& Co. Limoges" mark. . . 30.00

Pink floral transfer with yellow and green accents, scalloped rim with gold spong-

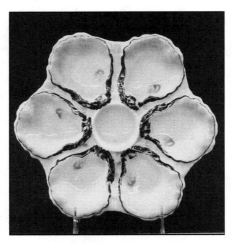

Oyster Plate, 8 3/4" d, purple shells, white ground, "Haviland & Company Made For Burley and Tyrrell Chicago" marks, set of 12, (A) $345.

ing, "green H & Co. L, France and red Haviland & Co. Limoges, Bailey, Banks & Biddle, Philadelphia" mark, (A) 20.00

Cup and Saucer, Demitasse

Brown, tan, and orange florals, "CFH/GDM" mark. 25.00

HP pink borders with gold splotches, gold rims and twisted sq handle, "CFH/GDM" mark, pr, (A) 20.00

Dish, Cov, 10 1/2" H-H, with undertray, lavender thistles, heavy gold handles 175.00

Oyster Plate

8 1/2" d, 5 wells, sprays of orange and brown flowers and stems from rim, gold trim, white ground 95.00

8 3/4" d, 5 wells, sprays of blue and brown flowers with white enameled accents, molded body swirls, gold streaked rim, "CFH/GDA" mark 115.00

Plate

7" d, pink and blue flowers with raised gold flowers and leaves, "CFH/GDM" mark. 10.00

7 3/8" d, band of red clover and green 3 leaf stems, indented gilt rim, "Haviland & Co." mark 10.00

7 5/16" d, pink and yellow scrolled floral design, gold scalloped rim, "green Haviland, France and red Haviland & Co. Limoges" marks, chips, set of 12, (A) 55.00

8 1/2" d

Gold and green wildflowers, rose ground 28.00

Seated white cat with green eyes, blue and beige shaded ground, gold scalloped rim 85.00

9" d, pink roses, gold and green garlands on rim 25.00

9" sq, handkerchief style, multicolored castle ruins in center, yellow centered pink and blue flowerheads on border, gold folded corners, "H & Co./L" mark 75.00

9 1/2" d, lg yellow centered white daisies, green stems at one side, gilt lined rim, "H. & Co." mark 18.00

9 5/8" d, "The Amiens" pattern, "red CFH and green GDA" marks 28.00

Platter

15" l x 10 1/4" w, oval, juice wells at ends, "Drop Rose" pattern, gold and green scalloped rim, made for Bailey, Banks & Biddle Co., Phila, Pa. 500.00

19" l x 12 5/16" w, border of gray, brown, yellow, and green floral transfer, scalloped rim, "H & Co., L, France" mark (A) 22.00

Ring Tree, 3 1/4" d x 1 3/4" h, pink floral transfer with green leaves and gold trim, saucer base with molded shell rim, "H. & Co. L. France" mark (A) 15.00

Soup Plate, 7 5/8" d, "Lorraine" pattern, scattered sprigs in center, border of 4 bunches of purple, blue, and dk red flowerheads and

leaves, yellow lined rim, "green Haviland France and red Haviland & Co." mark
. . . . 25.00

Teapot

5 1/4" h x 6 3/4" l, vert ribbing with gold accented shell and scroll designs, HP purple and yellow violets and green leaves, yellow ground, gold scrolled handle and knob, "H & Co., L France" mark (A) 55.00

9" h, brown, green, and red thistle type flowers on sides, gold veined spout, gold outlined ribbon terminal at handle, gilt and blue bamboo shaped knob, "Haviland & Co." mark 68.00

Vase

5 1/2" h, cylinder shape with sm base, oval cartouches of Art Deco style lady in long red dress and lg black hat, baskets of red, brown, pink flowers and garlands, tan ground, "CFH/GDH" mark
. . . . 265.00

11" h, circ, shape, flat sides, rect ft, multicolored nude after Francois Boucher, green, blue, and brown mottled ground, "imp Haviland Limoges" mark, pr (A)
. . . . 2,000.00

Vegetable Bowl, 10" l x 8 1/8" w, oval, border of sm blue flowers and green leaves with garlands of sm pink roses and green leaves, band of gold stenciled florals on int, gold stripe on rim, "green Haviland, Limoge and Haviland & Co., Limoges for Nathan Dohrmann Co." mark, (A) 25.00

c1882   c1909

HEUBACH

Thuringia, Germany
1840s to Present

History: Christoph and Philip Heubach founded the Heubach factory to manufacture decorative and household porcelains, figures, dolls heads, and dolls. Their dolls heads, animals figures, and piano babies were their most famous products. There was no connection between this factory and the Ernst Heubach factory in Koppelsdorf.

After World War II, the company was nationalized and experienced several name changes. The present company name is VEB United Decorative Porcelainworks Lichte.

Figure

3 1/2" l, cat, white with green eyes
. . . . 98.00

Figure, 5" h, blue shades, "imp sunburst" marks, pr, $395.

8" h, white owl on gray rock, mkd . 175.00

8 1/2" h, dancing girl holding dress at sides, lt green and aqua dress, white collar 195.00

9" h, dog seated on haunches, white body, tan collar, tinted eyes, nose, and mouth, imp mark 325.00

11 1/2" h, standing clown, hands in pockets, pink costume, gold buttons, tan brick support in bk, printed mark
. . . . 600.00

11 3/4" h, bisque, standing little girl, leaning to side, holding edge of green skirt in hands, white stockings, green shoes, white lace collar, brown hair, tambourine on base, imp mark 495.00

12" h, bisque, standing boy in mauve pants, blond hair, med green hat, hand on hip, fighting chickens at feet, imp mark 695.00

12 1/2" h, bisque, standing farm boy, mauve vest, brown pants and red banded brown hat, holding sickle, standing young girl, flowered white apron, blue vest, mauve skirt, leaning on farm implement, molded green leaves in bkd, brown and green molded circ base, unmkd, pr 750.00

Plaque

6" h x 4 1/8" w, rect, HP multicolored Wagner style half portrait of young woman with bow at waist, scarf around neck, star in hair, (A) 488.00

8" d, white cameos of Indian with bow and arrow, birds in foliage, green jasper ground, mkd 245.00

Vase

3 1/8" h x 5" l x 3 1/2" w, oval, white outlined incised white iris and green leaves, mottled blue-green ground, printed mark
. . . . 48.00

4" h, pink roses and green leaves, lt green ground, gold rim, green mark . . . 55.00

6" h, emb Dutch girl in blue dress, pink and green ground, mkd 75.00

Vase, 6" h, white, green, yellow, and blue enameled bird, black waves, matte red-orange ground, white int, printed mark, $95.

8 5/8" h, pink anemones, pale gray ground, green mark 88.00

9 3/4" h, purple iris with green leaves, orange-yellow butterfly, pearl luster finish, mkd 310.00

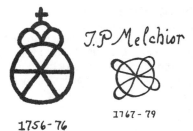

1756-76   1767-79

HOCHST

Hesse, Germany
1746-1796

History: Though in existence for a short time, the porcelain factory at Hochst produced a high quality product. Johann Goltz and Johann Clarus, his son-in-law, founded the porcelain factory together with Adam Friedrich von Lowenfinck, a decorator, who came from Meissen. The group did not work well together and soon split up. By 1750, Johann Benchgraff from Vienna joined Glotz and Clarus to produce porcelains.

After Benchgraff left in 1753, Goltz had financial difficulties. The Prince-Elector, Friedrich Carl von Ostern, from Mainz, took over. Johann and Ferdinand Maass were appointed managers of the factory, now known as the Prince-Electoral Privileged Porcelain Factory, from 1756 to 1776. Tablewares, decorative porcelains, coffee and tea sets, and figures were made. Oriental, rococo, and neo-classical decorative themes were used. Piercing and fretwork were common design elements.

Hochst porcelain was probably best known for the figurals that were modeled under the supervision of Johann Melchior. These painted and biscuit figures showed a high degree of artistic ability. Religious and pastoral groups, figures of children, and mythological characters were modeled with special attention to detail. Pinks and light rose tones were most prominently used by Melchior on his figures of children.

The new Prince-Elector, Breidbach-Burresheim, converted the company into a joint stock company in 1776. The factory was renamed the Prince-Electoral Fayence Manufactory. With the departure of Melchior to the Frankenthal factory in 1779, a gradual decline in quality occurred, although attempts at modeling continued. The factory ceased operations in 1796.

Reference: George Ware, *German & Austrian Porcelain,* Crown, Inc. 1963.

Museums: Dixon Gallery, Memphis, TN; Metropolitan Museum of Art, New York, NY; Museum fur Kunsthandwerk, Frankfurt, Germany; Schlossmuseum, Berlin, Germany; Seattle Art Museum, Seattle, WA.

Reproduction Alert: Following the closing of the Hochst factory, many of the molds were sold to the Muller factory in 1840 at Damm near Aschaffenburg. Muller produced many of the more popular items including the figures. The Hochst mark was used, but these new copies lacked the subtle coloration of the earlier Hochst originals.

The Fasold & Stauch Company of Bock-Wallendorf and Dressel, Kister & Co. of Volkstedt employed a mark which often is confused with Hochst. The quality of their products differs significantly from the high quality of the Hochst material.

Bowl

   6" d, polychrome scene of cottages, steeple, and people, scattered insects, lady bug on int, gilt rim, "blue crowned wheel" mark, c1765-74, (A) 800.00

   10" d, purple, orange, green, and gilt flower sprays on ext, sm sprays on int, gold rim, "gold wheel" mark, (A) . . .4,600.00

Cabinet Plate, 10" d, gilt accented border, neo-classical reserve, pr 55.00

Coffee Can, 2 1/4" h

   Hanging swags of polychrome floral garlands and sprigs, gilt rim, "blue wheel and incised IC" marks, c1762-96, (A) 300.00

   Painted sq of flowers on table top, blue wild flower border, "blue wheel" mark, c1762-96, (A) 300.00

Figure, 7 1/2" h, 12" l, brown and black highlights, green accents, "blue wheel" mark, $3,500.

Cream Jug, Cov, 4" h, raspberry red floral spray, berry knob, "blue crowned wheel and incised IN" mark, c1765-74, chip on cov, (A) 700.00

Cup and Saucer

   Cup with cassic ruins, saucer with ruins in landscape setting, c1750-62, (A) 375.00

   Painted scattered roses and gilt swirls, relief of flower and leaf on handle, gilt rim, "red wheel" mark, c1750-58, (A) 300.00

   Polychrome ruins with flying birds and insects, scrolled handle with floral and leaf relief design, "blue crowned wheel" mark, c1750-96, (A) 650.00

   Purple floral decoration, scrolled handle, "blue wheel" mark, c1762-98, crack and chips, pr, (A) 500.00

   Red, blue, green, and purple floral sprays, gilt rim, scrolled handle, "red wheel, 3 dots, and imp IH" marks, c1750-58, (A) 600.00

Cup and Saucer, Demitasse, ribbed body, blue and white floral design, "blue wheel" mark, c1764-96, set of 6, (A) 700.00

Cup and Trembleuse Saucer, HP multicolored woman and child on horse and cavalier on cup, saucer with seated gentleman in landscape 3,000.00

Dish

   7 3/8" l, oval, reticulated leaf design with puce lines and gilt "VS" on puce medallion edged in green laurel leaves in center, "blue wheel" mark, c1770, (A) 165.00

   9" w, shell molded, painted loose bouquet and scattered sprigs, "blue wheel" mark, c1770, (A) 160.00

Figure

   4" h, young girl in flowered dress, blond hair, little boy in pink suit, holding pink hat in hand, green and brown rock base, "blue wheel" mark, c1762-98, (A) 1,500.00

   4 1/8" h, young barefoot girl with white scarf and pink, yellow, and white sashed dress, holding water pitcher,

"blue wheel" mark, Johann Melchior, c1762-95, (A) 3,700.00

   4 1/4"h, young boy with hand on hip, cape on back and shoulder, polychromed, "blue wheel" mark, (A) 1,000.00

   4 1/2" h, young blond haired girl, laced bodice, whit apron, striped skirt, basket of fruit on arm, hand holds apron with spilled fruit, sq plinth, "blue crowned wheel" mark, 1765-74, hairline, (A) 800.00

   5" h, infant Hercules strangling snakes, natural skin colors, brown rock base, Johann Melchior, c1765-74, "blue wheel" mark, (A) 2,000.00

   5 1/4" h

      Standing little girl in pink blouse, white skirt, gray hair with blue ribbon, holding basket of toys, fan in hand, Johann Melchior, c1762-98, "blue wheel and imp N and HM" marks, (A) 1,900.00

      Young girl in pink polka dot dress, yellow shoes, and brown muff, "blue wheel" mark, Johann Melchior, c1762-98, repairs, (A) 800.00

   5 3/4" h, young girl wearing pink bodice, flowered apron, lg brimmed hat, green and brown rock base, "blue wheel and incised dots and 76" mark, c1762-1798, age crack, (A) 1,300.00

   6" h

      Standing young girl in flowered mauve vest, cream apron with sm red flowers, cream hat with green band, sm flowerpot at side, green and brown rock molded base 2,500.00

      Young girl in bonnet, striped skirt and shawl, holding basket of fruit, polychrome, 19th C, (A) 125.00

   6 1/8" h, standing Moorish woman in flowing robes, hand on hip, other outstretched, polychrome, late 19th C 225.00

   6 1/2" h, woman carrying goose in basket on back, holding dead rabbit, man with parcel on stick over shoulder, polychrome, blue wheel mark, pr, (A) 100.00

   6 7/8" h, Chinoiserie, standing young girl in pink hat, white blouse and apron, pink skirt, Chinese boy with ribbon-tied knot, yellow suit, pink sash, raised green and brown rock base, "blue wheel" mark, Melchior, c1770, (A) 3,450.00

   8 3/4" h, Chinoiserie, standing Chinese empress wearing yellow lined pink robe, green-striped flowered tunic, yellow and pink plaid dress, standing attendant in gilt trimmed white robe, pink striped tunic, yellow trousers, holding parasol overhead, dk and lt green rock base, "blue wheel" mark, c1760, (A) 7,475.00

   11 5/8" h, Juno, naked goddess in puce lined yellow drapery, seated on pink and blue clouds, tree in bkd, open peacock above and at feet, crown in

clouds, raised shaped base with puce and gilt rocaille scroll trim, "gray wheel" mark, c1760, chips, (A) 8,625.00

Jar, Cov, 8 3/4" h, graduated round bowl shape, stepped ft, domed lid with fruit knob, enamel floral sprays with gilt trim, "blue crowned wheel" mark, c1765-74, hairline, (A) 900.00

Jug, Cov, 7 1/4" h, orange, ochre, green, and raspberry red flowers, fruit knob, "blue crowned wheel mark," c1765-74, repairs, (A) 1,100.00

Plate

9" d, polychrome scene of ruins and man fishing with 2 figures, floral sprig border, indented rim, "blue wheel and LM" mark, chip on table ring, (A) . .1,000.00

9 1/2" d, polychrome scene of cottages and 3 figures on path, floral sprigs on border, "blue wheel" mark, c1762-96, (A) 900.00

9 3/4" d

Enameled landscape with castle and 3 figures near river, figure in boat, "blue wheel and imp M" mark, c1762-96, (A) 1,400.00

Polychrome scene of thatched hut and 4 workers in field, sprigs on border, "blue wheel and M" mark, c1762-96, chip on table ring, (A) 1,000.00

Platter, 12" l x 9 1/2" w, polychrome tulip and sprigs in center, scalloped emb flange with 4 floral sprigs, "blue crowned wheel" mark, (A) 1,200.00

Tea Caddy, 5 1/2" h, rect shape, domed cov, raspberry red, blue, green, and gold landscape of ruins and buildings, "blue wheel" mark, c1762-96, (A) 900.00

Teapot

4 1/2" h x 6 1/2" w, oblate shape, scrolled handle, shaped spout, flower knob, polychrome floral decoration, "blue wheel and incised IN" mark, repaired lid, (A) 700.00

5 1/2" h x 6" w, polychrome floral design, mythological animal spout, twisted handle formed from serpent, acorn knob, "blue wheel mark," c1762-98, repairs and hairline, (A)
. . . . .1,500.00

Tureen, Cov, 5 1/2" h x 7 1/4" d, with undertray, polychrome enamel hanging floral garlands, flying insects on cov, gilt accents, sq handles, reglued acorn knob, "blue wheel" mark, c1762-96, (A) 1,750.00

Vase, Cov, 11" h, oviform, neo-classical, bisque allegorial medallions over yellow drapery swags from gilt loops, fluted cov and waisted neck with puce and gilt stripes, bracket handles, sq base with band of gilt

ovals, "blue wheel" mark, c1775, chips (A) 5,750.00

1755 - 1773   1897

HOLLAND-GENERAL

Porcelain
1757-1819

History: Porcelain by Dutch manufacturers was not as well known as the country's Delftware. Dutch porcelain factories at Weesp, Oude Loosdrecht, Amstel, and The Hague produced some wares, although production was limited and frequently imitated styles from other areas.

Hard paste porcelain was made at the **Weesp** factory near Amsterdam beginning in 1757. The factory was sold to Count Diepenbroick in 1762. The factory used French and German styles for inspiration, e.g. white porcelains decorated with flowers and other motifs in relief. Perforated baskets were made along with rococo relief decorated wares featuring landscapes in cartouches or adorned with birds or flowers. The factory did not prosper and was sold in 1771. The mark used by Weesp was a copy of the Meissen crossed swords in underglaze blue with the addition of three dots between the points of the blades on either side.

De Moll bought the factory, and the company moved to **Oud Loosdrecht** between Utrecht and Amsterdam. The wares exhibited more Dutch characteristics. Landscapes were especially popular. The mark used at Loosdrecht was "M.O.L." either incised or in underglaze blue, black, or colored enamels.

The company moved again in 1784 to **Ouder-Amstel** and was taken over by Frederick Daeuber. The wares now imitated the Empire style wares from Sevres.

In 1800, the factory belonged to the firm George Dommer and Co. It was moved to **Nieuwer-Amstel** in 1809 and was closed in 1819. Sometimes the "M.O.L." mark was used with the word Amstel. Other wares were marked "Amstel" in black.

Lynker, a German, established a porcelain factory in 1775 at **The Hague.** It produced hard paste porcelain similar to Meissen. The pieces were decorated with landscapes, seascapes, and birds. The

factory also decorated china from other sources. It closed in 1786. The Hague mark was the stork from the city arms in blue underglaze. When other blanks from other firms were decorated, the mark was painted on the glaze.

Pottery

The earliest pottery in Holland was made before 1609, long before Holland became an independent nation state. Tin glazed wares of the early sixteenth century that were made in Antwerp, Haarlem, Rotterdam, and Amsterdam were similar to Italian wares known as majolica. Mid 16th century dishes made in Antwerp utilized the "blue-dash" around the edges that was later a design element found on 17th century English wares. Drug jars and spouted drug pots painted in high temperature blue tones similar to Italian wares were quite popular in the Netherlands.

With the founding of the Dutch East India Company in 1609, trade flourished with both China and Japan. As the Dutch potters became familiar with Far Eastern porcelains, they imitated the oriental designs on the earthenware. By the early 17th century, Delftware had developed.

When English salt-glazed stonewares and cream colored earthenwares were imported from England in large quantities about the 1760s, Dutch potteries experienced a decline. Customers preferred the English goods over the tin glazed wares made in Holland.

Museums: Gemeente Museum, The Hague, Holland; Municipal Museum, Amsterdam, Holland.

Additional Listings: Delft, Gouda, Maastricht, and Rozenburg.

Cup and Saucer, painted multicolored finches perched on shrub, gilt line dentil rims, "blue stork" marks, Hague, c1770, (A) 300.00

Cup Cov, 3 3/4" h x 3 3/4" w, cobalt floral panels, notched open handles, domed cov, sm finial, 18th C, repaired crack, (A) 25.00

Spoon Rest, 6 1/2" l x 5" w, oval, center multicolored bouquet, 4 sm border bouquets, The Hague, c1770 . . . . 235.00

Teapot, 6 1/2" h, dk blue fan flowers, gold stripes and zigzags, blue-green flowers and stems, cream ground, matte finish, Arnham 250.00

Vase

7 1/4" h, oviform, wide mouth, mottled irid maroon glaze on dk brown wavy ground, dk maroon running luster glaze on shoulder, "ST. LUKAS-HOLLAND" mark 300.00

9" h, ftd baluster shape with swollen neck and lug handles, green, yellow, and gray painted stylized butterflies above

yellow flowerheads and foliage, Brantjes & Co., damages, pr, (A)
.............................1,475.00

11 3/4" h, ftd baluster shape with everted rim, painted polychrome allover snowy winter scene of farmer feeding sheep at trough, sgd "N. Nauve," chip, (A)
.........................1,705.00

16 7/8" h, tapered cylinder shape, brown shaded oval portrait of 18th C woman reserved on purple, green, and blue ground with stylized flowers and foliage, (A) 308.00

HUNGARY-GENERAL

Holitsch
1743-1827

History: The Holitsch pottery factory was established in 1743 by Francis of Lorraine, consort of the Empress Maria Theresa. Decorative motifs followed the popular Strasbourg style. Tureens were made in the form of birds. Most of the painting favored a Hungarian peasant pottery style. When the firm started to produce English style earthenwares in 1786, they used workers from the Vienna factory. It continued in operation with State support until 1827.

The early faience wares were marked with the "HF" monogram for "Holitscher Fabrik." Later creamwares bear the full name "HOLICS" or "HOLITSCH."

References: Tivadar Artner, *Modern Hungarian Ceramics,* Art Foundation Publishing House, 1974; Gyorgy Domanovszky, *Hungarian Pottery,* Corvina Press, 1968.

Additional Listings: Fischer and Zsolnay.

Bowl
7" d, "Blue Garden" pattern, gold trim, Herend........................ 55.00
11 1/2" d, bird, leaf, and branch on int with scattered butterflies and insects, relief molded basketweave int border, insects on ext, gold rim, Herend 160.00
Cache Pot, 6" h x 10" d, red painted floral spray on molded lattice ground, 2 scroll handles, gilt scalloped rim, Herend, (A)
.............................260.00
Cup and Saucer, "Printemps" pattern, Herend
.............................40.00
Figure
4 7/8" h, HP gray squirrel eating nut, Herend......................... 225.00
7" h, seated young girl, turned torso, hand holding leg crossed, rect base, white glazed terra cotta, sgd "Komlos"
.............................400.00

Plate, 9 1/4" d, raised gray swans, brown cranes, green and gray water plants, multicolored floral border, gilt rim, Herend, "gold crest and cross" mark, $450.

7 1/2" h, Art Deco style bust of woman, blond hair, blue tam hat, lg blue bow tie
.... 375.00
10" h, kneeling nude woman, brown hair, green sash across lap, looking in gold mirror in hand, artist sgd, Herend
.... 595.00
Jardiniere, 7" h, baluster shape, alternating maroon and gilt bands, centered gilt geometric design, paw feet, plinth base, Herend, early 20th C, (A) 161.00
Pitcher, 8" h, applied piping forming stylized fish and horiz ribs, black glazed ground, Geza Gorka, c1935 .... 650.00
Pot, 5" h, 2 sm loop handles on shoulder, crackled reptile skin finish, Geza Gorka, c1930 .... 650.00
Salt and Pepper, 2 1/2" h, egg shape, roses design, Herend 45.00
Tea Service, pot, 9" h, creamer and stand, sugar bowl and stand, 12 demitasse cups and saucers, painted fruit and flowers, molded basketweave borders, molded magenta flowerhead on pot, green vine handle on pot and creamer, Herend........... 1,800.00
Tea Set, pot, 10 1/2" l, creamer, sugar bowl, blue stylized flower sprig on sides, blue bands of geometrics, gold outlined handle, spout, and accents, blue rose knob, Herend
.... 250.00
Vase
7 1/2" h
Cream glazed surface blisters, burnt orange ground, Geza Gorka, c1935
.... 475.00
Narrow base, wide tapered body, 8 architectural shaped feet from rim, runny green glaze with black crackle surface, Geza Gorka, c1930
.... 550.00
10 7/8" h, terra cotta, tapered cylinder shape, Art Nouveau style incised tall stemmed green stylized flowers
.... 225.00

HUTSCHENREUTHER

Hohenberg, Bavaria, Germany
1814 to Present

History: Carl Magnus Hutschenreuther established a German porcelain factory, Hutschenreuther A.G. at Hohenberg, Bavaria in 1814. When Carl Magnus died in 1845, he was succeeded by Johanna, his widow, and Christian and Lorenz, his sons. Lorenz was not satisfied simply to carry on the family business. He was bought out by his partners and established his own porcelain factory in Selb. The Lorenz Hutschenreuther and Carl Magnus Hutschenreuther porcelain factories co-existed as two totally independent businesses. When Lorenz Hutschenreuther died in 1856, Viktor and Eugen, his sons, took over his company.

The Lorenz family enlarged their firm through acquisitions and the creation of new factories during the first part of the 20th century. In 1906, they acquired the porcelain factory Jaeger, Werner & Co. in Selb. In 1917, Lorenz Hutschenreuther bought the Paul Muller Porcelain Factory in Selb. In 1927, they purchased the Tirschenreuth Porcelain Factory and Bauscher Brothers Porcelain Factory in Weiden. The following year the Konigszelt Porcelain Factory was added.

Both branches of the Hutschenreuthers were noted for the high quality of their tablewares and figures. In 1969, all branches of the Magnus and Lorenz firm were united under the group name Hutschenreuther AG.

A merger with Porzellanfabrik Kahla AG of Schoenwald in 1972 brought the Arzberg and Schonwald brands of porcelain along with two earthenware factories into the Hutschenreuther group of enterprises. The company is still in business today producing limited edition plates, figures, dinnerware, and other china. Distribution companies have been established in France, the United States, Canada, Scandinavia, Belgium, and Italy.

Bowl
5 1/4" d, 2 bunches of pink, purple, and blue flowers and green leaves on border 6.00
7" d, green grape transfer on green to brown shaded ground, scalloped rim, "LHR, Hutschenreuther, Selb, Bavaria" mark, (A) 20.00

Gravy Boat, 11 1/4" l, Platter, 17" l, multicolored florals, white ground, burnished gold borders, "CM Hutschenreuther and blue scepter" marks, gravy boats, pr, A-$920; platters, set of 5, (A) $2185.

Cake Plate, 12" H-H, HP 3 lg purple plums, lg white blossoms, shaded green ground 58.00

Figure

    4 1/2" h, 2 brown and tan running deer, white base 145.00

    7 1/2" h, seated Siamese cat, white with brown trim, blue eyes 295.00

    8 1/2" h, kissing budgies, yellow and green, sgd "Tutter" 295.00

    8 1/4" h 3 young girls playing ring-around-the-rosy, white glaze, rd base, sgd "K. Tutter," "Hutschenreuther, Selb and lion" mark, (A) 180.00

    9" h, Art Deco style nude woman standing on gold ball 175.00

    10" h, walking elephant, gray, brown accents, white tusks 495.00

    12" h x 12 1/2" l, dancing girl, flowing hair, arm raised, knees bent, white glaze, #1814 . . . . 650.00

Plate

    7 3/4" d, Black Eyed Susans, shaded green leaves, lt yellow shaded ground 12.00

    8" d

        Gilt lined yellow border band with 3 bunches of pink clematis, green leaves, gilt trim 10.00

        "Margarette" pattern, red, yellow, and blue daisies, gold trim 10.00

    8 5/8" d, center with pumpkin, plums, and grapes, gold lined rim 15.00

    10" d, 2 exotic birds and foliage in center, blue ground border with white florals and 3 ovals of exotic birds, gold sq design rim 55.00

    10 3/4" d, wide gold border with scrolling design, "Hutschenreuther, Selb, Bavaria in oval and lion and LHS" mark, set of 12, (A) 180.00

    11" d, multicolored floral design on cream border, etched gilt rim, set of 10, (A) 1,495.00

Tea Service, Pot, 9 3/4" h, creamer, cov sugar bowl, 8 plates, 7 3/4" d, painted fruit design, molded swirl bodies, gold lined rims 895.00

Tray, 12" H-H, 11 3/4" w, rounded corners, black outlined "Tratoria" with people seated at cafe table, lady walking dog, fountain and church, yellow and pink accents, "Hutschenreuther Selb Bavaria" mark 25.00

INDIAN TREE

English
Mid 1800s to Present

History: Indian Tree is a popular dinnerware pattern that was made by English potters such as Burgess & Leigh, Coalport, John Maddock & Sons, S. Hancock & Sons, and Soho Pottery from the middle of the 1800s until the present. The main theme is an oriental landscape with a gnarled brown branch of a pink blossomed tree. The remainder of the landscape features exotic flowers and foliage in green, pink, blue, and orange on a white ground.

Bouillon Cup and Saucer, dbl handles, "green Coalport England" mark 55.00

Butter Dish, Cov, 8 5/8" d x 2 3/4" h, Copeland 75.00

Cake Plate, 10" H-H, "green Coalport England" mark 175.00

Creamer, "Johnson Brothers" mark . . . 17.00

Cream Soup, with underplate, "Johnson Brothers" mark 20.00

Cup and Saucer, Demitasse, Coalport 35.00

Dinner Service, Part, 12 plates, 10" d, 12 plates, 9" d, 8 plates, 8" d, 6 lg cups and saucers, 6 sm cups and saucers, 2 cookie plates, pitcher, reamer, sugar bowl with undertray, butterdish with insert, 2 oval cov vegetable dishes, sauce tureen, gravy tureen with undertray, oval open vegetable bowl, rd cov vegetable bowl, 2 ftd cake plates, lg junket bowl, Minton 1,450.00

Dish, 7 1/2" H-H, pierced handles, Coalport 25.00

Jar, Cov, 4 1/2" h, Sadler 49.00

Pitcher

Vegetable Bowl, 10" l, "green Coalport" mark, $110.

    6 3/4" h, Burgess and Leigh 45.00

    7" h, Coalport 155.00

Plate

    8 3/4" d, wavy rim, "green Coalport England" mark 35.00

    10" d, "Johnson Brothers" mark 16.00

Platter

    12 1/4" l, "Johnson Brothers" mark . 26.00

    13 1/2" l, "Johnson Brothers" mark . 35.00

    14" l, "Johnson Brothers" mark 35.00

    15" l, Meakin 40.00

Sauce Tureen, 5 1/2" h x 8" l, with undertray, 8 1/4" l, "Spode Copelands China England" mark 120.00

Soup Bowl, 7 1/4" d, "Johnson Brothers" mark 13.00

Soup Plate, 9 1/8" d, Enoch Wood 12.00

Sugar Bowl, "Johnson Brothers" mark . 22.00

Tray, 10 1/2" l, oval, Maddock 28.00

Vegetable Bowl, 8 1/2" d, "Johnson Brothers" mark 25.00

IRISH BELLEEK

County Fermanagh, Ireland
1857 to Present

History: Pottery production using native clay deposits began in 1857 in Belleek in County Fermanagh, Ireland. Although David McBurney and Robert Armstrong, the founders, started with earthenwares, they soon produced Belleek parian china, a fine porcelain. William Bromley brought some workers from the Goss factory at Stoke-on-Trent when he moved to Belleek about 1860.

Native marine motifs, such as seashells, corals, marine plants and animals, seahorses, and dolphins were the subjects of early Belleek pieces. The Irish shamrocks also were a favorite subject. Many of these motifs continue in production. From its beginning, the factory produced both utilitarian and decorative wares.

Belleek porcelain is extremely thin and light with a creamy ivory surface and iridescent luster. Probably its most distinctive quality is its delicate cream or pastel tone with a pearl like luster. All pieces are hand crafted.

William Henshall's introduction of basketwork and flowers in 1865 gave Belleek porcelains a world wide audience. Each basket was woven out of fine rods of clay, not cast; each leaf and flower was made by hand. These intricate and highly decorative pieces are most sought after by collectors. Belleek baskets were dated according to whether they were three strands or four strands. Also, the pieces were identified with strips of Belleek parian with various impressed wording to indicate the date.

The company's first gold medal was won at the 1865 Dublin International Exposition. Irish Belleek parian china still is hand crafted, just as it was more than one hundred years ago. Each piece is made by one craftsman from start to finish; there is no assembly line technique.

References: Richard K. Degenhardt, *Belleek: The Complete Collectors' Guide & Illustrated Reference*, 2nd Edition, Wallace-Homestead, 1993; Marion Langham, *Belleek Irish Porcelain*, Quiller Press, Ltd. 1994; Walter Rigdon, *Illustrated Collectors' Handbook*, Wilkins Creative Printing, 1978.

Marks: Belleek pieces are marked with the Belleek backstamp consisting of an Irish Wolfhound, a Harp, a Round Tower, and Sprigs of Shamrock. This first mark was used from 1863 to 1890. The marks were either printed or impressed into the china. Early marks were usually black, but could also be red, blue, green, or brown.

With the second mark, 1891 to 1926, "Co. Fermanagh, Ireland" was added along with a ribbon. The third mark was used from 1926 to 1946 and included a round scroll with three Gaelic words "Deanta in Eirinn" and Celtic design with circle. The fourth mark in green from 1946 to 1955 was the same as the third. The fifth mark in green from 1955 to 1965 was the same as the fourth, but with the addition of the letter "R" in circle. The sixth mark in green from 1965 to 1980 was the same trademark reduced in size, ribbon shortened, and "Co. Fermanagh" deleted, leaving only "Ireland." The seventh mark from 1993 to the present is similar to the second but in navy blue. The current change reflects the 130th anniversary of Belleek.

Museums: National Museum, Dublin, Ireland; Ulster Museum, Belfast, Ireland; Victoria & Albert Museum, London, England; Visitor's Center, The Belleek Pottery, Belleek, Co. Fermanagh, N. Ireland.

Collectors' Club: The Belleek Collectors' International Society, 9893 Georgetown Pike, Suite 525, Great Falls, VA 22066. Membership: $35.00, Society journal newsletter.

Collecting Hints: Specialty shops and department stores usually carry contemporary Belleek wares. These are good sources for comparing the new examples with the older ones. In the modern pieces, the paste has a creamy white appearance and the high, brilliant glaze has a yellowish color tone. Modern pieces usually have more color used in the design than their older counterparts. Every genuine Belleek piece carries the company crest. Christmas collector plates were started in 1970. Reed and Barton is now exclusive distributor of Belleek products in the United States.

Basket

6 1/2" d, shamrock shape, 4 strand, applied roses and leaves 375.00

10 3/4" d, 4 strand, painted applied florals on border, pearl glaze, "imp BELLEEK R. IRELAND" mark, (A) 690.00

Basket, Cov

11 1/4" d, 3 strand, applied floral decoration on cov, 1st black mark, chips, (A) 1,955.00

12 1/4" d, 3 strand, applied floral decoration on cov, 1st black mark, chips, (A) 2,185.00

Bowl, 6 1/2" l x 5 1/4" w, white molded seashells, pink coral on base, 2nd black mark 295.00

Candelabrum, 14" h, Cherub, 2nd black mark 3,000.00

Cup and Saucer

"Limpet" pattern, 3rd black mark . 100.00

"Mask" pattern, 3rd black mark . . 155.00

"Neptune" pattern, 2nd black mark 110.00

"Shamrock" pattern, basketweave body, 3rd black mark 165.00

Cup and Saucer, Demitasse, "Celtic" pattern, green and red trim, gold edging, ring handle, 2nd black mark 245.00

Figure

5 3/4" h, leprechaun seated on mushroom, pot of gold at feet, white with lt yellow luster trim, "For Luck, Sonar Ort, and Irish Leprechaun," 2nd black mark 425.00

8" h, harp, 2nd green mark 195.00

Flower Pot

3 1/2" h, "Octagon" pattern, 2nd black mark 140.00

4" h x 4 1/4" d, applied flowers, 3rd black mark 285.00

6 3/8" h x 11" H-H, "Finner," harp handles, ribbed body with applied floral design, 2nd black mark, chips, (A) . . . 1,265.00

Mug, 2 1/2" h, "Grasses" pattern, yellow grass, 2nd green mark. 50.00

Pitcher

3 1/2" h, "Lotus" pattern, 3rd black mark 88.00

4 1/2" h

Dbl shell, 3rd black mark 110.00

"Ivy" pattern, 3rd black mark. . . 65.00

5 1/2" h "Grasses" pattern, 3rd black mark 300.00

6" h, harp handle, 1st black mark 325.00

Plate

6" d, "Lily" pattern, green trim, 2nd black mark 45.00

6 3/4" d, blue ribbon, yellow roses, cobalt floral garlands, 3rd black mark 260.00

7" d, "Shamrock" pattern, 3rd black mark 70.00

8" d

"Limpet" pattern, 3rd green mark 50.00

"Tridacna" pattern, 2nd black mark 98.00

9" d, hex shape, 3 woven strands, imp mark 850.00

9 1/4" d, pink and white florals and blue forget-me-nots in center, open work border with gold and aqua trim, 2nd black mark, pr 695.00

Salt, 1" h x 2" w x 3 1/4" l, emb shells with green shamrocks, 2nd black mark 65.00

Tea Kettle, 5 3/4" h, "Grass" pattern, 1st black mark, (A) 517.00

Teapot, 10 1/8" l, "Shamrock" pattern, 2nd green mark 235.00

Tray, 17" l x 14 1/2" w, "Neptune" pattern, orange tinted rim, 2nd black mark . . . 1,400.00

Tumbler, 4 3/8" h, vert ribbing on lower section, natural color, 1st black mark 110.00

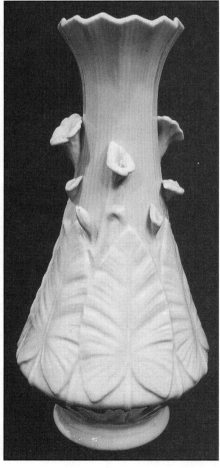

Vase, 13 1/2" h, "Nile" pattern, 3rd black mark, $575.

Vase

  6" h, trumpet shape, "Daisy Shamrock" pattern, green shamrocks, 3rd black mark 95.00

  6 1/8" h, figural tree trunk with branches, brown wrapped vine, 1st black mark 155.00

  7" h, "Sunflower" design, 2nd black mark 175.00

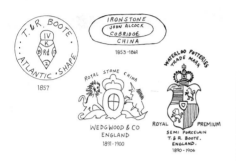

IRONSTONE, PATTERNED AND WHITE

Staffordshire, England
Early 1840s-1891

History: White ironstone in Gothic shapes was first produced from Staffordshire in the early 1840s. Gothic shapes already had been used by Staffordshire potters for cobalt and mulberry transfer wares. Roses, lilies, and human profiles comprised the finials or the trim under the handles.

The firm of James Edwards of Burslem made a tremendous variety of designs in white ironstone. T.J. & J. Mayer designed "Prize Puritan" and "Prize Bloom." "Adam's Scallop," "Line Trim," and "Scalloped Decagons" by J. Wedgwood and Davenport all used scallops in the pottery design. "Fluted Pearl" by J. Wedgwood and "Fig" by J. Wedgwood and Davenport are among the most collectible patterns.

William Adams, John Alcock, E. Challinor & Co., Davenport, C. Meigh & Son, and J. Wedgwood were some of the firms making white ironstone in the 1840s and '50s. Thomas and Richard Boote's "Octagon Shape" in 1851 was the forerunner of the famous "Sydenham Shape" from 1853. Many potters then copied these popular shapes.

"President" by James Edwards and "Columbia" made by six different companies were registered in 1855. The potters of "Columbia" used the same borders on the plates and platters, but used varied finials and foliage decorations. "Dallas," "Mississippi," and "Baltic Shapes" also were registered in that year. Many other shapes appeared from the Staffordshire Potteries during the 1850s.

Many white ironstone patterns used corn, oats, and wheat in their designs such as "Corn & Oats" manufactured by J. Wedgwood and Davenport from 1863, "Wheat & Blackberry" by J.& G. Meakin from 1865, "Prairie Shape" from 1862, and "Ceres" by Elsmore and Forster from 1859.

During the 1860s, gardens and woods inspired the designers of white ironstone. Patterns such as "Sharon Arch," "Hanging Arch," "Winding Vine," and "White Oak and Acorn" are just a few that developed. Flowers also influenced the Staffordshire potters during the 1860s in such patterns as "Morning Glory" by Elsmore & Forster, "Moss Rose" by J.& G. Meakin, "Bordered Fuchsia" by A. Shaw, and "The Hyacinth" by J. Wedgwood.

Ribbed patterns also were popular as in Meakin's "Ribbed Raspberry with Bloom" and Pankhurst's "Ribbed Chain" during the 1860s. A classical revival was seen in "Athens Shape" by Podmore Walker & Co. and "Athenia" by J.T. Close.

Rectangular shapes became popular during the 1870s and 1880s. After 1891, ironstone diminished as the demands for porcelains increased.

References: Dawn Stoltzfus & Jeffrey B. Snyder, *White Ironstone,* Schiffer Publishing, Ltd. 1997; Jean Wetherbee, *A Look at White Ironstone,* Wallace-Homestead, 1980; Jean Wetherbee, *A Second Look at White Ironstone,* Wallace-Homestead, 1984; Jean Wetherbee, *White Ironstone: A Collectors' Guide,* Antique Trader Books, 1996.

Collectors' Club: White Ironstone China Association, Inc. Jim Kerr, R.D. #1, Box 23, Howes Cave, NY 12092, Membership: $25.00, Quarterly newsletter <u>White Ironstone Notes.</u>

Patterned

Bowl, 12" d, Imari palette in floral geometric borders, Turner, 19th C, (A) 220.00

Chamber Pot, Cov, 6" h x 8 1/2" w, oct, ftd base, "American Marine" pattern, blue transfer, "FM & Co, drapery" mark, c1870, cracks and chips, (A). 302.00

Comport, 13" l, blue, pink, and orange florals, unmkd 695.00

Dish

  9 1/2" l x 7" w, oct, "Real Old Canton" pattern, blue transfer, "blue ASHWORTH BROS crown, HANLEY, drapery, ENGLAND" mark, c1890, (A) 110.00

  9 3/4" l, leaf shape, "Japan" pattern, cobalt stem with orange-red flowerheads and lg cobalt leaves and fencing, cavetto of compartments of orange-red crisscross and flowerheads or orange-red flowerheads on cobalt stems, blue stem handle, "Japan, Stone China in banner" mark 135.00

Dish, 11" l x 7 1/2" w, cobalt, yellow, turquoise, iron red and gilt, c1800, $595.

Jug, 10" h, "Oriental Pheasants" pattern, multicolored, white ground, handle with maroon line and specks, "red ASHWORTH BROS. crown, HANLEY, drapery, ENGLAND" mark, 1890-95, (A) 522.00

Pitcher

  6 1/4" h, paneled, reed peonies, blue, yellow, and red birds on branches, yellow and blue leaves, yellow lined rim, snake handle, Ashworth 175.00

  7" h, tapered shape, blue underglaze flowers and bands, iron red accents, pewter lid with knob, "B & L England" mark 150.00

  8" h, white lobed body, blue wheat and leaves around shoulder and handle, chip and crack 125.00

  13" h, blue and white "Blue Pheasant" pattern, cobalt serpent handle, Ashworth, rim chip 295.00

Plate

  6 1/4" d, underglaze blue, polychrome and gilt chinoiserie design of water lily under willow tree in foliage cartouche, band of sqs on rim, Turner, c1800, pr, (A) 293.00

Pitcher, 7 3/4" h, purple transfer, hunting scene of hunters and horses, England, $100.

7 1/2" d, "Bandana" pattern, bandana surrounded multicolored center scene of figure looking out window, black band on inner rim, border with black and white dragons on orange ground, "imp ASHWORTH" mark, (A) 110.00

9" d, floral pattern, blue printed with red and yellow enamels, c1850 . . . . . 65.00

9 1/2" d
"Nangpo" pattern, black outlined multicolored center scene of 5 figures with Indian tree and flowers, floral design with black and white swirls, "black MASON'S crown, PATENT IRONSTONE CHINA, drapery and ASHWORTH NANGPO, drapery, and imp ASHWORTH REAL IRONSTONE CHINA crown" marks, c1890, (A) 192.00

"Singan" pattern, black transfer, "T. Goodfellow" mark 45.00

10 1/2" d, oriental style brown vase on table with lg brown leaves, iron red flowerheads and blue leaves, inner border band of brown with gold overlay and yellow cartouches with white flowerheads, border of brown leaves, red, blue, and mauve flowerheads, Ashworth 85.00

Platter
13 1/4" x 9 3/4" w, blue "Snowflake" pattern, (A) 330.00

16 1/4" l, Imari palette polychrome floral spray reserve, gilt accented diaper border, late 19th C, (A) 374.00

19" l, cobalt, iron red, salmon, and yellow "Japan" pattern, Staffordshire, c1820-40 . . . . .350.00

20" l x 16 1/4" w, iron red, cobalt, tan, mauve, and gilt pagoda in center with fencing, palm and willow trees at sides, border of alternating panels of iron red and cobalt peony flowerheads, c1850 . . . . 595.00

Sauce Tureen, Cov
6 1/2" h x 8" l, with undertray, oriental style black, puce, and iron red flowers and banding, Ashworth 330.00

7" h, with undertray, enamel and gilt accented blue transfer of oriental florals, blue handles and knob, c1825, pr, (A) 748.00

8" h, ftd, Chinese figures, trelliswork, and gilded foliage, Famille rose palette, English, c1850s, restorations, pr, (A) 432.00

8 1/2" l x 8" h, with undertray, oval, "War Bonnet" pattern, blue and white, c1835 . . . . 350.00

Soup Plate
9" d, oct, center with iron red, green, and brown oriental willow tree, cobalt trim, rust peony and green leaves, inner rim with blue geometric shapes, border of 4 compartments of cobalt, rust, and gilt designs, 4 compartments with oriental flowers, pr 975.00

10 1/4" d, black, red, and gold oriental flower vase in center, chinoiserie border design, Ashworth, pr 350.00

Trivet, 61/2" d, ftd base, 2 olive green, brown, peach, and yellow overlapped oriental landscaped scenes in sqs in center, gilt and orange bands on beveled edge, "imp ASHWORTH" mark, (A) 165.00

Tureen, 11" l x 8" w x 5 1/2" h, "Real Old Canton" pattern, blue transfers, bird knob, dog head handles, "blue ASHWORTH BROS. crown, HANLEY, drapery, ENGLAND" mark, (A). 495.00

Waste Bowl, 5 1/4" d, blue "Snowflake" pattern, (A) 330.00

White

Bowl, 14" d, "Sydenham" shape, "T. & R. Boote" mark 65.00

Butter Dish, Cov, 4 1/2" h x 5 1/2" d, with drain, ftd, "Wheat and Blackberry" shape . . 195.00

Coffeepot
9 1/4" h, ovoid shape, ftd, "Lily of the Valley" shape, flower finial, "J Edwards, Fenton, Manufactures" mark, (A) 130.00

10 1/4" h, oval, "Wheat" shape, "Ironstone China J.E." mark 45.00

Creamer, 7 1/8" h, "Wheat" pattern, "Ceres" shape, "imp Elsmore & Forster, Ceres Shape, Tunstall" mark, (A) 95.00

Milk Pitcher, 8 1/4" h, "Fuchsia" shape, "J.G. Meakin, Ironstone China" mark, (A) . . . 60.00

Mug, 3 1/2" h, ribbed body, "Johnson Bros. England, Royal Ironstone" mark 55.00

Pitcher
6" h, "Wheat" shape, W. Adams . . . 29.00

7 1/2" h, melon ribbed body, copper luster cattails and leaves on neck, Wilkinson 35.00

7 3/4" h, plain body, "W.E. Corn Burslem" mark 92.00

8" h, "Wheat" shape, Wilkinson. . . . 55.00

8 7/8" h, "Wheat and Clover" shape, scrolled handle, Turner & Tomkinson, (A) 65.00

9" h, "Sydenham" shape, Boote . . 265.00

Tureen, 8 1/4" h, 13" H-H, "Ribbed Chain" shape, "J.W. Pankhurst Stone China Hanley, Royal Arms" mark, $225.

Tureen, 11 3/4" H-H, 8" h, "J.F. Ironstone China, Royal Arms" mark, $225.

9 3/4" h, "Chinese" shape, "Stone China, Anthony Shaw, Burslem" mark, (A) 85.00

11" h, "Ceres" shape, Elsmore & Forster 195.00

12 1/2" h, "Corn and Oats" shape, "J. Wedgwood Ironstone China" mark 250.00

Plate, 9 5/8" d, "Atlantic" shape, "T. & R. Boote, Atlantic Shape" mark, (A) 15.00

Platter
11 3/4" l x 5 3/4" w, "Basketweave With Band" shape, rect, "Royal Ironstone China, Alfred Meakin, England" mark, (A) 28.00

16 1/2" l, "Wheat" shape, "J. & G. Meakin Ironstone China" mark 145.00

17" l, "Ceres" shape, "W.E. Corn, Burslem" mark, c1864 . . . . 95.00

Sauce Tureen, Cov
7 1/2" h x 8 3/4" H-H, "Blackberry and Wheat" shape, unmkd 125.00

9" h, with undertray and ladle, "Sydenham" shape "T. & R. Boote" mark, pr 950.00

Soup Plate
8 1/2" d, "Sharon Arch" shape, "J. Wedgwood, England" mark 34.00

10 1/4" d, "Virginia" shape 42.00

Sugar Bowl, Cov
7 3/8" h, "Trent" shape, "S. Alcock & Co." mark, c1854 . . . . 175.00

7 1/2" h, ovoid shape with paneled band at base, "Lily of the Valley" shape, pear knob, "Ironstone China, J.E." mark, (A) 65.00

Teapot
9 3/8" h, "Wheat and Clover" shape, "Pearl Ironstone China, G.W. Turner & Sons" mark 125.00

9 3/4" h, "Lily Shape 2," "W.E. Corn Bursley Eng." Mark 185.00

11" h, "Potomac" shape, "W. Baker & Co., Fenton, England" mark 225.00

Toothbrush Holder, 5 1/2" h, cylinder shape, flared base, J. & G. Meakin 85.00

Tureen
8 3/4" H-H, oval, "Vintage" shape, Challinor 150.00

10 3/4" h, 14" H-H, "Cable and Ring" shape, John Maddock 265.00

12" d x 11 1/2" h, "Sevres" shape, "imp J. Edwards, Burslem, England" mark 425.00

16" h, with undertray and ladle, "Sydenham" shape, "T. & R. Boote" mark 1,225.00

Vegetable Bowl, 11 3/4" l x 8 1/4" w, oval, "Corn and Oats" shape, "Davenport Ironstone China" mark, (A) 15.00

Vegetable Bowl, Cov

8 3/4" l, "Corn & Oats" shape, "J. Wedgwood, Tunstall England" mark . . 195.00

9" d x 10 1/2" h, "Sydenham" shape, "T. & R. Boote" mark 275.00

9 1/2" l, "Sevres" shape, "J. Edwards, Burslem, England" mark 225.00

9 3/4" H-H, "Chain O' Tulips" shape, J. & G. Meakin 120.00

9 7/8" l, "Bordered Hyacinth or Lily" shape, "W. Baker & Co., Fenton, England" mark 150.00

10" l, "Wheat" shape, "R. Cochran & Co, Glasgow" mark, c1860 . . . . 150.00

10 3/8" l x 6" w, oval, "Tulip" shape, "Royal Stone China Wedgwood & Co. England" mark, (A) 25.00

10 3/4" l x 7 3/4" h, "Laurel Wreath" shape, Elsmore and Forster 175.00

11" l x 6 3/4" h, "Wheat" shape, "Stone China, Anthony Shaw, Burslem" mark 195.00

12" h x 10 1/2" l, paneled body with scallops, T. & R. Boote 150.00

12 1/4" l x 7 1/2" w x 6 3/4" h, "Grape and Medallion" pattern, "Vintage" shape, "imp Ironstone China, E. & C. Challinor" mark, hairline, (A) 30.00

12 1/2" l x 8 1/2" h, "Fuchsia" shape, "J. & G. Meakin Ironstone China" mark 155.00

13 1/8" l x 9 3/8" w, oval, "Fluted Pearl" shape, "imp J. Wedgwood, Ironstone China" mark, (A) 75.00

ITALY-GENERAL

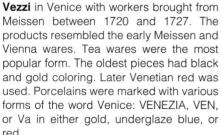

ITALIA
1901

Venice
1727-1812

History: Hard paste porcelain was made by Francesco and Guiseppe **Vezzi** in Venice with workers brought from Meissen between 1720 and 1727. The products resembled the early Meissen and Vienna wares. Tea wares were the most popular form. The oldest pieces had black and gold coloring. Later Venetian red was used. Porcelains were marked with various forms of the word Venice: VENEZIA, VEN, or Va in either gold, underglaze blue, or red.

After the Vezzi factory closed, a new factory was established by Friedrich Hewelke in 1758. His china was marked with the letter "V." The factory failed in 1763 during the Seven Years War.

A more successful factory to manufacture hard paste porcelain was established by Geminiano **Cozzi** from 1764 until 1812. Both utilitarian and ornamental wares were made and exported throughout Europe. Cozzi's wares featured pouring spouts on coffeepots molded with leaf decorations. Figures from the Italian Comedy were made along with colored and white tea sets, services, and vases. Pieces were marked with an anchor in red, blue, or gold.

Le Nove
1750 to Late 19th Century

Pasquale Antonibon established a porcelain factory in Le Nove in 1750. He took Francisco Parolini as a partner in 1781. The painter Giovanni Marconi was the factory's most prolific decorator. He signed several Meissen type examples of harbor scenes and rural romances. The factory was leased to Baroni in 1802, reverted to the Antonibon family in 1825, and continued to produce until the late 19th century. Its principal production was tableware. Special pieces included fish shaped tureens. The Sevres influence was strong. The mark used was a comet or a star in red, blue, or gold.

Naples
1771-1807

King Ferdinand IV, son of Charles IV, established the Royal Naples Factory in Naples in 1771 to manufacture porcelain and fill the gap left by the transfer of Capodimonte to Buen Retiro in Spain in 1759. Neo-classical wares were made along with the rococo styles formerly used by the Capodimonte workers. Domenico Venuti became director from 1779 until 1807. Filipo Tagliolini modeled figures of people from Naples in the fashions of the day. The factory was taken over by the French in 1807 and then closed in 1834.

The marks used were "FRF" under a crown until 1787 and then a crowned "N" impressed or painted in underglaze blue.

Vinovo
1776-1840

Gian Brodel from Turin and Marchese Birago of Vische, assisted by Peter Hannong, established a hard paste porcelain factory in Vinovo in 1776. It went bankrupt after a few years. Dr. Victor Gioanotti and Tamietti, a modeler, reopened the factory in 1780. They made mythological figures in colored and white porcelain, services with rococo decorations, vases with rural landscapes, groups and statuettes in the Capodimonte style, and busts of famous people in biscuit ware. The factory remained in operation until 1815 when Gioanotti died.

Giovanni Lamello, after working there as a sculptor from 1798, bought the factory in 1815. The factory marks imitated those of Sevres and the Meissen swords. The marks were either impressed or painted in underglaze blue or in red, gray, or black on the glaze.

Maiolica or Faience
1400 to Present

The earliest maiolica was produced by potteries located near Florence at Orvieto, Faenza, Siena, and Arezzo and used manganese purple and copper green decoration on pieces made for everyday use. These wares were inspired by earlier Spanish examples. Early in the 15th century, a cobalt blue was introduced from the Middle East. About 1450 new colors of yellow, turquoise, and orange appeared.

The rise of Faenza coincided with the brilliant colors used in the istoriato or pictorial style of Urbino. The entire surface of the piece was covered with historical, classical, mythological, or biblical scenes. Subjects included heraldic lions, birds, portraits, and foliage designs. Large drug jars (albarelli) with strap handles were made. Grotesques and arabesques were introduced in the 16th century. Faenza wares were at their finest from about 1480 until 1520.

Pictorials in the istoriato style were done at Castel Durante and Urbino. Venetian maiolica exhibited an oriental influence due to trade with the East. Large globular jars were a favorite shape.

Savona in Liguria made maiolica in the 17th and 18th centuries. A wide variety of wares was made including tea wares and figures. Castelli near Naples, made maiolica in the 17th and 18th centuries, reviving the istoriato style.

During the 17th and 18th centuries, many factories produced maiolica wares. Eventually they turned to the production of lead glazed earthenwares in the English style. Manufacturing of tin enamel wares still continues in Italy. Some of the production is directed toward making souvenirs for tourists.

Cantagalli
1878-1901

Cantagalli, an Italian potter, opened his faience factory in Florence in 1878 and used the crowing cock as its mark. The firm traded as Figli di Giuseppe Cantagalli. This factory manufactured imitations of early Italian maiolica, similar to pieces from Urbino, Faenza, Gubbio, Deruta, and at the Della Robbia workshop. The factory also imitated tin glazed earthenwares in the Isnik and Persian styles. Art Nouveau style is found in vases decorated with elongated plant motifs. Vases and dishes designed by William De Morgan were manufactured. Among its original products were decorative tablewares.

References: A. Lane, *Italian Porcelain*, Faber & Faber, 1954; B. Rackham, *Italian Maiolica, 2nd Ed,* Faber & Faber, 1963; John Scott-Taggart, *Italian Majolica,* Hamlyn Publishing Group, Ltd. 1972.

Museums: Bargello Museum, Florence, Italy; Birmingham Museum of Art, Birmingham, AL; British Museum, London, England; Gardiner Museum of Ceramic Art, Toronto, Canada; Musee National de Ceramique, Sevres, France; Museo Civico, Turin, Italy; National Museum of Wales, Cardiff, Wales; Seattle Art Museum, Seattle, WA; Victoria & Albert Museum, London, England; Wadsworth Atheneum, Hartford, CT.

Additional Listings: Capodimonte, Deruta, and Ginori.

Albarello

7" h, majolica

Ochre and green painted stylized scrolling foliage, lt blue ground, Sicily, 17th C, restored, (A) 339.00

Polychrome biblical scene flanked by blue scrolling foliage, late 18th C, chips, (A) 546.00

9 3/8" h, majolica, waisted shape, yellow and blue painted oval cartouche of saint on front, panels of scrolling foliage, Palermo, late 17th C, damaged rim, (A) 585.00

Basin, 23" H-H, majolica, multicolored center scene of Perseus and Andromeda, border of masks and foliage, figural snake handles, late 19th C, (A) 1,265.00

Basket

5" h x 12" l, cutout sides, cream ground, int with red flowers and green and yellow leaves, applied pink, yellow and blue flowers on ext and edge, brown trimmed base, top and ends, 4 green feet, "Made in Italy Milano" mark 75.00

22 1/4" h, oval, earthenware, free form purple and yellow flower with shaded green leaves in relief on front, arched handle, "F. & B. 17-H436, Italy" mark, (A) 200.00

Bowl, 4 3/8" d, blue, white, yellow, and red flowers in center, woven basketweave open sides 10.00

Bowl, Cov, 8" H-H, globular shape, flared ft, rosette scroll handles with anthemion terminals, domed cov with painted multicolored panels of "Cascata di Caserta" and "Marina di Casamicciola" on gilt ground chased with bands of flowers, bowl with "Terraferma d'alla Marina di Procida" and "Molina di Bottara" reserved on gilt ground, gilt int, gilt acorn knob, c1820, (A) .2,760.00

Charger

15 3/8" d, majolica, Renaissance style profile portrait of woman in center with scrolling ribbon inscribed "PIATA TETRENDA," border with alternating panels of scales or stylized palm and flowers, lustered, reverse green washed with black squiggles, (A) 690.00

18" d, majolica, Istoriato, multicolored biblical scene of king kneeling before warrior and troops near walled city, orange lined rim, Urbino, late 19th C, restored, (A) 693.00

19 1/2" d, majolica, central armorial, bands of winged cherubs, cherubs, and satyr masks in foliage, cobalt and lt blue glazes 850.00

22" d, majolica, blue and gray foliate patterned ground, mid 17th C, (A) 920.00

24" d, majolica, center polychrome scene of Neptune riding 2 dolphins, border of grotesques and scrolling with hanging swags of flowered urns, 19th C, (A) 805.00

Coffeepot, 9 1/2" h, black transfer of old map on side, map of Loire on reverse, black transfer of grapes and leaves on border, black outlined animal spout 100.00

Compote, 10" h x 7 1/8" d, blue ground, lustered silver overlay of leaves, geometrics, and zigzag, rooster mark 600.00

Cup, 2 5/8" h, puce painted flower sprays, Doccia, c1770, pr. 95.00

Dish

9" d, majolica, enameled ochre grasshopper on green leafy branch with red buds in center, band of red, ochre, orange and green interlaced floral sprays, shaped ochre rim, Pesaro, c1770, (A) 184.00

9 5/8" d, majolica, istoriato, painted multicolored scene of sleeping Venus in landscape with Cupid at side, Castelli, (A) 748.00

11 1/2" d, majolica, gadroon-molded basin, istoriato painted Renaissance style multicolored Biblical scene, (A) 230.00

12 1/4" d, majolica, exotic birds, florals, and leaves in center, banded feather border, blue and white, early 18th C, hairline, (A) 230.00

Figure

4" h x 6 1/2" l, stylized Persian blue donkey, purple base, "Gambone, Italy" mark, (A) 440.00

11 3/8" h, Art Deco style standing partially nude woman with gold hair, gold trimmed deer at each side, oval gilt trimmed base, "gold Made in Italy" mark 150.00

19" l, faience, reclining lion, white mane, blue glazed body, (A) 345.00

13 3/4" h, young baby leaning against dachshund puppy, brown and pink, gilt accents, "C.R.E.A. Made in Italy Torino No. 360" mark 123.00

Flask, 6 3/4" h, molded arches with blue Chinoiserie design and iron red scrolling florals, pendants, and tassels, gilt accents, Vezzi, c1727, cracks, (A) 21,850.00

Jar, Cov, 8 1/2" h, urn shape, tin glazed multicolored flowers, cream ground, blue lined trim on rim and base, blue knob, "Made in Italy" mark, c1930s. 75.00

Mug

2 1/2" h, yellow bird with blue tail, green grass and tree, white ground, c1800 . . . . 38.00

6 1/2" h, majolica, multicolored Bacchus scenes, gold lined trim, white int, figural satyr handle 85.00

Pilgrim Bottle, Cov, 17 3/4" h, majolica, satyr mask handles, painted portrait of doge and prince, or doge and winged lion of Venice holding book, blue ground with yellow-gold and dk red curlicues and scrolling, faux marble base, 19th, pr, (A) 1,150.00

Pitcher, 4 3/4" h, center band of blue outlined squares of stylized blue and green flowerheads, brown buds, blue X's over orange-brown diamonds and green dots on shoulder, orange and blue stripes, lt blue band on neck with dk blue dots 18.00

Plaque

9 7/8" l x 4 3/4" w, rect, painted seated Madonna and Child before crimson fringed hanging, branch of rosemary and oranges at left, "inscribed Quasi Oliva Speciosa in Campis/Profe N Berabino and Ebianchini" on reverse, (A) 207.00

12 1/4" h, round rect form, relief of busts Madonna and Child, yellow hair and halo, pink dots, gilt accents, white ground, Lenci, (A) 265.00

Plate

7 1/4" d, pink, blue, and yellow stylized roosters in center, band of blue leaves and dots on border, "rooster, Made in Italy" mark 15.00

8" d, enameled yellow, magenta, and green birds on brown branches, tan ground, scalloped edge with raised green swags and blue drop design, "imp Made in Italy, A P and starred staff" mark 38.00

8 1/2" d

Multicolored reserve of ducks with radiating rifles and branches, set of 11, (A). 195.00

Painted trainer and performing bear or man playing violin in orange and blue rococo scroll cartouche, fluted border with flowers and oval diaper panels, shaped brown line rim, Turin, c1760, pr, (A) 1,695.00

10" d, black outlined woman in pink, blue, and yellow gown standing next to staircase, mint green border with black band of leaves, gold lined rim . . . 30.00

Storage Jar, 8 1/8" h, oviform, majolica, "SANTAURUBRI" on yellow banner, blue scrolling ground, 18th C, (A) 462.00

Sugar Bowl, Cov, 5" h, hanging swags of mauve, orange, and red garden flowers suspended from green branches, red lined rim, molded apple knob, c1780........950.00

Tureen

12 1/2" H-H, silver shape, lobed body, majolica, painted loose sprays of flowers and scattered sprigs, orange lion's mask handles, late 18th C, (A) 770.00

13" H-H x 12" h, majolica, oval, body with 4 peg feet with applied and relief molded flowers and twigs, green and yellow molded leaf handles, overall painted floral and branch design, relief molded blue oval medallion on base, cov with painted scene of dog watching cat eating fish or dog chasing deer, yellow and green floral form knob handle, 19th C, (A) 633.00

Urn

13 3/4" h, campana shape, 2 vert handles, sq base, lg red, mauve, blue, pink, and yellow flowers in bouquet on white center band, gold everted rim, handles, and base 75.00

15 1/2" h, majolica, underglaze blue Italian village landscape scene, molded snake handles with male mask head terminals, Savona, c1781, (A) 978.00

29" h, majolica, campana shape, painted classical figures with temple in bkd, blue and yellow winged griffin handles, orange lined rim, c1820, chips and repairs.....................1,800.00

Vase

4 1/2" h, bulbous shape, blue and green drip on gray ground, dk red splashed rim 20.00

6 3/8" h, squat shape, HP pink and white roses on shoulder, dk green base, "Made in Italy" mark 125.00

8 5/8" h, majolica, ftd ovoid shape, sm cylinder neck, painted Renaissance-style mythical beasts, masks, and scrolling foliage on blue or yellow panels
.........................275.00

10 1/4" h, tapered shape with spread circ ft, scattered polychrome circus scenes of clown, horseback riders, and jugglers with stars and moon crescents, black ground, orange striped rim, Lenci, (A)...................4,928.00

10 5/8" h, baluster shape, shoulder gilt with anthemion and foliate scrolls, rosettes reserved on matte blue lozenges, white ground, swan handles, 19th C, pr, (A)
.........................1,150.00

63" h, baluster shape, flared everted rim, flared base, majolica, painted Bacchic putti drinking and playing in swag of grape leaves and vines, reverse with griffin in cartouche, applied winged female griffins on shoulders, painted plaster base with molded masks and swags, (A) 21,000.00

Wet Drug Jar, 8 1/2" h, majolica, blue and olive green designs, yellow stripe and spout, gray ground, late 17th C, repair to spout, (A) $550.

Wall Mask, 10 7/8" h, modeled as young woman with green curly hair, yellow and green scarf on neck, (A)..............185.00

Wet Drug Jar, majolica

8 1/4" h, black outlined cartouches of blue landscapes, foliate designs on body, 18th C, spout ground, (A)..... 230.00

8 1/2" h, ".M:ROSAT." below half portrait of woman in yellow dress holding mirror, flowering branches at sides, flat handle with ".G.N.," Castelli, mid-18th C, repairs, (A)..................616.00

JACKFIELD

Staffordshire and Shropshire, England
2nd half 18th century

History: Jackfield was a generic term used for black glazed earthenware made during the second half of the 18th century. The red clay body was covered with a blackish glossy slip that was ornamented with scrollwork and relief flowers, oil gilding, and unfired painting. Jackfield was named after the Shropshire Pottery Center.

From c1750-1775 the Jackfield factory was managed by Maurice Thursfield. John Rose of Coalport assumed control of the firm about 1780. Staffordshire potters such as Astbury and Whieldon also produced Jackfield wares.

References: R.G. Cooper, *English Slipware Dishes, 1650-1850*, Tiranti, 1968; *The Jackfield Decorative Tile Industry,* pamphlet, published by Ironbridge Gorge Museum Trust, England, 1978.

Museum: British Museum, London, England.

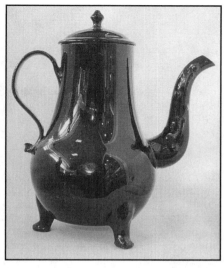

Teapot, 9" h, unmkd, c1760-80, $1,250.

Coffeepot, 9 3/4" h, mask and paw feet, Staffordshire, chips, (A) 75.00

Cream Jug, 5" h, baluster shape, 3 sm feet, 18th C, chips, (A) 158.00

Cream Jug, Cov, 6 3/4" h, 3 feet, flower knob, traces of gilt florals, chips, (A) 155.00

Figure

6" h, standing rooster, pr 150.00

6 1/4" h x 7 1/4" l, standing cow, seated milkmaid, gilt accents 225.00

8 1/2" h, seated cat, gilt trim, pr...275.00

9" h, seated spaniel, pr 695.00

Jug, 6 5/8" h, gilt scroll framed "JH 1765," (A)
.........................160.00

Pitcher, 6 1/2" h, traces of enameled birds, initials, and "1763," (A) 110.00

Salt Cellar, 1 3/4" h, oval lobed body, worn gilt accents, (A).....................100.00

Teabowl and Saucer, applied and gilded vine and florals, c1765, (A)............275.00

Teapot

3 1/2" h, miniature, restored, (A) ..230.00

4 3/8" h, ball shape, branch handle, 18th C
.........................195.00

4 1/2" h, globular shape, 3 feet, traces of gilt floral design, chips and hairlines, (A)
.........................160.00

7" h, oviform shape, printed and painted oriental figures, (A) 100.00

Waste Bowl, 5 1/2" d, ftd, everted rim, applied and gilded vine and florals, c1765, regilded, (A) 375.00

JASPER WARE

Staffordshire, England
Continental
1774 to Present

History: About 1774, Josiah Wedgwood perfected a hard, unglazed stoneware whose body was capable of being stained throughout its substance with metallic oxides. Shades of blue, lavender, sage, olive green, lilac, yellow, and black could be used. With jasper dip, the color was applied only on the surface.

Many firms, in addition to Wedgwood, produced jasper wares. Adams made jasper from the early 1800s into the 20th century. Adams blue jasper was distinguished from that of Wedgwood because it had a faint violet shade. Initially Adams modeled many of the designs for his jasper ware. In 1785, he employed Joseph Mongenot from Switzerland as a modeler. Together they designed the bas-reliefs and border decorations that were applied in white jasper to the colored bodies of vases, urns, tea and coffeepots, plaques, medallions, and candelabra drums. Most of the Adams jasper is marked.

Another producer of jasper ware was Spode. Other Staffordshire manufacturers produced marked jasper ware. Unfortunately, many examples do not include a maker's mark. Several continental potters, e.g. Heubach also manufactured jasper ware.

Museums: British Museum, London, England; Memorial Hall Museum, Philadelphia, PA; Museum of Fine Arts, Boston, MA; Victoria & Albert Museum, London, England.

Bottle, 5 1/2" h, white cameo of couple toasting on blue jasper ground, green jasper body with cameos of cherub and hanging swags, missing stopper, (A) 45.00

Bough Pot, 5 3/4" h, sq form, white cameos of classic figures in rect panels framed with foliate borders, beading and flowerheads on base, arched rim with bead and fan design, cov with textured ground and foliate relief, solid blue jasper ground, Turner, c1775, pr, chips, (A). 3,738.00

Bowl
  3 3/4" d, white cameo bust of queen wearing crown on dk green ground in oval gold cartouche, lt green jasper ground, undulating rim 20.00
  5 1/2" d, white cameos of classic scenes and flying insects, engine turned base, Turner, c1785, (A) 978.00

Box, Cov
  3 3/4" l, shell shape, white cameo of mermaid blowing horn on cov, green jasper ground 50.00
  4" l x 2 1/4" h, rect, raised white oval cameo of seated woman and flowers, white swags on base, female heads at ends, blue jasper ground 85.00
  4 1/2" l, oval, white cameos of 2 seated cherubs, one with fan on cov, lavender jasper ground, green tinged rim
  . . . . 150.00
  4 3/4" d, white cameos of standing classical woman holding flower garland, cherubs at sides, base with white vert

stripes and flowerheads, med blue jasper ground, unmkd 58.00
Bud Vase, 7" h
  Bulbous base, tall neck, white cameos of 2 cherubs lifting baby Bacchus, stiff leaves at center and border, med blue jasper ground, unmkd 28.00
  Slender shape with side twist handles, white cameo of Art Nouveau woman, green jasper ground 28.00
Cake Plate, Cov, 9" h x 10" d, white cameos of cherubs on sides of cov, white flowerheads and geometrics, white acorn knob, med blue jasper ground, Dudson 395.00
Coffeepot, 7" h, white classic cameos of Greek figures, festoons, lt green jasper ground, "Dudson Bros. England" mark 50.00
Creamer, 2 3/4" h, pink cameos of Kewpies and floral designs, green jasper ground, "Copyrighted Rose O'Neill, Kewpie, Germany" mark, (A) 20.00
Cup and Saucer, white cameos of 2 muses and Cupid, children on reverse, dk blue jasper ground, Adams 115.00
Egg Cup, 2 5/8" h, white cameos of florals and stiff leaves, sawtooth band on rim, rope band on ft, solid blue jasper ground, Adams, late 18th C, set of 4, (A) 2,185.00
Ewer, 8 3/4" h, white cameo of Grecian woman holding flowers in apron, white medallions, med blue jasper ground, unmkd 26.00
Hair Receiver, 3 1/2" l x 1 3/4" h, heart shape, 2 white cameo female figures flanking hole, white drapery and florals, green jasper ground 58.00
Humidor, 5 3/4" h, lg molded white roses on side, green basketweave jasper ground, unmkd 160.00
Jug, 7" h, white cameos of classic figures in clouds, engine turned base with white stiff leaves on rim and base, leaf molded handle and spout, solid blue jasper ground, c1785, Turner, (A) 1,150.00
Match Holder, 3" h, white cameo of winged cherub holding bow and arrow, white curlicues, reverse with cherub holding arrows and flaming heart, green jasper ground . . . 65.00
Pin Dish, 4 1/2" d, white cameo of Indian with braids smoking pipe, scalloped rim with feathers and curls, blue jasper ground
. . . . 125.00
Pitcher
  2 1/2" h, white cameo of angel blowing trumpet on dk green jasper ground in gold molded cartouche, gray-green jasper body with molded leaves top and base 30.00
  3" h
    Molded cartouche of white cameo of bust of young woman with lg hat on dk green ground, lt green jasper body 25.00
    White cameo of Cupid on green ground in gold outlined cartouche, lt green jasper ground, raised floral border and base 14.00

3 1/2" h, white cameos of Rosie O'Neill Kewpies, blue jasper ground. . . 445.00
9 3/4" h, bulbous shape, white body, blue band on neck with white cameos of grape leaves and tendrils, beaded band at middle. 500.00
Planter
  3 5/8" l x 5" l, oval, Art Nouveau style, white cameo bust of woman on dk green ground, lt green jasper body with white flowerheads, wishbone handles, full figure nude attached to end, unmkd
  . . . . 45.00
  4 1/2" h x 5 1/2" w, white cameos of cherub heads, green jasper ground 40.00
  5" h
    Oval shape, white cameos of seated classical woman holding lute or book, shell design on rim, white scroll handles, med blue jasper ground, Germany 85.00
    White rococo scrolling border and 4 feet, green jasper ground. . . . 37.00
  7 1/4" l, oval, continuous pink cameos of reclining classic woman holding bird, medallion feet, dk green jasper ground
  . . . . 95.00
Plaque
  4" d, white cameos of Venus and Cupid, green jasper ground, unmkd. . . . 40.00
  4 1/2" d, white cameo of cherub and dog in center, white floral border, scalloped rim, blue jasper ground, (A) 30.00
  4 5/8" l, white cameos of half busts of 2 winged cherubs kissing on rose bed, border of leaves, green jasper ground, pierced for hanging 42.00
  5 3/8" d, white cameo of Cupid with bow and hat, heart target with arrow, leaf and flower scroll border, green jasper ground, Germany. 65.00
  5 1/2" d, white cameo of man in toga holding dead game on stick and grapes, dog at side, seated woman nursing baby, pink jasper ground, pierced for hanging 32.00
  5 5/8" l x 3 3/4" w, white cameo of woman sitting in garden playing guitar, man placing wreath on her head, flying birds, blue jasper ground, Germany 25.00
  6" d
    White cameos of man with mandolin and woman, blue jasper ground, Germany. 40.00
    Wrapped cattail border
      White cameo of child with anvil and hammer, holding 2 iron rings, green jasper ground, Germany
      . . . . .145.00
      White cameo of fisherman in slicker, smoking pipe, standing on dock, green jasper ground
      . . . . .145.00
  6 1/2" h x 4 3/4" w, white cameos of 2 flying putti kissing, white scrolled inner border, white rococo shaped rim, green jasper ground, pierced for hanging 65.00

7" h x 5 1/2" w, oval, white cameos of man seated on brick wall, woman leaning into well, white scrolled border, med blue jasper ground, pierced for hanging, Germany 68.00

9 1/2" h, white molded cavalier on med green scroll jasper base, unmkd. 75.00

13" h, rect, white cameos of Art Nouveau woman with whiplash stems and flowers, green jasper ground and floral shaped rim, Germany, pr, (A) . . 340.00

Plate, 5 1/2" d, white cameo of Indian with headdress, beaded swag border, green ground, unmkd 40.00

Sugar Bowl, Cov, 4 1/4" h, white cameos of putti playing games, stiff leaves on cov, solid blue jasper ground, engine turned lower section, Turner, c1800, (A) 633.00

Teapot, 5" h, white cameos of classic figures, engine turned base, stiff leaves on base and cov, band of circles on rim, leaf molded handle and spout, solid blue jasper ground, Turner, c1785, finial repair, (A) 1,840.00

Toothpick Holder

1 7/8" h, cylinder shape, 3 handles, white cameo of City of London seal, dk blue jasper ground, Adams 85.00

2 1/4" h, white cameo of Seal of United States and "E Plurbus Unum," dk blue jasper ground, Adams 110.00

Tray

6" l, oval, white cameos of buffalo and Indian on horseback, dk blue jasper ground, Heubach 145.00

7 1/4" l, oval, raised black swags suspended from flowerheads, dk green jasper ground, unmkd 45.00

Urn, 6" h, dk brown classical scene of putti in landscape, beaded border, yellow jasper ground, unmkd, (A) $75.

Vase

3 1/2" h, white cameos of lady and Cupid, blue jasper ground, Germany. . . 30.00

5 1/2" h, cone shape, white cameos of classic woman holding grapes, hanging leaf swags on rim, leaf border on base, dk blue jasper ground 20.00

6 1/4" h

Campana shape, 2 white classic figures dancing, blue jasper ground with molded stiff leaves, 2 horiz handles 55.00

Triangle shape, white cameo of classic woman holding branch with bird, white floral and grape border with urn on pedestal, green jasper ground 125.00

Two sm handles, white cameos of woman playing lute, cherub holding music, lilac jasper ground, unmkd 30.00

9 7/8" h, campana shape, white cameos of classic scenes on body, white band of acanthus leaves on shoulder, stiff leaves on rim, lower body and sq base, band of beading on rim and circ ft, blue jasper dipped body, white scrolled leaf molded handles, Adams, c1790, (A) 920.00

JOHNSON BROTHERS

Staffordshire, England
1883 to Present

History: Henry, Robert, Alfred, and Fred, the four Johnson brothers, founded a pottery in 1883 in Staffordshire, England. Although begun on a small scale, it soon expanded. Its principal success was derived from earthenware tablewares that were quite successful in both England and the United States.

By 1914, the Johnson Brothers had five factories scattered throughout Hanley, Tunstall, and Burslem. Some popular patterns included "Granite" made for the overseas market, "Green & Golden Dawn," and "Rose." Johnson Brothers' wares originally were white ironstone. It was replaced by a lighter weight ware known for its uncommon lightness and finish.

Johnson Brothers became part of the Wedgwood Group in 1968.

Reference: Mary J. Finegan, *Johnson Brothers Dinnerware*, Marfine Antiques, 1993.

Berry Set

Master bowl, 9 1/4" d, 6 bowls, 4 7/8" d, "The Florentine" pattern, polychrome transfers 58.00

Master bowl, 9 1/2" l, 6 bowls, 5 3/4" l, oval, "Tally Ho" pattern, polychrome transfers 65.00

Bowl

5" d, "Old Britain Castles" pattern, blue transfer 6.00

6" d, "Old Britain Castles" pattern, blue transfer 7.00

7" d, "Friendly Village" pattern, multicolored transfer 16.00

7 5/8" d, "English Chippendale" pattern, red transfer 12.00

8" d, "Friendly Village" pattern, multicolored transfer 46.00

9 3/4" d, "Castle on the Lake" pattern, red transfer 30.00

Butter Pat, "Convolvulus" pattern, dk blue transfer 6.00

Casserole, Cov, 10" H-H, "English Village" pattern, blue transfer 65.00

Celery Dish, 8" l, "Rose Chintz" pattern, multicolored transfer 24.00

Cereal Bowl

6" d, "Bradbury" pattern, red transfer 9.00

6 1/2" d, "Old English Countryside" pattern, brown transfer 6.00

7 1/8" H-H, "Historic America-St. Louis, Missouri," blue transfer 9.00

Charger, 10 1/2" d, "Victorian" pattern, spray of multicolored leaves and flowers in center, molded flowerheads and leaves on border, cream ground, shaped rim 28.00

Coffeepot

8 3/4" h, "English Chippendale" pattern, red transfer 175.00

11" h, "Bonjour" pattern, red and green transfer 60.00

Creamer, "English Chippendale" pattern, red transfer 25.00

Cup and Saucer

"Bradbury" pattern, red transfer . . . 12.00

"Castle on the Lake" pattern, red transfer 2.00

"Day in June" pattern, multicolored transfer 5.00

"English Chippendale" pattern, red transfer 6.00

"English Village" pattern, blue transfer 12.00

"Old Britain Castles" pattern

Blue transfer 9.00

Red transfer 12.00

"Olde English Countryside" pattern, brown transfer 6.00

Platter, "Friendly Village" pattern, polychrome transfer, $30.

"Sheraton" pattern, multicolored transfer
.... 10.00

"Strawberry Fair" pattern, red transfer
.... 7.00

Cup and Saucer, Oversize, "Historic America-The Alamo," blue transfer 25.00

Egg Cup, "Friendly Village" pattern, multicolored transfer 10.00

Fruit Bowl, 5" d, "Bradbury" pattern, red transfer 7.00

Fruit Dish, 5 1/4" d

"English Chippendale" pattern, blue transfer........................... 8.00

"Strawberry Fair" pattern, red transfer
.... 10.00

Gravy Boat, "English Chippendale" pattern, red transfer 45.00

Pitcher, 5 1/2" h, "Friendly Village" pattern
.... 35.00

Plate

6" d

"English Village" pattern, blue transfer
.... 6.00

"Friendly Village" pattern, multicolored transfer..................... 6.00

6 1/4" d, "English Chippendale" pattern, red transfer 5.00

6 3/8" d, "Camellia" pattern, polychrome transfer........................... 6.00

6 1/2" d, "Olde English Countryside" pattern, brown transfer 8.00

7" d, "Old Britain Castles" pattern, red transfer.................... 18.00

7 1/2" sq

"Castle on the Lake" pattern, red transfer 11.00

"English Chippendale" pattern, red transfer 6.00

"Strawberry Fair" pattern, red transfer
.... 10.00

8" d, "English Village" pattern, blue transfer............................. 8.00

8" sq, "Castle on the Lake" pattern, blue transfer........................... 19.00

10" d

"Bradbury" pattern, red transfer. 14.00

"English Chippendale" pattern, red transfer 15.00

"English Village" pattern, blue transfer
.... 12.00

"Friendly Village" pattern, multicolored transfer 12.00

"Old Britain Castles" pattern

Blue transfer 10.00

Red transfer................. 13.00

"Olde English Countryside" pattern, brown transfer 12.00

"Strawberry Fair" pattern, red transfer
.... 10.00

"The Old Mill" pattern, multicolored transfer 12.00

Platter

11 3/4" l, "Road to Windsor" pattern, dk brown transfer.............. 15.00

12" l

"Olde English Countryside" pattern, brown transfer 20.00

"Rose Chintz" pattern, multicolored transfer 30.00

14" l, oval, "Friendly Village" pattern, multicolored transfer............. 90.00

16" l

11 1/8" w, rect, "Columbia" pattern, brown transfer 38.00

Oval, "Friendly Village" pattern, multicolored transfer 120.00

20" l x 15 1/2" w, oval

"Friendly Village" pattern, multicolored transfer 125.00

"Historic America-Thanksgiving" pattern, blue transfer 125.00

"Old Britain Castles-Stafford Castle" pattern, blue transfer..... 125.00

20 1/2" l, "Tally Ho-The Kill" pattern, multicolored transfer............. 240.00

Soup Plate, 8" d

"Old Britain Castles" pattern, red transfer
.... 10.00

"The Old Mill" pattern, brown transfer with yellow-gold and maroon 22.00

Teapot

5 3/4" h, "English Chippendale" pattern, red transfer................ 165.00

7 1/2" h, "Cotswold" pattern, brown transfer 65.00

Tea Service, teapot, creamer, sugar bowl, 6 cups and saucers, "Grey Dawn" pattern, blue 95.00

Tureen, 17 1/4" H-H, 9 3/4" h, "Harvest Time" pattern, polychrome transfer, $250.

Vegetable Bowl

8 3/8" l, "Coaching Scenes" pattern, blue transfer.................... 46.00

8 1/2" d, "Bradbury" pattern, red transfer
.... 32.00

8 1/2" sq

"English Chippendale" pattern, red transfer 35.00

"Olde English Countryside" pattern, brown transfer 30.00

9" l, oval

"English Chippendale" pattern, red transfer 60.00

"Historic America-Tow Path, Erie Canal" pattern, blue transfer.... 48.00

"Paisley" pattern, red transfer .. 20.00

9 3/4" d, "Olde English Countryside" pattern, brown transfer............ 50.00

9 3/4" l, "Castle on the Lake" pattern, red transfer.................... 30.00

KELLER AND GUERIN

Luneville, France 1778 to Present

1788 - 19TH CENTURY

History: Keller and Guerin bought the old faience factory of Jacques Chambrette from Gabriel, his son, and Charles Loyal, his son-in-law, in 1778. The factory made blue decorated faience similar to that of Nevers, and rose and green faience that imitated old Strasbourg motifs.

Schneider was the most celebrated of the potters that worked at Keller and Guerin. The company commissioned designs from sculptors Ernest Bussiere and E. Lachenal among others. Biscuit porcelain figures, especially of large animals, were a specialty.

The company switched from faience to English style earthenware at the end of the 19th century. Majolica and transfer printed wares entered the product line. The company still is in operation.

Bowl

5 3/4" d x 3" h, pedestal base, dk blue floral sprig in int center, hanging blue lambrequins on inner border, ext with dk blue flower and leaf sprays with gilt accents
.... 28.00

6 3/16" d, black oriental genre transfer with red, green, yellow, and irid brown accents, red striped rim and base, "K & G, Luneville, France" mark, (A) 20.00

9" d, lg red tinged white roses and green leaves in center, shaded blue-green ground 30.00

9 1/8" d, blue oriental figure on int center, int border of blue and red oriental figures in gardens repeated on ext, red lined rim 30.00

12" d, center with magenta florals and greenery, florals interspersed on int and ext sides, magenta scalloped rim, "K &

G. Luneville, Made in France" mark
. . . . 80.00

Cup and Saucer, "Timor" pattern, blue, rust, green, and orange oriental design, "Keller & Guerin, Luneville, France" mark 38.00

Dish, 11 3/4" H-H, rect, 3 section, Art Deco style blue sailor in center section, side sections with blue dressed woman holding brown basket of fish. 65.00

Plate

7 1/4" d, dk red roses, blue and yellow flowers, green leaves, red outlined molded basketweave inner border
. . . . 45.00

8" d, "Timor" pattern, iron red and cobalt
. . . . 34.00

8 1/4" d

Border of blue stenciled flowerheads
. . . . 10.00

Center with pink flower and green leaves, inner border of pink flowers and lt orange leaves and 3 geometric shapes with lt orange star-type design, sm black dots and zigzag rim 20.00

8 3/4" d, stenciled brown and blue windmill and village in center, sqs, dots, and dashes on border 45.00

9" d, standing peasant woman in red jacket, blue dress, white apron, border of blue hanging lambrequins, "blue K. & G., St. Clement, France" mark. . 165.00

9 1/8" d, brown and blue overall checkerboard pattern. 22.00

9 5/8" d, HP blue, green, yellow, red, and brown rooster in center, green clover on border, scalloped rim with painted shell design, "green Les Coos, K & G, Luneville, France" mark, set of 4, (A) . 200.00

9 3/4" d, 3 clowns and shadow figure in shades of blue-green and white, gilt rim, pierced for hanging, "Keller & Guerin, Luneville, France" mark 35.00

10 1/4" d

Red and white roses, leaf and bud shadow ground, blue indented rim, "K. & G. Luneville" mark. 38.00

Stylized black, red, and blue peasant dancers, cathedral in bkd, black dash rim, pierced for hanging
. . . . 22.00

Planter, 14" l, 8" w, 6" h, brown and black stylized foliage, white ground, "Keller & Guerin, Monterey" mark, (A) $110.

Vase

7 7/8" h, faience, bulbous body, leaf molded spread ft, green and blue stiff leaf molded body, 4 apertures around central opening, late 19th C, (A). . . 231.00

10 1/2" h x 9" d, pillow shape, pierced handles, purple and gray tin glazed body with silver lustered geometrics, "KG" mark 895.00

KING'S PORCELAIN MANUFACTORY (KPM)

Berlin, Germany
1763 to Present

History: The King's Porcelain Manufactory (KPM) was purchased and controlled by Frederick the Great. He ran the factory according to his own ideas and was responsible for its successes and failures, even though he employed Johann Grieninger as director.

The early porcelains were characterized by a dense, clear glaze over a fine white body. Many of the more talented German painters were employed by Frederick, resulting in products that competed with the highly successful Meissen factory.

The 18th century at KPM was characterized by technically superior figures in the glazed and biscuit state that showed a critical attention to details. However, the mainstay of the company was a line of popular, fine tablewares and ornamental pieces. Large quantities of tablewares were decorated with detailed florals and period and pastoral paintings. These early pieces showed a discriminating use of gilding, often used to highlight rather than to decorate. The later periods saw an increase in the use of gilding to the point of excessiveness. After the death of Frederick the Great in 1786, the factory continued to produce dinner services and other utilitarian and decorative porcelains.

The King's Porcelain Manufactory also was known for the fine miniature plaques in porcelain, which featured copies of popular paintings of the period. KPM, along with other major European houses, kept up with the times and changing styles, adopting the rococo, neo-classical, and Empire styles as each became fashionable. KPM was among the first to produce lithophanes. During the 19th century, the emphasis shifted to simple, clean designs.

From its beginnings, KPM was under the control of the Prussian monarchy. With the abdication of William II, the last of the kings, in 1918, KPM became the property of the Prussian state. It was renamed the States Porcelain Manufactory Berlin. Severe damage from bombings during World War II resulted in the factory being moved to Selb where it leased the porcelain factory of Paul Muller.

After WW II, the factory in Berlin was reconstructed. Since the two factories were in separate occupation zones, both branches remained legally separated until 1949. When the Federal Republic of Germany was established in 1949, the factory in Berlin became the property of the City of Berlin (West Property). The branch in Selb returned to Berlin in 1957. Products from Selb have an "S" beneath the scepter.

References: Winfred Baer, *Berlin Porcelain,* Smithsonian Institution Press, 1980; George W. Ware, *German and Austrian Porcelain*, Crown, Inc.1963.

Reproduction Alert: This mark is one of the most frequently copied and reproduced marks on china and porcelain. Imitations and modern reproductions have little or no hand painting; they are transfer printed. Other factories used similar marks to KPM. A mark without the scepter is not authentic. KPM must appear in combination with scepter, orb or eagle on authentic marks.

Cabinet Cup and Saucer, int painted with scene of The Royal Palace in Berlin, lt blue ground, gilt borders, "blue scepter and iron red K.P.M. and orb" marks, (A). . . . 1,610.00

Cane Handle, 4 1/2" w, modeled as lady's head with cap and black veil, yellow bodice, rococo scroll molded base, painted and gilt scrolls on border, (A) 500.00

Coffee Set, pot, 11 1/2" h, creamer, cov sugar bowl, baluster shape with scrolling handles, urn knobs, multicolored armorials on sides with inscriptions, gilt trim, (A) 633.00

Cup and Saucer

Cup painted with reserves of battle scene and royal meeting in C-scroll and acanthus borders on blue ground, gilt cornucopia handle, raised base, saucer with 2 reserves of coronation, (A) . 3,220.00

Coffee Set, pot, 11 1/2" h, cream jug, cov sugar bowl, multicolored armorials, gilt accents, 19th C, (A) $605.

Painted multicolored goldfinch in branches in gilt roundel gilt scrolling leaves, dk blue ground, "underglaze blue eagle, KPM, and iron red orb" marks, (A) 308.00

Painted named topographical scenes, gilt int and loop handle, "blue scepter" mark, c1820, pr, (A) 2,070.00

Cup and Saucer, Demitasse, molded flutes, painted gilt line and blue dash band suspending blue scale diapers with gilt flowers alternating with pendant flower sprays, gilt line rim, "blue scepter, iron red K.P.M. and orb" mark, c1915, set of 12, (A) 2,070.00

Dinner Service, Part, 2 platters, 13 3/4", 17 1/2" l, 2 bowls, 8 1/2" sq, 11 plates, 9 1/2" d, 12 plates, 8 1/2" d, 10 plates, 7" d, 5 soup plates, 9 1/2" d, 3 condiments, 7" d, lg dk pink florals and foliage, white ground, raised design on borders, scalloped edges, "rust KPM, orb, blue scepter " marks, late 19th C . . .2,800.00

Drinking Vessel, 10 1/2" h, tapered cylinder shape, relief of gold outlined shields on upper section above German inscriptions in arches, relief band of green leaves around middle, relief band of purple radishes below, white ground. 1,275.00

Figure

5" h, parrot on tree stump, red head, blue-green plumage, later decorated, "blue scepter" mark, (A) 127.00

5 3/4" h, young boy holding cage, flute in pocket, "red KPM" mark, c1832, (A) 700.00

7 5/8" h, "Terpsichore," marked on reverse, dancing woman in pink and yellow flowing gown, holding tambourine, scrolled and gilt base, "underglaze blue trident" mark, late 18th C, (A) . . 462.00

7 3/4" h, "Gabriel," standing man with crown of thorns on head, olive green sash across waist, sq base, "red sword, cross, crown, KPM, blue scepter, imp 322" marks, (A) 175.00

8 1/2" h

"Fortitude," female warrior in draped lion skin, seated on column, holding burning brazier, polychrome, "underglaze blue scepter, printed red orb" marks, late 19th C, (A) . 200.00

Young man in classic brown trimmed waistcoat, holding cocked hat, long boots, female in Empire style dress, fancy hat, holding fan, brown trimmed, gold accents, circ base with gold trim, pr 350.00

16" h, Venus and Cupid embracing, cylinder plinth, applied flower swags, white glaze, "blue scepter" mark, 19th C, (A) 246.00

16 1/2" h, oriental male in peaked hat, striped tunic, orange shoes, playing cymbals or oriental female in white kerchief, green lined yellow flowered robe, striped underskirt, holding cockatoo, 19th C, pr, (A) 1,725.00

Luncheon Service, Part, teapot, 6" h, hot water pot, 9" h, 10 teacups, 11 saucers, 10 coffee cups, 11 saucers, 7 demitasse cups, 12 saucers, 11 plates, 8 3/8" d, HP floral bouquets, gilt accents and rims, basketweave molded borders, chips and repairs, (A) 2,415.00

Plaque

5 1/2" d, Madonna and Child with John the Baptist, after Raphael painting, c1920, (A) 690.00

6 1/4" h x 9 1/4" w, rect, "Liebe," winged Eros embracing nymph, sgd "F. Tenner," "imp scepter and K.P.M." mark, (A) 3,450.00

7 3/8" h x 4 3/4" w, rect, young maiden seated on bench reading book, 2 children at side, "imp scepter and K.P.M." mark, (A) 2,760.00

7 1/2" h x 9 7/8" l, rect, painted 17th C tavern scene of cavalier having palm read by gypsy, "imp scepter and K.P.M." mark, (A) 3,680.00

10" h x 7 1/2" w, rect, 3 maidens holding putto, wheatfield bkd with putti faces, "imp scepter and K.P.M." mark, (A) 2,990.00

12 1/2" h x 9 3/4" w, rect, "Theodore," half profile portrait of blond woman with wreath of roses in hair, sgd "H. Meisel," "imp scepter and K.P.M." mark, (A) 9,775.00

16 5/8" h x 13 1/4" w, oval, "The Sistine Madonna" after Raphael, "imp scepter and K.P.M." mark, (A) 4,025.00

Plate

7 3/4" d, polychrome transfer of soldier seated on cannon in center, "KPM, scepter, cross" mark. 100.00

8 3/8" d, painted with various lg loose bouquets, ozier molded border with painted flower sprays, gilt scalloped rim, "blue scepter" mark, late 19th C, set of 24, (A) 690.00

8 3/4" d, reserve painted with various fruits and vegetables, gilt rim, 20th C, set of 12, (A) 1,955.00

9" d, painted loose bouquets of Deutsche Blumen with gilt in center, wide reticulated border with flowerheads at joins and 4 gilt cartouches with painted flowers, "blue scepter, iron red orb and KPM" marks, late 19th C, set of 12, (A) 4,025.00

9 1/2" d, painted couple in 18th C dress in landscape, dk blue band and shaped gilt line rim, "KPM, blue scepter, iron red orb" marks, (A) 215.00

Platter

19" l x 13 1/4" w, oval, center with red and purple flowers and foliage, molded, painted and gilt rim, late 19th C. .650.00

21 1/2" l, 3 lg pink roses and green leaves in center, green and gold twist ribbon on border, 2 gilt bands on rim, "blue scepter" mark, (A). 375.00

Punch Bowl, 22" l, oval, int and ext painted with water lilies, irises, and garden flowers,

green and gilt accented rocaille molded scroll handles and terminals, "blue scepter, iron red orb" mark, (A) 1,978.00

Serving Dish, 13 1/4" l, center floral spray reserve, gilt accents, pierced handles, shaped gilt accented body, 19th C, (A) 50.00

Stein, .5 L, relief, white standing stylized king holding beer stein, leaf and floral sides, cobalt glazed ground, porcelain inlaid lid with figural hunter head, hairlines 100.00

Sweetmeat Stand, 8 7/8" h, figure of woman in yellow rustic dress, grapes in apron, standing before basket, arched scroll molded trefoil base, gilt accents, "underglaze blue scepter" mark, damage, (A) 370.00

Teapot, 7 3/4" h, relief molded vines and flowers, white, gilt accented spout, handle, knob, and rims, "blue scepter, red K.P.M orb" marks. 250.00

Tureen

10 1/4" H-H, lobed oval shape, scroll handles, painted scattered pink roses under green ribbon entwined around gilt line, pine cone knob, "blue scepter" mark, c1830, pr, (A) 1,265.00

13 1/2" H-H x 12 1/2" h, swirled molded oval shape, gilt band and vines over solid gilt lined rims, gilt accented figural knob of putti holding cornucopia of flowers, gilt accented molded cornucopia handles, "blue scepter, brown cross and KPM" marks, (A) 1,093.00

Vase

6 3/4" h, ball shape on circ base with short scroll arms, intaglio molded lt pink and gray stylized flowering trees, applied yellow jeweling on rims and base, sgd "H. Lang," (A) 715.00

8 1/2" h, Art Deco style incised figural landscape design, white glaze, "KPM, blue scepter" mark 500.00

10 1/8" h, baluster shape, streaked crystalline sea green and yellow, "blue scepter" mark, (A) 250.00

Vase, Cov

23 1/2" h, painted continuous frieze of Aurora, cobalt ground with raised gilt flowers, ribbons, and leaves, swirled design on cov and socle, sq base with cut corners, ring handles, (A) 4,887.00

41 1/4" h, baluster shape, flared neck and rim with molded serpent scales, winged serpent handles, molded stiff leaves on ft, sq base with molded classical masks, white glaze, (A) 2,875.00

KING'S ROSE AND QUEEN'S ROSE

Staffordshire, England
c1820-1830

History: The King's Rose pattern, decorated on a soft paste body, was related closely to Gaudy Dutch in form as well as in the colors used in decoration. A large orange or red cabbage rose with green, yellow, and pink leaves surrounding it as accents formed the center of the design. Many plates also featured relief motifs.

The Queen's Rose pattern had a pink rose as the center with the accent colors in more delicate tones.

Bowl, 6 1/4" d, pearlware, lg pink rose, dk red and green sm flowers and leaves, dk brown lined rim. 275.00

Creamer, 4 1/4" h, pearlware, oval with sq handle, lg iron red rose and red and yellow polychrome flowers with green and yellow leaves, red and green vine border with sm pink roses, unmkd, (A) 275.00

Cup and Saucer, Handleless

Lg iron red flower and green leaves, pink rims 265.00

Sm pink and green flower in center, brick red line, alternating pink, green, and brick red florals, (A) 75.00

Cup Plate, 4 1/2" d, soft paste, lg iron red flower, floral and vine luster rim. 165.00

Pitcher, 6 3/4" h, lg iron red flower with green and blue trim, basket of flowers on side .85.00

Plate

5 1/4" d, pearlware, sm pink rose and red and yellow polychrome flowers with green and yellow leaves, red and green polychrome vine border with sm pink roses, scalloped rim, unmkd, (A)
. . . . 200.00

5 3/8" d, lg iron red rose, "Oyster" pattern, repairs, (A). 180.00

5 5/8" d, pearlware, lg iron red rose and red and yellow flowers with green and yellow leaves, wide pink banded border with diamond design, plain rim, (A)
. . . . 270.00

6 1/8" d, lg pink rose, yellow centered red petaled flowers, iron red banded border with sm pink roses 155.00

6 1/4" d, lg iron red flowerhead

Pearlware, red and yellow polychrome flowers with green and yellow flow-

ers, pink polychrome banded border with diamond design and 4 reserves of blue and red floral sprigs and green leaves, plain edge, unmkd, (A). 110.00

Pink border with red accents . 145.00

6 1/2" d, pearlware, sm iron red rose and red and green polychrome flowers with green and yellow leaves, wide pink banded border with diamond design and red and blue floral sprigs with green leaves, plain rim, unmkd, (A)
. . . . 100.00

7 1/4" d, pearlware, lg pink rose, red and yellow polychrome flowers with green and yellow leaves, wide pink banded rim with diamond design, plain edge, (A) 125.00

7 1/2" d, lg iron red rose

Green leaves, vine design on rim, chip on rim, (A) 95.00

Sm pink flowers and green leaves, molded purple luster leaves and painted green leaves on border
. . . . 110.00

7 5/8" d, lg red rose in center with red and yellow flowers, molded basketweave border with purple luster lines on each side, c1810 . . . . 115.00

8" d, lg iron red rose in center with greens, 2 red border bands. 130.00

8 5/8" d, sm pink and green flower in center, pink and blue scalloped and feathered outer design, wide pink and narrow yellow border bands, (A) 85.00

10 1/4" d, iron red flowerhead, dbl red line border 165.00

Platter, 11" l x 9 1/2" w, lg iron red rose, red edged yellow flowerheads, yellow and green leaves in center, pierced canary yellow border, iron red lined shaped rim, hairline, (A)
. . . . 825.00

Soup Plate, 9 7/8" d, pearlware, lg iron red rose and red and yellow flowers with green and yellow leaves, wide pink border band with diamond design, plain rim, unmkd, (A) . . .400.00

Sugar Bowl, Cov

4 5/8" h, pearlware, oblong shape, sm pink rose on side, red and yellow flowers, green and yellow leaves, red vine border with sm pink roses and green leaves, red stripe on base and ring handles and knob, (A) 130.00

6" h, tapered barrel shape, sm pink rose, pink panels with dk pink X's around lid and border, molded flat handles
. . . . 110.00

6 1/2" h x 6 1/2" H-H, rect, sm pink rose, continuous band of dk pink X's around lid and base, 2 ear handles, rect knob, c1820 . . . . 115.00

Teapot

4 3/4" h, creamware, globular shape, intertwined ribbed handle with molded floral ends, lg iron red flowerhead on side, scattered leaves and intertwined flowerheads, flower knob, (A). 3,025.00

5 3/4" h, pearlware, dk brown outlined molded shell design with rect reserves on sides with lg iron red rose with yellow and red flowers and yellow and green leaves, red vine border with sm pink roses and green leaves, repairs, (A)
. . . . 440.00

LEEDS

Yorkshire, England c1757-1878

HARTLEY GREENS & CO.
LEEDS POTTERY
c1781-1920

History: The original Leeds factory was located in Yorkshire and was founded by John and Joshua Green about 1757. Among its products were saltglaze, basalt, and stoneware, plus a very fine pearlware using a bluish glaze similar to that of Wedgwood. Figures, transferwares, lusters, and mottled wares, similar to Whieldon's, also were produced.

Probably the most recognized Leeds product was yellow glazed creamware, first produced about 1760. This creamware was characterized by its soft yellow-cream color and the extensive use of perforations and open work, especially evident in the border treatments.

All types of utilitarian and decorative items were made in creamware from the simplest plate to elaborate, multi-sectioned fruit coolers and figural groups. The basic body often was augmented with painted and printed designs. Floral and fruit finials were a Leeds trademark.

The Green brothers had several different partners in their enterprises; shortly after forming the company, it traded as Humble, Greens & Co. Financial difficulties beset the Yorkshire pottery. After several additional owners and attempts at resurrection, the company failed and closed its doors in 1878.

Only a small amount of Leeds wares bore factory marks.

References: Heather Lawrence, *Yorkshire Pots and Potteries*, David & Charles, 1947; Donald Towner, *The Leeds Pottery*, Cory, Adams & MacCay, 1963.

Museums: City Art Gallery, Leeds, England; Everson Museum of Art, Syracuse, NY; Fitzwilliam Museum, Cambridge, England; Museum of Fine Arts, Boston, MA, Victoria & Albert Museum, London, England.

Bowl

5 1/2" d, pearlware, multicolored transfer of milkmaid and cow or maidens at well washing clothes, farm in bkd, pink and green luster banded border, pr . 285.00

9 1/4" d, int painted with mustard, blue, and green flowers and foliage, (A)
. . . . 633.00

Plate, 8 1/4" d, lg mauve flower, yellow and green leaves, border with iron red and mauve flowerheads, green leaves, iron red lines, c1840, $150.

Coffeepot, 10" h, blue grapes, green leaves, brown tendrils, c1818-20, chips 450.00

Creamer

3" h, green and yellow sprigs, yellow and brown bands, handle chip, (A) . 105.00

3 1/4" h

Leaf handle, gaudy blue floral design, hairlines, (A) 80.00

Pearlware, ribbed handle, blue oriental pagoda and willow tree design, (A) 220.00

Creamer and Sugar Bowl, Cov, creamer, 5" h, sugar bowl, 4 3/4" h, brown granite surface, bands of brown and white checkering, rope twist handles with leaf terminals, (A). . 546.00

Cup and Saucer, Handleless

Band of blue and yellow flowerheads, brown and green leaves, (A). . . 605.00

Blue, tan, yellow, and brown bird on branch, green and brown foliage, (A) 1,238.00

Lg cobalt 8 petal flowerhead, green foliage, mustard accents, (A). . . . 330.00

Yellow and brown acorns, green foliage, cobalt leaf and bands, (A). . . . 523.00

Yellow flower with blue center and brown accents, green, orange-brown, and brown leaf and foliage design, (A) 550.00

Cup Plate

4" d, oct, brown, yellow, green, and blue floral and foliage design, brown lined rim, (A) 1,128.00

4 1/4" d, blue and yellow flowers with brown accents, green fern-type leaves with brown accents, green feathered scalloped rim, (A) 1,485.00

Milk Jug, Cov, 4 1/4" h, baluster shape, scalloped pierced rim, inset spout molded with laurel garlands, reeded dbl twist handle with flower and foliage terminal, beaded ft, green vert stripes and brown dotted stripes, c1765, repairs .1,550.00

Mug, Cov, 4 7/8" h, fluted and beaded cov border, neck, and ft, grooved ear handle, flattened turned knob, green translucent vert striping, c1775 . . . . .1,975.00

Pepper Pot, 4 1/2" h, blue feather edge 200.00

Pitcher

4 1/4" h, bulbous, wide blue band in center over blue, green, and orange-brown foliage, (A) 358.00

5" h, bulbous, blue floral and leaf running vine around body, blue lined rim and handle, (A) 193.00

6 3/4" h, brown agate surface, bands of brown and white checkering, loop handle, repairs, early 19th C, (A) . . 805.00

8 1/4" h, bulbous, meandering blue, green, and brown floral and vine decoration, (A) 990.00

Plate

6 1/4" d, oct, pearlware, yellow, orange, blue, green, and brown peafowl in tree

with leaves, green feather edge, (A) 660.00

6 5/8" d

Pearlware, exotic oriental palace in landscape, blue transfer, molded basketweave border, blue outlined pierced rim, c1810, pr, (A) . 100.00

Polychrome single strawberry, tendrils, and leaf in center, hanging 3 leaf plants and swags on inner border, blue feather edge, c1770 . . 395.00

7" d, HP blue, yellow, orange and green peafowl bird in branch, blue feather edge 395.00

7 1/4" d, lg orange-brown, blue, and yellow flowers, green foliage, border of green, yellow, and orange brown running vine, blue feather rim with floral and foliate design, (A) 440.00

7 1/2" d

Oct, blue, yellow, tan, and brown peafowl on brown branch with green sponging, green feather edge, (A) 1,210.00

Tan pineapple and urn in center, green foliage, brown accents, green feather edge, hairline, (A) 1,073.00

7 3/4" d

Blue and yellow flowers, tan buds, blue, green, and brown foliage, emb tassel border, blue lined shaped rim, "imp Stubbs and Kent" mark, (A) 1,760.00

Blue on white floral acorn and foliate design, blue scalloped leaf and fish scale border, (A) 330.00

8 1/4" d

Blue, tan, and yellow peafowl on branch, green fan foliage, green scalloped feather rim, (A) . . 468.00

Lg orange-brown, yellow, and blue flowerhead, lg green and brown leaves and tendrils in center, border band of orange-brown squiggle and blue vining, brown lined rim, (A) 935.00

Oriental scene of house, boats, lake, and landscape, blue transfer, "imp Leeds Pottery" mark, rim chip, (A) 50.00

8 1/2" d, blue and tan flower and brown and green foliage in center, band of blue and tan flowers with brown and green foliage on border, (A) . . . 220.00

8 3/4" d, blue, green, yellow, tan, and brown flower and foliage in center, emb leaf and basketweave border, green feather edge, (A). 1,705.00

9" d, pierced diamond and demilune border, c1790. . . . . 195.00

9 1/8" d, pearlware, blue, yellow, orange, green, and dk brown peafowl in tree, blue feather edge, (A). 632.00

9 7/8" d, brown, blue, and ochre eagle and shield in center, green feather edge, (A) .1,045.00

10" d

Lg orange-brown and blue flower with lg fern leaves in center, emb rose and foliage border, blue feather edge, "imp S. Tams & Co." mark, (A). 2,860.00

Molded flutes and edge design, reticulated rim, "imp Leeds" mark, pr, (A) 230.00

Platter

10 1/4" l x 7 1/4" w, blue 6 petal flowers with mustard buds, blue and green foliage, (A) 523.00

15 3/4" l x 12 5/8" w, pearlware, blue molded feathered rim, unmkd, (A). . . . 85.00

17" l, green feather edge, c1830s . 350.00

18" l x 13 1/2" w, molded and feathered green rim 245.00

18 3/8" l x 14" w, green feather edge, glaze flakes, (A). 220.00

19 1/4" l, green feather edge 195.00

19 1/2" l, blue feather edge, (A). . . 125.00

20 3/4" l, oval, pearlware, blue and white oriental scene of woman with parasol in garden setting, blue feathered edge, repair, (A) 495.00

Spill Vase, 6 1/2" h, pearlware, modeled spiral fluted cornucopia and rocaille scroll, blue accents, Chinese landscape on reverse, round base with blue diaper border, c1780, restorations, (A) 320.00

Strawberry Dish, 10" H-H, oval shape, molded ribs, feather borders, scalloped edge, stalk feet, c1780 . . . . 1,800.00

Teabowl and Saucer, pearlware, blue, yellow, orange, green, and dk brown peafowl in tree, (A) 1,155.00

Teabowl and Saucer, Miniature, iron red, green, and black flowers, beaded rim on teabowl, central beading on saucer . . 550.00

Teapot

2 1/2" h, miniature, iron red, green, and black flowers on front, fruit on reverse, beaded cov, should, and ft, reeded entwined dbl strap handle with flower and foliage terminals, flower knob, c1785, restruck spout 3,450.00

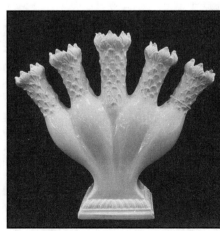

Vase, 8" h, sq gadrooned base, pr, (A) $900.

5 1/4" h, Bataviaware, blue transfer landscape design with oriental border, brown ground, dbl entwined handle, c1800, repairs, (A) 316.00

5 1/4" h

Cylinder shape with concave shoulder, reeded spout, entwined strap handle ending in flower and foliage terminal, overall iron red, black, blue chintz pattern, gilded roping on cov, shoulder, and ft, blue flower knob, c1770 . . . . .6,850.00

Vert ribbing, galleried top, spread ft, acanthus molding on spout, grooved dbl strap handle with foliage terminal, flower knob, vert green stripes, c1775, repairs . . .11,800.00

7 1/2" h, squat shape, wishbone handle, blue leaf and branch design, blue dashes on spout and handle, "imp L. Wood" mark 275.00

Toddy Plate, 4 1/2" d, black transfer of hen and chick, emb lime green and rust shell border with blue dots, lime green lined rim, (A)
. . . . 550.00

Wall Pocket, 8 1/4" l, cornucopia shape, relief of urn and ribbons, white, c1780, pr . 2,713.00

LIMOGES

Limousine region of France
c1770 to Present

History: Limoges' first hard paste porcelain dated from about 1770 and was attributed to the company of Massie, Grellet, and Fourneira. Permission was granted to make porcelain by the Council of the Court. The company came under the patronage of Comte d'Artois, brother-in-law of King Louis XVI, in 1777. Since the company was financed and supported by the court, the products were marked with the initials "C.D."

Due to financial and technical problems, the company was sold to the King in 1784. He used the factory as a branch of Sevres. Whitewares were made at Limoges and sent to Sevres for decoration.

Grellet served as manager from 1784 until 1788. J. Francoise Alluaud followed as manager and remained until 1794. About that time, the factory was sold to Joubert, Cacate, and Joly, three of the workers.

At the end of the French Revolution, c1796, the progress of porcelain making continued at Limoges with the addition of many new factories. Alluaud, Baignol, and Monnerie were among those establishing their own factories during the 1790s.

Additional factories developed between 1800 and 1830, among which were two factories begun in 1825 at Saint-Leonard, the Recollet factory, which remained in production until 1963, and the Pont de Noblat factory, still in production. These factories responded to the growing demands of a large export market for Limoges porcelains, with America as the largest customer. The mid to late nineteenth century was the golden age for Limoges porcelain.

David Haviland also established himself in Limoges during the 1850s. Many of the other factories imitated his techniques. Limoges porcelain is usually more bold than Haviland. With the tremendous amount of porcelain produced, the market could not absorb all the wares. After World War I and the economic crises of the 1920s and 1930s, many older companies were forced out of business. There was some revitalization after World War II. Today Limoges still is the center of hard paste porcelain production in France.

A wide range of objects was made with vivid decoration of florals, fruit, figural, and scenic themes that were embellished with gold. Decorative pieces included vases, large plaques, trays, tankards, mugs, bowls, plates, paintings, and jardinieres.

Smaller accessory pieces such as dresser sets, trinket boxes, cache pots, candleholders, baskets, and inkwells added variety. In addition, a whole range of dinnerware sets, compotes, coffee, tea, and chocolate sets, and fish and game services bore the Limoges mark.

Early Limoges porcelain whiteware blanks were sent to Paris for decoration over the glaze. Decoration under the glaze did not begin in Limoges until the late 1800s. Transfer decoration was used mostly on tablewares. Hand painting usually appeared on accessory art pieces and decorative porcelain pieces. Mixed decoration, where the transfer outline was filled in or trimmed with hand painting, was used primarily on tablewares. The decoration was found on both over and under the glaze styles.

Floral decor was most prominent on Limoges porcelain. Fruit themes of berries, cherries, and grapes were next. Oyster, fish, and game sets had birds and marine life subjects. Figurals of either allegorical subjects or portraits also were used, but in a more limited context.

Most of the Limoges colors were deep and vivid. The lavish gold embellishments had a rich patina.

References: Mary Frank Gaston, *The Collector's Encyclopedia of Limoges Porcelain,* Collector Books, 1980; *2nd edition*, 1992, Values updated, 1996.

Museums: Limoges Museum, Limoges, France; Musee National Adrien Dubouche, Limoges, France; Sevres Museum, Sevres, France.

Additional Listing: Haviland.

Collecting Hints: Limoges porcelains are still in production. Marks aid the collector in determining the age of a piece of Limoges. The quality of the craftsmanship and decoration on the older pieces was superior to the new examples. Less gold decoration is used on newer pieces. The newer marks usually are found over the glaze. Many pieces have factory whiteware marks in addition to marks to indicate whether the piece was decorated at the factory or at another decorating studio.

Asparagus Set, server, 15" H-H x 7 1/2" w, 12 plates, 9" d, scattered lavender violets, gold shaped rim 1,650.00

Biscuit Jar

6" h, white daisies and foliage, cream and green ground, gold trim and handles, "T & V France" mark 325.00

6 1/2" h, vert ribbing, HP gold enameled flowers and stems on cream ground, Redon 275.00

Box

6 1/2" d, HP violets and leaves, lt blue ground, Elite 135.00

8 3/4" d, HP white and brick red Art Deco flowers, black ground, metal mts, (A)
. . . . 400.00

13" l, oval, blue, violet, yellow, and pink flower sprays on int and ext, gilt trim, ormolu mts, "Pate de Limoges, Couleuvre, France" mark, hairline 895.00

Bureau Box

1 5/8" d, transfer of woman gleaning wheat with gold border on cov, wide gold band on sides, "blue Limoges, A.J. Co. France" mark, (A) 28.00

4 3/4" d, HP pink rose design with green leaves, blue banded borders, gold line on base, "T & V France" mark, (A).40.00

Cache Pot, 4" h x 6" d, hex, HP blue parrot with red wings and gray feathers in yellow circle with red fruit on ext panel, med blue ground, white int 175.00

Candlestick, 9" h, molded shell design with beaded scalloped base, molded shell design on socket, brown floral transfer accented with orange and gold, gold banded rim and base, "A.K. Limoges France" mark, (A) 30.00

Candy Dish

7 1/2" d, gold loop handle at end, blue luster ground, "PL Limoges" mark . . 18.00

8 1/2" d, gold loop handle at end, purple violets and green leaves on shaded blue to lt green and pink ground, gold lined rim, "green PL Limoges France" mark. 35.00

Casserole, Cov, 11" H-H x 5 1/2" h, oval, inner border of pink roses and green leaves, gilt handles and rim, "M. Redon, Limoges, PL Limoges, France" marks 35.00

Chocolate Pot, 11 3/4" h, scroll handle, scrolled an beaded ftd base, scalloped rim, scrolled knob, HP floral design, shaded beige ground, "Limoges, France" mark, (A) . . 95.00

Cracker Jar, 4 1/4" h, HP pink and red roses and shaded green leaves, shaded green and yellow ground, lt blue molded scrolling on rim and base, gold rim, gold molded scroll arched handles, "J.P. L., France" mark, (A) 85.00

Creamer, 4 1/8" h, HP blue and purple floral design with green leaves, lt peach colored ground, scrolled handle and scalloped rim, gold shell and scrolled decoration, "T & V Limoges France" mark, (A) 20.00

Cup and Saucer, pink roses, shaded pink to white ground, gold trim, J. Pouyat, set of 6 . . . . 260.00

Cup and Saucer, Demitasse

HP roses, gold trim and handle 45.00

Molded swirl body, scalloped rim, gold twisted arch handle, gold banded rims, pink, yellow, or lt blue ground, "red Elite, Limoges, and green Limoges, A L Depose" marks, set of 3, (A) 40.00

Vert pleating, HP gold and red florals, gold banded rim, gold scrolled handle, "LS & S, Limoges, France" mark, (A) . . 20.00

Custard Cup, 5" d, with underplate, pink, white, and yellow floral swags on border, gold accented rim, "green Elite, L, France and red Elite Works, Limoges France" mark, set of 6, (A) 85.00

Dinner Service, Part, cov vegetable dish, 12" l, 2 platters, 11 1/2" d, platter, 13 1/2" l, oval, 21 plates, 9 7/8" d, 11 soup plates, 9 1/2" d, printed and enameled Chinese style figures, birds, and animals, flowering branch on border, (A). 863.00

Dresser Set

Tray, 11" l, ring tree, cov jar, 5" d, hair receiver, 5" d, painted brown centered white daisies, shaded yellow to green ground, "green T & V Limoges" marks 175.00

Tray, 11 5/8" l, cov powder jar, 2 1/2" h, hair receiver, 2 1/2" h, HP green and black accented red poppies with green leaves, shaded blue ground, dbl gold striped rims, "T & V Limoges, France" marks, (A) 70.00

Dresser Jar, 4 7/8" d, HP polychrome cherubs and holly on cov, "T & V France" mark, (A) 165.00

Dresser Tray, 11" l x 8" w, HP Cupid with pink lilies and butterfly, gold trim 160.00

Ewer

5" h, raised gold flowers, beige ground, c1892 . . . . 125.00

10 1/2" h, HP pink dogwood blossoms, green leaves, lt blue to cream to green shaded ground, gold fancy handle and rim, "T & V Limoges" mark 125.00

Glove Box, 13" l, white enameled forget-me-nots, green foliage, pink ground, "T & V Limoges" mark 350.00

Hatpin Holder, 5 3/8" h, elongated egg shape, 4 gold scroll feet, HP pink and yellow roses and green leaves, yellow, purple, and brown shaded ground, (A) 55.00

Ice Cream Set, tray, 16 1/4" l x 9 1/4" w, 10 dishes, 8" H-H, molded and scalloped rims with blue forget-me-nots and pink rosebuds, gold trim, molded handles 450.00

Jar, Cov, 15" h, painted nasturtiums, ivory ground, reticulated lid, gold knob, "Wm. Guerin & Co." mark 395.00

Loving Cup, 7 1/4" h, multicolored florals, 3 gold handles 140.00

Mug

5" h, HP bust of man in blue-green jacket, brown vest, smoking long stemmed pipe, green to brown to cream ground, brown handle, "A.K. France" mark 125.00

6" h, brown and tan monk drinking wine from uplifted bottle, cream to brown shaded ground 150.00

Nut Dish, 2 7/8" h, with attached undertray, band of yellow, white, and pink transfer roses on side and tray, green stenciled floral band below rim, gold beaded scalloped rims, (A) 55.00

Pitcher

4 3/4" h, squat shape, flared rim, scroll handle, band of HP red, purple, yellow and green fruit, gold painted body, "T & V Limoges" mark, (A) 155.00

6" h, Art Deco style platinum mistletoe berries and leaves, gray and pink ground, platinum handle, "J.P. Limoges" mark 175.00

6 3/4" h, applied gold leaves, shaded lavender ground, twisted gold handle, Lanternier, c1875 . . . . 135.00

11 1/2" h, painted flowers and leaves in colors, green and lavender shaded ground, figural dragon handle, molded mask spout, (A). 100.00

Plaque

10" d

Multicolored pastoral scene with seated man and woman in period dress, pastel bkd, gold rococo border, pierced for hanging. 150.00

Oyster Plate, 9 1/8" d, multicolored floral transfers, lt blue fan molded border, "Limoges, France" mark, $165.

Seascape with mother and child in colors, heavy gold border, sgd "Puisoyer" 395.00

10 1/2" d, multicolored Victorian courting scene, gold rococo border, artist sgd 150.00

12 1/4" d

HP peaches and pears, green and beige ground, gold rococo border, pierced for hanging 225.00

HP purple plums and seed pods, pastel shaded ground, gold rococo border, pierced for hanging . . . 225.00

Multicolored pastoral scene, woman and sheep, church in bkd, irreg gold rim. 185.00

12 3/4" d, painted scene on man on horseback next to lady at fence, house in bkd, molded gold rococo rim, pierced for hanging, artist sgd. 295.00

13" d, multicolored scene of woman sitting on stone wall with ladder, gentleman with tricorn hat behind, gold rococo border, pierced for hanging, artist sgd 450.00

13 1/4" d, HP purple grapes, yellow and green peaches, flowers and leaves on lt brown ground, shaded green bkd, irreg molded gold border, pierced for hanging, sgd "Golse". 265.00

13 1/2" d, 3 lg yellow roses, 2 sm red roses, tan shaded ground, gold rococo rim, pierced for hanging, artist sgd 250.00

Plate

6 1/2" d, pink floral garlands, gold reticulated border, Pouyat, set of 6 . . . . . 90.00

8 3/8" d, HP white dogwood design on yellow to white shaded ground, gold striped rim, "T & V Limoges" mark, (A) 10.00

8 1/2" d

Pink roses on lt green ground, gilt outlined crimped rim, T & V Limoges 75.00

Raised gold flowers, splashed gold trim, cobalt border, gold lined shaped rim, "green J.P.L. France" mark 35.00

8 5/8" d, bluish-purple forget-me-nots in center, green leaves spread to border, lt yellow to cream ground, gold lined rim, "CA Limoges" mark 25.00

9" d, multicolored crawfish and florals, white ground, gilt rim, set of 6, (A) 90.00

9 1/8" d, HP florals with green and brown leaves, shaded cobalt ground, "Limoges, France and Ovington Brothers" mark, pr, (A)................ 25.00

9 1/2" d

HP yellow, white, and pink roses, sgd "Segur," "Jean Pouyat, Limoges" mark 225.00

Medieval pastoral scene with man, woman, lamb, emb border, scalloped rim, "T & V Limoges" mark 95.00

Sprays of pink and lavender orchids in center, green and yellow accents, gilt swag border, orchid named on reverse, sgd "L. Moage," "T & V Limoges, Ovington Bros. New York" mark 250.00

9 3/4" d, pink floral transfer design with green leaves, gold accented scalloped rim, "green Elite, L, France and red Elite Works Limoges, France" mark, set of 12, (A) 130.00

10 1/2" d, HP oranges, peaches, and gooseberries, gold rococo border, pierced for hanging 135.00

11" d, center with polychrome floral bouquets, gilt stylized trellis, scrolling foliage, ribbons, and floral swag cavetto, gilt rim, cream ground, set of 8, (A) 288.00

Platter

14" l, scattered brown, gold, yellow, and olive green blossoms, "T & V Limoges" mark....................... 75.00

16" l, oval, scattered bunches of sm pink roses and green leaves, molded gold outlined handles, paneled border, "CA and Charles Ahrenfeldt" mark ... 55.00

Powder Box, 5 1/2" d, cobalt and white enameled relief flowers, artist sgd 135.00

Punch Set, bowl, 14" d x 6" h, 8 pedestaled cups, HP grapes, gold outlined int and ext, "T & V Limoges" marks 1,195.00

Salt Dish, 4 1/2" d, lt to dk pink pearlized int, gilt and pearlized swirl rim 65.00

Serving Dish

11 1/4" d, 3 section, vert molded ribbing, pink and peach roses, sm lavender flowers and green leaves, gold shaded ground, gold overhead hand, gold irreg border, unmkd............. 145.00

Tray, 12 /4" H-H, pink, red, blue, and green, gold trim, "J.P.L. & J. Poyet Limoges" marks, $35.

13 1/4" l, scattered red floral sprays, molded brushed gold border, J.P.L. France dbl marks 70.00

Tankard

13 1/2" h, cherries and leaves on burgundy and ivory ground, bands of scalloped gold, dbl loop handle, "J.P.L. Limoges" mark 395.00

15" h, HP grapes, gold dragon handle, "J.P. Limoges" mark 500.00

Teapot, 6" h x 9" l, HP lg pink roses and green leaves, mint green handle, spout, and scroll foot, gold trim, flower knob, "AL anchor and Limoges France" marks 150.00

Tray, 13 1/2" H-H, gold drop cavetto, border of gilt leaves and stems and puffy green leaf heads, molded gold rim, molded handles, "green J.P. Limoges" mark 95.00

Tureen, Cov, 11" l, ftd, scattered pink roses, green leaves, scrolls, tree trunk handles, "J.P. Limoges" mark 315.00

Vase

12 1/2" h, shouldered cylinder shape, Art Nouveau style pink, green, blue, and gray 3 vert flowering and fruiting stems, leaves on base, shaded blue ground, "D & Co. Limoges" mark, (A) .. 392.00

13 5/8" h, tapered cylinder shape, sm ft, trumpet shaped throat and rim, oval gilt lined cartouche of multicolored transfer scene of classic lovers, cobalt body, sgd "Fragonard" 180.00

20" h, ovoid shape, multicolored courtly figures in garden in molded gilt foliate cartouche, reverse with river landscape, rose and cranberry red ground, pr, (A) 5,750.00

Vegetable Bowl, Cov, 12" H-H x 7" h, ftd, scalloped base, raised handles, overall purple, blue, coral, and yellow florals, gilt trim, "green T & V France" mark 105.00

Vegetable Dish, Cov, 8 1/4" d, overall pink rose and green leaf transfer, gold stripe on rims, gold scroll molded handles, "red GDA Limoges and green GDA France" marks, (A) 35.00

c 1833-1836

c 1796-1833

LIVERPOOL

City and port of Liverpool, England
c1754-1840

History: During the 18th century, a group of potteries in Liverpool were producing mostly tin-glazed Delft type wares and some porcelains. Utiliarian wares usually were made without distinguishing factory marks. Among the Liverpool potteries were:

Richard Chaffers & Co.
c1754-65

Made soapstone-type porcelain. Chaffers' blue and white and enameled pieces featured oriental designs.

Samuel Gilbody
c1754-61

Took over his father's earthenware pottery and switched production to enameled porcelains.

William Ball
c1755-69

Used a soapstone body with a glossy glaze that gave a wet appearance to his Chinese designs in underglaze blue.

William Reid & Co.
c1755-61

Also used underglaze blue oriental motifs on an almost opaque body.

Philip Christian & Co.
c1765-76

Took over Chaffers' factory and made soapstone-type porcelains, mostly with underglaze blue designs.

Pennington & Part
c1770-99

Produced lesser quality wares decorated with underglaze blue prints. Their enameled pieces exhibited simple decorations.

Thomas Wolfe & Co.
c1795-1800

Made hard paste porcelains.

Herculaneum-Liverpool factory at Liverpool
c1796-1840

Established by Samuel Worthington. Most of the workers were brought from the Staffordshire Potteries. At first only earthenwares and stonewares were made.

"Herculaneum Pottery" was the name of the factory. Some pieces were marked with an impressed "Herculaneum." About 1800, porcelains were introduced. Some Empire style vases were manufactured, but the principal production focused on teawares. Extremely large jugs were a specialty.

References: Dr. Knowles Boney, *Liverpool Porcelain of the 18th Century and Its Makers*, B.T. Batsford, 1957; H. Boswell Lancaster, *Liverpool and Her Potters*, W.B. James & Co.1936; Robert McCauley, *Liverpool Transfer Designs on Anglo-American Pottery*, Southworth-Anthoensen Press, 1942; Alan Smith, *The Illustrated Guide to Liverpool Herculaneum Pottery 1796-1840*, Barrie & Jenkins, 1970; B. Watney, *English Blue and White Porcelain of the 18th Century*, Faber & Faber, 1936; Bernard M. Watney, *Liverpool Porcelain of the Eighteenth Century*, Antique Collectors' Club, Ltd. 1997.

Museums: City of Liverpool Museum, Liverpool, England; Henry Ford Museum, Dearborn, MI; Potsdam Public Museum, Potsdam, NY.

Reproduction Alert: Modern imitations of old marine decorated Liverpool jugs 8 1/2"-11" high are decorated in black transfer on one side with "The Shipwright's Arms," reverse with ship flying the American flag in colors on a green sea entitled "Ship Caroline," and under the spout with the name "James Leech" in a wreath. These have been showing up at various auctions. Some have artificially produced age cracks and glaze crackle.

Bottle

    10" h, Delft, painted blue, yellow, green, and manganese diaper and pendant grapes on mouth, flowers and insects on shoulder and reverse, front with painted castle on island in scalloped surround, c1760, (A) 6,325.00

    10 1/4" h, Delft, blue bouquet of garden flowers on base, scattered sm bouquets, c1760, (A) 460.00

Bowl

    7" d, int with black transfer of ship, presentation verse and sailing motifs on ext, (A) 345.00

    10 1/2" d, int blue painted with 2 men standing next to ale cask, border of blue alternating panels of trellis and half flowerheads, ext blue painted vignettes of Chinese houses and rockery, c1754, (A) 9,200.00

Charger, 13 3/4" d, black drawn iron red, yellow, green, and blue Fazackerly floral pattern, scattered florals on rim, (A) 825.00

Coffee Cup and Saucer, pearlware, multicolored enameled buffalo and Chinese figure in stylized landscape, iron red and black cell pattern borders, Herculaneum, c1790, (A) 180.00

Coffeepot, 8 7/8" h, pear shape, blue printed Chinese lady holding bird in garden in diaper panels and foliage scrolls, foliage molded scroll handle, reeded spout, cov blue printed with 2 oval panels of Chinese figures in landscape in stylized diaper, domed cov with spire knob, Seth Pennington, c1775, (A) 1,840.00

Cream Jug, 3 1/4" h, spiral fluted base with rocaille scrolls, iron red, blue, turquoise, green-yellow, and back painted Chinese man beside tree, another holding stick, scalloped rim, C-scroll handle, c1776, (A) 460.00

Cup and Saucer, oct, blue "Jumping Boy" pattern, Chaffer's, (A) 475.00

Cup and Saucer, Handleless, bust of George Washington and "Washington, His Country's Father" on saucer, bust of Washington and Lafayette on cup, black transfers, hairlines, (A) 330.00

Cup and Saucer, Miniature, adults and children in period clothes, black transfers, black line trim, hairline 30.00

Jug

    6 1/4" h, black transfer of machine and women and "...come here ye toothless lame with gray come and be ground

Canister, 4 3/8" h, tea party on front, fishing scene on reverse, black transfers, pewter cov, Sadler & Green, c1770, $380.

without delay," "The Bird's Nest" on reverse, polychrome accents, (A). 345.00

    7 7/8" h, black transfer of Masonic symbol of side, temple on reverse 900.00

    9 3/4" h, black transfer of standing "JEFFERSON" in leaf cartouche, reverse with bust of "HANCOCK," HP polychrome and gilt sprigs on body and rim, early 19th C, repairs, hairlines, chips, and wear, (A) 20,700.00

    10" h, "Map of East Coast" with Washington and Franklin, reverse with dancing villagers, polychrome transfers, "T J 1799" under spout, turquoise rim with purple and green swags, cracks 2,850.00

    10 7/8" h, black transfer of "Proscribed Patriots" on one side, 3 masted ship on reverse, "Smugglers" under spout and handle, polychrome accents, chip on base, (A) 1,840.00

    11 1/4" h, black transfer of Washington, 7 angels, and "Apotheosis, Sacred to the Memory of Washington," implements of war, eagle, American Indian, shield, Great Seal of United States under spout, "imp Herculaneum" mark 4,200.00

Pickle Dish, 3 1/8" l, leaf shape, porcelain, blue painted flower sprays, serrated rim, c1770, (A) 205.00

Pitcher

    4 1/2" h, "The United States and Macedonian" and "The Enterprise and Boxer," black transfers, copper luster rim 1,750.00

    8 1/4" h, creamware, The Chain of Sixteen States Surrounding The Seal of the U.S. on side, reverse with "United We Stand+Divided We Fall," wheat and grapevine wreath with "GHH" under spout, black transfers, (A) . . . 2,090.00

    9 1/4" h, black transfers of "The Packet of Boston" and "A chain of sixteen states

Pitcher, 5" h, Commodore Bainbridge on front, Commodore Lawrence on reverse, black transfers and trim, restored, $650.

surrounding a seal of the United States," (A)...............1,760.00

9 1/2" h, creamware, President "JOHN ADAMS" in circ cartouche, reverse with "THE CONSTANT," ship flying American flag, "IWM" in wreath under spout and figure of Hope, American eagle and wreath under handle, band of vines and leaves around rim and spout, black transfers, (A) 15,400.00

Plaque, 5" h, oval, creamware, George Washington bust, black transfer, Herculaneum
....................................2,500.00

Plate

7 3/4" d, creamware
Dancing dog design, black transfer, black lined rim, Turner 165.00
Nelson's Monument in Liverpool harbor, black transfer, black lined rim
.... 165.00

8 7/8" d, Delft, Fazackerly polychrome design of floral blossoms and fencing in center, floral sprigs on border, c1760, pr, (A)...................... 374.00

9" d, Delft, blue painted flowering prunus and peonies from urn on table, border of flowers from stylized rockwork, stylized foliage on reverse, white ground, c1760, (A) 77.00

10" d, creamware
"Hope," black transfer of woman seated under tree, sailing ship in bkd, liverbird border, polychrome enamel accents, c1800, (A) 173.00
Transfer of American 3 masted ship in center, 6 floral transfers on border, shaped rim, "imp Herculaneum" mark, chips, (A) 522.00

Puzzle Jug, 7 1/2" h, neck pierced with blue outlined hearts and ellipses, body inscribed with rhyme and Chinese landscape in blue, c1760, (A) 2,185.00

Tankard, 5 7/8" h, "United States Ship Flying the Flag," black transfer, rim chips . .1,200.00

Teapot

6 1/2" h
Globular shape, underglaze blue and iron red oriental landscape, gilt accents, Pennington, c1775, chips and hairline 925.00
Oval, molded basketweave body with oval cartouches of puce transfer printed coastal landscape or shepherd boy, "imp Herculaneum" mark, c1805, spout damage, (A) .1,265.00

6 3/4" h
Globular shape, ribbed body with raised scroll molding, painted polychrome Chinese Export style floral sprays grooved C-form handle, pointed knob, Christian, c1775
....................1,600.00
Ribbed body with raised scrolling leaf panels surrounding enameled floral sprays, Christian, c1775, (A)
.... 805.00

Underglaze blue and polychrome enameled landscape scene with stags, geometric band on shoulder, Pennington, c1785, repairs, (A)
.... 207.00

8 1/2" l, multicolored enamel scene of seated and standing oriental figures, Christian, c1775, (A) 835.00

LLADRO

Almacera, Spain
1951 to Present

LLADRÓ
HAND MADE IN SPAIN
1951

History: The Lladro brothers, Juan, Jose, and Vicente, started their small studio in 1951 in Almacera, Spain. They built their own kiln and began making small flowers for decorative lamps. All three brothers shaped the porcelains. Only Juan and Jose decorated them; Vicente supervised the firing.

As their business expanded, they formed Lladro Porcelanas in 1958 and produced their first porcelain figurine of a ballet dancer. Their distinctive style emphasizes the elongated look in porcelain sculpture. The figurines were hand painted in a variety of pastel colors.

Salvador Furio was one of the most senior and prolific sculptors at Lladro. His "Clown with Concertina" was the first figurine he designed for Lladro. Furio has become the Lladro sculptor specializing in particular thematic subjects such as historic characters, figures of literature, and personalities in public life.

Today the Lladro complex is located in Valencia, Spain and is known as "Porcelain City."

In the late 1960s a new line titled Nao by Lladro was added to respond to different aspects of the marketplace. The logo features a sailing ship in tandem with the company name. The three bothers are involved in Nao as they are in Lladro, but there are two separate manufacturing facilities.

There are some shared design themes, but differences in the detail work and palette of colors applied. Some sculptural lines are similar.

Nao retired in 1992.

Reference: Dr. Glenn S. Johnson, *The Official Lladro Collection Reference Guide, First Edition*, Clear Communications, 1996.

Museums: Lladro Museum, Los Angeles, CA; Lladro Museum, New York, NY.

Collectors' Club: Lladro Society, 1 Lladro Drive, Moonachie, NJ 07074, Membership: $45.00, Quarterly magazine Expressions.

Newsletter: *Lladro Antique News,* Lladro Mail Center, Dept. 909, 41 Jackson Street, Worcester, MA 01608.

Figure

2 1/4" h, Beagle Puppy, #1072... 135.00

2 1/2" h x 3 1/2" l, Lladro Society Plaque, #7601........................ 25.00
3" h, Fox and Cub, #1065 .... 475.00
4" h, Attentive Bear, #1204 ..... 75.00
4 3/4" h, All Tuckered Out, #5846 . 128.00
5" h
Angel Praying, #4538........ 45.00
Heather, #1359............ 150.00
5 1/4" h, All Aboard, #7619 ..... 125.00
5 1/2" h, School Days, #7604..... 375.00
5 3/4" h, Little Riders, #7623 ..... 169.00
6" h
Pekinese Sitting, #4641 ...... 325.00
Skye Terrier, #4643 ....500.00
Swan, ball shape, #4829, (A) .. 125.00
6 1/4" h, Sweet Scent, #5221..... 115.00
6 1/2" h
Eskimo Riders, #5353........ 125.00
Little Bo Peep, #1312........ 250.00
6 3/4" h, Young Mozart, #5915.. 1,000.00
7" h
Angela, #5211 .... 165.00
Angel Tree Topper, #5719 .... 125.00
Evita, #5212 .... 140.00
Flower Song, #7607........ 550.00
Tinkerbell, #7518 .... 2,200.00
7 1/4" h
Littlest Clown, #5811 ...... 155.00
Pick of the Litter, #7621 ..... 269.00
7 1/2" h
Beth, #1358 .... 150.00
Dog in the Basket, #1128..... 225.00
Fishing With Gramps, #2351 1,025.00
Girl with Child, #4636........ 125.00
Jolie, #5210 .... 165.00
Ten and Growing, #7635 ..... 275.00
7 3/4" h
Bowing Crane, #1613...... 245.00
Fragrant Bouquet, #2305 ..... 229.00
Love Boat, #5343 .... 950.00
Summer, #5219 .... 111.00
Wedding, #4808 .... 139.00
8" h, My Buddy, #7609......... 300.00
8 1/4" h
Spring Bouquets, #7603, (A) .. 360.00
Starting Forward, #7605...... 195.00
8 1/2" h
Boys Meets Girl, #1188 ...... 240.00
Courting Time, #5409........ 350.00
Fisher Boy, #4809........... 150.00
Little Traveler, #7602 .... 995.00
Picture Perfect, #7612 .... 225.00
8 3/4" h, Little Pals, Club piece, #7600
.... 3,200.00
9" h
Eskimo Playing, #2097....... 265.00
Peter Pan, #7529 .... 698.00
Snow White, #7555 and 7 dwarfs, #7533-39 .... 1,750.00
Summer Stroll, #7611....... 175.00
The Voyage of Columbus, #5847
.... 950.00
9 1/2" h, Basket of Love, #7622 ... 225.00
9 3/4" h, Prissy, #5010 .... 100.00

Figure, 9 1/2" h, #1255, $695.

10" h, One More Try, #5997 . . . . . 469.00
10 1/4" h, Racing Motorcyclist, #5270
. . . . .1,175.00
10 1/2" h
  Lost Love, #5128 . . . . 800.00
  Mimi, #4985 . . . . 550.00
  Roses For My Mom, #5088. . .1,450.00
  Venetian Carnival, #5658 . . . . . 650.00
11" h, Susan and Her Doll, #1378 . 475.00
11 1/4" h, Young Bach, #1801 . . . . 639.00
11 1/2" h
  Chrysanthemum, #4990, (A) . . 190.00
  Hebrew Student, #4684 . . . . . . 350.00
  Lady From Majorca, #5240 . . . 250.00
  Valencian Boy, #1400. . . . . 475.00
11 3/4" h, Rest in the Country, #4760
. . . . 325.00
12 1/4" h
  A King is Born, #2198. . . . . 700.00
  Cathy and Her Doll, #1380. . . . 450.00
  Jockey, #1341 . . . . 315.00
  Soldier With Gun, #1164. . . . . . 225.00
12 1/2" h
  Cinderella and Her Fairy Grandmother,
    #7634 . . . . 789.00
  Daughters, #5013. . . . . .1,250.00
  Garden of Dreams, #7634 . . .1,150.00
12 3/4" h
  Fairy Queen, #5068 . . . . 600.00
  Pharmacist, #4844 . . . . .1,200.00
  Sorrowful Mother, #5849 . . . . . 995.00
13" h, Eskimo Boy and Girl, #2038 495.00
13 3/4" h, At The Ball, #5398 . . . . . 525.00
14" h, Little Girl, #2024. . . . . 520.00
14 1/2" h
  Baggy Pants, #1749. . . . . . . .1,495.00
  Jester's Serenade, #5932. . . .1,100.00
15 1/2" h, The Doctor, #4602, (A) . 250.00
15 3/4" h, Winter Wonderland, #1429
. . . . .2,125.00
16" h, Languid Clown, #4924. . . . . 600.00
16 1/4" h, First Date, #1393 . . . .5,300.00
16 3/4" h, Car in Trouble, #1375 .7,500.00

17 1/4" h
  Harlequin With Dove, bust, #1717
. . . . 995.00
  On Our Way Home, bust, #1715
. . . . .2,500.00
17 3/4" h
  Clown With Concertina, #1027
. . . . 695.00
  Romeo and Juliet, #4750. . . . . 465.00
  The Hunt, #1308 . . . . .7,600.00
19 3/4" h, Peace Offering, #3559 . 450.00
21 1/2" h, I Am Don Quixote, #1522
. . . . .3,550.00
22 3/4" h, Venus and Cupid, #1392
. . . . .2,500.00
Vase
  4 1/4" h, emb children playing, #5262, (A)
. . . . 125.00
  10 1/4" h, Sparrow design, #5564. 245.00

LONGTON HALL

Staffordshire Potteries, England
c1750-1760

1749 -55

History: Longton Hall existed for the ten year period between 1750 and 1760. There were several different partnerships during the factory's short production period.

Longton Hall porcelains featured an underglaze blue design in the oriental style. Some pieces exhibited a streaky blue glaze. Most wares were thickly potted and finished in a crude fashion. Some leaf shaped tablewares were produced.

Most Longton Hall soft paste porcelain was unmarked. Although production was brief, the amount of production was large. Many examples survived to attract the attention of today's collector.

Reference: B. Watney, *Longton Hall Porcelain,* Faber & Faber, 1957.

Teapot, 7 1/2" h, polychrome florals, c1770, $1,850.

Museums: Fine Arts Museum of San Francisco, CA; Walters Art Gallery, Baltimore, MD.

Dish
  7" l, leaf shape, painted bouquet of flowers and flowerheads, molded veining, green shaded rim, c1755, (A) . . 920.00
  9 5/8" l, molded overlapping lettuce leaves with puce veining and stem handle, c1755, cracks and repairs, (A) . 863.00
Soup Plate, 9 1/8" d, centered painted with birds in landscape, border molded with trailing strawberry vine and green edged leaves and puce veining and stems, and iron red berries, c1755, (A) 550.00
Sauceboat, 8 1/4" l, molded overlapped lettuce leaves with puce veining, 2 scrolling branch handles with foliage terminals, c1755, cracks and repairs, (A) 2,875.00
Sweetmeat Dish, 5 1/2" l, molded strawberry leaf edged in brown, painted tulips and roses in center, twisted green handle, c1755
. . . . 1,250.00

LONGWY

LONGWY
20TH CENTURY

Lorraine, France
1798 to Present

History: A French faience factory, known for its enameled pottery which resembled cloisonne, was established in 1798 at Lorraine. Utilitarian wares were made in addition to the enameled pieces.

About 1875, Emaux de Longwy introduced wares that were decorated with Persian inspired motifs. His designs were first outlined with black printed manganese resist and filled in with brightly colored glazes, especially the turquoise color for which the pieces are most famous. The company achieved its greatest fame for pieces with Art Deco motifs featuring bold colors and geometric designs.

Marks used on Longwy examples incorporate "LONGWY" either impressed or painted under the glaze.

Bowl
  8 1/4" d, ftd, enameled white and pink cherry blossoms, green leaves, Persian blue ground, "LONGWY FRANCE" mark, (A) 275.00
  10 1/8" d, ftd, pink, blue, and rust enameled flowers, blue ground, dk blue rim, inner rim with pink flowers and green leaves and dk blue trim, "Longwy, Kenilworth Studios" mark 675.00
  11 3/8" H-H, oval, cream, red, and purple iris, brown stems, turquoise ground, "LONGWY FRANCE" mark 400.00
  15" H-H, int with turquoise outlined vert bands of blue flowerheads on lt blue ground, raised gold diamonds and sqs, cream crackle ground, turquoise ext with gold crossing lines, gilt accented turquoise scroll handles 1,545.00

Box

3 1/4" d, red flowerheads with cream centers, scattered cream dots, turquoise ground, dk blue rims, "Longwy France" mark 225.00

4" d, dk blue and white bird and tree, turquoise ground, (A) 125.00

4" l, rect, pink and blue flowerheads, black ground, (A) 150.00

5" l x 2 1/2" h, multicolored and gold florals and flowerheads, tan geometrics, brown ground 165.00

Bud Vase, 9 1/4" h, pale rose and yellow flowerheads, dk blue stems, turquoise ground, "Longwy France" mark 295.00

Charger, 14 1/2" d, enameled yellow and peach shore birds in center, mauve, red, and blue flowerheads with yellow streaks on border, turquoise ground, dk blue rim, "Longwy France" mark 450.00

Compote, 9 1/2" d, center chinoiserie scene of red thatched tan hut by lake in roundel, blue, red, and yellow enameled prunus blossoms, brown branches and green leaves, med blue ground, dk blue lined rim, (A) 220.00

Dish, 6 1/4" sq, central dk blue lined cartouche of red enameled flowers and green leaves on cream ground, turquoise ground with orange, blue, and yellow flowerheads, curlicue border, dk blue enameled rim 110.00

Knife Rest, 3 1/4" l, triangular, pale rose and yellow flowerheads, dk blue stems, turquoise ground 75.00

Pitcher, 5 3/8" h, red and yellow flowerheads, green leaves, dk blue branches, turquoise ground, dk blue rim and handle, cream int 275.00

Plate, 7" d, oct, blue open basket with stylized purple and red flowerheads and green leaves, white ground 35.00

Powder Box, 6 1/8" d, stylized yellow iris, pale green and black leaves, white crazed ground, black int, "Longwy France" mark 265.00

Tea Tile, 8" sq, Art deco lady in yellow dress with purple trim, tan ground, purple and white trees and flowers, rust red bkd, 4 sm feet, "Longwy France Primavera, crown and shield" mark 395.00

Tete-a-Tete, pot, creamer, cov sugar bowl, 2 cups and saucers, tray, 13" l, 12" w, pink and cream enameled blossoms, brown branches, turquoise ground, dk blue handles, med blue and brown knobs, marsh bird in cartouche on tray, $795.

Tete a Tete Set

Teapot, 5" h, cov sugar bowl, creamer, 2 cups and saucers, enameled pink dogwood blossoms, dk brown stems and branches, turquoise ground, dk blue rims, handles, and knobs, "Longwy Kenilworth Studios France" marks 895.00

Teapot, 5 1/2" h, milk jug, sugar bowl, 2 cups and saucers, tray, enameled green outlined flowerheads with green stems, orange-red dots, white crackle ground, dk blue rims and handles, (A) 770.00

Trivet, 8" sq, Primavera, standing woman in lt brown dress, dk brown trim, stylized dk blue leaves, sm red flowers, dk brown blossoms, tan crackle ground, dk blue lined rim 525.00

Urn, 12 1/4" h, 4 sides, red, yellow, green, and brown flowers, leaves, and stems, Persian blue ground, dk blue applied elephant head handles with rings 750.00

Vase

4 3/4" h, white nudes with black hair in brown and yellow tropical seascape, crackle glaze, (A) 385.00

5" h, paneled, pink, red, and yellow flowerheads, dl blue leaves, brown branches, turquoise ground, cream int, "LONGWY FRANCE" mark 310.00

6 1/2" h

Cylinder shape, black outlined white bird and trees, blue enameled ground, black rim, "LONGWY PRIMAVERA" mark 600.00

Oct cylinder shape, dk red and mauve flowers with yellow petals with white edges joined by dk blue stems, turquoise ground, dk blue rim, cream int 500.0

7" h, compressed, oct, white outlined lt blue stylized flowerheads with orange centers, dk blue leaves, turquoise ground, brown and dk blue banding 525.00

8" h, cylinder shape, 2 green and red enameled parrots on brown branch, white crackle ground, brown lined rim 200.00

8 3/8" h, enameled lg cream star shaped flowerheads with tan swirled centers and yellow dots, dk brown outlined tan leaves and dk brown stems, med blue ground, dk blue base, turquoise and tan stripes on rim 575.00

11" h, Primavera, dk brown monkeys and palm trees, med brown crackle ground 1,045.00

11 1/4" h, flattened form, tapered neck, wide base on straight ft, dk blue horiz handles, mauve centered white petaled flowers, green leaves, turquoise stems, dk red ground, dk blue rims, cream int, imp "Longwy" mark 595.00

LOWESTOFT

Bell Lane, Lowestoft, England
c1757-1799

135
7913
✕ ☽
c1775-1790

History: Soft paste porcelains were made in Lowestoft beginning about 1757 and ending in 1799. The principal production was utilitarian wares for the local community. Until 1770, all the designs used blue and white oriental motifs. Sales were direct from the factory.

Later, formal floral patterns were introduced. During the 1770s, blue-printed designs, copied from Worcester and Caughley, were produced. Lowestoft's enameled wares of the 1780s resembled the Chinese Export figure and flower painted wares imported by the English East India Company. Rarer examples of Lowestoft have naturalistic flower painting and English views.

No Lowestoft factory marks were used.

References: G. A. Godden, *The Illustrated Guide to Lowestoft Porcelain,* Herbert Jenkins, 1969; W.W.R. Spelman, *Lowestoft China,* Jarrold & Sons, 1905.

Museums: Castle Museum, Norwich, England, Christ-church Mansion, Ipswich, England; Fitzwilliam Museum, Cambridge England; Lowestoft Museum, Lowestoft, England; Museum of Fine Arts, Boston, MA; Victoria & Albert Museum, London, England.

Cup, cylinder shape, ftd, ear handle, blue painted peonies and scrolling foliage from rockwork, inner border of quarter round ovals, c1790, chips and stains, (A) 70.00

Cup and Saucer, pink, green, purple, and orange polychrome floral design surrounded by floral vine on orange dbl line, wide purple diamond design on border with orange stripes, gold rims, (A) 55.00

Pickle Dish, 4 1/4" l, blue and white, c1775, $395.

Cup and Saucer, Handleless, sm pink rose design surrounded with alternating pink and floral sprigs, wide pink border with pink rose floral swags, yellow band on rim, (A) . . 85.00

Sauce Boat, 6 1/8" l, molded body, blue floral design on sides, blue geometric band on int trim, repairs, (A) 150.00

Sugar Bowl, Cov, 5 3/4" h, purple, red, and green floral sprig design, wide pink diamond design band flanked by orange striping, applied entwined branch handles with sm floral rosettes and leaf designs, vert pleating, berry knob, hairlines and chips, (A) 65.00

Teapot

- 5 3/4" h, globular shape, underglaze blue, iron red, and gilt flowerheads and stems, c1780, repairs, (A) 230.00
- 6 1/2" h, painted red rose and green leaves on sides, iron red swag and dot band, mauve compartments on shoulder, mauve painted flowerhead on cov 685.00
- 6 3/4" h, polychrome enamel floral spray on sides, scattered sprigs, c1780, chips, (A) 345.00

MODERN MARK   1756-1824

LUDWIGSBURG

Wurttemberg, Germany
1758-1824

History: Karl Eugen, Duke of Wurttemberg, founded a hardpaste porcelain manufactory in 1758 at Ludwigsburg, twelve miles north of Stuttgart. A faience factory was established two years later. Joseph Jacob Ringler directed the porcelain factory from 1759 to 1799. Initially copies of Meissen wares were made.

The peak period of production was between 1758 and 1776. Utilitarian wares decorated with birds and ornamental wares, e.q. candlesticks, were produced. Riedel, the major designer and modeler during this period, crafted mythological and classical figures. Berger, another sculptor, made small figural groups comprised of peasants, work and ballet groups. These figures did not match the quality of the figurines from Meissen, Nymphenburg, or Frankenthal.

Initially the Ludwigsburg shapes and decoration were in the rococo style. The factory changed its forms and designs as tastes changed. Rococo gave way to neo-classical followed by Empire styles. Ludwigsburg porcelain started to decline after 1770. The enterprise never really was profitable or highly successful. Duke Karl

Eugen died in 1793. Production deteriorated even more after his death. The factory struggled on for thirty more years; it closed in 1824. During the 19th century, the Ludwigsburg molds were sold to Edward Kick, at Amberg in Bavaria. Kick reissued a number of the pieces.

References: George W. Ware, *German and Austrian Porcelain,* Crown Publishers, Inc. 1963.

Museums: Cincinnati Art Museum, Cincinnati, OH; Museum fur Kunst und Gewerbe, Hamburg, Germany; Shloss Museum, Berlin, Germany; Wurttembergishes Laesmuseum, Stuttgart, Germany.

Cream Jug, Cov, 6 1/2" h, baluster shape, painted loose bouquets and scattered sprigs, C-scroll handle with serpent head, spiral scroll knob, "blue crowned interlaced C's" mark, c1765, (A) 125.00

Figure

- 5 3/4" h, Turkish man in pink and yellow robes with flowers, seated on tree stump, scroll molded base, 19th C, pr 462.00

Figure, 7" h, purple dress with green leaves, yellow bodice, "blue interlocking C's" mark, spoon missing, $475.

6 1/2" h, young man with basket of fruit standing beside keg, polychrome, old repairs, 1758-93, (A) 400.00

6 3/4" h, standing beggar in red lined yellow uniform, arm in sling, feeding dog at side, gilt accents, green base, "blue interlaced C's" mark, late 18th C, restored 250.00

10 5/8" h, Minerva modeled as standing woman wearing magenta edged white bodice, yellow gown, leaning on shield on plinth, helmet on oct base, "blue interlaced C's" mark, c1770, restored 1,500.00

11" h, classic man playing violin, female in ball gown lifting skirt, circ base with leaf shaped feet, polychromed, pr . . 875.00

13 3/8" h, Mars modeled as standing nude man, red sash wrapped around waist, leaning on shield, helmet on brown rocky base, "blue interlaced C's" mark, late 18th C, (A) 493.00

Plate, 9" d, polychrome florals, white ground, scalloped rim, rim chip, (A) 300.00

LUSTER

English
19th Century to Present

History: The exact beginning of luster decoration on British pottery cannot be dated accurately. The first pieces dated from the first quarter of the 19th century; the luster process still is used today.

Luster decoration was achieved by applying thin metallic films to earthenware or china bodies. Gold luster comes from gold oxide, copper luster from copper oxide, silver luster from platinum, and pink or purple luster from "purple of cassias."

All over lustering imitated metallic wares made in gold, silver, or copper. Luster decorations also were used on rims, details, and decorative highlights.

The "resist" process involved keeping parts of the object white through temporarily resisting them with wax or paper cut-outs so that when the luster solution was applied to the object it would not affect the resisted portions. Reserved panels could be left plain, painted, or transfer printed. Stenciling also was used. Overglaze enamels could be added to the lustered ground.

Sunderland or "splash luster," a mottled type of pink luster used on a white body, was very popular. The splash effect came from spraying an oil on the wet luster that had just been applied to the white ware. The oil expanded in the kiln to form bubbles and splashes. Manufacturers who used this technique were Southwick, Dixon & Austin, and Ball's. A large portion of Sunderland luster was produced at Newcastle-upon-Tyne.

Jugs, mugs, tea, and tablewares were among the most popular luster forms. An enormous variety of jugs was made, some featuring mottled pink with verses and others silver or other colors. Inscriptions on luster ware varied greatly. Events, landmarks in history, and popular sentiments, were commemorated. Plaques had either mottos or verses, sailing ships, or landscapes within painted frames. Staffordshire and other potteries that made a wide variety of luster ware types included: Spode, Wedgwood, Lakin & Poole, Ralph & Enoch Wood, Davenport, New Hall, and Minton.

References: John Bedford, *Old English Lustre Ware*, Walker & Co.1965; W. Bosanko, *Collecting Old Lustre Ware*, George H. Doran Co.1916; Jeanette R. Hodgon, *Collecting Old English Lustre*, Southworth-Anthoensen Press, 1937; W.D. John & W. Baker, *Old English Lustre Pottery*, Ceramic Book Co.1951; J.T. Shaw, *The Potteries of Sunderland & District*, Sunderland Library, 1961.

Museums: Art Institute of Chicago, Chicago, IL; Cincinnati Museum of Art, Cincinnati, OH; City Museum & Art Gallery, Stoke-on-Trent, Hanley, England; Cleveland Museum of Art, Cleveland, OH; Laing Art Gallery & Museum, Newcastle, England; Potsdam Public Museum, Potsdam, NY; Sunderland Museum, Sunderland, England.

Reproduction Alert: Portmeiron Potteries Ltd., a Stoke-on-Trent firm, produces jugs which are reproductions of older luster types in museums and private collections These new pieces have the maker's mark and are not intended to confuse the collector. Sometimes the mark is removed, and these reproductions are offered as old pieces.

Copper

Bowl, 5 3/4" d, yellow band with enameled raised flowers, (A) 50.00

Compote, 3 1/4" h, pedestal base, flared sides, wide blue band with copper luster house design, (A) 55.00

Creamer

   3" h, arched handle, wide sanded copper luster band, (A) 15.00

   4 1/8" h, ftd, wide orange-brown band with relief of baskets of flowers with yellow, green, red, and pink enameled accents, scroll handle, (A) 35.00

   4 1/2" h, ftd, wide sanded copper luster band, scroll handle, (A) 15.00

Figure

   7 1/2" h, seated Whippet dog, overall luster body, c1830, pr 875.00

   10" h x 7" w, hen on nest, Italy 225.00

Goblet, 4 3/8" h, purple and blue florals, green leaves, copper luster body, $75.

Goblet

   3 1/8" h, ftd, band of HP pink, blue, yellow, and green polychrome flowers on sides, beaded rim, copper luster body, (A) 25.00

   3 3/4" h, ftd, blue center band with red and brown enameled flowerhead, beaded ring on stem, copper luster body. .88.00

   5" h, ftd, red centered yellow enameled flowerheads, enameled green leaves, copper luster body 85.00

Jug, 8 1/2" h, flared cylinder shape, beak spout, scroll handle, relief molded dancing couple between foliate scrolls, overall copper luster, mid-19th C, (A) 45.00

Mug

   2 1/2" h, yellow center band with lustered stylized leaves and fruit, copper luster body 88.00

   3 1/8" h, blue band with white polychrome cherubs and classical figures at play, copper luster body, scroll handle, (A) 25.00

   3 1/2" h

      Cobalt band with green, orange, yellow, and pink painted relief florals, molded beaded rim, scroll handle, (A) 20.00

      Med blue center band with multicolored children and goat or pony, copper luster body 60.00

   5 1/4" h, applied colored pears and fruit, copper luster body 375.00

Pepper Pot, 4 1/2" h, ftd, domed top with flattened knob, wide yellow band on waist, (A) 75.00

Pitcher

   3" h, yellow band with luster leaves and flowers on neck, beaded outline, copper luster body, "Allerton" mark 45.00

Pitcher, 4 3/8" h, yellow and red enameled fruit, green leaves, copper luster body, $65.

   3 1/4" h, multicolored transfer of "Ye Olde Jug Inn," copper luster trim, Gray's Pottery 24.00

   3 1/2" h, blue bands with yellow berries, copper luster body 55.00

   3 7/8" h

      Red-orange band with oval reserves of black transfers of Surrender of Cornwallis or Lafayette on reverse, horiz ribbing on neck, molded beaded rim, scrolled handle, ftd, copper luster body, (A) 240.00

      Wide pink luster band with yellow, pink, and green floral design, narrow white band with pink luster vines on neck, beaded rim, copper luster body, (A) 30.00

   4 1/4" h

      Cobalt lower band with yellow and brown enameled scene of dog, boy, and trees, copper luster body 85.00

      Cream ground with lg dk red flowerhead, band of chevrons on neck, pink int on neck 55.00

   4 3/8" h, brown transfer of farmer watering horses at trough, inn in bkd, green and red accents, cream ground, copper luster rim and handle, "A.J. Wilkinson, Ltd Staffordshire" mark 27.00

   5" h

      Polychrome badminton scene on canary band, copper luster body, unmkd. 125.00

      Sanded band, copper luster body 49.00

   5 1/8" h, white center band with pink luster flowers, narrow white band on neck with pink luster dashes, copper luster body, (A) 150.00

   5 1/2" h

      Cream center and neck band with pink luster streaks, copper luster body 110.00

      Med blue band in center with stylized leaves, med blue band on neck, copper luster body 75.00

5 3/4" h, wide orange bands with copper luster floral designs, ftd, scroll handle, (A) 20.00

6" h

Blue and mauve bluebells, copper luster body 75.00

Pink bubble band, beaded rim, pedestal base, copper luster body 125.00

White center band with red transfer of youth in forest setting, purple luster and red floral enamel trim, beaded rim, copper luster body, (A) . 100.00

6 1/2" h, molded dancing couple, blue enameled feathers on rim, raised English reg mark 48.00

7 1/4" h, wide center blue band with relief of cow and horse with pink luster accents, molded beaded rim, molded crisscross pattern on handle and spout, c1840, (A) 201.00

7 5/8" h, ovoid shape, molded snake handle, yellow, blue, and white polychrome florals, copper luster body, (A) . . 50.00

7 3/4" h, scalloped ftd base, HP white, blue, and yellow polychromed florals, copper luster body, scalloped rim, scrolled snake handle, (A) 35.00

7 7/8" h, molded lustered tree trunk body, green accented molded ivy and human figures on body, scrolled knurled handle, (A) 25.00

Plate, 6 1/2" d, polychrome florals on blue stripe, copper luster body 45.00

Salt

2" h, pedestal base, yellow band with stylized luster leaves, copper luster body 65.00

2 1/4" h, pedestal base

Cobalt band with copper luster florals, copper luster body, (A) 25.00

Pink luster band of house design, pink int, copper luster body 85.00

Teapot

5 3/8" h, lt blue band on shoulder with copper luster leaves, copper luster body, Price Brothers 145.00

8 1/2" h, paneled body, pink center band with copper luster leaves and flowers, copper luster rim 225.00

Vase, 6 1/2" h, flat sides, trumpet shaped neck, rect base, 2 sm curled handles, enameled puce transfer of clock face on front, oriental figures in courtyard on reverse, copper luster body 70.00

Pink

Bowl

6 1/2" d, ftd, pearlware, wide pink luster floral band with 2 oval reserves of woman reclining on couch, young girl holding dog, purple transfers with blue, green, and red accents, pink luster stripe on rim and ft, (A) 230.00

8 5/8" d, Crimean War commemorative, int center with red and green trimmed gray-black transfer of lad reclining under tree, int border of panels with sailors and guns or man, woman, and child saying farewell, or poem, pink luster squiggles, ext with Crimean War emblem of lion, eagle, shield, and guns, pink luster squiggles, and pink luster rim 595.00

Creamer

3 7/8" h, lt blue ground with alternating molded green acanthus leaves and pink and green floral sprigs, molded green grapevine border band, pink luster spout, rim, and handle, (A) . 120.00

4 1/2" h, transfer of woman in magenta dress, gold skirt, holding flower basket, magenta and blue flowerheads, pink luster rim band and dashed handle 48.00

Creamer and Sugar Bowl, Cov, creamer, 5" h, sugar bowl, 5 3/4" h, globular shape with vert ribbing, wide pink luster band with pink luster florals, pink luster band on rim and ft, scroll handle with pink luster trim, hairline, (A) 90.00

Cup and Saucer

Cup with steamship Clermont, saucer with American frigate, anchor in harbor, red transfers, pink luster rims, (A) . . . 30.00

Temperance star, banner, and crest, pink transfers, pink luster trim 125.00

Cup and Saucer, Handleless

Band of blue, red, green, and yellow polychrome stylized flowerheads and leaves, pink luster rims 125.00

Pearlware, pink luster reserve of picket fence and trees, pink luster stripes at sides, pink luster banded rims, (A) 20.00

HP pink, yellow, purple, and green floral design, pink luster leaves and stems, pink luster rims, (A) 35.00

Pink transfer of reclining classic woman, pink luster border band with red and blue flowerheads 110.00

Cup and Saucer, Oversize, black transfer of man and woman fishing at river, church in bkd, pink luster rims 55.00

Cup and Saucer, pink luster chinoiserie scene and banding, (A) $55.

Dish, 8" d, scallop shell shape, overall pink luster, "imp WEDGWOOD" mark 475.00

Figure, 10 1/2" h, bust of John Wesley, black robe, white collar, flesh, red, yellow, and brown face, splashed pink luster tapered base, c1825, (A) 1,035.00

Jug, 4 7/8" h, relief molded running hunting dogs, berried vine border, pink luster accents, Staffordshire, c1825, (A) 460.00

Mug

2 1/8" h, pink luster flowerheads, green dot leaves, pink luster border and handle 95.00

2 3/8" h, mustard yellow and blue bands, beaded rim, pink luster body 65.00

4 3/4" h, pink luster church pattern with fencing 495.00

5" h, birds and floral design, black transfer, pink luster trim, hairline 495.00

Pitcher

3 1/4" h, magenta flowerheads, green leaves, pink luster accents and rim 55.00

6" h

Black transfer of 2 men before manor house, black transfer flowers on border, pink ground, pink luster rim 85.00

Pink luster "House" design, quilted apple green ground, c1815 . . . 795.00

6 1/4" h, "Coursing," hunt scene, black transfer, sculpted base, black transfer of florals on handle and int rim, dk pink luster rims on top and base, c1830 . . . . 220.00

7" h, white ground with pink luster design on neck, base, and handle, polychrome floral garland with "Harriet Le Bas, 1845" under spout, pink luster foliate frame of verse or sailing ship on sides, (A) 633.00

Plate

6 3/4" d, wide pink band with pink luster floral designs, pink luster band on rim, (A) 15.00

7 3/8" d, black transfer of oriental scene of figures by fence, red, orange, pink, green, and yellow accents with pink luster sky, border of HP pink roses and green centered red flowers, black stems with green leaves and blue florets, dk brown rim band, (A) . . . 100.00

9 1/4" d, pink luster flower buds and fan leaves on border, scalloped rim, unmkd 20.00

Quintal, 7 3/4" h, pink resist luster, fluted spouts with blue trimmed scalloped rims, raised fan form leaf design on center with leaf and floral design, c1815, (A) 575.00

Sugar Bowl, Cov, 6 3/8" h, pink and purple luster flowers with green an red accents, leaf shaped handles, (A) 72.00

Teabowl and Saucer

Black goat and cherub transfer, red, blue, and green polychrome accents, wide pink luster rim bands, (A) 40.00

Landscape scene with villa, pink luster, pink lustered rims, c1825, (A) . . . 50.00

Lg iron red flowerheads, green and pink luster leaves, pink luster rims . . . 65.00

Luster "House" pattern 35.00

Pink luster reserve with picket fence flanked by trees, wide pink luster band on rims, pink luster stripe on side, (A) 100.00

Pink transfer of bird in nest, red, blue, green, and yellow polychrome accents, pink luster band on rims, (A) 30.00

Tea Service, Part, 19 piece, pot, 9 1/2" h, creamer, cov sugar bowl, waste bowl, 5 1/2" d, 8 cups and saucers, 7 plates, 8 3/4" d, oct shape, acanthus leaf scrolled handles, "Gothic" pattern, pink lustered molded grapes designs, (A) 175.00

Silver

Bough Pot, 9" w, pearlware, demi-lune shape, pierced cov, urn knob, silver luster central panels of fruit flanked by molded columns and leaves, reserves of stylized flowers, ball feet, Staffordshire, c1820, pr, (A) 2,070.00

Coffee and Tea Service, Part, coffeepot, 10 1/4" h, teapot, 7 1/4" h, milk jug, 8" h, cov sugar bowl, 6 1/8" h, 8 cups and saucers, Empire style silver luster band of stylized foliate scrolls suspending vines, France, 19th C, (A) 230.00

Coffee Pot, 12 1/4" h, fancy handle with thumb rest, domed cov, molded vert reeding, overall luster, repairs, (A) 100.00

Creamer

2 5/8" h, silver resist design of bird, lion, trees, and "C.A. 1812," chips and repairs, (A) 85.00

4 3/8" h, helmet shape, overall luster, (A) 45.00

Cup and Saucer

Gray-green bat printed transfers of putti and "Louis XVIII" and "PEACE" on saucer, "Wellington for Ever" on cup silver luster rims 285.00

Hanging red painted flowerheads from green dots, silver luster scrolling leave, silver luster borders 110.00

Overall silver luster abstract floral design, Wedgwood, set of 12, (A) 350.00

Figure

10 1/2" l, standing lion, ft on ball, buff ground, overall silver luster, Staffordshire, c1820, repairs, (A) 489.00

13 1/2" h, bust of Madonna, flared circ base, Staffordshire, c1820, (A) 1,150.00

Flower Font, 14 1/4" h, 3 graduated rect form pots with corner spouts, flared cov with mask knob, overall silver luster, Staffordshire, (A) 748.00

Jardiniere, 7 1/2" h, tapered, silver resist, imp dice banded borders with scrolled leaf designs, blue surface agate, c1820, (A). 288.00

Jug

4 1/4" h, silver resist of leaves and stems, carouches of black transfers of robins

with red, blue, yellow, and green polychrome enamels, Staffordshire, c1815, (A) 805.00

5 1/4" h, white quilted body, dk red flowerheads with silver luster leaves, band of dk red and silver luster leaves on shoulder, black lined rim, c1800. . . . 225.00

5 3/8" h, roundel with red and yellow owl seated on brown branch, silver resist leaves on body 750.00

5 1/2" h

Blue, yellow, and purple enameled exotic bird standing on green ground on front, reverse with running bird, silver luster body, c1820 . . . 165.00

Ovoid shape, white relief of sporting figures, silver luster ground, Staffordshire, c1810, (A) . . . 230.00

6" h, cream ground, dk red flowerheads and silver luster leaves, band of dk red and silver luster squiggles on shoulder, silver lusted lined rim and handle, c1800 . . . . 165.00

10" h, silver resist, floral and foliate designs, banded border, Staffordshire, c1815, chips, (A) 633.00

Loving Cup, 5 1/4" h, silver resist, birds in landscape, Leeds, restored handle, (A) 285.00

Mug, 3 3/4" h

Black transfer of woman with book and "Ann Moore of Tutbury Staffordshire. Born 1761 who has lived without food since July 17, 1807" in silver luster roundel on front 525.00

Silver resist, floral design surrounding HcW monogram, Wedgwood, 1950, (A) 517.00

Pitcher

4 1/2" h, silver resist

Bird and floral design, "Grey's Pottery, Stoke on Trent" mark 59.00

Pear shape, grapes and leaves design 95.00

4 3/4" h, bulbous shape, silver resist farm implements design, repairs . . . 195.00

Pitcher, 4 1/4" h, silver resist florals, leaves, and geometric loops, $265.

5 3/8" h, bulbous shape, silver resist, seated bird with flowerheads, bands of chevrons on rim 175.00

5 1/2" h, silver resist, ftd, grape vine designs, scroll handle, repair to ft, (A) 25.00

5 5/8" h, bulbous shape, black transfer of farmer's arms with polychrome accents, silver luster bands, (A). 220.00

6" h, globular base, straight neck, ftd, scroll handle, overall luster, (A) . . 25.00

6 1/2" h, ftd, loop handle with thumb rest, molded shell body, overall luster, (A) 90.00

7 1/2" h, silver leaf design, Myott . . . 85.00

Potpourri, 4 5/8" h, basket form, pierced cov, silver resist, leaf and berry design, Leeds, (A) 275.00

Plate, 7 7/8" d, silver resist design of leaves and twisted tendrils, band of flowers, leaves, and tendrils on border, (A) 85.00

Relish Tray, silver luster leaf design, Myott 55.00

Teabowl and Saucer, scattered sm silver luster apples, floral sprigs and leaves. . . 250.00

Teapot

5 1/4" h, squat shape, molded reeded borders, overall luster, (A). 138.00

6 1/4" h x 10 1/2" l, rect, silver ground with resist white leaves, berries, and tendrils, dk red outlined rim and knob. . . 325.00

11" l, silver resist, figural rooster, tail forms handle, George Jones, c1875, repairs, (A) 690.00

Tea Set, pot, 7" h x 11" l, squat shape, creamer, open sugar bowl, "Silverine" pattern", overall silver luster, raised scrolling on base, black wood handles and knob, "S.F. & Co. Silverine" mark 125.00

Tumbler, 3 3/4" h, tapered, 2 polychromed molded masks, silver resist leaf design, Staffordshire, c1815, (A) 633.00

Vase, 7 1/4" h, bulbous shape, silver floral design on wide black band, cream ground, Wedgwood, 1920, (A) 373.00

Sunderland

Bowl

10 1/8" d, Masonic, polychrome enameled black transfers of farmer's arms, "God Speed the Plow," sailors fairwell and verse, and Masonic emblems on ext, pink luster trim and berries on int border with center int figural landscape and "Thomas & Susanna Gray," "Dixon, Austin & Co. Sunderland" mark, (A) 633.00

11 3/4" h, transfers of Odd Fellows and verses, splashed and wavy pink luster designs 1,250.00

Creamer, 2 7/8" h, Sunderland band on collar and front oval reserve with black transfer of floral wreath and "Ladies all I pray make free And tell me how You like your tea," arched handle, (A) 220.00

Jug, 4 1/2" h, black transfer of Iron Bridge, verse on reverse, splashed pink lustered body, $175.

Cream Pitcher, 3 1/2" h, paneled body, overall splashed pink luster 115.00

Figure, 8 1/2-8 3/4" h, allegorical "Four Seasons," titled on base, polychromed with pink luster, "imp DIXON, AUSTON, & CO." marks, set of 4, (A) .1,955.00

Goblet, 5 1/4" h, overall splashed pink luster, c1830 . . . . 195.00

Jug

6" h, "Iron Bridge" under spout, black transfer with red, yellow, and green accents, splashed pink luster panels and rim 495.00

6 1/2" h, "Battle of Wasp and Reindeer," "Constitution" on reverse, black transfers, pink luster trim, chips, (A) . 402.00

7 1/2" h, black transfer of "Say if no more in converse sweet..." in red flowerhead and green leaf cartouche, iron bridge on reverse, pink luster wavy lines, pink luster bands on neck and spout 595.00

8 1/2" h, pink "Commodore Perry" under spout, pink luster cottage scene with burst clouds on one side, pink luster mill scene with burst clouds on reverse, band of pink luster flowers on neck 975.00

Mug, 2 3/4" h, overall splashed luster . .125.00

Jug, 5 3/4" h, black Masonic transfer, verse on reverse, pink luster clouds and rim bands, $450.

Pitcher

3 1/8" h, "Commodore Bainbridge," black transfer, pink splashed body, cream rim with pink luster stars 48.00

8 1/2"h, transfers of ships, compass, and "The Sailor's Tear" poem, luster trim 1,025.00

8 3/4" h, transfers of the ship "Opthumerland" and Masonic symbols, pink luster trim, (A) 715.00

9 1/2" h, "West VIEW of the IRON BRIDGE over the WEAR under the Patronage of R. BURDON Esq. M.P." and "FRIENDSHIP, LOVE AND TRUTH" and verse on reverse, verse under spout, black transfers, splashed pink luster surrounds and rim, c1800, (A) 1,035.00

Plaque

6 1/2" d, black transfer of "THOU GOD SEE'ST ME" in floral cartouche with trumpeting angel at top, pink luster border 350.00

6 3/4" d, black transfer of "The Total Society," splashed pink luster border, (A) 115.00

7 3/4" d, black transfer of "THOU GOD SEEST ME," pink luster trim . . . 350.00

8" sq, black transfer of "PREPARE TO MEET THY GOD," pink luster trim 350.00

8 5/8" l, rect

"FLYING CLOUD BOSTON," black transfer, pink luster border, copper luster rim, pierced for hanging 450.00

"PRAISE YE THE LORD" in oval floral wreath, pink luster leaf sprays, pink luster border, molded copper luster rim, pierced for hanging . . . 195.00

8 3/4" l x 7 3/4" w, "FOR MAN DIET'L WASTETH AWAY: YEA, MAN GIVETH UP THE GHOST AND WHERE IS HE, Job 14," black transfer, pink luster border, copper luster rim, pierced for hanging 475.00

9" l x 8" w, black transfer of "West View of Bridge Over River Wear Begun 24 Sept. 1793," green, yellow, and rust splashes, framed border of lavender, green, and pink luster 3,315.00

9 3/8" l x 8 1/4" w, rect, "VICTORIA AND ALBERT YACHT," black transfer, green water, pink splashed border, molded brown rim, pierced for hanging. 450.00

9 1/2" l, rect, "PRAISE YE THE LORD" in center in green wreath with trumpeting angel at top, pink luster border, scrolled copper luster rim. 195.00

Plate, overall splashed luster

6" d 20.00

6 5/8" d 35.00

7" d, molded swirls, Charles Allerton 22.00

Puzzle Jug

6 1/2" h, pink luster house and landscape scene, lustered rim and nozzles, chips, (A) 747.00

9" h, overall pink splash, "G C 1829" under rim, chips 1,200.00

Salt, 2 1/8" h x 3 1/8" d, ftd, overall splashed luster, (A) 40.00

Shaker, 4 1/4" h, overall pink splash, (A) 75.00

Watch Stand, 11" h, figural tall case clock flanked by 2 classical children, black, yellow, red, and green enamels with splashed pink luster on base, "imp Dixon, Austin" mark, (A) 1,093.00

c1836-1878

c1878

MAASTRICHT

Maastricht, Holland
1836 to Present

History: Petrus Regout founded a glass and crystal works in 1834 in Maastricht, Holland. In 1836 he expanded his operation to include the De Sphinx Pottery that had a work force recruited from England. It was Regout's desire to introduce the manufacture of ironstone, a ware that had greatly reduced the market for Delftware.

From 1836 to 1870, Petrus Regout manufactured dinnerware in the style of English ironstone decorated with transfer printed patterns with scenic or romantic themes. Pattern names were back stamped in English for wares exported to English and American markets. Patterns included: "Amazone," "Mythology," "Pleasure Party," "Ruth & Boaz," "Wild Rose," and "Willow." Until about 1870, Regout's decorations had been printed only in one color, either blue, black, violet, or red. If a second color was desired, the piece was first decorated with a printed black transfer and the second color then hand applied. In 1870, lithographic decalcomania made possible multicolor printing on china. Brightly colored dinnerware became the rage until the end of the century.

When Regout died in 1878, his sons reorganized the company. They adopted the Sphinx trademark. During the 20th century, tastes became more conservative. Today the firm is called "N.V. Konmklijke Sphinx." Since 1974, it has been part of the British conglomerate Reed International.

Pieces usually had a printed back stamp. Most dinnerware was marked with a pattern name. The company also made blanks for others to decorate. The phrase "Royal Sphinx" was authorized in 1959 and used on decorative tiles.

Other potteries in Maastricht during the 1840s and 1850s included N.A. Bosch, W.N. Clermont and Ch. Chainaye, and G. Lambert & Co. who merged with Sphinx in 1958.

References: John P. Reid, "The Sphinx of Maastricht," <u>The Antique Trader Weekly</u>, December 20, 1984.

Collecting Hints: Early Regout pottery always had a heavily crazed glaze. After the 1870s, the glaze was free of crazing. The tan luster did not wear well. The quality of the printing varied with the different transfers.

Bowl

7 3/4" d, "Pajong" pattern, black transfer with orange and luster trim 75.00

6" d, ftd, "Honc" pattern, green transfer with polychrome accents 40.00

7 3/4" d, ftd, "Slamat" pattern, orange and green oriental scene of young boy, "green Petrus Regout sphinx" mark 45.00

8 5/8" d, "Honc" pattern, green transfer with polychrome accents 35.00

9" d, ftd, "Honc" pattern, green transfer with polychrome accents, (A) . . . 28.00

Charger

13"d, rose, blue, and green florals and lines in center, brown and yellow inner circles, blue triangles on border, cream ground, "Maastricht, Made in Holland" mark 45.00

15 1/2" d, blue and white Delft-type design 60.00

Cup Plate, 4 1/2" d, "Lasso" pattern, horse hunting scenes, red transfer, "Petrus Regout & Co. Maastricht, Made in Holland" mark 20.00

Cup and Saucer

"Honc" pattern, blue-black oriental design with orange accents 18.00

"Oriental" pattern, overall floral design, red transfers, "Societe Ceramique Maastricht" mark 10.00

"Pekin" pattern, red, green, and orange, "Petrus Regout sphinx" mark 35.00

Bowl, 6" d, 3 11/4" h, "Abbey" pattern, green transfer, orange accents, $35.

"Timor" pattern, green, iron red, blue, and luster 38.00

Cup and Saucer, Demitasse, "Oriental" pattern, pink transfer, "Societe Ceramique, Maastricht, Oriental" mark, (A) 25.00

Pitcher

5" h, "Timor" pattern 100.00

7 1/2" h, "Siam" pattern 75.00

Plate

6 1/2" d

"Belus" pattern, orange, gold, and green oriental scene 10.00

"Pajong" pattern, black oriental scene with orange luster trim 18.00

7 1/16" d, "Tea Party" pattern, brown transfer, "M. Maastricht and rampant lion" mark 25.00

7 3/4" d, "Potiche" pattern, iron red and black oriental items, set of 6 . . . . 50.00

7 7/8" d, "Fruit" pattern, black transfer of fruit on branches in center, raised white diamond border, gold lined rims 26.00

8 3/8" d, "Vlinder" pattern, multicolored butterfly in center, insects on border, "Petrus Regout sphinx" mark . . . 15.00

8 1/2" d

"Canton" pattern 38.00

"Lasso" pattern, black transfer, "Maastricht, Made in Holland" mark . .45.00

"Pompeia" pattern, iron red, orange, and cobalt oriental style scene of jug, bottle, and flowers, Petrus Regout 35.00

Red, blue and lt and dk green stick spatter gaudy floral pattern, (A) 30.00

8 5/8" d

"Alpine" pattern, bands of geometrics, brown transfer 65.00

"Honc" pattern, green transfer, orange-red accents, orange luster trim, "green Petrus Regout, sphinx" mark 15.00

8 3/4" d

"Honc" pattern, green and orange-red, orange accents 24.00

Maroon tulip in center with green leaves and dk purple-gray design flowerheads, border of red and blue flowerheads with design dk purple-gray design flowerheads and red wavy lines, red striped rim 38.00

"Pekin" pattern, green transfer with iron red florals 25.00

9" d, "Pajong" pattern, oriental scene of man and woman with umbrella, black transfer, orange luster, "Petrus Regout, sphinx" mark 35.00

9 1/8" d, border band of red, blue, and yellow half flowerheads, "Petrus Regout, sphinx" mark 18.00

9 1/4" d, border of stylized red flowerheads and blue crosses between bands of purple crisscross design, "Maastricht, Made in Belgium" mark 48.00

10" d, "Honc" pattern, red, green, and yellow, "Petrus Regout sphinx" mark 48.00

Soup Plate, 7 1/2" d, "Flora" pattern, "Petrus Regout sphinx" mark 22.00

1874-1924
GEORGE JONES

1890 - 1939

MAJOLICA

English and Continental 1850 to Present

History: During a visit to Rouen in 1849, Herbert Minton saw flower pots with a green glaze. When he returned to England, Minton instructed Leon Arnoux, his firm's art director, to copy these wares. Arnoux introduced English Majolica, an opaque tin-glazed earthenware, in 1850. The name Majolica originally came from the Spanish island of Majorca. Its popularity in England remained strong through the second half of the 19th century.

Minton's early majolica wares closely imitated Palissy ware, a pottery made by Bernard Palissy at Saintes, France between 1542 and 1562 and later in a workshop on the grounds of the Palais des Tuileries in Paris.

Palissy ware was characterized by relief figures and ornaments that were covered with colored glazes, mainly yellow, blue, and gray highlighted with brown and manganese. Palissy was known for naturalistic designs of leaves, lizards, snakes, insects, shells, and other natural objects in high relief on plates and dishes. He also made vases, ewers, and basins. The reverse of his wares was covered with a mottled glaze in brown, blue, and manganese. Palissy developed the appliqué technique which consisted of making plaster casts resembling the natural objects separate from the main body and applying these later.

Early Minton majolica wares were modeled by the French sculptors Emile Jeannest, Albert Carrier-Belluse, and Hugues Protat. Protat made the models from which the wares were cast. Leading artists from the Victorian period who decorated the wares included Thomas Allen, Thomas Kirkby, and Edouard Rischgitz.

Early majolica wares by Minton also attempted to emulate Italian majolica, basic earthenware, that was coated with an opaque white glaze or covering slip. English majolica meant earthenwares that were decorated with deep semi-transparent lead glazes. Typical Victorian majolica examples included large garden ornaments such as seats and jardinieres plus many types of plates and dishes for utilitarian and decorative use.

Daniel Sutherland and Sons of Longton established a pottery in 1863 to manufacture the majolica wares. A tremendous variety of articles was made. Other manufacturers included: Brown/Westhead, W. Brownfield and Company of Cobridge, Holdcraft, George Jones and Sons, Moore and Company, and Wedgwood. George Jones, who was employed by Minton until he established his own Trent Pottery in Stoke in 1861, made lidded vases, ornamental bowls, candelabras, and wall plaques, along with more ordinary everyday majolica wares.

Wedgwood's majolica took the form of molded leaves and vegetables that were decorated with a translucent green glaze. Other Wedgwood majolica wares were covered with colored glazes on a white body that was molded with high quality relief ornamentation. Vases, umbrella stands, wall brackets, candlesticks, compotes, plates, and a variety of dishes were made.

Majolica wares were made on the Continent by Sarreguimes in France, by Villeroy and Boch and Zell in Germany, and by companies in Austria, Bavaria, and Italy. Nineteenth century majolica was different from the earlier Italian majolica wares.

References: Victoria Bergesen, *Majolica: British, Continental and American Wares, 1851-1915,* Barrie & Jenkins, 1989; Leslie Bockol, *Victorian Majolica,* Schiffer Publishing, Ltd.1996; Helen Cunningham, *Majolica Figures,* Schiffer Publishing, Ltd. 1997; Nicholas M. Dawes, *Majolica,* Crown Publishers, Inc.1990; Marilyn G. Karmasn with Joan B. Stacke, *Majolica: A Complete History and Illustrated Survey,* Harry B. Abrams, 1989; Marshall P. Katz & Robert Lehr, *Palissy Ware: Nineteenth Century French Ceramists from Avisseau to Renoleau,* Athlone Press, 1996; Mariann Katz-Marks, *Collectors' Encyclopedia of Majolica,* Collector Books, 1992; D. Michael Murray, *European Majolica,* Schiffer Books, 1997; Julia E. Poole, *Italian Majolica,* Cambridge University Press, 1997; Mike Schneider, *Majolica,* Schiffer Publishing, Ltd. 1994; Jeffrey B. Snyder & Leslie J. Bockol, *Majolica: American & European Wares,* Schiffer Publishing, Ltd. 1994; Alan-Caiger Smith, *Tin-Glaze Pottery in Europe & the Islamic World,* Faber & Faber, 1973.

Collectors' Club: Majolica International Society, 1275 First Ave., Suite 103, New York, NY 10021, Membership: $35.00, Quarterly newsletter, Majolica Matters.

Museums: British Museum, London, England; Cooper Hewitt Museum, NY; Henry Ford Museum, Dearborn, MI; Cleveland Museum of Art, Cleveland, OH; City Museum and Art Gallery, Stoke-on-Trent, England; Metropolitan Museum of Art, New York, NY; Minton Museum, Stoke-on-Trent, England; J Paul Getty Museum, Los Angeles, CA; Strong Museum, Rochester, NY; Victoria & Albert Museum, London, England; Wadsworth Atheneum, Hartford, CT; Wallace Collection, London, England; Wedgwood Museum, Barlaston, England.

Reproduction Alert: Original majolica always was thick walled with smooth interior walls showing no sign of the pattern. Most new majolica is much lighter in weight than Victorian counterparts. Check the glazes since new ones are not as rich or deeply colored. Some marks have also been reproduced.

Reproductions coming from China are now close copies of some of the original Victorian majolica. The Chinese examples have hollow handles, unglazed bottoms, dull, rough surface glazes, and poorly molded details. The dark background colors are predominately yellow-brown or gold-brown. Patterns on the outside of vases and pitchers can also be seen and felt on the inside of these pieces. Many Chinese examples have a matte finish, while original pieces utilize bright colors and shiny glazes. Old examples have solid handles that were made separately and applied to the body of the piece so there are no firing holes. With the hollow handles, these pieces were cast as a single piece so there is a firing hole by the handle.

Some reproductions from China can carry dangerous amounts of lead and should not be used to serve food.

To complicate matters, some reproductions are better made and have shiny, smooth glazes and bright colors, but they are generally heavier than the originals they are copied from.

Continental

Asparagus Server, 16" H-H, rect, red striped white asparagus on brown leaf, yellow basketweave border, green rope twist handles, France, (A) 440.00

Candleholder, 11" h, green and brown mottled figural deer head, orange and green flower in mouth, 2 orange and green sockets on top of head, (A) 521.00

Candlestick, 6 1/2" h, figural girl in pink dress, yellow hat, brown and green candleholder, (A). 110.00

Charger
    11 3/4" d

    Gold sunflowers, dk green leaves, matte lt green and gold ground, Germany. 200.00

    White water lilies, dk green leaves, turquoise ground 105.00

  13" d, center relief of nude woman, children, dog, birds, and trees, green, blue, rust, and yellow, gold reticulated rim, Italy 125.00

Ewer, 13 1/2" h, middle eastern style black outlined brown, ivory, and blue arabesques 1,050.00

Figure

  5" l x 3 1/2" h, reclining black child, aqua hat, white blouse, purple bodice, yellow apron, France 95.00

  21" h, standing heron, gray-brown and white feathers, brown cattails and vert green leaves in bkd, (A) 770.00

Humidor, 5 1/2" h, figural fox in blue coat with red collar, (A) 358.00

Jug, 11" h, yellow flowers, green leaves, Austria. 250.00

Oyster Plate, 10" d, 6 gray and white shells, brown center well, green ground, France, (A) 220.00

Pitcher, 8 1/2" h, red striped, green tipped white asparagus, red int, France, (A) . 440.00

Planter, Hanging, 10" d, pink and yellow calla lilies, green leaves, turquoise ground, France, (A) 990.00

Plaque, 12 1/4" d, red and yellow pears or red cherries, green leaves, brown branches, blue, cream, green, and brown shaded ground, pierced for hanging, France, pr 395.00

Tobacco Jar, 7 1/4" h, dk red jacket, gray-green suit, brown pipe, unmkd, $895.

Plate

6 1/2" d, red poppy, chartreuse ground, Germany 20.00

8" d, red-headed yellow birds, purple grapes and green leaves, turquoise ground, Germany, set of 7, (A) . 165.00

Vase

10 1/2" h, modeled as yellow ear of corn with green leaf handles and base, c1890, (A) 747.00

17 1/2" h, polychromed and decorated with pink and yellow flowers in relief, shaded teal blue ground, purple graduated neck, open vine handles, (A) 225.00

20" h, waisted shape, brown glazed ground with applied irises, Oonaing, c1890, pr 1,500.00

English

Bowl

11" l, brown and green mottled figural shell, turquoise int, brown shell feet, Holdcroft, (A) 330.00

11 1/2" d, white water lilies, green lily pad ground, ftd base, "J. Holdcroft" mark 475.00

Cache Pot, 8" h, white strawberry blossoms and green leaves, cobalt mottled ground, Minton, (A) 1,100.00

Candlestick, 16 1/4" h, turquoise Italian Renaissance designs on cobalt ground, scrolled feet, Minton, dtd 1876, pr, (A) 3,450.00

Center server, 9 1/2" h, pink tinged white egg supported on 3 green and brown dolphin, base of turquoise and green shells, 3 pink leaf feet, George Jones, (A) 3,680.00

Cheese Keeper

10" h, white and green primrose on cobalt ground, brown basketweave base, brown branch knob, Wedgwood, (A) 2,860.00

12 1/4" h, figural castle turret, brown stonework, applied lt and dk green ivy leaves, blue draped flag knob, George Jones, c1873, (A) 4,600.00

13" h, green leaf pads, yellow and white water lilies, brown cattails, dragonflies on cobalt ground, brown base, figural kingfisher knob, George Jones, repairs, (A) 11,000.00

Condiment Dish, 8 1/4" d, handled, white bird on green oak leaf, multicolored sides, Minton 1,200.00

Dish

10" l, green and yellow figural fish with brown fins, Minton, (A) 385.00

10 1/2" l x 7 1/4" w, green leave, brown basketweave border, Wedgwood 305.00

Figure, 8 1/2" h, tan standing lion with dk brown mane, green and brown rect base, Minton, c1890, (A) 1,840.00

Fish Server, molded gray and white figural salmon on molded green ground, dk brown basketweave base, George Jones, c1871, (A) 2,875.00

Game Tureen, 10 1/2" l, hanging game on sides, brown ground, figural rabbit knob, Wedgwood, (A) 770.00

Jardiniere, 12" h x 14" d, basketweave ground with ribbon and bow, med blue, Minton, (A) 275.00

Jug, 8 1/4" h, figural pineapple, yellow base, green molded leaf top and handle, Minton, c1867, (A) 575.00

Match Holder, 8" h, seated maiden in brown jacket, green skirt, brown basket with turquoise int, brown and green base, Minton, (A) 715.00

Nut Dish, 6" h x 11" l, scalloped turquoise dish, figural bird handle, Holdcroft 650.00

Oyster Plate

7" d, 5 turquoise wells, raised white center well, brown coral and green seaweed, George Jones, (A) 1,430.00

9" d, 6 pink wells, turquoise center well, Minton, (A) 990.00

9" l x 7 1/2" w, rect, 4 mottled shells, pink center well, green leaf base with white water lilies, Minton, (A) 990.00

10 1/2" d, 6 pink shells separated by yellow, green, and brown coral, seaweed, and shells, turquoise center well, George Jones, c1872, (A) . . . 2,070.00

11" d, 6 figural brown fish shells, brown ground with green seaweed, Minton, (A) 1,870.00

Pitcher

6 1/2" h, gourd shape, mottled brown ground, figural cobalt and black bird handle, George Jones, (A) . . . 1,430.00

7" h, green fern around vert brown bamboo body, Wardle, (A) 175.00

7 1/2" h, brown, green, and pink, flowers, leaves, and rope design 190.00

8" h, white and orange irises, white water lilies with green leaves, lavender ground, brown wrapped handle, George Jones, (A) 4,840.00

9" h

Red accented white nautilus shell, green ivy leaves on brown mottled ground, dk brown twisted vine handle, Wedgwood, (A) 1,045.00

White stork on turquoise ground, cobalt top and base, brown bamboo rim, foot, and handle, turquoise int, (A) 880.00

14" h, figural duck, gray back, white breast, yellow beak, brown figural monkey handle, Brownfield, (A) . . . 1,430.00

Plate

8" d, green pond lily design, pr, (A) 220.00

8 3/8" d, molded sunflower design, basketweave border, brown glaze, Wedgwood, pr, (A) 25.00

8 1/2" d, figural grape leaf, green, "WEDGWOOD" mark 45.00

Tray, 12" d, brown and yellow butterfly, yellow wheat with green leaves, turquoise ground, brown border, George Jones, $2175.

9" d

Green cauliflower, yellow border, "imp WEDGWOOD" mark 160.00

Orange-yellow pineapples with green stalks, dk green ground, George Jones, (A) 275.00

Sardine Box, 8" l, 3 molded gray-black fish on cov, green ground, yellow and pink edge, green vert stiff leaves on cov sides, base with green stiff leaves, pink and yellow rim, George Jones, c1872, (A) 1,265.00

Sauceboat, 5" h x 8" l, figural fish on waves, dk green body, turquoise int, med green waves, (A) 990.00

Tankard, Cov, 12 3/4" h, center band of Medieval peasants running against gray stone wall, upper and lower bands of brown and green entwined ivy, gray shell cov with figural jester head knob, brown and green entwined vine handle, Minton, dtd 1874, (A) . . . 920.00

Teapot

6" h x 8 1/2" l, yellow coconut body, brown figural monkey with cobalt jacket and red fans, Minton, (A) 4,400.00

7 1/2" h x 10" l, white figural bulbous fish with red eye, blue-green waves, green seaweed handle, Minton, (A). 2,475.00

Toothpick Holder, 2 1/2" h, white open egg, 2 figural brown mice, green leaf base, Royal Worcester, pr, (A) 1,650.00

Vase

9 1/2" h, figural standing woman in green dress, blue ribboned yellow hat, brown trimmed cream skirt, leaning on turquoise lined yellow basket, green and brown circ base, Minton, c1870, (A) 1,035.00

31" h, standing figural gray and white heron with leg raised, holding fish in mouth, tall molded green leaves and brown cattails at side, rocky base, Minton, c1880, (A) 9,775.00

Walking Stick Stand, 40" h, figural white stork standing on one leg, green snake in beak, green vert leaves and lily pads, frog under ft, Minton, chips and cracks, (A) 18,700.00

LATE 19TH CENTURY   LATE 19TH CENTURY

MALICORNE

West of Paris, France
Last Quarter 19th Century to 1952

History: Pouplard established his Malicorne factory in the Sarthe region west of Paris during the last quarter of the 19th century. He was making fine quality reproductions of the typical Quimper patterns, especially those of the Porquier-Beau factory.

To add to the confusion, Pouplard used the "P" from his own name and the "B" from his wife's name Beatrix to form a "PB" mark of his own. Though the design differed from the "PB" mark of Porquier-Beau because the letters were separated and followed by a small "x," Porquier-Beau still brought suit against Pouplard. When the suit was settled in 1897, Malicorne was ordered to cease production and forced to destroy all of his remaining pottery molds. He continued to sign pieces with the PBx mark, only he no longer used the Breton designs. He ceased doing business in 1952.

References: Sandra V. Bondhus, *Quimper Pottery: A French Folk Art Faience*, privately published, 1981, *Rev. Ed.* 1995; Millicent S. Mali, *French Faience*, United Printing, 1986.

Museum: Sevres Museum, Sevres, France.

Ashtray, 5" l, rect, crowned crest in center with green olive branches, blue streaked border, unmkd, (A) 20.00
Asparagus Plate, 9 3/4" d, yellow raised asparagus with green top in middle, seated peasant man leaning on bag above, yellow and green florals below, blue dash inner border, scalloped rim, "P.B.x" mark 225.00
Doll Platter, 4 1/2" l x 3" w, oval, peasant man in cobalt jacket, green shirt, rose pantaloons, yellow stockings, blue streaked border, (A) 44.00
Doll Porringer, 2" d, female peasant knitting or male peasant playing bagpipe, blue single stroke rim and handles, "P.B.x" mark, set of 3, (A) 200.00
Jardiniere, 13" l x 10"h, figural swimming fish, red, yellow, and green face, tail, and fins, standing peasant man holding flower on side, fence and forest in bkd, flying butterfly and

Bowl, 9 1/4" sq, tan scarf, green blouse, red apron, blue dress, yellow flowerheads with green and iron red accents, $245.

scattered flowers, crowned crest on reverse with berried branches and blue bow, (A) 675.00
Letter Tray, 9" sq x 3 1/2" h, center multicolored scene of man pushing child in wheelbarrow, dk blue stylized flowerhead border on med blue ground, overhead handle with cartouche of windmill and ocean, "P.B.x" mark, (A). 930.00
Melonniere, 13 1/2" H-H, multicolored scene of Breton man with 2 children, lt and dk blue decor riche border, crest of Brittany at top, multicolored confetti handles, (A) . . . 605.00
Pipe, 11 1/2" l, multicolored flowers on bowl, blue decor riche rim, yellow stem with "Malicorne (Sarthe) 15 Aout 1913," repaired chip 750.00
Pitcher, 8" h, peasant woman seated on bench, blue flowerheads, blue and red stripes, fleur-de-lys shaped rim, rim chips 150.00
Plate
    6" d, male peasant in center, blue striped border, "P.B.x" mark 25.00
    9 1/2" d
        Mother holding baby, waving to sea, child at side, blue, red, purple, green, and yellow, dk blue "Italiante" border with crest of Brittany, "P.B.x" mark, (A) 520.00
        Peasant woman wearing green vest, red dress, pink apron, feeding pigs, border with 6 cartouches of blue shaded fleur-de-lys and green lattice work and red dot designs, indented rim, "P.B.x" mark, (A) 770.00
        Seated peasant woman, child at knee, hanging clock on wall, blue stylized flowerheads on border, "P.B.x" mark. 490.00
    9 3/4" d
        Breton legend scene in center, Devil stealing peasant man's cow, red and green flowers and leaves on border, lt blue lined shaped rim,

"Qu'est-ce que cela" on reverse, "P.B.x" mark 720.00
Cobalt, yellow, green, brown, and purple bird drinking at fountain, border of blue leaves and sm green leaves, crackle ground, "P.B.x" mark, (A) 195.00
10" d
    Frontal view of peasant woman in white coif, blue skirt, green blouse, pink apron, basket of radishes and leeks in hand, basket on arm, stylized fruit and floral border, "P.B.x" mark, (A) 210.00
    Oriental style red and blue chrysanthemums on leafy branches, butterfly, inner border of green lattice and red blossoms and scrolls, blue lined shaped rim, (A). 150.00
    Portrait bust of Carnot, black hat, red plume and band, white shirt, yellow cravat, blue toned jacket, "Carnot 1793" across top, single stroke leaves and flowerheads on border 125.00
    Seated peasant woman in red skirt, blue apron, green blouse, and pink coif, little girl in red cap, pink striped dress, orange boots, standing on stool eating bread, toys and pitcher and bowl on floor, dk blue acanthus border on blue ground with crest of Brittany, (A). 675.00
Platter
    11 1/4" l x 8 1/4" w, oval, seated male peasant in blue coat, magenta pants, green sash, orange stockings, wooden shoes, holding bagpipe, border with rust, yellow, green, and blue flowers, scalloped rim, unmkd 375.00
    13" l, oval
        Center scene of peasant couple in open field, forest and church in bkd, border of blue croiselle and red dots alternating with 4 panels of black ermine tails, "P.B.x" mark, (A) . 550.00
        Frontal view of female peasant in orange blouse, blue skirt, mauve apron, holding 2 baskets, yellow and blue flowerhead border, crackle ground 275.00
    15 1/2" l x 11" w, center scene of 2 peasant couples in bridal party, wood fence in bkd, purple, blue, green, yellow, pink, and red, dk blue acanthus border on lt blue ground with 4 panels of pink and blue daisies, (A). 1,600.00
Porringer, 7 1/4" H-H, male or female peasant, vert red, yellow, and green flower, blue and yellow striped rim, red and blue striped handles, "P.B.x" mark, pr 300.00
Puzzle Jug, 5" h, grape vines and purple grapes at reticulated top, figural grape spout, "Buvez je le veux bien Mais sachez placer votre main" round base, (A) 300.00

Snuff Bottle

3" l, figural bagpipe, female peasant, red and yellow roses, and bluets, dk and lt yellow bow at top, lt blue pipes with yellow accents, floral sprays and 4 blue dot design on reverse, (A) 220.00

3 1/2" h x 3" w, female peasant in lt blue skirt, red apron, gold skirt on front, rust, blue, yellow, and green single stroke flowers on reverse, blue rim with brown stripe, unmkd 275.00

4" l, figural shoe, peasant woman, sm blue and red floral sprigs, "Cregastel" on top, "P.B.x" mark, (A) 240.00

Tray, 12" H-H, female peasant in white coif, green blouse, blue skirt, pink apron, purple vest carrying basket, male peasant in purple hat and pantaloons, green shirt, blue vest, scythe over shoulder, blue wavy line on border with blue dots, blue sponged twisted handles, "P.B.x" mark, (A) 425.00

Vase

6 1/2" h, fleur-de-lys shape, seated female peasant holding distaff on green ground, blue skirt, rose apron, green coif, yellow curlicues with green X's and rust lines, crest on base, "backward P.B. x" mark 425.00

8 1/2" h, cylinder shape, seated peasant woman with distaff, fence and forest in bkd, crest of Brittany on reverse, sprays of bleeding hearts, pink and blue roses on rim and base, ermine tails on sides, (A) 250.00

Vegetable Bowl, 10" d, standing peasant woman holding bottle and glass, green blouse, mauve skirt, red apron, floral and 4 blue dot border, "P.B.x" mark 118.00

Wall Pocket

7 1/2" h, stylized basket shape, frontal view of peasant man seated on rock, crowned crest of Brittany on int with laurel leaf branches and blue bow, blue, green, and yellow with red accents, (A) 350.00

11" h, cornucopia, female peasant holding dbl basket of eggs on each arm, green blouse, pink apron, blue skirt, lt and dk blue fleur-de-lys at opening, (A) . 185.00

MARTIN BROTHERS

c 1895

Fulham, England
1873-1877

London and Southall, England
1877-1914

History: Robert, Walter, Edwin, and Charles Martin, the first of the English "studio potters," were four brothers who produced salt glaze stoneware called "Martinware." The Martin tradition evolved around ornately engraved, incised, or carved designs on salt glazed ware. Glazes usually were mottled with colors including, gray, brown, blue and yellow in muted tones.

Robert initially worked for the Fulham Pottery of C.J.C. Barley. He and his three brothers established their own workshop in 1873 at Pomona House in Fulham. They fired their wares in the kiln at Fulham Pottery. When that kiln was no longer available, they leased a kiln at Shepherd's Bush.

Robert, known as Wallace, was the sculptor and director of the Martin team. He received his training at the Lambeth School of Art. He was an experienced stone carver and modeler of figures. Wallace modeled grotesques, now eagerly sought by collectors, for over thirty years. Grotesque birds were called "Walleybirds" after their maker.

Walter was in charge of throwing the large vases, mixing the clays, and the firing process. Edwin decorated the vases and other objects with naturalistic forms of decoration. Often he used incised or relief designs of fish, florals, and birds. Charles handled the business aspects of the concern.

In 1877, the brothers founded a pottery in Southall and built their own kiln. They opened a shop in London the next year. The Southall Pottery declined in 1910 with the death of Charles Martin. When Walter died in 1912, production ceased.

All pieces of Martinware were signed with their name, the place of production, and numerals and letters signifying the month and year. The information was incised into the soft clay before firing.

Between 1873 and 1883, the pottery was incised "R.W. Martin" followed by "Fulham" if fired at the Fulham Pottery, "London" if fired at Shepherd's Bush, and "Southall" if made at their own works. From 1879 when the shop was operating, the words "and London" were added to "Southall." From 1883 the full mark was "R.W. Martin & Bros. London & Southall."

References: C.B. Beard, *Catalogue of the Martinware in the Collection of F I. Nettleford,* privately published, 1936; Malcolm Haslam, *The Martin Brothers Potters,* Wittenborn Art Books, 1978; Hugh Wakefield, *Victorian Porcelain,* Herbert Jenkins, 1962.

Museum: Victoria & Albert Museum, London, England.

Bowl, 4 3/4" h x 3 1/4" d, carved vert lines, charcoal and gunmetal, "carved Martin Bros., London & Southall, 10-1905" mark . . 475.00

Bud Vase, 4 1/2" h, fluted, thick brown and white runny glazes, (A) 300.00

Dish, 7 1/2" H-H, incised dk brown swimming fish, tan ground, "Martin Bros, London & Southall, 6-1906" mark 500.00

Ewer, 8 1/4" h, bulbous body, cylinder neck, brown and blue stylized leaves on gold-brown and cobalt ground, sq handle, "incised Martin, Southall, 4-64" mark 450.00

Figure

3" h, sculpted standing bird, blue, brown, and oatmeal glazes, (A) 950.00

3 1/2" h, grotesque figure grappling with writhing snake, oatmeal, gunmetal, and lt green glazes, "incised RW Martin, London, Southall, 3-1890" mark, (A) 1,800.00

Humidor, 8 1/2" h, figural grotesque bird, lg brown beak, blue outlined feathers, wood base, "inscribed Martin Brothers, London & Southall, 9-1890," mark, (A) 10,000

Jar

8 1/2" h, seated gargoyle, holding legs, lt gray glaze, R.W. Martin, 1904 . . . . 22,750.00

9" h, figural standing bird, gunmetal brown beak, cobalt, mauve, and green feathers, mtd on stand, R.W. Martin 10,400.00

Jug

5 1/2" h, smiling face on each side, curly hair, brown and caramel flambe glaze, "incised R. W. Martin & Bros., 10.6.1913, London & Southall" mark, (A) . . 1,900.00

6 1/4" h, stoneware, modeled smiling face on each side, gunmetal and brown glazes, "incised R.W. Martin and Brother, London, Southall" mark, (A) 1,600.00

6 1/2" h, stoneware, ovoid, incised and surface decorated with brown and green smiling quarter moon and sun, beige ground 4,900.00

7 1/4" h, stoneware, modeled smiling face to each side, brown, 1898, restored rim chips, (A) 1,495.00

9 1/2" h, 4 sides, dk brown sea creatures and plants, mottled chocolate brown, gray, and lt blue ground, 1896 . . . . 3,250.00

Mug, 4 1/2" h, molded stern face and smiling face, matte dk brown glaze, R.W. Martin, 1911 . . . . 2,750.00

Paperweight, 4 1/2" l x 2 1/2" h, figural dragon with open mouth, dk brown and green textured scales, 1882 . . . . 2,600.00

Pen Stand, 5" l x 3 1/2" h, figural turtle with open mouth, green and cream body, brown faceted shell, 1910 . . . . 3,900.00

Pitcher

6 3/4" h, bulbous shape, Renaissance style incised and painted white animal faces and acanthus leaves, dk blue ground, 1895 . . . . 1,300.00

7 1/2" h, 4 sides, brown and black iguanas and lizards, apple green ground, 1875 . . . . 2,300.00

8 1/4" h, tapered cylinder shape, incised and painted brown and yellow long-legged birds, gray ground, 1895 . . . . 3,100.00

Urn, 7 1/2" h, brown and tan, "R.W. Martin Bros. London & Southhall" mark, $1,950.

Spoon Warmer, 4" h x 6 1/4" l, figural gargoyle, long brown beard, raised spine and pointed ears, open mouth, dk blue and green glazes, R.W. Martin, 1879 . . . . .7,800.00

Vase

3 1/2" h, 4 sides, incised blue outlined grotesque fish, gray ground, "incised 2-1901/Martin Bros./London/Southall" mark, (A) 750.00

8" h, tapered cylinder, brown incised and painted swimming eels and fish, mottled pink and brown-green ground, 1903. . . . . .2,300.00

8 1/2" h, flat bottle form, gunmetal and brown incised prehistoric fish, lt brown ground, 2 handles on shoulder, "incised Martin Brothers, London, Southhall, 5-1905" mark, repaired rim chip 1,550.00

9" h, bulbous shape, flared rim, brown and green incised and painted crabs, jellyfish, and lobsters, wavy blue and cream ground, restoration to body, 1897 . . . . .3,600.00

9 1/4" h, gray and blue painted jonquils, natural ground, "incised Martin Brothers, Southall, 4/82" mark, repaired base chip, (A) 550.00

10 3/4" h, olive, med blue, and oatmeal incised and sculptured fern design, figural frond handles, "incised R.W. Martin, London, 1-1876" mark, repaired rim chip, (A) 550.00

MASON

Lane Delph, Staffordshire, England c1804-1848

History: Although ironstone is the most familiar product associated with Mason's name, Miles Mason actually began his business career as an importer of china wares, specializing in matching pieces for incomplete sets. After studying the manufacturing methods at Worcester and Derby, Mason joined with Thomas Wolfe in Liverpool in 1780 to manufacture Chinese-style porcelain tablewares.

After the dissolution of the Wolfe-Mason partnership in 1804, Mason started a second concern at Lane Delph in Fenton, Staffordshire. The Fenton factory was devoted to the manufacture of quality blue and white transferware. Within a short time, the factory was relocated at Minerva Works and expanded to incorporate the Bagnell factory. The new factory was known as the Fenton Stone Works.

Charles and George, Miles' sons, eventually became the managers. In 1813, they patented the ironstone formula and manufacturing technique. They were not the first to produce this hard and durable earthenware, but they certainly were the most successful. Mason's Patent Ironstone China became dominant in the market. Ironstone, designed to meet the middle class needs for utilitarian, durable china tablewares, was produced at Fenton from 1813 to 1848.

The first designs were Oriental in nature. The most common method of applying the design was by transfer. Areas were highlighted with touches of enamel. Hand painting and gilding of the ironstone blanks was not uncommon, especially in floral and scenic patterns. Every conceivable form was fashioned in ironstone, from common tableware to fireplace mantles.

Economic difficulties beset the works in 1848. Charles was forced to sell the family business to Francis Morley. Morley, in partnership with Ashworth from 1849 to1862, acquired the Mason designs and molds. Ashworth reissues of Mason's original shapes and decorative patterns were hard to distinguish from those produced at the Fenton works.

For over one hundred years, Ashworth and Brothers, Ltd. have been selling vast quantities of their Mason's type ware with the traditional oriental-styled patterns. In 1968, the firm took the new name "Mason's Ironstone China, Ltd." The old mark was re-instituted.

References: Geoffrey A. Godden, *Godden's Guide to Mason's China & Ironstone Wares*, Antique Collectors Club, Ltd.1980; Geoffrey A. Godden, *The Illustrated Guide to Mason's Patent Ironstone China,* Barrie & Jenkins, 1971; Reginald Haggar & Elizabeth Adams, *Mason Porcelain and Ironstone 1796-1853*, Faber & Faber, 1977; R.G. Haggar, *The Masons of Lane Delph*, Lund Humphries, 1952.

Collectors' Club: Mason's Ironstone Collectors' Club, Susan Hirshman, 2011 East Main Street, Medford, OR, 97520; membership: $25.00; six newsletters per year.

Museums: City Museum & Art Gallery, Hanley, Stoke-on-Trent, England; Potsdam Public Museum, Potsdam, NY.; Victoria & Albert Museum, London, England.

Reproduction Alert: Mason's has reissued 19th century transfer patterns such as the "Quail pattern" on old shapes such as two handled soups, mugs, teapots, and creamers in brown and blue with similar backstamps. However, "Made in England" appears in the cushion part of the mark and this was not done on pre-1900 examples.

Mason's reproductions are also being made in China with the crown mark. Some have paper labels identifying their China origin, but these are easily removed.

Collecting Hints: Don't overlook the Ashworth reissue pieces. They qualify as true antiques.

Bowl

8 3/4" d, "Vista" pattern, pink transfer 19.00

14 1/8" d, printed and painted overlapped panels of fishermen and islands, dk blue ground with flowerheads and gilt scrolls and dots, repeated on int, c1845, (A) 493.00

Bud Vase, 5 3/4" h, bulbous base, slender neck, ftd, "Hobob" pattern, multicolored florals and fence design, "brown MASON'S crown, HOBOB and MADE IN ENGLAND" mark, (A) 44.00

Card Rack, 5 1/8" w, rect, 2 sections, painted and gilt Imari palette with peonies and prunus, lustered buff leaf and scroll molded rims and feet, c1820-25, (A) 500.00

Coffeepot, 9 1/2" h, rect, "Vista" pattern, brown transfer, "brown MASON'S crown,

PATENT IRONSTONE CHINA, drapery, VISTA, ENGLAND" mark, c1890-1900, (A)
. . . . 412.00

Creamer

3 1/4" h, "Vista" pattern, red transfer, "red MASON'S crown, PATENT IRONSTONE CHINA, drapery, VISTA and ENGLAND" mark, c1890-1900, (A) 99.00

4 1/2" h, "Vista" pattern, blue transfer, "blue MASON'S crown, PATENT IRONSTONE CHINA, drapery, VISTA, ENGLAND, GUARANTEED PERMANENT & ACID RESISTING COLOURS" mark, c1925-30, (A). 99.00

Cup and Saucer

"American Marine" pattern, red transfer, "red MASON'S crown, PATENT IRONSTONE CHINA, drapery, ENGLAND, and AMERICAN MARINE" mark, set of 4 (A) 99.00

"Wood Pigeon" pattern, multicolored bird on maroon branch, multicolored flower heads, "maroon MASON'S crown, PATENT IRONSTONE CHINA, drapery, ENGLAND" mark, c1900-20, (A) . 66.00

Dinner Service, Part, ironstone, 2 hex tureens with stands, 13 1/4" d, 3 hex sauce tureens with stands, 7 1/2" d, bowl, 9 7/8" sq, drain, 14" l, 2 platters, 17" l, 2 platters, 14 1/4" l, 4 platters, 12 1/2" l, 4 platters, 10 1/8" l, 3 platters, 8 7/8" l, 19 soup plates, 9 5/8" d, 46 soup plates, 9 1/2" d, 15 plates, 8" d, pink peonies and bamboo from blue rocks in band of gilt spears, borders with clusters of pink, green, blue, and iron red flowering branches, water lily knobs, gilt animal head handles, c1820, (A) 34,500.00

Dish

7" l x 6" w, oval, multicolored center scene of bird and flowers, brown scroll design around center, scattered cobalt leaves, floral design on border, scalloped rim, "brown MASON'S crown, PATENT IRONSTONE CHINA, drapery, ENGLAND" mark, (A) 99.00

10 1/4" H-H, sq, fruit basket in center in colors, lt green twist handles, "red MASON'S crown, PATENT IRONSTONE CHINA, drapery, ENGLAND" mark, c1891-1900, (A). 137.00

10" l x 9" w, pagoda with long windows, 2 roof peaks, figure at door, 2 figures on bridge, lt blue transfer, gilt band around scene, gilt rim, unmkd 137.00

11" H-H x 9" w, "Vista" pattern, blue transfer, "blue MASON'S crown, PATENT IRONSTONE CHINA, drapery, VISTA and ENGLAND" mark, c1890-1900, (A) 110.00

Dish, Cov, 10" l x 8 1/2" w, rect, "Vista" pattern, brown transfers, "brown MASON'S crown, PATENT IRONSTONE, drapery, VISTA, ENGLAND and GUARANTEED PERMANENT & ACID RESISTING COLOURS" mark, c1925-30, (A). 275.00

Egg Cup, 2" h, "Vista" pattern, brown transfer, "brown MASON'S crown, VISTA and EN-

GLAND" mark, c1890-1900, set of 4, (A)
. . . . 88.00

Flower Boat, 10" l x 2 1/2" w, gilt lined front panel oriental basket with florals, reverse with floral panel, marine blue ground with gilt swirls, gilt outlined rim and scalloped base, "brown MASON'S crown, PATENT IRONSTONE CHINA, drapery" mark, (A) . . 990.00

Fruit Bowl, 10 1/2" l x 8" w x 5 3/4" h, with undertray, ftd and scalloped base, reticulated sides and undertray, 2 scalloped handles, "Napoleon's Battles-The Revolt of Cairo," green transfer, "green NAPOLEON BATTLE crown, NEW STONE CHINA C.J.M. & Co." mark, chips, (A) 715.00

Gravy Boat, 5 1/2" l, with undertray, "Persiana" pattern, multicolored florals, cream ground, "red MASON'S crown, PATENT IRONSTONE CHINA, drapery, ENGLAND" marks, c1930, (A). 137.00

Inkstand, 5" h x 6" l, shell shaped compartments, gilt outlined marine blue and orange floral design, gilded handle, green base, "imp MASON'S PATENT IRONSTONE CHINA", c1815, inner wells missing, (A) 1,100.00

Jug

4" h, ironstone, Hydra, paneled, iron red, cobalt and orange oriental floral design, stylized dragon handle 300.00

5 1/4" h, ftd, scalloped base, "American Marine" pattern, flowers on handle, mulberry transfer, c1890-1900, "mulberry MASON'S crown, PATENT IRONSTONE CHINA, drapery, ENGLAND, AMERICAN MARINE" mark, (A). 412.00

5 1/2" h

Oct, "Pheasants" pattern, polychrome, cobalt serpent handle with gilt scales, "black MASON'S crown, PATENT IRONSTONE CHINA, drapery" mark, (A) 660.00

"Persiana" pattern, multicolored florals, cream ground, "red MASON'S crown, PATENT IRONSTONE CHINA, drapery, PERSIANA and ENGLAND" mark, c1930, (A). . . 88.00

6" h, oct, "Red Scale" pattern, multicolored oriental scene, white ground, branch handle, "black MASON'S crown, PATENT IRONSTONE CHINA, drapery" mark, c1813-29, (A) . .550.00

6 1/2" h, oct

"Japan" pattern, multicolored, white ground, serpent handle, "blue MASON'S crown, PATENT IRONSTONE CHINA, drapery" mark, c1818-20, (A) 467.00

"Vista" pattern, brown transfer, "brown MASON'S crown, PATENT IRONSTONE, drapery, VISTA, ENGLAND and GUARANTEED PERMANENT & ACID RESISTING COLOURS" mark, c1925-30, (A). 137.00

7" h, oct, "Vista" pattern, red transfer, "red MASON'S crown, PATENT IRONSTONE CHINA, drapery, VISTA and ENGLAND" mark, c1890-1900, (A) 220.00

Plate, 9" d, cobalt, iron red, green, and gilt, "imp Mason's Patented Ironstone China" mark, $295.

8 5/8" h, oct body, printed Chinese scenes reserved on orange geometric patterned ground, green and yellow sprig handle, c1820, crack, (A) 277.00

Pancake Dish, Cov, 8" d x 5" h, "Dragon around Urn, Floral Branches, Chinese Landscape" patterns, multicolored, fruit knob, "maroon MASON'S crown, PATENT IRONSTONE CHINA, drapery, ENGLAND" mark, c1900-20, (A) 165.00

Pitcher, 4 5/8" h, paneled, "Ascot" pattern, red floral transfer 75.00

Plate

7" d, "Napoleon's Battles-The Alps" pattern, center scene of figure on horse in mountains, floral and scroll design around center, green transfer, "green NAPOLEON BATTLE, crown, NEW STONE CHINA C.J.M. & Co." mark, hairlines, set of 4, (A). 77.00

7 3/4" d, "Oak Vista" pattern, green transfer, "green MASON'S crown, PATENT IRONSTONE CHINA, drapery, OAK VISTA ENGLAND U.S. PAT NO 78017" mark, (A) 22.00

9" d, "Double Landscape" pattern, rect pink outlined green, orange, and gold, oriental landscape overlapping rect white outlined oriental landscape on green ground with gold flowerheads and stems, inner border of lt orange with white flowerheads, outer border of cobalt compartments with multicolored flowerheads, separated by pink panels with red centered white flowerheads, shaped gold rim, c1830, pr 750.00

9 1/2" d, "Long Tailed Bird" pattern, shades of blue, pink accents, c1820, set of 8 . . . . 1,750.00

10" d

"American Marine" pattern

Black transfer with gold and green accents, "black MASON'S

crown, PATENT IRONSTONE CHINA, drapery, ENGLAND, and AMERICAN MARINE" mark, (A) 137.00

Brown transfer, " brown MASON'S crown, PATENT IRONSTONE CHINA, drapery, ENGLAND, and AMERICAN MARINE" mark, (A) 88.00

Floral design with 2 birds in flowers in center, polychrome, "maroon MASON'S crown, PATENT IRONSTONE CHINA, drapery, ENGLAND" mark, (A) 88.00

"India Grasshopper" pattern, polychrome, "blue MASON'S crown, PATENT IRONSTONE CHINA, drapery, REGENCY, ENGLAND" mark, set of 6, (A) 192.00

"Vista" pattern

Mulberry transfer 18.00

Red transfer, "red MASON'S crown, PATENT IRONSTONE CHINA, drapery, VISTA and ENGLAND" mark, set of 6, (A) 165.00

10 1/2" d

"American Marine" pattern, red transfer, "red MASON'S crown, PATENT IRONSTONE CHINA, drapery, ENGLAND, and AMERICAN MARINE" mark, c1890-1900, (A) 99.00

Center scene of monkey holding cat at stove, 2 kittens in basket in bkd, black transfer, cream ground, raised basketweave design around center, scalloped rim, "black MASON'S crown, PATENT IRONSTONE CHINA, drapery, ENGLAND, and imp MASON" marks, c1820, set of 3, (A) 165.00

"Pagoda" pattern, 3 figures on bridge, 2 birds overhead, polychrome with green and brown accents, "brown MASON'S crown, PATENT IRONSTONE CHINA, drapery, ENGLAND" mark, (A) 88.00

"The Politicians" pattern, center design of 2 dogs in suits and hats around table, 2 dogs in bkd, black transfer, cream ground, raised basketweave around design, scalloped edge, titled "THE POLITICIANS," "black MASON'S crown, PATENT IRONSTONE CHINA, drapery, ENGLAND, and imp MASON" marks, set of 3, (A) 165.00

Platter

11" l x 8 1/2" w, oval

"Manchu" pattern, brown and yellow shades, "brown MASON'S crown, PATENT IRONSTONE, drapery, MANCHU, ENGLAND and PERMANENT DETERGENT PROOF, drapery, mark, c1925-30, (A) 77.00

"Prunus Bush" pattern, multicolored with yellow accents, "brown MASON'S crown, PATENT IRONSTONE CHINA, drapery" mark, (A). . 247.00

13" l x 10" w, rect, "American Marine" pattern, mulberry transfer, "mulberry MASON'S crown, PATENT IRONSTONE CHINA, drapery, ENGLAND, and AMERICAN MARINE" mark, (A) 330.00

13 1/2" l x 11" w, oval, "Vista" pattern, mulberry transfer, "mulberry MASON'S crown, PATENT IRONSTONE CHINA, drapery, VISTA and ENGLAND" mark, c1890-1900, (A) 110.00

15 1/2" l x 12 1/2" w, oval, "Vista" pattern, red transfer, "MASON'S crown, PATENT IRONSTONE, drapery, VISTA and ENGLAND" mark, (A) 165.00

17 3/8" l, ironstone, "Two Pheasants" pattern, iron red, cobalt, and orange-pink, c1840, pr. 1,500.00

17 1/2" l, "Vista" pattern, blue transfer, c1900 .... 295.00

18" l x 15" w, rect, "American Marine" pattern, red transfer, "red MASON'S crown, PATENT IRONSTONE CHINA, drapery, ENGLAND, and AMERICAN MARINE" mark, (A) 495.00

18 1/4" l, "Napoleon's Battles-The Battle of Marengo," purple transfer, c1829-45 .... 425.00

20 1/2" l, 16 1/2" w, oct, "Pheasant" pattern, blue transfer, "blue MASON'S crown, PATENT IRONSTONE CHINA, drapery, and imp MASON'S PATENT IRONSTONE CHINA" mark, c1818-20, (A) 1,210.00

21" l, well and tree, "Peonies and Bird" pattern, blue transfer 895.00

Serving Bowl, 10" d, "Vista" pattern, red transfer, "red MASON'S crown, PATENT IRONSTONE CHINA, drapery, VISTA, ENGLAND and GUARANTEED PERMANENT & ACID RESISTING COLOURS" mark, (A) 137.00

Soup Plate, 9" d, "American Marine" pattern, blue transfer, "MASON'S crown, PATENT IRONSTONE CHINA, drapery, AMERICAN MARINE" mark, (A). 88.00

Sugar Bowl, Cov, 5" h, sq shape, "Black Chinese" pattern, pink flowers, aqua and lt green leaves and tan branches, black ground, dog head handles, bird knob, "black MASON'S crown, PATENT IRONSTONE CHINA, drapery, ENGLAND, and BLACK CHINESE" mark, c1890, (A). 137.00

Teapot

4 1/4" h, squat shape, blue and iron red flowers and leaves with blue vase, gilt accents, blue handle with gilded scale pattern, floral design with green leaves on spout, blue and gilt knob, "blue MASON'S crown, PATENT IRONSTONE CHINA, drapery" mark, (A). 385.00

6 3/4" h, rect paneled shape, "Vista" pattern, blue transfer, "MASON'S PATENT IRONSTONE CHINA, PERMANENT & ACID RESISTING COLOURS" mark 165.00

7" h, "Vista" pattern, red transfer, "red MASON'S crown, PATENT IRONSTONE, VISTA, ENGLAND, and GUARANTEED

Potpourri Jar, 5 1/4" h, 6 3/4" d, cobalt, orange, and gilt Imari pattern, "imp Ironstone China Patent" mark, pr, (A) $632.

PERMANENT & ACID RESISTING COLOURS" mark, (A) 192.00

Tureen

7" l x 4 1/2" w x 3" h, "Pheasant" pattern, blue transfers, dog head handles, scroll knob, "blue MASON'S crown, PATENT IRONSTONE CHINA, drapery, and imp MASON'S PATENT IRONSTONE CHINA" marks, c1818-20, hairline, (A) 220.00

7 1/2" l, oct, Chinese export style painted loose bouquets of flowers, blue handles and knob, c1820, (A) 285.00

Vase, 8" h

Cylinder shape, "Applique" pattern, multicolored, "blue MASON'S crown, IRONSTONE MADE IN ENGLAND, drapery and APPLIQUE" mark, (A) 137.00

Flared rim, "Brown Velvet" pattern, multicolored florals, "brown MASON'S crown, PATENT IRONSTONE, drapery, BROWN VELVET" mark, (A). 88.00

Vegetable Dish, Cov, 10 3/8" sq, "Pheasant and Peony" pattern, blue transfer, pr 1,750.00

Water Pitcher, "Bible" pattern, orange, blue, and mauve flowers, green striped handle and spout 125.00

MASSIER

Golfe-Juan, France 1881-1917

C. M
Golfe-Juan:
(A.M)
1845-1917

History: Clement Massier, who started work in 1881 in Golfe-Juan, France, was an artist and potter who produced earthenware with metallic luster decoration. He used plant motifs and other nature themes on shapes that were Art Nouveau in style.

Massier's wares usually are marked with an incised "Massier" or have his initial or the location of the pottery.

Museums: Musee d'Art Moderne de la Ville de Paris, Paris, France; Musee d'Orsay, Paris, France; Musee Municipal de Ceramique et d'Art Moderne, Vallauris, France.

Bowl, 8 1/2" d

Irid blue, green, and red flower and stem design, "Clement Massier" mark, (A) 207.00

Tapered shape, int with irid red and blue geometric and spot designs, (A) .185.00

Charger

12 1/2" d, lustered gold tall pines and lakeshore, burgundy glaze, "CLEMENT MASSIER/GOLFE/JUAN" mark 1,600.00

13" d, Mediterranean bay scene with pine trees, lustered gold and burgundy glazes, "imp CLEMENT MASSIER, GOLFE JUAN" mark, (A) 1,300.00

16" d, irid gold, scarlet, emerald green, and blue windswept tree on mountainous shore, "painted Clement Massier, Golfe-Juan" mark, (A) 3,250.00

Ewer, 15 3/8" h, tapered cylinder shape, figural female handle with flowing hair, streaked claret red and green glazes, Clement Massier, (A) 352.00

Plaque, 15 3/8" d, relief molded profile bust of Art Nouveau woman with headdress, poppies on border, lustered green glaze, "Delphin Massier & Cie. Vallauris" mark, (A) . .1,158.00

Vase

2" h, ovoid, flared lip, oil spot irid purple and green, sgd "C.M.," (A) 230.00

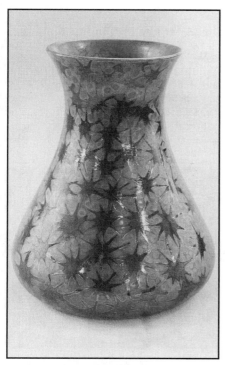

Vase, 6" h, starburst design, irid purple, red, gold, and blue, "Clement Massier, Golfe Juan A.M." mark, (A) $502.

Vase, 15" h, daisies and leaves, irid gold, blue, and red, "D.M. Vallauris A.M." mark, repairs, (A) $605.

4" h, tapered shape, 4 ribbon handles , irid green and gold dandelions, magenta ground, "incised Clement Massier, Golfe Juan" mark 400.00

4 3/8" h, cylinder shape with squared rim, stylized foliate motifs, irid maroon glaze, Clement Massier, (A) 200.00

5 1/2" h, ovoid shape, irid red, maroon, green, blue, and gold abstract flowers, "C.M." mark, (A) 460.00

6" h

Center band of brown, green, and yellow exotic fish on cream ground, Greek key borders, "Jerome Massier et Fils" mark. 155.00

Sq form neck on flared body, irid gold, blue, and green drip, Clement Massier, (A) 460.00

Swollen cylinder shape, 4 applied 3 prong handles, irid blue, orange, and green stylized floral designs 633.00

7 1/2" h

Cylinder shape, flared base, 2 sq handles on base, gold snails and marine plants, burgundy ground, "painted Clement Massier, Golfe-Juan" mark, (A) 800.00

Flared with rolled rim, green and pink enameled flowers and stems, blue lustered ground, (A) 300.00

9" h

Bulbous body, flared ft, base, and rim, 10 circ openings, irid blue and red cloisonne type stylized flowers, gold-brown ground, "painted C.M. 1888, Golfe Juan, (A.M.)" mark 1,250.00

Tapered cylinder shape, squared cylinder neck, irid olive and pewter shaded fruit, rose-violet and blue-green irid ground, sgd "M. Clement Massier, Golf Juan, .M.," (A) 1,380.00

10" h, swollen cylinder shape, maroon, red, green, and blue irid landscape design, "D.M." mark, (A) 345.00

12" h, wide base, globular cylinder neck, applied female form on neck, irid gold, green, blue, and red surface with butterflies, "Delphin Massier Vallauris A.M." mark, (A) 1,150.00

12 7/8" h, pink and orange applied flower and green leaves, streaked black to gray shaded ground, chips, "Massier, Golf Juan France" mark. 1,200.00

14 1/4" h, bottle shape, flared ft, raised gilt cartouche of woman in shear dress and long brown hair on cream ground, green and blue irid body 2,000.00

c 1890   c 1891

MEAKIN

Hanley, England
Alfred Meakin
1873 to Present

History: Alfred Meakin was a Staffordshire potter who made a wide range of earthenware and ironstone china at his Royal Albert Works in Tunstall starting in 1873. Beginning in 1877 the firm traded as Alfred Meakin Ltd. a name it still uses today.

The earthenware was marked with a crown and "ALFRED MEAKIN/ENGLAND."

J. & G. Meakin
1845 to Present

History: James Meakin established a pottery in Longton in 1845 and transferred it to Hanley in 1848. When he retired in 1852, James and George, his sons, succeeded him. The firm traded as J.& G. Meakin.

The Meakins built the Eagle Works in 1859 and enlarged it in 1868. Later there were branches of the factory at Cobridge and Burslem. Both earthenware and granite ware were produced. The wares were decorated in the style of French porcelain and made for export to the American market.

Meakin also produced romantic Staffordshire and flow blue decorated pieces.

J.& G. Meakin joined the Wedgwood Group in 1970.

Reference: Bernard Hollowood, *The Story of J. and G. Meakin,* Bemrose Publicity Co. Ltd. 1951.

Berry Bowl, 5 3/8" d, "Romantic England-Willy Lott's Cottage" pattern, red transfer, J. & G. Meakin. 7.00

Butter Dish, Cov, 4 1/2" h x 7 1/2" d

Border band of black palm trees, khaki colored links, white and blue flowers and green leaves, J. & G. Meakin 22.00

"Severn" pattern, blue-black floral transfers, gold accented raised molded design, Alfred Meakin 45.00

Cereal Bowl, 6 5/8" d, "Tudor Rose" pattern, red transfer, J. & G. Meakin 18.00

Creamer, 5 1/4" h, "Moss Rose" pattern, rose with green and brown leaves, "Alfred Meakin, Royal Ironstone China" mark. 36.00

Creamer and Cov Sugar Bowl, creamer, 5 3/4" h, sugar bowl, 7" h, "Essex" pattern, florals and ribbons, brown transfers, J. & G. Meakin 130.00

Cup and Saucer

"Fair Winds" pattern, brown transfer, Alfred Meakin 8.00

Multicolored transfer of village scene, J. & G. Meakin 10.00

"Spring Fields" pattern. 10.00

"Vanity Fair" pattern, sheet pattern of sm red flowerheads, J. & G. Meakin . . 8.00

Dinner Service, 4 plates, 10" d, 4 plates, 7" d, 4 soup bowls, 6 1/2" d, 4 cups and saucers, "Lucerne" pattern, green florals and sprigs, J. & G. Meakin. 100.00

Gravy Boat, 8" l, ironstone, 2 pink roses, brown and green ferns and leaves on sides, gilt lined rim, Alfred Meakin. 20.00

Pickle Dish, 8 1/4" l, sm blue flowerheads, green ferns, gilt spotted rim, J. & G. Meakin 10.00

Sugar Bowl, 7" h, ironstone, "Moss Rose" pattern, pink flowers, blue and green leaves, gold trim, Alfred Meakin, (A) $28.

Plate

6 3/4" d, "Dresden Hopfen" pattern, green hops and gold trim, Alfred Meakin 3.00

9" d, red and blue Union Jack in center, pink banner with "THERE'LL ALWAYS BE AN ENGLAND," gilt trim, J. & G. Meakin 16.00

9 1/2" d, oct, "Riverdale" pattern, river, windmill, cottage, blue transfer, Alfred Meakin 20.00

Platter, 14" l, oval, "Cambridge" pattern, brown-red florals, swags, and curlicues, Alfred Meakin 24.00

Soup Bowl, 6 3/4" d

"Chatsworth" pattern, multicolored pattern, J. & G. Meakin 15.00

"Home Pastures" pattern 14.00

Soup Plate

8 7/8" d, rim band of pink and white roses on cream and brown ground, green rope twist outline, Alfred Meakin 10.00

9" d, "Eulalie" pattern, brown transfer, J. & G. Meakin 8.00

Sugar Bowl, Cov, 6 3/4" h, "Moss Rose" pattern, "Alfred Meakin Royal Ironstone China" mark 48.00

Vegetable Bowl

9 3/8" l, oval, gold outlined cobalt leaves, green stems, mauve, orange, yellow flowerheads in inner purple band, border of gold outlined cobalt leaves, gold outlined molded handles 46.00

9 1/2" l, "Medway" pattern, blue floral transfer, Alfred Meakin 55.00

Vegetable Bowl, Cov, 10" H-H

"Garland" pattern, blue transfers, Alfred Meakin 325.00

Platter, 12 1/2" l, "Gleneagle" pattern, cobalt, orange, mauve, green, and gold, Alfred Meakin, $62.

Lobed body, scattered sm blue bachelor buttons, gold molded curlicues, J. & G. Meakin 50.00

MEIGH

Staffordshire, England c1805-1834 Job Meigh

1835-1901 Charles Meigh

History: Job Meigh operated the Old Hall Pottery at Hanley in the Staffordshire District beginning around 1805 and ending in 1834. Charles, his son, joined the firm. Charles operated the pottery under his own name between 1835 and 1849. The factory produced earthenwares and stonewares.

Charles Meigh was famous for his firm's white stoneware jugs with relief decorations. The decorations were part of the mold from which the pieces were cast. During the 1840s, jugs with gothic details were made. The "Minister" jug of 1842 was the most famous. Classical jugs featuring designs of sporting events and drinking scenes were produced during the 1840s and '50s.

For two years, 1850 to1851, the firm operated as Charles Meigh, Son & Parkhurst. For the next eleven years, 1851 to 1861, the company was known as Charles Meigh & Sons.

Museum: Potsdam Pubic Museum, Potsdam, NY.

Dinner Service, Part, ironstone, 11 soup plates, 9 1/4" d, 9 soup plates, 10 1/4" d, 25 plates, 10 3/4" d, 7 plates, 9 1/4" d, 8 oval platters, 10 3/4" l to 20 3/4" l, cov soup tureen with undertray, cov sauce tureen with undertray, 2 cov vegetable dishes, ftd fruit compote, 2 oval vegetable bowls, 10 1/4" l, 6 shaped serving dishes, 10" l to 11" l, gravy boat, 7" l, 2 shaped dishes, 5 /4" l, 4 coffee cups, oriental style urn

Platter, 15" l, 11 3/4" w, ironstone, cobalt, red, and gold Imari pattern, "Royal Arms and Stone China" mark, (A) $110.

with florals on table, puce transfer with orange and blue enamels, Hicks and Meigh, c1830, restorations, (A)................4,025.00

Plate

9 1/4" d

Blue pinwheel pattern in center, pinwheel waves around inner rim, emb green flowers and scrolls border, scalloped and swirled dk yellow rim, c1851 .... 150.00

"Susa" pattern, med blue transfer, "C.M.S. & P." mark 35.00

10" d, "Oriental Shells" pattern, blue and white, Hicks, Meigh, and Johnson, hairlines 125.00

11" d, ironstone, oriental style bird and insect design with floral bunches on border, shaped rim, Imari colors, "crowned Stone China" mark, c1820-30 . . 155.00

Platter

20" l, bridge and flowers design, blue transfer, gadrooned scalloped rim, Hicks and Meigh 995.00

21" l, well and tree, "Zoological Sketches-Elephant," blue and white, Job Meigh.................1,400.00

Soup Bowl, 9 1/2" d, Imari, iron red peony in center, cobalt leaves and branches from tan ground, gilt initials and iron outlined panels with iron red, gilt, and cobalt flowers on border, Hicks and Meigh, c1825 .... 330.00

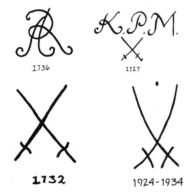

Royal Dresden China
1938 - Present

1736   1727

1732   1924-1934

MEISSEN

Saxony, Germany
1710 to Present

History: The history of Meissen porcelain design falls into distinct periods which were determined by the director of the company and the kings who appointed and controlled them. Located in the Saxon district of Germany, the Meissen factory, or Royal Saxon Porcelain Manufactory, was founded in 1710 by Frederich August I and first directed by Johann Boettger. It was Boettger who developed the first truly white porcelain in Europe. His white porcelain

was exceptionally plastic and could be molded into a variety of applied decorations. Silver shapes were most popular.

After 1720, Meissen porcelain was decorated with fine enamel painting, even surpassing some of the Chinese porcelains. During this period, most of the Meissen tablewares were of relatively simple form which provided ample backgrounds for the beautiful painted decorations. The original crossed swords factory mark was adopted in 1723.

When Johann Horoldt was manager during the last ten years of the reign of Augustus the Strong (1694-1733), the porcelain was a brilliant pure white. Horoldt did pseudo-Chinese scenes in scrollwork of red, gold, and luster plus other adaptations of Chinese, Japanese, and other oriental wares and motifs. Johann Kirchner (1727-1733) made life-size figures of animals and birds for Augustus the Strong's Japanese Palace.

When Joachim Kaendler, a modeler, came to Meissen in 1731, he began producing figures, especially the Crinoline figures and groups. About 1738 Kaendler created numerous miniature figures used for lavish banquet decorations for the court of Dresden. He designed the world famous swan set for Count von Bruhl. Kaendler also introduced tablewares with low relief borders in the style of silver.

The rococo influence occurred after 1740. The famous onion pattern appeared about that time. The factory was severely damaged during the Seven Years' War (1756-1763) and was occupied by the victorious Prussians.

Following a major reorganization, the master modeler Michel Victor Acier came to Meissen in 1764 and became the dominating influence. He moved the factory into the neo-classical period with emphasis on mythological figures. Pictorial decoration was copied from Sevres. Under the directorship of Marcolini (1774-1813), the style shifted to that of Louis XVI. The Marcolini Period ended with the cessation of the Napoleonic Wars in 1814.

The factory experienced a decline in production under the management of Von Oppel from 1814 to 1833. The wares during this phase often imitated other successful European concerns.

The period from 1833 to 1870 is called the "Kuhn Period," after a director of the factory. The company's fortunes improved, both technically and economically. A revival of production of the great pieces from one hundred years earlier was carried out. Many figures were copied in the rococo style, which was the popular taste of the times. Sales of the china wares continued to increase.

The "New Period" at Meissen started in 1870 when Kuhn died and Raithel became director. Exports of china to America increased during this time. Utilitarian wares in blue underglaze grew in popularity. Improvements continued to be made in the china production process.

From 1895 to 1901, the factory was managed by Brunnemann. A conflict developed between the supporters of old and new ideas of china manufactory. Between 1901 and 1910 there was increasing success artistically and financially, culminating with the two hundredth anniversary Jubilee year of 1910. Many reforms were carried out. New buildings were constructed for furnaces and studios. A new drawing school was established at the factory.

Following World War II, the factory was reorganized. Today it operates as the State's Porcelain Manufactory. New models are made as close as possible to the old shapes. Ornamentation also tends to follow the old models. In addition, some new forms are made. The Meissen factory also manufactures various commemorative wares for coronations, Christmas plaques, and Easter plaques.

References: Dr. K. Berling, Editor, *Meissen China, An Illustrated History*, Dover, 1972; Yvonne Hackenbroch, *Meissen & Other Continental Porcelain Faience & Enamel in the Irwin Untermeyer Collection*, Harvard University Press, 1956; W.B. Honey, *Dresden China: An Introduction to the Study of Meissen Porcelain*, Dresden House, 1946; Ingelore Menzhausen, *Early Meissen Porcelain in Dresden*, Thames & Hudson, 1990; Robert E. Rontgen, *The Book of Meissen*, Schiffer Publishing Co.1984; Otto Walcha, *Meissen Porcelain*, G.P. Putman's Sons, 1981.

Museums: Art Institute of Chicago, Chicago, IL; Cincinnati Art Museum, Cincinnati, OH; Cummer Gallery of Art, Jacksonville, FL; Dixon Gallery, Memphis, TN; Dresden Museum of Art & History, Dresden, Germany; Gardiner Museum of Ceramic Art, Toronto, Canada; Meissen Porcelain Museum, Meissen, Germany; Metropolitan Museum of Art, New York, NY; National Museum of American History, Smithsonian Institution, Washington, DC; Robertson Center for the Arts and Sciences, Binghamton, NY; Schlossmuseum, Berlin, Germany; Stadtmuseum, Cologne, Germany; Wadsworth Atheneum, Hartford, CT; Woodmere Art Museum, Philadelphia, PA; Zwinger Museum, Dresden, Germany.

Collecting Hints: Collectors must distinguish between the productions from the greatest period 1710-1756 and later works.

During the 19th century, Meissen reproduced some of its 18th century molds in addition to making new ones.

Numerous Dresden factories also reproduced Meissen wares and figures, some copying the original marks. One should be aware of Helena Wolfsohn's decorating shop in Dresden who used the Augustus Rex (AR) monogram which was not used by Meissen after 1730, but was applied by Wolfsohn to reproductions of much later works. About 1833, the Royal Porcelain Manufactory in Meissen obtained a court decision against Wolfsohn ordering her to cease and desist using the AR mark.

Helena Wolfsohn operated the decorating shop, but probably did not produce her own porcelain. However, most of her AR pieces have the AR mark underglaze. Since this mark was applied before glazing and final firing, Helena Wolfsohn must have ordered the white porcelain blanks with the AR mark from some porcelain factory. The manufacturer is not known. Wolfsohn sold many thousands of pieces with the "AR" mark.

The Meissen factory itself used the "AR" mark in 1873 as a trademark and still uses it on special pieces. Therefore, every "AR" marked piece must be studied very carefully.

Beaker and Saucer, 5" h, 2 handles, upper section and saucer with painted chinoiserie scene in gilt, iron red, and purple laub-und-bandelwerk cartouche, lower section molded with gilt or blue vert gadroons, int rim with gilt pendant scrolls, "blue X'd swords" mark, c1725, (A) 4,830.00

Bowl, 14" l x 10" w, blanc de chine, apricot outlined raised grape vines, "blue X'd swords" mark 450.00

Box, Cov

4 1/4" d, blanc de chine overall molded flowering prunus, modern gilt mts with paw feet, c1760, (A) 483.00

4 3/8" w, flower and insect encrusted, polychrome, twisted branch handles, "blue X'd swords" mark, late 19th C, restored, (A) 770.00

Charger, 11" d, HP cherub resting chin in hand, white ground, raised gold relief flowers on border, scalloped rim, "blue X'd swords" mark 250.00

Coffee Can and Saucer, bouquet of red, purple, and green flowers, scattered sprigs on saucer rim, early 19th C 325.00

Coffee Cup and Saucer, painted young girl in garden with fountain, flanked by trellis joined at top with shuttle cock, hats, musical instruments, and racket, green ear handle, "blue X'd swords, imp 17 and 14" marks, (A) 575.00

Coffeepot, 10 1/2" h, painted pink rose design, white ground, rosebud finial. . . . 500.00

Compote

6 1/2" h x 9" d, gilt and HP floral sprays, reticulated border, "blue X'd swords" mark, c1895. . . . . 1,050.00

8 1/2" h, "Indian Purple," reticulated border 595.00

Cream Jug

3 1/2" h, oviform, green encrusted stems with multicolored flowers, 3 sm feet, "blue X'd swords" mark, late 19th C, (A) 465.00

4 1/2" h, pear shape, puce and turquoise beak spout, turquoise loop handle, painted vignettes of gallant serenading companion under tree, "blue X'd swords" mark, c1760, (A) 552.00

Cream Pot, Cov, 5 1/4" h, quatrefoil cartouche of multicolored enameled seated period lovers in landscape, gilt ground, white ozier-molded body, scroll handle, gold trimmed pineapple knob and 3 paw feet, c1750, repair to ft, (A) 1,840.00

Cup and Saucer

Blue and white fishing scene 110.00

Green leaf design on rim 35.00

Loop handle, multicolored enameled cup with gilt surround of Turk with barrels at shore, saucer with oriental figures in landscape in gilt surround, scattered florals, "blue X'd swords, puce 69, imp 17" marks, 1745, (A) 2,000.00

Multicolored topographical view of Konigsbruch on cup, topographical view of Camenz on saucer, gilt cartouches, gilt strapwork borders, hausmalerei decorated, "canceled blue X'd swords" mark, (A) 340.00

Painted and encrusted forget-me-nots, "blue X'd swords" mark, late 19th C, (A) 125.00

Puce painted fruit and flowers, "blue X'd swords" mark, (A) 400.00

Multicolored enameled Chinese figures holding trays, waving incense, and kneeling on cup, Chinese woman holding infant, children at side with shrubs on gold scrolling bracket on saucer, ozier-molded borders, scattered Indian flowers, "blue X'd swords" marks, c1750, chips, (A) 1,725.00

Cup and Saucer, Cov, trembleuse saucer, multicolored painted flowers reserved on gilt ground, "blue X'd swords" mark, c1760, (A) 633.00

Dessert Dish, 8" sq, painted red rose and foliage in center, sm bouquets at corners, c1770 . . . . 225.00

Dish, 9 5/8" d, 4 gilt lined quatrefoils of puce painted battle scenes on border, ozier-molded ground, gilt shaped rim, "blue X'd swords and imp 24" mark, c1745 . . . . 1,800.00

Ecuelle, Cov, 5 1/2" d, painted bowl with scene of woman seated at table spinning wool, child at side and gentleman, reverse painted with lady seated in garden with tennis racket, ball, and shuttlecock, boy at side, cov painted with couple in garden with atten-

Figure, 10 1/4" h, 7 1/2" w, man in blue coat, brown pants, woman in magenta lined yellow dress with rust, blue, and green flowers, multicolored raised floral on base, "blue X'd swords" mark, c1920, $4,500.

dants, entwined branch handle and floral terminals, pink rose knob, "blue X'd swords" mark, c1750, (A) 2,300.00

Figure

2 1/4" h x 6 1/4" l, figural slipper, underglaze blue and overglaze iron red and gilt floral decor, white ground, gilt rim, "blue X'd swords" mark, pr . . 1,500.00

4" h, yellow canary with head turned on high base, "blue X'd swords" mark, (A) 200.00

4" l, crouching cat, black and white, c1740, (A) 9,200.00

4 3/8" h, swan with wings spread, white with black and red accents on head, black feet on brown base, "blue X'd swords, imp 93" mark, late 19th C, (A) 540.00

4 1/2" h, seated young boy in red jacket, black hat, blue striped floral trousers, holding grapes and rod, seated on gilt accented trunk base, "blue X'd swords" mark, c1910 . . . . 550.00

4 3/4" h, Autumn modeled as seated boy holding grapes, hat with grapes, rockwork base, white glaze, "blue X'd swords and dot" mark, c1765, (A) 748.00

5" h, woman in yellow outer gown, flowered skirt, seated before harpsichord, gilt trim, "blue X'd swords" mark, (A) 403.00

5 1/8" h, peasant woodcutter, man with ft on wood, ax in hands, black hat, white waistcoat with gold buttons, iron red breeches, black shoes with yellow rosettes, "blue X'd swords, puce triangle" marks, Kaendler, c1745, repair to ax, (A) 1,840.00

5 3/4" h, seated Dalmatian, black and white spots, mound base with applied

flowers and foliage, c1750, "blue X'd swords" mark, repairs, (A)....3,220.00

6 1/2" h

Shepherd leaning on tree stump playing recorder, yellow hat and brown edged coat, turquoise breeches, iron red rosette on knees and hat, black spotted hound at feet, raised mound base with applied flowers and foliage, "blue X'd swords" mark, Kaendler and Reinicke, c1747, restored, (A) 1,265.00

Woman in purple bodice, green stripes and floral skirt, yellow collar, white apron, tray on top of head, holding clam shell, gold trimmed base, "blue X'd swords" mark........450.00

6 5/8" h, dancing peasant, rt foot out, arms open, white chemise with inverted iron red triangle, puce jacket, white mound base with rock support and applied flowerheads, "blue X'd swords" mark, Kaendler, c1740, repairs, (A)......3,220.00

6 3/4" h, old woman selling fruit, stooped position, white kerchief, white blouse, green bodice, puce skirt, white apron, black belt, apple in hand, basket on arm, raised mound base with applied flowers and foliage, c1747, chips, (A) 1,695.00

7 1/2" h, young man and woman gathering eggs from under tree, white glaze, "blue X'd swords" mark, late 19th C, (A) 275.00

8 1/2" h, seated red squirrel, nut in teeth, black collar, chain on neck, oval molded green and yellow base with applied flowers and foliage, "blue X'd swords and black 9" mark, Kaendler, c1750, repairs, (A) 6,325.00

8 5/8" h, dancer holding apron in hands, blue trimmed hat, ruffled collar, blue trimmed dress, blue shoes, pierced gilt accented rocaille base, "blue X'd swords and dot" mark, c1765, restored, (A) 976.00

9 1/5" h, cockatoo perched on tree stump, white body, orange-red and yellow feather accents, "blue X'd swords and incised 57a" mark, (A).......493.00

10" h x 7 1/2" w, "Queen of Ocean," queen seated on throne, med blue gown, red drape on base, 2 cherub attendants presenting treasures, "blue X'd swords" mark, (A) 3,220.00

10" w, crinoline group, seated court lady in flowered yellow skirt, pug in lap, holding chocolate cup, kneeling gallant kissing her hand, red coated Blackamoor at side holding biscuit tray, flower encrusted mound base, "blue X'd swords" mark, (A) 3,335.00

14 1/2" h, "The Bliss of Sleep," gray winged standing Cupid wearing blue drape, leaning on brown lion skin strewn column, overturned flaming torch on base, lizard on column, hanging garland of roses, "blue X'd swords,

incised J13, imp 141, C.G. Juechtzer" mark, (A) 2,875.00

Perfume Tray, 15 1/4" w, oval, white ground, molded crenelated band and applied with ribbon-tied oak garlands entwined at handles, fluted tapered sq columnar feet, "blue X'd swords and star" mark, Marcolini, c1780, (A) 2,300.00

Plate

8" d, pink floral pattern, white ground, gold scalloped rim, "blue X'd swords" mark, late 19th C, set of 5, (A) 150.00

8 1/4" d, "Indian Purple," c1880, set of 10 ....850.00

8 1/2" d, HP florals, emb green border with gold scrolling, "blue X'd swords" mark, set of 6 .... 450.00

8 3/4" d, painted center of boys pulling in fish nets from boats, forts and rocks in bkd, border with entwined green ribbon with 3 bouquets of flowers, gilt circlet rim, "blue X'd swords" mark, pr, ...978.00

9" d, center multicolored floral bouquet with ladybugs and butterflies, scattered floral bunches, gilt patterned shaped lobed rim, set of 4 .... 500.00

9 1/16" d, painted multicolored center of 2 birds in branches on brown mound, molded woven border with painted insects in 4 panels, "blue X'd swords" mark, late 19th C, set of 12, (A) 6,900.00

9 1/2" d

Enamel painted exotic birds in center, scattered insects on border, gold draped shaped rim, set of 11, (A) 1,150.00

Painted scattered sprigs of Indian flowers, brown line rim, "blue X'd swords" mark, c1730, rim cracks, (A) 146.00

9 5/8" d, painted bouquets and scattered flowers, border of molded band of forget-me-nots, brown rim, "blue X'd swords and imp 22" marks, (A) ..320.00

Platter, 13 1/2" l, 9 3/4" w, lg mauve and yellow flowers, yellow, blue, and red pansies and garden flowers, multicolored insects, gilt lined rim, "blue X'd swords" mark, $550.

9 3/4" d, painted still life of fruit, open work pierced border, gilt rim, late 19th C, pr, (A) 690.00

11 3/4" d, HP orange tulip, magenta chrysanthemum, yellow and orange daisies, pink zinnia, blue and magenta floral sprays, green and turquoise leaves, gilt leaf border, scalloped gilt rim, c1860-80 .... 985.00

Platter, 20" l, rect, blue painted blue flower bouquet, scattered sm sprays, and insects, 19th C, (A) 355.00

Potpourri Vase

10 1/2" h, flattened ovoid shape, neo-classical style, oval cartouche painted with European harbor scene suspended from molded gilt floral swags and band of raised pink roses, pink and mint green molded acanthus leaves on base, squared handles, ftd tripod base draped with pink swag, pierced cov with putto finial, "blue X'd swords, imp 67, incised F.48, gilt 16" marks, late 19th C, pr, (A) 10,350.00

25" h, painted vignette of seated young gallant with guitar and kneeling woman in forest, applied red, yellow, blue, and orange flowerheads on body, gilt outlined molded leaves, applied putti with basket of flowers on ft, applied putti with holding flowers on ft, pierced cov with applied green flowerhead knob, sq base with curved feet and applied flowerheads 11,500.00

Sauceboat, 8 1/2" l, dbl lip, branch handles with flower terminals, 4 branch feet, painted scattered flowers, "blue X'd swords and star" mark, Marcolini, c1775, (A)........ 690.00

Sauce Tureen, Cov, 6 1/2" l, oval, fluted body, painted multicolored branches of fruit and flowers, blue bouquets in molded gilt rocaille cartouches, blue flower knob, "blue X'd swords and dot" mark, c1765, (A) ... 633.00

Snuff Box, 3" l, rect, molded and painted scattered sprigs, int of cov painted with still life of birds pecking fruit on table and basket, gilt metal mts, c1750, (A) 5,175.00

Soup Plate, 8 7/8" d, multicolored enameled scattered German flower bunches, ozier-molded border, gilt lined rim, "blue X'd swords & imp 16" mark, c1755, pr, (A) 552.00

Stand, 9 5/8" d, 4 quatrefoil panels of puce painted equestrian battle scenes, ozier-molded ground, gilt dentil rim, "blue X'd swords" mark, c1745, (A) 1,840.00

Sugar Bowl, Cov, 4 1/4" d, puce painted putti on grass mounds, green floral swags and diapering with scrolls, gilt rims, rosebud knob, repairs, "blue X'd swords" mark, c1760, (A) 2,185.00

Sugar Box, 4 3/8" l, oval, chinoiserie scenes of Chinese figures in gardens in shaped gilt cartouches, iron red and puce scrolling foliage, stepped domed cov with gilt dbl button knob, "blue X'd swords" mark, 1730, crack, (A) 4,370.00

Sweetmeat Dish, 5 1/2" d, shell shape, HP vines and pears design in center, c1774-1814, set of 6 . . . . .450.00

Tazza, 12 1/2" d, "Indian Purple" pattern, "blue X'd swords" mark. 550.00

Tea and Coffee Service, Part, coffee pot, 9 1/2" h, cov hot milk jug, 5 1/2" h, teapot, 4" h, cov sugar bowl, 3 3/4" h, waste bowl, 6 3/4" d, spoon tray, 6 3/4" w, 5 coffee cups, 10 tea-cups, 15 saucers, puce painted hunters and travelers in stables, rivers, and camping in gilt chain surrounds with puce and green trailing roses and blue ribbon-tied ivy, puce and gilt scattered sprigs on sides, gilt dentil rims, floral knobs, "blue X'd swords and star" marks, c1770, (A) 12,075.00

Teabowl and Saucer

Kakiemon palette, bowl with iron red purple and green flowering shrubs, int with moon in iron red circle, flying phoenix and stylized shrubs on saucer, brown line rims, "blue X'd swords" mark, c1735, (A) 805.00

Three purple flowers and green leaves, early 19th C, chip 325.00

Teapot

4 1/2" h, polychrome rose and floral bouquet, scattered sprays, gold accents, flower knob, "blue X'd swords" mark, hairlines and chip, (A) 100.00

5" h, globular shape, gilt accented dragon spout and wishbone handle, painted vignettes of peasants in village landscapes, border and shoulder with green trellis diaper edge with purple rocaille scrolls suspending flower sprigs, silver mts, "blue X'd swords" mark, c1760, (A) 2,990.00

5 1/8" h, Bottger, squat baluster shape, loop handle, curved spout with molded mask, multicolored enameled chinoiserie scene of Chinese figures holding parasol and fan, fenced garden with flowering shrubs, insects, and bird, gold knob, "black X'd swords" mark, c1723, restored cov rim, (A) . .4,255.00

9 5/8" h, quatrefoil gilt scrolling cartouches of multicolored oriental scenes, pale blue ground, figural flower knob and leaf terminal 1,450.00

Tea Service, Part, teapot, 4 1/2" h, gilt figural bird's head spout, gilt pineapple knob, hot water jug, cov, 6 1/2" h, gilt spout and pineapple knob, sugar bowl, cov, 4 1/4" d, branch knob with applied flowerheads, tea caddy, 5 3/8" h, gilt pineapple knob, 5 cups and saucers, puce painted scenes of period people in landscape settings, ozier-molded borders, gilt rims, "blue X'd swords" marks, c1740, chips and repairs, (A) 7,675.00

Tete-a-Tete, teapot, creamer, cov sugar bowl, 2 cups and saucers, 6 sm feet on cups, tray, 16" l, lobed bodies, encrusted polychrome flowers and leaves, white ground, "blue X'd swords" marks, (A) 3,300.00

Toothpick Holder, 2 1/2" h, "Red Dragon" design 250.00

Tureen, 11 3/4" H-H, 9 1/4" h, painted polychrome bouquets, gilt accented molded handles with asparagus sprigs, gilt rims, polychrome figural knob, "blue X'd swords" mark, c1755, (A) $1,800.

Tray

16" sq, rose and greenery in center, 2 floral cartouches on border, molded shells at corners, cobalt and gold border, open handles 900.00

17 1/4" H-H, painted German flowers and scattered sprigs, ozier-molded border with gilt accents, molded closed handles, "blue X'd swords and imp 54" marks, c1745, (A) 3,680.00

Tureen, Cov, 11" h, circ shape, painted oriental style flying dragon, exotic birds, and scattered floral sprigs between molded Sulkowski or crisscross basketweave ozier borders, artichoke knob, gilt metal mtd mask handles with rings, ft, and rims, "blue X'd swords" mark, c1740, repairs, pr, (A) 23,100.00

Vase

3 1/8" h, Kakiemon painted flowering prunus branch and butterfly, winged lion and bird on reverse, S-scroll handles with puce dashes, "blue X'd swords and dot" mark 700.00

7 3/4" h, painted scene of amorous couple in garden, leaf handles with encrusted flowers and strawberries, scattered floral bouquets on back, neck, and ft, "blue X'd swords" mark, late 19th C, pr, (A) 3,220.00

11" h, campana shape, reserve of HP polychrome flowers, cobalt ground, "blue X'd swords" mark, c1920 . . . . 1,450.00

Vegetable bowl, Cov, 10 1/2" l, bombe shape, shell handles with molded asparagus and cauliflower, kneeling child with cornucopia knob, painted loose bouquet and scattered flowers, brown line edge, "blue X'd swords" mark, c1760, (A). 1,725.00

MINTON

Stoke-on-Trent, Hanley, England
1793 to Present

History: Thomas Minton established his pottery in Stoke-on-Trent. During the early years, he concentrated on blue transfer printed earthenware, cream colored earthenware, and plain bone china. By 1810, production expanded to include stoneware, Egyptian black and printed and painted bone china. A tremendous number of shapes, styles, and decorations with printed, enameled, or gilded designs was manufactured. Many nineteenth century Minton patterns resembled those of Spode, Miles Mason, New Hall and Pinxton, the company's principal rivals. Most pieces were unmarked.

Between 1816 and 1824, production at the Minton factory was concentrated on earthenwares and cream colored wares. Bone china production resumed in 1824. A large selection of figures and ornamental wares augmented the traditional tableware line.

Much of Minton's success could be attributed to the decorations applied by the staff of painters. French porcelain artists and ex-Derby decorators were employed by Minton. By the late 1830s, Minton had achieved a quality of modeling and decoration on bone china that was unequaled in Europe.

In 1836, Herbert took complete charge when his father died. Herbert Minton, Thomas' son, gradually changed the factory from a small scale producer into one of the greatest Victorian potteries in Europe. By 1858, Minton employed more than 1,500 people utilizing new technologies and decorative styles. Encaustic floor tiles and Parian porcelain were developed under Herbert's jurisdiction.

Leon Arnoux became art director at Minton's in 1849. He encouraged many French artists to move to Stoke-on-Trent and introduced a revival of the Renaissance styles. Arnoux also developed a series of colored glazes for a "majolica" line.

Colin Minton Campbell took control in 1858. The acid gold process was developed, allowing rich gold decorations in bas relief. Louis Marc Solon came to Minton from Sevres in 1870 and brought with him the technique of pate-sur-pate decoration. Pate-sur-pate became a major contribution by Minton to the 19th century English ceramics heritage. After Campbell's death in 1885, Minton continued to be the leading English pottery manufacturer of the 19th century.

In 1968, Minton became a member of the Royal Doulton Tableware Group. Minton china still is being produced today. The company retains its reputation for high quality, hand painted, and gilded tablewares.

References: Paul Atterbury & Maureen Batkin, *The Dictionary of Minton, Rev. Ed.* Antique Collectors' Club, Ltd. 1996; G.A. Godden, *Minton Pottery & Porcelain of the First Period. 1793-1850,* Herbert Jenkins, Ltd.1968; G.A. Godden, *Victorian Porcelain,* Herbert Jenkins, 1961; Joan Jones, *Minton: The First Two hundred Years of Design and Production,* Antique Collectors' Club, Ltd. 1993.

Museum: Minton Museum, London Road, Stoke-on-Trent, England.

Breakfast Service, Part, feldspar, sq dish, 10" H-H, rect dish, 10" l, 8 plates, 7 5/8" d, waste bowl, 7" d, 3 egg cups, 9 breakfast cups, 8 breakfast cups and saucers, mismatched cov sugar bowl, "Chinese Tree" pattern, multicolored urns of flowers, pattern #2067, c1820, (A) 276.00

Cup and Saucer

"Golden Heritage" pattern 30.00

HP bird vignettes and flower blossoms, aqua borders 55.00

Shell design reserves of multicolored florals, overall gold accents, pink borders, (A) 30.00

Cup and Saucer, Demitasse, scrolling reserves of HP and gilt flowers, cobalt ground, c1900 . . . . 295.00

Cup Plate, 3 7/8" d, central design of flowers, zigzag lined rim, med blue transfer, c1830 . . . . 98.00

Dinner Service, Part, bowl, 12 1/2" H-H, ftd, cov dish, 10 1/4" H-H, cov sauce tureen, 7" H-H, 6 graduated platters, 62 plates, 10 3/8" d, 21 soup plates, wide turquoise border band with 6 gilt chased oval medallions between gilt laurel bands, ribbon tied ring handles and knobs, c1865-66, (A) 4,025.00

Figure

4 1/8" h, bone china, seated man holding pear, basket of fruit in lap, puce jacket, flowered waistcoat and trousers, seated woman holding flower garland, green bodice, flowered blouse and skirt, gilt accents, later turned ivory stand, c1830, restored, pr, (A) 339.00

4 3/8" l, recumbent greyhound, black with gilt collar, puce rect pillow with yellow and gilt corner tassels, c1830-40, (A) . . . . . . \ 462.00

Jardiniere, 9" h, ovoid shape, everted rim, Secessionist, tube lined blue cornflowers with green and yellow trim, brown stems, (A) 750.00

Jardiniere and Stand, 42 1/2" h, Secessionist, painted stylized pink and yellow poppies, green ground 2,852.00

Jug, 13 3/8" h, molded geometric interlaced serpents on black vermicular cross ground, lt blue rope borders, dtd 1878, (A) 77.00

Mug, 3 1/2" h, "Genevese" pattern, alpine chalets, blue and white, hairline. 135.00

Planter, 10 5/8" h, sq, black and yellow printed English historic scenes on side panels, gilt accents, pr, (A) 750.00

Plate

8 1/2" d, HP multicolored bird in center, gilt border with green enameled jewels, different bird on each, dtd 1898, set of 6 . . . . 1,600.00

8 5/8" d, molded raised swirls, bunch of purple lilacs tied with red ribbon, gilt shaped rim, "imp Minton" mark . . .75.00

8 7/8" d, multicolored fable scene of tortoise and hare in field near lake, basketweave molded border, loop pierced rim, Bernard Rischgitz, (A) 75.00

9" d

Bone china, center painted in colors with circ cartouche of Venus and Cupid, ivory ground, tooled gilt borders 150.00

HP lg apple blossom spray tied with russet brown ribbon, gold rim, made for Shreve Crump Low, Boston 28.00

9 1/8" d, multicolored portrait of young woman in Victorian dress, plique-a-jour border, sgd "A. Bouilemier," pr 1,800.00

9 1/4" d, center with multicolored landscape scene surrounded by gold bands and lacy design, scalloped border with

Plate, 9" d, cream Grecian maiden on maroon ground, gold inner border, cream border, gold and maroon twist rim, "crowned Minton, Tatman Chicago, Made in England" mark, set of 12, (A) $400.

gold bands and raised gold dots, gold lacy inner border, pr 150.00

9 1/2" d, HP multicolored bird in foliage in center, border with gilt trellis over cobalt ground with 3 reserves of floral sprays, c1830 . . . . 595.00

10" d

Cobalt and gilt vase on yellow tray, oriental mauve and red flowers from cobalt and gilt stems, cobalt border with yellow bundles of flowers and tan scrolling, Minton and Hollins 165.00

Oct, "Denmark" pattern, floral design, blue transfer 55.00

10 1/2" d, cream center, border of parcil gilt cornucopia, husk, and swag draping, retailed for Tiffany, set of 12, (A) 1,840.00

Platter, 18 1/4" l, rect with cut corners, "Amhurst Japan" pattern, iron red, cobalt, yellow, and peach 850.00

Tea Service, Demitasse, teapot, creamer, sugar bowl, 6 cups and saucers, "Bird of Paradise" pattern, dtd 1863 . . . . 300.00

Tureen, 14 1/4" w, with undertray, oriental garden scene, black transfers with enameled accents, ribbed handles and loop knob, c1882, (A) 403.00

Vase

6 1/8" h, gray, rust, pink, and green feathers, turquoise ground, gilt rim, Joseph Bancroft 425.00

11 1/2" h, tapered cylinder shape, spread ft, flared rim, Arts and Crafts style green and yellow flowerheads and stems, blue ground, (A). 403.00

12 1/2" h, slender, swollen ovoid shape, Seccessionist, painted yellow and green stylized flowers and stems, lt blue ground 625.00

13 1/2" h, pilgrim shape, painted bust of young woman on front surrounded by orange, white, and green orange blossoms, steel blue sides, cobalt reverse, studio line, dtd 1872 . . . . . . 2,500.00

MOCHA WARE

Staffordshire, England
1760-1939

History: Inexpensive utilitarian wares with tree-like, feather, moss, and worm designs, known as "Mocha" wares were made during the 19th century. The name came from the mocha stone or moss agate which the design resembled.

William Adams made the first examples at his Cobridge factory in 1799. Since these wares were mainly used in public houses, jugs, tankards, coffeepots, porringers, and butter dishes were the principal shapes that were manufactured.

Basically the decorative portion of a piece consisted of a broad band of colored slip, usually blue, gray, or coffee colored in tone, upon which was the design itself. To achieve the "tree" design, mocha ware potters utilized a mixture called "tea" that was put into the slip while still damp, thus causing the color to spread out into tree-like fronds that contrasted with the white earthenware beneath. On some examples, black rings were added.

Mocha ware exhibited a large variety of patterns. Arboration was made with an acidic solution, forming patterns such as Tree, Shrub, Fern, Seaweed, and Landscape. Cat's Eye and Worm patterns evolved from the use of a three-chambered slip bottle. Marbled and splotched pieces were made by using a blow pipe.

When the background was green, brown, cream, or orange, the designs usually were brown or black. Ale mugs, chamber pots, jugs, pitchers, and shrimp and nut measures are the forms most frequently found with mocha decoration.

It is rare to find a piece with a maker's mark. Among the known manufacturers of Mocha ware are Edge and Malkin in Burslem between 1871 and 1890 and T.G. Green & Co. in Derbyshire from 1864 to 1939. Additional mocha ware makers included Adams of Tunstall, Cork and Edge of Burslem, Broadhurst of Fenton, Tams of Longton, Macintyre of Cobridge, Pinder and Bourne of Burslem, Green of Church Gresley, and Maling of New Castle-on-Tyne.

Museum: City Museum and Art Gallery, Stoke-on-Trent, England.

Bowl

5" d, flared shape, ftd, wide med blue center band flanked by 4 black stripes, cream ground 70.00

6 3/8" d, flared shape, ftd, wide lt blue center band flanked by 3 black stripes top and base, (A). 160.00

8 1/2" d, blue, white, and dk brown earthworm design on blue band, hairline on base, (A) 385.00

12" d, int with 8 spiraling opaque white, tan, and brown earthworms on blue-gray ground with brown dots, ext with band of earthworm between dk brown squiggle and straight lines, orange-brown rim, (A). 11,550.00

Chamber Pot

5 1/2" d, white spots on dk brown band, blue and white stripes, applied leaf handle, chips, (A) 715.00

8 3/4" d, 2 tone blue bands, black stripes, black and white earthworm design, leaf handle, (A). 121.00

Creamer

2 5/8" h, bulbous shape, black seaweed design on amber center band, brown and white stripes, ribbed leaf handle, (A) 220.00

4 1/8" h, with undertray, black seaweed design, pink-beige ground, hairlines, (A). 1,265.00

Jar, Cov, 5" h, wide lt blue center band with black, blue, and white earthworm and 2 bands of blue, black and white cat's eyes, black border stripes, repairs and hairline, (A). 495.00

Milk Pitcher, 4 5/8" h, dk gray-blue band with black stripes, emb band with green and black seaweed, leaf handle, (A) 440.00

Mug

2 1/4" h, brown seaweed on white ground, brown rim stripe, (A) 200.00

2 5/8" h, black seaweed design on ochre band, brown stripes, leaf handle, repairs, (A) 275.00

3" h, gray-yellow center band with blue, white, and brown cat's eye design, brown stripes, leaf handle, repaired, (A) 330.00

3 1/2" h, center cream band with dk brown vert stripes, dk brown ground, band of brown and cream circlets on rim, applied acanthus leaf handle 325.00

3 5/8" h, gray band with brown and white stripes, black seaweed design, leaf handle, (A) 165.00

4 1/4" h, tan band with blue and white earthworm design, blue, brown, and white stripes, leaf handle, (A) . . 550.00

4 1/2" h, pearlware, earthworm design, blue ground 450.00

4 3/4" h

Blue and gray-blue bands with 2 bands of brown and white earthworm designs, brown and white stripes, (A). 605.00

Orange center band with blue, brown, and white earthworm design, emb lt green band on rim, white and dk brown stripes, leaf handle, hairlines, (A) 550.00

5" h, dk tan center band with blue, white, and dk brown earthworm design, dk brown and white stripe, leaf handle, hairlines, (A) 495.00

5 3/4" h

Black and white checkerboard pattern with ochre stripes, molded green bands on rim and ft, (A) . . 1,155.00

Tan band with black seaweed design, dk tan, blue, white stripes, hairlines, (A) 495.00

Mustard Pot

2 1/8" h x 2 7/8" d, black seaweed design on olive gray center band, dk brown stripes, leaf handle, (A). 385.00

4 1/8" h, bulbous shape, blue, tan, and white earthworm and cat's eye design on blue-gray center band, tan and white stripes, leaf handles, chips (A) . .220.00

Pepper Pot

3 5/8" h, black seaweed design on orange-tan band, brown stripes, (A) 990.00

3 7/8" h, white, brown, and beige earthworm design on ochre band, brown stripes, (A) 1,100.00

4 1/2" h

Band of dk brown, tan, and white cat's eyes on lt blue band flanked by tan and dk brown bands, domed top with blue and dk brown bands, chips, (A) 990.00

Brown, tan, and white earthworm design on gray band, black stripe, blue dome, (A) 825.00

Dk brown seaweed design on ochre band, white, green, and dk brown stripes, (A) 825.00

4 7/8" h

Black, tan, and blue stripes, (A) 330.00

Lt blue, tan and white earthworm on lt blue-gray band, dk blue dome with dk brown stripe, (A) 935.00

Pitcher

4 7/8" h, bulbous shape, wide blue and white bands, white and black stripes, leaf handle, hairline, (A). 220.00

5" h, dk brown wavy bands, emb green band on shoulder, blue band with tan and white stripes, leaf handle, hairlines, (A) 550.00

5 5/8" h, lt blue, tan, and white earthworm design on tan band, dk brown and tan stripes, applied leaf handle, repairs, (A) 715.00

6" h

Bulbous shape, white band with brown seaweed on one side, blue seaweed on other, brown ground with black stripes. 850.00

White polka dot and leaf design on olive green center band, blue top band, dk brown and white stripes, leaf handle, chips and hairlines, (A) 935.00

Pitcher, 7" h, orange center band with brown and white earthworm design, lt green band on neck with black seaweed design, dk brown stripes, $450.

6 1/8" h, blue, white, tan, and dk brown earthworm design on light brown center band, dk brown band on neck, emb green band, white stripes, applied leaf handle, repaired, (A) 1,485.00

6 1/4" h, blue and white squiggle band on blue band with black and white stripes, teal bands above and below, leaf handle, (A) 137.00

6 5/8" h, dbl band of brown, blue, and white earthworm design on brown band, blue tooled bands top and base, dk brown stripes, applied leaf handle, chips and hairlines, (A) 1,925.00

6 3/4" h, brown and white earthworm design, emb green band, beige band, and gold and white stripes, leaf handle and spout, rim chips, (A) 192.00

7" h, brown, white, and tan earthworm design on lower band, brown, white, and tan cat's eye design on neck band, brown-gray, blue, and emb green bands with dk brown and white stripes, leaf handle, spout repair, hairlines, (A) 1,540.00

7 5/8" h, black seaweed design, orange-tan bands with black and white stripes, repairs, (A) 825.00

7 3/4" h, brown, black, and white earthworm design, lt blue ground, white handle, rim, and spout. 875.00

8" h, brown, blue, black, and yellow earthworm design, lt blue and black banding, leaf handle 1,095.00

8 3/4" h, blue, teal, and black bands and stripes, white ground, (A) 357.00

13 1/4" h, yellow, white, blue and black bands and stripes and marbleized and polka dot cat's eye designs on center band, applied leaf handle under spout, (A) .2,530.00

Waste Bowl

4 1/2" d, white, orange-tan, and dk brown earthworm design on beige band, rim chips, (A) 220.00

5 5/8" d, white, blue, and dk brown earthworm design on red-orange band, dk brown stripes, emb green rim, hairlines, (A) 275.00

6 1/2" d, blue, brown, and white earthworm design on brown band with dk brown and black stripe, hairlines, (A). . 165.00

MOORCROFT

Burslem, Staffordshire 1897 to Present

W. Moorcroft

c1919

History: William Moorcroft was first employed as a potter by James Macintyre & Co. Ltd. of Burslem in 1897. Moorcroft believed in ornamentation which enhanced rather than disguised the shape of the ware. Most pots had to be hand thrown. He created his designs on the pot itself, rather than on paper, achieving an extraordinary marriage of shape and design.

Moorcroft's early works included vases, bowls, and biscuit jars that were decorated in blue, red, and gold plant forms called "Aurelian" ware.

Moorcroft also made "Florian" ware in a wide variety of shapes and types of decorations. "Florian" ware featured poppies, violets, or cornflowers applied in relief or portrayed in slip trail outlines or tube lining techniques. It was marketed under various trade names such as: "Claremont," "a toadstool design; "Hazledeen," a landscape with trees; "Honesty;" "Pansy," "Pomegrante," and "Flamminian" luster wares. The principal markets were in London, New York, Paris, and San Francisco. The signature "W. Moorcroft" appeared on each piece along with the standard Macintyre printed mark. In 1913, Moorcroft built his own small factory, the Washington Works, at Burslem, employing potters and decorators with whom he worked at James Macintyre & Co. A line of "Powder Blue" speckled tableware was designed in 1913 and continued in production for almost fifty years.

"Persian" was introduced in 1914, which was followed by "Late Florian," with orchid designs, narcissus, damson plums, and cornflowers. In 1921, Moorcroft experimented with trees in blues and greens on a powder blue ground called "Moonlit Blue." This was followed by "Eventide" and "Dawn."

Moorcroft continued the floral styles, but now used simpler and bolder designs. Dark colored exotic flowers adorned many pieces. Landscapes were done in the trailed outline technique. Monochrome luster glazes were produced until the 1920s, followed by flambe glazes in the decade that followed. The flambe or transmutation glazes provided the most interesting for Moorcroft.

W. Moorcroft was appointed potter to Queen Mary in 1928. The impressed phrase, "Potter to H.M. The Queen," was added to his mark. During the 1930s, fruits, fish, birds, and boats joined the traditional decorative motifs. Matte glazes found favor. When Moorcroft died in 1945, Walter, his eldest son, continued the Moorcroft company.

At first Walter used his father's designs. In the 1950s, he developed a more personal style with exotic designs and more dramatic use of color, especially with the eccentric Caribbean and marine life designs. He continued the flambe experiments and increased the range of flambe colors until 1973.

Walter was in charge for more than forty years. Changes during that time included the use of electric kilns, and casting replaced throwing. They still utilized William's styles and basic methods. During the 1970s, Walter designed the magnolia range.

In 1984, Walter's brother John became managing director, and the Moorcroft family sold a controlling interest to the three Roper brothers. This relationship lasted only two years, and the Dennis and Edwards families took over. Walter retired in 1987, and Sally Tuffin became Moorcroft designer along with Phillip Richardson.

Since 1994, Rachel Bishop has been Moorcroft's designer. Today Moorcroft is selling more of its wares all over the world than it did in its heyday in the mid-1920s.

Marks: Various types of marks include the Moorcroft signature or initials, printed or impressed factory marks, retailers' marks, design registration numbers, and pattern or shape marks. Some paper labels with printed factory marks also were used starting in the 1920s. Rectangular ones were used first. After the awarding of the Royal Warrant in 1928, circular paper labels were used until 1978 when the Royal Warrant expired.

References: Paul Atterbury, *Moorcroft: A Guide to Moorcroft Pottery 1897-1993, Rev. Ed.* Richard Dennis and Hugh Edwards, 1990; A. W. Coysh, *British Art Pottery, 1870-1940*, Charles E. Tuttle, 1976; Richard Dennis, *William & Walter Moorcroft, l897-1973*, an exhibition catalog, 1973; Francis Salmon, *Collecting Moorcroft Pottery*, Francis Joseph Publications, 1994; Susan Scott, *Moorcroft*, Antique Trader Weekly, March 29, l995.

Museums: Everson Museum of Art, Syracuse, NY; Moorcroft Museum, Stoke-on-Trent, England; Victoria & Albert Museum, London, England.

Collectors' Club: Moorcroft Collectors' Club, Lipert International Inc. 2922 M. Street, NW, Washington DC, 20007. Membership: $30.00, 3 newsletters per year. Collectors' Club pieces issued yearly.

Ashtray

5" sq, red hibiscus, mustard yellow ground, "By Appointment Potter to the late Queen Mary" mark 58.00

6" l, apricot orange hibiscus, dk green ground 65.00

Bowl

3" d, "Dogwood" pattern, yellow ground, imp mark 100.00

4 1/2" d, "Fresia" pattern, yellow, rose red, green, and pink flowers, green ground, blue pedestal base 185.00

6 1/4" d, "Hibiscus" pattern, peach flowers, olive ground, "imp MOORCROFT, ENGLAND" mark, paper label, (A) 200.00

8" d, "Pomegranate" pattern, cobalt ground, "Wm. Moorcroft" mark, c1916 . . . . 850.00

Bowl, Cov, 6" d x 4 1/2" h, "Orchid" pattern, shaded rose, blue, and yellow orchids, green ground 350.00

Bud Vase, 6 1/2" h, squat shape with tall slender neck, "Aurelian," painted and printed stylized flowers and foliage, red and green with gilt accents, white ground, repaired rim, pr, (A) 495.00

Candlestick

3 1/2" h, squat, tapered cylinder shape, "Clematis" pattern, pink, purple, and green on green ground, imp factory mark and paper label, pr, (A) . . 150.00

6" h, Tudric, plum, yellow, and red fruit design, blue ground, hand hammered pewter base, bobiche, and socket, "stamped Made in England, Tudric Moorcroft, 01513" mark, pr, (A) 750.00

7 3/4" h, tapered shape, Tudric, "Pomegranate" pattern, red, ochre, and pink fruit, cobalt ground, hand hammered pewter base, bobiche, and socket, "imp H, TUDRIC, MOORCROFT, 01362, MADE BY LIBERTY & CO." mark, pr, (A) 1,700.00

8 1/2" h, squeeze bag design of lt blue landscape on dk blue ground, "blue painted WM and imp MOORCROFT/MADE IN ENGLAND" marks, pr, (A) 750.00

Charger, 13 3/4" d, "Finches" pattern, blue and pink finches, rose red apples, green leaves, blue and purple berries, blue ground 495.00

Dish, Cov, 6 1/2" d, "Clematis" pattern, cobalt ground, "W. Moorcroft" mark, c1940s 425.00

Figure, 6 5/8" h, figural bear seated on haunches, running yellow and flambe glaze, paper label, (A) 3,365.00

Inkstand

2 3/4" h, "Moonlit Blue Landscape" pattern, silver mts, c1920s 750.00

8 7/8" l, "Eighteenth Century" pattern, painted pink, green, and blue, gilt accents, white ground, incised signature, (A) 850.00

Mustard Pot, 2 1/8" h, Macintyre, blue painted flowers and foliage over lt blue band, green ground, (A) 445.00

Pitcher

5" h, bulbous shape, yellow and pink irises, shaded blue to green ground, "imp MOORCROFT, MADE IN ENGLAND, glaze signature" marks, (A) 350.00

6 1/2" h, pink and purple berries, green, yellow, and rose red leaves, green ground, blue handle, c1949 . . . 795.00

18 1/4" h, tapered cylinder shape, "Pomegranate" pattern, red fruit, dk purple ground, "stamped MOORCROFT, MADE IN ENGLAND and blue script" marks 1,200.00

Plate

8" d, "Hibiscus" pattern, dk blue ground, c1950 . . . . 245.00

10 1/4" d, blue and maroon "Hibiscus" pattern, dk olive green ground, paper label, signature mark 310.00

Potpourri Jar, 3 1/4" h x 3 1/2" d, heart shaped leaves in circle, red-brown glaze, script signature, chips, (A) 400.00

Sugar Sifter, 6 7/8" h, "Florian," blue and green painted frieze of poppies between bands of scrolling foliage, white ground, green signature mark, (A) 2,302.00

Tobacco Jar, 3 3/4" h, Florian, blue poppies, screw lid, painted William Moorcroft mark, (A) 1,650.00

Vase

4" h

Orange luster glaze, 3 handles 425.00

"Pansy" pattern, late 1920s . . . 225.00

3" h x 4" d, squat shape, "Anemone" pattern, blue, white, and pink flowers, "imp signature and POTTER TO HM THE QUEEN," (A) 175.00

3 1/2" h, pomegranate, grapes, and leaves, dk blue ground, "W Moorcroft, potter to HM the Queen, England" mark 250.00

3 3/4" h, "Landscape" pattern, brown trees, orange sky, black ground, "stamped MOORCROFT, MADE IN ENGLAND" mark, pr, (A) 950.00

4 1/2" h, squat shape, Hazledene, squeeze bag design of celadon trees on lt celadon ground, "painted W. Moorcroft/XII/1913" mark, (A) 700.00

5" h, ovoid shape, everted rim, "Moonlit Blue" pattern, blue and green shades, blue ground, painted green signature, (A) 2,657.00

5 1/4" h, bulbous, "Anemone" pattern, blue and red flowerheads, lt to dk green

shaded ground, paper label, (A) 175.00

5 1/2" h, raised design of 2 brown kissing birds with blue-green tails, strawberries and green leaves, yellow flowers, blue ground, "MOORCROFT, MADE IN ENGLAND" mark 225.00

6" h, corset shape, blue landscape, lt celadon ground, "painted W. Moorcroft and red Made for Liberty and Co." marks, 1903-1913, (A) 700.00

6 1/4" h

Bulbous, "Hazledene" pattern, squeeze bag design of blue trees, green and lt yellow ground, "painted W. Moorcroft/des and stamped Made for Liberty and Co." marks, (A) 950.00

Ovoid shape, collar rim, "Weeping Willow" pattern, pink and ochre, white ground, salt glaze finish, painted blue signature, (A) 1,948.00

6 1/2" h, bulbous shape, ftd, flared rim, "Pomegranate" pattern, squeeze bag design of red and burgundy pomegranates and green leaves, celadon ground, "painted W. Moorcroft" mark, (A) 500.00

6 5/8" h, squat ovoid shape, short cylinder neck, "Pansy" pattern, pink, purple, and

Vase, 5 1/4" h, Pomegranate design, dk blue ground, blue mark, $495.

Vase, 11" h, Florian, blue shades, "JAS Mcintyre & Co. Lt. and imp Wm. Des" marks, (A) $2,100.

It green, dk blue ground, painted blue signature, (A) 975.00

7" h, "Hibiscus" pattern, green ground 175.00

7 1/4" h, baluster shape, "Pomegranate" pattern, red fruit, cobalt ground, "imp MOORCROFT, MADE IN ENGLAND, 72" mark, (A) 400.00

7 1/2" h, wide flat ft, purple grapes, yellow leaves, shaded green to blue ground, "stamped Moorcroft, MADE IN ENGLAND, ink signature" marks, (A) 600.00

7 7/8" h, ovoid shape, 2 handled, "Peacock Feather" pattern, painted blue and green, lt green ground, (A) . . .3,542.00

8" h, cylinder shape, Tudric, "Eventide" pattern, puffy green trees, blue mountains, red sky, hand hammered pewter rim and base, "stamped Made in England, Tudric, Moorcroft, 01335" mark, hairline, (A) 1,000.00

8 1/4" h, bulbous body, corseted neck, "Claremont Toadstool" pattern, red and lt blue toadstools, lt blue gloss ground, "painted W. Moorcroft and imp MOORCROFT/MADE IN ENGLAND" marks, (A) 1,800.00

9 1/4" h, baluster shape, "Spanish" pattern, pink, purple, green, and ochre, green ground, painted green signature, (A) .3,896.00

9 3/4" h, narrow base tapered to wide shoulder, rolled rim, "Pomegranate" pattern, squeeze bag design of orange and purple fruit, blue flambe ground, "stamped MOORCROFT/MADE IN ENGLAND and ink signature" mark, (A) 850.00

10" h

Bulbous base, corset neck, squeeze bag black peacock feathers, ruby luster glaze, "imp Moorcroft and inked WM" marks, (A). 650.00

"Big Pansy" pattern, white, magenta, and dk magenta flowers, cobalt ground, c1929 . . . . 595.00

10 3/4" h, cylinder shape, collar rim, squeeze bag stylized cobalt, celadon, and olive green peacock feathers, "painted Moorcroft, DES" mark 950.00

11 1/2" h, wide ft, tapered base, flared body, spread rim, Florian, squeeze bag relief of blue flowers, celadon leaves, cobalt ground, "W Moorcroft/Des" mark, (A) 1,200.00

11 3/4" h

Florian, squeeze bag relief of yellow iris blossoms and celadon leaves, cobalt ground, "W. Moorcroft/Des." mark, (A). 2,900.00

Slender profile, Macintyre Florian, "Lilac" pattern, periwinkle blue flowers, white ground, 1898, (A) . . .1,400.00

12" h, squeeze bag and painted landscape of white trees on lt blue mountains, "blue Moorcroft, stamped MOORCROFT/Made in England" mark, (A) 1,900.00

12 3/4" h, blue plums, yellow flowers, purple-blue ground, "imp MOORCROFT, MADE IN ENGLAND, signature" mark, hairline on rim, (A) 1,100.00

13" h, bulbous shape, red orchids, blue irises, white blossoms, cobalt ground, "stamped MOORCROFT, MADE IN ENGLAND" mark, (A) 1,100.00

14 1/4" h, "Anemone" pattern, lg squeeze bag flowers under ruby luster glaze, "painted W. Moorcroft and imp MOORCROFT/MADE IN ENGLAND" marks, (A) 1,900.00

MULBERRY WARE

Staffordshire, England
1835-1855

History: Mulberry ware was made by many of the same Staffordshire potters that produced Flow Blue. In fact, many patterns with identical design and name are found on both types of wares. The bulk of the Mulberry ware production occurred during the early Victorian period, 1835-1855.

The mulberry color was achieved by a chemical combination of red, brown, gray, and purple dyes. Mulberry referred to the color of berries from the English black mulberry trees. Some mulberry patterns on earthenware or ironstone were "flown," producing a soft, hazy effect. Most were presented with a sharp, clear design.

Mulberry ware was a response to the public's need for something new and different. Its popularity did not last. Few pieces were made after 1855.

References: Petra Williams, *Flow Blue China & Mulberry Ware, Similarity and Value Guide, Rev. Ed.* Fountain House East, 1981.

Collecting Hints: Previously, mulberry prices always had been priced higher than Flow Blue examples. However, in the past few years, there has been a reversal. Mulberry ware now sells for about one-third less than the prevailing price for a comparable Flow Blue piece.

"Allegheny" pattern

Bowl, 10 1/2" d 62.00

Plate, 9 1/4" d 75.00

Platter, 15 3/4" l x 12" w 260.00

"Athens" pattern

Pitcher, 6 1/2" h, heat crack 125.00

Plate

8 1/2" d, "W. Adams & Sons" mark 60.00

9 1/4" d 55.00

10 1/2" d 55.00

Platter, 15 1/2" l, Meigh 175.00

Plate, 8 5/8" d, "Abbey" pattern, "W. Adams & Sons" mark, $95.

"Beauties of China" pattern

Plate, 8 1/4" d, Mellor, Venables . . . 80.00

"Bochara" pattern

Plate

9 1/8", oct, "J.E." mark 65.00

10 1/2" d 85.00

Vegetable Bowl, 10 1/2" l x 8 1/4" w 160.00

Waste Bowl, 5 1/4" d 115.00

"Bryonia" pattern

Plate, 9 1/2" d 30.00

"Calcutta" pattern

Cup and Saucer. 80.00

Plate, 9 1/2" d 35.00

Teapot 275.00

"Castle Scenery" pattern

Plate, 10" d 115.00

Platter, 15" l 175.00

"Coburg" pattern

Plate, 9" d, "imp J.E. Real Ironstone" mark 165.00

Platter, 11" l 150.00

"Corea" pattern

Plate

6 1/4" d 55.00

8 1/4" d 75.00

9" d 40.00

10 3/4" d 85.00

"Corean" pattern

Creamer. 175.00

Cup and Saucer, Handleless. 65.00

Cup Plate, 4" d 80.00

Gravy Boat. 55.00

Pitcher

8" h 295.00

10" h 300.00

Plate

5 1/4" d 60.00

7 1/4" d 26.00

7 3/4" d, paneled 60.00

8" d 50.00

8 7/8" d, "P.W. & Co." 45.00

9 5/8" d, paneled 95.00

9 3/4" d 55.00
10" d 80.00
10 1/4" d, paneled 110.00
Platter
12 1/2" l 185.00
14" l 250.00
16" l x 12" w 225.00
17 5/8" x 13 3/4" l 350.00
18" l x 14" w 325.00
Sugar Bowl 175.00
Teapot 300.00
Vegetable Bowl, Cov, 9" d 435.00

"Cyprus" pattern
Creamer 200.00
Cup and Saucer, Handleless 125.00
Charger, 11" d 55.00
Honey Dish, 5" d 50.00
Plate
7 1/2" d 60.00
9 1/2" d 45.00
Platter
13 1/2" l 175.00
18" l 250.00
Soup Plate, 10 1/2" d 90.00
Teapot 275.00

"Delhi" pattern
Plate, 7 1/2" d 44.00

"Flora" pattern
Creamer 170.00

"Foliage" pattern
Cup and Saucer, Handleless 95.00

"Genoa" pattern
Plate 10 1/2" d 85.00

"Heath's Flower" pattern
Platter, 14" l 275.00

"Hong" pattern
Teapot, 9 5/8" h 650.00

"Jeddo" pattern
Creamer 215.00
Cup Plate, 4 1/8" d 80.00
Pitcher, 7 1/2" h 325.00
Plate
6" d 35.00
9 1/4" d 35.00
10 1/4" d 100.00
Platter, 15 1/2" l x 12" w 225.00
Sugar Bowl 195.00
Teapot 375.00
Vegetable Bowl, 11" l x 8 1/2" w . . . 148.00

"Kan Su" pattern
Plate, 9" d 60.00

"Leipsic" pattern
Platter, 14" l x 10" w 145.00
Vegetable Bowl, Cov, 13 1/2" l, 6 sides,
Clementson, chips 195.00

"Loretta" pattern
Pitcher, 6" h, Alcock 115.00

"Medina" pattern
Sugar Bowl, Furnival 195.00

"Monterey" pattern
Plate, 9 1/2" d 29.00

Platter, 13 5/8" l, "Orpheus" pattern, Davenport, $370.

"Montezuma" pattern
Plate, 7 1/8" d, Goodwin 22.00

"Moss Rose" pattern
Plate, 10" d 65.00

"Nankin" pattern
Creamer 225.00

"Neva" pattern
Platter, 10" l 95.00

"Ning Po" pattern
Pitcher, 8" h 195.00

"Palestine" pattern
Plate
7" d 40.00
8 1/2" d 35.00
10 1/2" d 45.00

"Panama" pattern
Creamer 225.00
Honey Dish, 4 3/8" d 90.00
Plate, 7 1/4" d 35.00

"Pelew" pattern
Charger, 11" d 50.00
Cup and Saucer, Handleless 75.00
Cup Plate, 4 1/8" d 80.00
Pitcher, 5 1/2" h 150.00
Plate
8 1/2" d 50.00
9 1/2" d 85.00
Platter
10" l x 7 1/2" w 125.00
13 1/2" d, rect with cut corners
. . . . 175.00
18" l 275.00

"Peru" pattern
Creamer, 6" h, unmkd 180.00
Plate 9 1/4" d 70.00
Platter
10 1/2" l x 7 7/8" w 125.00
13 1/8" l x 10 1/8" w 150.00
Sugar Bowl, Cov, 8 1/2" h, "Holdcroft &
Co." mark, c1848 . . . . 350.00
Teapot, 9 3/4" h, "Holdcroft & Co." mark,
c1848 . . . . 400.00
Waste Bowl, 5 1/4" d, "Holdcroft & Co."
mark, c1848 . . . . 100.00

"Peruvian" pattern
Plate
9" d 55.00
10 5/8" d 75.00
Teabowl and Saucer 65.00
Teapot 650.00

"Rhone Scenery" pattern
Plate
7 1/2" d 60.00
10" d 45.00
Platter
13 1/2" l, rect with cut corners . 195.00
18" l 275.00

"Rose" pattern
Bowl, 10" l, rect 150.00
Creamer 225.00
Platter, 14" l x 11" w 185.00

"Scinde" pattern
Plate, 7 1/2" d 40.00
Vegetable Bowl, 11 1/4" l, oct, "P.W. & Co."
mark 225.00

"Shapoo" pattern
Platter, 14" l x 10" w 225.00

"Singan" pattern
Teabowl and Saucer 72.00

"Susa" pattern
Plate, 10 1/2" d, "CMS & P" mark . . . 65.00

"Tavoy" pattern
Plate
7 1/2" d 60.00
10" d 80.00
Platter, 15" l 130.00

"Temple" pattern
Plate, 8" d 50.00
Platter, 10 7/8" l x 8 1/4" w 125.00
Toddy Plate, 5 1/2" d 85.00
Vegetable Bowl, 8" l 3,335.00

"Tonquin" pattern
Vegetable Bowl, 9 1/4" l, "Heath" mark
. . . . 200.00

"Undina" pattern
Platter, 18" l x 14 1/4" w, rect, Clementson
. . . . 225.00

"Venture" pattern
Creamer 95.00

"Vincenes" pattern
Creamer 200.00
Cup and Saucer, set of 6, ... 550.00
Plate 9 3/8" d 75.00
Platter
15 1/2" l x 11 3/4" w 265.00
18" l x 14" w 300.00
Sugar Bowl, Cov, 7 1/2" h, pagoda shape
. . . . 295.00

"Washington Vase" pattern
Creamer 200.00
Cup and Saucer 80.00
Plate
7 1/2" d 70.00
8" d 35.00
9" d 55.00
10" d, "P.W. & Co." mark 80.00

Platter
  11" l x 8" w 150.00
  12 3/8" l................ 225.00
  16" l x 12 3/8" w 295.00
Sauce Tureen, w/ladle 595.00
Soup Plate, 9 1/2" d 75.00
Sugar Bowl, lion's head handles .. 240.00
Teabowl and Saucer 95.00
Vegetable Bowl, 9 3/4" l x 7 3/4" w
  .... 275.00
"Whampoa" pattern
  Platter, 15" l 245.00
"Wreath" pattern
  Vegetable Bowl, Cov, 11" l...... 425.00

MUSTACHE CUPS

English, Continental
1830 to Present

History: The mustache cup was a Victorian innovation that owed its origin to Harvey Adams, a Stoke-on-Trent potter who introduced the design in 1830. It was a drinking cup used for imbibing tea or coffee, featuring a raised lip guard attached to the rim of the cup to keep the mustache and beard from touching the liquid. Originally called "Napoleons and Saucers" after the small beards popular at the time, mustache cups reached the peak of their popularity in the 1890s when wearing a mustache was the rage.

Mustache cups were first sold singly. Some had matching saucers, but most stood alone. As their popularity increased, they were included in dinnerware sets. Gift sets that included a cup with a mustache rim for the gentleman and an identical rimless cup for madam were common. Right and left handed cups were produced. Left handed examples are scarce. Although originating in England, the manufacture of mustache cups quickly spread to other areas including France, Germany, and Austria.

Many different media were used for the body including earthenware, porcelain, and bone china. Free hand painting by artists along with transfer printing and other decorative techniques were used. Heavy raised and burnished decorations and rich gilding proved popular. These are the most frequently encountered pieces today.

Some mustache cups employed several techniques in order to catch the fancy of the buyer.

Many of the major houses produced mustache cups and marked their products accordingly. Crown Derby, Wedgwood, Meissen, and Limoges all provided cups for the mustached gentleman. However, many of the examples found in today's market are unmarked.

The size of mustache cups ranges from demitasse to quart. The eight ounce size is most commonly found.

References: Dorothy Hammond, *Mustache Cups,* Wallace-Homestead, 1972; Thelma Schull, *Victorian Antiques,* Tuttle, 1963.

Reproduction Alert: Reproduced matching left-handed and right-handed mustache cups have found their way to antique shops. Since matched sets are very rare, collectors should by careful to make sure the matched set is old, not a reproduction.

Collecting Hints: Sayings and mottos are fairly common but do not add significantly to the value of the piece. Advanced collectors seek out Majolica, Imari, Rose Medallion, Sunderland, Luster, and Belleek cups.

Note: All listings are for right handed cups unless indicated otherwise.

Cup

Blue flowers, gold trim, wide base.... 25.00
Bulbous base, spiral fluting, blue flowers, brown leaves, unmkd.............. 25.00
Decal picture in colors of "Race of the Century," white body 12.00
Gold scrolling on rim, white ground... 22.00
HP
  Blue flowers, edged with raised gold
    .... 40.00
  Castle on snow covered ridge with trees and lake, gold trim 45.00
  Left handed, scene of 2 angels in clouds, multicolored pastels, pale peach and gold border, gold handle 135.00

Mauve, orange, and purple flowers, raised gold designs, "green C.T. eagle" mark, (A) $25.

Lg size, man, woman, and dog scene in colors, gold flowers, black speckle, pink ground, gold feet, twisted rope handle
  .... 40.00
Mug, white roses, pink luster and gold rose trim, white ground 25.00
Oct shape, blue and white leaf pattern, gold trim, angular handle 40.00
Orange flowers, gold trim, white ground, flowers on int 25.00
Oversize, purple lilacs, white roses, emb design, white ground............... 30.00
Pink rim, lg violets, white ground 20.00
Pink and white lilies, gold rim and handle, white ground 25.00
Portrait of boy and girl in garden, pink ground, sq handle 30.00
Raised blue "Father," gold grass ground, "Made in Germany" mark 25.00
Raised gold flowerhead in pink molded shield........................ 28.00
"Remember Me" in gold, gold band at top, white ground, gold on bridge 25.00
Red apples on green shaded ground, molded beaded base, "Made in Bavaria" mark. 32.00
Textured raised gold flowerhead, swirls with raised gold dots, dk pink ground 18.00
"To My Husband" in blue wreath, white ground....................... 25.00
White fluted body, rippled lip, gold trim on lip, bridge, and base, "C.T. eagle" mark .. 35.00

Cup and Saucer

Angel handle, imp gold flower and leaf design, purple berry branches, white ground
  .... 75.00
Applied gold flowers and leaves, wide gold band on int, gold accented bridge, white ground........................ 40.00
Band of pink roses, 2 bands of gold flowers, "eagle, C.T. Germany" mark 65.00
Bell shaped cup, white ground with forget-me-nots bouquet, scalloped rims .. 45.00
Blue and yellow butterfly handle, gold "Present," gold bands, removable nickel plated bridge..................... 100.00
Blue-gray luster band on rim, lg red rose, white ground, 3 crowns Germany 35.00
Blue luster base shaded to white, gold trim, roses on int and ext, "Made in Germany" mark 25.00
Blue outlined raised gold "PRESENT" and gold wheat sheaf................. 28.00
Blue spiderweb design with trailing flowers, white ground, gold trimmed scalloped edge
  .... 50.00
Brown and pink flowers, gold "Remember Me," scalloped saucer 35.00
Cobalt centered iron red flowerheads, cobalt leaves with copper luster trim, blue handle with luster stripe 65.00
Convoluted hex shape, pink violets, gold trim, lt blue ground, scalloped rims 40.00

Cup with 4 feet, pink luster, gold daisies, gold trim, scalloped rim on saucer, unmkd. . 60.00

Decal of wild raspberries, white ground, Germany 30.00

Dk green with roses, unmkd 50.00

Farmhouse scene surrounded by red and blue daisies, green ferns, gold trim on saucer 20.00

Flower swirls on rim, lt lavender ground, "Carlsbad Austria" mark 35.00

Frosted green band, floral bouquet, gold trim, "eagle and C.T. Germany" mark 0.00

Garland of roses with gold leaves at rim, roses on saucer, white ground, "Imperial Crown China, Austria" mark 45.00

Gold branches with blue dot fruit, peach band at base, "T and lion" mark 35.00

Gold "Friendships Gift," white ground, unmkd 35.00

Gold outline raised maple leaf design, white ground, "Manufactured in Germany" mark 40.00

Gold "Papa" and flowers, pink ground . 40.00

Grapes on yellow and dk green shaded ground, gold luster trim, "Handpainted Made in Germany" mark 40.00

Green luster, gold flowers, stylized red leaves 35.00

HP sm purple flowers, speckle gold trim, white ground. 30.00

Ivory ext with pink and yellow roses, white int with pink roses, Bavaria 60.00

Left handed
  Capodimonte, painted cherubs in colors, pedestal base 75.00
  Cobalt and pink flowers. 60.00
  Gay Nineties couple, gold trim, scalloped base 25.00
  HP flowers, heavy gold trim, R.S. Prussia 50.00

Lg red rose, pink trim, white ground, unmkd 30.00

Lilac and blue dogwood, frosted gold trim, white ground, "Germany" mark 50.00

Lime yellow luster, raised pink flowers, blue leaves, Germany 40.00

Lobed cup and saucer, brown transfers of hanging leaves from borders, gold lined rims, England. 48.00

Miniature, shaded yellow border , gold accented rim and handle, "A.K." mark, (A) 55.00

Molded flute design, blue luster with heavy gold trim, 4 sm feet 60.00

Molded leaf design, white, removable bridge, "Copeland England" mark 65.00

Oversized
  Dutch windmills on pink ground, sq handle, Germany 50.00
  Gold shamrocks, white ground, unmkd 15.00
  HP flying hummingbird and flower . 35.00
  HP red poppy, blue and brown leaves, line drawn butterflies, white ground . . 45.00

Maroon and gold border, wide pink band, "gold Forget Me Not," gold and violets flowers. 40.00

Pink overspray band on rims, blue chrysanthemums on cup 35.00

Purple and white floral design, gold trim, white ground, R.S. Prussia 65.00

Raised dove and flower design, gold luster, "Made in Germany" mark . . . 50.00

Yellow and pink flowers, raised pattern 70.00

Orange pumpkin shape with pedestal base cup, gold trim and handle, white rim . . 45.00

Pansies in colors, gold leaf chain on rim, green luster at base of cup and on saucer, gold handle, ornate shape 50.00

Patterned gold leaves on cup and saucer, violet rim on cup, white ground, Limoges 50.00

Pink airbrushed cup base, garland of forget-me-nots, "C.T. eagle, Made in Germany" mark 45.00

Pink and yellow luster, gold flowers and leaves, wide base, narrow middle 35.00

Pink daisies, blue band at top, gold trim, unmkd 35.00

Pink lilacs, gold filigree, white ground . 30.00

Pink luster banner with gold rose, spiral ribbed base, unmkd. 35.00

Pink luster, blue flowers, "Love The Giver," "Made in Germany" mark 47.00

Purple and red raised geometric design, heavy gold trim. 25.00

Purple flowers, gold trim, petal shaped saucer 50.00

Purple primroses, molded ground, white body, ornate handle, gold trim. 35.00

Radiant grooves, gold band on rim, bamboo handle, "Made in Germany" mark 30.00

Raised bough pattern and pink flowers on int and ext, white ground, Rosenthal 35.00

Raised gold flowerheads and buds, scattered purple flowers. 55.00

Raised gold flowers and berries, fluted cup base, white ground, unmkd 40.00

Raised orange leaves and violet flowers, spattered blue bkd, cream cup and saucer, "Made in Germany" mark. 50.00

Red and white wild roses, gold violets, lt molded design, fancy handle, unmkd 35.00

Red ground, white relief of flower bouquet, gilt on bridge 35.00

"Remember Me" on white panel, gold trim and flowers, dk green ground, Germany . . 50.00

Shamrock pattern, Irish Belleek, 2nd black mark 300.00

Sm red roses and branch, gold band, gold decorated bridge, white ground, gold band on saucer, Elite, Limoges, France 30.00

Spiral fluted, gold trim, gray-blue base, "Made in Germany" mark. 22.00

Straight flutes, blue ground with raised pattern flowers, heavy gold trim on handle and bridge 40.00

"Think of Me," gold in gold floral surround, white ground 60.00

Three roses and lilacs, fancy handle, white ground, saucer with 4 gold bands, unmkd 30.00

Transfer of clipper ship and motto, Sunderland luster 125.00

Tridacna pattern, Irish Belleek, 1st black mark 125.00

Two multicolored birds and nest with eggs, gold trim, white ground 35.00

Two women in garden setting, blue ground, gold trim, unmkd 70.00

White roses on peach ground, gold trimmed inner and outer borders, 3 crown Germany 40.00

Yellow bow, pink flowers, brown branches and handle, lt blue-green ground, artist sgd 60.00

Demitasse

Decal of red rose bouquet, raised ground pattern. 30.00

Gold "A Present" and flowers, molded pattern, white ground 35.00

NEW HALL

Staffordshire Potteries, England c1731-1735

1812-35

History: A group of partners purchased Champion's patent to make translucent porcelains and in 1781 established the New Hall China Manufactory at Hanley in Staffordshire to make hard paste porcelains based upon the patent. Tea and dessert sets, along with blue and white wares showing Chinese influences, were characteristic products at New Hall. Gold was used in both simple and elaborate designs. Many early pieces only had elegant gilt borders.

Fidelle Duvivier, who had been employed at Worcester and Derby, worked at New Hall from 1781 to 1790. He did figure and landscape compositions and flower subjects on presentation jugs. Early New Hall teapots were globular in form. Pieces made during the hard paste period were not marked. Pattern numbers were used instead.

About 1812-14, bone china that was lighter and whiter was introduced at New Hall. The pieces were marked "New Hall" in a double-lined circle along with a pattern number. Work declined after about 1820. The factory was put up for auction in 1831. Various firms using the original site continued the name until 1836.

References: David Holgate, *New Hall & Its Imitators, Rev. Ed.* Faber & Faber, 1988;

G.E. Stringer, *New Hall Porcelain*, Art Trade Press, 1949.

Museums: City Museum & Art Gallery, Stoke-on-Trent, Hanley, England; Victoria & Albert Museum, London, England.

Creamer

    4 1/2" h, paneled body, dk red floral spray on sides, border of band of dk red bundles 165.00

    4 5/8" h, molded swirled ribbing, sm polychrome florals on sides and rim, (A) 100.00

Cup and Saucer

    Fluted, cup with band of garden flowers on ext, int with scattered garden flowers and red dot drape, saucer with mauve and red garden flowers, green leaves, scattered sprays 195.00

    Gold outlined cobalt and orange-red pagoda, willow tree, and flowering tree, band of gold leaves and flowerheads on borders 425.00

    "Window" pattern, orange, green, and puce orientals in windows, pattern #425, c1790. . . . . 225.00

Plate, 8 1/2" d, multicolored scene of 2 oriental gentlemen standing in garden setting, brown rocks, pattern #421, c1795 . . . . 450.00

Teabowl and Saucer

    Multicolored scene of 2 oriental gentlemen standing in garden setting, brown rocks, pattern #421, c1791 . . . . 300.00

    Rose design, pearlware, (A) 65.00

Teapot

    5 3/4" h, with undertray, paneled oval shape, gilt florets and bands, yellow banded border, pattern #206, c1790, (A) 402.00

    6 1/2" h, pearlware, molded swirl body, pink and green floral bouquet on sides, scattered sprigs, c1790-1810 . . 375.00

    6 3/4" h, scattered bouquets of sm red flowers and green leaves, meandering red ribbons, dk red rims, red pointed knob. 550.00

Teapot, 8 1/4" h, with stand, "Boy in the Window" pattern, orange, blue, and green, white cartouches, $1,200.

7 1/8" h, oval shape, swirled ribbing, enamel and gilt florets on body, floral banded border, c1785 . . . . 350.00

Tea and Coffee Service, Part, teapot, 6" h, lobed body, stand, 7 7/8" w, coffeepot, 10 3/4" h, cream jug, 4 1/2" h, 2 waste bowls, 6 1/8" d, 2 saucer dishes, 8 1/2" d, 12 teabowls and saucers, 2 cake plates, 7 1/4" d, polychrome painted "Boy and Butterfly" pattern, pattern #431, c1820, (A). 4,370.00

Tea Service, Part

    Pot, 6 1/2" h, with undertray, lobed body, creamer, 4 3/8" h, helmet shape, sugar bowl, waste bowl, plate, 8 1/2" d, 6 teabowls and saucers, polychrome scattered floral sprays, dot and swag rims, (A) 1,430.00

    Pot, 7" h, squat shape, creamer, cov sugar bowl, waste bowl, 6 1/4" d, 5 demitasse cups, 8 teacups, 10 saucers, blue transfer of stone bridge over river, gilt leaf and berry borders 1,200.00

    Eight cups and saucers, milk jug, slop bowl, 2 saucer dishes, printed and enameled chinoiserie figures seated in front of urns of flowers, (A) 308.00

Waste Bowl, 5 1/4" d, enamel decorated vine design, (A) 135.00

MODERN MARK   1754 - 65

NYMPHENBURG

Near Munich, Bavaria, Germany 1747 to Present

History: The Nymphenburg Porcelain Factory, located in Neudeck ob den Au, near Munich, was founded in 1747 by the Bavarian Elector. As production increased, the factory was moved to the grounds of Nymphenburg Palace in Munich.

As with many German porcelain firms, Meissen pieces strongly influenced the types of wares produced at Nymphenburg. By 1765, under the guidance of the Elector, Nymphenburg became the most renown hard paste factory in Europe. Shortly thereafter, a series of wars and economic reversals created a decline in the popularity of the porcelain. By 1770, the Nymphenburg factory was hard pressed for markets in which to sell its products.

During the early years at Nymphenburg, production was devoted to table services, accessory pieces, and household wares that were painted in a rococo style featuring birds, fruits, flowers, and the popular pastoral scenes. However, it was the modeling of Franz Bustelli, the Swiss craftsman who worked at Nymphenburg from 1754-1763, that contributed the most to the success of the company. Bustelli's figures were modeled in a light, graceful rococo style that found a ready market with the gentry.

The Nymphenburg pottery was transferred to the control of the Elector of Palatinate, who also owned the Frankenthal factory, a competitor of Nymphenburg. With more emphasis placed on the Frankenthal pottery, Nymphenburg experienced a period of neglect and subsequent decline. When the Frankenthal Factory closed in 1799, many of the workers and artisans were moved to Nymphenburg to revitalize the ailing concern.

Melchoir, who achieved fame at Hochst and Frankenthal, was chief modeler at Nymphenburg between 1797 and 1822. He produced many biscuit portraits and busts.

When Melchoir died in 1822, Friedrich Gartner was appointed artistic director. He preferred to produce vases in a variety of decorative motifs. Gartner showed little interest in producing tableware. As a result, the factory declined economically. Royal commissions for Ludwig I (1825-1848) did result in the manufacture of several outstanding state services.

When Eugen Neureuther assumed control as director in 1848, the factory's finances were poor. Ludwig I abdicated in favor of Maximilian II, his son. Maximilian II had almost no interest in the pottery factory. Economies were taken. Popular wares such as paperweights, toothbrush racks, and cigar holders were made to attract working capital. Tablewares regained favor. The factory still lost money. In desperation, the factory switched to industrial porcelains.

In 1862, the Royal Manufactory was leased to a private concern. The new managers produced art porcelain and reissued some of the earlier rococo figures. The pottery again became profitable.

Albert Keller from Sevres and Louis Levallois, a student from Sevres, developed an Art Nouveau line for Nymphenburg based the underglazed painting of figures. When Theodor Karner, a sculptor, came to Nymphenburg, he introduced a number of successful animal sculptures that were modeled after the animals and birds in Bavaria and the Munich Zoo. Animal motifs also were used on modern tablewares. Other tablewares were produced in the Art Nouveau style that encompassed linear decorations, stylized designs, and angular handles.

The popularity of the neo-classical, Empire, and Biedermeier movements that swept across Europe during the late 19th

Figure, 4" h, blue shield, white ground, pr, $225.

century achieved the same success at Nymphenburg. In 1887, the Baum family from Bohemia gained control of the company and still guide its fortunes today. Recently the company reproduced a number of pure-white figures from its old models. The company still has not regained the position of prominence it enjoyed in the past.

References: S. Ducret, *German Porcelain & Faience*, Universe Books, 1962; George W. Ware, *German & Austrian Porcelain*, Crown Publishers, Inc., 1963.

Museums: Bayerisches Nationalmuseum, Munich, Germany; Gardiner Museum of Ceramic Art, Toronto, Canada; Metropolitan Museum of Art, NY; Schlossmuseum, Berlin, Germany; Victoria & Albert Museum, London, England.

Box, Cov, 3 3/4" h, paneled, painted purple, yellow, and orange fruits and flowers, gold geometric designs on rims, figural orange and leaf knob 75.00

Butter Dish, 5 1/2" d, 12 sides, gray domed lid with berry and leaf knob, beaded rim . . 20.00

Figure

6" h, white regal lion seated on haunches, holding blue and white shield, "black

Figure, 4 3/4" h, 6 1/4" l, white glaze, imp mark, (A) $150.

crown over shield, Nymphenburg" mark 275.00

7" h, standing mourning Madonna, head to right, hands clasped at breast, white glaze, "imp shield and 4" mark, c1760, firing crack, (A) 21,850.00

8 1/2" h, man playing flute, woman seated on bench, child at feet, pierced scrolling arbor and pillar, rocaille base, white glaze, "green crowned C.T." mark, (A) 316.00

8 5/8" h, standing soldier wearing pink tricorn hat, turquoise lined pink jacket, upper body turned looking over shoulder, "imp shield, incised 169, & 3" marks, (A) 460.00

9 1/2" h x 18" l, wild boar chasing figure in 18th C dress, 20th C, (A) 518.00

12 3/4" h, cockatoo perched on branch of cherries, rococo base, polychromed, (A) 633.00

Soup Plate, 9 1/2" d, 12 sides, central castle landscape cartouche in black framed gilt banded blue enameled ribbon, raised beaded rim, late 19th C, set of 12 . . . . . . 1,150.00

Stein, .5 L, HP scene of Bavaria and lion, pewter base ring, relief pewter lid with leaf design and coin of bust of Ludoficus Bavarie Rex., lion thumblift, c1840 . . . . 2,000.00

Teapot, 4" h, globular, dbl scroll handle, bearded serpent spout, painted Indian style flowers in border of iron red scrolls and purple flowerheads, "imp shield" mark, c1757, chips 850.00

Vase, 13" h, campana shape, rect reserve of painted lions in mountain scene with palm trees, gilt lyre and stylized foliage scrolls on reverse, gilt socle, brown rect faux marble base, c1813, (A) 18,400.00

Figure, 5 3/4" h, 5 1/4" l, green leaf hat, lt yellow gown with lilac trim on rt figure, iron red trimmed pants, blue flowered top, gray hair on lt figure, gilt trimmed base, "imp shield" mark, $500.

OLD IVORY

Silesia, Germany

Late 1800s

History: Old Ivory dinnerware was made during the late 1800s in the pottery factories in Silesia, Germany. It derived its name from the background color of the china.

Marked pieces usually had a pattern number stamped on the bottom. The mark also may include a crown and "Silesia."

References: Alma Hillman, David Goldschmitt & Adam Szynkiewicz, *Collector's Guide to Old Ivory China,* Collector Books, 1997.

Collectors' Club: Old Ivory Porcelain Society, Jo Ann Hamlin, Route 3, Box 18B, Spring Valley, MN 55975. Membership: $25.00, *Elegance of Old Ivory* 3 times a year newsletter.

Berry Bowl
5" d
#11 pattern, Clairon mold 25.00
#84 pattern, Empire mold 25.00
5 1/2" d
#7 pattern, Clairon mold 25.00
#16 pattern, Clairon mold 20.00
#73 pattern
Clairon mold 30.00
Empire mold 30.00
#75 pattern, Empire mold 25.00
#82 pattern 25.00

Berry Set, master bowl, 9 1/2" d, 10 bowls, 5 1/2" d, #27 pattern, "Ohme Silesia" marks
. . . . 300.00

Biscuit Jar, 8" h, #16 pattern 525.00

Bowl
5" d, #84 pattern 35.00
5 1/2" d, #15 pattern 20.00
5 3/4" d, #7 pattern, Clairon mold . . 25.00
6 1/2" d, #84 pattern 50.00
8 1/2" d, #124 pattern 60.00
9 1/4" d
#15 pattern 195.00
#84 pattern 95.00
#200 pattern 195.00
9 3/8" d, #11 pattern 150.00
9 1/2" d
#15 pattern 135.00
#16 pattern 75.00
#22 pattern, Holly 225.00
#75 pattern 80.00

Butter Pat, #16 pattern 150.00

Cake Plate
10" H-H, open handles
#15 pattern 110.00
#16 pattern 80.00
#75 pattern, Empire mold 125.00
11" H-H, #84 pattern, Empire mold
. . . . 115.00

Cake Plate, 10" H-H, #XXII pattern, (A) $155.

Celery Bowl, 11" l, #84 pattern 150.00
Cereal Bowl, 6" d
    #7 pattern, Clairon mold 50.00
    #9 pattern. 32.00
    #10 pattern, Clairon mold 40.00
    #15 pattern, Clairon mold 40.00
    #16 pattern, Clairon mold 55.00
    #33 pattern, Empire mold 45.00
Charger, 13" d
    #11 pattern, Clairon mold 215.00
    #15 pattern, Clairon mold 225.00
    #16 pattern, Clairon mold 215.00
    #32 pattern, Empire mold 175.00
    #203 pattern, Deco mold. 200.00
Chocolate Pot, 9 1/2" h, pedestal base, #11
pattern. 498.00
Chocolate Set, pot, 6 cups an saucers, #16
pattern. 800.00
Chop Plate, 13" d, #11 pattern 135.00
Coffee Cup and Saucer
    #11 pattern, Clairon mold 85.00
    #15 pattern, Clairon mold 85.00
    #16 pattern, Clairon mold 80.00
Coup Plate
    7 1/2" d, #15 pattern, Clairon mold
    . . . . 65.00

Cracker Jar, 7 3/4" h, 8 3/4" l, #84 pattern, (A) $310.

Creamer and Sugar Bowl, creamer, 4" h, sugar bowl, 5 3/4" h, #84 pattern, (A) $410.

9 1/2" d
    #7 pattern, Clairon mold 200.00
    #10 pattern, Clairon mold . . . 200.00
    #11 pattern, Clairon mold . . . 200.00
Creamer
  3 1/4" h
    #9 pattern 35.00
    #16 pattern 90.00
    #15 pattern 35.00
Cup and Saucer
    #7 pattern 50.00
    #11 pattern, Clairon mold 65.00
    #15 pattern 40.00
    #16 pattern, Clairon mold 65.00
    #32 pattern, Empire mold 65.00
    #75 pattern 65.00
    #84 pattern 75.00
    #200 pattern, Deco mold 65.00
    #202 pattern, Deco mold 65.00
Cup and Saucer, Demitasse
    #28 pattern 60.00
    #75 pattern, Clairon mold 125.00
Gravy Boat, 8 1/2" l, with attached undertray,
#16 pattern. 595.00
Plate
  6" d, #118 pattern, Empire mold . . . 35.00
  6 1/8" d
    #11 pattern, Clairon mold 35.00
    #16 pattern 75.00
    #84 pattern 75.00
  6 1/4" d
    #7 pattern, Clairon mold 35.00
    #8 pattern, Clairon mold 35.00
    #10 pattern, Clairon mold 25.00
    #12 pattern, Clairon mold 25.00
    #16 pattern, Clairon mold 35.00
    #84 pattern, Empire mold 20.00
    "Holly" pattern 50.00
  6 1/2" d
    #12 pattern, Clairon mold 32.00
    #16 pattern
      Clairon mold. 35.00
      Empire mold. 35.00
    #73 pattern, Empire mold 35.00
    #75 pattern, Empire mold 35.00
    #202 pattern, Deco mold. 25.00
  6 3/4" d, #11 pattern, Claron mold . 35.00

7 1/4" d, #9 pattern 32.00
7 1/2" d
    #7 pattern, Clairon mold 45.00
    #10 pattern, Clairon mold 40.00
    #11 pattern, Clairon mold 35.00
    #15 pattern 20.00
    #16 pattern, Clairon mold 30.00
    #118 pattern, Empire mold 55.00
    #200 pattern, Deco mold 40.00
    #202 pattern, Deco mold 35.00
7 3/4" d
    #7 pattern, Clairon mold 45.00
    #15 pattern 95.00
    #16 pattern 37.00
8" d
    #28 pattern 30.00
    #82 pattern 85.00
    #200 pattern, Deco mold 65.00
8 1/4" d
    #7 pattern 85.00
    #16 pattern 44.00
8 1/2" d
    #11 pattern, Clairon mold. 55.00
    #15 pattern, Empire mold. 55.00
    #28 pattern, Modern mold 65.00
    #32 pattern, Empire mold 55.00
    #75 pattern, Empire mold 65.00
    #203 pattern, Deco mold 40.00
8 3/4" d, #84 pattern 48.00
9 3/4" d, #7 pattern, Clairon mold
    . . . . 200.00
Platter, 11 1/2" H-H
    #7 pattern, Clairon mold 115.00
    #10 pattern, Clairon mold 115.00
    #11 pattern, Clairon mold 110.00
    #16 pattern. 130.00
    #33 pattern, Alice mold 175.00
Salt and Pepper
    #11 pattern. 100.00
    #16 pattern. 125.00
    #75 pattern. 85.00
Tea and Toast Tray, 8 1/4" l, #202 pattern
. . . . 45.00
Teapot
  7" h, #15 pattern. 395.00
  7 1/8" h, demitasse, #16 pattern . . 395.00
Toothpick, #84 pattern 285.00
Tray, 11 1/2" l x 8 1/4" w, oval, self handles,
#11 pattern 150.00
Waste Bowl, 9" l x 7" w, #7 pattern 22.00

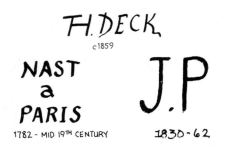

OLD PARIS AND PARIS

**Paris, France
18th and 19th Centuries**

Old Paris

History: Old Paris referred to porcelains made in the 18th and 19th centuries by various French factories located in and around Paris. Shapes were usually classical in design, decoration were elegant, and gilding was popular. Although some examples were marked, many were not.

Paris

History: Most of the early porcelain factories of France were located in and around Paris. Without marks it was difficult to differentiate between the various factories because their shapes and designs were similar. Strewn flower sprigs, especially the cornflower, and lots of gilding were favorite decorative motifs.

Fabrique du Conte d'Artois was founded by Pierre-Antoine Hannong in 1773. Hannong's polychrome flower painting was similar in style to that of Sevres. Coal was used to fire the ovens since the woods around Paris had been depleted by earlier porcelain manufacture. In 1787, Hannong was granted the rights to make figures in biscuit, paint in color, and use gilding. Production ended about 1828.

Hannong used the letter "H" as his mark.

Fabrique de la Courtille was founded by Jean-Baptiste Locre de Roissy, a potter from Leipzig, in 1773. He imitated German porcelains, including those of Meissen. Large vases were a specialty. The factory was taken over by Pouyat of Limoges about 1800. No exact date is known for its closing.

The factory mark was a pair of crossed torches that closely resembled the Meissen crossed swords.

Fabrique de la rue de Reuilly was established by Jean Joseph Lassia of Strasbourg about 1775. He used an "L" mark. Production ceased in 1784. Henri-Florentin Chanou had a factory nearby from 1779 to 1785. His mark was a "CH."

Fabrique de Clignancourt was founded by Pierre Deruelle in 1771. Porcelains rivaling Sevres were made. The decorative motifs included polychrome flowersprays and landscapes along with gilding. Some figures also were made.

The first mark was a windmill, a tribute to the windmills of Montmartre located nearby. A later mark was "LSX," a monogram for Louis XVIII.

Fabrique de la Reine was organized by Andre-Marie Leboeuf about 1778 under the protection of Marie-Antoinette. Products were called "porcelaine de la Reine."

The decorations included small sprigs of cornflowers, daisies, and roses, bird paintings, and some gilding. The factory was sold by Guy in 1797.

Fabrique Duc d'Angouleme was established by Dihl in 1780. Guerhard became his partner in 1786. The firm's main pattern was called "Angouleme Sprig," strewn cornflowers. The pattern was copied by many other factories. Biscuit figures were made. Dihl introduced the painting of portraits on porcelain. The favored decorative motif was designs in the Empire style. The factory was transferred to Fabrique rue du Temple in 1796.

Marks included "GA," "Dihl," "Guerhard and Dihl," or "Rue de Bondy."

Fabrique de la Popincourt, founded by Lemaire, was bought by Johann Nast in 1782. He moved it to Popincourt in 1784. Biscuit porcelains, biscuit clock cases, and Wedgwood imitations were made. The factory's marks were "Nest a Paris" or "N."

Fabrique du Duc d'Orleans was started by Louis de Villers and Augustin de Montarcy in 1784. Its mark was a monogram "MJ." In 1786, the factory changed hands. The mark became "LP." A single rose, decoration appears on some pieces.

Factory of the "Prince de Galles," the "Prince of Wales" factory, was established in 1789 by the Englishman Christopher Potter. He was the first in Paris to use the transfer printing method. The factory changed hands several times. The first mark was "Potter Paris," then "EB" for E. Blancheron, the manager in 1792, and finally "PB."

Fabrique de Petit rue Saint Gilles was started by Francois-Maurice Honore in partnership with Dagoty about 1785. They made vases in the style of Wedgwood. The names "Honore and Dagoty" were used in the marks.

Fabrique du Jacob Petit was established by Jacob Petit Fontainebleau in 1834. Much of Petit's porcelain was inspired by eighteenth century French and German examples. His animal tureens and figurals all looked to the past for inspirations; he used English shapes for his tea services. Many pieces contained relief ornamentation in the form of flowers, jewels, and fruit. The factory closed in 1866.

Reference: George Savage, *Seventeenth & Eighteenth Century French Porcelain*, Spring Books, 1969.

Museums: Musee National Adrien-Dubouche, Limoges, France; Musee National de Ceramique, Sevres, France; Munson-Williams-Proctor Institute, Utica, NY; Victoria & Albert Museum, London, England.

Basket, 8 1/2" l x 5 3/4" h, multicolored garden flowers in center, shaped reticulated border with gold rays to center, overhead handle with molded gilt trumpet flowers and stem, Old Paris 185.00

Cabinet Cup and Saucer, painted panel of peasant woman and peg leg soldier in int scene, claret ground, gilt banding with geometric designs, named on base, Darte Freres, c1820, (A) 1,495.00

Cachepot, 4" h x 6 1/4" H-H, cartouche of multicolored birds, cartouche of multicolored flowers, rose red ground, gilt trim and handles, white int, Paris 195.00

Celery Dish, 11 1/2" l, boat shape, scattered sm red and blue daisy heads, green leaves on int and ext, gilt lined rim, c1860 . . . . . 125.00

Centerpiece, 14" h, bisque figure of kneeling winged angel holding gold ext pierced flared basket, gold tasseled cushion on gold and green rect base with molded female masks and scrolls, paw feet, c1830, pr, (A) 5,750.00

Coffee Can and Saucer, en grisaille designs of young girls playing with birds, gilt rims, Petit Carrousel factory 350.00

Coffee Cup and Saucer, scrolling loop handle, band of gilt stylized lily buds and topiary on wide white band reserved on gilt ground, Dagoty & Honore, c1815, crack, (A). . 322.00

Cologne Bottle, 6 1/2" h, sq, 2 panels of raised gilt designs, 2 panels of gilt designs and multicolored florals in raised gilt cartouches, floral top, Old Paris 125.00

Comport, 6 5/8" h, multicolored scene of castle and river, pink borders with gold accents, Old Paris 250.00

Cup, 3 1/2" h, cartouche of multicolored bust of Lajos Kossuth, raised gilt design, gilt lined base 1,500.00

Coffee Service, Part, pot, hot water pot, creamer, cov sugar bowl, 7 cups and saucers, multicolored landscape scenes, gilt accents, (A) $467.

Cup and Saucer

Cylinder shape, en grissaille coastal scenes and portrait medallion reserved on gilt ground, Dihl & Guerhard
.... 450.00

Figural white biscuit swan form cup, gilt beak and int, gilt saucer with border band of white biscuit leaf tips, P.L. Dagoty, c1810, (A) 2,070.00

Dessert Plate, 8 3/4" d, floral spray in center on white ground, cavetto of floral sprays, gilt rim with blue band, set of 12, (A) 200.00

Dessert Service, Part, bowl, 10" d, coffee pot, 8 1/4" h, cov sugar bowl, 7 1/8" h, cream jug, 7 3/4" h, 10 dessert plates, 8" d, 6 teacups, 5 saucers, painted iron red and gilt classical figures, border of vine with pendant husks, P.L. Dagoty, cracks, chips, and repairs, (A)
.... 3,680.00

Dish, 8 1/2" l, oval, white ground with raised ribbon design and gilt lines and dots, open handle, scalloped rim, unmkd. 35.00

Ewer, 6 1/8" h, figural shell, purple, lt brown, and cream shaded ground, coral red figural handle, gilt rim, Edouard Honore, c1830, (A) 2,070.00

Figure, 27 1/2" h, gallant and companion in 18th C dress, polychrome, "blue X'd torchere" marks, pr, (A) 4,370.00

Flower Pot, 8" h, with stand, tapered cylinder shape, painted bouquet of loose flowers in gilt rocaille cartouche, green ground, gilt reeded bandstop and base, molded gilt lion head handles, Paris, c1830, pr, (A) 2,530.00

Jar, Cov, 6 5/8" h, turquoise glazed body and scroll handles, gilt metal rims with incised foliate banding, Theodore Deck, (A) 148.00

Luncheon Service, Part, 28 plates, 9 1/4" d, 18 plates, 8 1/4" d, 11 plates, 6 5/8" d, 12 sauce dishes, 7 1/8" d, 11 soup plates, 9 1/4" d, oval serving bowl, 12 1/2" l, oval platter, 17 1/2" l, 2 shaped dishes, 9 3/4" l, 2 circ cov vegetable tureens, 7 3/4" d, cov sauce tureen, oval cov tureen with undertray, 12 1/4" l, cov jam jar with undertray, 7 1/4" d, lt blue ground banding with gilt and iron red cartouche and monogram, mid 19th C, (A) 1,610.00

Perfume Bottle

4 3/4" sq, green ground with raised turquoise stones on shoulder corners, gilt cartouches with birds and butterflies in scrolls, mushroom stopper, 19th C
.... 350.00

9" h, figural, male or female historic figures in period dress or armor, multicolored and gold trim 545.00

Plaque, 13" d, central bust of black bearded Persian king in red helmet with yellow horns, blue costume, border of panels of warriors or script on yellow ground, "imp T. Deck" mark, (A) 1,693.00

Plate

8 1/4" d, gold chain cavetto, cobalt border with chain of gold Green key design, pr 395.00

8 5/8" d, painted center rural landscape scenes in wide gold inner band, peach border with Empire style stylized flowers in colonnades, gilt rim, c1835, set of 8, (A) 2,940.00

8 3/4" d, painted named scene of "Palais des Beaux Arts," claret red border with gilt diapering, gilt rim, Paris, mid 19th, (A) 690.00

9" d, painted reserve of various flowers, gilt accented pink border, 19th C, set of 5, (A) 184.00

9 1/2" d

Painted bouquet of flowers and scattered flowers in center, gilt dentil rim, "blue X'd torches" mark, c1780, set of 11, (A) 1,610.00

Painted center scene of Samson and Delilah in room setting, gilt border with chased flowering branches and reserves of putti or trophies, Paris, c1810, (A) 2,075.00

9 3/4" d, body painted with polychrome floral sprays, scalloped shell molded border, late 19th C, set of 11 (A) .. 261.00

Sauceboat, 11 1/2" l, with attached undertray, purple neo-classical band and strawberry roundels, gilt rim and rose band, (A)
.... 195.00

Sauce Tureen, 11 1/2" l x 4 1/2" h, with attached undertray, oval, band of red roses and green leaves, band of purple and dk purple geometrics, gilt accents, repeat design on undertray ext, sm floral sprays on int of undertray, gilt rect knob, c1815 .... 495.00

Sugar Bowl, Cov, 6 1/2" h x 7 1/2" d, bands of gilt bronze fruit and foliage on borders, scroll handles, Old Paris, pr 700.00

Teapot, 6" h, cov, shoulder and base with alternating rose wreaths and blue gilt panels, cream center band with roses, gilt oval panel with painted winged putti on side, Paris, 19th C, (A) 230.00

Tea Set, pot, 8 5/8" h, cream pitcher, 7 3/4" h, cov sugar bowl, 5 1/2" h, enamel decorated floral bouquets and banding, gilt ground, Paris, 19th C, cov damage, (A) 460.00

Tete-a-Tete Set, chocolate pot, 6 1/8" h, cov sugar bowl, 2 cups and saucers, tray, 11" sq, painted iron red, med blue, and gilt sprigs, border of flowering foliate garlands and blue ribbon entwined with blue ribbon enclosing single rose reserved in gilt scroll cartouches, "iron red crowned M" marks, c1773, (A)
.... 3,680.00

Tobacco Jar, 10 1/2" h, raised polychrome tobacco leaves, pipes, pouch, cards, dice, and gentleman smoking, twist handles, c1850
.... 1,250.00

Tureen, 6 1/2" h x 7" H-H, with underplate, multicolored exotic birds in raised gilt leaf type cartouches on sides, turquoise ground, white panels with multicolored flower chains, gold outlined flowerhead knob and scrolled

Urn, 7 5/8" h, multicolored florals, gold banding, c1820-30, $375.

leaf handles, gilt dentil rims, c1840, pr
.... 1,400.00

Urn, 11 1/2" h, campana form, cartouche of polychromed enameled landscape scene with figures, green body ground, gilt jeweling and trim, vert handles on ides, 19th C, pr
.... 1,700.00

Vase

6" h, flared flattened oval form, painted tulip and other flowers, green ground, "iron red JP" mark 600.00

7 1/4" h, Jack-in-the-pulpit shape, polychrome enameled floral bouquet on front, gilt trim, c1880, pr....... 425.00

7 1/2" h, flat shape, applied gilt and puce trimmed cartouche with bisque bust of George or Martha Washington, dk pink scattered roses, gilt accented fin type handles, molded wavy gilt outlined rim, band of dk pink dots on ft, c1890, pr
.... 425.00

9" h, rect shape, front panel painted with classic woman in yellow gown or woman in red gown holding umbrella, classic ruins on reverse and sides, platinum ground, gilt outlines and ear handles, c1878, pr, (A) 4,600.00

11 1/2" h, lg gilt lined sq panel of multicolored garden flowers on front, sm gilt lined sq of multicolored garden flowers on reverse, cobalt body, gilt neck, rim, socle, and sq base, figural chimera handles, c1880, pr, (A) 805.00

13" h

Baluster shape, painted birds on branches with open flowerheads, platinum ground, chased gilt rim and foot rim, c1878, pr, (A)
.... 8,625.00

Rococo form, foliate handles, shell molded ft, painted multicolored flower bouquet in gilt scrolling foliage, Paris, late 19th C, pr, (A) . . . 385.00

14" h, flattened flowerhead form, painted tulip and garden flowers in petals, green ground, applied cobalt and gilt flowerheads and gilt stems, "iron red JP" mark, 19th C, (A) 345.00

14 1/2" h, shield shaped body, flared ft, sq base, ruffled rim, figural goat and fruiting grapevine handles, gilt floral carouche of 18th C women in garden setting, reverse with floral carouche, blue enamel ground, 19th C, restorations, pr, (A) 575.00

15" h, baluster shape, front panel of painted 17th C int courtship scene, gold ground, gold winged female herm handles, (A) 2,645.00

17" h, multicolored scene of woman playing mandolin reserved on cobalt ground, gilt accents, applied gilt handles 100.00

PARIAN

English/Continental Early 1840s to 20th Century

1862

History: Parian had a slightly translucent, natural creamy white body fired to a matte finish. It was introduced in the early 1840s and remained popular during the entire Victorian era. Parian's strong resemblance to marble appealed to the Victorians since it suggested elegance, opulence, and wealth.

The best parian examples were characterized by the delicacy of the ware's texture. Its excellent molding versatility made it suitable for figures, utilitarian wares, and even floral jewelry pieces.

Among the many firms that have made parian china from the 1840s to the present time was Copeland. Pieces often were marked with an impressed "Copeland." After 1862, Minton impressed its parian with the name of the company and occasionally added the impressed year mark.

Parian also was manufactured by Belleck in Ireland and Coalport, Goss, Robinson and Leadbeater, Wedgwood, and Royal Worcester in England. Gustavsburg and Rorstrand in Sweden carried parian wares as part of their line. Most leading firms marked their parian wares. Smaller firms were less likely to do so.

References: Paul Atterbury, Editor, *The Parian Phenomenon*, Shepton Beauchamp, 1989; G.A. Godden, *Victorian Porcelain*, Herbert Jenkins, 1961; C.& D. Shinn, *The Illustrated Guide to Victorian Parian China*, Barrie & Jenkins, 1971.

Museum: Victoria & Albert Museum, London, England.

Figure

4 3/4" h, bust of young girl wearing ruffled bonnet, cross on chain around neck, (A) 35.00

5 3/4" h x 7 1/4" l, standing greyhound, head turned toward tail, shaped flat base, repaired crack, (A) 600.00

6" h, torso bust of Gladstone, "imp R & L" mark, c1880 . . . . 275.00

6 1/2" h, bust of laughing boy, tapered pedestal, sq base, "imp J. Teissonniere, Limoges, France" mark. 95.00

7 1/2" h, Bust of Bismark, sgd "Warth," dtd 1879 . . . . 125.00

7 3/4" h, "Matchmaking," 2 owls seated on tree log, England, dtd 1871 . . . 195.00

8 1/4" h
Bust of Sir Walter Scott, raised circ base, Copeland, (A) 230.00
"The Veiled Bride" bust, "J & T B" mark 250.00

8 1/2" h, bust of Charles Dickens, circ base, "imp Dickens," c1900 . . . 125.00

9" h, young girl carrying wheat, unmkd 65.00

9 1/2" h
Bust of Clytie, unmkd 450.00
"Winter," standing bearded old man in cloak, wood under arm, Copeland, (A) 100.00

9 3/4" h
Beethoven, seated on couch, molded sprigs on base, unmkd, (A). 220.00
Young boy standing on pedestal holding harp, wearing knee breeches, flowing cape, unmkd, (A) . . . 25.00

Figure, 9 1/2" h, Queen Alexandra, Robinson and Leadbeater, $375.

10" h
15" l, wild boar with dog under foot, rocky base, Sevres 2,500.00
Three standing woman, one holding child, center woman on brick wall with "Faith, Hope, Charity" on face 110.00

10 1/4" h, bust of Sir Walter Scott, circ base, unmkd, (A) 175.00

10 3/4" h, bust of Charles Sumner, circ base, "Equality of Rights is the first of Rights" on bk 650.00

11 1/4" h, bust of Dickens, raised circ base, Robinson & Leadbeater, (A) 259.00

11 3/4" h, farmer seated on rocky base, holding bagpipe, Copeland, repairs, (A) 172.00

12 7/8" h, bust of Charles Sumner, raised circ plinth, imp title and verse, Robinson & Leadbeater, c1880, (A) 345.00

13 3/4" h, standing muse holding mask, circ stepped base, c1880, chips 250.00

14" h
Bust of Sir John Campbell, "J. Ridgway, Bates & Co." mark, 19th C 475.00
Standing figures of Caster and Pollux, stepped base, "blue X'd swords" mark, c1814 . . . . 2,850.00

14 1/2" h, bust Milton, circ base, Wedgwood 875.00

14 3/4" h, bust of Stephenson, raised circ base, England, dtd 1853, (A) . . 517.00

15" h, standing figure
Canova holding floral garland, titled circ base, Minton, chips, (A) 747.00
Miranda seated on rocks, shells and waves at base, titled base, Minton, c1866, (A). 431.00

15 3/4" h, girl seated in chair, making lace, book in lap, unmkd 695.00

16" h, standing female peasant holding mandolin, ivory shades, Robinson & Leadbeater 550.00

16 1/2" h, kneeling maiden, hands in lap, raised circ base, Gustavsberg, late 19th C, (A) 575.00

17" h, goddess and winged Cupid, Minton, c1868. . . . . 625.00

18 1/2" h, standing nude female wearing arm bands, shackled wrists, draped column at side, Copeland, mid 19th C, (A) 748.00

20" h, young woman reading book, sgd "Detrier," chip on base 550.00

20 1/2" h, "Solitude," seated classical semi-nude lady, bird at side, "imp Art Union of London 1852" mark, Copeland 1,550.00

Oil Lamp, 11" h x 13" l, nude young scribe sitting on Greek style oil lamp, unmkd, chips 1,650.00

Pitcher

6 1/4" h, mask spout, scrolled ram's head handle, molded putti at spout, molded rounds of children as "Four Seasons" in acanthus leaf scrolls, British reg mark 195.00

11 1/8" h, relief of cherubs picking grapes from branches and tendrils, twisted branch handle, Copeland 550.00

Vase, 6" h, modeled as upturned hound's head, cornucopia at side, wrapped in cloth, England, c1860. . . . . 395.00

PATE-SUR-PATE (PASTE ON PASTE)

Austria, England, France, Germany
c1860 to 1900s

History: During the early 1860s, several Sevres potteries attempted to copy the Chinese technique of pate-sur-pate. In pate-sur-pate, the design exhibited a cameo-like decorative motif achieved by using tinted parian as the background and adding layers of white parian slip that then were carved into the design before the firing. When fired, the layers of white parian slip became semi-translucent and vitrified. The dark ground showed through the thinner parts.

Marc Louis Solon, who trained at Sevres, brought the Victorian pate-sur-pate process to England in 1870 when he began employment at Minton. At first he depicted tall, thin, classical female figures in diaphanous drapery. Later he expanded his repertoire to include children and cupids. Each creation was unique and signed.

Solon enjoyed a great reputation for his pate-sur-pate pieces. Since the painstaking pate-sur-pate technique was exceptionally slow and the market demand was great, Solon trained a series of apprentices while at Minton, the most talented of whom were A. Birks and L. Birks. Solon worked at Minton until 1904. After retirement, he worked free lance until he died in 1913.

Not all pate-sur-pate examples were made at Minton. Royal Worcester, Grainger-Worcester, the Crescent Potteries of George Jones, and several other firms manufactured pate-sur-pate pieces. F. Schenk produced many examples for Crescent Pottery at Stoke. These pieces were inferior and repetitive when compared to those made at Minton and Worcester.

Meissen, Berlin, and Vienna on the Continent were known for the production of pate-sur-pate. Pieces from these factories lacked the finesse of Solon's works and tended to be heavy and Germanic in style.

References: Paul Atterbury & Maureen Batkin, *Dictionary of Minton,* Antique Collectors' Club Ltd. 1996; Bernard Bumpers, *Pate-Sur-Pate,* Barrie & Jenkins, 1992; G.A. Godden, *Victorian Porcelain,* Herbert Jenkins, 1961.

Museums: National Collection of Fine Arts, Smithsonian Institution, Washington, DC; Victoria & Albert Museum, London, England.

Collecting Hints: Collectors should be aware that some George Jones wares are being sold as Minton products in today's marketplace.

Box, Cov

5 3/4" d

White female portrait, blue ground, Limoges, late 19th C, (A) 690.00

White garden flowers on blue ground in gold scrolled cartouche on cov, cream body with gold flowers, artist sgd, Limoges. 85.00

6" l, 3 white cherubs playing in clouds on dk blue ground in gilt cartouche, white body, France. 50.00

6 1/4" d, cov with white bust of woman wearing hooded cloak, holding holly branch, med blue ground, gold outlined dk blue border and body bands separated by cream ground, Limoges 975.00

Center Bowl, Cov, 14" h x 10 1/2" d, black ground field with teal blue ground trim, white slip panels of reclining maidens and putti, scrollwork border and base, Albione Birks, Minton, c1900, restored ft chip, (A) 5,462.00

Compote, Cov, 9 1/2" h, white slip design of chained putti, blue ground, med brown overglaze, buff and green slip trim, gilt accents, sgd "Louis Solon," Sevres, c1865, (A) 6,325.00

Flask, 10 1/4" h

Pilgrim, terra cotta and green slip center medallion of seated classical male, white slip cartouche of putti and scrolled foliate design, dk blue ground, gilt handles, Minton, c1881. . . 1,500.00

White slip design of seated angel releasing cherubs from sack, blue ground, polychrome slip borders, gold trim, sgd "Louis Solon," Minton, c1870, (A) 8,050.00

Plaque

5 3/4" h x 3" w, white slip design of standing maiden holding candlestick, 3 putto overhead, brown ground, France, (A) 1,840.00

6" h x 4 3/4" w, oval, white slip design of Cupid breaking chain with hammer on anvil, dk blue ground, sgd "Louis Solon," gilt wood frame, (A) 1,840.00

6 1/2" h x 4 1/2" w, oval, white slip figure of Cupid standing on globe holding chains, dk brown ground, Louis Solon, 1907, mtd in frame, (A) 2,645.00

8 1/2" h x 15 1/2" l, rect, white slip design of 5 female warriors with shields, swords, and helmets, reclining Cupid on trellis above, brown ground, sgd "Louis Solon," dtd 1880, wood frame, (A) 9,200.00

9 1/2" h x 5 1/2" w, oval, white slip design of flying angel with stars overhead, dk blue ground, sgd "Louis Solon," England, c1908, ebonized and gilt wood frame, (A) 3,737.00

16" h x 11" w, oval, "La Nouvelle Psyche," colored slip design of maiden holding lantern, putto with torch, mottled blue-gray ground, France, 1870, (A) 2,760.00

Plate, 9 1/8" d, white slip design of nude child behind net strung from 2 trees, dk brown ground, gilt geometric rim, Moore Brothers, c1885, (A) 748.00

Tray, 13 1/2" l, rect, center panel of white slip design of 2 putti flanking urn, brown ground, gilt trim, gilt field of circ dots on cream ground, silvered molded handles, Louis Solon, Minton, c1878, (A) 6,325.00

Vase

5 1/4" h, Pilgrim, white slip design of 3 flying putti, ribbon tied floral border, black-brown ground, enamel and gilt shoulder, Minton, chips on ft, pr, (A) 2,990.00

5 5/8" h, cylinder shape with circ ft, white slip design of egrets in water foliage, gray ground, gilt trim, cobalt ft, Pillivuty and Co., c1870, (A) 747.00

6" h, gilt trimmed oval cartouches of white slip design of classical figures fishing, brown ground, gilt band of leaves on border, gilt ring handles, George Jones, c1885, pr, (A) 1,610.00

Vase, 8 1/2" h, white cameo on lilac ground, pink and blue enameled flowers, green leaves, med blue ground, gilt trim, "Made in Germany" mark, $850.

6 7/8" h, ovoid shape, flared rim, white slip design of young girl seated in garden facing rt or lt on mauve ground oval cartouche, blue ground, 2 gilt trimmed handles from shoulder to rim, Germany, pr, (A) 748.00

7 1/4" h, white holly berries and leaves, celadon green ground, gold twisted serpentine handles, unmkd, pr 995.00

7 1/2" h, white neo-classical scene, black ground, late 1800s 485.00

8 1/2" h, white slip bust of male or female mythological figure, med brown wash, dk blue ground, stylized column and urn border with gilt trim, loop handles with coil bases, sgd "Miles," Sevres, c1865, pr, (A) 7,475.00

9 1/2" h

Brown ground, white slip florals tied with ribbon, gilt flowerheads on base, gilt shaped rim and coiled handles, Albione Birks, Minton, late 19th C, pr 4,312.00

White slip scene of maiden in rainstorm, green ground, gilt trimmed base, neck, and ring handles, Albione Birks, Minton, (A) 1,725.00

14" h, Pilgrim, circ panels of white slip design of oriental figural courtyard, reverse with oriental furniture, gilt and brown enamel designs on celadon green border, mtd on base, Minton, c1876, (A) 3,737.00

16" h, white slip design of maiden standing among putti, reverse with putti supporting seated Cupid, blue ground, gilt trimmed neck, base, and knot formed handles, sgd "Louis Solon," Minton, c1892, neck restored, (A) 4,600.00

20 5/8" h, white slip design of "The Creation of the earth," putti playing with orbs, reverse with female holding torches and orbs, dk blue ground wide gilt borders and starburst handles, sgd "Louis Solon," Minton, c1889, (A) 20,700

PEARLWARE

English
c1780-c1865

History: Pearlware, a variation of white creamware body, had a slightly bluish tint due to the addition of a small quantity of cobalt to the glaze. Pearlware was closer in general appearance and whiteness to porcelain than creamware. Wedgwood first made pearlware about 1779.

Pearlware was made mostly in tablewares. Among the leading Staffordshire manufacturers were Herculaneum, Phillips Longport, Davenport, Clews, T. Mayer, Enoch Wood, Rogers, and Stubbs. Potteries at Leeds and Swansea also produced pearlware.

Polychrome floral decorations on pearlware became popular about 1800 and continued for approximately twenty years. These designs, usually in yellow, green, orange, or on silver luster resist, were most commonly found on pitchers and jugs. Mocha decoration also was used on pearlware bodies.

Vast quantities of pearlware were shipped to the United States between 1790 and 1830. Some firms, such as Enoch Wood, produced pearlware specifically for the American market. Shell edge plates were decorated with the American eagle and shield in polychrome; other plates depicted prints of American ships with polychrome flags. Later blue transfer prints of American landmarks were applied to pitchers, plates, and chamber pots.

Museum: Victoria & Albert Museum, London, England.

Bird Feeder, 4 3/4" h, domed pedestal, seated draped figure on top, sponged blue, ochre, yellow, and brown surface, Staffordshire, c1800, (A). 575.00

Candlestick, 10 1/4" h, modeled as standing classical youth holding dog, blue robe, rt hand holding reeded foliate stem with green acanthus bobeche and nozzle, sq base with canted sides, molded with petals, "NEALE & CO." mark, c1780 . . . . 1,500.00

Chestnut Basket, 7 3/4" h, with undertray, "Mared" pattern, molded intersecting scrolls, husks, and acanthus leaves, cov pierced, flower and foliage finial, twisted dbl entwined handles with briar terminals, stand pierced with Greek key pattern, blue overall accents and blue buds, "WEDGWOOD" mark, c1790 . . . . 5,500.00

Coffeepot

9 1/4" h, dome shape, oriental scene of building in landscape, flying birds, blue transfer, rope twist handle, early 19th C, (A) 316.00

12" h, oriental scene of fisherman at lake, mountains in bkd, flowerheads on cov, blue transfer, Staffordshire, c1820 . . . . 750.00

Creamer

3 3/4" h, barrel shape, cobalt and yellow leaf design at rim, sm green leaves, cobalt banded rim, blue striped base, blue leaf design on handle, molded foliate design on handle, chips, (A) . . 100.00

4" h, oval shape, 4 sm feet, black dashed dolphin handle, red, green, and black flowers with underglazed blue buds, black stripe on shoulder, (A) . . . 55.00

Creamer and Cov Sugar Bowl, creamer, 4 1/2" h, sugar bowl, 5" h, meandering blue stems with orange-brown flowers, bunches of green leaves at terminals, brown lined rims, blue herringbone pattern on handles, c1820 . . . . 1,100.00

Cup and Saucer

Couple having tea in garden with servant and dog, red transfer, (A) 50.00

Red cabbage rose flowers, green leaves, blue buds and blue flowers with yellow centers, red stripes on rims, hairlines, set of 4, (A) 350.00

Cup and Saucer, Handleless

Black, rust, and yellow feather pattern 100.00

Border of brown line loops with hanging single stroke yellow flowers, blue leaves, and red drops, yellow and blue flowers in center of saucer, gray-green lined rims 375.00

Cup and Saucer, Miniature, vert lt blue, green, and brown stripes, (A). 210.00

Handleless

Blue floral sprig with green leaves, red buds, and black stems, (A) . . 25.00

Sm green floral sprig in center of saucer and cup bottom, green stripes on sides, green band on rims, (A). 60.00

Cup Plate, 4 1/8" d, HP red rooster with black accented yellow wing, green, red, and yellow foliate ground, lt blue rim stripe, unmkd, (A) 60.00

Dish, 7 3/4" l, oval, blue painted bouquet in pierced gallery, Staffordshire, c1820, pr, (A) 210.00

Figure

3 1/4" l, bird pecking at wheat, mound base, dk brown and olive splashes, (A) 375.00

3 1/2" h, standing bird, yellow, blue, and ochre wings and spots, green circ base, Yorkshire, c1800, restored base, (A) 633.00

Figure, 8 3/4", 9 1/4" h, Minerva and Poseidon, yellow and white clothes, turquoise dolphin, green lined base, pr, (A) $380.

3 7/8" l x 2 1/8" h, hooded Christening cradle, figure of sleeping child in long dress in blue, green, and orange accents, molded basketweave cradle, yellow body with brown line rim, chips, (A) 510.00

4 1/4" h

Hessian soldier standing and holding rifle, brown, yellow, ochre, blue, and green splashed glazes, sq base, Staffordshire, c1760, pr, (A) 1,265.00

Spring, woman seated in armchair, brown and green accents, Staffordshire, repaired, (A) 220.00

4 3/8" l, recumbent lion, brown mane, dk ochre fur, green grass base, Yorkshire, c1780, (A) 1,265.00

5 3/4" h, standing figure of Apollo holding lyre, books at feet, sq base, blue accents, England, 1780, restored chip, (A) 115.00

6 1/8" l, recumbent sheep, ochre spots, 3 brown stripes on back, green mound base, c1820, (A) 1,955.00

Hot Water Plate, 10" d, blue feather edge, (A) 248.00

Jug, 4 3/4" h, globular, yellow, ochre, brown, and green accented relief of hounds running in woods with fruiting vines, blue rope twist rim, Yorkshire, c1810, (A) 650.00

Loving Cup, 7 1/2" h, blue transfer printed scattered florals and *Love Feast*," mid-19th C, (A) 200.00

Mug, 4 5/8" h, cylinder shape, arched handle with acanthus terminals, 3 dk brown bands, top and base bands with yellow rosettes and dots, center band with yellow foliate design, orange and green scattered sprigs on body, (A) 100.00

Pepper Pot, 4 1/2" h, ftd, domed top, bulbous base, wide green band at waist, green stripe on collar, and ft, unmkd, (A) 150.00

Pitcher

6 5/8" h, red, blue, green, and black gaudy floral design, molded acanthus leaf handle, repairs, (A) 110.00

9 1/8" h, stylized blue and rust flowerheads and meandering brown stems and green leaves on sides, brown lined base, brown lined rim with hanging blue zigzag and yellow drop leaves and orange-brown leaves 675.00

Plaque

7" d, relief of Bacchus, Venus, and Ceres with attendants, blue, ochre, brown, and green accents, Staffordshire, c1810, (A) 1,380.00

7 3/8" d, relief of cow herder in blue jacket, yellow pants, brown hat, yellow spotted cows, brown spotted dogs, brown and green trees, yellow beaded border, brown reeded rim, Yorkshire, c1810, (A) 1,495.00

Plate

6 3/4" d, 2 ochre flowerheads and brown leaves in center, border of hanging brown drops with stylized blue and yellow flowerheads, brown lined rim 175.00

7" d, lg red cabbage rose, sm red and yellow flowers with green leaves, red striping on scalloped rim, (A) 150.00

7 3/4" d, blue and white oriental scene of house on hill, flanked by trees, rocks in front, blue rim with wavy line, "imp Turner" mark, (A) 165.00

9 1/4" d, black transfer inscription of "Sir Philip Musgrave Bart and the Constitution 1820" over crossed flags, repaired rim chip, pr, (A) 690.00

9 3/8" d, red, blue, and green floral sprig with black stem in center, border with band of yellow, blue, and black pansy flowerheads and green and red leaves and black stems, scalloped red lined rim, (A) 75.00

9 3/4" d, blue center scene of oriental man with umbrella near pagoda, blue outlined molded feather border, England, c1800, (A) 201.00

9 7/8" d, lg yellow-orange cabbage rose in center with yellow-orange buds, green and yellow leaves, dk brown stem, sm floral sprigs on border, dk brown banded rim, (A) 150.00

10" d

Bust of Napoleon Bonaparte, named in flowing ribbon under portrait, blue transfer, early 19th C 150.00

Polychrome center scene of musician with couple in garden ruins or man and dog in landscape, floral sprays on spirally fluted border, basketweave outer border, gilt shaped rim, France, c1790, pr 650.00

10 1/16" d, border band of red berries, green leaves, and black stems, "imp Wedgwood" mark, (A) 50.00

Platter

17 5/8" l x 14" w, rect with cut corners, sprig design, scattered red buds, green leaves, black stems, (A) 200.00

19" l, oriental scene in center, butterfly border, med to dk blue 535.00

Potpourri Vase, 7" h, relief of white floral swags over engine turned flutes, blue ground, Wedgwood, c1800, restored, married cov, (A) 230.00

Quintal, 7" h, underglaze blue and ochre, brown, and green enameled birds and foliage, silver luster accents, pr, (A) 495.00

Sauceboat, 5 1/4" l, figural swan, loop neck, tail spout, sponged ochre and brown body, blue tail feathers, Yorkshire, c1800, (A) 1,265.00

Sauce Tureen, Cov, 8" l, oval, "Mared" pattern, molded shell edge on cov and body rims, bands of blue buds around body and cov, twisted dbl entwined handles ending in briars and applied florets, pedestal base molded with overlapped shells, underglazed

blue accents, figural seahorse knob, "WEDGWOOD" mark, c1790, pr 7,200.00

Spill Vase, 5 1/4" h, modeled spiral molded cornucopia with rocaille scroll, brown, ochre, and green accents, Yorkshire, c1800, (A) 625.00

Sugar Bowl, Cov, 5 1/4" h, underglaze blue floral wreath and blue striping, button knob with blue floral swags and striping, molded ring and shell handles, scalloped rim, chips and hairlines, (A) 100.00

Sugar Box, Cov, 6 1/2" h, sq, pattern of tulip, peony, rose, coreopsis, and sweet William bouquet in vase, bird and flowers in bkd, med blue transfers, arched leaf form handles, sq knob, Staffordshire, c1830 .... 595.00

Tankard

4 1/2" h, HP brown, black, yellow, and green enameled farm and agricultural equipment and haystack, (A) .. 412.00

4 3/4" h, cylinder shape, loop handle, enameled polychrome Chinese woman holding parasol, attendant at side, Staffordshire, c1775, (A) 460.00

Teapot

5" h, parapet shape, HP enamel oval reserves of shepherd and 2 females with book, shepherd with 2 females and instrument on reverse, fruiting grapevine border, Wedgwood, c1790, (A) 2,185.00

5 3/4" h, oblong, paneled, blue painted basketweave body, blue wheel border, figural swan finial, c1800 .... 1,150.00

6 7/8" h, molded cartouche of putto, molded floral and stiff leaf designs, green and pink luster highlights, repaired, (A) 247.00

Toddy Plate, 4 3/8" d

Blue feather edge, "imp Alcock" mark, (A) 65.00

Pink sunflower with cobalt leaves and gold accents, scattered pink buds and green leaves, pink lined scalloped rim, (A) 150.00

Tureen, 5 1/2" h x 8" l, with ladle and undertray, green edge 2,200.00

Vase, 7" h, white applied drapery festoons, tan colored slip ground, gilt accents, "Wedgwood" mark, restored, (A) 161.00

Vegetable Bowl, 9 7/8" d, blue accented molded beaded rim, chips, (A) 50.00

Waste Bowl, 4 3/8" d, "Opium Smokers" pattern, men smoking long pipes by river on ext, cell and diaper border, floral int border, brown transfer "clobbered" with blue, yellow, orange, and dk brown, Yorkshire 350.00

Water Pitcher, 8 1/4" h, bulbous shape, sq handle, band of blue swags from shoulder with foliate pendants, foliate band on shoulder and handle, blue banded rim and base, (A) 260.00

Whistle, 3" h, figural bird, blue and manganese wings, round base, Staffordshire, c1800, chip, (A) 375.00

PIANO BABIES

England and Germany
19th Century

History: Piano babies, primarily in bisque, ranged in size from two to twelve inches long. They were popular additions to Victorian parlors, usually found on the top of a piano.

Piano babies were produced in a variety of poses from crawling, sitting and lying on their stomachs, to lying on their backs playing with their toes. Some babies were dressed; some were nude.

The most popular manufacturer was Heubach Brothers of Germany. Other identified makers include Hertwig and Company and Royal Doulton.

4" l x 2 1/2" h, bisque, crawling, blue trimmed white gown, blond-brown hair, Germany, (A) 30.00

5 3/4" h, bisque, seated, legs crossed, arms raised, blond hair, open white nighty with pink trim 395.00

6" h, bisque, seated child, blond hair

Pink nighty, gold buttons, blue ribbon on shoulder 185.00

White nighty with blue ribbons and bows, hands outstretched 55.00

6" l, bisque

Lying on back holding toe, blond hair with headband, blue trimmed pink nighty, unmkd 40.00

Lying on stomach, foot raised, leaning on elbow, lt blue nighty with white and pink trim 65.00

10" h, lt brown hair, pink underdress, lime green nighty, gold trim, $525.

6 1/2" h, bisque, seated, yellow dress, red accented bow, HP red and white floral rosettes, Germany, (A) 45.00

6 1/2" l, bisque, baby crawling on stomach, ft raised in air, blond hair, lt blue nighty with blue ribbon on bk, imp Heubach mark . . . 495.00

7" h, bisque, seated girl holding pear, yellow dress with raised gold dots, pink and blue trim 370.00

7" l, bisque, baby lying on back, blond hair, white nighty with blue collar trim and bow, holding gold ball in hands 255.00

7 1/2" l, crawling baby, white gown with blue ribbon and bow, Heubach 195.00

8" l x 5" h, bisque, baby lying on stomach, blue dress, Germany 125.00

8 7/8" h, bisque, seated baby holding toes, white nighty with blue ribbon and bows 275.00

9" l, bisque, blond baby on back, one hand holding toe, turquoise trimmed white nighty, unmkd 750.00

9 1/4" l, bisque, crawling on stomach, blond hair, white nighty with pink bows on shoulder 200.00

9 1/2" l, bisque, baby lying on stomach, white dress, pink ribbons, dimpled face . . . 175.00

10" l, bisque, baby crawling on stomach, brown hair, relief molded lace outlined nighty with red trim, holding tan basket in hand, unmkd 495.00

PITCHER AND BOWL SETS

English/Continental 19th and Early 20th Centuries

History: Pitcher and bowl sets or washstand china were popular during the 19th and early 20th centuries. A typical set consisted of a pitcher (ewer) and basin, soap dish, sponge dish, toothbrush tray, and slop pail. Additional specialized pieces, e.g. hair receivers and comb box, also were available. Wash sets allowed an individual to complete washing up in the privacy of the bedroom. The availability of piped water put an end to the Victorian and Edwardian jug and basin sets.

The list of manufacturers of washstand china was large. Principal English manufacturers included Minton, Wedgwood, George Jones, Doulton, Clarice Cliff, and Ridgway. Many continental companies also made washstand china.

Collecting Hints: Not every set has the same number of pieces. Many sets featured only the pitcher and bowl.

Two Piece

Pitcher, 3 1/8" h, bowl, 3 1/2" d, miniature, gold banding and striping, white ground, Staffordshire, (A) 65.00

Two piece, pitcher, 9" h, bowl, 10" d, orange flowerheads, orange-brown, tan, and green leaves, black stems, tan shaded ground, Charlotte Rhead, Crown Ducal, c1905, $500.

Pitcher, 6" h, bowl, 9 1/2" d, sponged multicolored swimming fish, green sponged seaweed, orange-brown rim and handle, Dartmouth 259.00

Pitcher, 8 7/8" d, bowl, 11" d, paneled, Willow pattern, blue, Mason 595.00

Pitcher, 9 1/2" h

Bowl, 12" d, overall blue spatter, chips, (A) 385.00

Bowl, 12 1/2" d, "Genevese" pattern, brown transfers, Minton 800.00

Pitcher, 10" h

Bowl, 12 3/4" d, "Chapoo" pattern, lt blue transfers 650.00

Bowl, 13 1/2" d

Family fishing and picnicking, dk blue transfers, England 1,275.00

Wide yellow-brown center band with enameled floral design, copper luster ground, unmkd 1,500.00

Bowl, 15" d, "Oceanic" pattern, sailboat and seashells, brown transfers, "Stoner, Hollinhead & Oliver, Henley" mark 145.00

Bowl, 17" d, wide blue flowerheads, raised gold swirl design, "W.H. Grindley" mark 875.00

Pitcher, 10 1/2" h

Bowl, 12 1/2" d, paneled, "Scinde" pattern, flow blue, J. & G. Meakin, c1840 . . . . 4,995.00

Bowl, 14 3/4" d, "Sado" pattern, cartouches of heads of oriental children, brown transfers, Brownfield 400.00

Bowl, 16 1/2" d, "Campion" pattern, flow blue, "W.H. Grindley" mark 1,200.00

Pitcher, 10 7/8" h, bowl, 14 1/2" d, "Etruria" pattern, red transfers of blossoms and leaves, Challinor & Mayer 200.00

Pitcher, 11" h

Bowl, 15 1/2" d, medallions of wild roses, deer, and waterfall, brown transfers, cream ground. . . . 200.00

Bowl, 16" d, lg HP roses and daisies, sponged gold accents 230.00

Pitcher, 11 1/4" h, bowl, 14 1/2" d, brown scattered dogwood blossoms, England
. . . . 150.00

Pitcher, 11 1/2" h

Bowl, 10 3/4" d, "Lafayette at Franklin's Tomb," dk blue transfers, Enoch Wood & Sons, (A) 1,610.00

Bowl, 13 1/4" d, white ironstone, "Scalloped Decagon" shape, John Wedgwood. 375.00

Bowl, 13 1/2" d, med blue sponging, blue striped bands around bases
. . . . 895.00

Bowl, 14" d, "Medici" pattern, blue transfers, "Mellor, Venables & Co." marks 850.00

Pitcher, 11 3/4" h, bowl, 17 1/4" d, "Primula" pattern, flow blue 1,475.00

Pitcher, 12" h

Bowl, 14" d, paneled, red and green Cluster of Buds design in white ovals, black spatter ground, repaired bowl, (A) 4,400.00

Bowl, 16" d, "Balls of Snow" pattern, lt blue sprays of hydrangeas, "Boules de Neige, Societie Ceramique Maastricht Holland" mark . . . 675.00

Bowl, 16 3/4" d, flow blue, molded scrolls, sponged gold, Wood & Sons 1,450.00

Pitcher, 12 1/4" h, bowl, 17" d, tea roses and leaves, white to tan shaded ground, gold trim, Royal Doulton 375.00

Pitcher, 12 3/4" h

Bowl, 14 1/8" d, "Whampoa" pattern, flow blue 1,575.00

Bowl, 14 7/8" d, tea leaf ironstone, Alfred Meakin 295.00

Bowl, 15 3/8" d, paneled pitcher, raised gold chrysanthemums, green leaves, brown stems, scattered magenta and turquoise flowers and stems, cream

ground, raised English registry mark
. . . . 195.00

Pitcher, 13" h

Bowl, 13 1/2" d, white ironstone, "Wheat" pattern, "Ceres" shape, Elsmore & Forster 395.00

Bowl, 14" d, "Peruvian Horse Hunt" pattern, green and brown transfers
. . . . 1,095.00

Bowl, 17 1/2" d, "Atlas" pattern, flow blue 1,200.00

Pitcher, 13 1/8" h, bowl, 17" d, flowing blue "Alexandra" pattern, (A) 300.00

Pitcher, 14 1/2" h

Bowl, 15" d, pink shading on borders, England 275.00

Bowl, 15 1/4" d, shaded orange to yellow ground, gold striped and sponged borders, "Semi-Porcelain, Johnson Brothers" marks . . 275.00

Bowl, 15 3/8" d, "Marguerete" pattern, florals and leaves, stylized flowerheads on borders, brown transfers, Clementson 175.00

Bowl, 15 1/2" d, lobed rect pitcher, tan and brown geometric band, border band of dk pink hanging florals on pink ground, molded dot and drape border, orange lined rim, England
. . . . 425.00

Bowl, 16 1/2" d, "Kensington" pattern, ext with hanging drape of mauve roses and blue leaves, Art Nouveau style vert lines with blue leaves, 6 mauve roses with blue leaves on inner border of bowl, vert intertwined stems on pitcher with hanging garlands, blue lines and leaves and mauve roses, gilt trimmed handle and rims, "Losol Ware, Keeling & Co." mark. 395.00

Three Piece

Pitcher, 15 1/8" h, bowl, 15 1/2" d, cov soap dish with insert, "Eagle" pattern, blue transfers, "Pearl Stone Ware, Eagle, P.W. & Co." marks, (A). . . . 260.00

Four Piece

Pitcher, 14" h, bowl, 16" d, toothbrush holder, 5 3/4" h, cov soap dish, 6" d, "Aubrey" pattern, Doulton. . . . 1,795.00

Five Piece

Pitcher, 11 1/2" h

Bowl, 14" d, pitcher, 6 1/2" h, mug, 3 1/2" h, cov soap dish, 6" d, gold outlined wide pink band, cream ground, gold rims, England 150.00

Bowl, 17 1/4" d, toothbrush holder, 6" h, cov soap dish, 6 3/4" d, chamber pot, 9" d, lg yellow and white flowerheads and buds, mint green ground, gold rims, raised English registry numbers 525.00

Pitcher, 11 5/8" h, bowl, 15" d, pitcher, 7 1/8" h, toothbrush holder, cov rect soap dish, brown floral transfers with pink and green shaded accents, molded ribbed bands on rims and bases, gold striped

bases and rim designs, "John Maddock & Sons, England, Royal Vitreous and crown" marks, chips, (A) 140.00

Six Piece

Pitcher, 12" h, bowl, 17 1/2" d, pitcher, 4" h, pitcher, 7" h, toothbrush holder, 5" h, chamber pot, cov, 10 3/4" d, molded curlicues, gold sponged accents, W.H. Grindley 275.00

Pitcher, 12 3/4" h, hairline, bowl, 16 1/2" d, hot water pitcher, 7 3/8" h, toothbrush holder, 5" h, cov soap dish, 6 1/2" d, cov chamber pot, "Atlas" pattern, flow blue, "W.H. Grindley" marks 3,500.00

Seven Piece

Pitcher, 11 1/2" h, bowl, 15 1/8" d, pitcher, 7 3/8" h, toothbrush holder, shaving mug, cov soap dish with insert, cov chamber pot, "Avon" pattern, brown transfers, "Avon, F. Winkle & Co., England" marks, (A) 350.00

PORTRAIT WARE

English/Continental
Mid 19th C to 1900

History: Plates, vases, and other pieces with portraits and busts on them were popular during the mid-19th century. Male subjects included important historical figures, such as Napoleon, Louis XVI, and James Garfield. However, most portraits featured beautiful women, ranging from the French Empress Josephine to unknown Victorian ladies.

Many English and continental firms made portrait ware. Makers included Royal Vienna, Limoges, Schumann, and MZ Austria. Most examples were hand painted and often bore an artist's signature. Transfer prints supplemented the hand painted pieces.

Reproduction Alert: Portrait plates were imported to the United States by reproduction wholesalers and giftware distributors during the 1970s and 80s. These utilized full color transfers that also appeared on urns, vases, and compotes as well as plates. Many carried Germany and Austrian backstamps as well as facsimile signatures. Beware of gold trim that is too shiny.

Bud Vase

4 3/4" h, multicolored bust of Marie Antoinette wearing lg green hat with pink feathers in tooled gilt cartouche, green paneled ground with gilt tooled leaves, "blue shield mark," Royal Vienna
. . . . 600.00

5" h x 5" H-H, squat shape, ribbed base, bust of woman with brown cascading hair, blue low-cut dress, mauve ground, Austria, c1915 . . . . 29.00

5 3/8" h, bust of woman, red turban in hair, black flowing hair, gold necklaces, blue print gown, brown shaded ground, 2 sm

Two 2 piece, pitcher, 9 1/2" h, bowl, 15 1/4" d, "Wamba" pattern, blue, yellow, and green Art Nouveau style florals, white ground, Wedgwood, (A) $200.

gold trimmed handles, Czechoslovakia 25.00

Cake Plate, 11" H-H, bust of smiling woman, lt brown hair, white and blue off-shoulder gown, brown shaded ground in gold stenciled cartouche, lt green to white shaded border with molded design and gold overlay, "Imperial Austria" mark..................... 55.00

Charger, 12 3/8" d, bust of von Hindenburgh in center, cobalt border, gold shaped rim, "RM Austria" mark................ 225.00

Plaque, 10 3/4" l x 8 3/4" h, rect, HP bust of woman with long brown hair, holding peacock feather, arm on pillow, Limoges 1,800.00

Plate

7 1/8" d, 10 sides, bust of woman with brown curly hair, star band on forehead, pale blue scarf on neck, white gown, blue border with molded hanging drape and gilt stenciled swirls, "Limoges France" mark................ 80.00

7 3/8" d, bust of woman facing left wearing middle eastern headpiece and necklace, white bodice, band of yellow stars on blue ground on sleeve, gold pattern border with 5 floral circles, C.T. Germany 45.00

8 3/8" d, bust of woman with brown curly hair, star band on forehead, cream gown with gilt trim, brown border with gold overlay, "C.T. Germany and eagle" mark..................... 45.00

8 3/4" d

Half bust of woman with white flowers in black hair, green dress, holding bunch of white flowers, raised gold outlined flowerhead border .. 45.00

"Martha," bust of woman, white collar and hat, blue trim, tan ground, gilt rim, "Johnson Bros. England, Tatler 572" mark................ 95.00

9 1/2" d

Bust of brown haired female, brown dress with white insert, white mantilla flowing from hair, holding paint

Plate, 8 1/2" d, "Amorosa," brown hair, mauve and blue gown, burgundy luster border, raised gilt accents, "Z.S. & Co. Bavaria, gold crown and shield" marks, $125.

brush and palette, shaded green ground, wide rust brown border, scalloped rim with raised gold trim, Royal Munich............. 75.00

Portrait bust smiling woman, lt brown flowing hair, lt blue gown from breast, lt brown ground, gold design inner border, lt green border with tooled gold rim, Austria 95.00

Thalia, painted bust of black haired woman with yellow roses in hair, dk red dress, border with Art Nouveau style gilt shaped cartouches and flowers on lt yellow and pink ground, Hutschenreuther, c1910, (A) 805.00

9 5/8" d, painted frontal bust of Euphemia in red cloak and green leaf crown, lt green ground, border with gilt heart-shaped cartouches with red ground, rect panels, and lappets, and gilt foliate scrolls, sgd "Wagner," Hutschenreuther, (A) 805.00

9 3/4" d

Bust of woman, brown hair, pale purple fringed lavender shawl on shoulder, gold stenciled inner rim, green border with raised molded and gilt overlay, "blue Victoria Austria" mark 125.00

Bust of woman with head turned red rose in brunette hair, red and white off-shoulder gown, gold drop inner border, cobalt outer border with gold overlay, "O. & E.G. Royal Austria" mark................ 95.00

Vase, 6 1/4" h, brown hair, lt blue gown, blue bkd, olive green and brown shaded lower section, "Austria" mark, $70.

Vase, 9" h, brown hair, purple sash, multicolored bkd, gold rim, Royal Bayreuth, $250.

Bust of woman with long brown curly hair, orange gown on shoulders, inner gold band with pink roses, pink and blue shaped border with gilt flowers and leaves and raised white enamel dots, gold rim, "blue shield" mark 435.00

10" d, Gibson Girl type bust, brown hair, blue-green ground, purple to pink shaded ground, shaped gold rim, artist sgd, Austria 49.00

10 1/8" d, frontal bust of brown-haired woman with gold-trimmed white dress and ruby jewel in diadem on gold ground, gilt border chased with rosettes and rect panels, Hutschenreuther, c1915, (A) 978.00

10 3/8" d, Gibson Girl type bust, green and rust dress, magenta hat, green and pink scalloped border with raised florals, artist sgd 80.00

11" d, center bust of Art Nouveau woman with swirling hair and gold crown of leaves, wide gold inner band, irid pearl white ground, "T & V Limoges" mark 125.00

Vase

3 1/8" h, bulbous base, slender neck, portrait of brown haired woman in plaid shawl, holding wine glass, green ground, Royal Schwarzburg 95.00

6" h, portrait of lady in pink gown, long flowing hair, gold handles, gold overlay on rim, artist sgd, Royal Bonn .. 695.00

7" h, ball shape, bust of woman with brown curly hair, flowers in hair, blue and red striped gown, shaded green ground, Heubach 195.00

8 1/4" h, spread ft, tapered flared body, narrow neck, flared rim, frontal bust of brunette woman with bunches of red flowers on each side of hair, blue-green off-shoulder gown, brown to yellow and green shaded ground, Austria
. . . . 125.00

10 1/2" h, portrait of brown-haired gypsy girl on shaded blue ground reserved on blue luster ground with gilt bands of foliate scrolls, trellis diapering, and jewels, sgd "H. Stadler, blue shield" mark, (A) 1,380.00

PORTUGAL-GENERAL

Ilhavo, Portugal 1824 to Present

1824 - PRESENT

History: Jose Ferreira Pinto Basto established a factory to make porcelain at Vista Alegre in 1824. Soft paste porcelains and earthenwares, based on English models, were made until 1832. Anselmo Ferreira, a modeler from Lisbon, and Joseph Scorder from Germany helped develop the factory. In the early 1830s, the ingredients to manufacture hard paste porcelains were found in the region.

Vista Alegre's golden period began in 1835 when Victor Chartier-Rousseau, a French artist, arrived. He remained until his death in 1852. During his tenure, an improved hard paste porcelain became the standard product. Sevres forms replaced the earlier English influenced pieces. Classical, Gothic, and Rococo Revival influences can be found among Vista Alegre's products. Gustave Fortier served as artistic director from 1851 to 1856 and from 1861 to 1869. French influences continued. The factory prospered.

During the late Victorian period, when the Portuguese Joaquim de Oliverra (1870-1881) was head painter, the factory experienced financial difficulties. These continued under head painters da Roche Freire (1881-1889) and Jose de Magalhaes (1889-1921). De Magalhaes was responsible for ornamental plates with high relief decorations that featured vibrant themes and Art Nouveau characteristics.

In 1924, the factory was reorganized. An emphasis was placed on the production of classical patterns. Some contemporary designs were introduced.

The factory still is controlled by the descendants of the original owner Jose Basto. The "VA" mark in blue has been maintained. A laurel wreath and crown symbolizing the royal patent of 1826 were added, but later abandoned.

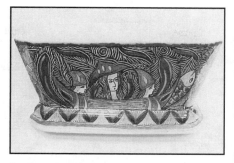

Bowl, 10 3/4" sq, cut corners, polychrome on black ground, yellow and green striped border, "Portugal" mark, $90.

Bowl

11" d, wide rim, tin glazed, lg blue star in center with stylized flowerhead, blue, red, and green leaves with crisscross design, border of stylized blue and green leaves with red crisscross centers, blue splashed dots 65.00

13" d, green molded leaf design with white veins, repaired chip 125.00

Cache Pot, 8" h, red and yellow garden flowers in scrolled gilt cartouche, lt yellow ground on body, gold rim, gold outlined handles
. . . . 185.00

Compote, 12" l x 5 3/4" w x 6 1/2" h, yellow flowers, cream leaves, green ground on ext, gold rim and circ ft, "ELPA Alcobala Made in Portugal" mark 45.00

Cup and Saucer, molded green leaf pattern
. . . . 10.00

Charger, 11 5/8" d, faience, brown outlined blue man on horse with sword chasing deer in woods, border of oval brown leaves . 185.00

Dish

8" l, figural shell, brown transfer of peasant and sheep, gold trim, "Artibus Fondeville Portugal" mark 40.00

12 1/2" d, figural red lobster on tromp l'oeil seabed, figural mussels, shellfish, and green seaweed on brown mottled border, Alvero Jose, (A) 425.00

Coffee Set, pot, 9 1/2" h, creamer, cov sugar bowl, blue design, white ground, "Mottahedah, Visa Alegre VA" marks, $160.

Dish, Cov, 11 3/4" H-H, relief molded grapes, leaves, and stems, twist handles, white glaze
. . . . 25.00

Figure, 16 1/4", 20" h, tin glazed, standing rooster, white body, red comb, blue-gray tail feathers, yellow legs, squatting hen, white body, red comb, lt blue-gray wings and tail, yellow legs, standing on brown branches, mottled green sq base, pr. 4,000.00

Plate

8 5/8" d, center bouquet of green and black flowers, border of molded basketweave and alternating green and black sprigs, gold lined shaped rim, "VA Portugal" mark, set of 840.00

10" d, stylized blue and green flowerheads with dk red stems on inner border, open lattice outer border 65.00

11" d, faience, primitive drawing of farmer and wife in center in colors, blue wave cavetto, border of blue centered red stylized flowerheads and yellow open diamonds, blue and red dash rim
. . . . 25.00

Teapot, 6 3/8" h, blue flowerhead and sm flowers, blue band of dk blue diamonds and blue band of circles, gold lined rims, knob, and handle, "VA Portugal" mark. 88.00

Tureen, 15" d, with undertray, figural cabbage, green and white, yellow and brown figural snail knob. 325.00

Vase, 16" h x 14" d, "Manta Ray," turquoise foam drip, gold outlined, med blue gloss ground. 185.00

POT LIDS AND RELATED WARES

Staffordshire, England c1840-1900

1850

History: Pot lids were defined as under the glaze, chromatic transfer printed Staffordshire pot covers. The pots were containers designed to hold foodstuffs, delicacies, and cosmetics, such as potted meats, relishes, fish paste, sauces, rouge, lip salve, hair pomades for women, and bear grease for men. First sold about 1840, they reached their popularity in the Victorian era. They were priced according to size. There were five basic sizes ranging from the smallest (under 1 3/4" diameter) to the largest (5 1/2 to 8 1/2" diameter).

The finest pot lids were made between 1850 and 1870. Production continued to the end of the 19th century. Although at least eight firms made pot lids, Pratt & Company was the major manufacturer.

In 1836, George Baxter patented his process to make an oil color printing from a number of plates and blocks. Ten years later the process was applied to ceramics. Pratt's

1847 "Grace Before Meals" was the first full chromatic transfer printed under the glaze on a pot lid. T.J. & J. Mayer followed suit in 1851. Chromatic transfer printing first involved painting a watercolor. Next a key plate was engraved. Prints from the key plate were then transferred to three other plates that held the three prime colors.

Pratt's master artist-engraver was Jesse Austin. His key plate color was brown. From 1852 to 1869, Austin engraved plates that portrayed portraits of royalty and famous people on pot lids. Between 1864 and 1873, eleven different views of London on pot lids were made. In addition to his own original watercolors, Austin also reproduced in miniature forms the paintings of famous artists.

Early Pratt lids frequently were flat topped. Shapes varied. The glaze had a bluish tint, especially before 1870. In the 1870s, the glaze was more gray-blue in tone. The glaze also featured fine crazing. Forty-seven pot lids had the line and dot border design. Large Pratt pot lids made before 1863 show three stilt marks on the underside. Pratt's chief competitor from 1856-1862 was Cauldon Place Pottery.

References: A. Ball, *The Price Guide to Pot-Lids & Other Underglaze Multi-Colored Prints on Ware*, 2nd Ed., Antique Collectors' Club Ltd.,1980; H.G. Clarke, *The Pictorial Pot Lid Book*, Courier Press, 1960; Ronald Dale, *The Price Guide to Black & White Pot Lids*, Antique Collectors' Club, 1978; Cyril Williams-Wood, *Staffordshire Pot Lids & Their Potters*, Faber & Faber, 1972.

Museums: County Museum, Truro, England; Fitzwilliam Museum, Cambridge, England. (Collection seen by appointment only.)

Collecting Hints: Full color lids are the most popular among collectors. Pot lids with broad gold bands that were either produced for display at trade exhibits or showrooms or as souvenirs for families and friends of the master potter are most prized.

Jar and Lid

2 3/8" d, "Calvert's Carbolic Tooth Paste," black transfer 49.00

2 1/2" d, "Cold Cream," geometric cartouche, black transfer 45.00

2 3/4" d

"Cracroft's Areca Nut Toothpaste," black transfer 65.00

"Cullwick's Skin Ointment," black transfer 115.00

"Oriental Toothpaste," black transfer 185.00

3" d, "Cherry Toothpaste," bust of Queen Victoria, black transfer, green and bronze 165.00

3 1/4" d, multicolored transfer of ice skater falling down, c1850 . . . . 250.00

3 1/2" d

"Burgess Genuine Anchovy Paste," black transfer 55.00

Two wolves on mountain ledge, multicolored transfer, rim chip . . 115.00

4" d, "Royal Harbour, Ramsgate," multicolored transfer 250.00

4 1/4" d

"I See You My Boy," multicolored transfer 175.00

"On Guard," multicolored transfer, chips 155.00

"Strasbourg," French street scene, multicolored transfer 195.00

"The Room In Which Shakespeare Was Born, 1564 Stratford On Avon," multicolored transfer 115.00

"The Shrimpers," multicolored transfer 175.00

"The Village Wedding," multicolored transfer, chips on inner rim 125.00

4 1/2" d, multicolored transfer scene of Victorians picnicking by stream, Gothic ruins in bkd, (A) 115.00

6" l, "War," "P. Wouwerman Pinx," multicolored transfer 225.00

Lid

2 3/4" d, "Little Red Riding Hood," multicolored transfer 295.00

3 1/8" d

"Artic Expedition," men hunting bear, multicolored transfer, (A) 50.00

"Cherry Tooth Paste-Patronized by the Queen," bust of Victoria, green and black 185.00

"Crane & Co., Cherry Tooth Paste," black and white 95.00

3 1/4" d, "Cherry Areca Tooth Paste," black and white 145.00

Pot Lid, 4 1/4" d, "Albert Memorial," multicolored, $45.

Pot Lid, 5 3/4" l, Dutch battle scene, multicolored, $80.

4" d

Fishermen at sea, multicolored transfer, (A) 58.00

"I See You My Boy," boys spying on sleeping peasant, multicolored transfer, (A) 50.00

"Letter from the Diggings," multicolored transfer, (A) 60.00

"New St. Thomas's Hospital," multicolored transfer, (A) 75.00

"On Guard," multicolored transfer, (A) 55.00

Peasants resting in field, multicolored transfer, (A) 58.00

"Uncle Toby," multicolored transfer, (A) 55.00

4 1/4" d

"The Best Card," couple playing cards, multicolored transfer 170.00

"The Late Prince Consort," Prince Albert seated by book and globe, multicolored transfer, (A) 45.00

"The Outs," tavern scene, multicolored transfer, (A) 45.00

"The Screwball Horse," multicolored transfer 140.00

5" d, "Royal Harbor, Ramsgate England," multicolored 225.00

5 1/16" d, "The Grand International Building of 1851," multicolored transfer, (A) 79.00

Miscellaneous

Comport

12 1/2" H-H, ftd, oval, "Highland Music," multicolored transfer of Scottsman playing bagpipes in stable with dogs, green marble border, "F. & R. Pratt Fenton Manufacturer's to H.R.H. Prince Albert" mark 950.00

13 1/2" H-H, ftd, oval, "The Blind Fiddler," polychrome 220.00

Cup and Saucer, "A Horse Drawing a Boat to Land" and "Halt Near Ruins" on cup, "Stall Woman" on saucer, multicolored transfers, blue-green ground, (A) 45.00

Jar, Cov, 4" h, vert designs of oriental figures or trailing flowers, cross-hatched design on rims, sqs on knob, blue transfers, "F & R. Pratt & Co. Fenton" mark 165.00

Plate, 9 1/4" d, multicolored transfer, dk pink inner border, mustard yellow rim, gilt accents, "F. & R. Pratt Fenton" mark, $125.

Plaque, 10 1/8" l x 7 1/8" w, oval, "Highland Music," multicolored transfer 200.00

Plate

> 7 3/8" d, multicolored transfer of "Shakespeare's House Henry Street, Stratford Avon," tomato red border, yellow rim with black pattern 155.00
>
> 8 5/8" d, "The Queen, God Bless Her," 2 seated boys eating and drinking in courtyard, dog at side, multicolored transfer, orange-red border, tan and black rim, unmkd 65.00
>
> 9 1/8" d, "Chatsworth," multicolored transfer, olive border with reclining classic figures, "Pratt Fenton" mark. . . . 145.00
>
> 9 1/2" d, "The Truant," multicolored transfer of child listening at doorway to woman and children in room, border of black oak leaves and acorns on yellow ground 145.00

Pot, 4" d x 1 3/4" h, "The Best Card," multicolored transfer, (A) 70.00

Teapot, 6" h, cartouches of "A View Near St. Michael's Mount" and "A Village Scene on the Continent," multicolored transfers, pink ground, (A) 100.00

Vase, 6 1/2" h, green body

> "Fording the Stream" and "The Red Bull Inn," multicolored transfers 175.00
>
> "The Trooper" and "Cattle and Ruins," multicolored transfer 175.00

PRATT WARE

Staffordshire, Shropshire, and other English pottery centers c1785-1840

Scotland
1750-1840

History: Pratt ware was relief decorated, high-temperature fired, under the glaze,

cream-colored earthenware and pearlware that was made between 1785 and 1840. William Pratt headed a family of potters who worked at Lane Delph and Fenton. William was the first of six generations of Pratts to make Pratt ware. Felix, John, and Richard, William's sons, managed the pottery after their father's death in 1799.

Jugs with relief-molded designs of sporting and bucolic scenes or commemorative subjects featuring naval or military heroes or royal figures were the most popular forms. Tea caddies, plaques, flasks, teapots, dishes, mugs, cow creamers, busts, and other forms also were produced.

The body usually was white or a pale cream color. The glaze consisted of lead oxide tinged with blue. The wares were decorated with relief designs pressed from intaglio molds. Colors used for the decorations included: yellow, orange, ochre, green, cobalt blue, brown, black, and mulberry. The under-the-glaze color technique that protected the colors under a transparent glaze retained the brilliance of the pieces.

The majority of Pratt's jugs were unmarked. Other potters that imitated the wares from Pratt's factory included Wedgwood, Leeds, E. Bourne, T. Hawley, and R.M. Astbury. Under-the-glaze colored figures of animal groups, Toby jugs, tall case clocks, money boxes, and watch stands appeared. Classical scenes were featured in relief decoration under the glaze on jugs. A number of relief decorations on Pratt ware duplicated the intaglio patterns found on jasper ware.

The Scottish East Coast Potteries made Pratt ware-style jugs and other forms from the mid-1700s until 1840. Some pieces contained motifs with a distinctive Scottish flavor.

Reference: John & Griselda Lewis, *Pratt Ware 1780-1840,* Antique Collectors' Club Ltd. 1984.

Museums: City Museum & Art Gallery, Stoke-on-Trent, England; Fitzwilliam Museum, Cambridge, England; Potsdam Public Museum, Potsdam, NY; Royal Pavilion Art Gallery & Museum, Brighton, England; Royal Scottish Museum, Edinburgh, Scotland; Victoria & Albert Museum, London, England, William Rockhill Nelson Gallery of Art, Kansas City, MO.

Cream Pitcher, 5 3/4" l, pearlware, head modeled as ram, torso as bird, cov as fish fin, underglazed brown and orange accents, late 18th C, (A) 1,380.00

Cup, 5 1/2" h, "Pope and Devil" pattern, relief molded face of Pope in yellow mitre and cross, yellow and green acanthus leaves, acorns and oak leaves on rim, green, brown,

Figure, 9 3/4" h, blue jacket, yellow vest, red, blue, and black spotting, c1800, $15,500.

ochre, and yellow accents, c1800, repairs and hairline, (A) 920.00

Dish, 3 1/2" d, relief molded quarter profile bust of Queen Caroline in laurel wreath, blue and ochre, c1820, (A) 100.00

Figure

> 3 1/2" l, mole, underglaze green, brown, and ochre glazes, c1800, (A) . . 489.00
>
> 4 1/2" l, figural cradle with sleeping child, blue and yellow, (A) 345.00
>
> 4 3/4" h, standing woman, ochre and brown underskirt, blue lined overdress and shawl, blue hat, circ base, c1810, (A) 365.00
>
> 5" h, 4 3/4" h, standing boy in brown lined green toga, rooster under arm, brown lined sq base, standing girl in brown spotted white toga, orange-brown mound, orange-brown striped sq base, c1810, pr 895.00
>
> 5 1/2" h, pearlware, Summer, standing woman holding cornucopia, green, brown, and ochre, sq base, chips, (A) 385.00
>
> 6" h x 7" l, standing horse, ochre sponged body, blue an white checkered saddle cloth, green base, ears re-attached 5,500.00
>
> 6 1/2" h, standing woman, mauve top, lt blue skirt, black sash, leaning against brown tree trunk topped with green bocage, sq base with black line, c1810 . . . . 395.00
>
> 7" h, "Demeter," standing woman, cream vest, yellow gown, holding black sickle, yellow wheat, green mound on red striped sq base, c1810 . . . . 695.00
>
> 7 1/2" h, "Hope," standing woman in green trimmed yellow robe, cream dress with blue and yellow circles, rust belt, brown sandals, c1800 . . . . 1,075.00
>
> 8" h, "Winter," standing man in black hat, yellow pants, mauve jacket, rust cape

with green and brown stripe, brown lined sq base, c1810 . . . . 895.00

8 1/8" h, standing woman wearing yellow dress with black dots, ruffled collar, holding orange roses, man's top hat on head, barefoot on translucent green base, c1790, reglued 950.00

8 1/2" h, "The Lost Sheep," shepherd in brown coat, dk green breeches, standing on rock base w/flower, fern, and orange, blue, and green waterfall, c1795 . . . . .1,950.00

Flask, 4 1/4" l, molded pectin shell, brown neck, yellow, blue, orange, and brown layers, white sides, c1790, hairline on neck
. . . . .1,250.00

Jug

4" h, molded basketweave base, center band of blue, red, yellow, and green dashes, relief of purple grapes and blue flowerheads, green vines on shoulder, painted mask spout, pink lines and rim 425.00

4 1/4" h, modeled Satyr mask, red and green scattered florals, late 18th C
. . . . 450.00

5 1/2" h, pearlware, faceted sides with blue and ochre festoons between molded bands of ochre and green berried vine and leaves, ochre and green band of stiff leaves on base, shaped handle, c1815, (A) 625.00

6 1/4" h

Ovoid shape, "Miser," relief figure of miser in black hat, mauve jacket counting money, another in brown hat, turquoise cartouche, blue feathered border with yellow dots top and base, rose red lined rim 450.00

Paneled, green and brown leaves, raised green leaf border, raised mustard yellow circles with blue centers and brown outlined leaves above base, cream ground, mustard yellow rims 265.00

8 1/2" h, relief molded heads with black beards, green hats, purple, mustard yellow, blue, and green geometrics between, green rim, green leaves, purple berries around spout 350.00

8 5/8" h, relief of sailor in blue jacket, green vest, ochre striped trousers returning from boat to woman in brown hat, white dress with dk brown spots, reverse with sailor and woman saying farewell, relief of dk brown tree branches and green leaves, molded stiff leaves on base
. . . . 1150.00

9" h, "Fair Hebe," relief molded standing huntsman in cobalt coat and brown boots, bottle at feet, dog leaping at side, reverse with man reclining in cobalt jacket handing basket of eggs to woman, green tree trunk body with yellow flowers, c1789 . . . . .1,250.00

Mug, 5 1/4" h, "The Miser," bust of gentleman in cobalt coat, black hat, ochre arched cartouche, ochre trimmed rim 220.00

Pipe

5" h, figural fish body, sailor form bowl, polychromed, c1800, restored stem, (A)
. . . . 805.00

7 7/8" l, figure-of-eight with multiple loops, underglaze blue foliage and ochre dots, figural female head bowl with brown hair, c1790, cracks 1,650.00

Pitcher

5 3/4" h, yellow scrolled branch and green leaf molded heart shaped reserves of 2 girls with dog and doll and "imp Sportive Innocence" or 2 girls fighting and "imp Mischievous Sport" on reverse, brown striped rim with blue and yellow molded chain and shell design, green accented leaf band at base, hairline, (A) 240.00

7 1/2" h, oval reserve of brown titled Duke of York, yellow, blue, orange, brown, and black rider on horse, reverse with brown titled Prince Coberg, yellow, blue, orange, brown, and black rider on horse, blue outlined molded shells on neck, lt green accented acanthus leaf design on front and back, C-shaped handle with molded acanthus leaf, dk brown banded rim, (A) 850.00

Plaque

6 7/8" l x 5 5/8" h, rect, relief of Venus riding olive green waves on yellow and blue shell, pulled by pr of yellow, orange, and brown dolphins and Cupid, molded green laurel garland frame, c1790
. . . . 1,550.00

10 1/2" h, circ with molded urn and swag hanger, molded bacchanalian scene, polychromed, late 18th C, hairlines and chips, (A) 402.00

Sauceboat, 6 3/8" l, modeled as swimming duck, ochre and blue sponging, brown eyes and beak tip, c1780 . . . . 1,250.00

Teapot, 6 1/4" h, relief design of woman in blue robe and cherubs, bands of relief ochre and green stiff leaves, cherub knob . 400.00

Watch Holder, 8" h, modeled as Father Time in blue robe with orange and green drapery, holding scythe, seated next to orange tall case clock with winged cherub's head, stepped green base, c1780 . . . . . . 1,950.00

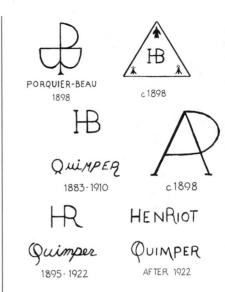

PORQUIER-BEAU 1898

c1898

HB Quimper 1883-1910

c1898

HR Quimper 1895-1922

HENRiot Quimper AFTER 1922

QUIMPER

Quimper, Brittany, France
1600s to Present

History: Quimper faience derived its name from the town in Brittany, in the northwest corner of France, where the potteries were located. Three of the major 17th and 18th century centers of French faience strongly influenced the early Quimper potters: Nevers, Rouen, and Moustiers.

Jean Baptiste Bousquet settled in Quimper in 1685 and started producing functional faience wares using Moustiers inspired patterns. Pierre, his son, took over in 1708. In 1731, Pierre included Pierre Bellevaux, his son-in-law, in the business. He introduced the Chinese inspired blue and white color scheme, the oriental subject matter, an intertwining border pattern of leaves and flowers, and the use of the rooster as a central theme.

From Rouen, Pierre Clement Caussy brought to Quimper many important features such as "decor rayonnant," an intricate pattern of stylized leaves and florals on the outer border and lacy designs that resembled wrought iron trellises. By 1739, Pierre Clement Caussy had joined with Bousquet. He became the manager of the faiencerie and expanded the works.

Francois Eloury opened a rival factory in 1776, and in 1778 Guillaume Dumaine opened a second rival factory. Thus, there were three rival faience factories operating in Quimper, producing similar wares by 1780.

Through marriage, Antoine de la Hubaudiere became the manager of the Caussy factory in 1782. The factory's name became the Grande Maison.

After the beginning of the 19th century, the essential Breton characteristics began to appear on the pottery-the use of primary colors, concentric banding in blue and yellow for border trims, and single stoke brushing to create a flower or leaf. Toward the end of the 19th century, scenes of everyday Breton peasants became popular decorative motifs. Artists such as Rene Quillivic joined Grande Maison in 1920 and produced figures.

Concurrently, the Eloury factory passed to Charles Porquier and later to Adolphe Porquier. In 1872, Alfred Beau, a master artist, joined the firm and produced Breton scenes and figures.

In 1884, Jules Henriot took over the Dumaine factory. He added the Porquier factory to his holdings in 1904. Mathurin Meheut joined the Henriot factory in 1925 and introduced patterns influenced by the Art Deco and Art Nouveau stylistic trends. Other noted artists at Henriot were Sevellec, Maillard, and Nicot.

During the 1920s, the HB concern introduced the Odetta line that utilized a stoneware body and decorations of the Art Deco period.

The Henriot factory merged with the Grande Maison HB in 1968, each retaining its individual characteristics and marks. Production ceased in the early 1980s. An American couple purchased the plant and renewed the production of Quimper.

Quimper pottery was made in a tremendous number of shapes and forms among which are utilitarian pieces, all types of figures and decorative articles, and in fact, just about everything imaginable.

Marks: The "HR" and "HR Quimper" marks were found on Henriot pieces prior to 1922. The "Hen Riot Quimper" mark was used after 1922. The "HB" mark covered a long span of time. The addition of numbers or dots and dashes referred to inventory numbers and were found on later pieces. Most marks were in blue or black. Consignment pieces for department stores such as Macy's and Carson Pirie Scott carried the store mark along with the factory mark. These consignment pieces are somewhat less desirable in the eyes of the collector.

References: Sandra V. Bondhus, *Quimper Pottery: A French Folk Art Faience*, published privately, 1981; *Rev. Ed.*1995; Millicent S. Mali, *French Faience*, United Printing, 1986; Millicent Mali, *Quimper Faience,* Airon, Inc.1979; Anne Marie O'Neill, *Quimper Pottery,* Schiffer Publishing, 1994; Marjatta Taburet, *La Faience de Quimper,* Editions Sous le Vent, 1979 (French Text).

Museums: Musee de Faiences de Quimper, Quimper, France; Musee Departemental Breton, Quimper, France; Victoria & Albert Museum, London, England; Villa Viscaya, Miami, FL.

Reproduction Alert: A line of pottery called "museum quality" has appeared on the market. These pieces featured a brownish wash over a crazed glaze surface. The marks were generally in brown as opposed to the blue or black factory marks of the earlier period. Originally these reproductions had paper labels, but the labels were removed easily. The reproductions sometimes are sold as old pieces.

The Blue Ridge Pottery and several Japanese firms have produced wares with peasant designs similar to those of Quimper. These are easily recognizable.

Peasant pottery similar in style and feel to Quimper has been produced by the Malicorne factory, near Paris. These pieces carry a Malicorne "PBx" mark. Examples have appeared on the market with the "x" removed and sold as genuine Quimper.

Modern Quimper pottery still is made and marketed in decorator shops, in china specialty shops, and in Quimper factory shops in Paris and Quimper in France, in Alexandria, VA, and in Stonington, CT.

An American couple, Sarah and Paul Jansen, now owns the Quimper factory. Many of the older patterns are being reproduced for an eager market. New pieces of Quimper are much lighter in weight than the older examples.

Collecting Hints: Most Quimper available to the collector comes from the late 1800s to the mid-1920s. Since so much was made, the collector should focus on pieces that are in very good or better condition. Missing covers to sugar bowls, teapots, inkwells, etc. greatly reduce the value of these pieces and should be avoided. Small flakes in the glaze are inherent in the nature of the pottery, and, for the most part, do not detract from their desirability.

Pieces from the Odetta period (c1920) are less desirable because of the emphasis on Art Deco designs rather than the country motif associated with the more traditional Quimper pottery.

Newsletter: Le Monde de Quimper, Quimper Faience, Inc.141 Water St., Stonington, CT 06378. Subscription: $10 for three years.

Basket, 8 1/2" h, "Scene Bretonne," child holding mirror, woman combing her hair on one side, reverse with mother holding child in arms, child at side waving to sea, crest of Brittany on front, crest of Quimper on reverse, fluted ribbon handle with lt and dk blue acanthus design on yellow ground, Porquier-Beau, (A)............................ 925.00

Bell

3 1/2" h, bagpipe shape, peasant woman with floral prays, blue bow and brown bagpipe handle, "HenRiot Quimper France 128" mark, (A)........ 165.00

4 1/2" h, figural female peasant, cobalt blouse, yellow apron with orange stripes, leg clapper, "HenRiot Quimper" mark...................... 310.00

5" h, figural female peasant handle, white coif, green blouse, purple vest, cobalt skirt, yellow apron, band of florals on bell, orange and blue striped borders, "HenRiot Quimper 120" mark, (A) 325.00

Biberon, 4 1/2" h, red starburst under spout, band of red, blue, and green florals and leaves, yellow an blue banded base, blue striped handle, blue sponged spout, "HenRiot Quimper France" mark 225.00

Bowl

5 3/4" d, stoneware, brown-yellow sunflower head in center, gray or white metallic triangles on border, metallic drip on ext, "HB Quimper Odetta 270" mark 195.00

8 1/2" d, oriental style fish and orange shells in center, sponged maroon, green, yellow, and rose, purple notched rim, "P. Fouillen, Quimper E." mark 265.00

12" d

Female peasant holding flowers, band of red and green florals and leaves, vert ribbing, scalloped rim, "HR Quimper" on int 450.00

Female peasant with distaff, leaning on brown fence, blue and red crisscross border panels separated by red and yellow flowerhead panels, orange and blue scalloped rim, pierced for hanging, "HenRiot Quimper France" mark..... 375.00

Butter Tub, 4 1/2" h, 5" d, with attached underplate, alternating panels of dogwood blossoms and red and blue dot crisscross design, female peasant on cov holding egg basket, seashell knob, "HenRiot Quimper" mark, (A) 215.00

Cake Plate, 11" H-H, female peasant with vert florals, bands of florals and 4 blue dot pattern on border, blue dash outlined loop handles, green ground, "HB Quimper France" mark 100.00

Cache Pot, 4" h, orange blouse, blue skirt and pantaloons, yellow and orange raised bunting, green sponged rim, "HenRiot Quimper France" mark, $275.

Candlestick

5 1/2" h, oct base with blue croisille and red dot designs and sprigs, male or female peasant on base, shaft with blue dots, sprigs and red dot designs, blue-green sponged lip, "HenRiot Quimper 116" mark, pr, (A) 425.00

7 1/2" h, lighthouse shape, male or female peasant on shaft, bands of green, blue, and red flowers, orange-gold and blue striped bands and rim, "HenRiot Quimper France" mark, pr. 550.00

8" h, figural peasant boy or girl with pot on head, boy wearing cobalt shirt, green vest, and orange pantaloons, girl wearing cobalt skirt, green blouse, purple vest, and pink apron, "HenRiot Quimper France" mark, pr (A) 1,073.00

Charger, 12 1/2, d, old peasant woman leaning on cane, lt blue coif, green blouse, cobalt skirt, orange trimmed purple vest, pink apron, border of 3 panels of blue croisille and red and dots, and 3 panels of stylized dogwood blossoms, shaped, indented rim, "HenRiot Quimper 159" mark, (A) 350.00

Clock, 8 1/2" h, steeple shape, man with horn and woman with distaff on front, view of Quimper in bkd, gold fleur-de-lys above and green decor riche ground, blue spread base with green relief scrolling and crowned crest of Brittany, stepped side handles, Porquier-Beau, chip on base. 3,200.00

Coffeepot

7 1/2" h, hex shape, top band of alternating stylized dogwood blossoms and red crisscross and blue dot panels, middle band of diamond shaped blue lattice and red "V's," bottom band of stylized flower buds, blue dash spout and wishbone handle, "blue HenRiot Quimper 33" mark, (A) 690.00

11 1/2" h, donut shape with hole in center, frontal view of female and male peasant, blue forget-me-nots and green leaves, blue dashed loop knob, handle, and spout, repair to knob, "HenRiot Quimper 71F" mark, (A). 402.00

Compote, 6" h x 8" l x 5 1/2" w, pedestaled, seated female peasant holding basket, male smoking pipe, yellow and blue molded cartouche, molded green leaf form feet with brown and yellow molded fleur-de-lys, "HR Quimper" mark 975.00

Crepe Server, 13 1/2" l, 5 1/2" w, scene bretonne of young girl in cobalt and pale blue dress with pink apron and yellow sash and boy wearing tan vest and leggings, green jacket, and purple pantaloons, cobalt on yellow acanthus border, blue sponged reverse, Porquier-Beau Quimper, (A) 930.00

Cruets and Stand, 8 1/2" h, bottle with frontal view of female peasant in blue dress, pink apron, and yellow sash, male peasant wearing blue jacket, yellow pantaloons, and blue stockings, playing bagpipe, yellow outlined blue dashed stoppers and handle, middle base with yellow lion paws and blue and orange dots, "HR Quimper" mark 950.00

Cup and Saucer

Heart shape, male peasant, band of multicolored florals, blue lined rim, blue dash handle, "HR Quimper" mark, (A) 198.00

Hex shape, band of red, yellow, and blue florals with green leaves, wishbone handle outlined in orange with blue dashes, "HenRiot Quimper France" mark .110.00

Dish, 10" w, sq on sq, male peasant with horn or female peasant with egg basket, red, blue, yellow and green vert flowers, blue and yellow line inner border, blue triangular border with red slashes, outer border with blue squares and red dashes, "HR Quimper" on front, pr 750.00

Doll Dish, 2 1/2" d, red 4 pointed star with blue stripes and 4 blue dot design, "HR Quimper 6," (A) 121.00

Egg Cup

2" h, figural hen, yellow ground, blue accented wings and head, band of rose red centered blue sponged flowerheads on base, "HenRiot Quimper, France 91" mark 75.00

2 1/2" h, pedestal shape, female peasant on body with florals, red 4 dot design on base, 3 blue bands on stem, "HR Quimper" mark, (A) 93.00

Figure

5 1/2" h, "Channik," female peasant holding basket, purple vest with yellow and red brush strokes, green blouse, cobalt skirt, blue-green apron with 4 blue dot design, name on base, "HenRiot Quimper 150" mark, (A) 330.00

6" h, St. Anne, standing figure, cobalt veil and mantle, red and blue brush stroke gown, Mary at side in blue "V" decorated gown, "Ste. Anne" on base, "HR" mark, (A) 300.00

8" h, bust of old peasant woman, navy blouse, yellow, orange, and black accents, white coif with green accents, sgd "J.C. Le Bozec," "HenRiot Quimper" mark 595.00

Fish Platter, 20" l x 10" w, multicolored wedding procession scene in center, dk blue acanthus border on yellow ground, crest of Brittany at top, scalloped and indented rim, "HenRiot Quimper" mark, (A) 2,255.00

Holy Water Font, 8" h, fleur-de-lys shape, young boy in blue jacket, yellow pants before cross on backplate, crest of Brittany on bowl, blue decor riche borders, yellow lined rim, "HB" mark. 656.00

Inkstand, 11 1/2" l x 4 3/4" w x 4" h, seated peasant woman with basket, seated peasant man with scythe, crests of Brittany and Quimper, border of green decor riche on yellow ground, Porquier-Beau, chips . . . 960.00

Jam Jar, 5 1/4" h, female peasant holding flowers, red flowerheads and blue and yellow forget-me-nots, blue dot borders, blue star knob, "HenRiot Quimper France 83" mark 225.00

Jug

5 1/2" h, stoneware, tan circle with man in hat smoking pipe, brown ground with black rim and base, brown and black striped neck with 2 blue circles, tan circle on body, "HB Quimper Odetta 395" mark. 355.00

11 1/2" h, stoneware, center white "V" band surrounded by black and brown "V" bands, thumb rest on handle, "HB Quimper Odetta 454-1270x" mark, (A) 605.00

Knife Rest

3 1/2" l, triangle shape, male or female peasant, florals on other sides, blue sponged ends, "HR Quimper" marks, chips, set of 6, (A) 210.00

4" l, figural male peasant lying on back, Modern Movement colors, sgd "MAILLARD" 75.00

Menu, 7" h, Breton youth holding scythe, one ft on brick wall, yellow raised fleur-de-lys, blue script "MENU," blue outlined wavy border, Porquier-Beau. 550.00

Oyster Plate, 9 3/4" d, 6 wells with various painted flowers, blue sponged diamond border, blue printed "Henriot Quimper" mark 295.00

Picture Frame, 9 1/2" h x 6 1/2" w, rect with cut corners, molded shield with black ermine tails frontal view of male or female peasant on sides with floral sprays and bluets, red linked "S" inner border, blue striped and sponged outer border, blue sponged and outlined bracket feet, "HR Quimper" mark, (A) 1,100.00

Pipe Rack, 11" l x 6 1/2" h, raised shield and crown with male peasant at top, floral garlands and bluets at sides, shelf with 5 slots, blue single stroke and red petal trim, molded yellow and red seashell at base, pierced for hanging, "HenRiot Quimper France 75" mark, (A) 375.00

Pitcher

7" h, Modern Movement, figural female peasant head, coif forms spout, ribbon formed handle, orange embroidered coif, brown hair, black lined base, "HB Quimper 228 with A15," (A) 110.00

8" h, bulbous body, female peasant woman holding flowers on front, lg orange and blue flowers on sides, wide yellow and 3 thin blue bands on border, blue sponged handle, "HenRiot Quimper France 436" mark under handle 170.00

Planter, 7" h, 8 1/2" l, figural swan, trefoil cartouche of seated male peasant on breast, blue sponged circles with yellow dots on body, yellow ground, "HenRiot Quimper St. Malo" mark, (A) 264.00

Plaque, 18 1/4" l x 15" w, rect with cut corners

Relief molded castle scene, black "Eglise de Pont Labbe" below, black and brown geometrics on border, Porquier-Beau 1,200.00

Plate, 9" d, blue jacket, red pantaloons, yellow stockings, red, yellow, blue, and green florals, blue dot and red dash border on yellow ground, blue striped rim, "blue HB" mark, $300.

Relief molded scene of village by sea, molded crest of Quimper at top, crest of Brittany on bottom, brown and black swirls on border, Porquier-Beau
. . . . .1,250.00

Plate

5 1/2" d, blue and orange flowers in center, green and yellow border bands, "HR Quimper 47" mark 40.00

7" d, Modern Movement, bust of male peasant in black hat and vest, blue shirt with yellow embroidery, blue banded border, "HenRiot Quimper France" mark, (A) 60.00

8" d, blue goose with red head feathers, red and yellow wings, greens and floral sprays at sides, conc blue and yellow border bands, "HR Quimper" on front, (A) 250.00

8 1/4" d, multicolored scene of peasant man with baskets of fruit, border with yellow arabesque design on lt blue ground, red inner and outer bands,

Plate, 9" d, yellow blouse, blue skirt, green apron, red, green, and blue vert florals, red and blue dash border, yellow and blue striped rim, "black HB" mark, $300.

Plate, 9 3/8" d, blue jacket, black pantaloons, yellow stockings, red, yellow, blue, and green florals, blue 4 dot design, "HR" mark, $285.

crest of Brittany, Porquier-Beau, c1875
. . . . 1,295.00

8 1/2" d, lg blue flowerhead in center, pink sponged border, "HB Quimper" mark
. . . . 35.00

8 3/4" sq, "black Brittany Ware from old France, Henriot Quimper" in center, multicolored floral border, blue striped rim, (A) 130.00

9" d

Male peasant wearing blue vest, brown pantaloons, yellow stockings, red, yellow, blue, and green floral bunches on border with 4 blue dot design, shaped rim, "blue HR" mark
. . . . 225.00

Yellow sun face in center with blue 8-pointed radiating star, red and green strokes and 4 blue dot design, blue and yellow banded border, unmkd, (A) 375.00

9 1/8" d, painted orange-red and blue nasturtiums, pale blue ground, yellow lined shaped rim, Porquier-Beau. . . 1,200.00

9 1/2" d, frontal view of female peasant in cobalt apron, green jacket, white blouse, jug on shoulder, red, blue, and green floral garlands at sides, band of red buds, blue forget-me-nots, and green leaves on border, blue outlined indented rim, "blue HR" mark, late 19th C, (A). 402.00

9 5/8" d, Art Deco style cobalt, red, and yellow scenes of fishermen and women, dk red inner border and rim, sgd "R.O.L." on front, "HB Quimper" mark, set of 4 . . . . 400.00

9 3/4" d, red, yellow, and purple tulip, green leaves, yellow outlined shaped rim, Porquier-Beau 1,200.00

10" d

Female peasant holding flowers in center, band of blue and orange flowers and green leaves on border, blue scalloped rim, "HenRiot Quimper France 162" mark 67.00

Modern Movement, blue and black dancing peasant couple, blue and black striped inner border, blue and black sponged border, "HenRiot Quimper France" mark 65.00

Profile bust of Anne de Bretagne, pink and blue coif, gold crown, blue ermine tails at rt, gold fleur-de-lys at lt, band of blue interlocking circles on yellow ground border, orange and blue striped rim, "blue HenRiot Quimper" mark 465.00

Platter

13" l, oval, seated female peasant holding distaff, walking male peasant blowing horn, fence and farmhouse in bkd, yellow and orange outlined hearts on red-brown border, black ermine tails in yellow shields top and bottom, "HB" mark 1,450.00

19 1/2" l x 14 1/2" w, female peasant drawing water from well, male peasant holding fishing net, smoking pipe, scattered floral bunches on border with 4 blue dot design, shaped rim with rolled edge, unmkd, (A) 1,073.00

22" h x 15 3/4" w, standing male peasant in blue jacket, yellow vest, brown pantaloons, purple hat holding hand of female peasant in pink trimmed white coif, red dress, purple swirled apron with yellow and red border, village in bkd, blue acanthus border with crest of Brittany at top, "Maries de Ploare, Porquier Beau" mark, repaired 4,000.00

Porringer

5 3/4" H-H, blue strutting goose on int, blue and yellow striped border, blue sponged handles, "HR Quimper" on front, (A). 90.00

7" H-H, male or female peasant in bowl, scattered florals, blue shades, "HB Quimper France" mark, pr, (A) . . 60.00

Puzzle Jug, 4 1/2" h, lady with distaff on body, vert flowers and blue forget-me-nots, blue sponged open lattice shoulder and rim, "HR Quimper" mark, (A) 325.00

Quintal

3 3/4" h, Ivoire Corbeille, red flowerheads, blue sponging, yellow stripes, pale pink ground, "HenRiot Quimper" mark
. . . . 115.00

4 1/2" h, seated peasant woman with basket at side, floral sprays and pink violets, leaves and buds on sides, side tubes with red salvia and 4 blue dots design, black ermine tails on center tube, blue rims, "HB Quimper" mark, (A) 160.00

Relish Dish, 8" l, oval, female peasant seated on rock, stylized roses and bluets, 4 blue dots on border, blue lined rim, "HB Quimper" mark, (A) 130.00

Salt

3" l, dbl, 2 figural swans with center loop handle, yellow beak, eyes, and tail, white ground with blue accents, "HenRiot Quimper France 90" mark 95.00

3 1/2" l, figural swan, blue feathers and blue speckled breast, female peasant on int, "HenRiot Quimper France," (A) 72.00

Serving Dish, 14" d x 8 h, 3 section, figural fisherman holding fish vert center handle, red, blue, and orange Ivoire Corbeille design on 3 molded shells, sgd "A.B.," "HenRiot Quimper" mark 450.00

Shoe, 4 1/2" l, female peasant with red and green floral sprigs, 4 blue dot and floral sprigs on heel, blue chain outline at opening, "HR Quimper 11" mark, (A) 55.00

Snuff Bottle, 3" d

Black outlined lt and dk blue fleur-de-lys on face, blue sponged rim and neck, "HR Quimper" on front, (A) 302.00

Blue rooster with red, yellow, and green plumage, red flowers and green leaves on each side, clock face on reverse, yellow and green bands on rim, unmkd, (A) 550.00

Spill Vase, 4 1/4" h x 5 1/2" l, blue and gold crown flanked by brown figural rampant lions, crest of Brittany on reverse, molded blue wave base, "AP" mark . 495.00

Teapot

5" h, standing male peasant with pipe in gold shaped cartouche, floral design on reverse, multicolored scattered florals and geometrics, blue striped wishbone handle, "HB Quimper" mark . . . 400.00

6" h, bulbous shape, standing male peasant with red and green vert flowers, blue and yellow striped rims, blue loop handle, "HenRiot Quimper, France" mark 130.00

Tea Tile, 5 3/4" sq, ftd, female peasant with red, yellow, and blue vert flower stalks, cut corners, red "S" lined rim, "HB Quimper" mark 175.00

Teapot, 8 1/2" h, blue blouse, red skirt, yellow apron, red, blue, and green florals, gold outlined blue striped handle, yellow ground, "HB Quimper" mark, $195.

Trivet, 8 5/8" sq, iron red and yellow flowerheads, blue sponged shaped rim, "HenRiot Quimper" mark.................. 65.00

Tulipiere, 11 1/2" h, bulbous body, fisherman and child on front, ajonc and pink bleeding hearts on sides, blue acanthus band on top, 3 green sponged figural dolphin feet, 5 flower petal openings, "HR Quimper" mark, (A) 1,375.00

Tureen

8" h, blue, yellow, and orange flowers, green leaves, blue banded rims, blue sponged handles and knob, cream ground, "HenRiot Quimper 73" mark 270.00

14" H-H, 6" h, lobed body, female peasant on base, male peasant on cov, red, blue, and green vert flowers, scattered 4 blue dot pattern, blue handles and open knob, "HR Quimper" mark, hairline on cov.................... 650.00

Vase, 15" h, bulbous base, narrow body, flared top, shaped rim, male or female peasant, blue cabbage rose and yellow and red flowerheads, vert red, blue, and green foliage, "HB Quimper" mark, c1930s, pr 895.00

Wall Pocket, 13 1/2" h, bellows shape, peasant man and woman near fence on blue circ cartouche, blue decor riche on yellow ground borders, "HR Quimper" mark....... 600.00

RELIEF MOLDED JUGS

England
1820-1900

History: During the 1820s in England, a new type of jug that was molded in one process with no additional decorations was made at numerous potteries. The main center was in the Staffordshire Potteries, but some relief molded jugs were made elsewhere.

The earliest jugs had hunting scenes, but by the mid-1800s, there was a wide range of designs including historical and commemorative subjects, classical figures, naturalistic patterns, biblical stories, religious architecture, scenes from literature and wildlife, and others. The best jugs were made during the 1840s and 50s. After that time, cheaper mass produced jugs resulted in a lesser quality product with mostly floral or geometric patterns.

Jugs were an essential part of everyday life in the Victorian era and were used for ale, water, cider, milk, wine, and toddy. Some were made with lids of Britannia metal, some had relief molded pottery lids, and some had strainers in the spout to feed invalids. There was a range of sizes, and some were made in sets. Jugs were produced in huge numbers, and the variety in shape, style, quality, size, decoration, and subject matter was vast.

To produce the master model for a relief molded jug, the modeler carved the original design, often in a block of alabaster. Casts were then made from the master to form reversed master molds. Further casts produced cases. Final castings resulted in the working molds. Approximately 25 jugs could be made from a master, and then a new mold was necessary.

At first jugs were buff colored, then pastel blues and green were used. White became the standard color. Jugs also were made in beige, gray, and brown. Some makers used enamel colors for highlighting certain aspects of the designs. After c1845, colored grounds increased in popularity.

Many relief molded jugs were marked with either impressed, printed, molded, or applied marks. Applied marks were the most common on relief molded jugs. They were formed separately and then attached to the body using slip. Applied marks were used mostly in the 1830s and 40s, and molded marks were used in the 2nd half of the century. Printed marks were used in the 40s and 50s. Some marks included publication dates which indicated when a design was first introduced. These were either applied or impressed. The diamond shape registration mark was used from 1842 until 1883. This mark designated when a design was registered, not necessarily when it was made. Registration marks provided protection for makers against copying by other makers. After the Patents, Designs and Trade Marks Act of 1883, marks were either "Rd." or "Rd. No."

There were numerous makers of relief molded jugs. William Ridgway and Company's most famous jug, Tam O'Shanter, was based on scenes from a Robert Burns poem. He worked with James Leonard Abington from 1831-1860 mostly at the Church Works in Hanley. At least twenty-six different designs were made during this thirty-year period in a wide range of subjects.

Another prolific maker of jugs was Herbert Minton who used model numbers on relief molded jugs to identify the designs. Charles Meigh's first relief molded jug was made in 1835. His famous Apostle jug was produced in huge quantities. This jug set the standard for others who made these jugs. William Taylor Copeland's first jug was "The Vintage Jug" made in 1844. After 1849, all his jugs were registered. Another important maker was William Brownfield who made a wide range of designs, mostly in naturalistic motifs to appeal to mid-Victorian tastes.

Additional makers included Ashworth, Doulton, Mason, Worcester, Wedgwood, Samuel Alcock and Company, and Mayer.

References: R.K. Henrywood, *Relief-Moulded Jugs 1820-1900, Rev. Ed.,* Antique Collectors' Club Ltd.,1996; Kathy Hughes, *A Collector's Guide to Nineteenth-Century Jugs, Vol. 1 & Vol. 2,* Routledge, Kegan & Paul, 1985.

Museums: City Museum & Art Gallery, Hanley, Stoke-on-Trent, England; Potsdam Public Museum, Potsdam, NY; Victoria & Albert Museum, London, England; Wadsworth Atheneum, Hartford, CT.

4 1/2" h, felspathic stoneware, "The Kill," hunting scene, white smear glaze, c1790 . 175.00

6" h, felspathic stoneware, "The Kill," hunting scene, white smear glaze, c1790 .... 375.00

6 1/2" h, relief of hanging water flowers and leaves, pebbly ground, pale blue, Edge Malkin 95.00

6 3/4" h, acorns and oak leaves, stippled ground, med blue 225.00

7" h

    7 1/2" h, 8 1/2" h, "Autumn and Winter" pattern, classical figures, med blue, Dudson, set of 3 .... 540.00

    7 3/4" h, 9" h, white relief of pineapples, grapes, leaves, and tendrils, med blue pebble ground, c1860, set of 3 . 525.00

    "Havelock," grapes and leaves, putty color, Walley 250.00

    Panels of reclining classical figures, lacy trim at top, trellis trim on base, white, c1862 .... 145.00

7 1/2" h

    8 1/2" h, 9 1/2" h, "International" pattern, figures of Art, Music, Commerce, and Science in panels, pale blue ground, Dudson, set of 3 .... 675.00

    Parian, paneled, scenes from Shakespeare, white, Kerr and Binns ... 695.00

    Relief scene of 3 dogs attacking boar, reverse with 3 dogs attacking stag, cream ground, Mason, c1890, (A) 357.00

    Stoneware, "Viking Masks" design, figural dolphin handle, gloss blue glaze, c1880 .... 395.00

    Tulips, relief of copper luster outlined tulips and stems, dk blue leaves, med blue pebble ground 170.00

7 3/4" h, "Eglinton Tournament," knights on horseback jousting, blue-gray ground, pewter lid, "imp Ridgway, September 1840" mark 195.00

8" h

    "Barley," putty color, Dudson 125.00

    "Cup Tosser," white, Worthington & Green 310.00

    Kneeling hunter with dog and gun, grape and leaf border, tan, black English reg mark 235.00

8 1/4" h

    Baskets on base with vert twisted stem ending in flowered urn in 3 lobed cartouche, pebble ground, white, raised English reg mark 125.00

7 3/4" h, "International," Science, Art, Music, and Commerce, white relief, med blue ground, William Brownfield, (A) $70.

Wheatsheaf, bundles of wheat on sides, pebble ground, off-white, Dudson 110.00

8 1/2" h

    Portland jug, white scene of "Wooing of Thetis by Peleus," reclining woman and seated man, lavender ground, metal cov, Samuel Alcock 365.00

    Relief of various leaf designs, cream ground, pewter lid, unmkd 245.00

    Wheat and Barrel, gray, "imp COPELAND" mark 235.00

8 3/4" h

    Pan, male masks and curlicues, grapes and leaves on shoulder, figure lying on handle, tan, John Ridgway 195.00

    "Silenus," gray, Minton 350.00

    Vine Border pattern, grapes, leaves, and tendrils on border, bushy leaves and flowers on body, med blue, Dudson 325.00

9" h

    Relief molded running stags, leaf and grape molded trim on base, trellis with heads on rim, white, c1840.... 225.00

    "Sylvan" pattern, lt green ground, pewter lid, Ridgway & Abington 475.00

10" h, woman seated with 4 dogs, house in bkd, white body with dk blue shaded top and base, hound handle, Burleigh 425.00

10 1/4" h, "Bacchanalian Dance" scene, grapes and leaves on shoulder, frolicking people and cherubs on body, khaki body, Meigh 795.00

10 3/4" h, paneled, "Apostle," cream ground 475.00

11 1/4" h

    "International," relief molded panels of classic artisans on pebble ground, cream ground, Brownfield 425.00

    Molded green vert fern leaves, off-white ground, rope twist handle with green stripes, metal lid 195.00

RIDGWAY

Shelton, Staffordshire, England c1808-1855

History: Job Ridgway trained at the Swansea and Leeds potteries. In 1808, he took John and William, his two sons, into partnership at his Cauldon Place Works at Shelton. At first the company only made pottery. Later porcelains were added to supplement the earthenware line.

The early porcelain pieces usually were unmarked. A few pieces done before Job Ridgway's death in 1813 are impressed "Ridgway & Sons." After 1813, the two brothers separated. John retained the Cauldon Place factory and made porcelains. William produced earthenwares at the Bell Works.

John Ridgway specialized in the production of fine porcelain tablewares, mostly tea and dessert services. He was appointed potter to Queen Victoria. Very few ornamental pieces were made. Most pieces remained unmarked. Hence, his wares often were attributed to other factories by scholars and collectors.

William Ridgway expanded the scope of his operation until he eventually owned six factories at Hanley and Shelton. Their principal production was utilitarian earthenwares, with a tinted bluish-mauve body. The earthenware products that were made between 1830 and 1845 had no mark, only a painted pattern number.

After 1856, there were a series of different partnerships with varying names. By 1962, the porcelain division of Cauldon was carried on by Coalport China Ltd.

The Ridgways used a distinctive system of pattern numbering, which is explained in G. Godden's *British Porcelain.*

Reference: G.A. Godden, *The Illustrated Guide to Ridgway Porcelains,* Barrie & Jenkins, 1972.

Museums: Cincinnati Art Museum, Cincinnati, OH; Potsdam Public Museum, Potsdam, NY.

Basket, 9 5/8" H-H, with stand, rect, pierced with band of scrolls and molded panels of fruiting vines, painted bouquets of flowers in dk blue and tan ground with gilt scrolling leaves, leaf molded handles, pattern #851, c1815-25, pr, (A) 2,156.00

Bowl

  8 3/4" d, fluted, "Devonshire" pattern, orange-red, yellow, and green transfer, c1885. . . . . 300.00

  13 1/4" d, "Columbian Star" pattern, farmer plowing in front of cabin, band of stars on border, blue transfer, hairlines, John Ridgway, (A) 1,430.00

Cake Stand, 5" h x 9 1/4" d, "Simlay" pattern, c1870-80 . . . . 95.00

Cup and Saucer, "American State Flowers-Iris Tennessee," polychrome transfers 20.00

Dessert Service

  Sixteen plates, 7 3/4" d, oct, 2 cov sauce tureens, 6 3/4" h, 2 reticulated berry bowls, 10" H-H, with undertrays, 4 sweetmeat dishes, periwinkle blue border with gilt flowers, scalloped gilt rim, gilt outlined molded grape and leaf handles, c1820 . . . . 7,850.00

  Teapot, 8 3/4" h, creamer, sugar bowl, 4 plates, 6 1/4" d, cake plate, 9 7/8" sq, "Alberta Tartan" pattern, "Royal Adderly" marks 100.00

Dinner Service, Part, 8 plates, 10 1/2" d, 8 plates, 9 1/2" d, serving bowl, 8 1/2" H-H, tureen, 12 1/4" l, with undertray, soup ladle, cov vegetable dish, 8" d, cov vegetable dish, 10 3/4" l, with underplate, "Simlay" pattern, black transfers with enamels, repairs, (A) . . 230.00

Mug, 4" h, "Coaching Days," black transfer, caramel ground, silver luster rim and handle, set of 4. . . . . 440.00

Teapot, 6 3/4" h, ironstone, "Blenham" pattern, iron red, blue, and gold florals, white ground, "Ridgway Ironstone England Blenham" mark, $85.

Pitcher

  4 1/2" h, "Coaching Days," black transfer, caramel ground, silver luster rim and handle. 40.00

  6 3/4" h, "Royal Vistas Ware-Sea Scene St. Heliers," dk tan, black overwash, gold handle and rim 95.00

Plate

  7 7/8" d, "Venice" pattern, transfer of boats in canal and Italian buildings, purple, green, red, and yellow, purple curlicue border 27.00

  9" d

    "Coaching Days-Henry VIII," caramel ground, "Scenes from Coaching Days & Ways" on reverse . . . 75.00

    Robert Burns, black transfer . . . 50.00

  9 1/4" d, purple hanging willow branches with green flowerheads, blue leaves, purple willow trees, orange, green, and blue flowerheads on border, c1834, William Ridgway 65.00

  9 3/4" d, "Clevedon" pattern, floral and leaf border, blue transfer 25.00

  10 1/2" d

    "Coaching Days," black transfer, caramel ground, silver luster rim . 50.00

    "Yeddo" pattern, black transfer, red ground, Ridgway, Parks, and Ridgway, c1878, pr 360.00

Platter

  14" l, oval, "Conway" pattern, blue hanging baskets of flowers joined by hanging swags, band of blue flowerheads on border, quiver and bow mark . . . 75.00

  21 3/4" l, strutting turkey in meadow in center, floral border, lobed rim, dk blue transfer 1,195.00

  22" l, well and tree, "India Temple" pattern, blue transfer 1,200.00

Punch Bowl, 10 1/4" d x 5 1/4" h, pedestal base, "Humphrey's Clock" pattern, man and woman sitting under tree by river, gray transfer. 195.00

Soup Plate, 10 1/2" d, "India Temple" pattern, blue transfer, c1815 . . . . 165.00

Tea Service, pot, 4 1/2" h, creamer, sugar basin, 2 cups and saucers, tray, overall black floral and geometric chintz type pattern with gilt accents, white ground, (A) 195.00

Vase, 7" h, painted multicolored homes in park, gilt scroll handles, wide gilt band on rim, gilt banded base and ft, c1820, pr, (A) 863.00

Vegetable Bowl

  9" l, ironstone, "Canterbury" pattern, yellow and purple flowers, band of yellow, green, and purple flowerheads on border 22.00

  10" l, "Chiswick" pattern, blue florals, gold accents 65.00

Vegetable Bowl, Cov

  11" H-H, hex, dk red peony, blue and pink oriental florals, molded rim, gilt molded handles, J. & W. Ridgway 275.00

11 7/8" H-H, "Indus" pattern, brown, dk red, and gray bird and temple, gold outlined leaf knob and terminals. . . 140.00

12" H-H, oval, lobed body, pink and yellow floral sprays, gray leaves, gilt outlined swirls 38.00

Rockingham Works
Brameld
c 1826 - 1830

ROCKINGHAM

Swinton, South Yorkshire, England
Pottery 1745-1842

Porcelain 1826-1842

History: The Rockingham factory was located on the estate of Earl Fitzwilliam, Marquis of Rockingham, near Swinton in Yorkshire. The first pottery was manufactured in 1745. The factory continued production under various owners who concentrated on brown and yellow wares, blue and white dinner, tea and coffee services, and white earthenwares. In 1806, John and William Brameld took over the business and used the name "Brameld Co." They made pottery from 1806 to 1842.

Brown ware was the best known variety of Rockingham pottery. Its common forms included teapots, coffeepots, jugs, and cadogans (a pot from which liquid will not spill). The thickly applied glaze was intense and vivid purple brown when fired. The interior of pieces often was left white. Sometimes the brown exterior was decorated with gilding, enamel colors, or classical figures in relief. During the 19th century, many companies copied the "Rockingham" glaze of a rich brown stained with manganese and iron.

The Bramelds introduced porcelain production in 1826. Rockingham bone china porcelain had a glaze somewhat prone to fine crazing. During the next sixteen years, until 1842, many ornamental wares and some utilitarian wares were made. Rockingham tea and coffee services in both simple and ornate decoration remained a mainstay of production. Finally the company also manufactured animal groups featuring dogs, cats, squirrels, rabbits, hares, deer, or sheep. Vases, ewers, baskets, scent bottles, candlesticks, desk pieces, trays and pieces for the dressing table constituted the principal ornamental forms.

The red griffin mark was used from 1826 to 1830 and the puce griffin mark from 1831 to 1842.

References: Alwyn Cox & Angela Cox, *Rockingham Pottery & Porcelain 1745-1842,* Faber & Faber, 1983; Arthur A. Eaglestone & Terence A. Lockett, *The Rockingham Pottery, Rev. Ed.* David & Charles, 1973; D.G. Rice, *Ornamental Rockingham Porcelain,* Adam, 1965; D.G. Rice, *Rockingham Pottery and Porcelain,* Barrie & Jenkins, 1971.

Museums: City Museum, Weston Park, Sheffield, England; Clifton Park Museum, Rotherham, England; Rotherham Museum, Rotherham; Victoria & Albert Museum, London, England; Yorkshire Museum, York, England.

Reproduction Alert: Rockingham brown glaze was copied extensively throughout the 19th century by many factories.

Figure

1 3/4" h, reclining dog, brown spots and face marks, white ground, c1810 . . . . 350.00

6 1/4" l, recumbent youth and hound, rocaille molded mound, (A) 173.00

Luncheon Set, Part, 9 plates, 9" d, 2 compotes, 5 3/8" h, 4 low compotes, gilt framed enamel landscape scenes, pink ground rims, hairlines, restorations, mid-19th C . . . 375.00

Plate

7 3/4" d, exotic bird, butterfly, florals, and foliage on honeycomb pattern, Roman key border, polychrome, "imp Brameld" mark, (A) 303.00

8 3/4" d, "Parroquet" pattern, blue and white 215.00

Dessert Service, compote, 15 1/2" H-H, 6 1/2" h, 2 cake plates, 10 1/4" l, 8 plates, 8 1/4" d, dbl open plate, 11 3/4" l, pink, orange, yellow, and purple florals, white ground, cobalt and gilt cartouche, almond brown border, almond brown, cobalt, white, and gilt pedestal bases, $2,400.

9" d, green cartouche and floral spray border, set of 10, (A). 220.00

Platter, 19" l, "India Flowers" pattern, blue and white 975.00

c1878   c1884

RORSTRAND

Near Stockholm, Sweden
1726 to Present

History: Rorstrand, established in 1726 near Stockholm, was the oldest porcelain factory in Sweden. Although formed for the production of tin-glazed earthenware, porcelain was the ultimate aim of the founder. A succession of German managers directed the production during the early years. The company made little impact on the ceramic world.

When Anders Fahlstrom became manager in 1740, the company began to flourish. Elias Ingman assumed control in 1753. The company immediately undertook to imitate the successful Sevres and Meissen wares. The company continued to prosper. Rorstrand absorbed the rival Marieberg factory in 1782.

Bengt Jeijer became manager in 1798. In the early 1800s, the fortunes of Rorstrand were altered by two major events: the introduction and popularity of Wedgwood's creamware, and the ban on the exportation of English clay. Rorstrand tottered on the brink of bankruptcy. Eventually the clay ban was relaxed. Workers from Stoke-on-Trent were imported. Rorstrand's products now had a finer clay body and strong English influence.

In the mid-1870s, a limited company was formed. Production flourished due to the infusion of the fresh ideas of talented Scandinavian artists employed at the factory. Between 1895 and 1914, Rorstrand's art director and designer was Alf Wallander. He produced a wide range of tablewares and decorative pieces in the Art Nouveau style using delicate, sculptural modeling of figures and flowers, often in deep relief. Tonal qualities included delicate greens, pinks, and violets on a grayish off-white background. Wallander also used pale flower decorations contrasted with black grounds.

Following World War II, the entire factory was moved to the port city of Gothenburg, its present location.

The company has used the mark of three crowns of Marieberg with "RORSTRAND" since 1884.

Reference: Bengt Nystrom, *Rorstrand Porcelain: Art Nouveau Masterpieces,* Abbeville Press, 1995.

Bowl

3 1/2" d, ribbed body, wavy rim, brown and black streaked glaze, Carl Harry Stalhane, "R. 3 crown, Sweden, ASH" mark, (A) 100.00

7" d x 3 1/2" h, tapered shape, cylinder ft, blue-green spotted glaze, Carl Harry Stalhane, "R. 3 crowns, Sweden, CHS" mark, (A) 110.00

7 1/2" d, Art Moderne, Laplander, reindeer, mountain, and stars, off-white ground 110.00

Jardiniere and Stand, 42" h, gold outlined lt blue raised leaves, cobalt ground with imp stylized star design, turquoise int 850.00

Stein, .5 L, porcelain, etched design of cavaliers in colors, base crack, (A) 40.00

Vase

5 3/4" h, dbl gourd shape, sand and gray overall glaze, Carl Harry Stalhane, "R. Sweden, CHS, CES" mark, (A) . . 88.00

Vase, 6" h, lilac spotting, pale green dragonfly, green ground, $1,200.

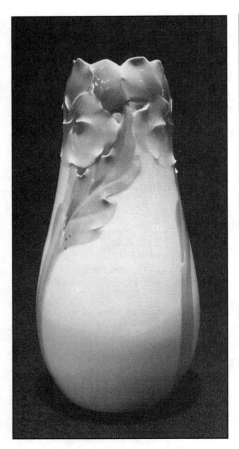

Vase, 8" h, mauve pansies, green stems, cream ground, $1,200.

7" h, swollen cylinder shape, purple and pale pink 3 leaf clovers, lt blue ground, 2 flower form handles from rim . 225.00

7 1/2" h

Flattened swollen cylinder shape, random black, red, and gray swirled glaze, Carl Harry Stalhane, "R. 3 crowns, Atelju, CHS, Sweden" mark, (A) 385.00

Globe shape, 6 sections, blue stylized florals and lines, white crackle ground, "Rorstrand, Made in Sweden" mark 65.00

8" h, kneeling bearded gnome holding steer horn on bk, cream with blue and gold accents 250.00

8 1/2" h, flared cylinder body, tapered shoulder, short neck, grid design on shoulder, dk gray glaze, Carl Harry Stalhane, "R. 3 crowns, CHS, Sweden" mark, (A) 330.00

9" h, gloss maroon and gray flambe glazes, 4 open handles 135.00

12" h, base shaped base, tall slender neck, indented body, green and irid streaks, brown ground, turquoise int 2,200.00

ROSENTHAL

Selb, Bavaria, Germany
1879 to Present

History: The Rosenthal factory was located in Selb, Bavaria. Philip Rosenthal started initially by purchasing whiteware from Selb's other potter, Lorenz Heutschenreuther, decorating it, and selling it from house to house. Rosenthal established his own factory in 1879.

Rosenthal's factory flourished, providing quality figure and tableware that was decorated tastefully. Simplicity of designs and high quality workmanship made Rosenthal a household word.

Several additional factories were constructed. Production rose steadily. Designers of dinnerwares included Theodor Karner, Karl Himmelstoss, Ferdinand Liebermann, Philip Rosenthal, and Walter Gropius. "Darmstadt," "Donatello," and "Isolde" originally were produced in plain white between 1904 and 1910. Heart-shaped motifs in the Art Nouveau manner were later added to "Darmstadt." "Donatello" was decorated with underglaze pate-sur-pate, painted cherries, or a geometric pattern.

Figures made during the 1920s and 1930s were shaped and decorated in the Art Deco style. Many were signed by the artists. Following World War II, most of Rosenthal's assets were destroyed or outmoded. Sources for raw materials mainly from the Eastern Block countries, were terminated.

Philip Rosenthal II assumed control, formed Rosenthal Porzellan AG, and began the restoration of the works. Many of the older designs, except for "Maria Weiss," "Moss Rose," "Sans Souci," and "Pompadour" were abandoned in favor of fresh ideas originated by designers familiar with the modern tastes, among whom were Tapio Wirkkala from Finland, Jean Cocteau from France, and Bela Bechem from Germany.

The U.S. market was the major goal. Raymond Loewy was hired to design medium priced dinnerware for the American market. Under Philip's supervision, Rosenthal regained its prestigious position and flourishes today.

References: Dieter Struss, *Rosenthal,* Schiffer Publishing, Ltd. 1997.

Candlestick, 6 1/4" h, white w/gold trim and base, pr, $595.

Bowl

7 5/8" l x 7" w, ftd, HP acorn and leaf design on shaded green, yellow, and peach ground, gold scalloped rim and gold feet, sgd "Elena Sage," "R.C., crown and X'd lines" mark, (A) . . 55.00

9 1/4" d, scalloped ftd base, pink rose transfer with green leaves, scalloped border with gold trim, "green RC Malmaison, Bavaria, crown and X'd lines" mark, (A) 25.00

9 1/2" d, burgundy florals, white ground, pleated rim. 55.00

Box, 4" sq, red, green, and brown leaves on cov and sides, 4 gold feet. 45.00

Cake Plate

9 3/8" H-H, "Donatello" pattern, wide pink and yellow floral transfer border with orange, yellow, and blue parrots on branches, gold band on rim and handles, "Rosenthal, Selb, Bavaria, Donatello, crown and X'd lines" mark, (A) 20.00

10 3/8" d, white camelias with yellow centers on int border, dk to lt green shaded ground, gold overlay rim 65.00

10 1/2" H-H, "Delft" pattern, windmill, horses and wagons, blue and white. 150.00

Cup and Saucer, "Devonshire" pattern 20.00

Figure

5" h

7" l, wild boar, white glaze 95.00

Laughing rabbit with lg floppy ears, white glaze, #510A 370.00

Seated kitten, black and white . 129.00

5 1/2" h, 2 winged cherubs with flute or mandolin, white glaze, "incised Lang" 95.00

7" h, seated woman in white clown suit with orange trimmed collar, cream shoes with orange bows, pointed hat with raised orange dots, hugging dog at side 1,200.00

7 1/2" h x 8 1/2" l, Poodle, gray, sg "Karner," #1211 . . . . 175.00

9 1/2" h, crane, black, gray, and yellow, sgd "Otto Eichw" 265.00

12" l, mother doe with nursing fawn, brown and white, sgd "A. Roehring" . . 495.00

13 1/2" l, 2 white pouter pigeons with black eyes and beaks, blue-green shaped base. 795.00

13 3/4" h, "Titania, Queen of the Fairies," mottled white dress with pink collar, holding blue flowers with green stem, gilt trimmed crown on head, sgd "Freidrich Growau," c1920s 695.00

18 1/2" h, stylized robed figure, white glaze, (A) 920.00

Fruit Bowl, 14" H-H, HP raspberries, gilt ram's head handles 575.00

Mug

5 1/2" h, lustered cascading grapes, gold trim, artist sgd 140.00

6" h, painted blackberries, green leaves and brown stems, stepped pink base, gold handle 95.00

Pitcher, 12 1/2" h, red-purple grapes, green leaves, shaded green, brown, and orange-brown ground, stepped base, fancy gold handle. 1,400.00

Plate

8" d

Tan and green wheat design, gold rim 10.00

Yellow, purple, and orange pansies on border, lt purple ground, shaped rim 48.00

8 1/2" d, HP lg yellow, blue, and salmon flowers, shaded ground. 27.00

9" d, "Cameo" pattern, purple bust of classic person in center, matte yellow ground 45.00

10" d, "Mon Bijou" pattern, border of scattered garden flowers into center, molded and gold rim, c1900 . . . . 13.00

10 3/8" d, multicolored center scene of 2 ladies dancing in meadow, raised gilt dot cartouche, pink border, gold overlay rim, "crowned RC, X'd lines, blue shield" marks. 75.00

Serving Bowl, 13 1/4" l, 4 lobes with multicolored sprays in each 32.00

Serving Dish, 10" H-H, oval, "Versailles" pattern, sm bunches of oranges flowers, purple rose, blue-green leaves, lt brown trailing stems, gold outlined handles 18.00

Tureen, 8 1/2" h x 13 3/4" H-H, oct, "Maria" pattern, band of pink roses and green leaves

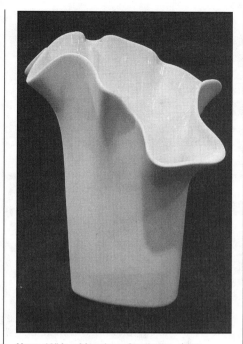

Vase, 10" h, white glaze, Studio line, $185.

on border, gilt accents molded flowerhead rims and handles 250.00

Vase

3" h, pillow shape, lg stylized orange birds with gold beaks, green, gold, and blue scrolling flowers, gold banded rim 25.00

9" h, tapered cylinder shape, 2 HP gray sandpipers on gray to green shaded ground 125.00

9 1/2" h, trumpet shape, wide flat base, painted bouquet of purple, blue, and white flowers and greens, red band top and bottom with silver overlay, gray rim and ft band with olive green swirls 295.00

11 5/8" h, tapered cylinder shape, sm neck, HP purple and magenta lilacs cascading from neck, mauve and purple lilac sprays on reverse, shaded green and orchid ground, c1907-20 . . . . 785.00

ROYAL AUSTRIA

Altrohlau, Bohemia, now Czech Republic 1889 to Present

History: In 1899 Oscar Gutherz joined with Edgar Gutherz, the former manager of the New York and Rudolstadt Pottery, to manufacture household, table, and decorative porcelains, mainly for export to the United States. The mark used was "O & EG" and "Royal Austria" until 1918.

The Austrian Porcelain Industry combine acquired the factory, named it Opiag, Branch Altrohlau, and operated it from 1918 until 1920. Between 1920 and 1945, the factory was called Epaig, Branch Altrohlau. It produced household and decorative porcelains, gift articles, and souvenir items. After World War II, the company was nationalized.

Bowl, 3 5/8" h x 6" d, lobed body, orange luster int, white ext, 3 gold feet, "O. & E.G. Royal Austria" mark. 75.00

Plate

7 1/2" d, 3 HP pink roses, buds, and green stems, raised gold beaded border, "O. & E.G. Royal Austria" mark 28.00

9" d

HP 4 lg yellow roses, buds, and green leaves in center, gold rim, "O. & E.G. Royal Austria" mark 69.00

White roses, brown shaded ground, gold rim, "O. & E.G. Royal Austria" mark 85.00

Yellow roses, brown stems, lt green leaves, wide gold border band, "O. & E.G. Royal Austria" mark. . . 60.00

9 1/2" d

Gold center medallion, band of pink flowers and green leaves on inner border, outer border of raised gold outlined red circles, "O. & E.G. Royal Austria" mark 15.00

Multicolored center scene of 2 classical maidens and Cupid in garden setting, wide magenta border band with blue circles and yellow and dk magenta diamonds, flanked by 2 cream bands with gold feather overlay, blue lined rim, "O. & E.G. Royal Austria" mark 75.00

9 3/4" d

HP border of lg red and yellow flowers, green leaves, gold shaped rim, "O. & E.G. Royal Austria" mark. . . 65.00

White lily of the valley flowers and green foliage, gold shaped rim,

Plate, 9" d, HP pink and lt green, gold rim, "O. & E.G. Royal Austria" mark, $35.

"green E. & O.G. Royal Austria" mark 25.00

Teapot, 5 3/8" h, with underplate, pink and red roses, brown stems, shaded green to mauve ground, gold loop knob, "O. & E.G. Royal Austria" mark 65.00

Tray, 13" H-H, oval, pink rose sprigs with green leaves, gold Greek key border, mint green rim 60.00

ROYAL BAYREUTH

Tettau, Bavaria
1794 to Present

c1903

History: Wilheim Greiner and Johann Schmidt established a porcelain factory at Tettau in 1794. They also maintained an association with the Volkstedt and Kloster Veilsdorf factories in Thuringia. The factory survived numerous wars, financial difficulties, and many changes in ownership until a great fire in 1897 destroyed most of the molds and early records. A more modern factory was built and operated until World War I.

The company operated under the name, Porcelain Factory Tettau, from 1902 until 1957. In 1957, the company adopted the name, Royally Privileged Porcelain Factory Tettau GMBH, which it still uses today.

Animal and floral forms, along with other unusual figural shapes, were made at Tettau between 1885 and World War I. Designs included fruits, vegetables, lobsters, tomatoes, and people. Shapes ranged from ashtrays to vegetable dishes. Individuals often bought them as souvenir and novelty items because of their inexpensive cost. Much of the production was exported.

Today the firm produces dinnerware and limited edition collectibles. The name, "Royal Bayreuth" is used in the United States to identify the company's products.

Rose Tapestry

Rose tapestry, similar in texture to needlepoint tapestry and called "matte finish" china, was made in the late 19th century. Rose tapestry had a rough effect that felt like woven cloth. It was made by wrapping the article in coarse cloth and then firing. The cloth was consumed in the firing, and the tapestry effect remained.

Decoration was added over the glaze. It varied from floral to scenic to portrait. The floral motifs included "rose tapestry," the most popular and prevalent design. The roses shaded from a pale pink to deeper red colors.

Occasionally pale yellow or white roses were combined with the pink or red roses. Rose tapestry also can be found in an apri-

cot and deep orange-gold shade. The rarest rose tapestry was "sterling silver." The roses were deep gray to a pale silver gray shaded into white.

The background of rose tapestry was off-white or had a grayish or greenish tinge. Pale green leaves and small faintly tinted flowers completed the decoration.

Floral, scenic, and portrait tapestries were made in plates, pitchers, cups and saucers, vases, pin boxes, trays, bells, and many other shapes.

Sunbonnet Babies

Molly and Mae, the Sunbonnet Babies, were created by Bertha L. Corbett, an American artist, in the early 1900s. Corbett had no confidence in her ability to draw faces so she hid them under the large bonnets. The Sunbonnet Babies were drawn to develop good character traits and teach children their daily chores, e.g. washing, ironing, sweeping, dusting, mending, baking, fishing, and going to church.

Variations identified as Beach Babies and Snow Babies also were made.

References: Mary J. McCaslin, *Royal Bayreuth: A Collector's Guide,* Antique Publications, 1996; Joan & Marvin Raines, *A Guide to Royal Bayreuth Figurals,* privately printed, 1973; Joan & Marvin Raines, *A Guide to Royal Bayreuth Figurals, Book 2,* privately printed, 1977; Virginia & George Salley, *Royal Bayreuth China* privately printed, 1969.

Collectors' Clubs: Royal Bayreuth Collectors Club, Inc. Judith White, 926 Essex Circle, Kalamazoo, MI 49008, Membership: $30.00, Quarterly newsletter; Royal Bayreuth International Collectors' Society, P.O. Box 325, Orrvile, OH 44667, Bi-monthly newsletter.

Babies

Bell, 3" h
　　Sandbabies, running on beach, blue mark 325.00
　　Sunbonnet babies, sewing, unmkd 400.00
Box
　　3 1/2" t, cylinder shape, Snowbabies sledding, unmkd 145.00
　　5 1/2" w, shell shape, Snowbabies 275.00
Bud Vase, 3" h, ball shape, overhead handle, Sunbonnet babies sewing 295.00
Candlestick, Sunbonnet babies
　　4 1/8" h,
　　　　Cleaning 235.00
　　　　Fishing, blue mark 200.00
Candy Dish
　　4 3/4" l, spade shape, Sunbonnet babies sweeping, blue mark 225.00
　　5" l, Snowbabies sledding 95.00

Candleholder, 4 1/2" h, Sunbonnet Babies washing and ironing, blue mark, (A) $575.

5 3/4" h,
　　Sweeping and washing windows, blue mark 595.00
Chamberstick, 4 1/2" h, Snowbabies sledding 250.00
Compote, 2 3/4" h x 6" d, Sunbonnet babies sweeping, blue mark 695.00
Creamer
　　3" h
　　　　Sandbabies running 138.00
　　　　Sunbonnet babies ironing 175.00
　　3 1/2" h, Sunbonnet babies
　　　　Fishing 220.00
　　　　Sweeping 225.00
　　　　Washing, blue mark 300.00
　　4" h
　　　　Snowbabies sledding 245.00
　　　　Sunbonnet babies
　　　　　　Fishing 235.00
　　　　　　Sweeping 225.00
　　4 3/4" h, corset shape, Sunbonnet babies washing 245.00

Creamer and Sugar Bowl, multicolored Ring Around the Rosie and girl pulling dog, blue marks, $335.

Cup and Saucer, mini, Snowbabies sledding
. . . . 150.00

Dresser Tray, 10" l, ruffled rim, Sunbonnet babies washing and hanging clothes . . . 995.00

Hair Receiver, 5" d, Sunbonnet babies, sewing, blue mark 595.00

Milk Pitcher, 4 1/4" h

   Jug shape, Sunbonnet babies washing
. . . . 325.00

   Pinched spout, bulbous shape, Sunbonnet babies fishing 225.00

   Sunbonnet babies sweeping, blue mark
. . . . 235.00

Pass Cup, 3 5/8" h, 3 handles, Snowbabies sledding, purple mark 395.00

Plate

   6" d

      Snowbabies sledding 150.00

      Sunbonnet babies mending . . . 140.00

   7 1/2" d

      Snowbabies sledding, blue mark
. . . . 275.00

      Sunbonnet babies washing . . . 100.00

   8 1/2" d, Sunbonnet babies sewing
. . . . 190.00

   9" d, Sunbonnet babies washing, blue mark 238.00

Toothpick, 2 1/2" h, pie crust edge, Sunbonnet babies sewing, unmkd 300.00

Tumbler, 3 1/2" h, handled, Snowbabies sledding 250.00

Vase

   3 1/8" h, squat base, barrel shape body, Dutch boy and girl playing with brown dog, 2 handles, green mark 55.00

   5 1/2" h

      Barrel shape, Sunbonnet babies cleaning 325.00

      Snowbabies sledding 245.00

General

Ashtray

   4 1/2" l x 4" w, figural eagle 495.00

   5 1/2" l x 4" w, figural mountain goat
. . . . 395.00

Berry Set, master bowl, 10" d, 6 bowls, 6" d, figural strawberries, blossoms, and leaves
. . . . 485.00

Bowl

   8" d, figural poppy, red 350.00

   9" d, figural grape 335.00

   9 1/2" d, wheat girl in apron with chickens
. . . . 395.00

Bowl, Cov, 4 1/2" h, figural tomato, red, blue mark 140.00

Box, 4" d, multicolored scene of 2 musicians on cov 110.00

Cake Plate, 10 5/8" H-H, Corinthian, white warriors, matte black ground, blue mark . . 65.00

Candlestick

   2 1/4" h, 5" l, Devil and Cards 350.00

   4" h

      Figural Basset hound 650.00

      Little Jack Horner, blue mark . . 250.00

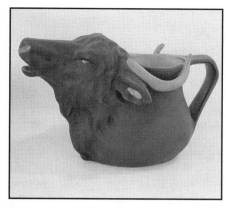

Creamer, 3 3/4" h, water buffalo, black, red trim and int, blue mark, $145.

   5 1/2" h, Corinthian, black ground, white classic figures, blue mark 195.00

   6 3/4" h, figural standing clown, blue mark
. . . . 1,700.00

Card Dish, 3 3/4" q, Devil and Cards . 100.00

Charger, 13" d

   Goose girl, polychrome 210.00

   Seated boy with donkeys, tan and brown shades 300.00

Cracker Jar, 6" h, figural strawberry
. . . . 250.00

Creamer

   Figural

      Apple, green 125.00

      Bell Ringer, green, yellow, and red
. . . . 325.00

      Bull, gray 235.00

      Butterfly, open-winged, orange, gray, and green, blue mark 325.00

      Clown, red 450.00

      Coachman, red and black 299.00

      Lamplighter, green and yellow
. . . . 375.00

      Lemon 200.00

      Pear 350.00

      Pelican 350.00

      Perch, white, green, and red . . 425.00

      Pig, gray 525.00

      Poodle, gray 275.00

      Poppy, white 295.00

      Robin 130.00

      Snake, blue mark 700.00

      Spikey Shell, murex 95.00

      Strawberry 150.00

      Water Buffalo 190.00

   3 1/2" h, "Babes in Woods" design, 2 children playing, blue shades, blue mark
. . . . 325.00

   3 1/4" h, Devil and Cards design, blue mark 225.00

Creamer and Sugar, creamer, 4" h, sugar bowl, 3 1/2" h, figural strawberry 450.00

Ewer, 8" h, stag and gazebo scene, polychrome 95.00

Fruit Bowl, 10" d, Jack and Jill series . 295.00

Hair Receiver, 3" h x 4" d, 3 legs, Jack and the Beanstalk design, blue mark 200.00

Hatpin Holder

   4 1/4" h, white figural poppy 675.00

   4 1/2" h

      Attached base, multicolored Arabs on horseback, blue mark 375.00

      Figural dachshund, lt brown . . . 900.00

   5 1/2" h, figural pelican 950.00

Humidor

   6" h, sailing skiff, matte gray ground
. . . . 255.00

   7 1/2" h

      Arab in desert scene, multicolored
. . . . 400.00

      Black and white penguins, lime green ground 475.00

      Figural lobster, blue mark 450.00

Milk Pitcher

   4 1/2" h, figural poppy, red 295.00

   4 3/4" h, figural Coachman, red and black
. . . . 325.00

   5" h, white figural cat handle, green body
. . . . 300.00

Mug, 5" h, Devil and Cards 350.00

Nappy, 5" l, white figural poppy 95.00

Pitcher

   3 1/8" h, Arab on horse in colors, gold handle, blue mark 55.00

   3 1/2, h, "Little Boy Blue" 210.00

   4 1/4" h, Spikey Shell, red coral handle
. . . . 195.00

   4 1/2" h, Arab on horse in colors . . 125.00

   5" h

      Devil and Cards 275.00

      Figural elk 245.00

   6" h

      Pinched spout, frogs and bees, red ground 275.00

      Portrait of woman in purple plumed hat, blue mark 275.00

   6 7/8" h, tankard shape, Corinthian, black, white, and gold figure, black satin ground, orange int rim 118.00

   7" h, multicolored man with pipe . . 150.00

Pitcher, 4" h, Corinthian Ware matte black ext, gilt trim on rim, lt orange to dk orange shaded int, $150.

7 1/2" h, full figured standing trout,
(A) 2,090.00

Plate

6" d

Apple leaf 85.00

Devil and Cards 500.00

Poppy, yellow 200.00

7 1/2" d, multicolored scene of 2 long
horned steers in meadow, blue mark
. . . . 90.00

8" d, sailing skiff, matte gray ground 85.00

8 1/4" d, satin apricot figural poppy
. . . . 150.00

9" d, multicolored scene of hunter and
dogs in stream, blue mark 100.00

Relish Dish, 8" l, Spikey Shell, mother of pearl
finish 85.00

Salt Shaker, 3" h, figural elk, brown shades
. . . . 75.00

Stamp Box, 2 1/4" h, 3 3/4" l, Devil and Cards
. . . . 600.00

String Holder, 6" h, figural rooster head
. . . . 600.00

Sugar Bowl, Cov

3 1/2" h, red figural poppy 160.00

4" h, figural lobster, blue mark 100.00

4 1/2" h, figural orange, blue mark
. . . . 375.00

4 3/4" h, figural lobster, blue mark
. . . . 125.00

Tankard, 4 1/2" h, 2 multicolored seated musicians, blue mark 125.00

Teapot

4 1/2" h, figural poppy, red 350.00

4 3/4" h, figural pansy, blue mark . 625.00

5" h, figural strawberry 350.00

Toothpick

2 1/4" h, 3 handles, multicolored florals
. . . . 150.00

3" h

Figural elk 175.00

Spikey Shell, mother of pearl finish
. . . . 120.00

Tray, 12 1/4" l x 9" w, multicolored scene of girl
and geese, shaped gold rim with molded
handles 320.00

Vase

3" h, "Babes in Woods-Girl Curtsying,"
blue shades 310.00

4 1/2" h

"Babes in Woods-Girls Under Umbrella," blue shades 425.00

Sailing scene, brown and tan shades
. . . . 135.00

5" h, hunting scene, multicolored . 175.00

6 1/4" h, multicolored scene of cows grazing in pasture, sun and trees . . . 365.00

7 1/2" h, cavaliers, green ground, sgd
"Dixon" 250.00

9 1/2" h, multicolored peacock in field, reticulated neck and base, gold scroll
handles 740.00

Water Pitcher

5" h, figural St. Bernard, blue mark
. . . . 1,300.00

6 1/2" h, figural geranium, blue mark
. . . . 1,250.00

6 3/4" h, figural seal, blue mark
. . . . 1,400.00

Wall Match Holder, 5" h

Devil and Cards 600.00

Elk, brown shades, blue mark . . . 550.00

Spikey Shell, white satin finish . . . 315.00

Water Pitcher

6" h, figural eagle 1,650.00

6 3/4" h, figural lobster, blue mark
. . . . 400.00

7" h, figural elk 325.00

7 1/4 " h, cows in pasture w/trees, multicolored, blue mark 245.00

Tapestry

Basket

2 1/2" h x 4 1/4" l, sterling silver roses
. . . . 950.00

5 3/4" h, 3 color roses 425.00

Bowl

10" d, 3 mountain goats on ridge . 525.00

10 1/2" d, 3 color roses, shell and leaf
molded rim 995.00

Box

2 1/2" sq, white rose 275.00

5 1/2" w, shell shape, 3 color roses
. . . . 450.00

Bud Vase, 4" h, stag in stream, multicolored
. . . . 385.00

Chocolate Set, pot, 8 3/4" h, 4 cups and saucers, 3 color roses, blue marks 2,800.00

Creamer

3 1/4" h, pinched spout

Pink roses 175.00

Three color roses 185.00

3 1/2" h, 3 color roses, blue mark
. . . . 225.00

4" h

Corset shape, pink roses, blue mark
. . . . 275.00

3 goats in meadow, multicolored
. . . . 250.00

**Tray, 10" l, 7 3/8" w, man in blue jacket, purple
pants, woman in orange gown, blue mark, $485.**

4 3/4" h, corset shape, 3 color roses
. . . . 225.00

Cup and Saucer, roses, blue mark . . . 325.00

Dish, 4 1/2" l x 2" w, 3 color roses, blue mark
. . . . 195.00

Dresser Tray, 10" l, rect, 3 color roses 375.00

Hair Receiver, 4" d, 3 color roses 295.00

Hatpin Holder, 4 3/4" h, pink roses, blue mark
. . . . 425.00

Plaque, 9 1/2" d, portrait of woman leaning on
horse, meadow bkd, gold outlined molded
border 770.00

Plate

7 1/2" d, 3 color roses, shell and leaf mold
. . . . 200.00

9 1/2" d, 3 color roses, gold rococo border
. . . . 375.00

Ring Tree, 3 1/2" d, pink roses 495.00

Shakers, 3 color roses, blue mark, pr
. . . . 525.00

Tray, 11 1/2" l x 8 1/4" w, courting scene in
colors 450.00

Vase

4" h, mountain goat design in colors
. . . . 265.00

4 1/2" h

Black cattle, ruffled rim, ftd, 2 side
handles 375.00

Reverse cone shape, 3 color roses,
blue mark 195.00

Swan design 265.00

8 1/4" h, bottle shape, bathers scene in
colors 435.00

ROYAL BONN

Bonn, Germany
1836-1931

History: Franz Anton Mehlem founded a
factory in the Rhineland in 1836 to produce
household, decorative, technical, and sanitary earthenware and porcelain. Between
1887 and 1903, the factory reproduced
Hochst figures in both porcelain and earthenware using the original molds from the
defunct Prince-Electoral Mayence Manufactory in Hochst. Villeroy and Boch from
Mettlach bought the factory in 1921 and
closed it in 1931.

Royal was added to the mark in 1890.
After that, products were marketed under
the name, "Royal Bonn."

Bowl

7" d, flanged, "Wildrose" pattern, blue transfer.................12.00

9 3/4" d, brown transfer of stag standing by stream in woodland setting, green border with molded designs.......95.00

Bowl, Cov, 5 3/4" h, with undertray, sm multicolored flowers, cobalt and gold trim on rims, cream ground..................170.00

Bud Vase

5 1/4" h, blue outlined mauve leaves with white and yellow irises, pale blue ground, brown rim...........395.00

5 1/2" h, bulbous, bouquet of red roses on white ground in raised gold cartouches around shoulder, med green ground 95.00

6" h, bulbous body, sm straight neck, flared rim, lg yellow roses, gray streaked ground 175.00

Charger, 11" d, brown basket on side, red fruit spilling out, green leaves in bkd, gray shaded ground, pea green lustered border with molded fans and beads 50.00

Ewer, 10" h, raised gold outlined purple and pink dogwood blossoms, gold outlined dk green leaves, cream ground with gold dusting, gold loop handle with 3 finger attachment 295.00

Plate

8 1/2" d, red and purple tulip, white rose, green shaded ground with purple accents, molded dash rim.......10.00

9 1/2" d, blue, yellow, red, and brown flower bouquet, blue-green leaves, molded scalloped border and rim 16.00

Stein, .5 L, blue Delft, transfer of bust of cavalier, leaves above and below, pewter lid, "Royal Bonn Delft" mark, (A)...........432.00

Vase, 7 3/4" h, magenta and yellow dahlias, blue, green, and yellow ground, gilt trim, molded leaf design on neck and base, $395.

Vase, 11 1/4" h, yellow roses, blue to lt green ground, raised gold overlay, shaded yellow neck, shaded green base, $595.

Vase

6 1/4" h, scene of 2 women picking wheat in colors, 2 handled 675.00

6 3/4" h

Ovoid shape with short cylinder neck, profile of Art Nouveau woman, white face, brown hair, red comb, horiz red ribbons, lg yellow sunflowers, mottled green ground, "Royal Bonn, Art Nouv, 214, 3889/4, 12" mark, pr, (A) 647.00

Yellow iris, dk blue leaves, brown and blue mottled ground 500.00

7 1/4" h, pink lilies, aqua ground, gold trim 175.00

8" h

Brown and gold oak leaves, green matte spotted ground, hex rim 175.00

Gold flowers and trim, pastel pink and blue ground..............65.00

8 1/4" h, moon shape, multicolored flowers in garden setting, tapestry finish 345.00

8 1/2" h, tapered cylinder shape, multicolored Persian style flowers and stems, sand tapestry finish..........295.00

10" h, ovoid shape, portrait bust of woman in white gown, flowing brown hair, multicolored landscape on reverse, yellow-brown shaded ground, raised geometrics on rim and base 350.00

11" h

HP birds with purple orchids, mkd 150.00

Vase, 12 1/4" h, blue birds, tulips, florals in colors, magenta and pink vert band, cream ground, gilt foliate design, (A) $150.

Narrow bulbous body, slim neck with flared rim, HP "Old Dutch" design of red flowerheads 325.00

11 1/4" h, pink and yellow roses, green and mustard-yellow ground, gold trim, c1900....................250.00

13" h, baluster shape, 2 branch handles, bust of brown haired girl in brown and green shaded dress, yellow roses on brown to green shaded ground, landscape on reverse, gold trim, (A) 518.00

13 1/2" h, tapered cylinder shape, gold outlined enameled pink, purple, and peach colored flowers, gold outlined blue-green leaves, cream ground with gold dusting...............795.00

13 3/4" h, bulbous shape, spread ft, sm flared rim, handles from ft to shoulder, HP red, yellow and white roses, dk rose ground at top, lt green ground in middle, dk green base, drilled base 425.00

14" h, cartouche with bust of brown haired woman, outdoor scene on reverse, pink ground with gilt scrolling accents 1,160.00

14 1/2" h, bulbous shape, red, white, and yellow hibiscus, shaded purple to yellow ground, molded floral handles, gold trimmed flower-form mouth 275.00

17 1/4" h, HP gold, rose and purple overall shadow flowers, tapestry finish, 4 gold curved feet, floral reticulated handles 885.00

20" h, ftd, HP lg multicolored floral sprays, green-gold band at base, raised gold flowers on neck, neck handles 270.00

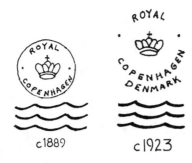

c1889   c1923

ROYAL COPENHAGEN

Copenhagen, Denmark
c1760 to Present

History: During the 1760s, the Danish royal family was interested in discovering the Chinese secret for white hard paste porcelain. Louis Fournier, a French ceramist, came to Denmark to conduct experiments in hopes of uncovering the porcelain formula.

In 1772, Franz Muller, a Danish pharmacist and chemist, produced the first genuine hard paste porcelain. Muller, with the Queen's support, founded the Danish Porcelain Factory in Copenhagen in 1775. By 1779, financial difficulties forced Muller to relinquish his hold to the Danish crown. The Dowager Queen Julianne Marie was the chief patron. Under her influences, the Copenhagen trademark of three wavy lines was established. Each wave represented a waterway from Kattegat to the Baltic.

Royal Copenhagen's Flora Danica, decorated with the native plants of Denmark, was a famous 18th century service begun in 1790. A total of 1,802 pieces was painted. The dinnerware was intended originally as a gift for Catherine the Great of Russia, but she died six years before its completion. All botanical illustrations were done free hand; all perforations and edges were cut by hand. The service still remains in the possession of the Danish crown. Flora Danica is still being produced today. Each piece is done entirely by hand by an individual artist who signs his work.

Royal Copenhagen's most famous pattern, Blue Fluted, was created in 1780. It is of Chinese origin and has three edge forms: smooth edge, closed lace edge, and perforated lace edge. It was copied by many other factories.

Although the quality of the porcelain kept improving during the early 19th century, and there was strong popular approval for the company's figures, vases, and accessory pieces in all pottery and porcelain compositions, the factory was not a financial asset for the crown. A. Falch, a private owner, purchased the factory in 1867. A condition of purchase was his right to con-

tinue to use the term "Royal" in the monogram. Philip Schou purchased the works from Falch in 1882 and moved to the present location at Smalzgade. Arnold Krog, who was appointed Art Director in 1885, was responsible for revitalizing Royal Copenhagen. The under the glaze painting technique was perfected under his control. Muller's early creations were reproduced as the "Julienne Marie Porcelain" line.

Dinner services, under the glaze painted figures, and vases were among the principal forms being made at Royal Copenhagen when Dalgas took over in 1902. The first Christmas plate was made in 1908. As at the Bing and Grondahl factory, the molds were destroyed each year after the holiday season to prevent restrikes in hopes of preserving the value of each plate for the collectors. During Dalgas' tenure, there also were experiments with stonewares and the renaissance of the overglaze painting techniques.

References: Robert J. Heritage, *Royal Copenhagen Porcelain Animals & Figurines*, Schiffer Publishing, Ltd. 1997; Pat Owen, *The Story of Royal Copenhagen Christmas Plates,* Viking Import House, Inc.1961; H.V.F. Winstone, *Royal Copenhagen,* Stacy International, 1984.

Museums: The Bradford Museum, Niles, IL; Rosenborg Castle, Copenhagen, Denmark.

Collecting Hints: Royal Copenhagen dinnerware sets are eager sought by collectors because of their high quality. The blue and white limited edition plates remain popular with collectors.

Basket
   9 1/4" l x 3 1/4" h, Flora Danica, painted ivy and berries on int base, openwork body with polychrome relief molded flowers and gilt decorated base, gilt rim, mottled brown and green handles, "Ribes alpinum, Royal Copenhagen, Denmark, 3 blue waves, #3536" marks, (A)
                     . . . . 748.00
   10" H-H, pierced sides, painted bouquets of flowers on int, ext with molded basket design entwined with forget-me-nots, painted floral bouquets, 2 twist handles, c1880, blue wave mark, chips, pr, (A)
                   . . . . 3,030.00
Bowl, 9 1/4" d, "Plain Blue Lace" pattern
     . . . . 58.00
Bud Vase
   4 3/4" h, green, brown, and white cactus flower, lt blue shaded ground, #2672
                     . . . . 65.00
   5 3/4" h, blackberries, flowers, and leaves, #288-43A 25.00
Candlestick, 4" h, "Full Blue Lace" pattern, pr
     . . . . 450.00
Chocolate Pot, 8" h, "Half Blue Lace" pattern
                                . . . . . 575.00

Bowl, 10 3/8" d, multicolored center scene, maroon and gilt banded int, gilt ext, "Royal Copenhagen 3 blue waves" mark, $385.

Coffeepot, 10" h
   "Half Blue Lace" pattern 250.00
   "Plain Blue Lace" pattern. 225.00
Compote
   5 3/8" h x 9 1/4" d, "Plain Blue Lace" pattern 295.00
   5 5/8" h x 8 1/4" d, "Full Blue Lace" pattern
       . . . . 375.00
Cup and Saucer
   Flora Danica, "Potentilla" design . . 595.00
   "Plain Blue Lace" pattern. 82.00
Decanter, 10 1/2" h, bottle shape, overall white glaze with raised flower on front, raised crown and 3 wavy lines on reverse, rd stopper 45.00
Dish
   7" sq, "Marselis" design, dk brown herringbone pattern on med brown ground matte finish. 75.00
   7 1/2" l, leaf shape, mauve rose, orange flowers, green leaves, scattered florals, brown stem handle with relief molded yellow and blue head at terminal, gilt lined rim 125.00
   11" l, molded overlapping leaves, top leaf with lt and dk green veins, white leaf with painted scattered florals, gilt dentil

Bowl, 11 3/4" l, 5" h, blue and white, "Full Blue Lace," (A) $250.

Compote, 9" w, 4 3/4" h, Flora Danica, "Potentilla Apaca L," or "Thymus Chamedrys FR," pr, (A) $920.

rim, blue wave mark, c1775, (A) 1,800.00

13 7/8" d, glazed blue floral reserves on red stoneware ground, (A) 25.00

Figure

4" h, walking polar bear, white glaze, #320 .... 235.00

4 1/4" h x 7 1/2" l, otter, lt brown, #2936 .... 270.00

4 1/2" h x 5" l, Boston Terrier, white and gray 165.00

4 3/4" h, girl sitting with doll, tan, white, and blue, #1938 .... 250.00

5 3/4" h, Amager girl knitting, blue, tan, and white, #1314 .... 250.00

6 3/8" h, school girl, long white dress and cap, book under arm, #922, (A) 85.00

7" h, washerwoman bent at waist, baby on bk, blue glaze with unglazed sections, sgd "Johannes Hedegaard" ... 345.00

7 1/2" h, seated boy in cap, tan, blue, and dk blue, #905 .... 185.00

8" h, seated hawk, blue, gray, and white, #263, (A) 200.00

8 1/2" h, Pan on gray column, rabbit on base, #456 .... 295.00

12 1/4" h, barefoot boy with peaked cap, holding stick, seated on rock, shaped base, blue, white, and tan, #1659, (A) 500.00

16 7/8" h, young peasant man holding scythe, leaning against corn sheaf, seated peasant woman holding pitcher, blue, gray, green, and brown, #1352, (A) 715.00

22" h, Agnette and Merman, blue, gray, tan, and cream 1,100.00

Jam Pot, Cov, 3 3/8" h, glazed blue stylized floral reserves on red stoneware ground, (A) 20.00

Jar, Cov, 5" h, scattered multicolored floral bunches, molded basketweave borders, gold dentil rims, gold outlined molded wave knob,

"Royal Copenhagen Denmark and 3 waves" mark 195.00

Mustard Pot, 3 1/2" h, with attached undertray, Flora Danica, relief molded flowers, pink and green foliage, gilt banding, raised handle on cov, "Royal Copenhagen, Denmark, crown, 3 blue waves, #20, 3515, dx" marks, (A) 403.00

Pitcher, 4" h, "Plain Blue Lace" pattern 80.00

Plate

6 1/8" d, "Plain Blue Lace" pattern 30.00

7 1/2" d, Flora Danica, "Violets" design, basketweave border........ 275.00

8 1/2" d, "Plain Blue Lace" pattern 58.00

8 3/4" d, "Plain Blue Lace" pattern 35.00

10" d, "Half Blue Lace" pattern.... 95.00

10 3/4" d, "Full Blue Lace" pattern 120.00

11 3/8" d, Flora Danica, "Black Raspberries" design, reticulated border, gilt serrated rim, (A)................. 895.00

Platter, 11 /4" l, "Plain Blue Lace" pattern 160.00

Sauce Boat, 10" l, with attached undertray, Flora Danica design............. 1,900.00

Soup Bowl

7 1/2" d, "Half Blue Lace" pattern 110.00

8" d, "Full Blue Lace" pattern 96.00

Teapot

5 1/4" h, "Plain Blue Lace" pattern 210.00

6 1/2" h, "Half Blue Lace" pattern 360.00

Tray, 10" l, oval, "Full Blue Lace" pattern 175.00

Vase

2 1/4" h, ball shape, blue butterfly over white daisy, dk green stem, shaded white to blue ground, #2688-4521 .... 35.00

2 1/2" h, ball shape, multicolored scene of rock formations in gilt dentil cartouche, rim of gilt floral drape 140.00

5" h, tapered cylinder shape

Brown flying hummingbird, white iris, blue shaded ground, #2676, 271 .... 30.00

Purple plums, green leaves, brown branch, gray ground, #907 88A 95.00

5 1/2" h, cylinder shape, tapered neck, dk red centered white dogwood blossoms, brown branch, green leaves, shaded blue ground 85.00

7" h

Bulbous bottle shape with collar rim, lg blue and brown eyes, white ground, (A) 75.00

Vase, 7" h, brown, blue, and tan design, "Royal Copenhagen Denmark, 870/3455" mark, (A) $110.

Gray and white flying seagulls over blue and green water, gray to blue ground, #1138 2289 .... 68.00

7 1/4" h, tan and blue sailboat, blue shaded ground, #101.2 56F 50.00

7 1/2" h, trumpet shape, green cactus, gray crackle ground 48.00

7 3/4" h, rect shape, purple and blue abstract flowers, white ground, (A) 60.00

8" h

Painted narcissus, pale blue ground 85.00

Sq shape, brown and blue stylized sunflowers, off-white ground, #436-3121 .... 185.00

9 1/2" h, shouldered cylinder shape, white, brown, and green flower blossoms, dk blue ground, #S337/132 ...... 315.00

11 3/8" h, swollen cylinder shape, green, blue, white, and brown wildflowers, hilly landscape bkd, blue shaded ground, #2549/1148, (A) 300.00

12 1/2" h, applied HP blossoms, cobalt ground 275.00

14" h, gray, brown, yellow, and white abstract faces, matte finish, (A).... 90.00

16 7/8" h, tapered cylinder shape, everted rim, blue, white, and gray continuous scene of sailing boats on sea, sgd "St. Ussing" 375.00

Vase, Cov, 19" h, urn shape, 2 bracket handles with gilt stripes, gilt band of stylized foliage over band of chevrons suspending hairbells on body, gilt chevron band on pedestal, gilt striped sq base, gilt flower knob, "blue wave" mark, late 18th C, restorations, pr, (A) 1,000.00

Vegetable Bowl, 10" l, oval, "Half Blue Lace" pattern 150.00

c1947   c1912

ROYAL DUX

Dux, Bohemia (now Duchow, Czech Republic) 1860 to Present

History: In 1860, E. Eichler established the Duxer Porcelain Manufactory in Dux, Bohemia. The factory was noted for its portrait busts and lavishly decorated vases. Much of the production was exported to America. After the turn of the century, the Art Nouveau style was used for large porcelain figures and vases.

Shortly after the conclusion of World War II, the factory was nationalized. The newly formed company produced household, decorative, and table porcelains, plus coffee and tea sets.

New figures are produced in many of the same subjects, colors and styles of the original pre-WWII pieces. The keys to dating are the impressed marks in the pink triangles and whether the pieces are marked "Czechoslovakia" or "Czech Republic."

Bookends, 8 7/8" h, Art Deco style, modeled as partly nude brown haired woman leaning backwards, holding up gilt flowered cobalt skirt, gilt trimmed triangle base, pink triangle mark, pr, (A) 372.00

Candlestick, 6 5/8" h, figural young boy or girl in gilt trimmed white clown suit holding fluted sconce, maroon edged shaped base, pink triangle mark, pr, (A) 310.00

Centerpiece, 16 1/8" h, modeled as maiden in pink gown, gold headband, pulling green nets between 2 lg nautilus shells, rocky base molded with seaweed and waves, pink triangle mark, (A) 930.00

Dish, 7" l x 5 1/2" h, oval, figural Art Nouveau woman in red gown seated on bk rim, 2 loop handles on corners, green-gold matte ext, cream int 525.00

Figure

7" h, young woman wearing low cut dress, leaning forward, holding edges of mottled orange and yellow skirt, pink triangle mark, (A) 170.00

7 7/8" h, Art Nouveau style woman reclining on conch shell, leaning on jug,

Figure, 11 1/2" h, gray, tan, and green, raised pink triangle mark, $350.

green, pink, cream, and gilt shades, pink triangle mark, (A) 462.00

8 1/4" h x 10 1/2" l, brown dog standing, rust dog seated, tan base, pink triangle mark 180.00

9" h, standing woman wearing burnt orange top, olive green skirt, jug under arm, standing boy wearing olive green hat, burnt orange shirt, olive green pants, holding jug and cup, pink triangle mark, pr 750.00

9 1/2" h

Art Nouveau woman holding jug, seated on rocky ledge above open shell, pink, cream, green, and gilt tones, pink triangle mark, (A) 250.00

Standing woman in swirling cobalt skirt, white hat, pink triangle mark 225.00

9 5/8" h, standing owl, white glaze, (A) 120.00

10 3/4" h

Art Deco standing nude woman, flesh tones with blue and gold trim, pink triangle mark 1,600.00

Brown haired 1920 standing woman in chartreuse dress with gilt trim, pink and rose red sash with gilt, white sleeves with yellow lines, round white base with gilt trim, pink triangle mark 165.00

11 1/2" h

Bust of Art Nouveau style woman smelling flowers, flowers in hair, tan and cream with gold accents, pale green sash on arm, matte finish 850.00

Standing peasant woman wearing lt mauve apron, green top, green sash around waist with gold trim, mauve hat with 2 white balls, wooden shoes, dragging brown streaked cloth, basket under arm, pink triangle mark 295.00

13" h, young hunter walking dog on leash, gold pants, lt pink shirt, cream dog, matte finish 595.00

13 3/4" h x 14" l, standing figural of blond haired shepherd, brown coat, green pants, blue shirt, 2 standing sheep and 2 lambs, dog at front, molded green leaf and rock mound base, c1864 . . . . 1,150.00

15" h

Cockatoo, white glaze with pink shading, pink triangle mark 185.00

Modeled as lg shell from organic scrolling, 2 Art Nouveau maidens modeled at sides, green, brown, cream, and gilt tones, (A) . . . 370.00

18" h, standing peasant man in pink shirt, brown trousers holding wheat bundle, kneeling woman in pink blouse, brown skirt, cream an green accents, oval base, pink triangle mark, (A) . . . 535.00

19" h, standing classic woman holding basket, ivory, gold accents, pr 1,800.00

19 5/8" h, standing peasant man in pink stocking cap, green tunic, pink sash with cup and jug, holding jug in hand, standing female peasant in green cap, pink robe, green sash with cup, holding jug in each hand, gilt accents, rocky base, pink triangle mark, damaged pot, pr, (A) 495.00

20 1/4" h, camel driver in red and green robes, leaning toward figure placing basket on mound, grassy oblong base, gilt accents, "ROYAL DUX BOHEMIA" and pink triangle marks, (A) . . . 690.00

21" h, young boy with fishing bag and hat, bronze and gold tones, pink triangle mark 450.00

23 1/2" h, 1930s brown haired dancing woman, mauve top, bare middle, pink flowered swirling skirt, gold bracelets on arm, white oval base with gold flowers 2,100.00

Vase

6" h, squat shape, 3 handles from base to neck, dk green swirls interspersed with red and yellow enamels with blue dots in center, lt green ground and tan leopard skin ground, acorn mark . . . 175.00

7 3/4" h, squat shape, 3 handles from base to neck, raised yellow marigolds and hanging yellow flowers, green and pink

Vase, 19 1/4" h, tan, green, and cream shades, gold handles, matte finish, $4,500.

raised leaves, gray and cream leopard skin ground, acorn mark 250.00

9" h, figural boy on nautilus shell, ivory with black and gold accents, (A) . . . 220.00

11" h, bust of Art Nouveau style woman resting chin on hands, tan brick wall in bkd with olive green leaves and gold accents, pink triangle mark . . .1,250.00

12" h, incised oriental woman design, ivory with gold accents 395.00

12 1/2" h, figural woman in olive green gown holding tambourine, seated on edge of cream sq base with pink blossoms molded brown branches, semi-matte finish, pink triangle and E mark 995.00

16" h, freeform design, lg orange poppies in relief, open asymmetric dbl handles, (A) 75.00

20 1/2" h, baluster shape, green-brown raised blackberries, leaves, and vines, gold accents, vine handles, scalloped leaf rim and ft, ivory body 385.00

ROYAL VIENNA

Vienna, Austria
1864 to Present

1749-1864

History: After the Imperial Porcelain Factory closed in 1864, some of the artists and workers established their own small shops. They produced the same forms and followed the same decorative motifs that they used at the Imperial Porcelain Factory. The quality of the pieces varied from shop to shop. Some were overdecorated; some cheaply done. Many of the pieces imitating the earlier Vienna porcelains were marked with the beehive mark.

The Vienna Porcelain Factory Augarten, that was established in 1922, considered itself the successor to the Imperial and Royal Porcelain Manufactory of Vienna which closed in 1864. This factory still makes decorative porcelain and figures.

A company started by Josef de Cente in 1793 as a tile and stove factory, made copies of the porcelain and figures from the Imperial Vienna factory after it closed in 1864. De Cente bought many of the original molds and used them. His reproductions always were marked with "de Cente," mostly impressed in the base. In 1902, the Alexandria Porcelain works in Turn-Teplitz bought the molds from the de Cente factory.

Bone Dish, center gilt dot cartouche of period courting couple in colors, wide gold border with gold flowerheads and gold drops, pale green ground, "Royal Vienna, blue shield" mark, set of 4 . . . . 100.00

Charger

15" d, Art Nouveau style bust of woman with orchid shawl and red and blue star designs, or bust with long blond hair and rose shawl, green shaded ground, cobalt border with gilt stylized lilies, blue beehive mark, pr. 3,200.00

16" d, multicolored scene of "Toilette der Venus" in center, dk green border with gold overlay 3,850.00

Compote, 3" h x 9" d, "Toilette der Venus," HP multicolored center scene of 2 maidens, Cupid, and basket of roses on terrace, mountains in bkd, gilt cartouche, cobalt border with scallops and raised gilt reserves and foliage design, white enamel accents, white pedestal with gilt design, cobalt border with gilt leaves, sgd "J. Riemer," blue overglazed shield and named scene on base, c1880 . . . . . 1,450.00

Cup and Saucer

HP green and purple grapes, gold rim and handle, sgd "P. Dauphin" 35.00

Painted Renaissance maiden holding bowl of fruit reserved in gilt rocaille cartouche on cobalt ground, c1900, (A) 175.00

Cup and Saucer, Handleless, HP scene of woman seated in garden, resting on wall in gilt cartouche, cobalt ground, gold int, cobalt saucer with gilt netting and scrolls, "blue shield, Austria" mark, (A) 330.00

Figure

8" h, standing woman in orange dress, holding fruit in outstretched apron, green bodice, white hat with blue ribbons, circ green paved base, "blue shield" mark, repairs 125.00

8 5/8" h, 18th C man in pink jacket, striped trousers, playing mandolin or man in yellow coat, purple trousers playing hurdy-gurdy, "blue shield" marks, pr, (A) 299.00

Mug, 4 1/4" h, polychromed relief molded face of Bacchus, gilt rim, base, and handle, "underglaze blue shield" mark, (A) 65.00

Pass Cup, 7 3/4" h, multicolored scene of women warriors and putto, 3 elaborate gold handles, gold animal-shaped feet, (A) 375.00

Plate

6" d, multicolored scene of seated Dido and Cupid, dk red and gold border 395.00

9 1/4" d, tooled gilt cartouche with multicolored scene of 2 classical figures, cobalt ground with gilt basket and floral and geometric design, gilt accented pierced border, "blue shield" mark 900.00

9 1/2" d

HP multicolored scene of 2 hunters and dog returning to beerhouse, border with alternating maroon panels with gilt foliates and sm gilt vase and florals, sgd "Wagner," blue shield mark, (A) 1,097.00

Multicolored transfer of Roman warriors and women with chariot in center, gold drop cartouche, green border with gold stenciled overlay, "blue shield" mark 45.00

"The Education of Bacchus," multicolored scene of 2 classical figures and young Bacchus holding spear, gilt tooled flowerhead inner border, dk red panels with raised gilt leaves and flowers and center gilt outlined red flowerhead on border separated by med blue stripes with raised enameled white dots 2,200.00

Charger, 13" d, center portraits of "Pierre le Grande" and "Catherine II" on pink and foliate ground, claret red and gilt border with blue reserves, inscribed on reverse, (A) $3,520.

9 5/8" d
 "In The Baths," multicolored center scene of 2 classical women lying next to pool, lg feather fan, emerald green border with raised gilt designs and white enamel accents, sgd "C. Heer," c1880-90 . . . . .1,600.00
 "Sylvan Nymphs In The Bath," multicolored scene of 2 classic women with arms round shoulders and attendants and urn in center, gold sawtooth inner border, maroon panels and red panels with raised gilt birds and geometrics separated by lt blue panels on border, dk green rim with gold dashes and dots, sgd "Ed. Baerschneider," c1885-90 . . . . . 1,550.00
9 3/4" d, center with multicolored scene of maiden and 3 shepherds, Tiffany burgundy border with gilt beading and accents 235.00
Potpourri Jar, 18" h, center multicolored band of titled "Bacchus Fest," gilt body and cov, gilt legs and paw feet, gilt circ base. . . .3,950.00
Powder Jar, Cov, 4 5/8" d, cov with multicolored scene of period couple fishing, deer in bkd, cobalt ground with gold overlay, "blue shield" mark 70.00
Punch Bowl, 6 1/4" h x 14" d, 2 circ panels of Napoleon at "Bataille de Friedland" and "Bataille d'Iena" on ext, green ground, gilt trim, 4 gilt claw feet, c1900, chips, (A). 715.00
Stein
 .5 L
 HP panel of 4 classical ladies, multicolored designs on sides and reverse, gilt diamond and dots borders, porcelain inlaid lid with cherub blowing horn on top, cherub and semi-nude woman on underside of lid, "blue shield" mark, (A). 2,656.00
 HP panel of Venus, ladies, man, and cherub swimming with dolphins, multicolored and gilt design on reverse, porcelain inlaid lid of 2 women and Cupid, 2 partially nude women on underside of lid, crown thumblift, sgd "Wagner," "blue shield" mark, (A). 2,541.00
 1 L, HP overall scene of lady sitting in cavalier's lap, gilt florals and birds and goat heads on reverse, gilt lid, (A). . 2,079.00
Urn, Cov
 11" h, pedestal shape, HP Jupiter and Calerti, red ground, dbl handles, sgd "K. Wek," "blue shield" mark 750.00
 12 1/2" h, center HP scene of nude woman sitting on rock, floral design on reverse, heavy gold frames, cobalt ground with gilt bands, dots, and leaves, gilt vert scroll handles, gilt knob, sq base with gilt floral design, "blue shield" mark, (A) .1,386.00
Vase
 9" h, painted scene of 2 children in garden setting, jeweled gilt trim, sgd "Wagner" 1,800.00

21 3/4" h, shield shape, painted scene of Bacchus and Ariadne on Island of Naxos on front, Juno and Aolus on reverse in gilt scrolling foliage cartouches, named below, cobalt ground, gilt curved scrolling handles ending in leaf terminals and suspended berry wreaths, sq base with canted corners, sgd "RICHTER PINX," "blue shield" mark, (A) 4,370.00

c1876-1891   1891

ROYAL WORCESTER

Worcester, England
1862 to Present

History: (See Worcester for early history). In 1862, Worcester Royal Porcelain Company Ltd. was formed by Kerr and Binns. Limoges-style enameled porcelains, figures, and many dessert services were manufactured. Vases and other ornamental pieces were painted with figure subjects. Among the factory's popular wares was Ivory porcelain, a glazed parian ware.

During the 1870s, magnificent porcelains in the Japanese style were produced. Many were modeled by James Hadley, one of the finest ceramic modelers. Hadley left Royal Worcester in 1875 to freelance, but almost all his work was bought by Worcester.

In 1889, Thomas Grainger's factory was bought by the Worcester Royal Porcelain Company. Grainger had started his own factory in 1801 at St. Martin's Gate. After having several different partners, George, his son, eventually took over.

George Owens made wonderful reticulated pieces for Royal Worcester in the 1890s. The piercing was done when the piece was still in the greenware stage before biscuit firing. Pieces were exceptionally delicate and fragile.

James Hadley started his own factory in 1896 to produce ornamental art pottery. It was located near Royal Worcester's main factory. Hadley modeled figures that were decorative as well as functional in the form of baskets, dessert centerpieces, and candlesticks. In addition to his Kate Greenaway children, he modeled a series of figures titled, "Countries of the World." By

1905, the Hadley firm was absorbed by the Royal Worcester Company. Binns retired in 1897, and Dyson Perrins took over.

Royal Worcester continued to make ordinary bone china patterns in the 20th century. Colored floral borders or blue and white transfer prints in the "Willow Pattern," "Royal Lily," and "Broseley Dragon," were most popular. Ornamental wares with a parian body were part of the product line. The ewer form was very popular at Worcester as were shell vases.

During the 1920s and 1930s, the company maintained its fine quality wares in a depressed world market with some degree of success. Around 1924, luster wares were introduced, inspired by Wedgwood's dragon and fairyland lusters. In 1928, an electrical decorating tunnel kiln was installed, causing a great improvement in firing decorated wares and raising the standards of china production.

World War II restrictions forced china manufacturers to cut back on their production. Rich ornamental and decorated wares came to an end.

Worcester carried on production of some wares, especially the Doughty Birds for the United States market as part of the war effort involved with lend-lease. Dorothy Doughty's bird figures were absolutely correct in size and color and even the foliage on which they were modeled. From the 1930s until 1960, thirty different bird sculptures were made.

Other figures also were produced during the war years including dogs by Doris Linder, Gwendoline Parnell's "London Cries," Miss Pinder-Davis's "Watteau" figures, and Eva Soper's series of small birds and children in wartime Britain. Freda Doughty modeled a series of children from foreign lands and nursery rhymes in the 1940s. She did an Alice in Wonderland series in 1957.

After World War II, things began to return to normal. A great number of young painters apprenticed to Royal Worcester. In 1948, Doris Linder modeled the first limited edition, equestrian model featuring Queen Elizabeth II on Tommy. It has become the most sought after of Worcester's equestrian models.

In 1950, the biscuit kilns were replaced by gas-fired tunnel kilns which produced even finer quality ware. The founding of the Dyson Perrins Museum at Worcester in 1951 marked the bicentenary of the Worcester Porcelain Company.

During the 1960s, Doris Lindner's equestrian models achieved great success. In addition to limited edition figures, Worcester produced tea, dinner and oven-to-table wares using both old traditional patterns, as well as new ones. Demands for Royal Worcester porcelain continuously increased. A new factory opened in 1970. Much of the current porcelain decoration still is done by hand. Hard porcelain ornamental wares are part of the product line. Royal Worcester commemorative pieces included mugs, jugs, and trays.

In 1976, the company was restructured and renamed Royal Worcester Spode Ltd.

Marks: Almost every piece of Worcester porcelain was marked. The principal mark on Royal Worcester was a circle containing intertwined W's with a crescent and the number 51. The 51 represented the original date of the first Worcester pottery. There was also a crown above the circle. From 1891-1915, the words "Royal Worcester England" were added around the circle. The mark could be impressed or incised instead of printed. The color could be green or purple.

References: John Edwards, *The Charlton Price Guide to Royal Worcester Figurines, Models by Freda Doughty,* The Charlton Press, 1997; Geoffrey A. Godden, *Victorian Porcelain,* Herbert Jenkins, 1961; Stanley W. Fisher, *Worcester Porcelain*, Ward Lock & Co. Ltd.1968; Susan & Jim Harran, *Royal Period Pieces Deserving of Worcester Name,* Antique Week, October 6, 1997; Henry Sandon, *Royal Worcester Porcelain,* Barrie & Jenkins, 1973.

Museums: Dyson Perrins Museum, Worcester, England; Roberson Center for the Arts and Sciences, Binghamton, NY.

Reproduction Alert: Both Austria and Rudolstadt made copies of Royal Worcester wares.

Biscuit Jar

6 1/2" h, ribbed body, gold outlined multicolored floral sprays and leaves, cream ground, gold band on rim and lid, gold handle 495.00

7" h, vert ribbing, cobalt bamboo leaves and stems 355.00

Bowl

6 3/4" l, enamel and gilt decorated floral sprays and butterflies on int, pierced gallery, molded leaf ext, scalloped rim, c1884, (A) 230.00

9" d, emb lavender and gold leaves around side, beige basketweave satin finish, gold open loop border, dtd 1896 . . . . 295.00

Butter Pot, Cov, 5 3/4" h, with drain, gilded multicolored florals, ivory ground, molded acanthus leaf rims, pine cone knob, c1890 . . . . 525.00

Cache Pot, 10" l, ovoid shape, reticulated neck, painted continuous scene of birds in oasis, (A) 2,185.00

Candlestick, 10 1/2" h, columnar shape with sq sconce and base, pink ground with spiral

Dinner Service, Part, 11 plates, 9 1/4" d, 8 salad plates, 9 bread and butter plates, 12 cups, 10 saucers, 4 teacups, 3 saucers, 4 oval platters, 3 cov serving bowls, gravy boat, 8 1/2" l, blue and white, dtd 1883, (A) $920.

band of yellow leaves, yellow hanging swags on base, c1894, pr, (A) 805.00

Cheese Dish, 9 3/4" h, Stilton type, molded bamboo body, relief of brown and gilt bamboo leaves, cream ground, bamboo handle, c1879, (A). 633.00

Cup and Saucer, pink, yellow, and blue flowers, gold trim, beige satin finish 85.00

Cup and Saucer, Demitasse, painted fruiting blackberry bushes, gilt handle and ft, gilt saucer well and cup int, pattern #C2886, 1935-40, set of 6, (A) 2,530.00

Dish

4 1/2" l, shell shape, tan to cream ground, gold serrated rim 50.00

9" d, 3 lobed, HP pink and yellow roses and green leaves, salmon pink ground, pierced for hanging, dtd 1908 . 135.00

Ewer

9 1/4" h, blue flowers and tan leaves, gold trim, cream satin ground, molded salamander handle with gold and purple accents, dtd 1887 . . . . 395.00

10 1/4" h, raised gold outlined rust and green leaves, matte cream ground, matte gold bamboo handle, gold rim, green mark 485.00

11 1/4" h, multicolored owl on branch with moonlit sky, gold serpent wrap-around handle, c1885 . . . . 930.00

15 3/4" h, raised gold leaf and red enamel flower design, satin ground, gold trimmed scrolled foliate handle, 1896, (A) 1,495.00

Figure

2 1/4" h, "China-Children of the Nations" series, Freda Doughty 125.00

5 1/4" h

"Burmah-Children of the Nations" series, Freda Doughty 200.00

Politician, white glaze, late 19th C, restored chip, (A) 288.00

5 3/4" h, "Down and Out," cream glaze 445.00

6 1/4" h, "Grandmother's Dress," pink gown with gold trim, puce mark 135.00

7" h, "First Dance," mauve gown, pink stole, #3629 . . . . 135.00

8" h x 9 1/2" l, "The Bulldog," brindle brown, gold studded collar, Doris Lindner 950.00

8 1/2" h, child in gold ruffled bonnet, mauve and gold dress, holding bowl on gold twist branch on cobblestones, sgd "Hadley" 1,375.00

10" l, "Hog Hunting," polychrome, Doris Lindner. 1,195.00

18" h, figural standing heron, off-white body with red outlined eyes, brown mottled tree stump, (A) 440.00

Ice Jug, 9 3/4" h, gilt and cream leaf molded neck, enamel and gilt floral sprays, gilt handle, dtd 1889, pr, (A) 690.00

Jar, Cov, 7 1/4" h, fluted body, multicolored enameled florals, raised gold spear head borders, satin ground, (A) 350.00

Jug, 8 1/2" h, lobed body, enamel and gilt garden flowers, gilt coral handle, scallop shell rim, late 19th C, (A) 130.00

Loving Cup, 6" h, painted purple and yellow flowers, shaded matte tan ground, gilt outlined handles, white int with flower sprays, purple mark. .395.00

Pitcher

2" h, HP still life of fruit, gold rim and handle, sgd "Harry Ayrton," c1938, (A) 250.00

4" h, mulberry floral decor, white ground, mask spout 125.00

4 5/8" h, bulbous shape, lt pink and yellow florals, rust and green leaves, tan ground, gold handle, purple flowers on shoulder, gold trim, purple mark 275.00

Plate

8" d, "Blue Dragon" pattern 20.00

8 1/4" sq, red, yellow, and blue oriental men with umbrella in yellow and green rect cartouche in center, blue and yellow hanging swags on border, purple mark. 65.00

8 1/2" d, polychrome floral bouquet in center, gilt scroll and foliate cavetto, cream ground, gilt rim, purple mark and retailer's mark, set of 12, (A) 207.00

8 7/8" d, painted pendant branches of peaches, green sponged ground, Townsend, (A) 116.00

9" d, yellow and orange florals on white ground in center, raised ribbed border with shaded lt blue and gilt edge 25.00

9 1/4" d, HP enameled fish in center, gilt lattice and foliate border, sgd "Harry Ayrton," c1940, set of 13, (A) 2,300.00

10 1/4" d, multicolored scene of Tewkesbury, gilt rim, sgd "Nicholls" . . . 225.00

Vase, 9" h, 12" H-H, gold outlined mauve and pink flowerheads, matte cream ground, gilt accents and handles, $450.

Quill Holder, 3 3/4" h, scrolled base, "blush" finish, "Royal Worcester Porcelain Co. Ltd, England" mark, dtd 1897 . . . . 325.00

Serving Dish, 10 3/4" d, 3 section, sm pink, yellow, and blue flowers, green leaves in each section, beige satin ground, overhead handle, lobed rim, dtd 1904 . . . . 250.00

Vase

  3 1/4" h, reticulated, florals in gilt trimmed oval panels, c1891, (A) 115.00

  5 1/8" h, reticulated, 3 rows of turquoise stones, scattered gold designs, ivory ground . . . . '. 785.00

  7 1/2" h, HP floral bouquet in raised gilt scrolling cartouche, red ground, ivory border with gilt accents, scroll handles, c1901, pr, (A) 1,955.00

  8" h

    Silver and gold stork in marsh, applied branches and flowers, ivory ground, 2 twist handles 320.00

    Stick shape with bulbous base, Hadley Ware, HP pheasant in field in colors, c1905 . . . . 895.00

  8 1/4" h, nautilus, coral stem, stepped circ shell molded base, burnished gilt and bronze, (A) 155.00

  8 3/4" h, bottle shape, Sabrina ware, cobalt landscape, lt blue ground, (A) 200.00

  9 1/8" h, moon shape, gilt angular bamboo handles and feet, enameled en grisaille design of Venus and 2 Cupids on front, gilt pendant ivy vines on reverse, gilt ivy arbor on shoulder, cobalt ground, artist sgd, c1880, (A) 1,035.00

  10 5/8" h, squat shape, tapered cylinder neck, Crownware, luster colored mythical castle in landscape, gilt accents, #CW297, hairline, pr, (A) 366.00

  12 1/4" h, pedestal base, gilt and enameled leaf, berry, and spider design, 2 sm gold handles on shoulder, late 19th C, (A) 725.00

  12 1/2" h, ovoid shape, trumpet neck, rd pedestal base, polychrome floral sprays on front and reverse, cream

ground, gilt handles on sides, purple mark, (A) 75.00

  15 1/4" h, flattened ovoid shape, tall spread neck and rim, circ ft, 2 sm handles, oval panel of HP red thistle and green foliage on white ground on front and reverse, yellow ground with pink tinges, sgd "Edward Raby, Junior," late 19th C, (A) 978.00

  15 3/4" h

    Bulbous base, narrow neck, flared rim, multicolored enameled floral sprays, satin ground, gold figural dragon handles on neck, 1888, (A) 748.00

    Spread stepped ft, bulbous body, flared rim, applied wing handles, gray, brown, black, and gilt marsh bird, brown and black marsh grasses, cream ground, gilt rim and trim, raised gilt beading on handles, c1885, pr 2,875.00

  16 1/4" h, bulbous body, spread ft and rim, sq base, HP cattle crossing stream on front, canyon and river on reverse, shaded lt blue ground, matte cream top and base, gold trim, leaf shaped handles, pr 900.00

Vase, Cov, 14 3/4" h, polychrome sprays of garden flowers, gilt trim, yellow ground, 2 side handles, c1893, finial repair, (A) 690.00

c1885

ROZENBURG

The Hague, Holland
1884-1914

History: W. van Gudenberg established an earthenware and porcelain factory at The Hague in 1885.

Rozenburg was best known for a line of exceptionally thin earthenware that was made during the late 19th and early 20th century in the Art Nouveau style. The delicate, translucent body had over the glaze decorations of flowers, foliage, and birds derived from the design of Japanese batik-printed fabrics from the Dutch East Indies, now Indonesia. Mauve, yellow ochre, orange, and shades of green were some of the vivid enamel colors used on the white ground. The decoration on later examples was stiffer and had less delicate colors. Shapes featured elongated handles and

spouts contrasted with the curved and flat surfaces of the body.

S. Juriaan Kok became director of the company from 1895 to 1913. He was responsible for a series of extraordinary Art Nouveau shapes. J. Schellink was employed as a painter who decorated his works with stylized flowers in brick-red, black, purple, green, and yellow on a bottle green ground. He also used sea horses and spiked leaves in his motifs. Schellink painted in a series of tense, nervous, spots and lines with subtle color combinations. The eggshell thin porcelain that Schellink used was unique to Rozenburg. M. N. Engelen, the firm's chemist, developed it. Production stopped with the beginning of World War I.

Pieces were marked "Rozenburg/den Haag" along with a stork that was copied from the mark of the 18th century porcelain factory at The Hague, and a crown.

Bowl, 7 1/4" d, pedestal base, multicolored Art Nouveau style flowers, pale green ground 325.00

Candlesticks, 7" h, wide circ base, blue-green ext with multicolored swirled Art Nouveau designs, green int, pr 1,500.00

Charger

  17 1/8" d, long stemmed purple irises, green leaves, yellow and brown ground, dtd 1901, (A) 2,000.00

  17 3/8" d, stylized lilac, ochre, and blue flowers and stems, yellow ground with red swirls, chips, (A) 1,694.00

Plaque, 12" l x 6 1/4" h, rect, 2 tiles, HP gray, brown, and green pastoral scene with white cow by stream, sgd "Rozenburg BK," artist sgd, framed 2,000.00

Vase, 12" h, dk red, pink, and brown flowerheads, green leaves, lt brown ground, dk blue base, "stork and Rozenburg" mark, c1895, $4,200.

Plate, 10 7/8" d, earthenware, painted vines, flowers and 2 birds, green, brown, black, yellow, and violet, "Rozenburg, anchor, and 911" mark, (A) 489.00

Urn, 14 1/2" h, squat body, ftd, 2 handles on shoulder, yellow, celadon, purple, blue-gray, and brown painted parrots and poppies, "stamped Rozenburg, den Haag, 441" mark, restored base chip, (A) 750.00

Vase

5" h, cabinet, eggshell, painted pink, violet, and yellow blossoms, white ground, "black Rozenburg, den Haag, B, Ibis, JWR" mark, repaired rim chip, (A) 500.00

6" h, eggshell

Art Nouveau shape, 2 handles, lt green with lilac accents, white ground, "Rozenburg den Haag, stork" mark, c1916 . . . . .4,400.00

Tapered shape, purple orchids design 4,000.00

6 1/2" h, shouldered ovoid shape, yellow and brown flowers with arabesque green foliage, chips, pr, (A). . . . 465.00

12" h, bulbous, green ext with brown, blue, and tan free style Art Nouveau design, streaked brown base, green int, artist sgd, "Rozenburg den Haag, stork" mark. 2,775.00

16" h, bulbous base, long tapered neck, blue and taupe flowerheads, lg green leaves, brown and gold ground, "ROZENBURG, 825, crown and Haag" mark, hole in body, (A) 1,100.00

Vase, Cov, 8 7/8" h, eggshell, sq tapered shape, 2 sm scroll handles, painted blue irises and foliage, white ground, dtd 1904, (A) 693.00

c1924   c1918

RUDOLSTADT

Thuringia, Germany
1720 to Present

History: Macheleid, with the patronage of Johann Friedrich von Schwartzbrug-Rudolstadt, established a Rudolstadt factory about 1720. During the factory's peak period, 1767-1797, the firm was leased to Noone. The arrangement lasted until 1800. Rococo style tableware and large vases were made. After 1800 the firm was sold to the Greiners. A series of partnerships followed.

Ernst Bohne Sons made decorative porcelain, coffee and tea sets, and figures between 1854 and 1920. Many products were similar to R.S. Prussia pieces. After 1920 the factory became a branch of Heubach Brothers.

Lewis Straus and Sons in New York were co-owners of the New York-Rudolstadt Pottery between 1882 and 1918. This firm received the right to use the Royal Rudolstadt designation. The firm produced household, table, and decorative porcelains and served as importers for the U.S. market.

The Rudolstadt-Volkstedt Porcelain Factory was nationalized in 1960.

Bowl

6 1/4" d, lg white rose in center, 4 sm white roses on int border connected by gold diamond chain, Beyer & Boch . . 65.00

7 1/4" d, white roses, green leaves with yellow centers, lt green to white shaded int, 3 gold feet, "Royal Rudolstadt Prussia, crown and B" mark 68.00

9 1/8" d, paneled, hummingbird with blue wings, yellow tail on green branch, chrysanthemums and peonies on int, black outlined blue luster border, yellow luster int rim 18.00

Cake Plate, 12" H-H, lg roses, open handles 195.00

Candy Dish, 6" d

Gold outlined wide brown border band, end handle, Beyer & Boch 15.00

HP red roses, green leaves, yellow shaded ground, stenciled gold geometric rim, gold end handle, Beyer & Boch 21.00

Celery Tray, 12 1/2" l, HP white daisies and purple violets with green leaves, blue shaded ground, wide matte gold rim 45.00

Charger, 12" d, HP pink and green sprays of apple blossoms, sgd "F. Kahn" 125.00

Chocolate Set, pot, 10 1/2" h, 4 cup and saucers, yellow and white roses, green leaves, cream ground, gold handles and trim, sgd "F. Kahn" 400.00

Figure, 3 1/2" h, girl in lt green lace dress, "crowned N and Dresden" mark, (A) . . 25.00

Nappy, 5 3/8" d, pink and white roses, green foliage, shaded pink to green ground, gold rim, "Royal Rudolstadt, Prussia, crown" mark 8.00

Pitcher

10" h, purple, orange, and mauve flowers, brown thorny stems and leaves, tan shaded matte ground, molded leaf border, gold handle, "RW in crowned diamond" mark 48.00

11 1/2" h, figural griffin, cream body with pink, gray, and gilt accents, tail handle 395.00

Planter, 6 1/2" d, yellow rose, 2 sm roses on border, lt green ground, 3 gold ball feet, sgd "Beyer" 55.00

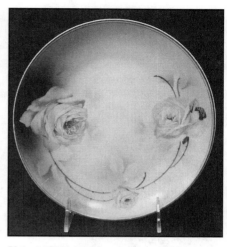

Plate, 8 1/4" d, transfer of pink and white roses with HP accents, brown, blue, and green shaded ground w/shadow leaves, gold rim, Beyer and Boch, $28.

Plaque, 12" d, HP center scene of woman in lavender dress, man in white holding tennis racket, woman in bkd holding tennis racket, purple border with gold stenciled floral swags and stars, (A). 130.00

Plate

8 3/8" d, 3 lg orange-red flowers on border, brown shaded and lt green leaves, dbl gold lined rim, Beyer and Boch 30.00

8 1/2" d, HP purple and yellow pansies, gold trim, sgd "Armand" 30.00

Salt, 1 3/8" h x 2" d, globular shape, overall relief of florals, "imp EBS" mark 15.00

Vase

5 1/2" h, figures of 2 children in Victorian winter clothes, stone wall in bkd, oval rocky base, polychromed, Ernst Bohne Sons, Rudolstadt, (A) 70.00

7" h, yellow poppies and buds, green foliage, sprayed dk brown to green to yellow ground, relief scrolls on ft, reticulated rim with spiral fluting. 90.00

9 3/4" h, center band of florals on cream ground, peach rococo top and base 135.00

10" h, gold outlined HP multicolored flowers, ivory sand tapestry finish, green scrolled handles, jeweled ft and rim 195.00

11" h

Center med blue band with painted purple flowerheads with raised enameled centers, molded gilt outlined shoulder and ft, 2 scroll handles, matte beige ground, c1910 . . . . 250.00

Molded swirl body, gold outlined puce clematis, cream ground, molded swirled neck, matte finish, gold fancy handles on shoulder 125.00

12 1/4" h, melon ribbed, gold outlined russet brown and yellow flowers and foli-

age, gold trim, pastel ground, draped rococo scrolled handles, leaf scroll neck and rim 135.00

13" h, molded gold and silver reticulated medallions, purple ground 69.00

13 3/4" h, center body enamel and gilt painted florets and scrollwork surrounding medallion with fruit, blue neck and base, gilt griffin handles, late 19th C, (A) 230.00

14 1/2" h, yellow, pink, and lavender chrysanthemums, oak leaves, 2 filigree handles 225.00

КорНИΛОВЫХЪ
Korniloff's factory
c1835

Завода
S.T.KУЗНЕЦОВА
63 Run 5
c1835

ВРАТЬЕВЪ
Baterin's factory
1812-1820

RUSSIA-GENERAL

Early 1800s to Present

St. Petersburg, now Leningrad, Russia
1744 to Present

History: The Kuznetsov family established a factory to manufacture porcelain and faience at Novocharitonowka in 1810. Their sons, trading as the Brothers Kuznetsov, managed the factory until the 1870s. They also operated other factories around Russia.

These factories produced powder boxes, vases, and toilet sets in blue and pink porcelain that was often enameled and gilded. Figures in biscuit porcelain were painted with regional costumes and other decorative motifs. Products from these Russian factories were exported to other European countries, the Far East, and India.

In 1891, the firm acquired the Francis Gardner factory near Moscow. Marks usually incorporated "Ms. Kuznetsov," along with the place of manufacture.

Native Russian porcelains developed during the 1800s due to the high duty on imported porcelains. The Kornilow Brothers established a factory to manufacture utilitarian wares in St. Petersburg in 1835.

The Yusupov Factory near Moscow operated from 1814 to 1831. White porcelain blanks for decoration were purchased from Sevres, Limoges, and Popov. Articles made at this factory were used as gifts for the members of the Tsar's family or for the friends and relatives of the Yusopovs.

The Popov Factory, established in 1806 at Gorbunovo, made dinner services, tea sets, and porcelain figures for an urban middle-class clientele. Popov's figures of

Russian craftsmen, peasants, and tradesmen, are eagerly sought by collectors. The factory closed in 1872.

Initially, the Imperial St. Petersburg porcelain factory enjoyed only limited success. Catherine the Great was associated with the factory by 1762. Her imperial patronage helped ensure success.

Most of the wares were basically French in form, but often were painted with Russian views. When Jean-Dominique Rachette became head of the modeling workshop in 1779, he increased the sculpture output by making porcelain statues, groups in bisque, and portrait busts.

Enormous dinner services were made for the Tsar's palace and the nobility of the court, e.g. the "Arabesque Service" of 973 pieces in 1784 and the "Cabinet Service" of 800 pieces. The War of 1812 disrupted production at the factory somewhat. Portraits of heroes and military motifs appeared on the porcelains during and immediately following the war.

Reorganization took place in 1901. The Art Nouveau style was utilized. About 1907, soft paste porcelains were developed. A series of figures titled, "Peoples of Russia," was designed by P. Kamensky and issued beginning in 1907. The factory's work continued after World War I and during the Civil War. The revolution inspired designs for porcelains reflecting industrialization of the country.

The factory was renamed Lomonosov Factory in 1925 in honor of M. Lomonosov, the Russian scientist. Production continues today.

Marks changed many times. Until 1917, the cypher of the reigning monarch was used.

References: R. Hare, *The Art & Artists of Russia*, Methuen & Co.1965; L. Nikiforova, Compiler, *Russian Porcelain in the Hermitage Collection,* Aurora Art Publishers, 1973; Marvin Ross, *Russian Porcelains*, University of Oklahoma Press, 1968; Ian Wardropper et al, *Soviet Porcelain,* The Art Institute of Chicago, 1992.

Museums: Hermitage, Leningrad, Russia; Russian Museum, Leningrad, Russia.

Bowl, 7" d x 3" h, ftd, gold outlined yellow panels with gold crisscrosses, blue and yellow leaves, gilt grapes and tendrils on mauve ground, white int. 275.00

Charger

12" d, center with pink, white, and purple rose bouquet with flowers and greens, border of alternating floral or animal cartouches on green, dk blue, and puce panels, gilt accents, Imperial Porcelain Factory 1,265.00

18" d, center with gilt dbl eagle, crown, scepter, and orb in gilt dotted cartouche reserved on cobalt ground, border

of painted multicolored natural flowers, gilt metal floral rim, Popov, repaired crack, (A) 1,840.00

Cream Jug, 5 1/4" h, baluster shape, gold monogram and crown, dk red top half, cream base, gilt line accents, late 19th C, (A) 920.00

Cup and Saucer

Panel of multicolored garden flowers in gilt dotted cartouche, 2 cartouches on saucer, blue ground with gilt scrolling, c1840 . . . . 385.00

Polychrome enamels of peasant dinner in log cabin, blue trim and gold leaves on saucer, Imperial mark for Alexander III, Soviet black mark, (A) 350.00

Dk red monogram on cup, dk red border bands, gilt accents bands, Imperial Porcelain Factory, c1909, (A) 545.00

Cup and Saucer, Cov, pink and green floral sprays, scrolling celeste blue cartouche borders, gold accents, flame knob, Kornilov Brothers, late 19th C, (A). 432.00

Dish, Cov, 8" l, figural bunch of grapes on grape leaf base, Kuznetsov, 19th C, (A) 385.00

Egg, 5" h, reserve polychrome portrait of St. Anne in gilt diaper and scroll border, cobalt patterned body, Imperial Porcelain Factory, (A) 3,450.00

Figure

5 1/4" h, old man wearing striped gray and white nightcap, striped and pieced brown overcoat, hand in coat, hand behind back holding boot, circ white base, (A) 253.00

8 1/4" h, young woman, hands on hip, short white jacket, purple stylized flowerheads, gold buttons and trim, standing on toe, black and white cat at feet, circ base with indentations, Imperial St. Petersburg 350.00

Jug, 5 1/2" h, pottery, printed and painted multicolored band of chinoiserie figures, 19th C 35.00

Plate

7 1/2" d, narrow cobalt border band with gold banding, gold monogram of Tsarevich Alexei Nicholaivich on bor-

Platter, 17" l, dk red eagle, gray and black birds, blue zigzag, dk red and brown border trim, Kornilov Brothers, (A) $700.

der, Imperial Porcelain Factory, dtd 1913, set of 12, (A) 8,050.00

8" d, gilt, green, and burnt orange geometric border, Kornilov Brothers, set of 7, (A) 345.00

9 1/4" d, multicolored Romanov crest on border between 2 gilt bands, Imperial Porcelain Factory, c1895, set of 12, (A) 7,590.00

9 1/2" d

Center scene of different birds in colors on gilt patterned ground, border of 3 rows of gilt triangles with 3 sqs of green and gold sqs, Kornilov Brothers, set of 17, (A) 5,520.00

"Etruscan" pattern, black female figure with dk red trim, burnt orange ground, Imperial St. Petersburg, Nicholas I period, pr 26,000.00

Polychrome dbl headed eagle in center, border of dbl row of alternating rectangles of yellow outlined blue, red, and green geometrics, Kornilov Brothers 895.00

9 3/4" d, red, orange, and black Constructivist geometric design, c1923, (A) 207.00

9 7/8" d, rose pink enameled flower spray in center and hanging husks on border, indented rim, Poskotchin factory, c1810, (A) 975.00

10 3/4" d, central gold and blue Gothic spandrel, border of blue and gold Gothic tracery in 2 bead and line bands, gilt rim, Kuznetsov, late 19th C, (A) 575.00

Soup Plate, Romanov crest on border, inner and outer gilt lines, dtd 1910 and 1913, pr 750.00

Vase, 12" h, blue, pink, and lavender leaves and flowers, brown branches, Imperial St. Petersburg, (A) $3960.

Teapot, 6" h, ball shape, cobalt grape-type flowers, pink flowerheads and blue tulips, gilt tendrils, gilt outlined rim and knob. . . 295.00

Vase, 4" h, painted polychrome gooseberries and strawberries, gilt banding, Petra-Fomin, Moscow, (A) 450.00

SALT GLAZED STONEWARE

Staffordshire, England 1671 through the 19th C

Rhineland, Germany 1500s to Present

History: Stoneware was pottery that was fired at such high oven temperature that the body had vitrified and became impervious to liquids. A salt glaze was achieved by throwing salt into the high temperature oven causing the salt to volatilize. The sodium in the salt combined with the alumina and silica in the clay to form a thin vitreous coating on the surface of the stoneware. The glaze layer also was impervious and had minute pitting.

English

In the late 17th century, potters in north Staffordshire around Stoke-on-Trent began experimenting in hopes of producing a purely English style of salt glazed stoneware. John Dwight was credited with discovering the technique. In 1671, Dwight was granted a patent for the manufacturing of salt glazed stoneware.

Six villages comprised "The Potteries" in Staffordshire. The greatest concentration of potters was in Burslem. Their salt glazed stoneware pieces were thin, lightweight, and made to compete with porcelain. A brown salt glaze stoneware was developed in the second half of the 18th century and was used for beer jugs, tankards, flasks, and industrial wares.

With the advent of mold making and slip casting, more complicated shapes could be made. A wide range of utilitarian and decorative articles was produced. Few pieces contained factory marks.

The Burslem families of Wedgwood and Wood manufactured salt glaze stoneware beginning in the late 17th century and trained a succession of master potters.

Enameled stoneware was introduced in the Staffordshire potteries about 1750. Enameled wares required a second firing, at a considerably lower temperature than the salt glaze oven, to "fix" the color to the pot. European and oriental porcelain decorative motifs were enameled on salt glaze pieces. Transfer printing also was done on white salt glazed stoneware.

The first salt glazed figures were animals. These were not marked and rarely dated. Most salt glazed figures were made by pressing slabs of moist clay into a two piece mold and then uniting the halves using a slip.

Groups of figures required the process of press-molding combined with hand modeling. A wide variety of salt glaze bird and animal figures was made between 1725 and 1755. Usually the figures were ornamental, but cow creamers and beer baiting jugs were useful exceptions.

German

Salt glazed wares were being manufactured in Germany by the early 16th century to fill the demand for drinking vessels for taverns. These brown salt glaze wares were also exported to England for more than 200 years.

References: J.F. Blacker, *The ABC of English Salt-Glaze Stoneware from Dwight to Doulton*, Stanley Paul & Co., 1922; Arnold R. Mountford, *The Illustrated Guide to Staffordshire Salt-Glazed Stoneware*, Barrie & Jenkins, 1971; Louis T. Stanley, *Collecting Staffordshire Pottery*, Doubleday & Co., 1963.

Museums-English: American Antiquarian Society, Worcester, MA.; City Museum, Stokeon-Trent, England; British Museum, London, England; Colonial Williamsburg, Williamsburg, VA; Fitzwilliam Museum, Cambridge, England; Museum of Art, Rhode Island School of Design, Providence, RI; Victoria & Albert Museum, London, England; William Rockhill Nelson Gallery of Art, Kansas City, MO.

Museums-German: Kunstgewerbemuseum, Cologne, Germany; Metropolitan Museum of Art, New York, NY; Rheinisches Landesmuseum, Bonn, Germany.

Basket, 11 1/2" l, with undertray, flared shape basket with woven reticulated sides, tray with woven center, reticulated border, hairlines, (A) 1,320.00

Bottle, 9" h, bulbous base, narrow neck, flared rim, England, mid 18th C, (A) 517.00

Bowl, 8 7/8" d, scratch blue chain and feather design on ext, 2 bands of waves on int rim, Staffordshire, c1760, (A) 3,220.00

Cream Jug, 3 3/4" h, baluster shape, enameled multicolored flowering branches and hydrangea, Staffordshire, c1755, (A) . . . 138.00

Cress Dish, 10 3/4" H-H, pierced center with molded hearts and swirls, border of molded

Creamer, 4 3/4" h, blue striping, white ground, Castleford, c1820, $750.

Plate, 8 1/4" d, drabware, c1840, pr, (A) $450.

fan shaped leaves, open rect handles, c1760 . . . . .1,150.00

Cup, 5 5/8" h, ftd, scratch blue design of flowering branches and "H/RE 1762," 2 scroll handles, Staffordshire, (A) 6,325.00

Dessert Basket

   8 3/4" H-H, with matching undertray, flared sides molded with basketry and pierced, molded hanging fruit, C-scroll handles, c1760 . . . . .1,550.00

   11 3/8" l, with matching undertray, molded basketweave base, open lattice work body, florets on rim, 2 rococo handles 2,450.00

Dish

   8 1/4" d, molded foliate scroll rosette reserved on basketweave ground, molded fruit in well, basketweave border, Staffordshire, c1760, (A) 800.00

   9 1/2" l, leaf shape, press molded, bird perched on leafy branch, circle and dot ground, feathered rim, Staffordshire, c1760, (A) 1,725.00

   10 1/4" l, oval, press molded raised dot and diaper, star, and basketweave in scroll bordered panels, England, mid-18th C, (A) 431.00

Ewer, 8 1/2" h, baluster shape, molded with grapevines on incised brown ground, pr, (A) 40.00

Figure, 4 5/8" h, seated cat, buff and brown solid agate, blue splashes, rect base, Staffordshire, c1750, (A) 2,530.00

Food Mold, 3 7/8" d, 6 pointed star shape, c1745 . . . . 950.00

Inkwell, 2 5/8" h, indented sides, 4 quill holes, screw top, "Alex: Ready Esq.r: 1745" on base, (A) 2,300.00

Jar, Cov, 3 1/2" h, cylinder shape, scratch blue stylized tulip design, spire knob, Staffordshire, c1755, (A) 805.00

Jug, 5 3/4" h, baluster shape, brown speckled band over cream ribbed body, (A) 60.00

Milk Jug

   5 1/8" h, baluster shape, sparrow beak, reeded handle, scratch blue flowerheads and leaves, c1750 . . . . 1,950.00

   5 1/4" h, pear shape, slip cast panels of woman on camel, hunters and hounds, birds, and beasts, and drunken Bacchus, hairlines. 3,200.00

Plate

   5 1/4" d, press molded seed pattern border, England, c1760, (A) 230.00

   8 1/4" d, oct, lilac printed water landscape in center, border of molded foliate cartouches between dot and star diapering, Staffordshire, c1760, (A) 1,093.00

Platter

   13 1/2" l, oval, border molded with hanging leaves, flowers, and fruit connected by stem swags, circle and dot ground, Staffordshire, c1760, (A). 1,725.00

   15" d, border panels of raised seed designs, shaped rim 800.00

   17 1/4" l x 13 1/4" w, oval, seeded paneled border, shaped rim, England, c1760 . . . . 650.00

Puzzle Jug, 8 1/2" h, scratch blue birds on flowering branches and a mound, rim applied with shells and berries, pierced neck, scroll handle, Staffordshire, c1760, cracks, (A) 1,725.00

Sauceboat

   6" l, scratch blue flowerhead and branches on sides, loop handle, shaped rim, Staffordshire, c1755, cracks, (A) 345.00

   6 7/8" l, dbl spout, oval, strap handles on side, cast pectin shell and floral vine designs, c1760, (A). 1,380.00

Soup Plate, 9 3/8" d, painted chinoiserie flowers and 2 partridges in center, iron red scalloped inner border, turquoise outlined molded seed border, scalloped lobe rim, c1760 . . . . .3,750.00

Sweetmeat Dish, 4 1/8" l, molded pectin shell with fluting, green glaze, Staffordshire, c1745 . . . . .950.00

Sweetmeat Tray, 9 1/2" d, 6 conjoined hearts, molded scrolls and anthemion, applied floret in center, sealed hairlines 3,850.00

Tankard, 6 3/8" h, scratch blue design of lg flowering branches, strap handle, Staffordshire, c1755, crack, (A) 345.00

Teabowl and Saucer, scratch blue stylized flowering branches, swags on rims, Staffordshire, c1750, restored chip, (A) 460.00

Tea Canister

   3 1/2" h, scratch blue design of flowers growing from rocks, diaper border, later wood cov, "Grace Leigh 1754" on base, Staffordshire, (A) 1,495.00

   5 1/4" h, rect, scratch blue tulips and "Joanne Ellis 1770," diapering on front, flowering branches on side and back, later wood cov, (A). 2,070.00

Teapot

  3 3/4" h

    Globular shape, crabstock handle and spout, puce, green, yellow, and manganese painted landscape with fort in harbor, reverse with tower beside ship tied to bank, Staffordshire, 1760, (A). 368.00

    Heart shape, relief of fruiting vines, serpent spout, c1750, (A) . . . 2,530.00

  4 1/8" h

    Flattened globular shape, curved spout, ear handle, turned knob, scratch blue bands of chevrons and multiple lined curves, c1750 . . . . 1,450.00

    Spherical shape, pink cartouche of King of Prussia with "Fred. Prussiae Rex" on side, reverse with crowned eagle and "Semper Sublimus" in pink cartouche on reverse, black ermine ground, black streaked crabstock handle, spout, and knob, c1765, restruck handle. . . 3,850.00

  4 1/4" h, hex form, leaf molded with green enamel leaves and red veining, green foliate spout, and handle with berries in relief, floral knob, Staffordshire, c1755, repaired chips, (A). 2,185.00

  4 1/2" h

   Globular body

    Dutch decorated, painted iron red and green baskets of flowers, gilt accents, shaped reserves, pebbled ground, ftd, c1780, (A) 1,610.00

    Incised cross bands on center band, applied lion, squirrel, acorns, cranes, flowers, and fleur-de-lys on shoulder, faceted spout, loop handle, acorn knob, Staffordshire, c1750, (A) 805.00

    Straight sides molded with masks, vases of flowering vines, and ga-

Tobacco Jar, 6" h, 5 1/4" l, 3 3/4" w, brown ground, "R.H. BRIDDON" mark, (A) $605.

drooning, lizard knob, serpent spout and handle, spread ft with molded fish, c1750, repaired spout tip 6,600.00

4 3/4" h, spherical body

Red and white enameled rose, yellow, red, and green leaves, overall blue ground, leaf molded handle and spout, Staffordshire, c1760, restored, (A) 2,530.00

Red enameled roses and green leaves on black dotted ground, green crabstock handle, spout, and circ knob, c1760 . . . . .5,500.00

5" h, figural recumbent camel, howdah on back with panels of Chinese subjects, fruiting vine handle, shaped rect base, rim chips, Staffordshire, c1750, (A) 5,463.00

5 1/2" h

Molded pectin shell body, serpent molded spout, notched handle, Staffordshire, c1750, chips and repairs, (A) 633.00

Spherical body, mold-applied scrollwork, crabstock spout and handle, figural bird knob, 3 mask and paw feet, England, c1735 . . . . .3,000.00

Tray, 10 3/4" l, leaf molded with stem handle, central vein, overlapped leaves on rim, 3 floret feet, c1750, sealed hairline 2,450.00

Tureen, 7 1/8" l, melon shape, molded veining on surface, multiple leaves on sides, leaf knob, c1750, repaired hairline 11,000.00

Wall Pocket, 10 3/4" h, cornucopia shape, molded foliate designs surrounding scroll formed figures of Flora, pierced border, William Greatbatch, c1760, repairs, pr, (A) 633.00

SAMSON

Paris, France
1845-1964

History: Samson made reproductions and copies of porcelains from famous manufacturers in hard paste porcelains. Some of the items they copied were originally only made in soft paste.

Edme Samson bought the Tinet factory in Paris. Until 1873 he decorated porcelains produced by other factories. Pieces he decorated had over the glaze marks, often duplicating the mark of the original factory.

Emile, his son, was the first in the family to make reproduction of decorative porcelains and figurals of the famous factories in England and the Continent. He started in 1873. The reproductions also contained a copy of the original mark under the glaze. Sometimes a small Samson mark was added over the glaze.

The Samsons owned more than 20,000 originals of Meissen, Sevres, Chelsea, Capodimonte, Chinese, and Japanese porcelains. They made molds from these originals to produce their copies. Frankenthal, Ludwigsburg, Furstenburg, Vienna, Derby, Bow, Worcester, Chantilly, Tournay, Vincennes, Mennecy, and Copenhagen pieces also were copied, as were the tin glazed earthenwares of Rouen, Sinceny, and Marseilles.

The company was operated by the Samson family until 1964 when C. G. Richarchere took over.

From about 1845 to 1905, the original marks were imitated on the pieces they copied. The company registered some trademarks after 1900 and used them underglaze after about 1905.

Reproduction Alert: Overglaze marks are removed easily. There is evidence that a large number of Samson marks have been removed so that the pieces would appear to be from the original manufacturers.

Candelabrum, 19 1/2" h, Chelsea style, 3 light, flower encrusted scrolling arms supported by seated woman and child on flower encrusted base, polychromed, restored, pr, (A) 460.00

Candlestick, 10 1/4" h, Chelsea style, polychromed tree trunk form with flowers and birds, kneeling dogs on raised rococo scrolled base, pr, (A) 690.00

Cup and Saucer, polychrome horse armorial, raised scrolled lines, orange border with gilt drops, dk red and gilt rims, set of 6 . . 195.00

Dish, 16" l, fan shape, emb yellow, green, and dk red florals and leaves, white ground, early 20th C 195.00

Figure

6 5/8" h, standing 17th C man looking at watch, scroll molded base, polychrome with gilt accents, (A) 100.00

7 1/4" h, long tailed gray, red, and green budgie perched on stump 95.00

7 1/2" h, classical maiden in flowing robe and coronet, holding lute, or holding jar with hound, scroll molded base, polychrome with gilt accents, "gold anchor" mark, pr, (A) 275.00

8 5/8" h, 18th C servant pulling sedan with mistress inside, oval base, polychrome with gilt accents, (A) 432.00

9" h, Meissen style busts of children representing 4 seasons, multicolored, raised quatrefoil columnar pedestal base, "blue X'd lines" marks, late 19th, set of 4 . . . . 1,200.00

11 3/4", 11 7/8" h, standing 18th C gentleman in puce coat, holding tricorn hat in hand, yellow rose in other hand, female in blue and yellow bodice, flowered skirt, scrolling base, "gold anchor" mark, late 19th C, pr, (A) 403.00

12 1/4" h, Derby style figure of Neptune standing on scallop shell with dolphin, polychrome, gilt scroll molded base with encrusted shells, "gold anchor" mark, (A) 155.00

Fruit Bowl, 9" H-H, flared shape, open basketweave body with molded purple, yellow and green flowerheads at intersections, painted floral bouquet on int, gold outlined handles on rim, pseudo chop mark 475.00

Ginger Jar, 6 1/2" h, magenta garden flowers, molded design on body, gold trim, gold foo dog knob, pseudo chop mark, pr 250.00

Plate, 9 1/4" d, Chinese Export style, polychrome and gilt armorial in center, floral border, set of 6, (A) 220.00

Platter, 16 1/4" l, oval, brown, black, and dk orange French ship of the line in center, blue wavy water, orange scroll and seaweed rim 1,150.00

Plaque, 8 5/8" d, puce, red, and blue birds, gold rim, "gold anchor" mark, (A) $175.

Tankard, 5 1/2" h, Worcester style painted exotic birds, "gold anchor" mark, (A)
. . . . 100.00

Urn, 29" h, baluster shape, polychrome painted florals swags and sprays, fitted as lamp, (A) 58.00

Vase, 9 1/4" h, dbl gourd shape, multicolored Chinese style decoration, central armorial crest, late 19th C 250.00

Vase, Cov, 13" h, shouldered ovoid shape, domed cov, painted panels of 18th C lovers and floral reserves, blue ground, pr, (A)
. . . . 862.00

c1770

SARREGUEMINES

Lorraine, France
c1770 to Present

History: The Sarreguemines faience factory, one of the most important manufacturers of French faience, was established in Lorraine about 1770 by M. Fabray and Paul Utzscheider.

During the 19th century, pottery and stoneware in the English style were manufactured. Transfer decorations were used frequently. Imitations of Wedgwood's cream-colored earthenware, black basalt, cane, cameos, wall tiles, agate, and marbled wares were made in addition to biscuit figures and groups. Mocha ware and majolica also were manufactured.

Modern production includes faience and porcelain wares.

Museums: Musee Regional de Sarreguemines, Lorraine, France; Sevres Museum, Sevres, France.

Cigar Holder, 8" h, tin glazed figure of seated monkey in turquoise jacket, cream trousers, red slippers, playing brown piano, brown base, c1890, (A) 2,070.00

Figure, 18" l x 10" h, walking fox, white glaze, (A) 192.00

Humidor, 7" h, figural comical man's head with black top hat, green and brown shoulders, majolica, (A) 577.00

Jug, 7 3/4" h, melon shape and ribbing, green ext glaze, turquoise int, "Sarreguemines" mark 330.00

Oyster Plate, 6 wells, pearl gray with peach colored accents 95.00

Pitcher
    3 1/2" h, "Face," man's face with green hat and pink ribbon and bow, (A) . . . 33.00
    6" h, "Face," man's face with rosy cheeks and chin, (A) 138.00

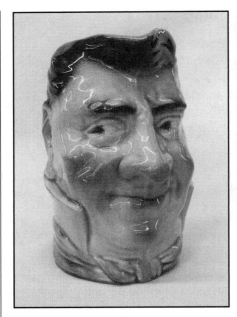

Pitcher, 8 1/4" h, brown, tan, and rose, turquoise int, mkd, (A) $90.

8 1/2" h, black and white figural cat on haunches, (A) 385.00

9 1/2" h, figural bust of pig, pink body with red trim, (A) 358.00

12" h, figural standing old woman, brown blouse, white apron, white hat with red ribbon, base chips, hairline, (A)
. . . . 440.00

Plate
7 1/8" d
    Black transfer of hunter and dog and "Chasse Aux Cailles," green basketweave border 45.00
    "Chasse Au Renarda L'Affut," shooter looking over house at running fox, black transfer, basketweave border
    . . . . 29.00
    "Juillet," 2 children fishing, black transfer, molded basketweave border
    . . . . 22.00
    "Sous Charles VI," portrait of woman in center, black transfer, green outlined basketweave border. . . 28.00
7 1/4" d, "MARS," 2 children with umbrella standing in rain, stone bridge and church in bkd, black transfer, basketweave border 55.00
7 1/2" d
    Bull fight scenes in center, black transfers, borders with leaf, floral and geometric brown transfers, set of 5 . . . . 50.00
    "La Romance," girl seated in meadow holding sheet music, male companion playing instrument, black transfer, border of cherubs and musical instruments, brown transfer 36.00
    "Soldat Ne Pouvant," military scene, black transfer, green

Plate, 9" d, dk pink floral, purple, blue, and green leaves, "Floret Vosges Sarreguemines" mark, $35.

transfer of Napoleonic symbols on border 20.00
7 5/8" d, "Chanson De Rousseaux" series, "Le Comedie Gratis," black transfer, purple transfer of street scenes on border 45.00
8" d, "Les Fleurs" series, green transfers, molded pink borders, set of 8 . . 180.00
8 1/4" d, 3 birds in colors on branches with flying insects, molded swirl border, gold rim 36.00
8 3/4" d
    French Foreign Legion cartoon, polychrome 35.00
    Multicolored opera scene. 35.00
Platter
    13 1/2" d, tin glazed, red, orange, and blue flowerheads, brown leaves, dk green ground, (A). 66.00
    13 1/2" l, oval, brown and blue basket in center with magenta and white flowers, gold striped border 20.00
Soup Plate
    10" d, cobalt and copper luster 8 pointed star in center, cobalt, tan, and copper luster half flowerheads on border with green leaves 150.00
    10 1/4" d, HP lg yellow flower surrounded by dk blue buds and tulips, red and green petaled flowers with red and green leaves on border, blue striped rim, "Made in France, Digion & Sarreguemines" mark, (A). 40.00
Stein, 1.5 L, stoneware, relief of festival scene on body, gray body, pewter lid with figural dwarf knob, "Sarreguemines" mark, pewter tear 125.00
Tureen, Cov, 12" l, figural fish, brown glaze, (A) 77.00
Urn, 11 3/4" h, 16" d, ftd, tin glazed cobalt ground with gilt trim, turquoise int, "Sarreguemines, France" mark 850.00
Vase
    10" h, bulbous base, long slender neck, green luster glaze, (A). 80.00

16 1/8" h, tin glazed, molded body with fruiting festoons, ribbons, and horned animal skull, mottled brown glaze, late 19th C, hairlines 350.00

SCHAFER AND VATER

Thuringia, Germany 1890-1962

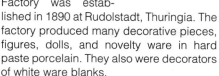

c1890
O & EG

History: The Schafer and Vater Porcelain Factory was established in 1890 at Rudolstadt, Thuringia. The factory produced many decorative pieces, figures, dolls, and novelty ware in hard paste porcelain. They also were decorators of white ware blanks.

Records of the company ceased in 1962.

Ash Receiver, 3 1/4" h, figural seated man with lg smiling feet 255.00
Ashtray and Match Holder, 3 3/4" h, couple under lg lavender hat, blue dress, black coat, green pants, holes in hat for matches, "Hidden Fire" 195.00
Bottle
    5 1/2" h, drinkometer, salt hour glass on reverse, relief bust of red coated tavern drinker, brown ground, (A) 174.00
    5 3/4" h, figural bust of woman with clasped hands on chest, fringed shawl, head stopper, brown glaze 125.00
    6" h, red, white, and blue Uncle Sam and "Your Health" on front, matte brown textured ground 195.00
    6 1/2" h
        Figural fat Dutchman astride barrel, pipe in mouth, cork stopper, hairline, (A) 264.00
        Handled, white cameos of troubadour and lady toasting, green jasper ground, mkd 175.00
    7" h, "Sir John Falstaff," blue figure of drinker, missing stopper, (A) . . . 319.00
    7 1/2" h, figural woman holding bottle, "I am always full!" on front, blue, (A) 440.00
    8 3/4" h, figural Uncle Sam seated on barrel with "What We Want," brown 578.00
Bud Vase, 3 1/2" h, seated figure of Chinese child with fan, sm vase next to child, gloss pink glaze 90.00
Chamberstick, 6" l, blue jasper ground with white scrolling, white cameo of woman's head on pink jasper ground at front, white handle 175.00
Creamer
    2 1/2" h, relief molded with 3 Dutch children's heads, pink brick ground, "imp crowned starburst" mark 140.00

Candlestick, 3 1/2" h, 5" l, green skirt w/yellow and orange trim, blue base, "imp crown and star" mark, $235.

3 1/2" h, figure with bulging eyes and claws, black 185.00
4 3/4" h, figural bust of Welshman, red jacket, white shirt, black hat . . . 190.00
9" h, figural man with bowling ball, med blue glaze 340.00
Dish, 5 1/2" d, white cameo of man and woman standing by barrel, green jasper ground, white wreath border 50.00
Figure, 5 1/2" h, standing green dog, red tongue, sign on neck, white eyes, white rect base 135.00
Hair Receiver, 4 1/4" l x 1 3/4" h, white cameo bust of woman on blue bkd, pink jasper body, imp mark 48.00

Hatpin Holder, 6" h, pink jasper ground, gold and green accents, "imp crown and star" mark, $395.

Pitcher, 5 1/2" h, orange jacket, black hat, lt green ground, tan handle, "imp crown and star" mark, $250.

Hatpin Holder, 5 1/2" h, pyramid shape, pink Egyptian motif, gray jasper ground, imp mark 495.00
Jam Pot, 5 1/4" h, flared rim, white cameos of 2 classic ladies, blue jasper ground, mkd 95.00
Jar, 4" h, Grecian relief figures, female bust, medallion cov, green, pink, gray, and white 125.00
Match Holder, 5" h, figural white dog, tan and brown ears, lt green ribbed holder, black base and "Scratch My Back," imp mark 150.00
Mug, 3 1/2" h, figural elk, white and green 70.00
Napkin Holder, 3 3/4" h x 4 3/4" H-H, white cameo of woman riding gazelle, med green jasper ground 175.00
Pitcher
    3" h, figural woman holding pink fan, pack on bk, white peaked hat, green handle, imp mark 150.00
    3 1/2" h, relief of 3 children, center one holding goose, reverse with 3 children, goose on ground, blue glaze, imp mark 350.00
    3 3/4" h, figural woman in green skirt, basket on bk, black keys on white apron, holding jug, imp mark 200.00
    4" h, figural oriental man in orange gown, holding goose forming spout, black hair forms handle, imp mark 200.00
    4 1/2" h, figural brown bear, green checked coat, hands in white muff, imp mark 250.00
    5" h, figural woman w/purse and jug, blue and white, mkd 135.00
    6" h
        Brown bearded figural gorilla spout with gray derby hat, pale yellow coat, holding red flowers at side, brown tail handle 295.00

Figural man in green coat, black hair, brown monkey on bk, imp mark 295.00

Shaker, 6 1/4" h, white cameos of classic figures, med green jasper ground, metal top, imp mark 195.00

Sugar Bowl, 3 1/4" h x 4" l, gold textured ground, green, pink, and blue raised stones on border 165.00

Teapot, 4 1/2" h, cartouches of white cameos of courting couples on blue jasper, green jasper body, molded fancy handle 190.00

Tea Service, teapot, creamer, cov sugar bowl, 4 cups and saucers, molded cartouche with jewels of white cameo bust of woman on green jasper ground, pink jasper ground, c1915 .... 875.00

Tobacco Jar, 4 1/4" h, relief molded bust of man with beard and pipe on front, pink jasper ground, gold trim, imp mark 450.00

Urn, 2 1/2" h, ball shape, white cameos of man and woman planting tree, wings on border, med blue jasper ground 49.00

Vase

2" h, blue-gray figural tree trunk, figural white bird on handle 45.00

4 1/2" h, cobalt base with emb lions, brown fence top forms vases 95.00

5 1/2" h, figural Egyptian woman holding jugs, tan and green 175.00

7" h, rect pillow shape, molded handles, white cameos of classical woman, blue jasper ground, mkd 110.00

9" h, elliptical shape, fancy white handles, white cameos of woman playing harp, white shell trim, green jasper ground, mkd 125.00

10" h, farm boy with dog, brown, green, and orange 68.00

10 1/2" h, triangle shape, white cameo of female figure on one side, hanging basket on other side, plain back, white mask at front, green jasper ground, imp crown mark 225.00

Wall Pocket, 7" h x 5 1/2" w, 2 figural green jasper slippers, relief cameos of white roses, ribbed front and back of slippers, imp mark 155.00

SCHLEGELMILCH PORCELAINS

History: The manufacturing of R.S. Prussia hard paste porcelains began when Erdmann Schleglemilch founded his porcelain factory at Suhl, Thuringia in 1861. Reinhold Schlegelmilch, Erdmann's brother, established his porcelain factory at Tillowitz, Upper Silesia in 1869. These two factories marked the beginning of private ownership of porcelain factories in that region.

The founding of these factories coincided with the time when porcelain items were experiencing a big demand, especially in the United States and Canada. The peak exporting years were from the mid-1870s until the early l900s. The brothers were able to supply large quantities of porcelains by utilizing new industrial production methodology and the availability of cheap labor.

c1900-1920s

E. S. Germany

Suhl, Thuringia
c1900 to c1925

Erdmann's factory at Suhl was associated with the E.S. marks. Some of the marks incorporated "Prov. Saxe," "1861," or "Suhl" in the mark.

The style and decoration of the porcelains were different in shape and decor from the "RSP" examples. Changes reflected fashions of the times. The porcelains had the elegant, flowing lines of the Art Nouveau period rather than the convoluted rococo shape between 1895 and 1905. A great number of "ES" pieces were totally hand painted. After 1905, the porcelain decoration returned to more classical, mythological themes, and to simpler forms. Many of the transfers were in the style of Angelica Kauffmann.

R.S. Germany

Tillowitz, Upper Silesia

c1910-1956

The forms and decorations of "R.S. Germany" were molded more simply, had more subtle decorations, and reflected the Art Deco period.

Reinhold concentrated on tablewares. Many examples were hand painted. Reinhold used a mark similar to the "RSP" mark at his Upper Silesia factory, except that "Germany" was included instead of "Prussia." The mark was usually under the glaze as opposed to the overglaze "RSP" mark. A number of large American department stores had special patterns created just for their use. Many of the porcelain blanks used for home decorating contain the "RSG" mark. Some exported blanks were decorated professionally by Pickard, a decorating studio for china in Illinois.

R. S. Prussia

Erdmann Schlegelmilch
Suhl, Thuringia
1861-1920

Reinhold Schlegelmilch
Tillowitz, Upper Silesia
1869-1956

Both Erdmann and Reinhold used the "RSP" mark. The famous "Red Mark" first appeared in the late 1870s and was used until the beginning of World War I. Decorative objects and tablewares were back stamped with the trademark featuring the initials "R.S." inside a wreath, a star above, and the word "Prussia" below.

There was a tremendous quantity of items produced with the "RSP" trademark. In addition to art objects, dresser sets, a large variety of tablewares (including complete dinner sets), and cake, chocolate, tea and coffee sets were all manufactured.

An endless number of "RSP" molds was made. Identical shapes were decorated differently; the same shape was made in a variety of sizes. Many molds produced pieces in the rococo style, including ornately fashioned scrollwork and flowers as part of the design of the blank. Some blanks were exported to the United States for the home decorating market.

Most "RSP" marked porcelains were decorated by transfer or a combination of transfer and enameling or hand applied gilt. Decorations were applied over the glaze. A few pieces were hand painted.

Decoration themes on "RSP" porcelains included: animals, birds, figural, floral, portrait, and scenics. Many pieces incorporated more than one theme. Floral themes were the most common; animal and fruit themes were the scarcest.

Background colors were part of the decorating scheme and not the finish or the glaze. These colors were applied over the glaze by the transfer method to highlight the central theme.

A variety of finishes such as glossy, iridescent, luster, matte, pearl, satin, etc. was used to complete an "RSP" piece. Gilt trim often was utilized on borders, bases, handles, feet, or to outline a particular design.

The Suhl factory stopped producing R.S. Prussia marked porcelains in 1920, unable to recover from the effects of World War I. The Tillowitz factory was located in a region where political boundaries kept changing. It finally came under the Polish socialist government control in 1956.

R. S. Poland

Poland
1945-1956

R.S. Poland pieces have predominately classical decorations or simple designs rather than the ornate or rococo decorations and designs of "RSP" porcelains. Art objects, such as vases and jardinieres, dominated production over common tablewares. After World War II, little export business was done. R.S. Poland examples are quite rare.

Reinhold Schlegelmilch's factory came under control of the socialist government in Poland in 1956.

References: Mary Frank Gaston, *The Collector's Encyclopedia of R.S. Prussia & other R. S. & E.S. Porcelains, 3rd Series,* Collector Books, 1994, *4th Series,*1995, *values updated 1997*; Leland & Carol Marple, *R.S. Prussia The Early Years,* Schiffer Publishing, Ltd. 1997; George W. Terrell, Jr. *Collecting R. S. Prussia, Identification and Values,* Books America, 1982; Clifford S. Schlegelmilch, *Handbook of Erdmann and Reinhold Schlegelmilch, Prussia-Germany & Oscar Schlegelmilch, Germany, 3rd Edition,* privately printed, 1973.

Collectors' Club: International Association of R.S. Prussia Collectors, Inc. Frances Coy, 212 Wooded Falls Road, Louisville, KY 40243, Membership: $20.00, Quarterly newsletter.

Reproduction Alert: Since the 1960s, R.S. Prussia collecting has grown rapidly. "RSP" pieces are being reproduced. There is a fake RSP red mark in the form of a decal which can be applied, glazed, and fired onto a piece of porcelain. This mark has an overall new appearance when compared to the old mark. There are many reproductions so marks should be checked carefully.

Japanese porcelain imports try and imitate "RSP" porcelains in type, decor, and mold. There are marked and unmarked examples. Most pieces initially have a paper "Made in Japan" label, but it is removed easily. The Lefton China Company manufactures reproductions.

There are many ways to spot the reproductions. The reproductions and Japanese imports are fairly thick. The scallops, scrolls, and lattice are clumsy rather than delicate. Often the decoration is too bright. The background colors are not subtle, and the transfers are applied poorly. The gold trim lacks patina. These porcelains are sold in gift shops and flea markets.

Collecting Hints: Not all "RSP" is marked. Examples usually can be identified by studying the mold and the decor of an unmarked piece to see if it matches a known mold or design.

E. S. Germany

Bowl

11" l x 8" w, oval, woman with holly wreath design, Tiffany finish 325.00

14" l, oval, lg red roses, orange shaded rose sprays, gold tracery, scalloped, "E. S. Germany Prov. Saxe" mark . 125.00

Cake Plate, 10 1/4" H-H, hunt scene in center with 3 men on horses and dogs, orange ground with orange and yellow trees, shaped rim, "E.S. Prov. Saxe" mark 125.00

Candy Dish, 7 1/4" d, gold handle at one end, lobed body, white camellias, green leaves, gold sponged rim, "red E.S. Germany Prov. Saxe" mark 18.00

Chocolate Set, pot, 9 1/4" h, 4 cups and saucers, lg pink rose and blue flowers on shoulders, hanging rose wreaths, heavy painted gold rims 325.00

Ewer, 7" h, pillow shape, multicolored scene of 5 maidens by brook, sapphire blue ground with raised gold accents, scalloped rim, ruffled base, "E. S. Germany Royal Saxe" mark 395.00

Hatpin Holder, 5" h, HP pink roses, blue to yellow shaded satin ground, "R.S. Suhl wreath" mark 85.00

Plate, 6" d, multicolored center, dk red border w/gold overlay, "E.S. Germany Prov. Saxe and shield" mark, $125.

Plate

7 3/8" d, multicolored center scene of classical maiden lying in forest, winged cherub in attendance, gold hanging swag cartouche, matte maroon border with gold overlay, shaped rim, "Royal Saxe E.S. Germany" mark 15.00

10 1/2" d, Madame DuBarry in center, luster burgundy border with 4 cartouches of women 400.00

10 7/8" d, multicolored center scene of three classical ladies in garden with musical instruments, relief molded wreaths, gold wreaths, gold crowned wreaths on border, shaped rim with hanging swags, "green E.S. Prussia Prov. Saxe" mark 52.00

Tray, 8 1/2" H-H

Goddess of the Sea design, green, gold, and maroon, "E.S. Germany Prov. Saxe" mark 125.00

Open handles, pink and white roses and green leaves, shaded tan to lt green ground, white and apple green floral line border, "E.S. Germany Prov. Saxe" mark 85.00

Urn, 6 3/4" h, 3 feet, 2 Victorian women with Cupid, gold beading, cobalt ground 195.00

Vase

6 3/4" h, bulbous shape, sm neck, multicolored scene of woman in blue gown standing in garden, birds flying overhead, orchid at base, raised gold car-

Vase, 7" h, brown bird, brown pine ones, tan ground, gold handles, "green E.S. Germany Prov. Saxe" mark, $200.

touche, pearlized ground with gold stenciled designs 495.00

7 1/2" h, full figure of Art Nouveau style woman and peacock, gold stenciling and beading, pearl luster finish, gold handles 395.00

9 1/2" h, "Lady with Swallows" design, turquoise and gold beading, white ground 475.00

11" h, oval scene of 3 colonial ladies playing music in colors, maroon ground, gold stenciling, 2 gold handles 495.00

R. S. Germany

Ashtray and Matchholder, 3" h, loop handle, brown acorns, green oak leaves, brown shaded ground, "blue R. G. Germany wreath" mark 120.00

Berry Set, master bowl, 9 3/4" d, 8 bowls, 5 1/4" d, 3 Art Nouveau style gold outlined white lilies and leaves, brown to yellow shaded ground, gold rims, green marks 300.00

Bowl, 9" d

Lilies on cream to lavender shaded ground, blue wreath mark 50.00

White roses with orange centers, green leaves and stems, gray shaded ground 45.00

Cake Plate, 10" H-H, cottage scene in woods with maiden and 2 yoked oxen 235.00

Celery Tray

10 /2" l x 5" w, pink flowers, green ground 65.00

12 1/4" H-H, 3 blue lilies, orange luster border, green mark 75.00

Charger, 11" d, HP magnolias, shaded gray-green ground, gold line trim 95.00

Chocolate Pot, 10 1/2" h, lg apricot and white flowers, shaded ground 115.00

Cup and Saucer, Art Deco, blue silhouette of dancing girl and scarf, beige luster ground with blue, black, and white bands 88.00

Dish

5" d, shell shape, ribbed body, band of pink flowers, green and gilt trim, raised molded rim. 37.00

13" H-H, oval, pink and yellow roses, open handles 68.00

Hair Receiver, 4 1/2" sq, peach and white flowers, tan, cream, and white ground 60.00

Hatpin Holder, 4 1/2" h, lg white rose at top, long green stem, shaded brown to green ground, green mark 150.00

Plate

6 1/2" d, HP white Shasta daisies 20.00

8" d

Acorns and oak leaves, dk green to cream shaded ground, gold lined rim, blue mark 22.00

Pink and white roses on border, shadow outlined green leaves, shaded

Relish Tray, 8" H-H, white and pink flowers, green shaded ground, gold lined rim, blue mark, $25.

green, brown, and cream ground, gold lined rim, blue mark. . . . 25.00

11 1/4" d, lilacs on white, green, and pink shaded ground, green and gold trim, gold rim. 110.00

Sugar Bowl, 2 7/8" h, pink and yellow rose transfer, sq handles, "R.S. Germany and wreath" mark, (A) 20.00

Syrup Jug, Cov, 3" h, HP pink roses . . .160.00

Tray, 15 1/4" H-H, lg green and white poppies 250.00

Vase

5 1/4" h

Ovoid shape, 2 handles from body to shoulder, HP blue violets on yellow to blue shaded ground, gold trimmed handles, "R.S. Germany and wreath" mark, (A) 65.00

Yellow birds on pink blossomed branches, lt blue ground, green wreath mark 45.00

7" h, lg roses, orange ground, "green R.S. Germany" mark 95.00

Wall Pocket, 7" l, slipper shape, flowing blue floral design, gold trim 150.00

R.S. Poland

Bowl

5 3/4" d, multicolored crowned cranes, forest setting, #90 mold 465.00

9 3/8" d, brown pheasant and blue and white pheasant, gray shadowed foliage, cream ground, unmkd 145.00

Hatpin Holder, 6" h, garland of red roses and green leaves on base, pale green band below with gold geometrics, pale green pierced surface with gold geometrics 125.00

Pickle Dish, 9" l, salmon pink and pink roses and foliage, shaded yellow ground, gold lined rim, offset closed handles 35.00

Server, 11" d x 8" h, center handle, lavender and orange roses 515.00

Vase

3 1/2" h, cylinder shape, multicolored crowned crane birds in forest setting 410.00

7 1/4" h, lg white roses with yellow centers, green foliage, shaded brown to cream ground 85.00

10" h, multicolored shepherdess and flock, mill in bkd, sm gold handles on shoulder, gold trimmed rim 640.00

Vase, 11" h, yellow, white, and pink roses, yellow to white ground, cobalt base with gilt, matte handles, "green and red R.S. Poland China, Made in (Germany) Poland" marks, $350.

11 3/4" h, white poppies with green, pink, and yellow accents, shaded brown-green ground, pr 705.00

R. S. Prussia

Bell, 3 1/2" h, sm purple flowers, white ground, ruffled edge, green twig and leaf handle, unmkd 285.00

Berry Set

Master bowl, 9" d, 6 bowls, 5" d, green leaves, pink roses, raised lily of the valley design, Leaf molds. 495.00

Master bowl, 11" d, 6 bowls, 5 1/2" d, "Pond Lilies Over Water" design, lcicle molds, red marks 650.00

Bowl

10" d

Lg yellow roses, pink and yellow ground 175.00

Bowl, 10 1/2" d, multicolored, red mark, $1,195.

Pink and white roses in center, gold stenciled frame, cobalt border with gold molded flowers and swirls, mold #57 . . . . 550.00

Roses and white snowballs in center, cobalt jewels, Point and Clover mold 575.00

10 1/4" d, pink and white roses, green leaves, shadowing, satin finish, mold #252. . . . . 230.00

10 1/2" d

"Water Lilies and Their Reflections" design, Lily Pad mold, med blue center, lt blue border, red mark 275.00

"Winter Season" design, satin finish, Iris mold 2,700.00

10 3/4" d, red, pink, and white flowers, lt blue ground, Iris mold, red mark 315.00

11" d

Hanging basket of roses with jewels, blue, brown, and green, mold #207, red mark 275.00

Pink and white poppies and lily of the valley in center, 4 swan medallions with swallows on gold tapestry border. 650.00

Cake Plate

9 3/4" H-H

"Spring Season" pattern, Fleur-de-lys mold, red mark 1,500.00

Yellow centered white daisies and greens, yellow to blue to green shaded ground, gold handles, "R.S. Tillowitz" mark 34.00

10" H-H, swallows, chickens, and ducks besides water and lilies, Swag and Tassle mold 1,010.00

10 1/4" H-H, dk pink and white roses, gold feathers, teal leaves, shadow flowers, Point and Clover mold 265.00

11" H-H, open handles

Lg pink and yellow roses, purple and yellow ground. 175.00

Pink and purple flowers and daisies reflecting in water, blue to aqua ground 175.00

Celery Dish, 12 1/2" l x 7" w, multicolored barnyard scene, Icicle mold 425.00

Chocolate Pot

9 1/2" h, swimming swans and water lilies, mold #508, unmkd. 50.00

10" h, lg roses, shaded ground, mold #507, red mark 250.00

Chocolate Set, pot, 10 1/4" h, 6 cups and saucers, Madame Recamier design, blue-green Tiffany finish 7,500.00

Cracker Jar, 7 1/2" h, pink, yellow, and white chrysanthemums, green border with shadow flowers and gilt trim, star mark 285.00

Creamer and Cov Sugar Bowl, creamer, 4 1/2" h, sugar bowl, 6" h, sm pink roses, leaf garlands, gold stenciling, blue trim, mold #601, unmkd 200.00

Cup and Saucer, Demitasse, pedestal, pink roses, mold #607, red mark 125.00

Dresser Tray

11" l, oval, white floral design, green and brown ground 90.00

11 1/2" l x 7 1/2" w, pierced handles, swans and flowers in relief on scalloped border, red mark, (A) 200.00

Hatpin Holder, 4 1/2" h, "Reflecting Poppies" design, mold #728, red mark 185.00

Plate

7 1/2" d, 12 sides, pink and yellow roses, lt green to white ground, gold trim, red mark 115.00

8" d, "Melon Boys" design, Point and Clover mold, unmkd 400.00

8 1/2" d, "Quiet Cove" pattern, Five Circle mold, red mark 695.00

9 1/2" d, "Dice Players" design, rose, cream, and green border panels with gold accents, emb gold beaded rim, pierced for hanging, red mark and blue shield mark 450.00

10" d

"Countess Potocka," Tiffany irid finish 1,800.00

Mill and water scene, shaded green and reds, round and wavy scallops, mold #341, unmkd. 425.00

10 1/2" d, white and pink roses in center, lavender and pink roses in 6 panels on border, pierced handles, Lily mold, unmkd 95.00

11" H-H, open handles, snow birds and sunset, Icicle mold 2,000.00

Relish Tray, 9 1/2" l x 4 1/2" w, "Melon Eaters" design, Point and Clover mold, red mark 695.00

Sugar Shaker, 4 3/4" h, sm pink roses, gold hanging garlands 260.00

Tankard, 9" h, "Chinese Pheasant and Evergreen" design, satin finish, mold #584, red mark 950.00

Teapot

5 1/2" h, Surreal Dogwood Blossoms, satin finish, red mark 175.00

6 1/4" h, pedestal ft, sm white flowers, green leaves, shaded white, green, pink, and beige ground, unmkd 135.00

Tray, 11 1/2" l x 8" w, pierced handles, red and pink roses and blossoms, mold #82, red mark 300.00

Vase

4 1/2" h, woman on swing design, mold #914, red mark 550.00

6" h, white and brown pheasants, shaded green ground, "R.S. Tillowitz, Silesia" mark 260.00

6 1/2" h, cottage scene, brown and gold tones, lavender accents, mold #910, red mark 600.00

7 1/4" h, cylinder shape with small neck and top, cobalt leaves, gold accents, cream ground, cobalt shoulder with

gold tracery, mold #909, red steeple mark 525.00

8" h, red and yellow parrots on leafed branch, satin finish, 2 sm handles on shoulder, unmkd 1,800.00

9" h, black silhouette of lady dancing with hoop in silver cartouche, yellow ground, SP handles, R. S. Tillowitz 375.00

SEVRES AND VINCENNES

Sevres
Paris, France
1738 to Present

History: The Dubois brothers started a small soft paste porcelain factory for the production of decorative flowers at Vincennes in 1738.. Encouraged by Madame Pompadour, the factory found favor with Louis XV who became the chief shareholder in 1753. Louis XV controlled most of the products manufactured at Vincennes as well as throughout the rest of France. Gilding and the use of colored grounds were reserved for his pet projects. The familiar interlaced "L" mark was used during his reign to signify his participation.

In 1756, the factory was moved to Sevres, coming under the watchful eye of its chief benefactor Mme. de Pompadour. The first products were soft paste porcelain pieces decorated in the oriental style. The soft paste porcelain lent itself well to the elaborate rococo style favored by the king and his court. In addition to decorated soft paste, exquisite biscuit porcelain figures were produced, much to the delight of Madame Pompadour.

After the late 1760s, hard paste porcelain gradually replaced the soft paste variety. Styles fell loosely into categories which had taken the names of the benefactors. The period of 1753 to 1763 was known as "Pompadour," 1763 to 1786 was "Louis XV," and 1786 to 1793 was "Louis XVI." The products of these periods ranged from small scent bottles to enormous dinner services to vases and urns of monumental size and decoration. The neo-classical styles were heavily favored. Jeweled or heavily enameled pieces first appeared about 1780.

Several directors influenced strongly the products from Sevres. During the directorship of Jean Hellot, about 1745 to 1766, several colors were introduced that have become associated with Sevres porcelain. The earliest ground color was gros bleu (1749) followed by bleu celeste (turquoise, 1752), rose pompadour (pink, 1756), and bleu roi (clear blue, 1763). The use of these colors during specific periods helped date Sevres porcelain.

Following the French Revolution, the company fell into disfavor and did not flourish again until the Napoleonic years. Alexandre Brongniart was appointed director by Lucien Bonaparte in 1800. The Empire style and scenics depicting Napoleon's campaigns and victories dominated the designs during the period. After 1804, soft paste was no longer made. Eventually the factory re-established itself as a leading producer of European hard paste porcelain.

A new range of colors was developed. Ground colors included dark blue, a pale blue called agate, and chrome green. These were seen most frequently in the First Empire Period, 1804 to 1815. Gilding was used extensively during this period. Painters were employed by Brongniart to paint miniature portraits on porcelain shapes that were modeled carefully by artists such as Theodore Brongniart and Charles Parcier.

Between 1800 and 1830, Sevres products included plaques, vases, table services, sculptures, and some very large special pieces. Porcelain plaques, made between 1818 and 1848, imitated oil paintings or frescoes. Some vases were made in a neo-classical style that imitated cameos. Napoleon revived the tradition of ordering large table services for his own use or for diplomatic gifts. Post Revolution monarchs had France glorified as the subject matter for services. Coffee, tea, or breakfast services also were made between 1800 and 1830.

The reign of Louis-Phillipe, 1830 to 1848, saw few changes at Sevres. Brongniart continued with the styles he was using from the early 1800s. White backgrounds were used more frequently for everyday table services. Decorations lessened. Decorations were printed, especially when gilding was used.

Brongniart died in 1847. Jules Dieterle became artistic director from 1852 to 1855; Joseph Nicolle took over from 1856 to 1871. Most of the output of the Sevres factory from 1852 onwards was for imperial residences and diplomatic gifts.

The most important decorative technique of this period was the pate-sur-pate process. This type of decoration was very popular in France and in England. The pate-sur-pate process ended at Sevres in 1897. (See: Pate-sur-Pate.)

The Second Empire style at Sevres provided a complete break with the preceding period. This was an eclectic period, 1850-1870, that utilized the Pompeian style to imitate decoration on classical vases with classical subjects. A return to the rococo forms and decorations of the Louis XV times also occurred during this period.

The Third Republic period, 1870 to 1940, began with difficult conditions at the factory. The factory moved to its present location by the Park of Saint-Cloud. In 1876, the sculptor A. Carrier-Belleuse became artistic director. He remained until his death in 1886.

Many experiments were carried out with different porcelain bodies. Flambe glazes were developed and became popular. During the Carrier-Belleuse period, many different decorating techniques, e.q. painted decoration, pate-sur-pate decoration, and copper glazing were used.

When Alexandre Sandier became director from 1896 to 1916, the factory was reorganized completely. He initiated new shapes and decoration techniques. Sinuous shapes were developed. The human figure was replaced as a decorative motif by painted vegetables, florals, and insects in the new Art Nouveau style. Winding tendrils appeared on vases and plates. Stoneware bodies often were used for the Art Nouveau decorated pieces. Sculpture regained prominence in biscuit porcelain as many busts were modeled.

Marks: For most of the 18th century, painted marks on Sevres porcelain consisted of the royal cypher (interlacing L's); the date mark, and the identifying insignia of painters and gilders. Marks usually were blue, but could be brown or purple. Initials below the mark indicated the artist. Artists signed their own works as a means of quality control. The Sevres crown was never seen on soft paste examples.

From 1753-1793, date letters appeared within the crossed L's. For example, A = 1753. R = 1st letter date used on hard paste. Any letter before R cannot be hard paste Sevres porcelain. From 1793-1800, the monogram of the Republic of France (RF) was used with Sevres and a painter's mark to replace the royal cypher. No letter dates were used. The marks were continually changing after that.

References: Carl Christian Dauterman, *Sevres*, Walker & Co.,1969; Carl Christian Dauterman, *Sevres Porcelain, Makers and Marks of the Eighteenth Century*, The Metropolitan Museum of Art, 1986; W.B. Honey, *French Porcelain of the 18th Century*, Faber & Faber, 1950; Linda Humphries, *Sevres Porcelain from the Sevres Museum 1740 to the Present*, Hund Humpries, 1997; George Savage, *Seventeenth & Eighteenth Century French Porcelain*, Hamlyn Publishing Co. Ltd.,1969.

Museums: Art Institute of Chicago, Chicago, IL; British Museum, London, England; Frick Collection, New York, NY.; Gardiner Museum of Ceramic Art, Toronto, Canada; J. Paul Getty Museum, Los Angeles, CA; Metropolitan Museum of Art, New York, NY; Musee des Arts Decoratifs, Paris, France; Musee du Louvre, Paris, France; Musee Nationale de Ceramique, Sevres, France; Victoria & Albert Museum, London, England; Wadsworth Atheneum, Hartford, CT; Wallace Collection, Hertford House, London, England; Walters Art Gallery, Baltimore, MD.

Reproduction Alert: A high percentage of pieces with the Sevres marks are fake or questionable. There are some clues to look for to help establish an authentic piece from a fake or reproduction. Nineteenth-century Sevres examples had more decoration and more gold than 18th-century pieces. Sevres examples were never marked on the lids. A marked lid indicates a fake. Many fakes had chateau marks. Soft paste was more often faked than hard paste since it is more valuable. Some Sevres white blanks were decorated by factory artists at home or at Paris porcelain dealers such as Peres and Ireland. Some blanks were decorated in England by Baldock and Mortlock.

There should be a hole underneath the rim in plates and saucers caused by the support used in the kiln with a black dot from iron oxide. If so, the piece dates from 1752-1803 or 1804 and was fired in the kiln at Sevres. If there are two marks, the piece was refired. If one sees black paint in a hole or a hole with no purpose, then the example is a fake.

The incised mark on a piece must date the same or earlier than the decorator's mark. If the mark on a blank was cut later, the piece was considered a "second" and never decorated at the Sevres factory. Check the painter's sign or symbol to see if it agrees with the letter date. Many Sevres painters produced fakes at home after stealing colors from the factory for decorating. Restorers in France reduced the value of huge quantities of Sevres and Vincennes pieces by regilding chips.

Many colors used on soft paste produced surface bubbles that look like holes, such as in purple due to the gum content. The turpentine used in making hard paste left carbon dots, and there was no bubbling in the colors. One can see scratches in the glaze if pieces of soft paste were used. If the scratches are molten out, the piece has been refired and is worthless.

Jewelled specimens with any date before 1780 are fakes. "Jewelled Sevres" has transparent raised enamels laid on gold that appeared like inlaid jewels on the surface of the porcelain.

Many Sevres copies were made by Samson. His mark was made to look like two L's. His glaze was yellowish, not white like Sevres soft paste.

Vincennes
Chateau of Vincennes, Paris, France
1738-1772

History: Gilles and Robert Dubois brought soft paste porcelain manufacturing to the royal chateau at Vincennes in 1738. They were assisted by Orry de Fulvy, Councillor of State and Minister of Finance. After two years, the Dubois brothers failed.

Francois Gravant took over and appointed Charles Adams the director. The king granted many concessions to Adams. The factory entered a period of prosperity.

Vincennes products made between 1745 and 1756 were prized by collectors. Jean-Jacques Bachelier took charge of painting and modeling in 1747. He introduced the use of biscuit porcelain for figure modeling. A Vincennes factory specialty was artificial flowers, popular in Paris around 1750.

In 1753, the king issued an edict giving the exclusive privilege of porcelain making in France to Adams. He sanctioned the use of the royal cypher, a pair of interlaced "L's."

The porcelain works were removed from the Chateau of Vincennes to a new building at Sevres in 1756. The firm became the Royal Porcelain Factory of Sevres.

Pierre Antoine Hannong, a Strasbourg potter, established a factory for hard paste porcelain in the vacated buildings at Chateau Vincennes in 1767. He was granted the right to produce porcelain as long as he did not infringe on the Sevres factory's designs. Only a small quantity of porcelains was made. In 1774, the factory was purchased by Seguin, whose patron was the Duc de Chartes. Seguin used the title "Royal Factory of Vincennes." His products duplicated those of many French factories.

Reference: George Savage, *Seventeenth & Eighteenth Century French Porcelain*, Spring Books, 1969.

Museums: British Museum, London, England; Gardiner Museum of Ceramic Art, Toronto, Canada; J. Paul Getty Museum, Los Angeles, CA; The Frick Collection, New York, NY; Victoria & Albert Museum, London, England; Wadsworth Atheneum, Hartford, CT.

Bowl, 5 3/4" d, flared shape, band of yellow roses and swags reserved in gilt line band suspending arcades of spearheads on gilt line ft rim, tortoise shell ground, c1830, (A) 155.00

Cabinet Cup and Saucer

Iron red and white outlined vert panels of oct cartouches of painted birds or en grisaille classic symbols, maroon ground with multicolored foliate arabesques, chased gold rims, ft, and saucer center, gilt scroll handle with palmette terminal, "blue interlaced L's and fleur-de-lys, iron red crowned eagle" marks, c1815, (A) 17,250.00

Painted continuous rural landscape with people between upper lilac band with purple band of foliate swags and gilt and lilac lower band with continuous band suspending swags, saucer painted with purple and gilt foliate rosette, gilt lined rims, "blue RF and *Sevres*" marks, c1793, (A) 1,078.00

Canister, 3 1/4" h, rect with domed shoulders and chamfered corners, painted loose bouquet in gilt rocaille scroll cartouches reserved on pink ground, gilt dentil rims, "blue interlaced L's and G" marks 2,500.00

Cheese Strainer, 9 1/2" H-H, with stand, rose painted flower sprays in gilt accented pierced foliate cartouches, pyramid of pierced holes below bow handles, star pierced base, stand painted with rose flowers in puce line and gilt dash bands, border with rose flying birds or flower sprays in molded gilt foliate cartouches, gilt dentil rims, "blue crowned interlaced L's and B" mark, Vincennes, c1754, (A) 13,225.00

Coffee Can and Saucer, gilt rocaille decoration of exotic birds and fountains in garden, gilt scrolled borders, Bleu Nouveau ground, "blue interlaced L's and L" marks, (A) 10,350.00

Cream Jug, 4 3/8" h, pear shape, 3 sm feet, branch handle, painted scattered bouquets, "sepia interlaced L's and AA" mark, 1778, (A) 518.00

Cup and Saucer

Bleu Lapis ground, painted flying birds in gilt foliage and flower cartouches, gilt dentil rim, "blue overglazed interlaced L's and incised 8 and 4" marks, Vincennes, (A) 920.00

Painted chinoiseries under gilt foliate vine reserved on blue band with gilt line and dot and dash borders, "blue R.F. Sevres" mark, c1797, (A) 4,600.00

Painted panels of exotic birds in landscapes, gilt peacock surrounds, green ground, gilt dentil rims, "blue interlaced L's and H" marks, (A) 9,200.00

Painted putto in clouds on cup, putto with arrow quiver on saucer, reserved on white ground in gilt foliate cartouches of grasses, flower sprays, and garlands, gilt dentil rims, "blue interlaced L's and B" mark, Vincennes, (A) 5,060.00

Painted scattered floral bouquets, blue line and gilt dash borders, "blue interlaced L's" mark, (A) 125.00

Painted turquoise ribbon interlaced with floral garland, "puce interlaced L's" mark, mid 18th C, (A) 125.00

Cup and Saucer, Demitasse, gilt Napoleonic crown between 2 cherubs, dk rose ground, 2nd Empire 395.00

Cup and Stand, 2 handles, rose painted musical putti in clouds in gilt cartouches of grasses and trailing flowers, reserved on Bleu Lapis ground, gilt dentil rims, "blue interlaced L's and B" mark, Vincennes, (A) 4,025.00

Cup and Stand, Cov, puce painted exotic birds in flight, perched on branches, and in landscape, gilt dentil rims, chrysanthemum knob, "blue interlaced L's" marks, Vincennes, c1753 . . . . 2,500.00

Dessert Service, Part, 2 fruit coolers, 10 1/4" h, 2 oval dishes, 10 1/2" l, oval dish, 9 1/2" l, 2 saucer dishes, 8 1/2" d, 2 octafoil dishes, 8 7/8" d, dish, 8 3/8" sq, shell shaped dish, 8 3/4" w, 30 plates, 9 5/8" d, painted flower bouquet tied with pink and blue ribbons, border of puce and gilt oeil-de-perdrix on blue ground, gilt rim, gilt lion mask and ring handles on coolers, "blue *Sevres*" marks, (A) 20,700.00

Milk Jug, 4 3/4" h, pear shape, branch handle, 3 gilt molded feet, painted flower sprays, gilt dentil rim, "blue interlaced L's and K" mark, dtd 1763, (A) 863.00

Paperweight, 3 1/2" d, white cameo of woman's profile, "FLORE" on rim, raised flowerheads in brown, blue, gray, and green matte glaze, "incised T DOAT, 1900, SEVRES" mark, (A) 1,800.00

Plate

7 5/8" d, painted exotic birds in landscape, gilt chased oak leaf, acorns, and oak root inner border, Bleu Celeste border, gilt lined rim, "blue interlaced L's and S" mark, (A) 9,775.00

9 1/2" d

Center painted in colors of bird perched on rocks in blue band with raised gilt beading, border of blue bands with raised gilt beading and gilt scrolling foliage between, "blue interlaced L's and PP" marks, (A) 1,265.00

Painted loose bouquets and scattered flowers, blue line and gilt dash shaped rim, c1772-3, set of 10, (A) 3,450.00

Three multicolored floral sprays, blue lined inner rim with gilt dashes, gilt lined shaped rim, dtd 1785, pr
.... 195.00

9 5/8" d, "Batailles" series, HP multicolored center scene of woman with flags on bastion or knights in armor, gilt tooled cavetto, cobalt border with gilt tooled designs with blue and red enameled jewels, gilt dentil rim, c1830, pr... 1,500.00

Solitaire Set, Part

Oval stand, 10 7/8" l, cup, cov sugar bowl, rose painted scenes of putti in clouds or trophies of love in gilt cartouches of foliate scrolls and flowers, reserved on Bleu Lapis ground, gilt dentil rims, "blue interlaced L's and A" marks, Vincennes, (A) 5,520.00

Rect tray, 7" l, ftd, teapot, 2 3/4" h, teabowl and saucer, rose painted putti in clouds, scattered birds, gilt dentil rims, flower knob, "blue interlaced L's and G" marks, 1759, chips, (A)
.... .3,450.00

Soup Plate, 9 3/8" d, painted scattered bouquets, blue line and gilt dash rim, gilt dentil edge, "interlaced L's and dates" mark, c1759-64, set of 10, (A) 2,070.00

Sugar Basin, 3" d, painted bouquet of flowers in gilt flower, rush, and fern cartouches, Bleu Celeste ground, gilt dentil rim, "blue interlaced L's and A" mark, Vincennes, (A)
.... .1,995.00

Sugar Bowl, Cov

2 1/2" h, puce painted birds in landscape, gilt dentil rim, "blue interlaced L's and E" mark, (A) 368.00

3 5/8" h, hard paste, painted rose garlands and floral swags in gilt edged pointed arched garlands, orange ground, c1780, chip, (A) 978.00

Wine Cooler, 4 3/8" h, 6" H-H, gilt framed multicolored panel of "Perseus Paying Homage To Gods Of Victory" on front, "Love Laying In Arbor With Nymphs" on reverse, dbl gilt banded rim, scrolled handles, dk blue ground, "interlaced L's and K" mark, (A) $1,500.

6 3/8" H-H, globular shape, bamboo handles, dbl walled, body pierced with stylized flowers on geometric trellis ground, cov pierced with half flowers and half loops on rim, c1865, (A) 850.00

Teapot

4 3/4" h, painted loose bouquet of cornflowers in floral and gilt surround, lavender ground with overall flowerheads, gilt flowerheads on spout, gilt accented handle, "blue interlaced L's and BB" mark, (A) 2,300.00

5 5/8" h, octafoil shape, ear shaped handle, molded prunus branches, blue painted scattered floral sprays, gilt dentil rims, gilt line on ft, "blue crowned interlaced L's and A" mark, Vincennes, 1753, cracks, (A) 2,070.00

Tray

6 3/4" l, blue painted putto holding mask in clouds in center, shaped gilt outlined

border, gilt dentil rim, "blue interlaced L's and F" mark, 1758, (A)... 1,265.00

11 1/4" l, lobed body, painted scattered flower sprays, blue line and gilt dash rim, gilt dentil edge, "blue interlaced L's and C, incised BP" marks, Vincennes, (A) 863.00

Vase

5 3/4" h, cylinder shape, white outlined brown toned geometric shapes and winged creatures, (A) 155.00

7 1/4" h, shouldered tapered cylinder shape, slender gilt and green flower sprays, yellow ground, (A)..... 445.00

9 1/4" h, narrow base to wide flat shoulder, enameled and gilded purple fuchsia flowers, green leaves, cream ground, gold lined rim and base, "stamped S1911/RF/MANUFACTURE NATIONALE/DECORE A SEVRES 1911/BELET" mark, (A) 1,100.00

17 3/4" h, oviform, flambe blue and yellow ground, band of gilt stenciled flowers on seeded ground on shoulder, c1917, (A) 3,680.00

22" h, Art Deco style stenciled blue enameled flowers and stems on yellow and green shaded ground, c1924, (A)
.... 1,150.00

34" h, campana shape, painted gilt lined cartouche of horsemen in canyon, Bleu-de-Roi ground with gilt bands of sheaves, and stiff leaves, gilt bronze mts, (A) 8,625.00

SHAVING MUGS

c1908

Austria, England, France, Germany c1850-1920

History: Many shaving or barber's mugs were manufactured of pottery or porcelain. Most mugs were shaped like coffee mugs; others had soap drainers and other features incorporated into the designs. Scuttles had double spouts. One spout was used for the razor, and the other for the shaving brush.

Many barber-supply companies in the United States imported blank shaving mugs from Limoges and Sevres in France, from Victoria Carlsbad and Imperial Crown China in Austria, from C.T. Germany and Felda China Company in Germany, from A.J. Wilkinson and Goddard in England, and other scattered sources.

The imported, plain white, unadorned pottery or porcelain mugs were decorated in the suppliers' workshops. Shaving mugs were not meant to be ornamental. They were designed for the owner's personal

Tea Service, teapot, 7" h, cream jug, 2 cov sugar bowls, 10 plates, 12 cups and saucers, multicolored portraits of French sovereigns, cobalt and gilt ground, (A) $5,720.

use at his favorite barber shop where he went for a daily or weekly shave. Some people viewed their private mug a status symbol; others felt it was more hygienic for each man to have his own mug reserved for his personal use.

Fraternal

Fraternal shaving mugs bear symbols of the various fraternal orders such as Masons, Elks, Moose, etc. In addition, the Industrial Revolution furnished an incentive for American laborers to unite in national organizations, e.g. the Noble Order of the Knights of Labor and the Grand International Brotherhood of Locomotive Engineers. Symbols of these labor organizations found their way on to shaving mugs just as did the symbols of fraternal groups.

General

Shaving mugs appeared in quantity after the Civil War and flourished during the Victorian age. One style of mug featured a photograph of the owner or his family or a favorite painting. It was made by adding a photographic emulsion to the ceramic body and then burning in the resulting image in a kiln.

Simple mugs with the owner's name added to a stock floral design were produced by all the decorating workshops. Scenes of the popular sports of the day also found their way onto shaving mugs.

Mugs with simply a number in gilt were used in hotel barber shops. The numbers corresponded to the hotel room numbers. Decal decorated mugs from Germany contained reproductions of either important people, such as Napoleon or Sitting Bull, well known works of art, or animals, e.g. horses, dogs, etc.

Character shaving mugs, introduced into the United States about 1900, were manufactured in Austria and Bavaria until the start of World War I. Animal and fish heads were among the popular forms. Some mugs also advertised shaving products, e.g. Wildroot.

Barber shop shaving declined after World War I. Safety razors had been invented and perfected. Returning soldiers had learned to shave themselves. In addition, the Blue Laws forced barber shops to close on Sunday, a popular pre-war shaving day. By 1930 shaving at the barber shop was nearly at an end.

Occupational Mugs

Occupational mugs, indicating the owner's type of work, existed for almost every business, profession, or trade. The mug had a picture featuring the owner's occupation and his name in gold, either above or be-

low the illustration. Lettering was usually in the old English style. Both indoor and outdoor trades were depicted. Some mugs had a scene portraying the owner working at his trade; others illustrated the working tools or emblem of the tradesman.

References: Keith E. Estep, *The Shaving Mug & Barber Bottle Book,* Schiffer Publishing, Ltd. 1995; Robert Blake Powell, *Antique Shaving Mugs of The United States*, published privately, 1978; W. Porter Ware, *Price List of Occupational & Society Emblems Shaving Mugs,* Lightner Publishing Corporation, 1949.

Collectors' Club: National Shaving Mug Collectors' Association, Penny Nader, 320 S. Glenwood Street, Allentown, PA 18104, Membership: $15.00, Quarterly newsletter.

Museums: Atwater Kent Museum, Philadelphia, PA.; Fort Worth Museum of Science & History, Fort Worth, TX; The Institute of Texas Cultures Museum, San Antonio, TX; Lightner Museum, St. Augustine, FL; The New York Historical Society, New York, NY.

Reproduction Alert: New shaving mugs are manufactured frequently as "replicas" of the past, but these should be recognized easily. Since they were used frequently, old shaving mugs should show definite signs of wear along the handle and the top and bottom rims.

Currently, Japanese companies are making reproduction "occupational" mugs in heavy porcelains similar to the earlier examples. Reproduction mugs from France and Germany appear to be hand painted but actually are printed by the silk screen process. An experienced collector can spot the difference.

Names on old mugs were larger, and the decoration left ample room for the name. On new mugs the picture is larger and the name looks crowded. Most old mugs were blanks from Germany or France. Old mugs never included the name of the occupation spelled out, only the person's name. Original occupational and fraternal mugs were hand painted and rarely showed wear on the scene. The gold trim does show wear. Perfect gold trim and lettering are rarely found on genuine old shaving mugs.

Collecting Hints: Many collections have been assembled that contain mugs representing more than 600 occupations. Uncommon jobs, such as deep sea diver, are difficult to locate. Mugs picturing obsolete occupations are prized highly by collectors. An occupational mug depicting a profession such as doctor or lawyer are harder to find since professionals were less likely

to advertise themselves than were tradesman or neighborhood merchants.

Fraternal

American Mechanics

    Compass and T-square in wood tones, Jr. O.U.A.M., gold name 350.00

    HP fraternal shield and arm holding hammer, compass and T-square and Jr. O.U.A.M., worn gold band on rim, (A) 35.00

Foresters of America, multicolored symbol, gold name 185.00

    GAR, gold letters on front, Meakin. . 58.00

    GAR, painted GAR medal on face, gold name above 325.00

    Gold U.C.T.C., white ground, unmkd 68.00

Fraternal Order of Elks, brown eagle with multicolored American flags, black F.O.E., gold name, "T & V Limoges France" mark . .475.00

Knights of Pythias, gold "FLT," gold chain, and gold "K P," multicolored triangle with FCB, skull and cross bones, gold name 175.00

Modern Woodsmen of America, gold axe in gold circle and "MWA," pearl luster body, blue luster border, "Germany" mark . . . 58.00

Multicolored shield with tent and crossed flags, eye above with gold scrolling, gold name 145.00

Odd Fellows

    Gold F.L.T. in gold chain over multicolored eye, gold name 195.00

    Tent with eye above, gold chain with F.L.T., "BAVARIA" mark 450.00

    Three gold chain links with "FLT," gold name at top 150.00

Order of Railroad Conductors, dk pink, green and tan interlaced letters, worn gold name, "V & D Austria" mark 56.00

General

Bird hunter and dogs scene, HP multicolors, unmkd 350.00

Black puffs with gold trimmed white name, T & V Limoges blank 135.00

Blue onion pattern, "Vienna, Austria" mark 58.00

Brown transfer of monk playing violin, "M1ade in Germany" mark 125.00

Bust of 18th C woman in gilt cartouche on side, olive, burgundy, and white horiz banding with gold overlay, Carlsbad 45.00

"Coburg" pattern, mulberry transfer, Edwards 250.00

Cov, with insert, enameled raised hunt scene, pink luster clouds, bands, and star design on cov, "black David Snowdon" on side, c1820, (A) 1,150.00

Eagle, flags, shield, and globe in colors, gold name, "T &V Limoges" mark 110.00

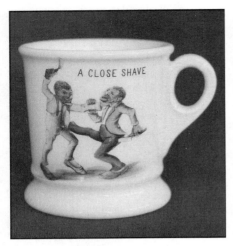

General, pink, blue, and brown, K.P.M., $550.

Figural, 3 1/2" h, elk, brown shades, Royal Bayreuth blue mark 600.00

Flow blue, "Marlborough" pattern 175.00

Gold horseshoe surrounded by red and green flowers, Austria 75.00

Gold "Howard B. Chapin" in gold wreath 50.00

Gold "51," barber shop or hotel mug, white ground 65.00

Gold oval cartouche with multicolored scene of little boy in blue jacket sitting on wall, watching ship at sea, gold side florals 225.00

Half panels of red rose or green fruit, gold striping, worn gold name and "1915," T &V Limoges 65.00

HP

    Brown pine cones, red branches, raised base 65.00

    Head of St. Bernard dog 65.00

    Wheat sheaves, Limoges blank, c1900 . . . . 85.00

Lavender and blue flowers, gold leaves, white ground, unmkd, pr, (A) 10.00

Left handed

    Molded gold ribbons, red roses, mirror on front 175.00

    Molded shell and coral design, orange coral handle, mirror on front 75.00

Multicolored scene of farm woman and goats in gold dot outlined oval cartouche, lt blue ground 25.00

Oval shape

    Arched brush holder, peach band at top, gold accents on rim and sides, scroll handle, (A) 20.00

    Red and yellow flowers, lavender to white shaded ground, gold and white dots, gold int rim, gold handle and lined snout, unmkd, (A) 15.00

    Pale pink roses on front, white ground with pale pink and yellow at top, gold trim on handle, brush rest on handle, (A) 35.00

General, multicolored transfer of horse scene, med blue ground mottled ground, gold rim, $80.

Pears on shaded green ground, gold beaded rim, (A) 15.00

Purple drape, red poppy, gold name, ivory and white round, (A) 95.00

Raised green leaves and lavender petals, raised red florals, raised gold "PRESENT," gold rim and lined handle 22.00

Scuttle

3 3/4" h, blue onion pattern 140.00

4" h

    Figural goose in pink shawl, yellow bonnet with pink ribbon, tan base and handle, Schafer and Vater 250.00

    Gold outlined relief molded veins and leaves, white ground, unmkd 45.00

    Lg red rose, green leaves, shadow leaves, Germany 40.00

4 1/8" h, bust of man with wig, blue glaze, Schafer and Vater 400.00

4 1/2" h, "Cottage" design, "A present for friend brother or son A shaving mug is

just the one," Watcombe Torquay 180.00

Ladies

    Bouquet of pastel flowers on side, sm flowers on reverse, green, peach, and gold base, top, and snout, Germany, (A) 10.00

    Dk blue and gold flowers and leaves, white ground, dk blue and gold handle, (A) 17.00

Shaded green top and base with shaded pink enter, raised outline of flowers, gold band at rim and snout, sq handle, (A) 15.00

Sm purple flowerheads, green leaves, lt purple sprigs, blue line on top and base . . 35.00

Squat shape, pink and white roses, green lustered roses on border, "red GERMANY" mark 33.00

Wide gold bands, gold name 25.00

Winter scene of birds in branches, barn in bkd, worn gold name 45.00

Occupational

Baker, 3 men working brick oven, gold name 595.00

Bartender, bar scene with 2 men at bar, bartender behind, multicolored enamels, gold name, (A) 315.00

Blacksmith, HP multicolored scene of man shoeing horse in shop, horseshoe overhead, gold name 225.00

Bricklayer, multicolored scene of man in lt blue shirt, blue trousers before red brick wall, black panels, gold name 895.00

Butcher

    Butcher shop in colors, gold "F.M. Bryant" name 180.00

    Steer's head flanked by cutting tools, no name, (A) 185.00

Cabinet Maker, multicolored scene of worker at table, gold name, (A) 393.00

General, red roses, green leaves and shadow leaves, "Germany" mark, $40.

Occupational, Baker, multicolored scene, gold name, gold trimmed handle, $950.

Carpenter, multicolored scene of carpenter sawing boards in workshop, gold name
. . . . 450.00

Carriage Driver, multicolored scene of carriage, horses, driver, and couple, black side panels, gold name 675.00

Doctor, man in derby seated in one horse buggy, whip in holder, gold name . . . 475.00

Drapery Maker, red velvet drapes and scissors, gold name, Limoges blank. 375.00

Farmer, multicolored scene of farmer plowing field behind 2 horses, gold name 250.00

Furniture Refinisher, multicolored scene of man painting chair, can of varnish on ground, gold name 825.00

Jockey

    HP scene of jockey sitting on fence, horse race in center, gold name, "C.T. eagle" mark, (A) 578.00

    Multicolored horse head flanked by red flowers and green leaves, pink flowers on sides, gold name 395.00

Lead Smelter, lt blue and black machinery, gold name 370.00

Livery Stable Operator, multicolored scene of livery stable, no name, (A) 248.00

Lumberyard Worker, multicolored scene on man with stacks of boards, horse-drawn wagon in foreground, gold name. 925.00

Machinist, black lathe, gold name . . . 440.00

Milkman, multicolored scene of driver in yellow and green wagon pulled by white horse, gold name 475.00

Mold Maker, multicolored scene of man making mold on stand, pile of dirt at side, gold name and stripes, (A) 478.00

Musician, gold cornet, blue asters, gold wheat ferns and green leaves, gold name
. . . . 425.00

Pharmacist, yellow-gold mortar and pestle in green leaf and red rose wreath, gold name
. . . . 595.00

Plasterer, multicolored scene of 2 trowels on pallet, gold scrolling, gold initials, Bavaria
. . . . 425.00

Railroad Engineer, multicolored scene of locomotive and tender, worn gold name
. . . . 265.00

Railroad Man, red caboose, gold florals at side, gold name, hairline on handle . . 395.00

Salesman, multicolored hand with cuff holding fancy gold calling card with name
. . . . 375.00

Scuttle, purple violets, green leaves, gold trim, $38.

Shoemaker, multicolored scene of man in blue apron, black shoe, gold trim and name
. . . . 750.00

Slaughterhouse

    Multicolored scene of butcher with raised axe and bull tied to metal ring, gold name. 585.00

    Multicolored scene of man holding steer by winch, butcher with raised mallet, gold name. 775.00

Sulky, sulky, cap, and horse, floral accents, gold name 325.00

Telegraph Operator, multicolored hand reaching for telegraph key, gold name
. . . . 675.00

Tinsmith, black tin shears and sheet metal, gold name 550.00

Trolley Operator

    Multicolored scene of electric trolley car with operator at front, gold geometrics at sides, gold name 650.00

    Paneled, multicolored scene of electric trolley car, wreath of roses and green leaves, sm blue flowers, worn gold name. 385.00

    Profile of modern electric trolley car in yellow and gray, gold name 990.00

Window Washer, multicolored scene of man in white on scaffolding before red brick wall washing windows, gilt trim, gold name
. . . . 1,175.00

1890-1910   1925-1945

SHELLEY

Longton, England
Mid-18th Century to Present

History: Members of the Shelley family manufactured pottery at Lane End beginning in the middle of the 18th century. In 1872, Joseph Shelley formed a partnership with James Wileman of Wileman & Co., operator of the Foley China Works. For the next fifty years, the firm used the name Wileman & Co. Percy, Joseph Shelley's son, joined the firm in 1881. Percy became an excellent potter. During his fifty years as head of the firm, he developed the lasting reputation of Shelley china.

During the 1880s, only average quality china was made. Pieces featured one color and poor quality transfers. Percy hired artists to produce dinner services with more elaborate decorations that were intended for the export market. During the 1890s, the wares were more varied, featuring finer patterns and better colorations.

When Joseph died in 1896, Percy assumed complete control and improved all aspects of production and decoration. The artist Rowland Morris modeled "Dainty White," the company's most successfully produced shape until 1966. The shape also was used for many pieces of commemorative ware.

Frederick Rhead, who trained under Solon at Minton and worked at Wedgwood, was employed as artistic director in 1896. Rhead introduced Intarsio, Spano-Lustra, Urbato, Primitf, and Pastello wares, a series of effects used on earthenwares. Intarsio was the most popular. A large number of patterns and styles was made.

Although the firm was still called Wileman & Co. in 1910, the mark utilized the Shelley family name enclosed in an outline shield shape. The art director now was Walter Slater, who had been an apprentice at Minton and spent twenty years working at Doulton.

A new series of Intarsio ware that reflected Art Nouveau motifs was introduced in 1911. Flamboyant ware with flambe glazes and Cloisello ware followed. Under Slater's direction, bone china was developed. Before World War I, Shelley's china dinner services were very popular in the American market.

After the war, Percy's three sons were involved in the firm. By 1922, miniature objects, heraldic and coat of arms, souvenir china and earthenware with engraved views of places of interest, and parian busts of military figures were produced in quantity. During the 1920s, many styles of teawares were made. "Eggshell china" referred to the thinness of the porcelain. Many styles of cups and saucers were made, some having from six to sixteen flutes.

In 1925, the firm's name was changed to Shelley's. Nursery wares decorated by Hilda Cowham and Mabel Lucie Atwell came to the forefront along with "semi-porcelain" domestic china.

The delicate teawares of the 1920s and 1930s established Shelley's reputation. The Queen Anne octagonal shape was one of the best known forms first made in 1926. More than 170 patterns based on about 80 distinct designs were applied to the Queen Anne shape.

More modern shapes such as Vogue and Mode were introduced during the Art Deco period. These shapes were a departure from previous teawares produced by Shelley. The Vogue shape had the wider and shallower teacup and a more definite foot, while the Mode teacup was more upright with a smaller foot. Both were introduced in 1930.

The Eve shape of 1932 had an open triangular handle. 58 patterns were applied to this shape until 1938. The Regent shape from 1932 had a flared trumpet shape cup. This shape continued unto the 1940s and 50s. Percy retired in 1932.

After World War II, earthenwares were discontinued. China dinnerwares remained in production. Lithographic techniques replaced the "print and enamel" decorations.

In 1965, the firm was renamed Shelley China Ltd. It was acquired by Allied English Potteries in 1966. The family connection with the firm finally ended. Allied merged with the Doulton Group in 1971.

References: Susan Hill, *The Shelley Style,* Jazz Publications, Ltd.1990; Chris Watkins, William Harvey, and Robert Senft, *Shelley Potteries,* Barrie & Jenkins, 1980; Muriel Miller, *Collecting Shelley Pottery,* Wallace-Homestead, 1997.

Collectors' Clubs: National Shelley China Club, P.O. Box 580, Chokoloskee, FL 34138, Membership: $25.00, Quarterly newsletter; The Shelley Group, 12 Lilleshall Road, Clayton, Newcastle-Under-Lyme, Staffordshire ST5 3BX, UK, Newsletter.

Ashtray, 3 3/4" d, "Blue Rock" pattern . 30.00

Bowl
   7 1/2" d, orange-yellow sunflower with gray center on int, mint green rim . . . 195.00
   8" d, oct, "Japanese Lake" pattern
   . . . . .350.00

Bud Vase
   5" h, blue and brown bird holding insect in beak, green grape leaves, grapes, and tendrils, gray luster ground, lt blue luster int 95.00
   6" h, ftd, flared body, narrow neck, flared rim, red roses and green leaves, white cascading vines, black ground
   . . . . 150.00

Butter Dish, Cov, 7 1/4" l x 2 1/2" h, rect, "Harmony," orange drip over tan ground. . 125.00

Cake Plate
   9 5/8" H-H
     "Garland of Fruit" pattern 115.00

"Woodland" pattern, multicolored florals and trees, white ground, gilt rim, blue raised handles, "Woodland 13348" mark 90.00
   9 3/4" H-H, "Ideal" pattern, Oxford shape, gray and black trees with yellow trim in landscape scene, yellow rim . . . 65.00

Candleholder
   2" h x 7 1/4" d, wide flat base, blue rings
   . . . . 110.00
   7" h, orange and blue mill scene
   . . . . 225.00

Candy Dish, 5" d, "Dainty White" pattern
   . . . . 25.00

Chop Plate, 13" d, "Castle Green" pattern
   . . . . 149.00

Coffee Pot, 5 1/2" h, "Begonia" pattern, Dainty shape 295.00

Creamer, 2 1/2" h, "Bridal Rose" pattern, 6 flutes 30.00

Creamer and Sugar Bowl
   "Blue Rock" pattern, 6 flutes. 85.00
   "Dainty Blue" pattern, 6 flutes. . . . 115.00
   "Lily of the Valley" pattern, 6 flutes
   . . . . 140.00

Cup and Saucer
   "Balloon Tree" pattern, Queen Anne shape
   . . . . 200.00
   "Begonia" pattern, 6 flutes 55.00
   "Bramble" pattern, Henley shape. . 75.00
   "Bridal Rose" pattern, 6 flutes. . . . 45.00
   "Bute" pattern, 6 flutes 30.00
   "Celandine" pattern, 6 flutes. 65.00
   "Cherries" pattern, #7923. . . . . . . 52.00
   "Cottage-2" pattern, Queen Anne shape
   . . . . 200.00
   "Dainty White" pattern, 6 flutes, gold rims
   . . . . 45.00
   "English Lake" pattern 63.00
   "Harebell" pattern, Oleander shape
   . . . . 65.00
   "Ideal" pattern, Oxford shape, gray and black trees with yellow trim in landscape scene, yellow rims 48.00
   "Japonica" pattern, Regency shape
   . . . . 62.00
   "Lily of the Valley" pattern, 6 flutes
   . . . . 45.00
   "Pansy" pattern, Dainty shape 75.00
   "Rose and Red Daisy" pattern, 6 flutes
   . . . . 45.00
   "Rosebud" pattern, 6 flutes. 45.00
   "Rose Pansey FMN" pattern, 6 flutes
   . . . . 40.00
   "Stocks" pattern, 6 flutes 40.00
   "Sunray" pattern, Vogue shape . . 375.00

Cup and Saucer, Demitasse
   "Blue Rock" pattern 45.00
   "Daffodil Times" 58.00
   "Morning Glory" pattern, 16 flutes . 65.00
   "Rosebud" pattern 50.00
   "Violeto" pattern, 16 flutes 62.00

Creamer, "Bridal Rose" pattern, 6 flutes
   . . . . 30.00

Dish
   4" d, handled, "Rose Spray" pattern
   . . . . 48.00
   4" H-H, "Primrose" pattern, 6 flutes
   . . . . 25.00
   5 3/4" d, "Residence of Tom Moore, The Poet, 1803-4, Bermuda," multicolored
   . . . . 12.00

Figure, 6 1/2" h, "The Bride," "The Groom," sgd "Mabel Lucie Attwell," pr 1,000.00

Marmalade Jar, Cov, 4" h, bulbous shape, "Harmony," orange and burnt orange splash, brown bands, textured surface. 75.00

Plaque, 12" d, faience, Dickens scene, multicolored enamels, "Shelley Foley" mark
   . . . . 195.00

Plate
   6" d, "Harebell" pattern 25.00
   7" d, "Rock Garden" pattern, green rim
   . . . . 60.00
   8" d, "Rose Pansy FMN" pattern, 6 flutes
   . . . . 45.00
   11" d, "Harebell" pattern, Oleander shape
   . . . . 70.00

Platter
   12 1/2" l, "Castle" pattern. 95.00
   13" l, "Dainty Pink" pattern, ribbed border
   . . . . 295.00
   15" l, "Castle" pattern. 125.00
   17" l, "Blue Rock" pattern. 200.00

Tea and Toast, 9 3/4" l, "American Brookline" pattern, 6 flutes 125.00

Tea Plate, 6 1/2" d, "Ideal" pattern, gray and black trees with yellow in landscape scene, yellow rim 22.00

Teapot, 5 1/2" h, mushroom shape, painted cottage, green doors and windows, red handle, spout, and knob, Mabel Lucie Attwell, (A) 215.00

Tea Service, pot, creamer, sugar bowl, 6 cups and saucers, 6 plates, 8" d, "Dainty Blue" pattern, 6 flutes. 695.00

Toast Rack, 2 1/2" h x 7 1/2" l, green and blue bars, green handles, mottled brown base
   . . . . 185.00

Tray, 14" l x 5 1/2" w, "Rambler Rose" pattern
   . . . . 110.00

Trio, Cup, Saucer and Plate
   "Art Deco" pattern, Eve shape. . . . 275.00

Teapot, 5 1/4" h, "Rosebud" pattern, $395.

"Bluebird" pattern, Dainty shape . . 160.00

"Castle" pattern 75.00

"Dainty Blue" pattern 135.00

"Floral" pattern, Dainty shape 395.00

"Hedge Row" pattern 90.00

"Regency" pattern, 6 flutes 50.00

"Sunset and Tall Trees" pattern 59.00

"Woodland" pattern 125.00

Vase

3 1/2" h, wide base, narrow top, "Harmony," orange drip on green and gray ground, irreg striped bands. . . . 110.00

5" h, "Balloons and Flashes" pattern, lustered 325.00

6 1/4" h, corset shape, blue kingfisher bird, orange and blue luster shaded ground 175.00

9" h, green flying exotic bird with black feathers, orange ground, band of black flowerheads on shoulder 225.00

9 1/2" h, cone shape, horiz ribbing, "Harmony," flat gray base, blue to gray shading, blue and white int 185.00

10" h, "Japanese Fruit" pattern, lustered 350.00

Vegetable Bowl, 10" l, oval, "Dainty White" pattern, 6 flutes, gold rim 65.00

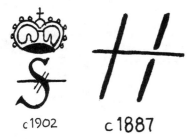

c 1902   c 1887

SITZENDORF

Thuringia, Germany
1845 to Present

History: A small porcelain factory was founded in 1845 in Thuringia. The Voight brothers managed the factory from 1850 until about 1900. They produced decorative figures and porcelains in the Meissen style.

At the turn of the century, the factory was called Alfred Voight AG. Within a few years, the name was changed to Sitzendorf Porcelain Manufactory, its earlier designation. In 1923, earthenware was added.

The company was semi-nationalized in 1957 and completely nationalized in 1972.

Bowl, 11" H-H, 6 1/2" h, int w/yellow and mauve flowers in gold circle and scattered flowers, applied pink, purple, and cream flowerheads, green leaves, gold scrolled feet, purple or red sashes on blond putti, Voight Brothers, (A) $150.

The current name is VEB Sitzendorf Porcelain Manufactory.

Center Bowl, 5" h x 11" d, painted roses and garden flowers in center int, applied polychrome flowers and hanging gilt ribbons on ext, feet as 4 figural cherubs in wearing sashes applied to ext of bowl, shaped gilt rim 550.00

Figure

4 1/2" h, standing boy holding grapes, standing girl holding lamb, polychrome, 20th C, pr, (A) 275.00

6 1/4" h, girl sitting on goat, boy playing instrument, white 650.00

8 1/2" h, polar bear seated on haunches, paws raised, white, black muzzle, eyes, and ear spots 295.00

15" h, bisque, standing period man in pastel clothes with gold trim, holding rosary in hand, standing period woman in pastel clothes, gold waistcoat, pr, . . .450.00

Figure, 13 1/4" h, male wearing magenta jacket, green pants, floral vest, female wearing blue vest, maroon and floral skirt, gold scrolled bases, pr, (A) $345.

SLIPWARE

Staffordshire, England
Continental
17th C to Present

History: Slip was powdered clay that was mixed with water until a cream-like consistency was achieved. The slip then could be used to decorate pottery in a variety of ways such as trailing, marbling, combing, feathering, and sgraffito.

Trailing was decorating by means of extruding slip or glaze through a nozzle onto the surface of the piece.

Marbling was achieved by trailing different colored slips onto a form that is then either shaken or twisted to produce the pattern.

Combing was done by applying slip and then wiping over the piece with a toothed or pronged instrument or by using the fingers.

Feathering occurred by trailing a line of slip onto a wet ground of a contrasting color. The tip of a feather or another flexible, thin point was then drawn back and forth across the trailed line.

Sgraffito was achieved by cutting, incising, or scratching away a slip coating to reveal the contrasting slip or body underneath.

Colored slips were made by adding a small amount of various oxides to the slip. Slip was an early method to embellish ordinary clay-colored pottery. After the slip decorations were done, the vessel was covered with a lead glaze in order to make it non-porous and to produce a shiny surface. Slip decoration was used from the 17th century until the present time.

Slipware was made mainly at Wrotham in Kent in Staffordshire. Other manufacturing centers included Essex, Sussex, Somerset, and Devonshire. The earliest piece from Wrotham was dated 1612.

Between 1670 and 1710, the most spectacular pieces of slipware made in Staffordshire were large chargers made by the Tofts, John and William Wright, George Taylor, William Taylor, and Ralph Simpson. Favorite subjects included royal scenes, portraits of popular figures, and cavaliers. Coats of arms, mermaids, Adam & Eve, and the Pelican in her piety were used. Borders usually had a trellis pattern. Human figures had minimal anatomical details and were painted in a naive fashion. Forms that were slip decorated included tygs, teapots, cradles, baking dishes, puzzle jugs, posset pots, whistles, etc.

Potteries in Devon made large harvest jugs using the sgraffito technique. Decorations included coats of arms, lions, unicorns, ships, mariners' compasses, and floral designs.

Wrotham slip decorated wares continued to be made until the end of the 18th century. Fleur-de-lys, roses, crosses, stars, and masks were frequent motifs. Tygs, posset pots, two-handled mugs and candlesticks were made. A distinctive feature of Wrotham ware was handles made by weaving different colored clays together.

Reference: R.G. Cooper, *English Slipware Dishes 1650-1850,* Tiranti, 1968.

Museums: Colonial Williamsburg Foundation, Williamsburg, VA; County Museum, Truro, England; Gardiner Museum of Ceramic Art, Toronto, Canada; Kansas City Art Museum, Kansas City, MO; Plymouth City Museum, Plymouth, England; Royal Albert Museum, Exeter, England; Sheffield City Museum, Sheffield, England.

Bowl, 8 1/2" d

White dots, red flowerheads with white petals and green leaves, red and white dot clusters on border, med blue ground, Germany 85.00

Yellow slip design of "LUCIA" and geometric dots, ribbons and dots on inner border, redware body, (A) 72.00

Bread Tray, 15 1/4" l x 12" w, rect, combed cream slip, raised sides, Staffordshire, 19th C 250.00

Dish

12" l x 9" w, rect, divided, graduated white slip squiggles, redware body, (A)
. . . . 50.00

13" d, reverse decorated cream flowing squiggles, redware body, 18th C, England 3,800.00

Hot Water Jug, Cov, 5 1/2" h, applied white slip birds, leaves, and flowerheads on glazed redware ground, beak spout, scroll handle, domed cov with acorn knob, c1740, (A)
. . . . 2,760.00

Loaf Dish, 16" l, tan, white, and brown comb pattern, England, late 18th C 1,650.00

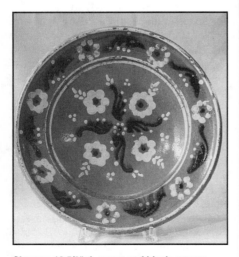

Charger, 13 5/8" d, cream and black, orange ground, France, c1870, $650.

Mug, 2 5/8" h, brown slip dots between brown slip lines, flat loop handle, chips, Staffordshire, c1700, (A) 2,070.00

Pitcher

5 3/4" h, cream slip vert zigzag lines with cream dots interspersed, burnt orange ground, France 295.00

7 1/4" h, black, green, and dk brown streaked slip designs on orange ground, yellow int, France, c1875
. . . . 195.00

Plate

5 5/8" d, redware, purple flowed slip, yellow slip ground, Continental, (A) 45.00

11" d, redware, white slip with blue glaze and sgraffito grapes and tulips and "1796," (A) 440.00

Pot

5 7/8" h, redware, rolled top, banded body, tooled handle, white slip curlicues and dots 750.00

12" h, redware body with cream lines and dashes, dtd "1873" in cream glaze, England 450.00

Puzzle Jug, 7 1/2" h, earthenware, yellow geometric slip design, pierced neck, inscribed "Gentlemen now try your skill. I'll hold your sixpence if you will. That you don't drink unless you spill," England, (A) 50.00

Teapot, 3" h, creamware, drum shape, vert fluting with brown slip vert bars, twist handle, c1780, (A) 863.00

SOFT PASTE

English/Continental 17th to 19th Centuries

History: Soft paste, or artificial porcelain, was made during the 17th and 18th centuries in Europe by using glass or a glass substitute that was ground up and mixed with clay. Over the years, the ingredients of soft paste varied.

The glaze was added in the second firing. This glaze was soft. It scratched and chipped easily. If the potter was careless, the glaze could wilt in the kiln and become uneven. The soft paste process was abandoned gradually during the early 19th century when the formula for hard paste porcelain became better understood.

Soft paste porcelain had the translucency of hard paste. It simply was softer and more porous. Since the melting temperatures of soft paste glazes and the colored enamels were similar, the overglaze enamel sank into the glaze and softened the outline of painted decoration. Essentially pigment and surface were melded together.

Soft paste was made in France at Rouen, St. Cloud, Chantilly, Mennecy, Vincennes, and Sevres. English factories making soft paste included Chelsea, Bow, Derby, Worcester, and Liverpool. Most European countries produced soft paste porcelain before switching to hard paste porcelain production.

Sugar Bowl, 8" H-H, 7" h, yellow centered mauve flowers, green leaves, purple stems, scattered small blue flowers, $75.

Cup and Saucer, red, blue, green, and purple flower design, unmkd, early 1800s 80.00

Cup and Saucer, Demitasse, cobalt and red swag design 45.00

Cup and Saucer, Handleless

Paneled, transfer of rose red flower with green leaves, blue ground. 85.00

Yellow and orange-brown flowers flanked by green and yellow leaves, cobalt band and scattered dot design, "imp Joseph Stubbs, Longport" mark, (A)
. . . . 495.00

Egg Cup, 4" h, yellow band on border with blue stripe and compartments with red flowerhead, hanging red flowerheads and blue dots below border, unmkd 185.00

Figure

7 1/4" h, standing peasant woman playing mandolin, blanc de chine, Germany, early 19th C, (A) 1,300.00

8" h, lady with outstretched hand, dog at side, blanc de chine, Germany, chips, (A) 1,400.00

Plate

7 3/8" d, multicolored transfer of farm house and trees in center, relief of yellow, magenta, and purple flowerheads and green and red dash leaves, dk red lined rim 135.00

8 1/2" d, rust, and green stenciled flowerhead in center, rust, green, and yellow insects and birds on raised border, shaped rim, England, early 19th C
. . . . 165.00

Platter, 15" l, rect, HP underglazed Adam's Rose style red flowerhead and green leaves in center, band of flowerheads and leaves on border 435.00

Teapot

6 1/2" h, oblong shape, band of mauve flowerheads, green and yellow leaves, mauve tendrils 65.00

8" h, sm red dot flowerheads with green dot centers, lt green leaves 135.00

EARLY 19ᵀᴴ CENTURY

1760-1804

SPAIN-GENERAL

Alcora, Province of Valencia
1726-1858

History: Count Aranda, assisted by Joseph Olerys of Moustiers and other French workers, established a faience factory in 1726. The original success of this factory was due to the skill of the French painters and the use of French models. The tin-glazed pottery that it produced was quite popular throughout Spain.

By 1737, all the workers were Spanish. Biblical or mythological scenes on large dishes or plaques were among its best pieces. The Count died in 1749. His son took over. A succession of Dukes of Hija owned the factory. When the factory was acquired by private owners, Francois Martin started to produce hard paste porcelain in imitation of Wedgwood's creamware in 1858.

Buen Retiro, near Madrid
1760-1812

King Charles III of Spain established Buen Retiro, near Madrid, using workers from Capodimonte in 1760. Soft paste porcelains were manufactured into services, tea sets, vases, bowls, and figures similar to Capodimonte wares. The factory also specialized in the porcelain tiles that were used to decorate palaces.

By the end of the 18th century, biscuit groups in the Sevres styles and medallions and plaques in the Wedgwood style were made. From 1765 until 1790 Giuseppe Gricci was the chief modeler. After his death, Spanish artists influenced the decorations.

Only hard paste wares were made at Buen Retiro after 1800. In 1808, the factory was transformed into a fortress that was destroyed by Wellington in 1812. In 1817, the factory was rebuilt at Moncloa in Madrid and remained in operation until 1850.

Hispano-Moresque, Valencia & Malaga
End of 13th Century to Present

Hispano-Moresque was white enamel, tin-glazed earthenware that was usually decorated with copper or silver metallic lusters. Moorish potters came to Spain, settled in Valencia, Manises, and Paterna, and made their lustered pottery.

Early luster colors were pale and filmy. Later pieces utilized a golden luster and deeper blue tones. As time progressed, the luster became more brassy and metallic in appearance.

Hispano-Moresque flourished for about 300 years. By the end of the 16th century, there was a steady decline, but the technique still continues today in Valencia.

All sorts of vases, drug pots, pitchers, covered bowls, large dishes, and wall tiles are made.

Talavera
15th Century to Present

Talavera pottery was decorated in a peasant-like style with birds, animals, or busts in a blue and dusty-orange motif outlined in purplish-black. Talavera wares were popular with all levels of Spanish society into the 17th century. Monastic coats of arms and the cardinal's hat were decorated in yellow, orange, and green. Shapes included large bowls and two handled jugs featuring sporting scenes, bullfights, buildings, trees, figures, and animals.

During the mid-18th century, Talavera adopted the styles used at Alcora which had copied the French style of Moustiers. Today only ordinary earthenwares are made.

Reference: Alice Wilson Frothingham, *Tile Panels of Spain: 1500-1650,* Hispanic Society of America, 1969.

Museums: Cleveland Museum of Art, Cleveland, OH; Hispanic Society of America, New York, NY; Musee Nationale de Ceramique, Sevres, France; Museo Arquelogical Nacional, Madrid, Spain; Seattle Art Museum, Seattle, WA; Victoria & Albert Museum, London, England.

Albarello, 5 3/8" h, waisted shape, majolica, blue painted arms over banner and scrolls, white ground, Talavera, early 18th C, crack and chips, (A) 500.00

Bowl

8 7/8" d, ftd, blue ground, gilt exotic bird in scrollwork medallion, border gilt with 5 griffins in silver shaped panels, Daniel Zoluaga, Segovia, set of 5 ... 1,500.00

12 1/4" d, majolica, yellow, green, and brown magpie on branch in center, band of foliage on border, pierced for hanging, c1780, rim chips, (A) 462.00

Candlestick, 10 3/4" h, bell shaped base, tin glazed, blue and white geometrics on base, scrolling on shaft, vert lines on nozzle, 18th C, (A) 55.00

Pitcher, 6" h, red and green florals, med brown bands, "imp Made in Spain" mark, $15.

Charger

15 1/2" d, Hispano-Moresque, copper lustered, central boss, overall lustered with doves and stylized vines, border with 3 blue stylized doves, reverse with conc bands of copper luster squiggles, (A) 345.00

16 7/8" d, Hispano-Moresque, center star design, fruit in rope framed panels, blue glazed and copper luster, 19th C, (A) 633.00

Dish, 13 3/8" d, pierced body, blue painted circ reserves of classical figures, 4 reserves of putti in scroll borders, Savona, early 18th C, restored, (A) 585.00

Drug Jar, 16 1/2" h, Hispano-Moresque, pink and copper luster overall foliate designs, 2 spouts on sides, (A) 288.00

Mug, Tin Glazed

2 3/4" h, blue-green circle flowerheads on black stems, red and green dash leaves, dbl stripes top and base, blue rim, c1800 .... 85.00

3 1/2" h, center band of stylized blue and green outlined yellow flowerheads, 2 orange stripes, 2 brown stripes, 2 yellow stripes, blue dash handle, c1800 .... 125.00

Pitcher, 5 7/8"h, 2 mauve stylized flowerheads, dk green and olive green stylized leaves on center band, black outlined brown bands, green stripe on handle 25.00

Vase, 7" h, 2 handles, compressed globular shape with hexafoil gadrooned neck, blue and white painted panels of stylized florals or foliate panels, Savona, late 17th C, (A) 695.00

SPATTERWARE

Staffordshire, England
c1800-1850s

Design

History: In design spatter there were small, shaped areas of spots or dots instead of large continuous overall spattered areas. Some design spatter was done with a stencil or template. Design spatter also was referred to as "structural spatter."

Colors used for design spatter were red, blue, green, and purple. Spatter techniques were combined with hand-painted decoration motifs. Decorative center motifs included: Adams Rose, Columbine, Dogwood, and Pansy.

Known makers of design spatter were: T.W. Barlow, Elsmore and Forster, and Harvey.

General

History: Spatterware was a decoration that appeared on a variety of body compositions including soft paste, creamware, pearlware, and ironstone. It appealed to "popular" tastes because of its inexpensive price and its cheery, colorful, and bright appearance. It was made primarily for export.

Spatter was a stippling or all-over design of color. One or more colors could be used. The color was applied in parallel stripes or concentric bands leaving a center of white for decoration. With spatter as a border, the center design could be either hand painted or transfer printed.

There were eight basic colors used for spatter: black, blue (the most common), brown, green, pink, purple, red, and yellow (the rarest). Most popular patterns were: Cannon, Castle, Peafowl, Pomegrante, Schoolhouse, and Thistle.

Few pieces of true spatter bore identifying manufacturer's marks. Among the known makers of spatter are: Adams, Cotton and Barlow, Harvey, and J.& G. Meakin.

References: Kevin McConnell, *Spongeware and Spatterware*, Schiffer Publishing Co. 1990; Carl F. & Ada F. Robacker, *Spatterware and Sponge*, A.S. Barnes & Co. 1978.

Museum: Henry Ford Museum, Dearborn, MI.

Reproduction Alert: "Cybis" spatter is an increasingly collectible ware made by Boleslow Cybis of Poland. The design utilized the Adams type peafowl and was made in the 1940s. Some pieces were marked "Cybis" in an impressed mark; some examples were unmarked. The principal shape was cup plates. The body of

the ware was harder than true spatter, and the glaze appeared glassy rather than soft. Many contemporary craftsmen also are reproducing spatterware examples.

Design

Bowl

5 7/8" d, ftd, painted red floral design with green and blue leaves and blue spatter florets on ext, red stripe on ext and rim, "Baker & Co., Made in England" mark, (A) 95.00

6 3/4" d, red and blue florets, black vines with green leaves on ext, red line on int rim, "Staffordshire, England" mark, (A) 95.00

10" d, conc brown circle in center, blue flowerheads, red and green fruit 135.00

10 1/2" d, inner band of red and green flowerheads and leaves, green int border 375.00

11" d, red and green flowers in center, green and red zigzag border . . . 75.00

13 1/2" d, lg HP flower with purple buds, green leaves and purple stems on int center in red band, red and purple painted swags with green design florets, border of design blue circles with red line through center, red stripes on rim and int, (A) 230.00

Charger, 13" d, group of red design spatter flowerheads in center, inner green band, lg painted red and green leaves and blue design spatter flowerheads, border of blue design spatter flowerheads 285.00

Coffeepot, 8 5/8" h, alternating red and green spatter holly sprigs on black stem, band of red spatter pussy willows on sides with lt blue stripes, rim, base, and spout with lt blue stripes, domed cov with onion shaped knob, (A). 400.00

Creamer, 3 1/2" h, bulbous base, lt and dk green vert ferns on throat, red striped rim, (A). 100.00

Cup and Saucer, Handleless

Band of green stylized design leaves with brown flowerheads, green striped rims, (A) 70.00

Blue, green, and black overall starflower design, (A) 880.00

"Camellia" pattern, red design flowerheads with green leaves, lt green striped rims, (A) 80.00

Red cornflower, green and blue foliage, red design spatter stylized flowerheads, blue lined rims, (A) 715.00

Miniature

Band of black leaves on green ground, polychrome sprig on saucer center, (A). 60.00

Blue florets on black stems with green and yellow leaves on saucer border and center band of cup, unmkd, (A) 25.00

Cup and Saucer, Handleless, ironstone, blue and red flowerheads, green leaves, "W.E. Oulsnau & Sons, Burslem" mark, (A) $25.

Red band of diamonds and dots and triangles on rim, lt green geometric band around middle, hairline, (A) 85.00

Mug, 2 5/8" h, ironstone, red, green, blue, and black wavy lines and dots, (A) 75.00

Plate

5 1/4" d, 2 bands of green daisies with purple centers, unmkd, (A) 250.00

6 5/8" d, purple columbine with red bud, green leaves, sm blue flowers in center, band of green centerless daisies on border, red stripe rim, unmkd, (A) 140.00

8 1/4" d, "Virginia" pattern, border band of HP purple, red, and green flowers with blue design florets, repairs, pr, (A) 115.00

8 1/2" d

Central purple columbine with red buds and blue lily of the valley, band of green daisies on border, dk red lined rim, (A) 200.00

Red, green, blue, and black painted cabbage rose and leaves in center, band of blue design leaf decoration between 2 red lines on border, (A) 275.00

8 5/8" d, red design leaf pattern on border alternating with yellow and green design florets, green striped int and ext rim, (A) 23.00

8 3/4" d, border with red star shaped design flowers and green leaves on blue stems, blue spatter rim, red lined edge and inner border, (A) 170.00

8 5/8" d, center and border band of red and green holly, (A) 22.00

8 7/8" d, center starburst design, scattered flowerheads, border of stiff leaves, red, green, and blue, "Auld Heather Ware" mark, (A) 72.00

Plate, 9 1/2" d, dk blue, dk red flowers and leaves, small green leaves, blue design spatter flowerheads, border of black rabbits on yellow-brown ground, red lined rim, $495.

Waste Bowl, 5 3/4" d, blue and red flowerheads, green leaves, "BB anchor, Royal Arms" mark, $50.

9 1/8" d

Border band of HP red flowers, green leaves, black stems, and blue design florets, red striped rim, "Made in England" mark, pr, (A) . . . 100.00

"Rabbit Ware," 3 rabbits sitting in field, brown transfer with yellow accents, border with blue design camellias, HP blue and red flowers, green design stars, blue int stripe, red line rim, (A) 340.00

9 1/2" d, group of red centered green design flowerheads in center, band of red centered green design flowerheads on border, set of 8, (A) 660.00

9 5/8" d, 10 sides, central pink flower outlined in black with green center and leaves, band of green bowknots on border, red lined rim, (A) 325.00

9 3/4" d

Four stylized red and yellow flowerheads, swirling green leaves, black stems, band of black diamonds on yellow-brown border, dk red rim
. . . . 225.00

Twelve sides, purple, red, green, and blue painted flower and foliage in center, green design spatter buckle pattern on border, blue inner and outer lines 510.00

9 7/8" d

Black lined pansy with purple and yellow petals, green leaves, black stem in center, band of blue bowknots on border, red line rim and inner border, chip under rim, (A) 400.00

Purple, green, blue, red, and black columbine in center, red design spatter loops on border, blue stripes, (A)
. . . . 275.00

Red painted flower with black stem and green leaves, border of dbl blue design loops, red striped rim, "imp

Cotton and Barlow" mark, (A)
. . . . 220.00

Platter

12 1/4" l, oval, 4 lg dk red flowerheads with scattered blue flowerheads and green leaves, dk red conch shells on border, yellow-gold rim 92.00

12 3/8" l, rect with clipped corners, green, purple, red, blue, and black painted columbine in center, border of red design circles, (A) 550.00

13 5/8" l, rect with cut corners, band of green leaves on int, red holly berries and green leaves on border, blue line rim 495.00

Soup Bowl, 8 3/4" d, 3 plums in center, dk blue flowerheads, green leaves, dk red line rim, Maastricht 55.00

Soup Plate

8 3/4" d, 5 sm design red florets with green leaves, black stems in center, blue spatter rim, (A) 130.00

9 3/8" d, group of stylized yellow-centered purple flowerheads in center, band of yellow-centered purple flower heads on border, (A) 190.00

9 5/8" d, border band of yellow rings with green florets in center, red striping, (A) 45.00

10 1/2" d, painted green, purple, red, blue, and black columbine in center, band of red design star-like flowerheads on border, (A) 330.00

Teabowl and Saucer, maroon and tan flowerhead, green leaves, red flowerheads on borders, blue lined rims 215.00

Teapot, 5 3/8" h, band of red flowers and leaves on body and cov, red striped ft and cov rim, (A) 225.00

Vase, 9" h, urn shape, bands of blue and red leaf designs, band of green flowers, black horiz lines, (A) 690.00

Vegetable Bowl, 9 5/8" l x 7 3/4" w, rect, red holly pattern, green leaves, blue striping, (A)
. . . . 240.00

Vegetable Bowl, Cov, 10 3/8" H-H, lg yellow centered flowers, blue leaves and stems, green leaves on cov, border bands of design

interlocking black rings on maroon ground, figural lion knob 350.00

General

Bowl

5 3/4" d, blue, orange, and black Peafowl design, green spatter foliage on reverse and int, black int rim stripe, white ground, (A) 850.00

12 1/2" d, everted rim, ftd, blue and purple Rainbow spatter, hairlines 215.00

Coffeepot, 8" h, red, blue, and green Peafowl on green ground design, red spatter body, repairs 1,050.00

Creamer

3 1/2" h, molded foliate top and base, red and green Cockscomb design, blue spatter ground, (A) 575.00

4 1/2" h

Band of blue spatter around shoulder and rim, arched handle with molded foliate design, (A) 45.00

Blue, green, red, and black Peafowl, design, red spatter rim, leaf handle, repairs, (A) 330.00

Yellow, blue, red and black Rooster design, blue spatter rim, chips and hairline, (A) 550.00

4 3/8" h, bulbous body, arched handle

Adam's Rose type flower under spout on wide blue spatter band, blue spatter rim, ft, and handle, unmkd, (A) 450.00

Red, blue, and green Dahlia design, red spatter body, (A) 450.00

5 5/8" h, oct, scrolled handle, scalloped rim, red, white, and blue Profile Tulip design, purple spatter ground, unmkd, (A) 1,500.00

6" h, paneled, blue and red Rainbow design, repairs and hairlines, (A)
. . . . 220.00

Cup and Saucer

Handleless

Black, blue, green, and red Peafowl design, green spatter ground, (A)
. . . . 412.00

Blue, green, red, and black Tulip design, blue spatter ground, (A)
. . . . 440.00

Brown, black, and red Fort design, green ground with spatter trees, blue spatter ground, hairlines, (A)
. . . . 75.00

Dk blue 8-pointed star, red spatter borders, (A) 375.00

Green, ochre, and red 6-pointed star design, blue spatter ground
. . . . 275.00

Green, red, and black Rose design, blue spatter ground, (A) 605.00

Ochre, blue, green, and black Peafowl design, red spatter ground, repair to cup, (A) 165.00

Purple and blue crisscross Rainbow design, (A) 1,980.00

Purple spatter body on cup, rim of saucer, dk red center dot in saucer and int of cup, (A) 700.00

Purple and black Rainbow design, black spatter band with purple center in saucer and cup int, (A) 1,075.00

Red and green Thistle design
  Red and yellow vert spatter, (A) 4,300.00
  Yellow spatter ground, (A) 605.00
  Red, blue, and green Rainbow design, "imp Adams" mark, (A). 495.00
  Violet, green, red, and black Peafowl design, blue spatter ground, (A) 165.00
  Yellow, blue, and red Peafowl design, red spatter ground, (A) . . .1,350.00

Miniature
  Adam's Rose type design on front and saucer, blue spatter band and saucer border, (A) 400.00
  Green, purple, yellow, and black Loop design, (A) 5,720.00
  Red and blue Rainbow spatter design, (A). 225.00

Milk Pitcher, 7 3/8" h, red, yellow, blue, black, and green Rainbow spatter design, scrolled handle, molded shell under spout, scalloped rim, cracks, (A) 2,200.00

Nappy, 8 1/4" d, red, blue, and green Peafowl design, red spatter ground, "imp Adams" mark 675.00

Pepper Pot, 5 1/8" h, purple and blue Rainbow design, (A). 5,500.00

Pitcher
  6 1/2" h, paneled, red and blue vert Rainbow spatter 1,155.00
  6 3/4" h, paneled, red, blue, green, and black Tulip design, blue spatter ground, hairlines on rim and handle, (A) 825.00
  10 1/2" h, red, green, yellow, black, and blue Rainbow design, emb scroll pattern on spout, (A). 14,850.00

Plate, 8 1/4" d, blue, yellow, green, and black Peafowl design, red spatter border, unmkd, (A) $460.

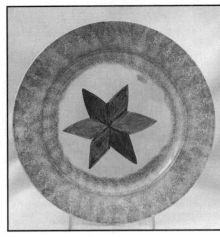

Plate, 9 1/2" d, blue, green, and dk red star, blue spatter border, $375.

Plate
  5 1/8" d, Wigwam design
    Brown spatter, plain rim, (A) . . 625.00
    Purple spatter, scalloped rim, (A) 330.00
  5 1/4" d, 12 sides, red, blue, and green Dahlia design, red spatter border, (A) 1,100.00
  6" d, Adam's Rose type flower in center, red, blue, and green conc banded Rainbow spatter border, "imp Adams 6" mark, (A) 300.00
  6 1/16" d, red and blue Rainbow spatter, rim chip, (A) 275.00
  6 1/8" d, blue, green, and red Peafowl design, green spatter ground, (A) . .400.00
  6 1/4" d, green, blue, and orange Peafowl design, red spatter ground. . . . 375.00
  6 3/8" d, blue, black, and green Morning Glory design, yellow spatter border, (A) 605.00
  6 1/2" d, red, yellow, and green Guinea Hen design, black comb and feet, green ground, blue spatter border, unmkd, (A) 900.00
  6 5/8" d, red, blue, green, and black Pomegranate design, blue spatter border, "imp Meakin" mark, hairline, (A) 825.00
  7" d, eagle and shield in center, blue transfer blue spatter border, paneled border, (A) 330.00
  8" d, 10 sides, purple, green, and black flower, blue spatter rim, chip on rim 95.00
  8 1/8" d
    Adam's Rose type design in center, blue and green variegated spatter border, (A). 275.00
    Brown acorns in center, purple spatter border, hairlines, (A) 425.00
    Purple and brown Rainbow spatter, repaired rim, (A) 180.00
  8 1/4" d, red and green Thistle design, blue spatter border, (A) 770.00

8 3/8" d
  Blue, red, and green Dahlia design, red and blue Rainbow spatter border, shaped rim, (A) 715.00
  Purple and blue Rainbow spatter, (A). 575.00
  Red Schoolhouse design on green spatter ground with green spatter tree and brown trunk, blue spatter border, (A) 2,800.00
  Yellow, blue, red, green, and black Tulip design, red spatter border, (A). 358.00

8 1/2" d
  Green, yellow, and red Peafowl design, blue spatter ground, (A). . . . 575.00
  Red Schoolhouse design on green and brown ground with green and brown spatter trees, red spatter border, (A). 1,800.00

8 5/8" d
  Red and yellow Profile Tulip design with green leaves and black stem, blue spatter border, "imp Cotton and Barlow" mark, (A) 350.00
  Red Wigwam spatter design, plain rim, unmkd, (A) 300.00

8 3/4" d, red, blue, green, and black Peafowl design, blue spatter ground, "imp Adams" mark, hairlines, (A) 330.00

9 1/4" d, lt blue, green, ochre, and black Peafowl design, red spatter ground, chip on ft rim, (A) 495.00

9 3/8" d
  Twelve sides
    Brown acorns with green caps and lt green leaves, blue spatter border, (A) 675.00
    Red, white, and blue Profile Tulip design, green leaves and black stems, blue spatter border, (A) 600.00
    Yellow, red, and black Peafowl design, green spatter rim, hairlines, (A) 450.00

9 1/2" d
  Blue "Target" pattern, conc bands of blue spatter 385.00
  Green, red, and black Adam's Rose design, blue and green Rainbow spatter border, hairline, (A) 660.00

9 5/8" d
  Brown, dk brown, and red Fort design with green trees and ground and brown accents, blue spatter ground, (A). 330.00
  Molded rim, blue, red, green, and black Peafowl design, blue spatter border, (A) 385.00
  Red and yellow Christmas Ball design, green spatter swag border, (A) 2,600.00

11" d, red, ochre, green, and black Peafowl design, blue spatter border, chips, (A) 578.00

Platter

10 1/2" l, blue transfer of fruits and berries in center, blue spatter border . . 245.00

13" l, horses and men in center, red transfer, blue spatter border 300.00

13 1/2" l x 10 1/2" w, blue "Peacock at Fountain" transfer, blue spatter border, (A) 250.00

14 1/2" l, blue eagle and shield transfer, blue spatter border, (A) 75.00

15 3/4" l, rect with cut corners, green, yellow, blue, and black Peafowl design, red spatter ground, (A) 962.00

16 1/8" l x 12 5/8" w, pink "Peacock at Fountain" transfer, blue spatter border, (A) 250.00

17 11/16" l x 13 3/4" w, brown eagle and shield transfer, blue spatter border, (A) 525.00

17 3/4" l x 14" w, oct, blue and purple egg shape spatter in center, blue and purple spatter border, (A) 2,310.00

Sauce Bowl, 5 1/4" d, paneled, black, green, and red Peafowl design, green and black foliage, blue spatter border, (A) 605.00

Sauce Dish, 5" d, red, yellow, green, and black Tulip design, green spatter border, "imp Davenport and anchor" mark, (A) 605.00

Soup Plate

9 3/8" d

Red, blue, green, and black Dahlia design, purple spatter border, shaped rim, repaired, (A) 275.00

Teal green, red, black, and blue Rose design, red spatter border, "imp N" mark, (A) 660.00

10" d, purple, green, red, and black Peafowl design, blue spatter border, (A) 1,375.00

10 3/4" d, red and green Tulip design, red and blue spatter border, "imp Cotton and Barlow" mark, (A) 1,320.00

Sugar Bowl

4" h, red Cluster of Buds design with green leaves, green spatter body, button knob, chips, (A) 325.00

4 3/8" h

Red, blue, green, and black Peafowl design, green spatter ground, chips, (A) 220.00

Two red Memorial Tulips with green leaves and black stems, blue spatter rims, hairlines, (A) 140.00

4 5/8" h, blue, green, red, and black Peafowl design, blue spatter ground, repairs, (A) 330.00

5" h, Fort design, blue spatter body an cov, (A) 200.00

6 7/8" h, paneled pagoda shape, green spatter band on center and rim, (A) 138.00

7 7/8" h, oct

Arched handles, domed lid with knob, red Carnation design and green

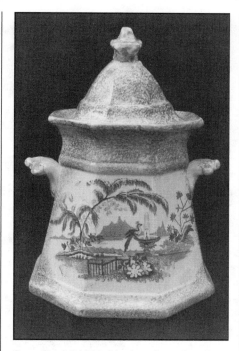

Sugar Bowl, 8 1/4" h, blue transfer, red spatter borders, $250.

leaves, red and yellow Rainbow spatter, chips and hairlines, (A) 2,050.00

Molded scroll handles, domed lid with floral rosette knob, brown and red Castle design with green spatter ground and trees, blue spatter body, repairs and chips, (A) 725.00

8" h, paneled pagoda shape, red and blue Rainbow design, repairs, (A) . . 150.00

Teabowl and Saucer

Blue, ochre, green, and black Peafowl design, red spatter ground, (A) . . 550.00

Purple 8-pointed star, brown spatter rims, hairlines, (A) 280.00

Teapot

5 1/2" h, squat shape, red, black, and green Adam's Rose design, blue spatter bands, flower knob, (A) . . . 1,485.00

5 3/4" h, squat shape, red and blue windmill, purple spatter bands, flowerhead knob, emb leaf handle, spout repair, (A) 2,750.00

6" h, blue, red, and purple spatter, (A) 100.00

6 1/4" h, blue, black, and yellow Morning Glory design, green spatter ground, chips, cracks, (A) 495.00

10 1/2" l, globular shape, red, blue, and yellow Peafowl design, blue spatter ground, button knob 250.00

Toddy Plate

5" d, blue and purple tulip, green and black foliage, blue spatter border, (A) 550.00

6 1/4" d, overall green spatter 125.00

Tureen, Cov, 8" h x 9 1/4" d, oct, black, red, and yellow castle, green spatter trees, overall blue spatter, base crack, (A) 4,600.00

Vegetable Bowl, Cov

10 1/8 sq, oct, ftd, 3 blue, green, and red peafowls, overall red spatter, rosette knob, (A) 4,400.00

10 1/4" sq, oct, ftd, band of design spatter red holly berries, green leaves, and black stems on cov and int of base, blue spatter borders, shell knob, (A) 950.00

Waste Bowl

5" d, red, blue, and green Dahlia design, red spatter ground, hairline, (A) 275.00

5 1/2" d, red, green, and blue Rainbow spatter, "imp A" mark, (A) 625.00

6 1/2" d, blue, green, red, and black Peafowl design, blue spatter ground, stains, (A) 1,100.00

SPODE

Shelton, Staffordshire, England c1797-1833

History: Spode was best known for two important contributions to the ceramic repertoire: the perfection of under the glaze transfer printing on earthenware and the introduction of the bone china formula. Josiah Spode I benefited from a five-year apprenticeship with Thomas Whieldon. By 1770, he was an established master potter at Stoke-on-Trent at the factory where his successors continue today. Josiah Spode II, 1755 to 1827, opened a showroom and warehouse in the City of London in 1778.

The perfection of transfer printing in blue under the glaze on earthenware enabled Spode to copy, at reasonable prices, Chinese blue painted porcelain. These new examples provided replacements and additions for services that had become increasingly difficult to obtain from Chinese sources.

Earlier English porcelain manufacturers had failed to make large dinner plates and platters with straight enough edges to be commercially saleable. By July 1796, Spode was selling dinnerware that he called "English China" at prices well below those of his established competitors. By 1800, a bone china porcelain containing up to forty percent calcined ox bone had emerged. The credit for perfecting this formula was shared jointly by the two Spodes. Josiah I developed the initial formula, and Josiah II refined it. Josiah Spode II marketed products made with the new formula with such success that within ten years bone china became standard English china.

Josiah II's successful promotion of bone china was achieved in part through the on-glaze decorating of Henry Daniel. The engraving techniques improved greatly. The zenith was reached in 1816 when, two years after the Tower pattern appeared, the pattern Blue Italian was introduced. Both patterns remain popular to the present day.

In 1813, Spode, responding to the demand for replacement pieces for polychrome Chinese porcelain services, adopted a stone china formula that was patented by J&W Turner in 1800. Turner's formula provided a superior body on which to decorate the more costly painted and gilded patterns. The body also matched the delicate gray color of the original Chinese porcelain. Over the years the formula was improved further and appears in today's market as Spode's Fine Stone China.

When Josiah II moved to Stoke in 1797 upon the death of his father, he left the management of the London business in the hands of William Copeland, who began his employment with Spode in 1784. Copeland worked with Spode as an equal partner. When Spode retired in 1812, Copeland assumed sole charge of the London house. His business acumen, augmented with the help of W.T. Copeland, his son, in 1824, contributed immensely to the success of the Spode enterprise.

(See: Copeland-Spode for a continuation of the company's history.)

References: Robert Copeland, *Spode & Copeland Marks,* Cassell Academic, 1993; Robert Copeland, *Spode's Willow Pattern & Other Designs After the Chinese*, Blanford Press, 1990; D. Drakard & P. Holdway, *Spode Printed* Wares, Longmans, 1983; Arthur Hayden, *Spode & His Successors*, Cassell, 1925; Leonard Whiter, *Spode:* A *History* of the *Family, Factory & Wares, 1733-1833,* Random Century, 1989; Sydney B. Williams, *Antique Blue & White Spode,* David & Charles, 1988.

Museums: Cincinnati Art Museum, Cincinnati, OH; City of Stoke-on-Trent Museum, Hanley, England; Jones Museum of Glass & Ceramics, Sebago, ME; Spode Museum, Stoke-on-Trent, UK; Victoria & Albert Museum, London, England.

Collectors' Note: Although there is no collectors' club, inquiries about Spode factory wares may be sent to: Historical Consultant, Spode, Stoke-on-Trent, ST4 IBX, England. All inquiries should contain good,

Dessert Service, Part, 2 biscuit bowls, 10 3/4" l, reticulated fruit basket, 6 plates, 8" d, reticulated cake plate, iron red and blue exotic bird, red and mauve flowers, olive green ground, gilt trim, "imp Spode" marks, c1810, $1,900.

clear photographs and full details on the marks.

Bottle, 9 1/4" h, pear shape, 2 molded ribs on neck, dk blue ground with enameled and gilt scattered sprigs, c1820-30, (A) 262.00

Charger, 13 1/2" d, red and blue enameled Imari style Chinese motif of vase and scroll in garden, floral border, gilt accents, New Stone China, c1810 . . . . 546.00

Creamer, 5 1/2" l, underglaze blue and polychrome floral design, gilt accents, "1645 Spode" mark, (A) 121.00

Dessert Service, Part

Two cov fruit coolers, 12" d, compote, 13 3/4" w, ftd, oval, cov sauce tureen, with stand, 9 1/2" w, dish, 11" w, lozenge shape, dish, 8 5/8" sq, 7 plates, 9 7/8" d, painted bird in landscape, green borders with painted birds in oval gilt cartouches, beaded and egg and dart lines, birds named on reverse, c1810, (A) 5,520.00

Two cov sauce tureens, 7 1/4" l, 3 oval dishes, 10 5/8" w, shell shaped dish, 9 1/2" l, lozenge shaped dish, 10 7/8" l, 16 plates, 8 1/2" d, black painted birds named on reverse in iron red landscape, scattered black and iron red feathers, gilt rims with X's and dots, pattern #1746, c1815, cracks and chips, (A) 2,300.00

Dish

9 1/4" H-H, oriental style yellow, dk red, and blue flowers from green outlined brown tree branch, open red and gray flowerheads and green branches on border, pattern #2861, c1800

. . . . 390.00

9 1/2" l, brown outlined molded single handle, mauve peonies, blue-green leaves, green stems, molded panel border with mauve and red outlined blue flowerheads on gray circled ground, c1820, pr. 345.00

Flower Pot, 5" h, HP panel of garden flowers, striped body, gilt sea serpent handle, rim, and paw feet, pr, (A) 2,185.00

Fruit Basket, 9 1/4" H-H, with undertray, pierced, blue transfer and enameled decorated oriental floral motif, (A). 575.00

Plate

8" d, cobalt, iron red, mauve, and orange-red oriental flowers in center, cavetto of 4 panels of flowers between blue band with geometrics, scattered flowers and flying exotic birds on border, c1784 . . . . 145.00

9" d, hex, center painted with titled titmouse or hoopoe, gray border with panels of molded white flowers alternating with panels of painted feathers, pattern #2059, c1825, pr 462.00

10" d

"Caramanian Series-Sarcophagia and Sepulchres at the Head of the Harbor," blue transfer. 325.00

"Hundred Antiques" pattern, blue transfer 165.00

Scattered bouquets and sprigs and molded flowers, gilt rim, pattern #1918, c1820, set of 12, (A)

. . . . 805.00

Platter

13" l, "Grasshopper" pattern, blue transfer 395.00

16" l, rect with cut corners, "Italian" pattern, blue transfer, c1820. . . . . . 550.00

18 1/2" l x 14" w, "Tower" pattern, blue transfer, c1815. . . . . 795.00

20" l

15 1/2" w, well and tree, multicolored exotic birds standing on pink and gray stones, orange cavetto with multicolored florals and peonies, inner border with 4 sections of florals, outer border with interspersed sections of blue designs or orange geometric shapes, "Spode Stone China" mark 695.00

"Gothic Castle" pattern, castle in oriental setting, blue and white

. . . . 750.00

21" l, "well and tree, "Tiber" pattern, river, castle, bridge, and St. Peters dome, c1811, blue transfer. 995.00

Porringer, 3 3/8" d, "Doll House" pattern, cobalt, iron red, med blue, and orange oriental-style house on side, flowerheads on reverse 195.00

Potpourri Vase

2 1/2" h, painted multicolored flowers on gilt scale blue ground, pattern #1166, c1810, (A) 253.00

5 1/2" h, flared shape, painted floral bouquets in gilt mirror and vase shaped cartouches, dk blue ground with gilt dots, and stars, gilt molded leaf designs, beaded sections on rim, 4 paw feet, pierced cov with flame knob, c1820, restored, (A) 277.00

9 7/8" h, with liner, oviform, reserve painted with pink, iron red, and gilt famille rose flowers, green ground, pattern #3087, rim chip 525.00

Tray, 9 3/4" l, cobalt, iron red, green, and gold, "imp Spode" mark, $175.

Serving Dish, 12 3/4" H-H, ftd, ironstone, rect, twig handles, enamel floral decorated black transfer, pattern #3125, (A) 375.00

Soup Plate

9 1/2" d, HP famille rose, green, yellow, and gold oriental flowers in center, 3 sprays of flowers on border, "SPODE-STONE CHINA" mark, c1806-17, pr 275.00

10" d, "Gothic Castle" pattern, blue transfer 225.00

Spill Vase, 4 1/8" h, cylinder shape, bands of multicolored urns and foliage scrolls under gilt accented blue band, pattern #409, c1820, pr, (A) 200.00

Tray

10" l x 7" w, rect, "Forest Landscape I" pattern, temple in trees, man in cov boat, blue transfer, c1810-20 . . . . . . 225.00

10 1/4" l, rect, green, yellow, and red pheasant on brown branch in center with magenta and red flowerheads, gold inner border, floral rim, "Spode Stone China" mark 395.00

Vase

4 1/2" h, black transfer of classical castle scene, stone bridge over lake, black lined rim and ft, c1820 . . . . 185.00

5 1/8" h, painted pink, mauve, red, and white garden flowers on gilt edged blue scale ground, white beaded rim and ft, gold handles with molded mask terminals, gold mons and flowerheads on base, c1805, pr 3,500.00

5 3/4" h, beaker shape, 3 paw feet, painted bouquet of flowers and smaller sprays, band of scrolling gilt foliage, (A) 195.00

6 1/2" h, Imari pattern, cobalt fencing and flowerheads, iron red and green flowers, gold veining, raised band of gold beads on rim, base, and ft 595.00

10 3/4" h, painted loose bouquets of flowers, green ground, reeded strap handles, metal plate on base, c1820, pr, (A) 1,840.00

Vase, Cov, 18 1/2" h, tapered oct shape, multicolored florals on gilt edged blue scale ground, 2 gilt horiz handles, gilt figural griffin knob, pattern #1166, repairs, pr . . . 38,000.00

Warming Dish, 9 3/8" d, New Stone China, oriental foliate landscape scene, blue transfer with polychrome accents, c1810, pr, (A) 200.00

SPONGEWARE

Staffordshire, England
Continental
c1840 to c1900

History: Spongeware, a cut-sponge stamped pattern decoration used on earthenwares and everyday tablewares, was achieved by dipping a sponge in color and applying it to the ware to produce a stamp of the pattern. A single dip of color produced about a dozen impressions. This accounted for the variation in shades.

The stamping technique was invented in Scotland and brought to England about 1845. It was a time-saving device used in decorating inexpensive china that was made mostly for export.

Cut-sponge border patterns included a variety of florals, leaves, scrolls, stars, triangles, hearts, and chains. Some borders supplemented the cut-sponge decoration with hand painting. The center motif also included combinations of cut-sponge and painted decorations.

William Adams and Son of Tunstall was one of the largest English producers of cut-sponge decorated pieces. W. Baker and Company of Fenton; Edge, Malkin and Company of Burslem; and Britannia Pottery of Glasglow were other leading manufacturers of spongeware.

Petrus Regout and Company in Holland, and Villeroy and Boch, in Germany were among the principal continental manufacturers.

References: Kevin McConnell, *Spongeware and Spatterware*, Schiffer Publishing Co. 1990; Earl F. & Ada F. Robacker, *Spatterware and Sponge*, A.S. Barnes & Co.1978.

Collecting Hints: Cut-sponge work could be identified by the uneven strength of the color in repeated motifs. Remember, the color supply lessened in the sponge as the pattern was repeated. An uneven interval or space between decorative motifs also indicated spongeware. Border motifs may be overlapped. A smudged effect often occurred because of too much pigment or a worn stamp. If a stamp had a defect in its design, it would be repeated throughout the pattern.

Bowl, 12 1/2" l x 10" w, oval, overall blue sponging, rolled lip, c1850 . . . . 650.00

Cereal Bowl, 7 3/8" d, molded vert lozenges, blue sponging, white ground 175.00

Cup and Saucer, child's size, blue sponging, (A) $25.

Cup and Saucer

Overall blue and white sponging 145.00

Oversize, ring handle, overall med blue sponging, gold rim, (A) 200.00

Cup and Saucer, Handleless, borders of blue and red sponging 400.00

Dish, 8 1/2" l x 6 1/2" w, overall blue sponging, serpentine rim, (A) 192.00

Figure

2 1/2" h, creamware, seated monkey, brown sponging, chips on base, (A) 248.00

3" l, pearlware, recumbent sheep, brown, blue, and ochre sponging, (A). . 275.00

Jug, 7" h, red and blue overall sponging, repaired chip, (A) 1,210.00

Milk Pitcher, 6 5/8" h, bulbous shape, flared rim, arched handle, overall med blue sponging, (A) 180.00

Pitcher

5 7/8" h, squat shape, gallery rim, blue and white sponging, crazed int, (A) . 165.00

6 1/2" h, cylinder shape, blue and white sponging, blue striped base and rim, (A) 440.00

9 1/2" h, cylinder shape, blue sponged ring pattern, white ground 385.00

11" h, dk blue and white center band, blue and white sponged body and handle 395.00

Planter, 8" d, hanging, blue sponging on white, (A) 17.00

Plaque, 11" d, molded figure of Victoria in yellow and blue trimmed white robe on black sponged horse, red and blue dot border, blue lined rim. 325.00

Plate

8 1/2" d, blue and red sponged border, (A) 88.00

8 3/4" d, overall blue sponging, (A) 55.00

9 1/4" d, dk blue sponging, shaped rim, pr
. . . . 165.00

9 3/4" d, black transfer of court dancing
scene, blue sponged border. . . 175.00

10 3/8" d, lt blue overall sponging, (A)
. . . . 170.00

Platter, 12 1/4" l x 8" w, oval, overall med blue
sponging, crazing, (A) 150.00

Vegetable Bowl, 9" l x 6 1/4" w, overall dk blue
sponging, scalloped and scroll molded rim,
(A) 85.00

STAFFORDSHIRE-BLUE AND WHITE

England
End of 18th C-1880s

History: Blue and white transfer printed earthenwares came to the Staffordshire district of England by the end of the 18th century. The transfer printing process was first used by Thomas Turner at Caughley in Shropshire.

At first patterns reflected Chinese porcelain designs, and the willow pattern was featured prominently in many examples. As the technique improved, scenics featuring abbeys, houses, castles, rivers, and exotic travel destinations were printed on wares. A tremendous export market developed since Americans were eager for scenes of American towns, sites, and historical events of interest.

Florals, birds, and animals also found their way to earthenwares, as did literary illustrations from prominent authors such as Sir Walter Scott and Charles Dickens.

Another area where blue printed wares were utilized was in children's' feeding bottles, pap boats, and feeding cups for use with invalids.

All blue printed wares were underglaze. Many makers used the same designs since there were no copyright laws to protect designs. Wares that were not marked were very difficult to attribute to a particular maker.

With the Copyright Act of 1842, copying of designs became much more difficult. Original designs were now registered to protect from copying for three years and then there was a renewal option. Makers could no longer copy engraving from literary works or other books. Since new sources were needed, designers turned to romantic scenes which were then quite popular.

By the 1880s, there were relatively few new patterns in use. White dinner services with printed borders became popular. Brightly colored dinnerwares also came into vogue.

References: Arthur Coysh, *Blue-and-White Transfer Ware 1780-1840,* David and Charles, 1970; A.W. Coysh and R.K. Henrywood, *The Dictionary of Blue and White Printed Pottery 1780-1880, Vol. II,* Antique Collectors' Club, 1989.

Collectors' Club: Friends of Blue, Mr. R. Govier, 10 Seaview Road, Herne Bay, Kent CT6 6JQ England. Membership: £12, Quarterly bulletins.

Museum: Wellcome Museum, London, England.

Basket and Tray, 13" l, "Fisherman's Hut" pattern, fisherman, seated woman and child, river, church in bkd, chip 1,250.00

Bowl, 6" d, man in sleigh, dk blue transfer
. . . . 250.00

Cider Tankard, 5 1/2" h, "Wild Rose" pattern, rustic cottage, boats, and bridge, flower border dk blue transfer, unmkd 475.00

Coffeepot

10" h, dome top, classic scene of ruins, flowerhead border, dk blue transfer, unmkd 1,000.00

11" h

Boy currying cow, med blue transfer
. . . . 1,250.00

Spread ft, wishbone type handle, scene of castle ruins, flowers on spout, ft, shoulder, and cov, med blue transfer, (A) 907.00

12 1/2" h, dome top, standing stag in forest setting between floral bands, blue transfers, c1830 . . . . 475.00

Creamer

4 1/2" h, molded spout, young boy on runaway horse, lt blue transfer, unmkd
. . . . 145.00

5 1/4" h, English cottage scene, flowerheads and foliage on border, dk blue transfer, (A) 165.00

5 1/2" h, lg and sm overall butterflies design, dk blue transfer, unmkd . . 350.00

Cup and Saucer

Dragon type pattern, dk blue transfer
. . . . 100.00

Thatched cottage with mother and child
. . . . 225.00

Young man and woman in garden with dogs, dk blue transfers, unmkd
. . . . 155.00

Cup and Saucer, Handleless

Vase of flowers, floral border, med blue transfers, (A) 110.00

White flowers, dk blue transfers, unmkd
. . . . 225.00

Cup Plate

3 3/8" d

Children milking goat, cathedral in bkd, dk blue transfer 160.00

Woman carrying baskets of fruit on yoke, loop and fleur-de-lys border, med blue transfer, c1835 . . 100.00

3 1/2" d

Acorns and leaves design, dk blue transfer 185.00

Basket of flowers design, dk blue transfer, Adams 155.00

3 5/8" d, beehive design, dk blue transfer
. . . . 185.00

3 3/4" d, leaves and flowers design, dk blue transfer, Stubbs 155.00

4" d,

Flowers and geometric design, dk blue transfer, Rogers 155.00

Lg flowerheads and leaves in center, flowerhead and bud border, Riley
. . . . 180.00

Overall leaves design, dk blue transfer, Stevenson 195.00

Drain, 12 3/4" l, "Visiting in the Churchyard" design, med blue transfer 400.00

Fruit Basket, 10 1/2" l, with undertray, reticulated, scene of shepherd and shepherdess and sheep, med blue transfer, (A) 650.00

Garden Seat, 15" h, ironstone, blue and white floral design, late 19th C, repairs, (A) . 300.00

Invalid Feeder, 3" h, still life of flower in vase, dk blue transfer, repairs 220.00

Jug, 8 1/4" h, bulbous shape, lg garden flowers from basket, scrolling leaves, dk blue transfer, Stevenson, (A) 748.00

Mug

2 3/4" h, floral design, dk blue transfer, unmkd 325.00

6 3/4" h, festival and harvest scene, lt blue transfer, unmkd 75.00

Pepper Pot, 4 7/8" h, ftd, dome top, oriental transfer scene, chips, (A) 50.00

Pitcher

8" h, overall floral pattern, med blue transfer 375.00

10 3/4" h, foliage and butterflies on body and handle, floral and foliate inner and outer rim, ruffled applied handle grip on front, med blue transfer, early 19th C, (A) 575.00

Plate

6" d, "Lakes of Killarney" pattern, med blue transfer, unmkd 110.00

6 1/2" d, deer and leopard design, med blue transfer 95.00

6 3/4" d, abbey ruins with man on donkey followed by woman, dk blue transfer, Davenport 160.00

7 3/4" d, hunter and dogs in center, birds on border, dk blue transfer 195.00

8" d, castle ruins and bridge, med blue transfer, unmkd 195.00

8 1/2" d

"Elephant" pattern, elephant and trainer in zoo setting, flower border, med blue transfer, beaded rim, "imp Rogers" mark 175.00

Fruit and flowers design, dk blue transfer, Stubbs, hairline 155.00

Oriental scene with people and horse, dk blue transfer, c1820-30 . . 120.00

Young man playing pipes, med blue transfer 145.00

Zebra in foreground, oriental buildings and figures in bkd, med blue transfer, Rogers, repaired chips . . 55.00

8 3/4" d, millwheel and waterfall, dk blue transfer, emb white border, Stevenson 125.00

9" d

"Fisherman's Hut" pattern, fisherman with nets on back, seated woman and child in foreground, river and church in bkd, dk blue transfer, unmkd 195.00

Young boy piping, unmkd 165.00

9 1/2" d, elephant walking in front of temple, mountain in bkd, flowerhead border, med blue transfer 145.00

9 3/4" d

Grazing rabbits, med blue transfer, rim chip 245.00

Royal lion in center holding sword, Persian style lobed cartouche, Persian style floral and geometric border, dk blue transfer 375.00

10" d

"Chinoiserie Ruins," med blue transfer 145.00

Donkey, ruins, and people scene, med blue transfer 195.00

"Fisherman with Nets," man in boat, 2 men holding net on tree 185.00

Fruit and flowers design, dk blue transfer, "Stubbs & Kent, Longport" mark 175.00

"Lakes of Killarney" pattern, med blue transfer, hairline, unmkd 125.00

Lg middle eastern building in bkd with overhanging tree, 3 people in foreground, flowerhead border, med blue transfer, maker unknown 125.00

"Parkland Scenery," country manor and water, quatrefoil frame, flower and net border, med blue transfer, Chetham & Robinson 285.00

"River Fishing," 2 boys fishing at river, mill, bridge and church in bkd, rose border, Meir 185.00

Swiss chalet in mountains with hikers, dk blue transfer 140.00

Two woman, man fishing, 2 cows along water, temple in bkd, floral border, med blue transfer, unmkd . . 165.00

Water lilies pattern, med blue transfer, unmkd 325.00

10 1/4" d, boy in boat fishing in river, 2 men poling boat on river, arched bridge and farmhouse at river's edge, buildings in bkd, flower border, med blue transfer, 1830 . . . . 165.00

Platter

9 1/4" l, "Lady of the Lake" pattern, med blue transfer, Careys 300.00

14" l, chinoiserie pattern, med blue transfer 275.00

14 1/2" l

Center with family and donkey before castle ruins and lake, floral and leaf border, med blue transfer, (A) 175.00

"Visiting in the Churchyard" design, med blue transfer 425.00

16" l, "Ornithology," Bald Eagle on cliff, eagle on river holding fish, waterfall in bkd, lt blue transfer, Meir & Son 595.00

16 1/2" l, ironstone, boat scene with house and trees, 6 oval reserves on border, med blue transfer 245.00

16 5/8" l x 13" w, with drain, pastoral scene of reclining sheep, thatched cottages, church in center, floral border, med blue transfers, (A) 400.00

17 1/2" l, center scene of pagoda and landscape bordered by panels of geometric designs, cavetto with scroll and geometrics, "G.R. & Co., crown, and STAFFORDSHIRE STONE CHINA" mark, pr, (A) 575.00

18" l

"Russian Palace" design, med blue transfer, unmkd, repaired . . 375.00

"Village Church" design, med blue transfer, unmkd 675.00

19" l, fisherman and nets, dk blue transfer, Hamilton 650.00

20 1/2" l, eastern scene with camels, palm trees, and buildings, med blue transfer, unmkd, (A) 770.00

20 3/4" l, "Chinese Fisher Boys" pattern, flowerhead border, unmkd 995.00

21" l, well and tree, deer in foreground, forest setting, dr blue transfer 895.00

Sauce Tureen, Cov, 8 1/2" h, with undertray, scene of castle by lake with trees, arabesque borders, med blue transfer, scroll handles, James Edwards 350.00

Soup Plate

7 5/8" d, oriental view with river and turreted buildings 125.00

10" d

Chinese junque and pagodas, med blue transfer, Hamilton 175.00

Springer Spaniel design, med blue transfer 245.00

Steeple and building in bkd with sailboat, man sitting on rock, donkey, woman with basket and dog, floral and fruit border, indented rim, med blue transfer, (A) 275.00

Sugar Bowl, Cov, 4 1/2" h, dog chasing stag, dk blue transfer, "Stone China" mark, chip 325.00

Tea Service, Part, pot, 6 3/4" h, 11" l, small pot, cov sugar bowl, waste bowl, 10 handleless cups, 11 saucers, "Vase and Flowers" pattern, (A) $1,955.

Teabowl and Saucer

Deer pattern, med blue transfer . . 195.00

Flowers in vase and geometrics, dk blue transfers, unmkd 225.00

Girl and calf design, med blue transfer, unmkd, repairs 285.00

Swan pattern, med blue transfer 225.00

Teapot

6 1/2" h, oblong shape, chain linked oval of bird's nest and eggs, flower border, med blue ground, early 19th C, (A) 460.00

11" h, 2 young women sitting in country setting, dk blue transfer, unmkd 650.00

Toothbrush Holder, Cov, 8" l, rect, "The Town Cottage" pattern, lg cottage, terrace, and urn, Carey 245.00

Tureen, 14 1/2" l, "Boy Piping," seated boy playing pipe to sheep, flower border, unmkd, c1820 . . . . 1,650.00

Vegetable Bowl, 16" l x 12 1/2" w, oval, chinoiserie scene of 2 men on bridge, butterfly border 495.00

Vegetable Bowl, Cov

11" l, floral design with still life of fruits and birds, dk blue transfers, molded leaf handles, flower knob, hairline, (A) 440.00

12" l x 7" w, "Sheltered Peasants" pattern, med blue transfer 875.00

Waste Bowl, 6" d, overall floral pattern, dk blue transfer 225.00

STAFFORDSHIRE FIGURES

Staffordshire, England
c1740-1900

History: During the 18th century, Staffordshire figures in salt glazed stoneware and Whieldon type earthenwares with translucent colored glazes were made by the family of Ralph Wood. (See: Ralph Wood).

Obadiah Sherratt's figures from the late 1820s displayed the rustic realism of true peasant art with humor, pathos, and brutality. The modeling was bold and crude; enamel colors were bright. Many figures were quite large. Usually Sherratt's figures were mounted on a table base. The name for the piece often was written on the front. Among his most famous pieces were "The Bull Baiting Group" and "Remus and Romulus." Sherratt also did classical and religious figures.

With the accession of Queen Victoria in 1837, simplicity of design appeared as well as restraint in the coloring of figures. Nineteenth century earthenware Staffordshire figures were made in a simple, uncomplicated manner, often mass produced at low cost for the cottage rather than for the stately home.

The figures featured a flat back, were compact in design, and were mounted on an oval base that was part of the figure. Figures were displayed on mantles, window ledges, bookcases, or Welsh dressers. Only the fronts were visible so decorations were restricted to the front of the figure. About 1840, potters made mantlepiece ornaments in under-the-glaze colors in great quantity. Cottage ornaments depicted the homey scenes characteristic of the people that bought them.

The most distinctive color used was the rich, dark, glossy cobalt blue. Additional colors included pink, green, orange, black, and some gold. After 1860, more colors were utilized including a pale flesh pink shade. The pottery was harder and whiter than in earlier pieces.

Both human and animal figures were molded. Just about every Victorian kitchen featured a pair of spaniels on either side of the kitchen clock. Greyhounds, poodles, Dalmatians, cats, and even zebras were memorialized in Staffordshire figures. Topical events, heroes and heroines of the times, members of the Royal Family, and theatrical characters appeared. Churches, cottages, and castles were popular. A unique form was the Victorian watch stand. Few figures were marked with a maker's mark.

Sampson Smith was the most prolific maker of the flatbacked figures and Staffordshire dogs. He worked from about 1847 to 1878. Others continued to use his molds to make figures long after his death. In addition to his famous dogs, Sampson Smith is known for figures of castles, churches, cottages, jockeys, Dick Turpin, Toby jugs, politicians, and royalty, including Queen Victoria.

References: T. Balston, *Staffordshire Portrait Figures of the Victorian Age*, Faber & Faber, 1958; Reginald S. Haggar, *Staffordshire Chimney Ornaments,* Phoenix House Ltd. 1955; Pat Halfpenny, *English Earthenware Figures:1740-1840,* Antique Collectors' Club, Ltd. 1992; J. Hall, *Staffordshire Portrait Figures,* Charles Letts & Co. Ltd. 1972; Adele Kenny, *Staffordshire Spaniels,* Schiffer Publishing, Ltd. 1997; B. Latham, *Victorian Staffordshire Portrait Figures for the Small Collector,* Tiranti, 1953; A. Oliver, *The Victorian Staffordshire Figures: A Guide for Collectors,* Heinemann, 1971; Clive Mason Pope, *A-Z of Staffordshire Dogs,* Antique Collectors' Club, Ltd. 1996; P.D.G. Pugh, *Staffordshire Portrait Figures & Allied Subjects of the Victorian Era, Rev. Ed.* Antique Collectors' Club, Ltd. 1987; H.A.B. Turner, *A Collector's Guide to Staffordshire Pottery Figures,* Emerson Books, Inc. 1971.

Museums: American Antiquarian Society, Worcester, MA; Brighton Museum, Brighton, England; British Museum, London, England; City Museum and Art Gallery, Stoke-on-Trent, England; The Detroit Institute of Arts, Detroit, MI; Fitzwilliam Museum, Cambridge, England; Victoria & Albert Museum, London, England.

Reproduction Alert: Lancaster and Sandlands are reproducing some of the old Staffordshire models, especially the animal and cottage figures. The colors match the old Staffordshire cobalt blue quite well.

Sampson Smith's figures were reproduced from his original molds from 1948 to 1962, but the colors are less vibrant than the originals.

While old figures were made in press molds, new figures are made in slip molds called slip casting. A large hole is a sign of slip casting. Many of the new figures are new slip casts with large holes to pour slip into the mold. Old figures had some fine strokes of a paint brush while modern ones are often colored by swabs or sponges. Old figures had some paint on the back while new ones have no paint on back. Old figures had more details in overall molding. The gold trim on the old figures was worn with a dull luster. New figures show no wear on the gold and it is shiny. Reproductions are usually exactly matched pairs, while old figures were seldom exactly the same. The underside of old figures had an even glaze while new glaze is intentionally "'aged" or "stressed."

Many reproductions are being made in China. More than 80 different figures and animals are now being made that are direct copies of old pieces found in standard reference books. Even the faults in the figures are being copied. These reproductions are heavier weight and are closer

Bank, 4 5/8" h, salmon pink and white sides, black and white windows, green grass base, gold trim, chip, (A) $125.

to the originals. They also have smaller firing holes.

Chinese reproductions have dark black crazing to make them look old. They are sprayed with dark colored transparent glaze. They have a rough surface overall, and have streaking in undecorated areas.

Abraham and Isaac, 10 1/4" h, standing Abraham in rose and iron red robe, raised dagger in hand, seated Isaac in purple tunic, bound to alter, wood stack in bkd, ram on base, flowering bocage in bkd, c1825 . . . . . . 1,650.00

Afghan Hound, 12 1/2" h, seated, white body, orange and black muzzle, prince or princess standing in front, brown hair, orange and blue trimmed clothes, black shoes, c1875, pr 1,300.00

Arabia, 8 3/4" h, standing female with black hair and red cheeks wearing gold trimmed gown, holding gold trimmed urn, brown and green rocky well shaped base, c1852 . . . . 295.00

Benjamin Franklin, 14 3/4" h, standing, holding pink tricorn hat under arm, scroll in other, beige face with red and black accents, grey coat over flowered white waistcoat, orange breeches, white stockings, black shoes, mottled green and brown oval base, early 19th C, (A) 259.00

Butter Tub, 5" l, reclining black spotted white cow, green grass ground, black striped brown oval base, c1870 . . . . 550.00

Cat, Seated

   3 3/4" h, black and white spotted, pink and green cushion base, c1890, pr
   . . . . 550.00

   4 1/4" h, black and yellow sponged spots, red collar 275.00

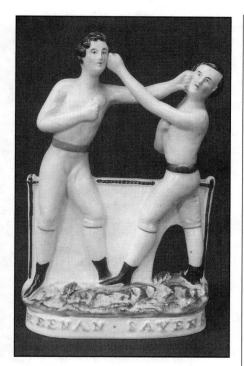

Boxers, 9 1/2" h, "HEENAN" and "SAVERS," yellow and blue or pink and orange, black hair, green-brown base, (A) $403.

Cat and Kitten, 2 3/4" h x 2 1/2" w, white bodies with black spotting, oval base, (A) 110.00

Cockerel, 9 1/4" h, removable head, standing, enameled iron red, brown, grey, yellow, and black modeled feathers, yellow spurred legs, brown base, c1820, repairs 3,650.00

Collie, 11" h, 10 3/4" l, standing, lt brown with white ruffs, face, and legs, black brows, pink and black muzzle, yellow and black eyes, gilt collar and locket, 19th C, pr, (A) 970.00

Comforter Spaniel

> 5 1/4" h, porcelain, dk brown splashes on white, black muzzle, separate front feet, hollow base c1845 . . . . 395.00

> 6 1/2" h, black splashes on white body, tan muzzle, gold chain and lock, "No. 5" mark 425.00

> 7 1/4, 7 1/2" h, red-brown splashes on white, orange muzzle, gold chain and lock, "No. 4" mark, pr 750.00

> 8" h, white body with painted face, molded and painted collar, cole slaw on ears, shoulders, and tail, pr 700.00

> 9 1/4" h, gold luster splotches on body, ears, and tail, white body, black and yellow facial features, gold molded collar, lock, and chain, pr, (A) 270.00

> 12" h, white body with molded collar and chain leash, black muzzle, tan paws 350.00

Cottage

> 5 1/2" h, arched front, climbing vines, seated lamb in front, white with black, tan, and red trim, c1860 . . . . 275.00

> 6" h, brown body, 2 red chimneys and doors, green foliage on roof edge, c1890 . . . . 295.00

Cow, 6 1/4" h, iron red and white standing cow, black and white spotted calf on green base, green bocage with flowerheads, c1825, repair to bocage, pr 2,850.00

Cow and Child, 6" h, brown and white cow with boy in cobalt jacket and flowered vest, gold striped hat standing in front or red-brown spotted cow with girl in cobalt jacket and flowered skirt, green and yellow oval base with grey road, c1880, pr 650.00

Crucifixion, 10 3/4" h, cross mtd on tree, Christ in blue loincloth, female in yellow lined red cloak, blue gown, another in ochre gown, both kneeling reaching before Christ, green base and bocage, c1825, repairs 7,000.00

Dismal Hound, 4 1/4" h, liver spots on white ground with bone, c1820 . . . . 475.00

Dove on Nest, 8 1/2" l, figural dove cov, brown wings, tail, and ruff, white face and wing tips, black circled brown eyes, oval brown and green nest base, 19th C, pr, (A) . . . 1,150.00

Dwight Lyman Moody, 11 1/2" h, standing figure in black coat and trousers, hand resting on book on red and green column . . . 975.00

Elijah and Widow, 10" h, man in lt orange coat, grey beard and hair, seated on stump with black bird, widow in lt green lined yellow gown, flowered underskirt, seated on brown barrel, dk brown jug at side, sq base with brown stripe, chips, pr 875.00

Equestrian, 9 3/4" h, flatbacks, man in green cape, orange hat, carrying crop, woman sidesaddle in tan hat, pink shawl, white dress with polychrome flowers, astride white horse with orange and blue trappings, black eyes and muzzle, green and brown knoll base, 19th C, pr, (A) 690.00

Evangelists, 9" h, standing, St. Matthew in red gown and yellow robe, grey apron, St. Mark in orange-red gown and yellow lined black robe, lion on base, St. Luke in puce robe and yellow robe, holding book, ox on base, St. John in purple gown and yellow robe, red chalice in hands, green oval bases with 3 leaf green bocage and red, yellow, and blue flowerheads, named rect bases, c1825, repairs to bocage, set of 4 . . . . 7,500.00

False Clock, 9 1/2" h, worn gold numbers, red and green open loops around dial, 2 children in pink blouses on each side, black spotted recumbent dog on oval base, c1875 . . . . 375.00

Fawn, 2 3/4" h, creamware, recumbent, brick red, ochre, and dk brown splashes, oval base, c1760, (A) 748.00

Fisherwoman, 7" h, woman in green kerchief on head, puce jacket, orange apron, green and orange striped dress, seated next to basket of fish, gilt lined oval base, c1860 . . . . 3,350.00

Forester, 8 1/2" h, standing man in green jacket with red sash, plumed hat, holding black

and white cross bow, brown and white seated dog on base, c1860 . . . . 350.00

Girl and Setter, 4 1/2" h, girl in pink dress, seated on reclining black and white setter, c1860 . . . . 375.00

Goat, 8 3/8" h, standing, white shaggy coat, brown horns, translucent green, ochre, and brown rocky base, c1810, cracks . . 1,850.00

Grandfather Clock, 7" h, mottled blue and rust design, c1820 . . . . 850.00

Grenadier, 5" h, ochre coat, brown plumed helmet and boots, sword at side riding lt brown horse, lt green support 650.00

Hedgehog, 2" h x 31/2" l, hollow, seated, ochre and brown spots, white body . . 650.00

Hen on Nest

> 6 1/4" h x 7" l, rust brown head and tail, white body feathers, 7 figural chicks on bk and base 1,325.00

> 6 1/2" h x 8" l, bisque, red comb, black head and tail feathers, tan body feathers, tan basketweave base 850.00

> 7" h x 7" l, bisque

>> Black, magenta, and yellow outlined feathers, white body, red comb, lt brown basketweave nest . . . 650.00

>> White hen, dk orange head trim, black beak, yellow basketweave base 525.00

Highland Couple, 12 3/8" h, woman with brown wood bundle on head, red and green accented dress, black haired man with pink luster trimmed vest and trousers 275.00

Hunter, 7 1/2" h, black hat, orange coat, white breeches, black and yellow boots astride tan horse with black mane, 2 black and white dogs chasing brown fox on base, floral encrusted raised background 850.00

John Solomon Rarey, 9 1/4" h, white standing horse with gold heart spots, purple or green saddle blanket, standing male in purple trimmed white clothing with yellow stockings, c1860, pr 850.00

Just a Peck, 12 1/2" h, standing man in black coat and removable tricorn hat, pink breeches, chip 850.00

King Charles Spaniel, 13 1/2" h, red-brown splashes, black muzzle, eyes, and lock and collar, separate front feet, grey paws, c1870 . . . . 875.00

Lamb, 2 3/4" l, pearlware, recumbent, black sponging, branch molded ochre base, c1810, (A) 275.00

Lion

> 4 3/8" h, recumbent, brown with black muzzle, green bocage w/florals, green oval base with blue scrolls, imp "WALTON" in banner on reverse, c1825 . . . . 2,850.00

> 8" h, standing, yellow body with black mane and face, yellow snake in green floral bocage, green rect base with blue painted heart, feather and scroll, c1825 . . . . 6,500.00

9" h

Seated, rust brown coat, glass inset eyes, oval base, (A) 127.00

Standing, brown glaze, paw on sphere, stepped plinth base, (A) . . . 195.00

Little Red Riding Hood, 5" h, red cloak, blue dress, brown wolf at side, c1860 . . . . 445.00

Palmer's House, 7 3/8" h, cream body, blue roof, orange outlined windows, red door, named on base 595.00

Pastille Burner

4" h, white cottage with brown-black cross timbers, tan thatched roof, 2 brown-red chimneys, 4 sm feet. 775.00

4 1/4" h, yellow and lt orange pavilion, gilt cross hatched roof, 8 columns, multicolored moss and flowers, gilded leaves, c1820, Coalbrookdale 2,450.00

4 1/2" h, earthenware, timbered Tudor cottage, yellow thatched roof, 2 red brick chimneys, 4 dormers, brown rocky base, 4 bun feet, c1820. . . . . . . 950.00

4 3/4" h

Bone china, lilac-blue cottage, gilded window sills, white moss edged gables, multicolored floral base with arch, c1835 . . . . .1,200.00

Hex cottage, peach building, grey roof 995.00

5" h, porcelain, pavilion, oct orange roof with gold trim, orange pillar supports, applied multicolored flowers, gold steps, Spode 2,000.00

5 7/8" h, oct pavilion, blue ground, gold outlined windows, blue encrusted flowers at windows. 1,500.00

6" h, Gothic gazebo, white body, applied blue floral swags on roof edge 495.00

6 1/2" h, bone china, Warwick castle, cream body, gilt-edged gothic windows, applied multicolored florals, c1835. . . . . .1,200.00

8 1/2" h, salmon pink shingled roof, flowered white body, pierced windows, applied florals and leaves on roof edge, 2 porch pillars, gilt lined oval base, c1870. . . . . 450.00

Pointer, 4 1/2" l, porcelain, black spotting and head marks, scroll molded base, 1840s 350.00

Prince Albert, 6 3/4" h, blue uniform jacket, yellow trousers, pink sash, orange robe, gilt lined base, c1841 . . . . 325.00

Prince and Princess

7 1/4" h, prince in cobalt jacket, white trousers, grey hat, princess in white jacket, pink gown, holding red ribboned yellow hat, gold lined base, c1862. . . . 325.00

11" h, prince in aqua jacket, holding tan hat, princess in pink jacket, holding yellow hat in hand, "raised black PRINCE & PRINCESS" on base 400.00

Prussian General, 11 1/2" h, equestrian, orange coat, yellow shoulder boards, puce sash, black maned brown horse, puce white

and green saddle and blanket, gilt lined oval base, c1870, pr 1,350.00

Queen Victoria, 17 1/2" h, standing with arms folded, blue eyes, brown hair, green ermine edged cloak and sash, gold trim, c1870 . . . . 895.00

Quill Holder, 6 1/4" h x 3 3/4" l, black and white Dalmatian dog seated on haunches, legs apart, oval cobalt base, c1860, pr 3,025.00

Rabbit, 3 1/4" l, prone, black splashes, white ground, brown and green raised base, (A). 302.00

Robinson Crusoe, 6" h, standing, puce and gold trimmed great coat, peaked cap, dead bird and gun on gold outlined shaped base 675.00

Romeo and Juliet, 10 1/2" h, lovers embracing, Juliet in gold trimmed white gown, Romeo in red and blue open shirt, black kilt, red shoes, Shakespeare quote on brown and green base, Thomas Parr, c1852. . . . 495.00

Royal Children

7" h, seated on ermine lined orange thrones, Highland dress, plumed hats, parrot on arm, sq base, c1845, pr 775.00

7 1/2" h, pony cart, prince in cobalt coat astride orange-brown pony, princess in cobalt top and tartan plaid skirt standing in cart, rococo molded base, c1845 . . . . 875.00

12 3/4" h, each mtd on horse, orange and blue striped hat, brown hair, red and blue flower wreaths in hand, child in orange dress on gilt lined oval base, pr 1,200.00

Saint Peter, 10 1/8" h, seated with hands clasped, orange robe, green mantle, multicolored cockerel and 2 keys at feet, green bocage with red and blue florals, flowers and foliage on med green base, "ST. PETER" on front, c1825 . . . . 1,550.00

Saint Roch, 7 1/4" h, white building, black trim, green arched windows, orange figure on roof 925.00

Samson and the Lion, 11 1/2" h, gray rearing lion w/red mouth and yellow muzzle, Samson wearing orange and green trimmed Greek garment, flowing red and green tartan plaid scarf, green and brown rocky oval base, c1880 . . . . 550.00

Scottish Highlander, 11" h, green and black kilt with orange fringed sash, cobalt coat, black hat with red plume, holding yellow and dk red wreath overhead, goat standing at side, oval base, (A) 140.00

Scottish Hunter, 16 1/2" h, standing hunter, black dash sash, holding brown rifle, green bocage bkd, ft on dead brown lion . . 585.00

Sebastapol, 8" h, 2 turret Russian fortress, grey ground with red and green accents, c1854 . . . . 525.00

Sheep, 4" h, recumbent on floral molded base, brown glaze, early 19th C, (A) 80.00

Sheep and Lamb, 5" h, standing brown spotted and incised sheep, black muzzle and eyes, reclining brown spotted lamb on brown and green base, green bocage bkd, Walton, early 19th C, (A) 288.00

Spaniel, 4 1/2" h x 8" l, reclining black and white dog on blue cushion base, Copeland and Garrett 2,500.00

Soldier and Sailor, 12 h, soldier on left, sailor on right, holding bags, orange, blue, black, pink, yellow, green, and gold, 1898 . . 925.00

Spill Vase

6 1/4" h, standing tan stallion, seated black colt with white face, green molded base, green and brown tree trunk in bkd, applied encrusted florals, lavender int, pr 3,500.00

6 1/2" h, figural tree trunks with musician and drum or musician and bagpipe, seated on rocky mounts, dog and duck at feet, streaked translucent brown, green, ochre, and blue, c1780, restruck heads, pr 2,100.00

6 3/4" h, seated boy in gilt trimmed white suit or seated young girl in gilt trimmed white dress and apron, milking black and white standing cow with coleslaw forehead, orange lined green tree trunk, pr 795.00

7 1/8" h, open tree trunk with black spotted dogs and iron red and white lambs in branches, scalloped scroll base, "WALTON" on reverse, c1825 . . . . 1,900.00

7 1/4" h, standing fisherman and woman, man in green jacket, lavender pants, black boots, brown net over shoulder, woman in lavender jacket, white skirt,

Spill Vase, 10 1/4" h, brown, black, blue, and yellow, pr, $1,750.

yellow apron, carrying basket of fish, orange int on spill, gilt lined white base 495.00

8 1/2" h, guardian angel wearing blue lined orange blouse and pink skirt sitting in white tree trunk with red int, sleeping royal children in Scottish dress on base, yellow and red parrot on branch 595.00

9" h, cottage, seated couple in cobalt, puce, and green seated before orange-red lined tan tree trunk, lg yellow cottage in bkd with applied red and green leaves and flowers on roof edge, grey-white winding steps to cottage, yellow ground base, c1860 . . . . 325.00

10" h, open tree trunks w/birds on branches, horse and cow on oval base, peach, yellow, pink, and blue enamels, pr 2,000.00

11 1/4" h, orange brown standing Apollo greyhound, recumbent grey Daphne on yellow lined green base, green tree trunk with red int, brown gate with red bands on side, c1860 . . . . . . .1,150.00

11 3/4" h, young girl in blue shirt, orange laced vest, cream skirt with pink and blue sprigs, pink scarf and apron, orange shoes, green and brown gnarled tree trunk, turkey and white basket on base, 19th C, (A) 345.00

12" h,

Standing brown and white cow with nursing calf, green tree trunk with red int, gold lined oval base, c1880 . . . . 595.00

White male and female figures in Greek dress w/gold trim, brown hair, white trunk with pink int and gold trim, "WINTERS TALE" on base, c1852 . . . . 475.00

13" h, seated white spaniel with gold spots and locket, black muzzle, orange-red lined green and brown tree trunk in bkd, green, brown, and yellow gilt lined oval base, pr 1,250.00

Squirrel, 7 1/2" h, standing, pink-brown fur, dk brown tail, yellow eyes and collar, holding nut, green raised circ base, c1810, hairline and repairs 4,100.00

Whippets, 7 1/4" h, 7 1/4" l, orange-brown body, black collar and muzzles, black and orange game on base, pr, (A) $400.

Tam O'Shanter and Sooter Johnny, 13" h, Tam wearing white jacket, gold hat and leggings, pink scarf, Johnny wearing white jacket, green apron, and red scarf, brown keg between, gold names on oval base 575.00

Terrier, 3" h x 4" w, hollow, seated, ochre and brown spots, green base 950.00

Victoria and Albert

6 1/2" h, seated, Victoria in cobalt bodice, green skirt, orange fringed robe, Albert in cobalt coat with yellow sash, white trousers, orange-grey fringed robe, c1840, pr 575.00

9" h, equestrian, Albert in cobalt uniform on brown horse, Victoria in cobalt gown with green, cream and pink hat, seated on brown horse, green molded base, raised gilt "ALBERT" or "QUEEN" on base, c1850, pr 650.00

Watch Holder

9" h, 2 Turkish soldiers in cobalt jackets in front of mosque, one seated smoking pipe, cannon and balls on base, green palms in bkd, red hanging flowers, c1854 . . . . 595.00

9 1/4" h, Urania seated on stone cube, classical gown enameled with flowers, floral sprigs, edged in turquoise, iron red lower gown, purple shawl, arm resting on globe, holding calipers, books at side, brown and green marbleized rect plinth, c1810 . . . . 1,950.00

11" h, St. George and the Dragon, blue clothing with orange cape on rearing tan horse, green, orange, and blue scattered florals on stand, orange sawtooth outlined opening, c1845 . . . . . . .475.00

Whippet, 5 1/8", 5 1/2" h, seated on haunches, tan body with blue accents, black base with gilt trim, pr, (A) 215.00

Windmill, 5 1/2" h, grey-green blades, white and orange cottage base with brown windows, water wheels at sides, c1860 . . . . 195.00

Winter, 9" h, standing man with arms folded, black hat, red jacket and cape, orange breeches, ice block base, c1830 . . . . 325.00

Youth and Dog, 5" h, standing barefoot boy in red coat, yellow breeches, black and white dog under arm, stepping into water 495.00

Zebra, 9" h x 8" l, standing, black and white, rocky mound base 675.00

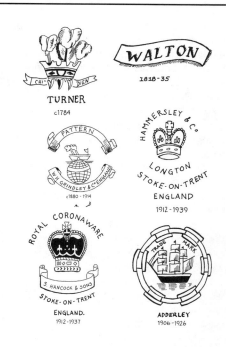

STAFFORDSHIRE-GENERAL

1700s to Present

History: In the Staffordshire district of England, numerous pottery factories were established that produced a wide variety of wares including figures, flow blue, transfer printed wares, historic blue, and ornamental pieces.

Samuel Alcock and Company established a pottery in Burslem about 1828 that was known for its parian figures, jugs, and decorative wares in the classical style. The pottery also made a wide range of blue-printed earthenwares and bone china. Sir James Duke and nephews took over the firm in 1860.

John and Edward Baddeley produced earthenwares at Shelton between 1786 and 1806. The company manufactured a wide range of tablewares, often enameled in red and black on a creamware ground.

Charles Bourne of Foley Pottery made bone china tablewares between 1807 and 1830. His factory equaled those of Spode, Coalport, and Davenport. Pieces could be identified by the pattern numbers and the initials "CB."

The Lane End factory of **Hilditch and Son** made teawares in under the glaze blue from 1822 until 1830.

Elijah Mayer established a pottery at Cobden Works, Hanley about 1705. In 1805 the name changed to Elijah Mayer and Son. Production continued until 1834. The Mayers manufactured black basalt wares, tablewares in cream colored earthenware, cane wares, and drab stonewares.

Humphrey Palmer was located at Church Works, Hanley in 1760. He produced wares popularized by Wedgwood such as black basalts, cream colored and agate ware vases, and seals and cameos that frequently were modeled by J. Voyez. Most of Palmer's wares were decorative. The pottery went out of business in 1778.

A.J. Wilkinson Ltd. was a Staffordshire pottery firm that operated several factories in the Burslem area beginning in the late nineteenth century. In 1885, Wilkinson took over the Central Pottery. The plant made white granite ware for the American market. Wilkinson introduced the use of gold luster work on granite ware.

Wilkinson operated the Churchyard Works from 1887 until the early 20th century and the Royal Staffordshire Pottery from c1896 until the present day. About 1900, Wilkinson gained control of Mersey Pottery, a subsidiary of Newport Pottery. The factory remained in production until the 1930s. Highly glazed stonewares, some of which were designed by Clarice Cliff, were made.

References: P.D. Gordon Pugh, *Staffordshire Portrait Figures & Allied Subjects of the Victorian Era, Rev. Ed.* Antique Collectors' Club, Ltd.1987; Bernard Rackham, *Early Staffordshire Pottery*, Faber & Faber, 1951; Louis T. Stanley, *Collecting Staffordshire Pottery*, Doubleday, 1963; John Thomas, *The Rise of the Staffordshire Potteries*, Adams & Dart, 1971.

Museums: City Museum & Art Gallery, Stoke-on-Trent, England; Everson Museum of Art, Syracuse, NY; The Henry Francis DuPont Winterthur Museum, Winterthur, DE; William Rockhill Nelson Gallery of Art, Kansas City, MO.

Biscuit Barrel, 8" h, lg yellow centered lavender flowers, green leaves, cream and lt yellow ground, emb flower design top and base, SP rim, handle, and cov with swan knob, "W. Wood & Co." mark. 200.00

Bowl

6 1/8" d, ftd, HP lg yellow sunflower with red petaled flowers, green leaves, black stems, red line on int, (A) 60.00

9" d, Franklin flying kite, pink transfer, repaired ft chip 495.00

Cake Plate, 10" H-H, bone china, "Pagoda" pattern, border of brown pagodas, red, yellow, and blue florals, gold handles, Ansley 20.00

Cheese Dish, Cov

7" h x 9 7/8" w, figural bull's head, tail shaped arched handle in center, triangle base, dk blue glaze, (A) 1,600.00

7 1/4" h x 12" l, 2 lobed slanted cov, yellow flowers, black leaves and stems, cream ground, molded border, black splashed base with rococo molded border, "Humphrey's Brothers, Tunstall" mark 85.00

8" h, dome shaped, "Calico" pattern, flowerheads and stems, brown sheet transfer 65.00

Coffeepot

11" h

Engine turned band of squares on base and domed cov, green glaze, band of gilt vines and leaves, loop 1,400.00

Scroll handle, dome lid with beehive knob, pink transfers of bands of flowerheads and scrolled foliage, spout repair, hairlines, (A) . . . 70.00

13" h, net and flowers design, brown transfer, beehive knob 595.00

Compote, 5" h x 8 1/4" d, "Tournay" pattern, brown transfer, T. & R. Boote 95.00

Cream Jug, 4" h, silver shape, lion paw feet and lion mask knees, blue, buff, and brown solid agate, c1760, (A) 748.00

Creamer, 4 1/4" h, squat shape, arched handle, HP purple and green sprig design, dbl incised line on shoulder, (A) 20.00

Creamer and Sugar Bowl, creamer, 3 1/2" h, sugar bowl, 2" h, "Springtime" pattern, orange poppies, yellow leaves, gold rim, Royal Albert 22.00

Cup and Saucer

Bat printed, Adam Buck type scene of mother and child, black, c1810 . . . . 120.00

Bone china

Fluted, "Periwinkle" pattern, blue transfers, Royal Albert t20.00

"Maytime" pattern, Crown Staffordshire 35.00

Cylinder shape, loop handle, buff, ochre, gray, and brown solid agate, c1760, (A) 805.00

Cup and Saucer, Oversize, "God Speed the Plough" and farm implements, polychromed transfer, ring handle, c1900 . . . . 125.00

Cup and Saucer, Handleless

Black, red, blue, and green arched floral sprigs, (A) 65.00

Cabbage rose design, chips on base, (A) 220.00

Floral pattern, black transfers, maker unknown 20.00

HP blue, yellow, and red peafowl on black branch with green leaves, int of cup with red buds, black stems and green leaves, "imp Stoneware, B & T" mark, (A) 130.00

Red, green, and black sprig design, (A) 22.00

Cup Plate

3 1/2" d, overall floral and geometric design, red transfer, unmkd, (A) . . . 30.00

3 3/4" d, giraffes design, pink transfer 175.00

Dinner Service, Part

4 plates, 10 1/2" d, 7 plates, 8 1/2" d, plate, 7 1/2" d, plate, 6" d, 7 soup plates, 8 1/2" d, "Chinese Tree" pattern, brown tree branch with yellow, blue, and pink flow-

ers, border of pink and yellow flowers, Booth 135.00

22 plates, 10 3/8" d, 12 soup plates, 10 3/8" d, 8 serving dishes, oval, 9 3/4"-17 1/8" l, 3 cov vegetable tureens, 12" l, cov sauce tureen with undertray, tureen undertray, 14 1/2" l, blue and iron red scattered florals, black transfer cell pattern bkd, cream earthenware ground, Brown-Westhead, Moore & Co., 1879, (A) 978.00

Figure, 5" h, blue and yellow bird on branch, applied flowers 130.00

Holy Water Font, 5" h x 2 1/2" h, shell-shaped base, arched back with Christ on cross, Virgin Mary and praying angels, cherub head and leaves on arch, green, blue, and pink polychromes with gold accents, (A) 50.00

Inkwell, 3" h, figural black and white dog in orange doghouse with red and green flowers on roof edge, gilt lined oval base with ink cup and gold chain 350.00

Milk Pitcher, 6 1/8" h, cabbage rose design, arched handle, (A) 700.00

Muffineer, 5 1/2" h, standing English gentleman, polychromed, c1860 . . . . 225.00

Mug

3" h, bird in flowers design, red transfer, c1900 . . . . 95.00

4" h, people in boat and palm tree, red transfer, unmkd 330.00

4 1/2" h, farmer and wife with cattle, brown transfer, unmkd 130.00

4 3/4" h, relief molded scene of 3 seated men in tavern, rust, blue, and green, blue lined rim and base 750.00

5 1/2" h, 2 elongated loop handles, painted black and white hound chasing yellow and brown spotted bird, reverse with

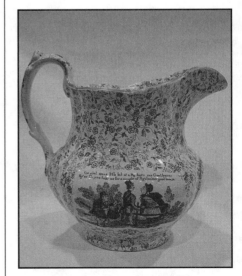

Pitcher, 8 3/4" h, pig stealers on one side, Farmers Arms on reverse, black transfers, sheet transfer of yellow centered blue flowers and green stems, "From The Experience Of Others Do Thou Learn Wisdom And From Their Failings Correct Thine Own Faults" on base, "gilt 1850 and initials" in black cartouche on front, $1,700.

black, brown, and white hound with bird in mouth, green and brown grass, relief molded yellow dots and flowers on band, int with molded mottled brown and green frog, 19th C, (A) 316.00

Pepper Pot, 5 7/8" h, figural standing jester, yellow cap, orange jacket, white ruffled collar with purple accents, green and brown accented shirt, black slippers, gold lined rd base, mid-19th C, (A) 240.00

Pitcher

5" h, man and woman in garden, black transfer 195.00

6" h, cows, horse, and peoples, purple transfer 130.00

7" h, overall floral pattern, purple transfer, unmkd 120.00

10" h, "Holy Bible," black transfer, Jackson, c1830 . . . . 325.00

Plate

7" d, Mandarin design, 2 figures seated at table with attendant holding umbrella in colors in center, red border with cartouches of oriental flowers, Rogers & Son. 165.00

7 1/2" d, "Harp" pattern, sailor playing lyre to woman on ship, purple transfer, R. Stevenson 225.00

9" d

Oriental scene of figures in barge on water, ornate border, brown transfer, unmkd 30.00

Red, yellow, and blue flowers, green leaves, brown transfer ground, maker unknown 55.00

9 1/8" d, cabbage rose design, scalloped rim, (A) 530.00

9 1/2" d

"East Indian Man Sailing From the Downs," black transfer 175.00

English country scene, red transfer, Hopkins & Vernon 160.00

10" d, chick watching butterfly on branch, "He That Will Not. When He May/Then He Will, He Shall Have Nay" on border, blue, green, yellow, and red transfer 485.00

10 1/2" d, flying dragons in overall flowerhead and stem bkd, red transfer. 95.00

Platter

13" l

9 1/4" w, rect, "Daffodil" pattern, scene of castle, man in front, lg florals, florals in border panels, brown transfer, "W.H. Grindley, Tunstall" mark 75.00

10 1/2" w, bunches of flowers and fruit, brown transfer, scalloped and beaded rim 115.00

13 1/4" l x 10 3/4" w, rect, scalloped rim, floral design with birds, black transfer with blue, red, and orange polychrome accents, chips (A) 95.00

19 1/8" l, center scene of people on shore, boat on lake, church in bkd, floral border, purple transfer, (A) 440.00

Soup Plate, 10 1/4" d, gold center design, red, blue, and gold border, gadrooned rim, c1820, $135.

21" l, castle and river scene, black transfer, cream ground, c1830 . . . . . 395.00

Relish Dish, 9 3/4" l, "Corea" pattern, brown transfer, Anthony Shaw 27.00

Sauce Tureen, 5 1/2" h x 7 1/2" H-H, "Tournay" pattern, lambrequin designs, brown transfers, "T.R. Boote, England Royal Premium" mark 38.00

Soup Plate

9" d, central urn, river, and buildings design, purple transfer 35.00

9 3/4" d, dog chasing bird, floral border, blue transfer, scalloped rim, (A) 220.00

Sugar Bowl, Cov

6" h, rect paneled body, open handles, floral design with birds, black transfer with blue, red, and orange polychrome accents, chips, (A) 85.00

6 1/4" h, oval shape, vert pleating, molded shell design base, scrolled handles, HP red and green 3 petal flowers and black stems and leaves, underglaze blue dots and buds, black striped shoulder and rims, rosette knob, (A) 40.00

Sweetmeat Basket, 6 3/4" h, trilobed body, applied multicolored flowers and bows, faux bamboo triple handle, George Jones, repaired, pr, (A) 1,000.00

Teabowl and Saucer, "Harp" pattern, sailor playing lyre to woman on ship, purple transfers, R. Stevenson 75.00

Tea Caddy

4 3/4" h, rect shape, green glazed fluted corners, mottled brown sponged body, late 18th C, chips, (A) 345.00

5" h, oct cylinder shape, sloping shoulder, rd foot, buff, blue, and brown solid agate, c1760, (A) 3,680.00

Tea Cake Stand, 14 3/4" h x 10 3/8" d, 3 tier, yellow, pink, and aqua plates with emb pink

roses and green leaves, center metal rod, Royal Winton Grimwades 225.00

Teapot

3" h, glazed redware, cylinder shape with engine-turned chevron bands, straight spout, loop handle, acorn knob, c1755, (A) 345.00

4 1/2" h, redware, hex shape, molded panels of Chinese figures on fretwork ground, hex form spout and handle with basketweave and ornaments, c1760, spout repair, (A) 2,645.00

5" h, pectin shell shape, dolphin handle, serpent spout, lion knob, solid buff, blue, and brown agate, c1760, (A) 7,475.00

6" h

Figural cottage, yellow ground, HP green and brown trim 75.00

Gold tooled outlined band of white, purple, red, and blue daisies on cream ground, brown mottled ground, gilt accents on spout, handle and knob, Arthur Wood . . 42.00

6 1/2" h

10 1/4" l, rect paneled body, arched handle, floral design with birds, black transfer with blue, red, and orange polychrome accents, hairlines, (A) 40.00

Pink, blue, and red oriental flowerheads, brown branches, blue and green leaves, gold trim, Sadler 38.00

7" h, deer with ruins in bkd, trees at side, black transfer, chip on side 150.00

7 5/8" h x 11 1/2" l, oval shape, curved spout, dolphin shaped handle, molded shell feet, vert pleated body, brown transfer of basket of flowers on sides with pink, yellow, and green polychrome accents, blue striped rims, unmkd, (A) 95.00

Tureen, 15" H-H x 9" h, oval, "Davenport" pattern, white ground, 4 panels of iron red and cobalt florals on body and cov, band of mauve triangles and dots on border, gilt accented scalloped rim and flower knob, Hollinshead & Kirkham, c1880 . . . . 195.00

Vase

6 3/8" h, trumpet shape, scalloped base, red and gold accented molded scroll and bullrush handles on sides, gold accented applied floral and leaf design, scalloped rim with gold band, pr, (A) 25.00

7 3/4" h

Fan shape, oct spread ft, Art Deco style orange poppy, buds, and green leaves, satin black ground, orange luster int, Crown Ducal 195.00

Figural seated woman with bird, cat on base, bench with bee keep at side, tulip flower form vase, blue, green, yellow, orange, purple, and black

polychrome accents, oval base,
(A). 220.00

9 1/2" w, Japanese style white exotic flaring orchids and plants, gold faux ormolu rocaille molded base, Moore Brothers, dtd 1892, pr, (A). . . .2,070.00

Vegetable Tureen, 6 1/2" h x 10 1/2" H-H, "Denmark" pattern, rose red transfer, cream ground, ribbed border on end and base, raised knob, "Furnivals Limited Trademark England" mark. 49.00

Waste Bowl, 7 3/8" d, blue, green, dk brown, and black gaudy floral design on ext, (A)
. . . . 85.00

STAFFORDSHIRE-HISTORIC

English and American Views 1818-1860

History: By 1786, there were 80 different potteries established in the Staffordshire district of England, the center of the English pottery industry. By 1800, the number had grown to almost 200. The pottery district included the towns of Burslem, Cobridge, Etruria, Fenton, Foley, Hanley, Lane Delph, Lane End, Longport, Shelton, Stoke, and Tunstall.

After the War of 1812, transfer printed Staffordshire pottery that depicted American historical events, views of cities and towns, tombs of famous individuals, portraits of heroes and other famous people, buildings of important institutions, patriotic emblems, and American landscapes were made for the American market. These historic view pieces allowed the British potters to recapture their dominance of the American market almost immediately upon the end of hostilities. Views were adopted from engravings,

paintings, and prints by well-known artists of the period.

Dark blue pieces were favored between 1820 and 1840. This color was inexpensive, easy to secure, covered flaws in the wares, withstood the high temperatures of the kiln, and retained its deep coloration. During the 1830s and 1840s, lighter colors of pink and blue along with black, sepia, and green became popular. Wares made included tea services, dinner services, sets of plates, jugs, etc. Canadian views also were manufactured.

Numerous potteries made the historic blue wares. Each firm had its own distinctive border design and characteristics. The border design was the chief means of identifying a specific maker of an unmarked piece.

English views also were popular. Transfers featuring old and famous castles, abbeys, manor houses, cathedrals, seats of the nobility, famous beauty spots, coastal subjects, English colleges, and London were used on the wares.

William Adams and Enoch Wood were the first manufacturers to produce the English views. Enoch Wood took the lead with the American views. Factories that were established after 1820 concentrated on American views.

William Adams
Stoke, 1827-1831
Tunstall, c1834 to Present

William Adams of Stoke was one of four potters with the name William Adams in the Staffordshire district. In 1819, a William Adams became a partner with William Adams, his father. Later his three brothers joined him. When the father died in 1829, William became the factory's manager. The firm operated as William Adams and Sons and controlled four potteries at Stoke and one at Tunstall.

Initially, English views, with a foliage border and the name of the scene on the back, were made. Two blue views were manufactured at Stoke. Views done at Tunstall had a border of baskets with roses. The Tunstall plant produced American views in black, light blue, sepia, pink, and green between 1830 and 1840.

William Adams died in 1865. All production was moved to Tunstall. The firm still operates today under the name, William Adams & Sons, Ltd.

Carey and Sons
Lane End, 1818-1847

Thomas and John Carey operated the Anchor Works at Lane End between 1818 and 1842. The firm changed names several times during its history. The factory pro-

duced English views, some of which were based on Sir Walter Scott's poem "Lady of the Lake."

James and Ralph Clews
Cobridge, 1819-1836

James Clews took over the works of Andrew Stevenson in 1819. Ralph, his brother, joined the firm later. In 1836, James came to the United States to establish a pottery in Troy, Indiana, but the venture was a failure. Clews returned to England but never re-established himself as a potter.

Clews made both English and American views. The company made a variety of borders, the most popular having festoons that contained the names of the fifteen existing states.

Thomas Godwin
Burslem Wharf, 1829-1843

Thomas Godwin produced both American and Canadian views in a variety of colors. His borders included nasturtium and morning glories.

Thomas Green
Fenton, 1847-1859

Thomas Green operated the Minerva Works in Fenton from 1847 until his death in 1859. His American view pieces contained variations of William Penn's 1683 Treaty with the Indians. The border was a simple, stenciled design. His printed wares were in green, pink, brown, black, and blue. After his death, his wife and sons managed the firm using the name M. Green & Co. It later became the Crown Staffordshire Porcelain Company.

Ralph Hall
Tunstall, 1822-1849

At the conclusion of a partnership with John Hall, Ralph Hall operated the Swan Bank Works in Tunstall. The firm exported many blue printed wares to America.

Joseph Heath
Tunstall, 1829-1843

Joseph Heath and Company operated a factory at New Field in Tunstall between 1829 to 1843. The company's border design was composed of large roses and scrolls with a beaded band and white edge.

Henshall and Company
Longport, 1790-1828

The firm consisted of a series of different partnerships with the only recorded mark being that of Henshall and Company. Both ·

English and American views were made. The border motif comprised fruit and flowers.

J. and J. Jackson
Burslem, 1831-1843

Job and John Jackson operated the Churchyard Works at Burslem between 1831 and 1843. Many of their American views were not copied by other manufacturers. Their border designs included sprays of roses, a wreath of fine flowers, a beaded band, and a white margin. Their transfer colors were black, light blue, pink, sepia, green, maroon, and mulberry.

Thomas Mayer
Stoke, 1829-1838

In 1829, the Mayer brothers, Thomas, John, and Joshua purchased the Dale Hall Works from Stubbs when he retired. Thomas produced the "Arms of the States" series at Dale Hall Works while the other brothers worked at Cliff Bank. Each factory produced fine ceramics.

Morley and Company
Hanley, 1845-1858

Until 1845, Morley was the sole owner of a pottery firm in Hanley. After that date, the firm experienced a succession of owners. Between 1847 and 1858, it was called Francis Morley and Company. Both American and Canadian views were manufactured.

J. and W. Ridgway and William Ridgway and Company
Hanley, 1814-1830

John and William Ridgway, sons of Job Ridgway, took charge of the Bell Bank Works in 1814 when George Ridgway retired. The brothers produced the "Beauties of America" series in dark blue with the rose leaf border. Their English views featured a border with flowers and medallions of children.

In 1830, the partnership was dissolved. John continued to operate Cauldon Place, Job's old manufactory, and William took charge of Bell Bank. John Ridgway continued the Cauldon Place Works from 1830 until 1858. In 1855, T.C. Brown-Westhead, Moore & Co. purchased the works.

William Ridgway and Company managed the Bell Bank Works from 1830 until 1859. Edward John, his son, joined the firm. By 1843, he was operating six potteries, mostly in Hanley. "American Scenery" and "Catskill Moss" were two series that were based on Bartlett's etchings. These series were issued in colors of light blue, pink, brown, black, and green.

John and Richard Riley
Burslem, 1802-1828

John and Richard Riley operated at Nile Street between 1802 and 1814 and at the Hill Works in Staffordshire between 1814 and 1828. Mostly they made English views and blue printed dinner services with a border of large leaf-like scrolls and flowers.

John Rogers
Longport, 1815-1842

John and George Rogers operated two factories in Longport in 1802. When George died in 1815, John took Spencer, his son, into the firm. The name changed to "John Rogers and Son," a designation used even after the father died. Rogers produced four American views, three of which featured the Boston State House with a floral border. English views also were made.

Anthony Shaw
Burslem, 1850-1878

Anthony Shaw founded Mersey Pottery at Burslem in 1850. He specialized in views of the Mexican War period.

Andrew Stevenson
Cobridge, 1808-1829

One of the pioneers among English potters to make blue historical, transfer printed ware with American scenes was Andrew Stevenson. W.G. Wall, an Irish artist, went to the United States and supplied the drawings for Stevenson. Stevenson's pieces had a flower and scroll border. English views were made with roses and other flowers on the border.

Ralph Stevenson
Cobridge, 1815-1840

Ralph Stevenson used a vine and leaf border on his dark blue historical views and a lace border on his transfers in lighter colors. British and foreign views were made.

Pieces from the works of Ralph Stevenson and Williams (R.S.W.) featured the acorn and oak leaf border design or the vases of flowers and scrollwork design. Williams was the New York agent for Stevenson.

Joseph Stubbs
Burslem, 1790-1829

Joseph Stubbs established the Dale Hall Works in Burslem in 1790. When he retired in 1829, he sold his pottery to the Mayer brothers. His American views used a border design of eagles with widespread wings among scrolls and flowers. Views included scenes in New Jersey, Boston, New York, and Philadelphia. Stubbs also made English views with a border of foliage and pointed scrolls.

Enoch Wood and Sons
Burslem, 1819-1846

Enoch Wood, sometimes called the "Father of English Pottery," made more marked historical American views than any other Staffordshire manufacturer. In 1819, his firm operated as Enoch Wood and Sons. Enoch died in 1840. Enoch, Joseph, and Edward, his sons, continued the firm with their father's name. The sons sold the firm to Pinder, Bourne, and Hope in 1846.

The company's mark had several variations, but each included the name "Wood." The shell border with the circle around the view was used most frequently, though Wood designed several other unique borders. Many of the views attributed to unknown makers probably were made at the Wood factory.

Enoch Wood and Sons also made British views, including the "English Cities" series, the "London Views" series, the shell border series, and the grapevine border series. In addition, they produced French views such as ceramic portrayals of Lafayette and his home in France, and the "Italian Scenery" series, and views of Africa and India. Many of the foreign scenes were copied from engravings after water colors by traveling artists such as William Henry Bartlett.

In addition to views of places, Enoch Wood made other designs including a Scriptural Series of biblical scenes, a Sporting Series of hunting scenes, and a Cupid Series showing a variety of cherubs.

William Adams did an Animal Series. Scriptural subjects were done by Adams, Mason, Jackson, Ridgway and others.

References: David and Linda Arman, *Historical Staffordshire: An Illustrated Check List,* privately printed, 1974, out of print; David and Linda Arman, *Historical Staffordshire: An Illustrated Check List, First Supplement,* privately printed, 1977, out of print; Ada Walker Camehl, *The Blue China Book,* Tudor Publishing Co. 1946; Elizabeth Collard, *The Potters' View of Canada,* McGill Queen's University Press, 1983; A.W. Coysh and R.K. Henrywood, *The Dictionary of Blue & White Printed Pottery, 1780-1880,* Antique Collectors' Club, 1982; *Volume II,* 1989; Ellouise Baker Larsen, *American Historical Views on Staffordshire China, Third Ed.,* Dover Publications, Inc. 1975; N. Hudson Moore, *The Old China Book,* Charles E. Tuttle Co. 1974; Jeffrey B. Snyder, *Historical Staffordshire Ameri-*

can Patriots and Views, Schiffer Publishing. Ltd. 1995.

Museums: American Antiquarian Society, Worcester, MA; City Museum & Art Gallery, Stoke-on-Trent, England; Henry Ford Museum, Dearborn, MI; The National Museum of History & Technology, Washington, DC; Wellcome Institute of the History of Medicine, London, England; Worcester Art Museum, Worcester, MA; Yale University Gallery of Fine Arts, New Haven, CT.

American Views

Adams

Cup, 2 1/4" h, "Log Cabin," view of cabin, cider barrel, American flag, int with medallions of William Henry Harrison in uniform, pink transfer, (A) 248.00

Plate

5 1/2" d, "Fort Edwards, Hudson River," black transfer 85.00

7" d, "Hartford, Monte Video," red transfer 35.00

7 3/4" d, "Virginia, Shannondale Springs," pink transfer 115.00

9" d, "New Hampshire, View Near Conway," red transfer 125.00

9 1/2" d, "Landing of Columbus-Indian Scene", Indians shooting geese, gray-black transfer 90.00

10 1/2" d, "Catskill Mountain House, U.S.," rose-red transfer 90.00

Platter, 20" l, "Falls of Niagara U.S.," red transfer 1,250.00

Soup Plate, "Head Waters of the Juniata," pink transfer 195.00

Ashworth

Vegetable Bowl, Cov, 11 1/2" l, "American Marine," brown transfers 995.00

Clews

Cup and Saucer, Handleless, "Landing of Lafayette," dk blue transfers, (A) 330.00

Pitcher, 9" h, "State House on Canal," med blue transfer, olive brown outlined rim and handle, unmkd, (A) $145.

Coffeepot, 11 1/2" h, "Lafayette at Franklin's Tomb," dk blue transfer, (A) $430.

Cup Plate, 3 3/4" d
"Landing of Lafayette," borderless, dk blue transfer, (A) 275.00
"Sandy Hill, Hudson River," brown transfer 125.00

Pepper Pot, 4 1/2" h, "Landing of Lafayette," floral and leaf border, dk blue transfers, (A) 1,155.00

Pitcher, 7" h, "Welcome Lafayette the Nation's Guest and Our Country's Glory," dk blue transfer, restored handle 1,600.00

Plate

5 1/2" d, "Fort Edward, Hudson River," black transfer, imp "CLEWS" mark 85.00

7" d
"Hadley Falls, Rapids Above," brown transfer 125.00
"Picturesque Views-West Point," black transfer 165.00

8" d
"Baker's Falls, Hudson River," purple transfer 130.00
"Near Sandy Hill, Hudson River," purple transfer 165.00

8 3/4" d
"Welcome Lafayette the Nation's Guest and Our Country's Glory," dk blue transfer 950.00
"Winter View of Pittsfield Mass.," church, medallion, and floral border, dk blue transfer, (A) 413.00

9" d, "Baker's Falls, Hudson River," black transfer 105.00

10" d,
"Fishkill, Hudson River"
Blue transfer 145.00
Brown transfer 135.00
"The Landing of General Washington at Castle Garden, N.Y.," dk blue transfer 450.00

10 1/8" d, "Landing of Lafayette," dk blue transfer, "imp Clews Warrented Staffordshire" mark, (A) 450.00

10 3/8" d, "Peace and Plenty," dk blue transfer, "imp Clews Warrented Staffordshire" mark, glaze wear, (A) 325.00

10 1/2" d, "Winter View of Pittsfield, Mass.," dk blue transfer 450.00

Platter

14 5/8" l, "Columbus, Ohio," flower border, dk blue transfer 2,500.00

14 3/4" l, "America and Independance," dk blue transfer, (A) 1,760.00

17 1/2" l, "Newburg, Hudson River," brown transfer 500.00

18 1/2" l, well and tree, "Lafayette, Landing of Gen. at Castle Garden, New York, August, 1824," dk blue transfer, (A) 1,600.00

Soup Plate

8 3/4" d, "States," university building in center, dk blue transfer, scalloped rim, (A) 248.00

10" d, "Peace and Plenty," dk blue transfer 495.00

10 3/8" d, "Winter View of Pittsfield, Mass.," dk blue transfer, "imp Clews" mark, (A) 440.00

Davenport

Plate, 10 1/8" d, "EXCHANGE HOTEL, NEW ORLEANS" in center, lt blue transfer, blue border with rope edge, (A) 440.00

Platter

14 3/4" l x 11 1/2" w, "Columbus," Cities series, dk blue transfer, (A) 1,600.00

16 1/4" l x 13" w, "Sandusky," Cities series, dk blue transfer, (A) . 2,200.00

18 1/2" l x 15" w, "Michigan, Detroit," Cities series, dk blue transfer, restored chip, (A) 2,600.00

Edwards, J. & T.

Plate, 8 1/4" d, "Boston Mails Series-Gentlemen's Cabin," black transfer . 135.00

Goodwin, Thomas

Plate

9" d, "Schuylkill Waterworks," brown transfer 195.00

10 1/2" d
"Capital, Washington," brown transfer 195.00
"The Narrows From Fort Hamilton-American Views," blue transfer 150.00

Green, Thomas

Plate

8 1/4" d, "William Penn's Treaty," brown transfer 95.00

9" d, "William Penn's Treaty," green transfer 200.00

Soup Plate, 10" d, "William Penn's Treaty," brown transfer 210.00

Goodwin, T.

Plate, 10 1/2" d, "The President's House, Washington," brown transfer, (A) 275.00

Hall, R.

Cup and Saucer, American eagle riding on shell with shield and arrows, brown transfers. 195.00

Heath, J.

Plate, 9 3/4" d, "Ontario Lake Scenery" pattern, med blue transfer 58.00

Soup Bowl, 8 3/4" d, "The Residence of the Late Richard Jordon, New Jersey," black transfer. 120.00

Jackson, J. & J.

Plate

6" d, "Girard's Bank, Philadelphia," black transfer 165.00

6 1/2" d, "Bunker Hill Monument," brown transfer 325.00

6 3/4" d, "Massachusetts, Harvard Hall," brown transfer. 85.00

7" d, "Hartford, Monte Video," black transfer 125.00

7 1/2" d, "Pass in the Catskills," dk blue transfer, (A) 500.00

8" d, "Virginia, Shannondale Springs," black transfer 135.00

9" d

"Battle Monument, Baltimore," red transfer 150.00

"Water Works, Philadelphia," med blue transfer 185.00

9 1/4" d, "Philadelphia, Race Bridge," brown transfer 165.00

Platter, 18 1/2" l, "Philadelphia, Pennsylvania Hospital," med blue transfer, (A) 1,375.00

Soup Plate, 10 1/2" d, "Hartford, Connecticut," red transfer 195.00

Knight-Elkins

Plate, 10" d, "Philadelphia," black transfer, c1830. . . . . 110.00

Maker Unknown

Cider Mug, 5 1/2" h, cylinder shape, "Famous Naval Heroes," dk blue transfer, blue feather/leaf handle, (A) 3,960.00

Chamber Pot, 5 1/2" h x 9 3/8" d, "Washington Independence," med blue transfer, chips, (A) 1,760.00

Creamer, 4" h, ewer shape, "Mount Vernon, Seat of the Late General Washington," dk blue transfer, hairline 695.00

Cup and Saucer, Handleless, "Yale College, New Haven Ct," border with 3 ovals of eagles and 3 rects of Wadsworth Tower, brown transfers, (A) 330.00

Drainer, 13 7/8" d, "The Death of General Wolfe," dk blue transfer 1,850.00

Gravy Boat, 7 3/4" l, "Catskill Mountains, Hudson River," med blue transfer 565.00

Honey Dish, 4 1/2" d, American eagle and shield, black transfer 175.00

Pitcher, 5 3/4" h, "Erie Canal-DeWitt Clinton Eulogy," dk blue transfer . 1,725.00

Plate

7 1/2" d, "American Villa," fruit border 85.00

9" d, "Hobart Town," dk blue transfer 225.00

9 7/8" d, "American Villa," dk blue transfer 225.00

10 1/4" d, "Catskill Mountain House, US," red transfer 195.00

10 1/2" d, "Episcopal Theological Seminary, Lexington, Kentucky," mulberry transfer 695.00

10 3/4" d, American eagle and shield, blue transfer, blue lined rim 175.00

Platter, 16 5/8" l, "Sandusky," dk blue transfer, (A). 8,525.00

Teapot, 11" h, "Virginia Church," dk blue transfer 650.00

Vegetable Bowl, 12 3/4" l, rect, "Columbus," dk blue transfer, chips and hairlines, (A) 660.00

Mayer

Plate, 9" d, "Arms of Rhode Island," dk blue transfer, chip on reverse. . 650.00

Platter

17" l x 13" w, "Arms of Delaware," dk blue transfer, crack and chips, (A) 1,300.00

19" l, "Arms of New Jersey," dk blue transfer 6,500.00

Toddy Plate, 5 1/2" d, "Arms of South Carolina," dk blue transfer 750.00

Meigh

Plate, 7 1/4" d, "Utica, NY," lt blue transfer 155.00

Platter, 18" l "Boston From Dorchester Heights," black transfer, rim cracks 125.00

Mellor Venables

Plate, 9 1/2" d, "Fort Hamilton, NY," Arms of the States Series, purple transfer 165.00

Ridgway, J. & W.

Cup Plate, 3 7/8" d, "Wilkes-Barre, Pa," lt blue transfer 155.00

Plate

7" d, "Insane Hospital, Boston," Beauties of America Series, dk blue transfer 275.00

8" d, Library, Philadelphia," Beauties of America Series, dk blue transfer 275.00

9 3/4" d, "City Hall, New York," medallions of rose and leaf border, med blue transfer, (A) 220.00

10 1/4" d, "View from Ruggle's House, Newburgh, Hudson River," Cities and Views Series, lt blue transfer 165.00

Platter

15 3/8" l, "View of Fort Putnam, Hudson River," lt blue transfer 375.00

16 3/4" l, "Alms House, NY," Beauties of America Series, dk blue transfer 995.00

Soup Plate

9 7/8" d, "Octagon Church, Boston," Beauties of America series, med blue transfer, "Beauties of America, Octagon Church, Boston, J. & W. Ridgway" mark, (A) 340.00

10 1/4" d, "Capital, Washington," mulberry transfer 160.00

Rogers, John and Son

Bowl, 9 3/4" l, oblong shape, "Boston State House," med blue transfer, (A) . 605.00

Cup and Saucer

"Boston Harbor," dk blue transfers, hairlines 365.00

"Boston State House," med blue transfer, hairline 175.00

Pitcher, 8 1/2" h, "Boston State House," med blue transfer, (A) 715.00

Platter, 14" l x 11" w, "Boston State House," med blue transfer, "John Rogers & Son" mark. 925.00

Shaw, Anthony

Plate, 9 3/8" d, "Texian Campaigne"

Purple transfer 185.00

Red transfer 295.00

Stevenson and Williams

Coffeepot, 9" h, "New Orleans," black transfer. 750.00

Cup and Saucer, "Hartford State House," med blue transfer. 995.00

Pitcher, 9 1/2" h, four medallions-Washington, Jefferson, Lafayette, Clinton, med blue transfer, crack, (A) 16,000

Plate

6 1/2" d, "Fort Gansevoort, New York," dk blue transfer, white beaded rim 1,200.00

7 1/2" d

"Columbia College," Acorn and Oak Leaf border, dk blue transfer 375.00

"The Capital, Washington," Shell border dk blue transfer 425.00

8 1/2" d, "City Hall, New York," "RSW" mark 375.00

9" d, "Hospital, Boston," vine leaf border, dk blue transfer 325.00

10" d

"Capital Washington," dk blue transfer 495.00

"Park Theatre, New York," dk blue transfer, acorns and oak leaf border 300.00

Platter

9 1/2" l, "Troy From Mt. Ida," dk blue transfer, Andrew Stevenson 1,695.00

10 1/2" l, "Brooklyn Ferry," dk blue transfer, (A) 3,800.00

12 1/2" l, "Village of Catskills," dk blue transfer, Andrew Stevenson, (A) 1,700.00

13" l, "Battle of Bunker Hill," dk blue transfer, Ralph Stevenson 3,850.00

14" l, "Junction of the Sacandaga and Hudson Rivers," dk blue transfer, Andrew Stevenson 4,800.00

14 1/2" l, "Almshouse, Boston," vine border, dk blue transfer, (A) 1,430.00

Stubbs

Plate

6 1/4" d, "Church in the City of New York," Eagle Border Series, dk blue transfer 1,050.00

7 3/4" d, "Hoboken in New Jersey," dk blue transfer, (A) 200.00

8 3/4" d, "Upper Ferry Bridge Over the Schuylkill," dk blue transfer 295.00

10" d

"Bank of the United States, Philadelphia," dk blue transfer 475.00

"City Hall, New York," dk blue transfer, (A) 275.00

"Fairmount Park, Philadelphia," dk blue transfer 350.00

Platter

18 3/4" l x 15 1/2" w, "Upper Ferry Bridge over the River Schuylkill," eagle and floral border, dk blue transfer, (A) 1,705.00

10 1/2" l, "Woodlands Near Philadelphia," dk blue transfer 850.00

Soup Plate, 10" d, "Fair Mount Near Philadelphia," with sheep, med blue transfer, "imp STUBBS" marks, pr, (A) .375.00

Soup Tureen, "Fairmount Park, Philadelphia," Spread Wing Eagle border, dk blue transfers, repaired hairline and chips 4,800.00

Tams

Soup Plate, 10" d, "United State's Hotel," dk blue transfer 895.00

Wood, E.

Coffeepot, High Dome

11" h,

"Wadsworth Tower," dk blue transfer, (A) 2,365.00

12" h, "Commodore MacDonnough's Victory," dk blue transfer, (A) 3,410.00

Creamer, 3 1/2" h, "Lafayette at Franklin's Tomb," dk blue transfer 1,400.00

Cup and Saucer, Handleless

"Chancellor Livingston," dk blue transfers, "imp Wood & Sons" mark, (A) 770.00

"Franklin's Tomb," dk blue transfer 485.00

"Washington Standing By His Own Tomb With A scroll In His Hand," dk blue transfers, "imp Wood" mark, (A) 350.00

Cup Plate, 3 3/4" d, "Castle Garden, Battery, New York," dk blue transfer, "Enoch Wood & Son, Peter Morton, Hartford" marks, (A) 325.00

Fruit Basket, 10 3/4" H-H, oval, "West Point Military Academy," dk blue transfer, (A) 1,895.00

Gravy Tureen, 4" h, with undertray and ladle, "Passaic Falls, State of New Jersey," dk blue transfer, (A) 2,750.00

Pitcher, 6 1/2" h, "Landing of the Pilgrims," dk blue transfer 1,495.00

Plate

5 5/8" d, "Hudson River View," shell border, dk blue transfer, (A) 880.00

6" d, "Entrance of the Erie Canal into the Hudson at Albany," dk blue transfer, (A) 688.00

7 1/2" d

"Pass in the Catskill Mountains," shell border, dk blue transfer, (A) 330.00

"Scudder's American Museum," dk blue transfer, (A) 900.00

"View of Trenton Falls," 3 figures on rock, dk blue transfer . . . 210.00

9" d, "Gilpin's Mills on the Brandywine Creek," shell border, dk blue transfer, (A) 400.00

9 1/4" d, "The Baltimore & Ohio Railroad-Inclined," shell border, dk blue transfer, "imp Enoch Wood," (A) 770.00

9 3/8" d, "Marine Hospital, Louisville, Kentucky," dk blue transfer, "imp Wood & Sons" mark, (A) . . . 138.00

10" d

"Cadmus," dk blue transfer 550.00

"Harvard College," black transfer 150.00

"Pine Orchard House, Catskill Mountains," shell border, dk blue transfer 325.00

"Table Rock, Niagara," conch shell border, dk blue transfer, "E. Wood & Sons" mark 475.00

10 1/4" d

"The Baltimore & Ohio Railroad-Straight," shell border, dk blue transfer, "imp Wood" mark, (A) 825.00

"Transylvania University, Louisville," Celtic Series, black transfer 195.00

10 1/2" d

"Harvard College," Celtic Series, brown transfer, white emb border 165.00

"The President's House," 4 panel floral border, lt blue transfer 175.00

"Union Line," dk blue transfer 375.00

Platter

13" l, "Military Academy West Point," med blue transfer, (A) . . . 2,200.00

14 3/4" l, "Niagara from the American Side," shell border, dk blue transfer, (A) 1,650.00

18 1/2" l x 15 1/4" w, "Bay of New York from Staten Island," black transfer, "Enoch Wood & Son" mark 725.00

"Castle Garden, Battery, New York," shell border, dk blue transfer, (A) 3,000.00

Soup Plate

10" d

"Boston State House," dk blue transfer 200.00

"Pine Orchard House, Catskill Mountains," dk blue transfer 695.00

10 1/4" d, "Table Rock, Niagara," dk blue transfer 495.00

10 1/2" d, "Transylvania University, Kentucky," purple transfer . . 175.00

Sugar Bowl, 6 7/8" h, "Commodore Mac-Donnough's Victory," shell border, dk blue transfers 785.00

Toddy Plate, 6 1/2" d, "Catskill House, Hudson," dk blue transfer, (A) 522.00

Plate, 6 5/8" d, "Hagley, Worchestershire," med blue transfer, "imp Enoch Wood and eagle" mark, (A) $60.

Vegetable Bowl, 9" l, "Eddistone Light," dk blue transfer. 1,200.00

English Views

Adams

Plate

6 1/2" d, "Coke Thorpe, Oxfordshire," dk blue transfer 175.00

7 3/4" d, "St. Pauls School, London," dk blue transfer 165.00

8 3/4" d

"Hawthornden Edinburghshire," dk blue transfer, "imp ADAMS" mark 300.00

"Villa in Regent's Park-The Residence of the Marquis of Hertford," dk blue transfer . . . 175.00

10" d

"Villa in Regent's Park-The Residence of G.B. Greenough," dk blue transfer 215.00

"Warleigh House, Somersetshire," dk blue transfer 225.00

"St. Phillip's Chapel, Regent's Street," dk blue transfer 225.00

10 1/4" d, "Blenheim, Oxfordshire," med blue transfer 115.00

10 3/8" d, "Gracefield, Queens County, Ireland," lt blue transfer 195.00

Platter

13 3/4" l, "Part of Regents Street, London," dk blue transfer. 650.00

15 1/2" l, "Denton Park, Yorkshire," dk blue transfer, chips 175.00

15 3/4" l x 11" w, "Bywell Castle, Northumberland," dk blue transfer, "imp ADAM" mark, chips, (A) 316.00

16 1/2" l, "St. George's Chapel, Regent Street, London," dk blue transfer 795.00

16 3/4" l, "Fonthill Abbey, Wiltshire," dk blue transfer 950.00

17" l, "Jedburgh Abby, Roxburgshire," dk blue transfer 760.00

Tureen, 15" H-H, 9 1/2" h, "Caius College Cambridge," cabbage knob, med blue transfers, "J.W. Ridgway" mark, chip on knob, (A) $1,955.

17 1/2" l, "The Regents Quadrant, London," dk blue transfer 950.00

19" l, "Cornwall Terrace, Regent's Park, London," dk blue transfer . 1,050.00

Vegetable Dish, Cov, 12" d, "Bywell Castle," Bluebell Border Series, dk blue transfers, 4 sm feet 795.00

Clews

Basin, 11 3/4" d, "Wansted House Essex," med blue transfer, feather edge, "imp Clews" mark, (A). 275.00

Plate

7 1/4" d, "St. Mary's Abbey, York," dk blue transfer 175.00

10" d

"Fonthill Abbey," Blue Border Series, dk blue transfer . . . 195.00

"St. Catherine Hill Near Guilford," dk blue transfer, c1830 . 190.00

10 1/4" d, "Canterbury Cathedral," dk blue transfer 175.00

Davenport

Dish, 7" l, fluted handles, "Bisham Abbey, Berkshire," med blue transfer, c1815, pr 700.00

Hall, R.

Cup Plate, 3 7/8" d

"Broadlands, Hampshire," Hall's Select Scenery Series, dk blue transfer 165.00

"Worcester Cathedral," dk blue transfer 165.00

Plate

6 1/4" d, "Dreghorn House, Scotland," Hall's Picturesque Scenery Series, dk blue transfer 155.00

7 3/8" d, "Cashiobury, Hertfordshire," Hall's Picturesque Scenery Series, dk blue transfer 165.00

7 1/2" d

"Eashing Park, Surrey," dk blue transfer. 175.00

"Gunton Hall, Norfolk," foliage border, dk blue transfer. . . . 145.00

8 1/2" d

"Fulham Church, Middlesex," Hall's Picturesque Scenery Series, dk blue transfer. 155.00

"Warleigh House," Hall's Select Scenery Series, dk blue transfer, chip on rim 165.00

8 3/4" d

"Barlborough Hall, Derbyshire," dk blue transfer. 165.00

"Wistow Hall, Leicestershire," Hall's Foliage Border Series, dk blue transfer. 175.00

10" d

"Llanarth Court, Monmouthshire," dk blue transfer 255.00

"Plains Hill, Surry," dk blue transfer 190.00

Platter, 13" l x 10 1/4" w, "Boughton House, Northamptonshire," Hall's Select Views, dk blue transfer, (A) 288.00

Pudding Bowl, 11" d, "Warleigh House, Somersetshire," Hall's Select Views, beaded rim, dk blue transfer, cracks 225.00

Soup Plate, 10" d, "Biddulph Castle, Staffordshire," Hall's Select Scenery Series, dk blue transfer 250.00

Tray, 10 5/8" l, "Castle Prison St. Albans, Hertfordshire," Hall's Select Views, dk blue transfer. 165.00

Henshall

Plate, 8 1/4" d, "Saxham Hall," fruit and flower border, blue transfer 155.00

Maker Unknown

Plate

6 5/8" d, "Falls of Killarney," lt blue transfer 79.00

7" d, "Tyburn Turnpike," blue transfer with "clobbered" polychrome enameled border 300.00

10" d

"Furness Abbey, Lancashire," med blue transfer 275.00

"Village Church," blue transfer 165.00

Tea Service, teapot, 7" h, teapot, 6" h, creamer, cov sugar bowl, 6 cups and saucers, "Gilrad House, Lancashire" and "Barlborough Hall, Derbyshire," flowerhead border, dk blue transfers, (A) 1,610.00

Morley

Compote, 10 5/8" d, ftd, "Chaudiere Bridge, Near Quebec," Lake Series, lt blue transfer. 550.00

Cup Plate, 3 7/8" d, "Georgeville," Lake Series, lt blue transfer 175.00

Soup Plate, 10 1/4" d, "Chaudiere Bridge, Near Quebec," Lake Series, lt blue transfer. 95.00

Ridgway, J. & W.

Plate, 10" d, Christ Church, Oxford," dk blue transfer, chip 135.00

Platter, 21" l, well and tree, "All Souls College, St Mary's College at Oxford," College series, med blue transfer, (A) 1,200.00

Soup Plate, 9 3/4" d, "Pembroke Hall, Cambridge," dk blue transfer . . 155.00

Soup Tureen, 12 3/4" h, "Caius College, Cambridge," med blue transfer 2,900.00

Riley

Plate

9" d, "Kingsweston, Gloucestershire," dk blue transfer 195.00

10" d, "Hollywell Cottage, Cavan," dk blue transfer 225.00

Stevenson, A.
Plate
9 3/4" d, "Edinburgh," dk blue transfer, "A. Stevenson, E. Pluribus Unum and American Eagle" mark
.........................245.00
10 1/4" d
"Culford Hall, Suffolk," dk blue transfer 165.00
"Faulkbourn Hall," med blue transfer, "imp A. Stevenson" mark
.........................275.00
Platter
15" l, "Tunbridge Castle, Surrey," dk blue transfer, wear 225.00
18 3/4" l, "Walsingham Priory, Norfolk," med blue transfer, (A) 1,210.00
20 1/2" l x 18" w, well and tree, "Windsor Castle," Lace border, brown transfer.................695.00
Vegetable Dish, Cov, 9 1/2" sq, "Audley End, Essex and Felix Hall," Wild Rose Border Series, dk blue transfers
.........................750.00

Wood, E.
Cup and Saucer, "Cliffs of Dover," dk blue transfer......................295.00
Cup Plate
3 5/8" d
"Castle Forbes, Aberdeenshire," med blue transfer 185.00
"Shirley House, Surrey," med blue transfer 185.00
4 5/8" d, "Bickley, Kent," grapevine border, med blue transfer .. 165.00
Plate
6 3/8" d, "Cowes Harbour," shell border, dk blue transfer, (A) ... 144.00
7 1/2" d, "Southampton, Hampshire," shell border, dk blue transfer
.........................125.00
8" d, "London Views, The Holmes, Regent's Park," dk blue transfer
.........................135.00
8 1/4" d, "Falls of Montmorenci, Near Quebec," shell border, dk blue transfer.................225.00
9 1/4" d, "Hanover Lodge, Regent's Park, London," dk blue transfer
.........................195.00
10" d, "The Holme, Regent's Park," dk blue transfer............195.00
10 3/8" d, "Worcester," Cathedral City Series, lt blue transfer, white emb border...................85.00
Platter
10 3/4" l, "Clarence Terrace, Regent's Park," dk blue transfer 575.00
14 1/2" l, "View of Dublin," dk blue transfer, seashell border ..1,100.00
16 5/8" l, "St. George's Chapel, Regents Street," dk blue transfer, (A)
.........................660.00
19 1/4" l, "Cornwall Terrace, Regent's Park, London," dk blue transfer
.........................795.00

Pudding Bowl, 9 1/2" d, "St. Phillip's Church, Regent's Park, London," beaded rim, dk blue transfer......495.00
Sauce Tureen, with undertray, "Cokethorpe Park, Oxfordshire," Grapevine Border Series, dk blue transfer ... 650.00
Soup Plate
8 3/4" d, "Guy's Cliff, Warwickshire," Grapevine Border Series, med blue transfer 165.00
9 1/4" d, "Liverpool," dk blue transfer
.........................450.00

Other Views

Hall
Plate
9" d, "Oriental Scenery-Mahomedan Mosque," dk blue transfer ..225.00
9 3/4" d, "Tombs Near Etaya on the Jumna River," dk blue transfer
.........................120.00
Platter
14 1/2" l x 11 1/4" w, "Oriental Scenery Below Patna on the Ganges," med blue transfer, "J. Hall & Sons" mark, (A) 431.00
19" l, "Tomb of the Emperor Shah Jehan," Hall's Oriental Series, dk blue transfer 795.00
Soup Plate, 9 7/8" d, "Klosterneuburg, Germany," dk blue transfer, (A)
.........................110.00

Henshall
Plate, 8 3/4" d, "Castle of Furstenfel," fruit and flower border, dk blue transfer
.........................155.00

Maker Unknown
Cup Plate, 3 7/8" d, "Batalha, Portugal," dk blue transfer 145.00
Plate
9" d, "City of Montreal," red transfer
.........................160.00
10" d, "Bridge Of Lugano Italy," blue transfer 175.00

Wood, E.
Plate
5 1/2" d, "Tivoli," Italian Scenery Series, dk blue transfer 165.00
7 5/8" d, "Cascade de Gracy Pres Chambery," French Series, dk blue transfer 155.00
8 1/2" d, "View Near Florence," Italian Scenery Series, dk blue transfer
.........................165.00
9" d
"East View of LaGrange, Lafayette's Home," dk blue transfer
.........................155.00
"Vue de LaPorte Romaine a Andernach," dk blue transfer
.........................195.00
9 1/8" d, "Moulon sur la Marne a Charenton," French Series, dk blue transfer
.........................145.00

10" d
"Castle of Lavenza," dk blue transfer 185.00
"Vue de Chateau Ermenonville," French Series, dk blue transfer
.........................250.00
10 1/4" d, "La Grange the Residence of the Marquis LaFayette," dk blue transfer, chips, (A) 143.00
10 1/2" d, "Oberwessel on the Rhine," brown transfer, yellow border
.........................185.00
Platter
13" l, "Moulin Pres. De Royal. Du Puy de Dome," French Series, dk blue transfer 395.00
14 3/4" l, "Hermitage en Dauphine," French Series, dk blue transfer
.........................695.00
20 1/2" l, "Christianburg, Danish Settlement Off the Gold Coast of Africa," dk blue transfer 1,200.00
Sauce Tureen, 6 1/4" h, "Italian Scenery-Terni," dk blue transfer, (A)
.........................440.00
Soup Plate, "Vue de Chateau Ermnonville," white emb border, dk blue transfer....................180.00
Tureen, 15 1/2" l, with undertray, "Northwest View of La Grange, the Residence of Marquis Lafayette," French scenes on tray, vintage border, dk blue borders, wear, (A) 6,160.00
Vegetable Dish, Cov, 9 1/2" sq, "Environs de Chambery," dk blue transfer, chips, hairlines, (A)...............862.00

STAFFORDSHIRE-ROMANTIC

England
1830-1860

History: Between 1830 and 1860, the Staffordshire District potters produced a tremendous number of useful dinnerwares intended for everyday dining that featured romantic transfer printed designs.

Romantic wares were printed in blue, red, green, black, brown, purple, and yellow. Some patterns were issued in only one color, while some were produced in a variety of colors. Within each color group, there was a great deal of color variation. Blues ranged from the darkest navy to a pale powder blue to shades of turquoise.

Designs used for romantic wares reflected the tastes of the Victorian age. Scenes with castles, alpine mountain peaks, and rivers evoked a fascination with European travel. Oriental scenery expressed the infatuation of the common man with dreams of far away places. English scenes were used, but they depicted homes of the nobility, castles, and other important locations.

Floral designs featured realistic flowers, leaves, fruits, and birds that reflected the English love of gardens. Some scenes added insects or butterflies in imitation of the Chinese patterns.

The Victorians loved the architectural and decorative styles of the past. Gothic elements, French designs from the Louis XV and XVI periods, and even Grecian and Roman designs became part of romantic transfer patterns. Classical designs often showed urns or vases in a garden setting. Some pieces contained allegorical stories.

Oriental designs utilized Chinese and Japanese flowers, baskets, exotic birds, flowering trees, pagodas, and urns. East Indian motifs depicted mosques, minarets, desert scenes, and men and women in Arabian or Turkish clothes. Elements of fantasy in these patterns reflected the love of far-off, romantic places, unseen by the common English resident.

Scenic designs were popular. Pastoral scenes showing the typical English countryside featured rolling fields, domestic farm animals, groves of trees, brooks, and ponds. Figures placed in these scenes usually wore Medieval, Elizabethan, or Empire clothing. Greyhounds were a common decorative element.

Although the names of rivers, countries, cities, or towns often were used as titles for these romantic views, the scenes themselves were imaginary. Most of the scenes appeared rather dreamlike in conception. Tall trees, rivers, castles, arched bridges, gazebos, ruins, or fountains were included in the scenes. Borders were either floral, geometric, or featured reserves with landscape scenes.

Some scenes showed local people in their roles as farmers, fishermen, warriors, dancers, etc. In these cases, the scenic background was less prominent. The figures were most important. Other romantic subjects included zoological, religious, moralistic, botanical, marine, or geometric transfers.

In many instances, the designers of the transfers were not known. Many pottery firms purchased their transfers from engraving companies such as Sergeant and Pepper of Hanley. The firm designed the printed patterns and also engraved the copper plates necessary for printing the wares. Popular designs were used by more than one pottery manufacturer.

Romantic transfers were made by many factories. The best known were Adams, Clews, Davenport, Dillon, Dimmock, Hall, Hicks and Meigh, Meigh, Ridgway, Rogers, Spode, Wedgwood, and Wood.

Commonly found patterns included: Athena, Andalusia, Asiatic Society, Asiatic Views, Caledonia, Cyrene, Ivanhoe, Mesina, Palestine, Tryol, Valencia, and Villa.

Hard to fine patterns were: Belzoni, Carolina, Columbia, Corell, Chinese Marine, Eastern Street Scene, Indian Chief, Italy, Ontario Lake Scenery, Oriental Birds, Temperance Society, and Texian Campaign.

Backstamps were used that reflected the romantic expressions of these Victorian potters. The backstamp was part of the sheet that contained the transfer pattern. When placed on the back of a piece, it indicated the pattern used.

References: Jeffrey B. Snyder, *Romantic Staffordshire Ceramics,* Schiffer Publishing, Ltd. 1997; Petra Williams, *Staffordshire Romantic Transfer Patterns,* Fountain House East, 1978; Petra Williams & Marguerite R. Weber, *Staffordshire II,* Fountain House East, 1986.

Museums: City Museum & Art Gallery, Stoke-on-Trent, England; Henry Ford Museum, Dearborn, MI.

Bowl

    7 3/4" d, rimmed, "Asiatic Pheasants" pattern, sepia transfer, "C.P.Co." mark 30.00

    8 1/2" d, "Italian Villas" pattern, red transfer, "J. Heath & Co." mark 60.00

    11" d

        "Canova" pattern, blue transfer 250.00

        "Napoleon" pattern, mulberry transfer, Charles James Mason 255.00

Charger, 15" d, "Valencia" pattern, red and green transfer, John Ridgway, c1834 . . . . 875.00

Coffeepot, 12 1/2" h, "Gothic" pattern, red transfer, "T. Mayer, Stoke" mark 535.00

Comport, 11" l, "Tyrolean" pattern, blue transfer, Ridgway 595.00

Creamer and Sugar Bowl, "Persian" pattern, brown transfers, William Ridgway, c1830 . . . . 240.00

Creamer, "Friburg" pattern, lt blue transfer 135.00

Cup and Saucer

    "Arabian" pattern, purple transfers, Dillon 65.00

    "Asiatic Pheasants" pattern, lt blue transfers 95.00

    "Brussels" pattern, purple transfers 65.00

    "Chinoiserie After Pillemont" pattern, green transfers, "Wm. Adams & Sons" mark 60.00

    "Cyrene" pattern, red transfers, "Wm. Adams & Sons" mark 65.00

    "Giraffe" pattern, brown transfers, hairlines 145.00

"Japan Flowers" pattern, red transfers, Ridgway, Morley, & Wear, c1840 . . . . 60.00

"Japonica" pattern, red transfers, maker unknown. 65.00

"Non Pariel" pattern, black transfers, "T. & J. Mayer, Longport" mark 65.00

"Rural Scene" pattern, red transfers 60.00

"Tyrolean" pattern, purple transfers, Wm. Adams 65.00

Cup and Saucer, Handleless

    "Gazelle" pattern, pink transfers, Adams, (A) 50.00

    "Paradise" pattern, green transfers, "J. & G. Alcock" mark. 20.00

    "The Sower" pattern, pink transfers, Adams, (A). 40.00

    "Tuscan Sprigs" pattern, magenta transfers 50.00

    "Venetian Temple" pattern, red transfer 65.00

Cup Plate, 3 3/4" d

    "Blenheim" pattern, brown transfer . 50.00

    "Caledonia" pattern, black transfer, Adams 100.00

    "Canova" pattern, green transfer. . . 95.00

    "Fountain" pattern, magenta transfer 45.00

    "Tuscan Rose" pattern, blue transfer, Ridgway. 95.00

Dessert Dish, 9 3/4" H-H, "Oriental Birds" pattern, blue transfer, Ridgway 245.00

Gravy Boat, ftd, "Antiquarian" pattern, magenta transfer 125.00

Pitcher

    6" h, "Pomerania" pattern, red transfer, J. Ridgway. 245.00

    7" h, "Canova" pattern, purple transfer, T. Mayer, sm hole 140.00

    12" h

        "Canova" pattern, med blue transfer, scroll handle. 650.00

        "Corinth" pattern, brown transfer 165.00

Plate

    6" d, "Mogul Scenery" pattern, red transfer, T. Mayer, chips 22.00

    6 1/4" d, "Florilla" pattern, purple transfer, blue, yellow, red, and green accents, (A) 20.00

    6 3/8" d, "Cleopatra" pattern, purple transfer with yellow, blue, and green accents, (A) 15.00

    6 1/2" d

        "Japan Flowers" pattern, red transfer, Ridgway, Morley, and Wear, c1840 . . . . 35.00

        "Pomerania" pattern, pink and purple transfer, Ridgway 70.00

        "Tonquin" pattern, brown transfer 9.00

    6 5/8" d, "Rosetta" pattern, purple transfer with yellow, red, green, and blue ac-

cents, "Rosetta, E. Challinor" mark, pr, (A) 45.00

6 3/4" d, "Canova" pattern, green transfer, T. Mayer 45.00

7" d

"Clyde Scenery" pattern, red transfer, J. & J. Jackson 85.00

"Davenport III" pattern, red transfer 40.00

"Mazara" pattern, pink transfer, "W. Adams & Co. Mazara, England" mark, (A) 20.00

"Mogul Scenery" pattern, red transfer, T. Mayer 40.00

7 1/4" d

"Canova" pattern, lavender transfer, "T. Mayer" mark 45.00

"Fisherman" pattern, blue and brown transfer, "Fisherman, E.W. & S." mark, (A) 20.00

"Medina" pattern, dk purple transfer, "Median, J.F. & Co." mark, (A) 25.00

"Palestine" pattern, med blue transfer 38.00

7 1/2" d

"Andalusia" pattern, red transfer, Adams 95.00

"Asiatic Scenery" pattern, red transfer, J. & J. Jackson 50.00

"Millenium" pattern, purple transfer, Stevenson 145.00

"Tuscan Rose" pattern, purple transfer, Ridgway 95.00

8" d

"Blantyre" pattern, red transfer, "J. & G. Alcock" mark, set of 10 .... 335.00

"Canova" pattern, red transfer, Mayer 85.00

"Indian Temples" pattern, red transfer, maker unknown 65.00

Plate, 8 1/4" d, "Palestine" pattern, red transfer, "imp Adams" mark, $85.

"Japan Flowers" pattern, red transfer, Ridgway, Morley, and Wear, c1836 .... 45.00

"Manhatten" pattern, purple transfer, R. Stevenson 75.00

"Venus" pattern, red, black, and green transfer 55.00

8 1/4" d "Lombardy" pattern, pink transfer, "Lombardy, J. Heath & Co." mark, (A) 45.00

"Suspension Bridges" pattern, pink and green transfer, "E.W. & S. Suspension Bridges" mark, (A). . 20.00

"Venus" pattern, lt blue transfer "P.W. & Co." mark 45.00

8 1/2" d

"Asiatic Views", purple transfer, Francis Dillon, c1834 .... 60.00

"Palestine" pattern, blue transfer, "Palestine, J. Ridgway No. 7184" mark, (A) 25.00

"Quadruped-Spotted Deer," med blue transfer 155.00

"Seaweed" pattern, purple transfer, J. Ridgway 50.00

"The Sea" pattern, red transfer, Wm. Adams 80.00

"Tyrol" pattern, purple transfer, red, blue, and green accents, "IRONSTONE CHINA, TYROL, J. WEDGWOOD" mark, set of 6, (A) . . 65.00

8 5/8" d, "Excelsior" pattern, purple transfer, red, blue, green, and yellow accents, "Ironstone, Excelsior, C. Woolscroft" mark, spider on base, (A) 40.00

8 3/4" d

"Marino" pattern, lt blue transfer, "C.E. & M. Marino" mark 65.00

"Oriental" pattern, red transfer, Wm. Ridgway 75.00

8 7/8" d, "Carrara" pattern, blue transfer, "Carrara, J. Holland" mark, (A). . 30.00

9" d

"Albion" pattern, pink transfer, (A) 50.00

"Arabian Sketches-The March" mark, pink transfer, W. Hackwood 85.00

"Canova" pattern, green transfer, "T. Mayer, Longport" mark 80.00

"Canovian" pattern, purple transfer, Clews 70.00

"Chinese" pattern, pink transfer, "Allerton, England Chinese" pattern, (A) 25.00

"Clyde Scenery" pattern, red transfer, J. & J. Jackson 80.00

"Indian Temple" pattern, red transfer 115.00

"Milanese Pavillions" pattern

Green transfer 65.00

Purple transfer, "J. Heath & Co." mark 65.00

"Millenium" pattern

Brown transfer, "R. Stevenson & Son" mark 100.00

Red transfer, "R. Stevenson & Son" mark 135.00

"Olympic Games-Bullfight" pattern, green transfer, "T. Mayer, Stoke" mark, c1827 .... 90.00

"Oriental Birds", brown transfer, Ridgway 125.00

"Palestine" pattern, blue transfer, Ridgway 65.00

"Quadraped-Antelope", blue transfer, Hall 210.00

"Railway" pattern, green and red transfer, "Enoch Wood & Sons" mark, c1840 .... 160.00

"Vista" pattern, blue transfer, "F.M. & Co. Vista" mark 125.00

9 1/8" d, "Gypsy" pattern, pink transfer, (A) 35.00

9 3/16" d, "California" pattern, blue transfer with red, green, and yellow accents, "California, F.M. & Co." mark, (A) 30.00

9 1/4" d

"Aurora" pattern, green transfer, red, yellow, green, and blue accents, chip, (A) 35.00

"Canova" pattern

Lt blue transfer, "T. Mayer Longport" mark 100.00

Pink and green transfer..... 85.00

"Milanese Scenery", purple transfer, "imp Stubbs" mark 75.00

Oct, "Abbey" pattern, med blue transfer, "L.P. & Co. Abbey Ironstone" mark 95.00

"Palestine" pattern, red transfer, Wm. Adams, repairs 55.00

9 3/8" d

"Italy" pattern, brown transfer, "imp Edge Malkin & Co." mark, (A) 25.00

"Tyrol" pattern, purple transfer, blue, green, and yellow accents, "IRONSTONE CHINA, TYROL, J. WEDGWOOD" mark, set of 4, (A) . . . 70.00

9 1/2" d

"Columbus" pattern, red transfer, Wm. Adams 105.00

"Corsica" pattern, red transfer, Wood & Challinor 75.00

"Florentine" pattern, lt blue transfer, "T.J. & J. Mayer" mark 75.00

"Gondola" pattern, red transfer, Wm. Davenport 85.00

"Mamora" pattern, med blue transfer 140.00

"Palestine" pattern, dk blue transfer, white rim, Stevenson 145.00

"Venus" pattern, green, red, and gray transfer 65.00

9 3/4" d, "Peruvian Horsehunt" pattern, green and brown transfer, Shaw 150.00

10" d

"Acropolis" pattern, lt blue transfer 85.00

"Adelaides Bower" pattern, blue transfer, maker unknown 85.00

"Antiques" pattern, lt blue transfer 80.00

"British Lakes" pattern, brown transfer, R. Stevenson 45.00

"Clyde Scenery" pattern, red and black transfer, J. & J. Jackson, c1831 . . . . 145.00

"Davenport" pattern, blue transfer 95.00

"Florentine Fountain" pattern, purple transfer, Davenport, c1832 . . 95.00

"Fruit Basket" pattern, dk green transfer, maker unknown 175.00

"Italian Buildings" pattern, purple transfer, R. Hall 110.00

"Millenium" pattern, red transfer, "R. Stevenson & Son" mark, c1832 . . . . 195.00

"Moral Maxims," brown transfer, Jacksons 195.00

"Napier" pattern

Blue transfer, "J. & G. Alcock" mark, c1839 . . . . 85.00

Brown transfer, "J. & G. Alcock" mark, set of 10 . . . . 340.00

"Olympian" pattern, blue transfer, J. Ridgway 95.00

"Olympic Games-Discus" pattern, green transfer, "T. Mayer, Stoke" mark, c1827 . . . . 95.00

"Oriental" pattern, lt blue transfer, Alcock 55.00

"Palestine" pattern

Dk blue transfer, Stevenson 145.00

Green transfer, Adams 90.00

"Persian" pattern, purple transfer, Wm. Ridgway, c1830 . . . . 95.00

"Rhone Scenery" pattern, med blue transfer 85.00

"Roselle" pattern, med blue transfer 85.00

"Tyrol" pattern, red transfer w/polychrome accents 45.00

10 1/4" d, "Asiatic Scenery" pattern, red transfer, "Jackson" mark 22.00

10 3/8" d

"Canova" pattern, purple transfer, "T. MAYER AND LONGPORT" mark 95.00

"Parisian Chateau" pattern, pink transfer, "Parisian Chateau, R. Hall" mark, set of 6, (A) 310.00

10 1/2" d

"Abby Ruins" pattern, blue transfer, "T. Mayer, Longport" mark, c1836-38 . . . . 95.00

"Aurora" pattern, red transfer, (A) 50.00

"Caledonia" pattern, green transfer, "Caledonian, RMW & Co." mark, (A) 40.00

"Cambrian" pattern, black transfer 65.00

"Canova" pattern, blue transfer 125.00

"Clyde Scenery" pattern, purple transfer, J. J. Jackson, chips chip in reverse 80.00

"Cologne" pattern, red transfer, "Ralph Stevenson & Son" mark 65.00

"Florentine" pattern, blue transfer, "T.J. & J. Mayer" mark 65.00

"Italian Villas" pattern, purple transfer, "Joseph Heath & Co." mark, c1838 . . . . 95.00

"Milan" pattern, lt blue transfer, "South Wales Pottery" mark 60.00

"Millenium" pattern, brown transfer, "R. Stevenson & Son" mark 105.00

"Oriental Scenery" pattern, black transfer, "T. Mayer Stoke" mark . . . 65.00

"Palestine" pattern, red center, green border, "ADAMS" mark 150.00

"Pomerania" pattern, brown transfer, Ridgway 115.00

"Sea Leaf" pattern, red transfer, Alcock 95.00

"Seasons" pattern, red transfer, Wm. Adams 75.00

10 5/8" d

"Pomerania" pattern, purple transfer, "Pomerania, J.R." mark, (A) . . 40.00

"Tyrol" pattern, purple transfer, red, blue, and green accents, "IRONSTONE CHINA, TYROL, J. WEDGWOOD" mark, set of 3, chips, (A) 40.00

10 7/8" d, "Brussels" pattern, blue transfer, "Ironstone, Brussels, J. Wedgwood" mark, (A) 40.00

Platter

11" l

"Canova" pattern, red transfer, T. Mayer, c1835 . . . . 210.00

"Spanish Convent" pattern, brown transfer, Adams, c1835 . . . . 160.00

11 1/2" l, "Tonquin" pattern, brown transfer 20.00

12" l, "Rhine" pattern, blue-green transfer 125.00

12 1/2" l x 9 3/8" w, "Tyrol" pattern, purple transfer, "IRONSTONE CHINA, TYROL, J. WEDGWOOD" mark, (A) 50.00

13" l, "Friburg" pattern, lt blue transfer 100.00

13 1/4" l, "Palestine" pattern, blue transfer, Ridgway 150.00

13 1/2" l, rect w x cut corners, "Luzerne" pattern, lt blue transfer, Challinor 185.00

14 1/2" l

"India Temple" pattern, blue transfer, Ridgway 475.00

"Scroll" pattern, black transfer, maker unknown 360.00

15" l

"Albion" pattern, blue transfer, Ridgway, Morley, & Wear 395.00

"Canova" pattern, blue transfer, "T. Mayer, Stoke on Trent" mark 350.00

"Jessamine" pattern, brown transfer 125.00

"Olympic Games-Chariot" pattern, green transfer, "T. Mayers, Stoke," c1827 . . . . 395.00

"Tivoli" pattern, blue transfer, Charles Meigh 250.00

"Tuscan Rose" pattern, blue transfer, Ridgway 450.00

"Tyrol" pattern, red transfer, J. Wedgwood, c1845 . . . . 235.00

15 1/4" l

12 1/4" w, "Caledonia" pattern, purple transfer, "imp ADAMS" mark, (A) 280.00

12 3/8" w, "Columbus" pattern, pink transfer, "imp ADAMS" mark, (A) 310.00

15 1/2" l x 12 1/4" w, "Venus" pattern, blue transfer 175.00

Plate, 10" d, "Quadrapeds" pattern, blue transfer, "R. Hall" mark, $250.

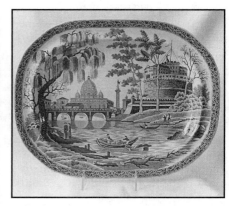

Platter, 14 1/4" l, 11 1/4" w, med blue transfer, "imp Stubbs" mark, $445.

15 3/4" l x 12 1/8" w, "Columbia" pattern, blue transfer, "Columbia, W. Adams & Sons" mark, (A). . . 200.00

16" l
"Asiatic Pheasants" pattern, lt blue transfer 245.00
"Baronial Halls" pattern, black center transfer, blue border transfer, T. Mayer, c1845 . . . . 280.00
"Canova" pattern, blue transfer, T. Mayers 340.00
"Spartan" pattern, blue transfer, "Podmore Walker & Co." mark . . . 250.00

17" l
"Andalusia" pattern, red transfer, Adams 525.00
"Columbus" pattern, purple transfer, Wm. Adams 495.00
"Napier" pattern, green transfer, "George Alcock" mark, c1839
. . . . 385.00
"Sea Leaf" pattern, green transfer, Samuel Alcock, c1835 . . . . . 295.00

17 1/2" l
13 5/8" w, "Jessamine" pattern, brown transfer, "Jessamine, J. Wedgwood" mark, (A) 45.00
14" w, "Rhine" pattern, gray-green transfer 285.00
18" l, "Parisian" pattern, red transfer, c1840s 320.00

19" l
"Palestine" pattern, blue transfer, Adams, c1830s 475.00
"Pomerania" pattern, brown transfer, J. Ridgway 350.00
19 1/4" l x 15 3/4" w, "Fairy Villas" pattern, blue transfer, "Maddock & Sedden" mark 600.00

19 1/2" l
"Antiquarian" pattern, brown transfer
. . . . 450.00
"Morea" pattern, blue transfer, maker unknown 410.00
19 3/4" l, "Florentine" pattern, brown transfer 385.00
20" l x 16" w, well and tree, "Oriental Flower Garden" pattern, brown transfer, Goodwin, Bridgewood, & Orlon 495.00
21" l, well and tree, "Japonica" pattern, purple-red transfer, unmkd 375.00

Sauce Dish, 5 3/8" d, "Alleghany" pattern, purple transfer, unmkd, (A) 25.00

Sauce Tureen
6 1/2" h, "Davenport" pattern, blue transfer 225.00
7" h, "Swiss Scenery" pattern, brown transfer, "John Swift & Co." mark . . . 265.00

Serving Bowl, 11 5/8" H-H, rect, "Asiatic Pheasants" pattern, lt blue transfer. . . . 95.00

Soup Plate
9" d, "Virginia" pattern, lavender transfer
. . . . 95.00
9 1/2" d, "Palmyra" pattern
Brown transfer, "W. & B" mark
. . . . 45.00

Lt blue transfer 49.00
9 3/4" d,
"Avon" pattern, black transfer, pink, yellow, and green accents, (A)
. . . . 30.00
"Versailles" pattern, purple transfer, "Versailles JG" mark, (A) 45.00
9 7/8" d
"Corintha" pattern, pink transfer, "Corintha, E. Challinor" mark, (A)
. . . . 55.00
"Venus" pattern, green, red, and gray transfer, "Podmore & Walker" mark
. . . . 70.00
"Valencia" pattern, blue and black transfer, J. & J. Jackson . . . 125.00
10" d, "Millenium" pattern, red transfer
. . . . 185.00
10 1/4" d
"Indian Temples" pattern, red transfer, Adams, rim chips 125.00
"Olympia" pattern, lavender transfer
. . . . 95.00
10 3/8" d, "Canova" pattern, blue transfer, "T. MAYER and STOKE UPON TRENT" mark, c1836-38 . . . . 125.00
10 1/2" d
"Aurora" pattern, red transfer, Francis Morley 75.00
"Millennium" pattern, purple transfer, (A) 160.00

Teabowl and Saucer, "Peacock" pattern, black transfers, unmkd 110.00

Teapot
7" h x 10" l, "Pompeii" pattern, brown transfer, John & George Alcock, c1839-46
. . . . 275.00
8" h, "Seasons" pattern, black transfer, Adams, restored spout tip 295.00
10" h, "Peruvian Horse Hunt" pattern, green and brown transfer, Shaw, c1850 . . . . 310.00

Tea Service, pot, creamer, sugar bowl, 6 cups and saucers, "Napier" pattern, J. & G. Alcock 940.00

Toddy Plate
4 1/8" d, "Canova" pattern, green and brown transfers 95.00
5" d, "Palestine" pattern, black transfer, Wm. Adams 50.00

Tureen, Cov
7" h, ironstone, "Asiatic Pheasants" pattern, lt blue transfers, hairline . . 150.00
8 1/2" h x 13" l, with undertray, "Italy" pattern, red transfers, "E. Malken & Co." mark 725.00

Vegetable Bowl
8 1/2" d, "Palestine" pattern, Ridgway
. . . . 135.00
9" l x 7" w, "Bologna" pattern, purple transfer, Wm. Adams 150.00
9 7/8" l x 7 5/8" w, rect with cut corners, "Gypsy" pattern, blue transfer, (A)
. . . . 75.00
10" d, "Oriental" pattern, purple transfer, Samuel Moore 135.00

12" l x 9" w, "Rhine" pattern, blue transfer, "John Meir & Son" mark, c1837
. . . . 80.00

Vegetable Bowl, Cov
10 3/4" H-H x 6 3/4" h, hex shape, "India Temple" pattern, med blue transfer, cobalt and gilt molded handles, J. & W. Ridgway 445.00
11" l, "Asiatic Pheasants" pattern, lt blue transfer 195.00

Wash Bowl, "Adelaide's Bower" pattern, red transfer, maker unknown 370.00

Water Pitcher, 10 1/2" h, "Palestine" pattern, blue transfer, scroll handle, (A) 170.00

ST. CLOUD

Seine-et-Oise, France
c1690-1773

History: About 1675, Pierre Chicanneau established a factory for the production of faience and soft paste porcelain at St. Cloud. Shortly after Chicanneau's death in 1678 Berthe, his widow, assumed control of the works.

St. Cloud porcelain was thickly potted with a yellowish color to the body. The glaze was very glassy with a somewhat orange peel texture to the surface. The pieces were decorated in strong polychromes or in the simple blue motifs similar to the faience examples from Rouen, especially in the use of the baroque diapering pattern. Many forms featured plain white and relief patterns. Fish scale-type embellishments were used as the method of decoration.

The variety of wares produced was quite large, exhibiting applied decoration. Accessory pieces, e.g. knife and cane handles, and novelty pieces, some of which were silver mounted, were made. Many of the designs incorporated elements from silverware such as reeding or gadrooning.

Family squabbles plagued the St. Cloud pottery. In 1722, Berthe Coudray died. Henri-Charles Trou II, backed by the sponsorship of the Duc d'Orleans, took control.

The St. Cloud factory ended its operations about 1773.

References: W.B. Honey, *French Porcelain of the 18th Century*,1950; George Savage, *Seventeenth & Eighteenth Century French Porcelain*, Hamlyn Publishing Co. Ltd. 1969.

Museums: J. Paul Getty Museum, Los Angeles, CA, Victoria & Albert Museum, London, England; Wadsworth Atheneum, Hartford, CT.

Beaker, 2 5/8" h, band of blue lambrequins on shoulder, vert fluting on base, c1730, (A) 60.00
Cane Handle, 1 1/2" h, green and gold enameled vert lambrequins, (A). 200.00
Egg Cup, 2 7/8" h, flared ft, blue lambrequins on rim and ft, molded gadroons on waist, c1735, pr, (A) 4,025.00
Teabowl and Saucer, molded and painted as chrysanthemum blossom, puce tipped overlapping petals, black stamen, c1740
. . . . 300.00

STEINS

Germany
1840s to Present

History: A stein is a drinking vessel with a handle and an attached lid that is made to hold beer and ale. The use of a lid differentiates a stein from a mug. Steins range in size from the smallest at 3/10 liters or l/4 liters to the larger at 1, 1 1/2, 2, 3, 4, and 5 liters, and even 8 liters in rare cases. A liter is 1.05 liquid quarts.

General

The finest steins had proportional figures with intricate details that made them appear real. The decorations were made in a separate mold and applied to the body of the stein, giving the piece a raised effect. Etched steins, with the design incised or engraved into the body of the stein, were the most desirable and expensive steins. Artisans used black paint to fill in the lines and then other colors to complete the motif.

The simplest steins to produce were the print under glaze (PUG). A decal or transfer printed scene was applied by the transfer method, the body was covered with an additional coat of transparent glaze, and the piece was refired.

Character or figural steins depicted life-like creations of Indians heads, skulls, animals, Satans, vegetables, buildings, and people. Ernst Bohne's firm produced

fine quality figural steins with realistic expressions.

Occupational steins were steins with a decoration or shape that depicted the owner's occupation. A slogan or the owner's name also may have appeared on the stein.

Thumblifts also came in a variety of designs on steins. Steins designed specifically for export to the United States had a United States shield as the thumblift. Other designs included a monkey, owl, jester, lyre, bust of a figure, twin towers, eagle, Munich maid, lion and shield, dwarf, or huntsman.

Mettlach Steins

The most prolific period in the history of stein production occurred in the second half of the 19th century, coinciding with the peak of Mettlach stein manufacture.

Chromoliths made by Mettlach were molded. The designs appeared to be etched by hand. Although the designs seemed three-dimensional, they were smooth to the touch.

Mettlach's cameos or phanoliths had portraits or small scenes in a translucent white clay set against a green or blue background. Even though these were three dimensional, the relief portions were blended into the background without showing seams.

When fire destroyed the abbey where Mettlach steins were produced in 1921, the company gave up production of chromoliths and cameos. Mettlach's stein competitors included Merkelbach and Wick, Albert Jacob Thewalt, Simon Peter Gerz, and the Girmscheid factory.

Regimental Steins

During the reign of Kaiser Wilhelm II, 1888 to 1918, German reservists frequently purchased souvenir steins that had information such as the owner's name, unit, garrison town, service dates, and rosters of comrades inscribed on them. Munich was the regimental stein capital. Most of the regimental steins date from the early 1890s.

Other European armies also issued regimental steins after the 1890s. A great variety of transfer scenes, finials, stein bodies, and lids was used for regimental steins. Lid varieties that included the finial type, screw off, fuse, flat, prisms, steeple or spindle, helmet, or crown have been identified. The thumblift on the stein usually represented the unit's state of origin or branch of service. Stein body size was usually the standard 1/2 liter. Maker's marks usually were found on pottery steins. Porcelain steins were rarely marked by the maker.

Mettlach military steins were only made in pottery. They were marked on the bottom with an incised stock or mold number and usually were dated.

References: J.L. Harrell, *Regimental Steins*, The Old Soldier Press, 1979; Gary Kirsner, *German Military Steins 1914-1945, 2nd Ed.,* self published, 1996; Gary Kirsner, *The Mettlach Book,* Seven Hills Books, 1983; Gary Kirsner & Jim Gruhl, *The Stein Book, A 400 Year History*, Glentiques, 1990; Dr. Eugene Manusov, *Encyclopedia of Character Steins,* Wallace Homestead, 1976; Dr. Eugene Manusov & Mike Wald, *Character Steins: A Collectors Guide*, Cornwall Books, 1987; R.H. Mohr, *Mettlach Steins & Their Prices*, Rev.4th Ed. Rockford, 1972; R.H. Mohr, *Mettlach Steins, 9th Ed.* privately printed, 1982; James R. Stevenson, *Antique Steins, A Collectors' Guide*, Cornwall books, 1982; Mike Wald, *HR Steins*, SCI Publications, 1980.

Collectors' Club: Stein Collectors International, Inc. Norman Pratore, P.O. Box 5005, Laurel, MD 20726-5005. Membership: $25.00, Magazine *Prosit*.

Museum: Milwaukee Art Center, Milwaukee, WI.

Reproduction Alert: For more than 20 years, several German firms have reproduced regimental type steins. The reproductions, usually made only in porcelain, have different physical characteristics and historical inaccuracies. The firms used only the finial type of lid and tapered bodies as opposed to the straight bodies on original regimentals. Smooth transfers appear on the reproductions. Lids on the reproductions are stamped from a single piece mold and have no seam line.

Collecting Hints: Regimental Steins: Collectors favor steins with inlaid lids. The inlay is a decorated stoneware disk that is set into a pewter rim. The design in the lid is an extension of the colors and designs on the main body of the stein. A few steins did come without lids or with an all pewter lid in a variety of designs. Steins with missing lids are generally reduced fifty percent in value.

After the destruction caused by World War II, locating regimental steins, became difficult. Occasionally some do surface from German attics or barns.

Journals: *The Beer Stein Journal*, P.O. Box 8807, Coral Springs, FL 33075. $20 per year. Quarterly, Publisher: Gary Kirsner; *Regimental Quarterly*, John Harrell, P.O. Box 793, Frederick, MD 21705.

Design

.25 L, stoneware, blue engraved cross in shield, flanked by vert leaves and stems, blue pendants hanging from border, salt glazed, pewter rim and base, (A) 185.00

.5 L

Pottery

Etched, Art Nouveau design with verse, ladies on sides, multicolored, pewter lid, chip on rim 80.00

Multicolored transfer of Bock verse and brewing ingredients, glazed surface, dented pewter lid, (A) . . 84.00

Munchener Burger Brau, multicolored transfer and enamels, engraved pewter lid with brewery logo, (A) 184.00

Relief band of cherubs and gargoyles, blue ground, (A) 68.00

Relief molded German verse in surround, scrolls and body and vert geometrics on base, blue ground, pewter lid, (A) 52.00

Stoneware

Art Nouveau style HP red tulips, blue leaves, blue wavy base, repaired pewter lid, "Merkelbach and Wick" mark, (A) 706.00

Bands of etched blue diamond patterns, salt glazed, metal lid, pewter hinge, (A) 128.00

Blue and purple salt glazed snowflake in circ and band of geometrics and scrolls, pewter lid, (A) 58.00

Brown glazed, relief teardrop design in center oval, geometrics on body, pewter lid, (A) 161.00

Engraved, Art Deco style blue drape with hanging flowerheads, pewter lid, (A) 200.00

Etched

Blue Art Deco swirls and scrolls, pewter lid, Merkelbach and Wick, #2101, (A) 231.00

Blue "HTP" on front, salt glaze, pewter lid with relief of crest of Munich, (A) 33.00

Blue repeating rose window design, salt glaze, flat pewter lid, (A) 118.00

Oct shape, blue vert panels, gray ground, pewter lid with beaded rim, (A) 133.00

Raised jewels, brown glaze, pewter lid, (A) 330.00

Relief and threading, blue German verse in circle on front, florals on side, salt glaze, pewter lid, (A) 55.00

Relief design of repeated circles, brown glaze, pewter lid, (A) 121.00

1 L, stoneware, blue etched florals and leaves arising from base, salt glaze, pewter lid, (A) 45.00

1.5 L, stoneware, salt glaze, engraved panel of vert stylized flower and stem on blue ground, panels of vert stacked circles on blue ground, pewter lid, (A) 208.00

12 L, white relief design of people drinking, grapevines, wine jugs, musical instruments, birds, cherubs, and verse, pale blue ground, interlocking vine handle, cavalier on tree stump knob, hairline and chips, (A) 2,887.00

Figural

.2 L, porcelain, figural Munich child on cream and black banded barrel, Schierholz, (A) 392.00

.25 L, pottery, Munich Child holding stein, inlaid lid, J. Reinemann, (A) 185.00

.3 L, Skull on Book, porcelain, inlaid lid, E. Bohne and Son, (A) 690.00

.5 L

Alligator, porcelain, white, green, and tan, Musterschutz 1,500.00

Bar Maid, pottery, inlaid lid, (A . . . 413.00

Black man in red striped jacket, pottery, inlaid lid, glazed finish, (A) 446.00

Boar's head with hat, brown, Schierholz, repaired chip, (A) 3,630.00

Bock Goat, porcelain, yellow, cream, and brown, inlaid lid, Schierholz, repaired tail, (A) 396.00

Bowling Pins, pottery, tan and green, figural inlaid bowling ball lid, (A) . . . 248.00

Cavalier, pottery, tan, green, brown, inlaid lid, (A) 236.00

Clown, pottery, inlaid lid, pewter repair, (A) 578.00

Devil, pottery, pottery lid with pewter rim, "Westerwalder Neukeramik" mark, lid repair, (A) 303.00

Drunken Monkey, porcelain, inlaid lid, Schierholz, (A) 667.00

Dutch Boy, porcelain, bust, red jacket, tan trousers, arms folded, porcelain lid, Schierholz, (A) 2,476.00

Fireman, stoneware, blue and purple salt glaze, inlaid lid, fireman thumblift, (A) 275.00

Gentleman Rabbit, porcelain, multicolored, (A) 2,990.00

Gooseman of Nuremburg, porcelain, polychrome, (A) 1,725.00

Happy Radish, tan and green, Musterschultz 950.00

Indian, porcelain, natural face, black hair, black trimmed headdress, chips, E. Bohne & Sohne, (A) 338.00

Iron Maiden, stoneware, black salt glaze, inlaid lid, (A) 462.00

Masquerade Lady, porcelain, polychrome, Schierholz, (A) 346.00

Military Monkey, pottery, inlaid lid, pewter repair, (A) 405.00

Monk, purple glaze, Merkelbach & Wicke, c1900 . . . . 285.00

Money Bag, porcelain, arm forms handle, porcelain lid with lid with coins falling out of bag, E. Bohne and Son, chip, (A) 1,560.00

Mother-in-Law, pottery, inlaid lid 656.00

Munich Child, pottery, full figure, tan, black, yellow, and green, inlaid lid, (A) 202.00

Newspaper Lady, porcelain, polychrome, Schierholz, (A) 286.00

Nun

Porcelain, brown-red robe, inlaid lid, (A) 182.00

Pottery, inlaid lid, chip (A) 154.00

Nuremberg Tower, pottery, tan and brown, pewter roof lid, goose man thumblift, (A) 281.00

Owl, stoneware, Mettlach #2036 . . 725.00

Pixie, porcelain, porcelain lid, Schierholz, (A) 1,016.00

Sad Radish, porcelain, Schierholtz 350.00

Singing Pig, porcelain, inlaid lid, Schierholz, (A) 578.00

Soldier, porcelain, tan, (A) 1,552.00

Skull, porcelain, cream-tan ground with black accents, inlaid lid, E. Bohne & Sohne, (A) 462.00

Stacked Pretzels, inlaid pretzel lid, #2388, Mettlach, (A) 578.00

Von Moltke, tan and brown, porcelain, Schierholtz 1,290.00

Wilhelm II, porcelain, tan and cream, porcelain lid, eagle finial, Schierholz, wings repaired 600.00

Mettlach

#24, 1 L, relief panels of Hunting, Drinking, Love, and Death, inlaid lid 495.00

#228, .5 L, white relief designs in 3 panels, German verse on reverse, gray ground, relief of silver grapes and leaves on ft, inlaid lid 395.00

#485, .5 L, relief of scene of musicians and people, tan, figural inlaid lid of kneeling dwarf, (A) 346.00

#812, 1 L, relief design of hunters, inlaid lid 425.00

#958-2181, .25 L, PUG of barmaid, pewter lid 200.00

#1467, .5 L, relief, tan, gray, and brown four seasons design, inlaid lid, (A) 417.00

#1526-595, 1 L, PUG, cavalier with drum, pewter lid, (A) 270.00

#1526-702, 3 L, PUG, parade in front of gasthaus, (A) 636.00

#1526-941, 2 L, PUG, people in front of gasthaus, pewter lid, (A) 693.00

#1526-1237, .5 L, PUG of Dutch children and dog, pewter lid, (A) 408.00

#1642, .5 L, tapestry, design of man drinking, pewter lid 395.00

#1675, .5 L, etched, castle at Heidelberg, inlaid lid, (A) 495.00

#1740, .25 L, relief design of florals, inlaid lid 250.00

#1786, 1 L, etched and glazed, St. Florian extinguishing fire, dragon handle, (A) 1,230.00

#1861, .5 L, etched and PUG, Wilhelm I, inlaid lid, (A) 578.00

#1909-726, .5 L, PUG, beer steins in line to be filled, pewter lid, (A) 523.00

#1909-942, .5 L, PUG, morning rooster meeting night watchman, pewter lid, (A) . . 200.00

#1923, .3 L, relief of scrolls and medallions, inlaid lid 100.00

#1987, .25 L, etched, wild rose design, inlaid lid. 225.00

#1997, .5 L, etched, portrait of George Ehret, inlaid lid. 595.00

#2001K, .5 L, glazed and HP book stein for banking, inlaid lid 650.00

#2002, .5 L, etched, City of Munich, inlaid lid 650.00

#2024, .5 L, etched and glazed Berlin shield, inlaid lid, (A) 715.00

#2025, .3 L, etched, cherubs, inlaid lid 325.00

#2044, .5 L, etched, drinking scene, inlaid lid 670.00

#2057, .3 L, etched, dancing peasants design, inlaid lid 375.00

#2065, 2.4 L, etched and glazed cavalier and bar maiden, jeweled base, inlaid lid 975.00

#2074, .5 L, etched, bird in cage, inlaid lid, (A) 3,335.00

#2077, .3 L, relief, coat of arms, inlaid lid, castle mark 110.00

#2085, 4.1 L, relief of dancing scene, inlaid lid 550.00

#2089, .5 L, etched, man receiving beer from winged barmaid, inlaid lid, H. Schlitt, (A) 1,292.00

#2099, .3 L, etched, man at club table, inlaid lid. 495.00

#2100, .3 L, etched, Germans meeting Romans and "Prosit", inlaid lid, Schlitt, (A) 495.00

#2126, 5.5 L, etched, Symphonia, pewter lid, (A) 5,060.00

#2130, .5 L, etched, soldiers drinking, inlaid lid, (A) 852.00

#2192, .5 L, etched, student joke, Etruscan style, inlaid lid 695.00

#2204, .5 L, decorated relief of Prussian eagle, inlaid lid 775.00

#2277, .5 L, etched design of Nuremberg castle, inlaid lid, (A). 826.00

#2373, .5 L, etched, St. Augustine, Florida, plain handle, inlaid lid 595.00

#2382, .5 L, etched, Thirsty Knight scene, inlaid lid, (A). 888.00

#2391, 1 L, etched, court scene, inlaid lid, (A) 2,541.00

#2441, .5 L, etched, men playing dice, inlaid lid, (A) 558.00

#2530, .5 L, cameo, boar hunting scene, inlaid lid, (A) 720.00

#2580, .5L, etched, "Die Kannenburg" design, inlaid lid 800.00

#2583, .5 L, etched, Egyptian motif, inlaid lid 850.00

#2652, .5 L, cameo, 3 white scenes of knights on blue ground, dk blue-gray tower body, inlaid lid, sgd "Stahl," (A) 693.00

#2727, .5 L, etched and glazed, occupational-printer, inlaid lid, (A). 2,830.00

#2730, .5 L, etched and glazed, occupational-butcher, inlaid lid 500.00

#2780, 1 L, etched, tavern scene, inlaid lid, (A). 814.00

#2802, .5 L, etched Art Nouveau design of wheat and hearts, inlaid lid, (A) 462.00

#2824, 3.8 L, relief molded design of castle, relief molded lid 4,000.00

#2828, .5 L, etched and glazed relief, castle at Wartburg, figural castle inlaid lid, (A) 2,541.00

#2831, .5 L, etched, owl on front, Siedel Science of Philadelphia, inlaid lid, (A) 5,290.00

#2833, .5 L, etched, students drinking, inlaid lid 630.00

#2951, 1 L, white cameo of Prussian eagle, green ground, pewter lid 795.00

#2958, 2.8 L, etched, boy bowling, inlaid lid 700.00

#3135, .5 L, etched, American flag and eagle, inlaid lid 1,250.00

2.2 liter, 15 1/4" h, boy with flute, brown glazes, pewter lid, #2786, (A) $575.

#3137, .5 L, etched, green and white Art Nouveau design, (A) 1,210.00

#3168, .5 L, etched, hunter on horse and dog, inlaid lid of horse, (A) 2,137.00

#3202, .5 L, etched, automobile and drivers, inlaid lid, (A) 3,465.00

#3236, .5 L, etched, blue and white Art Nouveau design, inlaid lid 575.00

#5021/5193, 5 L, faience, man drinking from goblet, floral design around body, pewter lid, (A) 952.00

Regimental

.5 L

Porcelain

"1 Eisenbahn-Baon, Munchen 1903-05," named "Pionier Paul Hukong," 4 side scenes and roster, winged wheel thumblift, skyline of Munchen, lithophane, pewter lid, (A) 871.00

"1 Foot Artillery, Neu Ulm 1901-03," named "Joseph Manr," 2 side scenes and roster, lion thumblift, prism inlaid lid with military farewell scene, (A). 616.00

"2 Bavarian Foot Artillery, Metz 1910-12," named "Res. Glanzmann," 2 side scenes, roster, stanhope in lion thumblift, (A) 751.00

"2 Chevauleger, Dillingen-Regensburg, 1907-10," named "Chevauleger Kronschnable," 4 side scenes, roster, lion thumblift, (A). 660.00

"4 Bad Feld Art Regt. No. 66 Rastaff 1899-1901" "Reservist Ott" at top, pewter lid with cannon and soldiers finial, crowned winged lion on handle, scrolled handle, man and woman lithophane on base, (A) 250.00

"4 Infantry Metz, 1900-02," named "Friedrich Triem," 4 side scenes, eagle thumblift, crown finial, (A) 347.00

"6 Chevauleger, Bayreuth 1911-14," named "Chevauleger Lucht," 4 side scenes and roster, lion thumblift with stanhope, pewter screw lid with relief scene and blue jewel, (A) 924.00

"9 Infantry, Wurzburg 1897-99," named "Andreas Wahler," 4 side scenes and roster, lion thumblift, pewter lid, (A) 302.00

"10 Field Artillary, Hannover, 1903-05," named "Gef. Dohmeier," 2 side scenes, roster, female thumblift, screw-off lid, (A) 515.00

"11 Infantry Rastatt, 1907-09," named "Res. Illig.," 4 side scenes, roster, griffin thumblift, lines in lithophane, (A) 396.00

"18 Bavarian Infantry Landau, 1893-95," named "Gef. Phil Frantz," 2 side scenes, Mason occupation on front, (A) 433.00

"20 Dragoon, Karlsruhe 1905-08," named "Gef. Roth," 4 side scenes and roster, eagle thumblift, lithophane, (A) 693.00

"22 Bavarian Infantry Zweibrucken, 1910-12," named "Infanterist Bauer," 4 side scenes, roster, lion thumblift with stanhope, (A) 605.00

"22 Infantry, Zweibrucken 1906-08," named "Gef. Gustav Schneider," 2 side scenes and roster, lion thumblift, wear, (A) 577.00

"23 Infantry, Saargemund 1909-11," named "Res. Schwarz," 2 side scenes and roster, lion thumblift with stanhope, (A) 401.00

"33 Field Artillery, Metz, 1911-13," named "Res. Thanscheidt," 4 side scenes, horsehead thumblift, (A) 402.00

"80 Susl, Wiesbaden 1910-12," named "Res. Hohler," 4 side scenes and roster, eagle thumblift, (A) . . 671.00

"110 Grenadier, Mannheim 1901-03," named "Grenadier Hutter," center scene and roster, lithophane, eagle finial on pewter lid, (A) 393.00

"115 Infantry, Darmstadt," named "Gardist Nold," 2 side scenes, roster, lion thumblift, (A) 462.00

"167 Infantry, Cassel 1901-03," named "Res. Trube," 4 side scenes and roster, relief on body, eagle thumblift, kneeling soldier finial, (A) . . . 629.00

Pottery

Third Reich, Panzer-Abwehr, Abtl. 10, Staubing 1935-36, multicolored transfer and enamels, flat metal lid, (A) 346.00

Stoneware

Etched, 11th Infantry 1909, crest of Bavaria, multicolored, relief pewter lid with crest, hairline and chip 100.00

"No. 1 Telegraph 1907-09," named "Richard Kirrbach," center scene and roster, eagle thumblift with pendant, initials and crown on pewter lid, (A) 484.00

"15 Infantry, Neuburg 1912-14," named Hans Leikauf," " In remembrance of the military bakery in Munich 1913-14," 4 sides scenes with 2 of bakery, roster, lion thumblift, prism lid, screw cov missing, (A) 808.00

"Garde-Schutzen-Batll., #1, Comp. Gr.-Lichterfelde, 1904-06," named "Garde Schutz Hermann Schmidt," 2 side scenes, roster, eagle thumblift, (A) 2,475.00

1L

Pottery

"S.M.S. Kaiserin, Keil 1912-15," named "Res. Grotke," 4 side scenes and roster, inscribed rim, replaced pewter lid, (A) 726.00

"S.M.S. Prinze Rgt. Luitpold Keil, 1912-15," named "Res. Bamweg," 2 side scenes, roster, ship on front, eagle thumblift, screw-off lid with porcelain inlay of woman, stanhope on finial, (A) 1,485.00

"S.M.S. von d. Tann, Wilhelmshaven 1912-15," named "Res. Schmidt," 4 side scenes and roster, inscribed top, pewter lid, replaced thumblift and finial, (A) 726.00

Stoneware, Third Reich, "Munchen 1934," blue transfer, pewter lid with "WR," (A) 302.00

Scenic

.25 L

Earthenware, HP genre scene titled "Zwischen Zwei Fevern," pewter lid, "imp R.H. Germany & 943" mark, (A) . 40.00

Stoneware, boy in soldier uniform riding stick pony, children in sm carriage pulled by goat, transfer printed and enameled, pewter lid, (A) 162.00

.3 L, pottery, etched scene of man being kicked out of gasthaus, multicolored, pewter lid, (A) 110.00

.5L

Faience

Manganese, green, blue, and yellow scene of woman holding fan, pewter lid with E.V.B." and emb, domed thumb piece, dtd 1793, (A) . 950.00

Polychrome man drinking from jug, lg shade trees, yellow, blue, and green, pewter lid with "G.M." and domed thumb rest, dtd 1810, (A) 1,000.00

Porcelain

Hunter and woman seated at table, multicolored transfer and enamels, lithophane, pewter lid, (A) . . 115.00

Hunter bidding farewell to companion, multicolored transfer and enamels, lithophane, pewter lid with blue glass jewel, pewter repair, (A) 82.00

Hunters and fox, multicolored transfer and enamels, lithophane, pewter lid, (A) 110.00

Occupational

Farming scene, multicolored transfer and enamels, named "Josef Fusseder," pewter lid, (A) 476.00

Jockey in racing scene with Munich skyline in bkd, multicolored transfer and enamels, named "F. Sonderhauser," pewter lid, (A) 808.00

Tyrolean couple standing in bar, multicolored transfer and enamels, lithophane, pewter lid, (A) 110.00

Pottery

Etched

Diana and Hunters, polychrome, inlaid lid, (A) 260.00

Frog dressed as hunter, multicolored, pewter lid, (A) 243.00

Lohengrin's arrival, relief pewter lid of lady in gown with shield, Hauber and Reuther, (A) 308.00

Scene of hunter at table with serving maid in colors, pewter lid, Hauber and Reuther, strap repaired, (A) 155.00

Franz DeFregger Gasthaus scene, multicolored transfer and enamels, pewter lid, (A) 200.00

Man smoking pipe, multicolored transfer and enamels, pewter lid, (A) 80.00

Multicolored relief of festive drinking scene, figural inlaid lid of standing man 100.00

Munich Child, multicolored transfer and enameling, pewter lid, (A) 112.00

Relief

Composers, tan, green, brown, and black, inlaid lid of books, lyre thumblift, (A) 231.00

Dwarfs playing instruments, tan, pewter lid, Diesinger, (A) 184.00

Lovers in castle setting in colors, castle form pottery lid, (A) 231.00

Man at table with barmaid in colors, pewter lid, (A) 92.00

Man riding high wheel bicycle in center panel, vines and leaves on sides, blue and brown, relief pewter lid with cherub and high wheel bicycle, (A) 440.00

Military marching band, multicolored, pewter lid, Hauber & Reuther, (A) 305.00

Three monkeys reading books and examining skull, figural monkey handle, multicolored, figural inlaid lid of skulls and barmaid, (A) 467.00

Scene of Deggendorf, multicolored transfer and enamels, "Greetings from Deggendorf," pewter lid, chip on base, (A) 173.00

Scene of Lindau, multicolored transfer and enamels, pewter lid, (A) 121.00

Scene of Linz, multicolored transfer and enamels, pewter lid, dented 75.00

Scene of bust of man with pointed hat seated at table, German verse, multicolored transfer and enamels, pewter lid, (A) 80.00

1 liter, 13 1/2" h, stoneware, blue and tan accents, gray ground, pewter lid, Simon Peter Gerz, c1900, $420.

Stoneware

Four panels of romantic scenes, red-brown, porcelain inlaid lid, Westerwald, (A) 108.00

Hofbrauhaus Munchen, multicolored transfer and enamels, relief pewter lid with Munich child, (A) . . . 347.00

Man drinking at table Munich child coming out of foam, multicolored transfer and enamels, pewter lid, (A). 346.00

Relief of dwarfs toasting, gray, porcelain inlaid lid, Westerwald, (A) 132.00

Relief of stag in forest, blue glaze, flat pewter lid, (A). 47.00

Transfer and multicolored enameled Munich Child and German "Greetings from Munich," sculpted pewter lid, (A). 254.00

1 L

Faience

HP scene of 2 men on hillside, buildings in bkd, pewter lid with pewter coin, pewter tear, c1920 . . . 150.00

Man playing mandolin, multicolored transfer, pewter lid and base, 1960 . . . . 139.00

Stylized c1770 European buildings in colors, pewter lid, (A) 1,760.00

Pottery

Relief design of drinkers in beerhall, multicolored, pewter lid 80.00

Scene of Berchtes gaden, multicolored transfer and enamels, "Greetings from Berchtes gaden," pewter lid, (A). 317.00

Stoneware

Dutch woman with 2 boys smoking, transfer printed and enameled, pewter lid, (A) 195.00

Fallen man with overturned cart, multicolored transfer and enamels, pewter lid, replaced thumblift, (A) 52.00

Relief of king with dwarf on front, geometrics on sides and base, gray, porcelain inlaid lid, Westerwald, (A) 200.00

STIRRUP CUPS

Staffordshire, England
c1770-1890

History: Whieldon made the first earthenware stirrup cups. They dated about 1770 and were in the shape of fox masks. Later animal shapes included deer, stag, hare, and bear heads.

The Staffordshire potters made a wide variety of stirrup cups, and they were rarely marked. Until 1825 the earthenware stirrup cups were well modeled and colored in naturalistic tones. After that date, quality decreased.

During the last quarter of the 19th century, stirrup cups were made in soft paste porcelain by Derby, Rockingham, and Coalport. In addition to wild animal heads, bull dog, bull terriers, setters and Dalmatian heads were manufactured.

Dalmatian, 5 1/2" l, pearlware, black splotches, gray nose, white and black ears, black rim, c1820 . . . . 1,800.00

Fox

3 7/8" l, porcelain, rust and brown body, white base with gray accents, "gold Tally ho," c1820. . . . . 1,450.00

4 1/2" l, pearlware, rust and white face, black nose and eyes, yellow band, c1810 . . . . 2,250.00

Greyhound

6 3/4" l, lt mustard yellow coat, gray muzzle, dk brown eyes, c1825, (A) 2,650.00

Hare

5 7/8" h, black basalt, 19th C, unmkd, (A) 1,495.00

7" l, pearlware, brown streaked glaze, c1760 . . . . 6,200.00

Hound Head

4 1/2" l, creamware, black eyes, nose, and whiskers, brown markings, Staffordshire, (A) 800.00

4 3/4" l, creamware, overall rust ground, c1800-10 . . . . 1,800.00

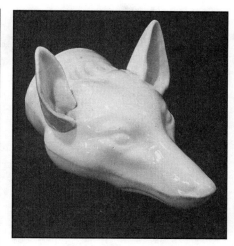

Fox Head, 4 5/8" l, pearlware, white glaze, $595.

5 1/8" l, porcelain, brown top and ears, blue eyes, gray nose, black muzzle, c1820. . . . . 1,800.00

5 1/4" l, pearlware, cream ground, black snout and eyes, tan band, early 19th C 1,650.00

5 1/2" l, pearlware, dk rust ears, black muzzle and eyes, lt rust ground, mustard yellow band 1,650.00

5 3/4" l

Porcelain, tan splotches, lt tan and white face, tan ears, black eyes, Derby 2,750.00

Treacle glaze, mottled brown with gray splotches in ears and eyes, England, c1830 . . . . 1,550.00

6" l, porcelain, dk gray floppy ears, white face, black eyes, salmon nose, black band with matte gold, Derby, c1820 . . . . 2,750.00

7 1/4" l, vert ears, Rockingham glaze, c1840 . . . . 1,550.00

Pug, 3 1/4" l, porcelain, dk tan body, black whiskers and eyes, gold band on neck, c1840 . . . . 2,800.00

Stag Head

4 3/4" l, gray ears and neck, black eyes, rust ground, c1820 . . . . 1,950.00

5" l, overall lt rust ground, yellow and dk brown accents, black and white eyes, c1800, Staffordshire, restored 2,500.00

5 1/8" l, creamware

Cream ground with brown sponging, black eyes 4,000.00

Green, yellow, and manganese streaks and accents, cracks and chip, (A). 665.00

5 1/4" l, earthenware, green and yellow streaks, brown nose, ears, and lashes, brown chevrons, cream ground, c1780 . . . . 2,650.00

STONEWARE

London and Staffordshire, England
c1670 to Present

History: Stoneware, made from clay to which some sand had been added, was fired at a higher temperature than ordinary earthenwares and became partly vitrified and impervious to liquids. Often it was glazed by throwing salt into the kiln at full heat. (See: Salt Glaze.)

Stoneware was first made in England in 1672 when John Dwight founded Fulham Pottery and received a patent. He started by making copies of German wine jugs called "graybeards" and also modeled portrait busts, jugs, mugs, and red clay teapots. Dwight died in 1703. Fulham Pottery was carried on by his family. Dwight's examples were unmarked.

In Staffordshire, John and Philip Elers made red stonewares and also introduced salt glazing and other improvements. Stoneware was made by firms throughout the Staffordshire Potteries district. Most stoneware was utilitarian in nature, but some of the useful wares were given a decorative treatment.

The Morleys made brown salt glazed stonewares in Nottingham between 1700 and 1799. Doulton & Watts were the best known and largest manufacture of commercial stonewares. English stoneware still is made, especially by present day studio potters like Bernard Leach, Charles Vyse, and Michael Cardew.

References: J.F. Blacker, *The A.B.C. of English Salt Glaze Stoneware from Dwight to Doulton,* Stanley Paul & Co. 1922; Jonathan Horne, *English Brown Stoneware,* Antique Collectors' Club, Ltd. 1985; Adrean Oswald, R.J.C. Hildyard & R.G. Hughes, *English Brown Stoneware 1670-1900,* Faber & Faber, 1982.

Museums: British Museum, London, England; Cincinnati Art Museum, Cincinnati, OH; County Museum, Truro, England; Victoria & Albert Museum, London, England.

Beaker, 4 1/2" h, etched red stylized bird with yellow beak and legs in yellow outlined dk blue roundel, dk blue rim, "Reinhold Merkelbach" mark, (A) 82.00

Bottle, 9 1/4" h, gray ground with blue traces, modeled mask on neck, 3 molded overlapped floral medallions on body, Rhineland, 17th C, (A) 1,380.00

Ewer

    10" h, blue relief of St. Hubert in circle on face, flowerheads and leaves on sides, ram's head handles, salt glaze, Germany, (A) 45.00

    11" h, donut body, flared ft, relief of geometrics on body, bird face on spout, tor-

so on handle, blue salt glaze
. . . . 100.00

    15 1/2" h, relief molded scene of St. Hubertus on side, molded grotesque head spout, rings on neck, applied lion heads on body, animal torso handle, blue salt glaze, (A) 248.00

    15 3/4" h, circ body, spread ft, figural mask on spout, loop handle, relief of blue crest on sides, leaf design on ft, (A) 139.00

    20" h, blue and gray, relief center band of king and subjects, lg face on spout with ring, figural boy handle 250.00

Flask, 7 5/8" h, globular shape, applied roundels of janus heads between leaves flanking band of horse heads, urns, and leaves, coat of arms of Amsterdam on neck, applied dbl handle, Germany, early 17th C, (A) . . 215.00

Garden Seat, 22 1/2" h, figural cushion with hanging tassels, cylinder body with lion heads and drapery, circ base with medallions, cobalt decorations 2,500.00

Jar, 6 3/4" h, cylinder shape, everted lip, side loop handles, imp stylized foliage between reeded bands, brown saltglaze, Nottingham, late 18th C, (A) 173.00

Jug

    4 1/8" h, baluster shape, brown body with turnings and floret reliefs, emb gilt metal cov and chain, Germany, 19th C
. . . . 350.00

    4 1/4" h, incised scrolling vines and tulip heads on manganese ground, blue glazed trim bands, Westerwald, 18th C, (A) 375.00

    6 1/2" h, bulbous base, slender neck, Bellarmine, bearded mask under rim, brown, Germany, c1590, (A) . 1,150.00

    6 3/4" h, bulbous shape, imp rosettes, cobalt ground, Westerwald, c1680-1710, handle repair. 450.00

    7 3/8" h, narrow base, bulbous body, narrow neck, rolled rim, bearded mask on neck, crest on body, mottled ground, Germany, c1600-68 . . . . 1,850.00

    8 1/4" h, flattened front and reverse, cobalt "GR" in radiating cartouche, scrolling leaves on cobalt sides, horiz threaded cobalt neck, Westerwald, c1740, hairlines. 575.00

    9" h, bulbous base, slender neck, rolled rim, Bellarmine, imp beaded mask on neck, imp crest on body, marbled ground, Germany 1,650.00

    9 1/2" h, bulbous body, flared ft, "Tigerware," brown glaze, Germany, c1600-50
. . . . 1,350.00

    12 1/4" h, incised and molded vert bands of diamonds and squiggles, "GR" on side, manganese threaded neck, Westerwald, c1720-40 . . . . 2,700.00

    14 1/2" h, ovoid, arched handle, mask spout, incised figural and branch decoration, England, 18th C 275.00

Loving Cup, 6" h, relief of toast to the hunt on front, taverners on reverse, stippled ground,

fluted base, leaf molded handles, white, Turner, late 18th C, (A) 748.00

Mustard Jar, 3 1/2" h, blue glazed dots and wavy base, 3 sm feet, pewter lid, Germany, (A) 40.00

Pitcher

    6 3/4" h, engraved blue flowerhead and swirling leaves on gray ground, purple threaded rim, c1840, (A) 462.00

    9 5/8" h, bulbous base, cylinder neck, blue glazed incised vert Art Nouveau motifs
. . . . 575.00

Tankard

    5 1/4" h, white body with relief of classical figures on textured ground, engine-turned foot rim, brown glazed band on upper section, metal mtd rim, Turner, c1800, (A) 375.00

    8 3/8" h, brown ground, top half dipped with dk iron brown, relief decorated central panel of paneled tavern scene surrounded by houses and trees over hunt subject, later metal rim band, Staffordshire, mid 18th C, (A) . . 575.00

Tobacco Jar, 9 1/4" h, relief, band of men around middle, hearts on cov, blue salt glaze, figural dwarf knob, Germany, chips and crack 55.00

Vase, 15 1/2" h, circ body, slender neck, spread ft, 2 rope twist handles with dog mask terminals, blue and gray relief of Justice holding scales on sides, stylized leaf border, flowerhead ft, Gerz, (A) 110.00

Pitcher, 8 3/4" h, brown ext, white int, "imp GERMANY" mark, $40.

Whistle, 3" h, figural bird, gray ground with blue and manganese accents, tapered circ base, Westerwald, 18th C, (A) 375.00

STRAWBERRY CHINA

Staffordshire, England
1820-1860

History: Strawberry china ware, a soft earthenware produced by a variety of English potteries, was made in three design motifs: strawberry and strawberry leaves (often called strawberry luster), green feather-like leaves with pink flowers (often called cut-strawberry, primrose or old strawberry), and the third motif with the decoration in relief. The first two types were characterized by rust red moldings. Most examples had a creamware ground and were unmarked.

Bowl, 5 3/4" d, red strawberries, green leaves, dk red tendrils on int, dk red lined rim, unmkd 75.00

Cup and Saucer, polychrome strawberries and leaves, hairline and chips, (A) . . . 250.00

Plate

7 1/4" d, pearlware, wreath of red strawberries, with yellow accents in green caps, red, yellow, and blue petaled flowers, blue and yellow buds with green and yellow leaves, pink border with red vines and stripes, (A) . . 130.00

7 1/2" d, strawberries in urn pattern in center, strawberries and leaves on border, polychrome 435.00

8 3/8" d, pearlware, pink polychrome basket in center with red and yellow strawberries, pink, rose, yellow, and blue petaled flowers and green leaves, border of green leaf swags and red and yellow strawberries and yellow and pink flowers, red-brown striped rim, (A) 75.00

Plate, 6 3/4" h, black transfer in center, red and green strawberries, relief molded border, $155.

8 5/8" d, center with red and yellow strawberries on vine and green leaves, pink and yellow roses, vine border with red and yellow strawberries and pink roses, red striped rim, (A) 90.00

8 3/4" d, pearlware, red and yellow strawberry and purple florets, ribbon, and green leaves in center, pink flowers with red and yellow strawberries on black and red vines on border, red lined rim 100.00

8 1/2" d, stoneware, 3 bunches of pink luster strawberries and leaves, Clementson Brothers, c1850, (A) 110.00

8 7/8" d, band of red, green, yellow, and black strawberries, leaves, and stems on border, black lined scalloped rim, "imp Rogers" mark, pr, (A) 165.00

Sugar Bowl, Cov, 6 1/8" h x 7 3/8" l, oval body with scrolled handles, flared scalloped rim, flower knob, polychrome strawberries and leaves, repairs, (A) 160.00

Teabowl, pearlware, orange-red strawberries, magenta flowerheads, green leaves, c1820, pr 225.00

Teapot

5 1/2" h, globular shape, Queen's Ware, enameled red strawberries, mauve flowerheads, and green leaves, leaf molded handle and spout, "imp Wedgwood" mark, c1770, restored chips, (A) 1,725.00

6 3/4" h x 11" l, oval body with scrolled handle, flared scalloped rim, flower knob, polychrome strawberries and leaves, repairs and chips, (A) 275.00

7" h x 11 3/4" l, pearlware, oval with vert pleating, gallery rim, dolphin shaped handle, curved spout, floral rosette knob, polychrome strawberries and leaves, repairs, (A) 360.00

Tea Set, pot, 6 3/8" h, creamer, open sugar bowl, vert fluted bodies, red strawberries, white blossoms, green leaves, gold banded rims, England 65.00

SUSIE COOPER

Burslem, Staffordshire, England
1932 to Present

A SUSIE COOPER PRODUCTION CROWN WORKS, BURSLEM ENGLAND c1932

History: Susie Cooper studied at the Burslem Art School in Staffordshire in 1922. She made jugs, bowls, and vases in stoneware with Art Nouveau style incised designs. When Cooper finished her studies, she became a designer for A.E. Gray & Co. Ltd. at Hanley, Staffordshire in 1925.

She founded Susie Cooper Pottery, Burslem in 1932. Cooper designed and

manufactured functional shape, earthenware tablewares with bright floral and abstract designs. Cooper introduced the "can" shape for the coffeepot, the straight sided shape that has become a universal design. Art Deco designs of bright oranges, greens, and browns were found on her later wares.

One of Cooper's most well known bird shapes was the Kestrel range of tablewares introduced in 1932. Coffee, tea, and dinnerware were all produced in the Kestrel shape which was so popular it remained in production until the late 1950s. Other bird shapes included Curlew in 1932, Wren in 1934, and Falcon in 1937.

Susie Cooper experimented with many decorating techniques for her wares. She developed the "Crayon Loop" pattern utilizing a crayoning technique where color was made up into sticks to draw on the wares. She used an aerographing technique for sgraffito patterns as in "Scroll" and "Astral." Cooper also utilized tubelining and "in-glaze" decorations.

For 30 years, Susie Cooper pottery was located at the Crown Works, Burslem. Patterns designed during the 1930s included "Bronze Chrysanthemums," "Scarlet Runner Beans," "A Country Brunch," "Orchids," "Shepherd's Purse," "Dresden Spray," "Nosegay," "Printemps," "Grey Leaf," "Cactus," and "Woodlands."

In addition to tablewares, Susie Cooper made vases, jugs, figures, wall masks, lamp bases, centerpieces, water and lemonade sets, cruet sets, cheese stands, candlesticks, ashtrays, hors d'oeuvres sets, and nursery wares during the 1930s.

She introduced lithography in 1935 to ensure both speed and accuracy. No. 1017 was a best seller for about 20 years. Other lithographed patterns followed which Cooper designed. Pattern numbers on pieces indicated whether they were before or after Dresden Spray which was so helpful in dating

Wartime slowed production as well as fires in 1942 and 1957. Bone china was introduced in the 1950s when Susie Cooper acquired Jason China Company, Ltd. Some of the same patterns were used for both earthenware and bone china. The last earthenware patterns were made in 1964. Bone china patterns in the 1960s included "Persia," "Venetia," "Assyrian Motif," and "Corinthian."

Susie Cooper died at age 92 in 1994. Her pottery eventually became part of the Wedgwood Group and patterns now decorate fine bone china tableware with the Wedgwood-Susie Cooper Design backstamp. The "can" coffeepot shape is still used.

References: Andrew Casey, *Susie Cooper Ceramics, A Collectors Guide*, Jazz Publications, Ltd. 1992; Ann Eatwell, *Susie Cooper Productions*, Victoria & Albert Museum, Faber & Faber, 1987; Reginald G. Haggar, *Century of Art Education in the Potteries*, 1953; Francis Salmon, *Collecting Susie Cooper, 1st Ed.*, Francis Joseph Publications, Ltd. 1995; Judy Spours, *Art Deco Tableware*, Rizzoli, 1988; Adrian Woodhouse, *Susie Cooper*, Tribly Books, 1992; Bryn Youds, *Susie Cooper: An Elegant Affair*, Thames & Hudson, Inc., 1996; Bryn Youds, *The Ceramic Art of Susie Cooper*, Thames & Hudson, 1996.

Collectors' Club: Susie Cooper Collector's Group, Bryn Youds/Allison Dobbs, P.O. Box 7436, London N12 7QF, UK. Membership: $15.00, quarterly newsletter.

Museum: Victoria & Albert Museum, London, England.

Bachelor Set, teapot, 4" h, milk jug, sugar basin, cup and saucer, side plate, "Gladioli" pattern, yellow, red, and green, Kestral shape, (A) 230.00

Biscuit Barrel, 6 5/8" h, "Moon and Mountain" pattern, red, blue, green, yellow, and black, Gray's Pottery, hairline 450.00

Bowl

    6 1/2" d, "Gardenia" pattern, Kestral shape 25.00

    8 1/4" d, yellow, red, brown, black, and green overlapping triangles, Gray's Pottery, rim chip, (A) 357.00

Box, 5 " l, rect, black, yellow, orange, green, and blue stripes, Gray's Pottery, (A) . . 713.00

Breakfast Set, teapot, 4 1/2" h, creamer, open sugar bowl, 3 bar toast rack, tray, 11" l, "Wedding Ring" pattern, narrow green bands over wide green band, Quail shape 595.00

Chocolate Pot, 5" h, "Dresden Rose" pattern 120.00

Coffee Can and Saucer

    Brown, yellow, and black overlapping rectangles, "A Susie Cooper Production" mark, (A) 267.00

Coffeepot, 7 1/2" h, "Tyrol" pattern, green crosses, green banding, yellow trimmed spout and cov, Kestral shape, (A) . . . 285.00

Coffee Service

    Pot, 6 5/8" h, milk jug, sugar basin, 6 cans and saucers

        "Everlasting Life" pattern, green and brown stylized foliage, Kestral shape, (A) 570.00

        Gilt outlined purple, yellow, blue, and orange luster band of sliced fruit, Gray's Pottery, (A) 230.00

    Pot, 7 1/4" h, milk jug, sugar basin, 4 cans and saucers, rust band with sgraffito dashes under wide beige band, Kestral shape, (A) 285.00

    Pot, 7 7/8" h, milk jug, sugar basin, 6 cans and saucers, Kestral shape

Coffeepot, 7 1/4" h, Kestral shape, coffee can and saucer, cream sgraffito crescents, orange ground, "Susie Cooper Crown Works England" marks, coffeepot, $795., coffee can and saucer, $225.

        Graduated black bands, red border bands, "A Susie Cooper Production" marks, (A) 678.00

        "Green Leaves" pattern, "A Susie Cooper Production" marks. . . . 375.00

Creamer and Sugar Bowl, creamer, 3 5/8" h

    Sugar Bowl, 1 3/8" h, Kestral shape, relief sgrafitto crescents on med blue ground, cream ints, running deer mark 125.00

    Sugar bowl, 2 1/4" h, painted blue, green, purple, and black lg flowerheads, cream ground, red rims, c1925 . . . . 165.00

Cup and Saucer

    Kestral shape

        Gardenia pattern 25.00

        Red and gray bands 25.00

Cup and Saucer, Demitasse, pink and green tiger lilies 18.00

Demitasse Set, coffee pot, 7 1/2" h, creamer, sugar bowl, 6 cups and saucers, conc pink and gray bands, scattered pink dots, pattern #475, Kestral shape 625.00

Dish, 4" sq, printed and painted "Pastoral" design of deer in colors, green banded, clipper mark, (A) 143.00

Ewer, 11 1/4" h, tube lined yellow and turquoise stylized orchids and foliage, buff ground, painted signature, (A) 392.00

Gravy Boat, "Gardenia" pattern, Kestral shape 40.00

Hot Water Pot, Cov, 5" h, "Horse and Jockey" design, yellow jockey, black horse, Kestral shape, "Susie Cooper Productions" mark, (A) 267.00

Jug, 4 3/4" h, yellow, gray, black, and brown overlapping geometric squares, "Susie Cooper Production" mark, (A) 500.00

Lemonade Jug, 7 1/2" h, "Cubist" pattern, black, red, blue, yellow, and green, red handle, Gray's Pottery, (A) 570.00

Lemonade Set, jug, 7 5/8" h, 6 beakers, green, blue, and yellow stylized flowerheads, gilt accents, Gray's Pottery, hairlines, (A) . . . 366.00

Plate

    5" d, oct, 2 bushy blue dot Lupins from black ground, blue rim, c1925, pr 175.00

    Kestral shape

        8" d, "Gardenia" pattern 15.00

        10" d, red and gray bands 25.00

    8 1/8" d, stylized red and purple tulips and green and yellow leaves in center, wide pink border band, set of 6 . . . . . 100.00

    10 1/2" d, silver luster "Persian Bird" design, exotic bird in flight, clipper mark, (A) 214.00

Sandwich Set, tray, 13" H-H, 6 oct plates, multicolored stylized flowers and foliage, "A Susie Cooper Productions" marks, (A) . . . 1,230.00

Shaker, 2 1/2" h, yellow, blue, red, and green "Cubist" pattern on black ground, black rim, Gray's Pottery 150.00

Soup Bowl, 8" d, red and gray bands, Kestral shape 30.00

Tankard, 5" h, tapered cylinder shape, bands of yellow and black under band of yellow chevrons and black circles, "A Susie Cooper Production" mark, (A) 195.00

Teapot, 6 5/8" h, "Dresden" pattern, green, Kestral shape, "A Susie Cooper Productions" mark, (A) 275.00

Tea Service

    Pot, 4 3/4" h, milk jug, sugar basin, 2 cups and saucers, side plates, "Pink Dresden Spray" pattern, Rex shape, (A) 535.00

    Pot, 5" h, milk jug, sugar basin, 2 cups and saucers, side plate, "Stars" pattern, rust and gilt, Falcon shape 175.00

Tray, 13" H-H, rect, yellow, orange, blue, green, and brown stylized flowers from grass 155.00

Vase

    6 1/4" h, ovoid shape with collar rim, incised fox stalking prey, matte blue glaze, incised signature, (A) . . . 357.00

    7 7/8" h, shouldered cylinder shape, lg yellow, green, and ochre stylized flowers, cream ground, (A) 392.00

    8 1/2" h, cylinder shape, yellow, gray, brown, and black overlapping squares, "A Susie Cooper Production" mark, hairline, pr, (A) 1,693.00

    9" h, waisted cylinder shape, painted gray spiral motif, painted signature, (A) 143.00

Vegetable Bowl, 10" l, oval, wide purple-brown, gray, and hair-brown bands
.... 65.00

CAMBRIAN POTTERY
c1783-1810

DILLWYN & CO.
SWANSEA
c1811-1817

BEVINGTON & CO.
c1817-1824

SWANSEA

Wales
c1814 to Early 1820s

History: Swansea potters produced a large variety of earthenwares during the 18th and 19th centuries. Their porcelains, like those of Nantgarw, were very translucent, had fine glazes, and featured excellent floral painting.

After experiencing a lack of funds in 1814, Billingsley and Walker came from Nantgarw to work with Lewis Dillwyn at Swansea. Billingsley and Walker made fine porcelains between 1814 and 1817 at Swansea and then returned to start again at Nantgarw. Production continued at Swansea until the early 1820s. Many Swansea wares were artist decorated.

Swansea Welsh porcelain blanks were quite popular with London decorators.

References: W.D. John, *Swansea Porcelain*, Ceramic Book Co. 1958; Kildare S. Meager, *Swansea & Nantgarw Potteries*, Swansea, 1949; E. Morton Nance, *The Pottery & Porcelain of Swansea & Nantgarw*, Batsford, 1942.

Museums: Art Institute of Chicago, Chicago, IL; Glynn Vivian Art Gallery, Swansea, Wales.

Reproduction Alert: Swansea porcelain has been copied for many decades in Europe and England. Marks should be studied carefully.

Coffeepot, 11" h, pearlware, "Buffalo" pattern, blue with ochre accents, c1810 ..... 795.00
Cup and Saucer, sq handle, purple and green sprig designs, (A) 25.00
Jug
   4 1/2" h, bulbous shape, lg red rose on side, sm flowers and greens, band of leaves on neck, c1820 .... 275.00
   5 3/4" h, bulbous shape, lg red and blue flowerheads, green leaves, wide red band on neck, red-brown lined rim
   .... 350.00
Plate
   7 1/4" d, pearlware, yellow, orange, brown, blue, and green bird on brown branch and green spatter tree, blue emb shell edged scalloped rim, (A) 775.00

Platter, 17 5/8" l, 13 1/8" w, "Long Bridge" pattern, blue transfer, "imp Dillwyn & Co." mark, $995.

7 1/2" d, polychrome floral bouquet in center, pea green and brown loop reticulated rim 350.00
Spill Vase, 10 1/2" h, figural standing dog in blue and white uniform with orange epaulets, blue and white striped pants, black hat with feather, holding drum, brown and green mottled rock spill holder and base with "imp Bibi Tapin," c1860-70 .... 395.00
Tea and Coffee Service, Part, teapot, creamer, 12 plates, 8" d, 3 trays, bowl, 7 1/2" d, 11 teacups, 11 coffee cups, 12 saucers, floral design, black transfer, underglaze blue, gilt accents, hairlines and chips, (A) 715.00

SWEDEN-GENERAL

Marieberg,
near Stockholm, Sweden
1758-1788

History: In 1758, Johann Ehrenreich established a factory at Marieberg, near Stockholm with the intention of making porcelain, but wound up producing faience instead. Pierre Berthevin, a porcelain expert, came to the factory and became director in 1766. Berthevin was the first in Sweden to make porcelain of the soft paste type. Pieces were decorated in the classical designs. Forms included cream jars, pitchers, small vases, and figures. Faience continued to be made and was decorated utilizing the transfer printing technique.

Henrik Sten took over in 1768. Hard paste porcelain was introduced during this period. Only small forms were made; no dinner services were produced. Custard cups, cream pots, and teapots were the most popular shapes. The decoration in-

cluded both classical and rococo styles. Some figures in Swedish rococo style costumes were made. Faience manufacturing continued. Strasburg faience was imitated in a table service for Baron Liljencrantz, the factory's owner. Around 1770 attempts were made to duplicate Wedgwood's creamware.

Marieberg was sold to Rorstrand in 1782. Sten resigned. Schumer took over until the works closed in 1788. Marieberg's faience and porcelain pieces were marked.

Gustavsberg

Island of Farsta, Sweden
1827 to Present

The Gustavsberg factory was established on the island of Farsta in 1827. The factory first produced faience and later made transfer printed creamware in the English style.

Samuel Gidenius enlarged and modernized the factory during the 1850s. Wilhelm Odelberg took control in 1869. During the 1860s, decorative majolica and bone porcelain were introduced. Parian was made from the 1860s until the late 19th century. After William Odelberg died in 1914, his two sons took over.

Between 1897 and 1914, G. Wennerberg was the artistic director. He made pottery decorated with simple floral designs in the sgraffito technique. In 1937 the firm was called AB Gustavsberg Fabriker.

The dinnerwares featured simple designs. "Blue Flower" has been made since 1870. "Allmoge" was introduced in 1905 and continues to the present day. "Elite" was very popular. "Amulet" in red, blue, or gray was designed by Stig Lindberg, the company's leading artist. Wilhelm Koge, another designer, modeled "Argenta" with silver and green backgrounds inspired by Persian wares. He also created "Pyro," "Praktika II," and "Carrara." Other sets included "Gray Bands" and "Marguente" in the Art Nouveau style.

Museums: American Swedish Institute, Minneapolis, MN; Gustavsberg Ceramics Center, Island of Varmdo, Sweden.

Ashtray, 8 1/4" sq, silver rampant lion, mottled green ground, silver line rim, "Gustavsberg Sweden" mark 385.00
Bowl
   6 1/4" d, silver fish blowing bubbles, mottled green ground, "Gustavsberg Argenta" mark 215.00
   8 1/2" d, ftd, green glaze, silver vine design on rim, Gustavsburg, c1930s, (A) 250.00
   12" d, green ext glaze with applied gold decoration, sgd "J. Ekberg," Gustavsberg, c1930s, (A) 50.00

Figure, 4 "l, 5 1/8" h, tan ground, black incised designs, "Gustavsberg Sweden" paper labels, (A) $50 ,left; (A) $75.

Box

5 7/8" h, sq, relief molded stem, leaf, and flowerhead on sides, draped flowerheads on cov, white glaze, Gustavsberg, (A) 217.00

6" l, rect, applied silver rampant lion, mottled green glaze, "GUSTAVSBERG, anchor, ARGENTA, 1230, made in Sweden" mark (A) 82.00

Candleholder, 6" h, figural man playing fiddle, yellow trimmed white coat, blue pants, socket in hat, woman in black and white striped skirt, yellow and rose striped apron, arm forms socket, Gustavsberg, pr 165.00

Dish, 9 1/2" d, silver rampant lion, mottled green ground, "GUSTAVSBERG, anchor, ARGENTA A24" mark. 365.00

Jardiniere and Pedestal, 35" h, sq jardiniere with raised cobalt and gold outlined blue panels of oriental scenes, shaft with molded blue leaves and gilt trim and figural griffin wrapped around shaft, base with 4 molded blue mermaids with white tails, scroll feet, artist sgd 12,000.00

Vase, 8 1/4" h, brown outlined circles, white ground, brown rim, brown clay body, "Gefle Porzlin Fabrikse AB" mark, $1,575.

Vase

4 1/2" h, cameo cut med blue flowers and leaves, mottled lt blue ground, sgd "Elsa Ergestrom," Gustavsberg . . 450.00

5" h, bulbous, Art Nouveau style carved frosted blue-gray leaves and flowers, lt blue ground, "Gustavsberg, 1913, Elsa Ergestrom" mark, (A) 220.00

6" h, silver florals and butterflies, white ground, "GRAZIA 218 DM Gustavsberg" mark 175.00

7" h

Cylinder shape, silver vert flower, stem, and leaf design, green mottled ground, Gustavsberg 295.00

Flat sides, silver swimming dolphins blowing bubbles, green mottled ground, Gustavsberg 1,250.00

7 5/8" h, cylinder shape, silver flower bouquet and spider, mottled green ground, Gustavsberg 490.00

8" h, flared form, silver fish chasing smaller fish, blowing bubbles, mottled green ground, silver line rim, "Gustavsberg Sweden" mark. 850.00

8 1/2" h, flared form, scattered small silver buds and stems, green mottled ground, "Gustavsberg Sweden" mark . . 395.00

10 1/2" h, blue relief florals, green ground, Gustavsberg, (A) 575.00

14" h, cylinder shape, black outlined brown, yellow, blue, and green stylized cityscape and figures, gray ground, Gustavsberg 275.00

17 1/2" h, dbl gourd shape, blue flowers and foliage, mottled green ground, Gustavsberg, dtd 1919, (A) . . . 277.00

Vase, Cov, 15 1/2" h, vert ribbed body, tin glazed blue and white panels of trees and florals, knob repair, 18th C, (A) 287.00

TEA LEAF IRONSTONE

Staffordshire, England
c1856 to Present

History: The tea leaf pattern started about 1856 when Anthony Shaw of Burslem began decorating his white ironstone with three copper luster leaves. At first it was called "Lustre Band and Sprig." Later names were "Edge Line and Sprig" and "Lustre Spray." The sprig eventually was viewed as a tea leaf, thus giving the pattern its name.

Tons of English tea leaf pattern ironstone china was sent to the United States where it greatly appealed to the American housewife. It was durable, white, and had a simple elegance.

More than 30 English potteries in Staffordshire manufactured wares decorated with the tea leaf pattern. The most prolific were Alfred Meakin Potteries and Anthony Shaw. The tea leaf pattern also was utilized at W.H. Gridley, Alcock Potteries, William Adams, Mellor, Taylor & Co., Wedgwood,

and many others. Each company used a slight variation of the tea leaf copper luster pattern. Since all decoration was applied by hand, no two designs were exactly alike, adding to the charm of the ware. Powell & Bishop and Bishop & Stonier also did the design in gold luster.

References: Annise Doring Heaivilin, *Grandma's Tea Leaf Ironstone*, Wallace-Homestead, 1981; Jean Wetherbee, *A Look at White Ironstone,* Wallace-Homestead, 1980.

Museums: Lincoln Home, Springfield, IL; Sherwood Davidson House, Newark, OH; Ox Barn Museum, Aurora, OR.

Collectors' Club: Tea Leaf Club International, 324 Powderhorn Drive, Houghton Lake, MI 48629. Membership: $20.00, *Tea Leaf Readings,* 5 times a year.

Reproduction Alert: Some recent reproductions are noted for their poor coloration, uneven copper luster decoration, and lower weight. Original ironstone examples are much heavier than newer ceramic pieces.

Bowl

5" d, unmkd 12.00

7 1/2" sq, W.H. Grindley. 20.00

8" sq, Meakin 48.00

9" d, paneled, Burgess 50.00

10" sq, "Royal Ironstone" mark . . . 110.00

Bread Plate, 12" H-H, open handles, "A. Shaw" mark. 45.00

Butter Dish, Cov

5 3/4" sq x 4 1/2" h, Powell & Bishop 145.00

6" d, Wilkinson 75.00

Butter Pat, 2 3/8" sq. 8.00

Cake Plate, 11 7/8" H-H, oval, "Mellor, Taylor, & Co. England Warrented Stone China" mark, (A) 75.00

Casserole, Cov

6 1/2" sq, Powell and Bishop 78.00

9 3/4" l, Anthony Shaw 200.00

Chamber Pot, 8 3/4" d, Mellor, Taylor 75.00

Compote

3 1/2" h x 9" d, ftd, "Anthony Shaw & Son, England" mark 270.00

5 1/2" h x 1/2" d, "Royal Ironstone China, Alfred Meakin, England" mark, (A) 310.00

Creamer, 6" h, Wilkinson 70.00

Cup and Saucer

Morning Glory shape, set of 4 . . . . 310.00

Straight sides, "A. Shaw" mark 55.00

Cup Plate, 4 1/8" d, Cloverleaf 20.00

Milk Pitcher

8 1/4" h, sq shape, Alfred Meakin. 125.00

8 1/2" h, Anthony Shaw 385.00

Pitcher, 5 1/2" h, Wilkinson 65.00

Plate

6 1/2" d, Meakin 7.00

Coffeepot, 9 1/2" h, Alfred Meakin, $125.

7" d, unmkd 10.00
7 7/8" d, "Royal Ironstone, Wedgwood &
    Co., England" mark, (A) 15.00
8" d
    Meakin 15.00
    Teaberry design 30.00
8 3/4" d, Meakin 7.00
9" d, unmkd 10.00
9 1/2" d 15.00
9 3/4" d
    Lily of the Valley shape 25.00
    Morning Glory shape 35.00
    Portland shape, (A) 15.00
10" d, Lily of the Valley shape, "A. Shaw"
    mark 18.00
Platter
    10" l x 6" w, Meakin 55.00
    12" l, Meakin 45.00
    12 3/4" l, rect, Meakin 30.00
    13 3/4" l, rect, Wilkinson 30.00
    14" l, rect, Anthony Shaw 50.00
    15" l, Meakin 55.00

Plate, 7 3/4" d, "imp Anthony Shaw" mark, $37.

16" l
    11 1/2" w, Anthony Shaw 239.00
    Raised border, Edward 125.00
Relish Tray, 7 3/4" H-H x 4 1/2" w, rect, scalloped rim, "Royal Stone China, Wedgwood &
Co. England" mark, (A) 25.00
Sauce Tureen, Cov, 5 3/4" h, with undertray,
Shaw 140.00
Soap Dish, 5 1/4" l x 3 1/4" w, rect, Meakin
. . . . 68.00
Soup Plate
    8 7/8" d, Bishop and Stonier 22.00
    9" d, Meakin 30.00
Sugar Bowl, 6 1/4" h, oblong shape, arched
handles, "Royal Ironstone China, Alfred
Meakin, England" mark 135.00
Teapot
    8 1/4" h, "A. Shaw" mark 165.00
    8 3/4" h, sq, Clementson 200.00
    9" h, sq shape, dotted handle, sq finial
        w/copper rays, "T. Furnival & Sons"
        mark 185.00
    9 1/2" h, Portland shape 495.00
    10 1/2" h, emb Lily of the Valley design,
        Chinese shape, "Anthony Shaw" mark
        . . . . 170.00
Tea Set, pot, 9" h, creamer, 6" h, sugar bowl,
7" h, "Cable" shape, Anthony Shaw, chips
. . . . 300.00
Toothbrush Holder
    5" h, Alfred Meakin 195.00
    5 1/2" h, "Anthony Shaw" mark . . . 195.00
Tray, 6 1/2" l, Wilkinson 25.00
Tureen, 8" l x 4 1/2" w x 6" h, with undertray
and ladle, Anthony Shaw 285.00
Vegetable Bowl, Cov
    9" l, ftd, Cable shape, "Anthony Shaw"
        mark 300.00
    9" sq, Meakin 110.00
    10" l, "Burgess & Leigh" mark 60.00
    12" H-H x 7 1/2" h, raised lg leaves outlined
        in copper luster around handles, copper luster outlined flower knob, Anthony
        Shaw 595.00
Waste Bowl, 5 1/2" d, paneled, "A. Shaw"
mark 110.00

TEPLITZ

**Bohemia,
Germany, now
Czech Republic
1892-1945**

History: Teplitz was
a town in Bohemia. Several companies in
the Turn-Teplitz area manufactured art pottery in the late 19th and early 20th century.
Amphora was one of the companies.

Ernst Wahliss of the Alexandria Works in
Teplitz manufactured and decorated pieces in the Art Nouveau style. In 1902, the
factory bought 600 molds from the Imperial
and Royal Porcelain Manufactory in Vienna

and made copies from them of earlier Vienna decorative porcelains and figures. After
1910, the firm manufactured faience wares.
In 1925, the firm was called Ernst Wahliss
AG. The plant ceased operation in 1934.

Additional Listing: Amphora.

Box, 4 3/4" d, squat baluster shape, stylized
white flowers and foliage, green ground, gilt
accents, Ernst Wahliss 100.00
Ewer
    15" h, bulbous body with pinched base,
        straight neck, shaped spout and handle, white outlined rust, pink, yellow
        enameled flowers and gold dots, scattered pink and white flowers, matte
        cream ground, olive green and matte
        gold spout and handle with curlicues,
        "Ernst Wahliss Alexandra Porcelain
        Works Turn-Teplitz Bohemia Austria"
        mark 275.00
    18" h, gold spider web on cobalt ground,
        reticulated top and handle 350.00
Figure
    14" h, bust of woman, reticulated shoulder
        panels, beige and tan 1,800.00
    16 1/4" h, bust of mid-19th C woman, hair
        piled with white plume and gold comb,
        pink neck ribbon, gold beaded necklace, low cut gown with pink and yellow
        molded scroll and beading, ruffled pink
        cape, shaded yellow and green lapels,
        gold accented lace shoulders, "E. Stellmacher, P St. K, Turn-Teplitz Bohemia"
        mark, chips (A) 575.00
    21 1/2" h x 17 1/2" w, "The Tulip Lady,"
        standing Art Nouveau woman with lg hat
        and bow, bird in hand, figural open tulips
        at sides on base, lt green glaze with gilt
        accents, Ernst Wahliss, c1890-1900
        . . . . 2,350.00
    24" h, "Des Liebes," polychromed standing nude Venus and Cupid at side, tripod pyre with applied roses and doves,
        squared base with molded leafed
        branches, sgd "A. Bank," "crowned
        EW" mark, (A) 1,700.00
Humidor, 6 3/4" h, center frieze of orange-brown classical figures, green ground,
orange-brown body, flower form knob
. . . . 245.00
Jug, 5 1/4" h, enameled Arab on horseback,
white robe, lt gray horse, dk gray ground,
Stellmacher, Teplitz 95.00
Milk Pitcher, 5 1/2" h, painted boy giving bouquet to girl, gray ground 250.00
Pitcher
    6" h, enameled young boy in lilac shirt,
        green pants, yellow hat, mottled gray
        ground 85.00
    9 3/8" h, multicolored scene of Madonna
        and Child in raised cartouche of white
        enameled flowers and blue and
        blue-gray leaves, mottled gunmetal
        ground, forked dbl handle
        . . . . 595.00

10 3/4" h, HP enameled bird, cream ground, green trim, Stellmacher 400.00

Planter, 5" h, 3 sm feet, sage green ground with imp vert panels, rect panel on front painted with Arab on horseback, dusted gold rim, Stellmacher 295.00

Plaque

11 1/4" d, relief of crabs, shells, and squids in waves, dk red glaze, relief of 2 lg gunmetal lily pads, Ernst Wahliss, (A) 90.00

18 3/4" h, oval shape, relief molded bust of Art Nouveau woman, cream face, tan hair with yellow flowers, border of molded long stemmed lilies, mint green ground, Ernst Wahliss, (A) 616.00

Sugar Bowl, 3" h x 5 1/4" H-H

Dk gray-brown bark ground, relief molded dk brown leaves with med green fruit 75.00

Relief molded green and gold dusted grape leaves, molded purple grapes, branch handles, gold lined wavy rim 95.00

Vase

5" h, twisted shape, applied yellow, red, and black cherries, irid blue ground, "EW" mark 200.00

6" h, gold leave and vines, cobalt and green ground, gold luster rim, "Turn Vienna" mark 325.00

6 3/4" h

Hourglass shape, 2 sm handles, lg yellow and green flowers, applied stones, dk green ground, Stellmacher 175.00

Portrait of woman with long black hair, cobalt and white enameled flowers, green and gold ground 395.00

7 1/4" h

Bulbous body, 2 sm loop handles from shoulder to rim, enameled cavalier,

Vase, 9 1/2" h, irid blue applied teardrops, red and green body, "stamped Turn-Teplitz" mark, (A) $385.

gold speckled brown ground, Stellmacher 195.00

Spread ft, wide body, flared neck and rim, applied child on shoulder, dog on base, swirled ribbon, lt taupe, dimpled surface with gold trim 275.00

7 1/2" h, tapered shape with rolled rim, raised gilt outlined enameled yellow, pink, blue, and purple flowers with raised dot centers, matte tan ground, matte gold top, magenta around neck and midsection 395.00

7 3/4" h, bulbous body, 3 sides pinched opening, enamel painted Arab on rearing horse, green mottled ground, yellow drip from rim, gilt accents, Stellmacher 150.00

10" h, 4 loop handles from bulbous base to mid neck, lg black outlined white and gold flowerhead and gold and green leaves, matte gold textured ground, "Turn-Teplitz" mark 385.00

11" h

Ewer shape, spiral molding with leaf and scroll designs, gold beaded outlined HP red, yellow, and purple floral sprays, lt olive ground, scrolled and beaded handle, reticulated ruffled collar 400.00

Urn shape with flower-form neck, hand enameled and gilt bands of grapevines and clusters, reticulated neck, gilt scrolled handles from shoulder to neck, Ernst Wahliss, c1895-1918 . . . . 695.00

12" h, Art Nouveau style, polychrome slip design of 2 Dutch girls in relief, (A) 145.00

12 1/2" h, flower form, modeled gold figure of woman on side, irid turquoise ground 875.00

13 1/4" h, bulbous body, flared neck flanked by gilt foliage over painted flowers 250.00

13 5/8" h, HP raised gold outlined purple flowers with white shaded edges, raised gold outlined green drip from top, cream to lt orange ground 595.00

14" h, gold outlined white enameled flowers, butterflies, cobalt and lt blue ground, E. Wahliss 650.00

25" h, standing figure of young maiden, standing lamb at side, tree trunk with applied leaves, berries, and stems, pale green glazes with gilt accents, (A) 250.00

Wine Jug, 6" h, 3 spouts, enameled Arab on horseback, matte green-gold ground, Stellmacher 160.00

c1872-1951

c1880

c1875

TILES

Bristol, Liverpool, London, England
Denmark, France, Germany, Holland, Italy, Spain, Portugal
1600s to Present

History: Tiles have been used for centuries on floors, walls, fireplaces, chimneys, and facades of houses, palaces, and castles. They even have been installed into furniture such as washstands, hall stands, and folding screens. Tiles cleaned easily and were quite decorative. Numerous public buildings and subways used tiles to enhance their appearances.

The earliest of the **Dutch** tin-glazed tiles featured polychrome figures, landscapes, flowers, and animals. Many used the fleur-de-lys motif in the corners. Additional subjects such as ships, sea monsters, mythical figures, fisherman, farmers, and biblical subjects appeared in the late 17th century. Tile pictures that were adapted from paintings and engravings of Dutch interiors or landscapes also were made.

Before 1629, at least 25 factories in Holland were making tiles with the Delft potteries the most prolific. After 1650 the Delft potteries became less important. However, all Dutch made tiles were generically called "Delft" tiles.

Even though the number of factories making tiles diminished during the 18th century, production increased throughout Europe. **Denmark, Germany, Portugal, and Spain** imitated Dutch tiles in their factories. The **Portuguese** tiles featured motifs in two tones of cobalt blue or polychromes. Flemish workers came to **Spain** and introduced the majolica technique. They used a tin oxide glaze for their decorated tiles.

French tiles were influenced by both Italian and Dutch styles of decoration. In **Italy,** majolica tiles were made in centers such as Florence, Sienna, and Venice.

Tiles made in **England** from the 16th through the first half of the 18th century generally followed the Dutch tiles in method of manufacture and design. Polychrome painting, blue and white motifs inspired by Chinese porcelains, birds, landscapes, and flowers all reflected the strong Dutch influence. Factories that produced tiles were centered in Bristol, Liverpool, and London.

In 1756, John Sadler from Liverpool produced the first transfer printed tiles and revolutionized the tile industry. The use of the transfer printing process on tiles allowed a far greater variety of designs and liberated the tile industry from the old Delft motifs. Transfer printing on tiles was responsible for the growth of the Victorian tile industry.

Herbert Minton was in charge of the production of tiles at Minton. In 1828, he produced encaustic tiles with inlaid decorations, reviving a technique use in medieval Europe. Minton bought Samuel Wright's patent for encaustic tiles in 1830. Minton specialized in tiles for wall decorations in public buildings. Minton began transfer printing tiles in 1850. Minton's Kensington Studio, which was opened in 1871, employed such designers as Moyr Smith, Henry Stacy Marks, and William Wise who made painted or printed pictorial titles. Many of Smith's tiles were based in famous literary series.

During the 1870s, decorative wall tiles were in use everywhere. By the 1880s, more then 100 companies in England were producing tiles.

Decorative tiles were a major industry in the Ironbridge Gorge in the late 19th century. Tiles were produced by Maw and Craven Dunnill for church floors, shop counters, public buildings, facades, porches, and many other uses. Maw's factory at Jackfield was the largest decorative tile factory in the world in the 1880s.

The Craven Dunnill firm was formed in 1871 and built its new Jackfield works in 1875. Many encaustic tiles were made for use in new and restored churches. With the revival of the gothic style, their reproductions of medieval tiles were in great demand.

George Maw and Arthur, his brother, bought the encaustic tile business of the Worcester Porcelain Company in 1850. In addition to floor tiles, they manufactured glazed tiles for walls, porchways, fireplaces, and washstands. Tiles were either hand painted, transfer printed, or stenciled. They also made ceramic mosaic tiles. The Benthall Works was added to the company in 1883.

In 1892, the Pilkington brothers established a pottery to manufacture tiles and other products at Clifton Junction, Manchester. Many experiments were done. The "Royal" prefix was granted to the company by King George V in 1913, and the company became known as "Royal Lancastrian."

Many designs used on tiles were copied from other fields of art. The Art Nouveau and Art Deco motifs were popular for tile designs.

References: Julian Barnard, *Victorian Ceramic Tiles,* NY Graphic Society Ltd., 1972; Anne Berendsen, *Tiles, A General History,* Viking Press, 1967; C.H. de Jonge, *Dutch Tiles,* Praeger, 1971; Jonathan Horne, *English Tinglazed Tiles,* Jonathan Horne, 1989; Terence A. Lockett, *Collecting Victorian Tiles,* Antique Collectors' Club, Ltd.,1979; Richard & Hilary Myers, *William Morris Tiles: Tile Designs of Morris and his Fellow Workers,* Antique Collectors' Club, Ltd., 1996; Anthony Ray, *English Delftware Tiles,* Faber & Faber, 1973; Anthony Ray, *Liverpool Printed Tiles,* Antique Collectors' Club, Ltd., 1994; Noel Riley, *Tile Art,* Chartwell Books, Inc.,1987; Hans van Lemmen, *Decorative Tiles Throughout the Ages,* Moyer Bell, 1997; Hans van Lemmen, *Delftware Tiles,* Overlook Press, 1997; Hans van Lemmen, Ed. *Fired Earth 1000 Years of Tiles in Europe,* Antique Collectors' Club, Ltd., 1991; Hans van Lemmen, *Tiles: A Collectors' Guide,* Rev. Ed. Intl. Spec. Bk., 1990; H. Wakefield, *Victorian Pottery,* Universe Books, 1965.

Collectors' Club: Tiles & Architectural Ceramics Society, Kathryn M. Huggins, Reabrook Lodge, 8 Sutton Road, Shrewsbury, Shropshire SY2 6DD UK. Membership: £24, *Glazed Expressions,* Twice yearly magazine, Quarterly newsletter and Journal.

Museums: Boymans-van Beunigen Museum, Rotterdam, Holland; City Museum, Stoke-on-Trent, Hanley, England; Ironbridge Gorge Museum, Teford, England; Lambert van Meerten Museum, Delft, Holland; Victoria & Albert Museum, London, England.

Reproduction Alert: English firms are making copies of 6-inch by 6-inch Victorian era ceramic tiles. Some even have the original artist's signature and 19th century dates. Old tiles are generally thicker, 3/4 inch or 1/2 inch, while reproductions are 1/4-inch thick. Old backs have ridges or grooves, while new backs are smooth. New tiles are also transfer printed.

More than sixteen DeMorgan original designs are being reproduced. Some designs are also copies from 18th century tiles as well as the Victorian tiles. Fireplace sets in five tile sets are also being reproduced.

Collecting Hints: Tiles are becoming increasingly more popular. They are difficult to identify as to manufacturer since they were mass produced and many were unmarked. Some firms only decorated tiles they received from another factory. The method of manufacture also may provide clues to the maker. Information on the back of a tile sometimes will indicate the manufacturer or the date that the tile was made.

5" sq, dk blue design, white ground, Dutch Delft, c1640-60, $850.

Condition is an important factor in determining price. Bad cracks, chips, and scratches definitely lower a tile's value. Crazing in the glaze is not uncommon in a tile and usually does not affect the price if it does not detract from the tile's appearance.

4 3/4" sq, faience, manganese man rolling hoop or lady with whip, Continental, pr, (A)
. . . . 30.00

4 7/8" sq, Delft, yellow and blue bird perched on branch, manganese cartouche and fan corners, framed, Liverpool, c1750, (A)
. . . . 275.00

5" sq,
  Delft
    Dk blue flowerhead and leaves, pale blue ground 95.00
    Man standing beside rock with pick, blue and white, England, (A) . 50.00
    Swan, tall grass in bkd, flowerheads in corners, manganese and white, England, (A) 60.00
    Two dogs on rocks at tree stump, manganese and white design, yellow, blue, and green scale an flowerhead border, England, (A). 50.00
    Winged cherub blowing horn in center, blue and white, England, (A) . 33.00
    Woman in long skirt, hands in muff, house in bkd, flying stylized birds, blue and white, England. 60.00
  Faience, polychrome bird in flowers or bent to ground, curlicues in corners, Continental, late 18th C, pr, (A) 80.00

5 1/8" sq, Delft
  Polychromed kneeling cavalier holding gun, blue scrolls at corners 75.00
  Sailboat in quatrefoil cartouche, joined flowerhead border, blue and white
. . . . 75.00
  Stylized scenes of children playing, blue and white, set of 8 . . . . 255.00

5 1/4" sq
  Delft, blue and white church, sailboats, and landscape in oct reserve, sponged

purple border with sprays in corners, (A) 50.00

Faience, various polychrome military figures, Continental, late 18th C, set of 13, (A) 300.00

5 3/4" sq, incised stylized brown and black flowers, brown ground, Martin Brothers, (A) 100.00

6" sq

Art Nouveau

Blue tulips from red pod, green stem, cream ground, "ENGLAND" mark 58.00

Profile of nude woman holding flower, pink and gray, Germany . . . 185.00

Blue printed scene of mother picking apples from tree, child holding apples in outstretched apron, Minton 150.00

Blue, yellow, and orange flowerhead and geometrics, printed cream ground, England 35.00

Brown printed scene of 2 grouse in field, flying birds overhead, Wedgwood 140.00

Cream daisies on brown ground, cream fenced border, printed 28.00

Green poppies and leaves, curlicue border, printed, white ground, England 24.00

HP dk brown scenes of Camelot, Minton, set of 8 . . . . 750.00

Oriental man shooting gun, ducks in flight, blue transfer, Minton 55.00

Pink fuchsia, green, blue, and yellow leaves, brown fan corners, printed, cream ground, England 35.00

Raised flowerhead and leaves, pebble ground, dk brown, England 45.00

Raised purple flower, swirling green stems, gold-brown raised curlicues, lt molded relief of leaves, lt green ground, England 48.00

Relief of black dog in brown doghouse, black crow in front, brown link rim, majolica glaze, Germany 295.00

Seated peasant woman near river, blue transfer, Minton 150.00

Standing stag, 2 seated deer in meadow, black transfer, Minton 90.00

"Taming of the Shrew," blue, gold, and yellow, sgd "J. Mayre Smith," Minton, c1880 . . . . 95.00

"The Cambridge Elm," George Washington and tree in circle, streaks and stylized leaves in corners, cobalt and white 160.00

Two dk green sqs, 2 sqs of raised stylized gold flowers from green pods, England 28.00

6 1/8" sq, olive green raised floral in center, dk green border, England 95.00

8" sq

Emb and carved intaglio seated bagpiper, clear burgundy glaze, Minton, (A) 385.00

Swallow and tulip design, lt and dk blue, Minton 95.00

8 1/4" sq, raised brown sprouting flower, flowerhead border, yellow ground, England 45.00

9" sq, green and brown painted country manor house in park, "molded Copeland Stoke-On-Trent" mark, 19th C, pr, (A) 748.00

12" l x 6" h, Art Nouveau style turquoise chrysanthemum, brown leaves, and peas, glossy green glaze, nick on rim, (A) 105.00

Tile Picture

6" sq, 6 tiles, yellow, brown, and green painted herd of deer in stylized foliage, Poole, chip, (A) 160.00

10" sq, 4 tiles, 17th C armed soldiers in shaped reserves, flowing leaf borders, blue and white, Dutch, c1660-90 . . . . 600.00

14 3/4" h x 9 3/4" w, 6 tiles, Dutch Delft, manganese cow in landscape, line and band border, (A) 1,150.00

15 1/4" h

10" w, 6 tiles, Dutch Delft, yellow canary in manganese cage with yellow finials and blue feeder, (A) 1,265.00

10 1/4" w, 6 tiles, Dutch Delft, manganese military figure or wife, green foliate border, pr, (A) 1,150.00

15 1/2" h x 10" w, 6 tiles, Dutch Delft, manganese mantle clock with Roman numerals and banner with "UTRECHT A:TUREL:1775," ochre and blue hourglass and birdcage, wood frame 1,265.00

15 3/4" sq, 9 tiles

Dutch sailing ship, manganese and white, pr 4,800.00

Three fighting sailing ships, Polar bears on ice flow, manganese and white, England 2,800.00

34" h, 22 1/2" w, blue design, yellow faux marble ground, Portugal, (A) $522.

20" h x 15" w, The Resurrection and Ascension of Christ, "UPSTANDING J.C." or "HEMELFAART J.C." on front, self framed with flowerhead corners, purple and white, c1800-50, Dutch, pr 7,500.00

TOBY JUGS

Staffordshire, England
1775 to Present

History: Toby jugs, first made by English potters from Staffordshire in the 18th century, were drinking vessels. Although they were at the zenith of their popularity from 1775 to 1825, Toby jugs still are being produced today. After they became outmoded as drinking mugs, they survived as ornamental pieces.

Some of the earliest Toby jugs were made by Ralph Wood and Whieldon at their Burslem potteries in Staffordshire. Some claim the name "Toby" originated with the Uncle Toby character in Laurence Sterne's *Tristram Shandy*. This is subject to debate.

The typical Toby jug featured a seated toper clasping a jug with both hands or holding a glass in one hand and a jug on a knee in the other. The seated figure was usually a male wearing a three cornered hat, each corner of which formed a spout. Figures were dressed in costumes of the period and usually had genial facial expressions. Toby jugs were designed for use in cottages and inns. Variations included standing figures and occasional female figures. Most were usually 10 inches tall, while miniatures, which were rarer, measured about 3 to 6-1/2 inches tall.

Some early Whieldon Toby jugs had the mottled and tortoiseshell underglazed effect. The Ralph Wood jugs had a somewhat whiter body and softer, translucent glazes. After 1780, some overglaze enamels were used. Wedgwood, Pratt, and Davenport, along with other English potters, made Toby jugs.

References: Desmond Eyles, '*Good Sir Toby*,' Doulton & Co. Ltd. 1955; Bernard Rackham, *Early Staffordshire Pottery*, Faber & Faber, 1951; Vic Schuler, *British Toby Jugs, 1st Edition*, Kevin Francis Publishing Ltd. 1986, Vic Schuler, *Collecting British Toby Jugs, 2nd Edition,* Kevin Francis Publishing Ltd. 1987; C.P. Woodhouse, *Old English Toby Jugs*, Mountrose Press, 1949.

Museums: American Toby Jug Museum, Evanston, IL; City Museum & Art Gallery, Stoke-on-Trent, England; Victoria & Albert Museum, London, England.

2 3/4" h, seated man, blue coat, yellow vest, red trousers, "black stamped Torquay Pottery England" mark 98.00

5 1/2" h

Blue Willow pattern, England 750.00

9 3/8" h, black jacket, pink vest, yellow breeches, yellow outlined black hat, brown and green base, c1840, $895.

Seated man, lt blue coat, yellow vest, red trousers, rosy cheeks, "Made in Torquay" mark 129.00

5 3/4" h, seated man, holding jug, rust vest, yellow trousers, flesh face and hands, "Staffordshire Ware England and bowknot" mark 425.00

6 1/2" h, seated figure of Elihu Yale, dk brown, blue, cream, or ochre, glaze, 1933, Wedgwood, set of 4, (A) 460.00

6 3/4" h, seated man, brown-red coat, green trousers, yellow stockings, holding foaming jug, black tricorn hat, "Wood & Sons, Toby" mark 45.00

8 1/8" h, standing man taking snuff, gray hair, red waistcoat, black trimmed green vest, yellow trousers, black shoes, black tricorn hat, green base with red accents and yellow stripe, (A) 165.00

9 1/8" h, cov, seated man holding foaming pitcher, gray hair, lt green waistcoat, orange vest, yellow trousers, black shoes, black tricorn hat and cov, black striped base, (A) 225.00

9 1/4" h, pearlware

Ordinary figure, blue, brown, and ochre striping on pants and jacket, Pratt, c1800, (A) 402.00

Seated Martha Gunn, translucent brown and ochre glazes, brim repair, (A) 1,265.00

9 1/2" h

Pearlware, seated man, pale green coat, ochre trousers, brown shoes, lt brown tricorn hat, holding brown foaming jug

and glass, Staffordshire, c1775, (A) 920.00

Seated man, iron red coat, mustard trousers, black shoes with yellow tassels, black dotted eyebrows, black outlined teeth, floral pitcher in one hand, pipe in other, iron red, green, and yellow striped base, c1840 Yorkshire 495.00

9 3/4" h

Lloyd George, dk blue naval uniform with gold trim, red seat, gray shell with "Shell Out!" Wilkinson, c1917 . . . . . . 400.00

Ordinary figure, blue trousers, brown splotched face, holding brown jug, mottled and translucent glazes, . Staffordshire, 18th C, rim chips, (A) . . . 460.00

Seated man

Blue hat, brown mottled coat, ochre waistcoat, blue trousers, frothing jug on knee, barrel between feet, pipe at side, Staffordshire, c1765, chips and repairs, (A) 403.00

Gray jacket, lime green trousers, black tricorn hat, orange face with warts, holding brown foaming jug, pipe at side 375.00

Standing man with lg belly, open hands, tricorn hat, rd base, Rockingham glaze 250.00

10" h, seated man

Black face, black tricorn hat, brown coat with green cuffs, cobalt trousers, red and black stockings, holding foaming pitcher, blue and green sponged base 1,250.00

11 1/2" h, blue coat, yellow vest, iron red breeches, black shoes and hat, $895.

Lt blue coat, gold trousers, black shoes with gold tassels, tan tricorn hat with black wavy outline, Toby jug in one hand, pipe in other, black, orange, and blue sponged base, c1800, Yorkshire 1,450.00

Stoneware, holding cup, black and caramel brown glaze, Martin Brother, 1903 . . . . 4,900.00

10 1/4" h, seated man holding flowered pitcher, orange jacket, mustard trousers, late 18th C 1,800.00

10 1/2" h, pearlware, seated man, dk brown tricorn hat cov, brown hair, lt blue face, yellow coat with brown spots, yellow trousers, brown shoes, holding brown and white foaming jug, brown and white spotted chair, chamfered brown streaked rect base, (A) 200.00

10 3/4" h, Field Marshall Haig, tan uniform, holding jug with Union Jack, seated on tank, Wilkinson, c1917, (A) 460.00

12" h, "H.M. King George V," seated king in blue uniform, black rimmed hat, black shoes, white molded lion throne, Wilkinson, c1919, (A) 431.00

TORQUAY

Torquay District, South Devon, England
1870s-1962

History: G.J. Allen discovered red terra cotta clay on the Watcombe House grounds, just north of Torquay in 1869. The pottery industry in Torquay owed its existence to this discovery.

Allen established the Watcombe Pottery. Charles Brock was appointed manager, and skilled workers were employed from Staffordshire. Watcombe Pottery was established during the peak of the art pottery movement, 1870 to 1900, and found a ready market for its products.

The appeal of the terra cotta wares was the natural color of the clay and the innovative shapes. A small amount of enamel decoration or gilt borders was added. At first, the style was classical, comprised of vases, figures, and busts imitating Greek and Roman originals. Later busts of contemporary and historical celebrities, vases, jars, architectural wares, garden ornaments, and tea services were made.

Watcombe Pottery also was known for its terra cotta plaques. Statues were made for advertising purposes. Enamel decoration of flowers, birds, and fish on ornamental wares was accomplished in a natural style on unglazed terra cotta.

In 1875, Dr. Gillow established the Torquay Terra-Cotta Company Ltd. at Hele Cross, just north of Torquay. Smaller decorative wares, such as statuettes, plaques, vases, figures, and busts were made. Some utilitarian examples also were produced. Products were similar to those made at the Watcombe Pottery.

Torquay Terra-Cotta Company declined. It closed in 1905 as a result of the decline in the Arts and Crafts movement and the shift to more modern styles. Enoch Staddon reopened the Torquay Pottery in 1908 to make pottery rather than terra cotta ware. The factory closed during WWII.

The Aller Vale Pottery, under the direction of John Phillips, started making terra cotta and other art wares in new forms and styles near Torquay in 1881. By 1890, the pottery was catering to holiday visitors who wanted something to take home as a souvenir. Designs were painted in thick colored slip on items prepared with a dip coat of slip of a uniform color. They were finished with a clear glaze. Usually rhymes or proverbs were scratched through the ground so the lettering showed up in the dark red color of the body. This "motto ware" gained tremendous popularity during the early 20th century, not only in resorts, but all over the country.

Watcombe Pottery combined with Aller Vale in 1901 to form the Royal Aller Vale and Watcombe Art Potteries. Watcombe started to manufacture the Aller type wares. One style of decoration showing the thatched cottage between trees was called "Devon Motto Ware" or "Cottage Ware." In addition to the motto, sometimes the place name was inscribed. Commemorative wares were made. The combined potteries eventually closed in 1962.

During the early part of the 20th century, several smaller potteries such as Longpark Pottery, Burton, and Daison were established in or near Torquay. Most were founded by men who had worked at one of the major potteries in the district. The designs tended to copy the styles used by Aller Vale and Watcombe. When Longpark closed in 1957 and Watcombe in 1962, the red clay pottery industry in Torquay ended.

References: Virginia Brisco, Editor, *Torquay Mottowares,* Torquay Pottery Collectors Society, 1990; D.& E. Lloyd Thomas, *The Old Torquay Potters,* Arthur H. Stockwell Ltd. 1978.

Collectors' Clubs: North American Torquay Society, 12 Stanton, Madison, CT 06443.

Membership: $20.00, Quarterly magazine *The Torquay Collector;* The Torquay Pottery Collectors Society, 5 Claverdon Drive, Sutton Coldfield, W. Mids B74 3 AH, UK. Membership: £12, Quarterly magazine.

Museums: Devonshire Museum, Devonshire, England; Exeter Museums, Exeter, England; Torquay Museum, South Devon, England.

Ashtray
- 3 1/4" sq, white polka dots, blue ground, Watcombe, 1935-62 . . . . 28.00
- 4 7/8" d, "Cottage" design and windmill, "Who burnt the tablecloth?" Watcombe, 1901-1920, flake on rim 55.00

Beaker
- 4 1/4" d, ftd, "Cottage" design on ext, thatched roof variation, "Daun 'ee try tu rin bevore yu kin walk," "black stamped Watcombe Torquay England" mark 40.00
- 4 1/4" h, "Cottage" design, "Time and tide wait for no man," "black stamped Watcombe Devon Motto Ware England" mark 58.00

Bean Pot, 3" h, ftd, "Lucky Devon Pixie" design, yellow shaded ground 65.00

Bouillon Bowl, Cov, 3 1/2" h, 6 1/2" H-H, with underplate, white polka dots, blue ground, unmkd, chip under lid 60.00

Bowl
- 4" d
  - 3" h, ftd, cream int, red and green stylized flowers, mottled blue ground 75.00
  - Ruffled rim, "Cottage" design, "Daun ee be fraid a it now," "black stamped Wat Torq England" mark 25.00
- 4 1/2" d, Kingfisher, dk blue ground, "Take a little sugar," "black stamped Torquay Pottery England" mark 40.00
- 5 1/4" h x 6 3/4" d, ftd, band of dk red and yellow flowerheads, junket motto on border 190.00
- 6" d, "Cottage" design, "Enough is as good as a feast," "black stamped Watcombe Torquay England Made in England" mark 76.00

Butter Shovel, "Cottage" design, "Cum me artiez eip yersels" and "From Perranporth," unmkd 80.00

Butter Tub
- 3 3/4" h, "Cottage" design, "To say well is good but to do well is better," Watcombe Torquay England, 1920-45 . . . . 149.00
- 4 1/2" d, "Shamrock" design, "From Killarney," Longpark 73.00
- 5" d, "Cottage" design, "Take a little butter," eared handles 67.00

Candlestick
- 3" h, "Shamrock" design, "None of your blarney," Longpark, 1926-1939 . . . . 70.00
- 4 1/2" h, Scandy, "Many are called but few get up," Aller Vale, c1891-1910 . . . . 95.00
- 6" h
  - Black cockerel and "Pleasent Dreams" 225.00
  - Dbl Scandy, Tormohun Ware, "Last in bed put out the light" 125.00
- 6 1/2" h, "Cottage" design, Torquay Pottery Co. 75.00
- 7 1/4" h, Scandy, "Daunt lite yer cannel at both ends," unmkd 145.00

Candy Dish, 5" d, "Cottage" design, "Where friends there riches," Watcombe. 45.00

Chamberstick
- 2 1/2" h, "Shamrock" design, "From Youghal Ould Irelands Native," Longpark, 1920-30 . . . . 135.00
- 4" h, "Shamrock" design, "Killarney Arrah now be aisy wid ye," Longpark 125.00
- 4 1/2" h, white Scandy design, green ground, red clay, Aller Vale, 1891-1902 . . . . 140.00
- 5 3/4" h, black Cockerel, "From Durham" and "Hear all. See all say nothing," "black stamped LONGPARK TORQUAY" mark 140.00

Coffeepot
- 6 1/2" h, Scandy, "Du'ee have a cup of coffee," unmkd 185.00
- 7" h, "Cottage" design, "take a cup of coffee it's very refreshing," Watcombe, 1920-1945, spout repair 175.00

Compote, 5 3/4" h, yellow, burgundy, and lavender iris, med blue ground, slip decorated, 3 twisted handles, unmkd 165.00

Creamer and Sugar Bowl, creamer 2 3/4" h, sugar bowl, 3 1/4" d, pink rambling rose design on black lattice work, cream ground, "Watcombe Torquay" marks 110.00

Creamer
- 2 1/4" h, brown polka dots, yellow ground, brown handle, Babbacombe 25.00
- 2 1/2" h
  - Black Cockerel, "From Morpeth, 'elp yerzel tu craim" 50.00
  - "Cottage" design, snow scene, "Help yourself to cream," Royal Watcombe 120.00
- 2 3/4" h
  - "Cottage" design, "Fresh from the dairy," "black stamped Longpark Torquay England" mark 25.00
  - Scandy, "Port Arthur, Ont", and "Take a little cream," "imp Watcombe Torquay Made in England" mark 43.00

Cup and Saucer, red, blue, and green scrolls, cream ground, "imp ALLER VALE" mark 98.00

Cup and Saucer, Demitasse, windmill, "Have another cupful," Watcombe, 1920-1945 . . . . 60.00

Dish, Cov, 5" d, Kingfisher, dk blue ground, "black stamped Longpark, Torquay" mark 110.00

Egg Cup

2 1/2" h, "Cottage" design with eggs, "New laid eggs," "black stamped Longpark Torquay England" mark 58.00

3" h, "Cottage" design, Watcombe 32.00

Ewer, 8" h, bottle shape, burgundy butterfly, green leaves and flowers on streaked rose ground, unmkd 85.00

Fruit Bowl, 10" d, "Cottage" design, "Say not always what you know, but always know what you say," Royal Watcombe, hairlines 90.00

Gypsy Pot, 3" h, Scandy, "If you can't be aisy be as aisy as you can," Longpark. 75.00

Harvest Jug, 7" h, Kerswell Daisy, "Do the work thats nearest Tho its dull at whiles Helping when you meet them Lame dogs over stiles," "imp Aller Vale H & H Co" mark 198.00

Hatpin Holder

4 1/2" h, colored Cockerel, "Keep me on the dressing table," "black stamped Longpark Torquay" mark. 130.00

6" h, cylinder shape, blue and white faience gulls and waves, "black stamped Lemon & Crute Torquay" mark. 120.00

Honey Pot, 4 1/2" h, "Cottage" design, "Yer's some honey for 'ee," "black stamped Watcombe Torquay England" mark 75.00

Hot Water Pot

4 1/4" h, black Cockerel, "Wishes never filled the bag," Longpark, c1930s 95.00

5" h, "Cottage" design, "Say little but think much," "black stamped Watcombe Devon Motto Ware" mark 98.00

6 1/2" h, "Cottage" design, "Newaway" on front, "Say not always what you know but always know what you say," Watcombe 135.00

7 1/2" h

"Cottage" design, "If your lips would keep from slips five things observe with care of whom you speak to whom you speak and how and when and where," Watcombe 188.00

Scandy, "Little duties still put off will end in never done By-and-by is soon enough has ruined many a one" 157.00

Humidor, 5" h, Scandy, "As Pan brot music from his vocal reed let us seek concord in the fragrent weed," Aller Vale 150.00

Inkwell

2" h, blue "Thistle" design, "Dip deep" 139.00

2 1/4" h, "Scandy" design, green ground, "Wa'al us be glad tu zee'e," white clay, Aller Vale, 1891-1910, chip on reverse 101.00

Jam Pot

3 3/4" h, "Cottage" design, "Boscastle" and "Take a Little Marmalade" . . 55.00

4" h, "Pixie" design, yellow shaded to cream 100.00

4 3/4" h, "Cottage" design, "Elp yerzel tu jam," "black stamped Longpark Torquay England" mark 75.00

5 1/4" h, Scandy, "Elp yerzel tu jam," "black stamped LONGPARK TORQUAY" mark 76.00

Jardiniere, 4" h, Scandy, orange wavy rim, "If you your lips would keep from slips Five things observe with care Of whom you speak. To whom you speak. And how and when and where," 2 handles, "imp Aller Vale Devon England" mark 155.00

Jug

Barrel shape

3 1/2" h, "Shamrock" design, "From Cushendall Arrah now be aisy wid ye," Longpark 5.00

5" h, "Cottage" design, "I cum from Torquay" on front, "May the hinges of friendship never grow rusty," Watcombe 165.00

8" h, black sailboats, rose red sunset, Royal Torquay 398.00

Junket Bowl, 7" d, Scandy, green seaweed border, "Take a little junket," Aller Vale 125.00

Match Holder

2" h, ship scene, "A match for any man" 55.00

3 3/4" h, geometric design, "A match for any man," "imp Watcombe Torquay" mark 88.00

Milk Pitcher

4" h, "Cottage" design, "Brendon" on front, "Help yourself to milk" on reverse, Watcombe. 75.00

4 3/4" h, sq shape, slip molded cottage, "inscribed *Bovey Art Pottery Devon*" mark 112.00

5 1/4" h, "Cottage" design, "Budleigh Salterton" on front, "Will 'ee 'elp yerzel tu milk," Watcombe. 110.00

Mug

2 1/2" h, "Shamrock" design, "The green immortal shamrock," Royal Watcombe 65.00

3 1/2" h, Kerswell daisy, "Never say die Up man and try," twin handles, "imp ALLER VALE DEVON" mark 67.00

3 3/4" h, "Cottage" design, "Drink like a fish Water only," "black stamped Longpark" mark 67.00

4 1/2" h, "Cottage" design, "Up to the lips and over the gums look out tummy here it comes," Royal Watcombe . . . 110.00

Pen Tray, 8 1/2" l, slip decorated yellow and violet irises, med blue ground, unmkd 95.00

Pin Tray, 5 1/2" l, "Cottage" design, "Every why hath a wherefore," Watcombe, 1920s 45.00

Pitcher

2" h, "Cottage" design, "For a good girl" 40.00

2 1/2" h, Scandy, amber ground, "H.M. Exeter" and "Put a stout heart to a steep hill" 66.00

3" h, side spout, Scandy, "Every blade of grass keeps its own draop of dew," Aller Vale 60.00

3 1/2" h, white seagull, med blue ground, Babbacombe. 29.00

4" h, side spout, Scandy, "Du'ee mak yerzel at home," Aller Vale, crazing 75.00

5 1/2" h, bulbous, "Cottage" design, "Tourley" and "When you've got the pip Don't squeak," "black stamped LONGPARK TORQUAY" mark 110.00

6" h, bulbous shape, Scandy, "Ride over all obstacles and win the race," paw handles, unmkd 135.00

Plate

4 5/8" d, black walking hen, "Hear all, see all, say nothing" 50.00

5" d "Cottage" design

"Bustle is not Industry" 45.00

"Lands End" and "Help yourself Don't be shy," "black stamped Royal Watcombe Torquay England" mark 30.00

"Masters two will never do," Watcombe 50.00

Scandy, "Better wait on the cook than the doctor," "imp Watcombe Torquay Made in England" mark 43.00

6" d, "Cottage" design

"Gude folks be scarce take care ov me," "black stamped Longpark Torquay England" mark 40.00

"The man that can't make a mistake Can't make anything," "black stamped Longpark Torquay England" mark 48.00

7" d, "Cottage" design, "He is well paid that is well satisfied," "black stamped Watcombe Torquay England" . . . 49.00

8 1/4" d, "Cottage" design, "Better wait on the cook than the doctor," Watcombe 110.00

Porridge Bowl, 6" d, "Cottage" design, "Better wait on the cook than the doctor," "black stamped Royal Watcombe Torquay England" mark 88.00

Powder Jar, Cov, 4 1/2" d x 2 3/4" h, faience peacock on cov, lt blue ground, "black stamped Lemon & Crute Torquay" mark 120.00

Salt Shaker, "Cottage" design, "There's no fun like work," unmkd 28.00

Scent Bottle, 2 1/2" h, Devon violets design, unmkd 50.00

Plate, 7" d, "Cottage," brown and cream, "After dinner sit awhile After Supper walk a mile" on border, $55.

Shakers, 3" h, egg shape, "Cottage" design, "Kind words never die" or "Hope well have well," pr 70.00

Sugar Bowl, 4 1/4" d, Scandy on green ground, "Sugar," Aller Vale, 1902-1924 . . . . . . .60.00

Sugar Bowl, Cov, 4" h, "Cottage" design, "There's a time for all things," "black stamped Royal Watcombe England" mark 48.00

Supper Tray, 7 1/2" d, 3 section, brown center handle, "Cottage" design, "If you can't be aisy be aisy as you can" and "From Lymouth," "black stamped LONGPARK TORQUAY" mark 140.00

Teapot

3 3/4" h

"Cottage" design, "We'll take a cup o' Kindness for Auld Lang Syne" on reverse 85.00

"Shamrock" design, "From Courtown Arrah now be aisy wid ye," Longpark, restored spout 130.00

5" h, bulbous, "Cottage" design, "Ladies all I pray make free and tell me how you like your tea," "black stamped ROYAL WATCOMBE TORQUAY" mark . . 98.00

5 1/2" h

"Burns Cottage" design, "Fae Land O' Burns" at top, "Burns Cottage" at bottom, "When freens meet hearts warm" on reverse 215.00

"Cottage" design, "From Herham" and "Du ee ave a cup a tay," "black stamped Longpark Torquay England" mark 155.00

Tea Tile

4 1/4" d, "Shamrock" design, "The chosen leaf o Bard and Chief," Aller Vale, 1891-1902, rim flake 85.00

6" d, "Cottage" design, green border, "imp Watcombe" mark 85.00

Tobacco Jar, 4 1/2" h, sailboat design in colors, cream ground, "Tobacco you are welcome", unmkd 135.00

Toast Rack, 5 bar, "Cottage" design, "Crisp and brown," unmkd 160.00

Vase

2" h, lg and sm white flowers, dk blue ground, unmkd 32.00

4" h

Barbotine, dk blue flower on ochre and brick red ground, slip decorated, unmkd 85.00

Lg pink flower, purple ground, ruffled rim, Watcombe 80.00

Ovoid shape, faience red cabbage rose, black vert stripes, cream ground, eared handles, unmkd 130.00

Pinched form, green irid finish, "imp Watcombe Torquay" mark . . . 35.00

Squat shape, pink and white rose blossom, streaked mauve ground, 2 twisted handles, "inscribed *Watcombe Torquay England*" mark 112.00

Waisted shape, Art Deco style, black streaks on yellow ground, "black stamped Watcombe Torquay England" mark 38.00

4 1/4" h, "Cottage" design, "RYE," and "It's better to wear out than rust out," "black stamped WATCOMBE TORQUAY ENGLAND" mark 88.00

4 1/2" h

Lg yellow and green petaled flower with red center, dk green ground, "imp Aller" mark 120.00

Ruffled rim, Ann Hathaway's Cottage in colors, "incised *WATCOMBE*" mark 115.00

5" h, applied amber flowers, dimpled front and back, Longpark, 1914-23 . . . . 131.00

5 1/2" h

Ruffled rim, faience red tea roses and green leaves on black lattice work on cream center band, purple top and base, "black stamped Watcombe Torquay" mark, pr . . 148.00

Scandy, "A fellow feeling makes us wonderous kind but I wonder if the poet would change his mind if in a crowd one day he were to find a fellow feeling in his coat behind," 2 handles, "Aller Vale 1900" mark 112.00

"Shamrock" design, "If you can't be aisy be aisy as you can," handled, Longpark 66.00

Tapered to shoulder, flared top, slip decorated yellow flowers, moss green ground, unmkd 130.00

6" h, tankard shape, Kingfisher on branch, white water lily, rose ground, "imp Devon Tors Pottery" mark 130.00

7" h

Cylinder shape, Scandy, "When down in the mouth think of Jonah He came out alright," Longpark 175.00

Trumpet shape with ruffled rim, "Cottage" design, unmkd 67.00

8" h, ovoid shape, Kingfisher, dk blue ground, brown eared handles, "black stamped Watcombe Torquay England" mark, pr 175.00

8 1/2" h, with saucer, relief molded red, blue, and yellow parrot on side, dk blue ground, 2 twist handles 225.00

9 1/2" h, waisted shape, white heather on rose, green, and ochre streaked ground, 2 twisted handles, "inscribed *Lemon* & *Crute Torquay*" mark . . 75.00

10" h

Bottle shape, yellow and blue Kingfisher, white water lily, lt blue ground, "black stamped Longpark Torquay" mark 148.00

Kingfisher, yellow flower, dk blue ground, "Longpark Torquay" mark 135.00

Waste Bowl, 2 3/4" h, timbered thatched roof cottage, "I'll take the dregs," unmkd . . . 35.00

VIENNA

Vienna, Austria 1718-1864

Du Paquier 1718-1744

State Factory 1744-1864

DU PAQUIER 1720-30

c 1760-1770

History: The Vienna Porcelain Factory, founded in 1718 by Claudius Du Paquier, was the second European factory to produce hard paste porcelain. Meissen was the first. Du Paquier developed high quality white porcelain. The privilege to make porcelain was granted to Du Paquier by the Emperor Charles VI. The decorations of the Du Paquier period fall into three categories: 1) 1725 in which the polychrome oriental theme was emphasized; 2) 1730-1740 in which polychromed scrolls, landscapes, and figurals in cartouches were dominant and black and gilt were used to highlight the themes; and 3) the final period which featured German florals or "Deutch Blumchen" designs similar to the Meissen treatment. The adoption of Meissen styles contributed to the rise of Vienna as one of Meissen's chief rivals. However, unlike Meissen, the Du Paquier factory did not produce a large number of figures.

Du Paquier sold his factory to the Austrian state in 1744. It became the Imperial Porcelain Manufactory and fell under the influence of Empress Maria Theresa. The quality of the porcelain reached its peak during this period, known as the State Period, 1744-1864. The Austrian coat of arms was used as the factory mark. Following the Seven Years' War, 1756-1763, which altered greatly the production at Meissen, Vienna porcelain assumed the undisputed leadership in European porcelain.

Between 1747 and 1784, Johann Niedermeyer, the chief modeler, contributed much to the success of the factory by creating rococo influenced figurals decorated in soft pastel colors. After 1765, the styles from Sevres greatly influenced the decorative styles at Vienna. Anton Grassi came to work at Vienna in 1778. He moved the factory's production away from rococo styles into the neo-classical influences.

Joseph Leithner concentrated on developing new background colors, especially a fine cobalt blue that was a match for Sevres' bleu roi. He introduced a special gold color. Leithner enhanced all the colors used at Vienna.

Under the management of Konrad Sorgenthal between 1784 and 1805, the factory produced richly ornamented dinner and tea services, vases, urns, and plates in the neo-classical and Empire styles. Emphasis was placed on the reproduction of paintings by famous artists such as Angelica Kauffmann and Rubens onto porcelain vases, plates, and plaques that were surrounded by gilt frames that often included the painter's name.

Flowers were the principal decorative element used on Viennese porcelains. Seventeenth century Dutch flower paintings were adapted or copied on plates, cups, vases, or plate sets. Many pieces had black backgrounds to make the flowers stand out.

When the Congress of Vienna was held, numerous participants placed orders for services. After this period, the factory experienced a period of stagnation. Competition from the Bohemian factories started to take its toll.

After reaching the very pinnacle of success in the highly competitive porcelain field, the state porcelain factory was forced to close in 1864 due to financial difficulties.

The Shield mark was adopted in 1749. The year was stamped on pieces beginning in 1784.

References: W.B. Honey, *German Porcelain*, Faber & Faber, 1947; George W. Ware, *German & Austrian Porcelain*, Crown Publishers, Inc.1963.

Museums: Art Institute of Chicago, Chicago, IL; British Museum, London, England; Gardiner Museum of Ceramic Art, Toronto, Canada; Metropolitan Museum of Art, New York, NY; Osterreiches Museum fur Angewandte, Kunst, Vienna, Austria; Smithsonian Institution, Division of Ceramics and Glass, National Museum of American History, Washington DC; Woodmere Art Museum, Philadelphia, PA.

Basket, 6 1/4" h, oval, pierced sides, puce and turquoise outlined strands, gilt wavy rim with molded shells, oval base, c1765, (A) 920.00

Beaker, 2 3/4" h, molded fluted collar, painted Kakiemon flower sprays on branches below, iron red indented lines, iron red lined triangles on int border, DuPaquier, c1730, set of 6 . . . . 1,925.00

Bowl, Cov, 5 1/2" h, lilac scale ground on upper half, printed bouquet on white ground on lower half, wavy gilt band between, gilt leaf borders, quatrefoil cartouche of painted flowers reserved on lilac scale ground, figural lemon knob, "blue shield" mark, date code for 1808, (A). 770.00

Coffeepot, 7" h, pear shape, painted scattered flowers, "blue shield, puce 44" mark, c1775, (A). 253.00

Cream Jug, 3 3/4" h, pear shape, 3 branch feet, puce painted seated shepherd playing flute in landscape, "blue shield" mark, c1780, (A). 345.00

Cup and Saucer, blue painted flying birds over stylized foliage from rockwork, white ground, banded and scalloped border, set of 4, (A). 125.00

Monteith, 13 3/8" H-H, oval, crenelated rim, 2 dbl handles, sea green bands and gilt bands of griffins, cornflowers, and foliate scrolls, molded and gilt horiz ribbing, "blue shield" mark, c1800, repairs, pr, (A) 7,475.00

Plate, 9 1/2" d, oct, painted en grisaille with classical figure in oval medallion surmounted by pink ribbon tied green laurel garland, band of gilt husks on inner rim, border with band of gilt trellis and sea green lozenges with stars, corners gilt with bellflowers and husk garlands, "blue shield" mark, c1805, set of 12, (A). 14,950.00

Solitaire Set, Part, tray, 8 1/2" H-H, cov milk jug, cream jug, cov sugar bowl, cup and saucer, painted vignettes of peasants at leisure, "blue shield" marks, c1788, (A) 2,070.00

Spice Dish, 5" h, molded rococo scroll bowl, flared, fluted socle and circ base, "incised shield" mark, c1749, chip, pr, (A) . . 1,610.00

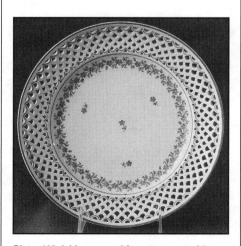

Plate, 10" d, blue enamel forget-me-nots, blue lined rim, "blue shield" mark, pr, $550.

Spoon Tray, 5 3/4" l, oval, painted polychrome man seated at table lighting pipe, companion smoking behind, barrel in foreground, gilt foliate scroll borders, "blue shield and puce JO" mark, c1770, (A) 1,035.00

Tete-a-Tete Set, coffeepot, 4 1/2" h, cream jug, cov sugar bowl, 2 cups and saucers, tray, 15" l, Sevres style enameled floral garlands suspended from laurel garlands, gilt overall bubble web design on blue ground, c1770, cracks and chips, (A) 5,980.00

Tray

12" l, 2 gilt handles, center painted with lg exotic bird on grassy mound at pond with water reeds and palm trees, flying bird and dragonfly, green chain border with pink flowerheads on gilt band, "blue shield, incised 2" mark, c1765, (A) 1,725.00

16 3/8" l, oval, 4 roundels of painted bouquets reserved on orange ground, white rim with band of gilt scrolling leaves, early 19th C, (A). 647.00

Urn, Cov, 37" h, ovoid shape, painted continuous scene of classical figures, gilt decorated cobalt neck, ft, and base, (A) 4,025.00

Vase, Cov, 21" h, shield shape, painted continuous frieze of classical figures, cobalt ground with gilt accents, sq base with half moon painted classical scene, sq gold handles, pr, (A) 8,625.00

VILLEROY AND BOCH

Mettlach, Germany 1836 to Present

History: Johann Franz Boch founded a dinnerware factory in 1809 in an old Benedictine abbey in Mettlach. This factory merged with the Nicholas Villeroy plant in Wallerfongen, Saar in 1836 to form the Villeroy and Boch company. The Luxembourg factory founded in 1767 by the Boch brothers also was included in this merger. Eventually there were eight Villeroy and Boch factories in other cities in addition to the main factory at Mettlach. August von Cohausen was the director who instituted the use of the old abbey tower as the factory's trademark.

Stonewares, original in both design and production techniques, were produced starting in the 1840s and were the most famous of the Villeroy and Boch wares. In addition to steins, punch bowls, beakers, wall plaques, beverage sets, drinking cups, hanging baskets, and vases were made.

Chromolith, colored stonewares, utilized two colors of clay worked side by side but separated by a black intaglio line. Raised decoration was done by applying the design and fusing it to the body of the stoneware pieces. This process was known as etched, engraved, or mosaic inlay.

Motifs included Germanic scenes depicting peasant and student life, and religious and mythological themes. Punch bowls featured garlands of fruit, while steins were adorned with drinking scenes, military events, folk tales, and student life scenes. About 1900, Art Nouveau decorations appeared on plaques, punch bowls, vases, steins, umbrella, and flower stands.

Phanolith stoneware plaques were given an initial coating of a delicate green matte color, glazed, and then fired. Figures to decorate the plaques were formed separately, applied to the pre-fired background, and then fired again. These applied decorations were ivory colored and stood out in relief against the green ground. Motifs on plaques included scenes from Greek mythology and Germanic legends.

Cameo stonewares had raised ivory colored decorations set on light blue or light green backgrounds. There was a less fluid quality to these applied decorations. The stoneware was more dense.

The pinnacle of stoneware production was between 1880 and 1910. Prominent artists at Mettlach were Christian Warth, Heinrich Schlitt, Fritz Quidenus, Mittein, and Johann Baptist Stahl.

Terra cotta for architectural use was made from 1850; mosaic tiles were made from 1852. Cream-colored earthenwares for domestic use were produced at factories in Dresden from 1853 and in Schramberg from 1883. Around 1890, artists at Mettlach manufactured plates and vases decorated in the Delft style and the faience of Rouen.

Around World War I, business had lessened due to unfavorable economic conditions and the lack of skilled labor. In 1921, a major fire destroyed all molds, formulas, and records of the factory.

Although the factory continued to produce tiles, dinnerwares, and plumbing fixtures, almost 50 years lapsed before the factory revived the production of steins and plaques.

Reference: Gary Kirsner, *The Mettlach Book,* Seven Hills Books, 1983.

Museums: Keramik Museum, Mettlach, Germany; Musee de l'Etat, Luxembourg; Munchner-Stadtmuseum, Munich, Germany; Rijksmuseum, Amsterdam, Holland; Sevres Museum, Sevres, France; Villeroy & Boch Archives & Museum, Mettlach, Germany.

Beaker
.25 L, PUG

#1023-2327, Violin Player 75.00

#1024-2327, Flute Player 75.00

#2327-236, man with pipe, brown shades, (A) 184.00

#2327-1302, American eagle and flag, chip, (A) 138.00

.5 L, PUG, #2327-1190, 2327-1191, men at seashore, pr, (A) 149.00

Beverage Set, pitcher, 12" h, inlaid lid, #2098, 4 tumblers, #2834, mosaic flower design, Mettlach 1,650.00

Bowl

6" d, oriental pagoda scene on int center, oriental buildings and peony flowers on inner and outer border, dk blue transfer, mottled tan ground, "V & B Wallerpangen" mark 30.00

7 1/4" d, ftd, orange, blue, and red oriental style design with figures on int, green, dk blue, pink, and orange oriental flowers and fencing on int border, green, dk blue, pink, and orange figures and pagodas on ext, brown lined rim . . 38.00

Candlestick, 8" h, etched, Art Nouveau design, #3339, pr 300.00

Chamberstick, 3 1/2" h, figural tree stump with match striker, brown shades, #114, Mettlach, (A) 115.00

Charger, 15 1/2" d, PUG, blue and white ships, Mettlach 225.00

Coaster, 4 3/4" d, PUG, drinking dwarfs in colors, Mettlach, pr, (A) 358.00

Creamer, 4" h, etched, Art Deco style white vert rect panels with black hearts, brown ground with black hearts and banding, #3052, Mettlach, (A) 174.00

Dish, 5" h, figural cream girl sleeping under lg cream shell on brown gnarled stump, platinum trim, #335, Mettlach, (A) 347.00

Figure

11 1/2" h, 3 stylized sailors walking arm in arm, sea green glaze 600.00

18" h, period brown haired standing man in gray hat, aqua jacket, red striped flowered trousers, pink shoes, blue cape under arm, holding bible, female companion wearing veil, pink trimmed blue bodice, flower trimmed white dress with blue checkered sash, brown and green base surface, pink, blue, and

Garniture, 8 1/2", 6 1/2" h, wheat colored ground, silver trim, "V & B Luxemburg" marks, $17,200.

gold striped circ base, "V & B, raised shield" mark, pr, (A) 2,426.00

Flower Pot

3 3/4" h, brown ground platinum relief bands of scrolling leaves, Mettlach 60.00

6 1/2" h, cylinder shape, brown, tan, and platinum marbleized finish with vines, Mettlach, (A) 93.00

8 1/2" h, etched, Art Nouveau style blue and yellow swirls on white ground, blue and yellow checkerboard border, #2908 II, Mettlach, (A) 670.00

23" h x 26" H-H, etched and glazed, multicolored scene of ladies in garden, one swinging, reverse with ladies standing and sitting, glazed figural cherubs on handles, glazed geometric rim, handle, and base, Mettlach, chips, (A). 5,500.00

Goblet, 7" h, Gambrinus, tan relief cameos of gentlemen seated at table drinking, vert panels of diamonds, brown ground, (A) . . 140.00

Jam Jar, Cov, 4 3/4" h, cylinder shape, painted relief design of strawberries and peaches, Mettlach. 100.00

Pass Cup, 7" h, PUG of Musicians, #2260-993, Mettlach, (A) 341.00

Pitcher

8 1/2" h, applied green leaves, brown stems, gray ground, brown birch handle 275.00

8 3/4" h, mustard and dk blue incised stylized berries and leaves, white ground, Mettlach, (A) 325.00

Planter, 11 1/2" l, etched, Art Nouveau style white panels with blue and brown buds on brown ground, white streaks, #2980, Mettlach, (A) 1,271.00

Plaque

6" sq, Phanolith, white cameo of classic woman holding mirror, child at side, med blue ground, #7066, Mettlach 275.00

Plaque, 14" d, PUG, "Stadthaus in Berncastle," "Mettlach mercury, Made in Germany" mark, (A) $85.

7 1/4" d, etched, oriental style scene of exotic birds near lake, #1417, Mettlach, (A) 462.00

7 3/4" d

Etched, cavalier holding tray with wine, jug, and glasses, Mettlach #2623 . . . . 200.00

PUG, dwarf being attacked by lg black beetle, mushroom and flowers in fore and bkd, #1044-1325, Mettlach, (A). 590.00

8" h x 6" w, rect, Phanolith, white cameo of classic woman in flowing gown, holding ribbons at side, white geometric border, med blue ground, #7072, Mettlach, (A) 416.00

12" d, PUG

"Porta Negra Trier," multicolored, #1044-481, (A) 289.00

Yellow flowers, dk blue leaves, med blue ground, #1044-110, Mettlach, (A). 208.00

10 1/4" l x 7 1/4" w, oval, white cameos of boys playing flute and mandolin, girl with fan, green jasper ground, Mettlach, #2445, c1898. . . . . 640.00

11" w x 13" h, shield shape, PUG and HP crest of Great Britain, #3225-1290, (A) 636.00

11 3/4" d, oct, PUG, woman in blue dress, white shawl, holding flower basket, or woman in red dress holding open fan, #9007, #9008, pr, (A) 352.00

12" d, PUG, "Remagen," #1044-158, Mettlach, (A) 176.00

14 1/2" d, etched

Cavalier and maiden, Cupid aiming bow and arrow, ribbon with German saying, #2322, Mettlach castle mark 950.00

Knight with weapon, blue ground, sgd "Schultz," dtd 1910, #1385, castle mark 925.00

15" d, etched

Etruscan scene, brown and cream, #2199, (A). 1,1040.00

Husaren on horseback, gold rim, #2081, Mettlach, (A) 792.00

17" d

Delft style, blue and white portrait of 17th C gentleman, #1044/5265, Mettlach 345.00

Etched

Castle on Rhine scene, gold rim, #1108, dtd 1907 . . . . . . 895.00

"Godesberg Castle," #2533, Mettlach, (A) 880.00

Town scene of Meissen, #2518, Mettlach, (A) 1,675.00

PUG

Hunting dog in field, #1044-127, Mettlach, worn gold rim, (A) 462.00

Old farm house scene, #1044/1067m Mettlach. 540.00

17" l x 11" w, etched, woman with basket of fruit. 1,470.00

17 1/4" d, etched, multicolored Rhine scene, gold rim, Mettlach castle mark, #1365 . . . . 995.00

17 1/2" d, etched, man and woman on bicycles in dark or daylight, multicolored, #2563, #2564, Mettlach, pr, (A) 15,400

17 1/2" l x 12" w, oval, PUG, "Spitzbergen; Advent Day Hotel," #2620-151, Mettlach, (A) 462.00

18" d, white cameo of Trojan warriors in boat, green ground, #2442, castle mark 995.00

27 1/2" d, etched and glazed, Imperial eagle in center, border of 14 city crests, #2013, Mettlach, (A) 11,000.00

Pokal, 9" h, cream colored relief of Gambrinus seated on throne holding tankard, heart shaped leaves and stems on base, dk brown ground, Mettlach, (A). 264.00

Teapot, 5 3/4" h, paneled, etched, blue, white, and gold Art Nouveau style design, #2946, Mettlach, (A). 375.00

Tray, 11 1/2" l x 6 1/4" w, etched, black and gold Art Deco geometrics on white ground, black and gold banded rim, #3055, Mettlach, (A). 462.00

Trivet

8" d, etched, green, yellow, and white wheel design, Mettlach, chip . . . 75.00

8 1/4" sq, lg orange flower, dk green leaves and stems, med green ground, Mettlach, (A) 35.00

Vase

3 1/2" h, ball shape, short straight border, etched and glazed red outlined white crosses on yellow ground, lt blue lined ft and rim with lt brown continuous intertwined loops, #1961, Mettlach, (A) 229.00

4" h, cylinder shape, indented rim, 4 handles, etched, gray, black and yellow leaves on dk brown ground, #2473, Mettlach, (A) 528.00

4 1/2" h

Brown figural tree trunk, panel of dk brown fox in hunter's coat and weapon, applied leaf design, Mettlach, (A) 204.00

Etched, Art Nouveau style, circ brown cartouche with white lily of the valley and gray leaves, mustard yellow ground, brown drip border with gray clovers, 2 molded scroll handles, #2472, Mettlach, (A) 597.00

9" h, PUG, orange iris, blue-green leaves, blue ground, gold rim, #2617-6090, Mettlach, repaired chip, (A) . . . 220.00

11" h, tan, brown, red, and blue mosaic, Mettlach 375.00

11 1/2" h

Tapered cylinder shape, flared rim, Delft, Dutch girl holding basket, repainted gold rim, #3014-5424, Mettlach, (A) 297.00

Tapered sq shape, white cameos of classic women in dk blue cathedral

shaped inserts, raised lt blue lines and squares, gray body, dk blue base, #3040, Mettlach, (A). . 366.00

12 1/4" h, ball shaped body, straight neck, spread ft, etched and glazed, white and brown stylized flowerheads and stems on blue ground, green molded dolphin handles and base, #2037, Mettlach, repaired, (A) 375.00

14" h, PUG, Munich child on globe, #2902-1014, Mettlach, hairline, (A) 462.00

25 1/2" h, relief of woman in white top, flowered blue gown, butterfly wings, sitting on vines, dk brown ground, #1611, Mettlach, chips, repaired hairline, (A) 1,238.00

48" h, etched, design of knight and maiden in colors, Mettlach, dtd 1900, (A) 46,000.00

MODERN MARK   1895   c1900

VOLKSTEDT

Thuringia, Germany
1760 to Present

History: The Volkstedt porcelain factory was started about 1760 under the patronage of Johann Friedrich von Schwartzburg-Rudolstadt. The peak of its fame occurred between 1767 and 1797 when the factory was leased to Christian Fonne. A succession of owners followed.

Until 1800, the factory produced mostly ordinary tablewares. These were usually massive in design and decorated in the rococo style. Some fine vases decorated in rococo or formal styles were made. Decorative motifs included small portraits, landscapes, and ornamental maps.

Between 1898 and 1972, Karl Ens occupied one portion of the Volkstedt factory. The firm made decorative porcelains, figures, and gift articles. The company was nationalized in 1972 and named VEB Underglaze Porcelain Factory. During the 20th century, Volkstedt manufactured tablewares, vases, and figures in the Meissen style.

Museum: Victoria & Albert Museum, London, England.

Center Bowl, 10 1/4" h, molded rim with pierced whiplash tendrils and 3 stalks with lilies, relief of white Art Nouveau maiden on

Figure, 9 1/4" h, brown, tan, cream, and gilt, pr, $650.

side, brown, peach, and gilt accents, Richard Eckert & Co., c1900, (A) 460.00

Figure

6" h, Art Deco style, 2 women swinging, holding hands, yellow dresses, artist sgd. 320.00

7 3/4" h, female flanked by cherubs, raised rect base, white biscuit, c1900, (A) 115.00

8 5/8" h, blue, green, and yellow parrot perched on white floral branch, Karl Ens, (A) 100.00

9" h, Toucan, white with black and rust accents, Karl Ens. 195.00

9 1/2" h

10 1/2" h, standing man in lt blue jacket, cream vest, lg pink bow tie, pink and white striped pants, holding hat, raised flower on shoulder, woman in cream skirt with gilt outlined pink band, white ruffled apron with lavender and blue trim, holding multicolored encrusted flowers, white and gilt headpiece with blue bow on top, multicolored sculptured base, Triebner, Ens, and Eckert, c1880, pr 750.00

Maiden in green jacket, white lace full skirt, bouquet of flowers and yellow hat in lap, lace chips 195.00

12 3/4" h, Cupid and Psyche mounted on rock molded circ base, white biscuit, restored, A) 230.00

13 3/4" h x 27" l, 8 figures in 18th C dress surrounding piano, dancing, or seated, rococo framed oval scroll molded base, overall white glaze, 20th C, restorations, (A) 1,495.00

Plaque, 13 3/8" h, white cameos of 2 Art Nouveau females floating above pond, or couple

Figure, 20" h, white glaze, sgd "Guitav Oppei," (A) $460.

embracing, blue jasper ground, white outlined shaped border, mkd, pr, (A) . . . 631.00

Salt, 5 5/8" h, figural draped putto seated on tree stump, leaf on head, polychromed, (A) 368.00

Tea and Coffee Service, Part, coffeepot, 8 1/2" h, pear shape, hot milk jug, cov, 6" h, teapot, 4 3/4" h, globular shape, tea caddy, 5" h, rect, puce painted loose bouquets, berry knobs, c1790, (A) 1,840.00

WEDGWOOD

Burslem, near Stoke-on-Trent, England 1759-1769

Etruria factory, England 1769-1940

Barlaston, near Stoke-on-Trent, England 1940 to Present

WEDGWOOD
c1759-1769

WEDGWOOD
c1900

History: By 1759, Josiah Wedgwood was working in Burslem, Staffordshire manufacturing earthenware. A partnership with Bentley was formed shortly after he moved

to his new factory in Etruria in 1769. The partnership lasted until 1780.

Black Basalt

Black Basalt was fine grained, unglazed black stoneware made between 1767 and 1796. This term was coined by Josiah Wedgwood to describe a refined version of "Egyptian black." In his 1787 catalog, Wedgwood described his ware as "a black porcelain biscuit (that is unglazed body) of nearly the same properties with the natural stone, striking fire from steel, receiving a high polish, serving as a touchstone for metals, resisting all acids, and bearing without injury a strong fire-stronger indeed than the basalts itself." "Egyptian Black" was used for utilitarian wares and for large relief plaques, vases, busts, medallions, seals, and small intaglios. It was a black clay body that resembled bronze when unpolished. Both historical and mythological figures and faces were produced.

Bone China

When Josiah II took over, he introduced the manufacture of bone china in 1812. Production continued until 1828. Josiah II was not satisfied with the product, so it was discontinued. Bone china was not manufactured again until 1878.

The 40-year period from 1840 to1880 was one of modernization. Solid jasper was reintroduced. Parian ware, a fine white body resembling marble, was produced. When Wedgwood introduced majolica in 1860, the company was the first to use a white body and semi-transparent colored glazes.

When Wedgwood began to manufacture porcelain again in 1878, the products were of very high quality in texture, color, glaze, and decoration. The printed mark with the Portland vase was used on this porcelain.

Fourth and fifth generations of Wedgwoods continued to operate the firm into the 20th century. An interest in late 18th century design was revived. Commemorative wares were made for the American market.

Creamware

Wedgwood's creamware utilized a Cornwall clay that created a lighter, stronger body of a more uniform texture. It became designated "Queensware" after Wedgwood supplied a breakfast set for Queen Charlotte in 1762.

Jasper

Jasper, probably Josiah Wedgwood's best known product, was started in 1774. Known as a "dry body" because it was non-porous and unglazed, this vitreous fine stoneware was made in several shades of blue, green, lilac, yellow, maroon, black, and white. Sometimes more than one color was combined. "Solid" jasper had the body colored throughout; white jasper "dip" was a white jasper body with the color laid on the surface. Raised figures and ornaments in white adorned the tremendous variety of jasper shapes. Classical motifs were most prominent. Wedgwood's replica of the Barberini or Portland vase was considered a high point in the production.

Pearlware

Pearlware, introduced by Wedgwood in 1779, was whiter than Queensware. Cobalt oxide was added to the glaze, reacting like a laundry bluing that whitened clothing.

After Bentley's death in 1780, Wedgwood worked alone until 1790 when his sons and Thomas Byerley became his partners. From 1769 until 1780, the firm was called "Wedgwood and Bentley." It was simply "Wedgwood" in the decade from 1780 to 1790. The name became "Wedgwood Sons and Byerley" between 1790 and 1793 and "Wedgwood & Sons & Byerley" between 1793 and 1795. Josiah Wedgwood died in 1795.

Redwares

Other "dry bodies" or redwares made that were manufactured between 1776 and 1870 included: a) cane ware (pale buff colored stoneware); b) rosso antico (dark red to chocolate colored unglazed stoneware); c) terra cotta (light red stoneware); d) drabware (olive gray stoneware); and e) white stoneware (pure white biscuit). Both utilitarian and decorative wares were made.

Wedgwood Lusters

Wedgwood lusters were formed by applying iridescent or metallic films on the surface of the ceramic wares. The effect was obtained by using metallic oxides of gold, silver, copper, etc. Lusters were applied as embellishments to an enameled object or as a complete or near complete covering to duplicate the effect of a silver or copper metallic object. The lusters were decorated by the resist method.

From 1915 to 1931, Wedgwood produced fairyland lusters from the designs of Daisy Makeig-Jones. Fairyland lusters were made in Queensware plaques and bone china plates and ornamental pieces, such as vases and bowls. The designs combined the use of bright underglaze colors, commercial lusters, and gold printing, often with fantastic and grotesque figures, scenes, and landscapes.

Pattern numbers were painted on the base of fairyland luster pieces by the artist who decorated them along with the Wedgwood marks.

A new factory was built at Barlaston, six miles from Etruria. Firing was done at Barlaston in six electric ovens. Production started at the new factory in 1940. Etruria eventually was closed in June 1950.

On May 1, 1959, the company commemorated its bicentenary. During the 1960s, Wedgwood acquired many English firms such as Coalport, William Adams & Sons, Royal Tuscan, Susie Cooper, and Johnson Brothers. Further expansion in the 1970s brought J.& G. Meakin, Midwinter Companies, Crown Staffordshire, Mason's Ironstone, and Precision Studios into the fold. Each company retained its own identity. The Wedgwood Group is one of the largest fine china and earthenware manufacturers in the world.

References: M. Batkin, *Wedgwood Ceramics 1846-1959*, Antique Collectors' Club, 1982; David Buten, *18th Century Wedgwood*, Methuen, Inc., 1980; Una des Fontines, *Wedgwood Fairyland Lustre*, Borne-Hawes, 1975; Alison Kelly, *The Story of Wedgwood*, The Viking Press, 1975; Wolf Mankowitz, *Wedgwood*, Spring Books, 1966; Robin Reilly, *Josiah Wedgwood, 1730-1795*, Pan Books, 1992; Robin Reilly, *The New Illustrated Dictionary of Wedgwood*, Antique Collectors' Club, Ltd., 1995; Robin Reilly, *Wedgwood Jasper*, Thomas Hudson, 1994; Robin Reilly & George Savage, *The Dictionary of Wedgwood*, Antique Collectors' Club, Ltd. 1980; Geoffrey Wills, *Wedgwood*, Chartwell Books, Inc. 1989.

Collectors' Clubs: The Wedgwood Society, The Roman Villa, Rockbourne, Fordingbridge, Hants. SP6 3 PG, UK. Membership: £7.5, Wedgwood Data Chart, Semi-annual newsletter; The Wedgwood Society of New York, 5 Dogwood Court, Glen Head, NY 11545. Membership: $22.50, *Ars Ceramic Magazine*, Bi-monthly newsletter; The Wedgwood Society of Boston, Adele I. Rogers, 28 Birchwood Drive, Hampstead, NH 03841. Annual Dues: $25.00; Wedgwood International Seminar, 22 DeSavry Crescent, Toronto, Ontario M4S 212 Canada; Wedgwood Society of Southern California, Inc. P.O. Box 4385, North Hollywood, CA 91617, Membership: $15.00, Monthly newsletter.

Museums: Birmingham Museum of Art, Birmingham, AL; The Brooklyn Museum, Brooklyn, NY; City Museum & Art Gallery, Stoke-on-Trent, England; Henry E. Huntington Library & Art Gallery, San Marino, CA; Jones Museum of Glass & Ceramics, East Baldwin, ME; Nassau County Museum, Sands Point Preserve, NY; R.W. Norton Art Gallery, Shreveport, LA; Victoria & Albert Museum, London, England; Wedg-

Candlesticks, 8 1/2" , 9" h, Cupid and Psyche, c1880, pr, $1,750.

wood Museum, Barlaston, Stoke-on-Trent, England.

Reproduction Alert: Two marks are currently in use on Wedgwood pieces. If neither of these marks appear on a piece, it is probably not Wedgwood.

Basalt

Candlestick, 9 3/4" h, figural kneeling Triton holding cornucopia sconce, pr, (A)
. . . . 2,415.00

Crocus Pot, 9 3/4" l, with undertray, figural hedgehog, c1800, chips, (A) 920.00

Cup and Saucer, Encaustic, orange and white band of running anthemion on borders, "imp wedgwood" mark, c1780, (A) 978.00

Figure, 8" h

    Bust of Robert Burns, raised circ base, mid 19th C, (A). 460.00

    Seated Cupid and Psyche on rocky oval base, titled, (A) 1,265.00

Incense Burner, 5 1/2" h, pierced cov, round bowl with leaf drape, 3 figural dolphin feet, triangle base with molded leaves, "imp Josiah Wedgwood Feb. 2, 1805," restored chips on cov, (A) 1,610.00

Inkwell, 3 3/8" l, lobed shape, relief molded baluster columns and dimpled ground, "wedgwood" mark, c1780, chip, (A). . 385.00

Jug, 11 1/4" h, helmet shape, relief of Bacchanalian boys over engine turned lower section with raised rope and dot foliate borders, Wedgwood and Bentley, c1780, chips, (A)
. . . . 3,335.00

Kettle, 6 3/4" h, flared cylinder form, reliefs of putti playing instruments under beadwork rim, trefoil shaped overhead handle, recumbent lion knob, Wedgwood and Bentley, c1780, (A) 2,530.00

Pitcher, 5 1/2" h, enameled flowers and stems on matte surface, polished int, (A) . . . 230.00

Plaque, 15 1/4" h x 12 1/4" w, oval, relief bust of Peter the Great, Wedgwood and Bentley, c1775, (A) 4,313.00

Teapot, 3 1/2" h, flat bulbous form, engine-turned body, straight spout, strap handle, ball knob, c1780, "imp wedgwood" mark, (A) 1,265.00

Vase

7" h, raised Grecian design, flower and grape band top and base, c1850 . . . . 550.00

8 3/4" h, Krater, side loop handles, Encaustic, iron red and black enameled classical figures to sides, Greek key border, (A) 2,070.00

9" h, Encaustic, white and black classical figures, iron red, blue, white, and black floral and geometric border, loop handles, early 19th C, (A) 2,990.00

11" h, hydra shape, 2 horiz handles, Encaustic, black outlined iron red, white, cream, and gray classical frieze on front, palmette and stylized foliage on reverse, late 18th C, (A). 5,463.00

Vase, Cov

9 3/4" h, fixed cov, engine-turned vert lines, molded drapery swags, applied Bacchus head handles, acorn knob, Wedgwood and Bentley, restored handles, (A) 1,092.00

12 3/4" h, scrolled foliate handles, gadrooned band over frieze of children playing, gadrooned socle set on sq plinth, Wedgwood and Bentley, c1775, (A) 4,313.00

Water Pot, Cov, 9 1/4" h, bulbous shape, flat ft, relief of Bacchanalian children over engine-turned base, cov with foliate molding,

Urn, Cov, 12" h, Wedgwood and Bentley, c1770, $4,750.

engine turnings, and figural sybil knob, "wedgwood" mark, c1780, (A) 1,265.00

General

Basket, 9" l, with undertray, Queensware, basketweave molded bodies with pierced galleries, green and black enameled oak leaves and trim lines, early 19th C, (A) 287.00

Coffee Pot, 8" h, Rosso Antico, multicolored enameled flowers and green leaves, gold trim, black basalt ground, "Wedgwood" mark 450.00

Candleholder, 6 1/2" h, surface agate body, applied creamware drapery swags, sq black basalt base, Wedgwood and Bentley, c1775, (A). 1,495.00

Cream and Cov Sugar Bowl, Queensware, emb cream grapes, celadon green ground 140.00

Cup and Saucer, Queensware
Emb cream grapes, celadon green ground 30.00
Gold wheat trim. 35.00

Dish

8" sq, bone china, black border with pink and red cherry blossoms, wavy rim, c1820, hairline, (A) 55.00

10 1/4" l, oval, Queensware, shell shape, enamel decorated bird and floral design, gilt trim lines, c1878, (A). 100.00

10 3/4" l, caneware, molded fern over molded banana leaf, "imp WEDGWOOD" mark, c1820, (A). 130.00

Epergne, 18 3/8" h, Queen's Ware, green and brown enameled accented 2 tier form, figural eagle at top, 3 shell molded dishes on fluted center column over lg sectioned dish on ftd circ base, c1790, repairs, (A) 4,025.00

Figure

7" h, "Fallow Deer," cream glaze, "imp J. Skeaping" mark, (A) 173.00

7 1/4" h, Rosso Antico, bust of Matthew Prior, raised circ base, imp title, late 18th , restoration, (A) 402.00

9 1/2" h, Yellow Shafted Flicker on tree branch, c1940, (A) 546.00

15 1/2" l, Queensware, "Taurus the Bull," cream ground, Arnold Machin, (A) 172.00

Fruit Compote, 7 1/8" d, Queensware, pierced basketweave body, scalloped rim, sgd "Hensleigh Wedgwood," c1930, (A) 575.00

Game Pie Dish, Cov, 7" l, with liner, caneware, oval, molded hanging dead game, rabbit knob, liner crack, 1865, (A) 431.00

Jug

4 1/4" h, caneware, reliefs of "Sportive Love" and "Charlotte at the tomb of Werther," engine-turned band on base, brown enameled "R" under spout, c1800, (A) 633.00

5" h, Doric, brown, tan, and blue agate on white ground, c1865, (A) 316.00

Mug, 6" h, cylinder shape, Queen's Ware, black transfer of figures playing blind man's

Soup Plate, 8 3/8" d, red and blue morning glory design in center, blue lined rim, "Morning Glory Wedgwood Patrician" mark, set of 6, $275.

bluff in landscape setting, "wedgwood" mark, c1775, (A) 1,610.00

Pie Dish, Cov, 12" l, with liner, oval, caneware, leaf molded cov, 1863, (A) 920.00

Pitcher, Cov, 10 1/2" h, Queen's Ware, black and red enameled Etruscan pattern borders, c1780, (A) 633.00

Plate

8 1/4" d, bone china, "Green Dragon" pattern, gilt trim, c1820, (A) 100.00

9 1/8" d, creamware, multicolored scene of little girl and mother buying buns from bun man, "Buns!Buns!Buns!" on reverse, sgd "Lessore" 325.00

10" d, Martha Washington, blue transfer 55.00

Platter

18 3/8" l x 15" w, oval, Queen's Ware, center scene of coastal landscape with figures, floral sprays on border, black transfers, molded feather rim, late 18th C, (A) 805.00

19" l x 17" w, "Harvard University," maroon transfer, c1941. . . . . 500.00

Teapot, 4 1/2" h, black outlined enameled flowers, terra cotta ground, (A) $70.

20 3/4" l x 15 3/4" w, Queen's Ware, Chelsea style polychrome bird and floral center, butterfly and floral border, 1871, (A) 373.00

Potpourri Basket, 4 1/4" h, caneware, relief band of black basalt fruiting grapevines on middle, early 19th C, (A) 575.00

Sauce Tureen, Cov, 7 1/8" H-H, with undertray, bone china, lg polychrome flowerheads, leaves, and stems, gold rims, handles, and open knob, (A) 345.00

Soup Plate, 9 3/4" d, Queen's Ware, underglaze iron red and blue Japan pattern with gilt accents, c1909, set of 6 . . . . 200.00

Teapot

   3 1/2" h, caneware, pentagon shape, figural bamboo body, handle, spout, and knob, Wedgwood and Bentley, c1775, (A) 2,070.00

   4 3/4" h, drabware, lion finial 275.00

   5" h, globular shape, Queen's Ware, "Exotic Birds" pattern, red transfer, leaf molded spout and handle, ball knob, "imp wedgwood" mark, c1775, repairs, (A) 489.00

   7" l, glazed caneware, white fruiting grapevine relief, c1830, (A) 172.00

Tea Service, bone china, teapot, 11" l, restored, creamer, cov sugar bowl, waste bowl, 5 1/2" d, cup and saucer, Chinese figural landscape scenes, blue transfers, c1820, (A) 431.00

Tureen, 8 1/2" h x 12" l, with undertray, oval, leaf molded handles, flower knob, Queen's Ware, band of brown and green enameled ivy leaves, stems, and berries, 18th C, (A) 690.00

Vase

   7" h, bone china, trumpet shape, "Kutani Crane" pattern, polychrome bird and peonies 38.00

   9 1/2" h, tapered cylinder shape, Vellum, gilt trimmed polychrome bird and floral design, cream ground, brown ground neck with gilt florals, c1885, (A) 345.00

   13 3/4" h, porphyry body, molded laurel creamware band on shoulder with gilt accents, rope twist creamware handles, black basalt sq base, Wedgwood and Bentley, c1775, restored rim, (A) 1,995.00

Vase, Cov, 9 1/2" h, solid agate body, figural sybil creamware knob with gilt accents, sq black basalt base, Wedgwood and Bentley, c1770, pr, (A) 7,475.00

Veilleuse, 3 3/8" h, with cov and stand, Queen's Ware, iron red and blue enamel vert loop banding, early 19th C, (A) 460.00

Wine Cooler, 10" h, redware, molded fruiting vines, raised mask handle, early 19th C, (A) 545.00

Jasper

Barber Bottle, 10 1/2" h, center medallions of white classic figures on lilac ground, dk blue

Candlesticks, 8" h, white cameos, blue jasper ground, "imp WEDGWOOD MADE IN ENGLAND" marks, pr, (A) $259.

center band, green base, shoulder, neck, and stopper, white cameos of stiff leaves, swags, and beading, figural Bacchus heads on shoulder, late 19th C, (A) 2,070.00

Biscuit Jar, 6 3/4" h, white cameos of ladies and 4 cherubs for 4 seasons, dk blue ground, SP rim, top, and bamboo handle, "WEDGWOOD" mark 235.00

Bowl, 5" d, white cameo bands of foliage and geometrics, solid blue jasper, polished int, c1800, (A). 546.00

Box, 3" d, white cameo bust of Winston Churchill, blue ground 95.00

Butter Dish, Cov, 6 7/8" d, white cameos of "Boys at Play" and "Domestic Employment," engine-turned foot rim and cov, foliate borders, solid blue jasper ground, "imp wedgwood" mark, (A) 1,265.00

Candlestick, 5" h, black cameos of classic figures and scrolled vines, floral border, white rim rings, yellow ground, c1930, pr, (A) 575.00

Centerpiece, Cov, 8 1/4" h, Diceware, lilac quatrefoils, white foliate borders, green ground, white figural knob, (A). 977.00

Cheese Dish, Cov, 9 1/2" d, white cameos of classic figures of muses and putti, floral and geometric bands on borders, dk blue ground, late 19th C, (A) 460.00

Chocolate Pot, 7 1/2" h, cylinder shape, lower band of white cameos of classic figures and cherubs, upper band of grape leaves and vines, stiff leaves on cov, "Wedgwood" mark 325.00

Coffee Can and Saucer, green jasper ground oval medallions with white cameos of classical and trophy reliefs between fruiting festoons hanging from ram's heads, lilac ground, c1870, handle restored, (A) 1,265.00

Creamer, 2 1/4" h, white cameos of classic figure, grapevine band on rim and handle, dk blue ground, "Wedgwood, Made in England" mark, (A) 40.00

Cup, 2 1/4" h, green jasper dip ground with engine-turned dicing on white ground and ap-

plied yellow quatrefoils, c1795, (A) 1,380.00

Figure, 5 1/8" l, white sleeping child, solid green jasper blanket, solid blue rect base with leaf molded rim and cut corners, c1785, (A) 3,335.00

Flower Pot, 5 3/16" h, flared shape, flared gallery rim, ftd, white cameos of classical figures and trees, grapevine band on foot, floral band below rim, removable bisque insert, pr, (A) 240.00

Jam Jar, 4" h, white cameos of classic ladies and trees, dk blue ground, SP rim, top, and handle, "WEDGWOOD ENGLAND" mark 145.00

Jardiniere, 7 3/16" h x 8" d, white cameos of classic figures on sides, grapevine swag with lion heads and rings, floral band on rim, dk blue ground, "Wedgwood, Made in England" mark, (A) 240.00

Jug, 5 3/4" h, white cameos of "Domestic Employment," stiff leaves on base, hanging swags of florals and leaves on throat, band of interlaced circles on rim, solid blue jasper ground, late 18th C, (A) 1,265.00

Medallion, 3 3/4" h x 2 7/8" w, oval, white relief of George IV, Prince of Wales, solid blue jasper ground, imp title, (A) 207.00

Mug, 1 3/8" h, white cameos of mythological figures, lt blue ground, "WEDGWOOD ENGLAND" mark 145.00

Pencil Box, 9" l, white cameo of walking maiden with basket on head, twist border, dk blue ground, mid 19th C, (A) 546.00

Perfume Bottle, 4 3/4" h, white cameo of woman and putto, drapery swags, beaded border, green ground, SP screw top, early 19th C, (A) 690.00

Pitcher

   2 3/4" h, white cameos of man, dog, and lady, dk blue ground, "WEDGWOOD" mark. 195.00

   7 1/2" h, white cameo bust of Washington or Franklin in starburst cartouche, cameos of grape leaves and vines on border, blue jasper ground, "WEDGWOOD, ENGLAND" mark. 375.00

Portland Vase, 10 1/4" h, white cameos of classic figures, half figure wearing Phrygian cap, solid black jasper, 19th C, (A) 2,875.00

Ring Tree, 2 1/2" h, white cameos of cherubs, acorn and oak leaf border, lt blue ground, "WEDGWOOD ENGLAND" mark 110.00

Sugar Bowl, Cov, 4" h, white cameos of classic ladies, bands of flowerheads, scroll handles, dk blue ground, "WEDGWOOD ENGLAND" mark 80.00

Teapot

   4 1/2" h, white cameos of classic ladies, dk blue jasper ground, "WEDGWOOD ENGLAND" mark 195.00

   5 1/4" h, cylinder shape, white cameos of "Charlotte at the Tomb of Werther" and "Domestic Employment," stiff leaves on cov, 18th C, (A) 977.00

Vases, 11 1/2" h, white cameos, lt blue jasper ground, c1825, pr, $7,000.

10" l, squat shape, white cameos of classic figures including muses and putti with trees, stiff leaf border on cov, crimson jasper ground, c1920, (A) 690.00

Tray, 10 1/2" l x 7 3/4" w, center with white cameos of facing classical figures, relief of acorns and oak leaves on border, dk blue border, unmkd, (A) 65.00

Urn, Cov, 9 1/4" h, white classic cameos, stiff leaves on cov, lavender jasper ground, "WEDGWOOD" mark 1,190.00

Vase

7" h, bulbous body, spread ft, straight neck, flared rim, white cameos of classical figures on side, white hanging grasses, stiff leaves on ft, piecrust rim, dk blue jasper ground, "WEDGWOOD ENGLAND" mark 225.00

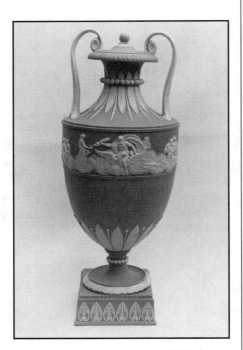

Vase, Cov, 11" h, white cameos, med blue jasper ground, c1800, $4,200.

10 1/4" h, cylinder shape, white cameos of vert stiff leaves on base, rams' heads and hanging swags on upper section, band of swags and stars on rim, lt blue jasper ground 275.00

Vase, Cov, 13 1/2" h, sq base, applied black central frieze of dancing hours, black bands of stiff leaves, white jasper Bacchus mask handles, yellow ground, early 20th C, pr
. . . . 2,300.00

Luster

Boston Cup, 5 1/8" d, Fairyland luster, "Leap-frogging Elves" pattern, (A) 980.00

Bowl

3 1/8" h, pedestal base, Fairyland luster, "Leapfrogging Elves" pattern, (A)
. . . . 1,158.00

4" d x 2" h, pedestal base, Dragon luster, blue ext, MOP int with multicolored oriental man on camel 375.00

4 3/4" d, Butterfly luster, mottled red ext, MOP int, c1920, (A) 200.00

5 1/2" d, Dragon luster, blue int, orange ext 425.00

6 1/2" d, Dragon luster, blue ext, MOP int with dragons 600.00

7" d

Butterfly luster, MOP int, mottled ruby red ext 325.00

Oct, Fairyland luster, "Gargoyles" pattern on ext, "Bird on a Hoop" pattern on int, #Z4968, (A) 3,925.00

8 1/4" d, Kang Hsi

Dragon luster, mottled green ext, MOP int with diaper and oriental landscape border, (A) 805.00

"Woodland Bridge" pattern on ext, "Woodland Elves I" pattern on int, black luster ground, (A) . . . 2,318.00

Vase, 7 3/4" h, Butterfly luster, gold butterflies, green/blue pearl luster ground, orange luster int, $750.

Vase, 8 7/8" h, Dragon luster, gold dragons, mottled blue ground, cream int with green line, "WEDGWOOD ENGLAND" mark, pr, $1,000.

8 5/8" d, Dragon luster, mottled blue ext, MOP int, c1920, (A) 546.00

9" d, oct, Fairyland luster, "Fairy in a Cage" pattern on int, "Castle on a Road" pattern on ext 4,625.00

10" d, Imperial, Fairyland luster, "Poplar Trees" pattern on ext, "Woodland Elves III" pattern on int, #Z4968 . . . 3,200.00

Candlestick, 7 1/2" h, Butterfly luster, powder blue luster with butterfly, MOP sconce dish, pattern #Z5095, pr, (A) 518.00

Coffeepot, 5 1/2" h, miniature, Moonlight luster, c1810, (A) 690.00

Cup and Saucer, Moonlight luster, c1810, hairline 200.00

Dish, 11 1/2" l, shell form, Moonlight luster, c1810, hairline, (A) 172.00

Jug, 5 1/2" h, bulbous body, Moonlight luster, c1810, ft chip 275.00

Plate

8 1/8" d, shell form, Moonlight luster, c1810, (A) 95.00

9" d, Dragon luster, MOP int, mottled purple, blue, and green ext, Chinese ornaments, #Z4831, (A) 373.00

Punch Bowl, 11 1/4" d, Fairyland luster, "Woodland Bridge" pattern on int, "Black Poplar Trees" pattern on ext, #Z4968, hairlines, (A) 1,380.00

Teapot, 3" h, drum shape, Moonlight luster, rim chips, c1810 (A) 575.00

Vase

5 1/8" h, bottle shape, Hummingbird luster, mottled blue ext with hummingbirds, orange mottled int rim, pattern #Z5294, shape #2350, pr, (A) 575.00

5 1/4" h, Butterfly luster, wine red ext, MOP int 400.00

7 7/8" h, trumpet shape, Fairyland luster, "Butterfly Woman" pattern, (A)
. . . . 3,030.00

8" h, horn shape, Butterfly luster, blue ext, orange int. 550.00

8 5/8" h, narrow base, wide shoulder, flared ft, Fairyland luster, "Candlemas" pattern, (A). 3,387.00

8 3/4" h, baluster shape, tapered ft, Dragon luster, blue luster ext with dragons, MOP int with diapered border and oriental landscape cartouches, pattern #Z4829, shape #2351, (A). 747.00

9" h, narrow flared base, bulbous body, Fairyland luster, "Imps on a Bridge" pattern, #Z5360, shape #2351, (A) 1,840.00

9 1/2" h, horn shape, Butterfly luster, blue ext, MOP int 650.00

12 1/2" h, shouldered cylinder shape, Fairyland luster, "Tree Serpent" pattern, flame luster ground, pr, (A) . .13,360.00

Wall Pocket, 10" l, figural nautilus shell, Moonlight luster, c1810, missing covs, repaired, pr, (A) 575.00

WHIELDON WARE

Fenton Vivien,
Stoke-on-Trent, England
1740-1780

History: Thomas Whieldon founded his earthenware factory at Little Fenton in 1740. He began potting small items such as boxes, cutlery handles, chimney pieces, and teapots. Whieldon introduced various metallics into the clay to alter the color of the earthenware body.

Whieldon experimented with colored glazes, attempting to imitate tortoiseshell. Most Whieldon ware is either mottled brownish or greenish in tone.

Several noted potters apprenticed with Whieldon. Josiah Spode is probably the most famous. In 1754 Whieldon took Josiah Wedgwood as a partner. While working for Whieldon, Wedgwood invented a green glaze which was used to decorate fanciful wares in the shapes of pineapples and cauliflowers. Together Whieldon and Wedgwood continued to make marbled, agate, and tortoiseshell pieces. Wedgwood left in 1759. Whieldon continued producing the variegated wares until the demand for these pieces diminished. He retired in 1780.

No Whieldon pieces were marked. Many earthenware potteries copied Whieldon's tortoiseshell wares between 1740 and 1780. Since no pieces were marked, it was impossible to attribute a piece to a specific factory. The term "Whieldon ware" is now generic.

Reference: F. Falkner, *The Wood Family of Burslem,* Chapman & Hall, 1912.

Museums: City Museum, Stoke-on-Trent, Hanley, England; Fitzwilliam Museum, Cambridge, England; Museum of Art, Rhode Island School of Design, Providence, RI; Sussex Museum & Art Gallery, Brighton, England; Victoria & Albert Museum, London, England; William Rockhill Nelson Gallery of Art, Kansas City, MO.

Butter Box, Cov, 4" d, creamware, cylinder shape, applied fruiting vines on body and cov, seated figural cow knob, mottled brown glaze, c1760, restored, (A) 690.00

Coffeepot, 10" h, molded cauliflower, cream florets at top, green leaves at base, green leaf molded spout with serpent head nozzle, c1770, (A). 7,475.00

Cream Jug

4 1/4" h, applied handle, modeled cauliflower, molded green leaves on base, clear glaze on upper section, repaired spout, (A) 385.00

5 1/2" h, baluster shape, scroll handle, flower knob, molded pineapple form, green base, yellow top, c1765, (A) 4,600.00

Figure

2 3/4" h, 2 nude children resting arm in arm on shrub, applied bird and foliage in foreground, translucent brown and green or brown, green, and gray-blue glazes, c1765, repairs to bases, pr, (A). 1,035.00

4 1/4" h, peasant woman, circ mound base, splashed brown and green translucent glazes, c1755, chips, (A) 345.00

4 1/2" l x 2 5/8" h, hooded christening cradle, sleeping child in red and green long dress, yellow blanket, cradle with red and green mottled molded woven ext, blue banded rim, (A) 650.00

5" h, creamware, standing cow on freeform base, translucent brown, yellow, and green glazes, c1780, repairs, (A) 2,300.00

Hot Water Jug, Cov, 5 1/4" h, loop handle, branch knob, masked paw feet, overall brown mottled glaze, c1765, (A). 575.00

Jar, Cov, 2" h, creamware, cylinder shape, mottled gray-green and blue glazes, c1760, (A). 1,265.00

Plate

8" d, brown tortoiseshell with green and yellow splashes, unmkd, (A). . . 138.00

9 1/4" d, overall brown on cream, green and yellow splotches, serpentine rim, (A). 700.00

9 3/8" d, border molded with trellis diaper pattern separated by prs of feathers, gray splashed glaze with yellow and green splotches, c1760, set of 9, (A) 3,105.00

9 1/2" d, blue, gray, and green splashes, emb rim, c1750 . . . . 395.00

9 3/4" d, overall brown on yellow, gold-yellow, green, and blue-green splotches,

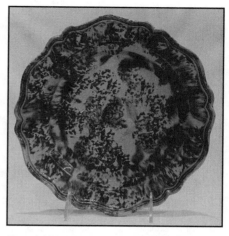

Plate, 9 1/4" d, brown, green, and yellow splashes, cream ground, c1750, hairline, $255.

scalloped emb feather edged rim, (A) 750.00

Platter

11 3/8" l, rect with cut corners, milled rim, splashed brown mottled glaze, c1770, (A) 225.00

14" d, border molded with ermine tails in compartments, splashed green and yellow glazes on mottled gray ground, splashed mottled brown on reverse, c1760, (A) 633.00

14 1/4" l, oval, border molded with ermine tails in panels, splashed green, blue, yellow, and gray glazes on mottled brown ground, c1770, (A) . . . 1,035.00

17 1/4" l, oval, paneled border, threaded rim, manganese-brown, green, and blue splashes on cream ground, (A) 288.00

Strainer, 2 5/8" d, creamware, pierced sides, masked paw feet, mottled gray, yellow, and green glazes, c1760 . . . . 1,380.00

Sugar Bowl, Cov, 3 5/8" h x 4 3/8" d, modeled cauliflower, green molded leaf base, clear glaze top, stains, (A) 3245.00

Teabowl and Saucer, Creamware

Green and yellow splotches on mottled lt brown ground, c1770, (A) 115.00

Mottled brown, ochre, green, and blue glazes, c1760, chips, set of 4, (A) . 1,035.00

Tea Caddy

3 3/8" h, cylinder shape, brown runny glaze, cov missing, (A) 275.00

3 1/2" h, rect shape, molded as mullion window, panels with raised star and domino patterns, splashed green and brown on dk buff ground, c1760, (A) 368.00

4 3/8" h, molded pineapple form, green glazed leaf base, yellow glazed pineapple top, c1765, (A). 4,312.00

4 1/2" h, molded lower body with green glazed leaves, cream glazed cauliflower on upper section, hairlines, (A) 403.00

Teapot

2 1/2" h, creamware, globular, straight spout, loop handle, mottled brown, blue, and green glazes, c1760, (A) 1,265.00

3 1/2" h, creamware, applied vines and leaves, brown tortoiseshell glaze, gilt traces, c1770, damages, (A). . . 230.00

4 3/8" h, molded cauliflower form, green molded leaves on base, white molded cauliflower top, cracks, c1770, cracks, (A) 1,200.00

4 7/8" h, globular, paw feet, applied vines, brown tortoiseshell glaze, bird knob, repairs, (A) 1,045.00

5" h, hex shaped body, molded overlapping cabbage leaves, blue-green translucent glaze, c1760, chips and restored handle 500.00

5 3/8" h, molded pineapple form, molded green leaf bottom, handle and spout, ochre pineapple body, c1770, restored cracks, (A) 1,035.00

5 3/4" h, tapered cylinder shape, green and brown runny glaze, figural widow knob, hairlines, (A)...........60.00

Wall Pocket, 8 3/4" h, figural mask of Bacchus crowned with vine, dolphin, and leaves, splashed green, gray, and brown glazes, buff ground, (A) 253.00

WILLOW WARE

English/Continental
1780s to Present

History: Blue willow china was the English interpretation of hand painted blue and white Chinese porcelain that was exported to England from China in the 16th century. The transfer method of decoration and the under the glaze decorating techniques introduced after 1760 provided the methodology to produce willow ware in large quantity.

The first English willow pattern was attributed to Thomas Minton at his Caughley Pottery in Staffordshire in the 1780s. The pattern was called Willow-Nankin.

Josiah Spode developed the first "true" willow pattern in the 1790s. Spode made three different willow patterns. The standard pattern developed in 1810 by Spode was the one that was considered the "true" willow pattern. It differed from the first two patterns in border design and the method by which the transfer pattern was engraved.

Spode's willow pattern had a willow tree in the center leaning over the bridge. A tea house with three pillars forming the portico and located near a large orange tree was behind the center willow tree. There was a bridge with three figures crossing towards an island. A boat with a man was on the lake. Two birds were flying towards each

other at the top center. Finally, a fence crossed the foreground. The outer border featured several scroll and geometric designs. The inner border consisted of geometric designs that framed the center pattern.

Many manufacturers used transfers that were variations of the Spode willow pattern. Some produced their own original blue willow versions. By 1830, there were more than 200 makers of willow pattern china in England. English firms still producing blue willow pattern china are Booth's by Royal Doulton, Burleigh, Coalport, Johnson Brothers, Meakin, and Wedgwood.

During the 20th century, other countries making willow ware included Belgium, France, Germany, Holland, Ireland, Mexico, Poland, Portugal, and Spain. Potteries in the United States and Japan also make pieces decorated with the blue willow pattern.

A tremendous variety of shapes was made in the blue willow pattern. Many pieces were not marked by the manufacturers, especially during the early period.

The color of the transfer varied with manufacturer. During the 1820s, a pale blue was fashionable. A whole spectrum of blues was used during the Victorian era. Although the most common color was blue, pieces can be found in black, brown, green, pink, yellow, and polychrome.

References: Leslie Bockol, *Willow Ware: Ceramics in the Chinese Tradition,* Schiffer Publishing, Ltd. 1995; Robert Copeland, *Spode's Willow Pattern and other designs after the Chinese,* Rizzoli International Publications, Inc. 1980; Mary Frank Gaston, *Blue Willow: An Identification and Value Guide, 2nd Ed.,* Collector Books, 1990; Veryl Marie Worth, *Willow Pattern China, Rev. 2nd Ed.* privately printed, 1981.

Collectors' Club: International Willow Collectors, P.O. Box 54681, Cincinnati, OH 45254. Membership: $20.00, Newsletters; The Willow Society, 359 Davenport Road, Suite 6, Toronto, M5R 1 K5 Canada. Membership: $15.00. *The Willow Transfer Quarterly, The Willow Exchange,* and *The Mandarin's Purse* (price guide); *The Willow Word,* Subscription: $25.00, Bi-monthly newspaper, Mary Lina Berndt, Publisher, P.O. Box 13382, Arlington, TX 76094; *American Willow Report,* Bimonthly newspaper, Lisa Henze, Publisher.

Reproduction Alert: Teapots, sugar and creamers are being reproduced.

Biscuit Barrel, 5 3/4" h, sq body, oct base, polychrome center band, dk blue top and bottom band, SP rim and cov, "Lancaster & Sons" mark, c1920 ....175.00

Bone Dish, 6 1/4" l, pink, Bailey Walker
............................20.00

Bouillon Cup and Saucer, red, yellow, green, blue, and brown "Chinese Willow" pattern, "Aynsley, England" mark, c1891.....40.00

Bowl

4" d, blue, "Societe Ceramique Willow" mark......................60.00

5 1/4" d, blue, "Allerton" mark 6.00

6" d, blue, Petrus Regout.........50.00

6 1/2" d, polychrome, unmkd, c1890-95, (A) 80.00

6 3/4" d, blue, "Allerton" mark 12.00

9" d, fluted body, scalloped rim, blue, Hollingshead & Kirkham, c1870-90
.......................235.00

9 1/4" d, blue, Petrus Regout......75.00

9 1/2" d, brick red transfer, red, green, cobalt, and gold accents, Ridgway
.......................150.00

10" l x 8" w, blue, "Booth's Real Old Willow" mark.....................125.00

Butter Dish, Cov, red, "Societe Ceramique" mark 90.00

Butter Pat, 3" sq, blue, "Booth's Real Old Willow" mark........................25.00

Cake Plate, 10" H-H, brown, "F. Bourne, Burslem" mark...................70.00

Cheese Dish, 7 3/4" l x 6 1/2" w, polychrome "Parrot" pattern 375.00

Children's Ware

Plate

1 1/2" d, blue 20.00

2 1/2" d, blue 24.00

3 1/2" d, blue 28.00

Platter

2 1/2" l x 2" w, oct, blue 45.00

4"l x 3" w, oct, blue, "E.M. & Co. England" mark 55.00

Coffee Cup and Saucer, blue, "Allerton" mark
............................30.00

Coffeepot, 7 1/2" h, blue, scalloped rim, "Allerton" mark....................250.00

Creamer, blue, "Allerton" 12.00

Cream Plate, 10" d, blue, gold etch, Mason
............................85.00

Cream Soup Bowl, 5" H-H, red, Swinnertons, c1930 ....30.00

Celery Dish, 8 5/8" l, multicolored transfer and accents, "Ashworth Bros. Hanley, England" mark, $185.

Cup and Saucer

    Blue, England 18.00

    Pink, England. 12.00

    Red, yellow, and green with blue shades, Crown Staffordshire 50.00

Cup and Saucer, Demitasse, blue, "Allerton" mark 12.00

Dessert Bowl, 6" d, blue 8.00

Dessert Service, serving plate, 10 1/4" H-H, 4 plates, 6 3/4" d, 4 cups and saucers, "Geisha" variant, rust, cobalt, yellow, and gold, Ford, c1893 . . . . 375.00

Dish, 6 3/4" l, shell form, floral terminal, blue, England, set of 4, (A) 138.00

Egg Cup, Dbl, blue, "Booths Real Old Willow" mark 40.00

Fish Platter, 21" l x 11 1/2" w, blue, Minton, dtd 1886 . . . . 650.00

Fruit Bowl, 10" d, blue 95.00

Gravy Boat

    Blue, "Grimwades" mark 30.00

    With undertray, green, "Royal Venton Ware" mark 75.00

Horseradish Dish, 5 1/2" h, blue, Doulton 110.00

Hot Water Plate, 11 1/2" H-H, blue, "Semi-China Warranted" mark, c1830 . . . . 475.00

Jar, Cov, 12 1/4" h, pearlware, sq base, blue, gilt accents, c1830, (A) 546.00

Jardiniere, 6 1/4" h x 8" d, horiz ribbing, brown transfer with yellow glaze 395.00

Jug

    5 1/4" h, blue, pewter lid, Royal Doulton, c1891-1902 . . . . 325.00

    6" h

        Oct, blue, serpent handle, "blue MASON'S crown, PATENT IRONSTONE CHINA, drapery" mark, (A) 357.00

        Polychrome, "black ASHWORTH BROS. crown, HANLEY, drapery, ENGLAND" mark, (A) 175.00

Meat Drain, 12 1/2" l, blue 250.00

Mug

    2 1/2" h, blue, hairline 85.00

    4" h, blue, Doulton 95.00

Pickle Dish

    5" l, leaf shape, blue, Spode 125.00

    6" l x 3 1/2" w, rolled handles, blue 145.00

Pitcher

    3" h, blue, "Made in Belgium" mark 18.00

    4" h, polychrome "Parrot" pattern, England 95.00

    4 1/2" h, blue, Allerton 95.00

    7" h, blue, "Booth's Real Old Willow" mark 120.00

    8 1/4" h, blue, scalloped rim, "Allerton" mark. 250.00

    9" h, stoneware, blue on tan ground, c1891. 395.00

Pitcher, 5 3/8" h, blue, Allerton, $125.

Plate

    4 3/4" d, center blue Willow pattern, "Schweppes, Indian Tonic" on border, "Luneville, France" mark 75.00

    5 3/4" d, blue, "Allerton" mark 8.00

    6" d

        Blue, "Allerton" mark 9.00

        Green, "Royal Venton Ware" mark 15.00

    6 1/4" d, red, Johnson Brothers 5.00

    6 1/2" d, blue, "Midwinter Staffordshire England" mark 9.00

    6 3/4" d, blue, "Woods Ware" mark . 8.00

    7" d, blue, "Midwinter Staffordshire England" mark 9.00

    8" d, blue, England 9.00

    9" d

        Blue, "Woods Ware" mark 9.00

        Green, "Royal Venton Ware" mark 30.00

    10" d

        Blue

            "Midwinter Staffordshire England" mark 12.00

            "Two Temples II" pattern, butterfly border, W.T. Copeland . . 38.00

        Red, Johnson Brothers 25.00

    10 1/2" d, blue, "Booths Real Old Willow" mark 25.00

    10 7/8" d, brown transfer with orange, green, yellow, and black enamels, molded woven border, gold rim, Adderley, c1930 . . . . 60.00

Platter

    9 1/2" d, blue, "Allerton" mark 58.00

    10" l, oval, red, Venton Steventon . . 89.00

    10 1/2" l x 8 1/2" w, stone china, blue, England. 175.00

    11 1/4" l x 9 1/4" w, blue, Allerton . . .125.00

    12" l x 9" w

        Blue, Ridgway 80.00

        Red, "Royal Venton Ware, John Steventon & Sons, Ltd" mrk. . 46.00

    12 1/2" l x 10 1/2" w, blue 150.00

    13" l

        Blue, "Allerton" mark 95.00

Serpentine shape, green, "Royal Venton Ware" mark, c1923, crazing 95.00

    13 1/2" l, blue 165.00

    13 3/4" l x 10 1/2" w, red, "Societe Ceramique" mark 175.00

    14" l x 11" w, blue, "Allerton" mark 135.00

    14 3/4" l, blue, scalloped edge . . . 165.00

    15" l x 11" w, blue, "Grimwades" mark 135.00

    15 1/4" l, blue 95.00

    16" l

        12 1/2" w, blue, "Warrented Staffordshire" mark 225.00

        13" w, blue 135.00

    16 3/4" l x 11 1/2" w, red, "Societe Ceramique" mark 225.00

    17" l x 14" w, blue, England 300.00

    18" l, blue, "Allerton" mark 150.00

    19 1/2" l, blue 210.00

Pudding Mold, 5 3/4" d, blue. 60.00

Ramekin, 4" d, blue, Booth, set of 6 . . 225.00

Relish Dish, 11" l, 3 section, blue, Booth, c1906 . . . . 275.00

Relish Tray, 8 3/4" l x 5" w, red, "Societe Ceramique" mark 75.00

Salt Dip, 1 3/4" h, urn shape, blue, Wiltshaw & Robinson, c1894 . . . . 175.00

Soup Plate

    8 1/2" d, pearlware, blue, scalloped rim 25.00

    10" d, med blue, "imp COPELAND" mark 35.00

Sugar Bowl, Cov, 5" h, blue. 55.00

Tankard, 6 3/4" h, blue 95.00

Tea Jar, 3" h, blue, Andrew Stevenson, c1790-1800 . . . . 135.00

Teapot

    5" h, blue, "Sadler, England" mark 100.00

    6" h, blue, Allerton 100.00

    6 1/2" h, blue, gold outlined handle, gold leaf knob, Sadler 65.00

    7 1/2" h, sq corset shape, blue, "Newcastle Upon Tyne" mark. 375.00

Tile

    5 7/8" sq, blue "England" mark 85.00

    8" sq, blue, "Steele & Wood" mark 145.00

Toothbrush Holder, 5" h, blue, "Willow Wedgwood Etruria England" mark 110.00

Tureen, 8" h x 12 1/2" d, brick red transfer with red, green, cobalt, and gold accents, cobalt scrolled knob and handles, Ridgway 950.00

Tray

    9 1/4" l x 7 1/4" w, pearlware, oval, blue, lattice border, blue line rim 200.00

    17 1/4" l, rect with cut corners, blue, gilt rim, Wedgwood 316.00

Vase

    5 1/8" h, shouldered, oval shape, blue, mid 19th C, (A) 75.00

10 5/8" h, cylinder shape with wide base, blue, Ashworth, c1891 . . . . 395.00

Vegetable Bowl

8 1/2" d, blue, "Green & Co. England" mark 40.00

9 1/4" l x 7 1/2" w, blue, "Allerton" mark 18.00

10" l, dk pink, "Royal Venton, John Steventon & Sons" mark 35.00

Vegetable Bowl, Cov

9" d, blue, "Brown & Stevenson" mark 160.00

9 1/2" d, blue, "Booths Real Old Willow" mark 200.00

9 1/2" l, blue, scalloped rim, "Allerton" mark 250.00

11" l x 9 1/2" w, rect, blue, Ridgway & Co. 180.00

11 1/2" H-H, rect, red, "Allerton" mark 85.00

Waste Bowl, 3 1/4" h, 6" d, aqua, England 50.00

WOOD, ENOCH

Fountain Place Pottery, Burslem, Staffordshire, England c1784-1840

ENOCH WOOD & SONS BURSLEM STAFFORDSHIRE 1818-1846

ENOCH WOOD & SONS BURSLEM 1818-1846

History: Enoch Wood came from an important pottery family that included Aaron Wood, his father, Ralph Wood, his cousin, and William Wood, his brother. After he completed his apprenticeship, Enoch entered a partnership with Ralph in 1784. They made enamel colored figures and Toby jugs using the new over the glaze decoration technique.

In 1790, Enoch wood entered into a partnership with Caldwell. The company's mark was Wood & Caldwell. Enoch bought out Caldwell in 1819 and formed a new partnership with Enoch, Joseph, and Edward Wood, his sons. The firm became known as Enoch Wood & Sons.

The company made under the glaze blue transfer printed dinnerware, much of which was exported to America. In addition to the blue historic wares, many romantic wares were printed in pink, purple, black, sepia, green, or mulberry. Views used included British, French, Italian, and American scenes. Although views were the most popular designs, biblical scenes, hunting scenes, and cherub motifs also were made. Many of the printed designs have the title marked on the back.

Marked pieces are impressed "WOOD."

References: A.W. Coysh & R.K. Henrywood, *The Dictionary of Blue & White Printed Pottery 1780-1880,* Antique Collectors' Club, 1982; *Vol. 2,* 1989.

Museums: Cincinnati Art Museum, Cincinnati, OH; Fitzwilliam Museum, Cambridge, England; Potsdam Public Museum, Potsdam, NY.

Bowl, 6 1/2" d

"Old Vienna" pattern, blue transfer, "Wood Burslem England" mark 12.00

"Seaforth" pattern, red transfer, "Wood Burslem England" mark 22.00

Charger, 11 3/4" d, center scene of geisha in green kimono seated, holding letter, gilt accents, black border, "Wood & Son" mark 1,800.00

Coffeepot, 11" h, bird pattern, blue transfer 950.00

Creamer, 5 3/4" h, man riding in horse drawn sleigh, floral borders, dk blue transfer, "imp Wood" mark, (A) 550.00

Creamer and Cov Sugar Bowl, creamer, 3 1/2" h, sugar bowl, 5" h, "Blarney" pattern, red transfers 100.00

Cup and Saucer

"English Scenery" pattern, pink transfer, smooth rims 10.00

"Woodland" pattern, blue transfer 40.00

Cup Plate, 3 3/4" d, HP pink rose, green leaves, blue bud, wide pink band on rim, (A) 35.00

Gravy Tureen, 6 1/4" h, with undertray, tureen with 3 country scenes, grapevine border, 4 dk blue peg feet, flower knob, undertray with classic castle scene, grapevine border, med blue transfers, (A) 1,210.00

Grill Plate, 10 3/4" d, "English Scenery" pattern, brown transfer with green, blue, red, and yellow accents 9.00

Pitcher, 5 1/2" h, "English Scenery" pattern, brown transfer with green and yellow accents, "Wood & Sons" mark 65.00

Plate

7" d

Dragonflies with oriental style chrysanthemums, multicolored, green lined rim, "Wood & Sons, England" mark 8.00

"On the Rhine" pattern, yellow and brown transfer 80.00

7 3/4" d

Blue molded floral swag and feather design on scalloped rim, "imp Wood" mark, set of 3, (A) . . . 95.00

"Enoch Wood's English Scenery" pattern, blue transfer, Wood & Sons 30.00

"Reubens," Castle Series, dk red transfer 22.00

8 3/8" d, hunter with gun chasing fox in woods, flowered border, med blue transfer, "imp Enoch Wood" mark 350.00

Platter, 13 3/4" l, "Hyde" pattern, green, red, yellow, magenta, and brown, $65.

8 1/2" d, dog in English countryside design, floral and scroll border, scalloped rim, dk blue transfer, "imp E. Wood & Sons, Burslem and eagle" mark, (A) 190.00

9" d

"Cupid Behind Bars" design, med blue transfer 265.00

"English Scenery" pattern, blue transfer 40.00

"Revelation-Scriptural Series," dk blue transfer, (A) 605.00

"Suspension Bridge" pattern, red and green transfer 150.00

10" d

Deer design, Zoological Series, dk blue transfer 245.00

"Seaforth" pattern, blue transfer, "Wood & Sons" mark 12.00

Platter, 16 1/4" l, "English Scenery" pattern, pink transfer, smooth rim 85.00

Soup Plate, 10 5/8" d, oriental scene of mosques, hanging willow trees at side, dk blue transfer, "imp Wood" mark, (A) . . 248.00

Sugar Bowl, Cov, 5 3/8" h, "Yuan" pattern, blue oriental bird and foliage 60.00

Teabowl and Saucer, pearlware, terra cotta Adam's Rose design, blue and yellow flowers and green leaves, red striped rims, (A) 100.00

Toddy Plate

5 1/2" d, "A TRIFLE FOR CHARLES" in oct line and floral wreath, dk blue transfer, dk blue rim, "imp Enoch Wood & Sons Burslem and eagle" mark, c1818-46 . . . . 185.00

5 3/4" d, ship at full sail, irreg shell border, blue transfer 525.00

Vegetable Bowl, 8 1/2" l, "Hyde" pattern, "Wood & Sons" mark 45.00

Vegetable Bowl, Cov, 10" sq x 7 1/2" h, "Yuan" pattern, peacocks and florals, patterned border, blue transfer, "Wood & Sons" mark 45.00

WOOD, RALPH

**Near
Stoke-on-Trent,
England**

RaWOOD

BURSLEM
c.1770 - 1801

**Ralph Wood
the Elder
1754-1772**

**Ralph Wood the Younger
1760-1795**

History: Ralph Wood and Ralph, his son, were the most important makers of earthenware figures and Toby jugs during the second half of the 18th century.

After his apprenticeship, Ralph Wood initially worked for Thomas Whieldon, making salt-glazed earthenware and tortoiseshell-glazed ware. Eventually, he founded his own firm. During the 1750s, Ralph Wood started making figures in cream-colored earthenware, with metallic oxide-stained glazes. He kept the colors separate by painting them on with a brush. The modeling of his figures was quite lively. Ralph's figures gained a reputation for portraying the mood and attitude of the character exactly.

Ralph the Younger was a skilled figure maker and joined with his father during the 1760s. Ralph the Younger continued the tradition established by his father and eventually produced even more figures than Ralph Wood the Elder. Since Ralph the Younger used many of his father's molds, it is impossible to assign a particular figure to the father or the son with certainty. Later in his career, Ralph the Younger switched to using enamel colors on figures.

Subjects included equestrian figures, contemporary portrait figures, some satyrical groups, classical figures, allegorical figures, and many different animals. All the molded human figures had large hands and well defined, bulging eyes. Ralph Wood is also credited with introducing the Toby jug form. These were very successful and copied by dozens of potters. (See: Toby Jugs).

In addition to figures and Toby jugs, Ralph Wood's factory also made plaques. John Voyez, a modeler, produced the plaques. Characteristics of Voyez's work were figures with bulging eyes, thick fleshy lips, slightly flattened noses, and a sentimental inclination of the head.

The Woods were the first figure makers to make their wares with an impressed company mark and sometimes mold numbers. However, some were not marked. "R.

Wood" was the mark of Ralph the Elder. "Ra Wood" was the younger's mark.

References: Capt. R.K. Price, *Astbury, Whieldon & Ralph Wood Figures and Toby Jugs*, John Lane, 1922; H A.B. Turner, *A Collector's Guide to Staffordshire Pottery Figures*, Emerson Books, Inc. 1971.

Museums: British Museum, London, England; Cincinnati Art Museum, Cincinnati, OH; City Museum, Stoke-on-Trent, Hanley, England; Fitzwilliam Museum, Cambridge, England.

Figure

3 7/8" h, seated cat, yellow and brown spots, green base, chips, hairline, (A) 550.00

4" h, standing man holding basket of eggs, black hair, blue coat, brown trousers, green base 250.00

5 1/8" h x 6 1/2" l, recumbent sheep, blue-gray coat, ochre ears and hooves, green ground, c1780 . . . . 1,150.00

5 1/2" h, standing man, head on hand, brown hat, blue coat, yellow trousers, green base 250.00

8 1/2" h

Standing Apollo, blue lined green drapery, green wreath, holding brown lyre, green and brown rocky base, "imp rebus" mark, c1780, (A) 1,840.00

Standing shepherd, lt brown coat, white shirt, green breeches, brown hat, brown sling bag, tree stump, spotted dog at feet, scroll molded green base, c1780, repairs, (A) 1,840.00

8 7/8" h, standing shepherd, black hat, green coat, yellow vest, gray breeches, white lamb over shoulder, c1785, (A) 6,325.00

12 1/4" h, standing Chaucer wearing white coat sprigged in red-brown over rose

Figure, 7" h, brown shaded deer, green base, unmkd, $2,750.

waistcoat, green breeches, leaning on stack of books, stone pedestal, or standing Newton in fawn brown coat over red-brown sprigged waistcoat, yellow breeches, holding telescope, raising green drape over globe on books with sheet with comet and "1680," marbleized sq bases, "imp Ra. Wood, Burslem," c1785, reglued, repairs, pr 7,200.00

Jug, 5 1/4" h, figural Bacchus head, fish form spout and handle, translucent and brown glazes, late 18th C, (A) 863.00

Spill Vase, 7 5/8" h, modeled as 3 entwined cornucopia supported by modeled dolphins and seaweed, green body, blue rim, brown shell base, c1780, (A) 1,380.00

WORCESTER

Worcester, England
1751-1892

History: The Worcester pottery was established in 1751. The pieces from the initial years of operation have decorations characterized by a strong dependence on oriental themes in under the glaze blue and on the glaze enamel. Production concentrated primarily on making excellent utilitarian wares, mostly tea and dessert sets. Very few purely ornamental pieces were made. The china was symmetrical and featured a smooth glaze. This initial period, 1751 to 1776, was known as the "Dr. Wall" period, named after one of the original stockholders.

After 1755, transfer printing was used extensively. By 1760, most of the best pieces had the typical Worcester deep blue cobalt under the glaze background, done either in a solid or scale motif. Panels were painted with beautiful birds, flowers, and insects.

The factory was managed by William Davis, one of the original partners from the Dr. Wall period. Davis died in 1783; Thomas Flight then purchased the factory. The middle period, also known as the Davis-Flight period, lasted from 1776 to 1793. Neo-classical designs were emphasized. Many of the whiteware blanks used for decoration were purchased from France. There was a limited quantity of fine clay for porcelain production in the area of the Worcester plant. The company received a Royal Warrant from George III in 1789.

Martin Barr joined the works in 1793. The period from 1793 to 1807 was designated the Flight & Barr period. Patterns continued to be rather plain. Barr's son joined the firm in 1807, resulting in the Barr Flight & Barr period between 1807 and 1813. Decorative motifs from this era were quite colorful and elaborate.

Martin Barr Sr. died in 1813. The time from 1813 to 1840 was called the Flight Barr & Barr period. Patterns continued to be quite colorful, finely painted, and gilded. The quality of porcelains made during the early 19th century was very high. Pieces were richly painted, often featuring gilt trim on a well potted body with a perfect, craze-free glaze.

In 1840, Flight Barr & Barr merged with the Chamberlain factory and took the name of Chamberlain and Company. The plant moved to Diglis. Quality of production declined during this time.

Kerr and Binns bought the firm in 1852. During the Kerr & Binns period, 1852 to 1862, the factory enjoyed a great artistic recovery. In 1862 R.W. Binns formed the Worcester Royal Porcelain Company Ltd. a company whose products then carried the "Royal Worcester" designation.

References: Franklin A. Barret, *Worcester Porcelain & Lund's Bristol, Rev. Ed.,* Faber & Faber, 1966; Lawrence Branyon, Neal French, John Sandon, *Worcester Blue & White Porcelain, 1751-1790,* Barrie & Jenkins, 1981; Anthony Cast & John Edwards, *Royal Worcester Figurines, First Edition,* Charlton Press, 1997; Geoffrey A. Godden, *Chamberlain-Worcester Porcelain 1788-1852,* Magna Books, 1992; F. Severne Mackenna, *Worcester Porcelain: The Wall Period & Its Antecedents,* F. Lewis Ltd., 1950; H. Rissik Marshall, *Colored Worcester Porcelain of the First Period,* Ceramic Book, 1954; Dinah Reynolds, *Worcester Porcelain 1751-1783: An Ashmolean-Christie's Handbook,* Phaidon-Christie's, 1989; Henry Sandon, *Flight & Barr: Worcester Porcelain 1783-1840,* Antique Collectors' Club, 1978; Henry Sandon, *The Illustrated Guide to Worcester Porcelain,* Herbert Jenkins, 1969; John Sandon, *The Dictionary of Worcester Porcelain, Vol. 1 1751-1851,* Antique Collectors' Club, Ltd. 1996; *1852-to the Present Day, Vol. II,* Antique Collectors' Club, 1997; John Sandon & Simon Spero,

Worcester Porcelain The Zorensky Collection, Antique Collectors' Club, Ltd. 1996.

Museums: Art Institute of Chicago, Chicago, IL; British Museum, London, England; City Museum, Weston Park, Sheffield, England; Colonial Williamsburg Foundation, Williamsburg, VA; Dyson Perrins Museum, Worcester, England; Fine Arts Museum of San Francisco, CA; Gardiner Museum of Ceramic Art, Toronto, Canada; Henry Ford Museum, Dearborn, MI; Seattle Art Museum, Seattle, WA; Sheffield City Museum, Sheffield, England; Victoria & Albert Museum, London, England.

Reproduction Alert: At the end of the 19th century, Samson and other continental artists copied 18th century Worcester examples. Booths of Turnstall reproduced many Worcester designs utilizing the transfer method. These reproduction pieces also contained copies of the Royal Worcester mark. Even though an earthenware body instead of porcelain was used on the Booth examples, many collectors have been misled by the reproductions.

Basket

    7" l, trellis pierced sides, blue printed "Pine Cone" pattern, blue crescent mark, c1770, (A) 100.00

    7 1/4" H-H, pierced sides, white int with painted flowers, yellow ext with painted flowers, brown crabstock handles and applied floral terminals, c1765
    . . . . 2,950.00

Bough Pot, 8 3/4" w, bombe shape, rococo scroll back and pierced top, sides printed and colored with scenes of classical figures in ruins in landscape in shaped cartouches, apple green ground, c1770, (A) 978.00

Bowl, 8" d, "Blind Earl" pattern, multicolored butterflies, dk and lt green foliage, gilt rim, "red Chamberlain & Co. 155 New Bond St." mark, pr, $1,750.

Cream Jug, 3 3/4" h, multicolored exotic birds and floral sprays, gilt cartouches, blue scale ground, (A) $160.

Bowl

    4" d, fluted, painted bird on branch and 2 insects, gilt rim, c1765, (A) 184.00

    6" d, blue printed "Peony" pattern, solid blue crescent mark 685.00

Butter Boat, 1 3/8" h, leaf shape, blue painted sprigs of flowers and insects on int, band of florals on int rim, c1760, pr, (A) 615.00

Cache Pot, 3 1/2" h x 5 1/4" l, tapered rect shape, Aesthetic design of cobalt oriental characters on turquoise ground, cobalt applied salamander to front, Hadley Worcester, c1875 . . . . 450.00

Caudle Cup and Saucer, gilt outlined surrounds of puce, iron red, gray, and gilt floral sprays on sides and saucer, wet blue ground, fluted gilt lined rims, ear handles, c1770, hairline 350.00

Coffee Cup and Saucer, iron red and gilt "Japan Star" pattern in cartouches on blue scale ground, blue sq seal mark, c1770, (A) 460.00

Coffeepot, 8" h, blue printed "Pine Cone" pattern, flower form knob, c1765, (A) 748.00

Creamboat, 4 5/8" l, silver shape, rococo shell form with 2 entwined dolphins and tridents under spout, lamprey eel handle, painted enameled flowers sprays with gilding, c1770 . . . . 1,250.00

Cream Jug, 4 1/8" h, "Queen Charlotte" pattern, scrolled vert panels of iron red and mauve flowers alternating with cobalt panels with gilt stylized flowerheads, Dr. Wall, c1780 . . . . 350.00

Cup and Saucer

    Blue forget-me-nots, gold leaves and stems, white ground, Flight, Barr & Barr .145.00

    "Jabberwocky" pattern, painted iron red winged dragon on blue flowering tree, iron red and gilt blossoms, turquoise

Cup and Saucer, Imari pattern, cobalt, iron red, and gold, c1815, $225.

border with scrolled gilding, diapered reserves an blossoms, "blind fret" scrolled handle, c1770 . . . . . .1,050.00

Dessert Basket

7 3/4" d, flared sides pierced as interlocking circles, green and gilt florets on ext, green foliage sprays and buds on int, gilt lined rim and center, c1775, pr
. . . . .2,500.00

7 7/8" H-H, sides with reticulated interlocking circles, central panel of painted urn and garlands, gilded surround of anthemion and lotus, burnished grapevines on dk blue body, twisted handles with flower and foliate terminals, crescent mark, c1770, reglued handles
. . . . .1,950.00

Dessert Dish, 7 1/2" w, shell shape, enamel painted pr of exotic birds in water landscape and flying birds, royal blue border with tooled gilding, crescent mark, c1770 . . . . .1,450.00

Dinner Service, Part, soup tureen, 2 sauce tureens, 7 1/8" d, 2 cov vegetable dishes, 10 5/8" d, 5 platters, 10 1/4"-18 7/8" l, 10 soup plates, 9 7/8" d, 29 plates, 10"-10 1/2" d, 7 plates, 8 1/2" d, plate, 7 1/4" d, "King's" pattern, lg flowering tree in iron red, cobalt, and gilt Imari colors, 19th C, (A) 5,175.00

Dish

6 1/2" d, gallant and companion taking tea in formal garden with servant, black transfer, c1770 . . . . 450.00

7 5/8" d, "Blind Earl" pattern, yellow shaded green leaves, bouquet with yellow-centered puce flower, 3 sm purple flowers, pink and purple sprigs on border, gilt shaped rim, c1760, pr, (A)
. . . . .1,725.00

8" w, shell shape, puce, purple, and yellow painted fruit, gilt line rim, c1770, (A)
. . . . 100.00

8 3/8" sq, center painted with bird in landscape in circ gilt surround, border of blue leaves reserved on gilt ground with angled stripes and scrolls, outside decorated, "imp crown" mark, Barr, Flight, & Barr, c1810, pr, (A) 658.00

Ewer, 7" h, pierced neck and handle, painted birds on flowering branches, pattern #473/G, Grainger & Co., dtd 1892, (A) 250.00

Fruit Cooler, 10 7/8" h, urn shape, center orange band with en grisaille crest, gilded acanthus leaves, sprays of foliage, foliate scrolls, and Greek key, inner lining, gilded satyr mask handles, gilded artichoke knob, "imp BFB and crown" mark, Barr Flight and Barr, c1810 . . . . 3,500.00

Mug

3 1/2" h, 2 landscape vignettes of milkmaid and companion, black transfers, c1770
. . . . 460.00

4 7/8" h, white reserves of polychrome birds and insects, blue scale ground, gold accents, repair, (A) 550.00

Mustard Pot, Cov, 4 3/4" h, with spoon, cylinder shape, blue printed trailing flowers, trellis diaper rim, scroll handle, knob finial, "blue open crescent" mark, c1770, (A) . . 1,035.00

Pickle Dish, 3 7/8" d, molded shell shape, blue painted bird in rockery with flowering branches, stylized flowers on rim, "blue shaded crescent" mark, c1770, pr, (A). 800.00

Pitcher, 9 1/4" h, gilt outlined cartouches of multicolored exotic birds, blue scale ground, c1770 . . . . 4,500.00

Plate

8" d, blue chinoiserie landscape and fisherman in center, blue oyster border, c1765, (A) 403.00

8 1/8" d, painted center with seashells in gilt-banded roundel, salmon ground border with gilt foliate scrollwork, Barr, Flight, and Barr, c1810, set of 6, (A)
. . . . 16,100.00

8 1/4" d, painted center with seashell in gilt band frame, gilt vermiculate border, gilt rim, Barr, Flight, and Barr, c1810, set of 4, (A) 8,625.00

10 1/2" d, polychrome floral sprays on white ground, shaped gadroon molded rim, Chamberlain, c1847-50, (A)
. . . . .70.00

Potpourri Vase

7 1/4" h, baluster shape, lobed cobalt ground with painted cartouche of bridge in mountain valley, faceted gilded ft, acorn knob, pierced cov, sgd "M. Davis," 19th C, (A) 126.00

7 1/2" h, flame finial, lobed baluster body painted with continuous scene of cattle grazing in mountains, pierced cov, 19th C, (A) 748.00

Sauceboat

7 1/4" l, shell shape, bracket handle, int blue painted with landscape vignette, rim with trellis and flower sprays, sides painted with chinoiserie landscapes of fisherman and boat, c1758, (A)
. . . . .650.00

7 1/2" l, floral molded body, blue painted floral sprays on body, rim, and int spout, c1765, (A) 316.00

8 3/4" l, molded cos lettuce leaf body, molded and painted fruits and leaves at curved handle base, enamel painted floral bouquets and flower sprays on ext and int, c1755 . . . . 1,250.00

Sauce Tureen, 8 1/2" l, with undertray, Imari style iron red and blue panels of stylized flowers and birds on branches, gilt accents, gilt lion mask handles, gilt recumbent lion knob, Chamberlain, c1820, pr, (A) 3,450.00

Soup Plate

8 1/4" d, blue butterfly in center with scattered gilt sprays, gilt outlined blue border with gilt leaves, scalloped rim, rim chip, (A) 165.00

9 1/2" d, polychrome seated cat in center with "A Cruce Salus," purple and gilt foliage border, "imp F.B.B. and Flight Barr

Cup and Saucer, "Royal Lily" pattern, c1800, set of 10, (A) $467.

& Barr, Royal Porcelain Works, Worcester" mark, (A) 275.00

10" d, painted coat of arms in center, salmon border with alternating gilt wreath tie wheat stalks or entwined garlands, gilt gadrooned rim, Chamberlain, c1815, (A) 403.00

Sugar Bowl, Cov, 4 3/4" h, "Jabberwocky" pattern, iron red dragon sitting on blue flowering tree with iron red and gilt blossoms and banded hedge, turquoise border with gilt scrolling and diapered reserves, c1770 . . . . . . 650.00

Tankard, 6" h

Blue ground with overall white floral design, 2 star shaped reserves of oriental woman seated in garden, damages, (A) 175.00

"Long Eliza" pattern in star shaped reserve, blue marbled ground with flowerheads, c1765, (A) 275.00

Teabowl and Saucer

Blue painted birds in exotic floral landscape, c1765, (A) 150.00

Fluted

Borders with black and white entwined lines reserved on turquoise ground in black edged gilt lines, Flight and Barr, c1800, (A) 100.00

"Rich Queen's" pattern, panels of banded hedges and chrysanthemums, dk blue panels of gilt diapering and reserved mons, crescent mark, c1770 . . . . 850.00

Lg exotic birds seated on foliate branches and flying birds, blue transfers, "blue hatched crescent" mark, (A) 95.00

Ribbed, "Hop Trellis" pattern, hanging red hops berries and green leaves, red and gilt vert trellises, scalloped blue and gilt rims, c1775 . . . . .1,250.00

Tea Canister, 6 1/4" h, ovoid shape, painted European flower sprays in gilt scrolled rococo cartouches, blue sale ground, flower knob, crescent mark, c1770, knob reglued
. . . . .1,450.00

Teapot

4 1/8" h, blue printed insects among flowers, crescent mark, c1780, (A)
. . . . 138.00

5" h

Globular, vert orange panels with gilt lattice and mons, puce and black enameled floral bouquets, c1765, chips and repairs 350.00

Ribbed barrel shape, blue printed willow pattern, floral molded knob, c1775, (A) 288.00

5 1/2" h, globular, C-form handle, S-form spout, florette knob, blue painted "Mansfield" pattern, cell and diaper borders, "blue open crescent" mark
. . . . 875.00

Tea Service, Part

Pot, 5 3/4" h, globular, fluted hex teapot stand, 6" d, sugar bowl, 4 5/8" d, milk jug, 5 5/8" h, 12 teabowls and saucers,

blue "Pine Cone" pattern, blue crescent marks, c1770, (A) 1,035.00

Pot, 6 5/8" h, cream jug, 4 1/4" h, cov sugar bowl, 5 1/4" h, waste bowl, 6" d, 8 cups and saucers, 3 cake plates, 7 3/4" d, gilt bands of stylized flowers on blue band, scattered gilt thistle, Flight, "blue crescent" marks, c1785, (A) 690.00

Pot, 7 3/4" h, creamer, cov sugar bowl, 4 teabowls and saucers, 2 teabowls, fluted bodies, gray roses and gilt leaves, gilt leaf design on handles and knobs, Chamberlain 2,050.00

Tureen

7" l, figural partridge on nest, brown shaded painted feathers, beak and head outlined in brown shades, white basketweave base with green loops, multicolored feathers, and leaves on rim, c1755, repair to cov 2,950.00

7 1/2" l, with undertray, oval, branch handles, painted multicolored flowers in mirror shaped cartouches, blue scale ground, "blue sq seal" mark, c1770, (A) 1,725.00

Vase

5 3/8, 5 1/2" h, flared base and top, raised lower ring, vert orange panels with gilt diapering or painted chrysanthemums and prunis, c1770, pr 1,300.00

5 1/2" h, 3 columns, each painted with seashells and seaweed in gilt frame, gray marbled ground, Barr, Flight, and Barr, (A) 18,400.00

9 1/2" h, ovoid shape with flared rim, painted rural landscape in chased gilt surround, turquoise ground, 2 gilt ring handles, Kerr & Binns, c1862, pr
. . . . 1,250.00

Vegetable Bowl, 8 1/4" sq, "Best Queen's" pattern surrounding central crest design, Chamberlain, c1800, (A) 863.00

Waste Bowl, 6 3/8" d, lg exotic birds seated on foliate branches and flying birds, blue transfer, "blue hatched crescent" mark, c1780, (A) 125.00

YELLOW-GLAZED EARTHENWARE

Staffordshire, Yorkshire, Liverpool, England/Wales c1785 -1835

History: English yellow-glazed earthenware was creamware or pearlware featuring an overall yellow glaze. The principal period of production was between 1785 and 1835. The color varied from a pale to a deep yellow. Yellow glazed earthenware also was known as "canary" or "canary luster" ware.

Most of the yellow-glazed wares were either luster painted, enamel painted, or

transfer printed. Sometimes two or three techniques were used on the same pieces. Silver luster was combined the most often with the yellow ground.

Enamel painting on yellow-glazed wares exhibited a wide range in subject matter and technique. The most popular enamel decorative motif was floral. Most flowers were stylized rather than naturalistic. Much of the decoration had a "primitive" or naive feel to the depictions. Iron-red and green were two of the most popular colors. Pastoral landscapes and geometric patterns also were used for enameled decorations.

Transfer printed yellow-glazed wares had the printing done over the glaze. Most patterns were in black, but brown and red were used occasionally. Landscape scenes were the most popular motifs, followed by scenes with birds and animals. Other themes included politics, historical events, sporting scenes, and some mythological figures. Sometimes the transfer prints were over painted in enamel colors.

Yellow-glazed earthenwares were made in nearly all shapes and forms except for complete dinner services. Jugs and pitchers were the most popular forms made.

Yellow-glazed earthenware figures of animals and birds enjoyed great popularity. Some utilitarian pieces such as children's mugs were made in quantity.

Most yellow-glazed earthenware does not contain a maker's mark. Among the identified Staffordshire manufacturers that made the ware were Josiah Wedgwood, Josiah Spode, Davenport, Enoch Wood & Sons, and Samuel Alcock & Co. Rockingham Pottery in Yorkshire made yellow wares; Leeds followed in the north. The Sunderland Pottery made yellow-glazed wares in addition to its more famous pink luster wares. Several potteries in New Castle and Liverpool contributed examples.

Cambrian and Glamorgan, two Swansea potteries, made a considerable number of yellow-glazed pieces. Another Welsh pottery, South Wales in Llanelly, also made yellow wares.

Reference: J. Jefferson Miller II, *English Yellow-Glazed Earthenware,* Smithsonian Institution Press, 1974.

Museums: Art Institute of Chicago, Chicago, IL; City Museum & Art Gallery, Stoke-on-Trent, England; National Museum of American History, Smithsonian Institution, Washington, DC; Nelson-Atkins Museum of Art, Kansas City, MO; Rose Museum, Brandeis University, Waltham, MA.

Beaker, 2 1/2" h, band of silver luster leaves, c1820, yellow ground, hairlines 295.00

Cache Pot and Saucer, 3 3/4" h, rust, blue, and green florals, pink luster accents, yellow ground, c1820..................3,200.00

Coffee Can, 2 5/8" h, green leaves, rust florals, yellow ground, c1820............650.00

Cup and Saucer, Handleless

Adam Buck scene of mother and child, orange-brown transfers, yellow ground, (A)....................358.00

Band of lg orange-brown flowerheads with green and brown foliage on cup and border of saucer, yellow ground, (A)
....................1,073.00

Fishing scene with castle and windmill in bkd, orange-brown transfer, yellow ground, (A)...............495.00

Figure

4 1/2" l, figural cradle, basketweave body, iron red and green accents, yellow luster body, Staffordshire, (A)....345.00

4 5/8" h, Winter, woman wrapped in cloak and hood, yellow ground, (A)..660.00

Flower Pot, 4" h, with stand, red, green, and brick red enameled flowers, vines, and leaves, dk brick red rims, England, (A)
....................1,045.00

Garniture Set, 3 piece, 2 vases, 4 1/4" h, vase, 4 7/8" h, flared body, wide flat rim, band of red, brown, and green flowers, leaves, and tendrils, brown stripes, yellow ground, (A)
....................1,430.00

Jug

3 3/4" h, silver luster and red enameled leaf and floral designs, yellow luster body, c1815, (A)............145.00

4 1/2" h, Satyr, black beard, red face, silver luster and rust red leaves, raised bumpy surface, yellow glazed ground, Staffordshire...............950.00

5 1/4" h, red enameled molded draped body with oval floral medallions, silver luster trim, yellow luster ground, (A)....................546.00

5 1/2" h, black transfers of "Charity" and "Hope" in silver luster roundels, silver luster bands, yellow body, (A)..230.00

Milk Mug

1 3/4" h, silver lines and squiggles, yellow ground....................450.00

2" h, silver bird design, yellow ground
....................550.00

2 1/4" h, silver leaves, yellow ground, c1820....................450.00

Mug

2" h, "A New Carriage for Ann," red transfer....................350.00

2 1/8" h, "A Trifle For Fanny" in frame, black transfer, copper luster rim and handle trim...............625.00

2 1/4" h

"Boys Balancing," red transfer, c1820
....................950.00

Blue florals, green zigzag design, pink luster rim, yellow ground, (A)
....................523.00

Green enameled leaves and pink luster scrollwork and trim, (A)....115.00

Red and green painted flower and leaves, yellow ground, leaf handle, (A)....................192.00

Wide band of red and green flowers and pink luster leaves, brown stems, around middle, pink luster rim, yellow ground, C-shaped handle, (A)
....................725.00

2 3/8" h

"A NEW DOLL FOR MARGARET," child in wreath, red transfer, (A)..489.00

Boy with sheep and "A Present for Mary," black transfer, pink luster rim, yellow ground, c1830, (A)..345.00

Red brown transfer of "My Son, if sinners entice thee, consent thou not lest disgrace come upon thee" in scrolled cartouche, yellow ground, leaf handle, (A).........413.00

Two musicians seated in field with fence, red transfer, pink luster rim and handle, yellow ground.395.00

2 1/2" h

Boy fishing, red transfer, pink luster rim, yellow ground, (A)....550.00

Brown stylized building, brown int lined rim, yellow ground.......525.00

"KEEP THY SHOP AND THY SHOP WILL KEEP THEE," shop int, red transfer, pink luster rim, yellow ground, (A)............175.00

Pink luster cottage design, applied handle, yellow ground, (A).330.00

"Remember Me," black transfer, yellow ground, c1825..........265.00

3" h, orange, brown, and black floral and foliage design, yellow ground, (A)
....................743.00

3 3/4" h, center band of silver resist florals and leaves, silver luster banding, yellow ground, (A)................115.00

4 1/4" h

Orange-brown leaves and bulbs with green and brown accents and tendrils, brown striped rim and handle, yellow ground, (A).......880.00

Relief molded with rust, green, and blue highlights, scattered black dots, yellow ground......650.00

6 1/4" h, cylinder shape, red transfer of man with gun and "Werter going to Shoot Himself," black stripe on rim and base, yellow ground, repaired, (A)
....................550.00

Pitcher

4 1/2" h

Black transfers of pastoral scenes, silver luster trim, yellow ground, (A)
....................135.00

Silver luster wheat and leaf design, silver luster rim, yellow ground, c1820
....................850.00

4 5/8" h, silver and rust red leaves, silver trim, yellow ground, chips on rim, c1820...............550.00

4 3/4" h

Bulbous shape, center band of silver luster stylized wheels and squiggles, silver luster bands, rim, and outlined spout, yellow ground
....................895.00

Red enamel rings centering silver resist band of florals and leaves, yellow ground, (A)..........175.00

5" h, panel with silver "W," overall leaf design, yellow ground, c1825....750.00

5 1/2" h

Black transfer of "Application" in silver luster circle, silver luster bands, spout repair, yellow ground, (A)
....................110.00

Painted lg red flowers with green centers, brown tendrils and rims, molded leaf and fruit border and handle, yellow ground...........485.00

Silver luster cartouche of romantic couple and animals in pasture front and reverse, yellow ground, c1820
....................750.00

6" h, bulbous shape, lg brown centered orange-brown flowerheads and sm orange-brown flowerheads, brown stems and leaves, band of brown and orange-brown stylized buds on border, yellow ground, (A)........1,485.00

7" h, silver luster lines, bands, and geometrics, yellow ground, c1825..795.00

7 1/4" h, 3 round reserves of "Toby Fillpot," "The Farmers Arms," and pastoral scene, black transfers with polychrome accents, silver resist band on leaves and berries on neck, yellow ground, c1815, (A)................920.00

Plate

6 1/2" d

Lg orange-brown beehive type flower in center with buds and green foliage, orange-brown relief of birds

Saucer Dish, 5 1/4" d, Adam Buck design, yellow ground, black transfer, $150.

Tea Set, pot and stand, 5 3/4" h, 10 3/4" l, creamer, sugar basin, black trim, yellow ground, England, c1810, $1,575.

and butterflies on border, indented rim, yellow ground, repairs, (A) 440.00

Orange-brown flowers, green leaves, brown tendrils in center, brown outlined yellow glazed border, (A) 248.00

8" d, rust, blue, and green floral design, yellow ground, c1820 . . . . . . .1,200.00

8 1/4" d, center with orange-brown shaded swirled flowerhead, sm flowerheads and green leaves, emb orange-brown fruit, flowers, and leaves on border, yellow ground, (A) 2,750.00

9" d, "Vu dans les environs de Dublin, en Irlande," floral border, black transfer, yellow ground 100.00

10" d, border of pink luster and polychrome enameled floral and foliate designs, yellow ground, (A). 145.00

Soup Plate, 8 1/4 d, lg iron red cabbage rose, green leaves, iron red buds on int, relief molded iron red and green flower sprigs on border, indented rim, yellow ground 400.00

Teapot

3 1/2" h, band of lg orange-brown flowerheads with green and brown foliage around body, yellow ground, hairline, repairs, (A). 633.00

5 1/2" h, squat shape, iron red transfers of "The Teaparty," iron red rims, yellow ground, hairline, chips. 850.00

Tea Service, child's size, teapot, creamer, sugar bowl, waste bowl, 5 cups and saucers, black and red sprig design, brown trim, yellow body 3,500.00

Vase

6 3/4" h, pinched flared rim, black transfers of "Charity" and "Faith," silver lustered bands, yellow body, c1815, (A) 230.00

7" h, ovoid shape, circ ft, flared rim, enameled raised floral medallions, raised swags with tied ribbons, silver luster trim, yellow body, (A). 1,840.00

Waste Bowl

5 1/2" d, rust and green flowers on ext and int, rust outlined crenelated rim, yellow ground, sealed hairline 895.00

6 3/8" d, pink luster and green enamel florals on ext, yellow ground, (A) . 150.00

ZSOLNAY

Pecs, Funfkirchen 1862 to Present

c 1828 - 1900

History: Vilmos Zsolnay established a Hungarian earthenware pottery at Pecs, Funfkirchen in 1862. Initially, utilitarian earthenwares were the main product. Ornamental wares decorated in Persian motifs were added to the line. The factory also produced reticulated and pierced highly decorative ornamental vases similar to those by Fischer. Enamel was used to paint designs onto porcelains, and they were fired at high temperatures.

At the turn of the century, vases and bowls with Art Nouveau decorations and boldly colored glazes were made. Many of the patterns were designed by J. Rippl-Ronai about 1900. An experimental workshop under the direction of V. Wartha produced some luster decorated pieces between 1893 and 1910. Vases in billowing, folded shapes decorated in shades of green, yellow, and blue lusters or in motifs of plants and cloud-like designs were manufactured. Zsolnay porcelains in fountains, sculptures, and tiles were used to decorate public buildings all over the old Austro-Hungarian empire.

Porcelain figurines were added to the line about 1900. These are in great demand today. The factory is called the Alfoldi Porcelain works today and produces Herend and Zsolnay porcelains.

The Zsolnay factory is still in business. It produces figures with an iridescent glaze.

The company's mark is a stylized design representing the five churches of Zsolnay. Sometimes the word "Pecs" also appears.

Museum: Zsolnay Museum, Pecs, Hungary.

Bowl, 7 1/2" d, reticulated flower and leaf design, steel blue, rust, yellow, and pink 260.00

Bud Vase, 3" h, squat base, slender, flared neck, bright red berry and leaf design, purple eosin glazed ground, c1900 . . . . . . 2,000.00

Cache Pot, 4 1/2" h x 5" d, relief of bulbous lined flower buds extending over rim, metallic eosin glaze, c1900. . . . . 950.00

Chalice, 6" h, 4 flower stems form handles, molded flowers and berry border, green and blue eosin glazes, red int, c1899, repaired chip 1,650.00

Charger, 15 7/8" d, yellow, blue, and mauve flowerheads on cream ground in raised gold lobed cartouche, pierced flower border separated by blue, pink, and purple molded shell designs, pr 575.00

Figure, 7 1/2" h, green-gold irid glaze, Pecs and castle mark, $325.

Ewer, 12 1/4" h, ftd bulbous shape, 2 scroll handles, applied brown speckling and florals on yellow glazed ground, (A) 90.00

Figure

3 7/8" h, peasant woman picking grapes, polychrome, sq base, c1910-26 . . . . 250.00

4 7/8" h, seated spaniel, blue-green eosin glaze, silver castle mark 265.00

5" h, 8" l, 2 polar bears walking on ice block, blue-green eosin glaze, brown castle mark 395.00

6 1/2" h, seated slender frog, blue-green eosin glaze. 61.00

9 1/2" h

Crouching bear with berries, blue-green eosin glazes. . . . 244.00

Kneeling female nude leaning backward, oval base, blue eosin glaze 103.00

15 1/2" h, standing female holding skirts, rect plinth, red flambe, (A) 375.00

Inkwell, 4 1/4" h, figural conch shell, crimson and black lustered glazes, repair to handle, (A) 300.00

Jar, Cov

7" h, ovoid shape, blue and cream snowflake design, coral ground, c1894 . . . . 1,650.00

11 1/2" h, ovoid shape, overall Persian floral design, lustered gold, red, and blue-green glazes, mkd, (A) . . . 800.00

Jug

6 1/2" h, applied female figures on sides, vert handle, green and gold eosin glazes 66.00

9 1/4" h, bulbous body, straight neck, sq handle with applied rosettes, 6 applied pierced geometric medallions, aqua bubble textured ground, gold trim, "imp ZSOLNAY PEC 763" mark 260.00

24" h, circ ft, bulbous body, straight neck, narrow tube spout, reticulated sides and beading, yellow glaze with gilt accents, c1882 . . . . 500.00

Pitcher

7 1/2" h, bulbous shape, wide spread lip, cream and lt brown flower and stem decoration, red-maroon metallic eosin ground, c1898 . . . . 750.00

15 1/2" h, tapered shape, overall modeled green and brown eosin glazed oak leaves and red beatles, c1893

. . . . .6,500.00

18" h, figural stylized crowing rooster, green metallic eosin glaze, raised steeple mark. 4,000.00

Plaque, 15 1/4" l x 10 1/4" h, rect, yellow, pink, green, and brown Dutch windmill and horse

Pitcher, 9" h, gold, red, and green irid glazes, $6,000.

scene, irid Art Nouveau border, mkd, (A)
. . . . 1,000.00

Stein

.5 L, relief design of shield on front, flowers and ribbons on sides, pink glaze, pink glass inlaid lid with crackled finish, "Zsolnay Pecs" mark, (A) 231.00

1.5 L, relief scene of people and lion heads with floral, pale tan glaze, pewter lid with gold paint, "Zsolnay Pecs No. 2661 16" mark. 150.00

Temple Jar, 7" h, oriental red glaze with black streaks, ball knob on cov. 84.00

Tray

10" d, figural crayfish on side, red, green, and blue eosin glazes. 220.00

11" d x 7" h, figure of woman bending filling jug at end of tray, blue, green, and red eosin glazes 232.00

Trinket Dish, 10 1/4" h, brown pouter pigeon perched on oval well 110.00

Vase

4 1/2" h, dull gold swirled Secessionist design, maroon ground, c1898 . 1,650.00

5 1/8" h, squat bulbous shape with cylinder neck, red relief molded seated figures of youth holding lyre and mermaid on gold luster ground molded with stylized flowers. 1,425.00

5 3/4" h, cylinder shape with 2 sm handles on shoulder, everted rim, blue and red eosin glazed dots, green gold eosin ground, c1900 . . . . 2,500.00

6 1/2" h

Bulbous shape, purple to red swirl irid
. . . . 325.00

Dbl walled, reticulated design, cobalt, beige, and gold. 325.00

8 1/2" h, "Tulip" form, metallic red, green, and blue eosin glazes, c1900
. . . . 7,500.00

9" h

Free form, 2 ribbon handles, dk red glaze 137.00

Molded lily pads on sides, 2 sm handles on shoulder, blue-green eosin glaze 76.00

Tapered lattice base, ball shape body, lattice vert flared neck, red marbleized glaze. 47.00

9 1/4" h, dbl gourd shape, blue, green, and silver "Labrador" metallic glaze, c1896
. . . . 1,350.00

9 1/2" h

Bulbous shape, rolled rim, relief of roosters an flowers, metallic eosin copper and green glazes, c1938-39
. . . . 1,500.00

Figure of woman leaning on side of vase, red-gold eosin glazes . .100.00

9 3/4" h, organic form, tulip shape with ribbon type handle, blue, green, and gold eosin glaze, c1899-1900 . . . . 6,500.00

10" h, carved yellow and red flowers with winding green stems, mottled putty colored ground. 6,000.00

10 1/2" h

Iznik design, red and putty colored leaf and vert tapered bush design, white glazed ground, c1893 . . . 2,750.00

Wide flat base, narrow neck, flared rim, 2 loop handles, blue eosin glaze
. . . . 203.00

10 3/4" h, stepped design, 3 spotted leopards around middle step, silver leaf and red flower design on upper step, red stylized ferns around base, mottled "granite" ground, raised steeple mark, c1912. . . . . 25,000.00

11 3/4" h, metallic gold and blue painted Secessionist flowerheads with serrated petals, dk burgundy ground, rim repair
. . . . 1,750.00

12 1/4" h, bulbous base with cream and gilt molded swirl design, cream glazed tapered cylinder body with raised apple blossoms and leaves, lobed rim, c1885
. . . . 540.00

16" h, architectural form, buttress handles, mottled blue glaze with gilt highlights, putty ground, c1910 . . . . 1,500.00

Water Jug, 15" h, bulbous, spout in overhead handle, faux cloisonne gold outlined multicolored flowerheads, burgundy ground, castle and Zsolnay castle mark, (A) 600.00

APPENDIX

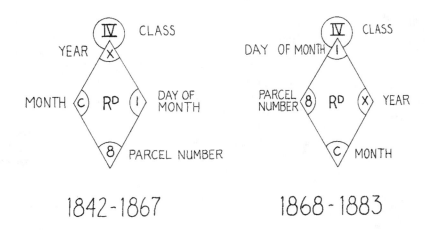

BRITISH REGISTRATION MARKS
1843 - 1883

1842-1867

1868-1883

THE BRITISH REGISTRY MARK

The British Registry mark or diamond is found on ceramics manufactured in Great Britain or handled by British agents for foreign manufacturers. The mark was used first in 1842 and continued in use in this form until 1883. The mark is usually found impressed or raised on the ceramic body and indicates that the shape or material was registered or printed when the decoration or pattern was registered.

Through registration of the shape or pattern, the manufacturer was protected from infringement for a period of three years before renewal was necessary. By examining and deciphering this device, the collector can determine the earliest date that a piece was registered, then place it in its proper time frame.

Deciphering the mark is not difficult. All ceramics are classified number IV as seen at the top of the diamond. Both examples bear this identification.

The 1842-1867 diamond is deciphered in the following manner: the top semicircle designates the year, the left one indicates the month, the right one indicates the day of the month, and the bottom one indicates the parcel number that identifies the manufacturer. The following is a list that corresponds to the semicircles in the 1842-1867 diamond:

Year	Month for Both Devices
1842-X	January-C or O
1843-H	February-G
1844-C	March-W
1845-A	April-H
1846-I	May-E
1847-F	June-M
1848-U	July-I

1849-S	August-R and September 1-19th, 1857
1850-V	September-D
1851-P	October-B
1852-D	November-K
1853-Y	December-A
1854-J	
1855-E	
1856-L	
1857-K	
1858-B	
1859-M	
1860-Z	
1861-R	
1862-O	
1863-G	
1864-N	
1865-W	
1866-Q	
1867-T	

From this chart, it can be determined that the sample diamond on the left dates the registration of the shape or decoration on Jan. 1, 1842.

In 1868, the British Registry mark was altered slightly to the form on the right. The following list corresponds to the diamond used from 1868-1883.

Year

1868-X	1877-P
1869-H	1878-W from March 1-6
1870-C	1878-D
1871-A	1879-Y
1872-I	1880-J
1873-F	1881-E
1874-U	1882-L
1875-S	1883-K
1876-V	

The diamond mark on the right dates Jan. 1, 1868. In 1888, the diamond-shaped device was replaced with the complete registration number filed in the London Patent Office.

PHOTO CREDITS

We wish to thank all those antiques dealers, auction houses, and collectors who permitted us to photograph their antique pottery and porcelain. Unfortunately, we are unable to identify the sources for all our photographs beneath the photos; nevertheless, we are deeply appreciative to all who have contributed to this price guide, and they are listed below by state.

California: Antiques & Art Glass, Santa Ana; McGee's Antiques, San Diego; Michael R. Newman, Woodland Hills; Squire Antiques & Fine Arts, Los Gatos.

Connecticut: Winsor Antiques, Fairfield.

Florida: Richard Newman, Ft. Lauderdale.

Illinois: Americana, Ltd. Chicago; Antiques & Porcelain by GK, Ltd. Glenview; Antique Warehouse, Grayslake; Browsatorium, Inc. Oak Lawn; Chalice Antiques Shoppe, Mt. Olive; Circa Antiques, Ltd. at Town & Country Antiques, Northfield; Country House, Lake Forest; Cynthia Hinman Antiques, Volo; Donald Stuart Antiques, Winnetka; Dunning's Auction Service, Elgin; Federalist Antiques, Kenilworth; Fermette Antiques, Downers Grove; Fly By Nite Gallery, Chicago; Grape & Cable Antiques, Lombard; Joel and Sue Kaufmann, Northbrook; Leslie Hindman Auctioneers, now Sotheby's, Chicago; Portobello Road West, Park Forest; Pumpkin Patch, Chicago; Red Bandana, Lincolnwood; Lucie and Bob Reichner, Wilmette; Smith & Ciffone Antiques, Kenilworth; Taylor Williams Antiques, Chicago; Volo Antique Mall, Volo.

Indiana: Crossroads Antique Mall, Seymour; The Antique Market of Michigan City.

Kentucky: Railroad Street Antiques, Midway.

Michigan: Silver Accents, Birmingham; Thomas Forshee, Stockbridge; Winding River Antiques, Fenton.

Minnesota: Bomar Antiques & Collectibles, St. Paul; C.L. Nelson, Spring Park; Gale Studio, Woodbury; Twin Owls Antiques, Inc. Alborn.

Missouri: Bonnie's Antiques, Raymore.

New York: Brickwood Antiques, Gloversville; Chelsea Antiques Building, Twelve Floors of Antiques & Collectibles, New York; E & J Antiques, Freeport; James M. Labaugh, Pound Ridge.

Ohio: AAA I-70 Antique Mall, Springfield; Lavonia Chait, Elyria; Mike Clum, Inc. Rushville; Patricia Pratt Antiques, Cincinnati; Seekers Antiques, Columbus; Springfield Antiques Center.

Oklahoma: Colonial Antiques.

Pennsylvania: Dorothy Lerner, Pittsburgh; Gillian Hine, Lancaster.

Virginia: Mimi & Steve Levine, Inc. Alexandria.

Wisconsin: Barnes Antiques, Milwaukee; Jeff Hembel Antiques, Milwaukee.

England: Jonathan Horne Antiques Ltd. London.

SPECIAL CREDITS

Our gratitude must go to the following people for exceptional help with either data for this third edition and/or photographs. Without their generous help and encouragement, we would have been unable to write this book.

AAA I-70 Antiques Mall, Springfield, Ohio; Americana Ltd. Judith Anderson, Chicago, Illinois; Antique Market of Michigan City, Indiana; Antiques & Porcelain by GK, Ltd. Glenview, Illinois; Chelsea Antiques Building, New York, New York; C.L. Nelson, Spring Park, Minnesota; Country House, Richard Norton, Lake Forest, Illinois; Dunning Auction Service, Elgin, Illinois; Federalist Antiques, Kenilworth, Illinois, Fly By Nite Gallery, Chicago, Illinois; Leslie Hindman Auctioneers, now Sotheby's Chicago; Mike Clum, Inc. Rushville, Ohio; Raven & Dove Antiques, Randi Schwartz, Wilmette, Illinois; Seekers Antiques, Columbus, Ohio; Smith & Ciffone Antiques, Kenilworth, Illinois; Taylor Williams Antiques, Chicago, Illinois; Wynn A. Sayman, Richmond, Massachusetts.

AUCTION HOUSES

The following auction houses cooperated with us by providing complimentary subscriptions to their catalogs for all pottery and porcelain auctions. Their help and cooperation is appreciated greatly. Without this help, it would have been impossible for us to produce this price guide.

Andre Ammelounx
P.O. Box 136
Palatine, IL 60078

Christie's East
219 East 67 St.
New York, NY 10021

Christie's
502 Park Ave.
New York, NY 10022

Christie's South Kensington
85 Old Brompton Road
London SW7 3LD, United Kingdom

Conestoga Auction Co. Inc.
768 Graystone Road
P.O. Box 1
Manheim, PA 17545-0001

Dargate Auction Galleries
5607 Baum Road
Pittsburgh, PA 15206

Dawson's
128 American Road
Morris Plains, NJ 07950

William Doyle Galleries
175 East 87th St.
New York, NY 10128

DuMouchelles
409 East Jefferson Ave.
Detroit, MI 48226

Dunning Auction Service
755 Church Road
Elgin, IL 60123

Flomaton Antique Auction
277 Old Highway 31
Flomaton, AL 36441

Garth's Auction, Inc.
2690 Stratford Road
P.O. Box 369
Delaware, OH 43015

Leslie Hindman Auctioneers
215 West Ohio St.
Chicago, IL 60610
(Now Sotheby's Chicago)

Horst Auctions
Clarence E. Spohn
114 West Orange St.
Lititz, PA 17543-1804

James D. Julia, Inc.
RT. 201
Skowhegan Road
Fairfield, ME 04937

Smith & Jones, Inc.
12 Clark Lane
Sudbury, MA 01776

New Orleans Auction Galleries, Inc.
801 Magazine St.
New Orleans, LA 70130

Phillips
406 East 79th St.
New York, NY 10021

Pook & Pook, Inc.
P.O. Box 268
Downington, PA 19335

David Rago Auctions, Inc.

333 North Main St.
Lambertville, NJ 08530

Remmey Auction Galleries

83 Summit Ave.
Summit, NJ 07901

Selkirk's

7447 Forsyth Boulevard
St. Louis, MO 63105

Skinner, Inc.

The Heritage on The Garden
63 Park Plaza
Boston, MA 02116

Skinner, Inc.

357 Main Street
Bolton, MA 01740

Sotheby's

1334 York Ave.
New York, NY 10021

Sotheby's London

34-35 New Bond St.
London W1A 2AA United Kingdom

Thomaston Place Auction Gallery

Route 1 P.O. Box 300
Thomaston, ME 04861

Wolf's Auction Gallery

1239 West 6th St.
Cleveland, OH 44113

SPECIALIZED AUCTIONS

Majolica

Michael G. Strawser
200 N. Main
P.O. Box 332
Wolcottville, IN 46795

Quimper

New England Absentee Auctions, Inc.
16 Sixth St.
Stamford, CT 06905

Steins

Andre Ammelounx Stein Auction Company
P.O. Box 136
Palatine, IL 60078

Gary Kirsner Auctions

P.O. Box 8807
Coral Springs, FL 33075-8807

Susie Cooper, Clarice Cliff, Moorcroft,

Christie's South Kensington
85 Old Brompton Road
London SW7 3LD, United Kingdom

ADDITIONAL NOTES ON MARKS

Bisque: see Heubach and Sevres for marks.

Creamware: see Leeds and Wedgwood for marks.

Delft: see Bristol and Liverpool for additional marks.

Flow Blue: see Staffordshire General for additional marks.

Majolica: see Keller and Guerin, Minton, and Sarreguemines for additional marks.

Minton: year cyphers were incorporated in some marks.

Mulberry China: see Flow Blue and Staffordshire General for marks.

Parian: see Copeland-Spode and Minton for marks.

Pate-sur-Pate: see Minton and Sevres for marks.

Pearlware: see Clews, Davenport, Ridgway, Staffordshire General, Wedgwood, and Enoch and Ralph Wood for marks.

Piano Babies: see Heubach for marks.

Pitcher and Bowl Sets: see Staffordshire General for additional marks.

Royal Worcester: year cyphers were incorporated in some marks.

Samson: no identifiable marks recorded. Used marks imitating those of Chelsea, Meissen, and Sevres.

Sevres: year cyphers were incorporated in some marks.

Staffordshire Blue and White: see Staffordshire General and Staffordshire Historic marks.

Tea Leaf Ironstone: see Ironstone marks.

Tiles: see Minton and Wedgwood for additional marks.

Toby Jugs: see Pratt and Enoch and Ralph Wood for marks.

Wedgwood: year cyphers were included in some marks.

Willow Ware: see Staffordshire general for marks.

GLOSSARY

Applied. Parts or ornaments attached to the body by means of liquid clay (slip). Also called sprigging.

Anthemion. A formal type of decoration in the shape of stylized honeysuckle flowers and leaves.

Bail Handle. Arched fixed or movable overhead handle.

Bargeware. Earthenware of narrow proportions for use on canal boats and barges. These pieces were decorated with florals and luster. Larger pieces featured modeled teapots on the covers or handles.

Bat Printing. The transfer of a design by means of glue-like slabs. Most often used on glazed surfaces.

Bellarmine. Stoneware jug or bottle featuring bearded mask and coat of arms under neck.

Bell-Toy Pattern. Oriental pattern featuring child holding toy composed of stick with bells. Popular pattern at Worcester.

Bianco Sopra Bianco. Decoration on tin-glazed earthenware in opaque white on a slightly bluish or grayish ground. It was employed on Italian majolica from the early years of the 16th century, and on English delftware in the 18th century.

Bird or Sparrow Spout. Modeled spout in form of open bird beak. These were closely associated with examples fabricated in silver.

Blanc de Chine. French term referring to a translucent white or ivory porcelain covered in thick glaze. Produced by several English and French companies after Chinese originals.

Bleu Lapis. Streaked or veined bright blue ground color often found in combination with gold accents. Used at Vincennes.

Bleu Persan. Dark blue ground color used on Nevers faience often in conjunction with white or yellow ornamentation.

Blind Earl Pattern. Low relief design of rosebuds, leaves, and insects which covers entire surface. Designed for the blind Earl of Coventry in 1755. The pattern was used at Worcester and Chelsea.

Bocage. Modeled foliage, branches, and flowers which form arbor or canopy background for figures. A method of covering unfinished backs of figures.

Bonbonniere. French term for small covered sweetmeat container.

Cachepot. Ornamental container designed to hold utilitarian flowerpot.

Cartouche. A method of framing or outlining a design, usually with elaborate borders. (See Laub-und-Bandelwerk)

China. Term frequently used to refer collectively to pottery and porcelain, but correctly applies only to porcelain.

Chinoiserie. European decoration utilizing pseudo-Chinese figures, pagodas, and landscapes. Used extensively in early 18th century England and the continent.

Crabstock. Modeled in form of branch or crabapple tree. Found on handles, spouts, and feet.

Dentil. Border treatment of small rectangular blocks giving appearance of teeth. Usually in gilt.

Diapering. Diamond or lozenge type pattern that is usually repetitive and connected.

Ecuelle. French term for small, covered shallow bowl with double parallel handles. Used for serving soup.

Engine-Turned. Machine-applied design that cuts into the surface of the clay.

Etched. Method of decoration using an acid-resistant covering in which the design is cut, exposed to hydrofluoric acid and pigment added to the etched recesses.

Famille Rose. Chinese-style design which incorporates opaque pink or rose-colored enamels.

Flambe. French term for red shaded glazes derived from reduced copper.

Fuddling Cup. Group of cups joined together internally and externally, usually with multiple handles.

Gadrooned. Continuous pattern or reeding or fluting used mainly as a border treatment. Inspired from silver examples.

Grisaille. French term for printing in gray shades on porcelain to give the effect of relief.

Hausmalerei. German term for ceramic decorators who literally worked at home. They purchased whiteware from factories such as Meissen and Vienna or finished partially decorated pieces.

Imari. Japanese style using designs based on native Japanese textiles. Colors of red and dark underglaze blue predominate.

Istoriato. Italian term for mythical, biblical, or genre historical scenes that were painted in polychromes on earthenwares. These paints often cover the entire surface of the object.

Kakiemon Style. Based on the Japanese decorations of the Kakiemon family. The main features include asymmetrical patterns of florals, birds, and Orientals in iron-red, yellow, and shades of blue utilizing large masses of white ground in the color scheme. Popular on 18th century Meissen, Chantilly, Chelsea, Bow, and Worcester.

Lambrequin. French term for a scrolled border pattern that consists of hanging drapery, lace and scrollwork, and leaves. This pattern reached its zenith at Rouen.

Laub-und-Bandelwerk. German term meaning leaf and strapwork. This elaborate type of design was used extensively in the cartouche borders at Meissen and Vienna.

Mon. Japanese inspired form representing circular stylized florals. Frequently incorporated in European interpretations of oriental designs.

Ozier. German term which describes a molded or painted woven basket-type treatment. Many variations exist including continuous and interrupted patterns.

Posset Pot. Multi-handled pot with center spout designed to hold mixture of wine or ale and milk.

Potpourri Vase. Designed to hold liquid, flower petals, and herbs. Pierced shoulder or cover allows for the escape of the aromatic scents.

Prunus. Plum blossom-type decoration which is based on the Chinese symbol for spring.

Putto. Italian term referring to nude or semi-nude young boy. Frequently used as accessory decoration.

Quatrefoil. Shape or design divided in four equal lobes or sections.

Reserve. An area of a design without ground color designated to receive a decorative panel.

Sheet Design. Repetitive design from border to border.

Silver Shape. Copies in porcelain and pottery of existing silver pieces. These usually were reserved for borders, spouts, and handles.

Slip. Clay in a liquid form.

Spill-Vase. A cylindrical vase with flaring mouth, used for holding spills (wood splinters or paper tapers for obtaining a light from the fire).

Transfer Printing. The transfer of a design from prepared copper plates by means of tissue paper. The design, once cut into the copper plates, was prepared with color. A thin sheet of tissue transferred the design to the dry ground of the piece prior to glazing.

Treacle Glaze. A thickly applied pottery glaze that gives the impression of being treacly and has often run down the side of the ware in much the same way as treacle would.

Trembleuse. French term used to describe a well or vertical projections found on saucers that were devised to keep the accompanying cups from shifting on the saucers. They were designed specifically for those with unsteady hands.

Tube Lining. A method of pottery decoration where a bag containing liquid clay (slip) is squeezed out of a narrow glass tube onto the surface of fired, but undecorated wares making a thin raised linear design as though icing a cake.

Additional glossary terms can be found in the following books: Louise Ade Boger, *The Dictionary of World Pottery & Porcelain,* Scribners, 1971; George Savage & Harold Newman, *An Illustrated Dictionary of Ceramics,* Thames and Hudson, Ltd. 1985.

BIBLIOGRAPHY

The following is a listing of general reference books on English and Continental pottery and porcelain that the reader may find useful. A list of marks books is also included.

CONTINENTAL REFERENCES

Paul Atterbury, General Editor, *The History of Porcelain,* Orbis Publishing, 1982; John Cushion, *Continental China Collecting for Amateurs,* Frederick Muller, 1970; Hugo Morley-Fletcher & Roger McIlroy, *Christie's Pictorial History of European Pottery,* Prentice-Hall, Inc. 1984; Reginard Haggar, *The Concise Encyclopedia of Continental Pottery and Porcelain,* Hawthorn Books, Inc. 1960.

ENGLISH REFERENCES

John A. Bartlett, *British Ceramic Art: 1870-1940,* Schiffer Publishing, Ltd. 1993; Victoria Bergesen, *Bergesen's British Ceramics Price Guide,* Barrie & Jenkins, 1992; G.A. Godden, *British Porcelain,* Clarkson. N. Potter, 1974; G.A. Godden, *British Pottery,* Clarkson N. Potter, Inc. 1975; G. Bernard Hughes, *Victorian Pottery & Porcelain,* Spring Books, 1967; Griselda Lewis, *A Collector's History of English Pottery, 4th Ed,* Antique Collectors' Club, Ltd. 1987; G. Willis, *English Pottery & Porcelain,* Guiness Signatures, 1968.

GENERAL REFERENCES

Emmanuel Cooper, *A History of Pottery,* St. Martins Press, 1972; John P. Cushion, *Pottery and Porcelain Tablewares,* William Morrow & Co. Inc. 1976; Antoinette Fay-Halle & Barbara Mundt, *Porcelain of the Nineteenth Century,* Rizzoli, 1983; Janet Gleeson, Ed. *Miller's Collecting Pottery and Porcelain,* Reed International Books, Ltd. 1997.

MARKS REFERENCES

W. Chaffers, *Marks & Monograms on European & Oriental Pottery & Porcelain*, William Reeves, 1965; J.P. Cushion, *Pocket Book of British Ceramic Marks*, Faber & Faber, 1984; J.P. Cushion & W.B. Honey, *Handbook of Pottery & Porcelain Marks, 4th Edition*, Faber & Faber, 1981; Ludwig Danckert, *Directory of European Porcelain Marks, Makers & Factories, 4th Edition,* N.A.G. Press, 1981; G.A. Godden, *Encyclopedia of British Pottery & Porcelain Marks,* Barrie & Jenkins, 1996; M. Haslam, *Marks and Monograms of the Modern Movement,* Lutterworth Press, 1977; Robert E. Rontgen, *Marks on German, Bohemian & Austrian Porcelain, 1710 to the Present*, Schiffer Publishing, Ltd.

INDEX

Y

Z

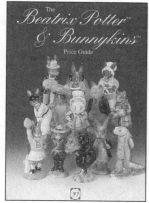

COLLECTORS WILL FIND THESE BOOKS AN INVALUABLE PART OF THEIR LIBRARY

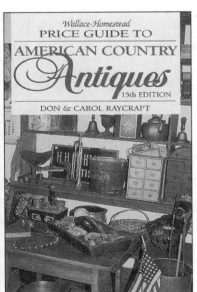
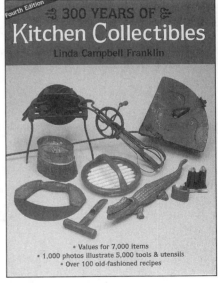

ADD THESE BOOKS TO THE SHELVES OF YOUR LIBRARY

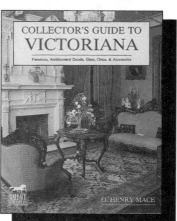